THE SECOND WORLD WAR

Also by Henri Michel

THE SHADOW WAR

Henri Michel

THE SECOND
WORLD WAR

Translated by Douglas Parmée

ANDRE DEUTSCH

First published 1975 by
André Deutsch Limited
105 Great Russell Street London WC1

First published in France under the title
LA SECONDE GUERRE MONDIALE by Henri Michel

Printed in Great Britain by
William Clowes & Sons, Limited
London, Beccles and Colchester

ISBN 0 233 95535 6

Contents

LIST OF MAPS   xvii
TABLES   xviii
PREFACE   xix
INTRODUCTION   1

I	The Antagonists: their Human and Economic Potential	1
II	The Navies	2
III	The Land Forces	7
IV	The Air Forces	8
V	Causes of the Democratic Countries' Shortcomings	11
VI	Moral Forces	13
VII	Strategic Plans	17
VIII	Italian Non-Belligerence	19
IX	The Insoluble Problem of Belgium	20

Book One   The War in Europe (September 1939–June 1941)

PART I   THE PRELUDE IN POLAND AND SCANDINAVIA

Chapter 1   The Obliteration of Poland from the Map of Europe

I	Hitler's 'Total War'	29
II	The Deployment of the German and Polish Forces	31
III	Blitzkrieg in Poland	33
IV	French Inaction. The Saar Offensive	35
V	The Partition of Poland	37
VI	Poland's Martyrdom Begins	38

Chapter 2 The Phoney War

I	Hitler and Peace	41
II	Relations between Germany and the USSR	43
III	The Finnish-Soviet Conflict	45
IV	Mussolini's Hesitation	49
V	Franco-British Determination	51
VI	Allied Relations with Belgium and Holland	53

VII   Allied Plans in the Balkans   58
VIII The Proposal to Attack Oil Sources in the Caucasus   60
IX   Allied Plans in Scandinavia   62
X   The War at Sea. The Blockade   64
XI   The Phoney War   66
XII   The Neutrals   68

Chapter 3   The War in Norway

I   The Opponents' Plans   70
II   The Occupation of Denmark   72
III   The Operations in Norway   73
IV   The Struggle for Narvik   76
V   The Norwegian Resistance   77
VI   Consequences of the German Victory in Norway   79

PART II   THE DEFEAT OF FRANCE

Chapter 1   Plans and Forces of the Antagonists in May 1940

I   Hitler's Views   83
II   The German Plans   84
III   The Allied Plans   87
IV   The German Forces   88
V   The Allied Forces   89
VI   Armoured Vehicles   92
VII   The Air Forces   94

Chapter 2   The Breakthrough at Sedan

I   The Invasion of Holland   96
II   The Belgian Forces and Plans   97
III   The *Chasseurs Ardennais*   99
IV   The Fighting in Belgium   100
V   The Crossing of the Ardennes   101
VI   The Battle of Sedan   103
VII   The Allied Counter-Attacks   105
VIII The Wehrmacht's Progress towards the Sea   108

Chapter 3   The French Collapse

I   The Changes in the French Command   111
II   Weygand's Plan   113
III   The Ypres Conference   115
IV   The Execution of Weygand's Plan   117
V   The Halt of the German Armoured Units   118
VI   The Belgian Capitulation   120
VII   The Dunkirk Evacuation   121
VIII The Battles on the Somme and the Aisne   124

Chapter 4   The Armistice

I	The Exodus	129
II	The Rout	130
III	The French Government's Deliberations	132
IV	Was the Armistice Unavoidable?	136
V	Pétain's Ideas	137
VI	Request for Germany's Terms	138
VII	Hitler's Ideas on the Armistice	139
VIII	The Signing of the Convention at Rethondes	141

PART III   BRITAIN STANDS ALONE

Chapter 1   The Battle of Britain

I	Hitler after his Victory	147
II	British Determination: Winston Churchill	148
III	Mers El-Kebir	149
IV	Operation 'Sea-Lion'	151
V	The Battle of Britain	152
VI	The Mobilisation of the Commonwealth	154
VII	The Exiled Governments – Free France	156
VIII	The Involvement of the United States	157

Chapter 2   The Birth of Hitler's Europe

I	Hitler's Ideas	162
II	Central Europe	164
III	Western Europe	167
IV	The Vichy Government	169
V	The Application of the Armistice Convention	171
VI	The Exploitation of France	172
VII	The Policy of Collaboration	173
VIII	The National Revolution	174
IX	Spain	175

Chapter 3   The Fighting in Africa and the Balkans

I	The Battle of the Atlantic	177
II	Naval Warfare in the Mediterranean. The Antagonists	179
III	The Problem of Malta	181
IV	The Naval Battles in the Mediterranean	182
V	The War in East Africa	183
VI	Italian Setbacks in Libya	184
VII	Italian Setbacks in Greece	186
VIII	German and British Intervention in Greece	188
IX	The Crushing of Yugoslavia	189
X	Greece Crushed	190

XI The Battle of Crete 192
XII The Successes of Rommel and the *Africa Korps* 194
XIII The War in Syria 195
XIV The State of the War in June 1941 196

Book Two   The World War
(June 1941–January 1943)

PART I   THE GREATER REICH

Chapter 1   The Break Between Germany and Russia

I Hitler's Decision 203
II German-Soviet Relations 205
III Hitler's Reasons 206
IV Was Stalin Caught Unawares? 207
V Hitler's Objectives 209
VI The Wehrmacht's Forces and Plans 211
VII Hitler as War Leader 212
VIII The USSR's Forces and Plans 214

Chapter 2   The Wehrmacht's Victories in the USSR

I The Surprise Attack 216
II The German Blitzkrieg 217
III The Battles of Leningrad and Moscow 219
IV Winter 1941–2 223
V The German Offensive of Spring 1942: Objectives and Disposition of Forces 225
VI The German Offensive and its Victories 227
VII The Caucasus and Stalingrad 229
VIII The German Occupation in the USSR. Principles and Organisations 230
IX The Administration of the Conquered Areas 232
X Economic Exploitation 234
XI Terror as a System of Government 236

Chapter 3   The Domination of Europe

I Consequences of the War in the USSR 239
II Political Domination 243
III The Status of Nazi Europe 245
IV The Greater Reich's Finances 247
V Economic Exploitation 249
VI The Security of the Reich 252
VII Poland's Martyrdom 255

Chapter 4   Concentration Camps and Genocide

I	Nazi Anti-Semitism	258
II	The ss	260
III	The Concentration Camps	262
IV	The Fate of the Jews	266
V	The Madagascar Scheme	267
VI	The Ghettoes	268
VII	The Final Solution to the Jewish Problem	269
VIII	Did the Jews Allow themselves to be Massacred?	271
IX	The Silence of the Vatican	273

Chapter 5   Collaboration

I	The *Volksdeutsche*	276
II	Goebbels' Propaganda	277
III	The Collaborators in Occupied Europe	279
IV	The Satellites	283
V	Collaboration in the Soviet Union	284
VI	The Vichy Régime and Collaboration	287
VII	The Friendship of Spain	290
VIII	Swedish Supplies	291

Chapter 6   Resistance Movements Begin

I	The Methods of the Resistance Fighters	293
II	The Allies and the Resistance	295
III	Resistance in Western Europe	297
IV	The French Resistance	299
V	Resistance in Central Europe	301
VI	The Resistance in the Balkans	304

PART II   JAPAN'S GREATER ASIA

Chapter 1   The Break Between Japan and the United States

I	Japanese Imperialism	309
II	The China War	310
III	Developments in Japanese Policy	312
IV	The Development of American Policy	315
V	The Japanese-American Negotiations	317
VI	The Attack on Pearl Harbour	321

Chapter 2   Japan's Lightning War

I	The Japanese Forces	326
II	Conduct of the War in Japan	328
III	The Allied Forces	329
IV	American Strategy and High Command	331

V   Nature of the War in the Pacific   332
VI   The Japanese Plans   334
VII   The Early Japanese Successes   336
VIII The Conquest of the Philippines   337
IX   The Conquest of the Dutch East Indies   338
X   The Conquest of Malaya and Singapore   339
XI   The Burma Campaign   340
XII   Japan's Defensive Perimeter Extended   341

Chapter 3   The Sphere of Co-prosperity

I   The Japanese Empire   345
II   Local Nationalist Movements   348
III   Indonesia   349
IV   China under the Chungking Government   352
V   Communist China   354

PART III   THE WATERSHED OF THE WAR

Chapter 1   A Balance of Forces in the War at Sea

I   The Organisation of the American Command in the Pacific   359
II   The Coral Sea and Midway   360
III   Guadalcanal   362
IV   American Submarine Operations in the Pacific   363
V   German Submarine Successes in the Atlantic   364
VI   Alarming Outlook for the Allies   366
VII   Convoy Protection   367
VIII Towards a Balance of Forces in the Battle of the Atlantic 369

Chapter 2   The Germans Halted in Africa

I   Italian Weakness   371
II   Rommel's 'Recovery'   372
III   The *Afrika Korps'* Offensive towards Egypt   374
IV   The Pause at El Alamein. The British Preparations   376
V   The Battle of El Alamein   378
VI   Operation 'Torch': the Allied Decision   381
VII   The Preparations in North Africa   384
VIII The Landing   387
IX   Results of Operation 'Torch'   393

Chapter 3   The Battle of Stalingrad

I   The German Offensive   394
II   Preparations for a Soviet Counter-Offensive   396
III   The Encirclement of the German Sixth Army   399
IV   Von Manstein's Counter-Offensive   401

V The Causes of the German Defeat 402
VI The Death Throes of Paulus' Army 404
VII The Soviet Winter Offensive 1942–3 406
VIII The Importance of the Victory of Stalingrad 407

Book Three   The Defeat of Italy

PART I   THE ALLIED WAR-MACHINE

Chapter 1   The Anglo-American War

I The British Conduct of the War 415
II The American Conduct of the War 416
III Anglo-American Co-operation 418
IV The Atlantic Charter 420
V The Adoption of a Combined Strategy 421
VI Unconditional Surrender 424
VII Italy, the Next Allied Objective 425

Chapter 2   The American Arsenal

I Choices and Programmes 428
II Economic Mobilisation 430
III Economic Stability 433
IV Manpower 435
V America's Might 436
VI Lend-Lease 439
VII Latin America 440
VIII British War Production 443
IX The Commonwealth 446

Chapter 3   The Soviet War

I The Conduct of the War 451
II Stalin's Role 453
III Russian Neo-Nationalism 455
IV The Dissolution of the Comintern 456
V The Soviet Union and the Communist Parties 458
VI Soviet Economic Losses through the Occupation 460
VII The Evacuation of Factories Eastwards 461
VIII The Human Effort 463
IX War Production in the USSR 467

Chapter 4   The Strange Alliance

I The Relationship between Churchill, Roosevelt and Stalin 470
II The Anglo-Russian Alliance 472

III	Lend-Lease and the USSR	474
IV	The Problem of the Second Front	477
V	The Polish Problem before Stalingrad	479
VI	The Polish Problem after Stalingrad	481
VII	Secret Negotiations?	483

PART II   THE ITALIAN SURRENDER

Chapter 1   The End of the War in Africa

I	French 'Indecision' in Tunisia	487
II	The Tunisian Campaign	490
III	Darlan's Reign	493
IV	General Giraud's Government	494
V	The French National Liberation Committee	496
VI	The Rebirth of the French Army	499
VII	Towards a French Recovery	501
VIII	The Empire: its Development	502

Chapter 2   Italy Surrenders

I	The Sicilian Campaign	507
II	The Collapse of Fascist Italy	509
III	The Italian Resistance	513
IV	The Plot against Mussolini	516
V	The Fall of Mussolini	518
VI	The Italian Surrender	520
VII	The War in the Italian Peninsula	524
VIII	The Liberation of Corsica	525
IX	The Division of Italy	527

Book Four   The Defeat of Germany

PART I   THE ALLIED OFFENSIVE

Chapter 1   The Bombing of Germany

I	The Financing of the Nazi War	535
II	The Organisation of the German War Economy	537
III	The Manpower Problems	538
IV	Speer's Priorities	540
V	German Aircraft Production	542
VI	The British and the Bombing of Germany	545
VII	The Americans and Carpet Bombing	546
VIII	The Effectiveness of the Bombing	548

Chapter 2   The Soviet Offensive. The Teheran Conference
(July 1943–May 1944)

I   Hitler and the War in the USSR   554
II   Soviet Warfare   556
III   Operation 'Citadel'   559
IV   The 'Affray' at Prokhorovka   561
V   The Soviet Summer and Autumn Offensive, 1943   562
VI   The 'Big Three' at Teheran   563
VII   The Decisions Taken at Teheran. The Second Front   565
VIII   The Polish Problem   566
IX   The German Problem   568
X   The Soviet Winter and Spring Offensive, 1944   569
XI   Partisan Warfare   571
XII   Soviet Espionage   574

Chapter 3   Soviet Victories. The Desatellisation of Greater Germany
(June–December 1944)

I   Alarm amongst the Satellites   576
II   The Committee for Free Germany   578
III   The Red Army Summer Offensive of 1944 – Finland   580
IV   Poland   581
V   The Warsaw Uprising   583
VI   Czechoslovakia   586
VII   Romania   588
VIII   Bulgaria   590
IX   Yugoslavia   590
X   Hungary   592
XI   The Agreement of October 1944 between Churchill and Stalin   594
XII   Greece   596

Chapter 4   The War in Italy (September 1943–December 1944)

I   The Military Operations   599
II   The Allies and Italy   601
III   The Salo Republic   603
IV   The Liberation Committees   605
V   The Partisans   607
VI   The dispute between British and Americans over Strategy   609

Chapter 5   The Liberation of France

I   The Allied Victory in the Atlantic   612
II   The Command of 'Overlord'   614
III   The Preparation of 'Overlord'   616
IV   The Disparity between the Forces Involved   618
V   Preparations for D-Day   620

VI D-Day 621
VII The Battle of Normandy 624
VIII The Battle of France 626
IX The Action of the Resistance 628
X The Advance to the Seine. Falaise 632
XI The Allies and the Provisional Government 635
XII The Liberation of Paris 637
XIII The Decision to Land in the Mediterranean 638
XIV French Participation 640
XV The Landing of August 15 641
XVI The Rhône Campaign 643
XVII Liberated France 645
XVIII The French Revival 647
XIX The Fighting of Autumn 1944 649

PART II   THE CAPITULATION OF GERMANY

Chapter 1   The Final Convulsions of the Nazi Reich

I German Opposition to Hitler 655
II The Putsch of July 20, 1944 657
III Nazi Fanaticism 659
IV Germany's Secret Weapons 660
V Hitler's Last Throw 664

Chapter 2   The Yalta Conference

I The Circumstances and Atmosphere of the Conference 668
II The Fate of Defeated Germany 670
III The Polish Problem 672
IV The War Against Japan 674
V The United Nations Organisation 675
VI Conclusions on the Yalta Conference 677

Chapter 3   The Death Throes of Nazi Germany

I The Soviet Offensive of January–February 1945 680
II The Anglo-American Discussions – the Malta Conference 683
III The Colmar Pocket – the Battle of the Rhineland 684
IV The Crossing of the Rhine – the Battle of the Ruhr 690
V The Battle of Budapest – the USSR and South-east Europe 691
VI Churchill's Anxieties and Proposals 693
VII The Battle of Berlin 697
VIII The End of the Fighting in Italy 698
IX The End of the Fighting in Germany 699
X The German Surrender 701

Chapter 4 The Potsdam Conference

I Matters of Dispute 706
II The Polish Problem 709
III The Potsdam Conference – the Polish Problem 711
IV The Fate of Germany 713
V The Ultimatum to Japan 716

Book Five The Defeat of Japan

Chapter 1 Strategy and Forces in Asia

I The Situation at the Beginning of 1943 722
II The Defensive Strategy of the Japanese 723
III The Search for an Allied Offensive Strategy 724
IV The Allied Command in the China–Burma Sector 726
V The American Command in the Pacific 728
VI American Naval and Air Superiority 730

Chapter 2 The War in China and Burma

I China's Weakness 732
II American Aid to China 734
III The War in China 736
IV Communist China 739
V Preparations for the Burma Campaign 740
VI The Reconquest of Burma 741

Chapter 3 The War in the Pacific

I The Fighting in Papua and New Guinea 745
II The Siege of Rabaul 748
III The Naval Battle in the Marianas 749
IV Formosa or the Philippines? 752
V Japan's Growing Weakness 753
VI The Battle of Leyte 755
VII The Reconquest of the Philippines 756
VIII Iwo Jima 758
IX Okinawa 759

Chapter 4 The Japanese Surrender

I Air Raids on Japan 762
II Japan's Exhaustion 764
III Conquest or Surrender? 765
IV The Atom Bomb 768
V The Red Army's Campaign against Japan 771
VI The Japanese Surrender 773
VII The Causes of the Japanese Defeat 776

Book Six   The World at the End of the War

Chapter 1   The Aftermath

I	The Bloodshed	781
II	Population Movements	784
III	The Material Havoc	785
IV	Moral Havoc	790
V	The Economic Consequences	793
VI	The Collapse of Germany	794

Chapter 2   The New Balance of Power

I	Great Britain	800
II	France	803
III	Italy	805
IV	The Arab World	808
V	Japan and China	811
VI	South-east Asia	813
VII	The USSR and the Communist World	815
VIII	The American Titan	819
IX	Problems and Disagreements	822

Chapter 3   The Task of Reconstruction

I	The United Nations Organisation	825
II	The New International Organisations	827
III	The Commitment of Writers and Artists	829
IV	Giant Strides in Physics	831
V	Giant Strides in Chemistry	834
VI	Disease during the War	835
VII	Immense Developments in Medicine and Therapy	836
VIII	The Age of Science and Technology?	839

CONCLUSION	842
APPENDIX	845
BIBLIOGRAPHY	851
INDEX	917

List of Maps

1   Europe on 1 September 1939   4–5
2   Defeat and Partitions of Poland   30
3   The Scheldt and Dyle-Breda Operations   55
4   The German Plans   85
5   The Battle of the Meuse   106
6   The Defeat of the French Armies   126–7
7   The Partition of France   170
8   The Jugoslav, Greek and Cretan Campaigns   191
9   The Battle for Moscow   221
10 The German Offensives in the USSR   226
11 Greater Germany   240–1
12 The Whole of France a Prison   253
13 The Scourge of Nazi Concentration Camps   263
14 Japan's Greater Asia   342–3
15 The War in Africa and in the Mediterranean   379
16 The Battle of Stalingrad   397
17 The Tunisian Campaign   491
18 The War in Italy   511
19 The Red Army's Offensives   557
20 The Normandy Landing   623
21 The Liberation of France   633
22 Resistance Activities in the Var   642
23 Montgomery's and Eisenhower's Plans   651
24 Hitler's Last Throw   665
25 The Campaign in Upper Alsace   686
26 The Final Assault on Germany   689
27 The War in China   738
28 The Burma Campaign   744
29 The American Offensive in the Pacific   746–7
30 The Ordeal of a French Department   788
31 The Occupation of Germany and Austria   796
32 Europe at the End of the War   806–7

List of Tables

Soviet and German forces engaged from June to December 1942   399

American forces schedule for 1942–3   430

us War Economy and Production   449

Summary Table of Soviet War Production   469

German Arms Production and Bombs Dropped on Greater Germany 549

Greater Germany's War Effort   551

Forces Employed in the Soviet Counter-Offensives   597

German Submarines   613

German Occupation Zones   797

France's Losses   798

Progress in the Production and Performance of Fighter Aircraft   846

Progress in the Production and Performance of Bomber Aircraft   848

Preface

HAS the time come to attempt a synthesis of the events of the Second World War? The vast number of books and articles on the subject, from all over the world, would seem to suggest that it has. In fact, the sheer quantity of works sets the historian well-nigh insoluble problems; it is no more possible for one man to read everything than it is for him to avoid leaving important gaps. The quality of these publications is most uneven; memoirs and accounts of spying and battles abound, but the sources are not always disclosed and in most countries the archives are not available for research. In short, the historian is gorged with details but the essential nourishment is often lacking.

The variety of languages in which these publications appear gives rise to further difficulties which are not always solved by the existence of a translation, more readily obtainable, incidentally, as a commercial publication than as a work of scholarship and all too frequently presented in mutilated form, generally shorn of its critical apparatus.

It must be added that historical research on the subject has reached different stages in different countries; some of the belligerents – Japan, for example – are only now beginning to make their voices heard. In other countries, political events have more than once changed the trend in historical writing – for example the repercussions of 'destalinisation' in the Soviet Union have enabled Soviet historians to inquire into an event of such major importance as the German-Soviet pact although not as yet to study it from the original documents. We can only form some idea of it through German documents. Finally, in every country, the younger generation sees the events from a different angle than those who lived through them.

It is obvious that, in such circumstances, any attempt at synthesis must be tentative and provisional. It is equally plain that it cannot be the work of one man but of teams who often have not yet completed their task. Thus *La Commission d'Histoire de la Résistance en France* has given itself ten years in which to draw up an exact chronology of the underground French Resistance movement, with some 150,000 index cards to deal with.

This book could not have been contemplated without the work accomplished during the last twenty years by the research team of the *Revue d'histoire de la deuxième guerre mondiale*,[1] which I am privileged to direct. The reader is requested to refer to this periodical to complete the selective bibliography placed at the end of the book. Through the specialists working on the *Revue* I have been able to acquaint myself with works which, either because of their technical nature or the language in which they were written, would otherwise have been inaccessible to me. It gives me pleasure to express my gratitude to them and I have been glad to quote them in my bibliography on every possible occasion.

It is obvious that the study of a conflict that set most of the world ablaze demanded a modicum of international co-operation. The *Revue d'histoire de la deuxième guerre mondiale* has often had occasion to devote special numbers to particular subjects, the result of co-operation of historians from various countries.

The recently created International Committee for the History of the Second World War[2] will no doubt lead to an increase in the exchange of books and documents which is so essential; it will enable various research organisations throughout the world to exchange information and, primarily, to make each other's acquaintance; it will help to bring to a successful conclusion the systematic card indexing of the sources of the Second World War, started by the French Committee for the History of the Second World War, and intended to gather together bibliographical information with card indexes providing guidance on the material held in archives.

In such a changing picture, the present work cannot claim to do anything but offer a provisional record of our present knowledge, an attempt to clarify rather than to explain, a factual account which poses more questions than it answers. No one will be surprised that a book written by a Frenchman and first published in France should lay stress on France during the war; certainly not with the intention of exaggerating the role of France, because everyone knows that it was a secondary one, but because it is plain that a French historian is most likely to produce something worthwhile when writing about France, even though he will find it more difficult to be impartial than on other matters. On the other hand, in the present state of historical research, it seemed necessary to stick close to the events and give an account of how they happened as well as how they were connected. I hope nonetheless that I have given the reader a picture of the Second World War that will enable him to understand its main features and follow its development.

Although the Second World War ended with the defeat of Germany and Japan, it began with successes for them on such a scale that, at the

1. Published by the Presses Universitaires de France.
2. With its Offices at 32, rue de Léningrad, Paris VIII.

time, it seemed these could be decisive. The first part of this book tells the story of the first half of the war, the success of the Axis powers.

From 1943 onwards, it seemed uncertain what course the war would take: the Wehrmacht had been checked, had indeed even begun to retreat, both in the USSR and in Africa, but deadly and destructive fighting was still taking place thousands of miles away from German territory. As for Japan, although she had not succeeded in extending her conquests, she still remained out of reach in her archipelago and could exploit 'Greater Asia' without let or hindrance. Of the three Axis partners, Italy had proved the frailest; her armies had suffered great setbacks, her fleet no longer dared emerge from its bases, her war economy had revealed its shortcomings and the Italian people were becoming more and more reluctant to fight.

On the Allied side, the USSR had made an extraordinary recovery, thanks to her vast resources and territory, the efforts and sufferings of her people and, finally, Stalin's iron fist and the solid structure of the Communist party; her successes had earned the Red Army the admiration of the occupied peoples; they had banished to oblivion the German-Soviet pact and Soviet imperialism. Everywhere the Communist parties, with unswerving loyalty to their ideological fatherland, were playing an increasing role in the secret Resistance or in the exiled governments. Britain had successfully extricated herself from the dramatic situation and isolation into which she had plunged after the defeat of France but her war effort had now reached its ceiling and would not be able to increase without American aid. The great event of the end of 1942 was the entry into the lists of an American army, as yet inexpert, of course, but possessing unequalled resources of war potential. The United States was struggling virtually alone against Japan; she was providing the Allies, including the USSR, with their lifeline of convoys, tanks, aircraft and dollar loans; through her industrial production and the expedient of lend-lease, she had become the arsenal of the Allied coalition. Thanks to the success of the convoy system, her munitions and men were reaching their action stations in the Pacific, Africa and Europe.

Up to now, the struggle had been on land and at sea; the air force had done no more than provide support for the army and the navy, often a decisive support; but it was not autonomous. Thanks to the massive American output of planes, the air force was from now on to play a strategic role, perhaps a major one, through its raids. Italy, Germany and Japan were to be ravaged long before the armies of their enemies approached their frontiers. One after another, the neutral powers – led by the South Americans – descended into the arena. The origins of the war were becoming lost in the past; were they still fighting for Poland or was she to be sacrificed to the Allied entente? What is more, since Roosevelt and Stalin openly displayed their anti-colonialism, was not the British Commonwealth itself under threat? The conflict had not only expanded beyond all measure, it had changed its directions and aims.

One thing which was however becoming certain was that victory would go to whichever of the two camps could manufacture the largest quantity of arms or discover soon enough irresistible new weapons. To invent or to produce these the belligerents strained every nerve and mobilised all their resources. Whatever their political régimes and ideologies, all the great fighting powers were transformed into 'companies for waging war'. Behind the strategist and the soldier and supporting or preparing their impetus, the scientist, the engineer and the working masses sustained their hopes of holding out and winning. Propaganda was still stifling any production of disinterested literary or artistic works; writers and artists were enlisting on both sides; research workers were being sent for, formed into teams and briefed; in every country the war really was becoming a total war; but in this unprecedented effort, it was the scientist who from now on was to play the primary role. He was, of course, working for war and destruction but each of his discoveries was equally full of promise for peace and the post-war period.

For the moment, at the beginning of 1943 soldiers and diplomats were still occupying the front of the stage. When things began to go wrong, would the Axis partners tear each other to pieces or would they manage to collaborate? Would the Allies produce a common strategy, and, if so, what? Would their alliance, forced on them by a common enemy, stand the test, and to what kind of post-war conditions would they lead? While ruin piled upon ruin throughout the world; while endless misfortunes, old and new, descended upon hundreds of millions of men and women; while hunger and disease were ravaging countries once rich and healthy; while millions of Jews were finding their way to gas chamber and crematorium; while further millions of human beings were being uprooted; while young people all over the world were sacrificing themselves, the whole planet was being shaken and convulsed. The power of nations was gradually falling into a new order and a new hierarchy; peoples who had been subjugated for centuries were feeling that the time had come for nationhood; those who had been defeated in the first round were preparing to reorganise themselves and, by fighting on, achieve freedom and rebirth; above all, in their laboratories, scientists were bringing forth the world of tomorrow, pregnant, if it should so wish, with the real victories of mankind over its real opponents: natural forces, famine, cold, ignorance, social injustice and poverty.

The Forces Involved in September 1939.
Strategic Plans

O N September 1, 1939, at 4.45 a.m. the German Army crossed into Poland. On September 3 at 11 a.m. Britain, and six hours later France, in fulfilment of their pledges to Poland, declared a state of war to exist with Germany. The Second World War had begun. What were the forces involved and what were the motives, aims and plans for bringing them into action?

I THE ANTAGONISTS: THEIR HUMAN AND ECONOMIC POTENTIAL

Superficially at least, the war was starting as in 1914: Germany was to have to fight on two fronts. In fact, however, on her eastern front she was protected by the German-Soviet pact and was faced, not as before by the Russian colossus, but by weak little Poland. To the west she had the same opponents as before: France and Britain, whose armaments, state of readiness and morale were, however, very different from in 1914. In addition, France had been forced to split up her armed forces; although not required to cover the defence of her frontier with Spain, as had once been feared, she still had to keep watchful guard against the blustering claims of Mussolini.

In human and economic terms, the democratic countries' potential was vastly greater than that of the Axis powers. It is true that by annexing Austria and Bohemia the Reich had increased its population from 70 to 85 million; with the Italians, the Fascist states were roughly equal in numbers to their opponents in Europe. In theory, the Third Reich could raise some 12 or 13 million soldiers and the Fascist propaganda machine had always boasted of the 8 million bayonets brandished in support of the Duce. But the democracies had at their disposal the limitless resources of manpower from vast colonial empires. In the event, apart from some reluctance on the part of South Africa, the Commonwealth showed no hesitation in faithfully following the mother country's lead into war; it was the same for the countries 'protected' by France.

At the outset, the Wehrmacht were able to deploy 54 first-line divisions and to reinforce them within a space of days by 59 reserve divisions. The French had 35 divisions, increased by mobilisation to 86 within a period of a few weeks; Poland had 30 divisions that could be brought up to 42; but Britain, which had recently reintroduced conscription, was able, a month after the declaration of war, to send over to France only two divisions. The French and Polish armies thus had to bear the brunt of the first attack alone. But even after leaving considerable forces on their Alpine frontier, in Corsica, in Tunisia, in the Near East and in Djibouti, the French army had a good chance of achieving numerical superiority on its north-eastern border. If the Poles were obviously going to be forced back on the defensive, the French army could, in theory, come to their help by taking the offensive. Did not the Franco-Polish convention of May 15 provide for a French attack a fortnight after mobilisation?

But mobilising large armed forces is not enough; you still have to provide them with officers, equipment and modern weapons. The democracies clearly had ample means to do this; their economic superiority was as striking as the weaknesses of the Axis powers were obvious from the statistics.

Although Germany had enough coal for her needs, she had to import iron ore from Sweden, in summer via the Baltic but in winter through the port of Narvik and via the more hazardous Norwegian territorial waters. On the other hand, despite the development of *ersatz* materials, synthetic rubber and petrol were far from meeting the needs of the war machine and though rationing had already been in operation for a number of years, massive imports of foodstuffs were required to feed the population. The Italians were in an even more parlous plight; they had no crude oil or iron whatsoever and their coal was imported – from England!

On the other hand, Britain had recovered from the economic depression; in 1938 her production was almost 20 per cent greater than in 1929. Though France lagged somewhat behind, the fact remained that the two allies together produced more steel than Germany. True, they were considerably dependent on imports, but the resources of raw materials in their empires were inexhaustible and their gold reserves would enable them to purchase anything they needed anywhere in the world, particularly in the United States.

II THE NAVIES

The shipment of men and materials presented few problems, since the democracies held complete command of the seas.

When Germany rearmed, she deliberately neglected the Navy. After the naval treaty signed with Britain in 1935, by which the tonnage of the German fleet was fixed at 35 per cent of that of the Royal Navy, Admiral Raeder had drawn up an ambitious programme of naval construction, providing for the launching over a period of twelve years of 13 battle-ships, 20 cruisers, 2 aircraft-carriers and 250 submarines. But by September 1939 this programme had barely started and its implementation had been greatly delayed. The naval strength of the Reich was only 3 pocket battle-ships, 2 heavy and 6 light cruisers, some 30 torpedo-boats and 57 sub-marines; 2 battle cruisers, the *Scharnhorst* and *Gneisenau*, were undergoing trials; 2 heavy battleships, the *Bismarck* and *Tirpitz*, were still being built and nearing completion.

What is more, when there were differences of opinion between the Kriegsmarine and the Luftwaffe, Hitler had come out in favour of Marshal Goering, the Air Force Commander, so that all naval air forces, be they land- or sea-based, remained subordinate to the Luftwaffe. Admiral Raeder had not even been allowed to have the reconnaissance aircraft which he wanted; in short, he had failed to obtain recognition of the necessity for all sea operations to be under the control of one single commander, in charge of both air and naval forces. The German Navy was thus in danger of being deprived of air support at the critical moment, the more so as Goering was convinced that command of the sea could be achieved by aircraft alone and land-based aircraft at that. 'I shall seek out the English fleet with the Luftwaffe,' he declared, 'and I shall drive it from one bay to the other all round the British Isles until it doesn't know where to find shelter next.' Good understanding between the chiefs of the services concerned could have reduced the gap between their two conceptions, but Raeder and Goering were at daggers drawn.

The Italian fleet was also of recent growth and possessed a number of very fast ships, but it, too, was not complete; its building programme had been based on the assumption of a war coming in 1942, so that in 1939, four 35,000-ton battleships were still under construction. The Italian Navy had been on a war footing since 1935 and this had resulted in premature wear and tear of material. Above all, fuel-oil stocks were com-pletely inadequate; in September 1939, they amounted to some 1,600,000 tons against a monthly consumption of the order of 200,000 tons. Finally, as in Germany, there were fundamental differences of conception between the Navy and the Air Force – and Mussolini had decided in favour of the latter. The Duce considered, in fact, that the Italian peninsula was 'one big aircraft-carrier in the middle of the Mediterranean'; consequently the Italian Navy had no need for aircraft-carriers or torpedo-carrying aircraft. It had at its disposal merely a few slow reconnaissance planes which were themselves provided by the Air Force; were the Navy to be attacked by enemy aircraft, it would have to call on land-based aircraft for support

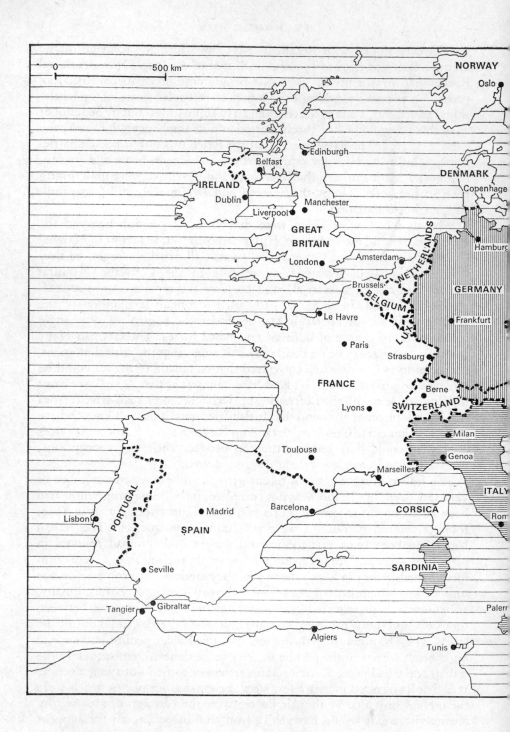

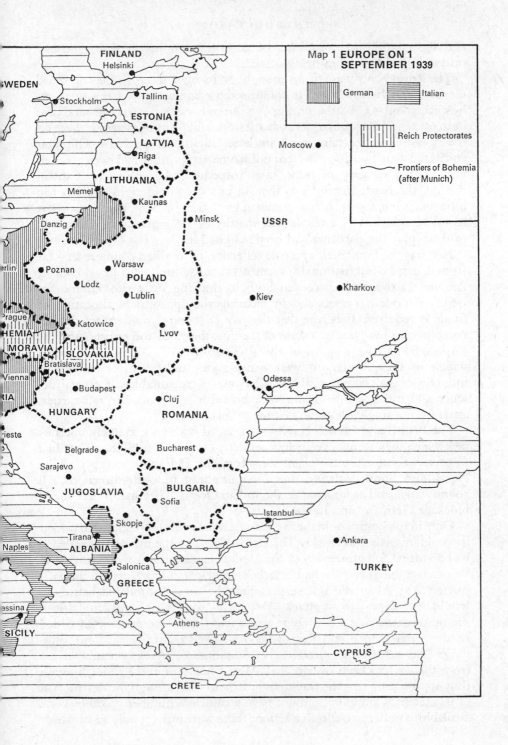

Map 1 **EUROPE ON 1 SEPTEMBER 1939**

German
Italian
Reich Protectorates
Frontiers of Bohemia (after Munich)

FINLAND
Helsinki
SWEDEN
Stockholm
Tallinn
ESTONIA
LATVIA
Riga
Moscow
LITHUANIA
Memel
Kaunas
Danzig
Minsk
USSR
Berlin
Poznan
Warsaw
Lodz
POLAND
Lublin
Kharkov
Prague
Katowice
Kiev
BOHEMIA
Lvov
MORAVIA
SLOVAKIA
Bratislava
Vienna
Budapest
Odessa
RIA
Cluj
Trieste
HUNGARY
ROMANIA
Belgrade
Bucharest
Sarajevo
JUGOSLAVIA
BULGARIA
Sofia
Skopje
Istanbul
Tirana
Ankara
Naples
ALBANIA
Salonica
TURKEY
GREECE
Messina
Athens
SICILY
CYPRUS
CRETE

and the complicated problems of co-ordination involved in such an operation were far from being solved.

The Royal Navy was strong enough, on its own, to crush the combined German and Italian fleets. It comprised 12 battleships – many of them, however, old – 3 battle cruisers, 7 aircraft-carriers, 64 cruisers, 200 destroyers and 60 submarines; 9 battleships and 6 aircraft-carriers were on the stocks. True, certain important bases such as Scapa Flow, Gibraltar and Malta were poorly protected; unfortunately, priority had been given to guns at the expense of mines and torpedoes. According to Captain Roskill, the battle instructions then in use were over rigid and left too little initiative to squadron commanders. But in September 1939 the Royal Navy taken as a whole was worthy of its glorious tradition and ready to play the part that had been assigned it.

Nor was the French Navy a pale reflection of its allied counterpart – far from it, despite international agreements that had limited its development, Admiral Darlan had succeeded both in drawing up a programme for building modern vessels and in securing the appropriate allocation of funds as required. It is true that the *Jean Bart* and *Richelieu* were not yet completed in 1939 but two ships of the line, the 7,600-ton cruisers and the torpedo-boats, were particularly successful. The submarines varied widely in size: the largest were ocean-going and powerful enough to intercept enemy convoys; the smaller ones were suitable for coastal defence and mine laying. There was, however, only one aircraft-carrier, apart from a single obsolete 'floating seaplane base'.

The British and French Navies were faced with an extremely onerous task which they were nevertheless perfectly capable of fulfilling. They had to protect some 7,000 merchant ships totalling 18 million tons plying the North and South Atlantic, the Mediterranean in both directions, all round Africa and as far away as the Indian Ocean. They had moreover to blockade Germany and Italy.

Only in the Baltic could the German fleet move about freely; to have left it would involve grave risks. The Italian fleet had the means to challenge its opponents for supremacy of the Mediterranean, but it was particularly vulnerable. Neither side had attached sufficient importance to aircraft-carriers; the Allies did not suspect that the most formidable battleship would be easy prey to air attack. Above all – somewhat surprisingly since the unrestricted passage of ships at sea was the prerequisite of an Allied success – the French and British Navies lacked escort vessels and long-range land-based strike aircraft; the techniques of attacks on submarines from the air had been overlooked. Meanwhile Admiral Raeder, though fully appreciating that the way to fight Britain was through the destruction of its merchant shipping, did not have a sufficient number of submarines available to undertake effective action; there were just 57, only 22 of which were ocean-going, whereas Admiral Doenitz, the submarine-warfare expert, considered that one thousand would have been required on the outbreak of hostilities. But if the Allies seemed in no danger of losing the war at sea, they could not win it there either. And the fact is that in September 1939, they were far from possessing on land and in the air the superiority they enjoyed at sea.

III THE LAND FORCES

The modern British Army was still in the throes of being born, the Polish Army's equipment antiquated. On the other hand, the reputation of the French Army, victorious in the First World War, was immense, even in Germany. But the reality did not match up with the memory. Individual infantry equipment was reasonably good and the basic artillery weapon was the well-tried 75-mm gun, but anti-aircraft defence was quite inadequate. The most serious deficiency, however, lay in the tanks. It is true that the manufacturing programme drawn up in 1936 had been largely completed. Provision had been made for 50 battalions equipped with light tanks and 12 with heavy tanks. In all, out of the 2,500 tanks that had been ordered, by September 1, 1939 the Army had received 1,770. These tanks were well armoured but, on the whole, rather lightly armed; for lack of radio equipment, their intercommunication was poor. Only the heavy tanks were powerful both in weapons and armour, with the accompanying drawback of low speed and high petrol consumption which reduced their range of action; above all, the Army had only 385 of them.

As for anti-tank weapons, the artillery's 47-mm gun was capable of penetrating the heaviest armour, but their manufacture had begun only in 1937, and out of the thousand ordered, only 411 were ready by September 1939. These guns were entirely unprotected against air attack and being horse-drawn they required a long time to set up, in contrast to the enemy's motorised and armoured equivalent.

All in all, when one considers that a German armoured division comprised some 350 tanks, it is plain that the French Army had the means to equip several armoured divisions, but in fact she was unable to raise even one against the six Wehrmacht divisions.[1] What was the reason for this discrepancy? After all, there were Frenchmen who had preached mechanised warfare; following General Estienne's lead, Colonel de Gaulle had conducted, in print and in conversation with political leaders, a campaign in favour of forming an armoured battle corps. It had been in vain.

1. France had two light mechanised divisions, which is not at all the same thing.

Hardly anyone had supported him, with the exception of Paul Reynaud who was clear-sighted enough to recognise that an offensive arm of this sort would enable France to fulfil its obligations towards her allies in Eastern and Central Europe. De Gaulle had caused dismay amongst other leading politicians by proposing to man this armoured corps by means of a professional army, the mere mention of which raised spectres of the Pretorian Guards or the Grenadiers at the time of the 19th Brumaire. Above all, at the technical level, he had failed to convince the military leaders, his superior officers.

Yet French military intelligence (the *Deuxième Bureau*) seems to have given fair warning to the French general staff. As early as 1935, it had pointed out the Germans' great innovation in using autonomous armoured units as a battering ram and it had described the composition of these units and their use of air co-operation. It had emphasised that hostilities might begin with a sudden attack; it had drawn special attention to the steady increase in the Wehrmacht's offensive strength. The articles by General Guderian, the German expert on tank warfare, had been translated into French.

Perhaps even the most intelligent people had been stultified by the precedent of the 1914–18 war and the prestige of its great – and victorious – military leaders. The French general staff listened more readily to the opponents of Guderian in Germany itself – Lieutenant-Colonel Boentsch, for example, who did not believe that a defensive front, solidly held, could be broken through by tanks alone. The Supreme Commander, General Gamelin, still convinced of the truth of the axiom that 'in battle, the infantry reigns supreme', had expressed the view of all his colleagues when he laid down in his directive of December 15, 1937: 'Tanks alone are unsuited to seize possession of any terrain or to occupy it for any length of time.' Consequently, 'their sole task is to act for the direct and immediate benefit of the infantry.' This is why, in September 1939, the French Army was not short of tanks but had only two light mechanised divisions; there was thus absolutely no possibility that France would attack the enemy in order to relieve Poland. But were the Allied air forces at least in a position to undertake effective aggression over German territory?

IV THE AIR FORCES

Between the two wars, the use of aircraft, a new weapon with unknown possibilities, had been the subject of passionate debate. Amongst all the military experts the Italian Douhet had stood out by reason of his coherent, indeed dogmatic, doctrine. According to him, as the aeroplane would in future make trench warfare impossible, the Army as well as the Navy would now have to step down in favour of the Air Force. Long-range bombers seemed to him capable of destroying the military and economic structure of an enemy so extensively as to paralyse its armed forces and demoralise its civilian population. Douhet used the metaphor of an eagle whose eggs are smashed by destroying its eyrie. All offensive operations would be the exclusive prerogative of the bomber aircraft; they would secure mastery of the skies not by air combat but by the destruction of enemy potential on the ground. As a result the Army and Navy were restricted to a purely defensive role; in Douhet's words, 'in order to put the full weight of attack in the air'.

In every country, there were three schools of thought. Some experts adopted Douhet's thinking, but they experienced great difficulty in imposing their revolutionary views on such powerful and traditionalist groups as the Army and Navy. Moreover, there had been no conflict to test the soundness of 'Douhet's doctrine'; in the Abyssinian war or the war between China and Japan, the superiority of the Italians and the Japanese had provided an immediate solution to a problem that would be posed in quite different terms in Europe; in the Spanish Civil War, the destruction of the enemy's potential was not to be contemplated. Other experts supported close participation in the ground fighting by the Air Force acting as a sort of long-range artillery or providing protective cover for the advance of armoured units. But there were many old-fashioned theorists who thought that an air force could never be anything more than an auxiliary service complementing the other two.

In Germany the Luftwaffe had enjoyed the benefit of unlimited funds since 1935; it had been provided with an organisation and material based on the most modern techniques; it had never been hampered by the need to preserve or adapt old, existing equipment. Although the air industry had been set up hurriedly and hastily equipped – mass production had not started until 1938 – in 1939 the total production of the German aeronautical industry had nonetheless reached 885 aircraft per month and in September the Luftwaffe possessed more than 4,000 aircraft, including one thousand fighters and 1,800 bombers.

Plans had been worked out for the close co-operation of aircraft with tanks; thus 450 bombers – Stukas – had been organised and equipped to dive-bomb enemy positions. The Germans had given priority to fast, light, twin-engined bombers, capable of carrying only one ton of bombs. These bombers were admirably suited for combined army/air operations, although they were not out of the range of enemy fighters. Their drawback was that Britain lay practically beyond their own range. Also they had been produced at the cost of neglecting the heavy four-engined bomber.

In general, the upper echelons of the German Air Force still lacked professional knowledge; many of them had come to it from the Army. Their supreme commander, Goering, had only had experience as a junior air force officer and former fighter pilot from World War I; he thought of the heavy four-engined bomber as a sitting target. The result was that the Reich possessed a powerful air force for waging a war of limited duration over a relatively restricted area; but it had no strategic aircraft.

The Italian contribution to the strength of the Luftwaffe was some 1,600 aircraft; they had been tried out over Spain but their quality was generally inferior and only 40 per cent of them were new.

France's industrial weakness was particularly noticeable in aircraft production. The aircraft ordered before 1937 were based on prototypes dating from 1934 and already out of date. In 1939, mass production of fighter aircraft had not yet started; there was no light bomber prototype and no dive bomber, although the *Deuxième Bureau* had drawn attention to the importance of this type of aircraft in the Luftwaffe. The most recent plan, called Plan V, called for the production of 4,700 aircraft which would provide a modern force of 2,600 front-line aircraft. In order to launch this programme, it had been necessary to purchase armament and equip new factories. By these means, the scheduled production had been maintained and starting from a monthly total of barely 35 aircraft in 1938, it had risen to 220 in 1939 and almost 300 at the end of the year. But the general staff had asked for absolute priority to be given to the fighter arm; bombers took second place and what was more, there was no good prototype.

To sum up, according to the files of the *Direction du Matériel aérien militaire*, on September 3, 1939 the exact situation was as follows: out of a total of 1,407 aircraft, 708 of the 1,157 fighters and 125 of the 175 bombers were with their squadrons, that is to say available for operations. Only part of these aircraft were equipped with the latest technical devices: variable pitch airscrews, superchargers, retractable undercarriage, radio and so on. Clearly, such an air force was incapable of attacking the military and industrial installations of the Reich; they would be at a disadvantage even over their own territory against the German Air Force. Could they at least expect the co-operation of a powerful British Air Force?

As the British had devoted their main efforts to the RAF, it was, after the Navy, their best service. Out of a total of 1,700 aircraft based in the UK, 1,100 of them were modern, more or less equally divided between fighters and bombers. The originality of the bombers lay in their variety. While most of them were medium bombers of limited range, there were also four-engined heavy bombers. Finally, by developing a theory that had been put forward by a Frenchman, Camille Rougeron, the British had begun manufacturing light bombers – Mosquitoes – which were as fast as fighters, so that defensive armament could be dispensed with; with this saving in weight, they could carry a payload of one ton for long distances – as far as Berlin. Britain was thus the only belligerent which by September 1939 had tried to provide herself with a strategic Air Force capable of carrying the war into enemy territory while still using the best of her Air Force in defence of her own territory. The question was whether there was anything left over to support the armies in the field.

For the moment, the French and British Air Forces together barely came to half the size of the Luftwaffe. But this figure was meaningless, for the whole RAF, planned basically for the defence of its national territory, would be needed to be deployed in France and the French general staff would have to find the best way to use the French Air Force. In any case, the planes of the Allies would no more be in a position to rush to Poland's aid than would their tanks, despite their promise of protection. It seemed likely to prove an empty promise.

V CAUSES OF THE DEMOCRATIC COUNTRIES'
SHORTCOMINGS

The democratic countries were thus in a position of inferiority on land and in the air. What was the explanation for this discrepancy between potential and reality?

Since 1936, Germany had been preparing for war. The Four Year Plan had set up an economy based on the principle of autarchy and imposed austerity on the living conditions of the population. In the metallurgical, chemical and electrical industries, Germany had, beyond any doubt, a technical lead; a lead that was equally marked in scientific research, theoretical as well as applied. From now onwards, Czech industry – and in particular the firm of Skoda – would be adding its own contribution. It was true that progress was sometimes slow, whether in the field of artificial silk or rubber production, industrial oils extracted from coal, the exploitation of ore with low iron content or, most important of all, in petrol production. But the Reich's political and diplomatic efforts had now succeeded in making available for use the Hungarian wheat lands, copper from Yugoslavia, crude oil from Romania and manganese from Turkey. The USSR could supply all the rest, even if it might have to come via the Trans-Siberian railway. Thus the whole of Germany's national effort had been controlled and disciplined with warlike determination. It was true that there were some parts of the machinery which were creaking and that economically the Reich was still vulnerable. But for the moment it had made maximum use of its potential. This was not true of the democracies.

In the case of Britain, the reason for this was simple. After the 1914–18 war, she had disarmed and reverted to a professional Army. Next, she had pursued a policy of conciliation towards Germany, which was reinforced by suspicion of France, who was accused of suffering from chronic germanophobia and inveterate imperialism. The British political leaders, above all Neville Chamberlain, had been slow to become aware of the danger of Hitler, despite Winston Churchill's warnings. Subsequently, in view of the protection from immediate German attack afforded by that impassable anti-tank ditch, the English Channel, Britain had looked first to her own defence at sea and in the air. The Royal Navy took charge of the first, and the fighter aircraft, which had been given priority, were responsible for the second. To fulfil her obligations towards her ally, France, Britain had reintroduced conscription, mistakenly perhaps, since the formation of armoured units doubtless deserved higher priority than the creation of a large Army. But although it was plain that hardly any other possibility existed and that action was proceeding as quickly as possible, there seemed every chance that, in time, a vast rearmament programme could gradually be implemented. But there was one condition: the enemy must not be in too great a hurry.

But why had France, whose Army had won the 1914–18 war, who had frequently viewed the intentions of the Weimar Republic with such a suspicious eye, and who had not really disarmed after 1918, why had France not rearmed in earnest after Hitler came to power? Was it the fault of her politics, her diplomacy, her lack of money, the short-sightedness of her general staff, the shortcomings of her economy – and, most important of all, of her industry? Or were all these things to blame? It is indeed surprising, to say the least, that the very same French government which on April 17, 1934 had refused to sign an international pact for the limitation of armaments, thus leaving entire responsibility for her defence to France alone, should at the same time have cut back its expenditure on armaments. On later occasions, it is true, the amount of this expenditure had been steadily increased and the French Parliament had never failed to approve it. The fact remains that, at certain moments which were decisive for the country's security, financial considerations – the stability of the franc or devaluation – did hamper French rearmament and that, in the ministerial discussions preceding the presentation of the Budget to Parliament, the French Treasury often cut down the amounts requested by the Defence Ministry.

It is equally true that the War Minister had taken a long time to work out production schedules and set up organisations capable of putting them into effect. Hesitation over which orders to place, rivalry between various organisations and the lack of flexibility in certain financial regulations no doubt explained the fact that, although complaining of being starved of funds, the War Ministry often found it impossible to spend even the resources which it had been granted, so much so that 60 per cent of the allocations for 1935 had had to be carried over to 1936; hardly the way to encourage the Finance Minister to be more open handed.

However, once the programmes had been drawn up, the prototypes chosen, the funds made available and the orders placed, if excessive delay then occurred in the production of guns, tanks or aircraft, it could no longer be blamed on the civil service or the government or the military but fairly and squarely on the armament manufacturers. The nationalisation of these industries, decided on by the *Front Populaire* more for political and moral than military reasons, had given rise to passionate debate; it had probably led in the first instance to confusion and further delay before achieving a streamlining of the industries, and later on it was not able to remedy all at once shortcomings which were common to much of French industry: antiquated plant, shortage of trained technicians, insufficient quantities of machine tools. In addition, the liberal economy was ill adapted to undertake the planning, authoritarian decisions and price control required for a proper mobilisation of industry.

Furthermore, the general staff, whose task it was, after all, to place the orders, needed a coherent theory of warfare and clear and stable ideas as to its needs. In fact, at no time did the military authorities ever work out an overall plan of rearmament; of course, they wanted to break new ground but, lacking precise aims, their discussions of prototypes were inconclusive. 'Not one single army man,' Minister Dautry told the Parliamentary Commission of Investigation, 'realised the extent of the industrial problems that the country would have to solve.' How did the country itself view the matter? Were the French fully aware of the threat from Hitler and did they really have the will to fight to dispel it?

VI MORAL FORCES

A professional army draws its strength from its professionalism. But a national army finds its justification and fighting spirit in the nation from which it springs. On this point, too, the situation was very different in the two camps.

In Germany the Nazis had fully imposed their harsh régime. The whole population had been drafted; public opinion was rigidly controlled; the civil administration was under close observation by the Party or else replaced by the Party's own officials. Never had a great people been more completely brought to heel or so powerfully coerced to follow its leaders with unquestioning obedience. It is true that the Führer's supreme authority, the strange ascendancy that he exerted over the masses, the blind obedience that he both demanded and received from all, did not prevent personal rivalries, sectarian strife or conflicts between competing branches of the armed forces. But nothing of this showed to the outside world and nothing was to show until after the first setbacks. To all appearances – moreover, in fact – the German nation was solidly behind its heaven-sent leader; they were grateful to him for what had been accomplished, the successes that had been achieved and a new-found sense of greatness.

The Weimar Republic now belonged to a discredited past; in any case, democratic ideas had never penetrated to more than a section of the German middle classes. Economic self-sufficiency had, of course, led to severe restrictions on everyone but it kept the wheels turning and it had got rid of unemployment. The higher ranks of industry were thankful to the Führer for having put an end to economic stagnation and the mass of the workers were grateful to him for having once more ensured them steady employment. As for the general staff, the reluctance and misgivings of some of its members at the time of the remilitarisation of the Rhineland, the annexation of Austria or the Sudeten affair, were now nothing but a memory. Hitler had put a stop to the humiliation suffered by Germany in 1918; he had managed to wipe out a large part of the Treaty of Versailles; he had given the Reich a powerful army once again and revived a sense of national duty in the people; in a word, the generals had gained too much from being obedient not to become submissive.

Did this mean that the whole of the German people were going to war with lively step and a song in their hearts? Goebbels' propaganda machine said so and the cinema cameras recorded it. All the same, foreign observers noticed more resignation than enthusiasm. But if there were qualms, they were not obvious, and the opposition said nothing. It is true that it had been roughly handled: Communists, Socialists, trades union leaders and sometimes Christian Democrats had been thrown into the concentration camps – Buchenwald or Dachau – that had been opened with them in mind; the police were keeping a watchful eye on those who for the moment had been left free. And the Churches, Roman Catholic or Protestant, were suspicious of Nazi paganism, all the more so since the Pope had condemned it. But the clergy who spoke out against euthanasia or the Nazis' ideas on education would then go on to ask the faithful to pray together for the Fatherland and its Führer.

The only possible active opposition would have to come from outside, from those who had emigrated. But the fact is that they were too dissimilar to unite or even to make contact. Communists and Socialists might be brothers but they were hostile ones and the German-Soviet pact had for the moment reduced the German Communists to silence, especially those who had taken refuge in Moscow. There was no common ground between early National Socialists who were followers of Otto Strasser and politicians like Brüning from the Weimar Republic: the latter, incidentally, had taken refuge in Switzerland and was lying low and saying nothing. The exiles wanted Hitler's downfall but they could not accept the only prospect that made this downfall seem possible: the defeat of Germany, their Fatherland.

Even the Jewish exiles showed little unanimity. Their desire to be assimilated and their sentimental loyalty to Germany amazed their co-religionists in the countries in which they had taken refuge. Some of them tried to settle down in their new homeland; others had thoughts of going to Palestine; nowhere did they form a coherent, active opposition group.

Willingly or passively, with enthusiasm or resignation, the German people were following their Führer on the path to war, and they would continue to follow him as long as that path led to victory. Did the same state of mind prevail amongst the population of Britain and France? In Britain there was a current of feeling that was anti-war, represented in Parliament by Lloyd George, but the traditional good citizenship and patriotism of the British was too strong for this trend to appear openly, except in certain circles. It was true that in the government itself, even if Churchill's determination was well-known, Neville Chamberlain's seemed less certain. But in fact, although the British faced up to their obligations with calmness and resolution, they did not consider themselves as being fully involved as yet; neither the fate of the British Commonwealth nor their security were at stake. In the first round, France versus Germany, they were rather like spectators.

On the other hand, the French knew that they were immediately and directly concerned. Mobilisation had taken place in an orderly manner according to plan, but instead of the enthusiasm of 1914 there was resignation, as is painfully plain in the films showing the expression on the faces of those leaving from the Gare de l'Est. In the French Parliament, no one had seriously questioned the necessity of declaring war; an end had to be put to the series of surrenders that had only encouraged Hitler's aggressive intentions. But the spirit of Munich had still not disappeared, nor its corollary, the attempt to find a diplomatic compromise that might avoid bloodshed.

From this and from other points of view, the German-Soviet pact assumed exceptional importance. For the traditionally anti-German right wing, it reinforced the militant anti-Communism aroused by the *Front Populaire* and led to the firm belief that the war would benefit only the USSR and international revolution. This point of view was represented by Pierre Laval.

As for the Left, its unity had already been compromised by the defeat of the *Front Populaire*, which was now only part of history. The Communist party had shown the most determined opposition to Nazism, both at the time of the Spanish Civil War and of Munich; it was certainly true that the disclosure of the German-Soviet pact had surprised and dumbfounded it; so much so that it voted in support of the military estimates shortly afterwards. Later on, its leaders had tamely knuckled under to the Comintern's instructions; as at the time of the occupation of the Ruhr the party had become pacifist once again, or at least, neutralist.

As a result the *Confederation Générale du Travail* was split from top to bottom. The mass of workers remained torn, obsessed by the cares of day-to-day existence and the desire to improve their standard of living in accordance with the splendid promises of the *Front Populaire*, or else imbued with deep feelings of pacifism. Despite Léon Blum's urgings, the Socialist party had not yet completed the swing which was to bring them round, after refusing to vote for the military estimates, to support, if not to request, a coalition government to set about the task of waging war in earnest. Even those intellectuals most strongly opposed to Fascism often disliked the thought of a conflict the first effect of which would be to restrict freedom in France. And in the minds of every Frenchman the new war aroused thoughts of the holocaust of 1914–18, the futility of which had been so frequently condemned and a repetition of which probably even more horrible than before, seemed in no way necessary. In a people that twenty years earlier had lost more than a million of its young men, there was a biological reflex to avoid further bloodshed. The result was a rejection of war, implicit rather than explicit, which took the form, for example, of trying to find 'special assignments' which in 1914–18 would have been called quite bluntly 'funk-holes'.

This firm belief in the absurdity of war was expressed by Albert Camus in his Diary. He condemns war as 'revolting, an inexcusable massacre'. He finds it difficult to excuse the conscripts who accept 'their obligation to go yet feel remorse that they were not brave enough to stay behind'. He refuses to let himself be caught up in the machinery of war; he states that 'this war is not inevitable' and concludes that 'there are means of stopping it that can be tried'. Many Frenchmen thought as he did and many conscripts wrote back to their families in similar vein.

In a country where economic stagnation had slowed down the production of armaments, where units had not received their proper complement of equipment, where the population were trying to persuade themselves that mobilisation did not mean war, how could the government and the general staff fail to favour a long-term strategy, defensive in the first instance, with the object of minimising the sufferings of the French people and avoiding unnecessary bloodshed, in short, with the object of letting them off lightly?

VII STRATEGIC PLANS

The strategies worked out by the antagonists were based not on abstractions but on the heartfelt feelings of the various peoples as well as on the actual possibilities allowed by their economies and armed forces.

Although partly protected from the hazards of a long war by his agreement with Stalin, Hitler wanted a short war so that the Reich should not be exposed to the danger of running out of steam; the armoured divisions and the Air Force intended to support them were to be instrumental in the rapid breakthrough into the enemy's positions and a total disruption of its forces. Having the advantage of the initiative and of short internal lines of communication, the Wehrmacht could choose its own time and place to attack. Hitler's plan was thus to crush Poland as quickly as possible; the Siegfried line and Belgian neutrality would provide a solid barrier in the west to any French counter-moves. What would happen next was not yet clear to the Führer but he could not fail to hope that, faced by a *fait accompli*, Britain and France would once again bow to the inevitable and, rather than become bogged down in a prolonged and costly war, of uncertain outcome, they would abandon Poland to its fate just as they had previously abandoned Czechoslovakia and Austria.

On the other hand, the democracies were anxious to gain precious time. Thus, while the blockade would be progressively weakening the German effort, the mobilisation of the unlimited resources of the two empires, which nothing could prevent in view of their command of the seas, would one day give them irresistible superiority in arms and men. The lesson of 1914–18 was surely quite conclusive. So why launch out on an offensive that could only be premature and bloody and for which, in any case, they lacked the attacking spearhead? Such an offensive could in any case reach enemy territory only by going through Belgium and Belgium refused to accept this at any price.

So a defensive strategy was essential, thus satisfying both the military mind that could not see beyond the lessons of World War I and the civil population for whom the greatest crime of all was the sacrifice of human lives. Fundamentally, Britain and France were without war aims; the former's colonial empire was not threatened by Hitler's ambitions and the latter no longer had to win back Alsace-Lorraine. More than one politician was inhibited by a guilt complex, the legacy of the 'Versailles Diktat'; after all, how could you fail to recognise the rightness of some of Hitler's claims, which had already been voiced by the Weimar Republic, such as those concerning the former German colonies, access to raw materials or the return of German minorities to the Reich? Was the destruction of the Nazi régime sufficient grounds for sacrificing millions of men? Surely it was the Germans themselves who had opted for that régime and it was the blunders committed by the democracies – French intransigence, thought the British, British weak-mindedness, thought the French – which had greatly facilitated Hitler's coming to power.

So the defensive strategy of the French supreme commander had the approval of the French and British politicians – Daladier and Chamberlain – as well as of the military pundits like Pétain and Weygand. A few heretics – Churchill, Paul Reynaud and de Gaulle – had spoken up strongly on the other side and warned that the democracies could not remain passive without falling into the danger of sluggish indifference. They were lonely prophets preaching in the wilderness. So we find Marshal Pétain accepting 'Douhet's doctrine' but not pursuing it beyond the first stage which required armies to remain on the defensive.[1] So the instructions of General Gamelin, the supreme commander of the Franco-British forces, laid down the principle that a sound defence 'must await the enemy and contain it on a continuous front of fortifications and trenches impossible to break through'. That was why priority had been given to the fighter arm in order to defend French airspace whilst no priority had been given to heavy tanks to lead an offensive.

Such notions were perfectly logical and coherent. They were based on glorious historical precedent and they corresponded to the will of the people. For the present, however, they left the initiative for the conduct of operations entirely in Hitler's hands and they condemned Poland to isolation and thus to disaster. The Allies were going to face the Germans in extended order; but in this sort of single combat, they ran the risk of throwing away all the advantages that accrued, on paper, from the numerical superiority of their forces. For basically the Allies could only achieve victory in three stages. First of all, their defences would have to be sound enough to withstand the enemy's first onslaught that would be intended to be decisive. Once this stage had been surmounted, the democracies would still need to maintain their lines of communication, increase their armaments on a massive scale and prevent the destruction of their convoys, harbours and factories, so winning the war at sea, in the air and in the arsenals. Only then would the time be ripe to take the offensive; the war would be carried into German territory, although no one knew exactly how; but in his heart of hearts, everyone was hoping, in fact, that Germany would admit defeat as a result of the blockade and the bombing before this stage was reached.

How many years would be needed to reach this successful outcome? Would the agreement between the Allies stand the strain for so long? Would the morale of the fighting soldier, so dubious from the very

1. See preface to Colonel Vauthier's book *La doctrine de guerre du Général Douhet*, Berger-Levraut, 1935.

beginning, hold out long enough? And above all, should Germany win the 'first round', that is should the French front be breached, would the French consider that the fate of France and of the war could be decided beyond its own frontiers – as they had imagined it could be in the case of Czechoslovakia and Poland – by means of the protection afforded by those 'big ditches', the Channel and the Mediterranean – perhaps even the Atlantic?

VIII ITALIAN NON-BELLIGERENCE

Such remote prospects seem never to have been examined, either by the governments or by the general staffs. But since, by definition, a defensive strategy leaves the time and place of attack to the adversary's choice, the Allied strategists were forced to draw up plans to allow for every possible contingency – a dangerous approach since it could only lead to a dispersal of forces that were weak enough already.

At first, one possible burden had, however, been removed, the entry of Italy into the war in the Alps and Tunisia. King Victor Emmanuel was not in favour of it and the Italian military leaders had warned Mussolini of the inadequate preparation of the Army and the Navy, both of which had been forced to make good the losses they had suffered in Abyssinia and Spain. The Minister of Foreign Affairs, Count Ciano, if he is to be believed, had been extremely irritated that Italy had, without any warning, been faced by Hitler's irrevocable decision to attack Poland. Although Mussolini was greedy for military success, as being the indispensable basis for his prestige and future ambitions, he acquiesced in his advisers' views.

The Italians' pretext to avoid entering the war was to make any such entry dependent on receiving very considerable quantities of arms and supplies from Germany, and Hitler found it difficult to meet this request.

So Hitler cut his losses, sent an 'understanding' letter to the Duce and declared in the Reichstag on September 1 that in the coming struggle he did not wish to call on any foreign power for help. 'This is our business,' he said 'and we shall settle it ourselves.' Italy invented a new diplomatic concept by declaring herself a 'non-belligerent'; Ciano explained to Hitler that it was not 'a strictly neutral attitude' but merely meant that Italy 'would not take the initiative in the west', thus complying with Hitler's desire to confine the conflict to the eastern front; in any case, had Italy gone to war, she would have been exposed to attack from Britain and France in the air, at sea and in her colonies, and the psychological effect might have been catastrophic. So Hitler agreed to restrain his irritation and recognise that this was all part of a 'subtle game between Germany and Italy'.

Italy's defection had, moreover, in fact provided Germany with the consolation of making the Allied blockade less effective; nor did it enable France to avoid keeping hundreds of thousands of troops immobilised in the Alps and Tunisia. As far as the French general staff was concerned, it had, however, removed two strategic possibilities: one was the not very formidable one of an Italian frontal attack, the other a violation of Swiss neutrality in order to link up the German and Italian armies. But it also destroyed a possibility that had appealed to one or two French generals: the chance of carrying the war into the Plain of Lombardy and putting the weaker of their opponents out of action.

IX THE INSOLUBLE PROBLEM OF BELGIUM

Since any attack against the French fortified lines on the Rhine and in Lorraine was improbable, the likelihood was that, as in 1914, the French and German armies would first join battle on the plains of Belgium. This had probably been thoroughly considered by the French high command; every possible contingency had been carefully examined and solutions drawn up to meet each of them. The fact was that the military and political problems were so inextricably intertwined that no single solution could be completely satisfactory.

The attitude most consistent with the general defensive approach that had been adopted was to await the German attack on French territory. But the Maginot line stopped short at the Ardennes and only improvised field fortifications could ever be built between the Ardennes and the sea, a fact which made the 'impregnable front' implied in the supreme commander's instruction a highly problematical affair. Militarily, to allow Belgium to be crushed meant depriving the Allied armies of valuable manpower at a time when British divisions were unlikely to appear on the Continent in strength for some considerable time. Diplomatically, leaving Belgium to her fate, after Czechoslovakia, would have had a most unfortunate effect on the neutral countries. Morally, such a course would be unworthy of France; it would amount to a confession of weakness and harm the morale of the troops.

So Belgium would have to be helped: but how? General Gamelin had indeed realised what the ideal solution would be: move the French armies as far forward as possible into Belgium, right up to the German frontier, on the line of the Albert canal where the Belgians had built good solid fortifications. In this way the Belgian Army, completely intact, would in due course be assimilated into the Allied defences; the Allied lines would thus be both shortened and more solidly held; the enemy threat to the northern industrial area would be largely averted; and Britain would not need to fear air and submarine attacks from aerodromes and bases set up in nearby Belgium. The possibility of aggression on Holland would also have to be taken into account and helping the Dutch would run the risk of overtaxing the strength of the Allied armies. In addition, there was an unfortunate gap between the Belgian and Dutch defences. But whatever these minor drawbacks, the 'Albert canal plan' provided a nice combination of the best immediate prospects of defence with considerable opportunities for future offensive action.

The Belgian authorities also shared these beliefs and desires. But by an extraordinary paradox they refused to consider taking the concerted measures required by such a plan of action. On September 3, King Leopold proclaimed Belgian neutrality, a decision taken by a national coalition cabinet and approved by Parliament and public opinion, with hardly one dissentient voice. It was the logical consequence of the policy adopted at the time of the remilitarisation of the Rhineland and described either as 'independent' or 'the policy of the free hand'; for Belgium, to start military talks with the Allies would have meant giving up her neutrality and provoking Germany.

Although the reasons behind King Leopold's decision and those of his very influential military adviser, General van Overstraeten, are not always very plain, it would seem that Belgian policy can be explained primarily by internal consideration and the desire to maintain national unity at all costs. It is true that the vast majority of the Belgians were ill-disposed to Nazi Germany; the German ambassador in Brussels estimated it at 90 per cent of the population. But a very active minority was violently anti-French: the *flamingant* group, representing the commercial element of the Flemish Nationalist movement, was the source of serious strain in Belgium's political and social structure. In order to assert their language and culture and obtain equal, or even larger, representation in the upper echelons of government with the Walloons, the Flemings, apart from a cultivated French-speaking minority, were almost unanimous in spurning French language, culture and influence in Belgium. Any attempt in peacetime to establish military links between Belgium and France would assuredly have inflamed Flemish nationalist feeling and given rise to unpredictably violent reactions. A policy of complete neutrality between the two camps thus seemed the only way to guarantee that Belgium would remain relatively united.

Perhaps the King of the Belgians and his government also imagined that they had some hope of saving Belgium from invasion. In fact, they were fully aware that the peril would come from Germany, not from France. But they were anxious not to arouse Hitler's wrath in any way whatsoever. It is also likely that the way in which the democracies had repeatedly given in to Hitler had not helped to inspire the Belgians with any confidence in their strength or determination; consequently any attempt to call in the Allies as a preventive measure would amount to inviting a crushing German counter-blast, the immediate result of which would be the invasion of the country followed by the destruction of its unity. In consequence, the Belgians refused to accept any secret military pact or technical agreement with the French. They recognised that, should the Germans violate their neutrality, the only source of help would be the French Army; they were prepared to agree to its crossing over into Belgian territory but only at their own request and at that time. Meanwhile, they refused to make any active preparations for such a contingency; they merely agreed to keep in touch, have discussions and exchange information on a limited scale.

The exchanges of views had been concerned with the time the Allied troops would require to reach the Albert canal after the Belgians had called them in. The Belgians wanted them to be in their positions, beside their own troops, within forty-eight hours. They were demanding the impossible. The French high command estimated that it would take at least five days but was very doubtful whether the Belgians, left to themselves, could hold out that long, in which case the Allied armies would find themselves having to fight a pitched battle, something which General Gamelin was anxious to avoid at all costs since he knew full well that they were totally unprepared for it. So Belgium's internal problems prevented the Belgian authorities from drawing up the plans which they recognised as being the only ones capable of protecting Belgium from invasion.

There was, of course, another possible solution: the Allies could take preventive action by advancing into Belgium in the hope that the Belgians would confine themselves to making a purely formal protest. Admiral Darlan was the only person to advocate this ruthless move, none of the consequences of which would impinge on himself. But no democracy, whose stated war aims were to defend the independence of small nations against that ogre Hitler, could possibly begin hostilities by violating the neutrality of their nearest small neighbour. Moreover, in such an event, one of the advantages of the manoeuvre – the incorporation of the Belgian and perhaps the Dutch armies into the Allied forces – would have been rendered very unlikely.

Thus any idea of moving the Allied armies up to the Albert canal had to be abandoned. The French strategists now had two alternatives: either to let Belgium be invaded in accordance with the defensive strategy that had been adopted – with all the unfortunate military consequences implied by such a passive attitude; or else to find some position in Belgium which the Belgians could hold long enough to enable the Allied armies to have time to come to their help, a position, in short, that would have the advantages of the Albert canal line without its drawbacks. The French drew such a line on the map: it joined the middle Scheldt to the Ghent canal and the sea. It had its advantages: the large urban industrial centres in the north would cease to be an embarrassment in the rear of the armies and the operation would only require part of the Allied forces to be committed; in addition, the Scheldt was quite a formidable barrier.

It was true that, in such an eventuality, a large part of Belgium would suffer invasion. And it would also require the Belgians to resign themselves to accepting such a situation, for their troops to withdraw in good order to the prearranged position, for a solid line of defences to be set up in good time and for the French troops not to be placed at risk by a more rapid enemy advance than was anticipated, and thrown into a pitched battle which would probably be disastrous from every point of view. All these were problems which, it was hoped, would be solved willy-nilly when the need arose. But would the Wehrmacht make its main effort in central Belgium, as in 1914? Nobody seemed to question it.

So in September 1939, the Franco-British Allies had unlimited economic and human potential at their disposal; their mastery of the seas was undisputed. But they were still ill-prepared for war – Britain even less well than France. They possessed sufficient quantities of the most effective weapons: tanks and aircraft; as for their use, they were still relying more on the lessons of the 1914–18 war than on the possibilities of new techniques. The will to fight was there; but it was not very keen. Thus the defensive strategy adopted was the least bad, in the circumstances; but in Belgium, its application was subject to special needs that made it difficult, if not unworkable. To sum up, in the face of Hitler's determination, backed by the discipline and even the warlike mood of the German people as well as by an army entirely planned for a swift and decisive victory, France and Britain found themselves in the awkward situation of facing an onslaught that might well overpower them, and of being forced to make last minute improvisations whose outcome would be quite unpredictable. But in the first instance it was only Poland, left entirely on her own, which was to bear the brunt of the attack by the formidable war-machine of the Third Reich.

BOOK ONE

THE WAR IN EUROPE

(September 1939–June 1941)

PART I

THE PRELUDE IN POLAND AND SCANDINAVIA

CHAPTER I

The Obliteration of Poland from the Map of Europe

---

1 HITLER'S 'TOTAL WAR'

THE Polish campaign allowed the Nazi Reich to show, at its very first attempt, its mastery of methods of warfare; the surprise and ruthlessness of the onslaught shattered the enemy's armed forces; terror paralysed the civil population; the 'Fifth Column' caused its opponent to disintegrate from within. These methods were to change but little in future operations.

The architect of victory on the ground was the armoured corps; the German Army had succeeded in solving the most awkward problems involved in its use: the difficulty of having thousands of motorised vehicles strung out over many miles; overall control combined with the independence of the constituent elements; direct communication with units which become dispersed in the course of the fighting. The Panzer division had already become a small army in its own right, combining speed and strength. Its reconnaissance groups, with their machine-gun carriers, anti-tank gun and pontoon sections, were sufficiently powerful in themselves to overcome any minor enemy obstacles placed in their path. The main body consisted of two brigades, one of tanks – between 250 and 320 per division – the other of motorised light infantry. The heavy tanks had the task of demolishing the enemy force as soon as it had been detected, assessed and located; their job was to break through the front. The medium tanks were to open up the breach, both to some extent on each flank to protect the advancing army, and above all in depth, to enlarge the breach in the enemy lines. 'They tear into the flesh of the defending force,' wrote Bauer, 'like the fingers of a steel gauntlet.' The rifle brigade with its artillery, its AA and anti-tank weapons, its guns, howitzers and trench-mortars, would mop up the isolated centres of resistance by-passed by the tanks. The rear sections, also completely motorised, could provide petrol supplies and repairs with minimum delay.

The Panzer division moved forward under the protection of the Air Force, which preceded it, bombing the opponent's positions as required. It would drop paratroops behind the enemy lines to capture and hold any

Map 2 **DEFEAT AND PARTITIONS OF POLAND**

- ▪▪▪▪ Polish Frontier on 1 September 1939
- German troop concentrations on 1 September 1939
- → The Wehrmacht's advance
- ⇐ The Red Army's advance
- First partition of Poland and Lithuania into zones of influence
- Second partition of Poland into occupied zones
- ▨ Polish territories occupied by the Red Army
- ▧ Soviet annexations after the Polish campaign

0   300 km

important point; during the attack itself, the aircraft would attack the enemy tanks, force any reinforcements coming to their aid to disperse and pound the defender's strong points with bombs. With his mobile command post, the Panzer division commander, equipped with two-way radio link could, in the thick of the fighting, give orders instantaneously according to the course of the operation.

This combination of tank and aircraft ensured the success of the German armies. But the Air Force had other roles. At the outbreak of hostilities, it could achieve command of the air by surprise attacks on enemy airfields, thus destroying its aircraft on the ground. It could paralyse any communication centres that might have enabled the enemy to regroup its forces. It could cause havoc and spread panic in defenceless towns: although Warsaw had been declared an open town, bombs were dropped on it as early as September 1, and it was bombed thirty-seven times within the week.

The Nazis' third weapon of the war was the 'Fifth Column'. As early as May 1939, thousands of young Poles of German extraction from the district of Poznan and Upper Silesia had gone to Germany to receive special training; hundreds of others, when called up for military service in Poland, deserted *en masse*. At the same time, German propaganda was loudly denouncing the 'persecutions' being inflicted on the German minority in Poland. The decisive phase was begun even before the end of August by German activities, described as 'Polish provocation': ss disguised as Polish soldiers set fire to buildings housing German organisations; after September 1, commandos of Polish 'German patriots' attacked radio stations, industrial establishments and even single Polish units.

On September 2 in Bydgoszcz (Bromberg) the Poles reacted by shooting 150 Germans in order to put down an actual uprising. As soon as the town was taken by the Wehrmacht, the ss retaliated by the mass execution of thousands of Polish civilians. The result of this initial subversive activity and subsequent terror was not only to increase the alarm and despondency of the civilian population, already sorely tried by the extent and suddenness of the tribulations that had overtaken it; it also heralded the important part that the ss was going to play in the territories conquered by the Wehrmacht, by working apparently independently of this but in agreement with it and, when necessary, with its help.

II THE DEPLOYMENT OF THE GERMAN AND POLISH
FORCES

Hitler had always thought – as he wrote in *Mein Kampf* – that a Polish state which had the impudence to cut into German territory and had annexed German territory offered unforgivable affront to the German nation. As early as April 1939, he had decided to smash Poland. At that time, it is true, he was convinced that the western democracies would show the same lack of response in Poland's case as they had for Bohemia and later on for Czechoslovakia.

When France and England had then pledged themselves to come to Poland's aid, Hitler had hesitated momentarily as to which course to take: should he attack first in the east or in the west? In any case, as he had specifically stated at a high-level conference of generals in May 1939, his war aims in Poland went far beyond the obliteration of the last clauses of the Versailles Treaty: 'Danzig,' he had emphasised, 'is not the real issue; the real point is for us to open up our *Lebensraum* to the east and ensure our supplies of foodstuffs.' Poland was condemned with no possible reprieve: 'she would not resist Soviet proposals'; she was 'a doubtful obstacle to Russia'.

In the end, it was Hitler himself who had failed to resist discreet approaches by Stalin. Ribbentrop's talks in Moscow had decided on 'concrete action' by the USSR in Poland. The German-Soviet pact signed Poland's death-warrant. It also finally decided in which direction Hitler would strike: Poland would be the Wehrmacht's first victim. Of course, should the western democracies come to her aid, the ultimate decision would have to be reached in the west and Hitler had not disguised from those close to him that it would be 'a fight to the death' and that a 'swift victory in the west was a matter for conjecture'.

This was not the case in the east. Leaving just sufficient forces in the west to man the Siegfried line, Hitler, gambling successfully on the hope that the Anglo-French forces would take up their positions ponderously and slowly, launched the main weight of his attack against Poland: sixty-three divisions, including five mobile army corps – with six armoured divisions, supported by 2,000 aircraft.

The German plan was to launch converging attacks from Prussia and Silesia, from each side of the Polish Poznan salient; General von Rundstedt's troops were to join up with those of General von Bock roughly on the Vistula–Nareth line, after disrupting the Polish forces.

The latter should, in theory, have amounted to some forty divisions; but at the request of the French and British ambassadors the Polish government delayed their mobilisation for twenty-four hours. Léon Noël has written that his British colleague and himself had suggested a delay of a few hours and that it was the Polish general staff which had decided on a whole day's postponement. General Anders is no doubt exaggerating the importance of this action when he says that it hastened the Polish defeat by a fortnight. In fact, it was the swiftness of the German advance, facilitated by the confusion created by this delay, that reduced the available divisions to twenty. The Polish Army had twelve cavalry brigades but only one of them was mechanised; out of 600 aircraft only 300 were modern; 500 AA guns, mainly old ones, were in service whereas the plans for the modernisation of the Army, which were not yet complete, provided for 2,000. The concentration of armaments factories in Warsaw made them particularly vulnerable. A few extra tens of thousands of badly armed conscripts would hardly have remedied such an inherent weakness.

The Polish defence also suffered from the country's geography: the immense plain did not lend itself to fortification but did offer great possibilities for the movement of motorised units: the tributaries of the Vistula opened up the road to Warsaw for any invader. Above all, the occupation by the Germans of Slovakia meant that Poland had to defend a frontier some 1,000 miles long.

Marshal Smigly-Rydz, the Polish Supreme Commander, had refused to shorten his lines of defence by withdrawing them towards the centre of the country; apart from the unfortunate psychological effect of a deliberate withdrawal of this sort at the very beginning of the campaign, it would have meant abandoning to the enemy the most fertile parts of Poland and the industrial area of Silesia. He decided, therefore, to make a stand on his own frontiers and even in the 'Polish corridor', which involved a dangerous dispersal of the meagre forces under his command.

III BLITZKRIEG IN POLAND

The ruthlessness and suddenness of the German attack made any concentration of Polish troops impossible; apart from a few squadrons camouflaged on secret airfields, most of the Polish aircraft were destroyed on the ground. Very soon the channels of communication were put out of action as well. As the Polish Army had no intermediate link between the Supreme Commander and his subordinate generals, from the start the fighting could not be controlled from above. Although the Polish troops were cut to pieces in every sector, there was no panic retreat. The Tenth German Army in the south, which advanced most rapidly, reached the outskirts of Warsaw on September 8 and was momentarily repulsed. No order for a general withdrawal of the Polish troops had been given until the 6th; but it was too late. Better news was a Polish counter-attack on September 9 in the central sector, towards Lodz, on the Bzura; but despite initial success and dreadful slaughter – Polish lancers were seen charging tanks – this attack was smashed.

The struggle continued in great confusion: large pockets of encircled Polish troops at Kutno and Radom resisted for some days before surrendering. In the battle area, the Polish state completely disintegrated - officials abandoned their posts and the civilian population fled in disorder. On September 5, the government itself decided to leave Warsaw. The capital was invested by the armies in the central sector and outflanked to the east by two pincer movements from north and south of the city; by September 14 it was completely cut off from the rest of the country.

On September 17, Soviet troops invaded Poland in their turn, meeting no resistance. The Russians seem not to have had time to prepare their intervention. They announced their intention to the Germans on September 9 but stated that they still needed two or three weeks to organise the invasion. They feared that the Wehrmacht might encroach on the zone allotted to them by the German-Soviet pact and Ribbentrop had to give full reassurance on this point. They were anxious to make the exact pretext for their intervention very plain and they disagreed with the Germans as to the wording. Now that Poland had collapsed, in order not to appear as aggressors, the Russians wished to base their case on 'the need to come to the help of the Ukrainians and White Russians threatened by Germany'. Ribbentrop objected that the two partners would then run the risk of appearing to be opponents. The Russians dug in their heels; they asked the Germans to make allowance for their embarrassment; 'up till now, they had shown little concern for their minorities in Poland'. At the end of the day, the Russian communiqué was a joint production; the Germans pledged themselves not to grant the Poles an armistice which would have the effect of making the Russian intervention seem pointless; they were eager for it to take place since it would obviate their having to pursue the remnants of the Polish army too far or too long. Every precaution was taken to avoid accidents or incidents.

Minister Potemkin, either through embarrassment or cynicism, justified the invasion by the Red Army to the Polish ambassador in these terms: 'The Polish state and its government has ceased to exist. Such a situation constitutes a threat to the USSR and makes it impossible to remain neutral any longer.' According to General Anders, the first result of the Russian intervention – which the Polish government seems not to have anticipated – was to prevent large numbers of Polish officers and men from escaping into Hungary and Romania.

From now on, the struggle was confined to a few isolated points, and the main thing now at stake, if not indeed the only one, was Warsaw. The city had been fortified in great haste, thanks to the short respite afforded by the Polish counter-attack on the Bzura. Any attempt to defend the suburbs was abandoned for lack of resources; in the city's historic centre barricades were put up, anti-tank ditches were dug and barrels of turpentine were set on fire when the German army approached. Hitler hoped to capture the town before September 21, on which date the American

Congress was due to meet; he was very disappointed. So that troop movements should not be impeded, he ordered that none of the civil population
should be allowed to leave. From September 24 onwards, Warsaw was
without gas, light or water; it was becoming impossible to fight the fires
caused by air raids; the food supply would hardly last a week, the ammunition two days. On September 26 German tanks and infantry launched their
attack. That afternoon, the Poles asked for an armistice which was not
granted until the following day; but during that time the Germans made
little progress. The Polish general Rommel was captured with all his
troops and granted military honours. On October 1, the German 10th
Division entered Warsaw. A few days later, Hitler went there to review
the victory parade.

Gdynia, the last Polish town to offer any resistance, capitulated on
October 2. The Poles had lost 450,000 prisoners to the Germans and
200,000 to the Russians. On March 8, 1940, Hitler put the German losses
at 8,400 killed, 28,000 wounded or taken prisoner and 3,000 missing.
The German victory was complete.

IV FRENCH INACTION. THE SAAR OFFENSIVE

While this victory was being achieved the French remained almost completely inert, although the Germans had left no more than forty-three
divisions in the west, only eleven of which were regular divisions, concentrated mainly on the French frontier. And yet France was solemnly
pledged to help her Polish ally, as was Britain, though in September there
were as yet no British troops on the Continent.

The protocol drawn up in May 1939 between the Polish Minister of
War, Krasprzynski, and General Gamelin, provided for immediate action
by the French Air Force, followed without delay by a limited attack by the
first available forces as soon as Poland found herself too hard pressed by
the German offensive; in any case, not later than the sixteenth day of the
war. In fact, on July 24, the instructions of General Georges, the commander of the French North-East Army Group, had stated that progressive action should be taken against the German system of fortifications
between Hardt and Mosel.

As a result, on September 8, the Fourth French Army made a small
advance from Sarreguemines; on the 9th it made contact with the forward
approaches of the Siegfried line. This line was several kilometres deep in
parts; more important, it was studded with small concrete defence-
works and the French troops did not attack it. Instead, they confined

themselves to methodically clearing the Warndt forest. On September 22, the attack planned by the Third Army towards Sarrelouis was called off because of the bad news from Poland. On October 1, when the Germans had started to bring back reinforcements from the east, the French advance came to a halt. On October 16, at the first German attack, the French troops withdrew to beyond their initial starting point and gave up Forbach.

Why did the French troops confine their activity to this futile demonstration against the enemy, in flagrant violation of solemn pledges? Liddell Hart put the blame on the slowness of the methods of French mobilisation, which he called 'obsolete'. But the French military leaders knew very well how long it would take when they pledged themselves to help the Poles in the formal military convention. Perhaps they had hoped for longer resistance on the part of the Poles. If such a calculation had been made, it would prove how greatly the French general staff were mistaken as to the Wehrmacht's fighting capacity and methods. If not, why was the date of the French intervention fixed for the sixteenth day following mobilisation when it was obvious that this was a promise that could not be kept? We are thus justified in wondering whether the French general staff had pledged itself to help the Polish army for psychological rather than military reasons – scared, in fact, that, if they did not know that their allies were supporting them, the Poles would give in to the German demands without a fight?[1]

Whatever may be the reasons for all this, the consequences of Hitler's decisive victory were plain to see on the map. As long as the German-Soviet pact lasted, Hitler was relieved of any concern in the east and of a war on two fronts. After having allowed Austria to be annexed and Czechoslovakia dismembered, France had proved incapable of preventing her brave Polish ally from being crushed or even delaying it; worse still, she had failed to keep her word. What a confession of weakness or pusillanimity! In the eyes of the world, Hitler's victory greatly increased his prestige; it placed central and eastern Europe at his mercy. The initiative was now his – whether he wished to proclaim his desire for peace or to launch his full strength against his western opponents. At the first crisis, cruel proof had been given that France's army was inadequate to meet her political obligations. Would it have improved sufficiently by the time the enemy turned its attention to her? And should some breathing space still be given, would she be able to take advantage of it?

1. After the war an argument arose on this point between General Gamelin and the Sikorski Institute in London. General Gamelin declared that in the absence of a political agreement binding France and Poland, France could have refused to carry out the military protocol. In that case, why sign it? It is true that the political agreement had *followed* and not preceded the military agreement. M. G. Bonnet, in his memoirs, acknowledges that he completed the political agreement *after* the declaration of war! Why not before?

V THE PARTITION OF POLAND

What would become of Poland now that she had been conquered and completely occupied by her two large neighbours? The first problem for these to settle was the careful marking out of the limits of their respective portions, a difficult task since their troops had overlapped in the course of the fighting; it was made even more laborious by Stalin's pettifogging and suspicious attitude during the preliminary talks. Once again, Ribbentrop had to go off to Moscow.

The difference of opinion concerned the extent of the territories due for partition. The Germans were inclined to the view that after each had taken his cut, there should remain a residual Polish state with 12 to 15 million inhabitants, all Polish – a sort of Grand Duchy of Warsaw. Such a state, the German ambassador Moltke considered, might provide the basis for discussions with France and England and facilitate a return to peace. Could such a Poland reasonably do anything but put itself under German protection, if only in order to obtain German help in recovering one day the territories the Russians had annexed? Moltke was already suggesting as the head of this rump state the name of General Sonskowski, who was known to be cool towards the USSR.

It seems that, though Hitler had quite firm ideas as to his aims in Poland, he was much less clear in his mind how to put them into effect now that victory had made their realisation possible. Had he not told von Brauchitsch on September 7, after the first brilliant successes, that he was ready to conclude peace with the Poles, thus assuming the survival of Poland?

But Stalin, at first agreeable, quickly detected the hint of anti-sovietism concealed by the plan for the creation of a Polish rump state. He was at pains to emphasise how important it was 'to avoid anything liable to create friction between Germany and the USSR'. During the discussion over the exact line of demarcation, he invoked the will of the Ukrainian people – who had never been consulted – and vehemently opposed the idea that the Germans should keep a small area of territory allegedly inhabited by Ukrainians. Stalin's major argument was that it would be unreasonable to partition the Poles between the two states. He suggested an exchange: Lithuania would be joined to the Russian zone whilst the province of Lublin and part of the province of Warsaw would be included in the German zone. If agreement were reached, he did not disguise the fact that 'the USSR would tackle the problem of the Baltic states without delay'.

It is probable that Hitler was most anxious at this time for a good understanding with Stalin. In the short term, he saw it as offering the immediate possibility of exerting strong pressure on France and England to induce them to make peace. Should they refuse and the war continue, the economic co-operation of the USSR would be indispensable. But by September 17, no start had yet been made in implementing the economic clauses of the pact and the German experts noted little eagerness on the part of the Russians to honour their contract. It was better not to irritate Stalin.

That was why in Moscow Ribbentrop in the end accepted all the Soviet's conditions. The German-Soviet treaty of 'delimitation and friendship' of September 28 partitioned Poland definitively in accordance with Stalin's proposals. It provided that Germans living in the zone of Russian influence[1] as well as the Ukrainians and White Russians living in the German zone would be free to emigrate from one zone to the other. Anxious to establish 'a solid basis of friendly relations' between themselves, the two parties pledged themselves 'not to tolerate any Polish agitation in their territories that might be liable to affect the maintenance of law and order in the other's territories' – a euphemism which condemned the Polish Communists who had taken refuge in the Russian zone to remain silent, if not to be interned. A programme of exchange of trade satisfactory to the Germans was drawn up. Ribbentrop achieved a small personal triumph: an area specially reserved for his hunting activities was left in Reich territory! On October 4, an additional agreement approved the line of demarcation drawn with the greatest accuracy by a mixed German-Russian commission.

VI POLAND'S MARTYRDOM BEGINS

Hitler despised the Poles. He used one word to define the reasons for their defeat: it was because their organisation for war had been *Polish*. He explained the 'dreadful opinion' that he had of Poland and of the 'wretched lot of the Poles' by quoting the silting-up of the Vistula as an example of Polish incompetence! However, even after the agreement with Stalin, he persisted for some time in his intention of allowing a residual Polish state to continue in existence and he explained to Count Ciano on October 2 'that the form [of that state] would depend on the way pacification would be achieved politically'. He could not yet say if Poland would be an independent state or a protectorate.

But when France and England refused to rise to the bait, Poland's fate was settled in accordance with the Führer's real feelings on the subject. By an order dated October 8, Hitler decided on the straightforward annexation by the Reich of the Polish territories that had formerly been German before 1918, i.e. east Prussia and the province of Poznan and Silesia,

1. That is, those living in the Baltic states.

which now became 'the incorporated Eastern Territories'. Four days later he made the rest of the German-occupied zone into the 'General Government' of the occupied Polish territories, under the rule of the Third Reich's legal expert, Dr Frank – a bargaining counter for later developments, perhaps, but meanwhile an amorphous state in which the victorious Germans could exercise completely arbitrary power. In a letter to Mussolini dated March 8, 1940, contradicting what he had said to Ciano five months earlier, Hitler explained to the Duce that, had he not assumed control of the 'General Government', Poland would have fallen into 'appalling chaos'. The country would have starved; 'the priests would have had their heads chopped off' – by the basically Catholic Poles presumably? 'The Poles could consider themselves lucky to have had to deal with the good-natured Germans!'

And here are the blunt terms in which this 'good nature' was expressed at a conference held on October 2, when Hitler met Bormann, Frank and a few minor aides. Hitler uttered one or two peremptory judgments on the Poles: the Pole was really made for dirty work. . . . You could not turn a Slav into anything but what nature had intended him to be. And the Pole was lazy by nature and had to be forced to work. As a result, there must be no question of mingling German and Polish blood; and the Poles should be given inferior status: 'Every chance of promotion should be given to the German worker but the Poles should be given no chance of this; it was, indeed, necessary for their standard of living to be low or kept down.'

Thus the 'General Government' would become a reserve of manpower for the Reich. It would be entirely under the control of 'a strict German administration'; it would not form a 'tight homogeneous' economic region, equipped with industrial plant. It would provide the Reich with 'cheap labour', which would be summoned to Germany for seasonal requirements and then sent back to live in Poland once the work had been completed. The 'General Government' would, in short, be 'one vast labour-camp'. The Poles would benefit 'since the Germans would look after their health and see to it that they did not go hungry'; but 'they must not move up in the world' and the Roman Catholic priests' task was to 'keep them in a state of ignorance and stupidity', in the interests of the Germans.

It is unlikely that the exploitation of slave-labour had ever been so systematically planned and cynically expounded. But beyond this exploitation there loomed an even more atrocious plan. It followed from the assumption of the inferiority of the Poles that they could have only Germans in control of them. As a result, Hitler said 'it was absolutely essential to ensure that no Poles remained in positions of responsibility; wherever this was the case, they would have to be executed, however brutal this might seem.' A little later on, Hitler stated that 'all the Polish intelligentsia must be executed'.

Experts in this field were already on the spot, following in the wake of the Wehrmacht and with its agreement, *Einsatzgruppen* – special action groups – of the Reich security police had moved into Poland. Their role was to 'counter any elements in the occupied territories that were hostile to the Reich'. They began by 'taking care of' the Jews. The latter were expelled from the territories annexed by Germany and forced to go back into the 'General Government' where, by the beginning of October, they were already being gathered into ghettoes. The same meeting on October 2 arranged that Viennese Jews should be transferred to the 'General Government', which was thus fated to become the 'Jewish reservation' of Europe.

Poland's martyrdom was beginning and the calvary of the Jews was already plain to see. Racialism was being confirmed as the most powerful motive force behind Hitler's policy.

CHAPTER 2

The Phoney War

(October 1939–May 10, 1940)

I HITLER AND PEACE

THROUGHOUT the Polish campaign, Hitler had instructed the Wehrmacht to exercise the greatest caution in the west, to remain indeed completely on the defensive. In his directive of August 31, 1939, he ordered that 'any hostile initiative should come from England and France'; in a further instruction, issued after some days of success in Poland, he allowed the Navy and Air Force to engage the enemy if necessary, but reiterated the injunction that 'any opening of hostilities must be made by the enemy'. The Führer was endeavouring to reduce to a minimum the disadvantages of a war waged on two fronts: his first and most urgent objective was rapid victory over Poland.

The manner in which this was achieved filled Hitler with optimism; by September 12 he was confiding to his aide, Colonel Schmundt, that he felt certain that France could be quickly conquered and England then persuaded to come to terms. On September 27, he made known his plans to the commanders-in-chief of the three services at a meeting in Berlin. Pointing out that time was working against Germany, he announced his intention of attacking in the west very shortly. Otherwise, the favourable impression created on the neutral countries by the triumphal success of the Wehrmacht in Poland would quickly fade; in addition, the industrial regions of west Germany which were particularly vulnerable had to be protected – according to Halder, Hitler was afraid that Belgium would enter the war. In addition, Italy could be brought into the war. Von Brauchitsch ventured a few timid comments which the Führer brushed on one side.

However, it was always possible that the democracies might climb down; anyway, it was worth trying. By occupying, under the terms of the agreement with the USSR, the whole area of Poland inhabited by Poles, Hitler had a trump card which he could play against the democracies, independently of Russia. So, on September 30, he made it clear to the

OKW (*Oberkommando der Wehrmacht*) that the restrictions applying to air warfare in the west were still operative.

Hitler and Goering received the Swedish industrialist, Dahlerus, probably in order to see how the land lay and told him that, if the present situation in Poland were accepted, Germany was ready to guarantee the *status quo* in the rest of Europe. A meeting with an English VIP was contemplated but nothing came of it. On October 2, Hitler suggested to Ciano that Mussolini might undertake 'an important mission by bringing the neutrals together' – keeping them well under control. But Mussolini was anxious to be a non-belligerent until something better turned up and he was irritated at being called a neutral. On October 3, Chamberlain firmly rejected any possibility of negotiation.

Next, Hitler called the world to witness his peaceful intentions. On October 6, in the Reichstag, he offered peace to his opponents, in vague terms. He did not put forward any concrete proposals and implied that the German conquests in Poland could not be challenged; in fact, he tried to put the blame for continuing hostilities fairly and squarely on the democracies. On October 10, Daladier declined the invitation, as did Chamberlain two days later: France and Britain could not accept any peace recognising an act of force.

Next the neutral countries, feeling themselves in jeopardy, were spurred into action. In the course of October and November, many offers of mediation were put forward by the sovereigns of Holland, Belgium, Norway, Sweden and Romania; Spain and the Vatican did the same. Nothing came of these offers.

Meanwhile Hitler did not halt his preparations for an offensive in the west; he confirmed his intentions in a minute of October 9, even before France and Britain had replied to his approaches of October 6! What is more, he revealed his real war aims: what was at stake was 'the destruction of the predominance of the western powers in order to leave room for the expansion of the German people'. Lifting the veil still more, on October 23, he told his generals that the object of the war was not 'to achieve the triumph of National Socialist Germany but to decide who should dominate Europe'. His peace proposals had thus no other purpose than to beguile his enemies and if possible to obtain the advantages which he so earnestly desired without having to fight for them.

The Führer's directives for the conduct of the war provided for two stages: first, the Franco-British army would be beaten in a straight fight; then 'an offensive would be launched against England's *economic power*', with submarines, mines and aircraft – there was no question at any time of contemplating a landing of any sort in the British Isles.

Hitler was now keen to attack. But autumn had come, with its rain and mud and low cloud, unsuitable for the movements of tanks or the operation of aircraft. Eleven times Hitler gave the order to attack and eleven times the weather forced him to cancel the order. And so, against Hitler's wishes, a truce set in between the belligerents and, as the sound of the guns died away, diplomacy and propaganda moved into the centre of the stage. How would the opposing parties use this lull before the storm?

II RELATIONS BETWEEN GERMANY AND THE USSR

And most important of all, how would the German-Soviet pact stand the test of time, in view of the fact that it had been concluded under the pressure of urgent needs on both sides: Hitler's desire to avoid fighting a war on two fronts, and Stalin's to channel the German onslaught away from the USSR? On the whole, both parties were showing a common desire to iron out difficulties so as to draw the maximum advantage from their agreement. But suspicion was rife on both sides and it was sometimes increased by mutual ignorance. The scope of the agreement was threefold: military, diplomatic and economic.

The Führer had been keen to keep the military credit for Poland's defeat for himself alone. He had been at pains to point out that at no time had the Reich requested military assistance from the Russians – sure proof of the vanity of a victor quick to take offence. Hitler had also made known to his generals his firm belief that the USSR would respect the conditions of the pact only as long as it suited their interests; but for the moment the weakness of the Red Army was a reassuring factor. Thus there had at no time been any question of a military alliance, however limited in scope. However, certain civilities had been exchanged, above all in naval matters. The Russians had asked for German ships to supply their submarines in the Baltic and this had been granted; the Germans had asked for and obtained the use of Soviet dry-dock facilities. The German Navy would have liked more: supplies for their cruisers and submarines in Russian ports, the possibility of acquiring Soviet submarines, the exchange of military information. The German documents published on this subject do not reveal what was the Russians' reaction to these requests.

Diplomatically, joint action had been taken against Turkey, to dissuade her from signing any agreement with the democracies. The Reich had recommended Japan to improve her relations with the USSR. At Germany's instigation, the USSR had protested against the British blockade. However, some friction had arisen in the occupied territories, particularly as the Germans had on several occasions gathered thousands of Polish Jews together close to the demarcation line and secretly smuggled them into the Russian zone. The Soviet authorities had confined themselves to pushing the poor wretches out again.

But it was primarily in the economic sphere that misunderstandings had emerged, although everything seemed quite straightforward, since the economies and needs complemented each other. But both sides were building up their armaments; as a result, the Germans needed the same machines or industrial products as the Russians and the latter were consuming a great deal of the raw materials that the Germans were hoping for. Above all, the Germans were hoping to obtain more than they handed over and wanted to pay off what they owed by staggering their deliveries of industrial products over a period of seven years. The Soviet government had other ideas. On the other hand, the Germans were growing impatient at the leisurely manner in which the cumbersome Russian bureaucracy was scrutinising their requests. And so, at the end of October, two months after the signing of the pact, nothing had yet been settled, even though a Russian purchasing commission had been roaming all over Germany showing an indiscreet curiosity that caused Keitel some concern.

The Russians had promised one million tons of grain, 900,000 tons of oil (including 100,000 tons of aircraft fuel), wood, manganese and 100,000 tons of cotton. They had authorised goods intended for the Reich to be transported via the Trans-Siberian railway, pointing out that such permission was quite exceptional. But they refused to hand over any iron or chrome.

In exchange, they asked for the delivery of the *Prinz Eugen*, the hulls of two cruisers, a training ship, the plans of the *Bismarck*, the most modern types of torpedoes and mines, Messerschmitt aircraft and 'more recent machines that they had not been shown', aircraft engines – they suggested that they should build them and sell them back to the Reich – AA equipment, in a word, almost exclusively equipment needed for modern warfare.

Goering, who had been put in charge of the Four Year Plan, was of the opinion that the Russian requests should be met. But on examination, the German experts discovered that the Russians were asking for twice as much as the Germans were prepared to offer, over a considerably longer period. Keitel was unwilling for the Wehrmacht to part with certain weapons which, to his mind, it could not do without. Ribbentrop himself, who had negotiated the pact, recognised that the Russian requests would need cutting down by half or even two-thirds. As he told the Soviet ambassador: 'It must not be forgotten that Germany is at war.'

The discussions now degenerated into something like a haggle between a couple of tough horse-dealers. Each protested that the other was not keeping to the terms of the pact. The Germans complained that the Soviet Purchasing Commission 'was poking its nose into everything' and behaving rather like the 'Interallied Control Commission during the years immediately following the First War'. Molotov upbraided the Germans for 'the exorbitant cost' of their aircraft. He recalled the promise that Ribbentrop had made on September 28: 'Germany would supply her *friend* the USSR with everything she wanted from her'. In short, there was deadlock.

However, no hint of these squabbles leaked out publicly. In the Soviet press, the attacks on Germany had ceased, even though, according to the report of the German ambassador in Moscow, public opinion remained suspicious. Above all, the Communist parties all over Europe had now stopped denouncing Nazism as the scourge of the age and were describing the current war as a conflict between imperialist powers which was of no concern to the people. Germany and the USSR had made a joint declaration laying all the blame for the conflict on to the democracies. On October 31, Molotov made a statement affirming the complete solidarity of the two states. 'The ideology of Hitler's Germany', he said, 'could not be destroyed by war,' and he spoke with a straight face of 'Germany's peaceful aspirations'![1]

Hitler accepted without a murmur the 'reorganisation' that the USSR was carrying out in its zone of influence. While the former Polish subjects, of White Russian or Ukrainian origin, were joined to their appropriate ethnic group in the Soviet Republic, Stalin forced 'mutual assistance pacts' on to Estonia, Latvia and Lithuania and made them grant him bases, while assuring them that he had no political ideological designs on them. Although Hitler had been bound by agreement ever since June 1939 to assist these three Baltic states, he made no demur. The USSR offered a friendship pact to Bulgaria, which King Boris declined; nor was it Hitler but Mussolini who was troubled by this Soviet approach and Ribbentrop had even informed Boris of Germany's assent. The spirit of the pact was being observed, therefore, on both sides and it was being implemented, albeit with some difficulty. Would the unexpected conflict between Russia and Finland raise new problems?

III THE FINNISH–SOVIET CONFLICT

The USSR wished Leningrad to be better protected; in other words, they meant to control that part of Finnish territory commanding the access to the city. Molotov simply summoned the Finnish Foreign Minister to Moscow; he did not go. And Finland discussed the Soviet 'proposals' word by word. In the course of talks held in Moscow with the Finnish Minister to Sweden, Stalin demanded that the Finns should hand over the

1. German news films had shown pictures of 'fraternisation': Guderian reviewing a parade of Russian tanks, German and Russian troops skiing together at Zakopane, etc.

Hankö peninsula and some islands in the Gulf of Finland as well as moving the Finnish frontier back in the Carelian Isthmus, receiving some Soviet territory in compensation. In addition, Finland was to destroy its fortifications in Carelia and the 'agreement' would form part of a treaty of mutual aid – the customary euphemism to disguise the status of protectorate imposed on a small power by a large one.

Finland was isolated; Sweden ignored her appeals and Hitler turned a blind eye. The appointment of a Socialist, Tanner, to the Ministry of Foreign Affairs hastened Russia's decision despite the fact that he was ready and willing to negotiate. Tanner was the epitome of the 'social traitor' loathed by the Bolsheviks; he had, moreover, committed the enormous indiscretion of reminding Stalin, in front of witnesses, that they were both old Mensheviks – which was, incidentally, not true as far as Stalin was concerned and was considered by him as an insult. Molotov did not mince his words: 'The Soviet government' he stated, 'expects nothing of any value to come out of the Tanner government.' Sweden and Norway made vain attempts to mediate; the Kremlin decided not to accept their communications. Roosevelt sent a message to Kalinin, the USSR President, and received from Molotov the friendly advice to apply his mind to Cuba and the Philippines.

On November 30, without declaring war, the Red Army began to move. Following a procedure that was to become standard practice, Stalin pretended that the only official Finnish government he now recognised was the one formed, at his instigation, by the Finnish Communist party representative to the Comintern, Kuusinen. Despite the great discrepancy between the two forces, the war lasted for three months. The Russians had probably underestimated their opponents and were using low-grade troops; they had made the mistake of starting the campaign at the beginning of winter and the bad weather soon cancelled out the overwhelming superiority of their tanks and air force. On the other hand, the shortness of the Carelian frontier prevented the deployment of large numbers of troops; and, finally, the vast areas of lake, marsh and forest hampered any military movement.

In short, all the Russian attacks in the Carelian Isthmus had foundered by December. Under the command of Marshal Mannerheim, a former Czarist guards officer and the 'liberator of Finland' in 1918, the Finns even went over to the offensive and carved a Soviet division to pieces north of Lake Ladoga; the Russians were also forced back on to the defensive in the extreme north. In the course of February, by dint of great efforts in the Carelian Isthmus, they overran the Finnish defences holding the 'Mannerheim line', thanks to the ice on Lake Ladoga which was thick enough to support the weight of tanks. On March 2, they were at Viborg.

Contrary to the diehard reputation which Soviet propaganda had been trying to pin on him, and which had led to his vilification by the whole Communist press in Europe, Tanner wanted to negotiate. On three occasions he went surreptitiously to Stockholm to meet the Soviet ambassador, Madame Kollontai, herself of Finnish origin. Marshal Mannerheim considered that it was no longer possible to continue fighting. The Soviets were less eager to stop but after Finland had accepted all their terms – those of the ultimatum of the previous November, plus the surrender of Viborg – the peace treaty was signed on March 12, 1940.

Stalin had given Hitler no warning of his intentions regarding Finland but the Führer refrained from embarrassing his partner in the tight corner in which he had been caught. However, Blücher, the German ambassador in Helsinki, was outspoken in his support of the Finns whom Mussolini had decided to help by sending arms; and Ribbentrop was subjected to loud expostulations from Molotov for this. But Hitler did not lift a finger; he withdrew the German ships from the proximity of the Finnish coast, persuaded Sweden not to go to her neighbour's help, rejected any suggestion that he might act as mediator, advised Finland to come to terms directly with her opponent – that is to say, to give in – and encouraged Sweden to offer to mediate discreetly.

The fact is that Hitler had absolutely no desire for the Finnish-Soviet conflict to spread, as the democracies were hoping (and their plans were an open secret), since this would open up a kind of second front at a time when he was concentrating his forces for a decisive attack in the west. Militarily therefore, Germany's interests coincided with those of the Soviet Union. But Russia's lack of success finally convinced Hitler of the deep-rooted weakness of the Red Army. The German delegates were able to exploit this during the difficult economic negotiations.

As a result, the Russians scaled down their claims; they had been asking for 26 two- or three-gun turrets: they now settled for 10; instead of 600 machines for making shells, they agreed to take 34; some requests they gave up altogether. Perhaps they were afraid of being deserted by their partners. In any case, while Hitler remained in the wings, Stalin was taking a direct part in the discussions and amazing the German negotiators by the extent and accuracy of his knowledge in his answers to their queries. The atmosphere was improved by certain conciliatory Russian statements: one from Stalin himself, who emphasised that it was not merely a question of 'a normal commercial treaty but of mutual aid'; another from Molotov who mentioned 'the *political* significance of the economic agreement'. At a critical moment when the talks seemed bogged down, Ribbentrop pointed out to Stalin on February 3 that 'the Soviet government had been able to realise its ambitions regarding the former Polish territories thanks to the German victory in Poland'. This 'represented a fairly considerable advance on the part of Germany' and 'a justification of her desire to obtain help'. He ventured 'to suggest to Stalin that he should reconsider the matter in the light of these factors'.

Stalin took the point at once and the commercial treaty was concluded on February 11, 1940. The Germans received satisfaction on the question of the time schedule for payments. They would be paying over a period of twenty-seven months for goods that would be delivered over a period of eighteen months. The Russians were to supply more goods than previously contemplated for a total overall payment of 1,000 million marks: copper, nickel, tin, molybdenum, tungsten and cobalt as well as the grain, crude oil and cotton as already agreed, but, in addition, the iron ore that had hitherto been withheld. Finally, the USSR granted a 50 per cent reduction on the freight charges for goods on the Trans-Siberian railway and agreed to make purchases on behalf of Germany from other countries and settle the accounts directly with them. The German negotiator Schnurre concluded that 'the USSR had pledged herself to provide Germany with far more goods than was justified merely from the economic point of view and that she would be doing so at the expense of her own supplies'.

On their side, the Russians also received satisfaction on a good number of points; rather than large quantities of plant, however, they were to obtain smaller amounts of high-quality specimens (armour-plating, boiler tubes, periscopes, mines and torpedoes, acoustic equipment, tanks, aircraft, samples of various types of ammunition, types of engine, equipment for the oil industry, locomotives and steel tubes). The Germans were providing them with a sort of scientific and technical object-lesson.

The interests of the two countries were now plainly closer together; in Finland the Russians had discovered by bitter experience certain grave military shortcomings which they must remedy without delay; and seeing that the war was going to be protracted, the Germans had a most urgent need of Russian foodstuffs and raw materials. Schnurre expressed this point when he noted that 'the effects of the British blockade have been *decisively* mitigated'. According to certain of Ribbentrop's statements, one of them made in Rome on March 10, the agreement had been extended to include co-ordinated action by various 'special services'.[1]

Certain points of friction still remained; the German negotiators complained of the 'continual distrust of the Russians'. Frequent incidents took place on the demarcation line in Poland, and sometimes even gunfire was exchanged. Each party reproached the other over delays in deliveries. These were minor blemishes; before committing himself in the west, Hitler was staking everything on agreement with Stalin; he wanted to be

---

1. Ribbentrop had jokingly said that 'a number of the clandestine Communist newspapers circulating in France are printed in Berlin'. This was doubtless a mere figure of speech of which there has never been the slightest shadow of proof.

certain that his rear was covered and he was now doubly reassured, both by the evident goodwill of the USSR and by the weaknesses revealed by her setbacks in Finland. So the gamble of the German-Soviet pact, achieved despite a massive history of past antagonism and despite its unnatural character ideologically speaking, was turning into a durable agreement, beneficial to both parties, so much so that Mussolini, feeling himself rather left out in the cold, was taking umbrage.

IV MUSSOLINI'S HESITATION

Hitler had been irritated by Italy's decision not to join in on August 26, 1939. Although he had made the best of a bad job, he had not concealed his view that Italian neutrality could only encourage France and Britain to urge the Poles to further resistance at the expense of the Reich. Later, while in the euphoric state caused by his victories in Poland, Hitler had come to realise to the full that keeping the Mediterranean out of the war and surrounded by neutral or friendly powers, would ensure that the clash between Germany and Poland could take place in isolation and the stronger quietly crush the weaker without interference. But once it had been decided to go over to the offensive in the west, it was clear – and the OKW was convinced of this – that Italy, whose military – and especially her air and naval – power were overestimated by Hitler, would, by entering the war, be useful in tying down French forces in the Alps and in Tunisia, thus reducing the forces available on the north-east frontier with Germany. But when the OKW approached the Italian high command to arrange for the necessary co-operation, they received no reply.

The fact was that Mussolini had not yet decided on active belligerence. His Minister of Foreign Affairs, Ciano, was urging him to take the lead in establishing a sort of neutral alliance, and become, as it were, 'the prince of peace'. Discreet feelers were coming in from Belgrade, Bucharest and even from Budapest and Sofia to do something of this kind. The Duce was, moreover, not happy about the German-Soviet agreement; 'it had,' he said, 'created an unfortunate impression'; he feared lest the USSR might encroach on central Europe, which he considered an Italian preserve. The fate of Roman Catholic Poland had caused anger among the Catholic Italians. Finally, the police were reporting unwelcome agitation on the part of the Germans in the South Tyrol, where the German victories were hardly conducive to encouraging the German-speaking inhabitants to leave their country.

So on December 16, to Ribbentrop's fury, Ciano made an important speech in which he emphasised the differences of opinion within the Axis. After which, the Pope, when receiving King Victor Emmanuel, openly expressed the wish that his country should continue to be neutral. On January 3, 1940, Mussolini took the liberty of offering Hitler some unsolicited advice to show moderation in Poland. He condemned the 'catastrophic repercussions' of the agreement between Germany and Russia 'where Germany would find her *Lebensraum*'. When asked for an explanation by Ribbentrop, Attolico, the Italian ambassador in Berlin, replied that 'should the war last five years, Italy will be unable to take any part in it before the second or third of them.'

The Germans' reaction to all this was not long delayed; in February 1940, Italy was informed that 'owing to the icy weather' they could not deliver more than 370,000 tons of coal; subsequently, the needs of the German economy would restrict further supplies to only 500,000 tons per month. And Italy was asking for 12 million tons of German coal a year! In his refusal, Ribbentrop stated, not without a hint of irony, that 'there was no difficulty in mining the coal'.

Had the two partners reached a critical stage in their relations? Whether or not they were aware of this, the British were working towards a rift between Italy and Germany by the use of sticks and carrots. In February, they asked Italy to sell them guns and aircraft; should Italy refuse, she would not get any English coal. This blackmail must have irritated the Duce. He flatly refused the bargain. Britain then decided to apply her blockade to the Italian ships loading German coal in Holland. Mussolini made a 'vigorous protest' and the moment of truth for Italian policy had come.

As if by magic, Germany promised Italy the 12 million tons of coal per year for which she had been asking, although expressing some doubts as to the possibility of shipping them to her. On March 8, two months after he had received it, Hitler replied to Mussolini's letter of January 3. He emphasised the fundamental solidarity of Nazi Germany and Fascist Italy; in spite of everything, 'fate would force them to fight shoulder to shoulder'. He minimised the Bolshevik peril because he said the Soviet Union was motivated more by a kind of 'Russian nationalism' than by Communism. When he went to Rome on March 10, Ribbentrop portrayed Stalin as a sort of modern Ivan the Terrible and promised that the USSR had no ambitions in central Europe. Although expressing scepticism and reiterating that 'for him the enemy was still Communism', Mussolini promised that 'Italy would enter the war at the appropriate moment and would fight on the same side as and parallel with Germany'. 'Parallel' implied that Italy meant to achieve her own ends, in her particular and limited sphere. But the pledge was made.

All the same, when Mussolini met Hitler on the Brenner on March 17, he still showed some scepticism as to the likelihood of Germany's beating the Allies before the end of the year. He reminded the Führer that Italy could not take part in a long war and that he still needed several months to make preparations for it. Hitler was very conciliatory: 'the final decision rested with the Duce'. At that time the latter had no knowledge at all of what Germany had decided; he knew that orders had been given for an offensive in the west but he did not know when or where it would take place. Imagining it to be imminent, he issued a memorandum on March 31 making known his final decision. While stating the principle that 'Italy could not remain neutral without putting herself beyond the pale, abandoning her rule and becoming a kind of larger version of Switzerland', when he tried to be more precise regarding Italian strategy, he found himself compelled by the weakness of his forces to decide to remain on the defensive everywhere except at sea and in Ethiopia.

So it was the Duce alone who took the decision to launch Italy into the fray. His pride had overcome both his caution and his certain knowledge of Italy's unreadiness for war. Had he not said to Ciano 'that he did not want to be the laughing-stock of Europe'? The Axis now seemed more closely knit than ever: the democracies had failed to detach Italy from Germany. Had they at least used the respite to make proper preparations for the inevitable and imminent confrontation?

The British and French had, in fact, in the first place co-ordinated their action and increased their forces; secondly they had tried to solve the irritating problem of Belgium; thirdly, they had planned a grand strategy of peripheral operations in Scandinavia and the Near East; and finally they had attempted to weaken Germany both by reaching an understanding with the opponents of the Nazi régime and by the use of the blockade. Was this going to be sufficient?

V FRANCO-BRITISH DETERMINATION

For the overall control of their coalition the British and French had set up a Supreme Inter-allied War Council which met for the first time on September 12. On November 17, this Supreme Council created a co-ordinating committee to pool the economic resources of the two countries; missions were to endeavour to negotiate group purchases abroad, but no real joint war production was agreed upon or even contemplated. The Reynaud-Simon agreements merely provided that one-third of the expenses of the war should be paid by France and two-thirds by Britain.

The British Expeditionary Force had taken up its positions on the Franco-Belgian frontier in the course of October. By January 1940 it consisted of five divisions. Its commander, Lord Gort, came under the Supreme Commander, General Gamelin but, as in every coalition, he had the right of appeal to his own government against any orders he might

receive. He was sandwiched between two French armies of the First
Army Group, but at Field Marshal Ironside's request he was not subordinated to that group but directly to General Georges. The RAF was
under strictly British control.

How strong was Great Britain's determination in fact? A Wilhelmstrasse document leaves some doubt on the subject. In the course of
October the Soviet ambassador in London met some British leaders.
Butler, who was certainly not speaking for himself alone, is stated to have
suggested that the British government would agree to making peace if
they could be assured that it would last for twenty years. If a guarantee
on the part of the USSR and the USA offered some hope of this, then the
British government would be prepared to make considerable concessions
in the matter of colonies. On his part, Chamberlain made no secret to
Sumner Welles of the fact that, in the final settlement, Great Britain
would not prove completely inflexible on the question of Poland and
Czechoslovakia.

It is true that Churchill, who had joined the British government as
First Lord of the Admiralty, and was supported by Eden, was criticising
Chamberlain for his lack of vigour. He was advocating that the democracies should take the initiative in the air and at sea and, to start with,
should lay mines in the Rhine. In France, Daladier's government had
fallen on March 20, 1940, because it had failed to 'make methodical and
energetic use of the resources of the nation'. Daladier had been succeeded
by someone whose energy was notorious, Paul Reynaud, but who was
merely the head of a coalition, not the leader of a team. Although powerless to bring about the changes that he would have liked to see in the high
command and to give the armed forces the weapons they needed, the
new Premier took every opportunity to assert his determination in the
well-turned phrases for which he had a special gift: 'Victory is salvation;
defeat, annihilation'; and 'We shall win, because we are strongest.'

Without consulting the President of the Republic or Parliament, Paul
Reynaud persuaded the English to sign a declaration saying that 'Great
Britain and France pledge themselves not to negotiate or conclude any
armistice or peace treaty except by joint agreement.' It was a way of
making Britain give public confirmation of her will to fight.

But armament production was getting under way slowly and with
difficulty; in January 1940, there were still only 21 heavy tanks coming out
of the factories as opposed to the 75 that had been planned. The fact was
that mobilisation had reduced the amount of skilled labour and this had
had to be put right by giving the status of 'reserved occupation' to highly
skilled factory workers. In May, the number of heavy tanks coming out
of the factories had gone up to 50 per month; this was still not enough
and did not help the formation of the armoured divisions as decided by

the high command in the light of the lessons of the war in Poland. This
decision had, in any case, not been taken until January; and the formation
of these units from scratch was very hurried; petrol supplies were badly
organised for lack of storage tanks; the three proposed armoured divisions were short of tracked vehicles, repair units and liaison cars; radio
communication links were either antiquated and clumsy or else non-
existent.

VI ALLIED RELATIONS WITH BELGIUM AND HOLLAND

The game of blind man's buff had gone on for seven months. Belgian
political leaders knew full well that Belgium could only be attacked by
Germany and defended by France and Great Britain, yet they turned a
blind eye by obstinately refusing to agree to the talks without which
any co-ordinated action was impossible. The declaration of war caused
them to withdraw slightly more into their 'policy of independence'.
King Leopold issued a message reiterating his 'firm determination to keep
the country out of war'. His influential military adviser, General van
Overstraeten, the real army leader, although not in name, interpreted this
imperative into terms of time: 'Gain time in order to arm ourselves to the
hilt without compromising our position.' The fear of calling down
Hitler's wrath on Belgium was so great that the numbers of troops and
obstacles (the latter could impede only the progress of friendly forces) on
the Franco-Belgian frontier were constantly changed; in order to give the
impression of impartiality between the two opponents, these forces and
obstacles were reinforced according to circumstances. Some Belgian
leaders – the Ministers Devèze and Spaak – were, indeed, more clear-
sighted and made some slight moves towards the French and English;
but they had no effect on the rigid attitude of other Belgians haunted by
the fear of jeopardising national unity and completely blind to the serious
danger from outside.

On the Allied side, General Gamelin considered that Belgian neutrality
was completely playing into the enemy's hands. He shrewdly weighed up
the advantage to be gained by advancing into Belgium and offering determined resistance to the Germans (after incorporating the Belgian Army
into the Allied defence positions) against the immense danger of a pitched
battle where German superiority in tanks and aircraft would have full
scope. But unless agreement had previously been reached, the Allied advance would depend entirely on how soon the Belgians asked for help.
There was serious risk of losing this fight against time and the real fight
that would then ensue.

So, after a further refusal on the part of the Belgians to engage in talks, even under the pledge of absolute secrecy, Gamelin adopted a plan of 'safety first': he would wage a defensive war in France on his own line of fortifications and their advanced posts; he would cross into Belgian territory only in response to a Belgian request and if adequate forces could be moved up, as and when required, to the chosen defence positions. It was the wisest thing to do until the Belgians showed a trifle more co-operation; there was little doubt on the French side that this would come willy-nilly through force of circumstances once the German threat became urgent. Meanwhile, no forcible entry into Belgium should be attempted, even though it seemed certain that the Belgians would offer only token resistance.

In October, the concentration of German troops in the Rhineland left no doubt as to the Germans' intention of launching a broad offensive. The Belgians realised this and concentrated the bulk of their forces on the Albert canal and along the Meuse. In his correspondence with Spaak, the Belgian Foreign Minister, Daladier confirmed that France 'would respond to any Belgian request' whilst emphasising the danger of being forced to improvise; he did not think that France would have a great deal of time. Gamelin in fact, with great shrewdness, considered that the German onslaught against Belgium would be ruthless, if not devastating. In consequence the French government and high command once again suggested general staff talks with the Belgians. Spaak turned down the idea, probably after consulting King Leopold. He believed that the emergency leading to German military action would last long enough for co-operation between the Allies and Belgium to be worked out. Everything suggested that the lessons of the Blitzkrieg against Poland had not been grasped in Belgium. Thus the directives of the officer commanding the north-eastern armies, General Georges, provided for the Allied troops in Belgium to advance only as far as the Scheldt. They were to advance further only if they had time to reach a prepared position where they could regroup. Meanwhile the weakness of the Allies can be deduced from their decision not to bomb the Ruhr for fear of German reprisals and not to attack the German ground forces from the air in order not to risk their small force of vulnerable bombers.

But in November, interest shifted from Belgium to Holland. The British were in fact greatly worried by the latter's situation; they feared that the Germans might set up submarine and air force bases and threaten the British Isles. An attack on Holland would also enable the Wehrmacht to outflank the Belgian defences on the west. It was thus important to be able to go to the help of the Dutch, that is, to advance as deeply as possible into Belgium.

Consequently the initial French plan of 'safety first', based on defence combined with a limited advance up to the Scheldt, was progressively

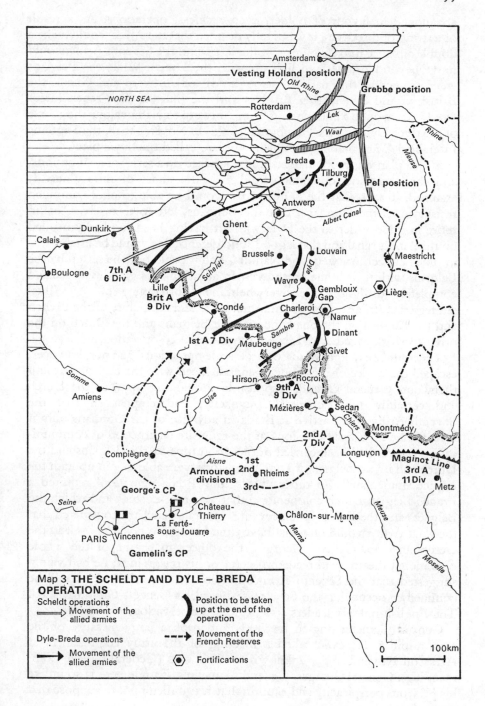

NORTH SEA

Amsterdam

Vesting Holland position

Old Rhine

Grebbe position

Rotterdam

Lek

Waal

Rhine

Meuse

Breda

Tilburg

Pel position

Antwerp

Albert Canal

Dunkirk

Ghent

Calais

Brussels

Louvain

Maestricht

Boulogne

7th A
6 Div

Scheldt

Dyle

Wavre

Gembloux
Gap

Liège

Lille

Brit A
9 Div

Condé

Charleroi

Namur

1st A 7 Div

Sambre

Dinant

Maubeuge

Givet

Somme

Hirson

Rocroi

Oise

9th A
9 Div

Amiens

Mézières

Sedan

Montmédy

2nd A
7 Div

Longuyon

Maginot Line

Compiègne

Aisne

1st
2nd
3rd

1st
Armoured
divisions

Rheims

3rd A
11 Div

Chiers

Meuse

Metz

George's CP

Seine

Château-
Thierry

Chalon-sur-Marne

Marne

La Ferté-
sous-Jouarre

PARIS Vincennes

Gamelin's CP

Moselle

**Map 3 THE SCHELDT AND DYLE – BREDA
OPERATIONS**

Scheldt operations
⟹ Movement of the
allied armies

Dyle-Breda operations
➔ Movement of the
allied armies

Position to be taken
up at the end of the
operation

- - - ▶ Movement of the
French Reserves

⬡ Fortifications

0   100km

abandoned in favour of bolder, even reckless, operations. As a result of a string of directives, it was finally decided that the Allies would make a double advance into Belgium. On the left wing, the Seventh Army would move beyond Antwerp to link up with the Dutch. While the Belgians were protecting the 'national strongholds' of Antwerp and Ghent, the British would be covering Brussels and the bulk of the French forces would move on to a line running from Antwerp to Namur along the course of the river Dyle and the Gembloux 'gap'. On November 17, the Supreme Interallied Council approved this new plan, called the 'Dyle plan'.

Such a plan was more than rash. It was based on a series of assumptions, and the successful outcome would be little short of miraculous. It assumed, in fact, that the Dutch army would be able to offer continued resistance to the Germans, that the Belgians, left to themselves, could retire in good order to the Dyle without having been too badly mauled on the Albert canal and that a good solid defence line would be established in time between Antwerp and Namur – and it could only be set up by the Belgians with their limited resources. In addition, this grand plan seemed completely to ignore the overwhelming shortcoming of the Allied strategy, i.e. its lack of large armoured units and the failure of the French and the English on the one hand and the Belgians and the Dutch on the other to work together to achieve the essential co-operation.

The immense danger of these 'large-scale operations' had not, however, escaped the notice of the French generals faced with the task of carrying them out. General Giraud, responsible for linking up with the Dutch and certainly not lacking in pugnacity, had emphasised that the Seventh Army could arrive at Breda in advance of the Germans only if it had three motorised divisions, if the requisite destruction of communication centres had been carried out in good time by the Belgians and the Dutch and if two Belgian or Dutch divisions were able to join up with the French immediately. In other words, the 'Breda operation' required a Franco-Belgian-Dutch co-operation that was non-existent and which the Belgians and the Dutch did not want. General Blanchard considered that the First Army would only just have time enough to position itself in the Gembloux gap. General Georges, the officer in charge of the whole operational theatre, had made no secret of his misgivings; he had vainly suggested that the Seventh Army's mission on the left flank should be confined to occupying the Scheldt seaboard, as General Giraud wished. The English military leaders also expressed reservations.

General Gamelin dug in his heels and took a large measure of the responsibility. He even called a meeting of the army commanders at Arras on November 23, unknown to their GOC (General Officer Commanding), General Georges. General Gamelin's attitude here is so unlike his previous perspicacity and caution that it is difficult not to suppose that it was forced on him by the Allied governments. It would thus seem that the 'Dyle operation' was political rather than military. By agreeing to it, Gamelin was surely showing meekness rather than character. At least he tried to reduce its risks by once more attempting to reach agreement with the Belgians, the only thing that could minimise the effects of failure even if it would not ensure success; but with a persistence worthy of a better cause, the Belgians still shied away from any such agreement.

Van Overstraeten had stated that the invasion of Holland would be a *casus belli* for Belgium, but this statement had not led to any agreement to link the two neutral countries, both equally threatened. Worse still, the Dutch Supreme Commander had decided to withdraw the bulk of his forces to the north of the main rivers, a decision which, by widening the gap between the Belgian and Dutch defence positions, made the Wehrmacht's attack all the easier.

It is true that in January 1940, after a German plane had been forced to land at Mechelen on the Meuse, and the German plans for the invasion of Belgium had been revealed, the Belgian authorities were extremely scared. 'Extracts' from the captured documents were communicated to the French. And the principle of neutrality was bent, if not broken: the obstacles facing towards the French side were removed! King Leopold declared his readiness to call in the French, not at once, despite the imminent danger, but merely after any invasion. Moreover he took the precaution of demanding that the Allies should guarantee Belgian frontiers and Belgian property in the Congo and grant financial assistance. The French troops were put at the ready; if Georges still had reservations, because of the Allies' shortage of aircraft and tanks, Gamelin was in favour of 'seizing the opportunity'. But there was no request from the Belgians; when the alarm had died down, they merely put back the barriers protecting them against an Allied advance into Belgium.

Henceforth the Allied requests, however discreet or trivial they might be, fell on deaf ears in Belgium. Yet these requests left aside the thorny questions of political and military co-ordination and were concerned only with technical problems of execution: the evacuation of the civilian population, the routes to be followed by the Allied troops or liaison with the local Belgian authorities. The Belgians even refused to disclose their demolition plans.

Nonetheless their attitude was changing slightly. They admitted that on the Albert canal they could at best undertake delaying action; they started to build an anti-tank defence line from Wavre to Namur, with little positive result, since its course was altered on a number of occasions and bad weather held up the work. On their side, the Dutch were contemplating defending Walcheren and Beveland islands jointly with the British and Breda and Tilburg with the French. But it was all rather vague;

nothing cut and dried really emerged. The Allied command was merely kept informed of troop movements and picked up hints as to the Belgian plans through contacts between officials, and from the fact that the French military attaché was able to move about freely, in mufti, all over Belgium.

One of the lessons of military history is the weakness of any coalition, however impressive the sum total of the forces of its constituent member states. In any case, though on the eve of waging a joint war, the French, British, Belgians and Dutch did not even form a coalition: they were not ready for anything, except to fight in extended order. Clearly, the failure of France to resist Hitler's demands since 1936 had hardly been conducive to inspiring confidence in potential allies. But on the other hand, every-thing pointed to the fact that the storm would break first on the Belgians themselves – and on the Dutch as well, although they had some faint hope of escaping it. The German troop concentrations seemed to forecast this, just as areas of low pressure forecast rain on a weather map; refusal to make the necessary contacts with France could not avert the danger for Belgium because she was the only door by which the Wehrmacht could enter France; but such a refusal was certainly signing her death warrant. Such arrant short-sightedness cannot be explained merely by worries con-nected with internal politics, however great.[1] It is probable that Belgian leaders had failed to gauge the speed of the German advance accurately; they thought that the overriding pressure of events would cause everyone to be both clever and co-operative and that all problems would be solved on the battlefield. This miscalculation seems to have been shared by Gamelin; as late as March 1940 he was still contemplating advancing as far as the Albert canal, after an initial 'leap forward', should the Belgians still be 'holding out'. In fact, once again proof was being offered that in 1940, as in 1936 or 1938, France had neither the military force or ideas required to fulfil her pledges. Nevertheless her army chiefs and the leaders of her government were not without aggressive intentions, as they were going to demonstrate by dreaming up vast hare-brained schemes.

VII ALLIED PLANS IN THE BALKANS

The French generals, particularly, were obsessed by the lessons of the First World War, because many of them had worked in close collaboration with the great commanders who had led France to victory. Hence the idea close to Weygand's heart and accepted by Gamelin, of creating a second front in the Balkans, based on memories of Salonica. In July 1939, Gamelin had envisaged it as a front of vast dimensions stretching from

1. On April 25, 1940, the Pierlot cabinet resigned in Belgium. The Liberal party had refused to approve the Education Budget as a result of language squabbles.

Poland to Turkey and Greece by way of Romania and Yugoslavia. It was with this prospect in mind that the 'Near East Expeditionary Force' was brought into being, under the command of Weygand with the ambitious title of 'Commander-in-Chief of the Eastern Mediterranean Zone of Operations'.

This vast scheme had its wings clipped by the German-Soviet pact. Henceforth, for the states forming the Petite Entente, the Red menace was either added to or replaced the threat from Germany. Poland's defeat removed any possibility of a really coherent second front. At best it was important to prevent central Europe from falling too quickly under the German or Italian yoke.

In the unfortunate situation now existing, Turkey seemed, if the most distant, at least the most solid sheet-anchor. The Anglo-French-Turkish treaty of October 17, 1939 provided for co-operation between the three countries 'in the case of aggression by any European power leading to war in the Mediterranean area'; but a separate agreement stipulated that Turkey could not engage in war with the USSR; thus Italy was the only country affected. In another agreement Turkey was granted a loan in order to purchase French or British war equipment; cautious to the point of inertia, the Turks had made it clear that they would not fulfil any of the pledges until they had received this equipment. This was the first brick, not very firm but still the most solid one there was, in the protective wall that the Allies wanted to build up in south-east Europe.

Yugoslavia was more afraid of Italy's ambitions than Germany's. At the outbreak of hostilities, it had mobilised 500,000 men and the unity of the country had been reinforced by an agreement with the Croat leader Macek. But it was tempting for Prince Paul, the Regent, to go to Berlin for protection against Rome, the more so as most of Yugoslavia's trade was between her and the Reich. Though the Army Chief of Staff, General Simović, made no secret of his hostility towards Germany, General Nedić, the War Minister, was at least prepared to wait and see.

As for Romania, she was more afraid of the Russians, the Hungarians and the Bulgarians than the Germans; would a guarantee from France and Britain be effective against this danger? Would it not be sensible to work for a counter-guarantee from Italy?

Nevertheless, at the Belgrade conference in February 1940, after Sarajoglu, on behalf of Turkey, and Metaxas on the part of Greece, had insisted on formulating a joint defence plan, Romania and Yugoslavia did not express their misgivings too openly and a joint plan was, in fact drawn up; but it was still necessary to prevent it from becoming a dead letter and this implied considerable help from France and England.

Weygand would very much have liked not to haggle over this support. His scheme was at the very least to create bridgeheads at Salonica and

Constanza in order to exclude the Germans from the Mediterranean and the Black Sea. The best scheme of all, he wrote, would be 'to go as far as Vienna' and hold the Save-Danube line 'in order to break out and attack when the moment came'. And he went on into fancies of 'one hundred Balkan divisions'!

But there was no co-ordination or even liaison between the countries concerned. On the other hand, the British were showing little enthusiasm; they were anxious to handle Italy gently and so the idea of a bridgehead at Salonica was abandoned for the moment. The Turks were asking for nine dozen 75-mm guns as well as tanks and aircraft. Where could they be found? Thus everything pointed to the conclusion that they would remain neutral. There were certainly splendid Allied plans on paper: in March 1940, it was suggested that command in the proposed operational theatres should be shared: Salonica would be a French responsibility and Thrace, Turkish, in order to neutralise the Bulgarians, while the British suggested taking over a theoretical front running through Afghanistan, Iran and Iraq, although it was difficult to see how the war would reach that far.

In any case, the spearhead of the operation remained the French army in the Near East. Although on paper it was inflated – each brigade was called a division – it never consisted of more than 80,000 men of whom 50,000 were to be in the Expeditionary Force. But this force had only two tank battalions and one fighter and one modern bomber group; since it had no motorised transport, it was without any strategic mobility; it possessed neither AA nor anti-tank guns. As for its transportation, for lack of shipping, three months were considered necessary to move three divisions from Beirut to Salonica. If the speed of the Polish campaign was anything to go by, should the Danubian countries be attacked by the Wehrmacht, they would cease to exist long before that time. The 'Weygand plan' in the Balkans was thus at best a psychological operation to boost the morale of friendly countries somewhat dismayed by the course of events. Yet even broader horizons were to be opened up.

VIII THE PROPOSAL TO ATTACK OIL SOURCES
IN THE CAUCASUS

Allied success in a long war demanded that the Wehrmacht should be deprived of that sinew of modern motorised warfare, oil, and Germany had taken over the Romanian oil, where joint German-Romanian companies were intending to increase the rate of flow for the Reich's benefit. In view of the Allied control of the Mediterranean, Romanian oil could only be shipped to Germany up the Danube. The Allies had thought of sabotaging the drilling and refining installations but as the effect would probably have been to push Romania completely into Germany's arms, these plans were never put into operation. There still remained the theoretical possibility of blocking the Danube. In April 1940, British experts disguised as sailors were supposed to sail up the Danube in boats laden with dynamite which they would then sink at the right spot; but the experts were detected and arrested by the Romanian authorities.

Even had this audacious plan succeeded, the Reich would still have had the oil from the Caucasus accruing to them by the trade agreement with the Russians. In January 1940, Daladier asked for various schemes to be investigated: the possible interception of oil-tankers in the Black Sea, direct intervention in the Caucasus and a liberation movement on behalf of the inhabitants of the Caucasus. It was finally decided to bomb the oil wells; this scheme seems to have been approved both by the British and the French, including Daladier, Reynaud, Gamelin, Weygand and even Vuillemin. But the execution of the plan was to be entirely in French hands.

Since Groznyy-Maikop was too far, it was decided that the raid should be made on Baku and Batum and include refineries, storage-tanks, harbour installations and railway lines. The first problem was one of distance; take-off airfields could certainly be found comparatively nearby, in Turkey and Iraq, but the chances of being able to use them were slight. This would mean that bases would need to be built from scratch in the 'duck's-bill' of Jezireh, in Syria, 400 miles from the targets, an area of sweltering heat in summer. The second problem was, of course, the question of aircraft. Since the American bombers which were going to equip the Near Eastern Air Corps had a maximum range of rather less than 900 miles, it would be necessary to convert French transport aircraft.

Once these preliminary tasks had been completed, what could the operation be expected to achieve? According to General Chassin not only were the most whimsical calculations made, they were actually accepted. The raid was to take place at night, at 16,000 feet, and, despite the absence of aerial photographs, it was assumed that the concentrated nature of the target would enable every bomb to hit its mark. Thus with 117 aircraft – which, by the way, had not yet arrived in the Near East by April 1940 – carrying 325 tons of bombs of just over 100 pounds apiece, it was hoped to stop the flow of oil from Baku within a fortnight. It was estimated that it would take the Russians six months to make good the damage. Even Douhet would hardly have been so optimistic.

However, there were other problems, this time of a diplomatic nature; the aircraft would have to fly over Turkey, who was determined at all costs not to come into conflict with the Russians: so Turkey's airspace would have to be violated, thus arousing her animosity at the very moment when she was the keystone of schemes for a Balkan front.[1] As for the USSR, a neutral power which would be suffering attack without warning in one of her vital regions, nobody seemed to be worried about her possible reactions, not even if they were to take the form of bombing in the Near East. The pleasant assumption seemed to be, on the contrary, that having received this sharp warning, Russia would withdraw into her shell and abandon Germany to its fate.

The 'Caucasus operation' never even began to get off the ground; one single French reconnaissance plane flew over Baku! Yet it was the most significant of all the hare-brained schemes in which fantastic targets were going to be struck at by the most pitiful means. It revealed the firm belief in the inherent weakness of the USSR. It was also evidence of the mixed feelings of hatred for the Russians and the Germans, prevalent amongst the French political leaders since the German-Soviet pact, feelings supported in part by public opinion.[2] The Finnish war provided the opportunity for another manifestation of the same attitude.

IX ALLIED PLANS IN SCANDINAVIA

Just as petrol was needed to keep engines running, so steel was necessary to manufacture armaments. And the Reich produced very little more iron ore than oil. Its ore was obtained from Sweden and it was of particularly high quality. The iron magnate Thyssen who, after helping Hitler to power had quarrelled with him and was now living in France, was confident that without Swedish iron, Germany was doomed to lose the war; he said that he had warned Hitler and Goering of this. Coming from such a pundit, such a categorical statement commanded respect and called for action: the 'iron-supply route' must be cut as well as the oil-supply route. This time the British showed greater keenness than for their allies' Balkan or Caucasian schemes; the point was that in winter, when the Baltic was frozen, the Swedish iron ore was shipped by rail to the Norwegian port of Narvik, which was clear of ice. From there, it was taken by freighter to Germany via Norwegian territorial waters, something which was anathema to the British who wanted complete control over the whole of the North Sea. As early as September 1939 Churchill had proposed laying mine-fields along the Norwegian coast – but the danger was that Norwegian boats would be the first to suffer. Next, the British government had

1. Turkey also controlled the railway line leading to the Jezireh 'duck's-bill'.
2. According to General Larminat (*Chroniques irrévérencieuses* p. 37–40), General Weygand said to him, after the German-Soviet collusion: 'Now all the swine are on the same side.' Germans and Russians both took the projected operation seriously: even today Soviet historians attribute far greater manpower and strength to the Near East Expeditionary Force than it ever possessed.

put pressure on Sweden to stop exporting iron ore via Narvik. They promised Britain's help should the Germans turn nasty and had suggested preliminary talks which the Swedes had declined, being anxious to preserve their neutrality.

The attack on Finland threw a new light on the matter. The Soviet Union was banned from the League of Nations and vilified by world opinion everywhere; certain French right-wing newspapers attacked her as if it was she who had become the true enemy of France. In France the Communists had to pay the price for the popular outcry; the party was dissolved, its press shut down, its leaders arrested or interned. Anxious to keep public opinion happy, Daladier saw that help to Finland could be the means of proving his aggressiveness and determination as well as of 'cutting the iron supply route'. It might be thought that it would be difficult for Norway and Sweden to refuse to help Finland; moreover, they would legally be covered by the League of Nations decision.

On December 19 Daladier prevailed on the Supreme Interallied Council to go to Finland's help, with the co-operation of Norway and Sweden. In fact, at the beginning of January, Sweden agreed to allow free passage over her territory of war materials intended for the Finns and even of 'technicians' provided they were volunteers travelling privately. But she refused to take any part in the conflict.

On March 2 the situation of the Finns seemed desperate. A further Franco-British approach was made to Oslo and Stockholm. If Finland were to ask for troops, the Allies would be prepared to send her them. Since the consent of Sweden and Norway was taken for granted, the Allies promised that they would support them against any possible German threat. Daladier told the Consul General Nordling that France could send 50,000 men to help Finland, via Narvik. The operation would begin on March 15, timed to coincide roughly with the bombing of Baku. The French even thought of landing in Finland, at Petsamo, but the British were opposed to this as it would certainly bring about a complete break with the Soviet Union. It was clear that as far as they were concerned, helping Finland was an excuse and an opportunity to obtain a solid foothold in Scandinavia.

Both Norway and Sweden were agreed in not accepting the Allied proposals. But Norway hinted that, while protesting in principle, she would put up only token resistance to any initiative the British might take on her territory. The Swedes' refusal was firmer. On March 12, the British made one final attempt to be granted right of passage; but on that same day, Finland accepted the Soviet terms.

The Allies had adopted a peripheral strategy that was logical in view of their inferiority: in doing this they would divert the enemy's effort from the one field of operation where it might be able to force a decision:

France. But their Finnish operation was just as makeshift as the air raid on the Causasus. Had not one British transport expert who went out to Sweden pointed out that Norway's and north Sweden's railway links could easily be cut, thus rendering the situation of any expeditionary force advancing into Finland completely untenable? In northern Europe, as in the Near East, the Allied plans had been dictated by the desire to weaken the German economy. Surely this was the only way for them to take the initiative in the only operational theatre where their superiority was obvious, namely at sea.

X THE WAR AT SEA. THE BLOCKADE

Franco-British naval co-operation had been worked out as early as May 1939, on a very flexible basis. The oceans and the seas bordering on Europe had been divided into operational zones depending on one or other of the two Admiralties. But these zones were not rigidly fixed and on several occasions they were modified by joint agreement. In addition, forces of one or other of the two countries passed under the command of its ally – the French 'X Force' of Admiral Godfroy in Alexandria, for example, under the command of Admiral Cunningham. Finally, any joint operations were handled by the two Admiralties concerned.

The Allied navies faced an immense task. They had to try to maintain a blockade of Germany and they had to protect their own merchant navies against enemy pirate ships and submarines.

The British government, overestimating the needs of the German war effort, anticipated that the enemy stocks of fuel and raw materials would be rapidly exhausted. As a result, they attached great importance to the naval blockade which would prevent these stocks from being replenished. However, during the 'phoney war', the methods adopted were still based on the experience of the 1914–18 war. Attempts were made to prevent Germany's neutral neighbours from becoming German warehouses by persuading them, in a friendly manner, to agree not to import produce that might be intended for Germany in greater quantities than usual. But the neutrals were only relatively amenable; Holland showed herself particularly recalcitrant.

On the other hand, apart from the fact that the German-Soviet agreement had opened a large gap in the blockade, the British were handling Italy gently in order to keep open a chance of wooing her away from Germany. As early as October 1939, they agreed to let her make considerable purchases abroad; they even supplied her with coal and raw materials. Even more, Italian violations of the blockade were dealt with very half-heartedly; in March 1940, 82 per cent of the cargoes held on suspicion were returned to their owners and big Italian firms were granted permission to increase the size of their purchases.

In these circumstances, the blockade could hardly be very effective. On March 4, 1940, Goering boastfully assured Sumner Welles that there would never be any famine in Germany; 'many school buildings and halls were piled roof-high with grain'. He did, however, confess to a slight shortage of raw materials – until such time as they could be obtained from the newly-won former Polish provinces or bought from the European countries which Germany now had in tow, after her victories. At roughly the same time, for Mussolini's benefit, Ribbentrop was painting in Rome a picture of the inhabitants of Berlin 'who had been shivering with cold during the winter'. But for the moment these difficulties were not producing any discontent on the part of the people or any fall in industrial production. If the blockade were going to prove effective one day, that day was still far off.

For its own part, the German Navy was not dealing Allied shipping any devastating blows, either. It is true that its pirate ships had caused some losses: the *Graf Spee* had sunk nine ships in the south Atlantic before three British cruisers had forced her to scuttle herself off Montevideo. In the spring of 1940, the German Navy despatched nine raiders, including six auxiliary cruisers, as far afield as the Pacific and the Indian Oceans to undertake operations which met with varying success – the *Hipper*, for example, sent sixteen ships to the bottom in the area round the Azores but was damaged and had to return home. More than by the losses they were inflicting on the British Merchant Navy, these pirate ships were a nuisance to the Royal Navy by obliging it to hunt them down and thus disperse their ships all over the world.

There were few German ocean-going submarines in September 1939: barely twenty-seven, of 500 to 700 tons. Lurking on the sea-routes which converged on the British harbours each side of Ireland meant covering vast distances, since the Straits of Dover were closed by an anti-submarine barrier; so they found it difficult to sail further than the fifteenth meridian and were never able to operate in force. The British Admiralty was content to operate as in 1918: convoys were escorted slightly beyond the fifteenth meridian. The submarines were located by means of ASDIC,[1] a device transmitting an ultra-sonic wave under water and picking up the echo sent back by any object: it was an accurate instrument but only up to a distance of ten miles. The anti-submarine weapon was a depth charge of some 300 pounds.

But the British were short of escort vessels and aircraft equipped with radar capable of dropping depth charges. Here again, they were relying on their experience of 1914–18, when aircraft rarely sank submarines;

1. Allied Submarine Detection Investigation Committee.

some had even been shot down by them. The advantage of aircraft was, however, in making the submarine exhaust its oxygen supply by forcing it to remain submerged. The British started to use their aircraft-carriers and this led to the first duels between aircraft and submarines. German submarines damaged a battleship in Scapa Flow, a great feat, and sank almost 410,000 tons of merchant shipping in 1939 – a smaller number than the British naval shipyards built over the same period; in retaliation, only nine submarines were sunk.

But the chief innovation in naval warfare during this time was when, from November 1939 onwards, the Germans started dropping magnetic mines by parachute: when a ship passed over the mine, lying at a depth of some five to eight fathoms, the mass of metal caused the mine to explode. The Thames was soon dotted with them. Their secret came to light when one of them was recovered from a mud bank, and ships' hulls were then demagnetised. Here again the Germans had shown the initiative. This new device cost Allied shipping some 200,000 tons in 1939.

If we add that the German aircraft attacks on shipping forced the British to concentrate their naval forces and Merchant Navy off the west coast of the British Isles, we are forced to the conclusion that, even at sea, where they were indisputably stronger, the Allies had not succeeded in establishing a clear advantage during the seven months following the defeat of Poland.

XI THE PHONEY WAR

These seven months had been nicknamed the 'phoney war'[1] because the French civil population had the impression of a long period of waiting for nothing to happen except a few private skirmishes in the No Man's Land on the north-eastern frontier and a large number of futile air-raid warnings. It had been a hard winter and if the nation's wealth seemed unaffected, a large number of families where conscription had taken its toll were financially embarrassed – only civil servants were having their pay made up. The population was living in fear of air raids which, as a result of a great deal of intense pre-war propaganda, either from pacifists or to boost the Air Force, were expected to cause a holocaust; the air-raid warning system was working badly and the sirens often dragged urban dwellers out of their beds for nothing. Cellars had been fitted up as air-raid shelters under the direction of *concierges*; works of art had found refuge in country houses; monuments were sandbagged; people walked about with First World War gas-masks slung over their backs. More as a warning than as a

1. In French, '*la drôle de guerre*'.

necessity, rationing of certain commodities had begun. In order to maintain production in the armament factories, certain skilled jobs had been made into 'reserved occupations', whereby the workers continued to exercise their trade, at their normal rates of pay, often working at home; the discrepancy in comparison with men who had been mobilised, as well as the fact that some 'reserved occupations' were unjustified, bred jealousy and bad feeling. Between fear of the future and the drab emptiness of the present, an insidious feeling of resignation or irritation grew up, instead of a will to action.

The public were thirsty for news and they wanted it to be sensational. So wild rumours spread. In the press there was strict censorship, everyone listened to foreign broadcasts and, particularly, to 'the traitor from Stuttgart', Ferdonnet, the spokesman of the skilful German propaganda machine, with the plausible leitmotif that France had been dragged into war by perfidious Albion and that the English would fight to the last Frenchman. The French government had formed their own propaganda machine, led by the subtle diplomat and novelist Jean Giraudoux, surrounded by a team of brilliant men – rather remote perhaps from the simple ideas and language of the mass of the people.

In the armed forces, the state of permanent inactivity relieved only by futile training exercises was slowly undermining morale. The commanders were aware of this and very properly attached great importance to the fair allocation of leave and to sport, theatre or film shows to alleviate the enforced leisure. Gradually, however, everyone was beginning to wonder just how necessary this war was, especially as, although it had been declared, it had not yet broken out. People were hoping against hope that, by some kind of miracle, it might come to an end before it really began perhaps by their opponents being starved out by the blockade or collapsing through internal dissension. Every night aircraft were unloading, not bombs, but tons of pamphlets on the sleeping Germans.

It was impossible for the politicians not to be infected by this feeling of lassitude and uncertainty amongst the people. Thus there grew up, not a peace *party* but a trend towards peace, unorganised yet heartfelt, with Pierre Laval as its spokesman in the Senate. The ambitious schemes in the Caucasus and in Finland had been partly conceived to whip up public opinion, and give the impression that the war had really started without disturbing anyone's peace of mind, because the operations were both remote and relatively trivial. Another facet of this disappointing Allied strategy was the attempt to disorganise the internal authority of the Nazis.

The fact is, the British believed in this more strongly than the French. On two occasions at least, Chamberlain stated solemnly that Britain was not waging war on the German people. He is reported as having said to his biographer, Sir Keith Feiling: 'What I am hoping for is not a military victory – I doubt very much if it is possible – but the collapse of the German home front.'

Thus numerous attempts were made to approach what was assumed to be the opposition to Hitler. The fact that no one ever really discovered what it was only made people try harder, so to speak, to invent it. Contacts were made in Berne, in Arosa (with the ambassador Ulrich von Hassel), in Lausanne-Ouchy (with the former Chancellor Wirth) and in the Vatican. The only semi-official contact took place by an indirect exchange of letters between the Secretary of State in the Foreign Office, Sir Robert Vansittart, and the Mayor of Leipzig, Goerdeler. The British government declared, almost in so many words, that it would be prepared to make concessions over colonies to a new German government but not to Hitler. But the 'German opposition' proved rather shadowy. After all the successes that he had achieved, Hitler had quite definitely rallied the German people behind him.

XII THE NEUTRALS

Hitler's successes, added to the confession of failure shown by the lack of activity on the part of the Allies, could only arouse fear, or even admiration, for the Nazi Reich in the hearts of the neutrals. It was true that they all felt that no final decision had been reached as long as the Wehrmacht and the French Army had not come to grips. But meanwhile Romania, Yugoslavia, Turkey, Norway, Sweden, Belgium and Holland clung desperately to neutrality, thus playing into Hitler's hands.

A few dissentient voices could indeed be heard in the camp of the natural friends of the Axis. Hungary, through its regent Horthy, had been troubled by the German-Soviet pact: 'If Germany were to weaken, the way would be open to revolution.' The German decisions as to Slovakia had deprived the Hungarians of any hope of expanding in that direction; the German desire to avoid any disturbance in south-east Europe provided a curb on Hungary's eagerness to regain Transylvania from Romania. So the Hungarians were dissatisfied and Count Teleki made no secret of his mistrust of the Reich. But Henrik Werth, the chief of general staff, was openly germanophile. In any case, if the worst came to the worst, the Hungarians might try to come to some arrangement with the Italians but never with the Allies.

Similarly, since the German-Soviet pact Japan seemed to be taking a malicious pleasure in falling in with British wishes concerning the blockade, so much so that the German ambassador in Tokyo wrote that Japan was offering better terms to England than to Germany. But the first round that everyone was waiting for would not be fought in the Far East.

In Europe, the only current theatre of war, the hint of a crisis between Germany and Italy had been overcome; but in April 1940, Serrano Suñer, Franco's Foreign Minister and strong man of the régime, informed the German ambassador, von Stöhrer, of his belief that 'the moment Italy entered the war, Spain would also have to decide on her attitude'. And he was already hinting at what might be the possible spoils of such an intervention: Gibraltar and Tangier.

As for the United States, she was slowly beginning to emerge from her inertia and indifference to European problems. True, Roosevelt, whom his Secretary of the Treasury Morgenthau called the 'keenest and boldest democrat of his age', could clearly see the danger which the Nazis presented for democracy and civilisation in the American sense, but he knew that he could do nothing without the support of public opinion. His advisers were themselves divided: Morgenthau and Ickes were thoroughly anti-Nazi and were doing all they could to facilitate the purchases made by the French mission in the United States. But the Secretary of State, Cordell Hull, although also an anti-Fascist, was unwilling to appear to be provoking the totalitarian states. The Secretary of War, Woodring, was a confirmed isolationist.

Overall, the Americans certainly wanted Britain to win but most of them failed to assess or realise the extent of the danger facing her. Some of them were even inconvenienced by the measures necessitated by the blockade: American ships had to put into British ports in order to be checked and this gave rise to complications and delays in their business dealings with Europe.

The United States had as yet no European policy and did not associate her lot with Europe's in any way. The war seemed to her the logical result of blunders committed by Europe, above all by France, after the First World War, amongst the first of which was the failure to pay war debts. Some sectors of the population of Jewish or Polish origin had indeed been roused by the Nazis' anti-Jewish measures and the subjugation of Poland; there were numerous refugees, some of them completely destitute. But these stirrings had not as yet made any impact on the collective consciousness of the American people.

However, as early as September 1939, Roosevelt had declared a state of pre-emergency. In November, he persuaded Congress to pass the 'Cash and Carry' bill allowing belligerents to buy equipment from America on condition that they paid for it and took it away themselves. Only France and Great Britain were able to do this. It was a first infringement of neutrality and acceptable because it kept business turning over; but it was stripping the Allies of their gold reserves.

CHAPTER 3

The War in Norway

THE Allies could not hope for very much from a blockade riddled with gaps; so, if it could hardly be expected to shut off the flow of Caucasian oil, might it not at least be possible to cut the supply route of Swedish iron? As for Hitler, the Finnish war had revealed to him the strategic importance of Scandinavia. The stage was set for a race between the opposing sides: the goal was Narvik.

I THE OPPONENTS' PLANS

On the military level, there is a striking parallel between the German and Allied preparations for a Norwegian operation: each wanted to forestall the other.

On March 28, the Allied Supreme Interallied Council decided to demand that Sweden stop exporting iron ore to Germany, to lay mines in Norwegian territorial waters and to send an expeditionary force to Norway which it was hoped to land without difficulty with the tacit agreement of the Norwegians. Churchill and Reynaud had engineered this decision and even carried Chamberlain with them since, according to Churchill, the latter suddenly became an enthusiastic supporter of the offensive.

All the same, the French and British did not quite see eye to eye. The French primarily emphasised the importance of the iron traffic via Narvik, the British were more interested in the Baltic theatre of operations. Now that the Baltic was about to thaw out, the British would have liked to bomb the shipping concentrated in the German Baltic ports; but the French were afraid of bombing reprisals which would hinder their re-armament effort.

On April 5, similar notes were delivered by the two Allies in Oslo and Stockholm; they showed obvious embarrassment because they had to justify the violation of a neutral state; this is why the arguments put forward may seem surprising. Attention was drawn to the possibility of a further attack by the Soviet Union on Finland, in order to obtain bases in Norway – no doubt the Allies wanted to exploit the feelings aroused in Scandinavia by the Finnish-Soviet war but for the Scandinavians their enemy seemed the Soviet Union, not Germany. On April 8, another note informed Norway of the mine-laying in her territorial waters, an operation that had started three days earlier.

In theory, the Allied Expeditionary Force was ready: it was the one that had been intended to go to the help of the Finns. There should have been no problem about shipping it since the Allies had command of the seas. In fact, there was a shortage of specially equipped units and the British had to call on one of their BEF divisions in France. According to the French commander, the whole thing was a makeshift operation; there was poor co-ordination between the Allies.

As a result, there were delays which the Germans were able to turn to advantage. In concentrating on his scheme for a decisive offensive against the west, Hitler had over a long period been determined to respect the neutrality of Scandinavia. The Kriegsmarine, the service most closely involved, were divided on the subject. Admiral Raeder was convinced that a British action was imminent and must be forestalled but the 'Operations Division' feared that unilateral action on the part of Germany, which would make Norwegian territorial waters an operational area, might result in greater difficulties for German shipping in using them as extensively as it was now doing under cover of their neutrality – a practice which had become universally known when the British Navy challenged the tanker *Altmark* which was carrying British prisoners of war. According to the German admirals, it was this incident that convinced Hitler of Anglo-Norwegian connivance and made him decide to act.

But he had taken his decision for three reasons which he confided to Mussolini on April 18. Militarily it was necessary to prevent Britain from spreading the war into the Baltic; should she succeed in doing this, it would be impossible for Germany to continue her counter-blockade of the British Isles in the North Sea and the Atlantic. On the other hand, large bases could be set up in Norway which would enable the Luftwaffe practically to exclude the Royal Navy from using the North Sea.

Economically, it was impossible for Germany to manage without a regular supply of Swedish iron ore; and if British power were established in Norway, how long would Sweden be able to withstand her pressure? Moreover, depriving Britain of Danish foodstuffs and Scandinavian raw materials was a counter-blow of some importance.

Finally, there were ideological considerations. Rosenberg, the upholder of Nazi philosophy, was the 'patron' of a 'Nordic Association' intended to bring together all pure Aryans. He had under his wing a Norwegian by the name of Quisling, leader of the *Nasjonal Samling*, a tiny Norwegian Fascist party which wanted to link Norway and Germany in a large 'German-Scandinavian community'. Quisling had received funds from Rosenberg, large enough to publish 25,000 free copies of each number of his paper; his party had sympathisers in the Norwegian Army and administration; he had set up an intelligence organisation which was working for the Reich, and the Germans had thereby discovered how useful it was, as the ambassador Brauer emphasised, 'to be collaborating with a political movement whose members are acting for reasons of conviction rather than with paid agents who are more easily detected'; and who cost more, anyway. Hitler had thought Quisling interesting enough to be worth meeting in the autumn of 1939, although he had made no promises nor disclosed any secrets. But on December 15, 1939, Hitler, backing up Rosenberg, dictated a minute emphasising the need to create 'a Greater German Federation of States'.

However, Hitler's conceited statement to Mussolini that 'he had left the Allies at the post' because he had learnt of their intentions through Churchill's and Reynaud's indiscretions and that, thanks to his outstanding qualities of mind 'the outcome of the war had perhaps been settled within the space of ten hours', was merely a boast. In fact, he had ordered the possibilities of operations in Norway to be investigated as early as January 1940. On March 1, he had issued his directives for the 'Weserübung operation', the occupation of Denmark and Norway, and on April 2, he ordered their execution. The Germans were the first to arrive in Norway because they had a start of a few days. But this short start was to upset the Allied plans completely and put them in an unexpectedly awkward situation.

II THE OCCUPATION OF DENMARK

Both for the Wehrmacht and Wilhelmstrasse the occupation of Denmark passed off without a hitch; it took place in the twinkling of an eye. Launched on April 9 before sunrise, four hours later the operation was all over. Whilst one armoured column crossed the Jutland frontier, paratroops were being dropped and ships were landing commandos at various strategic points, even in the very centre of Copenhagen. As he got up that morning, the King was handed the thirteen-point ultimatum from the German minister, von Renthe-Finke. At 6 a.m., after a dramatic session, the Danish Cabinet accepted the ultimatum and the King ordered his guard, which had been resisting the German patrols, to lay down their arms. At 8 o'clock, the bewildered Danes heard a German officer reading out on the radio an appeal from Hitler – written by the officer himself since by some mistake he had been handed the message intended by the Führer for use in Norway.

The Danes had been completely taken by surprise. It would seem that the government, made up of a radical-socialist coalition, although anti-Nazi in its views, had given no heed to the alarming reports emanating from their naval attaché in Berlin. In any case it could hardly have done anything, except prolong the fighting in order to save face – but at the sacrifice of human lives.

Under protest, the Danish government therefore agreed to 'place its neutrality under the protection of the Germans'. The Germans had thus completely achieved their aim, which was a peaceful occupation. Their troops were ordered not to interfere in the administration of the country, except in case of dire necessity; strict measures had been taken to ensure that there would be no looting or even excessive purchases of commodities on the part of the soldiers. The German government guaranteed the integrity of Danish territory; consequently, the German minority in Schleswig had been strictly advised not to indulge in any action of a provocative nature or in any victory celebrations and to behave with complete propriety towards the Danish authorities – they were not yet 'liberated'.

The Danish economy was to be entirely integrated with that of the Reich, which would supply limited quantities of coal and fuel. It was agreed that Danish industry should work 'indirectly' for the Reich, in 'friendly co-operation'. The maintenance of law and order and stable prices was declared to be 'highly desirable' by the two parties. In Denmark the German authorities seem to have perfected the methods adopted in their occupation of the western European countries which they conquered, with the one exception that on this occasion the occupation costs fell on the Reich, although the Danish National Bank did agree to advance the necessary amount in kronen. But the occupation soon showed its other face – the face of the Nazi Third Reich; as in Poland, from May onwards, ss units started to move into Denmark, following in the footsteps of the Wehrmacht 'in search of volunteers so as to interest them in the idea of a Germanic community'. A 'Danish National Socialist Party' immediately asked for representation in the government. For the moment it was not included in the unified coalition cabinet formed by the King from the four main traditional parties. So Denmark would still be running her own affairs, at least in appearance. Anxious to appear willing, the government even announced its 'full understanding and co-operation'. But Nazi Germany was holding other cards up its sleeve – *Volksdeutsche* in Schleswig, local Nazis – which she would be able to play when the need arose.

III THE OPERATIONS IN NORWAY

Events followed a very different course in Norway because the German troops landed there had to fight a force composed of French and British and also because the Norwegian authorities preferred fighting and exile to submission.

The speed of the Germans took the Allies by surprise. Whilst the first mines had been laid on April 5 and the British began embarking their troops on the 7th, on that same day the squadron under the command of Admiral Lutjens, whose movements had escaped detection by the RAF, put detachments ashore in the chief Norwegian ports. The German forces were not very considerable: seven cruisers, fourteen destroyers and about 10,000 men; at no point were more than 2,000 men landed initially. A parachute battalion had seized the Oslo and Stavanger aerodromes. But the decisive factor was the German Air Force, which terrified the Norwegians and was to paralyse the Allied counter-attacks.

Although lagging somewhat behind, the Allies had at least partly achieved one of their aims: they were engaging German forces in a remote theatre of operation. Were they going to take advantage of this to seize the initiative in Belgium, the main scene of operation? Admiral Darlan strongly supported this idea and suggested that the Allied troops should cross into Belgium if possible with the agreement of the Belgians but, if necessary, without it. But the government could not agree to violate Belgian neutrality. On April 9 another urgent appeal was thus made to the Belgians emphasising their 'weighty responsibilities'. General Gamelin pointed out that, given time, he could still move the bulk of his forces up to the Albert canal. He emphasised that it was a suitable moment, since the Luftwaffe was tied down in Norway. But once again the Belgians replied in the negative, and the Dutch followed suit. At this point, the French government's short-lived desire for action faded. Gamelin's only decision was to go to the aid of the Dutch, should they be attacked, whether the Belgians agreed or not. For the moment, the only result of the emergency was that, once again, Belgian troops manned the frontier facing France, since it was from that side that danger of invasion threatened!

It seems likely that the Allies had thus relinquished their last chance of taking the initiative and conducting the defensive battle that they desired in the most favourable circumstances: they were now reduced to conducting their first military operations in Norway but not in the circumstances they would have chosen. For one thing, instead of landing unopposed, they were forced to attack an enemy already established; for another, they were obliged to modify their plans; whereas they had intended to operate only in Narvik, they had to come to the help of the Norwegians, now under attack, and had to move the bulk of their landing forces into central Norway.

Nor was Allied co-ordination very good. The coalition lacked a permanent controlling body that could make decisions and ensure that they were carried out. Each government made known its views to the other at meetings of the Supreme Council, which were inadequately prepared and too infrequent. All that had been arranged was that, since the Norwegian sea area was the preserve of the Royal Navy, the expedition was under British command, overall control would thus be in the hands of a British admiral and, consequently, the expeditionary force would be under an English general.

It would seem that, at the start, the British Admiralty committed the blunder of seeing the whole operation with blinkers. It was obsessed by the idea of destroying the German squadron that had incautiously ventured within its reach. While the main British force was off Bergen, instead of trying to make a landing which at that time might have enabled the town to be recaptured, the Admiralty gave the order to seek out and destroy the enemy cruisers – thus losing the opportunity of intercepting the troop-carrying vessels, which were of minor importance in their eyes. This decision, which involved abandoning a military expedition that had been carefully prepared, was taken, according to Mr Derry, by the British Admiralty alone, which probably means by Churchill.

In fact, the only major naval battle took place in the north, in the Narvik fjord, where on April 13, the battleship *Warspite* pursued and disabled ten German destroyers. It was a good beginning but a shortlived triumph. Later, the English learned by bitter experience one important new lesson of this war, namely that the best armed warship was an easy victim for aircraft and that it was pointless to have mastery of the seas if you did not have mastery of the skies at the same time.

To avoid endangering its ships, the British Admiralty abandoned the idea of a landing at Trondheim and replaced it by landings to the north and south at Namsos and Aandalnes, points not occupied by the Germans; however, they had to be abandoned a fortnight later as a result of heavy Luftwaffe attacks, against which the troops which had been put ashore had no defence.

The struggle in Norway, wrote Admiral Barjot, became one between 'Britain, a maritime power almost without aircraft and an air power supported by weak naval forces'. The British had too few planes – their heaviest raid comprised a hundred aircraft whereas the Germans had sent a thousand to Norway. Their planes often proved inferior to their opponents', with the exception of the Hurricane fighters. Above all, the conditions were uneven: the German Air Force was home-based on well-equipped Norwegian aerodromes; the British aircraft had to come from at least 300 miles away; providing them with intelligence required many hours of flying time with the result that the intelligence (when it reached them) was often out of date. Moreover, the area covered was immense. It was a task that only naval aircraft could have undertaken successfully but all aircraft-carriers except one were in the Mediterranean.

Until they arrived, it was necessary to make do with makeshift airfields in Norway. But no provision had been made to protect the engines against the cold, the only remedy being to keep them running all the time; the aircraft had to be refuelled with jugs and buckets and as a result, patrols could not always take off when required. When the *Ark Royal* and the *Glorious* arrived from Alexandria on April 24, the Luftwaffe had been established for fourteen days. Thanks to the long period of daylight, aircraft were able to fly almost continuously but the aircraft-carriers proved vulnerable when they kept too close to land. The *Courageous* was sunk; the Royal Navy had now lost two out of their five aircraft-carriers since the beginning of the war.

To sum up, the RAF destroyed a few ships; it damaged a hundred or so aircraft but it lost many more itself; it failed to interrupt enemy communications; it proved unable to protect the expeditionary force that had been landed at Namsos, whose equipment was partly destroyed by Heinkels while it was still on the quayside. Reluctantly and with great difficulty, the force had to be taken off; it was a pitiful failure.

IV THE STRUGGLE FOR NARVIK

In the extreme north, however, the fight had gone better for the Allies, although not without providing some awkward problems. The first of these, unlikely as this may seem, was the rivalry between the naval and army commands of the Allied Expeditionary Force, despite the fact that both were British. They had received different orders! General Mackesy was instructed not to attempt a landing if the risk was too great; Admiral Cork, on the other hand, had been ordered to seize Narvik quickly, without counting the cost.

The first plan, hastily worked out by the Admiral, was rejected by the General, who pointed out that naval guns, with their flat trajectory, would be unable to reduce the German machine-gun nests and that since there were no proper landing craft, his men would have to be landed in open boats without protection. What is more, the ground was covered in snow and the British soldiers had not been provided with skis or snow-shoes.

French *chasseurs alpins*, better equipped, arrived at the end of April. Their commanding officer, General Béthouart, had the dual advantage over his British colleague of knowing Norway and being familiar with mountain warfare in winter. He suggested landing on the peninsulas to the north and south of Narvik. Two battalions of the Foreign Legion and two Polish battalions having arrived at the beginning of May, it proved possible to launch the attack in the night of May 27–28. At the spot chosen, the German machine guns were not protected from the British naval guns. The operation was successful; Narvik was captured and its German defenders pushed back eastwards.

But the situation in France had by that time become catastrophic. As a result the victorious troops were taken off from June 2 to 7. The operation went off without hitch, thanks to air cover helped by bad weather. But it was nonetheless a retreat. The expeditionary force had at last succeeded in providing itself with a well-equipped airfield, with wire-mesh landing strips and camouflaged shelters! But these efforts had all been in vain.

V THE NORWEGIAN RESISTANCE

The German victory was, in fact, complete. Contrary to Paul Reynaud's clarion call, the 'iron-supply route' had not been cut. But their military victory had not solved the problems of the occupation and administration of Norway for the Germans.

Although Norway was economically and sentimentally linked to Great Britain – 'public opinion', so ran a telegram from the German ambassador Brauer, 'is entirely on the side of the British' – nevertheless, before the German attack the Norwegian government had decided not to relinquish its attitude of neutrality. According to Brauer, the Norwegian Minister of Foreign Affairs, Koht, was irritated by Churchill's alleged offensive preparations and he called him bluntly 'an inconsistent demagogue'. All the same, it was probable, in Brauer's estimation, that merely passive resistance would be made to a British landing. But the Germans had arrived first. How were the Norwegians going to react?

It was a hostile response, above all because of Hitler's psychological error in allowing Quisling to come to power, despite the continual warnings of Brauer who had long been emphasising that Quisling's party had no great following and its leader no political influence. On the morning of April 9, Brauer handed the Norwegian Premier an ultimatum; the latter took his time in replying and finally rejected it. In the ensuing confusion in Oslo, Quisling seized power, made a broadcast appeal denouncing all resistance to the aggressor and tried to paralyse the mobilisation of the Norwegian army to the best of his ability. Militarily, he had thus rendered good service to the Germans, even if the German military blamed him for some of his rather muddled measures – he had not been informed of their intentions. But politically he was a failure; he had formed a makeshift and inexperienced government, some of whose members had not even been consulted; most of the civil servants considered him a traitor to his country and refused to recognise his authority. King Haakon, who had left Oslo, also refused to recognise him or have any contact with him.

Realising that the Germans were barking up the wrong tree, Brauer took energetic action; he too withdrew his recognition from the Quisling government; he even had guards posted in front of the Ministry of Foreign Affairs to prevent Quisling from entering. But Hitler himself, not wishing to have anything to do with 'Marxist politicians' – the Norwegian cabinet was socialist – gave instructions from Berlin that Quisling was to remain in power and Brauer was forced to obey. As a result of his actions, he was relieved of his post.

King Haakon was certainly greatly shocked by the 'Quisling manoeuvring'; what is more the Germans had tried to kidnap him and use him as a hostage. From that moment, his decision was irrevocable and unanimously approved by his government: Norway would resist invasion; and Norwegian troops did, in fact, fight side by side with the French and the British, particularly in Narvik. As for the King, when his position in Norway had become untenable, he left with his government for Sweden and then London and a large part of the Norwegian Merchant Navy took refuge in British harbours. Norway was an example both of the legal government of a small country refusing to submit to the right of conquest and of an illegal government of collaborators trying to hold power against the will of the people, with the backing of foreign troops. The name of Quisling became synonymous with this sort of behaviour.

But this did not solve the problem of governing Norway. Seeing Quisling's inability to assert himself with his compatriots, General von Falkenhorst declared himself unable to support him, as did even the special envoy sent by Ribbentrop. As a result of this, Hitler decided to appoint a 'Reichskommissar for occupied Norway', Gauleiter Terboven, a Nazi of long standing. Contrary to what they had done in Denmark, contrary to their intentions and their own interests, the Germans had been forced into the position of governing Norway directly.

A bitter power struggle now ensued between Terboven and Quisling. As his authority was steadily being eroded, Quisling appealed to Berlin. He was ill-advised to do so, for Hitler, although offering him bouquets, turned against him. He decided that Quisling should not take over the government again until his party had become stronger; in a word, the Norwegians were being advised to become collaborators in order to put an end to the direct control of the Reichskommissar. Meanwhile, Quisling was made commissioner for demobilisation – a pure sinecure, since there had been no mobilisation. The Germans then set up a 'Directory' with the 'Norwegian Supreme Court'; but they were forced to admit that, for the Norwegians, their legal government was in London. Their political failure was patent for all to see.

Economically, however, Hitler was pleased at having brought the whole of Scandinavia into his orbit. Sweden had done nothing to help Norway;

her co-operation with the Reich, under cover of neutrality, was more complete than ever. The Reich would not go short either of iron or timber.

VI CONSEQUENCES OF THE GERMAN VICTORY IN NORWAY

Diplomatically, Germany benefited from her military success; the small countries had been shown that it was inadvisable for them to oppose the Führer of the German nation. Romania took the hint and agreed to let the Germans have more and cheaper oil. The Soviet Union was glad to see the disappearance of any Franco-British threat to the northern regions of her immense territories.

Above all, although kept in the dark as to his partner's intentions until the very last moment, Mussolini showed effusive approval. He immediately cast his eyes on Croatia. Ciano refused to accept a 'special French envoy' – Pierre Laval – and on April 27 Mussolini made a very tart rejoinder to a letter from Paul Reynaud. Better still, the Duce wrote to the Führer that 'the Italian fleet had been put on a war-footing'. He called up the 1916 class on May 15; by the summer, he said, Italy would have 'two million men under arms'. In his metaphorical style, in tune with what he considered his mission, Mussolini stated that 'he could not stand by with his arms crossed while others were making history'. The defeat of Norway was the invitation to go into the kill against France.

The fact was that once again Hitler had achieved complete success in a Blitzkrieg. Another area of Europe had come under German control. Their failures had taught the Allies what were the chinks in their armour: their co-ordination was faulty; their plans were makeshift ones; they had been unable to conduct combined operations where success depended on the close co-operation of the three services; above all, their equipment had been shown to be inadequate in quantity and in quality and their air force grievously inferior. This was why the British Admiralty decided not to send naval surface units into the Skagerrak or the Kattegat, although that would have been the only way to halt the flow of German reinforcements into Norway.

The Allies had shown aggression disproportionate to their limited means and a lack of skill in using them to the best advantage: but although their failure left them rather discomforted, the final result was not entirely disastrous. The Norwegian Merchant Navy would enable them to increase both the number and the frequency of their Atlantic convoys; Iceland and Greenland, now separated from Denmark, would provide valuable sites for naval and air force bases. Above all, the German Navy had suffered such losses that it was practically impossible for it to expose its surface ships to further risk. Yet the immediate need was that the now imminent

German offensive in the west should not lead to another complete victory for Germany. The replacement of Chamberlain by Churchill gave British policy a determination which had been lacking but it did not increase the size of the Allied armed forces. How would they stand up to the German onslaught? And how were they deployed to meet it?

PART II

THE DEFEAT OF FRANCE

CHAPTER I

Plans and Forces of the Antagonists in May 1940

I HITLER'S VIEWS

WE know Hitler's ideas concerning France and England because he confided them to his generals and to Mussolini. He made no attempt to minimise his personal role, which he described quite simply, 'without any false modesty, as irreplaceable'. He was 'fully aware of his gifts of intelligence and decision that were, he supposed, not to be found anywhere else. Nobody had yet achieved what he had achieved. He had led the German people to its apogee.' Having said his piece, Hitler had proceeded to give an accurate analysis of the situation and reached the conclusion that present circumstances were exceptionally favourable for a German offensive. Nothing need be feared from the USSR 'for a year or two'; Italian support was certain 'as long as the Duce was alive'; the weakness of the British Army made it 'a token force'; the superiority of the German over the French forces was indisputable, in personnel, AA, aircraft, armoured corps, anti-tank guns, artillery and the 'quality of the men'; Hitler had confided to Mussolini 'that it had been easier to boost the morale of the men than of the generals'.

But though the balance of forces was for the moment in Germany's favour, this might not always be the case. What worried Hitler was not France but 'the steadily increasing power of England– a tough opponent'. So the attack must be made at once, remembering that 'wars have always ended by the total destruction of the adversary'. Pompously Hitler delivered himself of the statement that, given the choice 'between victory and destruction, he preferred victory'. Once this decision was taken, the direction of the offensive could be seen from the map: since Germany's Achilles' heel was the Ruhr, the French and British must not be allowed to approach it; for that reason it was important to forestall them in Belgium and Holland. When Germany had won, nobody would worry whether it had violated Belgian and Dutch neutrality. At the end of these singularly cynical monologues, Hitler placed the fate of Germany firmly 'in the hands of Providence'!

Neither Mussolini, to whom Hitler had imparted some of his doubts (which he kept from his generals, particularly those concerning the hypothetical importance of the role devolving on the Luftwaffe), nor the German general staff were entirely convinced. Still impressed by the memory of the tenacity of the French and British Armies in the First World War, the commanders of the three German Army Groups in the west, von Leeb, von Rundstedt and von Bock, had expressed reservations, not to Hitler but to von Brauchitsch. Von Leeb's judgment was particularly pessimistic: 'it was impossible to hope to break England's and France's military power in such a way as to make them sue for peace.' Hitler does not appear to have been directly informed of these reservations. Von Brauchitsch timidly tried to give him some idea of their gist but retired into his shell when Hitler expressed in violent terms his dislike of being contradicted. The German generals followed their Führer.

II THE GERMAN PLANS

It remained to be decided how Belgium and Holland were to be invaded. The first plan drawn up by the OKH (*Oberkommando des Heeres*) went back more or less to the Schlieffen plan of 1914. The main role devolved on the German army's right wing, von Bock's Army Group B. After breaking Belgian resistance on the Albert canal, forty-three divisions, nine of them armoured and three motorised, would pour through towards the Somme. The limited objective was to destroy as many as possible of the enemy's armed forces to ensure a broad base for action against England whilst providing better protection for the Ruhr. But the possibility of totally destroying the whole of the French Army in one single battle never entered the German generals' heads. As von Leeb had written, France was not Poland – and, moreover, even in Poland, despite the final triumphal victory, some disturbing weaknesses had been revealed in the leadership and training of the German troops.

Barely was the plan drawn up than the critics began to let fly: some said that the French would not allow themselves to be taken in by the Schlieffen plan a second time; others pointed out that the Belgian Army was stronger than in 1914. Hitler himself, when he studied the plan on the map, was struck by the large number of natural obstacles in the way of Army Group B north of Liège. His conclusion was that it was necessary to break out both north and south of Liège; the main weight of armour could then be directed in accordance with the development of the fighting.

This modification opened up fresh possibilities. For example, as Hitler suggested to General Jodl, why should not an armoured detachment be

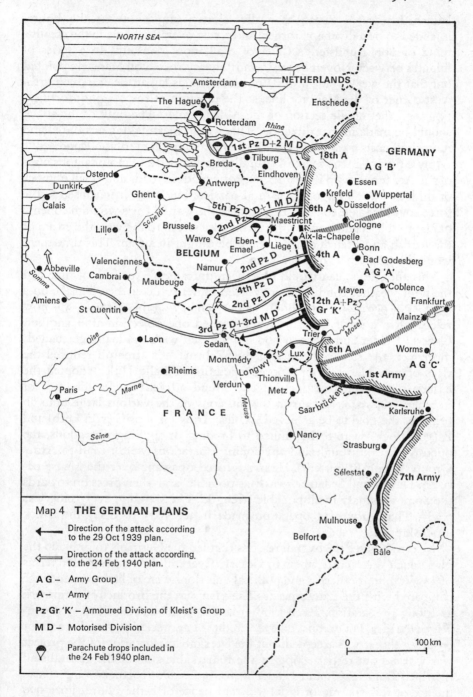

Map 4   **THE GERMAN PLANS**

← Direction of the attack according to the 29 Oct 1939 plan.

⇐ Direction of the attack according to the 24 Feb 1940 plan.

A G – Army Group

A – Army

Pz Gr 'K' – Armoured Division of Kleist's Group

M D – Motorised Division

Parachute drops included in the 24 Feb 1940 plan.

0   100 km

launched towards Sedan as a diversionary move? What the Führer intended to be a diversion turned into a vast overall scheme in the creative mind of von Rundstedt's Chief of Staff, von Manstein. In a series of minutes between November 1939 and January 1940, von Manstein pointed out that the weak point in the French positions lay at the extreme north-west corner of the Maginot line, at the junction of the Maginot fortifications and the mobile section of the Allied armies. The bulk of the attack should be made in that direction. This would mean taking armoured and motorised units away from von Bock and giving them to von Rundstedt's Army Group A in the centre. Naturally the wooded and mountainous mass of the Ardennes, with its gorges, narrow winding roads and small number of bridges was an imposing natural barrier; but if the mechanised strike force could manage to get through, then the way to Paris would lie open – or else to the Channel and with an immense sweep to the west the cream of the British and French armies would be caught in a trap. This time there would be no miracle of the Marne.

This audacious plan would have been unrealisable for lack of time had the poor weather conditions not forced Hitler to defer the offensive on a number of occasions. Von Bock, who, from having the star part, was now relegated to a secondary role, vainly raised one objection after another. General Halder and General von Brauchitsch were gradually persuaded; moreover, the steady increase in the Wehrmacht's strength reduced the risks of von Manstein's proposed operation. Finally Hitler adopted the latter's plan, which instinctively he found attractive. His directive of February 18, 1940, laid down the missions of the various large units in terms of the goal to be achieved. Whilst Army Groups C (von Leeb) and B (von Bock) were to be limited to holding or spoiling operations, the offensive breakthrough and enveloping operations were to fall to Army Group A (von Rundstedt). He must 'force a passage over the Meuse between Dinant and Sedan as swiftly as possible' and 'then press on towards the Somme estuary in all possible strength'. On March 7, everything was ready. The Norwegian operation made it necessary to delay the attack until May 10.

We can thus see the overall reasons that led the Germans to draw up the plan which was to carry them to victory. Everything was planned in terms of a swift military success and political questions were of little consequence compared with the army's needs. The plan was the product of teamwork and long preparation. Even though it was von Manstein who first conceived the idea, Hitler must take the credit for appreciating its value and for ensuring that it was accepted. But the later intricate gearing of the project was worked out to perfection by the remarkable skill of the general staff in which Brauchitsch and Halder were the leading partners. One consequence of this sharing of tasks was that henceforth the Führer imagined himself to be a strategist of genius; the unfortunate effects of this were not to be seen until later.

The Allies had no premonition of the enemy plans whatsoever. The French Intelligence Service had certainly detected movements of units from the north to the south as well as bridging operations in the region of the Middle Rhine, measures which hardly seemed consonant with a repetition of the Schlieffen plan; but this information was submerged in a welter of other intelligence leading to different conclusions. It did nothing to make the French general staff alter its plans. On the other hand, the German command had had little difficulty in identifying and locating the French units by listening in on the communication links and decoding the French messages, since the French general staff was incautiously relying on transmission by radio.

III THE ALLIED PLANS

The Allied plans were given their final form on March 12, 1940. In theory, every eventuality was covered; the advance of the French armies would vary according to whether Belgium and Holland were attacked together or singly, while another variant depended on the speed of the enemy advance into Belgium. One thing was certain: the Allied troops would not stay in their positions to await the enemy attack; for psychological and diplomatic rather than military reasons, they would move out to meet their foe in such a way as to absorb the retreating Belgian army. It makes no difference that this scheme had been decided on by the government and imposed on the high command: the supreme commander, General Gamelin, and General Georges, the GOC on the north-eastern front, had agreed to it – the latter with some reluctance – and prepared for it after very little discussion. It was, however, a very risky scheme, first in its conception and even more so in its execution.

It had been agreed, in fact, that on the probable assumption that Belgium and Holland would be invaded simultaneously, the British forces with the Ninth and First French Armies would move up to the line assumed to be fortified by the Belgians and running from Antwerp to the Meuse via the Dyle and the Gembloux gap. The Seventh Army on the left wing was to advance much further to Breda and Zeeland, or even as far as Tilburg to provide the final link in a theoretical Franco-Belgian-Dutch front. However, the distance that this army would have to cover was 150 miles, much further than the mere 65 miles that the Germans would require to reach the same objectives. The winner of this race therefore seemed obvious before it started.

The movements involved had indeed been carefully analysed and exact details of the routes worked out on paper. But success depended on factors which had not been fully assessed and on circumstances difficult to foresee. In the first place, information was lacking as to the Belgian plan of operations – their troops, timetables and routes. Above all, the phasing of the operation was very critical: everything depended on how long the Belgians could hold the Germans on the Albert canal, how many troops would be able to withdraw and how fit they would still be to fight. In any case, the incorporation of the Belgian and Dutch forces into the Allied coalition was bound to be a makeshift affair. Finally, the Allies were going to risk sending their strongest forces into the plain of Belgium almost on trust, over unknown, inadequately prepared terrain and on the assumption that it was there that the decisive battle would be fought, whereas the von Manstein plan envisaged this as a purely secondary operation. The Allied armies were going to be like a tree loosening its own roots in order to fall more easily to the storm. They were going to advance towards the enemy so as to be more rapidly encircled. In any case, for an army to launch an offensive when it was planned and equipped for defence was, to say the least, a wager. Did the Allies have sufficient forces at their disposal – or did they think they had – to have any chance of winning?

IV THE GERMAN FORCES

For any valid comparison of the forces involved, we must consider not only their total strengths but also their deployment and how it was proposed to commit them.

On May 10, the Germans had mobilised 5 million men, 3½ million of them under arms. They had 157 front line divisions, including 12 armoured, 7 motorised and 3 ss divisions (one of them motorised). Included in this number were 2 incomplete armoured divisions armed with captured Polish equipment and 37 infantry divisions as garrisons in occupied territory, fighting in Norway or under training. There were only 10 divisions on the USSR frontier, consisting for the most part of reserve troops; this gives some idea of the significance of the German-Soviet pact and of the Germans' confidence in their Russian partners.

The bulk of the German forces were thus concentrated in the west. On May 10, the situation was: 114 divisions (this was going to rise to 137), including 10 armoured divisions, 6 motorised divisions and 46 regular divisions. It was far from being an entirely motorised army; it had only 120,000 lorries and, according to General Halder, it was due to receive only 1,000 lorries per month. It had been recognised that it would require the addition of 180,000 horses and the general staff deduced from this that each operation would have to be followed by a long pause, unless, of course, the armoured and motorised units were able to achieve success on their own.

The supreme commander was the Führer as head of the Wehrmacht, assisted by the *Oberkommando der Wehrmacht* (OKW), a combined services general staff under General Keitel, with General Jodl as his deputy. The ground forces were under the command of General von Brauchitsch and General Halder was in charge of its general staff, the *Oberkommando des Heeres* (OKH).

On the western front, there were three Army Group commanders. In the south, the troops manning the Siegfried line opposite Lorraine, Alsace and north Switzerland were in Army Group C, commanded by General von Leeb and comprising only 20 infantry divisions. In the north, facing Holland and north Belgium, was Army Group B, under General von Bock, consisting of some 30 infantry divisions and 3 armoured divisions.

The main striking force was thus concentrated in the centre, in Army Group A, under General von Rundstedt. He was commanding roughly 50 infantry divisions and, most important, 7 armoured and 3 motorised divisions. As we have seen, it was he who had been entrusted with the task of breaking through towards Sedan; it had been arranged that, as the fighting developed, further powerful units would be brought under his command.

V THE ALLIED FORCES

France had mobilised 5,700,000 men, 5,100,000 of whom were French. In 1939–40, 1,400,000 were allotted to 'special duties' (reserved occupations). Army units and ancillary services absorbed 2,700,000 men, plus some 100,000 foreigners – the embryonic Polish and Czech Armies. Of these, 2,240,000 were engaged in the defence of the north-western front. Every attempt had been made to avoid any dispersal of forces. There were 7 divisions guarding the Alps, 8 in North Africa and 3 in the Near East, while 3 others were still fighting in Narvik; this still left 94 divisions, plus 10 British divisions, massed against the Wehrmacht.

On paper, the Germans were thus only slightly superior in numbers; if one adds the 22 Belgian and 9 Dutch divisions to the Franco-British forces, the German numbers were even numerically inferior. But one disturbing difference was immediately visible: 3 French armoured divisions – a fourth was in the process of being formed – as opposed to 10 German Panzer divisions. Another disparity lay in their 35 regular divisions as against the Germans' 46.

The French infantry was well armed but certain units were not yet fully equipped. The artillery lacked shells heavy enough to destroy concrete defence works; half of the AA equipment was old; as for the transport, it consisted mainly of requisitioned private vehicles and its heterogeneous nature was matched by its inadequacy in numbers; horses were still the main means of locomotion. A number of large units were under strength because training had been held up for want of modern equipment. Finally, the 'B' series of units were made up of older conscripts, rather like the 'territorial' divisions in 1914. In short the 'phoney war' and the time which it had gained had been insufficient to make good the fundamental short-comings of the French Army.

In May 1940, the English had only 1,500,000 men mobilised. The dis-crepancy between the French and British war efforts was blatant. The British Expeditionary Force was certainly in no way able to compensate for the inadequacies of the French. Its troops were insufficiently trained – some units had even completed their training at the front. Their equip-ment was incomplete and inadequate; they were short both of AA and of anti-tank weapons and of motorised and armoured units – there were only two tank battalions. The British had despatched practically all their officers and all their equipment to France, with the exception of one armoured division being formed. It was understandable that their govern-ment should be particularly concerned about its expeditionary force – it was the only force it possessed.

How were the Allied troops commanded? Even the French forces had no single supreme commander-in-chief. General Gamelin was in command of the land forces; in addition, as chief of the national defence staff, his duties were confined to co-ordinating the general staffs of the three ser-vices; the Navy under Admiral Darlan, and the Air Force under General Vuillemin were practically autonomous. Combined operations were worked out by regular but slow liaison between the widely dispersed command posts of the three Commanders-in-Chief. The Supreme Com-mander, General Gamelin, had four areas of operations under him, although, in fact, only the north-eastern one had any real importance. He had put General Georges in command of this, together with the appro-priate general staff; however, the logistical services that he needed did not come under him but under the chief of staff of Gamelin's GHQ. The net result was a tangled web of responsibilities and a dilution of authority.

Unlike the Germans, the Allies thus had no really unified command, combining authority and responsibility and clear thinking with swift execution. Moreover, as the Allies were waiting for the Germans to attack, they were obliged to take various possibilities into account and run the risk of tying down large numbers of units in areas of secondary importance at the expense of the main operational area, which would only become clearly identified after the enemy's offensive had been launched. So we find fifty-nine divisions concentrated opposite Switzerland, along the Rhine and behind the Maginot line; this Third Army Group, under General Besson, and Second Army Group, under General Prételat, were confined to a purely defensive role and were intended, in part, to be transferred as the battle developed.

The First Army Group, which had the task of advancing into Belgium, and was commanded by General Billotte, contained almost all the powerful and mobile Allied units, that is 4 out of the 5 cavalry divisions, the 3 light mechanised divisions and one of the 3 armoured divisions. But his force totalled only 41 divisions in all, 15 of them regular divisions – *fewer in fact, than those stationed behind the Maginot line.* They were far from being the equals of the German strike force intended for the breakthrough.

As for the Sedan hinge against which the Germans were proposing to exert their pressure, it was very badly defended. The solid Maginot line had been extended just short of Montmédy onwards with defensive outposts of light concrete bunkers protected by barbed wire and anti-tank ditches. At this point, which was to prove decisive, the French forces were particularly badly placed, since the French military leaders had seen the Ardennes as providing an insurmountable barrier; thus General Huntziger had stationed three divisions, one of them a regular division, at Montmédy, which was a moderately well fortified sector, but only one division, and a B class reserve division at that, inadequately equipped with anti-tank weapons, at Sedan. This was, in fact, a badly fortified sector where the bunkers which had been hastily built during the winter months were often still without any doors or firing-slits.

It is true that, once the fight was on, the Allied command could always in theory bring up reserves to plug any gap at critical points or to support any massive strategic advance. In fact, there were 25 infantry divisions (4 of them still being formed), as well as 2 armoured divisions in reserve, dispersed over a vast area extending from Rethel to Saverne and Besançon. It was intended that they would be moved to any sectors that might be threatened, but only by rail. It had been calculated that it would take four days for a unit of division-size to be assembled, entrained, transported, detrained, regrouped and brought into the line. Did not this show a complete disregard of the speed of the enemy's armoured and motorised forces and of the destructive effect of the Luftwaffe on the French rear transport communications? In other words, what were the respective resources of the antagonists in tanks and aircraft? What provisions had the French command made for resisting the battering-ram effect of the German Panzer divisions, whose success in the Polish campaign had shown that they were no figment of the imagination but a formidable war-machine?

VI ARMOURED VEHICLES

There has been passionate argument in France concerning the number, quality and method of use of armoured vehicles. As far as total numbers were concerned, the French and German experts are now more or less agreed: the quantities were roughly the same on each side; the French and British could put up 2,280 modern armoured vehicles; the Germans 2,800. But in fact in Belgium, the main operational theatre, the Wehrmacht could throw 2,600 tanks and 720 self-propelled machine guns against the Allies' mere 1,520 tanks and 750 self-propelled machine guns.

Between Dinant and Sedan, the odds were everything to nothing, because the French had no armoured vehicles facing von Rundstedt's seven Panzer divisions.

The quality of the tanks was also roughly similar in the two camps; each of them was using some old and some recent models. The Germans had four types; Marks I and II were faster than the French light tanks but inferior in weight, armament and armour. At a conference called by the Führer on February 18, 1940, it had been agreed that this type of armour could be used only against a demoralised enemy. The German Mark III was more or less the equivalent to the French D type medium tank; but the French Somua, although slightly less well armed than the German Mark IV, was faster and had a wider range of action. Finally, the French army had the B model battle tank, very heavily armoured and armed, of which the German army had no real equivalent.

So each command could bring to bear armoured vehicles roughly similar in numbers and quality, with the reservation, however, that their battle order was different; but on the other hand – and this was the crucial point – the conceptions of the use to be made of armoured vehicles were miles apart. The Panzer division was thought of as a sword, sharp as well as heavy, to be used to slice through the enemy front and turn a tactical success into strategic victory. Consequently, it enjoyed considerable autonomy in action and the other units were subordinated to it. To achieve a breakthrough, several Panzer divisions would be grouped into an armoured corps and concentrated on a narrow front; they were supported by motorised divisions and equipped with all the combat resources necessary to hold on to essential positions until the arrival of the infantry. This had been amply demonstrated in Poland.

But the French general staff, blinkered by the lessons of World War I, had not succeeded in conceiving modern warfare in this way; they had not fully come round to it even after the defeat of Poland with all its obvious lessons. It is futile to try to allocate and assess individual responsibility in this matter. Pétain and Weygand showed the way through the weight of their immense prestige, but this was no reason for Gamelin or Georges or anyone else meekly to follow their views. And Gamelin had said to François-Poncet in 1935: 'Armoured divisions are too heavy and clumsy an instrument. They may break through our lines but the lips of the wound will then close up behind them and we shall smash them with our reserves. We have a more judicious approach. *We shall use tanks as an auxiliary for the advance of the infantry.*' And he added: 'When we want to form armoured divisions, we can always collect our tanks together and make them into units.' Since that time Gamelin's ideas had not greatly changed.

So the French Supreme Commander, like his colleagues, was living in a different age from the present, which was the age of machines and speed. Whether it was a question of advancing into Belgium, moving reserves or forming armoured corps, he always thought he would have time to spare. What is more, he failed to understand the complexity, or even the real nature, of tank warfare.

The French armoured division was, in fact, conceived as a *defensive* weapon, a sort of blunt instrument to knock out any adversary who had put himself at a disadvantage, to plug a gap and to make a local gain of no great consequence for the general outcome of the battle – which, it was thought, could only be really definitely won by the infantry. So the armoured division was at the service of the infantry; it could only be committed in the framework of an army corps, on a limited terrain. It had no means of reconnaissance, no AA or anti-tank defence adequate for it to exploit its success; such a task, in the battle instructions of the French high command, would fall on the light cavalry divisions, with their self-propelled machine guns and light tanks. So the creation of armoured divisions was vitiated from the start, in its very conception; what was more, they were not ready.

At the Parliamentary Committee of Investigation, this lack of readiness was denounced again and again. General Dufieux asserted that there were no proper instructions as to their operational role and that neither their transport nor their use was properly organised. They had been assembled with elements taken from all over the place and their cohesion left much to be desired. They were refuelled by unprotected tank lorries which were unable to 'stick close to the tank' on the battlefield. The anti-tank guns were drawn by old tractors which were slower than the tanks. Radio transmission quickly became impossible as the batteries in the tanks ran down; as a result, the unit commander soon found himself unable to command his unit.

So, in tank warfare, men and ideas from 1914–18 were fighting against opponents thinking in terms of 1940. What was the situation in the air?

VII THE AIR FORCES

Here the disparity between the forces was, of itself, catastrophic. The French hoped to be able to have 1,500 operational aircraft by May 1940, 1,300 of them modern ones; but they had barely more than 1,000, of which 600 were fighters and about 100 bombers. Certainly, some of these aircraft were based on excellent prototypes, particularly the fighters; but their numbers were dramatically inadequate. Britain might have remedied much of this shortage because she had, in fact, 1,500 aircraft, most of them modern; but only 350 of them were based in France. The British government and the British high command, having despatched all their ground forces on to the Continent, intended to hold back the greater part of its air forces for the defence of the homeland. The French knew this and had accepted the situation.

On the other side, the Luftwaffe could call on more than 4,000 combat aircraft, more than 3,600 of which were on the north-eastern front – 1,500 bombers, 1,000 fighters and 340 Stukas.

This potential and real disparity of forces was matched by very different ideas on how they should be used. The Luftwaffe was organised into large units – air fleets and air divisions. Part of it, entirely autonomous, had the task of seeking out and bombing enemy targets in its home territory, at the head and fount of its operations. But the tactical air force was at the disposal of the Commander-in-Chief of the armed forces to make possible close collaboration between the two services; so the armour, with tactical and other intelligence provided by air reconnaissance, could quickly receive help from fighters or dive bombers. On the other hand, the extremely powerful German flak was brought right up into the front line so that defence groups could be set up rapidly at strategic points, where there was tank fighting or a position to be held. However, the method of using the Luftwaffe was exposed to great risks; in order to achieve quick success, in accordance with the conception of the Blitzkrieg, the German Air Force was thrown into the attack against ground targets before they were sure of having complete control in the air.

The battle order of the French Air Force was, superficially, not very different from that of the Luftwaffe; one part was kept in reserve under the orders of the Commander-in-Chief of the Air Force; the other part was allotted to the various operational zones, each corresponding to that of an Army Group. But because of the obvious German superiority, the French Air Force commander was primarily anxious to avoid too rapid a wastage of his forces. Thus, day bombing was severely restricted. On the other hand, even though the British Air Force based in France, while retaining its autonomy, worked in close co-operation with the French Air Force, the larger forces stationed in Britain came under the RAF. It took longer to call on it for help, and refuelling was more difficult; consequently, its action was less effective and more spasmodic. Above all, the dispersal of aircraft between army groups made it difficult to achieve the concentration of aircraft that the course of the fighting might require; it was entirely understandable that generals commanding armies on the ground wanted nothing better than to cling to the air forces that had been allocated to them. Finally, the armoured divisions and the air force had no theory or practical means of co-operation.

The question is whether the Wehrmacht could have been beaten in May 1940. General Halder pointed out certain disturbing factors: in April 1940, only 50 modern tanks had been manufactured, while for the whole of 1940, only 3,600,000 tons of steel had been allocated for the use of the Army instead of the 6,800,000 that had been requested. For Christmas 1939, the Führer had granted, as an exceptional treat, one pair of stockings to every German woman and a tie for every German man. Future economic prospects were gloomy.

But at this moment of time there existed a German war-machine under unified command, with modern equipment and organised in such a way as to ensure inter-service co-operation, which could launch a fierce offensive whose risks and effectiveness had been carefully assessed, against an enemy coalition inferior in numbers, in tanks and, above all, in planes. This coalition was composed of four countries speaking three different languages, and their armies would have to work out their liaison on the spur of the moment on the field of battle. The Wehrmacht had the advantage of the initiative and of surprise, while the French army would leave its fortified hideouts and advance to meet it. In such circumstances, could the clash turn out to be anything else but a sledgehammer against a pin?

CHAPTER 2

The Breakthrough at Sedan

I THE INVASION OF HOLLAND

ONCE the Germans had decided to direct their main thrust against Sedan, Holland moved out of the main orbit of battle. Her neutrality was still going to be violated at the request of Goering who was afraid that she might be used as an aircraft-carrier for the RAF.

The Dutch had an army of 400,000 men, short of officers, equipment and training. Half the population, the large cities and almost the whole of her industry lay between the three large rivers of the Meuse, the Waal and the Rhine. The Dutch were aware of the dangers threatening them, thanks to the intelligence supplied by their military attaché in Berlin, who had obtained it from the most reliable source possible – the Abwehr. Even before 1939, they had decided that only the vital area of the country would be properly defended; but they thought it possible to hold out there for several weeks, as the Belgians had done in the First World War. Reynders, the Supreme Commander, had even had hopes of giving battle outside this area, thus keeping open the possibility of linking with the Belgians. But the War Minister thought otherwise and when agreement with the Belgians proved impossible, Reynders was replaced by Winkelman.

The new generalissimo decided, in the event of German aggression, to abandon the north and east of the country entirely and the south in part. The Dutch Army would fight delaying actions on the Grebbe line, on the border of the provinces of Guelder and Utrecht; then it would retreat into 'old Holland' and protect it by the traditional method of flooding. The east to west movement of the Dutch forces would certainly not bring them towards the Seventh French Army which, according to the Allied plans, was coming to their help. On May 10, even before Holland had been handed the declaration of war, the German troops attacked. The Dutch had learnt what had happened in Oslo and, in expectation of para-chute drops, had placed barriers on the roads and airfields; but these turned out to be not strong enough and too few in number. Thus, even though a daring surprise attack on the Royal Palace was frustrated, the German paratroops had little difficulty in seizing aerodromes around the Hague. General Winkelman succeeded in recapturing them but only by commit-ting his reserves.

In the south, resistance became impossible after the bridges crossing the Meuse at Dordrecht and Moerdyk had fallen into the hands of German soldiers wearing Dutch uniform – some of them Dutch National Socialists trained in Germany. The disorderly retreat of the southern Dutch units towards the north and west caused a general collapse of morale. Also, German paratroops dropped over Waalhaven, close to Rotterdam, had succeeded in digging themselves in. They received reinforcements from gliders, transport aircraft and even seaplanes which landed on the Waal, in Rotterdam itself.

On May 13, the Panzer division of the Eighteenth German Army began its assault on the 'Dutch stronghold'. The night before, Winkelman had informed the Queen and her ministers that there was no chance of resisting. On May 13, Queen Wilhelmina embarked for England on a British torpedo-boat destroyer and her ministers followed suit. Like Norway, Holland would still remain in the war, together with her merchant fleet and the Dutch East Indies. General Winkelman had been given full powers to surrender when he thought fit.

On May 14, the German commander demanded the surrender of Rotterdam but the ultimatum was unsigned and rejected by the Dutch command, although the latter had decided to cease hostilities: a further ultimatum was then despatched; immediately afterwards, probably as a result of faulty liaison between the German services concerned, Rotterdam was bombed. The centre of the city became a mass of flames fanned by the wind; there were a thousand deaths and 25,000 houses were destroyed.

On May 15, at 9.30 a.m., General Winkelman ordered fighting to cease on all fronts, except in Zeeland. The promised Allied help that was expected proved illusory although the Dutch authorities had requested it in most urgent terms. General Vuillemin had not found it possible to detach one single squadron to go to the aid of the Dutch. The Seventh Army had indeed moved into Holland according to prearranged plan, occupying Walcheren and then pressing forward as far as Breda. But it was impossible to establish any link when the Dutch Army had ceased to exist and only a few small units were in fact able to join up with it. Moreover, the demolitions carried out by the Dutch had not been co-ordinated with the French advance. The Seventh Army's progress had above all had to be halted because its headlong advance had jeopardised its right flank as a result of the withdrawal of the Allied troops that had moved forward into Belgium.

II THE BELGIAN FORCES AND PLANS

On May 10, the Belgian Army comprised 650,000 men, and rose to 900,000 after mobilisation. Amongst the 18 infantry divisions, there were only 6 regular ones; 2 of the cavalry divisions were motorised; there was one heavy artillery division but no tanks, little AA and only one regiment of fighter aircraft.

These troops were relying on a system of fortifications in depth. An emergency line with roads blocked or blown up ran from Antwerp to Arlon. The Albert canal position, depending on the fortification of Antwerp and Liège, consisted of fieldworks with machine-gun posts along the line of the canal, each containing two machine guns and a good 500 to 800 yards apart!

The fortified towns of Liège and Namur provided mutual support by means of a line of pill-boxes, equally rudimentary, on the left bank of the Meuse. But ever since 1930, the Belgians had thought of withdrawing to a line running from Antwerp to Namur. It was the shortest defence line; it could serve equally well as a second line of defence and as protection for a 'national stronghold', if the main French forces were committed elsewhere than in Belgium. It was this line to which the French had eventually decided to advance and had called it the 'Dyle plan'. The Belgians called it the 'KW line', after the names of the two villages at each end: Koningshoyet and Wavre. But even if flooding the Scheldt, the Lys and the Maulde might make some sectors of the 'national stronghold' difficult of access, there was no natural obstacle between Wavre-Gembloux and Namur. The Belgians had, in fact, started work in November 1939 on that part of the gap that ran from Antwerp to Louvain and had speeded it up after March 1940; two lines of pill-boxes had been built there. But they had overlooked the section between Louvain and Namur that the French were supposed to be occupying, although no previous agreement had been made with them, nor indeed any real contact. The final course of the line had not been settled until April 9. In all, on May 10, 520 pill-boxes had been built, only 20 for the British and 5 for the French; they had been planned for use by Belgian weapons and proved unsuitable for either the French or the British.

On May 10, the Belgian Army's order of battle was as follows: 4 divisions in covering positions; 12 divisions on the Albert canal; about 6 divisions could be detached for the defence of the KW line. It would seem, therefore, that the Belgian high command had not finally decided on its conduct of operations and that it was leaving its choice of defence positions open, to be modified according to the strength of the German attack, with the Albert canal defence line having the advantage of covering the whole national territory. But if there was to be a retreat, the whole Belgian Army was to withdraw into the national stronghold.

Even after the German attack, the Belgians, forced into a coalition against their will, were going to try to wage their own war. General van Overstraeten resisted any suggestion of subordinating the Belgian Army to any foreign army; it had merely been agreed, according to custom, that an Allied army fighting in any sector would incorporate the Belgian troops already in the line. Having made this concession, the Belgian command tried to safeguard the autonomy of its forces to the fullest possible extent. This gave rise to numerous misunderstandings, the first and not the least of which was caused by the behaviour of the *chasseurs ardennais*[1] who were unfortunately stationed at the very point chosen by the OKW for their breakthrough.

III THE *CHASSEURS ARDENNAIS*

The Belgian plans included a 'K detachment', comprising one cavalry division and one division of *chasseurs ardennais*, to undertake demolition and blocking operations in the Ardennes before doubling back over the Meuse as soon as the enemy could no longer be contained; this detachment would then take up its allotted position on the KW line – that is to say, it would retreat north-westwards. The Belgians had expected a German attack in the Ardennes but they did not wish to protract the fighting there for fear of weakening the forces required for the 'national stronghold'. As a result, they were leaving this zone of operation entirely to the French.

The latter had received some warning of the intentions of their potential partners. General van Overstraeten had exchanged a few words on the subject with the French military attaché, General Laurent. But the fact was that on one hand the direction of the *chasseurs'* withdrawal made liaison with the French unit advancing to meet them impossible and on the other, General van Overstraeten had refused to disclose what demolitions were intended. Finally, the *chasseurs ardennais* had been given no orders to defend those points where demolition or blocking operations had been carried out, whereas the only way to delay the German advance was, in fact, to defend them. Acting in accordance with their orders, the Belgian *chasseurs* thus left without waiting for the French, whose morale was not a little shaken when they arrived and discovered that the allies whom they had come to help were no longer there.

This incident would have been of minor importance had it not happened at the exact spot where the German thrust was due to take place. For this reason, it provided the most significant example of the damage caused by the lack of co-operation between the Belgians and their allies. But it also shows that, without any consultation between themselves, they both overestimated the defensive value of the wooded mountain country of the Ardennes and underestimated the possibility of an enemy advance

1. Light infantry units.

through that area. As General Wanty wrote: 'We were thus laying ourselves open to the biggest shock of all, being caught out intellectually.' As
a start, 'being caught out' in this way completely invalidated, in the space
of a few hours, all the plans laboriously drawn up in Belgium itself, by the
Belgians as well as by the French.

IV THE FIGHTING IN BELGIUM

How was the link-up going to be made between the retreating Belgians
and the French who were advancing to meet them? It had, of course, to be
most carefully timed and its success depended on the combination of many
factors. In order to cross the Ardennes – General Halder thought that the
odds were ten to one against – the Germans needed to overcome with all
possible speed the Belgian frontier posts. But the three bridges over the
Albert canal were well defended as well as mined and the approaches to
them were dominated by the impressive fort of Eben Emaël, which rose
some 130 feet sheer above the canal and whose concrete defence works
extended over an area of 1,000 yards by 750 yards. The whole position was
all the more formidable since the Belgians had been in occupation as early
as the night of May 9–10.

However, they were taken unawares by gliders which landed 300
German soldiers on the west bank of the canal, with such dispatch that
two bridges were captured intact. As for the fort of Eben Emaël, in the
space of a few minutes a hundred or so pioneers, after landing from
gliders, hurled explosive charges and bombs into its guns, against its protective covering and down its ventilation ducts. Not surprisingly these
pioneers went to work swiftly and accurately, for they had previously
practised the manoeuvre on a full-scale model. The fortress garrison was
isolated but continued to keep the canal itself under fire. However, in the
course of May 10, the Belgian forces, possibly deceived by a dummy parachute drop behind their lines, made no attempt either to recapture the
bridges or to relieve the fort. On the morning of May 11, German assault
parties clambered up into the fort and with explosive charges silenced the
last batteries that were still firing. At noon the fort surrendered. This
brilliant German exploit ushered in the Belgian campaign.

On May 12, the Belgians abandoned their positions on the Meuse and
withdrew. Although harassed by Stukas, they had managed to avoid any
catastrophic disaster and eight almost intact Belgian divisions took up their
positions on the KW line between the Seventh French Army on their left
and the British Expeditionary Force on their right. Perhaps the defensive
battle planned by General Gamelin was to be fought in favourable conditions and on the positions anticipated.

Unfortunately, to enable the French operations to be carried out properly, the Belgian withdrawal should have been spread over four days whereas in fact it had taken only two. At the Gembloux gap, which was the critical sector, the French mechanised divisions were only just beginning to arrive, having been delayed because they had only started to move on the evening of May 10. It would perhaps have been wiser to withdraw to the Scheldt; but this emergency operation would have made the link-up of the Allied forces even more difficult. So battle was joined at Gembloux on May 13. Although inferior in tanks, without any good intelligence and insufficiently supported by their Air Force, the French held out, although some units, such as a Moroccan division, were thrown into battle almost immediately they arrived, and this was after forced marches. The battle was desperately hard but it finally enabled the First French Army to take up its position between Gembloux and Wavre on May 15.

Would the combined Allied forces have time to organise themselves, once having occupied their field positions? A meeting took place at Le Casteau, near Mons, between Edouard Daladier, Lord Gort's Chief of Staff, and King Leopold. Agreement was reached whereby General Billotte, commander of the First Army Group, would become the 'deputy for the Commander-in-Chief of the north-eastern front with the task of co-ordinating the operations of the Allied forces on Belgian territory'. This was not quite a single unified command but it was better than complete lack of unity and a free-for-all.

On May 15, the Germans attacked again. They were held at Louvain and at Gembloux. But in the afternoon the Allied armies received the order to disengage. They were threatened with being outflanked in the south. It was elsewhere, in the Sedan gap, that the enemy forced a decision.

V THE CROSSING OF THE ARDENNES

The Sedan sector was held by two French Armies; on the right, the Second Army under General Huntziger and on the left the Ninth Army under General Corap. The junction between the two Armies was downstream from Sedan, where the Ardennes canal joined the Meuse.

The 'Dyle plan' had provided for the Second Army to remain where it was. Its task was the defensive one of resisting any attempt to thrust westwards round the Maginot line. As for the Ninth Army, whilst its right wing was also to remain where it was, its left wing was to move up to the Meuse from Namur to Givet.

The battle started badly for the French: in the early hours of May 10, their airfields were bombed and many planes destroyed on the ground. At 8 a.m., French reconnaissance groups crossed the frontier; these were cavalry units whose task was to delay the enemy advance in order to give the main body of the Army time enough to move up into new defensive positions. It was considered that five days would be needed to reach these positions, as part of the Ninth Army was on foot. General Corap proceeded with more thoroughness than despatch; he gave orders for the operation to proceed only 'after the Meuse was adequately held'. The French expected their opponents to move with equal deliberation. As General Georges had stated, 'on any assumption, whatever the concentration of enemy forces involved, operations are expected to develop comparatively slowly by reason of the poor rail and road communications.'

In any case, contact was made between the French and the Belgians under General Kayaerts. But although the French were uncertain what attitude to adopt towards their new allies – whether they should merely make contact or support them or incorporate them into their own forces – the Belgians had received very strict instructions which their leader carried out most religiously. Despite French objections, he gave orders for demolition operations to be made according to plan and then beat a retreat in accordance with the timetable laid down, completely ignoring the existence of the French. The first result of this demolition was to delay the progress of the French by cutting their road communications. The Belgians' object had been to hold up the German advance for one day, whereas the French estimated that they would need five days to come to their support. Lack of co-ordination could not be more damaging.

The whole operation was starting off on the wrong foot and the rapid and unexpected advance of the German armour was soon seriously to aggravate the situation. General von Kleist had ordered this group 'not to rest or relax; to move forward night and day, looking neither left nor right, always on the alert; the group must exploit its initial surprise and the enemy's confusion; take him everywhere unawares, harass him relentlessly and have only one aim in mind: to get through.'

But it was not easy to put these vigorous instructions into practice, in view of the large number of vehicles – General Guderian's advanced units alone had 10,000 – and the narrowness of the roads, which were few and far between. In fact, the von Kleist group stretched out like a long snake with its tail still trailing behind over the Rhine when its head had already reached the Meuse. This long winding body, forced to stick to the twisting mountain roads, could easily have been chopped to pieces by any air force that had control of the skies. But the Allied air forces were engaged elsewhere.[1] In this sector the sky was filled only with the throb of German aircraft.

Along all the roads there were countless gorges and many villages that

1. The raids by French and Belgian aircraft on the Albert canal bridges had failed and all the aircraft engaged had been lost.

could be converted into defensive 'plugs'; and the Belgians' demolition operations, both on the frontier itself and afterwards at Neufchâteau did, in fact, slow down the enemy advance. But with some exceptions, these demolished areas were not defended and the German engineers proceeded with the necessary repairs swiftly and quite undisturbed, so much so that Guderian made up one whole day on the timetable that he had set himself.

The fact remained that the crossing of the Meuse, which was the objective of von Kleist's group, was a tricky task. The river was deeply embanked. But the French were not yet firmly established at any point; they were neither in sufficient strength nor numerous enough to prevent the crossing. Two German Panzer divisions were facing one French light cavalry division – that is, one horse brigade and one motorised brigade, possessing thirty-three anti-tank guns in all.

Before they were even in position, the French were blown to pieces. At dawn on May 10, the Germans crossed the Our and the Sure without any difficulty. On May 11, the 5th Light Cavalry Division failed to blow up all the bridges over the Semois as it withdrew. In the night of the 11th–12th, the Germans crossed the Semois. Throughout, their air force provided cover for their armour and their complete mastery in the battle area enabled them to open up the way and demolish with devastating force any of their opponent's centres of resistance whose existence they detected or even suspected. The vertical dives and ear-splitting noise of the Stukas took the French soldiers by surprise and destroyed their morale.

By the evening of May 12 – Guderian's timetable had been the 14th – the German troops had reached the banks of the Meuse. The eastern suburbs of Sedan had been captured but all the bridges over the Meuse had been blown up in time. The 'battle of the Meuse' was about to begin. What were the forces facing the Germans and what defensive positions did they hold? How were the French commanders going to react to this early defeat, serious and totally unexpected as it was?

VI THE BATTLE OF SEDAN

The brunt of the attack fell on Huntziger's Second Army. It comprised 5 infantry divisions, some cavalry, 3 artillery regiments – and 3 tank battalions. Its front extended over fifty miles, so that, on average, each division had to cover a sector ten miles long. In addition, two of these divisions were B divisions and were not ready to be thrown headlong into hard fighting. While each division was planned to have fifty-two 25-mm and eight 47-mm anti-tank guns, the divisions stationed at Sedan each had a few dozen 25-mm guns to fight the German tanks – that is, eight per mile. It is true that they were in fortified positions but these were stronger on paper than in reality. The block-houses varied greatly in type and were incomplete; there were not enough steel doors, loop-hole shutters or trenches. By a strange paradox, the Second Army, much less well protected by concrete defence works, had received fewer anti-tank mines than the armies concentrated behind the Maginot line.

The task of the Second Army was of vital importance as it provided the hinge for the whole French Army, and if that hinge gave way, all the French armies on its left would be in danger of being attacked from the rear or even encircled. First and foremost amongst these was the Ninth Army that had advanced into Belgium. General Huntziger was well aware of the gravity of the situation; new plans had to be improvised at a moment's notice to meet the situation that had arisen; reserve units were hurriedly thrust into the front line without any organised means of communication while aircraft were thrown in regardless of heavy losses. The grave planning blunders of the French strategists were plain for all to see. The Ardennes which they had considered impassable for large motorised units had been crossed without difficulty. They had estimated that at least nine days would be required to mount any attempt to cross the Meuse and the Germans were there in three. However, it was not certain that the gravity of the situation had been fully appreciated by the French high command even as late as May 12. They had not halted the armies advancing into the plain of Belgium; obsessed by the lessons of the 1914–18 war which had taught the absolute necessity of a continuous front they were to endeavour to plug the gap at Sedan by committing units piecemeal. They also thought that, having covered seventy-five miles at one stretch, the German troops would be forced to regroup, that a slight respite would thus be gained and that the Germans would use artillery to prepare a fresh leap forward. On May 13 General Gamelin had, in fact, telephoned to General Georges that the cavalry which had been pulled out of Luxemburg were to be sent into Belgium in the rear of the First Army. At that time, he still saw the decisive fighting as taking place in Brabant.

General Guderian lost no time in disillusioning him. Drifting barges that were blocking the Meuse provided a convenient support for footbridges; and bridges on the canal which ran alongside the river were captured undamaged. At 11.00 a.m. on May 13, the German Air Force started bombing the French command posts, pill-boxes, gun positions and communications networks. In accordance with Guderian's directives, the raids were short and relatively light; but they were repeated over a period of several hours in order to protect the German sappers and infantry-men as they crossed the Meuse in rubber dinghies. The 1st Panzer Division broke through the French front line and established a pocket three miles deep at Chemery but the 2nd and 10th Panzer Divisions had greater difficulty in advancing. The engineers were hastily constructing bridges behind the infantry.

On the evening of May 13, the situation for the French was serious but not desperate. However, one alarming phenomenon was observed; at Bulson in the course of that afternoon some units were seized by panic and stampeded, as a result of fatigue, jarred nerves and the demoralisation caused by the overwhelming enemy air superiority which was turning the troops into sitting targets; also perhaps under the influence of the pitiful exodus of the civilian population which was now getting under way.

However, even though the Germans had achieved the bridgehead that they wanted, their situation remained difficult and even hazardous. Only the infantry had crossed the river; the armour was still on the other bank; their area of penetration into the French positions was a narrow pocket open to flank attack. It was true that the Meuse had also been crossed further north at Dinant and at Monthermé; but the left bank was not strongly occupied.

VII THE ALLIED COUNTER-ATTACKS

So on May 14 everything depended on the speed and weight of the Allied counter-attacks. The lack of bombers was cruelly apparent; the task of destroying the pontoon bridges over the Meuse was given to French and British fighter aircraft. They pressed home their attack and out of sixty-five British planes only thirty-two returned to base; even those were in bad shape. But only three bridges over the Meuse had been damaged and they were quickly rebuilt.

Would armoured divisions succeed where aircraft had failed? The 3rd Armoured Division was, in fact, thrown into the attack but in a way that plainly showed up the French command's inability to adapt to the new methods of warfare that they were now beginning to experience. First of all, the operations of the tanks and the aircraft were unco-ordinated. Next, in accordance with the lessons of the 1914–18 war, before counter-attacking, General Huntziger spent time taking steps to plug the gaps, even though the lightning speed of the German advance had made it impossible to do so. But as Colonel Le Goyet has written, consolidation and counter-attack are two mutually exclusive operations: 'In order to consolidate, you have to spread out, lengthen your line and disperse; to counter-attack, you must concentrate, group and act as one force; to delay counter-attacking until you have consolidated means wasting time and during that time, you will lose opportunities that will not occur again.'

A favourable opportunity presented itself, in fact, on that very afternoon of May 15. Carried away by his own daring, realising that his first

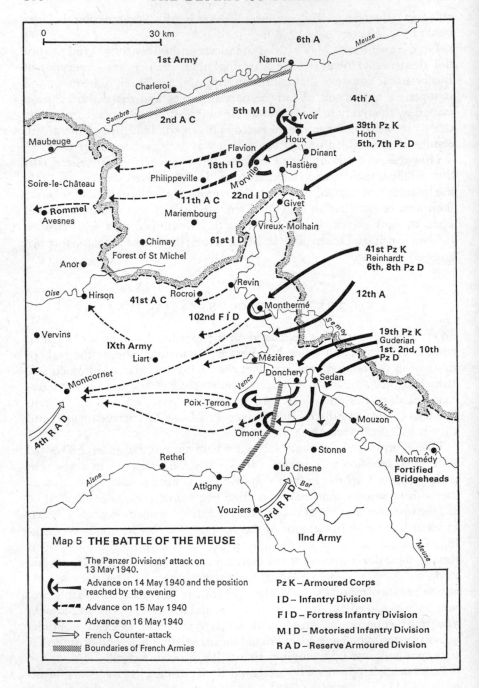

0 ——————— 30 km

6th A

1st Army

Namur

Charleroi

4th A

Sambre

5th M I D

Yvoir

2nd A C

Houx

39th Pz K
Hoth
5th, 7th Pz D

Maubeuge

Flavion

Dinant

18th I D

Hastière

Soire-le-Château

Philippeville

Morville

Rommel
Avesnes

22nd I D

Givet

11th A C

Mariembourg

Vireux-Molhain

Chimay

61st I D

Forest of St Michel

Anor

41st Pz K
Reinhardt
6th, 8th Pz D

Hirson

Revin

12th A

Oise

Rocroi

41st A C

Monthermé

102nd F I D

Semoy

Vervins

19th Pz K
Guderian
1st, 2nd, 10th
Pz D

IXth Army

Liart

Mézières

Montcornet

Donchery

Sedan

Chiers

Vence

Poix-Terron

Mouzon

4th R A D

Omont

Rethel

Stonne

Montmédy
Fortified
Bridgeheads

Aisne

Le Chesne

Attigny

Bar

Vouziers

3rd R A D

IInd Army

Meuse

Map 5   **THE BATTLE OF THE MEUSE**

The Panzer Divisions' attack on
13 May 1940.

Advance on 14 May 1940 and the position
reached by the evening

Advance on 15 May 1940

Advance on 16 May 1940

French Counter-attack

Boundaries of French Armies

Pz K – Armoured Corps

I D – Infantry Division

F I D – Fortress Infantry Division

M I D – Motorised Infantry Division

R A D – Reserve Armoured Division

task had been fulfilled before the date fixed and that he had broken through the French front line, General Guderian decided not to wait before carrying out the second part of his task, which was to swing round and thrust westward towards the sea. He did not know at that time that he was exerting pressure on the most vulnerable spot in the French defences; he struck while the iron was hot. He needed, however, to convince his superior officer, von Kleist, who thought him rash and was afraid of French counter-attacks. General Guderian condemned von Kleist's shortlived defensive reaction so vehemently – he said that it would amount to 'giving away victory on a plate' – that von Kleist allowed himself to be persuaded.

But it was a risky manoeuvre. To the south, Guderian had only the weak protection afforded by the Gross Deutschland regiment which had just spent an exhausting few days. Would General Huntziger seize his chance? He does not seem even to have realised that it existed; blinkered by the fear of leaving the road to Paris undefended, he carried out the defensive measures which he thought necessary. Of his own accord, he gave ground in order to regroup more effectively. Thus, without a fight he abandoned to the enemy a hundred or so small forts between the Chiers and the Meuse, in order to draw back towards the 'Inor junction'. This certainly had the advantage of shortening his line by a few miles, but this advantage was nullified by the greater weakness of his defence positions. By his own action, he had enlarged the German pocket south of the Meuse.

In these circumstances, would General Brochard's 3rd Armoured Division which was proceeding from Rheims be strong enough to deal with this pocket? As it turned out, this division was not sent into action. General Flavigny, the commander of the Tenth Army Corps to which the 3rd Armoured Division was attached, had been unfavourably impressed by certain shortcomings – various 'technical incidents' – and the division had already been deprived of part of its tanks by a German attack. Flavigny called the counter-attack off and dispersed the elements forming the division to provide 'plugs' at various points to hold up the enemy advance.

However, on May 15 the French command had at last realised and located the area of greatest danger. Whilst Gamelin decided to halt and then pull back the armies that had moved into Belgium, Georges, with Gamelin's agreement, gave orders for the armour to counter-attack towards Sedan. Huntziger then issued orders for the operation to be conducted 'with all possible vigour'. Mere words. The French 3rd Armoured Division no longer existed; it was spread out over a distance of twelve miles or more. It soon became clear that it was impossible to regroup and refuel it in time to be of any use. And so, perhaps not over-reluctantly, they went back to the old 1914–18 methods; it was decided to launch a traditional infantry attack, backed by tanks. 'All possible vigour' had been reduced to a snap of the fingers. Fighting was restricted to an artillery duel, at a range of half a mile, between sixteen French tanks and the German anti-tank guns. At a moment when action by a powerful armoured force was all the more urgent because it had some chance of being effective, the only available French armoured division had been more or less destroyed not so much by the enemy as by its French commanders, first through their delay in committing it but above all by dispersing its elements when they could only be effective as a whole. It is true that, in any case, the striking power of this 'armoured division' had been blunted from the start: it had only been formed in March 1940 and it had no AA, no engineers, no breakdown services and no anti-tank batteries.

VIII THE WEHRMACHT'S PROGRESS TOWARDS THE SEA

By May 15, the French front line had been finally broken. The road to the North Sea was free. Would the Germans take it? They had planned to do so in order to 'roll up' and destroy the large Allied units committed in Belgium. But would they press on straightaway? Once more, Guderian's impetuosity clashed with von Kleist's caution. The latter wanted to leave time for the infantry divisions to catch up with the armour. Reluctantly, he gave Guderian permission to continue on his way for one more day, May 16. On that day, Guderian reached Marle and Montcornet. There he was attacked by the hurriedly formed 4th Armoured Division, under Colonel de Gaulle, who had assumed command of it the day before. The three tank battalions which composed it took up their positions during the night, using their own resources. The infantry was unable to follow them, owing to lack of transport. Action began before the terrain had been sufficiently reconnoitred and some of the tanks became bogged down. Nonetheless, there was hard fighting, but at nightfall, in view of threats to both flanks, the 4th Armoured Division had to pull back to its assembly points north of Laon.

Although Guderian's advance had not been seriously delayed, once again von Kleist would have liked to slow it down and Guderian had to appeal over his head to General List for permission to press on towards St Quentin. On May 19, he had reached Péronne and on the 20th he took Amiens and was thrusting towards Abbeville. The northern group of Allied armies – French, British and Belgian – was cut off from the rest of the French armies. The Allied forces were now all condemned to fight a defensive action on terrain that, on the whole, had not been prepared for it in any way. All the prearranged plans had to be revised on the spot, in a fluid situation. The complete futility of the Maginot line was apparent. It was a heavy, if not irreparable, defeat.

Yet the French weapons were not inferior in quality to the Germans'. General List has described how when captured French 25-mm anti-tank guns were immediately tried out against German armour plating, they went right through it. The morale of the ordinary soldier was not always as high as that of the preceding generation in 1914-18; but on the whole, the front-line troops fought well. The German successes were, of course, favoured by circumstances – misunderstanding between the Allies and the Belgians, the placing of weak French units just at the decisive point where they met the brunt of the German attack, the fact that Guderian, who played a vital personal role, was in command of the German spearhead.

In fact, the Germans had been allowed to fight in their own way; they combined speed and power; their rate of advance, the co-ordination of their forces – above all of their tanks and aircraft – their concentration of resources enabled them constantly to take the initiative and enjoy the benefit of surprise. They themselves seem sometimes to have been surprised by the extent and speed of their victory. In February 1940 General Halder had estimated that nine days would be required to cross through the Ardennes and over the Meuse, and this was the same time as the French high command had allowed.

In the event, the German Army had proved itself irresistibly superior in the field. Colonel Goutard was surely right when he drew attention to and deplored the 'lost opportunities' of the French command which, in E. Bauer's well-chosen words, was 'overtaken by events every day, throwing divisions about like small change on a card table and ordering consolidation at points generally too close to the point of breakthrough. Most of its orders were based on inadequate or belated intelligence for want of proper liaison and a communications system suited to the speed of the Blitzkrieg, and it seemed impossible to carry them out from the very moment they were issued.'

France certainly lacked an army to match her greatness and her policy. True, it was her governments – and their frequent changes were no help, either – which were mainly responsible for not having provided it. But basically they had provided the means required for the sort of army suggested by the general staff. And the general staff, all intellectually hidebound, could see no further than the 1914-18 war. No better proof of this arid and anachronistic attitude on the part of the French military pundits could be given than the use of reserves during the fighting. On May 16, Winston Churchill who had gone over to Paris because of the bad news, asked Gamelin: 'Where are your reserves?' And Gamelin replied: 'There aren't any.' Then he bitterly attacked General Georges whom he considered responsible for this piece of incompetence. 'I would never have thought,' he said, 'that a commander-in-chief defending a 500-mile front could have left it without a main striking force.'[1]

In fact, at the start some twenty divisions were available; but it was impossible to use them effectively at the right time. They needed at least four days to move anywhere and having achieved its success, the enemy had long since left the critical point where each division should have been thrown in. Thus the 14th Division under Delattre de Tassigny, which on May 12 had been ordered to proceed urgently to Sedan, did not reach Rethel until the night of May 16–17, by which time the German armour had already reached the bank of the Oise, fifty miles to the west. The French generals were still thinking in terms of moving foot-soldiers or horses; the German army, or at least its spearhead, was advancing at the speed of its motorised elements and its aircraft.

It is correct to say that this failure to keep up-to-date was just as much the fault of French industry as of the Army, and that the French people themselves had also failed to realise the danger in time. But this would not have prevented the Army from equipping itself for modern warfare – it had indeed partly done so – and above all, from adapting its methods to use modern equipment, if it had had a clear idea of what was required. But for want of armoured forces, of a powerful air force and of suitable planning, as Colonel Lyet rightly says, 'the battle of France was lost even before the surprise attack on Sedan'. In view of this, could and would the battle still be continued in France?

1. In his *Mémoires* General Gamelin wrote that his reply to the British Prime Minister was: 'There aren't any left.' This variant does not really make much material difference.

CHAPTER 3

The French Collapse

I THE CHANGES IN THE FRENCH COMMAND

DURING these sad days in the history of France, Paul Reynaud had been steadily broadening his government in an attempt to provide the country with the widest possible spectrum of national unity – but not including the Communists. Camille Chautemps, Campinchi and Queuille, the Radicals surviving from Daladier's government, were joined, in minor posts, by Serol and Georges Monnet, two members of the Socialist party which had hitherto been content merely to support the government. On May 10 this opening towards the left was counter-balanced by the admission of two right-wingers, Louis Marin and Ybarnegaray – the latter a member of the *Parti social français* with Fascist sympathies and opposed to the republican régime. On June 5, another batch of politicians was added thereby making the government more cumbersome, without any apparent motive unless the change was based on arithmetical calculations that were now hardly relevant. More original was the invitation extended to certain experts, Dautry, Bouthillier, Prouvost, Paul Baudouin and General de Gaulle, who were all certain to support the French Premier and likely to strengthen his hand. But in fact, this very broad cabinet was lacking in homogeneity and did not add up to a proper team. Ever since Munich, if not before, all parties had been divided as to the necessity of the present conflict and the way to end it. In theory, Paul Reynaud, who throughout kept asseverating his determination and energy, had called on men who were as resolute as himself; but the course of events now split this conglomeration into warring elements.

In order to whip up public opinion, Paul Reynaud, justifiably worried, had called in Georges Mandel, Clemenceau's right-hand man, and, above all, Marshal Pétain; two names which recalled to every Frenchman the victory in 1918 and seemed to promise a repetition. Indeed, Mandel had never ceased advocating a firm attitude towards Nazism. Pétain's position was more ambiguous. At the age of 84, the Marshal had been appointed French ambassador to Spain by Daladier and Georges Bonnet, in order to try to patch up France's relations with Franco. He had never played an important part in politics or come to terms with any party, although, perhaps without his knowledge, a few trouble-makers had launched a campaign to bring him to power. After February 6, 1934, he had entered the Doumergue government but only in the cause of national unity. Later on he had refused to become a candidate to succeed Albert Lebrun as President of the Republic. Paul Reynaud announced that the Marshal 'was putting his wisdom and strength at the service of the country' – in fact, he had remained very vigorous despite his great age – and on May 21, the Senate rose as one man to give a prolonged ovation to the great soldier when he honoured them with a visit. What did Pétain really think of the situation? The dispatches of the German ambassador in Madrid often represent him as being opposed to the continuance of the war but they were based on impressions and hearsay and not on actual statements by the Marshal. According to General Laure, his biographer, Marshal Pétain was convinced as early as May 18 that the war was lost and that all that remained was to try to conclude an honourable peace. But the Marshal, like a mysterious sphinx, said not a word. One thing is certain: he had not intrigued to get into the government but had been approached by them. If, in Paul Reynaud's mind, it was mainly a psychological operation, in the eyes of the public, Pétain was already assuming the role of saviour of the fatherland and his prestige and fame completely over-shadowed his Premier.

The latter would have liked to dismiss the Supreme Commander Gamelin as soon as he came to power in March 1940 but Daladier had opposed this. The near-disasters now brought him down and General Weygand, another national hero full of years and glory – he was 72 years old – was recalled from Syria on May 19 to replace him. Weygand had been outstanding as Foch's right-hand man; he, too, was identified with the victory of 1918 in the eyes of the public. Nobody wished to be reminded that the two great military heroes who had in fact been in charge of the French Army between the wars, Pétain and Weygand, were largely responsible for its adoption of the out-of-date ideas and methods that had been at the root of its present setbacks and the misfortunes that had over-taken the country. Did Weygand have any illusions as to the military situation? It would seem not. But he accepted the difficult task offered him out of a sense of duty: 'To refuse,' he wrote, 'would have been cowardly.'

It seems that Paul Reynaud had not consulted the British over Weygand's appointment. And indeed, although his official titles were rather different from Gamelin's – Reynaud and Weygand were going to argue this point later on – the new French Supreme Commander wore more or less the same uniform as his predecessor. Even although he took the title of 'Commander-in-Chief of all theatres' and not merely that of 'Commander-in-Chief of the ground forces', Weygand still did not take precedence over Admiral Darlan or General Vuillemin. He was not an interallied commander-in-chief either; indeed, there was no interallied general staff. His appointment did nothing to improve the co-ordination of the Allied forces; yet this was more than ever necessary now that defeat, always a bad counsellor, was pulling the coalition asunder.

II WEYGAND'S PLAN

On May 19 General Weygand knew nothing about the front at all. He knew only that the enemy had penetrated deeply but he did not know accurately the forces or the movements and less still about the intentions of the British and the Belgians. On that day, he met Gamelin, who, in his own words, 'put him briefly in the picture', but curiously enough did not show him the report on the states of the armies that he had drawn up for the French Premier.

Gamelin, a very poor man of action but a remarkable armchair strategist – 'we needed a soldier,' Jules Romains wrote, 'and we got a philosopher' – had sent General Georges instructions which, although he may have had grave doubts about their effectiveness, laid down the only obvious tactics, namely, for the armies in the north to break out of their encirclement and for a continuous front to be reformed along the Somme and the Aisne.[1] But these were the ideas of Gamelin the strategist; and in his capacity as Commander-in-Chief, this same man, even whilst stressing that 'it was a question of hours', was content merely to express them clearly on paper without ordering them to be carried out! Perhaps he wished to avoid committing his successor since he knew that he was in disgrace at the time. In any case, this strange behaviour serves to emphasise the extent to which this changing of horses at this moment of grave crisis was to increase rather than solve the difficulty of crossing the stream.

It was logical for General Weygand to wish to receive the fullest possible information from General Georges and General Doumenc – as Chief of Staff, the latter was able to reveal the Allies' shortage of tanks and aircraft and the wastage of their reserves. But the new generalissimo's notion of going by plane to discover the state of the encircled armies on the spot was not perhaps based on an accurate assessment of the speed at which the battle was developing. Finally, after having considered certain other possibilities, General Weygand adopted Gamelin's plan; but a good many 'valuable hours' had been lost and the situation had seriously deteriorated.

1. Amazingly, Gamelin also recommended an offensive 'towards the Mézières bridges'; which was completely unrealistic at that date but which would have been very useful – on May 14.

By this time, in fact, 27 out of the 137 large units of the Allied coalition as a whole had disappeared. In General Billotte's First Army Group, 13 French divisions, 9 British divisions and the whole of the Belgian Army were encircled. The British had formed a very accurate idea of the gravity of the situation and they had begun to take precautions to extricate themselves from the mess. The RAF had heavy losses; out of 474 planes operating in France, 206 were shot down in the evening of May 13. The Air Ministry calculated that at least 25 fighter squadrons must be kept on British soil in order to provide adequate air defence for the United Kingdom. So Churchill allowed Weygand only ten further squadrons for use in France; he refused to release the 600 fighters for which he was asked and which might perhaps have provided the only possible means of equalling the Luftwaffe in the critical battle that was about to ensue. This decision, based on national self-interest, may be thought to have saved Britain later on and, in addition, the whole Allied cause. But in the short run 'for the sake of an uncertain eventuality,' as E. Bauer properly points out, 'an effective fighting weapon was being held back from the main battle area'.

Britain was worried by the thought of her own defence and could not fail to be concerned at the fate of her Expeditionary Force on the continent – the only army that she possessed at that time and which could certainly not be replaced by the 'local defence volunteer' force which Eden had just decided to form. For his part, Lord Gort, realising that the situation was becoming hourly more serious and having little confidence in the judgment of General Billotte,[1] who had been his superior officer since May 12, had informed London via his CGS (Chief of Staff) that it was important to keep in mind a possible evacuation of the BEF under his command. In reply, on May 20, the British government, far from acceding to his request, instructed him, through General Ironside, his CGS, to move south-west, via Béthune and Arras, and place himself on the left of the French Army – a decision which was in line with General Weygand's wishes. But in anticipation of the worst, at the same time the British Admiralty began to assemble a large number of small craft and on that same May 20 held its first meeting to examine the urgent evacuation of 'very considerable forces' across the Channel. As Adrienne Hytier very properly points out, the French were not informed of this decision.

Lord Gort obeyed but without much conviction. His view was, in fact, that since he was outflanked on his right and his left flank was threatened, the only reasonable decision was to retreat towards the coast. The British general was aware that the Germans had reached Abbeville and Montreuil and that the 2,000 tons of ammunition and stores required by his army

1. General Billotte had refused Lord Gort's request to replace British by French divisions on the Scheldt, suspecting that this request might be a hidden preparation for an evacuation.

every day would now have to be shipped entirely through the North Sea ports. These supplies would be gravely jeopardised by the air attacks to which these ports were now being subjected. From May 20 onwards, Lord Gort was disinclined to undertake any actions of more than limited scope in the south. He was obeying but with mental reservations that made it only token obedience. Whether he decided on this himself or whether he had the more or less explicit approval of the British government is not clear. In any case, it was certainly neither willingly nor with any determination in his heart that General Gort took part on May 21 in the Interallied Conference called by General Weygand in Ypres.

III THE YPRES CONFERENCE

General Weygand has related the circumstances of his journey to Ypres, which might well have been dramatic. He wanted to meet King Leopold and General Gort in order to put forward his plan to them because, although both of them, through General Billotte, were in theory his subordinates, they were still in fact independent supreme commanders free to make their own decisions whenever they chose. Realising that for the moment the Allies still had numerical superiority in the Péronne–Abbeville–Cambrai triangle and anxious to take advantage of this while there was still time, General Weygand was, in short, adopting the broad outlines of Gamelin's 'personal and confidential order no. 12'. This provided for eight Franco-British divisions to attack from Arras–Cambrai southwards towards Bapaume; to protect themselves on the north, the Belgian Army would narrow its front by moving from the Scheldt to the Yser, where it would consolidate its defensive positions by opening the locks. General Frère's Seventh Army would advance northwards to link up with the encircled units. On the map, it seemed a simple and obvious manoeuvre; should it succeed, the Allies would once again have a continuous front line, the best of the Allied troops would avoid being either smashed or captured – and the British would continue to fight on French soil.

The Ypres Conference might thus have offered a last chance. In fact, a number of unfortunate incidents, together with the mental reservations of some of the participants, turned it into rather a confused and incoherent series of talks during which the necessary decisions were not taken as clearly and firmly as was desirable. First, General Weygand put his suggestions to King Leopold and General van Overstraeten, who pleaded the difficulties of the withdrawal and the tiredness of the Belgian troops. In reality, both of them shrank from the idea of relinquishing another square inch of Belgian territory.

With the arrival of General Billotte, commander of the First Army Group, another conference began. He painted a frankly gloomy picture of the state of the French armies that was not likely to allay King Leopold's misgivings or those of his military adviser. However, the Belgian ministers Pierlot, Denis and Spaak, who were not taking part in the military talks, were very keen for political reasons not to cut Belgium off from her allies. They even thought that the Belgian Army should simply withdraw south without further ado, something which for the moment was impossible. Their views were thus rather ahead of their sovereign's. The latter was shaken but unconvinced and accepted Weygand's suggestions.

The approval of General Gort, whose behaviour, to say the least, was surprising, had not been obtained. He claimed that he did not know the exact time of the meeting and it is true that communications were chaotic; he could never be reached personally, he was always 'out reconnoitring'. Van Overstraeten and Admiral Keyes, head of the British mission to the Belgian Army, were obliged to go and fetch him and when he eventually arrived, Weygand was no longer there! He had left without meeting the British commander who was to play the major role in the proposed operation and knowing nothing about his intentions. The Commander-in-Chief seems also not to have attached sufficient importance to Admiral Keyes' obvious hostility to his plans; the Admiral had not, of course, any real authority but his significantly cautious attitude increased the hesitations of the Belgians and the doubts of the British. The only thing we are told by Weygand is that the Admiral's knowledge of French had not improved.

Once Weygand had left, the real interallied conference began, without the Supreme Commander. Lord Gort made no secret of his lack of confidence in Weygand's plan; he is even reported as saying to King Leopold 'It's a bad job'. However, General Billotte and his deputy Fagalde insisted on decisions being taken in accordance with the Supreme Commander's wishes: the attack from the north southwards would take place as planned and the Belgians would withdraw to the Yser. So Weygand could prepare his equivalent attack from south to north.

But on his way back, King Leopold changed his mind. Perhaps he thought, on reflection, that the withdrawal to the Yser was not possible. Perhaps he was afraid that, with the English thrusting south, the Belgians would be left to fight a hopeless battle all by themselves. Or else, in accordance with his 'policy of independence', which was certainly a hardy growth, he wanted to create a purely Belgian bridgehead, as his Premier Pierlot accused him of doing. In any case, on May 22, King Leopold issued orders which limited the proposed withdrawal; only the first stage would be carried out; the Belgian Army would pull back, not to the Yser, but to the branch-canal of the Lys. This would leave a blank space at the southern end of their positions, at the point of junction with the BEF, through which the Germans would be able to pour. It is clear that this personal decision by Leopold was an extremely grave one.

To cap it all, General Billotte was killed in a car accident as he was on the way back to his headquarters; he was replaced by General Blanchard while General Prioux took over as commander of the First Army. But General Blanchard was obliged to find out about the plans and settle in, so that forty-eight valuable hours were lost – by the Allies, not by the Germans, whose own operations, though entirely predictable, do not seem to have received much attention from those taking part in the Ypres Conference.

IV THE EXECUTION OF WEYGAND'S PLAN

Weygand's plan was thus likely to get off to an inauspicious start, although, on May 22, the Interallied War Council meeting at Vincennes, with Churchill and General Dill present, gave it its blessing. Enthusiastically, Churchill sent Lord Gort instructions that even went beyond General Weygand's own scheme: he talked of an attack in the south by 'the Third Army Group'. Either because he was less optimistic or more realistic, General Weygand had fixed neither the date of the operation nor the size of the force to be employed, leaving this to the discretion of the commander concerned, General Blanchard.

But on May 20, Lord Gort had commented pessimistically on the proposed operations to Ironside: 'Neither the First Army nor the Belgians were in a position to fulfil their part in the operation . . . the supply position would make any prolonged operations difficult.' And in fact, from May 23 onwards, the British troops had to be rationed. It was plain that in these circumstances the British general, pressed for time, would be tempted to take his own decisions on the spot, whatever the results of talks 'at the highest level' might be. And on May 22, the Germans reached Boulogne which resisted for two days.

Meanwhile, on May 21 the limited operation agreed on by Generals Billotte, Ironside and Lord Gort at Lens, on May 20, as a sort of preliminary to the Weygand plan, had started. Although the forces involved comprised only one French light mechanised division, one infantry division and a tank brigade, the Allies advanced beyond Arras but were soon halted; the attackers had been counter-attacked by German Panzers, from the south, the west and the east. Despite its relative lack of success, this positive action had nonetheless caused the German command concern by showing the vulnerability of the flanks of its excessively and dangerously strung-out positions.

Weygand wanted to launch the operation a second time on a larger scale. But was this still possible on May 23? Would the English be able to deploy half their forces southwards whilst *at the same time* containing the Germans to the east? Would the French units, tired out by their marching and fighting and short of tanks and air-cover, have sufficient strength and morale for offensive action? The French command believed or made believe that this was the case, since on May 23 General Georges issued the order 'to continue to effect a link-up between the First Army Group and the Third Army Group' – a link-up that had not even begun. General Gort had, in fact, estimated that he could only throw in two divisions for this operation and not before May 26. In the south, at the other end of the pincer, General Frère had not yet been able to make any move.

So General Gort was thus forced to act on his own responsibility. Two of his divisions were surrounded in Arras and were in danger of annihilation. On May 24 a violent bombing raid on Dunkirk showed how frail and tenuous were the links on which the supply position of the BEF depended. On May 25, the Germans breached the Belgian lines at Courtrai. Thus threatened on his left, on his right and in the rear, obsessed by the fear of being responsible for the loss of the only army available to the British Commonwealth at that time, on May 25, on his own initiative, Lord Gort ordered the withdrawal of the divisions threatened in Arras. He took this decision without either asking or waiting for permission from the French command. Any hope of implementing Weygand's plan had now evaporated. It had never even been started.

V THE HALT OF THE GERMAN ARMOURED UNITS

Lord Gort had not taken his decision hastily or without knowledge of the facts; it was the result of a careful deliberation, based on a clear and accurate assessment of the deterioration in the situation. All the same, he did not know all the factors involved; he had moved a pawn on the board in the hope of saving it; but this affected a whole game of chess. He had made the first tear in the delicate fabric of the Allied coalition which Reynaud and Churchill were striving to knit together; and it led to its being slowly but inexorably torn to shreds.

To begin with, Lord Gort's decision condemned the First French Army to be annihilated or captured. He was also abandoning the Belgians to their fate for the British withdrawal forced them to provide their own protection both on the west and on the north-west, by throwing their last available forces into the melting pot. With one flick of his finger, Lord

Gort had brought about a completely new orientation of the front lines. On May 26, Weygand as it were obeyed him by ordering a withdrawal towards Dunkirk, 'whilst fighting to save anything that could be saved', but the retreating troops were abandoning their heavy weapons and ammunition as they fled.

But Lord Gort had at least saved the BEF at the last moment, just when the German noose was about to tighten around its neck; he saved it but only by withdrawing it from the fighting; he preserved it for an uncertain future but in so doing turned the present situation that was merely alarming into a hopeless one.

If he had not taken this decision, would the BEF have necessarily been doomed? This is a question of vital importance, because the actions of the French, Germans and perhaps the Belgians were governed by those of the British. The French were, in fact, preparing to launch their V Army Corps into battle towards the north. On May 26, General Weygand gave the order to reduce the Somme bridgeheads and on May 27, the 4th Armoured Division under General de Gaulle launched a spirited attack on Abbeville on a ten-mile front; this time, it was supported by an infantry division. On the first day it achieved its objectives; on the second, it held off an enemy counter-attack. At the end of three days, the battle had been a partial success for the French. Next the 2nd Armoured Division took up the attack but it, too, was brought to a halt. The French were short of tanks; the 2nd Armoured Division was able to mass only 150 tanks on a front one and a half miles long. Above all, as always, the French command had failed to understand armoured warfare, by splitting up its forces and sending them into battle in successive waves rather than massing them for one concentrated attack.

But would this attack have succeeded had it been made towards Arras and if, *at the same time*, the British had taken the offensive in their sector on May 26 as arranged, even if only with two divisions? Would the Germans have continued their progress along the North Sea when they had, *before this*, decided to halt their armour? The reason for this halt is not very clear, since order no. 12 which, to judge by the war diaries of General Jodl and General Halder, probably issued the instructions, has not been recovered amongst Hitler's battle orders. But it is certain that the Führer was acting in agreement with the general in charge in the field, General von Rundstedt, and that he was merely underwriting the latter's decision.

Von Rundstedt had not taken his decision for political or even for general strategic reasons – such as Hitler's fear, based on his experience of the 1914–18 war, that the armour might become bogged down in Flanders or his desire to offer Goering's Luftwaffe a spectacular success at the expense of the Army, considered as being 'reactionary'. As Colonel Bernard rightly says, von Rundstedt had become aware of the need to give the tanks a breathing-space through the British attack on Arras on May 21 (which had pushed forward ten miles with three battalions and sixteen tanks), the French preparations on the Somme and the arrival of British reinforcements at Calais, a series of actions that would seem to make no sense unless it was intended to launch an attack in strength on the extended flanks of the German forces.

It is also known that the decision to renew the advance of the tanks towards Dunkirk was made on May 26 and implemented on May 27, *after* Lord Gort had ordered his troops to retreat north-westwards. In doing this, like a fish trying to slip away, Lord Gort was only inviting the fisherman to draw his net closer round him. He was thus dragging all the Allied forces in his wake – towards evacuation or surrender.[1]

VI THE BELGIAN CAPITULATION

After the German success at Courtrai on May 24, the Belgians had temporarily succeeded in restoring the situation by themselves. But as a result of Lord Gort's decision, their appeal for help to the British had remained unanswered. On May 25, the Sixth German Army, rested and refreshed, renewed its attack north of Lille. The Belgians succeeded in stopping them on the Scheldt but were unable to prevent a breakthrough on their southern front.

On May 26, the Allies were several times informed of the gravity of the situation. In particular, King Leopold warned Lord Gort: 'The moment is rapidly approaching when the Belgian troops will be no longer able to fight on.' That same day, an identical note, foreshadowing that the Army would capitulate to avoid a catastrophe, had been handed to General Champon, head of the French mission attached to the Belgian Army. In fact, the situation had become even more dramatic since there were 600,000 Belgian civilians caught in the fighting area and no evacuation by sea was conceivable. The only support from Lord Gort, as he continued his withdrawal, was to send two brigades, which were quite inadequate to plug the gaps in the Belgian positions and only sufficient to protect the rear of the British Army's retreat.

On May 27, King Leopold decided to surrender. He sent an envoy to parley with the enemy, without seeking the advice of the Allies and without even informing General Champon. The latter was in fact violently attacked by General van Overstraeten, who blamed the Allies 'for having

1. The idea that Hitler wanted to spare the British in order to come more easily to a settlement with Britain has never received an atom of proof. It was a hare started by Abetz' vivid imagination.

deserted the Belgians' and concluded 'The time is coming when the strain is so great that the rope will break.'

Hitler made known his desires: he would accept nothing but an unconditional surrender. King Leopold gave in – and the French were only advised of his acceptance an hour after it had been communicated to the Germans. However, steps had been taken by the Belgians to save one French division, which was moved out of the Belgian battle area on Belgian lorries. The surrender became effective from 4 a.m. on May 28; the French had rather less than one night to deal with the new and serious situation that had arisen.

The Belgian surrender had, indeed, become inevitable and the Belgians had fought as long as they could. All the same, following in Lord Gort's footsteps, King Leopold, influenced by interests which were purely national interests, or at least considered as such, had taken a unilateral decision that spelled the doom of the coalition which, in fact, Belgium had never wholeheartedly supported. King Leopold, whom German pamphlets dropped over the Belgian lines accused of wanting to abandon his army, took the view, contrary to the King of Norway and the Queen of Holland, that he should consider himself a prisoner, like the soldiers he commanded. But why was he not content to play a purely passive role when he surrendered after the fighting? Perhaps he was anxious to avoid further suffering for his troops. Perhaps it was in order to avoid arousing the Germans' wrath that instructions were issued not to destroy all the equipment but to collect it and hand it over to the victors. But this surely was helping the enemy at the expense of the Allies.

VII THE DUNKIRK EVACUATION

On the same day that the Belgians surrendered, General Béthouart's troops took Narvik; this Allied success, the only one at this stage of the conflict, was to have no influence on its course; the divisions in Norway would have been better employed in France; in short, it proved that any operation on the periphery was of interest only if the main front was sound.

On May 28, the 'pocket' in which the Allied troops were shut round Dunkirk was rather less than sixty square miles. By the evening of May 26, the British Admiralty had given the signal for the evacuation – Operation 'Dynamo'. Churchill had informed Paul Reynaud; but Admiral Abrial, who was in charge of the Dunkirk defences, and General Blanchard did not receive official instructions to arrange for the French troops to be taken off until May 29, when the British troops had been embarking on the craft that had been coming to pick them up for the last three days. Moreover, Blanchard had made plans to hold the line of the Lys and he was still relying on British support. These misunderstandings and the resulting acrimony could not fail to make Franco-British co-operation more difficult at a time when it was more necessary than ever.

The preliminary calculations were pessimistic. 45,000 men seemed the maximum number that could be expected to be evacuated from the one single port of Dunkirk. This was why Weygand would have liked to re-take Calais and Churchill even contemplated landing troops at Ostend. Both these plans had to be abandoned as impracticable.

From May 27 onwards, German bombers began to raid Dunkirk; but the RAF threw in all its reserves of fighters to defend the bridgehead, the embarkation points and the ships. If they took the shortest route between Dover and Dunkirk, at the end of the crossing the ships came under fire from the German batteries between Calais and Gravelines. Thus they were obliged to take a longer course by first steering north-east and their round trip took longer. Moreover, they were having to sweep for mines. On the first day only 7,700 men were landed in Britain, a disappointing performance.

By May 28, the operation was working more smoothly. Men were being taken off both in Dunkirk harbour and from the beaches; 17,000 men were saved; but 20,000 men were awaiting their turn, huddled together on the beaches and they had to be supplied with provisions by boat.

From May 29 onwards, the number of small craft rose considerably as yachts, launches, dredgers, trawlers and destroyers joined in; 47,000 men were taken off. But the arrival of the French troops produced some confusion, since in order to reach the sector allotted to them, they had to cross the approach paths being used by the British. Also communication between the various beaches was possible only by motor-car or motor-cycle. It was very fortunate that the weather remained fine throughout the operation.

By May 30 the whole of the BEF had withdrawn within the perimeter, which was now defended only by French troops who sacrificed themselves for their British brothers-in-arms. By now, 120,000 British had left as compared with only 6,000 French. The British government decided that from now on French and English should be taken off in equal numbers. The operation was to be concluded on June 1. At the request of the French government, it was extended until June 4.

Its success exceeded all expectations. In all, 330,000 men reached England – 200,000 British, 130,000 French and a few Belgians – almost twice as many British as French. Two French divisions had been sacrificed; 40,000 French soldiers were captured after the last boat had left. The

French had lost six torpedo-boat destroyers, sunk or damaged, while the British had lost nine. The British had left behind 1,200 artillery guns and 1,250 AA and anti-tank guns, 6,400 anti-tank rifles, 11,000 machine guns and 75,000 motorised vehicles – all their heavy equipment. The British Army would have to start again from scratch. One hundred and eighty RAF aircraft had been shot down in the course of the evacuation; but it was consoling to see, as a promise for the future, that the Luftwaffe had suffered even heavier losses and had been unable to prevent the embarkation. Its bombers had been an easy target for the British fighters, who had often won their dogfights with their German counterparts.

Though the result of Operation Dynamo was remarkable, it nonetheless represented the final act of a series of setbacks that would be difficult to reverse. To all intents and purposes, the British had vanished from the Continent with little idea of returning; the French would have to meet the second impending offensive on their own. And they were not very pleased with the British.

It is arguable whether the Allies could have acted in any other way. If the evacuation had been decided on earlier, several other ports would certainly have been available, in particular Ostend, Nieuport and Calais; some part of the equipment, at least the infantry weapons and perhaps some guns and lorries, would have been saved. But such a decision would have entailed abandoning the counter-attack that had been advocated by Gamelin and organised by Weygand.

It is true that it had not been possible to carry out the Weygand plan. But for a number of days it provided a sufficient threat to the German troops to make them slow down and even stop their advance. And when von Kleist's tanks in the von Rundstedt army group stopped, they were much nearer to Dunkirk than Lord Gort's infantry divisions and much better placed to occupy the whole of the North Sea coast than the tanks of von Bock's army group. The relative success of Dunkirk, or rather, its success in avoiding disaster, was, of course, due to the continued resistance of the Belgians until May 27, the competent logistical organisation of the British and the courage and self-sacrifice of the French. But what would have been achieved by all this if von Kleist had arrived at Dunkirk first? And if the Allies had not launched a counter-attack at Arras, however limited in extent, and if their units had given unmistakable signs of intending to embark, in other words if the Germans had not been worried about exposing their flanks, why should they have ceased their headlong advance, which, if successful, would have prevented any evacuation? The success of the evacuation was in any case not a victory; it enabled Britain, of course, to keep something of an army, although this army had hardly any weapons; above all, it meant that the French Army would stand alone against the impending assault by considerably superior forces.

VIII THE BATTLES ON THE SOMME AND THE AISNE

On June 4, General Weygand issued a terse and peremptory order: 'The Somme. To be held until June 15, by which date I shall have my reserves in position.' So the Commander-in-Chief did not completely despair of the situation. It seemed possible that a new 'miracle of the Marne' was on the cards. Weygand asked Georges to form 'two strike forces with the mechanised divisions and the majority of the reserve divisions, one in the area of Beauvais, the other in Argonne'; he was thus contemplating launching future counter-offensives, this time with concentrated forces.

But these forces no longer existed. In fact, Weygand had, on paper, only seventy-one divisions available, including four armoured divisions – in theory, at least, because they each had only fifty to eighty tanks apiece. The British still had one infantry division in France and one so-called armoured division, consisting of 3,000 men with 180 tanks, no artillery, no AA or anti-tank weapons, no ancillary services – and some of the tanks had no ammunition. Thus a fundamental difference between France's and Britain's conception of the meaning and conduct of their joint war was now apparent for all to see. France was fighting *her* battle which might be the last on French soil. Britain was only engaged in the first stage of the war; for her, France was merely the first line of her battle, the Channel was the second and, at a pinch, the Atlantic and her American cousins would be the final bulwark. Basically, Britain's attitude to France was rather like France's towards Poland; she urged her on and then dropped her to ensure her own safety since, at the end of the day, her own success would mean that of her ally.

The French saw things differently. The Germans noted an improvement in their fighting spirit. The French Premier took every opportunity of asserting his unconquerable determination, so much so that Churchill referred to him as 'indomitable'. However, this deliberate optimism was not shared by all the French leaders. While lunching with the American ambassador, Bullitt, on June 4, Pétain made no secret of his misgivings; he considered the war had been lost, through the fault of the British, who were willing to fight to the last Frenchman; then, safely ensconced behind the impassable anti-tank barrier of the Channel and protected by their fighter squadrons, which they had held back for their own selfish purposes, they would reach a negotiated peace at France's expense.

What was the true situation in the field? With 130 divisions, the Germans had overwhelming superiority; their armour had been regrouped into four corps of unequal sizes, according to the functions they had been assigned; now that its tasks in Flanders and Dunkirk were over, the Luftwaffe could concentrate on the one single objective of supporting the ground forces – and it had complete mastery of the skies. However, in order to demoralise the back areas, without encountering the slightest opposition, long-range bombers were raiding factories, aerodromes and communication centres in the Paris area, in Lyon, St Etienne and even as far afield as Marseilles, to the terror of the civilian population who saw them pass overhead. In France itself, the struggle was one-sided, if indeed the French had not already lost.

General Weygand had, however, restored a continuous front from Montmédy at the mouth of the Somme, along the Aisne, the Ailette and Crozat canals and the Somme. Defence positions had been built in depth. Would they hold out long enough? They had been improvised and to make up for the lack of anti-tank weapons, the French artillery – which in E. Bauer's words 'had an enormous technical and tactical superiority over its German counterpart and completely terrified the German infantryman' – had been dispersed to the various vulnerable points. On the other hand, the French counter-attacks had failed to eliminate the enemy bridgeheads south of the Somme.

At dawn on June 5, battle was joined on the Somme, in the area of von Bock's army group. On June 6, Weygand still showed a certain optimism, more stubborn than rational: the enemy had been held up by the 'French strongpoints'; but on June 7, the French defence line was pierced on the watershed between the Oise and the Somme. By June 9 Rommel had reached the outskirts of Rouen and the French Tenth Army had been 'rolled-up' at St Valéry-en-Caux – a second Dunkirk. South of Péronne, General Frère's Seventh Army had to pull back towards Paris as a result. On June 8, the Germans captured an important bridgehead on the Aisne round Soissons.

On June 9, von Rundstedt attacked in Champagne. On June 10, General Guderian succeeded in putting his armour across the Aisne; General Buisson's armoured group counter-attacked on the same day but it was held and then forced back. The battle for Champagne had been lost, as had the battle for Picardy; between the Maginot line and Le Havre, General Weygand had, at most, twenty-four divisions available.

On that same day June 10, Mussolini decided to enter the war. Roosevelt had vainly appealed to him on May 29 to 'save the Mediterranean from war'; and the French ambassador, François-Poncet, had made a final unavailing approach to the Duce offering considerable concessions – 'there's nothing we can't discuss', he had said. These approaches had been sharply rebuffed. On May 30, Mussolini informed Hitler that he would attack on June 5 with seventy divisions. The Führer asked his partner to delay for three days – he was doubtless not displeased to trim back the laurels that the Duce was anxious to place on his own head.

On June 2, Mussolini decided to declare war on the 10th and to attack

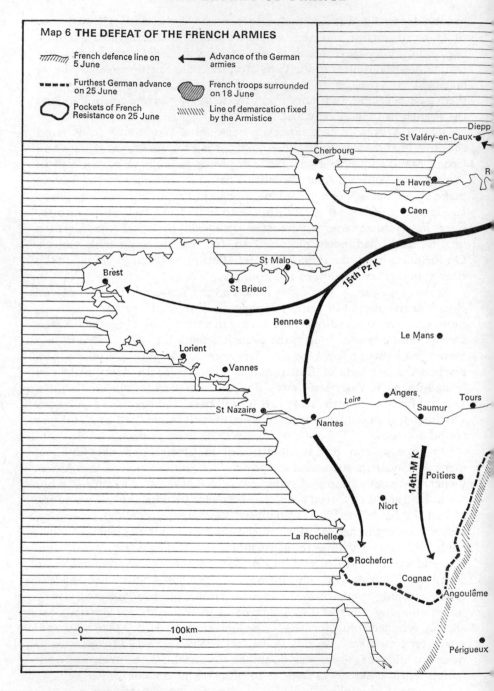

Map 6 **THE DEFEAT OF THE FRENCH ARMIES**

French defence line on 5 June

Furthest German advance on 25 June

Pockets of French Resistance on 25 June

Advance of the German armies

French troops surrounded on 18 June

Line of demarcation fixed by the Armistice

Dieppe

St Valéry-en-Caux

Cherbourg

Le Havre

Caen

15th Pz K

St Malo

Brest

St Brieuc

Rennes

Le Mans

Lorient

Vannes

Loire

Angers

Tours

Saumur

St Nazaire

Nantes

14th M K

Poitiers

Niort

La Rochelle

Rochefort

Cognac

Angoulême

0   100km

Périgueux

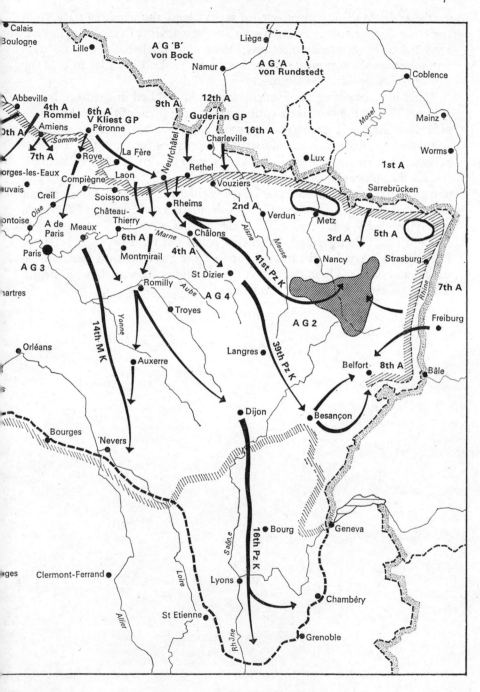

on the 11th. At this moment, according to Ciano, the whole of Italy, from the King downwards, was bursting with rage against France. Badoglio is reported to have raised objections; Mussolini brushed them aside with an unanswerable argument: 'I need a thousand dead in order to take my seat at the table with the victors.'

The Allies, or rather the French, were thus stabbed in the back by the Italians. Would they receive a counterpart in the form of timely American aid? Paul Reynaud urgently requested it on several occasions. Bullitt suggested to Roosevelt sending the American fleet into the Mediterranean. The American President's hands were tied by the law of neutrality. He did, however, offer to let the French have 2,000 75-mm guns and 150 aircraft. But they would not be ready till June 17. As for Congress, it had voted $50,000,000 to provide foodstuffs for 'refugees' in France – a purely charitable act, of no military significance.

The French Premier had stated that he would fight on outside Paris, in Paris and beyond Paris. But on June 10, the government evacuated the capital and declared it an open city. A dramatic week was about to begin. There was already talk of an armistice.

CHAPTER 4

The Armistice

FROM June 10, the French government was on the run, roaming and dispersing from one château to another, first in accordance with a prearranged plan but soon driven on by the enemy advance. It had expected to settle in Tours but it could only stay there four days. On June 15, it reached Bordeaux. During this fateful week, when the gravest of decisions had to be taken, the ministers were cut off from each other and from their staffs; they were no longer young, and suffered anguish and exhaustion on the roads or anywhere they could find to lay their heads; they were starved of news; sometimes they knew only what they could hear from the odd radio bulletins or the chance rumours picked up from their distraught compatriots; hardly had they taken a decision when it proved impossible to implement it, either because it had been overtaken by events or else because it had failed to reach the people supposed to carry it out.

The flight of the government was paralleled by the exodus of a whole nation. Starting from the north and from the north-east, from Belgium onwards, a flood of humanity, flowed in their millions towards the west and the south, people of every age and condition, flung headlong on to the roads by the dreadful fear of what the morrow might have in store. It was a vast tidal wave, washing away large swathes of humanity from the streets through which it poured; cars, motor-cyclists, cyclists and horse-drawn carts all moving at a snail's pace because of the congested roads. It dragged everything helter-skelter in its wake. The authorities went off either before or after those whom they had been appointed to govern; towns lost their mayors, councillors and clerks, their dustmen, policemen and firemen. Exhausted crowds camped out wherever they could, on guard against rioting and looting. When the enemy troops arrived they found a vacuum which their propaganda was not slow to exploit: 'We are coming in order to help civilians deserted by their leaders.'

At first this wave of panic caused a real collective trauma. France was deprived of any national or local government and the French left at the mercy of their obsessions and weaknesses. The sight was a demoralising one for the members of the government and President Albert Lebrun has told how deeply it affected him. On all sides the feeling was that every-thing was falling apart and that the state and all authority had ceased to exist. It would have been impossible not to be obsessed by all this when making these grave decisions.

The hordes of refugees mingled with the retreating army convoys. The chaos amongst the civilians infected the soldiers, and vice-versa; their panic rush took them along the same roads. Soldiers threw away their weapons and desertion became commonplace. German aircraft flew over and machine-gunned civilians and troops indiscriminately. The tanks forced their way through. In the general chaos, it was obvious that there was no longer any possibility of co-ordinated resistance.

II THE ROUT

Indeed, the German troops were advancing in all directions without meeting anything but local resistance. General Weygand – whom Paul Reynaud had thought of replacing by General Huntziger but then decided otherwise – had, of course, issued his instructions: the Tenth Army was to block the way west by digging in on the Perche hills; the Paris Army and the Seventh Army were to hold the Loire between Tours and Cosne; the Sixth, Fourth and Second Armies were to block the valleys of the Yonne, the Seine and the Marne; and finally the Second Army Group would leave the Maginot line and take up positions on the Swiss frontier. These positions were well dispersed but not continuous; and they were never to be held or even occupied, because the Supreme Commander no longer knew the whereabouts of the armies supposed to occupy them. All that remained were a number of isolated pockets of resistance under a few determined leaders at bridges, crossroads and communication centres. Some mayors were opposed to defending their towns for fear that they would be destroyed.

Premier Paul Reynaud conceived one last grandiose operation: the formation of a 'Breton stronghold' so that the struggle could be con-tinued on some part of French territory and links maintained with his British ally; control of the seas would enable supplies to be brought in. Without great conviction, Weygand issued the necessary instructions on June 10. Generals Fagalde and Altmeyer were to regroup the divisions saved at Dunkirk and repatriated from England in order to man the stronghold. The collaboration of the British was obviously indispensable; on June 11, they began landing a Canadian division in France. On June 14, agreement was reached between Weygand and General Alanbrooke, the new commander of the BEF. Weygand made no secret of his pessimism to Alanbrooke; he called the stronghold a 'romantic idea' and confessed to him that the French Army was no longer capable of organised resistance. Alanbrooke was concerned at this and reported the real state of affairs to his government. The British government then took decisions which confirmed their intention to cease playing any part in the struggle on the Continent: they released Alanbrooke from his commitments, kept the BEF under their control, stopped sending reinforcements and prepared to re-embark the last British troops still on French soil.

On June 15, Sir John Dill, the British CIGS, informed Weygand that the BEF was no longer subordinated to him, but that he would help the French troops to embark if they so wished. In fact, the British now proceeded to undertake a second evacuation, this time very successfully (150,000 men including 20,000 Poles, and 310 guns). By June 18, there were no British soldiers left in France, except a few hidden stragglers looked after by French civilians.

By that date, moreover, the Germans had reached every objective within the range of their rate of advance. Guderian took St-Dizier, Langres and Besançon one after the other. On June 17, he had reached Pontarlier and had completely isolated the eastern army group. On the 18th, Belfort fell.

The Hoeppner group had crossed the Marne and then the Seine; one Panzer division had reached Auxerre, Avallon, the Jura and then moved on to Bourg, Lyon and the Dauphiné, where it was preparing to join up with the Italians; another, starting from Semur and Dijon, was fanning out towards the Rhône valley via Chalon-sur-Saône and Mâcon.

The Kleist group was making for Clermont-Ferrand via Provins, Sens, Montargis and Moulins. Finally, in the extreme west, the Hoth group with Rommel in the lead had captured the remnants of the Tenth Army in Rennes, took Cherbourg on the 17th, had almost reached Brest and was advancing on Niort.

Apart from a few isolated heroic feats, such as that of the Saumur cadets on a bridge over the Loire, the French had stopped fighting except in the north-east and in the Alps. According to General Prételat, General Weygand, against his advice, took too long to order the withdrawal of the Second Army Group. The latter had opposed the German attack in the Saar; when it pulled back, the enemy had been able to cross the Rhine; then it had been encircled by Guderian's advance; however, the struggle was still continuing and many units were offering stout resistance, particularly on the Maginot line – some of its forts did not surrender until ordered to do so, between June 25 and July 7.

In the Alps nothing happened on June 11, 12 or 13. On June 14, 'local' attacks were launched by the Italians on easily accessible points; these attacks were pressed home on June 15 and 16, but were halted by a French counter-attack on the 17th. Not until June 20 did the Italians attack in strength but only a few French advanced works were lost or by-passed on June 21 and 22. The struggle for Menton began in the evening of the 23rd, but the Italians succeeded in occupying only the old town. 450,000 Italians were pinned down by less than 180,000 French. The French considered that they had not been beaten by the Italians, in fact quite the reverse.

But in the pitiful state of France this was meagre consolation. How could the deterioration in the situation and the disintegration of the French Army fail to affect the determination of the members of the govern-ment and the military leaders?

III THE FRENCH GOVERNMENT'S DELIBERATIONS (JUNE 13–16)

The government proved to be divided as to the answer to be given to the one question that faced them: should fighting continue or should hostili-ties be brought to an end by suing for peace?

This question, on which hung the present as well as the future of France, split the ministers into two groups, one led by the Premier, Paul Reynaud, the other by Marshal Pétain. The decision was taken in the course of discussions spread over four dramatic days and only after some violent clashes.

In the War Committee of May 25, 1940, the cessation of hostilities had been mentioned by the President and by Campinchi, the Minister for the Navy, as one of a number of possibilities that must be considered. In the Interallied Supreme Council held at Briare on June 11, Paul Reynaud informed Churchill that Marshal Pétain had expressed himself in favour of asking for an armistice but that he had not yet sent him a minute on the subject.

On June 12, at Cangé, it was General Weygand himself who, after re-porting on the military situation, had concluded that fighting must be brought to an end, to the great consternation of the French cabinet, whose members had not imagined that the situation was so serious. Almost all the twenty-four ministers present rejected Weygand's proposal that Paul Reynaud described as 'completely inacceptable'.

The new factor in Weygand's approach to the matter was that he was speaking as much in political as in military terms. He considered that 'the country could not be allowed to drift; some troops would have to be kept in reserve in order to maintain public order which might shortly be gravely jeopardised; if an armistice were not requested without delay, the Army as well as the local civilian population and the refugees would get out of control.' In a word, the Supreme Commander was not confining himself to advising the government; over and above his very persuasive urgent military reasons, he was putting forward considerations of internal policy and even raising the question of defending a particular social order. He was going beyond his brief in order to indicate to the government the policy that they should follow. The only person to support Weygand was Marshal Pétain.

In face of this alliance of two great soldiers, what possible weight could the civilian ministers' opinions have, when their names were practically unknown to the French people and most of them were in any case incapable of forming an independent judgment for themselves? How could they avoid the natural inclination to cover themselves by siding with those who seemed to speak with indisputable authority and prestige?

And so, on June 13, Paul Reynaud's assistants, the 'experts' Bouthillier and Baudouin joined the ranks of those supporting an armistice. The politician Ybarnegaray followed suit, with the remark that he was a soldier and would follow his leaders.

Marshal Pétain now came out openly without reservation as the leader of the peace party. He read out to the Cabinet a memorandum whose contents went far beyond any request to cease hostilities. He brushed aside any idea of continuing the struggle beyond the frontiers of metropolitan France, not for military but for moral reasons: 'Abandoning French territory would amount to desertion. To deprive France of her natural defenders in a period of general confusion would mean delivering her into the hands of the enemy.' He wanted France's revival to be the work of the French themselves and not through 'the conquest of our territory by Allied guns'. Moreover, he did not see this French revival as taking place through military success but as the result of 'suffering imposed on the fatherland and its sons'. He concluded by describing an armistice not as a punishment for a defeat, with its incalculable consequences, but as the first stage in a fresh start, 'a necessary condition to ensure that immortal France should continue to exist for all time'. Thus while Marshal Pétain considered any military and political reasons for the government's decisions as clearly important, he took his stand on a quasi-religious level. As for the government, it may be wondered how far he recognised its authority; he had no desire to submit to a majority decision; his own decision had been taken once and for all: 'He would not leave France . . . and he would leave the government if necessary.'

No decision was reached that day. But Pétain's determination to act outside the government if he did not become its leader had already been shown when, without informing the Premier, he summoned General Weygand that afternoon to ask him to attend the cabinet meeting at Bordeaux on the following day. It was Weygand himself, correct to the last, who told Paul Reynaud of Pétain's request.

In Bordeaux, where the government arrived on June 14, two new-comers made their appearance on the scene. Laval, who was not a member of the government and who had hitherto played no part at all, had installed himself in the Hôtel de Ville. By exerting influence on the members of Parliament who were also in Bordeaux, he was able to provide the group of ministers who were behind Marshal Pétain with some incipient parliamentary support. In fact, a number of deputies informed Herriot, the leader of the Chamber of Deputies, that they wished to approach the government to suggest suing for peace.

Till now, Admiral Darlan had shown himself determined to continue the fight at the head of the Navy, whatever happened. The defeat of the Army had made the Admiral the senior French military commander and the Navy had become the last remaining organised force in France. His actions had thus suddenly become extremely important; but on June 12, Pétain succeeded in winning him over: he told him of 'his disgust at the government's wavering'; he emphasised 'the need to change the régime'; he forecast 'that a sort of Consulate would be necessary' and said 'that he saw him as a First Consul'.[1] Although on other occasions he still expressed himself in favour of continuing the fight – for example, on June 15 to Edouard Herriot – the Admiral had definitely made up his mind, so the opponents of an armistice could no longer rely on the Admiral of the Fleet. How would it then be possible to continue the fight overseas?

At the cabinet meeting on June 15, it was, however, still Weygand who held the limelight. Paul Reynaud asked him to put an end to hostilities, on land and in the metropolis, following the Dutch precedent, by surrendering the Army. In this way, the government would remain free to continue the war with the fleet and the Air Force in the French colonies. The general's reply gave a strange twist to the problem. He categorically refused to surrender, on the grounds that 'what was right in a monarchy was not right in a democracy in which governments follow one another in rapid succession'. When Paul Reynaud suggested giving the Supreme Commander a written order to cover him, Weygand replied that he would refuse to obey any such order. He considered that it would be dishonourable for the Army.

It was now no longer merely a question of a confrontation of forces, the sufferings of the civilian population or choosing the lesser evil. What had suddenly and dramatically emerged was the pre-revolutionary conception, held by a great Republican army leader, of his relationship with the French government. In reality, it was no more 'dishonourable' to order all the

---

1. Darlan has given three roughly identical accounts of this meeting: one to Henri Béraud (*Gringoire*, May 5, 1941); one to Matteo Cornet, Campinchi's principal private secretary (Parliamentary Investigating Committee, vol. VII, p. 2188); and one in a letter to Marshal Pétain dated October 5, 1942 (Admiral Fernet: *Aux cotés du maréchal Pétain*, p. 282).

units which were continuing a hopeless battle to lay down their arms together than to let them surrender piecemeal, one after another, as had been the case with the 40,000 men who had been left behind at Dunkirk. Once again, it was a political or even an ethical point of view that the Supreme Commander was trying to force on the government; at the very least, he was intent on protecting the Army from any share in the responsibility for the disaster and ensuring that the government should assume full responsibility for suing for peace, which is a political act.

Supported by Frossard, Camille Chautemps now put forward one of those compromise solutions which were his speciality. He suggested that an armistice should be requested and Germany sounded as to her peace terms. These, he said, would be so outrageous that public opinion would refuse to accept them; this would restore unity in the government, which would thus be stronger and more able to continue the struggle in North Africa. According to Paul Reynaud, thirteen ministers voted for Chautemp's suggestion and only six against. This 'classical lobby compromise' as it was correctly termed by W. Langer, would in fact make Hitler 'the saviour of French unity', as Robert Aron pointed out. In any case, it could not really lead to much, since the 'unacceptable conditions' had not been defined. But some of Paul Reynaud's supporters had been lured away, although Chautemps afterwards denied that he had been in any way working hand in glove with the Pétain–Weygand faction.

In the morning of June 16, the ministers met again. Judging that further hesitation was impossible, Pétain brought matters to a head: he stood up and read a prepared letter of resignation, giving as his reason the delay in suing for peace. He even attempted to leave the room and President Lebrun was obliged to restrain him.

That afternoon, the government was informed of a staggering British proposal – in fact, thought up by General de Gaulle, Jean Monnet and René Pleven, the members of the co-ordinating committee for the purchase of armaments in London, and approved by Churchill. It suggested quite simply a complete political union of France and Britain. Its real purpose was, in fact, to gain time and prevent the supporters of an armistice from carrying the day. Paul Reynaud was the first to be surprised but he nonetheless put the proposal to his colleagues; they did not examine it closely. Chautemps and Ybarnegaray even thought that Britain meant to reduce France to the status of a dominion and expressed indignation.

That evening, without seeking the advice of any of his ministers, Paul Reynaud handed in his resignation to President Lebrun, proposing Marshal Pétain as his successor. When the leaders of the two houses, Jeanneney and Herriot were consulted, as is customary in a ministerial crisis, they concurred in the choice. To everyone's surprise, the Marshal pulled out of his pocket a readymade list of ministers. The new cabinet met at once and, in the night of June 16–17, Paul Baudouin, the new Minister of Foreign Affairs, asked the Spanish government to agree to act as intermediary with the Germans.

IV WAS THE ARMISTICE UNAVOIDABLE?

That the French Army, victorious in the First World War, had been crushed in less than forty days' fighting was an unprecedented disaster for the French nation, and as dramatic as it was unexpected. And the fact that suing for peace was also to involve occupation and resistance, collaboration and national revolution, was bound to lead to passionate heart-searching amongst the French as to its reasons and causes. Thus we find that those directly involved have offered long, often violently conflicting explanations – particularly Paul Reynaud and General Weygand.

On both sides, the arguments put forward were equally strong. Paul Reynaud, Mandel and Louis Marin have pointed out that France was bound to Britain by treaty and Hitler wanted the total destruction of France – as Paul Reynaud had said, 'he's Gengis Khan'; and, even although the army was beaten, France still had her fleet intact and an immense empire. Pétain and Weygand's retort was that France had done its utmost and that Britain had failed to do the same; that, on the other hand, it was despicable for those governing a country to leave it to its fate when the battle had gone against it. Weygand had added his personal interpretation of the honour of the Army and he had not disguised his apprehension that defeat might lead to social revolution.

In this way, the nub of the problem has frequently been strangely shifted so that the real question is concealed. This was to decide whether France could and should continue the fight outside metropolitan France, on the seas and in the colonies. In point of fact, no one had given the matter serious thought and no plans had been drawn up. General Weygand had never concealed his belief that any such project was doomed from the start because it was impracticable. But Truchet has shown that in French North Africa there were still 400,000 men and means were available to supply them with further manpower and equipment; that above all the whole population – Europeans, natives, civil servants and the military, with General Noguès at their head – were unanimous in wanting to continue the struggle. It is true that there were many unknown quantities, not least the attitude of Spain. But all in all, if no decision was reached, it was because no one had even begun to make any preparations for further fighting and the question was never examined, because after June 16 the new political leaders of France under Pétain and Weygand wanted nothing to do with it. What were their reasons?

V PETAIN'S IDEAS

The ideas which motivated the Marshal at this crucial time were communicated to the French people in a series of messages from June 20–25.

The prime cause of France's irretrievable defeat was, he stressed, the disparity of forces. Pétain considered that the British were especially responsible for this state of affairs.

To this inferiority in numbers there must be added a still greater inferiority in equipment. 'The French Air Force,' said the Marshal 'had to fight against odds of six to one.' Curiously enough, no mention was made of tanks, of tank–aircraft co-operation or of German Panzer tactics.

The truth probably was that for him the real causes went deeper, since they were moral rather than military: 'Love of pleasure was stronger than the spirit of sacrifice. People claimed things as their right rather than being willing to serve. They shirked effort and so they have fallen on evil times.' So it was the whole French people and no chance disparity between the armies involved that was responsible for France's defeat. By their bad conduct, the French people had called down condign punishment upon their heads. 'Our defeat had its roots in the laxity of our conduct.'

The conclusion followed inevitably from these premises: for the moment the harm was irreparable and the defeat irredeemable; by recognising this, 'the French were showing more greatness . . . than in meeting it with empty words and vain schemes' – a reference to Churchill's expressed determination that Britain would continue the fight alone and a reply to General de Gaulle's prophetic appeals from London.

There was nothing for France to do but to submit to her unhappy fate. That way lay wisdom and salvation, at least for what might still be saved. Seen from this viewpoint, it might moreover be a shrewd move to beat the British in the race to see who would give up first. For Pétain thought that Churchill's call for resistance at all costs was futile and perhaps even empty words.

This resigned pessimism had been expressed by Pétain even before the battle of the Somme had started. All that had happened since had only confirmed him in his conviction that Germany had won the war; so without losing a minute, the least unpalatable terms possible must be obtained so that no more French soldiers' lives should be uselessly sacrificed and also in order to preserve what little strength France still retained.

Thus when he took power Marshal Pétain was not concerned that fighting should stop, as he felt it must, for military reasons only, nor did

France's diplomatic obligations towards her British ally weigh with him
either. Looking beyond the catastrophe which, grave as it was, was only
an accident in the life of a people, he was seeing into the future of France;
and this future would only be assured if she could drag herself out of the
morass into which she had been plunged by bad leadership and evil
habits, and enter into the path of revival in which he would show the way.
He did not look upon himself as merely taking over the tiller in a difficult
moment but as the saviour for whom the country had been longing for
many years. So it was pointless to consider continuing the struggle in
Africa. Nor could France's task be dealt with by means of a mere suspension of hostilities which was always precarious and would inevitably
be denounced. Moreover, since it was France who was responsible for the
ills that had befallen her, it was for her alone to turn the tables on herself,
in the due course of time.

VI REQUEST FOR GERMANY'S TERMS

It may thus be wondered whether it was really a truce that the Spanish
government was to request from the Reich on France's behalf or whether
it was not in fact Germany's peace terms.

Paul Baudouin relates in his memoirs that he handed M. de Léquérica,
the Spanish ambassador to Paris, a handwritten note but he does not
reveal its contents. He writes that the 'government had decided to ask
Germany her terms for the cessation of hostilities'. Charles-Roux has
come to his minister's help: 'It is possible,' he writes 'that M. Baudouin
on one occasion used one word instead of another' – peace instead of
armistice – 'but the overall gist of his message left no doubt as to what
request he was making.'

Paul Baudouin was a makeshift Foreign Minister and a novice, and his
emotion at having such a grave step to take as his first act of diplomacy is
understandable; but it is difficult to imagine that he displayed such confusion of mind and casualness of approach as to fail to distinguish a
temporary armistice and a definitive peace, especially as he was implementing a vital decision which had been reached at a cabinet meeting that
had only just ended.

In any case, the German ambassador in Madrid, von Stöhrer, had no
doubts at all: Paul Baudouin had told Léquérica – the Spanish government had just informed him – that 'the French government wishes the
Spanish government to transmit to Germany, with all desirable speed, a
request for the immediate cessation of hostilities and that it should be informed of Germany's proposed *peace terms*'. When Léquérica asked the
French minister if he was talking about an armistice or peace or both,

Baudouin replied: 'Armistice terms were always, obviously, a temporary expedient and the French government was interested in knowing the peace terms.' So it is hardly a question of its being a slip of the tongue in a hurried conversation; Paul Baudouin had been perfectly explicit. And Hitler was not mistaken, either; in his order of the day to the Wehrmacht, he had stated: 'The newly formed French government has informed the German government that it intends to cease hostilities and wishes to be informed of our peace terms.'

Moreover, hardly had the request been made than Pétain made a solemn proclamation to the troops on June 17, that 'while recognising the heroic nature of their struggle', they must 'cease fighting'. A confession of this sort that he was abandoning the struggle, even if it was made 'with a heavy heart', not only placed the French envoys in an awkward position in their negotiations with the Germans over the conditions for an armistice and, if possible, peace terms; it also incurred the risk of encouraging the enemy to think that it was pointless to engage in talks with a government which, of its own accord, was ordering its armed forces to cease fighting, leaving the commanders to decide for themselves the best way to set about it; it considerably limited any possibility the French might have of rejecting or even of discussing the enemy's terms.

The first immediate result was that whole regiments of troops ceased fighting, since they had been ordered to do so.

What would have happened had Hitler demanded something 'unacceptable', that is, if he had made claims on the French empire and the French fleet? How could the Bordeaux government have been able to take up the fight again in view of the fact that it had deprived itself of any possibility of doing so? But Hitler did not place the Bordeaux government in such an embarrassing position, which would doubtless have caused its downfall. He was careful not to demand anything 'unacceptable' and he gave Mussolini his reasons.

VII HITLER'S IDEAS ON THE ARMISTICE

Whilst ordering the Wehrmacht to 'pursue the beaten foe energetically in every sector', Hitler was above all concerned to weaken Britain decisively by preventing the remaining French forces – the empire and the fleet – from casting their lot in with her.

On June 18 and 19, he met Mussolini and Ciano in Munich. The latter wrote: 'He spoke with a moderation and clearsightedness which were really surprising after such a victory . . . At that moment, I greatly admired him.' What was it Hitler said to his allies? He explained to them that it was important, during the negotiations, for a French government to continue to function in French territory. 'This would be far preferable to the situation that would arise if the French government fled to London to continue the war.' In addition, an agreement with a legal French government remaining in France would relieve the occupying powers of the 'unpleasant responsibility' of running the country directly. It was obviously more convenient to have the German decisions implemented by a government of French officials who would be more readily obeyed by their compatriots than foreigners, who were also their enemy. The Reich officials wanted to use again the methods which had proved their worth in Denmark and avoid the troubles they were encountering in Norway. The Bordeaux government knew nothing, of course, of these concerns of the Führer and had no suspicion that its decision to remain in France was playing directly into his hands.

Hitler was, above all, perturbed at the thought of what the French fleet might do. He had calculated that should it go over to Britain, it would in some cases double the strength of the Royal Navy. It was, therefore, necessary to come to an agreement with a French government that would remain in France and neutralise the fleet. 'This might be done by disarming the fleet in French ports under German and Italian supervision' with the guarantee that 'France's entire fleet would be returned to her when peace was finally concluded'. But Hitler doubted whether 'France would have the slightest confidence in any guarantee given by himself'. So he was thinking of impounding the fleet in a neutral country such as Spain or Portugal. In any case, it would be better to prevent the fleet from leaving for the United States, because they might, at a later date, hand it over to Britain; but he did not completely exclude the possibility of its going to America. A good solution would be for the fleet to scuttle itself.

Consequently, Hitler thought that, rather than the whole of France being occupied, the French government should be left with an area of theoretical sovereignty. Nor should any request be made to hand over the fleet; since it would be impossible to lay hands on it, it would escape and the French government would have no further interest in signing an armistice. Similarly, no demands should be made at the moment concerning the French colonial empire; this would be equally impossible to enforce and the only foreseeable result would be that France's colonial territories would go over to the British side.

Thus, far from being intoxicated by victory, Hitler was displaying surprisingly statesmanlike common sense. In a monologue which lasted for several hours, he had, in fact, given an outline of what his policy in France would be for the next four years: to exploit to the full, for Germany's benefit, a French government still retaining a semblance of authority. Graziani's notes report him as saying, 'all things considered, I prefer an enemy like France, whose forces are thickly concentrated, who

can be got at and beaten, to enemies that are weaker but more dispersed.'
But similar caution prevented Hitler from informing his opponents of his
peace terms which the Bordeaux government was so anxious to learn.

Mussolini fully realised that his own views carried little weight since it
was Hitler who had won the war. On June 22, he wrote to his colleague
that he would make 'minimum' demands on the French. According to
Ciano, Mussolini was even afraid that, by pressing his claims, he might
compromise not only the current negotiations but even the good relations
between Italy and Germany.[1]

But Hitler's 'moderation' did not include making France any gifts. He
intended to take over the whole of the Channel and Atlantic coasts; to
occupy France down to the Loire and the Swiss frontier; to include in the
occupied zone the railway line to Spain in order to control the rail traffic
with that country. Above all, the German economists had drawn up a
plan for 'all the economic resources of France and her colonies' to be
placed at Germany's disposal, an embargo on all cargo-vessels and German
control of the press and the radio. Hitler had indeed been quite explicit to
Mussolini: apart from the question of the French fleet and the French
colonies, he was ready to make concessions on matters of detail 'which
might seem of great importance to the French' but he would not concede
any points of substance.

VIII THE SIGNING OF THE CONVENTION AT RETHONDES

Hitler wanted the signing of the armistice to be as spectacular and symbolic as possible; he ordered it to take place at Rethondes, where Marshal
Foch had dictated his terms to the German delegates in 1918.

On June 21 at 3.30 p.m. the Führer received the French delegation in
Foch's own carriage; he was accompanied by Ribbentrop, Goering,
Keitel and the commanders-in-chief of the various branches of the
Wehrmacht. After Keitel had read the preamble to the armistice terms in
German, followed by a translation in French, Hitler stood up and left.
For him, the matter was settled.

Keitel handed the French delegation the text of the German terms,
emphasising that 'the basic conditions were not open to discussion and
must be accepted or rejected as they stood'. It was a *Diktat*. The area for
manoeuvre was not very large.

1. In the course of his talks with Ribbentrop in Munich, Ciano had informed him of Italy's
claims: Nice, Corsica, Tunisia, French Somaliland; 'an outlet to the Atlantic' through French
North Africa; redrawing the Tunisian frontier to include the Algerian iron and phosphate;
Malta; and Italy should replace Britain in the Anglo-Egyptian Treaty and the Sudanese
condominium! Not a bad price for ten days' unsuccessful participation in the war and
hardly any fighting at all.

When the meeting reassembled, Jodl was in the chair. General Huntziger described the German terms as 'harsh and pitiless'. He asked whether the demarcation line of the occupied zone was unalterable.

To ensure the maintenance of law and order and to 'prevent the country drifting into Communism' – a phrase echoing Weygand's fears – Huntziger made it plain that France would need an army of 120,000 to 130,000 men. On this point Keitel gave his assent without difficulty 'for a provisional period'. Keitel then promised that the occupying troops would be limited to the needs of the war against Britain and that only 'a force sufficient to maintain law and order' would be stationed in Paris.

The Bordeaux government decided to request Germany to make some modifications to the original text. Two minor concessions were made by the victors: it was agreed that the French military aircraft need not be handed over to the Germans – General Bergeret considered this would be an insult to the honour of the French Air Force; the aircraft would merely be disarmed, under German supervision. Also, 'the German government would take into consideration the essential needs of the population of the non-occupied zone'.

But Keitel showed no flexibility with regard to another problem. When Huntziger made the point that the extradition of German exiles who were enjoying the right of asylum would be a shameful act on the part of the French people, Keitel replied unequivocally that they were 'warmongers and traitors to Germany' and that 'the extradition of that type of person would be demanded at all costs'. There was nothing further to be said.

The most important discussion, however, was on Article 8 of the convention. This laid down that naval vessels which were not under the control of the French government, that is, almost all of them, were to be disarmed in their pre-war home ports. Germany pledged herself not to seize them.

Huntziger proposed an amendment: 'After demobilisation and the removal of ammunition under Italian and German supervision, the French warships should proceed to French North African ports with half their peace-time establishment.' Huntziger gave as the reason for this request the fear of British air raids. For the proposed amendment to be fully effective, it ought also to have asked for the assurance that during the disarmament of the fleet under enemy supervision no attempt should be made to seize possession of it. But the question did not arise, for Keitel refused any discussion. He stressed the 'very generous' terms of Article 8 that the French did not seem fully to appreciate. The protection of the fleet against air attack was a question of detail that concerned the armistice commission. 'The German delegation rejected the French request'; Huntziger did not insist. So Article 8 placed the French fleet in danger of being seized by the enemy.

In the evening of June 22, orders came from Bordeaux to sign, which Huntziger did, as the only French signatory, after stating that 'the French government felt justified in expecting, having accepted such very onerous demands, that Germany would approach the ensuing negotiations in a spirit that would enable the two great neighbouring peoples to live and work in peace'. But although the Germans listened politely, they made no kind of pledge of this sort.

The French were very apprehensive about the Italians. But on June 23 in Rome, everything went off very well. The Italians put forward no claims likely to cause a breakdown in the negotiations. No mention was made of occupying the left bank of the Rhône or of occupying Corsica or Tunisia. They confined themselves to demanding the demilitarisation of a thirty-mile strip along the frontier and occupying those areas that had been conquered by the armies of the Prince of Piedmont. Instead of increasing their demands, as the French had feared, the Italians even made some concessions.

Admiral Le Luc tried to raise once again the question of disarming the fleet under Article 8. He asked for 'the idea of home port to be considered purely as a suggestion'. The Italians were conciliatory and said that they did not want the French ships to be exposed to the danger of being sunk. But these kind words did not lead to any change in the wording of the text. Neither in Rome nor at Rethondes was any improvement made in the wording of the armistice agreement and this article, if implemented, would seriously jeopardise the greater part of the French Navy.

France was beaten and had accepted her defeat. Britain was standing alone. Was she ready to withstand the blow?

PART III

BRITAIN STANDS ALONE

CHAPTER I

The Battle of Britain

I HITLER AFTER HIS VICTORY

A T Rethondes, Hitler danced a joyful little jig on leaving Foch's carriage. There seemed no end to his hopes after such a swift succession of un-qualified victories.[1] Although he took great care not to reveal his war aims either to Mussolini, because of the slight rivalry between them, or to those he had conquered, in order not to arouse them from their paralysing stupor, to his intimates the Führer made no secret of his grandiose schemes; all the lands seized from Germany in the last 400 years would be handed back, not counting other gains.

In this immense plan to recover lost territory, Britain was only directly threatened with having to hand over some mandated territories, the former German colonies which she had been administering since 1918. Was it worth continuing the war for their sake? Chamberlain had dropped one or two hints concerning them on a number of occasions. Hitler con-sidered the British Commonwealth an institution worth preserving – after all, it was Aryan stock that was governing these vast territories.

So he was probably convinced that Britain would be quite happy at being asked for almost nothing and that, willy-nilly, she would accept the new situation that the Wehrmacht's victories had created in Europe. Ciano wrote: 'Hitler's desire to conclude peace as quickly as possible is obvious from everything he says.' On August 3, at the same time as he was giving orders to reduce the number of army divisions – and annexing Eupen, Malmédy and Alsace-Lorraine – the Führer made advances to the British government, through the King of Sweden.

Churchill's reply was an emphatic no. Possibly Hitler then had the thought of driving a wedge between the people of Britain and their Prime Minister. This may have been the meaning of the peculiar approach that was made to the Duke and Duchess of Windsor who were just getting ready to leave for the Bahamas, where the Duke had been appointed governor. Through the mediation of some Spanish friends, the Duke was

---

1. His prestige was enormous everywhere, even in Britain. The Afghan ambassador in Ankara had told von Papen that 'Germany had a large number of friends, more than she might think'.

warned that Churchill was planning to assassinate him; he was advised
not to go and, in order to prevent him, his luggage was 'mislaid'; they
even went so far as to hint that 'changes might possibly be made in the
British constitution' – this is said to have made the Duchess 'look thoughtful'. But while not concealing the fact that he was no keen supporter of
the war, the Duke refused to enter into 'negotiations against the instructions of his government': there was no fifth column in England.

II BRITISH DETERMINATION: WINSTON CHURCHILL

Nonetheless, the disparity between the two forces was discouraging. The
British Army now had only 500 guns and 200 tanks; American arms were
only just beginning to arrive, carefully packed in grease, because they
dated from 1917–18. There were a few well-trained brigades but they had
to defend thousands of miles of coastline. The Home Guard was being
hurriedly drilled, using sticks and poles. The strike force consisted of 700
fighters and 500 bombers which were awaiting the Luftwaffe's onslaught.
No one could say if and when Britain would take the offensive; for the
moment and for a long time to come, she would have to 'stick it out' under
attack from an opponent superior in numbers and free to choose the time,
place and manner of its offensive.

It was at this dramatic moment that one morning, at breakfast, Winston
Churchill, that amazing man who was leading the country, put forward
the novel idea of 'prefabricated harbours' that would enable vast forces to
be landed at any point on the coastline of the Continent. From this time
onwards Churchill appears, in all his glory, as a unique personality, riding
high above the storm. Journalist, serving officer, historian, MP and
minister, his political career had hitherto been extremely controversial; in
1919, he had been one of the supporters of 'cordoning off' the Soviet
Union; in 1925, as Chancellor of the Exchequer, he had been responsible
for revaluing the pound, thus heading for the slump; he had been almost
the only politician to side with Edward VIII at the time of the latter's
abdication; as Colonial Secretary, he had crushed the nationalist movements; in 1935, he had disapproved of sanctions against Italy and as late as
1936 he had thought that Britain should keep out of any European war.

But the dismemberment of Czechoslovakia had opened his eyes to the
peril of Hitler and from then on no one was more resolute in his determination to thwart it. With a touch of eccentricity in his dress, always
smoking a cigar, a glass of whisky handy at crack of dawn, working to no
systematic timetable, liable to go to bed at 2 a.m. and drag his advisers out
of their own beds a couple of hours later, finding it hard to resist childish
pranks such as going for a bathe on a beach in Libya in front of all his

staff only a few miles away from the front line, Churchill displayed an equanimity and optimism in the direst adversity that were of the greatest comfort to his compatriots. He was able to hit on words and attitudes that galvanised them into action and stung their pride: 'I can offer you,' he said 'nothing but blood, sweat and tears.' But when announcing an impending German landing, he could make his hearers relax and laugh when he said: 'We are waiting for the Germans' – pause – 'so are the fish.' In the smoking ruins of London, he would walk about making the V for victory sign and with a word or a gesture, raise a cheer from those who had been bombed out. Tireless, ubiquitous, a glutton for punishment, imaginative, impulsive, with a gambler's pleasure in taking a risk, capable of playing fair *and* of hitting below the belt, putting the safety of the British Commonwealth above everything else, an orator, poet and man of action, Churchill was also an inexhaustible source of ideas, anecdotes, questions and schemes. Lloyd George used to say of him that he had ten ideas a day but that he didn't know which was the right one. Marshall considered that one of the main tasks of his general staff was to stop him making strategic blunders. But this unorthodox visionary was able to build for the future as well as living intensely in the present. The British people felt at one with their leader; they admired his youthful spirit, his sturdy vitality, his courage and even his childishness. An extraordinary man, a specimen of humanity the like of which has rarely been seen over the centuries, an anachronism fully in touch with his times, exasperating yet irresistible, Churchill flourished in the dramatic atmosphere in which he came to power and responded with all his bulldog pugnacity.

He had no intention of running the war through endless committees. Within the government he formed a war cabinet of five members, including the Labour opposition leader, Attlee. He himself was Prime Minister, First Lord of the Treasury and National Defence Minister. It was he who really directed the war effort and British strategy with the help of the Chief of Staff's committee: John Dill and later Alanbrooke for the Army; Dudley Pound for the Navy; Charles Portal for the RAF; his military adviser was Lord Ismay.

III MERS EL-KEBIR

The Royal Navy was the most reassuring factor in the United Kingdom's defences. But the defeat of France had deprived it of the co-operation of the French fleet, whose future filled it with apprehension. If by some mishap the French fleet were to fall into the hands of the Germans, the Axis powers would seize control of the Mediterranean; the Atlantic convoys – Britain's life-line – would be even more seriously jeopardised; a German landing would no longer be an empty threat.

Throughout those tragic days when France's request for German peace terms had first of all exaggerated and then shattered the relationship between the Allies, the British had been worried about the clauses imposed by the victors regarding the French fleet. Yet they had received every possible reassurance – from Reynaud, Pétain and Darlan; the French fleet, they had been told again and again, would never be handed over to the enemy; it would scuttle itself rather than fall into their hands. But the British had noted that the Bordeaux government had refused to allow the fleet to sail for British harbours and that the French Admiralty had taken certain steps to separate the two navies. They were doubtful whether the government of France would be able to prevent the enemy seizing the French ships; they wondered whether it might not be persuaded to hand them over of its own free will, if the Germans were to offer substantial advantages in exchange – the release of the prisoners of war, for example, as Churchill suggested.

In short, on July 1 the British government decided to eliminate the possible danger represented by the unknown quantity of the French fleet. It was particularly concerned about the implementation of Article 8 of the armistice convention, whereby the French ships were to return to their pre-war home ports – in the ports situated in occupied France they would be a tempting and easy prey for the enemy. The Bordeaux government had not transmitted to the British the veiled promises that it had obtained, suggesting that the dangerous stipulations contained in this clause might be judiciously modified.

On July 3 Operation 'Catapult' was launched. French ships at anchor in British harbours were treacherously attacked by British boarding parties, to the great indignation of their crews. Fortunately, in Alexandria talks between Admirals Cunningham and Godfroy led to an agreement to neutralise the latter's squadron without resort to arms. But at Mers el-Kebir where the bulk of the French fleet was at anchor a dramatic tragedy took place.

With the French Admiralty's full approval Admiral Gensoul rejected pointblank Admiral Somerville's four-point ultimatum. The British then launched an attack in which the odds were bound to be uneven; only one French battleship, the *Strasbourg*, managed to escape; the rest of the fleet was sunk or seriously damaged; and 1,300 French sailors were killed.

Although a reversal of alliances was only just averted – Marshal Pétain soothed Darlan's and Laval's wrath and decided to exercise a minimum of retaliation – the outrageous attack at Mers el-Kebir nonetheless set the seal on the break between France and England; it thus played into Hitler's hands and opened up the way for the French policy of collaboration.

However, these unfortunate consequences, plus the odium incurred by the aggression, were outweighed by the feeling that Britain was determined to fight to the last ditch, which impressed every country, not least the Axis powers. Churchill anticipated that this would be so and Ciano confirmed it when he wrote, 'this action by the British proves that their fighting spirit is unimpaired and that His Majesty's Fleet still has the toughness of the captains and pirates of the seventeenth century'. But the immediate danger to the British Isles from Germany was not in any way thereby reduced.

IV OPERATION 'SEA-LION'

In his directive no. 16, dated July 16, Hitler laid down outline plans for an attempted landing in England. It would be a surprise operation over a broad front stretching from Ramsgate to the west of the Isle of Wight. The air fleets based in Norway, the Netherlands, Belgium and France – 3,000 aircraft in all – would overwhelm the defences, shoot down the RAF in air combat and neutralise the Royal Navy; under the protection of powerful coastal artillery, the German convoys would sail through a channel between mine-fields on either side. Hitler contemplated landing between twenty-five and forty divisions on the broadest possible front so that they would have an extensive field of operations. Von Brauchitsch and Halder meekly prepared the plans demanded by their Führer.

But Admiral Raeder, who would have the responsibility for the operation, quickly realised its risks and the inadequacies of its preparation. The German Navy had suffered heavy losses in Norway which were far from having been made good, even assuming that they could be; all the necessary shipping – barges, tugs, motor-boats – would have to be requisitioned in Germany and the occupied countries and brought up to the French Channel coast; this could not be done overnight.

The Army was asking the Navy to carry a first wave of 100,000 men with heavy equipment and AA weapons, followed by 160,000 men in the next three days.

The Navy had calculated that its preparations would not be completed before September 15; it considered that success could only be expected if air supremacy had been achieved in the first place and it asked for reassurance from the Luftwaffe on this point. Above all, it stated that it would be unable to provide effective protection for the convoys unless the landing area was narrowly circumscribed. But the general staff of the Army, who would take over in the event of a successful landing, realised that where the Channel was narrowest, the terrain was ill-suited to tanks because of swampy ground and hills. Consequently, it hoped to land its troops over a wide front in order to make a broad enveloping movement round London, the nerve centre of the British defences.

These divergences of view between the Navy and the Army were matched by similar divergences between the Army and Air Force. Among other things, the Luftwaffe did not want to drop its paratroops until the bridgehead was well established, while the military considered that these paratroops must be dropped in order to achieve the bridgehead. In fact, Marshal Goering was not really interested in the projected landings; he thought that the Luftwaffe was strong enough to bring Britain to her knees on its own. As the British on their part were losing no time in bombing the ships concentrated on the French coast, Admiral Raeder found himself forced as a result of all these unresolved problems to suggest to Hitler that the operation be put back till October or till next year or indefinitely. In any case, since control of the sea was impossible, success would depend on control of the skies. It was up to the Luftwaffe.

V THE BATTLE OF BRITAIN

A battle was thus about to begin on the lines imagined by Douhet, fought out purely in the air, with soldiers and sailors playing no part, almost like spectators. The Germans had more aircraft but they had not had the time to set up airfields close to the British Isles in the occupied territories and the distance out and back had thus not been shortened; on the other hand the home-based British planes could carry out several sorties over the same period, so that in the air the balance was restored. In addition, the manoeuvrability and armament of the British fighter planes confirmed the experience of Dunkirk, and soon proved superior to those of their German opponents. As the Stuka dive-bombers were so vulnerable that they had to be withdrawn from the fighting and since the German bombers, because of the limitations of range of their fighters, were unable to receive the necessary fighter protection, the two sides seemed equal.

But the British were to turn the situation to their advantage by means of a completely new system of defence, thanks to a technical invention they alone possessed: radar. In fact, in addition to the easily penetrated barrage provided by 2,200 balloons and their excellent AA artillery which in July 1940, according to Churchill, consisted of some 1,800 guns, including 1,200 heavy ones, the British, thanks to the inventiveness of Sir Edward Appleton and Robert Watson Watt, were able to erect a chain of radar stations capable of detecting enemy aircraft and their strength, at a distance of sixty miles. In addition, they had decoded the control system of the German day and night bombers and had found ways of upsetting it. Intrigued by air photographs showing defence preparations along the British coast, the Germans had in fact sent the airship *Graf Zeppelin* on two reconnaissance missions but they had achieved nothing and Goering had decided not to attack the radar stations whose importance he failed to assess correctly. This blunder was the Luftwaffe's death warrant.

The Battle of Britain began on July 10, with attacks on Channel convoys and harassing attacks on south-coast harbours. The Luftwaffe wished to lure the RAF away from its bases and destroy it; but the British fighters refused to rise to the bait. To their great surprise, from July 10 to August 10, the Germans lost 286 planes and the English fighters only 150. August 15 was a decisive day; four successive waves, each of 100 aircraft, were launched against south-east England and the Germans lost 290 aircraft. Yet the radar stations were not yet completely ready and the aircraft were being located acoustically, that is to say, inaccurately and comparatively late.

At this juncture Goering decided to attack the British fighters on their airfields, in accordance with the old method that had shown its worth in Poland and France. But the situation was now very different. In eighteen days, the Luftwaffe made 7,500 sorties, 790 of them on August 31. The British AA proved powerful enough to disperse part of the aircraft before they reached their targets. The Spitfires looked after the rest and shot down nearly 500 enemy aircraft.

The Germans now realised that their aircraft were being lost thanks to some technical device of which they were unaware. A plotting and listening detachment between Calais and Boulogne succeeded in deciphering the riddle of the directional control system of Fighter Command and in reading the conversations between the British pilots and their ground installations. The Germans were thus enabled to discover the strength and location of British squadrons in the air and sometimes to warn their bombers that they were being stalked. In this way, by the end of August and in early September, the Luftwaffe's losses had dropped. From now on, the Germans' chances of success in the fighting depended on persistent jamming of their opponents' radio links.

Goering now decided on a 'terror offensive' against London, thus giving psychological warfare priority over the destruction of the enemy's armed forces. It is possible that, by giving it a short breathing space, this decision saved the British fighter force, whose planes were as worn out as their pilots. It was now the Londoners' turn to be sorely tried. They were to be pounded for two whole months; day after day, night after night, an average of 250 bombers came over and showered tons of high explosive and incendiary bombs over London; hundreds of fires were started and whole quarters devastated; this was the Blitz. Londoners took to sleeping in their cellars, while restaurants and night clubs opened up theirs, too. There was no lack of humour. A story went the rounds of a tailor who stuck up a notice on his door after every raid, reading 'Open as usual'. One night, the front of his shop was blown out and the notice read: 'More open than usual.'

Since the threatened destruction of their capital had not daunted British determination, the Luftwaffe turned to the industrial centres, with priority for aircraft factories. On November 15 Coventry was razed to the ground and Goebbels' propaganda machine found a new bogey word: 'coventrysation'. But from October onwards there were radar stations all along the coast and what is more, thanks to the use of electronics, they were working perfectly in converting acoustic plotting into images on a tube. In addition, by December 1940, British AA consisted of 2,100 guns – more than before the air raids started. On October 12, Hitler drew the logical conclusion of his failure; the planned invasion of Britain was called off. According to Air Marshal Johnson, had the Luftwaffe persevered in its intensive attacks for another fortnight, the RAF would have had to admit defeat; but the British had won the first round.

VI THE MOBILISATION OF THE COMMONWEALTH

Before the war, the dominions made a point of leaving their defence in the hands of the metropolis; but now they found themselves in the position of having to come to its aid; they had been its debtors and they were now going to become its creditors. They were not prepared for this change; they had no soldiers, no armament factories and practically no metallurgical industry. Nor were they all equally aware of the gravity of the danger; some of them did not even feel themselves concerned. It is true that they had immense resources but exploiting them would be an extremely slow process. And for these resources to reach Britain or the various operational theatres, it was still necessary for Britain, having won the war in the air and thus saved her national territory, not to lose the war at sea.

Canada had declared war on Germany a few days after Britain, in order to obtain the greatest possible amount of American war equipment; but her army comprised only 4,500 men and her economy was a strictly agricultural one; reserve officers and men were forbidden by law to serve overseas. The French Canadians were against the war effort since they were not keen on being defenders of the British Commonwealth. But Mackenzie King, who had been Premier for twenty years, looked on Canada as Britain's rear area. He put through Parliament a bill requiring 'all Canadians over sixteen years old' to sign on and in June 1941 this became military conscription for all men. Canada became the training area for pilots from the British Commonwealth. She linked her defences with those of the United States; she provided Britain with a merchant fleet of 300,000 tons which was to increase tenfold in the course of the war. From early in 1940, she began to build aircraft factories and naval shipyards and from 1941 onwards, Canadian troops were being sent to Britain and Hong Kong.

Australia and New Zealand were even less well defended than Canada and more deeply affected by the slump; and all activity in the military field had been suspended in Australia in 1929. The Conservative Prime Minister, Menzies, introduced compulsory military service as early as 1940. He forbade strikes and set up compulsory arbitration in labour disputes; consumption was restricted, starting with petrol. At the end of 1940, one New Zealand and four Australian divisions arrived in Egypt to guard the Suez Canal. Churchill had the shrewdness to keep Menzies closely in touch with the British war cabinet's decisions. Australian co-operation never wavered.

Things did not go quite so smoothly in South Africa. German propaganda had gained a lot of ground with the Afrikaner nationalists under General Herzog. Nazi racialism found supporters and Fascist organisations formed themselves into 'Grey shirts' or 'Black shirts'. In South-West Africa, the Germans had kept their nationality, while still being citizens of the Union. Nevertheless, Field Marshal Smuts succeeded in getting South Africa to declare war on Germany. But he was forced to accept one reservation: South African troops were not to fight outside Africa. Henceforth, Smuts, who had fought on the side of the Boers, was Churchill's faithful comrade in arms.

The nationalist leaders of India, whether they were members of Gandhi's Congress Party or of the Muslim League, were not pro-Nazi. But they were only willing to take part in the struggle against Germany if India would thereby achieve full dominion status as a pledge of future independence. Churchill refused: 'He would not dig the grave of the British Empire.' He was thus reduced to using strong-arm methods by imprisoning the nationalist leaders. As a result, some of them began to wonder if the way to liberate their country was by open revolt and alliance with the enemies of Britain. This climate of opinion made it impossible for Britain to raise large forces amongst the enormous population of India; only eight divisions were eventually sent to Egypt, from February 1941 onwards. Furthermore, troops and arms were tied down in India in order to maintain law and order.

On her western flank, Britain was hampered by Eire's neutrality; this prevented her using Irish harbours and turning Ireland into an outpost in the battle of the Atlantic. In addition, a German landing was on the cards and British troops had to stand guard in Ulster in order to intervene swiftly if need be.

Despite these black spots, on the whole the enormous machine of empire had swung into motion to help the mother-country. She could thus consider the possibility of loosening the enemy's grip by opening up operational theatres on the periphery; this thought was to provide food for Churchill's fertile imagination.

VII THE EXILED GOVERNMENTS – FREE FRANCE

Other possibilities of action in Europe could well arise from the fact that London had become a sort of free capital of occupied Europe as a result of the arrival of the legal governments of the conquered countries. King Haakon of Norway, Queen Wilhelmina of Holland, President Beneš of Czechoslovakia and General Sikorski from Poland had found asylum with their governments, either because they had followed them there or had formed them in exile. Even if King Leopold III thought fit to consider himself a prisoner of war in Belgium, there was no doubt that Hubert Pierlot was the head of the legal Belgian government in London. The only exceptions were Denmark and France; the Vichy government had been recognised throughout the world as the legitimate French government; General de Gaulle had merely set up the dissident 'Free French' movement in London.

True, none of these governments could continue to exist without largesse from the British. None of them had much to offer, so their sum total did not amount to a great deal. However, the Dutch and Norwegian merchant fleets, the territories of Indonesia and the Belgian Congo and the Polish and French troops represented a substantial contribution and in her almost desperate isolation, England could not afford to turn away any ally in her struggle. From the psychological point of view, the presence in London of authorities from the occupied countries, albeit almost a token presence, was an encouragement for their peoples not to despair and not to submit passively to the occupying power's demands; it was to be hoped that, in the long run, this attitude would give rise to a whole network of underground resistance movements, like a Trojan horse in the heart of the enemy fortress.

However, the British did not recognise the right of the exiled governments to any real say in the conduct of the war; at the very most, they allowed them to sit on international commissions drawing up post-war plans of minor importance; all that the foreign leaders and troops had to do was to contribute to the British war effort by filling the role assigned to them.

Most of these governments, well aware of their weakness, accepted this control by the British without difficulty; but this did not apply to General de Gaulle. An advocate – unheeded in his own country – of tank warfare, a gifted writer, commander of the French armoured division that had fought most determinedly and with the greatest success against the Germans, a secretary of state in Paul Reynaud's government for a few days and one of the begetters of the plan for complete Anglo-French union, General de Gaulle had left for England on an English plane when Pétain had formed his government. From June 18 onwards, Churchill, who looked on him as the 'Constable of France', had encouraged him to use the BBC to appeal to the French to continue the fight. The general's appeals were prophetic in more ways than one, notably when he said: 'France has lost a battle, but she has not lost the war . . . because this war is a world war.' Few people heeded his words. General de Gaulle failed either to prevent the signing of the armistice or to arouse dissidence amongst the rulers and military leaders of the French colonies, or even to persuade anyone of the first rank or any large bodies of men to rally round him. Thus the British, anxious not to throw the Vichy government and the forces which it still retained into the arms of the Germans, refused to recognise General de Gaulle as the French representative, but merely as the leader of a group: Free France.

But General de Gaulle's view was that the Vichy government was the catspaw of Germany and that he alone would be capable of effectively defending France's interests, even against his own allies. There were thus frequent collisions: the General's stock was at its lowest when, in September 1940, off Dakar, he failed to rally French West Africa to his cause. Nonetheless, as considerable territories had come over to Free France (the French Pacific Islands, the Indian trading stations, French Equatorial Africa and the Cameroons) and he had a small army of soldiers, sailors and airmen under his command (the Free French merchant fleet amounted to 700,000 tons and French pilots took part in the Battle of Britain), General de Gaulle formed an embryonic French government called the French National Committee. A regular stream of volunteers joined his movement, although the attack at Mers el-Kebir considerably reduced the flow even if it did not make it completely dry up.

VIII THE INVOLVEMENT OF THE UNITED STATES

The exiled governments were keeping the flame alight, but the appearance of any national resistance movement in occupied territory was still only a hope and not yet a power to be reckoned with. So the help that Britain so sorely needed to withstand an enemy so much more powerful than herself was even less likely to come from the national resistance movements than from the Commonwealth. Possibly the United States would be willing to help.

American public opinion was shifting, though slowly. The defeat of France had caused great dismay and in the autumn of 1940, a survey showed that 75 per cent of Americans wanted to aid Britain although a greater number, 83 per cent, expressed itself as against taking part in the war. There were two minority groups that were trying to influence the mass of Americans. The members of the 'Committee for the Defence of America by Aiding the Allies', better known as the White Committee, after the name of its first chairman, were either pro-British through a feeling of kinship, or anti-Nazi, or else convinced that a Nazi victory in Europe would jeopardise the United States by placing them abruptly, and perhaps at too late a stage, in the front line of defence of democracy. Preparations must be made to meet such an eventuality.

But this committee was less powerful than its isolationist opponent, the America First Movement, founded in September 1940, which had as many as 850,000 members. America First considered that war must be avoided at all costs. It was not manoeuvred by the Nazis, it was not even pro-Nazi and the German ambassador to the United States urgently advised it not to compromise itself by organising sabotage or even pro-German demonstrations which would, in his view, have quite the opposite effect. America First was the voice of the strongly felt views of the Middle West of indifference towards Europe and suspicion of its tortuous Byzantine problems. Its centre was in Chicago. 'Ideas' it maintained 'cannot be destroyed by wars'; it was pointless to send 'our boys' to their death in an attempt to prevent National Socialism from expanding in Europe. It showed the same lack of interest, moreover, in Russian Communism. America First was recruited mainly from Republicans but also included some Democrats. Its protagonists were industrialists such as Henry Ford, Catholic bishops, senators and state governors, well-known academics and personalities such as the pilot Charles Lindbergh, the hero of the Atlantic crossing.

Roosevelt had to show the greatest consideration for the divisions and lack of awareness in the American public. He was a complex character, paralysed and authoritarian, an aristocrat and a politician; a mixture of idealism and artfulness, kindness and obstinacy (he never spared his opponents), familiarity and earnestness. His co-operation with Wilson had left its mark on him; but he was above all anxious to avoid the older man's mistakes. He was deeply convinced of the evil nature of Nazism. The German ambassador to Washington deplored 'his determined and obstinately anti-German sentiments that would be unlikely to waver'.

Roosevelt was to act with consummate skill, showing perfect understanding of his powers and of his compatriots. There were no dramatic sessions in the House of Representatives or in the Senate, as in Paris and London; relations between Congress and the White House are traditionally based on distrust, if not hostility. The best method for a president was to reach agreement with a few influential leaders. But the most effective way of influencing the man in the street is to talk to him directly on the radio, using language he can understand. Roosevelt excelled in friendly little 'fireside' chats, almost as if talking to his family.

He stressed, above all, the defence of the United States, something to which no American would remain indifferent. Public-opinion polls had shown him beforehand exactly how far he could go. He had a freer hand after being re-elected in November 1940, when he took the unprecedented step of seeking office for the third time, although in order to succeed, his election campaign had contained solemn assurances that he would maintain United States' neutrality: 'As I have already said and shall repeat again and again, our boys will not be sent to fight in any foreign war' – a clever formula that did not exclude committing the United States to a war for the defence of their national interests, as this would then no longer be a 'foreign war'.

In simple language, Roosevelt kept putting forward three sorts of argument to his compatriots, so that, in the words of his trusty lieutenant Hopkins, 'he would be pushed into war by them'. The Nazi leaders, he would explain, wanted to reduce Europe to slavery and then dominate the rest of the world; and the interests of the United States would be seriously jeopardised if Germany and Japan ruled the roost in the Atlantic and the Pacific; hence the need to help Britain, America's advance guard. On a more down-to-earth level, he would show how a victory of the Axis would be the Waterloo of the American economy; European markets would be closed to the American producers who would also have to meet at home the competition of lower-priced foreign goods produced by cheaper foreign labour. Finally, talking to people used to the Sunday sermons of their priests and pastors, Roosevelt would stress the moral values inherent in a firm attitude towards Fascist aggression; the defence of freedom, democracy and the American way of life thus became part of the defence of national and material interests.

One consequence of all these efforts with their very deliberate pattern of advance followed by cautious retreat, was the progressive rearmament of the United States. In July and August, two laws were passed doubling, on paper, the tonnage of the American war fleet; in September 1940, by the expedient of having 'selective military service' and army training, conscription was introduced. The President arranged for the necessary powers to be voted requiring industrial firms to produce manufactured goods, ordered by the Federal State, at predetermined prices in fixed quantities and with fixed delivery dates. Thus by July 1, 1941, the American Army numbered 1,400,000 men with thirty-three divisions, four of them armoured, supported by 6,000 aircraft. But, above all, the conversion of the greatest industry in the world had been started; E. Stettinius, Vice-President of General Motors, was made responsible for the mobilisation of industry. Roosevelt had succeeded in gaining acceptance for the idea that the United States was to become 'the arsenal of democracy'.

Churchill, whose mother was American, showed admirable skill in exploiting Roosevelt's favourable attitude and he maintained a regular correspondence with the President, increasingly cordial in tone. In September 1940, he asked for American destroyers: 'At the present rate of loss,' he wrote, 'we shall not be able to hold out for long.' Against the advice of Admiral Stark, who was the commander of the American Navy, Roosevelt, with General Pershing's public approval, decided to send fifty old destroyers in exchange for the lease of bases in the Caribbean – 'to turn it into an American lake', in the words of Knox, the Secretary of State for the Navy. These bases were situated in Newfoundland, in Bermuda, the Bahamas, the West Indies and British Guiana. Aid to Britain was thus disguised as an improvement of the United States defence system.

On December 8, 1940, Churchill wrote Roosevelt a letter which he called 'the most important in his whole career'. In it he painted a broad picture of the military, political and economic situation. He ended with an urgent appeal for help: once her dollar reserves had run out, Britain would soon no longer be in a position to pay for the indispensable American equipment that she had been able to buy under the Cash and Carry law. Roosevelt showed ready understanding and seems to have hit on a solution to the problem, of his own accord. Stating that it was important to get rid of the 'superstition of the dollar', he explained to the Americans that war equipment must be lent to the British; they would return it at the end of hostilities. This was the 'Lend-Lease' bill, of incalculable importance for the course of the war. In theory, the system was based on reciprocity; in fact, the Americans were giving something in exchange for a theoretical deferred payment and were receiving nothing. Not only was the bill passed without difficulty by the legislative assemblies in March 1941 but Roosevelt managed to acquire at the same time a new and important power, that of distributing the war material produced in the States according to his own choice; a further shrewd move was that the bill did not contain the names of the countries benefiting from Lend-Lease, thus enabling the list to be extended as events might dictate.

This equipment still had to be shipped and the British Navy was in danger of not being equal to the task. Left to itself, it was even less able to prevent it all going to the bottom through enemy submarine attack. Ever since January 1941 the British and American general staffs had been examining together on a world scale their joint strategic problems. In April 1941, Roosevelt took a great step forward; he extended the 'American security zone' to the western part of the Atlantic from Greenland to the Azores. American vessels would report the presence of German ships to the British. By the end of May, the Americans were providing protection for their convoys all the way to Britain. In June, British ships were allowed to join American convoys. In July, the Americans established a naval base in Iceland.

So, little by little, Anglo-American co-operation became closer and closer. But although the United States were moving towards probable entry into the war, no date for this had yet been fixed, nor could it be guaranteed with complete certainty. Meanwhile, Hitler was extracting from the occupied countries of Europe the resources which he lacked at the outbreak of the conflict, in preparation for the long war that now faced him after the defeat of the Luftwaffe in the air by the British.

CHAPTER 2

The Birth of Hitler's Europe

I HITLER'S IDEAS

UNDER the *Führerprinzip*, in Nazi Germany nothing could happen unless Hitler had himself decided or approved it. But even though he had expressed in *Mein Kampf* and repeated in speeches a few slogans that he had inflated into political or military objectives – the overthrow of the humiliating Treaty of Versailles, the grouping of all the Germans together into one Fatherland, the acquisition of *Lebensraum* – Hitler and his lieutenants had never drawn up the appropriate detailed plans. Victory had, in any case, opened up unexpected vistas – the domination of Europe by Germany. How was this domination, based on conquest, to be reconciled with the needs of the war that as a result of Britain's obstinacy was now bound to be protracted?

Although Hitler often changed his plans, being a thoroughgoing opportunist who veered unexpectedly in accordance with the turn of events – Halder compared him to a 'political kaleidoscope' – there were still some constant notions influencing his behaviour: racial inequality and the supremacy of the Aryans; a system of education and upbringing that E. Vermeil described as 'soldierly'; an individual morality far removed from Christian principles and close to nature, subject to the overriding demands of the national good; the 'breeding' of human beings inspired by Darwinism; complete freedom of action for the strongest, based on a misinterpretation of Nietzsche's theory of the Superman.

But in the autumn of 1940 the very magnitude of his victory took Hitler rather by surprise; now he could indeed build for the future but he also had to look to more urgent matters. Diplomatically, he needed to isolate Britain and to extract the greatest possible benefit in Europe from his victory over France. Economically, he had to ensure a rational development of the conquered territories in order to provide for Germany's subsistence and the Wehrmacht's armaments.

Diplomatically, in accordance with the lessons taught by political geography, Hitler's aim in H. A. Jacobsen's words 'was to set up a regional system on a continental basis as opposed to the universal approach of the Anglo-Saxons'. Such was the object of the tripartite pact of

September 27, 1940, between Germany, Italy and Japan. The world was carved up at Britain's expense and to the exclusion of the United States: Japan's zone of influence was to be the Far East; Europe and Africa would be Germany's and Italy's. The latter was given the Mediterranean, although no very exact definition was given of the term; Hitler merely thought that below a certain latitude and outside a certain specified climate, conditions were not favourable for the establishment of a sound Aryan civilisation, although this did not prevent him from competing with Mussolini in certain areas; but the two partners in crime avoided mentioning this.

In this division of the world, a Greater Germany could arise in Europe. In Rosenberg's presence, Hitler once compared the birth of this *Grossreich* to that of Bismarck's Empire in 1860. He was, in a word, reviving Naumann's old conception of *Mitteleuropa*. On November 28, 1940, Himmler declared at a meeting of Gauleiters: 'I believe in a community of Germanic peoples, in which each will retain its own language and cultural heritage, which does not mean that they will be able to decide their own external economic or military policies.' Were one to look for the roots of such an empire, they would be found in the Germanic Holy Roman Empire. Thus Richard Ganzer, the Nazi philosopher of history, even though uncertain whether he was really expressing the ideas of the Master, who had been known to disown those who expounded his thought, saw it as a central nucleus (the Reich) around which would be grouped states in the process of being annexed, 'buffer' states, autonomous vassal states with specific tasks and independent states associated with the Reich.

One thing was certain: the exploitation of the entire resources of Europe could take place only under the system of autarchy foreshadowed in the Four Year Plan, which W. Schussler, another theorist, called 'returning to the Continental idea which existed before the discovery of America'. Germany would control production, technology and scientific research in every country; goods would be exchanged by a barter system so as to save the export of currency; working conditions would become uniform and this would lead to the appropriate movements of population.

Meanwhile – and this was not in contradiction to these gigantic plans – everything must be subordinated to satisfy the war industry's needs in order to complete and consolidate the victory. So the Steering Committee for Trade Policy was set up in Berlin, an organisation containing representatives from all the ministries concerned, to assess the contribution of each of the occupied countries, make an inventory of the raw materials and products most useful for the war economy, ensure increased production and protection and organise the financing of purchases and the movement of goods. The long-term policy was to keep heavy industry, the source of power, as a monopoly in German hands; the other countries were to be forced to become suppliers of foodstuffs and raw materials. In each sector of the economy, guile was to be used to achieve these ends: the velvet glove was to be used in preference to plundering or requisitioning and attempts were to be made to reach agreement with the political and industrial leaders of the occupied countries.

This was the overall political pattern of Europe under Nazi domination, both for the present and the future. While based on a unified conception, it was liable to variation in accordance with local conditions.

II CENTRAL EUROPE

Since March 1939, Bohemia and Moravia had become a protectorate of the Reich, with the diplomat von Neurath as the 'Protector'. However, the chiefs of police and of the ss were not subordinated to him but were directly under Himmler. This dual authority was to be the regular policy in German-occupied Europe. The running of the country had been taken over by the Germans; the Protector governed by decree. However, there was a Czech government with limited administrative powers.

In March 1939 Slovakia broke away from Bohemia and proclaimed her independence; although she had a treaty with the Reich granting her the latter's 'friendly protection', Slovakia ran her own affairs. Josef Tiso, a priest, became President of the State on October 26, 1939; he appointed A. Tuka as his Prime Minister. Slovakia was the launching pad for the German armies marching against Poland; she became a signatory to the 'tripartite pact' and voluntarily put her own economy at the service of the Reich's war economy and placed her press and radio at the latter's disposal.

Germany's exceptional role in the country was constantly being stressed by Bernard, the German ambassador in Bratislava, who considered Slovakia's status as a tempting bait for the smaller Slav nations, since it showed them, in his view, how they might themselves prosper by placing themselves within the German orbit. But if any Slovak minister chanced to imagine that he really was independent, Bernard took care to call him to order or denounce him to Berlin.

The situation in Poland was completely different. The 'incorporated territories' – containing 9 million inhabitants, 600,000 of whom were German before the war – had simply become German. Their government was in the hands of Germans from the Reich or the Baltic countries; the mark replaced the zloty, German law Polish law and so on. The problem was to discover who was or became German and who stayed Polish. To this end, a 'German national list' was drawn up containing the names of the ex-Polish German subjects and the Poles who were to be 'germanised' in the interests of Germany; they received total or partial citizenship. All the rest, that is to say the majority of the Poles, were placed in the category of 'protected citizens' and although enjoying some protection – apart from Jews and gypsies – they had no property-owning rights, no right to any education above primary level, no right of association, no right to go to theatres, museums or libraries, or to fill any posts or professions at managerial level.

Polish workers and employers were the least well paid – albeit better paid, in some cases, than in pre-war Poland – and then only for days actually worked and not for rest days or holidays. They could not sue their German employers – that would have been insulting behaviour. They received no family allowances and their rations were only about three-quarters of those of the Germans. There were countless police regulations restricting their freedom of movement – they had to have a special pass in order to travel by train or even bicycle. Very heavy penalties were inflicted for the various crimes they could commit; they could be condemned to death for showing ill-will towards Germans.

The status of the 'General Government' – 12 million Poles, including Warsaw but with its capital in Cracow – was more amorphous. The Governor General, Frank, was directly responsible to Hitler and administered the territory through a government comprising 'divisions', which replaced ministries. Municipalities were in charge of German or Ukrainian and occasionally Polish mayors. Parallel to the German courts there existed Polish courts which were competent to deal only with civil cases between Poles and Polish law remained partly operative. There even existed a Polish police, strictly under German control, of course. The 'General Government' took over the Jews and Poles considered as undesirables in the incorporated territories.

The problem of the nationality of the inhabitants of the 'General Government' remained pending: the 'German national list' was not introduced there, even though excessive privileges were granted to the resident German minority – special residential districts, restaurants and railway carriages. The German authorities adopted the principle that, as a consequence of the war, the Polish nation had ceased to exist; as a result the inhabitants of the 'General Government' had become stateless. The consequence was that Poles living there retained certain benefits or liberties that were denied their compatriots in the incorporated territories. In the first few months, only the large firms were confiscated; and Poles could enter the liberal professions. But Polish associations were forbidden, education was restricted to primary level, racial discrimination was rife and the Gestapo ruled the roost.

Although not having taken part in the war, Romania was treated as a conquered vassal state. After receiving an ultimatum from the USSR she was forced to hand over Bessarabia and North Bukovina on June 26, 1940; while expressing some reservations about the Russian claims on Bukovina and watching over the lot of the Germans residing there, Hitler had advised King Carol to give in, although the latter had suggested 'co-operation in all fields' and stressed his willingness to 'speak the same language as Germany'.

Indeed, the Romanians, surrounded as they were by hostile neighbours, now saw German protection as their only salvation. They proclaimed their acceptance of Hitler's New Order in Europe. They expelled the French engineers working for the oil companies. But when Hungary claimed Transylvania from them and Bulgaria claimed Dobruja, Hitler and Mussolini both advised them to come to an agreement on these two requests directly, for, as Hitler wrote, 'Hungary and Bulgaria are old friends of Germany'. It was not as easy as that to join the winning side and there was a stiff entrance fee.

When direct negotiations failed, Ribbentrop and Ciano imposed their own 'arbitration' but Romania had to pay the piper. On August 30, Romania handed over to Hungary nearly 17,000 square miles and 2,300,000 inhabitants of Transylvania, including Cluj; and on September 7, 1940, it was Bulgaria's turn to be given Dobruja.

King Carol was forced to abdicate in favour of his son Michael, after having called on General Antonescu to form a government, with the approval of the German ambassador Fabricius. Antonescu took the title of 'Conducator'; he set up a Romanian Fascist movement, dissolved the political parties and included in the government Horia Sima's 'Iron Guard', which gave total allegiance to the German Nazi party. Their 'legionaries' immediately seized posts of power in the state and exacted vengeance on their opponents: house searches, arrests and forced suicides followed thick and fast. During the night of November 26–27, they massacred sixty-four prisoners held in their gaols; the well-known historian Iorga was also murdered.

Antonescu's authority began to weaken and in January 1941 he came into direct conflict with the Iron Guard. After standing by and watching this incipient civil war for a while, the Germans came down in favour of Antonescu against Horia Sima. They preferred their decisions to pass through a popular national leader rather than through someone only too well-known as dependent on them; but they held Horia Sima in reserve to keep Antonescu under pressure; this was another regular method of their policy in territories they occupied.

In any case, Antonescu was entirely subservient to them. He signed the tripartite pact; he applied the discriminatory measures against Jews demanded by the Reich; he allowed German troops into Romania on the pretext of training the Romanian Army and protecting the oil installations. He signed a ten-year plan of economic collaboration with Germany.

So the whole of central Europe, where Mussolini had been obliged to forego making any claims, had come under German sway. Either by direct control as in former Poland, by the expedient of protectorates as in Bohemia, or through puppet governments, Hitler's New Order reigned supreme; all the resources of every country were being fed into the German war-machine.

III WESTERN EUROPE

Germany's behaviour in the west was less harsh than in the east. Himmler recognised the Norwegians, the Dutch, the Swedes and the Flemings as branches of the Germanic race; Hitler was interested in Burgundy, the homeland of the fifth-century Burgundians, and in Normandy, the land of the Vikings. As for France in general, economic necessity required her to be granted special treatment for the time being.

In Norway the 'Administrative Council' set up by the Reich's High Commissioner, Joseph Terboven, which numbered amongst its members such important persons as the President of the Supreme Court and the Governor of Oslo, was striving to limit the powers of the Germans to the best of its ability, in the firm belief that King Haakon would approve. But Terboven refused to be taken in; he wanted a docile government to deal with. In June 1940 he asked the Legislative Assembly, the *Storting*, to replace the Administrative Council by the *Riksraad* or State Council. The *Storting* demurred for a few months and then gave in. But King Haakon refused to recognise the *Riksraad* and denied its legal competence to undertake the new responsibilities foisted on it by the occupying power.

With one accord, all the Norwegian political bodies and personalities now refused to collaborate with the Germans. Only Quisling approved everything; his newspaper *Fritt Folk* merely repeated German propaganda. Terboven had to acknowledge failure. He decided to dissolve the political parties and had some members of Quisling's party appointed to the *Riksraad*, although not Quisling himself as yet. Henceforth, Norway was allowed one single party, the *Nasjonal Samling*; Quisling remained its leader. This party tried to introduce its members into the various state, university and workers' organisations. The chance of a good job, the lure of power and various forms of pressure swelled the ranks of the party to some extent but it never achieved more than 100,000 members. For want of anything better, in February 1942 Terboven was led on logically to the next step of entrusting power to Quisling himself, though without altering the powers of the *Riksraad*.

Quisling revived the pattern of trade that existed in Norway at the time of the Hanseatic league, that is, Norwegian trade was exclusively directed towards the Baltic, and no longer via the North Sea. In any case, circumstances forced such a course; as a beginning, electrical power from Norway was fed to Germany.

Like Norway, Holland was for the Nazis a 'free National Socialist Germanic people'. It too had a National Socialist party whose leader was Mussert; it too was provided with a Reich High Commissioner, Seiss-Inquart. Like the Norwegians in their attitude to Quisling, the Dutch considered Mussert and his faithful followers as traitors. This was the reason why the Germans had felt it unwise to let them take over power.

Hitler had stated that Holland 'would remain politically and economically united so as to provide a gateway to the outside world'. There was thus no question of forcing a National Socialist régime on her nor of integrating her into the Reich, but it was hoped that she would join of her own free will. Executive power was exercised by Seiss-Inquart, assisted by four general commissioners – the one in charge of the police came directly under Himmler. But the government of the country was left to the Dutch, through the secretaries general in the ministries and the whole body of civil servants.

The Dutch people were wondering about their future and some important persons were not, *a priori*, averse to the idea of setting up a new government, distinct from the one in London. Their view was that people should accept the inevitable and adapt themselves to a long period of German domination. A very well-known politician, Hendrikus Colijn, expressed this point of view in a pamphlet entitled 'On the border of two worlds'.

But even though the membership of Mussert's party considerably increased, the population as a whole held itself aloof. Mussert took the view that Belgium should disappear in order to create a Greater Holland, closely linked with the Reich. The Germans used his supporters to spread their propaganda and to carry out their unsavoury police operations, but they kept Mussert himself in reserve.

The Dutch economy was nonetheless integrated with Germany's. Between December 1940 and April 1941, customs duties between the two countries were abolished and the Reich's wage-structures and conditions of work were introduced into Holland.

In Belgium, King Leopold's presence was both a hindrance and a promise. It prevented the Germans from forcing new institutions on the country but it was clear that if the King were to be won round to accept the occupation and speak out in favour of collaboration, he would be of inestimable value to the Germans. Leopold declared that 'he meant to avoid giving the Belgians the impression of wanting to reign at all costs under German pressure'. He proposed to withdraw to a small country house. Under the pretext that 'he ought to be granted special consideration', the Germans suggested, as a bait, the castle of Laeken as being 'more suitable and practical'. Leopold continued to consider himself as being held there as a prisoner of war.

Belgium formed a national government working under the responsibility of the military commander, General von Falkenhausen; it was administered by the secretaries general of the various ministries. Through resignations, lowering the age limit of retirement and the establishment of new posts, the Germans introduced into the administration people on whom they could rely. But the political, administrative and economic structures of Belgium were not changed.

IV THE VICHY GOVERNMENT

Of all the countries conquered by Germany, France was the only one whose legal government had signed an armistice putting an end to hostilities. The government had left Bordeaux and installed itself in Vichy because this small spa could provide accommodation for the administrative services in its many hotels and also because it was close to the occupied zone.

The Rethondes convention was harsh but it did not contain anything ignominious and it appeared to leave the French government with a number of not unimportant trump cards. The northern half of France was occupied by German troops but it had been agreed that the French government's authority should extend there – it being understood, of course, that the French authorities would act strictly in accordance with the directives issued by the Germans. The French government was even left free, in theory, to 'transfer its seat to Paris'.

In the so-called 'free' zone, the French government had, theoretically, complete authority. It retained all the attributes of a sovereign power. This meant that it could maintain diplomatic representation throughout the world and have ambassadors attached to it from every state, starting with the Soviet Union, the United States and the Vatican. On the other hand, although the French troops had been demobilised, their weapons collected up and handed over to the conqueror, the French government had kept an 'armistice army' of about 100,000 men to maintain its authority in the territories that it still retained. The war fleet, almost intact before the British attack at Mers el-Kebir, was no longer a fighting force because it was to be disarmed but it remained a valuable asset for any eventual peace negotiations.

The economic clauses were very harsh; occupation costs were to be

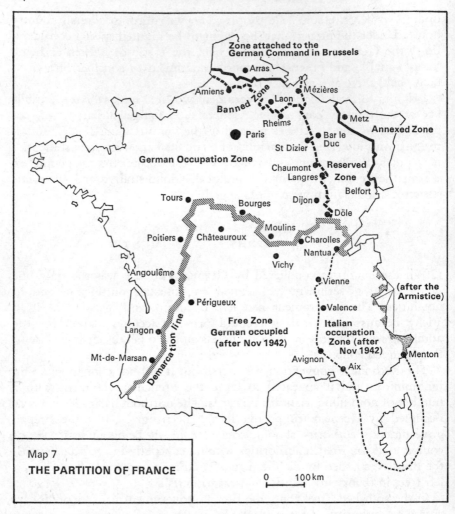

Zone attached to the
German Command in Brussels

Arras

Amiens

Banned Zone

Laon

Mézières

Rheims

Metz

Annexed Zone

Paris

St Dizier

Bar le
Duc

German Occupation Zone

Chaumont

Reserved

Langres

Zone

Belfort

Tours

Bourges

Dijon

Döle

Poitiers

Châteauroux

Moulins

Charolles

Nantua

Vichy

Angoulême

Vienne

(after the
Armistice)

Périgueux

Valence

Free Zone
German occupied
(after Nov 1942)

Italian
occupation
Zone (after
Nov 1942)

Langon

Mt-de-Marsan

Demarcation line

Avignon

Aix

Menton

Map 7
THE PARTITION OF FRANCE

0   100 km

charged to the French and France's external trade was blocked; to all
intents and purposes the assets and stocks held in the occupied zone
passed into German hands, and their haul of captured goods was immense. But France still held on to her loyal colonial empire; some of the
territories were of particular strategic importance – Tunisia, which had
Bizerta, and French West Africa, which had Dakar.

    After a number of reshuffles, the government under Pétain's leadership
now contained no deputies from the former Third Republic except Pierre
Laval. On July 10, 1940, the National Assembly meeting in Vichy unhesitatingly and by a large majority – only eighty members voted against –
gave Marshal Pétain unlimited powers and the brief to provide France

with a new constitution. At that time Marshal Pétain's popularity was immense; his dignity, noble bearing, unselfishness, plus memories of 1914–18 and the public conviction that he had saved the country from even greater misfortune meant that he had almost all the French people behind him. In fact, the Marshal was a capricious old man, easily tired, and his political experience was both recent and crude.

V THE APPLICATION OF THE ARMISTICE CONVENTION

The armistice terms were harsh and they were going to become even harsher because of the way in which the Germans applied them. The whole of the occupied zone was directly under the control of the military commander General von Stulpnagel; he issued directives to the *préfets*, he fixed prices, he requisitioned goods and labour, he gave direct orders to industrialists, he took over the French police and he interfered with the workings of justice; the press and radio were run by his departments. The Vichy government was, indeed, represented by a delegate in Paris but he was merely a go-between who passed information back and made known his government's wishes to the German military commander.

On their own authority the Germans modified the armistice convention in their favour. Thus they simply annexed the three *départements* that formed Alsace-Lorraine. After moving the customs posts back to the ridge along the Vosges, they introduced the German language and forbade the use of French: using the word 'bonjour' led to a fine on the spot. They expelled the French officials and replaced them by Germans; the French-speaking Lorrainers were forced to leave their district at a few hours' notice, taking with them only the bare necessities. The population of Alsace was organised into Nazi youth groups, labour groups and welfare groups; whole villages were transplanted into Germany. The Vichy government protested against this unilateral action but it did not think that its protests would have any effect except to arouse Hitler's wrath and so it did not make them public, thus rendering them quite ineffective.

Similarly, the Germans had joined the two northernmost *départements* (Nord and Pas-de-Calais) to their Brussels military command; this was done for military reasons – the Straits of Dover had great strategic importance – but no one knew what thoughts of dismemberment might lie behind the action and as a first result the coal of the area produced in such large quantities was now no longer available to the rest of the country. Another 'forbidden' zone was marked out in north-east France and it was disturbing to see that its borderline followed approximately that of the Holy Roman Empire.

The Germans turned the demarcation line between the occupied and free zones into a real frontier; neither goods nor mail nor travellers were allowed over it. Even Vichy ministers were turned back when they wanted to go to Paris. Thus France was cut into two sections, without any links between them, whereas in fact the one could not exist without the other. From the autumn of 1940 onwards, living conditions in the poor and mountainous free zone began to become difficult.

Finally, the Germans interfered in the southern zone; they sent many agents there and the members of the armistice commission poked their noses into everything; they tried to do business direct with the French living in the free zone; and they forced the Vichy government to submit its more important decisions, such as senior administrative appointments, for their approval.

VI THE EXPLOITATION OF FRANCE

On September 20 Keitel summed up Hitler's views thus: 'Upheavals in the French economy are a matter of indifference to us; any concessions granted to France must be balanced by deliveries from the non-occupied zone or the colonies.' Although left deliberately vague the intention plainly was to squeeze France till the pips squeaked.

Requisitioning of every sort continued in the northern zone after the signing of the armistice and the troops which had penetrated into the southern zone did not leave it without train-load after train-load of goods and industrial equipment. Thanks to a particularly favourable exchange-rate for the mark, the German soldiers throughout the occupied zone were able to strip all the shops on the cheap – with such eagerness that the Parisians called them 'Colorado beetles'.

The armistice convention provided the German authorities with more convenient and infinitely more effective methods. The occupation costs were fixed by the Germans unilaterally at 400 million francs a day. The French objected that such a sum would be enough for them to maintain 10 million soldiers and they tried to draw the distinction between occupation troops and those operating against Britain, who were more numerous and expensive. The Germans refused to accept any distinction or compromise and demanded payment of the indemnity in ten-day instalments. Such a constant drain on French finances could lead only to galloping inflation.

The armistice convention provided the Germans with many other means of extortion and further economic advantages. With the money which they did not spend they acquired not only goods and French assets but also shares in large French industrial and commercial firms. They were buying up the French economy with France's own money.

Thus the military Waterloo was completed by an economic Waterloo which became even more disastrous after the signing of the Franco-German compensation agreement. Its wording made it another *Diktat*; it provided, in fact, that the French Compensation Bureau should pay French exporters without taking any account of the receipt of German goods; and as the Reich was buying and not selling anything, very soon all the expenditure and transfer of funds turned into a one-way traffic, from France to Germany. The French protests fell on deaf ears; Hemming, the head of the economic section of the German Armistice Commission in Wiesbaden, was blunt and unbending: 'France declared war on Germany; any risks arising from the situation must be France's responsibility.'

VII THE POLICY OF COLLABORATION

Germany's harsh attitude had dismayed the Vichy government; but after having made some gestures of refusal and not without its delegates having disputed every inch of the way with the German Armistice Commission in Wiesbaden, it had duly knuckled under. The fact was that it considered that Germany had won the war and that the only thing left was to come to terms with reality. It had been greatly surprised that, left on her own, Britain had not surrendered; but Vichy continued to believe that even though Britain might still persist in fighting on she would find it impossible to return to the continent of Europe and win the war there.

Despite the British attacks at Mers el-Kebir and Dakar, and despite the support being given de Gaulle, who had been condemned to death in France as a traitor, Marshal Pétain did not want any reversal of alliances that would take France into war against her former ally. He wished to establish a *modus vivendi* with her in the hope that she would relax her blockade. However, he was anxious to recover the dissident colonial territories which had joined de Gaulle, and this operation did entail the risk of coming into conflict with Britain.

Pierre Laval and Admiral Darlan accepted this risk and even hoped it would come to pass. Their view was that, in the interests of France, the collaboration at administrative level laid down in the armistice convention and the economic collaboration that would be the inevitable consequence of that convention must be followed by political collaboration as the only way in which France could carve out for herself a less uncomfortable niche in Europe under German control, make Britain stand the bill for all the damage when peace came and perhaps replace Italy as Hitler's blue-eyed boy.

Pétain adopted this policy as his own and it was at his own request that he met Hitler at Montoire on October 24, 1940. At that time, Hitler was contemplating setting up a Mediterranean coalition against Britain. He thus needed the Vichy government's collaboration in order to gain a foothold in North Africa without trouble. At Montoire, the principle of collaboration was approved but no details of ways and means were worked out. Hitler very soon gave up his plan as a result of Franco's inflated demands and, above all, of Mussolini's attack on Greece. Consequently he felt no need to grant France any concessions; the armistice convention, interpreted as he pleased, was perfectly adequate to extract from her everything he wanted.

First Pierre Laval and then, after he had been ejected from the government on December 13, 1940, Admiral Darlan made repeated but fruitless advances; the only person to lend a favourable ear was Otto Abetz, who made Franco-German collaboration the mainstay of his policy. In May 1941, Admiral Darlan went as far as to grant the Germans bases in the French colonies, at Bizerta and Dakar, whilst German aircraft were permitted to land on airfields in Syria in order to help the Iraqi uprising against Britain.

VIII THE NATIONAL REVOLUTION

The new gentlemen of Vichy were for the most part old opponents of the Third Republic which they held responsible for their country's misfortunes. An intensive propaganda campaign was launched against the parliamentary system, the political parties and the leaders of the vanished régime. In order to 'restore' France and in the hope of currying favour with Hitler, the Vichy government set out to introduce certain reforms, some of them Fascist in spirit, under the name of 'National Revolution'.

One of the hobby-horses of this national revolution was 'the myth of the leader'. As leader of the country, Pétain became the object of a veritable cult, his messages were glossed, not discussed; the word went out 'think Pétain'. The premise was that power does not come from below and that the people need to be told what to do: 'schools of leadership' became widespread.

Marshal Pétain had not drawn up the constitution, as the National Assembly had requested; his political views were thus veiled in some mystery; but as a result of his past experience he had an entirely military conception of power, in the shape of a pyramid. He appointed and dismissed ministers as he pleased; it was he alone who took the decisions affecting the whole country – the policy of collaboration, for example. He declared: 'History will judge *me*.' In this way he established a monarchy in fact but not in name, to the great delight of Charles Maurras, the *Action française* political thinker.

However, the Marshal refused to accept those mainstays of Fascism, the single party and single youth movement. On the other hand, he grouped all the ex-servicemen into one 'Legion' and hoped that it would provide a body of disciplined, uncritical supporters. As for the machinery of state, elections were abolished; mayors were nominated, not elected. In the country, an important role was to be played by 'notables', and provincial squires deserted their manor houses in order to serve their country. Admiral Darlan appointed naval officers to many important posts; their loyalty would be guaranteed by their anglophobia and conservatism.

In theory the national revolution was anti-capitalistic. It rejected the class struggle and abolished all the syndicalist central committees of employers and workers. In practice, no serious action was taken against capitalist structures, even though their abuses were attacked; on the other hand, strikes were banned and wages frozen. The régime was not sympathetic towards the worker, who was considered revolutionary because he lacked roots, but towards the peasant, whose traditional virtues were praised. It was intended gradually to introduce a corporate régime to provide the framework of the whole economy.

The 'constructive' measures were matched by repressive and discriminatory action. Amongst the state corporations, the universities were particularly suspect and the subsidies to independent educational bodies, the reform of the syllabus and the influence given to the Minister of Youth were intended to limit their importance. From the French citizen himself, no opposition was tolerated; the press was strictly controlled; 'bad Frenchmen' – Communists, Socialists, Freemasons, free-thinkers – found themselves moved elsewhere, dismissed, placed under house arrest or interned. Those 'responsible for the defeat' were to be brought before a special court. Finally, the Vichy government anticipated the Germans' wishes by issuing decrees against the Jews.

IX SPAIN

Despite a certain reluctance on some issues and occasionally digging in its heels, on the whole the Vichy government was moving in the direction that Hitler wanted, although this did not prevent him from greatly distrusting it – especially its military leaders; his pet aversion was General Weygand.

Franco's Spain had, on the other hand, in theory, been allied to the Reich since the Spanish Civil War. However, Franco refused to go to war when Hitler asked him to do so in Hendaye on October 23. Or rather, the Caudillo, while stating that he was ready to pay off his debt of gratitude, asked for time to prepare and put forward claims that Hitler considered excessive and in any case was not in a position to satisfy – wheat, artillery, Catalonia, French Morocco and the province of Oran. How could these ambitions be reconciled with France's participation in a Mediterranean coalition against Britain? Not forgetting that Hitler and Mussolini also coveted a share in Morocco.

Hitler did not like Franco; he identified him with his Wehrmacht generals and considered him lacking in the political sense and gifts of a real leader. For his own part, Franco had been deeply shocked by the German-Soviet pact: Moscow, he said, was the Antichrist with whom no compromise was possible. On the other hand, he was being both wooed and threatened by Britain, with the strong support of the United States; and only the Anglo-Saxons could supply Spain with the wheat and petrol she so urgently needed.

But above all, Spain had only just emerged from civil war and was still recovering from its effects; she was exhausted almost to the point of famine and incapable of embarking on a new conflict; remobilisation would be tantamount to putting weapons back into their opponents' hands; in the event of any conflict, moreover, the Canaries would speedily be occupied by the British fleet. Hitler saw what was happening; he thought that Franco was using Germany as a catspaw and afterwards, at the eleventh hour, just like Mussolini, he would do the absolute minimum necessary to win a seat at the victory table and pick up his share of the spoils from the losers.

Hitler took away a very bad impression from his Hendaye meeting. He told Ribbentrop that, rather than go through it again, he would prefer to have several teeth out. So he made little further effort to influence Franco and the ensuing talks between Serrano Suñer and Ribbentrop came to no practical conclusions. Satisfying Franco would in any case have certainly worried the Vichy government and perhaps prompted the rulers of the French empire to secede under the shadow of the impending threat, something that Hitler wished to avoid at all costs. Mainly, however, Hitler had not toyed for long with the scheme of campaigning in the Mediterranean, which Raeder had been trying to sell him. Ever since July 1940, he had been contemplating launching out once more on the age-old path of German expansion eastwards. From this viewpoint, it was certainly not desirable to open up another theatre of war. What the Führer needed was a western Europe where everything was quiet – and being suitably squeezed by Germany. A neutral Spain fitted in with these schemes; a belligerent Spain would raise more problems than it would solve.

CHAPTER 3

The Fighting in Africa and the Balkans

BOTH now and later, the war continued its course at sea, in Africa and in the Balkans.

I THE BATTLE OF THE ATLANTIC

The battle of the convoys was vital for Britain. There was no point in the Commonwealth's mobilising its resources and the Americans becoming actively friendly if the men and their weapons were going to Davy Jones' locker.

At the start of the struggle Britain was not really short of freighters. Even though entering the war had greatly reduced the number of foreign ships coming into her harbours compared with peacetime, since their owners were anxious not to jeopardise them, German victories since the summer of 1940 had had the happy result of increasing the British Merchant Navy by some 1,600 Norwegian, Dutch, French, Greek, Belgian and Polish vessels, comprising some 7 million tons in all.

But the advantages gained from this extra tonnage were greatly reduced by new difficulties. First of all the ships usually had to travel much longer distances; things which before the war had come from the occupied countries of Europe now had to be provided from outside Europe, round Africa via the Cape, rather than through the short cut of the Suez Canal. As it was impossible to use the east coast ports, the west coast harbours were heavily congested since they were obliged to accept types of cargoes which they were not equipped to handle. Such operations as unloading and despatching inland took much longer in rudimentary harbours like Freetown or others on the West African coast, for example, which were now in constant use.

With its centuries-old experience, the Royal Navy was indeed well placed to cope with any task, however difficult, thanks to its complex qualities of tradition, instinctive reactions and powers of decision, backed by a thorough knowledge of all the problems of sea warfare. But it had to face unforeseen dangers. Thus, in order to deal with the vast quantities of mines, in November 1940 it had been obliged to bring more than 700 mine-sweepers into operation. It was also suffering from certain shortages.

For example, for want of sufficient escort vessels, it was still very difficult for it to provide protection for convoys. These moved in cumbersome groups of thirty or forty vessels, at the speed of the slowest, that is at ten knots on average; sailing in four or five lines, they were defended against possible attack by only one corvette or destroyer to every ten freighters or more.

However, the question of air support had been satisfactorily solved as far as the Navy was concerned, since it had its own naval air force; moreover, it had been given priority in the use of the squadrons of Coastal Command. But the fighting in Norway had shown the vulnerability of ships to air attack; ship-mounted AA was an inadequate defence; in any case, there were not enough guns to arm merchant shipping. German bombing raids reduced the output of the naval armament factories and dockyards and hampered the working of the ports.

Also German submarines now had additional facilities which they would be able to exploit to the full. Their bases had been extended to Stavanger, Trondheim, Lorient, St-Nazaire, La Pallice and Bordeaux; they thus held the whole of the British Isles inside their net and they could go through the Straits of Dover with impunity. Whereas in June 1940, there were on average only twelve German submarines operating in the Atlantic, which were joined by some Italian submarines, in May 1941 there were forty. The largest of them was 800 tons and had a range of 15,000 miles.

Most of the submarines could go faster than the convoys, thus enabling repeated attacks to be made at different points. Since the Luftwaffe had provided Admiral Doenitz with an air force, spotting convoys had become easier.

Thus British shipping losses became alarming. From a maximum of 340,000 tons per month in 1940, they rose to 650,000 tons in April 1941, more than was being built by the British and Canadian shipyards combined. When Hitler extended the area of his blockade as far as Greenland, convoys were being attacked south of Newfoundland. In these circumstances, the fifty destroyers, old as they were, that were handed over by the United States, and the help given by the American Navy in protecting convoys were more than merely token gestures.

In accordance with Douhet's doctrine, the British tried to destroy the submarine bases by bombing from the air. While the towns all around suffered plenty of raids, the submarines remained unharmed in their massive concrete pens. So it proved more rewarding to seek them out close to the convoys round which they were lurking. For this purpose, from 1941 onwards the aircraft of Coastal Command were equipped with radar which could detect a submarine thirty miles away, although then sinking it was another matter.

A further hazard was that, in the winter of 1940, the German Navy again started despatching auxiliary cruisers and heavy vessels to attack convoys from Brest and Lorient. The Royal Navy was obliged to disperse its ships throughout the seven seas in order to hunt them down: in the Indian Ocean the *Admiral Scheer* was attacking British freighters on their voyage between Australia and the Cape. Even the heavy battleship *Bismarck* was put into service in May 1941. She was quickly spotted but succeeded in sinking the battleship *Hood*; she was then pursued by the British aircraft-carriers *Victorious* and *Ark Royal*; after being damaged, she was sunk by the guns of the cruiser *Norfolk*. It was then that their mistake in failing to build aircraft-carriers was fully brought home to the Kriegsmarine. Admiral Raeder was temporarily forced to stop sending his warships into the Atlantic. But the submarines continued to be very successful and things were no better for the British in the Mediterranean.

II NAVAL WARFARE IN THE MEDITERRANEAN. THE ANTAGONISTS

'Thanks to aircraft, submarines, mines and small fast vessels,' wrote Admiral Assman, 'the Mediterranean had become merely an inland sea offering no possibility for deploying a powerful navy.' British possessions had become particularly vulnerable 'even for an opponent without a navy'. After the French fleet had withdrawn from the war, British control of the Mediterranean was all the more seriously jeopardised because the Royal Navy was heavily involved in protecting convoys in the Atlantic. And in the Mediterranean, Italy occupied a strategic position of paramount importance, by reason of her central geographical situation and her advanced bases in Sicily and Pantellaria. There was, however, one link missing in the Italian transversal chain running from north to south: Tunisia. Mussolini would have liked to occupy it as early as June 1940 but Hitler had persuaded him to leave it to the Vichy government in order not to create discontent in the French empire; in any case, Bizerta had been neutralised.

What place did the Mediterranean occupy in Hitler's overall conception of the war? Despite Admiral Raeder's suggestions, he refused to consider it an important operational theatre. According to General Halder, he thought that it would be impossible to prevent Britain from asserting her superiority there. All that could be done was to wage 'a war of attrition', taking care to ensure the 'greatest possible economy in the use of their forces', so as to postpone the day when British superiority would achieve its full effect – and it would then be pointless, because Britain would have been conquered elsewhere. In General Halder's view, the German Navy, which had different views on the matter, 'was dreaming in terms of continents'.

It was true that when the Axis partners were being assigned their specific tasks, it had been agreed that the Mediterranean would be Italy's preserve; Mussolini was very keen on this and he referred to it continually. These 'parallel interests' did, indeed, leave the two allies with one common 'enemy' but they prevented them from drawing up any plans for concerted action. Liaison had been established at staff level but each partner was jealous of his own independence and disinclined to reveal his schemes; the situation would need to become serious before the two dictators agreed to take joint decisions.

It was obviously Italy who had the greatest interest in driving the British out of the Mediterranean. Mussolini had frequently asserted that Italy was held 'prisoner' there and that she would only free herself by breaking open the two 'locks' of her prison, Gibraltar and Alexandria. And in fact, on July 11, 1940, the Duce had issued instructions in extremely determined and aggressive terms, to smash these 'locks'. But two days later these instructions had been withdrawn, with no explanation given. The fact was that the Italian Navy had confessed that it was powerless to carry them out and the high command had supported it; to seek out and destroy the British fleet was a task beyond their ability and any attempt to do so would be 'playing into the hands of the British'.

The Italian Navy was, in fact, gravely deficient in very many ways. Two promising additions had been made to it in August 1940, when the two battleships *Littorio* and *Vittorio Veneto* were brought into commission, because they were as good as any of the warships in the British fleet. But, like the older ships, these new ones were giants with hulls of clay, since they would be lacking any aircraft-carrier escort or effective cover by land-based aircraft. Experimental radar had been tried out in Leghorn but no ships had actually been equipped with it; so the Italian fleet was blind and deaf and while it could be spotted by the enemy, it would itself know nothing of its opponents until it was attacked. The lack of proper gunlaying equipment precluded any use of naval guns at night; at such times, they were not even kept loaded. The fleet also lacked submarine chasers and boats to undertake amphibious operations. Out of 108 submarines, 20 had been withdrawn from service as obsolete; 33 had been despatched into the Atlantic where 11 of them were lost in the space of a fortnight, from June 14 to 29. Barely 50 or so remained in service in the Mediterranean; their noisy engines made them liable to be picked up by listening devices; they were unable to turn quickly; they dived slowly and were thus very vulnerable to enemy aircraft overhead.

If we add that its mines were old and inefficient and that the Spanish war had disrupted its logistics, it was clear that the Italian Navy was a second-rate force, able to play a part when supported by powerful allies but incapable of any independent large-scale initiative when left to itself. Moreover, its fuel-oil supplies were in a parlous state; it had been calculated that stocks would run out by June 1941; as a constant link with North Africa was essential to supply the troops fighting there, priority had to be given almost exclusively to the ships and the oil being used for convoy protection.

Accordingly, the Italian supreme command, and first and foremost the naval high command, saw the Italian war fleet as too valuable an asset to be lightly squandered. This fear paralysed any initiative because it induced the Italian Admiralty – *Supermarina* – to interfere in the most minor details thus depriving the executive officers of all chance of initiative.

Yet the British Mediterranean fleet, towards which the Italians felt something of an inferiority complex, was by no means unbeatable. It had evacuated Malta and divided its forces into two squadrons, based on Gibraltar (Admiral Somerville) and Alexandria (Admiral Cunningham). In many respects, the attack on Mers el-Kebir had been merely a confession of weakness and fear. However, unlike the Italian fleet, each British squadron formed a formidable fighting force, thanks to the combination of battleship and aircraft-carrier. The battleship with its escort of cruisers and torpedo-boats provided the aircraft-carrier with the support of its AA, and the latter's fighters gave overall air cover. But whereas the strength of the Italian Navy in the Mediterranean remained more or less constant, the number of units in the British squadrons were sometimes dangerously reduced by the requirements of other operational theatres. The Italian Navy usually failed to exploit this temporary weakness of their opponents.

The great problem for the British was to avoid the 9,000-mile-long voyage round the Cape for their convoys. Shipping was escorted by the Gibraltar-based squadron until off Bizerta; in the eastern Mediterranean, they were taken over by the Alexandria contingent, while in between, the island of Malta had the vital role.

III THE PROBLEM OF MALTA

Malta lies only about sixty miles away from Sicily. Even before the beginning of the war, the Italian Navy had realised that troop supplies to Africa could only be ensured by bombing Malta into submission or to destruction. The British for their part had considered that it would rapidly become impossible to hold Malta and as soon as the first Italian air raids were launched in June 1940, they had withdrawn their ground forces, submarines and aircraft; so the Italian convoys on their way to Libya passed by the island unmolested.

In November 1940, having realised that the Italian air raids were not serious, the British returned to Malta in force in order to use it as a sort of aircraft-carrier; the result was that Italian shipping suffered its first losses.

The Italian Air Force could deploy only about a hundred aircraft to raid Malta. But in December 1940, the Germans based a squadron of 400 aircraft in Sicily, which from January 1941 onwards started pounding the air and harbour installations of Malta. The result soon showed; fewer Italian freighters were sunk and for a while the Malta-based British bombers stopped raiding Naples, Messina, La Spezia, Tripoli and Benghazi; in addition, one British aircraft-carrier was badly hit. The 'Malta problem' seemed by way of being solved in Italy's favour.

IV THE NAVAL BATTLES IN THE MEDITERRANEAN

Although for Hitler the Mediterranean was a secondary operational theatre, Churchill had not taken long to realise that in view of the Wehrmacht's successes, the Mediterranean was now the only possible front where injury could be inflicted on the weakest of his opponents, to ward off the grave threat menacing the British Isles. The most immediate way to achieve this aim would have been for the French colonies to stay in the war or come back into it. But Pétain, Weygand and Noguès remained deaf to all Churchill's invitations and pleas and the attack on Dakar, intended to win French West Africa over to the Allies, had ended in failure.

Meanwhile, the Italian Navy was being vigorously harried by the British fleet. On July 9, a brush took place at Punto Stilio, south of Calabria; an Italian battleship and a cruiser were hit; the Italian bombers did not arrive until the fighting was all over and then dropped a few bombs on their own fleet. On July 19, off Cape Spada in Crete, there was another clash: one Italian cruiser was sunk; the Italian bombers arrived on the scene in time to attack the British ship that was picking up the survivors.

The British then tried a bold move. On November 11, 1940, a large naval force managed to sail right across the middle of the Mediterranean without being spotted. At night, from a distance of fifty miles, the aircraft-carrier *Illustrious* launched twenty-four aircraft in two waves against the Italian battleships anchored off Taranto and seriously damaged three of the six of them; in addition two cruisers were disabled. 'So all the pheasants had gone home to roost,' Admiral Cunningham wrote. At the same time, part of the British fleet had undertaken a related operation against merchant shipping in the Straits of Otranto. The British force had escaped observation by the Italian Air Force for the whole of November 12.

The Italians were forced to move the rest of their fleet to Naples which still allowed them to operate in the western Mediterranean but not in the eastern Mediterranean. The victory at Taranto was a great boost for British morale. The First Sea Lord wrote to Admiral Cunningham: 'Just before the news of Taranto, the Cabinet were rather down in the dumps; but Taranto had a most amazing effect upon them.' The balance of power in the Mediterranean had been completely transformed.

Encouraged by this first success, another British squadron set off from Gibraltar on February 6, 1941; after feinting to move out into the Atlantic, it sailed towards Genoa and on the morning of the 9th, without being detected, it shelled the harbour and the industrial area. Nearly 200 Italian aircraft searched for it in vain.

The only Italian successes were in transporting arms and ammunition to Libya by submarine without loss; but restricting submarines to such a role meant greatly diminishing their importance. Proof had been given that, without German support, the Italians did not constitute a very formidable threat. They had provided further evidence of this in Africa.

V THE WAR IN EAST AFRICA

On the map, the Italian armies could take Egypt and the Sudan in a pincer movement, starting from Libya and Ethiopia. Indeed, in August 1940, they had no difficulty in seizing British Somaliland, which was undefended, and then invaded the Sudan and Kenya. In Ethiopia, the Italians had large forces under the command of the Duke of Aosta but their antiquated equipment included very few anti-tank weapons, meagre stocks of fuel, six AA batteries and thirty Caproni fighter aircraft which, according to General Pesenti, were 'splendid museum pieces'. Some native units were armed with guns dating from the Austro-Hungarian Empire.

The natives were, on the whole, unreliable; under the Italian occupation little respect had been shown for local rank and this meant that general revolt was simmering below the surface, above all in Choa and Harar. The return of the Negus Haile Selassie in January 1941 galvanised the opposition; stirred up by the British, guerrilla warfare gradually spread and the Askari deserted *en masse* to join up with the 'patriots'.

In these circumstances, the Duke of Aosta's 70,000 men were placed in a situation that was all the more precarious because they were completely cut off from their homeland and throughout the whole course of hostilities received only one cargo of rice and fuel oil. Although protected by the neutrality of the Djibouti territory which General Le Gentilhomme had not succeeded in winning over to the Free French cause, the fastness of Ethiopia was invested from the Sudan and Kenya by a mixed force of British, Indians, Afrikaners and Free French. In the north, General Platt penetrated into Eritrea, broke Italian resistance at Keren in March 1941 and occupied Asmara and Massawa, picking up 15,000 prisoners. In the south, General Cunningham invaded Italian Somaliland, moved diagonally north-west, broke through the Italians' defences in February 1941, taking 20,000 prisoners, and reached Addis Ababa in April. The Duke of Aosta took refuge on the Amba-Alagie plateau, where he surrendered in May 1941.

The King of Italy had not been Emperor of Abyssinia for very long. Once again, the Negus sat on the throne of the King of Kings and a treaty was signed forging close links between Ethiopia and Britain. In this sector, the war died down except for the blockade of Djibouti, until that town went over to the Free French in December 1942.

For their part, a handful of Free French under Leclerc had set off from the Chad and after crossing 1,000 miles of desert had brought France back into the war by capturing, on their own ground, the better armed and more numerous Italian garrison of Kufra. In the oasis which he had just taken, General Leclerc made the vow not to lay down his arms until he had succeeded in having the French flag hoisted once more over Metz and Strasbourg. These seemed empty words, when the Germans were parading through Paris.

VI ITALIAN SETBACKS IN LIBYA

Egypt occupied a position of paramount importance for the whole of the Middle East: she controlled the Suez Canal, the British Commonwealth's major artery; any power occupying it could influence Arab opinion in its favour, though not perhaps Turkey. Thus Egypt had the power to provide access to the rich sources of oil which were crucial for motorised warfare and she was also the key to the Italian *Impero*.

The belligerents on both sides were aware of her importance. Even on the eve of a possible German landing in the British Isles, Churchill had despatched to Egypt one-third of the few tanks that the British Army had salvaged from Dunkirk. A Commonwealth army was gradually being assembled there, with Australians, Indians and New Zealanders predominating. In early January 1941, General Wavell had 150,000 men under him.

For his part, Mussolini had ordered Marshal Balbo to launch an offensive towards Egypt with the 175,000 men under his command and Ciano had confirmed this decision to Hitler on July 7, 1940. But Balbo's reaction had been unfavourable on the grounds of lack of motorised transport and of the inferiority of the Italian tanks, armed only with machine guns, in comparison with the British tanks. At this moment of time, the Wehrmacht clearly had ample means to make good these shortcomings. But Mussolini was most reluctant to ask for this and the OKW would not have been very keen to grant it. Even after the defeat at Taranto, at the Italo-German military conference held at Innsbruck on November 15, 1940, the first of its kind, the two Axis partners kept their distance from each other. The result was a statement by Ribbentrop announcing that Germany was seeking no political advantage in the Arab world and, secondly, a sort of neutralisation of the Wehrmacht, which was going to rest on its laurels for the next nine months; the result of this was to allow the Italians to give blatant evidence of their alarming weakness and the British gradually to recover from their original inferiority.

However, in the Middle East a vast anti-British Arab conspiracy was being plotted, with its centre in Iraq and the Grand Mufti of Jerusalem as its leader. The conspirators had informed Rome and Berlin of their desire to 'settle the Jewish question in Palestine in accordance with the Arabs' national and racial interests'. They were planning an uprising in Transjordan and Palestine and hoping to arm 10,000 men in Syria from French army depots.

But in order to spur the Arabs on, it was still necessary for the Italians to achieve some spectacular successes. In September 1940, General Graziani had finally grouped his forces and stocked up with supplies. But he found himself up against some inconvenient geographical facts; his reinforcements would have to move over hard ground, across a steppe-like semi-desert, with only one road and an occasional urban settlement along the coast. Accordingly Graziani made a slow, cautious and strictly limited advance.

He took Sollum and Sidi-Barrani where he stopped and built field fortifications and a pipeline for drinking water. By so doing, he dawdled for three months and the British used the time to their advantage. In December, it was they who attacked with a small motorised army of 30,000 men. The Italians were taken violently by surprise and their ensuing disorderly retreat was equally violent. Three of their divisions were put out of action and their air force disappeared completely from the skies. The British advanced some 450 miles, took Bardia in January 1941, followed by Tobruk, the strongest naval base in Cyrenaica, which was defended by a double ring of concrete fortifications. It surrendered two days after being attacked by the Australians on January 21. The British reached El Agheila on the Tripolitanian border, having taken 100,000 prisoners.

Here they halted for both logistical and political reasons. For the first time the 'law of desert warfare' clamped down on them with full force: at a certain moment one army must call a halt to its victorious advance because it has outstripped its supplies; on the other hand, the loser regains strength as his supply route becomes shorter. Thus the balance was restored. Another feature of the war at this time was that Britain was powerless to meet all her commitments; thus, paradoxically, Italy's other setbacks in Greece were going to palliate the full effect of those that she had suffered in Africa.

VII ITALIAN SETBACKS IN GREECE

On October 15, 1940, Mussolini decided, in fact, to attack Greece. This apparently trivial move was to turn out to be one of the most important decisions of the Second World War. Mussolini's motives seemed as petty as his ambitions were grandiose. It was plain that conquering a few bare mountains could not begin to solve the problem of Italy's over-population or the poverty of her economy. In terms of the war, passing through Epirus was not the shortest way to Alexandria. And finally, attacking Greece meant giving the British a chance of regaining a foothold on the Continent. Entirely absorbed in his schemes for crushing England, when talking with Ciano in July 1940, Hitler had made no secret of his anxiety not to see another theatre of operations in central or southern Europe. Similarly he had never ceased advising the hotheaded Hungarians to restrain their desire to have a go at the Romanians in order to recover Transylvania – advice that was as good as an order to sit still and do nothing.

Mussolini's action would seem to have been motivated by jealousy of Hitler's victories. He was anxious to achieve, like Hitler, on his own initiative and under his own steam, political and military successes that would rescue him from his passive, secondary role and give him a seat at the victory table in the final settlement. According to Count Ciano and the diplomat Alfieri, the monotonous series of failures that had hitherto greeted all his schemes had filled him with a morbid sense of humiliation that was beginning to turn into a chronic state of depression. He was particularly embittered by the dominant position of Germany in Romania – a Latin land and his private preserve – and by the moves that Hitler had made, though fleetingly, to establish closer relations with Vichy France, a beaten country. To break out of this evil spell, the Duce must gain glory in a parallel war, one that he would win on his own, thus making his dream of Italian supremacy in Mare Nostrum come true.

But the operation could not have been worse prepared. Whereas the

Fascist party leaders saw it as a mere formality, Marshal Badoglio made reservations; he considered the proposed forces inadequate; he asked for time to examine all the aspects of the campaign; his first point was met, his second not – Mussolini insisted on its starting immediately. As for the Navy, according to Bragadin it had not even been consulted, although it was to be required to occupy the Greek islands and transport three divisions across the Adriatic in one single night. The first obstacle was the disparity between the amount of shipping space required, 10,000 tons daily, and the amount that could be handled by the Albanian ports, which was 3,500 tons at the most. On November 1, Durazzo harbour was completely jammed with more ships than quayside space and 30,000 tons of goods already landed which it was impossible to move inland. But nobody had dared to gainsay the Duce or even to point out that his directives and his calculations were based on a confusion between the various schemes that had been submitted to him.

The Italians threw eleven divisions into their first attack, later increasing them to sixteen and then to twenty-five. Against them the Greeks could at first put up only four first-line divisions. By the end of October, the aggressors won some early successes but they were soon brought to a halt by the state of the roads, which were narrow, few in number and washed away by the autumn rains. The whole Greek population rallied round its government; the mountain villagers, men and women, supplied their troops with provisions. In the middle of November, with their rear protected from any intervention on the part of Bulgaria by a statement from the Turks that would certainly preclude her entry into the war, the Greeks counter-attacked and forced the Italians to retreat all along the line. In less than ten days, the aggressors had been pushed back beyond their starting-point. Italian propaganda put out the story that the Greeks were unsuccessfully attempting to prevent the strategic retreat of the Bersaglieri; the whole of occupied Europe was splitting its sides with laughter. Placards were put up outside Menton, facing towards Italy: 'Greeks, please stop here: this is France.'

On December 4, the Greeks were pouring down towards Valona, one of the main Albanian harbours. Badoglio was made the scapegoat and replaced by Ugo Cavallero but this did not change the situation. While British submarines penetrated even into the Otranto channel and sank Italian ships and the Albanians were becoming restless, in January 1941 General Papagos was endeavouring to force the Italians to go back to Italy. Thrashed in Epirus and thrashed in Libya, Mussolini could think of nothing better to do than to appeal for help to Hitler. He saw him on January 10, 1941, although he had at first put off the meeting in the hope that he could have arrived crowned with victory. 'I shan't have blood enough for all my blushes when I see him,' he said to Ciano. Hitler's

pitying tone stung him to the quick and after he had left he showed his
vigour – by sending ministers and high-ranking Fascists off to fight in
Greece.

VIII GERMAN AND BRITISH INTERVENTION IN GREECE

The Duce's action had been an unpleasant surprise for the Führer. It was,
indeed, difficult for him to show annoyance at his partner's not divulging
his intentions, since he himself had behaved in the same way towards him
previously. But he could blame him for not succeeding, and this he did
not fail to do. He explained his fear that the British might bomb the
Ploesti oilfields and he despatched fighter aircraft to protect them. He was
not, however, very keen on sending troops to Albania and his generals
did not urge him to do so. Nevertheless, consideration was given to an
attack on Greece through Bulgaria, under the cover-name 'Marita'; such
an attack would also serve the purpose of keeping the Bulgarians in hand
who were rather disturbed by the Italians' lack of success.

In December 1940, when Mussolini's setbacks at sea, in Albania and in
Africa had become obvious and even disastrous, Hitler felt that Axis
solidarity and his friendship with Mussolini forbade him to remain
passive any longer. The OKW worked out a plan to inject mountain troops
and armour into the Italian-Greek front, one army corps in all, to help the
Italians stabilise their front and mount a counter-attack. Subsequently, if
need arose, this army corps would support the German Twelfth Army in
an attack launched from Bulgaria in the direction of Salonica. General
Paulus, who was given the task of examining the project, concluded that
the troops would not be ready until the middle of February; the fluctuating
front as well as the mountainous terrain would preclude a war of movement and would require a frontal assault that would be so costly in men
and equipment that the Führer hesitated. Eventually, he cancelled the
scheme.

Churchill had been similarly most hesitant before deciding to help the
Greeks. He felt that it was politically and morally impossible to leave in
the lurch a brave little nation whose stubbornness was arousing the
enthusiasm of the populations of the occupied countries and the admiration of the Americans from Roosevelt downwards. On the other hand,
his War Minister, Eden,[1] as well as Wavell, considered that the defence of
Egypt was paramount; they did not want the reinforcements intended for
the African front to be diverted to Greece. The Prime Minister's im-
pulsiveness and his eagerness to take risks, together with memories of

1. When he became Foreign Minister, Eden changed his mind and sided with Churchill!

Marathon and Salamis, made him decide in favour. The Greeks had appealed to the British on February 8; from March 4 onwards, at the rate of two convoys a week, 68,000 men were taken out of the Libyan front or from the reserves in Egypt and ferried over without mishap to Greece. It was a makeshift expedition and inadequately equipped.

Yet at the start everything went well. As there were indications that the Italian fleet was making ready to try to intercept the convoys on their way to Greece, the naval force stationed at Alexandria put out to sea and on March 28, 1941, having spotted an Italian squadron in the night, it moved in to within less than two and a half miles without being observed, close to Cape Matapan. The Italian guns were blown to bits before they had time to fire. Three Italian cruisers and two destroyers were sunk. 'You could see whole turrets being blown skyhigh,' wrote Admiral Cunningham, 'and great lumps of metal; the ships soon turned into flaming torches.' And yet before the action started the British admiral had been wondering whether the inferiority of his forces would not make them an easy prey for the enemy. But the damaged 35,000-ton battleship *Vittorio Veneto* had been happy just to get away without a fight.

IX THE CRUSHING OF YUGOSLAVIA

Returning more or less to Weygand's 1940 plans, the British wanted two things: to avoid involving the Germans in Greece – and so their troops remained strictly in central Greece – and, secondly, in the course of time to form a coalition combining Yugoslavia, Turkey and Greece. Eden undertook the preliminary diplomatic approaches. But the Turks were evasive and in Yugoslavia, the Regent Prince Paul refused to let himself be drawn by the bait of obtaining Istria, which the Britishd angled in front of him. The only result was to worry Hitler who ordered Yugoslavia to become a signatory to the tripartite pact.

The Yugoslavs first turned to the British but on March 8 and 9 in Athens, Eden and Dill were unable to promise them any immediate help. Approaches to the Soviet Union were equally unrewarding; the Soviet ambassador in Belgrade went off to Moscow with lists of equipment that Yugoslavia would have liked to have but he did not come back. However, after momentarily toying with the idea of occupying Salonica, on which they asked the Germans their view without receiving any reply, the Yugoslavs began to help Greece by sending her food and ammunition.

Hitler then insisted on their signing the tripartite pact; and on March 25 Prince Paul and the government of Tsvetković and Marković gave way. In return, Germany and Italy pledged themselves not to send troops through Yugoslav territory and, in a secret clause, promised to hand Salonica over to Yugoslavia.

In Belgrade the news of the signing of the tripartite pact aroused popular indignation which was fanned by British and possibly American agents, even if they had not been entirely responsible for creating it. Eden moreover had not returned to London but was waiting in Malta. On March 27, a military coup got rid of the regency and the government. Young King Peter proclaimed himself of age and General Simović became Prime Minister.

If the British had hoped to provide an obstacle to Germany's advance southwards, Hitler lost no time in destroying their illusions. On April 6, 800 aircraft pounded Belgrade and the main Yugoslav communication centres with bombs. Using Bulgaria as their starting base, German troops swiftly cut Yugoslavia off from Greece. Before the Yugoslavs had even completed their mobilisation the Germans had taken Skopje on April 7 and Zagreb on the 11th. The Italians, Hungarians and Bulgarians all rushed in together for the kill; on April 12, Belgrade fell.

The British barely had time to pick up King Peter and the Yugoslav government and take them away to England, where the King joined the growing band of exiled sovereigns. Hitler decided to deal with Slovenia separately and set her aside for the moment. The Hungarians occupied part of the Banat; the Italians took possession of Dalmatia and the islands; Croatia and Montenegro were proclaimed independent; Yugoslavia was reduced to the tiny territory of Serbia and placed under German occupation. It was highly inadvisable for little states to rebel against Hitler's Reich or oppose it. Greece was about to learn the same lesson.

X GREECE CRUSHED

Only the RAF had fought in Albania and then with a mere fifty aircraft; the Greeks complained that even these were not used very freely. As for the Expeditionary Force, it had advanced no further than Larissa and was now marking time. It demonstrated the ambiguity of the Anglo-Greek alliance. The British merely wanted to set up a bridgehead in preparation for better days to come; they wished to avoid arousing too much alarm in the Germans so that the latter should not pounce on them before they were properly established, and they were encouraging the Greeks, who by this time had fifteen divisions, to fall back on to their positions. But the Greeks did not want to give up Thrace and Macedonia without a fight and they could not make up their minds to withdraw from the Albanian front, where they were winning and hoping to link up with the Yugoslavs. The

Map 8 **THE JUGOSLAV, GREEK AND
CRETAN CAMPAIGNS**

Axis countries or allied

Limits of Greek advance on 31 Dec 1940

Advance of the German, Italian and
satellite armies

German parachute drops

0   200km

British themselves had decided to move back as far as Thermopylae in the event of a German attack. In these circumstances, any joint action of the Allied armies was out of the question.

On April 6, the same day as the offensive in Yugoslavia, the Germans launched their attack on Greece from Bulgaria, which was the springboard of the whole of this Balkan operation. The Greeks in Albania did not think of falling back until the 9th, when it was too late; the German forces, including an armoured division, had moved down from Monastir and were blocking their way. One after another the Greek units, under attack from the direction of Thessaly as well, were cut up, flung back into the mountains and ordered by their leaders to scatter. On April 20, General Papagos asked the Germans for an armistice; by then the Italians had still not succeeded in crossing the Greek-Albanian border and the Greek rearguards during their retreat had never ceased their local counter-attacks against them. But these minor successes could do nothing to affect the fate of Greece. On April 27 Athens was occupied and the swastika was hoisted on the Acropolis. While King George left with his government for Cairo and a large part of the Greek Navy and merchant fleet took refuge in Alexandria, the British were carrying out a difficult evacuation of Greece and the Peloponnese almost without a fight. Once again they had lost face in a repetition of Dunkirk, saving their troops but leaving their equipment behind. Once more they had shown that the available forces were not adequate for the vast schemes which were planned for them. Of course they still held the island of Crete; but for how long?

XI THE BATTLE OF CRETE

From the beginning of the war, the British had realised the importance of Crete for the control of the western Mediterranean; they were particularly attracted by the sheltered roadstead of Suda Bay, in the west of the island, which they wanted to turn into a naval base, a sort of Mediterranean Scapa Flow; but there had never been any serious attempt to defend Crete, nor had one ever been contemplated. In any case there were insufficient means to do so and the fleet seemed capable of ensuring the protection of the island. At the start of the intervention in Greece, Crete had been considered as an advance supply base; but it suddenly became a last stronghold held by 22,000 Commonwealth troops, including General Freyberg's New Zealand division.

But the island was defenceless; all the harbours and airfields were on the more exposed north coast; in the south, a better protected plain which might have been used to provide an excellent airfield could now not be got ready in time. Crete became the scene of operations between the German Air Force and the Royal Navy – an uneven contest, as the Norwegian expedition had already demonstrated. In addition, recent precedent could have shown how the Wehrmacht would carry out its attack; paratroops had been dropped on the isthmus of Corinth to forestall British troops as they were withdrawing towards the Peloponnese. And the Luftwaffe was employing a vast concentration of forces: 716 aircraft, including 430 bombers which, with 500 troop-carrying aircraft and 72 gliders, dropped a whole airborne division, comprising three mountain-infantry regiments, one armoured battalion and a motor-cycle battalion. In one sudden move, the attackers established themselves in strength, in the heart of their opponents' defences, like some fifth column falling from the heavens. The defenders who had been facing outwards to the sea had been caught in the rear.

When every attempt to retake the airfields and stem the flow of reinforcements had failed, it was apparent that any attempt to remain on the island would be doomed to failure. But the evacuation proved difficult. In the first place, it was held up by Churchill's stubborn optimism. On May 20, 1941, while the paratroops were showering down on to the island, he cabled to Wavell: 'Victory in Crete essential at this turning-point in the war. Use every exertion to achieve it by all possible means.' Not until May 26 when the New Zealand General Freyberg announced that the struggle was hopeless, was the order given, once again, to evacuate the men without worrying about the equipment. But the British fleet had in the last few days been greatly weakened; for example, the aircraft-carrier *Formidable* had lost every single one of its fighters. The men could only be taken off at night, on exposed beaches, between midnight and 3 a.m. so as to allow the ships to avoid the German Air Force attacks under cover of darkness. During the four nights from May 28 till June 1, the tremendous feat of embarking 16,500 men was accomplished; but three cruisers and six destroyers were sunk and two battleships and one aircraft-carrier damaged and put out of action for several months.

The Greek operation ended in pitiful failure; in Admiral Cunningham's words, 'a disastrous episode in the history of the Royal Navy'. Britain's weakness had been cruelly exposed for all to see. 'To save Crete,' wrote Cunningham, all that was needed were 'three long-range fighters and a few bomber squadrons'. Mastery of the seas was clearly of no use without control of the skies. Moreover, while the New Zealanders and Australians who had born the brunt of the fighting were showing their dissatisfaction, the depletion of the British units in Africa, plus the arrival of German reinforcements, was to lead to further galling setbacks for the British Commonwealth.

XII THE SUCCESSES OF ROMMEL AND THE *AFRIKA KORPS*

In January 1941, Hitler had decided to help the Italians in Libya as well as in Malta and Greece. He thought that the loss of North Africa, though acceptable militarily, would cause strong psychological repercussions in Italy that were better avoided. Against Admiral Raeder's advice, who wanted to 'clean out the Mediterranean in 1940–41', the proposed reinforcements for Africa were not intended to take the offensive but merely to stabilise the Italian front. Accordingly, first of all, a light division was sent; it was followed by a Panzer division; together, the two made up the *Afrika Korps* under the command of Rommel, one of the German tank commanders who had sped along the French roads in June 1940.

Hardly had Rommel arrived when, on his own initiative, he launched a lightning war which, once Cyrenaica was reconquered, was to take him right up to the gates of Egypt. Tireless, indifferent to hunger or climate, wilful and imaginative, equally swift to think and to act, always in the forefront, Rommel believed in pouncing without giving his foe a moment's respite. His rashness sometimes cut him off from his units and once nearly led to his capture; he was never at his command-post and he frequently embarrassed his subordinates by leaving them without instructions, especially when he went off with his chief of staff. But to compensate for this, he was in a position to exploit any favourable chance in the field. As he was constantly up with his men, sharing their life and all its dangers, he very quickly became extremely popular. His brilliant successes made him a legendary hero in his own lifetime; he became 'the desert fox'.

The British generals facing him gave the impression of being anxious not to miss their tea-break. They were having great difficulty in adapting themselves to desert warfare, in establishing close co-operation between the three services – the fighting was taking place in areas less than forty miles from the coast, so the Navy often intervened. They were outclassed in every field; they could only regain the upper hand if they achieved enormous superiority in equipment.

Taking advantage of the gap left by the departure of the British troops for Greece, Rommel hustled his enemy out of his positions. He pressed on, disregarding the objections of the Italian leaders to whom he was supposed to be subordinated. But he was unable to take Tobruk which remained as a thorn in the flesh of his north flank for 200 days. When he reached the Egyptian border, shortage of petrol and Hitler's orders, since the Führer did not wish to have to send large numbers of troops to Africa, brought Rommel to a halt when he thought Suez was in his grasp.

The British were able to organise their defence at Mersa Matruh, well in front of the vital zone of the Nile delta. The tables had, however, been totally turned in favour of the Axis. At the same time, Malta was neutralised by the Luftwaffe in Sicily and the British found their way across the Mediterranean barred. In addition, reinforcements were reaching Rommel, aided and abetted by the Vichy government and the use of Tunisian territorial waters by Italian freighters, in accordance with the terms of the 'Paris protocols'. In addition, encouraged by German successes, Arab nationalists were becoming restless and were making no secret of their hatred of the British, in Egypt as well as in Syria.

XIII THE WAR IN SYRIA

In April 1941, a military coup in Iraq had abolished the regency and brought General Rashid Ali to power. He had secretly formed an anti-British and anti-Jewish conspiracy with the Grand Mufti in Jerusalem. Rashid Ali dismissed Parliament, proclaimed Iraqi independence and on May 2 attacked the British garrison in Baghdad. The Germans did not want to miss the opportunity but, in order to help the Iraqi rebels, they needed to pass through Syria. In Berchtesgaden on May 11, 1941, Admiral Darlan who had been head of the Vichy government since Laval's dismissal accepted the terms of the 'protocol' dictated by Hitler. More convinced than ever of the invincibility of Germany, Admiral Darlan could at last see the possibility of achieving the collaboration with Germany which he had been pursuing in the hope of some relaxation of the harsh clauses of the armistice and of future benefit to France. The negotiations took a broader form. It was agreed that the Germans would use the Syrian harbours and airfields to send help to the Iraqi rebels, who would be given weapons stockpiled by the French in accordance with the armistice terms. In addition, Rommel would receive supplies via Tunisian territorial waters as well as by land, rail and road, with France providing the necessary lorries. Finally, the Germans would be granted bases in Dakar and Bizerta. Once again, the possibility of winning back the dissident equatorial African colonies was considered.

On his return to Paris Darlan signed the protocol, which was ratified by the Vichy government, and instructions were given to implement it. But this implementation required the collaboration of General Weygand, Commander-in-Chief in Africa, and of the Governor, General Boisson. On being summoned to Vichy, they protested vigorously and expressed the view that the army in Africa would not accept the terms of the protocol. They suggested that France should ask for concessions in exchange – the release of prisoners of war, a reduction in the occupation costs – to which the Germans could not agree. Implementation of the protocol which had already begun in Tunisia was now stopped, and, because of the swift defeat of the Iraqi rebels and of Rommel's successes, both of which rendered French collaboration no longer necessary, the Germans did not insist on its strict enforcement.

But in France there had been great indignation at the Vichy government's violation of the armistice. Pastor Basdevant, the legal adviser to the French Ministry of Foreign Affairs, vigorously condemned it. There had been even greater indignation in London where Free France violently denounced it as 'Vichy treachery'. There were hopeful indications that General Dentz's troops, who were opposed to the 'protocols', were only awaiting the opportunity to break away from Pétain. General de Gaulle persuaded the British to attempt to capture Syria; they did so rather reluctantly because they knew to their cost how limited their resources were. The attempt degenerated into a deplorable conflict between Frenchmen, because the hoped-for break with Vichy did not take place or at least only partially.

Despite American pressure – Admiral Leahy told Pétain that 'resistance to the English in Syria would work in Hitler's favour and not France's' – the Vichy government decided to fight. Pétain replied to Leahy: 'The British have attacked us. We know that we shall lose Syria but we are determined to fight to the bitter end.' After a few weeks' fighting in the course of which there were some thousand casualties on each side, General Dentz signed an armistice with the British. Contrary to General de Gaulle's expectations, only a small number of French officers and men joined Free France; the majority, on the other hand, showed him bitter animosity. General Catroux had proclaimed the principle of independence for Syria and the Lebanon; but this principle became a reality only after the war.

Meanwhile the British had recaptured Baghdad and put men on whom they could rely back into power in Iraq. The Middle East had been sealed off against Axis interference and British control re-established in the Arab world as well as over its vast resources of oil. It was a faint glimmer of hope in the gloom which enveloped Britain in June 1941.

XIV THE STATE OF THE WAR IN JUNE 1941

In June 1941, it was clear that, following her early successes in the Battle of Britain and then those at sea and in Africa, Britain had been striving to achieve a state of readiness that had been neglected so long that it could hardly be quickly attained. She had suffered one setback after another. True enough, her territory was now more adequately defended; she had raised and trained thirty-seven divisions, though they were short of tanks.

But rather than a landing in the British Isles, the danger now seemed to lie in attacks in the direction of Gibraltar – whose defences had been hurriedly strengthened but still gave cause for alarm – but above all in the direction of Alexandria. The happy ending to the Syrian problem guaranteed Egypt's rear and excluded any possibility of attack from the north; but on the borders of Cyrenaica the situation was fraught with danger. Threatened with being cut off from her Asian empire, Britain was in the still greater peril of being cut off from the United States by the mounting curve of merchant shipping sinkings in the Atlantic. Even in the Mediterranean, the Royal Navy had its back to the wall.

Britain was without doubt going to be forced back on the defensive for a long time to come. Churchill chafed at this but what else could be done? The Wehrmacht's victories and the German submarine successes, together with the fact that the German-Soviet pact was working smoothly, had changed the blockade of Germany into a blockade of the British Isles. While the British fleet continued to keep watchful guard over the coastline of Europe and issued a niggardly quota of importation permits, the gain from all this was little more than the pressure it exerted on the Vichy government which, however, still continued to maintain an attitude of benevolent neutrality towards the Reich. True, Churchill had thoughts of showering tons of bombs on German territory and had called for an immense programme of aircraft production: 14,000 aircraft in two years. But these aircraft did not exist nor did he know when he would get them, and meanwhile the air raids on German towns, communications and synthetic-petrol factories had more a token effect than a real one. As for a British landing in Europe, it was just a pipe-dream.

In these circumstances, how could one escape the conclusion that, even if Britain could no longer lose the war, she still had no chance of winning it? This was the firm belief of the Vichy government's leaders. Although Italy had shown herself surprisingly weak, did Germany not seem more unbeatable than ever? Any initiative could only come from Hitler. What would he do? The Mediterranean offered him vast vistas; Alexandria and Suez were within reach of the Luftwaffe; the unstable Arabs had only just settled down and could easily be roused again; with more tanks and petrol, Rommel could continue his victorious advance and this time reach Cairo. Even faced with such gloomy prospects as these, it is possible that Churchill would still not admit defeat; but how long could he hold out if the whole of the available German forces were then hurled against the British Isles?

But Hitler had chosen another path. There was now no going back on his decision to attack the Soviet Union; on June 1, 1941, the armoured divisions and most of the Air Force left the Balkans. On June 22, 1941, the USSR was invaded. At once, through Hitler's deliberate choice, the war assumed worldwide proportions. Full of self-confidence, Hitler seemed to have lost his fear of fighting on two fronts, although the diversions that he had been forced to make as a result of Churchill's enterprising operations all round the Mediterranean had cost him valuable time. The war was moving into a new phase; it was also going to change its scope, its nature and even its objectives.

BOOK TWO

THE WORLD WAR

(June 1941–January 1943)

PART I

THE GREATER REICH

CHAPTER I

The Break Between Germany and Russia

THE German-Soviet war is one of the phases of the Second World War which raises the greatest number of questions for the historian. Not that he lacks sources, which are plentiful enough. On the German side, the most important documents are known; but in their memoirs the Wehrmacht generals are inclined to dissociate themselves from their Führer and lay at his door all the sins of Germany – after the war. On the Soviet side there is also a mass of publications, but they repeat each other; changes of government have modified the official approach to the writing of history, but without sharpening the writers' critical faculties or allowing them full scope. Dissension and weaknesses tend to be glossed over in a continual eulogy of the Soviet people, the régime and the Communist party, which finds convenient expression in propagandist slogans. With this goes a systematic suspicion and disparagement of works published in 'the West', whose authors they choose to regard as enemies of the USSR and describe as 'falsifiers of history'. Soviet historians of the Second World War, often epic or lyrical in tone, still observe strict taboos – for example, concerning the motives and working of the German-Soviet pact. Hence there are embarrassing gaps and omissions.

I HITLER'S DECISION

If we trace the development of Hitler's attitude towards the USSR through the diaries of Generals Halder and Warlimont, he seems to have shown a peculiar singleness of purpose. It all began on July 21, 1940, when Hitler ordered von Brauchitsch, the head of the Army, to prepare for an attack on the Soviet Union. At this time, the Battle of Britain had only just begun, orders had been given to attempt a landing on the other side of the Channel, and Hitler had recently decided to reduce the number of infantry divisions. A puzzling decision, if ever there was one, ascribed by E. Bauer to a 'sudden illumination'. However that may be, from now on Hitler's resolve was to unfold with faultless logic. On July 29, during a conference at headquarters, the date for the attack was fixed for the spring of 1941; it was to be another Blitzkrieg, a 'lightning war'. The task of drawing up the preliminary plans was given to General Marks, commander of the Eighteenth Army stationed near the USSR. The following day, Halder set to work himself.

The German military leaders do not seem to have raised any serious objections. Admiral Raeder voiced the fear that the operations under consideration might prejudice the submarine war by cutting down the submarine-building programme. Marshal Goering showed some anxiety lest the Luftwaffe's commitment in the east might rob German territory of some of its protection from British bombers. The sole aim of these reservations was to point out beforehand the possibilities of failure so as to anticipate any blame should the occasion arise. But those who were really responsible, the OKW and OKH, without raising any fundamental objections, confined themselves to demanding facilities for the immense task that they were called upon to perform at very short notice.

On August 9 General Warlimont, the general in command of the operations, drew up the preliminary directives. The plan was called the *Aufbau Ost* (reconstruction of the east). His aim was to prepare for the attack by setting up the necessary services: roads, railways, bridges, hospitals, stocks of equipment, provisions, etc.

On August 26, Hitler began to transfer infantry and artillery divisions to the east. The reason given – probably a pretext – was to protect the Romanian oil-fields, which were in no danger. In his instructions on the methods to be employed, General Jodl insisted on the need for concealing the operation: 'We must not give the Russians the impression that we are preparing for war,' he said.

The crucial conference of the general staff took place on December 5. Hitler gave his approval to the plan which von Brauchitsch and Halder put before him and which had been drawn up by Paulus. He pompously announced that 'he would not make the same mistake as Napoleon'. It was on December 18 that the immense operation was given its final code-name of 'Barbarossa'. The same day, Hitler issued his 'order no. 21' which fixed the beginning of the operation for May 15. The Balkan campaign forced him to postpone it until June 21 – like Napoleon, Hitler was setting out for Moscow later than he would have wished.

Thus, from the summer of 1940 onwards, the whole of Hitler's train of thought and consequently the whole of Germany's political, diplomatic and military activity seems to have been geared to one major, if not single target: to ensure the most favourable situation for a decisive battle against the USSR. The operations of the *Afrika Korps* in Yugoslavia and Greece were only minor ones, carried out more or less reluctantly as the occasion required.

II GERMAN-SOVIET RELATIONS

Hitler's decision was perhaps the result of a deterioration in German-Soviet relations. The pact was certainly not working entirely to his liking. The Russians were showing some ill-will towards Finland and they were at odds with the Germans over the exploitation of nickel mines at Petsamo. On both sides there were complaints about delays in commercial transactions.

Hitler had been annoyed by the USSR's unexpected annexation of Bukovina, and Molotov, for his part, was complaining that 'the arbitration of Vienna' had reshaped central Europe to the detriment of Romania, without anyone having consulted the USSR or even giving her proper notice of it.

On September 2, 1940, the USSR had also been concerned at the signing of the tripartite pact between Japan, Italy and Germany. Although obviously directed against the United States and Britain, did the agreement not perhaps include a few secret clauses against herself? Was it not, in fact, a revival of the anti-Comintern pact? But on this she had been given all possible reassurance since she had even been invited to join it and in the gigantic partition of the world outlined by the pact she had even been offered a vast area as her share – the Persian Gulf and India.

On November 12, 1940, Molotov came to Berlin to discuss these grand prospects. His response to the temptation of the wide open spaces of Asia was very down-to-earth: he asked about Finland, which he regarded as belonging to the Soviet sphere of influence; Bulgaria, to whom the USSR, in order to emphasise her dominant role, would have liked to give a guarantee similar to the one which the Reich had given Romania; and the 'convention of Montreux' on the Dardanelles, which the USSR wanted to modify in her favour, in a way which Molotov described as 'not just on paper'. Molotov also mentioned Swedish neutrality, the Danish straits and Japan – the latter might be a trifle less interested in China since Indonesia had fallen into her lap through the Dutch defeat.

In short, each talked about himself and turned a deaf ear to the other. But although he made no effort to convince him, Hitler paid no attention to his companion's *desiderata*. German troops entered Bulgaria to attack Greece, and Bulgaria joined the tripartite pact, without the USSR making any protest. Furthermore, the very day that the USSR signed a friendship pact with Yugoslavia the latter was attacked by the Wehrmacht and conquered in a matter of days: not only did the USSR make no attempt to go to her 'friend's' aid, but she allowed her to be carved up by her neighbours without breathing a word. The Yugoslav minister was expelled from Moscow, without ceremony, since Yugoslavia no longer existed.

The USSR thus seemed to have resigned herself to surrendering the Balkans to German influence. There was nothing in her behaviour to worry the Führer to the extent of provoking him to declare war.

III HITLER'S REASONS

So on June 22, when Goebbels' propaganda machine declared that the Wehrmacht's invasion was a preventive measure to forestall Soviet aggression, it was clear that these implausible reasons were meant for the record and it is difficult to see why Stalin should have gone to so much trouble to exonerate himself from the sinister schemes attributed to him unless it were also for the record. But what then were the Führer's real reasons?

It is probable that although Hitler had been examining it as a possible course of action, until the autumn of 1940 he had not taken any definite decision. But the development of the war had gradually forced him to do so. His failure in the Battle of Britain, the difficulties he had encountered in forming a Mediterranean coalition and above all Mussolini's initiative in Greece had shifted the 'map of the war' from western to south-east Europe. The British offensive in Greece and the Belgrade putsch finally determined Germany's choice of this area for her new victory. Beyond stretched the boundless horizons of the USSR.

To say that Hitler was seeking victory over Britain in Moscow does not seem quite true. It was from the United States that Britain was hoping for an injection of new blood; of course, though it was not a matter of indifference to her whether the USSR became a partner of the Reich or was attacked by her it was less important to her than whether or not her cause was taken up or deserted by the United States. But the withdrawal of Britain from the Continent and the obvious impossibility of beating her on her own ground automatically brought Hitler back to his familiar fantasies: the fight against Bolshevism and the conquest of land in the east. For the time being the overthrow of Britain took second place.

On March 30, 1941, at a conference attended by the generals of the three forces and lasting two and a half hours, the Führer fell quite naturally into the tone of *Mein Kampf*. 'The Communists,' he said, 'never have been and never will be our friends. The fight which is about to begin is a war of extermination. If Germany does not embark upon it in this spirit she may well defeat the enemy but in thirty years from now they will once again rise up and confront her.'

A few weeks earlier he had confided to his closest colleagues: 'The vast expanses of Russia contain inexhaustible riches. Germany must, if not appropriate them, at least exploit them politically and economically. In this way she will be able to present a triumphant challenge to the whole world.'[1]

The pact with the USSR did of course give the Reich access to this wealth but only a little at a time and on the humiliating condition that Stalin was agreeable. From this viewpoint, Fabry is correct in writing that the German-Soviet pact contained the seeds of its own destruction; it had blown up the Polish dividing wall which the treaties of 1918 had set up between Germany and the Soviet Union; it had brought into contact two opponents whose temporary readiness to come to an understanding had not overcome their fundamental hostility, while their possession of a common border now made a direct confrontation possible.

Moreover the moment seemed well chosen for the Reich; Britain's weakness made it improbable that she could create a second front for a long time; the opportunity must be seized to strike in the east as a continuation and extension of the Polish campaign. Hitler also had very little doubt about the USSR's weakness; had this not been unmistakably proved by her defeats in Finland and her failure to speak out when the German invasion of the Balkans threatened her sphere of influence?[2] Hitler wanted this new victory to be entirely his own; he did not inform Mussolini until the very day of the attack and it was only at the Duce's entreaty that he agreed to the latter's proposal to send an Italian expeditionary force to the USSR, for it was Mussolini's opinion that 'Italy could not remain out of the war against the USSR' and he promised that this would not result in any withdrawal of troops from the African front.

IV WAS STALIN CAUGHT UNAWARES?

We now know that Stalin did not lack warning. Cordell Hull tells us in his memoirs how the American commercial attaché in Berlin used to receive intelligence in a cinema from a quite high-placed anti-Nazi German. It was in this way that knowledge of the plan for the attack against the Soviet Union reached the USA; 'it was so detailed', said Cordell Hunt, 'that at first I didn't believe it'. The plan was communicated to

1. On August 26, 1941, in a circular to the German legations abroad, Ribbentrop defined the importance of a victory over the USSR in the following terms: the control of the Ukraine would guarantee a permanent source of food supplies; Russian materials would bring about a considerable improvement in the German war economy; and victory in the east would enable the Reich to turn and face their last enemy, Britain.
2. In the controversies stirred up in the USSR by 'de-Stalinisation', great importance has rightly been attached to the 'purges' ordered by Stalin in the Red Army. They had convinced the French general staff that the Soviet forces were disorganised and they thus provided a partial explanation for the Franco-British reluctance to enter into a pact with the USSR. On the other hand, they had prompted Hitler to attack an army which he considered to be 'eighty per cent decapitated', and which he reckoned would take two years to recover.

Moscow at the beginning of 1941. In March the USSR was provided with more information from the same source – including the indication that wads of ruble notes had been printed in Germany. On April 19, Churchill warned Stalin that German troops were 'massing in Poland'.[1] It seems that Stalin thought this intelligence was exaggerated or even invented in order to cause dissension between the USSR and the Reich.

Yet it was confirmed by other more confidential sources. The Russian authors of the *History of the Great Soviet War* write:

From Soviet intelligence agencies – among them Sorge in Tokyo – from frontier guards, from diplomatic representatives, from foreign friends of the USSR, particularly from Poland, Romania, Czechoslovakia, Finland, Hungary and even Germany, there came indisputable information testifying to the extremely serious situation on the Soviet borders.

Even more explicit was the evidence disclosed in the USSR, where several hundred Abwehr agents were captured in 1940–41. Questioning revealed that spy-training centres had been set up in several German towns and that their members were provided by groups of Ukrainian, Baltic, Armenian and Georgian emigrants. In addition, battalions of exiles were being raised and trained to form embryonic national armies and civilian governments. The brain behind the undertaking was the 'Russian section' of the 'Geopolitical Institute'. Neither had the concentration of several million men on their borders escaped the notice of Russian intelligence; in April it was ascertained that there had been eighty violations of Soviet territory by aircraft, and the USSR complained to Berlin about it.

Obviously, all these reports were swamped by many others of a different and contradictory nature; their importance could be exaggerated or minimised, according to the way the facts were presented. And the Soviet intelligence chief, involved as he was, like all the Soviet top men at the time, in the 'personality cult', wanted above all else to please Stalin; he thus had his own reasons for describing as 'questionable' the intelligence concerning Germany's hostile designs against the USSR, since Stalin did not like to hear about them.

Perhaps Stalin was determined not to let himself be convinced. It seems difficult to believe that the wary Georgian should have placed absolute confidence in Hitler; even more difficult to accept that he had all of a sudden come round to the idea of coexistence with the Fascist states and that he believed that this coexistence could last, and Russia give up her revolutionary mission in the world. A certain number of decisions seem to show that Stalin had seen through Hitler's intentions or at least that he

1. Information confirmed by Sumner Welles, *The Time for Decision*, pp. 170–171, New York, Harper & Row, 1945.

was uneasy about them; he became President of the Council of Ministers on May 7. In June, the port of Leningrad was closed. Above all, on April 13, 1941, when Matsuoka, the Japanese Foreign Minister, was passing through Moscow on his way back from Berlin, the USSR and Japan signed a non-aggression pact. Stalin attached sufficient importance to it to go to the station and bid farewell to the Japanese minister on the platform as he was leaving, a rare gesture which attracted a great deal of comment; the fact was that this pact covered the USSR in Asia, should she be attacked in Europe.

It seems therefore likely that, foreseeing the storm and knowing that he was not fully protected against it, Stalin worked things so as not to hasten its outbreak at his expense. This is why on March 20, after the invasion of Bulgaria by German troops, a circular from the Soviet Foreign Office to its officials, while asking them to warn the Balkan states against falling too completely under the German yoke, concluded that 'the German-Soviet treaty was essential to the successful achievement of the most urgent objective, namely, the destruction of the British Commonwealth'. This is why on June 13 the Soviet government recognised Rashid-Ali's government in Iraq, while the Tass Agency, in a communiqué widely broadcast by the whole Soviet and Communist press, denounced the British officials who, for purposes which were not difficult to fathom, were spreading 'false rumours' about disagreements between the Germans and Russians.

In any case the Wehrmacht's aggression was a complete surprise for the Russian people, just as it was for the Red Army, insufficiently on its guard; and also, it seems, for Stalin himself, who thought that he had at least gained time, if not even warded off the danger. According to Ambassador Maisky, he shut himself up for three days in the Kremlin, during which time the Soviet government remained without a leader and its members were given no instructions. The question now automatically springs to mind, what would have been the result if Hitler had sent an ultimatum to Stalin, if he was so anxious for peace? To what extent would he have stood his ground? But this time, although he had shown that he could win victories simply by brandishing dangerous threats, Hitler had announced to his generals 'that no agreement was possible with a Communist'. He was at last embarking on his war of religion and extermination. He was going to justify Paul Reynaud's assessment of him as the Gengis Khan of modern times.

V HITLER'S OBJECTIVES

In the east, Hitler's objectives were practically unlimited. It was not merely a question of destroying the potential threat of the Red Army or even of gaining possession of a certain amount of territory, however extensive it might be. He had to obliterate the USSR, wipe her off the map of Europe, like Poland, and split her up into independent states. In order to do this the Wehrmacht would have to reach the Volga and the Caucasus; from there raids would be launched against the most remote strongholds, as, for example, the Urals. Once this total victory had been won, Romania, the 'General Government' and Finland would be enlarged and 'buffer states', whose area could then be accurately fixed, would be set up in the Ukraine, White Russia and the Baltic countries. The rest would remain a Slav block, 'Muscovy', which they would take care to leave in a reassuring state of chronic underdevelopment.

These objectives were to be achieved in the first instance by military victories but also by a deliberate policy of terror. The aim was not only to protect the Wehrmacht's rear but to destroy the achievements of the existing Bolshevik régime root and branch and to exterminate the Jews and Communists who had accomplished them. The population would thus be brought to heel with a single blow and firmly established in a state of permanent bondage.

So the directive on 'the jurisdiction of an exceptional court in the Barbarossa region' ordered 'complete ruthlessness' towards the civilian population and the immediate execution of all individuals or representatives of communities suspected of hostility towards the invaders. Political commissars in the armies and top-ranking officials of the Communist party were to be shot as soon as they were captured. As the USSR was not a signatory to the Geneva Convention, Soviet prisoners of war would not benefit from its protective clauses and would be subjected to forced labour.

A programme for the economic exploitation of the conquered territories, called 'the Green File', provided for the German seizure of industry, raw materials, crude oil and foodstuffs. The best land would be colonised by Aryan settlers – including room for the Scandinavians and the Dutch.

The *Aufbau Ost*, the eastern plan, looked further; after the war, German domination in eastern Europe would be established by a reign of terror – Hitler liked to forecast that it would last 'for a thousand years'. The subjugated peoples would receive only primary education, restricted to simple sums, learning how to write their name and to learning 'that, by divine ordinance, they should obey the Germans and be honest, hardworking and submissive'. Their state of health would be kept at a rudimentary level so that any population increase would be checked from time to time by epidemics. As for 'Muscovy', that sewage dump would be visited by punitive expeditions as a warning and a reminder to its subhuman inhabitants that the Germans were their masters. Seventy per cent of the Slav population would be transported to Muscovy, which could very well begin west of the Urals, although its exact location was not yet fixed.

Such were Hitler's grandiose and monstrous 'ideas'. Goebbels was to paraphrase them by brandishing the slogans 'crusade' and 'total mobilisation of Europe against Asian Bolshevism'. Himmler was to denounce any consideration shown to the Russians as a sentimental aberration. The war against the USSR was thus essentially an ideological and a racial war. But it required vast resources and, of course, most important, the victory of the Wehrmacht.

VI THE WEHRMACHT'S FORCES AND PLANS

On June 22, 1941, the German armies along the Soviet frontiers were concentrated in four operational areas: on the Finnish front, from Petsamo to north of Leningrad, General Dietl's mountain troops were fighting shoulder to shoulder with Marshal Mannerheim's Finnish army. Their target was Murmansk and the Carelian territory covering Leningrad. The northern army group, under the command of Marshal von Leeb, consisted of three armies, one of which was armoured; its target was Leningrad. The central army group under Marshal von Bock would advance on Moscow; it also contained three armies, but two of them armoured. In the south, the group of armies under von Rundstedt was to advance towards Kiev, Dnepropetrovsk and Odessa; this group was more heterogeneous; in addition to the four German armies, one of which was armoured, there were Hungarian and Romanian contingents – between which German units had had to be sandwiched – and later on the Italian expeditionary force. Each group of armies was supported by an air fleet. Naval support was provided in the Baltic.

In all, the German forces numbered 150 infantry divisions and 30 armoured divisions, added to which there were 15 Finnish divisions, 20 Romanian divisions, 10 or so Hungarian and the same number of Italian divisions; the non-German units were inferior in the quality of their officers, their training and equipment. About 60 German divisions were left to guard Norway, Denmark, Belgium, Holland and France; 7 were stationed in the Balkans; 2 were operating in Libya. Plainly, the Germans had not exhausted their reserves of manpower; but Hitler refused Halder's request for 40 supplementary divisions, so as not to jeopardise the output of the war industries.

About 4,000 tanks were engaged in the USSR; this included 2,400 heavy tanks – the Germans were convinced that their Mark IV Panzer was superior to any other. The Luftwaffe comprised 3,000 aircraft, two-thirds of its total force, 1,000 of which were bombers and 900 fighters. In point of fact, 3,000 aircraft on a front 1,250 to 1,900 miles long was hardly more than two aircraft per mile, whereas in the Polish and French campaigns the density was ten per mile. But the quality of the German equipment was superior to the Russians'; the majority of the Soviet fighters could fly only as fast as the Nazi bombers.

The OKH had realised that the great Russian plain between the Baltic and the Black Sea was divided from west to east by two areas difficult to negotiate by ground forces: the Pripet Marshes between Kiev and Minsk, and the Valday plateau between Leningrad and Moscow. These two obstacles left three wide corridors of approach to Leningrad, Moscow and Kiev, and this geographical factor had influenced the Wehrmacht's grouping and objectives. However, realising that the armies advancing on Leningrad and Kiev would have to cross numerous rivers and that Moscow was the point where most of the main Soviet railway lines converged – and rail was the only method of transport which could be used all the year round – General Halder had suggested that the Soviet capital should be made the chief target. Since the Russians were aware of this and would mass the bulk of their troops to its defence, the decisive battles would be fought and the Red Army destroyed in front of Moscow. But Hitler attached equal importance to the capture of Leningrad and Stalingrad, the names of which, wrote General de Cossé-Brissac, 'fascinated him'. It was in these 'sacred cities of Communism' that he wanted to 'overthrow the hydra-headed Red monster'. And Hitler had found little trouble in forcing his views on his generals.

VII HITLER AS WAR LEADER

For to an increasing extent, it was Hitler and Hitler alone who conducted the war, in the political and diplomatic field, in armaments production and in strategy. He alone took the decisions, disclosing them in dribs and drabs to small committees which were gradually extended in size as his decisions required a greater number of people to carry them out. At these meetings Hitler would of course, listen and try to understand, but above all he held forth and forced his wishes on his colleagues, whether they found them congenial or not. Since each of them knew only part of what was in the master's mind, they fell over one another to agree by paraphrasing his decrees. The generals were the last to offer any real criticism of the Führer's decisions, except when they had very serious objections to put forward on technical grounds; but these objections concerned only the execution, not the idea or the decision itself. 'The Führer had informed Jodl and me once and for all that politics were none of our business,' wrote Keitel; '. . . we were not always in agreement with his decisions at the operational level, yet we always carried them out to the letter.'

How good was Hitler as a strategist? It is a fact that he had studied the works of the great German war theorists from Frederick the Great and Clausewitz to Moltke and von Seekt. According to Speer, 'in matters relating to army equipment, the characteristics of weapons and various types of ammunition, he knew more than his chief of staff.' Guderian had often been struck by the Führer's extraordinary memory, his gift of persuasion and his immense will-power. He possessed in addition an outstanding sense of when to take strategic advantage of a situation and showed an amazing flair for discovering the most unorthodox and unexpected solutions.

He thought that the qualities which made up a military leader were intelligence, tenacity and iron nerves and that he possessed these qualities more than his generals. This conviction of his superiority led him to intervene in every detail; but he lacked the necessary professional knowledge and he paralysed his subordinates and caused confusion.

Above all, Hitler had become intoxicated with the extraordinary successes he had achieved. He believed quite simply that he was a genius. He wrote to Mussolini: 'Above the world of mediocrities, there is the fraternity of exceptional beings'; he considered himself irreplaceable and this filled him with a feverish desire always to see things bigger and better and to go faster and faster. He allowed himself to be taken in by the fulsome flattery of his lieutenants, who extolled him as 'the greatest military leader of all times'. But he was self-taught and his mind was often cluttered and confused. With the arrogance of the upstart, he would dismiss his opponents in a few contemptuous and peremptory phrases – as when he described the British soldier as 'so lazy that he would almost rather die of cold than build himself a shelter'. He was swift to abuse and swift to anger; he quickly lost all sense of proportion, whether he was talking about 'degenerate parliamentary scoundrels' or about the United States, whose 'production was the biggest fraud in the world'. He often allowed himself to be carried away by his emotions and he was superstitious: he advised Mussolini not to enter the war on June 7 because it was a Friday. He was thus often unable to distinguish between what was possible and what was not. His lack of moral sense, his cruelty, his instability, his morbid sensitivity and his manic reactions which made him pass from hysterical rage to blind obstinacy and despondency were to reveal their destructive nature when the tide turned against him. On the other hand, the boldness and originality of this novice were going to help the German Army as long as it retained its superiority.

VIII THE USSR'S FORCES AND PLANS

In June 1941 the German Army's superiority over the Red Army was beyond any shadow of doubt. With 170 million inhabitants, the USSR could of course raise larger armies than Germany and her economy would be able to equip them; but in 1941, the modernisation of the Red Army, although under way, was far from being complete.

There was, however, no shortage of soldiers; the age of conscription had been lowered and the length of service increased, so that in 1941 4 million men could be mobilised; what is more, nearly 10 million men, 6 million of them young, had undergone a course of intensive military training. The training of officers and NCO's was proceeding apace under Timoshenko, the new War Commissar; about a thousand officers had been initiated in modern methods of warfare at the Military Academy. Large numbers of militant Communists had been made to join the Army, in which 55 per cent of the cadres were card-carrying Party members; the political commissars had, however, been withdrawn, so as to allow greater responsibility to the military leaders. The Red Army contained 209 infantry and 32 cavalry divisions.

But in June 1941 a large number of the young recruits had not yet completed their training and above all the units' equipment was for the most part antiquated. Some excellent prototypes had been produced: a rifle with telescopic sights and automatic loading; a machine gun and an automatic pistol, anti-tank weapons. But the units had not received their full allocation; for example, the majority possessed nothing more than anti-tank grenades.

The artillery had the advantage over the German artillery, particularly with regard to their mortars; they were being equipped with recoilless guns; rocket-guns (*Katiuschas*) were already in existence before the war and aircraft armed with rockets had been tried out in the Finnish war. But only twenty per cent of the artillery was mechanically propelled and then only by under-powered agricultural tractors. The tanks were good and well armed, but the medium tank, the T.34, which Soviet military historians consider the best in the Second World War, was as yet being produced only in small numbers; above all, although some independent armoured divisions had been formed, the available equipment had been distributed amongst all of them, so that the majority of the armoured forces were not at full strength. Moreover, the Red Army did not have any large engineering unit; its ancillary services were inadequate and its means of communication unreliable because they operated through the peacetime telephone and telegraph systems. Finally, the 6,000 Russian aircraft belonged to a type that was now out of date – the I 16 fighter had a speed of 290 miles an hour and carried 224 pounds of bombs, while the Messerschmitt 110 could fly at 340 miles an hour carrying 1120 pounds of bombs. None of the new aircraft whose prototypes were still being developed were yet being mass-produced.

The USSR's military experience was confined to the civil war, the Spanish war, the fighting against Japan in 1938-9 and above all to the war against Finland. Theories based on inadequate experience led to serious blunders, such as the useless employment of large armoured units, or the use of the air force in purely tactical operations. The Russian strategists thought that the infantry still had the chief role in war and that armies could be mobilised and deployed long before the operations proper took place. They could envisage attacks only on limited fronts and never on fronts that might be 95 miles and sometimes more than 190 miles long. Basically, they were not so very different from the French generals of 1939.

However, by developing branches of industry linked with national defence – special alloys and machine-tools – and by moving centres of industry and armaments factories to the Urals, or establishing new ones there, the USSR had braced herself for a long war. The Comintern and the national Communist parties also provided her with effective 'revolutionary dynamite'. But the effectiveness of these methods would not show itself until later on.

So although the Germans had misjudged the Soviet forces by under-estimating their manpower and the number and quality of their tanks as well as by their belief that the non-Russian population would revolt, at the beginning of the war they commanded great superiority, which was still further enhanced by the fact that their opponents were inexperienced and taken by surprise. The Germans were to achieve successes of such magnitude that any power smaller in area, population and economic potential than the USSR would have been forced to admit defeat.

CHAPTER 2

The Wehrmacht's Victories in the USSR

I THE SURPRISE ATTACK

AT the Nuremberg trials Generals Halder and Jodl asserted that in attacking the USSR, Hitler had done no more than forestall her; to justify this preventive war they adduced Soviet concentrations on the frontier, the distribution of maps of Poland to the commanders of the Russian tanks, the construction of airfields close to German territory, etc. Soviet historians have vigorously and indignantly denied these allegations and by way of refutation they stress the shortcomings of the Red Army, for which Stalin is today held responsible. Besides, these allegations are contradicted by the statements of other German leaders. On June 21, while inspecting his front-line troops – his task was to seize the stronghold of Brest-Litovsk – Guderian smugly noted that the Russians suspected nothing, for they were drilling and marching to the sound of military music.

In actual fact, on the first day the Germans' only unpleasant surprise was the power of the Soviet T34 tanks, which General Reinhard compared to 'great lumbering bears', which 'made his tanks flare up like tinder'. But it was the Russians who had the most painful surprises in store for themselves.

In the first place, since the Soviet airfields were not large enough to take the new types of aircraft, the latter had all been assembled on a small number of bases; and as the order to disperse them arrived too late, by noon on June 22 the Soviet Air Force had lost 1,200 aircraft as a result of raids on 66 airfields or of heavy air fighting.

Then again the German attack surprised the Soviet troops scattered along the frontier. Their guns had been removed from the fortified positions along the old line; along the new one, work was not yet finished and there were gaps of several miles sandwiched between solid fortifications. There were forty-four divisions, forty of them infantry, deployed along a 1,250-mile-long front; each division was therefore defending a sector thirty miles long on average – at best fifteen miles, at worst sixty – whereas in theory a sector was only five to eight miles long. The covering troops on the frontier were even occupying salients whose flanks were not manned. No operational units had been concentrated or positioned in such a way as to meet a surprise attack; the bulk of the covering units was fifty miles to the rear. These defence positions meant that the enemy started with a local superiority of four or five to one. The Soviet soldiers were sometimes extremely inexperienced: the drivers of some of the tanks had been introduced to their machines only a few hours previously.

Nevertheless, on June 21 the Soviet authorities had had wind of impending German aggression, without giving it too much credence. Precautions had been taken, but in some places – in the region of Kiev, for example, as General Purkaiev reported – the alarm had not been given until June 22 between 4 and 6 a.m., when the enemy onslaught had already begun. As in Poland and France, the Wehrmacht had benefited from a surprise attack which gave them a great advantage from the very beginning.

II THE GERMAN BLITZKRIEG

Hitler thought that the USSR would admit defeat in six months and the Red Army disintegrate in eight weeks. Counting his Moscow chickens before they were hatched, he forecast that from July 14, 1941 onwards he would be able to reduce the strength of the Army and transfer these extra resources to the Navy and Air Force, in order to launch them against Britain and, if need be, against the United States. At the end of September, he gave orders that forty infantry divisions were to be disbanded in 1942, with the appropriate reduction in the manufacture of armaments for the Army. His roving imagination was already mapping out a vast pincer movement against Suez and the Persian Gulf for the same year, via Libya and Turkey. Nor were these schemes mere bombast.

Indeed, in the USSR everything was working out according to plan. The lessons of the Polish and French campaigns were bearing fruit. Once again the Germans, after gaining mastery of the air, developed their attack by the combined action of very large forces in the first stage of the offensive; the attack was then intensified at the enemy's weak points by armoured columns supported by the Air Force; the breakthrough was enlarged by scattering the enemy forces and then surrounding them. The most frequent method of encirclement was that of 'pincer movements', whose claws would start more than sixty miles apart and join up in the enemy's rear to encircle a whole army, or what was left of it. Once again the day had been won by meticulous preparation, the rapidity with which the forces were able to regroup, the attempt to smash the enemy by breaching gaps more than sixty miles wide and the ability to change the direction of attack according to the way the fighting was going.

The Luftwaffe was fully engaged in every sector; its sorties amounted to some 2,500 or 3,000 every day, which meant several for each fighter. On June 25, the first raid on Moscow took place. The first unpleasant surprise here was that the city's air defence proved so effective that further raids could be carried out only at night, in reduced strength.

This partial defeat in the air was amply compensated for by the victories achieved on the ground. On the evening of June 22, misinformed about the state of the forces and the course of the fighting, the Soviet Chief of Staff had ordered counter-attacks based on a misunderstanding of the Red Army's offensive potential. Although lines of attack were well chosen, owing to hasty preparation these attacks resulted only in considerable losses, through lack of air cover, adequate artillery support and motorised traction. As a result, by the evening of June 25, the German troops had advanced 145 miles towards Minsk and 125 miles from Brest-Litovsk. On July 3, Halder noted in his diary that the campaign against the USSR had been won in a fortnight. The Soviet Chief of Staff then decided to give up fighting 'along the frontiers' and join battle on a Narva–Pskov–Polotsk–Dnepr–Kherson line, where the natural defences in several areas had been strengthened by fortified works. Would the retreating armies retain the necessary cohesion and strength to stand their ground there?

Though cut off from their adjacent units and sometimes surrounded, many Soviet units continued fighting on their own. The majority of them surrendered when their ammunition, food-supplies and fuel gave out; everywhere their stocks had been captured or destroyed. In the north Riga had fallen, although Tallin held out until August 15. In the centre, the enemy had crossed the Beresina on July 4, broken through the Stalin line and conquered Vitebsk. In the south, Lvov was captured on June 30 and the Romanians advanced as far as Czernovitz. On July 6, the Germans reached the outskirts of Zhitomir and von Rundstedt's right wing was advancing between Kiev and Mohilev. After a war lasting eighteen days, the German Army leaped forward 280 miles; Latvia, Lithuania, Byelorussia and a large part of the Ukraine had been conquered; the Russians had lost 2,000 lorry loads of ammunition, 300,000 prisoners, 3,000 guns, 1,500 tanks and 2,000 aircraft.

Although they had suffered widespread defeat, they were nevertheless not crushed; the large scale of the German operations, which was out of all proportion to the number of troops employed – as Jodl said at Nuremberg, 'We really needed 300 divisions' – left gaps through which a good many Soviet units escaped encirclement. The Soviet Chief of Staff then adopted certain measures which Marshal Yeremenko listed as follows: incompetent leaders were removed and replaced; discipline was restored; morale was boosted by a few local victories (for example, concentrated raids by the few available air squadrons); intelligence and fortifications were improved; better collaboration between the various services was organised; more concentrated use was made of armour; and the technique of tank-warfare was improved. In short, the Russians were being initiated into modern warfare in and through their very experience of defeat. Would they have enough time?

They anticipated that the Wehrmacht's chief target would be Moscow. Timoshenko was given the task of delaying its advance as much as possible outside Smolensk. The battle began on July 10 and lasted until August 10. As a result, in August the Germans advanced less rapidly. Another stiff delaying action was fought at Briansk. Whereas on July 23 the German commander was hoping to capture Leningrad and Moscow on August 25, and reach the Volga in October and the Caucasus in November, he had to change his tune and envisage a winter campaign which he had not bargained for. He thus realised that the size of the USSR was liable to turn what had been an unqualified triumph in France into a Pyrrhic victory.

The Russian resistance led Hitler to take a closer interest in the fighting. Unlike Halder, he considered that they should concentrate their main energies not on Moscow, but on the wings, Leningrad and Kiev. He preferred economic targets to the political objective of Moscow. He wanted to capture the Donetz basin before the autumn rains set in by mid-September. The centre group of armies should therefore halt their advance towards Moscow.

Events seemed to prove Hitler right. On September 2, the external fortifications of Leningrad were under German fire; on September 8 the Neva was crossed and the following day the Germans captured Tikhvin 125 miles east of Leningrad. The Finnish Army, for its part, had seized Viborg. But the most spectacular victories were in the south: at Uman, Boudienny's troops were encircled and left behind 150,000 prisoners; Kiev fell on September 24; in this operational area the Russians lost 600,000 prisoners and 1,700 guns. But autumn had arrived; the Red Army had suffered heavy defeats but she had not been crushed. The Soviet government had not the slightest intention of admitting defeat.

III THE BATTLES OF LENINGRAD AND MOSCOW

In the summer the German soldiers marched on and on, often without water and without a proper route, guided by maps which proved more and more inaccurate the further eastward they penetrated, until, as Hossbach relates, it reached the point where 'a place shown as a large village would turn out to be an industrial town of 60,000 inhabitants'.

In the autumn, they came up against another enemy, the mud, which prevented supplies from coming through. Hossbach states: 'When they ran into the mud our machines had to admit defeat; infantry and mounted units were now the most mobile part of the army.' There was no longer any trace of the conditions so favourable to a Panzer Blitzkrieg. Besides, the tanks were much the worse for wear after their trek across the Russian steppes. One fact had emerged which was frequently to recur: the Wehrmacht's supply lines had been strung out and were sometimes cut off by Soviet troops who stayed behind, more or less organised and armed, in territories which in theory had been conquered. Fuel supplies were running short while consumption was rising.

It is true that Soviet economic potential had suffered tremendous losses which to all appearance were irreparable. The Germans had seized industrial areas producing 63 per cent of the country's coal, 68 per cent of the cast iron and 58 per cent of the steel as well as fertile land which produced 38 per cent of the wheat, 84 per cent of the sugar and 60 per cent of the livestock. On top of these losses, there was the systematic destruction caused by the Russians 'scorched earth' tactics, inherited from Kutusov and advocated by Stalin. Railways, bridges and factories were blown up, including the gigantic Dnepropetrovsk dam, the pride and joy of the first Five Year Plan; barns, stocks and warehouses were set on fire. Could the USSR hope to receive any help from outside? Since the German aggression Churchill, the man who had wanted to use the blockade to force the Bolshevik state into submission in 1920, had declared Britain's total solidarity with the USSR. 'Russia's danger,' he had stated 'is our danger, just as the cause of every Russian fighting for his home is the cause of free men and free peoples all over the world.' The British government had contemplated sending convoys via the North Cape to Murmansk, but it was at too low an ebb itself to be able to send very much and Stalin was very dissatisfied. Relations between the new allies showed signs of strain.

In the extreme north, in Lapland, fighting was between only isolated units, separated by vast, impassable areas cut off by forests and marshes. The only way of getting provisions through to the forces was on the backs of men or mules; a day's march of ten miles was an athletic feat. The Germans failed to reach the Murmansk railway line and in the autumn of 1941 the front settled down.

In Finland, Marshal Mannerheim's troops were carrying on their own war. No joint command had been set up with Germany and each stuck to his ideological guns. After winning back the part of Carelia which had been handed over to the Russians, Mannerheim refused to take part in the siege of Leningrad, since the Finnish Parliament had decided not to commit the army beyond the frontier.

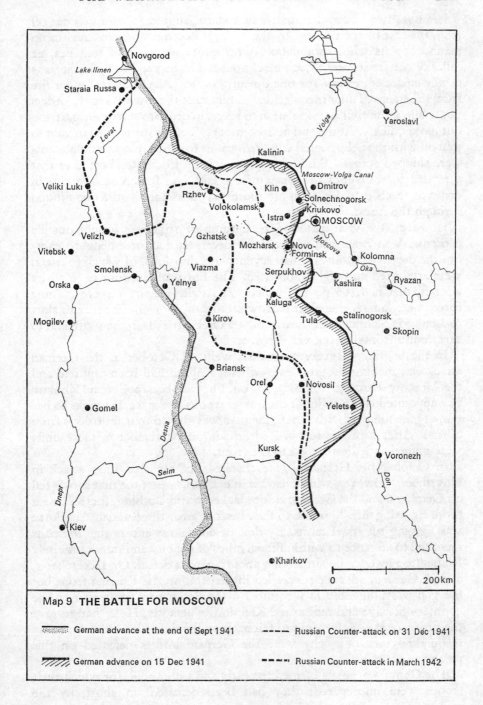

Map 9 **THE BATTLE FOR MOSCOW**

German advance at the end of Sept 1941   ----- Russian Counter-attack on 31 Dec 1941

German advance on 15 Dec 1941   - - - Russian Counter-attack in March 1942

Leningrad had been threatened ever since August 20, and was cut off from the rest of the country by the 30th; it became an entrenched camp manned by its whole population, who built 390 miles of trenches, 22 miles of barricades and 15,000 blockhouses. On September 8, the city was totally encircled, except for one opening on to Lake Ladoga. Under fire from the enemy, Hitler then decided to blockade the town and gave orders not to allow the civilian population to leave, in order to starve the garrison out more quickly. At the end of September a Russian army tried in vain to join up with the beleaguered city. Provisions for the 2,500,000 inhabitants were shipped across Lake Ladoga by water up till September; after that they had to wait until the water of the lake had frozen sufficiently; in order to reach the lake, a supply route 125 miles long had to be plotted through the forest.

However, the vital battle of the autumn of 1941 was fought outside Moscow. Von Bock had received the necessary reinforcements to carry out the decisive assault. He had seventy-five divisions, of which fourteen were armoured and eight motorised. The Luftwaffe let him have all its aircraft, that is 1,500 planes, which left it without any reserves. These forces were launched against narrow sectors of the front in order to skirt Moscow via Kalinin in the north and via Orel and Tula in the south and to carry out a frontal attack via Vyazma.

In the beginning, everything went well: on October 2, the German attack was making progress everywhere; Kalinin had been captured and the Moscow–Leningrad railway cut off. On October 10 General Zhukov was appointed commander of the Soviet troops in the west; thanks to her non-aggression pact with Japan, the USSR was able to transfer troops from Siberia. After a procession in Red Square on November 6, these units were immediately despatched to the front.

In October the Germans were checked but renewed their attack in November. However, winter had set in early that year; the first snows fell on October 6 and the German troops lacked warm clothing, fuel and even food. By using airfields close to the Moscow area, the Russian Air Force was fighting on equal terms. By dint of enormous efforts the Germans managed to advance to within fifteen miles of the city and rather unwisely Ribbentrop lost no time in talking about a Soviet defeat. On December 2, a fresh German advance succeeded in penetrating the Russian front but the gap was plugged. On December 6 the Red Army went over to the counter-offensive and recaptured Kalinin. Reluctantly, Hitler had to give the order for the Wehrmacht to fall back on the defensive. After so many resounding victories, why were the German armies defeated on this particular occasion?

The German generals blamed the early and bitter cold, for which their troops were unprepared; they had been defeated, in short, by the winter. But Soviet historians make the point that the Soviet soldiers were not all that well off either. Although the Russian troops were more accustomed to the cold and it was chiefly the attackers who were put out of action by the engines freezing up, it is a fact that even before the first snowfall, the German troops had shown signs of fatigue. It was on the field that they were brought to a halt. Whatever the cause, the German defeat, which was their first, came as a great shock and it left its mark. The results were not slow to make themselves felt; dissension was sown in the German camp. In quick succession Hitler dismissed von Rundstedt, discharged General Hoepner from the Army for having ordered a with-drawal and himself replaced von Brauchitsch as commander of the ground forces. The Führer thus became at one and the same time Head of State, President of the Council, Secretary of War, Supreme Commander of the German forces and Chief of the Army. Every soldier, sailor and airman was bound to him by an oath of personal allegiance. In addition, Hitler persuaded the Reichstag to bestow on him the title of 'Supreme Master of Justice'. But this accumulation of powers and responsibilities had no influence on the rigours of the Russian winter and the dogged resolution of the Red Army.

IV WINTER 1941-2

Hitler had pretended to treat the Russian cold with scorn. Basing his policy on his experiences in the 1914–18 war, he ordered Guderian to use gun-fire to dig individual holes for the front-line infantry. The frozen earth was so hard that it was impossible to carry out the order. Neverthe-less Guderian was relieved of his command a few days later.

The cold caused the radiators of the tanks and lorries to burst, through lack of anti-freeze; the petrol solidified, for they had no apparatus to heat it before filling the fuel-tanks. The frozen oil no longer lubricated and the synthetic rubber lost its elasticity.

Because of the enemy or the bad weather, the Wehrmacht had been deprived of a large part of its resources. Halder stated that out of 500,000 vehicles, 30 per cent were beyond repair, 40 per cent needed a complete overhaul and 30 per cent required minor repairs. Rail transport was growing steadily more inadequate at the very moment when the roads were becoming impassable. The centre group of armies were receiving sixteen trains of provisions per day instead of the thirty-one it needed. With its 1,700 aircraft, the Luftwaffe could no longer provide air-cover for the retreating troops; the planes were forced to perform acrobatics, such as landing on frozen lakes; some squadrons had to be taken away from the Mediterranean front. The cold was making itself felt especially among the Italian troops, and their leader General Messe reported that their morale was seriously affected.

However, Hitler was obsessed by the fear that the loss of a few bits of land might demoralise his troops. On January 2, 1942, he refused von Kluge's request for permission to withdraw. On January 15, rather than disobey, Marshal von Leeb asked to be relieved of his command.

Life was hard for the Russians. In Leningrad the besieged inhabitants were eating bread made of 10 per cent cellulose, 10 per cent cattle feed, 2 per cent paper dust, 2 per cent flour dust, 3 per cent cornflour and 73 per cent rye flour; they ate it with sausage containing 40 per cent soya flour. In December 1941, they had to bury more than 50,000 dead; in order to obtain water they burned furniture and books to melt the ice.

The Germans worked out a plan for setting up small scattered centres of resistance in the occupied villages, covered by outposts and capable of defending themselves long enough for the tanks and aircraft to come to their support. The most important points formed self-contained independent fronts, generally where lines of communication intersected. These were the 'strong-points' of Staraya Russa, Vyazma, Orel, Kharkov, etc. But the Russians made the most of the vacant spaces which were left; they slipped in between the centres, surrounded them, shelled the mud-walled houses and captured whole regiments. The Germans tried to hang on to the river banks but the rivers were frozen and no longer provided an obstacle.

In the north the Red Army recaptured Tikhvin, to the east of Leningrad. Outside Moscow the Germans were driven back some sixty miles from the city; at the end of January they had been forced back to their starting points of October 15. In March the Russians penetrated the outskirts of Vyazma, some sixty miles from Smolensk; they skirted the 'strong-points' which were still holding out, as for example, at Rzhev. In the south Timoshenko, who had replaced Boudienny, had crossed the lower Donetz. While beleaguered Sebastopol continued to defend itself, the Russians, who held Kertch, had moved over to the offensive in the Crimea.

In April 1942 Halder totted up his winter losses: they amounted to 900,000 men, for whom his reinforcements of 450,000 men offered poor compensation; 74,000 vehicles were unserviceable and only 7,400 new ones had arrived; 1,847 new tanks were no replacement for the 2,340 put out of action. The southern group of armies now possessed only 50 per cent of its original fire-power and the centre and northern groups only 33 per cent. It was in these circumstances that Hitler, after stating 'that the war would be won or lost in the south', decided to launch a crucial offensive in the spring.

V THE GERMAN OFFENSIVE OF SPRING 1942:
OBJECTIVES AND DISPOSITION OF FORCES

However, Hitler lacked the resources to advance over the whole of the vast front. The objective was determined by one of the Reich's urgent economic needs: it was to be an offensive to obtain oil by conquering the Caucasus. At the end of 1941 the Reich's fuel stocks had fallen to 800,000 tons; that is, about one month's supply. Speer was hoping that the output of *ersatz* fuel would rise from 4 to 6 million tons in 1942. But stepping up the air and submarine war against Britain, which was expected to be resumed as soon as the Soviet Union had been destroyed, would require a considerable increase in the amount of oil, which Raeder estimated at 200,000 tons per month for the German Navy alone, whereas it was actually receiving only 84,000. Supplies of Romanian oil were now static, for the Romanian army in the USSR had to meet its own needs. In short, the dilemma was simple; according to the evidence of General Paulus at the Nuremberg trial, in June 1942 Hitler described it to the general officers of the southern group of armies as follows: 'If I do not get the Maikop and Groznyy oil, I shall be forced to stop the war.'

Hitler's orders on April 5, 1942, thus had the following aims: the capture of Sebastopol and mopping up the Kertch peninsula in order to protect the Germans' right flank from attack; to the north of these German defences, Voronezh, a key position, must be neutralised to protect the left flank; the destruction of the enemy armies between the Donetz and the Don, by a pincer operation starting from Voronezh on one side and from the Don estuary on the other; and, when these preliminaries had been successfully completed, an advance with all available forces towards the oil of the Caucasus. This time, although the Germans' plan was vast in scale it was simple and relatively limited in scope. If it succeeded, it would enable them to retain and exploit both the industrial basin of the Donetz and the wheat supply of the Ukraine and to add to these the oil from the Caucasus. Once this had been achieved, there would no longer be any fear of a long war.

Marshal von Bock, who was responsible for the operation, had about a hundred German infantry divisions, supported by 20 Panzer and 10 motorised divisions, in addition to which there were 22 Romanian, 13 Hungarian, 11 Italian, 1 Slovak and 1 Spanish divisions. The quality of these troops varied. The Hungarian Army, under the command of General Jany, had only rudimentary equipment and logistical resources, so much so that its supplies were uncertain from the start; it consisted mainly of poor peasants to whom this Russian campaign meant nothing, plus 20 per cent of foreigners who had settled in Hungary.

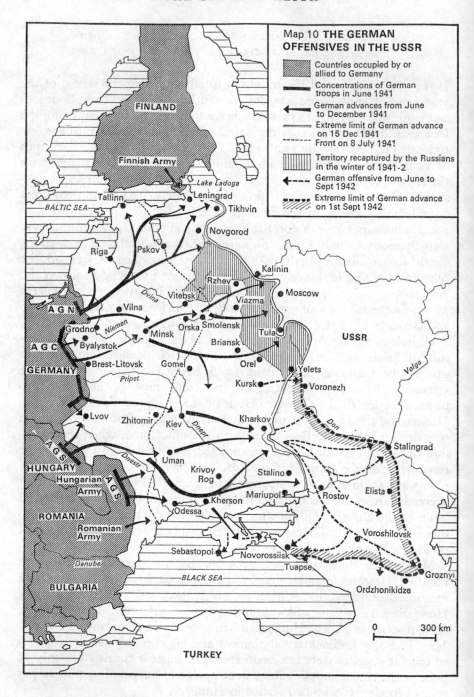

Map 10 **THE GERMAN OFFENSIVES IN THE USSR**

Countries occupied by or allied to Germany

Concentrations of German troops in June 1941

German advances from June to December 1941

Extreme limit of German advance on 15 Dec 1941

Front on 8 July 1941

Territory recaptured by the Russians in the winter of 1941-2

German offensive from June to Sept 1942

Extreme limit of German advance on 1st Sept 1942

FINLAND

Finnish Army

Lake Ladoga

BALTIC SEA

Tallinn

Leningrad

Tikhvin

Novgorod

Riga

Pskov

Kalinin

Rzhev

Moscow

Dvina

Vitebsk

Viazma

A G N

Vilna

Orsha

Smolensk

Tula

USSR

Grodno

Niemen

Minsk

A G C

Byalystok

Briansk

Volga

GERMANY

Brest-Litovsk

Gomel

Orel

Yelets

Pripet

Kursk

Voronezh

Lvov

Zhitomir

Kiev

Dnepr

Kharkov

Don

Stalingrad

A G S

Dnestr

Uman

Krivoy Rog

Stalino

Elista

HUNGARY

Hungarian Army

A G S

Kherson

Mariupol

Rostov

ROMANIA

Romanian Army

Odessa

Voroshilovsk

Danube

Sebastopol

Novorossiisk

Tuapse

Groznyi

BLACK SEA

Ordzhonikidze

BULGARIA

0   300 km

TURKEY

The Italian force, at first under the command of General Messe and then of General Garibaldi, comprised 11 divisions, one of them 'Black shirts'; although it had been given an *armata motorizzata*, fitted out with the best Italian equipment, its resources could not compare with those of the German units and it suffered in consequence. Messe had frequent clashes with von Kleist; the one complained that they were asking too much of the Italians; the other accused his allies of lacking aggression.

The Luftwaffe was in no condition to support the armies as it should have done. It had to leave a large number of fighters in the west to defend German territory against increasingly daring British raids. Instead of the 3,000 aircraft of June 1941 it could now muster only 2,000 to 2,500 in the east. Its equipment had not been substantially improved, apart from the emergence of a new Focke Wulf fighter. The Soviet Air Force, on the other hand, had made enormous strides; it had replaced nearly all its old aircraft, had received some British Hurricanes and was operating with Stormoviks which devoured tanks by the dozen. Far from merely surviving in the air, it could now even achieve mastery of the skies. Thus on the eve of its great advance, which Hitler hoped would be decisive, the German Army was in danger of being without air cover; this was hardly likely to strengthen the troops' morale.

VI THE GERMAN OFFENSIVE AND ITS VICTORIES

The German offensive began, as arranged on May 8, in the Crimea, a natural aircraft base which had to be neutralised in order to prevent possible raids on the Romanian oil wells. Von Manstein's Germans and Romanians 'mopped up' the Kertch peninsula and then launched an all-out attack against Sebastopol, which had been under siege since the end of October 1941. The fortress was defended by 600 guns and 1,000 mortars, which were able to take full advantage of the difficulties of the terrain and the large number of small natural positions. In mid-June the defenders were beginning to run out of ammunition. On July 2, the fortress surrendered; Soviet submarines managed to evacuate only a certain number of people. Sebastopol had held out for 250 days; the Russians had gained valuable time.

Timoshenko also attempted a delaying action by taking the initiative and attacking the Germans in the direction of Kharkov; after a few initial victories he was threatened with encirclement and had to withdraw.

But as a result the major German attack, the crucial one, could not begin until June 28, which was already late. According to the Germans, the Russians had guessed the enemy's plans: Halder said that the Soviet press had even published articles on the German intentions. They had prepared themselves by setting up a lightly occupied front, holding back powerful armoured and motorised units ready to move forward in support.

In the north von Weich was attacking on three fronts, Kursk-Voronezh, Byelgorod-Svoboda and Kupyansk-Rossoch. Hitler intervened in the conduct of operations. His orders were to try not to capture Voronezh at all costs, so as to concentrate the greatest possible weight of forces in the south, and he fell into a blind rage when he learnt that von Bock, whom he dismissed on the spot, had detached a Panzer division in order to capture the city.

Further to the south, Paulus, at the head of the Sixth Army, crossed the Don at Kalach and advanced towards Stalingrad; the Russians fell back systematically and Paulus was unable to press home his success as Hitler had taken some of his armoured and motorised units away from him in order to give them, logically enough, to Army Group A, whose task it was to carry out the great advance to the Caucasus. However, the Don was occupied along its whole length, although the Soviets retained a few bridgeheads on the south bank, which were to prove valuable. Nevertheless, the Germans had won a resounding victory, comparable to those of June–July 1941; the Russians had after all lost almost 600,000 prisoners.

Until now, in spite of a few inevitable hitches, the German plan had worked out as arranged; but once again Hitler became intoxicated with the taste of success; he now talked of a lightning advance towards the Persian Gulf. And even, according to Halder, of vague operations in the direction of the east coast of South Africa. Now that he had reached the boundless open spaces of Russia the Führer seemed to have lost his head; he was no longer able to choose one direction and stick to it; as on previous occasions, he wanted everything at once. On July 13, he dictated his directive no. 45, which laid down, *at one and the same time*, two equally important lines of attack: Army Group A, as agreed, would advance southwards towards Rostov and the east coast of the Black Sea, so as to seize the harbours; from there it would strike out for the mountains of the Kuban and the oil wells, including those of Baku, which meant crossing the Caucasus, another great leap forward; as if this grandiose scheme were not enough, Army Group B, instead of confining itself to protecting Group A's advance by tying down as many of the enemy forces as possible, would also advance, in order to take Stalingrad and the whole of the lower course of the Volga. Hitler was thus trying to do two things at once. He was dispersing his forces at a time when they most needed to be concentrated. He was waiting to see whether circumstances – or his mood – would require him to move his forces from one line of advance to the other. He had lost any notion of adapting the ends to the means. Colonel Bernard was quite right in concluding that it was his lack of moderation at that moment of time that 'clinched his downfall'.

VII THE CAUCASUS AND STALINGRAD

Army Group A under von List first of all advanced rapidly towards the Caucasus. Von Kleist captured Rostov on July 27 and Krasnodar on August 9. On August 22 the swastika was hoisted over the El'brus. The Russians had been overrun as in the heyday of the Wehrmacht. But once again the vast open spaces exhausted the assailant and gave the defenders a new impetus. The various Caucasian fronts had been brought under the single command of Boudienny, who set up defensive positions in depth on all routes leading to Transcaucasia: six outside Ordzhonikidze and ten outside Baku, the strongest ones in the immediately threatened sectors of the Groznyy and Maikop oil-fields. More large units had been raised in Georgia, Azerbaidzhan and Armenia. As everywhere else, the local population played an active part in defending its land.

The German armies had covered 500 miles in clouds of dust and in 50 degrees centigrade. Its supplies were taking longer and longer to get through; after all, the round trip from the Ruhr took eight weeks by rail. On the road, the tank-lorries consumed a considerable amount of their cargo of fuel on the way. Hitler was annoyed at the consequent slow speed of advance. But since he was even more exasperated by the Russian resistance outside Stalingrad and since he appeared to be obsessed by the name, he forgot the original objectives and after giving von List the Fourth Armoured Army, he took it away from him again to give it back to Paulus, and von List was unable to do anything about it. This did not prevent the Führer from dismissing him at the beginning of September – this really seemed to be Hitler's only way of solving his difficulties.

On the Stalingrad front the Russians had not in fact been content merely to put up a stubborn resistance; they had made a successful counter-attack and driven back the weakest elements of the enemy forces – the Hungarians and Italians. General Messe concluded that it was time to cut the costs and told Mussolini so. Even the Germans were shaken; General von Wieterheim wanted to pull back the spearhead which he had pushed forward on the Volga; General Schmidt had ordered a withdrawal on his own initiative. 'The command had had all it could stand,' reported Halder.

In September, although Novorossiysk had been captured, the first snows put a stop to the German offensive in the Caucasus; an attempt to capture Ordzhonikidze failed. There remained the Stalingrad front. Hitler stubbornly insisted on pursuing the offensive there. A plan was worked out on September 11: the attacks would begin on the 15th, and last for ten days. After violent street fighting the German LI Army Corps succeeded in reaching the Volga at three points. But the Russians were fighting every inch of the way.

In October the line showing the extent of the German advance looked impressive on the map. From Leningrad, the Valday hills and the upper course of the Volga, it skirted Moscow and Tula to the west, followed the Don, touched the loop of the Volga and formed a large curve between the foothills of the Caucasus and Tuapse on the Black Sea. The proposed objectives, however, had not been achieved; the oil wells were out of reach and intermittent and half-hearted raids had done little to reduce their output. Above all, the German defences were strung out dangerously over a distance of 2,165 miles, where 220 divisions were fighting – an average of ten miles per division. These defences were open to enemy counter-attack for something over 625 miles. 'It was a strategic heresy,' wrote Colonel Bernard, 'for to an increasing extent this front also represented a thinly held flank.'

On September 24, 1942, Halder noted in his diary: 'After the daily conference, I was relieved of my post by the Führer; my nerves are worn out and his are not much better; it is time for us to part company.' The time was past when Hitler and his generals worked hand in glove to achieve victory. At the same time Goebbels, in his own diary, was expressing his anxiety about the abnormal life which the Führer was leading, always under strain; he noted his nervous tics and was alarmed at how quickly he was aging.

At least Hitler was not mistaken in thinking himself protected from attack in western Europe. Although Stalin was clamouring for Churchill to attack, the latter was in no position to do so, and the experimental Dieppe raid on August 19, 1942, ended in complete disaster, though offering a wealth of lessons for future attempts, for which no date could yet be fixed. It is true that the Anglo-Saxons were supplying the USSR with modern equipment, via the Arctic Ocean, Iran and even Trans-Siberia. But on his visit to Stalin, Churchill could only reply to his demand for a real second front with fine words, promises – and a treaty of post-war friendship.

So, it was in the USSR that the war was being fought. The problem for the Germans was to retain their conquests against the impending Soviet attacks; but they lost the initiative for the whole winter, which the troops dreaded for its harshness and dangers; but Hitler had lost none of his optimism. Were the Germans' minds at least at rest about their rear areas? How were they running the vast Soviet territories which their armies had conquered and how did they treat the population?

VIII THE GERMAN OCCUPATION IN THE USSR: PRINCIPLES AND ORGANISATIONS

The Wehrmacht's conquests enabled Hitler to orientate the German expansion in the direction he had indicated in *Mein Kampf*: the new Reich continued on the path mapped out by the Teutonic Knights so that 'the German sword shall guarantee the German plough its furrows and the nation its daily bread'. The USSR was merely an extension of the prospects opened up in Poland.

Hitler's intention of destroying the centre of international Communism, first of all eliminating its shield and buckler, the Red Army, and then exploiting its wealth 'for a thousand years', was plain and clear; but although certain ways and means had been tried out in Poland, they had not been worked out in every detail and now that the war was being protracted, it might prove inadvisable to implement certain decisions. There were a number of discernible trends in the generals' ideas as to the right attitude to take. One group of officers who were experts on Russian affairs (Gehlen, Herre, Stauffenberg, Kostring and Wagner), and who were apparently supported by Goebbels, considered it good policy to declare war on Communism but not on the Russian people; some of them were even convinced that Germany and Russia must be reconciled. For the time being, therefore, it was important not to take any excessively harsh measures which would force the Russians to put up a desperate resistance and to adopt an attitude of uncompromising hostility. These soldiers did not have the ear of the Nazi politicians nor even of their leaders, the Wehrmacht general staff.

Rosenberg, the Nazi theorist from the Baltic, the author of one of the régime's bestsellers, *The Myth of the Twentieth Century*, had reached similar conclusions by different means. He proposed splitting up the USSR into a certain number of 'buffer states', to prevent any recrudescence of a powerful Russia. This policy entailed giving support to the separatist movements of the Byelorussians, Caucasians, Ukrainians and peoples of central Asia and treating the conquered peoples with relative moderation.

For Himmler, however, the Slavs were a backward people, subhuman (*Untermenschen*), Asiatics whose vast territories should be colonised by pure Aryans. Moreover, these subhumans were, by their very nature, criminals. An ss pamphlet accused them of 'aspiring to conquer the world', and concluded: 'Europe, defend yourself.' This 'point of view' was supported by Martin Bormann, who had Hitler's ear. The Führer was fond of saying that the frontier between Europe and Asia was not a geographical one but the dividing line between the Germanic world and the Slav. 'For him the Slav, whether he lived under the Tartars, Peter the Great or Stalin, was born to bear the yoke.'

In theory, it was Rosenberg whose responsibility it was to work out German policy in the east. When he announced the forthcoming attack against the USSR, Hitler received him in his office with these words: 'Well, Rosenberg, your great hour has come.' After being given at first a purely planning role, on July 17, 1941, Rosenberg was promoted Minister of the

Occupied Territories in the East. But his powers became operative and grew only as the military government handed the conquered territories over to him. In the area called 'the army zone', the army retained all its powers and the extent of this zone was elastic, depending on how operations were going.

This duality, together with the Red Army's resistance, certainly did not much help the formulation of a definite German policy. Matters were to be further complicated by a third power: Himmler's ss. Both because the OKW had given them the responsibility of establishing a Draconic order in its own zone and ensuring that it was observed, and because Rosenberg, too, was quite willing to let them take repressive action against Jews and Communists in his own territory, the ss became the virtual masters everywhere. Consequently, German behaviour in the conquered territories was at first characterised by a ruthless and indiscriminate terror; and later on, or, more accurately, at the same time, by economic exploitation in which the desire for output was hampered by the equal desire to destroy Communist institutions. In these circumstances, any policy could only be arbitrary and pretty incoherent.

IX THE ADMINISTRATION OF THE CONQUERED AREAS

The Minister of the Occupied Territories had his seat in Berlin. The territories under his administration were divided into Reichscommissariats, which were subdivided into *Generalbezirke* (general regions) and then into *Kreisgebiete* (districts). A German was placed at the head of each division, responsible to Rosenberg but virtually omnipotent. Two Reichscommissariats were set up, one for the Ukraine, the second for the other territories – it was christened *Ostland*, which was no indication of its real boundaries for the future and could only have temporary significance.

In the *Ostland*, Byelorussia, Lithuania, Latvia and Estonia formed relatively autonomous districts, each provided with a capital and an administrator under the supervision of the Commissioner-General, Heinrich Lohse. This method of organisation seemed to indicate that the different nationalities would be respected.

In Rosenberg's mind the Ukraine was to be the largest of the 'buffer states', with a population of 60 million, covering an area of nearly 400,000 square miles and combining the Russian Ukraine with the Polish Ukraine and Czechoslovakian Ruthenia. In actual fact, although established as a Commissariat of the Reich under Erich Koch, the Ukraine had been divided into four. North Bukovina and the Odessa region had been placed under the administration of Romania; Romanian historians had discovered, most opportunely, that the region between the Dniestr and the

Bug had at odd times been under the domination of Moldavian princes; Odessa was thus merely a former Romanian city, so Romania received her reward for her part in the war against the USSR by annexing a new province, Transnistria, from which she immediately gained a considerable item of loot: the Odessa trolley-buses were dismantled and put into service in Craiova.

West Ukraine, with Lvov, was incorporated into the Polish 'General-Government', under Hans Frank; East Ukraine, with Kharkov, remained in the army zone, because of its proximity to the fighting area. The Reichs-commissariat was therefore confined to central Ukraine, including Kiev; in addition there was the territory of Pinsk and that part of Byelorussia which was formerly Polish.

In the territories under Rosenberg's authority only the minor officials were locally recruited, and kept under close German control. In the towns, municipal corporations were in charge of rubbish collection, public order and the registration of births, marriages and deaths; the 'agricultural offices' and 'labour exchanges' made it easier for the Germans to exploit the available resources. Burgomasters and, in the villages, elders were appointed by the German authorities, to whom they were responsible.

In all the territories the German authorities pretended that there was no governing class. On principle, no 'native' was appointed to any political or economic, or even less to any cultural office of importance. Exceptions to this rule were made only in the case of the Baltic states, where nationalist elements had taken part in the Red Army's defeat and enabled the Wehrmacht to advance towards Leningrad.

The inhabitants were everywhere else subjected to systematic humiliation by the occupiers and had to register with the police. They were forbidden to leave their homes without prior permission; they had no right to use the water from the wells and tanks near the German garrisons; they were free to go out only in daytime; at night, the patrols automatically opened fire on anyone infringing these regulations.

All these measures were, of course, partly explained by the proximity to the front with all its fluctuations; they did not necessarily represent the policy which the Germans intended following or would have followed after the war, a policy which they did not have time to work out in detail or even less to put into practice. It was nevertheless in keeping with the ideas which Hitler had always expressed. For the time being, the inhabitants could scarcely see it as a war of 'liberation'; it was hardly calculated to make them friendly towards the Germans; it nullified the effects of the Wehrmacht's propaganda about collaboration. Moreover, its harshness was intensified by economic exploitation and repression which was both indiscriminate and systematic. The USSR gave the Germans the chance of extending the methods first used against the Poles to a greater number of potential slaves.

X ECONOMIC EXPLOITATION

The task of developing the occupied territories in the 'capitalist' manner was entrusted to experts and technicians formed into *Wirtschaftskommandos* (economic control groups). Soviet citizens were thus given the chance of seeing capitalist societies – of which they knew nothing – at work – the Eastern General Coal Board, the Eastern Iron Company, etc.

However, the rational exploitation, already complicated by the setting up of new structures, was first of all hindered by the destruction carried out by the Red Army as it withdrew and even more by the demands of the military, which was being forced more and more to live from hand to mouth in the occupied territories. In order to harmonise the points of view, the economic authorities appointed representatives – *Referenten* – to the military commands. But the standpoints were too diverse to make concerted action always possible.

The result was that plundering became the rule and the economy could not be restored, let alone transformed. The armies were the more inclined to use local resources as supplies were experiencing greater difficulty and delays in arriving from Germany. So the soldiers did not go short of meat and bread but they were provided by killing off livestock and sometimes by requisitioning seed crops. Thus agricultural production decreased. It was the same for industrial production. The factories were generally not reopened because future plans made no provision for them in vassal states reduced to a strictly agricultural economy. But when, as was rare, reparations were decided upon, they came up against power shortage and lack of raw materials or machinery, so the Germans confined themselves to seizing stocks and dismantling equipment that could be salvaged and sent back to the Reich. This practice of continually helping themselves to produce completely paralysed any commercial activity.

On the financial plane, German purchases caused prices to rise and the issue of an occupation mark brought inflation; officials and employees particularly suffered from this. New taxes were levied: per head, per household and according to the number of windows, as well as on dogs and cats. The few banks which remained open were aimed at siphoning off the inhabitants' savings towards Germany.

All these badly co-ordinated measures could but impoverish the population; in the long run they would have proved detrimental to the occupier himself by exhausting his source of supplies. It was probably this consideration which determined the Germans' agrarian policy. A few sovkhozes were broken up and the land given to German settlers. Russian historians mention the names of 'barons' of the former Czarist régime who recovered their estates – such as Baron von Bilderding in the Volodanskoe sovkhoze and the big landowner Beck in the sovkhozes of Gari, Vichenka and Iskra, in the Don regions. These ghosts from the past were given the freehold of thousands of acres and sometimes several villages. According to Soviet historians, they seized cattle and agricultural machinery and reintroduced forced labour.

Similarly, the first intention had been to break up the kolkhozes and to distribute the land among the peasants, the amount depending on their degree of submissiveness. But to avoid the risk of poor harvests, it seemed wiser to follow an intermediate system, the *obscina* (commune). In actual fact, this organisation revived the kolkhoze under another name; it allocated seed, horses and agricultural equipment, and assigned the chief tasks. The peasants kept only their houses and a piece of land of something over an acre. These communes gradually changed into co-operative farms, supplemented by 'centres of agricultural progress' under the control of German agronomists.

This may have been a wise measure in order to avoid too rapid a change but it was not understood by the peasants: on the one hand, they had been promised land and not been given it; on the other hand, requisitioning took away their cattle and crops. General Messe tells how this disappointment was expressed in the disillusioned phrase: 'At least Stalin left us with a cow, but Hitler has taken that away from us.' Moreover, preserving institutions meant retaining the technical experts. By this device the Communists who were formerly managers of kolkhozes or sovkhozes, retained or regained a small degree of power.

However, the most serious and dramatic procedure and the one arousing the keenest and most lasting resentment, was the requisitioning of labour. Thus in Orel, in November 1941, horses and smithies were confiscated and boilermen and carpenters commandeered to work to fight the cold. Then special services, *Arbeitsämter*, were gradually set up everywhere to organise forced labour. At the beginning they made attractive propositions to persuade people to go to Germany of their own free will. It very quickly became apparent that a systematic mobilisation of labour was necessary by combing whole regions; each place had to supply its own contingent and the burgomasters or elders were made responsible for seeing that they were provided.

Thus workers from Krivoy Rog and the Donetz were sent to the industrial centres of the Ruhr. To make up for the lack of tractors, peasants from Northern Ukraine were transferred to Southern Ukraine. Places left deserted by their inhabitants when they retreated with the Red Army were forcibly repopulated by taking people from elsewhere. These compulsory migrations affecting millions of men and women were accompanied by brutal and coercive measures, including harsh sanctions against anyone refusing to comply or against their relatives. They were in themselves already the first step towards a reign of terror.

XI TERROR AS A SYSTEM OF GOVERNMENT

Both before and after the invasion of the USSR, a series of decisions had been taken by the highest authorities of the Reich to safeguard the troops and also to exterminate Communists and Jews. To this end, in March 1941, before the invasion of the USSR, Himmler had been given 'special responsibilities . . . arising from the final decisive struggle between two opposing political systems'. This euphemism was a cover for the following measures.

In May Keitel had ordered that 'no pity' should be shown to civilians guilty of acts hostile to the German troops; they were to be shot on the spot, at the discretion of the officer in charge. On the other hand, German soldiers who committed offences against these civilians would be treated with great leniency: 'They will not necessarily be liable to punishment, even if they have committed a military crime.' On July 16, 1941, Hitler had spelt out this unlimited power of arbitrary punishment with his usual laconic ruthlessness: 'Shoot everyone who gives you a black look.'

On July 17 Himmler took over all security in the occupied territories. Each high official in Rosenberg's ministry was given an SS deputy appointed by Himmler and answerable to him.

The same day the Gestapo issued the order to exterminate those Soviet prisoners of war who 'represented a danger to the Reich'. On the instructions of the OKW it had been clearly understood as early as May 10 that political commissars would not be regarded as prisoners of war: 'They were liable to the death penalty in transit camps . . . without worrying about unnecessary considerations.'

On July 23, Keitel added a gloss to his ruthless decision of May. 'The army,' he said, 'must spread terror so as to nip in the bud any temptation to resist.'

The territories near the front were not the only ones to be affected by these measures, which might have been explained there as a safeguard for the army. On August 22, Rosenberg extended them to the territories under his allegedly civil jurisdiction. 'Any crime against the Reich and its army,' he decreed, 'the creation of any sort of atmosphere hostile to the Germans or any refusal to obey the orders of the military authorities . . .' would be punishable by death.

Thus all the occupying authorities, civil and military, in all the territories were unanimous in setting up a reign of terror. In his order of October 10, 1941, General von Reichenau defined the reasons for it as follows: 'It is to obliterate Asian influence on European culture; it is in this way that we shall fulfil our historic mission by liberating the German people for ever from the Jewish and Asian peril.'

The system was now established. The man responsible for these odious tasks was Heinrich Himmler and his ss. He was to be a thoroughly efficient executioner of a people.

The Soviet prisoners of war were the first victims of the harsh treatment which had been decreed; they were crowded together into improvised camps where, dying of starvation, they were doomed to destroy, if not even to devour, one another; later on they were sent to Germany and many of them vanished without trace in concentration camps – notably in Auschwitz. But Soviet deserters were treated no better; instead of separating them from the other prisoners and giving them preferential treatment, the Germans looked upon them with the greatest contempt.

All the conquered regions were the scenes of coldly premeditated acts of extermination. Countless examples were quoted at the Nuremberg tribunal. The Gestapo had drawn up lists of people condemned out of hand. A 'special' battalion called 'Nightingale' and belonging to the Brandenburg regiment was put in charge of the executions. According to one witness, 'the men burst into houses, dragged out the inhabitants and killed them in the backyard. In this way 3,000 lawyers, engineers and doctors were massacred.'

Operations of this kind were entrusted to special units, the *Einsatzgruppen*, who had already learned their trade in Poland. These units were attached to the armies; they were not dependent on them but they received any help they required from them. Their leaders were men from the criminal police and the Gestapo, the soldiers of the ss. They had served their apprenticeship in a police barracks at Pretsch on the Elbe, near Leipzig. Heydrich, the chief of the security forces of the Nazi party, had given them his orders in person. The *Einsatzgruppen* were instructed to carry out the 'liquidation of Jews and political commissars'. They recruited 'local volunteers' on the spot.

It was these *Einsatzgruppen* who started the gassing of the 'Reich's enemies' in the USSR. R. Hoess, the commander of the Auschwitz camp, explained how they set about it. The victims were first of all suffocated in lorries by the exhaust gases from the engines. They then acted as guinea-pigs to try out the gas *Zyclon-B*, which had been developed by the Reich's chemists. 'The Russians,' wrote Hoess, 'were made to undress in an entrance-hall and then they went into a specially fitted-out room under the pretence of being deloused.' The bodies were afterwards burnt on huge pyres.

General Messe, the commander of the Italian expeditionary force, had watched the Germans' harsh behaviour in the USSR all the more closely because by denouncing it he could have the pleasure of revenging himself for the way in which his German colleagues had wounded his pride. He concluded a report to Mussolini by noting a 'clear split between the conquerors and those they were dominating'. But he added this justifiable condemnation:

> If the will for power, perfect military organisation and a spirit of discipline enabled the Germans to conquer vast territories, only a sense of justice and an understanding of the needs and mind of the people could have guaranteed that they would consolidate them. Up to now, on the eastern front the German people has shown that it possesses the first qualities in the highest degree; they cannot be said to have given any sign of possessing the second to an equal or sufficient extent.

Although the Soviet peoples thus had the spectacular privilege of providing Nazi Germany with the greatest number of martyrs, the fate of the Poles and Yugoslavs was no better. To varying degrees, all the peoples of occupied Europe were realising, to their cost, what the future had in store for them at the hands of the master race, whose slaves they would become as a result of the Wehrmacht's victory.

CHAPTER 3

The Domination of Europe

I CONSEQUENCES OF THE WAR IN THE USSR

THE German–Soviet confrontation involved numbers of men and quantities of equipment which were without equal in the Second World War and historically without precedent. It brought about a complete change in the character of the war because of the vastness of the operational area, the high casualties and the long duration and relentlessness of the struggle. It was goodbye to the Blitzkrieg, which had started off with such jubilation, and to total and decisive victory won at the cost of slight losses which were amply compensated for by the immense spoils obtained, the territories conquered and the opponents who had been defeated. Nowhere else had the German soldier been exposed to such intense and prolonged suffering against an opponent tougher than himself. If the corps of general officers had been alarmed by the difficulties encountered and initial failures, the German soldier was even more demoralised by the 'Russian hell', and envied his comrades who had remained in the west waiting for a hypothetical British attack against the 'fortress of Europe'. Replacements had to be found for those who had fallen in battle or were exhausted. It was necessary to renew, increase and improve equipment and weapons which were always quite insufficient for their needs and quickly became unserviceable because of the vast distances they had to cover in summer and the bad winter weather against which they were helpless. In short, it had become a war of attrition, uncertain in its outcome and of unforeseeable duration.

Germany could no longer depend on winning it in a short, sharp and successful sweep with irresistible Panzer divisions supported by an all-conquering Luftwaffe. She had to mobilise all her resources and send into action all her able-bodied men. She thus came face to face with a contradiction: every German worker in uniform and up at the front was now one less in the factory producing her armaments. There was only one possible solution: maximum exploitation of the territories which had been conquered by the Wehrmacht or which its victories had forced into the Reich's orbit. So much, then, for the great plans for the future and the differential treatment of subjugated peoples. Everything had to be sacri-

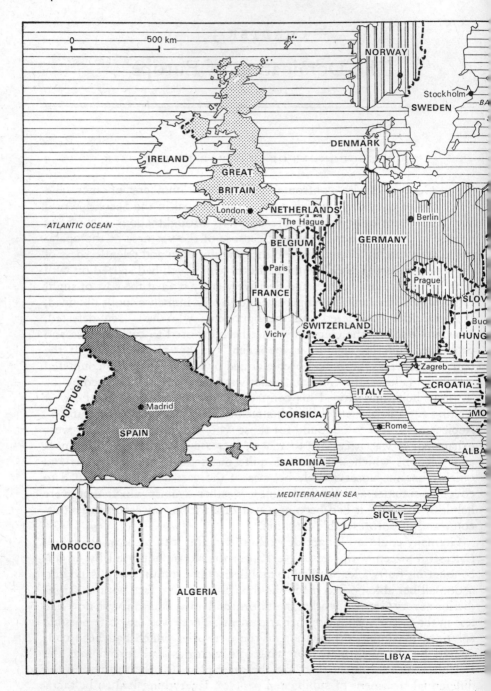

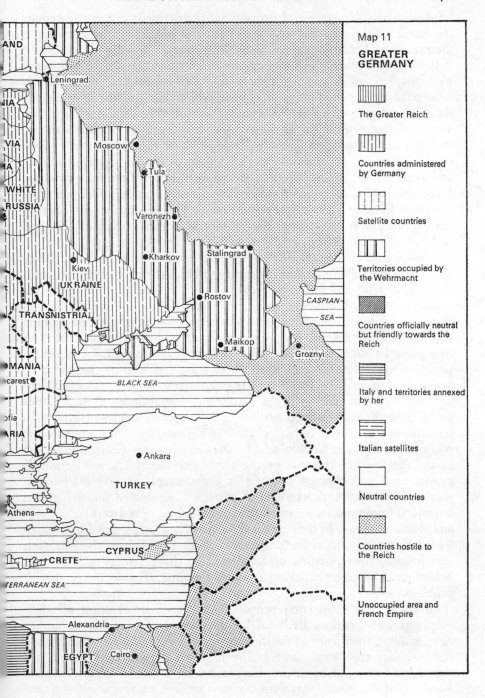

Map 11

GREATER GERMANY

The Greater Reich

Countries administered by Germany

Satellite countries

Territories occupied by the Wehrmacht

Countries officially neutral but friendly towards the Reich

Italy and territories annexed by her

Italian satellites

Neutral countries

Countries hostile to the Reich

Unoccupied area and French Empire

ficed to victory. If necessary, Europe would be drained of its raw materials, foodstuffs, machinery and manpower for the benefit of the conqueror. Germany was becoming an insatiable Minotaur.

It was consequently an inopportune moment to pander to the occupied peoples and to put on a show of 'correctness' and benevolence. Goebbels' propaganda was, of course, still trying to win over to the Reich volunteers who were in favour of anti-Bolshevism, anti-Semitism and the Europe of the future. In every country, groups of collaborators, motivated by conviction or by self-interest, were recruiting men to fight on the Russian front, repeating all the slogans of the *Propaganda-Abteilung* and assisting the various German police forces in their infamous tasks. Frenchmen were denouncing other Frenchmen; French policemen were arresting Jews or French resisters; French businessmen were offering French produce to the enemy. No country in Europe completely escaped collaboration except Poland; yet in no country did the collaborators succeed in convincing and rallying the great mass of the population. They remained everywhere in the minority, filling their countrymen with surprise, distrust and finally hatred.

Nazi domination was now showing its true colours. It came down on the conquered peoples with a system of repressive measures first suffered by the German people, but now extended and intensified. The first foreigners to suffer were the Poles and Russians but all the occupied peoples were affected in their turn. Fines were followed by the taking of hostages; warnings by shootings; imprisonment by deportation to concentration camps. The growing extent and importance of their duties made Himmler and his men no longer just 'special troops', confined to ignominious and secret tasks, but the real and undisguised masters of the régime. The Abwehr was replaced by the Gestapo, the Wehrmacht by the ss and the military tribunal by the torture-chamber. Europe became a prison, until such time as it would be a graveyard. Among the peoples thus terrorised certain categories of pariahs were singled out for special attention: Communists, the ever-growing numbers of resisters of all kinds and above all, Jews. In the first flush of victory, which seemed to guarantee impunity and then in fear and anger at their first defeats, the Nazis put into practice their doctrine of racialism, the driving force behind their behaviour. They were working towards the final solution to the Jewish problem.

However, the subjugated peoples were gradually shaking off their inertia and resignation. Reduced by the occupier to a state of underdevelopment, their very existence threatened as individuals, families and nations, they took new heart at the news of the stubbornness of the British, and above all of the Soviets' unshakeable determination. All over Europe, the Resistance was forming into groups, arming itself and preparing for action in the war of liberation. Europe was indeed being built but in suffering and in hope, not in accordance with the Nazis' orders but in defiance of them.

II POLITICAL DOMINATION

Hitler may have been clear in his own mind how the world would be organised as the result of German victory, but either deliberately or from expediency, he disclosed only fragments of his plans. Since they were often apparently contradictory, and even incoherent, there is every reason to believe that they were somewhat confused and far from being properly thought out. It is true that various German organisations set about drawing up plans, arguing fiercely about who had originated the ideas and what was to be gained from implementing them. In practice, everyone took part in a more or less co-ordinated way: Ribbentrop as Foreign Minister; Goering as Economic Director of the Reich; Rosenberg as Party theoretician and Minister for the Occupied Territories in the East; Himmler as the man responsible for ensuring the purity of the race; and also Goebbels, who had to give some substance to his propaganda arguments by providing tangible evidence of their application.

In June 1942, the ss Oberführer, Professor Dr Konrad Meyer, completed a very detailed plan to ensure Nazi domination in eastern Europe, the *Generalplan Ost*. The whole scheme was envisaged from the German viewpoint: rural colonisation and the creation of a 'healthy peasantry', involving the 'appropriate biological selection'; urban colonisation, leaving the Reich with 'complete freedom of planning'; and the creation of colonised districts in which the administration of justice was in the hands of German authorities and 'ss tribunals'. The estimated cost of the prospective 'reconstruction' took all possible factors into account, including removal, propaganda and 'supervisory' expenses. For example, 'the cost of providing space for one worker' was estimated at 'between 6,000 and 10,000 marks', depending on the type of industry. It is true that costs were to be met partly by 'reparations exacted from defeated enemies', and by 'the creation of a special capital fund formed from all the economic assets of the region to be reconstructed' – that is, from the contributions of the conquered people themselves. As for labour, a broad appeal was to be made to the forcibly tamed or naturally servile masses of prisoners of war, common-law criminals and those commandeered for forced labour. At no time were the rights of any communities or individuals to be taken into account and even less were their own requests to be met or even given a hearing. The whole thing was governed with pseudo-scientific rigour by a geopolitical law which Dr Meyer stated as follows: 'To re-

concile the space to be colonised with the available human resources.'
This would require a period of five 'lustres'.

This splendid scheme concerned, it is true, only one part of occupied
Europe – the east. But Dr Meyer, in his far-sighted wisdom, stressed that
it could be realised only if the whole Reich – including the countries of
western Europe – worked towards it. What the Nazis wanted to impose
on Europe was thus a colonial type of domination, systematised and based
on the principle of deliberate toughness.

It is probable that on the whole Hitler shared this way of thinking, even
if it had not been inspired by the ideas which he had expressed or was
supposed to have expressed. But because of lack of time it proved impossible for this vast project to be fully carried out. The alarming way in
which the war was developing was also forcing the Führer to give most
of his time and thought primarily to the conduct of operations. In short,
the political and administrative organisation of occupied Europe was,
except in a few points, less the result of plans for the future than of
present demands.

Thus, although generally convinced that it would be a source of strength
and an advantage to Germany to expand eastwards, Hitler had not completely given up the idea of a colonial empire overseas; but apart from the
Reich's recovery of the colonies lost in 1918, thus making reparation for the
harm that had been unfairly inflicted on her, he avoided speaking about
colonies, either because he did not wish to cause the French generals to
defect to de Gaulle, or because in certain areas – notably in Morocco – he
was competing with the ambitions of Franco or Mussolini or because he
wanted to maintain the chance of a peaceful compromise with Britain.

Some light is thrown on the Führer's motives by, among other things,
the monologue which he inflicted on some of his generals, as was his wont,
on July 1, 1943. He put forward the principle that force was not enough to
establish total domination; of course, it remained the crucial factor, but
equally important was the intangible psychological factor *required by a
tamer to dominate his animals*. This circus image showed Hitler's elevated
ideas about the relationship between vanquished and vanquishers in their
true light. At no time were the national interests of the conquered territories to stand in the way of the vanquisher's vital interests. For the
Ukraine, for example, the Führer made it clear that if necessary he would
say that he would build an independent state there; he would say it
deliberately, but this would not mean that he would do it. Then, paraphrasing *Mein Kampf*, Hitler concluded: 'It is living space which is at stake
in our fight.' According to him, it was not possible to have a great army
and a powerful industry within a confined area. What constituted the
strength of the Russian empire was not purely human strength, either in
quantity or above all if one considers the personal quality of individuals;

it was the strength of her gigantic empire. This nonsense did at least lead to one practical conclusion: Germany would not hesitate to seize those territories whose annexation seemed necessary for her greatness and power or simply for her well-being.

The inequality of rights and the temporary differences in status in Nazi-dominated Europe at the end of 1942, when it had reached its greatest extent, were not necessarily any indication of its future fate. They were nevertheless in keeping, as a whole, with views which had been expressed many a time by the Führer or his faithful henchmen.

III THE STATUS OF NAZI EUROPE

At the heart of Europe, as if its convenient geographical position was an invitation to her mission, lay the German Reich, that is the Germany which had emerged from the Treaty of Versailles, with the addition of Austria, the Sudeten Germans, the western part of Poland (Wartheland), Luxemburg, Alsace-Lorraine and Eupen and Malmédy; a small part of Slovenia had been taken from Yugoslavia and the former Polish district of Bialystok was again attached to east Prussia. All these territories were under German law and administration. They were both Germanised and Nazified. However, all the *Volksdeutsche* were not yet united; for those in Schleswig and Transylvania it was obviously only a matter of time; those in the Volga area would join the mother country once the USSR had been defeated. The Tyroleans had begun to leave their region; but after the Italian surrender it seemed more advisable to ask them to remain where they were and to annex their territory. As for those Alsatians who had taken refuge in France, even in the so-called free zone, the occupying authorities did not rest until the Vichy government had either handed them over or forced them to return to Alsace, whether they were Strasbourgers who had retreated to the Dordogne, young people from the work camps or legionaries. There were plans to make Brazilian Germans return to the bosom of the nation. On the other hand, foreigners who had settled on German territory without permission were expelled – Poles from the Poznan district and Silesia, or Lorrainers.

Hitler seems to have toyed with the idea of widening somewhat the concept of the Germanic race. In the course of a conversation with Goering on June 19, 1940 he had quoted Norwegians, Flemings and *Burgundians* as Germanic peoples. In his *Table-Talk* he one day added the Normans. According to Dr Globke's cross-examination at Nuremberg, Hitler had given Stuckart, an official from the Ministry of Internal Affairs, the task of drawing up a scheme to divide France up in this way. Nazi geopolitics was not an exact science.

It was obviously to serve this German 'nucleus' of the master race that the territories without any clearly defined status, the 'General Government', Cracow, the *Ostland* and the Ukraine were 'kept in reserve', and marked out for German colonisation in the footsteps of the Teutonic Knights.

In theory, Italy was Germany's fully-fledged ally and equal. In fact only comparatively small and economically unimportant territories had been annexed by her and had come into her sphere: a few high French Alpine valleys and part of Menton; a section of Epirus and Thessaly and the Dalmatian coast and its islands. In addition the Italian armistice commissions dictated what was to be done on the left bank of the Rhône, in North Africa and the Near Eastern states. Croatia was to become a kingdom with a member of the House of Savoy as its king. But Hitler no longer had confidence in any Italian except Mussolini. And in most of Europe there was no part left for Italy to play.

Next to the Germans were the protected states: Bohemia–Moravia, Norway and Holland. In a Slav world doomed to slavery Bohemia-Moravia had a special place, for she belonged to Greater Germany; although it was intended that she should be progressively Germanised, she retained a diplomatic representative in Berlin and her president had the right to the honours accorded a foreign head of state. As for Norway and Holland, they had the privilege of governing themselves under the supervision of a German civil administrator, but they too were to play a part in the 'colonisation of the east'. The 'Dutch Company for the East' was set up in the Hague. Since 1941 peasants and artisans had been settled on the Vistula by a 'Dutch Company for providing Directors of Development for Eastern Europe'. In military-occupied Belgium, the Flemings, whose prisoners of war had been released, were recruited, to the same end, by the 'Belgian-European Syndicate for Agricultural and Industrial Expansion'.

However, as Quisling in Norway was most definitely not succeeding in winning the support and confidence of the Norwegians, Terboven was gradually induced to replace incompetent Norwegians in senior administrative posts by Germans. The same thing happened in Holland, where under the control of Seyss-Inquart, the Nazi system of compulsory grouping of peasants, fishermen, workers, etc., in one single corporation was introduced.

The territories of great strategic importance were answerable to the military authority. This was the case in the occupied zone of France, in Belgium (to which the Nord and the Pas-de-Calais were attached),[1] in Greece (with control shared between Germans, Bulgarians and Italians) and in the Channel Islands, which were treated according to the laws of war since a state of hostility existed between Britain and Germany.

1. In July 1944 Belgium was given a civil high commissioner – but not for long.

Denmark and the so-called free zone in France, even after its occupation in November 1942, retained governments theoretically independent but more or less subject to the German military authority.

The Greater Reich was surrounded by a circle of satellite states, which either by choice or by force had thrown in their lot with Germany in the war against the USSR. Slovakia, Romania and Croatia had slightly differing Fascist régimes – in Slovakia it was rather like Italian Fascism, in Romania there was no single party, and in Croatia the government was dependent on Italy until September 1943. The German minorities there enjoyed special rights. Only Hungary and Bulgaria had succeeded in retaining their own institutions, although there had admittedly never been anything democratic about them.

Finally, Spain was the ideological ally of the Greater Reich, and Sweden, which Rosenberg regarded as the Aryans' land of origin, had moved into its economic orbit.

Thus the Greater Reich was like a harlequin's coat tailored out of shreds and patches. The multiplicity of German authorities wrought the greatest confusion. In two particular ways, however, urgency brought about unity; throughout, the main factor was to achieve success for Germany and everywhere there reigned the same repressive system of supervision and punishments.

IV THE GREATER REICH'S FINANCES

In every country to which they came as conquerors, the German armies did not scruple to live off the inhabitants by levies, looting and commandeering. The occupying authorities did not continue these ruthless methods; they handled matters more subtly by making large purchases and then leaving the inhabitants to whistle for their money. On every occasion it proved a lucrative operation, and always ended by sending to Germany all those products which were considered useful while her own products never left the country. Psychologically, the occupied peoples were under the mistaken impression that they were not being plundered, and the behaviour of the Germans appeared to them correct in commercial and human terms.

One of the first methods consisted in over-valuing the mark in relation to the currency of the conquered countries. Generally this rate remained stable, like that of a strong currency; but now and again it was regularly increased, as, for example, in Romania. One result was to restrict the purchase of German goods, which became more expensive; a second, linked with this, was to allow the Germans to purchase more at lower prices in the occupied countries. The German soldiers were the first to benefit and they were able to strip the shops with impunity.

The cost of supporting the occupation troops fell on the conquered countries (except in Denmark, which had not taken part in the fighting). The amount was fixed not in terms of the number of German soldiers in a country but according to her supposed wealth; in France, at 400 million francs per day, it was out of all proportion to the size of the occupation troops. Naturally, once the expenses of the troops' upkeep had been met, the occupiers still had considerable amounts left over. These they used to buy everything that there was to buy; what is more, they paid those foreign workers who had come to work in the Reich in the currency of their own country. Finally, with the national currency they bought shares in the national economy of every country. There was, of course, some awareness of the dangers of inflation; but the principle had been established that nothing should stand in the way of goods being sent to Germany; it was merely a question of making sure that inflation did not rise too steeply. At the end of February 1944 the Reich's Finance Minister, Schwerin von Krosigk, estimated that Germany had received about 47 thousand million marks through occupation charges alone – and of those about 25 thousand million came from France.

However, this was not the only way in which money was raised. Added to this were the costs of billeting the troops and of improving their quarters. In every country, for a mere trifle, fines were regularly inflicted on the occupied cities – in January 1941 Stavanger had to pay 100,000 crowns.

Unlike her opponents, Germany had entered the war without any currency reserves to finance her purchases. However, even before the war she had perfected an ingenious method of managing without them: this was the clearing-system. She continually extended it while at the same time distorting it so that it worked only one way – to her advantage. The purpose of the clearing-system was, in fact, to balance purchases and sales between two countries. Now, in all the occupied countries Germany quickly contracted widespread debts; the goods of the contracting party went to Germany but it received nothing in exchange; trains set off full and returned empty – assuming that even the engines and coaches returned at all. Germany promised to settle her debt but only after the war. In the meantime, the occupied countries had to find a way of paying their own exporters. In the summer of 1944 the same Minister of Finance, Schwerin von Krosigk, estimated the German debt at some 36 thousand million marks.

Finally, in order to nip inflation in the bud, or to prevent deliberate inflation in a specific country of the kind practised by the Weimar Republic, the Reich kept a watchful eye on the institutions issuing national currencies; sometimes, as in Holland, it appointed a fervent and reliable

Nazi national at the head: sometimes, as for the Bank of France, it insisted on appointing a German comptroller with the right of veto.

As for private banks, either they played along with the occupier of their own accord in order to remain in existence, or else they came under his control. The Czech banks, for example, had to merge into four large institutions, in which German banks took over the majority of the shares. The intention was to restrict normal credit operations in order to keep them exclusively for fulfilling the needs of the Reich.

Thus in financial matters the whole of occupied Europe came under the same law, which looked forward to the post-war period when the mark would become international currency. The machinery for sucking the European economy dry was now ready.

V ECONOMIC EXPLOITATION

In every occupied country, the Germans' practice of requisitioning goods of all kinds by exercising the rights of the stronger continued virtually throughout the whole war. Generally speaking, it was more ruthless and cynical in eastern Europe. But on September 23, 1940, the French delegation to the Armistice Commission denounced the 'removal from factories and warehouses of plant or of goods'. At Pétain's trial a reliable witness estimated the number of French machine-tools which had been dismantled and taken away to Germany at 25,000.

Now that the financial machinery was working smoothly, looting of the occupied countries gave way to apparently normal trading. To pay for their purchases, the occupying authorities were able to add to the national currencies, which continued to swell their coffers, the assets in precious metals and jewels which they had seized from the banks, as well as the occupation marks printed by the *Reichskreditkassen* – in the summer of 1942 there were fifty-two in Europe – a currency which totally lacked any surety and could be increased indefinitely as the Germans wished, without the financial authorities of the occupied countries even being informed. Germany thus absorbed vast amounts of produce through the standard type of commercial transaction. All kinds of agencies and shady organisations, as well as many middlemen attracted by the profit, offered their services to German firms, so that the producers did not always realise who their real customers were nor their nationality.

To make the transactions even more profitable the occupying authorities fixed prices in such a way as to benefit Germany alone. Thus Romania let her have oil at the pre-war price but had to pay 50 per cent more for German imports.

All the economic transactions of occupied Europe were channelled into the Reich or her satellites. For France this meant a basic reshaping of her foreign trade. Germany had become dominant in central Europe even before the war, but this now turned into a monopoly. Thus Romania's exports to Germany rose from 63 per cent of her total exports in 1940 to 90 per cent in 1941 and 98·77 per cent in 1943; this included in particular the whole of her oil.

To the extent in which large-scale plans for the future were contemplated, it could be seen that Germany was aiming at a virtual monopoly of European industry after the war, especially in the field of metallurgy and chemistry; Berlin would also become the centre of the arts, letters, fashion and entertainment, radiating German culture. The remainder of Europe would be reduced to an agricultural economy and deprived of all intellectual prestige.

For the time being it was essential to direct the output of the various countries towards satisfying the needs of the German war economy and if possible increasing it. To this end, German experts were despatched more or less everywhere, particularly to Romania. All over Europe orders placed by the German authorities were eagerly sought after on the market, even in the so-called free zone of France. To avoid stagnation the manufacturers had to try to satisfy them before anything else, since they otherwise ran the immediate risk of not receiving the raw materials and the power supplies which they needed.

It was more difficult to command obedience from the agricultural producers, because there were so many of them. The occupying authorities encouraged them to form corporate groups, so as to have men at the head who would be answerable to them. In this way they bought up most of the foodstuffs; almost the whole of the poultry and dairy produce from Denmark and Holland made their way to the Reich. But it was easier for the peasants than for the manufacturers to use guile and trickery and keep a part of their crops for themselves.

The Germans' wealth of paper currency enabled them to attempt a vast programme of expropriation. In the field of agriculture, this was carried out by establishing settlers, a prerogative which was not restricted to eastern Europe, since huge experimental collective farms were set up in Holland and in the Ardennes in France. In the sphere of industry, mining, banking and commerce, it consisted of buying large shares in industrial or other concerns. They began with foreign interests in the satellite countries – for example, French interests in the mines at Bor in Yugoslavia or in Romanian oil. But they quickly extended their interest to the largest and most varied concerns within the country itself. Thus in France German firms came to own 51 per cent of the shares of Francolor, the Société vinicole de Champagne, Carburants français, Gazogènes Imbert, and many others. The shares were paid for at above the quoted price in order to attract sellers. The biggest firms were 'sounded': Schneider, Westinghouse, Rhône-Poulenc, insurance companies, Saint Gobain and Hutchinson. The horrified General Hutziger one day remarked in the presence of the German Hemmen: 'You can buy up the whole of France.' To another Frenchman who was alarmed at German demands during some hard bargaining and who, in exasperation, eventually asked, 'Look here, what do you want?', another German replied, with the most brutal frankness, 'We want the lot.' So the German seizure of industrial and commercial property in Europe began.[1]

Naturally, the ever-increasing specialisation of the European economy along the lines desired by the Reich and the fact that it was so closely subjected to the latter's needs necessitated considerable movement of labour. The occupying authorities generally fixed wages and conditions of work – not always on terms unfavourable to the workers, if the comparison is based only on the nominal wages of the pre-war period. Besides, labour very quickly came forward of its own accord, for in the general slump almost the only guaranteed employment was with the Germans. The latter took advantage of this to send volunteers to work in Germany. Then, as the result of the enormous increase in the Germans' needs, volunteers were no longer enough, despite the appeal to humanitarian feelings by operations like 'relieving prisoners of war' which Laval engineered in France. It therefore became necessary to use force. This task was given to Gauleiter Sauckel. He set up 'Compulsory Labour Service' throughout Europe. Those commandeered were sometimes employed in their own country working for example, in the Todt organisation, on fortifications such as the 'Atlantic Wall'. But more often than not they were sent to Germany, where several million workers found themselves all living together – there were 600,000 from France – from every nation in Europe, with a majority of Soviet and Polish nationals. Most of them were workers and young men, but there were women also.

The exploitation of Europe, however disguised, was nonetheless tantamount to actual looting. It had disastrous consequences for the people. Despite every effort to nip it in the bud, monetary inflation was inevitable; it resulted in an 'unofficial market' and a rise in prices. Scandalous fortunes were made through collaboration with the conqueror. But the majority of the population lived in increasing hardship: food was rationed and sometimes there was none at all. Vital products – medicines, for example – became scarce and as a result public health and hygiene suffered. It was the workers and employees with fixed salaries who were most badly affected. But the ruling classes were not always satisfied either; although certain businessmen were able to speculate and grow

1. The 'Aryanisation' of firms for racialist reasons offered excellent possibilities for expropriation. Cf. the section 'The Fate of the Jews', page 266.

rich, many were capitalist property-owners who had been dispossessed or were in danger of being so. In every walk of life the occupiers' financial and economic policy thus aroused discontent which could only be increased by the severity and harshness of their police.

VI THE SECURITY OF THE REICH

As long as the people remained passive and resigned and the Germans continued to be successful in battle – these two factors were interdependent – the occupying authorities behaved correctly, at least in western Europe, for in the east they were brutal from the beginning. Things changed, or became worse, at the first setbacks and the first signs of opposition.

In order to forestall any danger, the Germans had taken the precaution of occupying solid positions of authority in the machinery of justice and the police services of each country. On the one hand, the German military tribunals had jurisdiction over everything concerned with safeguarding the German Army or the behaviour of German groups and nationals. On the other hand, the occupying authorities put pressure on the national judiciaries to take matters out of their hands or make them release protégés of theirs who had been charged.

In accordance with the Hague conventions, the police of the occupied countries were to maintain law and order: they were therefore serving the occupier. However, the latter employed them for unpleasant operations which aroused the inhabitants' indignation and hostility: for guarding military establishments, arresting Jews, suggesting hostages, identity checks, etc.

Above all, throughout every country, the Germans established their own police network and one which was particularly formidable and complex. The military commands had their own police services, whose task it was to maintain liaison with the national police – the *Geheime Feldpolizei* and *Feldgendarmerie*. For the purposes of intelligence and counter-espionage they had 'special services' – the Abwehr.

However, the duality of the police services, which had been an established fact in the Reich since 1938, did not take long to emerge in occupied Europe, too. The RSHA (*Reichssicherheitshauptamt*), under Heydrich, which combined the normal state security police with the security service of the ss (*Sicherheitsdienst*), wanted to establish itself in the territories occupied by the Reich to carry out the racialist tasks required of it. It intended supplanting the Abwehr and forcing itself on the Army. Of the seven departments of the RSHA, two were particularly important;

Map 12 **THE WHOLE OF FRANCE A PRISON**

Each dot represents a political prison or internment camp

counter-espionage, which included the teams of men who had the task of tracking down those guilty of crimes against the security of the state (*Geheime Staatspolizei*, or Gestapo), and the department (called *Amt VI*) which claimed the sole right to obtain and exploit military intelligence, at the expense of the Abwehr.

The nationals of the occupied countries who seemed indisposed to accept the new state of affairs soon discovered, to their cost, what the German police forces – who were agreed on this point – had in store for them.

Polizeihaft, or police detention, was the punishment for those who, by reason of their possible Communist, anarchist or Resistance – in France, Gaullist – activity, were considered so dangerous that their arrest and confinement in a German detention camp were necessary in the interests of the occupying power, it being understood that they could also be arrested as a form of reprisal. In France police detention took place in the camp at Compiègne.

Sicherungshaft, or security detention, was the punishment for acts jeopardising the interests of the Reich. This was a punitive and administrative measure, not a legal one; but at the end of legal proceedings it could be given to a man who had been accused and acquitted or to one who had been convicted and had completed his sentence.

Article 19 of Section III of the International Convention of Tokyo laid down that 'if, for exceptional reasons, the occupying state should find it absolutely necessary to take hostages, the latter should always be treated humanely. They should not, under any pretext whatsoever, be put to death or submitted to corporal punishment.' This rule of international law was unilaterally modified by the German authorities. As early as September 2, 1940, the military commander in Paris informed all *Feldkommandaturen*: 'Hostages are inhabitants of the country and their life is a guarantee for the good behaviour of the people. Their fate is thus in the hands of their countrymen. Consequently, the people must be clearly threatened that hostages will bear the responsibility for acts of hostility committed by anyone at all.'

The campaign against the USSR made these conditions worse. In December 1941, Marshal Keitel issued the decree poetically called '*Nacht und Nebel*' (Night and Fog). It laid down that persons arrested for hostility to the Reich's armies would be deported to Germany. They were to live there in complete solitary confinement and receive neither parcels nor correspondence. They were to be guarded by Himmler's ss.

In this way the practice of deporting the Reich's opponents to concentration camps was being extended. The ss and the Gestapo thus saw their responsibilities increasing and of course they did not demur. The Abwehr and the military tribunals were gradually deprived of power and the Reich's security ensured by more summary and brutal methods – the torture and immediate execution of suspects.

Amongst the groups of collaborators and from the prisoner of war camps the occupying authorities also raised special units to look after security, in their own way, in the occupied countries; there was a vast increase in the number of house searches and shootings and the burning of houses and villages. Sometimes these improvised policemen were given normal administrative powers, like Pavlevic's Ustashi in Croatia or Darnand's militia in France. The militia was allowed to hold courts martial; in 1944, its leader became a member of the Vichy government with control of all the police forces and the responsibility for 'maintaining law and order'.[1]

1. Cf. the chapter entitled 'Collaboration', page 276.

VII POLAND'S MARTYRDOM

Of all the occupied countries, it was Poland, together with the territories of the USSR, which suffered most. In the eyes of the Nazis she was doubly guilty: she was peopled with Slavs, with a strong Jewish minority, and she had annexed German territories in 1918. Unfortunately for her, she fell under the Reich's yoke at an early stage and remained there for a long time. Hers was a true martyrdom, for in Poland there was time for some of the schemes for 'the eastern countries' to be carried out.

On May 28, 1940, in Hitler's special train, Himmler put forward to the Führer a few ideas which the latter 'found fair and reasonable'. It was a potted version of the great SS master's 'racial ideas'. After explaining that, in the 'little Slav tribes' of Poles or Byelorussians, it was essential not to create 'a national culture and a national consciousness', Himmler suggested 'breaking up this jumbled mass of people in the *Ostland*'. After this, 'racial screening' would begin, involving a 'racial examination' which would enable them to send to Germany all those children 'who proved to have some positive element from the racial point of view'. There they would change their name and it would be forbidden to treat them as 'Polacks', so that the Nazi ideal 'would find an echo in their soul'. After 'systematic application of these measures', all that would remain in the 'General Government' would be 'the lower elements of the population ... human material without a Führer and fit to be navvies in Germany'. In short, a slave-dump.

However, the fact remained that, on the one hand, even the 'General Government' would become a land for Germanic colonisation and on the other, as Dr Wentzel, head of the Central Office for Racial Policy, expressed it in April 1942, 'the Polish people was the most hostile to Germany, the most dangerous and the most prone to conspiracy'. For the security of the Reich, it was therefore necessary to remove these undesirable Poles. And Dr Wentzel envisaged both an 'organised' emigration to South America, whence, in compensation, those Germans who had settled there could come back, and the deportation to Siberia of 20 million Poles over a period of thirty years, at the rate of 700 to 800 trains per year, 'which was feasible from the technical point of view'. They would be 'slowly spread out over the expanse of Siberia'.

These loathsome plans could not be carried out, except in a few instances. The Polish historian Madajczyk has described how, in a few days, 100,000 Poles were driven out of the Zamosc region. Since a few Germans had settled there in the twentieth century, their presence was considered sufficient justification to call the country a 'Germanic land'. The expulsion of the Poles took place in the autumn of 1942, at the very moment when, on the Volga, other subhuman beings, Russians this time, were beginning to pin down the army of their lords and masters.

It is astonishing that the Germans, who were famed, and rightly so, for their organising ability, were so bemused by racial hatred that they succeeded in bringing nothing but chaos and poverty to Poland. They confiscated the possessions of Jews and 'absentees', or large estates and concerns which were important for the German war economy and the 'consolidation of Germanism'. Mines, foundries, various factories and large farms were taken from their rightful owners, with a view to being handed over later to German settlers, particularly ex-servicemen, who, however, never arrived. In the meantime, the system of 'temporary government' which had produced such chaos continued.

Dr Wentzel had foreseen that 'the Polish question could not be resolved in such a way that the Poles would be exterminated like the Jews'. However, 'in conjunction with the operation to exterminate the Jews', Gauleiter Greiser put forward his own suggestion of killing off 35,000 Poles who were suffering from consumption 'in order to eliminate the danger of contagion for the Germans'. We are thus led to wonder what would have been the ultimate fate in store for the Poles: to be reduced to a race of slaves in their own country, to be gradually exterminated or to be transferred to Siberia? Or all three at once?

In the meantime, every measure was taken to lop off the whole of Poland's élite. First of all, its members were systematically removed from positions of responsibility in the 'General Government' and elsewhere. Thus Vilna, which in 1943, according to German statistics, contained 104,000 Poles and 29,000 Lithuanians out of a non-Jewish population of 146,000, was administered only by Lithuanians and they alone had a cultural society. The Poles had only one primary school to which they could send their children and were not united in any organisation, even for charitable purposes. Even in the Wartheland the Roman Catholic Church was regarded as a possible source of resistance and treated with extreme harshness. In October 1941, out of 681 parish clergy and 147 monks in the archdiocese of Poznan, 451 were in gaol or in concentration camps, 120 had been 'expelled' to the 'General Government' and 74 had been shot. There remained 34 to minister to the Poles' religious needs.

The most extensive looting of works of art took place in Poland. Indeed, the Germans considered that non-Polish works of art were a product of the west and that those of any value produced in Poland were due to Germanic influence. So they carried off everything, since, to their mind, the Poles were fundamentally incapable of making any contribution to culture or art. In six months they managed to loot museums and palaces, collect the works of art together and list them in a voluminous carefully printed catalogue, bound in linen and decorated with a swastika.

Watteau's *La femme polonaise* was found in Goering's villa at Berchtesgaden.

The Germans' behaviour became harsher and harsher, for with all the bludgeoning they received, the Poles still did not give in. Furthermore, all attempts to encourage a collaborationist movement among the leaders of political parties or the representatives of well-known families met with failure. As the battle front came nearer and the Wehrmacht's fortunes reached their lowest ebb, the military and political authorities became even more ruthless and the shootings and deportations increased.

The Germans had never been exactly gentle. The instructions of the organisation *Bund deutscher Osten* bore the reminder: 'Germans, the Pole is never your friend. He is inferior to every German on your farm or in your factory. Remember that you belong to the master nation.' When they were questioned after the war, the Polish workers employed by 'German masters' told how they were treated like cattle; their teeth were inspected and they were made to run and jump. After which the buyer, having weighed up his goods, paid a specified sum to the *Arbeitsamt* and took them away.

Forced-labour camps were set up in Poland very early on. The Polish Commission for War Crimes counted 435 of them. Living conditions there were very hard. In the camp at Skarzysko-Kamienna, for example, the effect on the workers of the chemical materials used was described by a witness in the following way: 'The men, dressed in paper held together by pieces of string, were yellow. Everything was yellow: the huts, the trees, the leaves. Women walked about, ginger-red from the action of the picric acid on their hair. Their bodies were yellow and even their eyes seemed yellow.'

But worse was still to come. Poland was to have the sad privilege of having the extermination camps of Auschwitz-Birkenau and Maidanek and the largest ghettoes in Europe set up on her territory. It was in Poland that the greatest number of Jews were done to death; it was she who, in proportion to her population, suffered the highest losses in human life from her merciless occupier.

The Germans who protested against these atrocities were few and far between. General Blaskowitz sent in a complaint which Hitler saw. General Ulex, the Governor of Cracow, condemned 'a situation which is dishonourable for the entire German people'. These isolated gestures made no difference when such ruthless behaviour was inspired by ethical and ethnic even more than by political motives.

CHAPTER 4

Concentration Camps and Genocide

HISTORIANS ask themselves what were the real motives behind Hitler's policy. Was he basically impelled by an urge for power as the Englishman Alan Bullock or the German Bracher think? In that case, the war would have been the Führer's way of extending his domination beyond the borders of Germany. As far as we can judge from the hotchpotch of ideas expressed in *Mein Kampf*, in his speeches and in *Table-Talk* in which, opportunist that he was, Hitler was swayed by current happenings and gave full rein to his fancies, that rapidly became ravings, it would seem that his ideas on mankind and nations were based on Darwin's notions of selection: in the struggle for existence the strong assert themselves; through their might, they achieve right; the weak can only acknowledge and accept their weakness. The law of life is thus the harsh exploitation of man by man and peoples by peoples. Woe unto the conquered, the degenerate, the weak, the decadent! Power was the sole driving force behind policy and it was to be achieved at the point of the sword. But what were its aims? The greatness of Germany, naturally, and the prosperity of the German people who would at last achieve their proper place in the world: on top. This objective required first of all that they rediscover their fundamental unity, that is to say overcome the various rivalries that had long hampered their power – the rivalries between parties, classes, religions and regions. But above all, it was necessary for Germany to remain pure, that is to say to avoid any contamination by impure racial elements – and first and foremost, by the Jews.

I NAZI ANTI-SEMITISM

Hitler's myth was the superiority of the Aryan master race (of which the Germans were the direct descendants) and the Aryan vocation for world domination; J. Billig rightly points out that the widespread firm belief in this myth grew out of exasperation which filled the Germans with wild rage and this rage would vent itself on any hostile elements until they were destroyed. There was no possibility of coexistence or coming to terms with them; the struggle must aim at their extermination. In the forefront of all these enemies, uniting them and personifying them, Hitler's mythology set the Jew.

Starting from Hegelian dialectics, which they transposed or deformed, Hitler and Rosenberg saw the Reich (of Hitler) opposing the Gegenreich (of Israel); one was the antithesis of the other and the two were irreconcilable. Nordic man was an imaginary type of man endowed with fictitious virtues (based on an intellectual content so feeble as to border on puerility) – courage, heroism, a simple way of life, loyalty, devotion to the community. The Jew is his opposite; he is to the Aryan what Satan is to God. 'The Aryan,' in E. Vermeil's words, 'is the German integrated into the national community and looking at race only from that point of view. The Jew is integrated into his racial community which he sets up in opposition to all the nations in which he exerts his disruptive influence.' For this reason, moreover, the Jew is not a race but the seed of racial destruction – in a word, anti-race.

Hitler's indictment created an imaginary Jew endowed with every physical, intellectual and moral shortcoming. In the loathsome caricatures of his *Stürmer*, Streicher popularised the image of the Jew as obese and flabby, his vices were written all over his face. In his propaganda, Goebbels described him as 'like pus in an abscess, ever ready to defile pure German girls'.

According to Hitler, the Jew was responsible for all the evils that afflict nations; it was he who had invented the false egalitarianism of democracy that emasculates the strong man. He excelled in pulling the strings of all movements of an international nature – Anglo-Saxon plutocracy, Manchester School Liberalism, Marxist Communism, Freemasonry; 'The Jew,' the Führer wrote, 'has always known how to unite princes, aristocrats and the bourgeoisie at the international level; it was he who first shouted: "Workers of the world unite."'

The Jew preached a purely destructive intellectualism which was like a poison. He deprived thought of its quickening elements without which it could only be arid and dead – race, the people, the soil. He epitomised rootlessness and used it as his stock in trade. When he settled anywhere, it was only to cause harm. He had only ceased being a wanderer over the face of the earth in order to make his home amongst the great nations like a canker and devour them from within for his own profit.

On the other hand, all the higher civilisations, including the Greek and the Roman, stem from the Aryan race 'which comes from the north'; in the twentieth century, this race had blossomed forth in the German people and had found a worthy setting in the Third Reich.

German power was only possible if the Jewish peril could be exorcised once and for all. Inversely, as its power grew, the German people would

become better able to achieve immunity against this virus that was in-
fecting it. Hitler's anti-Semitism was thus both an idea leading to action
and a reality governing a policy. Racialism and power were basically one
and the same thing.

II THE SS

Starting with the task of protecting leading National Socialist personalities and then of keeping other parties under observation, in fact as a sort
of spy and counter-espionage organisation, the 'Protection Sections'
(*Schutzstaffeln der Nationalsozialistischen Arbeitspartei*) were given responsibility for internal security in the Reich when the Nazi party came to
power and became one with the state. By 1934 it already numbered 50,000.
The logical conclusion of this conglomeration of tasks was the appointment in 1936 of Reichsführer ss Heinrich Himmler to be head of the entire
Reich police forces, completely independent of the Minister of the
Interior. From 1933 onwards, a special branch, the 'Death's Head ss', had
been put in charge of running the concentration camps. The war was to
give the ss ever-increasing powers and turn them into the architects of the
Nazi world created out of Germany's conquests.

Himmler, a small, insignificant-looking man with a neat moustache and
receding chin, was in fact a fanatic; he sought neither the satisfactions of
power, fame as an orator nor worldly success; as a zealous and blindly
obedient supporter of Hitler, he believed in the Messianic mission with
which he was entrusted. He devoted all his energies to the formation of
a Nazi élite, the ss, which was to be an 'order' within the party and
the state.

It was to be a racial order. As early as 1937, Himmler asserted: 'Our
Nordic blood confers on us an inventive genius far above that of other
nations.' Preserving the purity of this blood demanded rigorous precautions: the ss had to obtain the permission of their superior officers
before they could marry; bigamy, the kidnapping of children as well as
procreating them outside marriage were considered legitimate means if
they were felt to be necessary. The ss were educated in special schools of
their own. The whole system reached its apogee in the organisation which
Himmler pompously called *Lebensborn*, the fountain of life, the source of
German expansion in the world.

The selection of the ss was governed by racial criteria, purporting to be
scientific but containing a great deal of nonsense. Himmler described
them in these terms: 'I started by requiring a certain height because I

know that people who are above a certain height have the right kind of blood. I examined photographs of each one and asked myself the question: are there traces of foreign blood?'.

Himmler also stated in 1937: 'The coming decades will see the extermination of the inferior beings who are fighting against Germany, the cradle of the Nordic race and torch-bearer of civilisation.' The conquered Slav territories enabled these words to become deeds.

Henceforth the ss would be able to operate not only as an instrument of orthodox racialism but as the founder of the Nazi social order on conquered soil. 'It was,' wrote J. Billig, 'the embodiment of the myth of the master race raised to its extreme pitch of violence.'

In this function, the ss was the protector of the German state and it had sole charge of criminal justice. But by its nature it existed on the fringe of the state. Its mentality was that of a devoted and ferocious servant ready to undertake any task it might be given. The ss relieved the state and its organisations such as the Wehrmacht of the responsibility for operations that were unworthy of them. Its role was to prepare the way, by violent methods, for the Nazi colonisation of eastern Europe and to reduce the 'sub-men' to the bondage for which nature had intended them.

Accordingly, the ss diversified its organisation. It was no longer merely a group of shock troops for internal political use. From the time of the invasion of France onwards, it included armed units. These divisions were under the orders of the Wehrmacht which considered them crack troops; but the Wehrmacht was also at the service of the ss when the latter had need of large numbers of men to enforce 'Nazi order in the rearward areas'.

The ss were answerable for their conduct only to their leaders. They set up their own courts which dispensed justice according to their own ideas of honour and duty. Thus, two ss men who had summarily shot down some fifty Jews in a Polish synagogue were condemned by a field court martial to a long term of imprisonment. But, like many others of a similar nature, the sentence was not carried out. The verdict was quashed on the grounds that 'at the sight of the Jews, the accused had become aware with extraordinary intensity of the hostility of the Jews towards Germany'. So their behaviour was quite excusable, if not even praiseworthy. The ss's only link with the rest of German society was the strict terms of the oath its members took to their leaders. The transformation of the ss into a state within a state was completed when it created its own economic services. However, Himmler had absolutely no intention of directing Nazi policy; he never intervened in discussions on major questions of strategy, war economy or diplomacy. He remained the faithful servant to implement Hitler's desires and he did nothing without the latter's approval. But in reality his role was much greater because he was shaping from within the German society of the present from which the society of tomorrow would spring.

So the ss had a triple task of combating those considered unworthy, exploiting their wealth and putting them to death; and they were given every licence to carry this out and, as it were, get it working smoothly, in the concentration camps which Hitler had placed under their control as early as 1933.

III THE CONCENTRATION CAMPS

Concentration camps started in Germany as soon as the Nazis came to power. At first they were intended for those Germans who were opposed to Nazism – Communists, Social Democrats, Christian Democrats and conscientious objectors – with the purpose both of ensuring that they could not harm the régime and of 're-educating them'. Thus Dachau in Bavaria was opened in 1934, Buchenwald near Weimar in 1937 and Mauthausen in Austria in 1938. At that time, the Nazis tended to look on these camps as model prisons and were proud of them – photograph albums of Dachau were distributed to affiliated Nazi parties in occupied countries as an example to be followed; Mussert's albums were discovered in Holland.

However, from the start the camps showed certain characteristics that were to be constant; on the one hand, political internees and common-law criminals were inextricably mixed, with the latter in charge of the former and holding all the minor administrative posts, thus bringing the detainees into immediate contact with them; on the other hand, 're-education' took the form of systematic humiliation and bad treatment, such as to break down all resistance by completely destroying the personality.

With the war, as foreigners were added to the internal enemies of the Reich, their number increased. Accordingly, new concentration camps were built in the conquered territories. The largest of them were set up in Poland: Auschwitz, Maidanek and Stutthof. A women's camp was built at Ravensbrück in East Prussia; other men's camps appeared at Neuengamme near Hamburg, Flossenburg on the Czechoslovak border and Natzwieler-Struthof in the Vosges. The central organisation was at Oranienburg-Sachsenhausen; this was where general directives were prepared and reports received from the camp commandants. Some of the camps were linked together: Buchenwald and Dora, Oranienburg and Grossrosen; and they all hived off large numbers of *kommandos* of various sizes, formed for varying lengths of time; teams of detainees would be sent there to carry out some particular job, while remaining under the administrative control of the main camp. The whole area of the Greater

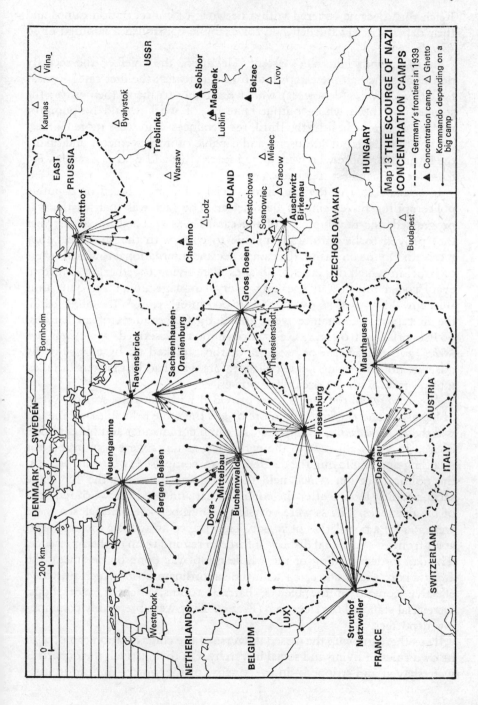

Map 13 THE SCOURGE OF NAZI
CONCENTRATION CAMPS

- - - Germany's frontiers in 1939
▲ Concentration camp △ Ghetto
━━━ Kommando depending on a
       big camp

Reich thus became covered with a network of concentration camps and their dependencies; Buchenwald for example controlled a hundred or so *kommandos*.

In 1941, with Himmler's assent, Heydrich, the chief of the security police, classified all the camps into four categories: the first category was for *Schutzhäftlinge* (deportees) who were likely to mend their ways; the second, for those whose output in terms of work would be poor for reasons of age or health; the third, for detainees who were more danger-ous for the Reich but still useful and capable of improvement; and finally the fourth, for those who were quite incorrigible and who as a result were to suffer the harshest treatment.

In actual fact, this division into special categories, based on a purely police approach, remained a dead letter. The fact was that, as the war progressed, the development of the camps was speeded up so fast that they proved to be chronically unable to cope with the work that they received. On the one hand, the camps became international towns, Towers of Babel in which detainees of all ages were living together, drawn from every social milieu and speaking every language under the sun; thus Buchenwald housed an average of 40,000 internees. On the other hand, the first types of detainee were joined by Communists of all nations, Soviet prisoners of war, Resistance fighters described as 'Nacht und Nebel' and the swarm of hostages or those picked up by chance or by mistake, not forgetting a few collaborators who had lost favour or fallen into disgrace with the occupying power.

Accordingly all the camps were provided with the same sort of system of hierarchy and organised on more or less the same principles. At the top was the *kommandantur*, comprising the camp commander and his deputies, housed in villas adjacent to the perimeter. ss units were responsible for guarding and employing the detainees; they comprised two main sections, the political section which held the prisoners' files and the economic section which looked after the commissariat and fixed the work required of the detainees. The ss were very few in number – at Mauthausen there were 260 for a population of 70,000. They stayed away from the detainees, apart from an occasional display of force to remind them of their presence. The day-to-day running of the whole camp was done by detainees, the *kapos* whom the ss entrusted with the subordinate posts which provided effective control of the blocks, barrack rooms, kitchens, workshops, secretarial staff and the sickroom (*Revier*). They were preferably common-law deportees.

Thus there grew up the closed universe of the concentration camp, with its own rules of living and social hierarchy. On their arrival, the deportees were shaved and stripped – in every sense of the word – dressed in cast-off clothing which made them look ridiculous, sometimes tattooed, given numbers and made to wear distinctive signs according to their nationality and the reason for their internment; these were different coloured triangles: green for 'common-law', red for 'political', pink for the antisocial, purple for conscientious objectors, and so on, with various letters on them, T for Czech, F for French, N for Dutch, etc. The *Nacht und Nebel* sometimes wore the letters NN; they were not allowed to receive any letters or parcels; they were forbidden to walk about the camp; and they lived in isolated blocks.

In fact, as the camps became more and more congested and their accommodation and services increasingly inadequate, the fate of all the detainees became very grim. At the mercy of their *kapos'* whims, liable to corporal punishment such as flogging on the slightest pretext, underfed, exhausted by unremitting toil, with little medical care, the wretched internees in order to survive were forced to resort to dreadful internecine strife which was only slightly mitigated by a few attempts at political organisation or group solidarity. Most of the time, these attempts came from the Communists, who formed the most homogeneous and disciplined element, and first and foremost from the German Communists who had been longest in the camps and were thus the most experienced, as well as occupying more of the minor administrative posts.

These living conditions, which became harsher and harsher as the war progressed, led to a high death-rate amongst the prisoners, which increased still further when they began to be employed in the German war industry. From 1942 onwards the organising of this employment was entrusted to ss General Pohl. It gave immense power to the ss: they could hire out to industrial concerns a labour force that cost them nothing, that was unable to make any protest and that could be continually renewed, as it was increased by recaptured prisoners of war or those unsuccessfully trying to evade forced labour. Several million men were thus taken on by the largest German firms – I. G. Farben, H. Goering, Krupp, Roechling; deportees were sent to work at Dora, Laura or Thekla in secret factories built underground to avoid enemy air raids. Some of them were even employed at Sachsenhausen in counterfeiting English pounds and American dollars that were put into circulation by an Austrian businessman, F. Schwend. These notes were used to buy men's consciences or other services such as those of the spy Cicero in Turkey, who was paid (and fooled) by them. Most of these fakes were good enough to be accepted by Swiss banks.

Through its concentration camps the ss thus managed to achieve all its objectives; the camps rendered Nazi Germany's opponents harmless and made them work for the glory of the Reich while condemning them to a lingering death; they became Germany's largest economic enterprise; as soon as war came, they moulded to their will the servile mass of 'sub-men' doomed to inescapable inferiority by reason of their racial or national origin or the fact that they had been defeated. The 'solution of the Jewish problem' increased their power still further.

IV THE FATE OF THE JEWS

Even before the war, the Jews in Germany, under the accusation of being stateless, had been subjected to discriminatory and humiliating measures; the Wehrmacht's victories now made it possible to extend these measures to the whole of occupied Europe.

The Jews were forbidden to work in the public services, to enter the liberal professions, to hold senior appointments in any organisation liable to influence public opinion – the cinema, radio, press, publishing, the theatre. Their names appeared on special census lists and they were forced to wear a yellow star; their identity cards and ration cards had to bear a distinguishing mark, as did their homes; they were not allowed to enter public places – cafés, parks, museums, theatres, cinemas or libraries. In Poland, they received reduced rations and required permission to move about.

The seizure of Jewish real estate steadily increased, on the pretext that they had themselves gained it by fraud from the countries in which they lived and which they would betray as a matter of course. This resulted in the immense swindle that went under the name of 'economic Aryanisation'; nationals of the various countries were put in charge of Jewish concerns. This transfer of property was a highly profitable business for the cover-men put up by the occupying authorities but also for the German firms which thus acquired considerable financial interests in the economy of the occupied countries.

The measures were accompanied by a campaign of vilification of the Jews through the medium of films – *Jud Süss* – lectures, exhibitions, pamphlets, newspaper articles and university teaching.

In addition to these measures designed to subject, expropriate or humiliate the Jews, they were made to form associations for the greater convenience of the German authorities. When they did not exist already, such associations were set up and the Jews were forced to join them – in France the General Union of Jews, in Holland the Jewish Council. They had the function of helping the occupying power in its decisions or implementing them. These associations sometimes published these decisions in special Jewish newspapers – the *Joodsche Weekblad* in Holland; they collected the funds required to pay the fines inflicted on the Jewish communities; they drew up lists from which the occupier would select the names of hostages to arrest, suspects to intern or those to be recruited for forced labour. These associations controlled by leading Jewish personalities inspired sufficient confidence in their co-religionists to encourage them to greater meekness but they had little power to alleviate their fate.

In the east, the *Einsatzgruppen* revived the tradition of the pogrom. They stirred up the local population, denounced Jews for more or less imaginary crimes and encouraged plunder, shop-looting and murder. They hoped in this way to gain support for collaboration. In Poland, at Lvov, in three successive pogroms organised by means of Ukrainian nationalists and the dregs of the population, there were 10,000 victims. In Yugoslavia, 2,000 Jews were shot as reprisals for partisan operations. In Jassy on June 29, 1941, 8,000 Jews were wiped out either on the spot or after being picked up and brought in. The list of crimes perpetrated in Poland, as established by a special commission, is terrifyingly long. But this small-town butchery merely offered the ss the chance to acquire the knack; it did not offer a solution to the 'Jewish problem'.

V THE MADAGASCAR SCHEME

The purely German solution to the problem for a while consisted in letting the Jews leave the country more or less voluntarily. Whilst life in the places where they lived was made increasingly unpleasant, no obstacle was placed in their way if they wanted to seek asylum elsewhere, on the understanding that they gave up most of their belongings. In this way, several hundreds of thousands of German or Austrian Jews left their country before the war and this explains the paradox that the proportion of German Jews who disappeared during the war was the lowest in Europe. The same policy seems to explain why, in the autumn of 1940, 7,000 Jews were sent without warning from the province of Baden into unoccupied France and why there were attempts to smuggle thousands of Polish Jews over the demarcation line between Germany and the Soviet Union.

But the size of the Polish Jewish population caused Hitler embarrassment, as he explained in March 1940 to an American of German origin, Colin Ross: 'It is the difficult question of finding enough room ... I would welcome any positive suggestion.' A solution had indeed been found to the problem of cleaning up the annexed Polish territories by transferring the Jews to the 'General Government' which became a sort of 'Jewish reservation'. But this was only a springboard for better things, sa Hitler confessed to Colin Ross: 'In Lublin, the Jews are already packed as tight as sardines.'

For a while in the summer of 1940, the idea was toyed with of expelling all the Jews from Europe at the end of the war. This 'solution' would be written into the peace treaty. After some research Madagascar was chosen to receive the Jews after the 25,000 Frenchmen living there had been evacuated. Sea and air bases would be held by the Reich; the Jews would administer the rest of the island under a German governor dependent on Himmler; their European assets would provide the basis for the development of the country and for creating the appropriate infrastructures. The Jews would lose their original nationality without becoming Germans; they would be 'citizens of the mandated territory of Madagascar'.

Although this scheme was the subject of thorough discussion between all the ministries concerned, it does not seem to have been put to the Vichy government who, in accordance with the armistice convention, retained complete control of the island. Heydrich seems not to have been entirely enthusiastic. Moreover, the invasion of the USSR was to create problems that the 'Madagascar scheme' would have been unable to solve; at the same time, this invasion opened up new horizons which were to suggest other solutions to Heydrich, including 'the final solution'.

VI THE GHETTOES

One good way of segregating Jews so as to be able to strike at them more easily by cutting them off entirely from the outer world consisted in shovelling them into the ghettoes that formerly existed in certain Polish and Lithuanian cities. Those who had not lived in them before the war, as well as the small local Jewish communities, were all sent there. Thus each ghetto formed an entirely enclosed Jewish world, surrounded by a wall through which the Jews passed only when they went to work in other parts of the town. Outside, the Germans set about reviving the anti-Semitism of the non-Jews; inside there were all the horrors of promiscuity – ten people to a room – forced labour, under-nourishment, raids and reprisals. When no ghetto existed, they were set up; Heydrich, the 'protector' of Bohemia, shut his Jews up in the old disused fortress of Theresienstadt; in Belgrade, Rademacher chose the gypsy quarter for the Yugoslav Jews, after rejecting the idea of an island in the middle of the Danube. More than 435,000 people were crammed into the Warsaw ghetto.

Inside the ghetto there still remained some semblance of family life and independent administration. 'Jewish councils' (*Judenräte*), appointed by the Germans, ran the community rather like municipal councils, with the help of Jewish police. They negotiated work contracts with the Nazis and issued the regulations governing the punishment of offences. Their role has been the subject of extremely diverse judgments, many of them very critical. Some of these councils were even said to have gone as far as to draw up lists of Jews sentenced to be hanged as reprisals; most of them, by meeting German demands as well as they could, had hopes of saving their own skins and the lives of their loved ones. But Mazor stresses that many of these reluctant Quislings did rebel at great risk to themselves; some of them stirred up revolt, or, in despair, committed suicide.

In Lodz, Rumkovski, a man of philanthropic bent and a former small manufacturer now in his seventies, took his position very seriously. He set up various institutions, indeed almost a small court. His picture hung in every office, like the Führer's. He toured the schools, conducted marriage ceremonies, printed a local currency and stamp bearing his own effigy. But he did not succeed in saving either the Jewish community or some of its members or himself, for the behaviour of the Nazis condemned their victims to come to tragic choices, none of which led to anything but despair.

The ghetto formed an economically closed world. In Theresienstadt, the population was divided into 'hundreds' of men and women from sixteen to sixty years old, forced to work ten or twelve hours a day under the control of a 'prominent person'. It was a caricature of joint management of the means of production. In theory, each inhabitant received free board and lodging in exchange for his work; but the shops were often empty and the ration cards rarely honoured. These extraordinary business concerns which paid their staff no wages, were hotbeds of all sorts of illicit trading. The German bosses and the 'prominent persons' took all the profits; the clever ones, the dishonest ones and the better-placed ones amongst the detainees managed to live off the black market. After November 1942, the Jewish workers in Lvov became the property of the ss, who hired them out to firms, sometimes run by Jews who were individually employers but collectively slaves.

In these communities doomed to slow extinction, the state of health of the population was deplorable and epidemics rife. Informers flourished in the atmosphere of suspicion. Yet some cultural life went on, pursued with desperate eagerness as the expression of a sort of will to live; newspapers were printed, concerts and theatre performances took place and even a grim humour sometimes appeared. At times the ss fancied themselves as patrons of the arts and supported them, even if they did send the writers and performers off to be killed next day. The ghettoes were in fact, only one stage in the 'final solution to the Jewish problem'.

VII THE FINAL SOLUTION TO THE JEWISH PROBLEM

At the beginning of 1942, Hitler announced in two speeches that the Jews would be exterminated; the scheme to transport them out of Europe had thus been abandoned. This change of heart in Nazi policy was the logical consequence of the behaviour of the ss in the ussr. Had they not been invited to 'protect the Wehrmacht' by immediately executing Jews and leading Communists – since to the Nazi mind, these were only two forms of the same enemy? After mass shootings – 34,000 in two days in Kiev – followed by cremating the bodies on vast funeral pyres, the ss had worked out a rough and ready system of itinerant gas-chambers; they asphyxiated their victims with the exhaust fumes from their lorries. But the ss found this method not very practical because the victims took too long to die and this restricted output. On request, the German chemists had produced a gas called *Zyclon-B* and its rapid effect proved most encouraging when it was tried out.

It was in these circumstances that, at Wannsee, near Berlin, apparently at Heydrich's suggestion, the decision was taken to exterminate the European Jews, a decision communicated in a letter from Heydrich himself to the Wilhelmstrasse apparently without their raising any objection. The operation began in Poland, a testing-ground for the ss, and was entrusted to Globocnik, the ss chief of the Lublin district; it was given the cover-name *Aktion Reinhard* in memory of the 'great' Reinhard Heydrich who had recently been executed by the Czech Resistance movement in Prague.

The method consisted of installing, in certain camps, gas-chambers camouflaged as shower-rooms, together with giant cremation ovens. At Birkenau, in open country a few miles from Auschwitz, a complete range of buildings was constructed, after expelling everyone in the vicinity to exclude any indiscreet observers; Himmler came to inspect the building personally. The same precautions were not considered necessary at Maidanek; the camp could be seen from Lublin and Jews still alive could observe from their ghetto the smoke produced by incinerating the corpses of their comrades, in full knowledge of the fate awaiting them.

In November 1942, a few Gauleiters raised objections to the 'final solution' on the grounds that it was depriving the Reich's war economy of a valuable labour force. A middle way was found: the healthy Jews would be sent out to work until they became exhausted; the others, after periodical 'selection', would be exterminated; those who for some reason or other were not exterminated, would be sterilised – an operation based on frightful experiments on human guinea pigs taken from the concentration camps.

All that remained was to drive the cattle to the slaughter-house door. Jews were rounded up in their thousands all over Europe, with the more or less willing co-operation of the authorities in the occupied countries; in Romania Antonescu, to his credit, delayed implementing the measures until they had become difficult to apply. In France, the poor wretches were crammed into makeshift internment centres, in the *Vélodrome d'Hiver* after the 'big round-up' on July 16, 1942, at Beaune-la-Rolande, Pithiviers and Drancy. In Holland, it was the Westerborck camp. Thence they were transported 'eastwards' – the trains deposited them at the very gates of Birkenau.

Gradually the ghettoes emptied of their inhabitants. On July 22, the *Judenrat* of the Warsaw ghettoes themselves announced the beginning of the 'big operation'; by July 1943 there were no longer any Jews officially living in Lvov. On September 1 in Lodz, Rumkovski had the hospitals evacuated and the patients handed over to the Nazis. On June 21, 1943, Himmler ordered all the Jews in the *Ostland* who were unfit for work to be sent to concentration camps. In Hungary Eichmann, the man in charge of the operation, was particularly keen on sending Jews to the gas-chamber; from March to June 1944, helped by the diplomat Wesenmayer, he succeeded in deporting 400,000 Jews, at a time when the Red Army was already approaching and the Wehrmacht was finding it impossible to obtain lorries to move their troops, whereas Eichmann had no difficulty at all. This same Eichmann tried to have Dutch Jews born of mixed marriages deported to Birkenau, when Himmler considered that sterilisation would meet the case. He even ordered 1,127 Jews to be transferred from Rome to Birkenau when Hitler himself wanted them to be confined in Mauthausen as hostages. The ss had been possessed by a lust for murder.

How many Jews died in this 'final solution'? L. Poliakov and B. Mark, who are specialists on this question, are agreed with Israeli statisticians in placing the figure at 6 million, i.e. more than 40 per cent of the whole Jewish people. It is the most atrocious crime in the history of mankind, in its grievousness and its wantonness, because the death of these wretched people contributed in no way at all to the success of the German armies. They were killed as a result of an ethos based on the will to power and on racialism and applied by one of the most highly developed countries in the world with all the vast organising ability and scientific knowledge at its command, because its sense of discipline and its patriotism had been completely perverted.

VIII DID THE JEWS ALLOW THEMSELVES TO BE MASSACRED?

The immense number of Jews who died raises the question of whether, in the vast majority of cases, the Jews allowed themselves to be massacred. Could they have done anything else? It is probable that a certain atavistic feeling based on memories of centuries and centuries of persecution, tended to produce meekness and resignation; they knew that a storm does not last for ever. By submission and prayer, the Jewish people lost many members of their race but they did continue to exist and hope for better days to come.

But in addition, the Nazis had taken all sorts of precautions. Fooled up to the very last minute, hundred of thousands of Jews went to the gas chambers still not realising what was happening; earlier on, they had left their homes or their ghettoes convinced that once they had been transferred in accordance with the orders issued by their present masters they would be allowed to live in peace. The 'solution' was so unthinkably bestial that their minds were bemused; and when their eyes opened it was too late.

The Nazis were also very skilful in their use of 'collective responsibility'. Dvorjetzky has analysed what 'the call of the woods' meant for those who were detained close to the Russian front: the promise of freedom and fighting; but their families were left behind in the towns as hostages so during the journey or in the camps and ghettoes, any attempt at escape or revolt would bring out the informer, for fear of reprisals.

And finally, the inhabitants of the concentration camps were never free from observation. As Wellers reminds us: 'The detainees lived night and day in public, slept in public, washed in public, performed their natural functions in public and died in public. In this sort of congestion, secrecy of any kind was impossible.'

It is all the more remarkable that nonetheless plots and revolts did take place, motivated by bitter despair but sometimes systematically prepared. Group communities in apartment-houses or ghettoes and national or political affiliation in the camps turned into resistance organisations. Though the insurrection at Lvov proved abortive, at Sobibor on the other hand, on October 14, 1943, 300 detainees managed to escape after killing nine ss. In Cracow, Bialystok and Treblinka, the ghettoes were 'liquidated' after fighting that sometimes lasted several days. Above all, in Warsaw the first German attempt in January 1943 was successfully opposed by four Jewish combat groups, out of the fifty that had been organised. In April they had to call in tanks, guns and flame throwers. Fighting lasted four weeks with the attackers compelled to reduce the underground bunkers one by one by blowing up blocks of houses with high explosive. Not until May 15 could ss General Stroop announce: 'The Jewish quarter no longer exists.'

So the Jews did fight their own war during the war itself and it was difficult for them to do more than they did. But there is another question: how much did the rest of the world know about the enormous crime that was being perpetrated and what did it do to try to stop it?

IX THE SILENCE OF THE VATICAN

In London, the Allies had been informed by the Polish Resistance of what was being concocted, albeit without realising its full horror, and through the BBC they had threatened the Reich with reprisals. Even during the war, they had decided to bring the war criminals before special courts when it was ended. These threats and decisions stemmed partly from considerations of psychological warfare.

It is a fact that nobody in Europe, and probably not even the German people, fully realised the immensity of the loathsome crime of genocide being committed against the Jews, as well as the gypsies, and which also threatened the Slavs. Such a crime was unprecedented and seemed incredible in the twentieth century. The International Red Cross said nothing and managed to gain entry into the camps only at the very end of the war; this inspection *in extremis* could not alter the state of affairs. The Vatican also said nothing, thereby incurring violent criticism as well as giving rise to extremely heated debate. Its policy towards Germany, wrote F. L'Huillier, 'has caused many Roman Catholics great qualms of conscience' and 'set a riddle for almost all thinking men'. What was this policy?

When he was papal nuncio in Germany, the future Pope Pius XII had been responsible for arranging the concordat whereby the Vatican gave the Third Reich international recognition at a time when the Nazi régime had not yet achieved, through its military successes, the prestige and power which made it unassailable. It is true that later on the encyclical *Mit brennender Sorge* condemned certain excesses of National Socialism but not the doctrine itself or its underlying racialism. Nevertheless, it aroused Hitler's wrath and was made the excuse for a violent anti-Catholic campaign in the Reich.

Ever since his election, Pope Pius XII had continually shown goodwill towards Germany by his constant display of affection for the German people, for whom he felt a particular regard. Between the lines, it was possible to read a distinction between the people and its régime but this distinction was subtle rather than overt. When war became imminent, the Pope asked the weaker power, the state that was threatened, Roman Catholic Poland, to make concessions to preserve peace. Later on, by appointing ecclesiastical dignitaries to dismembered Poland, the Pope seemed to recognise the *fait accompli* that had been achieved by violence.

If we add that the Vatican never directly intervened with the German government but always confined its approaches to the Italian government and that, while continually making peaceful declarations and canvassing in favour of peace, it refused to make any concrete proposals that could only lead to a condemnation of the aggressor, it is plain that the Vatican did little to stand in the way of Nazi policy. The invasion of Holland, Belgium, France, Yugoslavia and Greece touched the Pope's heart but called forth no protest. Faced by a constant stream of entreaty on behalf of the victims of Nazism, the Pope used every effort to mitigate the lot of the Roman Catholics, above all the priests and specifically those interned in Dachau; but he kept silent on the dreadful treatment that was being meted out to Jews. Yet it seems that by the end of 1942, he must have known all about it.

Pius XII thus showed the greatest caution in his relations with Hitler. True, this caution did not amount to pretending ignorance or, even less, showing approval. Many people who were threatened or persecuted, including many Jews, found asylum in the Vatican or in religious communities in Italy. Privately the Pope frequently referred to his concern and even to his distress. The voice of the Vatican was sufficiently outspoken in its broadcasts to inspire some of the earlier Resistance tracts circulated in France. And finally, Pius XII firmly refused to recognise the attack against the Soviet Union as any kind of crusade. But the fact remains that the only international authority that could raise its voice against the monstrous crimes of the Nazis was the Vatican, and the Vatican kept silent.

We can only surmise about the motivation behind such behaviour. Was the Pope imprisoned in a doctrine which forbade him to intervene in the affairs of another state – in fact, to give unto Caesar those things which are Caesar's? Was it this same doctrine that led him to give de facto recognition to the scandalous Ustashi régime in Croatia which professed Catholicism and set out forcibly to convert the orthodox Serbs living in the new state? Did Pius XII fear that he might aggravate the lot of the German Roman Catholics and priests? This meant putting the preservation of the Church before elementary principles of humanity that are fundamental to Christianity.

One is thus led to wonder whether the Vatican did not think that it was best to choose the lesser of the two evils. With his aristocratic temperament and social background and with the prevailing feeling in the Curia at the time, it is probable that Pius XII was led to find the true or most formidable enemy of Roman Catholic dogma and the Roman Catholic world in the materialism and atheism of Communism. By opposing it, in however wrong-headed a way, Germany represented western civilisation and was perhaps even its bulwark against Asia, since the Church still existed in Germany. After all, it was not all that long since the 'Red' barbarians in Spain had committed atrocities against churches and monasteries.

As for saying that the Pope's silence can be explained away as a calculation based on the likelihood of obtaining a 'real peace', this would mean expecting too much or too little from the international hearing that the Pope's utterances could command. Whatever it did, the Vatican was entirely powerless to establish a 'real peace'. On the other hand, a firm protest by Pius XII against the extermination of the Jews, published in the Catholic Press all over the world, would not perhaps have prevented or slowed down the massacre, although in this matter there can be no certainty. What is certain is that such a protest would have been a revelation for most people and that it would have turned Roman Catholics away from collaboration and perhaps made the German Catholics less submissive, quite apart from the relief that it would have provided for millions of troubled consciences.

CHAPTER V

Collaboration

T H E Hitler régime needed to keep the German people well in hand and to win the greatest possible support abroad; its prestige required this as did the successful conclusion of the war. Propaganda, inspired and controlled by Goebbels, was thus one of the pillars of its policy. Helped by the Wehrmacht's successes, the pre-war European Fascist parties gained many members, and hopes of victory as well as subsidies from the victor brought others into being. In the occupied countries, these parties acted as henchmen for the German authorities; in the satellite countries, if they were not themselves in the seat of power, the threat that they represented to their governments made the latter more ready to submit to the Germans' requests. Only in Poland and the Soviet Union did Nazi policy do nothing to play down its determination to exterminate its ideological and racial opponents and thus sow discord in their ranks. In those two countries collaboration was a dismal failure.

I THE *VOLKSDEUTSCHE*

In various countries, the German minority, the *Volksdeutsche*, provided the spearhead for Nazi penetration. Hitler insisted on their being granted autonomous status, so that they should keep their 'Germanity' by retaining direct links with the Reich. Thus F. Karmasin in Slovakia made no secret of the fact that he was a German agent and took his orders from Ribbentrop. The Slovak Germans were represented in the government by a Secretary of State and they levied their own taxes for their own purposes.

In Croatia, Dr Branimir Altgayer had been granted authority in all matters concerning the Germans; but those Germans who were officials in the Croat state took their oath to Hitler. The Germans had the right to wear Nazi insignia, to use the Nazi salute and to sing Party songs.

In Romania, the status of the German minority in Transylvania had been settled on August 30, 1940, in Vienna by a special protocol. It was completed by an agreement between Antonescu and A. Schmidt, leader of the minority, which gave it the status of a public corporation having the right to issue its own laws.

In Hungary there existed a 'National League of Germans', with Franz Basch as its leader; it had its own schools and was proportionally represented in the government service. But the Hungarian government, jealous of its own authority, had refused to grant it special status and its members were not allowed to wear the swastika.

II GOEBBELS' PROPAGANDA

In theory German propaganda was shared between various organisations. The Führer had made foreign propaganda the preserve of Ribbentrop and the Wilhelmstrasse; Dietrich was in charge of the press; Max Amann, one of the Führer's most trusty lieutenants, was responsible for the Party press; and finally, the Wehrmacht had its own propaganda service. In theory, that left very little for Dr Goebbels, who bore the title of 'Propaganda Minister' – merely the cinema and the radio, for internal use only. But in fact, it was he who set the tone and in practice he finished up, if not in complete control, at least guiding everything along his own lines.

This half-failed intellectual – he had not succeeded in achieving fame despite having published thirty or so books and pamphlets – was one of Hitler's earliest companions. He had greatly contributed to fabricating Hitler's legend and the latter had to some extent modelled his attitude on the image of himself popularised by Goebbels. An efficient propagandist, a brilliant speaker and orator and a splendid actor, capable of pleading the most conflicting causes in quick succession, Goebbels had more cleverness and ambition than real conviction; he thought Rosenberg a complete and utter idiot. Cultured and intelligent, he was also a mass of complexes, vain and unscrupulous. He had defined his function in one sentence: 'I had to keep up German morale.' It was a good pretext for poking his fingers into every pie – the shortage of warm winter clothing for the troops in Russia, the size of the potato crop or racial purity.

Goebbels regularly wrote the editorial for the weekly *Das Reich*. But above all, he had the radio and he knew how to use it; his broadcasts went out for eleven hours every day to the North Americans; there were eight hours for Africa and a whole programme for the British in preparation for a landing in the British Isles. In the occupied countries he introduced propaganda services to replace those run by the embassies or the Wehrmacht. They purged the libraries; controlled the press – 'an armful of directives every day', Bonnafous, the Vichy Minister of Information used to say; founded or backed newspapers; supervised the cinema news programmes; acquired interests in publishing houses, cinema and gramophone-record firms, news agencies and even printing presses; formed large numbers of cultural associations to spread the good (Nazi) word; produced films and organised anti-Masonic, anti-Semitic or anti-Bolshevik exhibitions; spread 'German culture' by means of weeklies, reviews, concerts and lectures; invited scientists, artists and men of letters to tour Germany; nor did they neglect fashion.

Goebbels was the inventor of the Nazi ritual; it was he who had perfected the giant Nuremberg rallies with rolling drums, flags, spotlights and endless parades of troops in uniform. For him, a human being was a collection of passions and instincts and it was to these he appealed and not to reason. On this point he was at one with Hitler, who considered the masses devoid of any sense of freedom, toleration or decency; they were unintelligent and needed to feel themselves dominated; it gave them a feeling of peace and security.

The scene of the mass rallies was carefully chosen for its historical associations or the possibility of cramming it with people, thus making it easier to create a collective spirit. Noises off-stage, marching songs, inspired applause amplified by loudspeakers, the march-past in columns ten deep, aroused and sustained enthusiasm so that the individual sank into the mass and lost his ability to think or criticise, all turned into uniformed automata caught up in a lasting delirious hysteria.

There was no question of telling the masses the truth. On November 10, 1938, Hitler had told German journalists in these explicit terms what their duty was: 'The rightness of the leaders' attitude must be continually stressed as a matter of principle.' Accordingly no matter was ever thoroughly explored; arguments were replaced by slogans of an alluring simplicity; by the continual hammering home of the same associations of words all the time, people came to believe what they heard.

Consequently, in order to be effective, propaganda restricted itself to a few well-chosen themes: extravagant praise of the Führer, and emphasis on the obnoxious nature of his enemies, the Jews and the Marxists. Before the war, Hitler had been presented as the great friend and comrade, a hero combining charm and strength, the modern Siegfried. When war came, he became a national symbol, the skilled statesman able to handle any political, diplomatic or economic problem, the infallible leader. When setbacks began to occur, he remained the protector, the shield and buckler of the people, the saviour. Thus Goebbels praised him as being the 'watchword of all who believe in Germany . . . the redeemer . . . the leader who understands the people and fights on their behalf'. The NS Frauenwarte, the official organ of the association of National Socialist women, wrote simply: 'You owe everything to the Führer, your wages, the blue sky above, life.' Children recited a prayer with these words: 'Führer, my Führer, my Faith, my Light, it is to you I owe my daily bread.' Even the Führer's style was considered as a model; Goebbels praised him as 'the cultivator of the German language'.

At first the Jew was put forward as a man without a country, a ferment of dissolution amongst peoples. Then, when the paradoxical alliance of the Communist Soviet Union and the capitalist Anglo-Saxon countries came into being against Germany, the Jew became the connecting link explaining this monstrous union. As part of its pretentious rubbish, German propaganda tirelessly brandished the spectre of the 'Jewish-plutocratic-Marxist-Masonic conspiracy.' There, too, Hitler had shown the way; he had the knack of tarring all his opponents, however different they might be, with the same brush so as to appear all the nobler by contrast. In *Mein Kampf* he had expounded his belief that the bigger the lie, the more likely it was to be believed.

III THE COLLABORATORS IN OCCUPIED EUROPE

The German 'New Order' was not without its attractions for various categories of people in the occupied countries. More than one captain of industry rejoiced in the elimination of social conflict, the banning of strikes and the vast market that might be expected from a German Europe. In every country anti-Semitism was glowing with a quiet fire that needed little to make it flare up anew. The property-owning classes and above all the petty bourgeoisie looked on Fascism as championing a social order based on private property. The Churches were tempted by the thought of the final elimination of atheistic and materialistic Communism. More than one aesthete was taken in by the virility, the martial look, the healthy physique and the splendid bearing of the victorious young German warriors: did not Drieu la Rochelle sing the praises of the 'tough Nazi fighter who can regenerate mankind and who is a combination of American gangster, Foreign Legionary and aircrew' in short 'a man who believes only in acts'? Even Nazi Germany's social achievements compared with those of the liberal democracies were not without attractions for trade unionists. And even when no ideological sympathy existed, the distribution of generous largesse by the occupying power was an excellent method of making converts and enlisting supporters. Thus the Gestapo found it easy to recruit auxiliaries sometimes even from the criminal classes. In a word, in every country groups of collaborators became legion, all fashioned more or less on the same model.

In all the groups the dominant figure was the leader, the infallible master of the masses; everywhere the attempt was made to enrol the whole of the population into territorial and co-operative organisations of a paramilitary type; everywhere there were myths, rituals and slogans rather than ideas; everywhere appeal was made to violence, fanaticism and terror; the virtues of discipline, blind obedience and sacrifice to the good cause were praised to the skies. The gestures, the dress – the coloured shirt – the ceremonial, the hierarchy and the vocabulary were all copied from the Nazis.

Thus in occupied Europe there appeared a sort of anti-Semitism that was imported and imitated from Germany rather than properly indigenous – for example, it did not exist in Italian Fascism. So we find such strange perversions as nationalist groups whose members had joined out of fear or even hatred of Germany turning into fanatical supporters of a German-dominated Europe. The first result of which was their acceptance of the occupation, exploitation and obliteration of their own country.

Yet each of these groups proclaimed itself 'national'. Was it a relic of patriotism, at least in words, or their desire not to alienate conservative elements? In any case, the 'programmes' of the various Fascist parties were singularly close to one another. They all demanded: a 'strong government' led by a 'strong man'; social order within a framework of political and economic stability; the 'solidarity' of all classes that was jeopardised only by the demands of the people, supported or incited by the workers' parties and trade unions; precedence of national over sectarian interests and of collective groups over individuals. Europe became the theatre of a 'Fascist international' where the same play was performed all the time, imported from Germany and having the same mass methods of indoctrination, the same enemies to be fought and the same passionate fury in shooting them down. The only national differences lay in the relative roles that German policy assigned to its puppets in each country.

In Norway, Quisling had the sad distinction of giving his name to a whole category of traitors. In fact his Fascism was, if such an expression is possible, the purest sort of all, because it sprang neither from economic uncertainty nor national emergency nor even from self-interest but from belief, a rather naïve belief indeed, in all the tawdry myths with which Nazism had decked itself out. Quisling believed in the Aryans, in the Germanic racial community which was to bring together the Scandinavians and the Germans. He was a missionary rather than a politician.

Quisling provided the occupying power with its first experience of collaborating with local pro-Nazi elements. It helped it to work out the appropriate methods of behaviour: use the Nazis to infiltrate the government services and win them over by eliminating the hostile elements within them, thus avoiding a direct takeover, which would be not only tricky but burdensome and dangerous; thus the unpopular measures put out by the occupying powers had a better chance of being acceptable to public opinion since they would appear to have been agreed upon and applied by fellow citizens. But should the collaborators fail to fulfil the role allotted them they would be ruthlessly swept aside, however loyal they might be.

Quisling learnt this to his cost in Norway as did Mussert in Holland. Both of them were either brought on or sent off the field according to whether they were still useful.

Thus Mussert had the notion that the Reich would help him to create a Greater Holland stretching as far as Flanders in France and which would be a sort of western marches of Greater Germany while retaining a certain amount of independence. But he ran up against thinly disguised German designs to annex Holland and learnt the sad lesson that a Nazi can always find someone more Nazi than himself. His acceptance of defeat did not prevent Seyss-Inquart from subsidising dissident groups supporting a straightforward annexation of Holland, led by Rost van Tonningen.

In Belgium the defeat of the democracies had led the Flemish nationalists to think that the death knell of French influence, under which they considered that they had been suffering for many years, had finally tolled. This ethnic and linguistic group which felt politically and economically bullied made common cause with Nazism as much to satisfy its claims as through ideological sympathy. In fact, it was really the inherently brittle nature of Belgium that was being confirmed and aggravated by events.

Paradoxically enough, the Walloon Fascists, the 'rexists' who predated the invasion, found themselves led by the internal logic of their action to the blatant aberration of proclaiming Belgium's 'Germanity of blood and soil'. The point was that, in the Nazis' eyes, Quisling, Mussert and de Clerk were Germanic; but Degrelle was not. Therefore he had to go further and shout louder and commit himself more deeply than the others. In every country, the Fascists found themselves caught up in a sort of inevitable spiral; faced by the threat of those who were more extreme and servile than themselves, they had steadily to increase their offers to the occupying power.

French Fascism was more complicated because there was no French Führer and it had split up into rival groups; on the other hand, it comprised elements from the traditional Left, the radicals and Socialists and sometimes the Communists. Indeed, the Vichy régime had drawn into its orbit the French right-wing reactionaries. So in the northern zone, we find the anti-militarist G. Suarez's *Aujourd'hui*, the anti-clerical Socialist sympathiser and radical R. Château's *La France au travail*, the syndicalist G. Dumoulin's *Atelier*, all denouncing the clericalism, the paternalism, the militarism and the jingoistic nationalism of the Vichy rulers and all subsidised by the ambassador Otto Abetz who used them to exert pressure on the Vichy leaders. The most powerful of these groups was the *Rassemblement national populaire* of the former Popular Front minister Marcel Déat, who in his *L'Oeuvre* attacked the Jews, the Anglo-Saxons,

the *Action française*, Communists and Liberals in the best Goebbels style
and advocated a planned economy, the protection of the race, the integration of France into a German Europe and French participation in the
war on the German side.

There were other groups more in line with pre-war French Fascism: the
ex-*Action française* R. Brasillach and his team who ran *Je suis partout*,
Deloncle's *Comité secret d'action révolutionnaire*, consisting of *cagoulards*,[1]
Bucard's *Parti franciste* and above all, Jacques Doriot's *Parti populaire
français* whose spokesman was the writer Drieu la Rochelle. Before the
war, the PPF had tried to win over the mass of workers by demanding
nationalisation of certain industries and calling itself socialist in order to
thwart the workers' parties. Under the occupation it became more and
more the defender of peasants and small property-owners, as well as
small traders and artisans, by espousing their grievances against the large
firms. It claimed that by doing this it was fighting against French decadence by attacking international capitalism or Marxism. But violence could
not add up to a programme. The 'physical revolution' preached by Drieu
la Rochelle – sport for all, holidays and back to nature – was not really
adequate either to provide a programme for industry or society.

Rommel's advance towards Egypt had aroused certain hopes amongst
the Arab nationalists. Hadj Amin al Husseini, the Grand Mufti of Jerusalem, had become a Nazi supporter and taken refuge in Berlin after the
failure of Rashid Ali's revolt. The Germans had acknowledged his right
to create a Palestinian state and solve the 'Jewish problem' there according
to ethnical and religious criteria similar to the solution that was being
achieved in occupied Europe. The Mufti delivered himself of fanatical
propaganda on the Berlin radio; he was the mediator between the Reich
and Italy on the one hand and Farouk in Egypt or Bourguiba in Tunisia on
the other.

All these Fascist groups developed in similar ways. Hitler intended them
to be his loyal henchmen or even slaves. They provided the men of action
to do the occupying power's dirty work; they carried out police or
reprisal operations against their compatriots – raids, arson or murder;
they were the purveyors of the future inmates of concentration camps.

Thus they came to an ever increasing extent within Himmler's purview
and they vied with each other in their eagerness to recruit volunteers for
the anti-Bolshevik crusade. They became Waffen ss, 'the shock troops of
the new order'. In France the 'Legion of French Volunteers against
Bolshevism' was formed in which Doriot served for a while. Twenty
thousand supporters of Mussert served in the German Army and several
thousand in the police; Mussert had suggested raising 300,000 men to be
sent to Russia, but Hitler refused for fear that they might not be amenable

1. Literally 'hooded men'; an extreme right-wing group.

enough. De Clerk became head of a 'Flemish Legion' officered entirely by Germans, and Degrelle of a 'Walloon Legion' which he took off to the Ukraine. Quisling divided the members of his anti-Bolshevik Norwegian legion between the Russian front and the internal front against his compatriots. The Grand Mufti recruited a Moslem Legion which goose-stepped in a Berlin parade together with Bosnians or Soviet prisoners of war from Azerbaidzhan and Turkestan.

All these volunteers wore German uniform and took an oath to Hitler, 'the Führer of Germanity'; the Flemings even took an oath to Himmler. These nationalists had become the mercenaries of the power that was occupying their country. The same fate was in store for the collaborators in the satellite states.

IV THE SATELLITES

In Romania, the Germans continued to maintain their trust in Antonescu, holding the 'Iron Guard' up their sleeve should need arise. Antonescu had set up a personal dictatorship accepted by young King Michael. His government consisted of officers, civil servants and experts, all of them responsible to him. But despite Goebbels' persuasion, the *Conducator* did not establish 'single party' rule, although the 'historical parties' remained banned – according to Mr Popescu-Puturi, Maniu and Bratianu, the leaders of these parties, had advised their members to accept the régime.

This régime was, however, in many respects a Fascist one. Popular assent was obtained by organised plebiscites. Freedom had been suppressed and there were thousands of arrests and internments. Nazi-type organisations – corporations, youth movements and 'Work and Light' cultural propaganda – brought the régime into line with that of the Reich.

Von Killinger, the new German ambassador, had been recommended to Antonescu by Hitler as an 'adviser'; in fact, no important measure could be passed without his approval. On the list of the staff of the German ambassador there was a 'police attaché'. The Romanian ministry of propaganda had been reorganised by Goebbels' 'experts', so that the press was tightly controlled and directed by the German ambassador and German culture became predominant in the theatre, music, literature and the fine arts. By meekly agreeing to send workers to Germany and allowing the Romanian units in the USSR to be used as the Wehrmacht generals saw fit, Antonescu had turned Romania into the perfect satellite.

In Hungary, the Germans had allowed the pre-war political régime under the Regent, Horthy, to continue. They felt some affinity with it in view of the veiled dictatorship it had set up and its anti-Semitism. But the independent spirit of the Magyars did not fail to cause them some concern. Accordingly, they were keeping note of Ferenc Szalassi's Arrow Cross movement.

Szalassi recruited his supporters from the lower ranks of the army and the lower middle classes. But he also made an impact on the industrial proletariat, which lacked any political or trade union organisation – particularly amongst the miners and unskilled workers. The movement had obtained twenty-five per cent of the votes in the elections and returned forty-nine members of Parliament. Compared with the conservative Hungarian ruling classes, the Arrow Cross seemed like a revolutionary mass movement.

As such, the movement gave Admiral Horthy and his associates cause for concern. They made no secret of the fact that they would forcibly oppose any attempt on Szalassi's part to achieve power. Although the Germans openly supported and subsidised Szalassi and succeeded in obtaining his release from prison, they did not immediately try to force this issue. They did not need to do so as long as the Hungarian government showed its loyalty as an ally in the struggle against the USSR.

On the other hand, in Croatia it was the Fascist Ustashi party that took over power under its leader Ante Pavelić, who had been the instigator of King Alexander's assassination and who was proclaimed *poglavnik* of the Croatian state. This was because Matchek, the head of the Croatian peasant party, had rejected the advances of the Italian occupying authorities. Pavelić instituted a reign of terror against the Serbs living in Croatia, the Communists, the Jews and the gypsies. He set up concentration camps at Jasenovać and Stara-Gadićoka, in which the inmates were regularly slaughtered. The entire populations of some localities inhabited by Serbs were massacred, such as those of the village of Suvaja in July 1941.

Pavelić, who was protected by Mussolini, recognised the Italians as owners of most of the Dalmatian islands and coastline; he even accepted an Italian protectorate over Croatia and it was intended that a member of the house of Savoy should become its king; but the Duke of Spoleto never ascended his throne. The fact was that the Ustashi's atrocities had finally disturbed and aroused the indignation of their Italian protectors themselves, despite the help that they provided them in their struggle against Tito's partisans.

V COLLABORATION IN THE SOVIET UNION

Collaboration in the USSR is a question which Soviet historians seem disinclined to treat; they restrict themselves to a wholesale condemnation

COLLABORATION   285

of it as treachery, while playing down its extent and its effects. However, although all the offers made to the Poles – apart from a few isolated neophyte Quislings, like the publicist Ladislas Studnicki – had been spurned, so much so that for example, even Poles fairly close to the Nazis ideologically fought against them in the National Military Forces (NSZ), it seems that on the contrary the Wehrmacht was not always entirely unwelcome in the USSR, especially in the western territories inhabited by non-Russians.

Thus a few thousand Estonians enlisted in the Wehrmacht or in the Finnish Army and fought outside Leningrad. In the Ukraine, national councils were set up which formed combat groups. Finally, in contrast to the fierce fighting spirit of most of the Red Army units, some of them, consisting of Armenians, Tartars, Caucasians and Moslems, proved much less keen, as was shown by the abnormally high number of prisoners captured.

On the initiative of General von Schekendorff, commanding the rear area of Army Group Centre, seven armed battalions and 200,000 auxiliary volunteers (*Hilfswillige*) were raised among the Soviet prisoners of war. The *Hilfswillige* were not armed but were employed in the Wehrmacht's auxiliary services, wearing German uniforms. In the course of the war, their number grew to 650,000 out of several million POWs; but these poor hungry wretches were impelled less by the idea of voluntary service than by the desire to escape their miserable fate.

By adopting these measures, the Wehrmacht was acting rather on its own. In the USSR the instructions of the occupying authorities were always to exercise extreme rigour to the point of collective extermination. The nationalists of other races were consequently caught between 'the hammer and the anvil'. Thus some Ukrainians, under A. Melnyk, continued to support collaboration despite everything; but others, such as Stephen Bandera and Mykol Lebed began to distrust Nazi Germany as much as Bolshevik Russia, the more so as their first moves – the proclamation in Lemberg of a provisional Ukrainian government combined with a sort of pre-Parliament – were disowned by the Germans. Some Ukrainian nationalists joined underground anti-German organisations, so that in June 1942 Hitler categorically forbade the formation of *Ostbataillons* and was reluctant to agree to the use of auxiliaries. He was afraid of putting arms into his opponents' hands.

However, some German leaders had the impression that a great opportunity had been lost. This was apparently Goebbels' view and above all, Sauckel's, whose efforts to recruit labour for the Reich were hampered by the severity of the occupation. In October 1942, Rosenberg's political deputy, Otto Bräutigam, who was in charge of relations with the branch of the Wehrmacht concerned with occupation matters, even spoke up against the way Soviet POWs were treated; he described it as 'a great tragedy'; he considered it the cause of 'the increase in the Red Army's powers of resistance' and as a result responsible for the 'death of thousands of German soldiers'. Bräutigam urged on Rosenberg the need to create a Russian 'anti-régime' consisting of native Russians of standing. He was backed by officers such as Colonel Stauffenberg and the head of the Wehrmacht's propaganda services, Colonel Martin. Then, at the end of the summer of 1942, General Vlassov was captured. This Soviet army commander had had a brilliant career. As a former deputy to Chiang Kai-shek's Russian military adviser, he had received the Order of Lenin at the age of thirty-nine and had ably defended Kiev in September 1941. Then he had been put in charge of the military government in Moscow when the capital was in grave danger. Finally, he had received the order to relieve Leningrad; his army had been surrounded and, famished and exhausted, had been forced to surrender. It seems that Vlassov had been revolted by Stalin's harsh directives and the great losses that they entailed; although he would not desert, he had refused to be taken out by the aircraft that had been made available for him after the rout of his army.

Vlassov accepted Colonel Martin's suggestion of forming an anti-Stalin 'Russian Committee'. At the beginning of 1943, he issued a manifesto from Smolensk containing fourteen points: the recognition of the freedom of the peoples composing the USSR, the reintroduction of private property and political and religious liberty, the return of the land forming the kolkhozes to the peasants; in a word, he was advocating something that was not Stalinism but not capitalism either. As for the Jews, Vlassov adopted Hitler's approach in all its severity and proclaimed that there would be 'no room for Jews in the new Russia'.

Vlassov was welcomed sympathetically by the German officers and often by the local population. Rosenberg gave him his support, albeit reluctantly, for he favoured the dismemberment of the USSR whereas Vlassov merely wanted to give greater autonomy to the various peoples, which did not win him the sympathy of the Baltic or Ukrainian nationalists.

At the end of the day, Hitler restricted his role to being an instrument of propaganda to increase the number of desertions from the Red Army. No important operation was ever entrusted to the Russian National Committee. Vlassov's propaganda was even kept under close watch: the Germans took the precaution of editing and publishing the newspapers representing his movement. Displeased by some of Vlassov's statements in the course of an official tour, Keitel even ordered the general to be transferred to a prisoner-of-war camp. The fact is that in the USSR, Nazi anti-Communism and racialism were not just propaganda but the expression, indeed the very heart, of German policy, even to the detriment of the military operations, where a Wehrmacht victory seemed, indeed, in hardly any doubt at the moment.

VI THE VICHY REGIME AND COLLABORATION

The almost limitless victories of the Wehrmacht reinforced the Vichy government in its conviction that Germany had won the war. It was true that the encroachments of the occupying authorities, such as the annexation of Alsace-Lorraine and forcible German participation in the French economy, still raised a tremendous stir, in Wiesbaden, however, rather than in Vichy. But the Germans had three infallible ways of bringing pressure to bear on the Vichy government: at the slightest hint of opposition, they closed the demarcation line, or used open blackmail regarding the fate of the million French prisoners of war, or set the subsidised press of the collaborators in the northern zone at the throats of the Vichy government.

Although he merely had the title of Vice-President of the Council of Ministers, Admiral Darlan had in fact been leading the government since February 1941. He had introduced three former members of the PPF into it – Pucheu, Benoist-Méchin and Marion; the first two made no secret of the fact that they were staking their careers on the success of collaboration and the third frankly advertised his Fascist views – and he was in charge of information and propaganda. As for Admiral Darlan, it would seem that he has, mistakenly, been considered as a sort of enigmatic sphinx. This naval man who had frequented Republican political circles – unusual behaviour for one in his position and regarded with suspicion – was indeed cold and cautious, despite being a southerner. He possessed great organising ability but was lacking in general culture and political experience and above all, his mind was already made up: the United States would not be ready to make war before the Germans had completed their victory. As for Britain, the Admiral's personal enemy, she was exhausted and in her final death throes. Marshal Pétain was aging and his natural tendency to let his collaborators take over responsibility at awkward moments, even if he then disowned or replaced them at the appropriate moment, left Admiral Darlan in charge of French policy.

Internally, the national revolution was touched up somewhat to bring it closer to Fascism, although neither the single party system nor the single youth movement was ever adopted. First of all, police repression was stepped up; at the beginning of 1942, 50,000 opponents of the régime were imprisoned and 30,000 interned in improvised camps; the Communists, the Gaullists, the foreign Jews and the 'unorthodox' were the main victims; the first of these in particular were despatched to twelve Algerian camps to be subjected to exhausting hard labour. When the Socialist Marx Dormoy, the former Popular Front minister, was assassinated by members of the PPF in July 1941, although a police investigation was ordered, it proceeded with leisurely caution. The murderers were arrested but their investigation took so long that two years later their trial had still not started.

Justice moreover now took its course in ways that were very different from those under the Republic. When attempts on the lives of the occupying troops began, a law on 'Communist plots' was applied retrospectively; instructions were issued that Communists who were already in prison when the attacks were made and thus had nothing to do with them, were to be sentenced to death by special courts. The Marshal set up a political Council of Justice; it was to advise him on bringing those responsible for the defeat before a Supreme Court of Justice at Riom; but on his own initiative the Marshal condemned those alleged to be guilty – Paul Reynaud, Léon Blum, Edouard Daladier and General Gamelin – to be interned before the Court of Justice had pronounced any judgment, in fact even before it had met.

In Fascist style, an oath of allegiance to the person of Marshal Pétain had to be taken first of all by the military, then by the judiciary – only one member refused – and finally by every official without discussion. The organisation of the economy became noticeably more corporative in nature. The *Charte du Travail* (Labour Charter) in its final form was different from René Belin's earlier scheme; *syndicats* (trade unions) continued to exist but they were unified and militarised, because the trade union delegates were no longer elected but appointed. Although not acknowledged as such, a sort of state control arose, partly through force of circumstance, partly because of the 'young technocrats' that Darlan liked to see around him. Thus, it was the government that fixed the minimum wage and appointed the members of the governing bodies of the professional organisations. As a first step towards government by notables that the national revolution was theoretically committed to setting up, an appointed National Council was created to advise the government; to avoid any similarity between it and a republican assembly it was to meet only in exceptional circumstances and would work mainly through its 'departments'. On the other hand, a further step was taken towards a totalitarian régime by forming, within the Ex-Servicemen's Legion, a *service d'ordre* (SOL), to maintain good order and discipline, whose uniform and function were an unfortunate reminder of the way in which the ss had come into being.

These internal Fascist tendencies of the régime went together with an outspoken desire to collaborate. Marion instructed the press to publish nothing that might stand in the way of collaboration.

One sign of this tameness was the stricter application of the anti-Semitic laws. A quota was fixed for the number of Jews to be admitted into the liberal professions – for lawyers it was two per cent. The 'Aryanisation' of Jewish concerns in the occupied zone proceeded according to the rules laid down by Vichy and under the supervision of French officials. A 'Legion of French Volunteers against Bolshevism' was raised in the northern zone; it was a private foundation, the work of the collaborationist movements but it received the blessing and the encouragement of the French head of state.

Would matters reach the stage of military collaboration? Admiral Darlan was still tending that way, despite the abortive 'Paris protocols'; and Weygand's recall from North Africa reassured the Germans. In January 1942, Rommel was once again in difficulties in Libya and he withdrew; Benghazi was recaptured by the British. It seemed the *Afrika Korps* might have to retreat to Tunisia. The Vichy government showed concern and negotiations were started between Abetz and Darlan's envoy, Benoist-Méchin. On the French side there exists no written evidence about them and they are known only through remarks made by the negotiator. But on the German side, the matter appears quite plain: Abetz communicated to Berlin a proposal from the Vichy government that it would enter the war against Britain. He stated explicitly that this proposal had been unanimously approved. But Rommel's situation recovered and Hitler, true to his principle of not creating a running sore in French Africa or, more accurately, of not opening the door to the British Army, did not proceed further with Vichy's proposal; once again, he did not need to.

So Darlan failed to reap any benefit from his policy of collaboration; he succeeded neither in obtaining the return of any large numbers of French prisoners nor any relief from the financial and economic burden imposed by the armistice convention. It seemed this was perhaps because he was *persona non grata* with the Germans, and especially with Abetz. For in Vichy they did not realise that the Germans were neither able nor willing to grant concessions to France, whatever leaders she might have. It was thought that Pierre Laval enjoyed their trust and that he was the one man to meet the situation; so in April 1942 he returned to power. The German leaders were so unenthusiastic, however, that Goering even urged him not to accept, although Abetz was delighted. This return made up for his personal failure on December 13, 1940.

Pierre Laval made no secret of the fact that he would intensify the policy of collaboration. He would have a free hand because the Constitutional Bill no. xi conferred on him 'effective control of France's internal and external policy'. Pétain had finally become the 'figurehead' that Laval had wanted him to be as long ago as June 1940. Pierre Laval brought new blood into the government; the Marshal's earlier ministers either resigned or were dismissed by him; two convinced supporters of collaboration, A. Bonnard and Bichelonne were appointed, one to 'condition' French youth, the other to control the economy in the way likely to prove most satisfactory to the Germans.

With the same purpose in mind, Laval took four crucial decisions. He used the whole weight of Vichy's information and propaganda services to requisition labour by luring Frenchmen to volunteer for work in Germany; he thought up the idea of older prisoners being 'relieved' by young workers; when the supply of volunteers for Germany began to run dry, he threatened and punished defaulters and set the French police on to them. He changed the 'Legion of French Volunteers' into the 'Tricolour Legion', thus giving it an official status. He instructed the French police to carry out massive round-ups of foreign Jews, both in the southern and in the occupied zones. Finally, he allowed the Gestapo to track down French resisters in the southern zone, especially those passing clandestine radio messages to the British believing that they were safe from the Germans.

Pierre Laval was a loyal supporter of Nazi Germany, and his loyalty never swerved. He expressed it in the plainest possible terms: 'I want Germany to win' he stated in June 1942. The next clause provides the explanation of this wish: 'since otherwise Bolshevism will triumph in Europe'; but this clause in no way reduces the gravity of his statement nor does it make his intention less obvious.

VII THE FRIENDSHIP OF SPAIN

During the war against France, the Spaniards had shown themselves actively friendly towards the Axis. Franco had been anxious to preserve the neutrality of his country exhausted by civil war and despite his fears that if the war were protracted the Anglo-Saxons might carry it into Spanish territory, he was bound to Germany and Italy by obligations that were too recent for him not to oblige them in his turn. He had agreed to allow German submarines to refuel in Spanish waters and for radio and meteorological stations to co-operate with the Luftwaffe. This had not prevented the Germans from expressing their dissatisfaction and Goering had sharply criticised the Caudillo for not entering the war.

After the defeat of France some Spaniards felt that the time had come to help themselves to some of the French colonies. Serrano Suñer became Foreign Minister instead of General Beigbeder, who was thought to be too neutral, or even anglophile. But in October 1940, in Hendaye, Hitler refused to pay the high price that Franco set as a condition of participating in a coalition to take Gibraltar from Britain and carry the war into Africa via the French colonies. As a result the relations between the Axis and their debtor cooled off.

The entry of the Wehrmacht into the USSR clarified the situation; the focal point of the war was now definitely moving away from the Iberian peninsula. Hitler was now no keener than Franco to see Spain turn into a battlefield where her weakness, like that of the French colonies, could only tempt the Anglo-Saxons to make a move.

This did not affect the question of ideological solidarity; the very day that the German-Soviet war started, a mass demonstration took place in Madrid in front of the British Embassy, shouting: 'Gibraltar'. Franco raised no objections to transferring workers to Germany; he merely negotiated on their behalf the most favourable possible terms. Since Bolshevism was for him the implacable enemy of Christian civilisation, of which Spain was the champion, in reply to Hitler's appeal for an 'anti-Bolshevik crusade', Franco sent the 'Azul Division' to fight in the USSR; its strength rose to 60,000 men. In addition, rare metallic ores, such as wolfram, were reserved for the Reich.

All this time, the Anglo-Saxons were working out more or less realistic schemes for occupying the Canary Islands; but at the same time, Churchill did not hesitate to hint at a future settlement with Spain after the war, at the expense of the French colonial possessions. Franco refused to be tempted; he remained true to his ideological friends and made the theatrical gesture of offering the 'breasts of a million Spaniards' to form a bulwark in Berlin should the need arise. Such grandiloquence made no positive contribution towards collaboration that was of a sentimental rather than an effective nature.

VIII SWEDISH SUPPLIES

The Swedes had been terrified to see the war coming closer as a result of the Finnish and Norwegian campaigns. They had succeeded in preserving their neutrality by failing to respond to their neighbours' appeals for help. Germany's victory had insured them against the risk of becoming an operational theatre but inevitably made them henceforth dependent on Germany. Being unable to refuse the Reich's requests, Sweden attempted merely to limit their extent and to obtain the best possible terms in return.

From 1940 onwards and throughout the whole of the war, Sweden supplied Germany with almost all the iron ore that she mined but did not herself smelt, that is, about 9,000,000 tons a year. After raising certain difficulties, she agreed that the Wehrmacht's equipment and troops on their way to and from Norway should be transported by rail over her territory or by ship through her territorial waters. Between July and December 1940, 130,000 men and more than 500 railway trucks passed through in both directions. In June 1941, when a whole German division

with all its men and equipment went over Swedish territory to take up its
positions in Finland on the Soviet tundra, Swedish neutrality became really
nothing more than a polite fiction, particularly as German aircraft were
flying over her air space without let or hindrance.

Nonetheless, Sweden set a limit beyond which she would not go; she
refused to sign a political treaty with Germany and she would not
accept the Reich's suggestions that she should become, officially and in
writing, an economic unit in Germany's Europe, even if, in fact, she was
one. Her policy brought her not inconsiderable advantages: she paid for
German coal at one-third the price paid by Switzerland; although, as
in other countries throughout Europe, her balance of payments with the
Reich was in deficit, it was quite a bearable one.

In compensation, Sweden did not pursue the British agents operating
in her territory with any great zeal; she gave shelter to Danish and Norwegian resisters; she gave asylum to Jews who were being hunted down
in Denmark. In short, she endeavoured to give the least possible dissatisfaction to the Allies, who alleviated the blockade somewhat in her
favour. This did not prevent the Baltic from becoming a German lake.

The same thing happened in the Black Sea. Although Turkey had been
a creditor in her clearing account with Germany even before the war, and
though she was afraid of supplying goods without receiving any equivalent return, she applied the clauses of the trading agreement signed in
June 1940 with scrupulous exactness. She provided the Reich with grain,
oil seed and scarce metallic ores. Von Papen, the German ambassador, was
extremely active and he laid down the law in Ankara. As long as the
Wehrmacht successes continued, it would be difficult for small states not
to submit to the law of the conqueror.

CHAPTER 6

Resistance Movements Begin

THERE was resistance to the occupying power throughout Europe. It could be found in every occupied country, but it was never unified or co-ordinated. This enormous Trojan horse in the heart of enemy territory was, of course, used by the Allies but with some mistrust. Yet in every country the resisters were much alike. First of all, they were anti-German; Italian occupation was relatively restricted and milder. All the resisters were motivated by two feelings: patriotism and the hatred of foreign or national Fascism; their war was at one and the same time a political struggle and military combat, ideological as well as patriotic. Consequently the resisters hounded down collaborators who were the friends of the enemy; resistance turned into civil war and sought to take over power.

Resistance warfare was ruthless; since the occupier had made terror a method of government, the partisans replied with counter-terror – the Germans, incidentally, called them 'terrorists'. It was a total war, based on a rudimentary sort of Manicheism: you were either for or against the occupier and those in between, the ones who were neutral or lukewarm, were fated to disappear because sooner or later they were forced to take a decision. Finally, the Resistance army was born under the sign of poverty; it lacked weapons, money and trained personnel; all it could do was to produce as many 'pin-pricks' as possible, without expecting to gain any real victory; it was incapable of winning the war and it was often merely an advance party that had to be sacrificed, doomed never to enjoy the victory for which its sacrifices had prepared the way; its losses were, proportionately, very high.

I THE METHODS OF THE RESISTANCE FIGHTERS

In every country the resisters found themselves in basically similar situations; they were all volunteers, often thrown entirely on their own resources. Their groups were always very unstable; for want of experience and precedents, they had to work out their own methods of fighting.

Passive resistance was an early form, before the resisters had gained any experience; it was shown in deliberately misunderstanding the occupiers' orders or by slowness in carrying them out, spreading witticisms or jokes which ridiculed the victor and cut him down to size. It was a spontaneous action of limited scope which worried the occupier because he sensed it rather than being able to weigh up its exact importance, except when it was shown by gatherings and demonstrations in places of historic importance – Wenceslas Square in Prague or the Arc de Triomphe in Paris.

This popular action fitted in with the psychological warfare that the Resistance movements discovered by experience. The distribution of occasional tracts, followed by newspapers that appeared more or less regularly, was another step forward, since it presupposed the existence of organised and stable groups – collecting news items, building up stocks of ink and paper, using printing machines, distributing the various broadsheets.

The underground press was in itself a form of action because though its aim was to inform, it sought even more to convince and stir up public opinion. The latter was also aroused by the behaviour of the occupying power, especially towards the Jews. Help for the enemy's victims – Jews and escaped prisoners – was highly dangerous for the helper; it thus implied a more determined commitment and it necessitated joint group action. One example of this was the escape channels which collected, sheltered and passed through to safety Allied aircrews who had been shot down over occupied territory.

All these early groups were formed by chance meetings, common sympathies or friendships, professional, ideological or family links. The networks were something different, especially the intelligence networks. They could not be satisfied with more or less active sympathisers; they necessitated learning a technique. The intelligence networks were rather like spy-rings, and their agents had to learn how to observe, select and pass on their information; but it was not professional spying nor was it practised in enemy country but in one's own national territory occupied by the enemy; many sections of the population were involved.

Informing the Allies as to the disposition, movements and intentions of the enemy was in itself a form of aggression against it. But sabotage and violence against persons were direct action; with the poor resources at its disposal, the subjugated population tried to paralyse the enemy war-machine. They began with acts that were in easy reach – cutting telephone wires, attacks on isolated soldiers. Later, sabotage became part of a strategy linked with the advance of the Allied armies. Thus in occupied territories, war turned to such things as destroying transport and factories working for the enemy. Corporate bodies such as railwaymen or post office workers were to play an important role in this because of the opportunities offered by their profession. Other forms of sabotage were working to rule or an open strike. The culmination of these tactics was the 'scorched earth' policy which caused the local population as much suffering as the enemy, if not more.

The logical outcome of all these operations was to take up arms again. It began with groups (called *maquisards* in France and 'partisans' in the USSR) which undertook harassing operations – attacks on depots, on patrols, on collaborators or raids against villages. These groups operated in inaccessible districts of the occupied territory, in mountains or forests. Their chief weapon was their mobility; the scope and force of the action depended on the amount of co-operation they found amongst the population itself; they could not exist if it were hostile. In this way the Resistance movements could form a proper front, as in Yugoslavia or Russia, or rouse a whole people, as in France and Poland.

II THE ALLIES AND THE RESISTANCE

In all their activities, the Resistance movements would be rendered powerless had they to rely on their own resources; they needed to receive arms, ammunition, money, instructions and sometimes even instructors from outside. They had to fit into Allied strategy and even more important not obstruct it; they were of tactical importance only and it was not for them to choose how they should be used. That at least was the view of the big Allied powers towards them; poor but proud, the Resistance movements felt restive under this control but were unable to shake it off.

Until June 1941, Britain was alone in the war; she carried with her all the hopes of the occupied peoples, as she was sheltering the legal governments driven out of their countries by invasion. Britain tried to inject something of her determination into the subjected peoples. Broadcasting thus proved to be a powerful instrument of psychological warfare. The BBC organised thirty-five hours' broadcasting a day, directed at eighteen countries in twenty-three different languages. In 1943, the German department of the BBC comprised more than a hundred people. Thus the populations of the various countries were no longer left in ignorance of the way the war was going; they learnt about British successes and German setbacks; they were told what was happening in their own countries, of the enemy's depredations at their expense or of the way in which they were threatened by its intentions. They no longer felt isolated and they could receive advice and even instructions. Resignation was replaced by hope and a feeling of impotence by the will to act. The skill of the BBC lay in not copying Goebbels' consummate technique of lying. The BBC showed complete and utter frankness; it did not hide British failures; it appealed to reason, to the critical faculties and the better feelings of its listeners. Its action was carried further by parachute drops of pamphlets, newspapers and miniature books, but the effect of these was infinitesimal compared with that of the radio broadcasts which at regular intervals spread the good word into every home.

But at the same time, Britain looked on the Resistance movement as a sort of rearguard on the Continent. They expected to receive intelligence information from them, as for example news of German preparations for a landing. Military intelligence sent agents over to the Continent to form intelligence networks by recruiting volunteers amongst the nationals whose position in society made them good sources of information – such as engineers working in naval dockyards. For its part, the Ministry of Economic Warfare had formed a subversive warfare branch – Special Operations Executive (SOE) – with the task of organising, in all the occupied countries, sabotage of the enemy war effort, limited in scope, at carefully selected places and with small groups of agents.

Britain thus perfected a whole technique of underground warfare: 'personal messages' on the radio giving direct instructions to agents hundreds of miles away, in language that could be understood by them alone; training camps for agents; despatching men or materials by submarine or air; the manufacture of the appropriate tools – explosives such as malleable plastic, devices for two-way radio transmission, clandestine transmitters that became more and more powerful and easy to handle.

But Britain's influence could be more easily and effectively exercised in western than in central and eastern Europe, because of the distances involved. On the other hand, she allowed the Resistance movements in each country only limited independence; she was even afraid that they might launch out prematurely; she counselled caution and warned them to await better days. The attitude of the USSR after June 1941 was quite different.

When the USSR was invaded, Stalin made an appeal for help to Communist parties all over the world. He wanted them to begin fighting the occupying power without delay by all the means in their power, however limited, so as to pin down as many troops as possible and prevent their being sent to Russia. Communists everywhere responded to this appeal. Until now, they had professed the belief that the war was being waged between two rival imperialistic powers and that whatever the outcome it did not concern the people. And now, suddenly, they were to preach a patriotic war, a war to the knife; the French Communist party took over the traditionally anti-German slogans of the nationalists: 'One man, one Boche.'

The Communists supported and practised what they called 'immediate action', consisting of violence and sabotage, without worrying about enemy reprisals and the losses they would entail. But at the same time, they found the right words to appeal to the mass of the people; they explained that their wretched state, although indeed brought about by monopolistic capitalism, had been rendered intolerable by Hitler's aggression. So the social revolution must be achieved through national liberation. Except in Yugoslavia, the Communists in every country stretched out the hand of friendship to all the enemies of the occupying power, even if overnight they had been their opponents. They advocated the formation of broadly based 'national fronts'.

With the Communists, the Resistance movements became more popular and more incisive; strikes, stoppages and sabotage increased in the factories. In return, the occupying power used sterner measures; it took to shootings and taking 'hostages'; the blood of these martyrs inspired further volunteers who were brought into the Communists' orbit. Despite this, they received no help from the USSR; the latter was too heavily absorbed in her own fight and too much concerned about her own fate to be able to share any of her own resources. Russia did not organise anything resembling the British SOE; she sent weapons and equipment only to her own partisans. She merely issued instructions via the Comintern and these instructions were obeyed.

III RESISTANCE IN WESTERN EUROPE

The legal governments of Norway, Holland and Belgium were in London and in the occupied territories nobody questioned their legality. But their weakness made them entirely dependent on the British, who practically controlled the Resistance movements in the occupied countries, and even sent them articles already written for inclusion in the underground newspapers. In all these countries the Communist party played little part. The situation in France was completely different.

In Norway, where a landing was one of Churchill's obsessions to which he gave a periodical airing, surprise attacks – notably on the Lofoten Islands – were carried out by Norwegian commandos from London, with information and help from local resisters. Since it was organised by officers the Resistance movement assumed a military nature and was formed into one single group, the *Milorg*, under the actual commander of the Norwegian Army, General Ruge. Communications were established with the Shetland Isles which functioned with such regularity that they became known as the Shetland bus. One of the exploits of the Resistance movement was the partial sabotage of the 'heavy water' factory in March 1943.

For their part, the Norwegian population offered unswerving moral resistance to Quisling's attempts to organise them in the Nazi manner; academics, officials, the young and the sportsmen all refused to be shepherded into single movements. The Lutheran Church spoke out condemning collaboration. The High Court ceased to function. The high commissioner, Terboven, retorted by mass arrests – 1,000 officers and 1,200 students were picked up in a single operation.

In Denmark the situation was different, as collaboration was official, since the German invasion had not changed either the régime or its leaders. But the Nazis were not very successful; in the 1943 elections 97 per cent of the votes went to democratic parties. Resistance started through the operations of the SOE; information for the British was communicated to Sweden by secret telephone. Then, as the war proceeded, the Danes gradually changed their attitude, especially after the measures adopted against the Jews, and the Danish authorities followed suit. Underground papers were circulated and organised sabotage began. Seven thousand Jews were saved and sent to Sweden. But the country was flat and unwooded and did not lend itself to guerrilla warfare.

Holland was no more suited to this type of warfare than Denmark. Her isolation in the middle of occupied countries with no outlet to the outer world was hardly conducive to underground activity. Yet it is remarkable that an underground was formed despite the attentions of the Germans and despite the activities of Mussert's movement. It was the arrest of Jews in Amsterdam that sparked off the first large-scale popular reaction in February 1941; it took the form of a sympathetic strike and some universities had to be shut down.

An underground press which had existed since the summer of 1940 published newspapers running to 80,000 copies (*I shall hold on, The Word, Free Holland*); in 1941, 120 secret newspapers were circulating; in 1943 there were another 150. At about the same date the first intelligence networks began to function; reports and messages reached London via Sweden or Geneva; escape organisations linked up with Belgian and French networks. But this activity was brought to a halt by a remarkable success on the part of German counter-intelligence services, who managed to take the place of the resisters, collecting the parachute drops intended for them and for some months transmitting false intelligence to the British. The harm thus caused was not made good until the end of 1943. But before then, many students and workers had refused to go to work in Germany. There were frequent brawls between Dutch Nazis and resisters.

In Belgium, memories of the occupation in 1914–18 were still very fresh in men's minds and the first underground newspapers took the titles of earlier days – *Libre Belgique* was a notable example. Escape networks automatically picked up the threads of the First World War; they extended their activities into France; thus 'Comète' had branches in Montauban and 'Pat O'Leary' in Marseilles.

From 1942 onwards, contact had been made with the government in London and there were thirty-five intelligence networks in operation, employing almost 10,000 people, including 300 agents who had been dropped by parachute. The Belgian government decided to let the 'Secret Army' have sole control of military Resistance while the 'Independence Front' was in charge of civil action. But there were other fringe groups that remained independent. In contrast with Holland, armed action had been contemplated, in the Ardennes.

IV THE FRENCH RESISTANCE

The French had no experience of underground warfare; they were utterly crushed by the defeat of their reputedly invincible army, without arms and condemned to a state of underdevelopment that produced privation, physical suffering and lack of spirit, and they were more than divided by their misfortunes. They were thus inclined to inertia, and this was encouraged by the Vichy régime's propaganda which asserted that it was the duty of every good citizen to obey Marshal Pétain – 'think Pétain' was their injunction.

In these circumstances, the first volunteers in favour of continuing the struggle gathered round General de Gaulle in London, and the volunteers who had remained in France were anxious to help or join him. General de Gaulle thus found himself commanding a small army which fought in the Atlantic, in the skies of Europe, in Ethiopia, in the Sahara and in Libya. This army was gradually increased by additions from territories that came over to his cause, either voluntarily, like Equatorial Africa, the Cameroons and the Pacific islands or else after a fight, like Saint-Pierre-et-Miquelon, Syria, the Lebanon and Madagascar. Now and again the British let General de Gaulle speak to the French on the BBC. They also allowed him to form a special organisation, the *Bureau central de Renseignements et d'Action* which was to make contact with the French underground Resistance movement and provide it with arms and officers.

Free France was a conglomeration of Frenchmen from every political and social sphere. Its intention was to be merely a fighting organisation and its leader pledged himself to leave the French to decide the fate of their country for themselves after the war. However, it categorically and vigorously condemned both the Third Republic, which they regarded as responsible for the defeat and which had now disappeared as a result of that defeat; and the Vichy régime which was considered illegal and guilty of abject and premature submission to the occupying power.

In France, the customary framework of society no longer existed – political parties, trade unions or societies such as the Freemasons. The French were thus open to form fresh allegiances. They discovered General de Gaulle through the British radio; few, however, followed him immediately; for a long time to come the French people continued to put their trust in Marshal Pétain, who was universally respected. In the 'armistice army', however, in violation of the terms of the convention, certain branches of the service were stockpiling arms and arresting German agents.

Meanwhile an underground press was developing spontaneously and attacking the occupier, though not always the Vichy régime; heterogeneous groups of 'Resistance movements' grew up round these newspapers. For a long time they were to remain rather weak, lacking both substance and experience, short of money and without any means of action. However, they differed according to the zones. In Alsace, which had been annexed, any opposition was considered treason by the Germans; if they did not want to return to their country, the Alsatians who were sheltering in France could only rely for help on the Vichy authorities. In the *départements* of Nord and Pas-de-Calais, memories of the 1914–18 occupation contributed to the early appearance of a Resistance movement; in December 1940 the Lille *Feldkommandantur* reported forty telephone wires cut and a dozen other acts of sabotage. But groups such as 'La Voix du Nord' could only find local recruits and could influence only a restricted area.

In the occupied zone, there was a good deal of enterprising activity and the presence of the occupying power was a constant provocation. Officers organised intelligence branches, in co-operation with the armistice army's own intelligence services. Young ethnologists at the Musée de l'Homme formed a Committee of Public Safety which started circulating a roneoed broadsheet, *Résistance*, as early as December 15, 1940. Students published and distributed the newspaper *Défense de la France*. 'Ceux de la Résistance', 'Ceux de la Libération', 'Pantagruel', 'Valmy' and 'Arc' were little groups that had difficulty in avoiding the attentions of the Gestapo. 'Libération Nord' and 'l'Organisation civile et militaire' were larger because the first of them drew its recruits from trade unionists and Socialists and the second from reserve officers' associations and government and industrial executives.

In the southern zone where the absence of any occupying power reduced the risk, there were three large movements that extended to every *département*: 'Franc-Tireur' and above all Emmanuel d'Astier de la Vigerie's 'Libération Sud' and 'Combat'. Henri Frenay, the leader of the latter, showed himself to be a remarkable organiser; he created the structures of underground Resistance – secret army, propaganda, intelligence, false papers, accommodation, parachute drops, help for those in trouble.

After June 1941, the Communist party as a whole joined the Resistance movement, whereas previously only isolated members had been active in it. The party started the 'Front national', widely open to the Right. It became solidly established in both zones and produced specialised newspapers for every trade or professional association and, in theory, welcomed into its ranks the Communist party's action groups – the 'Francs Tireurs et Partisans' who, while preaching and seeking the collaboration of all the opponents of the occupying power, in fact preserved their independence.

Thus the Resistance developed an even greater tendency to form rival splinter groups, because the reappearance of the Communist party as an active force gave new life to the Socialist party. General de Gaulle's achievement was to be to unify it. His agents had already created intelligence networks, the most active of which was the 'Confrérie Notre-Dame'. But the General entrusted Jean Moulin, a former *préfet* who had joined him in London, with a far bigger political mission. With stubborn determination that was crowned by success, Jean Moulin set out first of all to co-ordinate the action of the Resistance movements in the southern zone and then those in the northern zone. By the middle of 1942 the non-occupied zone had its 'United Resistance Movements', all of whose volunteers were enlisted in one single 'Secret Army', under General Delestraint, who was appointed by General de Gaulle. At the same time, Jean Moulin provided the Resistance with joint organisations: a 'Research Committee', a department in charge of parachute drops and landing grounds, an underground press service, and a 'Solidarity Committee'.

Thanks to Moulin's activities, the Socialists, Communists and various moderate politicians acknowledged General de Gaulle's authority. Moreover de Gaulle's attitude had changed. He had promised to introduce a certain number of social reforms after the Liberation and thus appeared as a leader of a broader 'Front populaire'. Correspondingly, Marshal Pétain's popularity declined, because of the policy of collaboration which he represented. The armistice army's Resistance activities were curtailed by Laval when he returned to power; in any case, it was the work of a few groups of expert technicians, with no appeal to the masses.

Thus 'Gaullism' arose in France. It was not obedience to a blind trust in one man, General de Gaulle, but acceptance of the cause he represented: a refusal to collaborate, a refusal to give in, a continuation of the fight by all possible means inside and outside the country and the liberation, rebirth and transformation of France.

V RESISTANCE IN CENTRAL EUROPE

The first country to experience German occupation was Czechoslovakia. After March 1939, the Resistance was directed by President Beneš from

France, where he had taken refuge. The problem was to maintain or re-establish communications with the country from outside and this had been achieved by August 1939. The first underground resisters were Czechs, soldiers and Communists, in two separate groups that were un-friendly but not enemies. Opposition to Germany was shown by mass gatherings – a strike of tramway workers on the anniversary of the Munich agreement, boycotting the feast of St Mathias, in spite of a thousand preventive arrests by the Gestapo. By January 1940, a 'Central Committee for Internal Resistance' (UVOD) was circulating underground literature and broadcasting thousands of messages a month to Paris and London by secret radio transmitters. Czechs enlisted in the German Army acted as informers and others organised sabotage in Germany itself.

The defeat of France was a 'second Munich'. Then, after the German-Soviet pact, the Communists broke violently with President Beneš' supporters, whom they even accused of helping 'the British colonial magnates in their dirty war'. For its part, the provisional Czechoslovak government in London started talks with the Polish government to form, after the war, a Polish-Czechoslovak confederation which could only mean once again creating a sort of 'cordon sanitaire' round the USSR.

When the USSR entered the war, everything changed. The Comintern's directives were followed to the letter by the Czech Communists; they called for national unity against the occupier. The USSR recognised the exiled Czech government and pledged itself to restoring Czechoslovakia to her former state after the war. For his part, President Beneš had drawn his conclusions from what had happened; he was now convinced that Czechoslovakia could in future only live with the backing of Soviet friendship. The wait-and-see attitude, more or less neutralistic, represented by President Hacha and his supporters was roundly condemned, both inside and outside the country.

On May 27, 1942, agents from London executed the 'protector' Heydrich. The occupying power's reprisals were appalling: the villages of Lidice and Lezaky were destroyed and their inhabitants exterminated; 10,000 people were arrested in Bohemia, 2,000 of them underground workers. The UVOD never recovered from these blows and continued to exist only in small ineffective groups. London issued instructions to go warily. The Soviet setbacks also forced the Communists to restrict their activities. But despite these momentary handicaps, Czechoslovakia herself was making a fresh start with her underground movement. Everyone had come to recognise that its existence was dependent on two factors: the need for better internal understanding between Czechs and Slovaks and a reconciliation with the Soviet Union.

The German occupation was nowhere harsher than in Poland, nor was any other people more united in resisting the occupier. Every political party, of both left and right, resisted. In 1939 the Communist party had played a very small part, both because its leaders had taken refuge in Moscow and because the party had been abolished by the USSR in the part of Poland that she was occupying; also the Moscow exiles had been prohibited from undertaking any political activity. The Polish people thus unreservedly recognised the authority of the exiled Polish government, which had moved from Angers to London and was under the presidency of a Liberal, General Sikorski. The composition of this government reflected concern for national unity but some of its members were very reactionary, both anti-Semitic and anti-democratic. For the exiled Poles, as for most of the Resistance workers inside the country, Poland had two enemies, both more or less equally loathed: Germany and the Soviet Union.

After the defeat of France, distance made communications between London and occupied Poland difficult. Between February 1941 and April 1942, the Polish government requested 104 air operations; only twelve were authorised, nine of which were successful. The British allowed the Polish section of SOE a certain freedom which the exiled government was able to use to good effect. But on the other hand, the difficulties of communication, even by radio – the relatively few receiving sets in Poland had been confiscated by the Germans – forced the underground groups to work out their own activities. The many early small groups mainly formed themselves into the 'Secret Army' (AK).

The Soviet entry into the war did little to change the Poles' feelings towards the USSR; but it did create a new situation for General Sikorski. He went to Russia to negotiate an agreement with Stalin whereby Polish prisoners of war interned in Russia would be released to form a new Polish army. Sikorski would have liked this army to fight with the Red Army in the USSR. But Stalin raised all sorts of difficulties; he refused to make any guarantee about the Polish frontiers; in December 1941 he formed Polish Communists exiled in Moscow, some of whom had taken Soviet nationality, into a 'Polish patriots' group which did not recognise the authority of the London government. In these circumstances, it seemed wiser to despatch the new Polish Army, on its release from Soviet captivity, to the Middle East where it would be trained under the command of General Anders.

The Polish underground Resistance showed great activity; it drew up schemes for widespread sabotage operations which it put into effect – particularly against the railways to hinder traffic going to the USSR. It transmitted information concerning very large areas, collected either by Poles who had been sent to work in the Ruhr or from Poles serving in the Wehrmacht and who accompanied it in its advance up to the Volga. But however hardy and determined the Polish Resistance might be, it could not ignore the fact that, geographically, it was in the Red Army's sphere of influence and that same Red Army had invaded Poland and dismembered her in September 1939.

VI THE RESISTANCE IN THE BALKANS

After the March 1941 putsch and the invasion of Yugoslavia, King Peter went to London with his government and they were entirely cut off from their country. But in this hilly country where communications were difficult, the Wehrmacht was content merely to disrupt the army without occupying the whole territory. In the mountains there still existed units that had barely had time to be mobilised. In the heart of Serbia, in the Ravna Gora, Colonel Mihailović was thus able to retain control of his troops; he called them *chetniks*, in memory of the struggle against the Turks. His reputation soon spread beyond the borders of his own country; the exiled Yugoslav government was glad to make him their representative, in the field, with the title of War Minister. The British wished to help him but he was a long way away.

However, when the USSR entered the war, the Yugoslav Communist party, in accordance with Stalin's instructions, formed a military committee headed by Broz, otherwise known as Tito; this Communist party had few members and those were mainly in the towns; but some of its members had gained valuable military experience while fighting in the international brigades in Spain. The leaders set out to spread the good word and to set an example by their actions; on July 4, 1941, they gave the order for a national uprising; they followed this by liberating towns and installing new officials, after executing those accused of collaborating. Far from sacrificing their revolutionary programme to national unity, Tito's supporters advocated it as well as practising what they preached. They made it known that after the war the new Yugoslavia would be a federal state, totally transformed economically and socially by the revolution.

Stalin was alarmed by this political propaganda, which he found far too flamboyant and likely to jeopardise the broad anti-German alliance that he was advocating. At his urgent suggestion, Tito tried, unwillingly, to come to an agreement with Mihailović. But the latter made no secret of his 'pan-Serbianism', following the tradition of Alexander I, and this caused concern to Tito who was a Croatian. On the strength of his title of War Minister and in pursuance of the orders from his government in London, Mihailović tried to take over the partisans into his command. Consequently, agreement between the two did not last very long and internecine strife began even in Serbia itself, Mihailović's own territory, when partisans tried to establish themselves there. The *chetniks* came off second best.

From this time onwards, Tito was a lone rider, despite Stalin's calls to order. He raised a 'proletarian army', without ranks, where fighting went hand in hand with training in Communist doctrine. Wherever he settled and however short his stay, Tito abolished the existing institutions and left only the party structure intact. On November 26 and 27, 1942, he called together a consultative assembly at Bihac, consisting of fifty-four delegates representing every area and every nationality in Yugoslavia; the 'Anti-Fascist Council of National Liberation' (AVNOY), which was directing the partisans' struggle, decided to introduce communal control of property, popular political education and the establishment of revolutionary Committees of Liberation.

This spectacular success resulted in the 'National Liberation Army' (ALNY), now about 80,000 strong, being attacked by a combined force of nearly thirty German, Italian, Bulgarian, Hungarian and Ustashi divisions. During the winter of 1942–3, the partisans were forced to keep on the move from Bosnia to Montenegro, fighting hard though ravaged by typhus. They were also attacked by the *chetniks* under Mihailović, who was scared by their revolutionary programme. In Yugoslavia, therefore, the struggle against the occupying power was also a civil war and a revolution as well.

The same thing happened in Greece and Albania. In Greece, the King and the government had taken refuge in Cairo and no longer had any authority over their country, which was governed by a group of collaborationist generals. As in Yugoslavia, the Resistance was born in the mountains; sometimes it was started by officers, at other times by the Communist party. All of them were enabled to arm and equip themselves thanks to the stores left behind by the British and to the equipment relinquished or hidden by the Greek Army. But though they were agreed in continuing the struggle and repudiating the monarchy, the two main organisations soon started to fight each other. The largest non-Communist group was the EDES under General Zervas; but there were other small fringe groups, such as Colonel Psaros' EKKA. The Communists formed the ELAS group.

In October 1942, the British sent a mission to Greece. Churchill considered that it belonged to the British sphere of influence and he intended to re-establish the monarchy there, if necessary against the will of the Greeks. The British mission tried to co-operate with all the Resistance movements, indiscriminately; they helped them organise acts of sabotage to hold up the supplies going to Rommel. The sabotage of the Gorgopotamos viaduct on the Athens–Salonica line on November 25, 1942 made a great stir. But this sort of co-operation between ELAS and EDES was short-lived; the British were powerless to do anything but sit back and watch their bitter struggles.

Later on General Davies' mission to Albania met the same disappointing fate. Enver Hodja's Communist 'National Liberation Movement' was opposed by the right-wing party's 'National Front' or 'Balli'. The two groups were as keen to eliminate each other in order to seize power after the war as they were to fight the Germans. The violent British objections and rebukes had no effect.

*

So, by the end of 1942, the European Resistance movements, though not as yet very strong, were growing everywhere. Except in Yugoslavia, they did not create any actual new operational theatre but their progress and increasing support from the people worried the occupying power. At the same time the Resistance movements were bringing about fundamental modifications in the structures of the countries where they appeared. They stood revealed as a powerful factor of political and economic change. Their divisions mirrored those of the extempore coalition fighting against Nazi Germany; their internecine strife pointed forward to the divisions that later became apparent in post-war Europe.

PART II

JAPAN'S GREATER ASIA

CHAPTER I

The Break Between Japan and the United States

JAPAN had been waging war against China since 1931; despite her successes, she was becoming bogged down. The defeat of France and Britain's almost desperate isolation were to open up unlimited vistas for Japanese imperialism which stemmed equally from economic necessity and xenophobic nationalism.

I JAPANESE IMPERIALISM

On her mountainous archipelago, Japan had difficulty in supporting her highly prolific population of 73 million inhabitants. She had looked for additional resources through industrial development copied from the West and she had been remarkably successful. But even in this direction, there were serious obstacles in the way of her expansion: on her own territory she could find neither the sources of energy nor the raw materials that she needed; in order to obtain them she was obliged to dispose of a large part of her manufactured goods to other countries at a low price. As her economic stability and progress was thus bound up with the size of her external trade, which had to be shipped by sea, her economy was vulnerable. It had already suffered from growing pains in 1919 and had been very seriously affected by the worldwide slump of the 'thirties.

Japanese nationalism, based on the firm belief in Japan's divine mission, had been greatly increased by legitimate pride in the happy combination of a recently acquired western technology and an original, jealously preserved, traditional culture. Though the principles of Shintoism, the national religion teaching the divine origin of the empire of the Rising Sun, were no longer blindly accepted by the Japanese ruling classes and though they knew that their country's material civilisation still lagged behind that of the white races, they would accept no suggestion of spiritual inferiority. Without exception, they believed that one day they would catch up with their rivals and then irresistibly outstrip them. They disagreed only in the means of winning this race for supremacy.

The emperor Hirohito, more interested in laboratory experiments than in politics, and the immense trusts that had arisen through industrialisation, were both supporters of peaceful methods; was not the whole of east Asia open to economic and political penetration that would be all the more easily achieved because of their proximity and racial affinity? But some powerful nationalist groups held diametrically opposed views. Thus the Kokuhonsha, the 'Society of the Foundations of the Country', with 200,000 members, based its action on the following four principles: Japan's unique religious character; anything that was contrary to this outstanding originality should be reformed; its special nature gave Japan a special mission in Asia; and anything standing in the way of this mission must be forcibly crushed.

These secret societies contained civil and military personalities of the highest rank, but more and more they were joined by active and lively young officers who, having risen from the poorer classes, were aware of the difficult material conditions in which the Japanese people were living and wanted to put an end to this state of affairs by victories and conquests which would show that the Japanese were invincible, a fact sufficiently obvious to them since the defeat of Russia in 1905. Any Japanese leaders considered too timorous by these fanatics were fit only to be murdered; amongst others, two Prime Ministers had met the dramatic fate of being shot down in their offices at pointblank range in 1930 and 1932.

Thus Japan had gradually become steeped in a Fascist mentality suited to their national temperament: the political institutions had not changed but the control of the state had to all intents and purposes passed into the hands of the Army and Navy, where the 'Young Turks' gradually imposed their extremist views. They were xenophobes and not anti-Semites; but as in Italy and Germany they preached the cult of violence, unswerving obedience and the conviction that only war could provide the solution to the country's difficulties.

In what direction should expansion take place and on which opponent should the blow fall? In this matter the two main ruling forces, the Army and the Navy, disagreed. The Army was tempted by the vast spaces within its reach, the immense areas of Asia; there it would come up against the USSR. The Navy, by its very nature, yearned for vast horizons over the seas; the colonial empires of the British, French, Dutch and Americans barred their way or were ripe for elimination.

II THE CHINA WAR

With her vast size and supposedly inexhaustible wealth of resources, China offered both the reserves of raw materials and the commercial outlet that the Japanese were seeking. Since 1930 they had been penetrating into China in two ways: their businessmen had invested all their available capital there, and, in the country itself, after a more or less deliberately provoked incident in 1931, their Korean-based Army had, on its own authority, occupied the north-eastern provinces. From there, whether Tokyo liked it or not, it had the firm intention of occupying Manchuria and advancing at least as far as Inner Mongolia; its only fault was being more royalist than the Emperor.

The war had got off to a good start as a result of China's great military weakness. The Japanese always adopted the same procedure; they shelled the towns and then went in with their armoured vehicles; unable to defend themselves, all that the Chinese could do was to abandon the town and withdraw inland. Thus Peking, Chang-kia-kow, Tai-yuan, Canton, Hangkow, Shanghai and other towns had fallen without striking a blow. By 1939 the Japanese army had conquered the richest part of China, her ports, communication routes and her few industrial centres; but in fact, a million Japanese were lost in the vastness of China. The Army had believed that it could deal with the 'Chinese incident' in a few months; but it was able to push out in any depth only a few tentacles in order to 'mop up' a region and remained unable properly to occupy the whole country. With a few exceptions, they found themselves facing an opponent who was elusive because he was non-existent. Japan was nibbling at China without digesting her.

In face of the Japanese threat, the Chinese government of Chiang Kai-shek, a disciple of Sun-Yat-sen, the founder of the republic and leader of the single party of the Kuomintang, had in 1937 become outwardly reconciled with its Communist opponent Mao Tse-tung. The Chinese government had moved its capital out of reach of the Japanese to Chungking in the mountains of the interior. It had sent its officers to be trained in Europe and it was trying its hand at guerrilla warfare, something which only the Communists showed themselves able to do. Mao Tse-tung had summed up its principles in four lines of verse:

> *When the enemy advances, I withdraw;*
> *When the enemy withdraws, I advance;*
> *When the enemy settles in, I disturb him;*
> *When the enemy is exhausted, I fight him.*

In fact, complete anarchy reigned in China. The Japanese had been able to play on her internal dissensions and her superficial unity. They had created the theoretically independent state of Manchukuo and set up a 'Chinese Republican Central Government' under a friend of Chiang Kai-shek's, Wang Tsin-wei, who had deserted to their side. They had raised troops of mercenaries and employed terrorist methods that the Chinese called 'the three Alls' – fire, massacre and loot.

In this way, China had lost many men and most of the territories on which she depended for her soldiers and her money. This ordeal had disrupted government and caused corruption and anarchy. If left to herself China would be unable to drive out the Japanese; she would have to receive arms and the necessary instructors from outside and these could reach her only via the Yunnan-Tonkin railway line and subsidiarily via the Burma 'road', which ran over high mountains. For her part, Japan was floundering in an endless war which was hindering the exploitation of the part of the country that she had conquered. Her blatant ambition was becoming a matter of concern to all the powers with interests in China. Germany's victories in Europe were going to create a new situation, favourable to Japan.

III DEVELOPMENTS IN JAPANESE POLICY
(September 1939–June 1941)

Chiang Kai-shek was being supplied by Britain and France, from the latter via Indochina. The United States, by virtue of their axiom of not recognising any monopoly situation of any sort in China, which in their view should be 'free for all,' were also opposed to Japanese imperialism. But before the war, Chiang Kai-shek had found his main support in the USSR; in particular it was Russian pressure that had induced Mao Tse-tung to recognise his authority, in theory.

The Japanese had joined the anti-Comintern pact against the USSR in 1936. It is possible, as the Japanese ambassador in Rome has claimed, that this pact contained a secret clause with Germany in which the two countries pledged themselves not to sign any non-aggression agreement with the USSR. In any case, the signing of the German-Soviet pact had been considered by Tokyo as violating a promise. But once her representations to Berlin had been rebuffed, Japan calmed down very quickly and drew realistic conclusions from the incident: the Soviet Union was now to be left in peace by her forces alone – an undeclared war on the Siberian frontier in 1938 had already given warning of this. She therefore immediately suggested to the USSR a diplomatic settlement of the frontier dispute between Mongolia and Manchukuo. She even contemplated a non-aggression pact with the USSR, if the latter stopped supporting Chiang Kai-shek. Germany offered her good offices to help this rapprochement.

For Japan this represented a change in her foreign policy and a hint of its future course. The rapid defeat of France and Britain's forced inertia confirmed this. Japan suddenly found herself with a free hand in southeast Asia, where the United States were now her only serious rival. On September 4, 1940, at a conference of the four chief ministers, the territorial limits of Japan's 'New Order', the area of her self-appointed mission in the Far East, were fixed not just to include China and Manchukuo but also French Indochina, Thailand, Burma, Indonesia, the Pacific islands and India. Siberia, which had previously been included, no longer figured in the list. Ever since July, the GHQ had been stressing that war with Britain and the United States might prove necessary to achieve these objectives.

As a start, there was the possibility of cutting off the supplies that Chiang Kai-shek was receiving via the Yünnan railway, which was French property. An ultimatum to the Vichy government was accepted after it had realised the impossibility of offering any resistance without American help, which was not forthcoming. Operational bases, aerodromes and the port of Haiphong were granted to the Japanese though not before they had bared their teeth – in September the Canton army attacked the French in Langson and it had called off the attack only on the express orders of the Emperor.

After this success, however, Japan adopted a hesitant policy. She was weighing up the pros and cons of caution and peaceful advance, advocated by the Emperor, the diplomats, the businessmen and part of the Navy which was worried by the shortage of fuel oil in the event of a conflict with the USA and of a sudden strike, which now seemed possible owing to an exceptionally favourable combination of circumstances; convinced of its invincibility, the Army was urging immediate action on these lines and was warmly supported in the government by the War Minister, General Tojo. The Prime Minister Prince Konoye was striving to satisfy the military without going as far as open war; but the military leaders were thoroughly determined to go their own way, in the best interests of the country.

The anti-American trend of Japanese policy was confirmed by the signing of the tripartite pact in September, 1940, whereby Japan received Germany's and Italy's agreement and support for the creation of a Greater East Asia Co-Prosperity Sphere in the vast area granted her in the proposed carve-up of the world. In October 1940, a Japanese mission went to the Dutch East Indies to arrange for supplies of tin, crude oil and rubber but found some difficulty in obtaining them.

Germany was very keen to reap the benefit of her agreement with Japan. By using the threat that Japan represented for the British Commonwealth in Asia, she thought that she might induce Britain to end the war. And by the prospect of a war on two fronts which this threat also offered, she hoped to persuade the United States not to abandon their neutrality. She thus encouraged Japan to confine her attentions to the weakest opponent, the British Commonwealth. In February 1941, Ribbentrop stated to the Japanese ambassador, Oshima: 'The Reich and Japan are both in the same boat. German defeat would mean the end of Japan's imperial ambitions, too. It would seem to be in Japan's interests to ensure that while the war is on she achieves the positions that she wishes to have when peace is concluded.'

This appeal did not fall on deaf ears; in January 1941, the Japanese General Staff was examining how to attack Singapore. But the German-Japanese agreement was not entirely free from suspicion and reservations. The immense expansion of a coloured people did not inspire great joy in the hearts of the racialist specialists amongst the Nazis. When Japan requested a completely free hand in Indochina and the Dutch East Indies, Germany expressed the wish that the *status quo* should remain unchanged: the German ambassador in Tokyo even described Japan's action in Indochina as 'a breach of trust'. Ribbentrop wanted to 'retain this bone of contention amongst the Pacific powers'.

On two occasions, a Chinese diplomat, followed by Kurusu, the Japanese ambassador in Berlin, and a Japanese general, asked for the Reich to mediate in order to settle the 'Chinese incident'. This idea was supported by Ott, the German ambassador in Tokyo. He considered that a peaceful bloc could be formed in Asia with Japan, China and the USSR. This would force the USA to remain very much on the alert in Asia and consequently reduce their freedom of action in Europe. But Germany refused to mediate between China and Japan.

Perhaps she was afraid that, once Japan had escaped from her Chinese wasps' nest, she would launch out on a war with the USA which would then inevitably fall back on to her. In any case, it is probable that the coolness of the support that she received from her ally confirmed Japan in her intention of pursuing her own policy alone by her own means. Failing peace with China, before embarking on any other venture, she needed to be covered in her rear by the neutrality of the USSR. Since Stalin was similarly concerned, the agreement which he and Matsuoka signed during the latter's brief visit to Moscow in April 1941, surprising as it might seem at first sight, stemmed very logically from the immediate interests of the two parties, as a not too remote consequence of the German-Soviet pact.

It confirmed that Japan had chosen to direct her expansion towards the South Seas. It left Japan and the USA a little more in direct confrontation, with the risk of a conflict accepted by the former. How, for their part, did the Americans see their policy in the Pacific and their relations with Japan?

IV THE DEVELOPMENT OF AMERICAN POLICY

The Americans had watched with concern Japan's takeover of Manchuria. They had condemned the treaty violations and had not recognised Manchukuo. However, they had carefully refrained from any gesture liable to lead them into a conflict for which they were unprepared. Businessmen were anxious for continued good relations with their Japanese customers or suppliers; before 1939, the Army was not strong and thinking only of defending its own continent, or at the most of defending the Philippines. The Navy, though better armed, wanted its strength to be increased and it did not want to fight on two fronts.

In these circumstances, the State Department followed a policy of extreme patience and caution. In spite of all their interests in China – capital investments, schools, hospitals, missions – which were jeopardised by the Sino-Japanese war, the United States confined themselves to making formal protests and advising their subjects to leave the country. The President even warned American citizens that they would transport weapons into China at their own risk. Passports were refused to airmen engaged as instructors by the Chinese.

Roosevelt was as conscious of the seriousness of the threat from Japan as of the danger from Germany. Grew, the American ambassador in Tokyo, recommended taking a tough line, to intimidate the Japanese, which was, in his view, the only way to avoid a trial of strength with them. Chiang Kai-shek's government was very popular in the States; it was spending enough money there to achieve that. Chiang was considered an American-style democrat and his wife's family, the Songs, as well as his wife herself, had a large number of friends in a wide variety of circles. In a word, it would have been quite easy to arouse American enthusiasm for China against the Japanese – the success of Pearl Buck's novels was a measure of this infatuation. In any case it would have been easier than arousing the Americans against Germany in favour of France. But Roosevelt was well aware the worldwide nature of his obligations and he declined to make any premature or precipitate choice between Europe and Asia.

Accordingly Churchill's pleas in July and September 1940 that American ships should be sent to Singapore fell on deaf ears, as did Chiang's appeals for help or the suggestion of the Dutch East India authorities to hold a conference to organise the joint defence of the archipelago. The Vichy government's approaches at the time of the Japanese ultimatum over Indochina were equally unsuccessful.

Roosevelt was convinced that war between the United States and Japan was inevitable but he was endeavouring to delay it in order to be in a better position to meet it. He undertook limited and cautious retaliatory measures aimed at convincing the Japanese that America was taking a firm line. The entry of the Canton Army into Indochina was thus met by a partial embargo on goods indispensable for Japanese industry, starting with steel and scrap iron. The list of these goods grew gradually longer, with crude oil being kept as the final trump card. At the same time, considerable loans were granted to China, who was allowed to join the lend-lease club in May 1941.

However, the President was inhibited in this course of action by Britain's difficulties which he wished to remedy first. In January 1941, he came to an agreement with the British Premier that in the event of America's entering the war, Germany would be enemy number one; Japan would come later. This decision was not made known to the American public, which, even if it was not interested in Singapore, was concerned about Manila. But the decision did not prevent the Navy from keeping its eyes firmly fixed on the Pacific, although it did force Roosevelt to proceed more gently with Japan.

On April 9, 1941, the Secretary of State, Cordell Hull, informed the new Japanese ambassador of the American conditions for the maintenance of good relations between their two countries: respect for the territorial integrity of nations; equal rights and the principle of the 'open door' in matters of colonial expansion; non-intervention in the affairs of other countries; the *status quo* in the Pacific. It was not a very conciliatory attitude; but there was no threat of breaking-off relations and the door was left ajar for a diplomatic solution. Moreover, these rules were to be valid for the future only; the failure to mention the past was an implicit recognition of Manchukuo. 'If the Japanese government accepts these principles,' concluded Cordell Hull, 'they can serve as a basis for fresh negotiations.'

Prince Konoye's view was to accept these proposals and start talks; 'the Chinese incident' he thought, could be settled only by agreement with the USA; any advance southwards by force of arms would be fraught with immense danger; successful talks would enable Japan's stocks of raw materials to be peacefully replenished. But the Foreign Affairs and War Ministers, Matsuoka and Tojo, had different views from the Prime Minister's and they carried the day. Japan merely offered the United States a non-aggression pact, which, considering the offer inadequate, they rejected.

Attitudes were hardening on both sides. However, on June 21 the Americans moved a step forward: if the Chinese matter could be settled satisfactorily for both parties, they said, normal trading could be resumed between the two countries.

V THE JAPANESE-AMERICAN NEGOTIATIONS
(June–December 1941)

Germany's attack on the USSR on that same day opened up a new phase in Japanese-American relations. Once again, Germany had acted without consulting and without even informing Japan. And now here she was inviting Japan to start a war against Russia too, when only a few months earlier she had been persuading her against it! Although the ink on the non-aggression pact with the USSR was hardly dry, Matsuoka was tempted by the prospect of an easy conquest of Siberia. But there the Japanese would find neither the raw materials nor the commercial outlets which they were seeking. The Army pointed out that it was an unhoped-for chance to lay hands on them where they could be found; Britain had her back to the wall and the Soviet Union, too, for the moment; the United States were not ready. Its decision was irrevocable and it carried the day. Japan would expand, by force of arms, into the South Seas.

Negotiations now began between Japan and the United States. It is difficult to say whether they were sincere or whether on both sides their only purpose was to gain time with each party hoodwinking the other. It is possible that they may have been complicated by misunderstandings that have been analysed by the American historian Butow: the inexperience and ignorance of English of Admiral Nomura, who did not communicate to his government until May American proposals that had been made the previous month; the intervention of certain officious emissaries who led the Japanese to believe that negotiations had started and thus that the Americans were prepared to be conciliatory whereas the latter were making the start of actual negotiations conditional on a minimum agreement on principles. One certain thing was that each side hoped to influence the other by a show of toughness and considered that the best way to bring the other round was to be highhanded. Was it not being said in Washington that Prince Konoye had a photograph of Roosevelt in his room?

However, in July 1941, after Konoye had got rid of the tiresome Matsuoka, a sort of compromise was reached between the opposing Japanese factions; it was decided that as a concession to the Emperor, Konoye and the Navy they would continue to negotiate but that at the same time certain precautionary steps must be taken in order to be in a favourable position should negotiations break down. The generals did not fail to take advantage of this. The importance of the views of the Army in the field had been frequently demonstrated by its tendency to act on its own initiative, so much so that before going to Washington Admiral Nomura had felt compelled to go the rounds of the Korean and Chinese headquarters. But the order to send troops into southern Indochina in July 1941 came from Tokyo. The Vichy government knuckled under all the more easily because this time it was under pressure from Germany who was anxious to see Japan going on the warpath. In addition, after urging the Siamese to claim part of Cambodia, Japan had placed herself in their good books by insisting on acting as mediator to ensure that they obtained it, despite the fact that their fleet had been smashed by a tiny French naval force from Indochina. It was clear that this new step was aimed at Malaya and Singapore and possibly Burma as well.

Coming as it did in the middle of the negotiations, this step persuaded the Americans of the bad faith of the Japanese, the more so as their secret services had succeeded in deciphering the secret code used by Tokyo in its messages to the Japanese embassy in Washington. Sumner Welles therefore informed Nomura that 'such acts were opposed to the spirit of the current discussions and would make any further negotiations point-less.' A few days later, Roosevelt took the gravest step that had ever been contemplated: he froze Japanese assets in the United States and imposed an actual embargo on fuel oil. At the same time General MacArthur was appointed commander of a new operational theatre, the Far East, the creation of which, as well as MacArthur's appointment, hardly seemed inspired by thoughts of peace. The revelation of Japan's duplicity appears to have made Roosevelt switch round completely in the space of forty-eight hours; he had just had the suggestion made to Nomura that Indo-china should be declared neutral when he learned that the Japanese troops had established themselves there with the agreement of the Vichy government. His threefold decision caused the situation to deteriorate without hope of recovery. In particular the Japanese leaders were con-vinced that being deprived of dollars amounted to a blockade and would doom the Japanese economy to bankruptcy within two years. A decision must therefore be taken without delay: should it be peace or war?

However, the German suggestion of attacking Vladivostok was dis-missed by the Japanese cabinet. Prince Konoye obtained permission to make one further attempt; he would ask for an interview with Roosevelt in person. General Tojo agreed to this only on condition that this ap-proach should not stand in the way of opening hostilities with the USA if it emerged that 'the President of the United States was unable to under-stand Japan's intentions'. And as speed was essential in order to avoid 'economic strangulation' on September 5, the Japanese cabinet took some very grave decisions: it would reach a state of readiness for war by the end of October and if, by that date, it had not received satisfaction, it would make 'the decision to prepare for war'. The Emperor showed some reluc-tance but allowed the Army to convince him that the Pacific would be conquered within three months.

From this time onwards, the bogus negotiations in Washington were to be paralleled by real preparations for launching a campaign, which, moreover, were kept from the Japanese negotiators Nomura and Kurusu, the latter having been despatched specially to assist the former; both of them were keen to continue the talks and bring them to a successful conclusion. But they had been instructed to communicate to the Americans proposals that were so uncompromising as hardly to be acceptable: non-intervention in China; closure of the 'Burma road' by the British; no further aid to Chiang Kai-shek; a pledge not to undertake hostile action against Japan; agreement to hand over to Japan 'the necessary raw materials'; American support for the 'establishment of close economic relations between Japan on the one hand and the Dutch East Indies on the other'. In a word, Japan was asking the usa to acknowledge her supremacy in the Pacific and in return for these enormous demands, Japan made no concescessions whatsoever; she would evacuate Indochina, the cause of the increased tension, 'only after a fair peace has been established in the Far East'.

Did the Japanese think that, in their concern over the major German successes in the ussr, the United States would show themselves more conciliatory in Asia? If so they had made a big mistake: Cordell Hull's reply merely recalled 'the fundamental principles that the American government and people had made their own'. It was clear, after such a reply, that Roosevelt would not now agree to meet Konoye and meanwhile the autumn deadline was approaching. Yet Konoye spoke out in favour of continuing negotiations; he then received a clear ultimatum from Tojo: 'Decisions are needed that can be taken only by another cabinet.' At the same time, as if fortuitously, an attempt was made on Konoye's life. He resigned and on October 18, General Tojo formed a government, seven of whose fourteen members were either generals or admirals; Admiral Tojo became Minister of Foreign Affairs. Ribbentrop urged them to be firm but they needed no urging.

On November 3, having obtained the assurance that, in the event of war with the United States, Germany would follow Japan, Tojo sent Nomura 'the final Japanese proposals'. At the same time, on November 5, without waiting further, Secret Operational Order no. 1 was transmitted to the Navy; its instructions were that the American Far Eastern Fleet should be destroyed as soon as hostilities began. What was the point then of Nomura's suggestion of evacuating the south of Indochina in exchange for unfreezing the Japanese assets? Cordell Hull replied that, in any case, the United States wished to be assured that 'Japan was adopting peaceful ways without any ulterior motive and was relinquishing her warlike aims.' This blunt refusal matched the Japanese hypocrisy.

The dialogue was at an end. Roosevelt sought the advice of his military

leaders; the Joint Army and Navy Board as well as General Marshall
and Admiral Stark were for pursuing the negotiations with a view to
gaining a few more months, whilst reminding him, however, that Germany was the main enemy to be brought down, something of which
Roosevelt was in any case personally well aware. The President had perhaps reached the conclusion that war was inevitable and that every effort
must be made to saddle Japan with the responsibility for breaking off
negotiations. He probably thought that the American public, whom he
wished to convince that the present war was *their* war and who were still
rather reluctant, would prove more keen on going to war if their first
enemy was Japan. In any case, between November 22 and 26, his attitude
hardened and he seems to have been aware that this hardening would
probably lead to a surprise attack by the Japanese. And anyway, although
General Tojo had couched the last proposals passed on by Admiral
Nomura in the form of an ultimatum expiring first of all on November 25
but then postponed till November 29, he had not waited for the American
reply to give Admiral Yamamoto the order to take up the positions
required for a state of impending hostilities.

It is difficult to imagine a breakdown more easily accepted by both
sides. Cordell Hull handed over his reply to Nomura on November 26,
when he knew perfectly well that the ultimatum had expired. In his
memoirs, Cordell Hull wrote humorously: 'The sword of Damocles
hanging over our heads was fixed to an alarm-clock.' On the same day,
Tojo was of the opinion that it was not possible to continue negotiations,
whereas Nomura thought that a new date had been fixed for the ultimatum, November 29. The Japanese negotiators, who had been kept in
ignorance until the very end, were only informed of the breakdown on
December 7. The Emperor had advised strongly against attacking without warning; but by the time the memorandum considered as a declaration
of war was handed in at Washington on December 8, the Japanese fleet
had started operations and the British were attacked in Malaya without
receiving any document notifying the opening of hostilities.

Both parties seemed to be glad to be going to war, which each either
wanted or thought inevitable. But the Japanese military leaders had
chosen their own time and place and they would benefit immensely from
their surprise attack. As for Roosevelt, he had indeed achieved the awakening of the American conscience which he had been seeking; but at the
cost of a tragic disaster, the destruction of the American fleet at Pearl
Harbour. It is true that Japan's partner, Hitler, had not been informed of
the decision by his ally any more than had their joint opponents. And so,
after starting a war with the firm resolve to fight only one front at a time,
the Führer had launched his people into a fight to the death with the three
greatest powers in the world.

VI THE ATTACK ON PEARL HARBOUR

The idea of an attack by carrier-based aircraft against the American fleet in Pearl Harbour in the Hawaiian Islands came from Admiral Yamamoto, who in 1941 commanded the 'combined fleet', the highest operational command in Japan. He had great difficulty in obtaining agreement for it. Indeed, earlier Japanese plans had provided for the quickest possible occupation of areas rich in raw materials – the Navy was thinking particularly of crude oil which was in very short supply. The means were not available to launch major attacks in two directions and for different, if not divergent, purposes.

In addition, an attack in strength on Pearl Harbour seemed an extremely risky operation to the naval general staff and their head, Admiral Nagano. It would indeed mean committing all the large aircraft-carriers in one single operation. Were it to fail it might prove an irreparable disaster. Or more simply, the American fleet might be at sea and the lengthy expedition, deprived of its target, would result only in delaying the rich conquests that were earnestly desired. Success also required complete surprise; how could one guarantee that the fleet would not be detected during the 2,800 miles that it would have to cover?

In Admiral Yamamoto's view, as long as the United States possessed a powerful fighting fleet, it would provide a formidable threat for the new Japanese empire; thus it was necessary to begin by rendering it harmless; in this way, there would be time to fortify a whole ring of islands before the fleet could be repaired or built up again; to these arguments Yamamoto added the threat of resigning if they were not accepted.

His stubbornness was rewarded; suddenly, in October 1941, the Navy adopted his plan. It was known that, during manoeuvres, the American fleet was accustomed to put in at Pearl Harbour on Friday and sail again the following Monday; this was why the attack was fixed for Sunday, December 7 (December 8 in Japan). The Navy kept its secret to itself; since it had decided to make war, its plan of campaign was its own affair and it is probable that the Prime Minister, Tojo, was not completely informed until the decision had been taken. The Emperor, the other ministers, the army leaders and the Japanese people learnt about it, like the Americans, once the attack was over.

The raid raised a number of problems. Its success depended on the use of air torpedoes, but the water in the Pearl Harbour roadstead was shallow; the torpedoes would explode if they hit the bottom; it was not until October 1941 that a method was developed of stabilising air torpedoes by means of special ailerons. On the other hand, all the ships engaged would need to have an extremely long range of action, greater than that of some of the aircraft-carriers and most of the destroyers. It was decided to refuel them at sea on the outward journey as close as possible to the target area and let them make the return trip under their own resources by using oil filled containers carried as cargo. The major obstacle to this procedure and one which was solved only after much discussion and cutting a good deal of red tape, was an article in the Navy regulations forbidding the use of bilges as cargo holds.

As the Americans often anchored their vessels in pairs in the Pearl Harbour roads, it seemed wise to supplement the torpedo operation with dive bombing. But there was a shortage of heavy bombs and so they had to be improvised by converting armour-piercing shells. All these preparations were concluded only at the last minute.

In addition, the aircraft-carriers taking part in the operation were short of aircrew and they could only be brought up to strength by calling on the pilots left in Japan. Once all these problems had been settled, the fleet had only one month in which to practise; it made use of it in the best possible conditions, in a stretch of water in the south of Kyushu which was shaped like the Pearl Harbour roads. The attacking technique of the torpedo-carrying aircraft and their height and speed were most carefully worked out.

And so, in a venture that was not devoid of danger, the Japanese deployed a combat fleet of unprecedented power, consisting of 4 battle-ships, 2 heavy cruisers, 6 aircraft-carriers and 10 destroyers; they had sent on ahead 22 long-range submarines and 5 midget submarines, armed with scaled-down torpedoes, each manned by one man which could penetrate into the outer harbour despite anti-submarine netting. It had been decided not to use landing troops, as much in order to avoid the extra burden and delay for the convoy as not to weaken the expeditionary forces intended for the Philippines and Malaya. The Pearl Harbour operation was thus, if complex in its detailed execution, extremely simple in its conception; it was merely a bombardment, lasting some hours, of a predetermined target by aircraft and warships; once the operation was completed, they would withdraw. It was a raid but on a massive scale and only of value if it proved decisive; in a word, a gamble.

What were the American defences? Lying some ten miles from Hono-lulu, Pearl Harbour is a roadstead entered through a narrow channel. As it was barely deep enough for large vessels, the latter were moored together at the most suitable spot. There was so little room that any manoeuvring could lead to a collision and the congested harbour could turn into a trap if a large vessel were sunk in the channel, some two miles long and a quarter wide. The anti-submarine detecting installations, the warehouses, arsenal, airfields, docks, workshops and oil-storage tanks, were completely uncamouflaged. From the top of the hills surrounding it, the outer harbour was clearly visible and nothing would be hidden from any close observers, of whom there was no shortage amongst the 100,000 Japanese on the island. So Admiral Yamamoto's squadron knew the enemy's defences with extreme accuracy; through observations transmitted by radio in an agreed code, he had learned that the Americans were not flying barrage balloons and had not put out any anti-torpedo netting; less pleasant was the news that three aircraft-carriers which had been expected to be at Pearl Harbour had left. But the attackers knew that at 7 o'clock every Sunday, the radar team left its post and was not replaced. The attack was timed to the minute.

It came as a complete surprise and achieved complete success. Out of 8 American battleships in the harbour, 7 were sunk and 1 damaged; 10 other ships were lost. Of the 394 aircraft in Oahu, 188 were destoyed and 159 others damaged. American casualties totalled 3,581 of which 2,403 were killed. In two whirlwind waves of aircraft, of which a mere 29 were shot down, the Japanese eliminated both the defences of the harbour and the major ships in the American Pacific surface fleet. Within the space of two hours naval superiority in the Pacific had passed into the hands of Japan.

The immensity of the disaster filled the American public first with stupefaction and then with anger; after the war, Roosevelt's opponents used it to blacken his memory. The ensuing large-scale inquest revealed incredible incompetence. First of all, it was discovered that Admiral Richardson had continually repeated his warnings against crowding the fleet into Pearl Harbour and had recommended its return to the US Pacific coast. In this, he came up against his superiors who were anxious to intimidate Japan; President Roosevelt had decided against Admiral Richardson's advice.

But in that case, since, against expert advice, the fleet was remaining in Pearl Harbour for diplomatic rather than military reasons, why was it not better protected? After the war Admiral Theobald undertook the role of public prosecutor. He drew attention to the many indications pointing to a raid on the harbour. In particular, it was known that twice a week the Japanese consul in Honolulu informed Tokyo regarding the ships' movements. On December 7 a Japanese midget submarine had been sunk in the channel. Was the incompetence of the naval and military authorities on the spot at fault? Admiral Kimmel and General Short pointed out that they had certainly been kept informed of the gravity of the situation but had never been warned that an attack was imminent. They had thus been unable to prepare for it; it had been detected at the very last minute and too late by two soldiers who had remained rather later than usual at their radar sets.

Responsibility, if responsibility there was, thus lay with the men at the top. When interrogated by the Investigating Commission, the Secretary of War, Stimson, and the Chief of Staff, General Marshall, stated that although they did indeed suspect a Japanese attack to be imminent, they were convinced that it would be launched against the Philippines. Accordingly they had given only a guarded warning to those responsible for the defence of Pearl Harbour on November 27 in order to avoid revealing to the Japanese that their intentions had been discovered because their diplomatic – but not their naval – code had been broken. All this demonstrated a rather alarming lack of preparation and excessive optimism on the part of the Americans.

Could one go further and imagine that President Roosevelt had knowingly let the Japanese have their head in order to shock American public opinion into awareness? He might, in a word, have been subtly provoking the Japanese who had then merely gone rather too far. The upsurge of American isolationism after the war lent force to the attacks on these lines which the Republicans made on their Democrat opponents, with the dead President providing the stick with which to beat his successor. But though there is no doubt that Roosevelt had very skilfully built up a pattern of acts irreconcilable with neutrality, above all against Germany, without declaring war, leaving the potential enemies of the United States the responsibility for the ultimate step, it cannot be proved that he had considered it necessary to expose the American fleet to such danger in order to set a trap for the Japanese. As M. Latreille has written, 'ever since politicians have been seeking means of preventing war, it has never been known whether it is better stubbornly to pursue a compromise that might be construed as weakness or to display very firm determination which might become foolhardiness.'

The Pearl Harbour attack did nonetheless have incalculable consequences. Militarily, the outcome proved less disastrous in the long run than might have been feared. Morison has pointed out that the departure of the three American aircraft-carriers and the fact that fortunately the dockyard was not destroyed still left the Americans with their most effective means of retaliation and the possibility of making good the losses. On the other hand the raid had revealed the Japanese's remarkable qualities of ingenuity, boldness and courage; but its success only partly disguised a relative weakness inherent in Japanese naval power, which had had to be mobilised almost in its entirety for this one single operation.

On the American side, this aggression roused public opinion much more than the loss of the Philippines would have done. The activities of the 'America First' committee stopped abruptly. Helped by racialism, national unanimity was reached much more easily and completely against the cowardly hypocritical Japs than against the Germans. President Roosevelt declared: 'We have to realise that modern war, as waged by the Nazis, is a repulsive business. We did not want to join in. But now we are in and we are going to fight with all our resources.' And the American nation backed him up completely.

Thus began the process which was to turn the greatest economic power in the world into the world's greatest military power. With his wide-ranging view of the world situation, his infallible understanding of his compatriots and his supreme skill in the choice of the appropriate means and arguments, President Roosevelt had succeeded in leading the United States exactly where he wished them to go. The United States was going to war without any predetermined aims; she had no territorial claims to make, no historic defeat to avenge and no hereditary enemy to destroy. She would, of course, be fighting in defence of her long-term national interests but above all for a certain conception of society, of freedom and of international law and morality. Her bitter initial defeat was not going to divert her from her main objective: the defeat of Germany. This view of the war, added to her lack of experience and inadequate preparation, was going to lead to a a succession of disasters against Japan.

CHAPTER 2

Japan's Lightning War

WITH the advantage gained by her aggression, for almost two years Japan was going to show herself superior to her opponents, on land and sea, and she used this superiority to carve herself out an immense empire.

I THE JAPANESE FORCES

With her 100 million inhabitants, 73 in the islands and 27 in Korea and Formosa, Japan possessed vast reserves of manpower; her troops were both well-trained and fanatically indoctrinated.

Her war fleet was almost as strong as the British Royal Navy. It consisted of some 15 battleships, 5 of them of more than 40,000 tons, 10 aircraft-carriers, 50 cruisers, 110 destroyers and 80 submarines. But the only really new warships were some of the aircraft-carriers; most of them – and in particular all the escort vessels – were converted passenger-ships or tankers; though the former were fast, the speed of the latter was less than 20 knots. The war fleet had 1,350 aircraft; the 450 ship-born aeroplanes were a formidable but limited striking force.

Despite the million men tied down in China the Japanese had large and formidable ground forces available; these men had experience in numerous landing operations and they were equipped for mountain and jungle warfare as well as being accustomed to monsoon conditions and great heat.

The land-based air force comprised 3,000 aircraft, rather few in view of the remoteness of the targets. A programme did exist to build 30,000 aircraft for the Army and 30,000 for the Navy but construction had been delayed and the Japanese aeronautical industry did not have the necessary equipment for mass-production.

These shortcomings throw light on the future difficulties of the Japanese war economy. It was true that mining output had increased threefold and steel production doubled between 1919 and 1939; the industry was highly concentrated and often modernised but by world standards, it was not very powerful. In addition, the country could not be fed from home production alone.

Moreover, all this potential had not been completely devoted to the war effort. While state control of foreign trade, currency, prices and wages had existed since 1937, the essential factor, that is heavy industry, remained outside the government's authority because of the immense power and the independence of the large trusts.

Above all, the Japanese economy was completely reliant on its shipping; it had to import 60 per cent of its raw materials, including 75 per cent of its iron ore, 60 per cent of its copper, 84 per cent of its lead and tin, 89 per cent of its bauxite and the whole of its rubber and nickel. In anticipation of an embargo, enormous quantities of crude oil had indeed been stockpiled, amounting to 43 million barrels which, it was estimated, would cover two years' consumption; but it was calculated that 16 million barrels would have to be imported in the second year of the war and 30 million in the third year.

If it is remembered that communication between the countless, unequally developed islands of the archipelago could obviously be maintained only by sea, the extent of the immense burden resting on the shoulders of the Japanese Merchant Navy can be fully appreciated. With a tonnage of six million, the merchant fleet was indeed largely modern – 38 per cent of its ships were less than ten years old; their average speed and uniformity of construction were the highest in the world; their quality was excellent – in particular, their enormous fuel capacity enabled very long distances to be covered.

This merchant fleet was entirely under the control of the Army and the Navy, thus ensuring that it would be used to the best possible advantage for the war effort; but on the other hand the war fleet had requisitioned a large number of freighters in order to convert them into auxiliary cruisers or transport vessels for men and equipment. In December 1941, only 37 per cent of the normal fleet remained available. It was questionable whether this would suffice to cover the enormous amount of freight transport required. One Japanese shipowner had estimated the need at 20 million tons.

Like Germany, Japan was thus condemned to win a war only if it was short. Her earlier successes, the raid on Pearl Harbour, the advantage of having the initiative, the discipline and self-sacrificing qualities of her troops, in addition to the inadequate preparation, dispersal and divided objectives of her opponents, seemed an earnest of victory. But her tasks were as many and varied as they were immense. She had to do the following and do them quickly: conquer an empire, organise it, protect its internal lines of communication, fortify its outposts against American counter-attacks, fight and win in defence of these outposts, convince the conquered peoples that their future must lie with their conquerors and harmonise their economies with Japan's. All this had to be done before the

Americans had converted their unlimited industrial potential into armament factories. And since Pearl Harbour, no new strike of any size could be made against the USA; now in their homeland, the Americans were out of reach of the Japanese forces; the latter, on the other hand, or at least, their forward positions, were not out of reach of the Americans.

II CONDUCT OF THE WAR IN JAPAN

The powers controlling the Japanese war effort consisted of a sham and a reality.

The sham was the theocratic and theoretically unrestricted authority of the Emperor as the combined political, military and religious head of the nation. In theory, he was assisted by advisers who, according to the constitution, bore the entire responsibility of the Emperor's actions and were answerable to the Diet. In fact, the latter had no authority; its functions did not extend beyond legislating and passing the Budget. Although free to behave as an absolute sovereign, the Emperor had chosen to be a constitutional monarch and follow the advice of his counsellors. He was, of course, kept informed and important decisions were taken only when he was present and with his approval; in fact, he listened and said nothing; he had the semblance of command but instead followed his subordinates who were the real holders of power. Bowing obsequiously they would present reports to him and he approved their conclusions, even when he sometimes expressed some reservations. Authority belonged to him and he could always recover it but he had relinquished his responsibility and took no active initiative.

The real power thus lay in the hands of the Emperor's advisers. In theory also, these were of two kinds: the government and the high command; in practice, they tended to form one only, the high command. Even before the war and more so throughout its whole course, Japan was subject to a military dictatorship and the general staff was, in fact, the government.

How had this come about? First of all, according to the constitution, the Army and the Navy were responsible only to the Emperor, which gave them considerable independence and shielded them from government interference. In consequence, the Prime Minister and his colleagues played no sort of role in working out the strategy and conduct of operations; they only knew what their military and naval colleagues saw fit to tell them; and these colleagues were never civilians but always an admiral and a general. They were appointed only with the approval of the high command and almost always at its suggestion. Thus there was no risk of disagreement between a minister and the Supreme Commander, as in most countries. But the result was that the conduct of a war became in practice the responsibility of the experts of the specialised military departments, above all the operations division, and even more of the military affairs division, which was in charge of national defence, mobilisation and international affairs.

This complete independence of the supreme command was personified, after Prince Konoye had been ousted, in General Tojo, at one and the same time Prime Minister, War Minister and the brains of the Army. Almost always he succeeded in getting his way. But he was hampered, if not sometimes even hamstrung, by having under him as colleagues not one proper combined general staff but two separate ones, the Army's and the Navy's. Co-ordination between the two was always difficult and often non-existent. On occasion, for want of agreement, an operation had to be delayed or cancelled. When agreement had been reached, the operation, necessarily an amphibious one, was not entrusted to one single leader but to two, of equal rank, a sailor and a soldier, and the two services each received their supplies in different ways. Similarly, in each operational theatre, covering enormous geographical areas, there would be found a naval and a military commander.

Japan's whole organisation for the conduct of war was thus faulty and badly co-ordinated; its efficiency could not fail to be adversely affected. But the full gravity of these weaknesses did not appear immediately.

III THE ALLIED FORCES

With 132 million inhabitants the United States was industrially an exceptionally powerful country, despite the aftermath of the slump of the thirties and a slight recession in 1938. In 1940, their level of production had caught up with that of 1929. The United States provided Europe with large quantities of cotton, cereals and oil; they had a near monopoly of rare metals, except for aluminium; they produced as much iron ore, cast iron and steel as the rest of the world put together. By means of capital investment and the political agreements they had concluded, they were able to carry Canada along in their wake, as well as the countries of Latin America where the 'Monroe doctrine' was not regarded as an empty phrase.

But for the moment, this extraordinary potential, estimated at more than one-third of total world industry and supported by unrivalled gold reserves and financial capital, was not yet adequately represented by the size of its armament industry, output of weapons or its armed forces.

At sea, though the Atlantic fleet was intact – but needing to be kept available for its own operational theatre (and the decision to help Britain would ensure that it must remain there) – the Pacific fleet had been reduced to the three aircraft-carriers which had escaped the disaster of Pearl Harbour and fifteen cruisers or destroyers in the Philippines. To these could be added the three Dutch cruisers at Surabaya and two British battleships that Churchill had decided to send to Singapore though they had no air cover. For an indefinite period of time therefore, the American fleet would be forced back on the defensive; its only possible aggressive action would have to be confined to submarine attacks on Japanese convoys. Their small number and remoteness from base would make defence difficult for the moment and attack difficult later on; the Hawaiian Islands were 2,500 miles from San Francisco, the Philippines were isolated to the west and the small Midway Islands of Wake and Guam were some 1,000 to 1,250 miles apart and none of them could be protected. Once they were lost, the Japanese archipelago would be invulnerable for many a long day.

The British flag flew over vast territories which were, however, practically cut off from the metropolis, and India and Australia had sent their best troops to the Middle East. The Hong Kong base was surrounded by Japanese-occupied Chinese territory. At what was likely to be the extreme limit of the Japanese advance, Free France provided Tahiti, the New Hebrides and New Caledonia; but the French forces were ludicrously small. The Dutch forces in Indonesia amounted to 100,000. The Americans had the same number in the Philippines.

After the Munich agreements, President Roosevelt had worked out ambitious plans for aircraft production; but the American aeronautical industry was still something of a cottage industry, despite the slight stimulus afforded by orders placed by France. Construction of the first batch of 5,500 aircraft had only just begun in July 1939. On December 8, 1941, the American air forces consisted of something over 2,000 land-based aircraft and 2,500 intended for the Navy.

So potentially the United States were enormously powerful; but they had to convert this power into a similarly powerful war-machine; the industrial realignment required to do this raised immense problems which would have to be solved as need arose. Time would be necessary and success depended on a complicated series of hypotheses: first and foremost, that the war should not be lost beforehand in Europe and Asia; that the hastily raised and hurriedly equipped armies should cohere to form a sound fighting force; that they should be wisely deployed; that the efforts of the Anglo-American coalition should be, if not jointly controlled, at least co-ordinated. Meanwhile, the only possible attitude was defensive; but how extensive would the withdrawal have to be and where could it be stopped?

IV AMERICAN STRATEGY AND HIGH COMMAND

The US general staff found itself faced by three possibilities: defending the Pacific at all costs, whatever the consequences for Europe, now that Japanese aggression had upset all the earlier plans; accepting the inevitable by resigning itself to the loss of the south-west Pacific and concentrating the maximum number of forces in Britain in order to achieve victory in Europe first of all, leaving the return match with Japan to some later date, as yet undetermined; or else defending the south-west Pacific using the greatest economy of means so as to proceed with the concentration of their forces in the British Isles.

The American military leaders chose the last solution – a compromise – for logistical reasons: evacuating the South Pacific would have been as complicated as reinforcing it. The British let themselves be easily convinced because they could glimpse the possibility of once again seizing the initiative on the continent of Europe without thereby relinquishing their Asian empire.

Thus a defensive position would need to be organised in the Pacific and this raised the problem of command, first of all with the Americans themselves and secondly with the Allies. Before Pearl Harbour there existed dual control, naval and military, of the American forces both in the Philippines and in the Hawaiian Islands. President Roosevelt decided that from December 17 all the Hawaii forces would come under the Navy and the Philippines forces under the Army.

The USA, Britain, Australia, New Zealand and the Dutch East Indies now found themselves suddenly all fighting in the same war together without any previous agreement other than general staff talks in April and these had ended in a discussion of offensive operations which were no longer valid. To deal with what was most urgent first, a unified Allied command was set up called ABDA; General Wavell was put in charge, assisted by deputies from the other nations in the alliance – an American for the Navy, an Englishman for the Air Force, a Dutchman for the Army; the French, whether they had joined the Free French or remained under Vichy, were left out in the cold. Wavell's authority was somewhat theoretical since each of his subordinates could appeal to his own government against his decisions. The fact was that interests differed: the British were primarily concerned with defending Malaya and Singapore, the Americans with maintaining their lines of communication, the Dutch with defending Indonesia and the Australians with defending their own country. This combination of weak partners could in any case never add up to one strong force.

On General Eisenhower's suggestion, General Marshall decided that a

convoy of seven ships, bound for Australia, would be the nucleus of a
force called, in anticipation, us Army Forces in Australia. Accordingly,
during the first three months of 1942, Australia received 55 per cent of the
troop transports and 33 per cent of the shipments of equipment from the
usa. Indeed, though Australia and New Zealand were rich in cattle and
agricultural produce, they were poor in tools and manpower; the north
Australian harbours lacked docks and cranes; there were few inland roads
and they were not really suitable for heavy lorries while the railway network was small and had the added inconvenience of five different gauges.
As the American soldiers were more difficult to please than the Australians – the standard rations of the former contained thirty-nine items as
against the latter's twenty-four – they had to be sent large quantities of
food – spaghetti, rice, fruit, milk, cocoa, etc. – in addition to the arms,
vehicles, ammunition and other items necessary for a campaign.

At the very moment when it was important to support the ussr, who
had been granted the benefit of lend-lease by sending them convoys via
Iran and the Arctic Ocean, the situation that had arisen in the Pacific, even
on the basis of a strictly defensive policy with minimum outlay, demanded
an enormous effort from the American Merchant Marine. Boats had to be
taken off the most important civilian services. But the American authorities were handicapped by their respect for free enterprise and reluctant to
place the whole of their private shipping under military control, so that
it was not used as rationally as might have been desirable – in May 1942,
there were on average seventy-eight ships immobilised and practically
useless in the South African area.

The war in the Pacific thus set the Americans problems that were almost
insuperable. The Japanese had similarly difficult ones to solve.

V NATURE OF THE WAR IN THE PACIFIC

The belligerents had first of all to overcome enormous distances. The war
was waged in the western half of the Pacific, that is over an area comprising one-eighth of the earth's surface. Tokyo was over 4,500 miles from
Hawaii and more than 3,000 miles from the Solomon Islands; from Midway to Burma was well over 6,000 miles and from New Caledonia to the
Aleutians just under 4,500. It took twice as long to go from San Francisco
to Brisbane as it did to go from New York to Liverpool. American experts estimated that 100,000 troops could be shipped to Great Britain
with the same tonnage that could carry only 40,000 to Australia. As the
distances increased, the number of problems and the difficulty of solving
them grew in geometric proportion.

On both sides, the first priority was to get convoys safely into harbour.

The American convoys had to leave from Pacific ports, which were fewer in number and less well equipped than those on the east coast. San Francisco was crammed to bursting point and the produce shipped from there had to come from thousands of miles away, food from the Middle West, arms and machinery from the Great Lakes and New England. As a rule, all troops sailing from America had to take with them a two months' supply of food; each soldier needed five to ten tons of equipment when he left and one ton per month afterwards.

The logistical services thus assumed paramount importance on both sides. Transports required long preparation, because it was important to work out how they should rotate, receive protection and then be replenished. Inevitably things arrived at the wrong destination and nothing could be done about it. Troops unaccompanied by their stores were as good as useless. Sometimes, a transport company would arrive safely but without its lorries, or bakers minus their ovens. But by adapting their big industrial techniques to the war, the Americans soon showed their superiority in assembling such delicate mechanisms, keeping them running easily and improving them.

In the Pacific war problems of equipment would thus be more complicated than elsewhere and the fighting troops correspondingly smaller in manpower. Above all, shipping was of paramount importance; but not just any kind of shipping; special craft of all shapes and sizes would have to be invented and then manufactured and despatched to their destinations. If one adds that the enormous size of the Asian continent was made even more formidable by the climate, the rugged nature of the terrain, the jungle, the lack of roads and railways and that, in a word, the sea was the shortest distance between two points, then clearly final victory must depend on victory at sea.

The Pacific war would thus be primarily an air and naval war, requiring organised fortified bases, closing in gradually on the enemy's strongholds and long-range naval and air transport and methods of warfare. To avoid dispersing their air forces after their widespread gains, the Japanese chose to fortify islands, thus turning them into unsinkable aircraft-carriers. In a few hours, aircraft could be fetched in from other bases in order to defend them. The Americans preferred mobile forces, squadrons in which battleships and aircraft-carriers gave each other mutual support. But on both sides, any offensive operation was an amphibious one, combining naval, ground and air forces. In such operations, surprise, minute attention to detail, secrecy and accuracy of execution were essential, and success depended on controlling the skies and the sea. This is the context in which this war was waged, a war rich in episode, when almost uninhabited islands were fought over ferociously and won at the cost of heavy casualties.

The furious, even ferocious nature of the fighting was going to be aggravated by a more or less overt racialism. The Japanese showed little respect for the provisions of the Geneva Convention governing the treatment of prisoners of war. H. James, an American historian and eye-witness, wrote, 'In my 40 months' captivity I cannot recall one single example of a Japanese civilian or soldier showing disgust or even sorrow when an act of brutality was committed in his presence.' The American and Philippine prisoners captured by the Japanese at Batan – 72,000 in all – had to walk long distances on foot under a tropical sun. Sick and wounded were finished off by their guards at the roadside, hundreds at a time. Out of 50,000 prisoners of many nationalities employed by the Japanese on the construction of a railway in Siam, 16,000 died of illness, exhaustion or torture; the celebrated film, *The Bridge over the River Kwai*, describes such an episode. When these horrors became known in the United States, they came as a bombshell; public opinion demanded merciless revenge. The Americans would often drive Japanese soldiers out of their shelters with flame throwers, turning them into human torches. It is not anticipating events to recall that the first atom bombs were dropped on Japan, certainly with less compunction than if they were to have been dropped on a white population. The fanatically indoctrinated Japanese soldiers preferred to be killed on their little islands rather than let themselves fall into enemy hands.

VI THE JAPANESE PLANS

Although waging the same war against the same adversaries – except the USSR – as Germany and Italy, Japan never concerted her actions with her Allies. She waged her own war to achieve her own objectives, which were both grandiose and detailed in their conception. The Japanese leaders, and first and foremost General Tojo, were all convinced of the legitimacy of their aspirations: Japan was suffocating in her islands and only powers who were opposed to her in principle would want to stop her breathing more freely. She was thus driven to break forcibly out of the vice in which she was being held. But at no time did the Japanese imagine that they would have to force the United States to their knees and that they would be able to dictate their peace terms to the White House. They wanted to build up their empire and were prepared to brush aside anything that stood in their way, first of all the American fleet; and then, once Japan's new position was well established and proof had been given that it was impossible to take her gains away from her, they would negotiate. The success of these schemes depended on a German victory in Europe or at least on Hitler's continuing for a long time yet to make the USSR incapable of any effective action in Asia; it also presupposed either that the United States would commit the bulk of her forces to the fighting in Europe or else that she would accept the situation as it was after her first defeats in Asia – a situation which entailed in fact losing only the Philippines, to which she had promised independence – rather an inadequate reason, surely, for waging a long and difficult war.

Having established these principles, the Japanese modified the extent and the limits of their future empire according to events. They also hesitated between several different schemes of how to conquer it. For the moment they had given up any designs on Siberia east of Lake Baikal and they had remained deaf to Germany's appeals to reach out towards her by a vast attack in the direction of India; nor had they any intention of occupying Australia and New Zealand, merely of isolating them. They thus had a threefold objective: to conquer the territories producing the raw materials which they lacked – oil, rubber and various ores which made the Dutch East Indies and Malaya particularly important; to fortify a line of small islands in the central Pacific so as to form a defensive barrier against the onslaught of the Americans; and to protect themselves in Burma and the key position of Singapore against a possible counter-offensive by Britain. After all this had been achieved, China would be completely isolated and her defeat and incorporation into the new political and economic area thus created would be only a matter of time.

The Japanese hesitated between three possibilities: a direct attack on the Dutch East Indies, considered too risky because it dangerously extended the lines of communication; a leapfrog advance from the Philippines to the Indian archipelago and Malaya, which was rejected because it was too slow; and a conquest of Malaya and the Indian Archipelago both together, leaving out the Philippines as no longer necessary by reason of the decision to attack Pearl Harbour. The Japanese adopted a plan finally involving simultaneous advances towards the Dutch East Indies, the Philippines and Malaya. The element of surprise would compensate for the dispersal of forces. The remoteness of the objectives required careful timing for the troop landings, the advance of the Air Force, the allocation of shipping and the bringing up of supplies. The vast scope of the scheme made it very bold and very hazardous, but as it suited the book of each of the parties concerned, the government, the Army and the Navy, it was adopted. And the Japanese knew all about their opponents' weaknesses.

The operation was to be carried out in two phases. In the first phase, Hong Kong, Wake and Guam would be occupied and troops landed in the Philippines and Malaya; in the second phase the Dutch East Indies, Singapore and Burma would be conquered. In the east, no advance would be made beyond a line joining the Kurile, Wake and Gilbert

Islands, the north coast of New Guinea, Timor and the northern Solomon Islands. In the south-west, the main stronghold would be Rabaul.

In these plans the attack on Pearl Harbour was in fact considered merely as an hors d'oeuvre, a preliminary tactical operation on a grand scale reserved for the Navy, the success of which would make it easier to carry out the rest of the scheme. And indeed for the first few months, everything took place as planned.

VII THE EARLY JAPANESE SUCCESSES

The Japanese repeated their tactics in almost identical fashion everywhere with the same success: enemy bases and airfields were bombed; troops were landed at selected points, never in great strength but sufficient to guarantee local superiority and ensure a swift victory; next, airfields were set up or brought back into action on the conquered territory; a fresh leap forward some hundreds of miles ahead was then made from this starting point with the least possible delay.

These combined operations imposed a great strain on the naval and air forces; but they carried out their tasks with extreme competence. The strike force of six fast aircraft-carriers, skilfully grouped and deployed, provided, whenever they were employed, air superiority of four or five aircraft to one. Between December 7, 1941, and April 1942, this force operated over an area extending from Hawaii to Ceylon, one-third of the circumference of the earth. In turn, they launched successive attacks on Pearl Harbour, Rabaul, Port Darwin, Tinjilap, Colombo and Trincomale, without losing one single ship.

The land-based air force showed similar mobility. Its 700 aircraft were divided into two air fleets; the first, based on the homeland, with advanced bases in the central Pacific, had the defensive role of covering Japan. The second had an offensive role: based at first on Formosa, Indochina and the Palau islands and later using island bases, its 350 aircraft and sea-planes flew from island to island, opening up the way for landings and destroying the enemy aircraft – 300 in all – that were launched against them in small batches.

On December 8, Guam and Wake were attacked; the 500 defenders of Guam surrendered thirty-six hours later. Wake, about 1,500 miles from Guam, was only an atoll; the garrison, without food or water, surrendered on December 22. The Gilberts had already been conquered since the 9th.

Hong Kong was defended only against attack from the sea. On December 8, the bombing raids began and the Japanese 38th Division crossed the border into the peninsula. The 15,000 Australian, Canadian and Indian defenders were forced back into the suburb of Kowloon and then, on the 17th, to the island of Hong Kong, where the Japanese landed on the 19th; having run out of water, the garrison surrendered on December 25. These were Japan's first great successes; there were to be others.

VIII THE CONQUEST OF THE PHILIPPINES

The American government had shown indecision in its policy towards the Philippines. It had granted them independence in principle, to start in 1946, but it still kept them somewhat under its wing. It realised that they would be impossible to defend by reason of their remoteness but it could not bring itself to abandon them to their lot. As a result of this half-hearted attitude the archipelago was inadequately defended.

Thus in December, the army, 100,000 strong, of whom 75,000 were Filipinos, was supported by only about 100 fighters, 34 bombers and some 100 tanks; for want of adequately equipped airfields, it had not proved possible to disperse or camouflage them; radio communications were very slow and, as at Pearl Harbour, the presence on the island of large numbers of Japanese had made spying easy. Although as a result of incompetence, on which American historians have had little to say, perhaps because General MacArthur's responsibility is involved, the attack on Pearl Harbour became known six hours after the opening of hostilities, the Japanese Air Force destroyed half the American aircraft on the ground at Mindanao without having been in any way detected or even, it would seem, expected.

On December 10 the Japanese began to land on the north coast of Luzon and at Lingayen on December 24. The Americans were able neither to repulse them nor even to delay their advance. Soon there were 150,000 Japanese on the islands. MacArthur withdrew to the Bataan peninsula and it was a miracle that the endless columns moving along the single road were not disrupted by Japanese bombing.

It was clear that the Philippines could no longer be defended, although MacArthur asserted the opposite. The few remaining aircraft were brought back to the Dutch East Indies; Admiral Hart's fleet received the order to seek refuge behind the barrier of Malaya before it was too late. General Yamashita's Japanese troops took possession of the islands one after the other without much difficulty. Lacking any support from outside, MacArthur's tiny army's first line of defence was pierced on January 22 at Bataan. Successive lines of defence only delayed the inevitable withdrawal to Corregidor on April 9 where it continued to fight; but, decimated by malaria and having run out of water, the last American garrison surrendered on May 7 having suffered fifty-three air raids. MacArthur left to take command of the forces that were beginning to be organised in Australia. He was unhappy to leave the Philippines and swore he would come back.

Like the British in Europe, the Americans in Asia had shown themselves unable to provide effective defence for the territories they had taken under their protection. The British and the Dutch were in no better plight.

IX THE CONQUEST OF THE DUTCH EAST INDIES

The Dutch Army totalled about 100,000 men of whom barely 35,000 were equipped with relatively modern equipment. Since they were spread out over an immense area and supported by 200 aircraft only 60 of which were of recent type, they were incapable of offering effective resistance anywhere. The creation of a unified Allied command and the arrival of General Wavell in Java produced little change. No amount of preliminary training could overcome the confusion created by the diversity of languages and, where the ships were concerned, by the absence of a common signals code.

Nonetheless, it had been possible to bring up some reinforcements – the American fleet from the Philippines, some American aircraft from Australia and the advance guard of an Australian division coming home from the Middle East. It did not amount to very much.

In accordance with their invariable tactics, the Japanese gradually invested Java, on the one hand by pouring down the Malacca peninsula towards Sumatra, on the other by landing in Borneo, in the Celebes and in the Moluccas, where from the island of Amboyna, they were able to start bombing the Dutch base of Surabaya. Wherever they went, they found the oil installations destroyed but this handicap did not hinder their advance.

Little by little the ring closed round Java, as the Japanese established their foothold in regions where no defence was possible. South Sumatra, Timor and Bali were occupied in February; so Java was cut off from Australia on the east while Singapore was falling on the west. At the same time, Batavia started to be bombed.

The battle for Java was waged at sea on February 27 and 28 and March 1, 1942. The Allied fleet under Admiral Doorman suffered an unfortunate mishap at the start of the fighting when the British cruiser *Electra* was sunk on the spot. Subsequently, the Japanese lost only one torpedo-boat destroyer but they sank two cruisers and three Allied torpedo-boat destroyers. It was a disaster, above all for the Dutch Navy, which had not fought for 150 years.

Without awaiting the outcome of a hopeless campaign, the Dutch authorities had evacuated Batavia. The Japanese landed on the plain in the north of Java and advanced swiftly. On the very first day they captured an airfield a few hundred miles from Bandung which had been made the capital. On March 6, they had reached the south coast of Java and entered Tjilatjap, which had been declared an 'open city'. Although fighting was still going on in Sumatra and on Timor, the Dutch authorities, having vainly attempted to negotiate a partial surrender, were forced to capitulate completely and unconditionally to General Hitoshi, who threatened to bombard the towns if they refused. The first thing that the Japanese did after their victory was to intern a large part of the white population of Java, in addition to the soldiers who had been captured.

X THE CONQUEST OF MALAYA AND SINGAPORE

For a long time the British had thought that the Japanese would not attack Singapore – this was the opinion of the Commander-in-Chief in the Far East. Churchill thought that at the worst they could not attack it before the spring of 1942. In any case, the British were relying on the American fleet to contain the Japanese, and the Pearl Harbour disaster was a bitter disappointment for them as well. All they could do was to face up to the situation with their own inadequate resources, that is about 90,000 men, lacking tanks, experienced officers and NCOs and even trained soldiers. To meet the Japanese squadrons based in Indochina the RAF had only 180 aircraft, most of them out-dated. The British government expected setbacks and was resigned to them because in their eyes the Asian theatre of war was a secondary one; but to save what it could, it nevertheless decided to send two modern battleships to Singapore. They arrived at the very last moment, on December 2.

The British high command had thought of moving into Siam to forestall the Japanese but was reluctant to violate that country's neutrality. The Japanese were less scrupulous. On December 8, they occupied Bangkok and the Siamese harbours close to the Malayan peninsula.

Could Admiral Philipps, the commander of the only respectable British force, possibly remain idle? He sailed to intercept the convoys that had been reported to him. He knew that the Japanese surface fleet was not there and that the danger would be aircraft and submarines. Warships had, of course, been sunk by aircraft in Norway and Crete but never a battleship. The British tended to underestimate their opponents and they did not know that the Japanese were the only people at that time to have perfected the technique of torpedo attack by aircraft. Completely without air cover or even reconnaissance planes, on December 10, despite their forty automatic AA weapons, the *Prince of Wales* and the *Repulse* were sent to the bottom in thirty-five minutes with all their crews. The British had now lost control of the seas as well as the skies.

With his lines of communication now protected, General Yamashita advanced into Malaya, both through the jungle and by means of a series of landings on the coast, along which ran both the railway line and the roads. The Indian and Australian troops, constantly attacked in the rear, could do nothing but retreat, until, demoralised, they finally took refuge in Singapore.

Well defended from the sea, where a number of little islands in the Malacca straits were powerfully fortified, Singapore was less well defended against the land, particularly since a causeway nearly two miles long joined it to the mainland. In the night of February 8–9 the Japanese made a surprise landing on the island, repaired the causeway and sent their tanks and artillery along it. On February 12, they were at the gates of Singapore; by the 14th they had taken the naval base and the water tanks. On the 15th, the garrison surrendered, handing over 80,000 prisoners. The Japanese had given themselves one hundred days to complete their programme and they had done it in seventy.

XI THE BURMA CAMPAIGN

Burma had separated from India in 1937 and the British had paid little attention to her defences, for one thing because the young Burmese intellectuals were very hostile. But it was important to protect the approaches to India and two divisions, one Indian and one Burmese, under General Hutton had been given this task.

For its own part, the Japanese general staff looked on Burma as a secondary operational theatre. But by despatching troops there, they were pursuing three aims: cutting China's last communications with the outside world (in January 1942 there were 100,000 tons of stores in Rangoon intended for Chungking), depriving long-range enemy aircraft of bases and guarding against an offensive from the direction of India. They possibly thought of making Burma a springboard for the invasion of India, but this is doubtful, although India did figure among the countries likely to form part of Greater East Asia Co-Prosperity Sphere. In any case, such a huge undertaking would have to be held over till later.

Burma was separated from India by mountains having no roads passable for vehicles; the lines of communication followed the valleys which lay north-south; from May to October the wet monsoon turned the tracks into torrents and the roads into quagmires; the only suitable season for campaigning was from October to May. These geographical conditions, aggravated by the low density of population and the paucity of resources, meant that though the fighting forces were small, the ancillary services were large and complex.

Now that they possessed airfields sufficiently close to Rangoon, the Japanese overran the hastily prepared British defences on the rivers and entered Rangoon in March 1942 – an important gain because of its harbour installations, oil refineries and stores of commodities which were only partly destroyed.

The second phase now began. The Japanese moved up the Irrawaddy. They pushed back the British as well as the Chinese, who had come to their help – somewhat to the mortification of the British. They took Lashio, where the 'Burma road' started, then Mandalay and the oil wells, while their Air Force bombed Ceylon. The boldness of this operation intimidated the British so much that they recalled their ships as far as the east coast of Africa. As the Japanese fleet had not gone beyond the Andaman Islands, there were no ships left in the Indian Ocean. But feeling themselves threatened in the rear, the British made a landing at Diego Suarez and occupied the whole of the island of Madagascar, which caused them difficulties both with Vichy and Free France.

In a third phase, the British troops evacuated Burma, not without great difficulty and considerable losses, and took refuge in India, while what was left of the Chinese troops returned home. The wet monsoon put a stop to the fighting. But how was China to be supplied now? Where would the Japanese advance stop? And who was to stop it?

XII JAPAN'S DEFENSIVE PERIMETER EXTENDED

In the spring of 1942, the Japanese had reached all their objectives with a minimum of loss and more quickly than they had anticipated. In each of them they had been able to take advantage of help from a native 'Fifth Column'. The British and Americans had been reduced to sporadic guerrilla activity in the Philippines and north Burma. China was completely isolated and could now be supplied only by air; a whole air lift had to be set up and its capacity could never be very large. India was in a ferment; although Gandhi and Nehru preached non-violence and refused any sort of co-operation with the British, Chandrah Bose, who had taken refuge in Burma, was preaching and preparing for armed revolt. Australia was withdrawing troops from the Middle East and Churchill was criticising her for not introducing conscription. In a word, the anti-Japanese coalition was in a bad way and its morale was low.

The Americans were reduced perforce to undertaking small-scale counter-attacks against the Gilbert, Marshall and Wake Islands. They had set up an advanced base in New Caledonia, not without friction with the

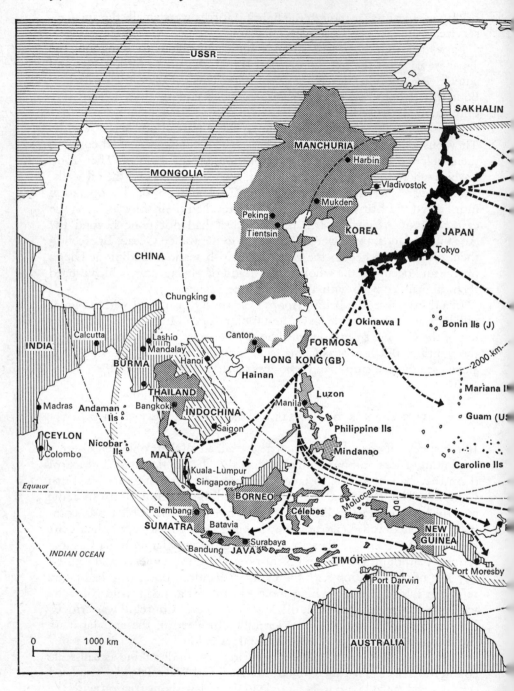

USSR

MONGOLIA

MANCHURIA

Harbin

Vladivostok

Peking

Mukden

Tientsin

KOREA

SAKHALIN

JAPAN

Tokyo

CHINA

Chungking

Okinawa I

Bonin Ils (J)

Calcutta

Lashio

Mandalay

Canton

FORMOSA

2000 km.

INDIA

BURMA

Hanoi

HONG KONG (GB)

Hainan

Mariana I

THAILAND

Luzon

Bangkok

INDOCHINA

Manila

Guam (US

Madras

Andaman
Ils

Saigon

Philippine Ils

CEYLON

Nicobar
Ils

MALAYA

Mindanao

Caroline Ils

Colombo

Kuala-Lumpur

Singapore

Equator

Palembang

BORNEO

Célebes

Moluccas

NEW
GUINEA

SUMATRA

Batavia

Bandung   JAVA   Surabaya

TIMOR

Port Moresby

INDIAN OCEAN

Port Darwin

0   1000 km

AUSTRALIA

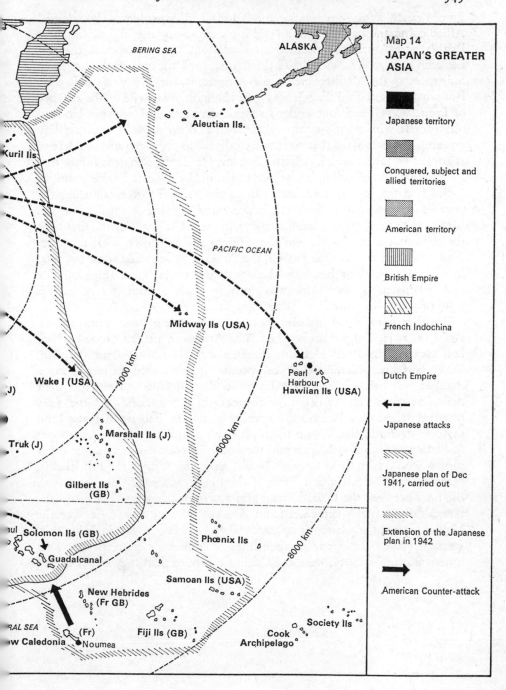

BERING SEA

ALASKA

Aleutian Ils.

Kuril Ils

PACIFIC OCEAN

Midway Ils (USA)

Wake I (USA)

Pearl
Harbour
Hawiian Ils (USA)

4000 km

(J)

Truk (J)

Marshall Ils (J)

6000 km

Gilbert Ils
(GB)

aul
Solomon Ils (GB)

Phœnix Ils

8000 km

Guadalcanal

Samoan Ils (USA)

New Hebrides
(Fr GB)

Society Ils

RAL SEA   (Fr)

w Caledonia   Noumea

Fiji Ils (GB)

Cook
Archipelago

Map 14
**JAPAN'S GREATER
ASIA**

Japanese territory

Conquered, subject and
allied territories

American territory

British Empire

French Indochina

Dutch Empire

Japanese attacks

Japanese plan of Dec
1941, carried out

Extension of the Japanese
plan in 1942

American Counter-attack

Free French high commissioner, Admiral d'Argenlieu. The unified Allied command had come to an end for want of any useful function. The British and Americans decided to share out the operational theatres between themselves. Wavell and the British took the area extending from Singapore to the Mediterranean; the Americans, the whole of the Pacific. But what forces could they deploy over these huge areas? For the defence of India, Wavell had four under-strength divisions and two squadrons of old aircraft with poorly equipped airfields and no radar. The Australian government estimated that twenty-five divisions were required to defend Australia and the Foreign Affairs Minister, Dr Evatt, was demanding that six whole weeks of Britain's war output should be allocated to his country.

But had the Japanese advance run out of steam? After capturing the port of Rabaul in the Bismarck Islands and turning it into a base, in March 1942 the Japanese landed troops in New Guinea. For the first time the mountains, the jungle and the climate slowed down their advance. And now for the first time as well, the Americans achieved some success: in March 1942 their bombers damaged twenty Japanese ships off Lae and Salamaua. In itself, this was nothing really serious but perhaps a taste of things to come.

Another unexpected incident caused the Japanese much concern: on April 18, 1942, Tokyo was bombed. The American aircraft-carriers which had escaped the Pearl Harbour disaster were responsible for the raid, which had a considerable effect on morale. It was a cold shower to put a damper on their elation. The Japanese then decided to enlarge their defensive perimeter in order to protect their homeland. At the very moment when they had come to realise that they had reached the limit of their strength, they found themselves contemplating further advances towards the Solomon Islands and the south of New Guinea; while other moves would take them towards New Caledonia, Samoa, the Fiji Islands, Midway and the Aleutians. True, if they had succeeded they would cut the lines between the United States and Australia, they would remove the threat of any attack launched from Alaska and they would deprive the United States of any base for operations west of Hawaii. But in doing this, were they not over-extending their lines of communication? In the sweet intoxication of victory, were they biting off more than they could chew?

CHAPTER 3

The Sphere of Co-prosperity

How were the Japanese going to administer and exploit their huge conquests? If truth be told, they had not worked out many detailed schemes, even fewer than the Germans. On the whole, they had been welcomed by the native populations but these were extremely diverse in race, religion and standards of living. Also, the war would force Japan to exploit their wealth for her own purposes straightaway and this desire to appropriate for her own use might mean that she would slip into the shoes of the colonising powers whom she had supplanted, to the detriment of the individual and national freedom towards which these populations aspired – or at least one section of their ruling classes and their educated classes. Finally, more than the previous occupying powers, Japan tended to impose on others the military way of life that she had adopted for herself. In any case, she was going to have insufficient time to consolidate her ascendancy and build her empire. But through her works, south-east Asia was going to be unsettled in a way that long outlasted her brief period of domination.

I THE JAPANESE EMPIRE

The Japanese empire ran down the whole coastline of Asia, from Manchuria to beyond Rangoon; it included all the archipelagos of the western Pacific up to a line running from the Aleutians to New Guinea, passing through the Gilbert Islands. It covered one-sixth of the earth's surface, that is, more than 32 million square miles. Most of it had been conquered from the Americans, the British and the Dutch but Siam was an ally of her own free will; Indochina had been occupied by virtue of agreements with the Vichy government recognising French sovereignty; Manchukuo was already a protectorate in which in theory there reigned a descendant of the Manchu dynasty, Pai-Yi; finally China was only partially conquered and still at war with Japan. The vast area of such an empire, added to its scattered nature, might be a weakness; the distance between Tokyo and the Solomon Isles was well over 3,000 miles. The empire would last as

long as the Japanese war fleet and Air Force could retain mastery of its seas
and its skies; Japan would be able to enjoy all its wealth only if her
Merchant Navy was large enough to ensure and increase the flow of goods.

Thanks to her empire, Japan now had all the sources of energy and raw
materials which she had previously lacked; coal, iron, oil; 70 per cent of
the world production of tin and almost all of the rubber; she had cut the
US off from her supply of natural rubber. Conversely, the conquered
nations formed a vast market for her manufactured goods. Her war
economy was thus able to work flat out; but the rational exploitation of
her empire would have to wait for the end of the war in order to expand,
on the supposition that Japan then possessed the necessary capital, industrial potential and structures as well as the necessary number of competent
technicians.

The Japanese – above all their soldiers – believed in their mission in
Asia; their task was to put an end to the domination of the white over the
coloured races, while borrowing the former's science and technology,
and to uproot the seeds of materialism and moral disintegration introduced by colonialism. Being more highly developed than other Far
Eastern peoples, Japan would lead them on to material progress while
still allowing them to retain their own cultures. The Japanese cabinet had
defined its political aims as early as July 1940: it would establish a new
order in eastern Asia. In February 1942, Tojo set up a 'Greater Asia
Council', composed of senior civil servants and industrialists. Then in
November 1942, a 'Ministry for Greater Asia' was set up under Aoki.

But the liberated peoples were not to be granted complete or immediate
freedom. Their strategic importance made it necessary for certain territories, such as Hong Kong, Singapore, Borneo, New Guinea and Timor
to be purely and simply annexed. A second type of country was to be
progressively led forward into theoretical independence, similar to that of
Manchukuo; thus on August 1, 1943, Burma was proclaimed independent
and, on October 15, 1943, the Philippines, both proclamations being
accompanied by the signing of military, political and economic alliances,
reducing them to satellite states – both countries declared war on the
United States. The Malay states and the Dutch East Indies were also to be
granted theoretical independence; but though the Ministry of Foreign
Affairs was inclined to let them have it without delay, the Navy and the
Army preferred it to be deferred till later on.

Finally, other countries became allies of the Japanese; thus Siam, when
she declared war on Britain and the United States, received the high
mountainous region of upper Burma in compensation, as well as the promise of Cambodia. The Chinese Nankin government under Wang
Tsing-wei also declared war on the British and Anglo-Americans and it
was likely to be given Tonkin. However, the future of Indochina was

not clearly defined; the French administration was still functioning and the Japanese were afraid of creating unrest if they got rid of it; in this way, the French stayed on in an equivocal position, on the one hand as representing a certain amount of independence *vis-à-vis* the occupying power, on the other as a colonial survival opposed by local nationalist feeling.

As far as India was concerned, plans were fairly vague. The British would naturally be driven out; but the Japanese did not consider the Indians ripe for self-government, although not feeling themselves capable of ruling them directly. Moderate support was given to Chandrah Bose who, when he came to take part in a Congress of Greater Asian countries in Tokyo, found himself treated as a guest and not as an active member. Nonetheless Chandrah Bose, a former member of the Congress party, formed a 'League for Indian Independence' in Bangkok, with Japanese backing; then, on October 21, 1943, in Singapore, he formed a 'Free Indian Government' which was to raise a national army from amongst the Indian soldiers captured by the Japanese.

All these schemes, the product of propaganda or of ideas for the future, found difficulty in facing up to the harsh reality. Even had they not so wished, the Japanese had too pressing a need for all the wealth of the countries they had conquered not to take it for themselves. They made a clean sweep of their foodstuffs and raw materials, which they bought for a song; their businessmen simply replaced the colonisers who had been expropriated; they had recourse to paper money in order to buy everything on the cheap, although this did not prevent the occupying troops from extorting and commandeering from the local population. The abject poverty of the masses was merely increased and food rationing had to be introduced.

Nor were the Japanese free from a superiority complex towards the natives. They were imbued with the feeling that they were military conquerors, established there by right of conquest. They often showed arrogance, contempt and even cruelty towards the natives. One of the Burmese nationalist leaders, Ba Maw, protested to Tojo against the excesses committed by the occupation troops but General Kimura, the Commander-in-Chief in Burma, took several months before he could bring himself to put down his subordinates' 'mistakes'. In every country, the inhabitants complained of the harshness of the *Kempeitai*, the Japanese military police.

The Japanese military or civil authorities rarely appointed natives to any senior governmental positions and when they did agree to do so, they reduced their powers. They dismissed officials imbued with western ideas and methods as being guilty of 'collaborating' with colonialism. They replaced them by younger men whom they hoped to win over by promoting them and whom they trained in Japan. They intended to make Japanese the standard language in south-east Asia. Even in religious matters, they were not free from a certain imperialism. In October 1943 they removed the two 'living Buddhas' from Mongolia and Tibet, carried them off to Japan, and set up a 'Greater Asian Society of Young Buddhists'.

Although the Japanese had no difficulty in rousing the native populations against their former white masters whom they systematically looted, maltreated and humiliated, on the other hand, after they had raised great hopes amongst the nationalist movements which were spurred on by their arrival, they then caused them great disappointment and even aroused antagonism against themselves.

11 LOCAL NATIONALIST MOVEMENTS

In Indochina, the Cao Daist sect openly professed sympathy for Japan, but in October 1941 the Indochinese Communist party under Ngugen Ai Quoi, who was the son of a scholar and had studied in Paris, was broadened to become the Independence Front or Vietminh. In 1943, Ngugen Ai Quoi became Ho Chi Minh, 'he who brings light'. The expressed aims of the movement were two in number: to destroy 'colonialism' but to destroy 'Fascist imperialism' as well; while the enemy was French colonisation, Japanese neo-imperialism was not necessarily the friend, at least as long as it did not give independence to Vietnam.

In the Philippines the natives felt themselves superior to the occupying Japanese. The latter found supporters amongst the ruling classes but met with great hostility from the population of the interior, the Huks. President Quezon had formed a 'free government' in the United States. Guerrilla forces were formed, officered by Americans, some of whom had not left the country, and were supplied by air or submarine; these gradually grew into a 'People's Army', which levied taxes from collaborators and adopted violent action and sabotage in the towns. In 1943 the Americans estimated its strength at 30,000 men.

In Burma the Buddhist-inspired *Wunthann*, the equivalent of the Indian Congress Party, was recruited from among the leading citizens; it adapted itself quite well to the Japanese occupation. But the mountain peoples in the north of the country were, by tradition, less docile. British agents, trained in a special camp in Colombo, were dropped amongst them by parachute to form guerrilla units.

In Malaya there was an aristocracy of recent growth based on the mineral wealth and rubber plantations of their country; they turned their back on the West, preferring to complete their studies in Cairo or Mecca. They had formed the Malay Union which in 1940 had asked the British authorities for their own minister, tax reform and the right of diplomatic representation. They welcomed the Japanese and provided the core of the 'Malayan Youth Movement'. However, the Sultan of Pahang refused to collaborate through fear of seeing his powers reduced.

Everywhere the Japanese came up against two groups who, because of their homogeneity, were particularly hostile: the colonies of Chinese and the Communists. In Malaya, they were one and the same thing. As soon as the Japanese attacked, the Malayan Communist party, led by Chinese, offered its services to the British who, however, were reluctant to give them arms, lest they might turn them against the British. The party seized them, however, from the stocks of arms left behind by the British troops during their hasty retreat. It formed carefully organised and strictly graded groups, patrols and regiments – seven anti-Japanese regiments – taking their orders from a 'guerrilla headquarters'. The British sent instructors whom the Communists accepted as advisers but without giving up hope of forming a Malayan Communist republic at the end of the war.

III INDONESIA

The situation was much more complicated in Indonesia, because of its considerable Moslem element, with which the Japanese endeavoured to ingratiate themselves.

Contrary to Dutch hopes, the natives had remained passive spectators of the Japanese attack and victorious occupation. The Japanese seemed in no hurry to talk of independence, even of administrative independence – Indonesia remained under military authority but it was divided; Java was controlled by the Sixteenth Army, Sumatra by the Twenty-fifth; Borneo, the Celebes and Timor were under the Navy. At the beginning, the Dutch administrative machinery was retained, no doubt in the interests of efficiency, in order not to introduce too rapid a change in an area so vitally important for the Japanese war economy.

The Dutch were all gradually interned, together with their wives and children, and replaced by Japanese and Indonesians both in the public and the private sector of government and industry. The main emphasis was placed on combating the aftermath of colonialism; foreign languages – Dutch and English – were banned and Japanese replaced them in the schools; the press was tightly curbed; all the professions and other collective bodies were organised as corporations in order to make stricter control possible. The Chinese, two million of them, who had shown signs of resistance, were forced to knuckle under after a number of them had been arrested.

Economic exploitation started at once. In order not to overburden their Merchant Navy, the Japanese had decided that the armies of occupation would live off the country; in addition, each one of the territories had the task both of exporting the maximum possible amount to Japan and of supplying its own needs by importing as little as possible. The result was that the country was squeezed dry of its wealth without receiving anything in return. This could not fail to disturb its economy and reduce the standard of living.

Ever since the eighteenth century most of the population of Sumatra and Java had been converted to Islam, an Islam adapted to the religious concepts already present; the Moslem priests and scribes were the spiritual leaders of the peasant communities and Moslem culture was retained by many of the élite who had no access to European education. The Dutch had done nothing to hinder the Moslem movement in so far as it was confined to religious, cultural or social matters; but they kept a very watchful eye on any possible political repercussions.

However, side by side with the traditional Moslem hierarchy, a nationalist party had grown up which wished for reforms in religious matters and independence at the political level. But it was torn between two factions according to whether the intellectuals who were its leaders had retained a Moslem culture, enhanced by study in Cairo, or else had acquired a non-religious, western culture.

The Japanese were not entirely without experience in Moslem matters. In 1930, for propaganda purposes, they had founded a Japanese Moslem Society which had organised a Pan-Moslem Congress in Tokyo in 1938 that had been attended by a delegation from Indonesia. The military government set up a 'Religious Affairs Bureau' whose members had spent some time in the Middle East.

The Japanese were aiming at winning over the enormous Moslem movement to their cause. They directed their effort towards the traditional hierarchy, rather like the French government in Morocco. Accordingly, they banned the two Moslem political parties which had been more or less tolerated by the Dutch and replaced them by new associations with themselves in control. The Moslems were formed into a 'Moslem Federation' which had existed earlier but had gradually disappeared. As for the small non-Moslem parties, they were also formed into a single organisation called *Putera*.

The Indonesian nationalist leaders were divided as to the attitude to adopt towards this Japanese policy. The most important of them, such as Soekarno or Mohammad Hatta, accepted it. Others, like the veteran nationalist militant Dr Tjipto Mangunkusumo, opposed it but were obliged to go into hiding and their insurrection never led to any subversive action or guerrilla warfare.

The two organisations *Putera* and the Moslem Federation were rivals, and this rivalry did not displease the Japanese, who wanted to divide in order to rule. But it did hinder the mobilisation of Indonesian resources for Japan's benefit. Accordingly, in 1943, the Japanese created an entirely new multi-racial mass movement *Djawa Hokokai* (Association for the Assistance of Java) which replaced all the others and in which they kept all the leading posts for themselves: at the risk of undermining their propaganda, they even introduced the cult of the Emperor into it.

It was not the best way to woo the Indonesians and this soon became obvious, especially as the granting of independence to Burma and the Philippines had aroused hopes in Java that quickly turned sour. In June 1943, General Tojo issued a decree allowing the Indonesians to participate, in a modest way, in the running of their country. A 'Central Consultative Committee' was set up in September 1943, with Soekarno as chairman; its power extended to the provinces in the form of local councils. This reform, however limited in extent, nonetheless strengthened nationalism at a time when it was still barely articulate.

Did the Japanese become aware of this and try to take back with one hand what they were giving away with the other? They doubtless felt closer in spirit to the traditional Moslem hierarchy than to the Europeanised nationalist leaders; they could see that the peasantry was still living in the social structures provided by its religious leaders and they considered these leaders more pliable as well as less dangerous than the nationalists. All these reasons led them to form in January 1944 a powerful Moslem association, *Masjumi*, covering the whole country, whereas *Djawa Hokokai*, as its name indicated, was restricted to Java. Control of *Masjumi* was placed in the hands of Moslems and not of the Japanese, as was invariably the case elsewhere. Moslems, too, formed most of the recruits of the volunteer force created by the Japanese as a sort of auxiliary military under the name of *Peta*.

Thus in 1944 Indonesia and especially Java became a Japanese protectorate, in which the occupying power allowed some say to national independence while basing its own authority on the Moslem hierarchy. Accordingly *Masjumi* loudly asserted that Japan's cause was the cause of Islam and its war a holy war. But the nationalists could find little satisfaction in a system which maintained and reinforced political, religious and social structures which they considered oppressive and out-moded and which made them serve a foreign power while indefinitely postponing any hope of independence.

Later, when Japan's military situation deteriorated, Tokyo considered it necessary to avoid unrest in Indonesia; the best method to achieve this seemed to be to gain the confidence of the nationalist leaders, who had moreover been actively and often successfully infiltrating and setting up

cells in the mass organisations sponsored by the Japanese, including
Djawa Hokokai.

IV CHINA UNDER THE CHUNGKING GOVERNMENT

Japan was thus experiencing great difficulties in organising and exploiting the vast empire which had come her way through the fortunes of
war. It was clear that any military setbacks or slackening of her military
or economic potential would only aggravate them. And she was still
engaged in a war in China that seemed interminable.

True, she controlled the richest and most populous regions and even
though she had not succeeded in arousing a really popular collaborationist
movement, her authority was accepted there and was undisputed. This
was not the case in the peripheral lands of the Middle Empire.

Now completely isolated in his mountains and deprived of all supplies
from outside, Chiang Kai-shek had ceased to be a serious threat for the
time being; conversely, the remoteness and height of his demesne meant
that it was well-nigh impregnable. But his army, slowly starved of modern
weapons, was falling apart. His administration was being reduced to
anarchy and in the absence of any proper central authority each local pot-
entate was acting as he thought fit. Corruption and muddle were rife
from top to bottom.

Moreover, the Chinese state had no resources; taxes were collected only
at irregular intervals and the provinces where they yielded most were
under the Japanese yoke; before the war, half its revenue came from
customs duties, which no longer existed. In contrast to this dwindling
income, the outlay due to the war was ever-increasing. Most fortunately,
the Chinese gold and silver reserves had found a safe haven abroad and
they provided security for the necessary purchases. But in China herself,
loans and the issue of government bonds had not prevented galloping
inflation. By 1941, prices had risen tenfold since 1937. The growing
increase in bank notes called for 150 tons per month of special paper and
ink, flown in from Burma.

The middle classes, the intellectuals and civil servants, were hardest
hit by this growing anarchy, even if some tradesmen and middlemen
were making good profits. Chiang Kai-shek's popularity suffered a good
deal as a result. And no aid was now being given to the Chinese by the
Soviet Union since she had been attacked; nor was Britain in any position
to replace her. Only the United States had the necessary means. But they
were asking themselves if the game was worth the candle. Although
practically at his last gasp, Chiang in fact continued to put forward the
most exorbitant claims. He haggled bitterly over his price for continuing

the fight and threatened to make a deal with the Japanese if he was not given satisfaction. He refused to allow the Chinese armies to be commanded by foreigners and he even requested that all the Allied forces fighting in Burma should be placed under his control.

In June 1942, despite misgivings and the immense difficulties involved in implementing its decision, the American government resolved to help Chiang Kai-shek. His collapse would indeed have grave consequences; Japan's prestige and aggressiveness would appreciably increase and considerable forces would be freed; she would be able to draw the resources she needed from China; it would never be possible again to bomb her from the continent of Asia; the defeat of China would also have the most unfortunate repercussions in the territories conquered by Japan.

In a word, without too many illusions, the Americans thought that China must be kept in the war. They suspected that Chiang or his associates would squander much of the aid supplied to him and that he would not use all the rest in the fight against Japan but would hold it back in order to appear stronger when peace came; perhaps he might even use it against his internal enemies? But a China that had relapsed into anarchy at the end of the war was not a very attractive proposition either. So President Roosevelt plied Chiang with friendly and flattering messages and endeavoured to calm him down when he was not able to satisfy all his requests.

From February 1942 onwards General Stilwell became Chiang's military adviser; he was an energetic and honest soldier who was appalled by the anarchy which he discovered and he was impervious to Chinese wiles. As a result he did not get on very well with Chiang, whom he called 'peanut' in his correspondence, and he was reduced to impotent rage when he learned that Chinese generals, suitably primed with dollars, were still not paying or feeding their troops.

As a first step – an expensive one and of limited value – 60,000 Chinese soldiers were flown into India to receive modern training and equipment and, if possible, a better fighting spirit. It would, however, have been more valuable to despatch equipment to China so that the fight might be resumed. But how could it be done? One possible route started from Karachi and reached Sin-Kiang via Russian Turkestan; but this idea never went beyond the planning stage. Flying over the mountains of India would need heavy long-range aircraft and of these the United States had only a limited number.

As a bait for the countries occupied by Japan, and in order to make them realise that the victory of the Anglo-Saxons would not mean an automatic return to the *status quo*, in January 1943 the British and Americans gave up their extra-territorial rights in China.

Finally, in order to put the finances of the Chungking government on a better footing, it was granted a 500-million-dollar loan. The Chinese refused to pay any interest and resisted any suggestion of restrictions on how it was to be spent; as for repayment, that could be left for discussion after the war; for the moment, this American action was looked on by the Chinese as long overdue recognition of the sacrifices that China had made for the common cause in the last five years. The Americans had thus no sort of guarantee that this life-line that was now being offered China as a last desperate chance would be adequate to reactivate her economy or the fighting spirit of her troops.

V COMMUNIST CHINA

It is true that another China was coming into being, using her own resources, in the mountainous districts of Chen-si and Kan-su, a Communist China under her leaders Mao Tse-tung and Chou En-lai, with her capital in Yenan. She was initiating a new form of fighting and working out the principles of a fundamental revolution.

Chinese Communism had its roots in an agrarian society; since its adversaries were occupying the towns, it had developed in a very poor rural community; in contrast to Russian Bolshevism, it drew its support from the peasant masses, masses composed of small farmers as much as real proletarians. A few intellectuals, some of them of bourgeois origin, succeeded in organising a real Communist state.

Following Stalin's directive Mao Tse-tung considered that before the revolution could succeed, Japan must be defeated. Once China had been liberated, the Revolution would spread to all colonial or semi-colonised countries. Nothing must stand in the way of victory and all men of good-will who were anti-imperialist, including even capitalists, were invited to co-operate in its realisation. Accordingly, the 'United anti-Japanese National Front' was set up, which implied an agreement with Chiang Kai-shek, however great the cost and even if Chiang's armies attacked the Communist Red Army.

The Chinese Communist party was thus led by economic pressures to abandon the idea of confiscating land in order to hand it over to poor peasants and to confine itself to reducing farm rents and land taxes in the areas which it controlled. It even declared its support for co-operation with capitalist industrialists if this could strengthen the war effort. So Mao Tse-tung condemned in vigorous terms those whom he called 'leftist deviationists' who thought that revolution could take place in one single operation and begin without further delay. Their attitude, he said, only succeeded in frightening many Chinese and isolating the Communist party. It would thus be playing into the hands of enemy number one: Japan.

The Communist state was self-sufficient; from the Soviet Union it received kind words but no material aid. The United States ignored it completely, at that time not so much because of hostility to its ideas as because she failed to realise its significance and underestimated the contribution it could make. In 1941, Mao Tse-tung arranged for the lessons he had delivered to the pupils of the Soviet Red Army Academy after 1936 to be printed, distributed and put into effect. It was his doctrine of revolutionary warfare, which starts from nothing and must lead to the victory of the revolution. Its essence is therefore aggression. But it must be applied in the light of a full knowledge of the real balance of forces; subversive warfare cannot succeed by means of a few decisive battles; it requires a long struggle and considerable suffering.

In particular, the enemy must be induced to penetrate deeply into the territory controlled by the Communist state; it is true that it would cause great devastation but it would also come up against a hostile population, controlled by the Party and determined to resist, in which guerrilla units would feel themselves at home as 'a fish in water'. So the Red Army should give as much ground as necessary, not in order to dig in behind some fortified line assumed to be impregnable but in order to wait for the situation to turn round in its favour; if no opportunity presented itself, it should disappear into thin air, melt into the population or else reform somewhere else. The favourable opportunity would be provided by the dispersal of the enemy's forces, which might give the partisans a temporary local superiority in numbers; and the enemy's troops which had been exposed in this way would then not be captured or obliged to withdraw but completely wiped out.

While the Chinese Red Army endeavoured to manufacture the weapons it needed in the territories under its control, it relied even more on seizing them from the enemy by plundering its transports, ransacking its stores and attacking its factories and arsenals.

In this way Mao Tse-tung defined the type of war which was for him 'one of the highest forms of the struggle to resolve the contradictions between classes, nations, states or political groups'. Victory would mean setting the seal on the identification of people, Army and Party. After that, the second stage, the revolution proper, could begin; to tell the truth, it had already begun because the forces that would bring it about were already in position. In this way the dictatorship of the proletariat would come about through the Communist party; and land, the banks and the big firms would be socialised.

This economic revolution would, however, be incomplete unless it was cultural as well. In his *Talks on art and literature in Yenan*, Mao emphasised still more strongly Lenin's refusal to accept bourgeois culture. He developed the theory, which was also Lenin's, that 'all art, literature and culture belong to a particular class and depend on a definite political line'. The proletarian party must fight on 'the cultural front'; revolutionary art must be 'useful for the revolutionary masses'. It is true that the artist remains creative; his value must, however, be assessed not by aesthetic but by political criteria; it is no use his 'expressing himself' if he does not speak the language that the masses expect.

Thus in 1942, Chinese Communism began to follow a line of thought different from that of Soviet Communism. At this time, the USSR was rediscovering her own historical, Russian values and extolling them in order to provide intellectual nourishment for her fight. On the other hand, even though for tactical reasons he had come to an understanding with Chiang Kai-shek, Mao Tse-tung never ceased denouncing the political and intellectual attitude of the Kuomintang as reactionary. For him, the class struggle was taking place at different levels – economic, political and ideological – at the same time. It must go on and on and would never be complete on the ideological level, even when the economic basis of bourgeois society had disappeared.

PART III

THE WATERSHED OF
THE WAR

At the end of 1942 and beginning of 1943, the map of the war became stabilised and then went into reverse on every front; the Axis armed forces were first checked and then pushed back. Yet this happy result was in no way the result of Allied co-ordination. In fact, the three operational theatres were separate and distinct: none of the belligerents was fighting in all of them. The Atlantic and North Africa were the lists in which the navies and air forces and to a smaller extent the armies of the British and Americans faced those of the Germans and Italians; the Russian steppes were the scene of a colossal single combat between Germany and the Soviet Union; in the Pacific, the United States were fighting it out with Japan; in all these theatres, there were the weaker brethren trying to cover themselves by joining in the fight of the larger powers.

The war had reached a turning point, but this was not the result of better organisation or strategy on the part of one or other of the two coalitions. But after having achieved almost unhoped-for success and attained their objectives, entirely in the first case and more or less completely in the second, Japan and Germany after their long series of victories had run out of steam. As they had not destroyed their opponents, the latter had gradually reformed and increased their strength, so that a balance of forces was reached. Victory had not yet decided whom she would eventually favour, but from now onwards she seemed to be more fickle.

The fact was that the American armament industry was beginning to turn out tanks, Flying Fortresses, aircraft-carriers, freighters, lorries, guns, submarines and tankers in large quantities. For her part, the Soviet Union found her wide open spaces working in her favour and she had completed the reconversion of her industry in the Urals and beyond. Thus the chances were becoming more even.

And so the Japanese expansion was halted at Guadalcanal and Midway whilst in the battle of the Atlantic the graph of the amount of shipping built intersected with that of the amount sunk, and the production of German submarines was balanced by the number of those lost. In Africa,

Rommel was brought to a halt at the gateway to Egypt and then pushed back; at the same time, the Americans gained a foothold in North Africa. Above all, the Red Army inflicted its first sharp defeat at Stalingrad.

In every operational theatre, hope changed sides.

CHAPTER I

A Balance of Forces in the War at Sea

After March 1942, the American Army and Navy planners had turned their minds to the problem of the necessary co-ordination between the services; the Navy and the Army were rivals and their views so divergent that all parties were agreed that a single command for the whole operational theatre was out of the question. It remained only to apportion the responsibility for each separate geographical area.

General MacArthur was made Commander-in-Chief of the Southwest Pacific Area, which included Australia, the Philippines, New Guinea, the Solomons, the Bismarck Islands and Indonesia. The rest of the Pacific came under Admiral Nimitz. These two commands were co-ordinated by the Joint Chief of Staff in Washington, which thus acted as GHQ for the Pacific. In fact, this headquarters had no head, except the President of the United States, and all its decisions were the result of compromise. In consequence, there were close-fought tussles, with few holds barred, over the allocation of ships, aircraft, units and supplies. But the first condition for success in each of the operational theatres that had been thus created and which were sufficiently large and separate for there to be little possibility of interference, was that the Commander-in-Chief had the ground, sea and air forces under his command: he chose his own deputies, decided on operations and had complete control in action.

In late 1943 the great strength of the Americans began to show itself by the appearance on operations of the B 29 bombers, splendidly adapted to the enormous size of the Pacific since they were able to carry nine tons of bombs for more than 3,000 miles at over 350 m.p.h.; each plane was a small factory with its six generators, its 170 various sorts of motor and fifteen miles of electric wiring. The American Navy had 9,000 landing craft and their naval shipyards were churning out submarines at the rate of one every five days. The battleships damaged at Pearl Harbour, now re-equipped and in some cases modernised, were gradually being brought back into service.

This military efficiency was shown in the introduction of a combat weapon as effective as it was flexible: the Task Force. Of varying size and composition, each task force represented at sea the equivalent of a tank corps on land. Using destroyers as scouts and submarines as escorts, its battleships and cruisers could fire by radar on an enemy twenty-five miles away. The aircraft-carriers provided the ships with intelligence, prepared their attack and protected them against enemy aircraft. Troop transports, workshop and hospital ships and supply vessels of all kinds and sizes gave the Task Force considerable autonomy of action and enabled it to concentrate its attacks on selected targets.

The American naval industry produced floating docks made of elements welded together which enabled the largest battleship to be repaired at sea. The dock was submerged by filling ballast tanks; the damaged ship was floated into it; then the ballast tanks were pumped out and the whole thing lifted out of the sea like an authentic dry dock. Valuable time was thus gained because, except in cases of really serious damage, ships no longer needed to travel all the way back to the American dockyards where they remained out of action for a long period.

II THE CORAL SEA AND MIDWAY

The Japanese were given their first warning in the Coral Sea from May 4 to 8, 1942. For the first time in history, the only units really engaged were aircraft-carriers; the warships did not join in but merely defended themselves against enemy aircraft. One aircraft-carrier was lost on each side. This indecisive battle had the result of averting any danger directed from Japan against the north of Australia and of inducing the Japanese to abandon the idea of taking Port Moresby by sea.

Another, more considerable, naval engagement took place on June 4 and 5, 1942, at Midway, an atoll situated 2,500 miles from Tokyo and something under 1,000 miles from Hawaii. After the idea of an attack on Australia had been rejected, since the Japanese Army was against it, Admiral Yamamoto, taking advantage of the feeling aroused by Doolittle's air raid on Tokyo, had succeeded in obtaining approval for a plan with a double objective: the remaining American fleet in the Pacific would be lured to Midway and destroyed.

Admiral Yamamoto had considerable forces at his disposal: nearly 200 vessels, including eleven battleships and eight aircraft-carriers with a strength of 700 aircraft. In order to disperse the American ships, Yamamoto concocted a diversionary operation against the Aleutians; he could not know that the American intelligence service had intercepted Japanese messages which left Admiral Nimitz in no doubt as to the real Japanese intentions. There was time to strengthen the air defences of Midway, notably with B 17 heavy bombers. But even when concentrated, the American naval forces were inferior, on paper, to their opponents, since they comprised only three aircraft-carriers, seven heavy cruisers and seventeen destroyers – and this despite the fact that Yamamoto had despatched two aircraft-carriers and four battleships to the Aleutians on a fool's errand.

Unfortunately for himself, the Japanese general also drew up his forces in a way calculated to reduce his margin of superiority: he made the blunder of fragmenting his forces into small vulnerable groups. In addition, as his aircraft-carriers had the task both of destroying Midway's defences and of attacking the American fleet, they were tied to a very exact timetable, which meant that they had little freedom of action. Also, Admiral Yamamoto was relying mainly on his battleships; the aircraft-carriers and submarines were intended to act merely as their advance guard and protective screen, thus failing to take advantage of the benefit that might accrue from using the ship-borne aircraft; finally, by mischance, the Japanese submarines had not reached their stations by the proper time and the Japanese were in the dark as to the movements of the closely concentrated American fleet.

Battle was joined on June 4, when a Japanese air raid on Midway destroyed their installations; if a landing had been made at once the island would have had to surrender on the spot; but the Americans had shot down forty-three enemy aircraft and these were going to be needed in the air and naval battle a few hours later. Indeed, the American squadron's aircraft attacked the Japanese planes as they were on their way back from Midway and short of fuel and ammunition. Three Japanese aircraft-carriers were destroyed as against only one American aircraft-carrier. One further tactical blunder was committed by Admiral Yamamoto during the fight: he formed his aircraft-carriers into a compact group, thus making them a target impossible to miss, whereas their American opponents were sufficiently far apart not to be hit by the same attack but close enough to help each other.

Without having had the opportunity of committing his battleships, and despite his superior armament, Admiral Yamamoto turned back since he totally lacked air support. For two days he was pursued by the Americans; guided by searchlight, their aircraft sank another Japanese aircraft-carrier, a battleship, a cruiser and three destroyers. On June 7 the chase was called off.

The aircraft-carriers had shown not only the crucial part they could play but also their vulnerability. When one of them was hit, its aircraft had to land on another one; there were many accidents, for instance one aircraft's machine guns went off as it was landing and killed many of the crew. The Americans had lost a large number of torpedo aircraft which lacked speed but had won the day partly because of the proximity of Midway, the aircraft which were based there and its airfields where the ship-borne aircraft were able to land as required.

The battle of Midway was in the best tradition of naval battles and it was a decisive one. Admiral Yamamoto had let slip an opportunity that would not occur again. The Japanese fleet was now only marginally superior to the Americans'. Above all, the Americans had won in spite of being the weaker side; they owed their victory to their better techniques, tactics and organisation and this augured well for the future.

III GUADALCANAL

After insistent demands General MacArthur had received his reinforcements: one Australian division which had been withdrawn from the Middle East and two American divisions. Although he considered this inadequate, he adopted the principle that Australia would have to be defended outside Australia, which meant that he was intending to take the offensive. A scheme to occupy and organise a good airfield close to Buna failed when the Japanese forestalled the Allies by three weeks.

Backed by Marshall, MacArthur reckoned that if the Navy 'did their stuff', it would be possible to make a direct attack on Rabaul straightaway. He would have liked to try in July 1942, but as the 700 aircraft collected in Australia could not now attack Rabaul from New Guinea, MacArthur asked the Navy for two aircraft-carriers. Admiral King thought the scheme was too ambitious and risky. His view was that they should advance more slowly and cautiously, starting by occupying Tulagi and Guadalcanal in the South Solomon Islands; the next stage would be the North Solomons, and Rabaul would have to be kept for the third stage.

As a result of this procrastination, the Japanese retained the initiative and in July 1942 landed on Guadalcanal, which could serve as an aircraft-carrier for advancing to New Caledonia. But a land attack on Port Moresby failed and a tough and costly series of actions was started by the Australians and Americans as they pursued the Japanese vigorously when they retreated. Then, although the Australians were poorly trained and not well equipped and the American artillery was inadequate, on August 7, 1942, 19,000 men were landed on Guadalcanal.

Success on the ground depended on supplying the troops and this could be done only by sea. A series of air and naval battles took place from August 8 to October 26, with fluctuating fortunes on both sides. The

Japanese had naval superiority but the Americans were stronger in the air. As a result the outcome remained uncertain.

The most important naval battle took place from November 12 to 15. It began with an unexpected engagement, haphazardly, because of an error in the functioning of the American radar; there were serious losses on both sides and two American admirals were killed. Shortly afterwards, eleven Japanese transports steaming towards Guadalcanal with inadequate protection were sunk. Finally, in the night of November 14–15, in thick fog, Admiral Lee's Task Force used its radar to destroy three Japanese cruisers and a Japanese battleship from a distance of nearly nine miles. 'The guns had been laid automatically on invisible targets,' Colonel Bernard wrote; 'allowance was made for the force and the direction of the wind, the speed of the ships, the pitching motion of the targets and the guns and the shells struck home with tremendous speed and accuracy.' As at Midway, this was a decisive American victory.

On February 8, 1943, Guadalcanal was taken. The Japanese succeeded in withdrawing part of their troops but their advance had now come to its end.

IV AMERICAN SUBMARINE OPERATIONS IN THE PACIFIC

Being forced to give priority to naval battles, the Japanese Navy did not have adequate means of protecting the convoys – troop-carriers and freighters – plying between the Japanese archipelago and its empire. There was no central authority to organise such a protection. And as Reussner wrote, 'it is not possible to improvise a convoy protection system; one needs the appropriate equipment, a coherent theory and personnel well-trained in anti-submarine warfare.'

On paper, the Japanese did indeed possess 300 escort vessels but they were old, slow and unarmed; later on, when the decision had been taken to build such vessels, there were no prototypes; suitable escort ships did not begin to be brought into action until 1943. These inadequate resources were distributed amongst the various port-admirals in the homeland and the territorial commands in the conquered countries. In such circumstances, any joint action was out of the question and each authority did as it pleased; it was practically impossible to co-ordinate the movements of convoys, reallocate escort vessels or draw up a regular list of priorities. The local authorities did not always know the arrival dates of the ships supposed to be on their way to them; if escort vessels happened to be available, everything was all right; if there were none, then the ships sailed away unprotected.

Accordingly, although precautions were taken to defend troop-carriers, which were as a rule always escorted by naval vessels, merchant ships were reduced to forming convoys to escort themselves, so that they could take advantage of each other's experience. American submarines had never had it so good.

The Americans had relatively few flotillas, but they used them to the best advantage. The Hawaiian flotilla's operations extended as far as Formosa and, with something over a dozen craft, it began to exercise an increasingly tight blockade over the east coast of Japan. The group based at Brisbane supported the surface fleet in hindering the Japanese advance towards New Guinea. The Fremantle flotilla had the task of cutting Japan's links with the Philippines, Indochina, the Indian archipelago and Malaya – the main sources of raw materials.

On December 31, 1942, Japan had lost a million tons of shipping through American submarine action, a loss barely made good by captured or newly built ships. Thus, in the Pacific, the Japanese thrust had, on the whole, been contained; inside its defensive perimeter, though Greater Asia was indeed still safe, the shadow of an American threat was appearing both in the air and at sea.

What was happening in the Atlantic Ocean during this same period?

V GERMAN SUBMARINE SUCCESSES IN THE ATLANTIC

In the Atlantic, the situation was reversed. It was the Allies who were experiencing the greatest difficulty in protecting their vital lines of communication against German submarines, which were enjoying considerable success and creating a critical situation for their opponents.

The Germans had been steadily increasing the number of submarines in service. In April 1942, Admiral Raeder reported the following situation to Hitler: the German Navy had 288 submarines, 125 of which were operational – 19 in the Arctic Ocean, 81 in the Atlantic, 20 in the Mediterranean, 5 at base. Since the beginning of the war, 304 new submarines had been brought into service and 105 had been lost; the average monthly loss was 2·9 per cent of the total number and 4·9 per cent of the number at sea; as the Reich's naval dockyards were turning out approximately 20 submarines a month at that time, the number of new craft was more than the losses. The future looked optimistic. By the end of 1942, there would be 400 u-boats actually in service.

In addition, the quality of the submarines had also been steadily improving. Trials of the *Walter*, with a gas-turbine engine capable of an underwater speed of 23 knots, had proved successful; an anti-Asdic device and a radar detector had been perfected; the submarines were armed with electric and acoustic T 5 torpedoes, with a range of 6,500 yards and a speed of 25 knots.

Methods of submarine warfare had also improved. From the beginning of 1941, Admiral Doenitz had ordered the general tactics of undertaking night attacks only; the submarines remained submerged during the day, surfaced in the dark, fired their torpedoes and then dispersed with all speed to reload their forward tubes. In order to counteract their weakness when submerged, they were grouped into 'packs' so as to launch an almost uninterrupted sequence of attacks against the convoys they had spotted. In March 1942, the introduction of 'milch-cows', large tanker submarines, enabled submarines to be refuelled at sea and doubled the range of the smaller craft. As a result, there was no part of the Atlantic now beyond their reach – they were even operating off the American coast, from Canada as far south as Venezuela.

Submarine reconnaissance was provided by long-range four-engined aircraft based on Trondheim, Cognac, Vannes and Mérignac. They reported convoys to the west of Ireland in time for submarines and bombers to go out and attack them. In 1941, 220 co-ordinated attacks of this type were made. They ceased in 1942 when the Luftwaffe's heavy commitments in the USSR prevented it from operating in the Atlantic.

All the same, the submarines' list of kills was impressive and its rising curve was alarming for the Allies. Between September 1939 and December 1941 nearly 8 million tons of Allied merchant shipping had been sunk and only one-third of this replaced. The gravity of these figures spoke for itself. The United States entry into the war, far from improving the position by adding fresh tonnage and considerably increasing the potential naval construction programme, merely made it worse. The German submarines calmly waited to pick off the American ships almost as they came out of harbour – the large urban centres along the coast had no blackout. The American Merchant Marine alone suffered losses described by Morison as 'terrifying': 500,000 tons from January to April 1942, 350,000 in May, 365,000 in June; it was like a second Pearl Harbour.

For the first seven months of 1942 the overall Allied naval losses amounted to 4,760,000 tons, that is 460,000 tons more than in the previous year. The month of June was particularly disastrous: 800,000 tons went to the bottom; one Allied merchant ship was being sunk every four hours. Things were not much better in the last five months of 1942, because more than 3 million tons of shipping were lost – 400,000 in the first week of July, as Churchill cabled to Roosevelt. In return, the Kriegsmarine had lost about 50 submarines, still less than were being turned out by its naval dockyards.

In addition, German surface ships began their raiding operations again. Between the North Cape and Spitzbergen, lurking in fjords or hiding behind the countless islands off the Norwegian coast, the battleship *Tirpitz* and four fast cruisers were constantly threatening the convoys that were carrying the promised equipment to Murmansk for the Russians. Other ships of the German Navy dealt a resounding, spectacular and humiliating blow to the pride of the Royal Navy. On February 12, 1942, the *Scharnhorst* and *Gneisenau*, which had been shut up in the outer harbour at Brest for the last six months and regularly bombed without sustaining any damage, managed to break out. After having momentarily toyed with the idea of putting the ships out of commission and transferring the crews to Norway, Hitler, ignoring Admiral Raeder's advice that the operation was too risky, had decided in fact to let them try to pass through the English Channel. The British Admiralty had anticipated this operation and were on the watch to foil it; they received regular intelligence from a French Resistance network called the *Confrérie Notre-Dame*, one of whose members was a naval officer in the Brest dockyard. The German ships left in the night of February 11, moving slowly because minesweepers were clearing the way for them. They were in fact spotted but a radar failure in two British reconnaissance aircraft caused delay in launching the formidable force that had been made ready to pursue them – 6 destroyers, 8 MTBS, 42 torpedo aircraft and 500 fighters. The attacks could not start until noon on February 12. Hampered by bad visibility, they were unable to prevent the *Scharnhorst* and *Gneisenau* from arriving safely at Wilhelmshaven, although each of them struck a mine. The British had been made to look ridiculous on their favourite element, the sea, in the Straits of Dover to boot, right under their very noses.

VI ALARMING OUTLOOK FOR THE ALLIES

It is not exaggerating to think, as does Chester Wilmot, that the gloomy prospect of steadily mounting shipping losses was to colour the whole of Allied strategy for many months to come and even dictate it. In fact, the German submarines – the Italians and the Air Force were of secondary importance by comparison – were jeopardising their entire war effort. Their hopes of success depended on their industrial superiority and these hopes would be reduced to nil if this industrial production was finding its way to the bottom of the sea. In assessing the total damage, as well as the actual loss of shipping, there must be added all its cargo which would never reach its destination, that is, for a 3,000-ton freighter, a score of tanks, a similar number of guns, thirty or so self-propelled machine guns and 1,000 tons of supplies and ammunition.

Britain's imports, indispensable if she was to be the springboard for a successful counter-offensive and without which she could only become progressively weaker, fell to 24 million tons by weight compared with 30 millions in 1941 and 54 millions before the war. Transporting troops also became more difficult now that units were more motorised and powerfully armed. Lorries and jeeps were shipped dismantled and men were crammed into transatlantic liners – 15,000 per trip were packed into the *Queen Mary* as compared with the 6,000 previously; but a successful enemy attack made the losses all the greater.

The Americans even began to wonder whether they would be able to maintain the European war effort as planned. It seemed it might be better to look to their own defence, such as ensuring the safety of the oil tanker traffic, without which their industry would grind to a halt. Should not priority be shifted to the Pacific until things improved in Europe? The Navy still found this solution tempting.

In any case, it was plainly impossible to meet all the obligations of the war at sea: a choice had to be made. In the autumn of 1942, the whole convoy system in the Atlantic was altered; those intended for the USSR and the Mediterranean were temporarily suspended, which called forth bitter protests from Stalin and well suited Rommel's book. The Home Fleet whose task was the protection of the British Isles had its destroyers taken away for convoy duty.

The Admiralty was at variance with the Air Ministry as to the best use of heavy bombers. Would it not be better to cease using them in raids on Germany and put them on anti-submarine patrols since there were not enough of them to fulfil both tasks at once? Admiral Pound pithily pointed out the principle on which Britain's power was based: 'If we lose the war at sea, we shall lose the war.' The RAF replied that by bombing the shipyards and submarine bases, they would win the war, by eliminating the opponent – it was Douhet's doctrine all over again. To this the Admiralty replied – and the admission must have been a painful one – that control of the sea had become pointless and indeed impossible without control of the air. In order to solve the problem, Churchill set up an interministerial committee on anti-submarine warfare with himself as chairman. At their first meeting in November 1942, the committee settled the squabble: they decided to transfer thirty Halifax bombers from Bomber to Coastal Command. Britain was in fact being thrust back on to the defensive. But however significant such a measure was, it did not solve the problem of protecting convoys.

VII CONVOY PROTECTION

The first important thing to be done – though it was unlikely to be achieved quickly – was to step up the output of freighters; yet it would not be sensible to do this at the expense of naval construction. In 1942,

British shipyards turned out 1,300,000 tons of merchant shipping; with the help of the Canadian and, above all, the US shipyards, it would be possible to launch something over 7 million tons – but this was less than the amount being sunk.

Another thing would be to change the type of ships being built. Thus in a moment of untimely optimism, the Americans decided to give priority to landing equipment over escort vessels. These priorities were reversed but the decision did not become fully effective until towards the end of the war, when the submarine threat had died down considerably. Out of a programme of 1,000 escort destroyers planned by the United States, 520 were completed, 420 fitted out and only 373 brought into effective service during the war.

So the most urgent thing was to cut down losses. A more elaborate co-ordination of convoys partly succeeded in doing this. Coastal shipping destined for New York was directed into two channels, with sailings at regular intervals, one from Key West, the other from Guantanamo, with branch lines for the Gulf of Mexico and the Caribbean; this enabled more effective protection and reduced losses, which were especially high for isolated ships. Thus between August and December 1942, 166 Allied vessels in convoy were sunk as against 256 sailing separately; between January and July, the respective figures had been 73 and 574.

The Atlantic convoys linked on to the coastal convoys with the punctuality and accuracy of a railway timetable. But there were vast areas of the Atlantic, off Trinidad for example, which were out of range of land-based aircraft; these 'air-gaps' left the enemy submarines free to surface and refuel; the Germans did not fail to discover them and concentrate their submarines there.

The only real solution, therefore, was to strengthen the convoys' defences to enable them to fight the submarines on equal terms and, better still, sink them. For a long time the measures undertaken to achieve this were rather tentative. Then the British fitted out their escort vessels with radar and this greatly reduced the attacks in 'packs', since the submarines were detected several miles away. Wellington bombers were fitted with a searchlight which enabled them to operate at night; the explosive power of depth charges was doubled by using a new type of explosive.

The fact remained that only aircraft were capable of detecting submarines easily, attacking them without risk and pursuing them for a sufficient length of time to put them out of action. Since they did not have an adequate number of escort aircraft-carriers, the Admiralty fitted out cargo ships with catapults for fighter planes; but the escort vessels then had to pick up the aircrews, because the aircraft were irrecoverable. The remedy cost as much as the disease.

The final and decisive solution was thus the aircraft-carrier, armed both with anti-submarine weapons and fighters. The first one, the *Audacity*, converted from a captured German liner, came into service in the autumn of 1941; she carried only eight aircraft and she was sunk by a submarine in December 1941; despite this unhappy beginning, in December 1942 for the first time the number of submarines destroyed was the same as the number of freighters sunk, whereas previously the proportion had been ten ships sunk for every submarine put out of action. The experiment was thus conclusive.

The first mobile protection group was formed in September 1942; it consisted of six naval vessels and a tanker; its task was to go to the aid of convoys under attack and to hunt down the submarines whilst the escorting vessels, the convoys' watchdogs, could only bark at their heels without moving very far away. But this sort of group could achieve maximum effectiveness only if it included aircraft-carriers and these did not come into general use until the spring of 1943.

VIII TOWARDS A BALANCE OF FORCES IN THE BATTLE OF THE ATLANTIC

On December 31, 1942, Hitler learnt through the BBC of the failure of a German naval operation on the Murmansk route. The heavy cruiser *Hipper*, one light cruiser and six destroyers had attacked a convoy without much effect. The Führer was furious and his rage was fanned by Goering, who complained at having to immobilise air squadrons in support of a navy which, he claimed, was not fighting with sufficient determination. Hitler echoed this complaint and held the Army up as an example to the Navy; when the former 'has once launched an operation, it sees it through to the bitter end'. In his irritation the Führer contemplated having the guns unbolted from the heavy naval surface vessels and installed on land. In the end, he took the decision not to send any more ships of the line out to sea; they would be restricted to operating in Norwegian waters and even in the Baltic.

Admiral Raeder bore the brunt of the Master's wrath; he was replaced as Commander-in-Chief of the Kriegsmarine by Admiral Doenitz, hitherto the Chief Submarine Commander. The logical conclusion was that submarine warfare was going to be intensified. But what with? On the one hand, as the Allied aircraft received their radar equipment, so it became more dangerous for the submarines to surface; in Doenitz's words, 'they had to keep their heads under water'. In October 1942, thirteen submarines had been sunk and in November, fifteen as against only eleven new ones built. The German naval construction programme was still suffering from

Hitler's earlier decisions in 1939 and 1940 to grant priority in the allocation of raw materials to the Army's needs – Admiral Raeder wrote that
he had been reduced to obtaining copper on the French and Belgian black
markets. Doenitz worked out an improved production schedule; thirty
submarines were to be built per month – but not until the end of 1944.

For their part, the Americans formed five mobile convoy protection
groups in March 1943. There were now also merchant ships coming
into service which had been converted into escort vessels and aircraft-
carriers each with a score of aircraft and a flying deck some 150 to 190
yards long. The Kaiser shipyards in the States were being equipped to
mass-produce them.

Results were soon forthcoming. In March 1943 the Allied shipping
losses still amounted to 500,000 tons, 97 ships in all. But then these
figures suddenly dropped. In April, one convoy lost 13 ships but sank 5
submarines. The amount of shipping built matched the shipping sunk;
the number of German submarines destroyed rose above the number
brought into service. As in the Pacific, a balance of forces was reached in
Britain's life-line, the Atlantic.

And the expectations of the British and the Americans were all the
greater since the vicissitudes of the war at sea had not prevented them
from taking the offensive in Africa with great success.

CHAPTER 2

The Germans Halted in Africa

SINCE April 1941, Rommel and his *Afrika Korps*, together with the Italian allies to whom he was subordinated, had been occupying the Bardia–Sollum Halfaya line in Cyrenaica. To enable the troops to hold their positions and if possible to strike out towards Egypt, the vital problem was their supplies. The only way they could get through was by sea and the Malta-based aircraft and ships were a constant threat to the convoys. After the Wehrmacht's attack on the USSR, the African front became even more of a side-show for the Germans; both for Mediterranean shipping and vital reinforcements, the Axis troops had to rely above all on Italy. And, as time went by, it emerged that the latter was very weak.

I ITALIAN WEAKNESS

In order to hold on to the conquests which she had had such trouble in acquiring, Italy had immobilised thirty divisions in Yugoslavia and Greece; eight others, one of them armoured, was on guard between the Little Saint Bernard Pass and the Mediterranean; there were two defending Sicily; and finally, there were Messe's troops in the USSR, some ten large units adding up to a total of 200,000 men and 22,000 motorised vehicles.

This Italian Army, seriously weakened as a result of being dispersed, had been unable to mobilise in the way which it had anticipated and which would have provided it with eighty divisions. The armaments factories were turning out seventy tanks and twelve self-propelled tracked guns per month, barely enough to form two armoured battalions every three months. The shortage of coal and electricity as well as the lack of raw materials meant that only 300 aircraft could be produced per month, for the most part inferior in quality to British aircraft.

At sea, since Kesselring's Luftwaffe had abandoned the airfields of Sicily for those of the USSR, the percentage of Italian convoys lost rose from 12 per cent in July 1941 to 41 per cent in July and 62 per cent in November; according to Bragadin, at the end of 1941 the proportion of ships sunk rose to 80 per cent. These losses were due mainly to the British

K' Force' in Malta, composed of light cruisers and destroyers supported by long-range torpedo aircraft.

After such a blood-letting, the Italian Navy was virtually defenceless; none of her ships was yet equipped with radar; only three destroyers possessed any device comparable to Asdic; there was only one escort vessel fit to carry out its tasks; the conversion of two liners into aircraft-carriers did not solve the problem. In December 1941, Mussolini drew the moral from his failure and wrote to Hitler: 'It is at sea that the outcome of the battle is being jeopardised.'

Indeed, from June to November 1941, even with less traffic than in the preceding six months, the Italian Navy lost forty-four ships, totalling 220,000 tons. On November 9, a complete convoy of nine ships was sunk; on December 14, ships totalling 100,000 tons were assembled to escort two ships carrying tanks – involving a prohibitive consumption of fuel, for a petrol shortage was looming up in the near future. Some ships were already having to empty their tanks to provide fuel for others.

It was in these favourable conditions that Auchinleck attacked in November 1941; in mid-December, after a tank-battle lasting a whole month, Rommel, unable to make good the gaps left by the fighting, was compelled to retreat as far as the Great Syrtis, abandoning Cyrenaica; he stopped on the El Agheila–Maranda line which he was able to hold thanks to the lie of the land and the opponent's exhaustion.

However, the Axis troops that managed to hold out there were in a sorry state. The *Afrika Korps* had lost 15,000 of its 45,000 men, 220 of its 250 tanks and some fifty guns. On the Italian side, things were much worse; their five divisions now numbered only 20,000 men, with 80 per cent of their tanks gone and half their artillery – 120 tanks and 180 guns abandoned or captured by the enemy. It is easy to see how Churchill was able to predict in the House of Commons 'the thorough destruction of the German-Italian army in Africa in the very near future'. But Rommel was tough and Churchill was counting his chickens before they were hatched.

II ROMMEL'S 'RECOVERY'

In fact, a series of mishaps severely handicapped the British Mediterranean squadron; the aircraft-carrier *Ark Royal* and one battleship were sunk and two cruisers were damaged by mines. On December 18 the Italians sent manned torpedoes into Alexandria harbour and put two battleships on their beam-ends, where they lay for several months. These losses, added to those that the Royal Navy was suffering at the same time in the Atlantic and off Malaya, resulted in the British Navy's sudden disappearance from the Mediterranean. The Commonwealth troops in Egypt had to be provisioned via the long route round the Cape.

Then again the winter truce in the USSR enabled Kesselring's Second Air Fleet to return to Sicily. Once more Malta was heavily pounded; the Axis MTBS and submarines preyed on the approaches to the island, so that she was again reduced to impotence. In February 1942, by a strange and rapid reversal of the situation, not one single ton of the Italian convoys to Tripoli was lost.

Rommel was not a man to let such an opportunity slip through his fingers and he seized it even before he had time to ascertain whether or not it was favourable. Seeing that the British were hesitating and marking time – Australian divisions had had to be withdrawn from the Middle East and sent to the Pacific – he took up the offensive again on his own initiative, barely eighteen days after retreating, and without waiting or asking for the permission of his Italian commander or even paying any heed to his advice. The British were caught unawares and withdrew in disorder. Without firing a shot, Rommel reconquered Benghazi, whose population was now becoming used to changing its master every so often, and in seventeen days he reached the area of Tobruk. General Ritchie, commander of the British Eighth Army, somehow managed to establish himself on the Gazala–Bir-Hakeim line, having lost in his turn 130 guns, 280 tanks and 2,000 lorries. This was the round trip to Libya.

In order to consolidate this unexpected victory, the Axis clearly had to take precautions in case the British returned to the attack, that is they had to neutralise Malta. This could be done diplomatically if the Italian ships were allowed to move in the shelter of Tunisian territorial waters and if the Axis was given control of the base at Bizerta. This was the course advocated by Marshal Cavallero, the Italian Chief of Staff. He emphasised that in this way the war in the Mediterranean would be finally won; he believed that, at a price, the Vichy government would not raise great difficulties; since Italy was neither able nor willing to give up Corsica, could not Germany promise France the Walloon area of Belgium and even Brussels? But Hitler refused to commit himself; being completely taken up with the eastern front, he wanted at all costs to avoid creating new problems in the Mediterranean.

In these circumstances, the only alternative seemed to be to capture Malta. This was also suggested by Marshal Cavallero, supported by Admiral Raeder, who wrote to Hitler in February 1942: 'It is a matter of urgency to seize Malta as quickly as possible and to launch an attack against the Suez Canal before the end of 1942.' Mussolini was all enthusiasm for this idea but he knew that the Italian forces were incapable of carrying it out on their own. As for Rommel, he had no desire to find himself deprived of the resources he needed for his long-awaited final victorious advance towards Egypt.

The decision depended, of course, on Hitler and he proved to be both attracted by it and yet hesitant. Finally, he remained faithful to the principle of not doing two things at once and the OKW approved: the date for the great offensive towards the Caucasian oil was drawing near; what did the sinking of a few Italian ships matter compared with this crucial target? Easy though it might seem in view of the dilapidated state of her defences, the capture of Malta would nevertheless mean taking aircraft and men away from the Russian front; moreover, once the island had fallen, it would be necessary to set up a solid defence on it and this would require regular reinforcements and supplies. In short, Hitler was for postponing the attack.

Moreover, the German Air Force seemed quite adequate for the task. Out of the 150 British aircraft based in Malta at the beginning of January 1942, in February only thirty remained. The British tried to reinforce them by Spitfires, which took off from aircraft-carriers and landed on airfields which German bombs had turned into craters. But the island also had to be kept supplied and only ships were capable of doing this. However, in March 1942, out of a convoy of 26,000 tons, only 5,000 reached their destination. June was much worse: a convoy coming from Egypt had to turn back while one from Gibraltar lost four of its six freighters on the way, at the hands of German aircraft and Italian cruisers.

Inversely, the shipping intended for the Axis troops in Africa was crossing as regular as clockwork. In the first quarter of 1942, only 16,000 out of 190,000 tons went to the bottom; in April, 160,000 tons got through with losses of 1 per cent and in May 170,000, with 7 per cent losses. Surely one could conclude from this that Malta had become harmless and did not require much more attention? Hitler informed Mussolini of his view that it would be better for Rommel to strike against Egypt. Perhaps the Führer, still fascinated by vistas of grandeur, had been attracted by the image of a gigantic pincer movement seizing the Middle East from Libya on one side and Turkey on the other. In any case, the time was past when the Duce had an equal right to put forward his point of view and his criticisms. He meekly acquiesced in the opinion of his ally and protector. 'The historic moment had come to conquer Egypt,' he said.

III THE *AFRIKA KORPS'* OFFENSIVE TOWARDS EGYPT

This was what Rommel had been waiting for. In the words of Bauer, 'the *Afrika Korps* had grown its claws again.' In January 1942 it had been reinforced by the arrival of 150 tanks followed by another 135; its strength had been increased by eleven battalions – ludicrous figures in comparison with those engaged in the USSR but sufficient to tip the scale of power in

Africa. The kindly spring weather had enabled this amount to be tripled. So Rommel was able to convince Hitler, with whom he was in correspondence over the heads of the Italian authorities, that he would reach Cairo in no time at all; once he was master of the rich Nile delta, it would supply him with his provisions, and, having lost her function, Malta would fall 'like a ripe fruit'. Marshal Cavallero showed some scepticism, but this Piedmontese general, whom Ciano branded as having 'the mentality of a Neopolitan parliamentarian', was used to bending to the Duce's wishes; and the Master had spoken. The fact remained, as Admiral Assmann stressed, that 'the attack on Malta would have ensured a solid base for one of the pillars on which the projected operation rested, while to go rushing off first to Suez was a major gamble which was completely unnecessary from the strategic point of view.' But the optimism and dash of Rommel, who had Hitler's ear and was liked by him, had won over even the OKW, which, following his example, suddenly changed from favouring cautious defence in Africa to a desire for an offensive at all costs. And Rommel was to come very close to winning his gamble.

His opponent, General Auchinleck, had a presentiment of the German attack. He insistently demanded replacements for the units which had been transferred to the Pacific and was promised eight divisions, though he estimated that he needed seventeen, or at the very least twelve. He vigorously denounced the behaviour of his troops, whom he described as 'amateurs', and of their officers, whom he saw as old style Bengal lancers. As he also considered his tanks and anti-tank weapons to be inferior to those of the Germans, Auchinleck was in no hurry to obey Churchill's orders, while the latter, seething with impatience, was urging him to take up the offensive.

But it was Rommel who attacked, on May 26. After a few days of indecisive fighting, the Eighth Army retreated, leaving the Free French brigade under General Koenig to delay the enemy advance and prevent it from carrying out an encircling sweep from the south, by clinging on to Bir-Hakeim for as long as possible; Koenig fulfilled his task. Nevertheless, after only fourteen hours of siege, Tobruk, which had held out for so long the previous year, fell on June 20, giving Rommel 40,000 prisoners, a large amount of equipment and above all stocks of provisions and fuel which there had not been time to destroy and which were very welcome to the *Afrika Korps* and its vehicles. A few days later, Rommel was at Mersa Matruh and then at El Alamein, where Auchinleck admitted that he was not sure of being able to hold on.

In London, emotion was running high. Egypt seemed lost and the fleet evacuated Alexandria. Egyptian nationalism reared its head at once. Fortunately Nahas Pasha, the head of the Anglophile group of the Wafd, who had been made Prime Minister by the British ambassador, Sir Miles

Lampson, proved absolutely reliable, even though his old opponent Ahmed Maher did not conceal his hostility towards the occupier. In order to ensure law and order, the British took the precaution of disarming the Egyptian troops. Nahas Pasha placed the emphasis on defending democracy, expelled dubious elements from his ministry and even dissociated himself from the secretary general of the Wafd. British law and order reigned in Egypt.

Churchill, however, had to face criticism in the House of Commons. He launched a dramatic and passionate appeal which recalled the worst moments of the summer of 1940: 'Every man in uniform must fight as if Kent or Sussex was going to be invaded. Egypt must be held at all costs.' He dismissed Auchinleck, who was the scapegoat for the defeats and especially for the loss of Tobruk, whereas the general had warned London in January 1942 that no stronghold could be held beyond the Egyptian frontier.

However, the inexorable law of desert warfare this time played in favour of the British and saved them. At the gates of Alexandria, while his opponents were in complete confusion, Rommel now had only twenty-six tanks with which to deal the final blow, and these were short of petrol; his soldiers were exhausted; his supply lines, which were too far extended, were being bombed by the RAF. Sick at heart, he was forced to halt. It would perhaps have been wiser to retreat again in order to put 250 miles of desert between the *Afrika Korps* and the British Army, which was taking on a new lease of life and increasing in strength as it reached Egyptian soil. But this was not Rommel's temperament, nor was it Hitler's orders.

Since the fighting in the USSR had made it necessary to recall the four German squadrons from Sicily, Malta had begun to breathe again; from August 1942 onwards she suffered fewer and fewer attacks and in November none at all. The number of bombers and torpedo aircraft based there could be considerably increased. Once again the Italian convoys found themselves exposed to alarming attacks: from August 1942 to January 1943 fifty-three ships were sunk; in October losses reached 44 per cent and in December 52 per cent. Rommel was suffering from the fact that the fronts were mutually dependent and from the difficulties facing the Wehrmacht in the USSR. Would he be able to resist the new attack which the British were preparing?

IV THE PAUSE AT EL ALAMEIN. THE BRITISH
PREPARATIONS

The *Afrika Korps* had come within forty miles of Alexandria. On August 31 its leader said to his troops: 'In three days we shall be at Alexandria.'

In actual fact the battle just lasted into September and the soldiers dubbed it the 'six day race'. It was the British superiority in the air combined with the *Afrika Korps*' lack of petrol which clinched the matter. The British aircraft made 18,000 sorties and dropped 930 tons of bombs on their opponents, who were concentrated in an area of less than sixty miles. Rommel had asked for at least 10,000 tons of petrol; he was promised 6,000 and received 600.

The only result of the German attacks was to make a small gap in the enemy lines which was gradually closed up again. Rommel did not like failure and for eighteen months he had spared no effort nor his health. He went back to Germany to rest. The first round of the battle had ended in a draw.

When he returned on October 24, he found a very different state of affairs. Churchill had completely recast the British command; in Cairo Alexander had replaced Auchinleck as Commander-in-Chief; Montgomery had been put in command of the Eighth Army. This son of a Tasmanian clergyman was a strange mixture of mysticism, austerity and careful determination; he had absolute self-confidence; in his mobile command post he kept a portrait of Rommel so that he could stare at it intensely in order to divine his opponent's intentions at his leisure. He demanded a great deal of himself and of his troops; he thought that they should lead a strict life and that comfort made them soft. No one was given home leave, only leave to go to Cairo. Some campaign veterans thus found themselves away from home for five years. Surprisingly, Montgomery enjoyed great popularity among his soldiers, who nicknamed him 'Monty'.

Despite his eccentricities, 'Monty' was a cautious and extremely careful leader. He had realised that the ups and downs which the Eighth Army had been experiencing since 1940 with their succession of victories and defeats, were demoralising the men. His intention was to muster enough resources to advance without afterwards being forced to retreat. He cancelled the orders involving further withdrawal, sacked some of his officers, supervised training and, in a way which was unprecedented in the British Army and seemed impossible in view of the independent traditions of each of the services, combined the Army and Air Force in a joint general staff. He formed an armoured force similar to the *Afrika Korps*. And he waited until a continuous stream of reinforcements had arrived in Egypt and given him ample and lasting superiority in men and equipment. Churchill, always impetuous, was irritated by this slowness and urged Montgomery to hurry. But the latter, although still unknown, was daring enough, according to his biographer Alan Moorehead,[1] simply to reply to the all-powerful Prime Minister: 'If the attack begins in September it will

1. *Montgomery*, London, Hamish Hamilton, 1965.

fail; if we wait until October, I can guarantee a great victory and the destruction of Rommel's army; am I still to attack in September?' And Winston, who liked men of character, approved the plan which Monty submitted to him.

The Nile delta was a far livelier jumping-off point for an army than the Cyrenaican desert. Montgomery received a further supply of American Sherman tanks and he soon had twice as many tanks as Rommel. He gained the mastery he needed in the air. Fresh troops, notably New Zealanders, put new life into his infantry. He united his various different units into a homogeneous force. At last, by the night of October 23–24, he considered that he was ready and he launched his offensive.

V THE BATTLE OF EL ALAMEIN

Montgomery's preparations had not gone unnoticed by the German-Italian command. They had wondered whether, after the fruitless attack of August 31, it would not be better to fall back to the west in order to reduce its line of communications and increase that of its opponents. Rommel had had several discussions with Kesselring about this. They concluded that the positions which they had reached, stretching from the sea to the Qattara depression, an area of many hundreds if not thousands of square miles which were completely impassable, were good and must be held. Kesselring had no difficulty in convincing Mussolini, who was obsessed with the long-delayed leap to victory in Egypt. Rommel, for his part, saw Hitler and he seems not to have suggested a withdrawal which he knew the Führer opposed on principle.

The lie of the land did not leave much chance for the opponents to show great imagination in their renewed attack; with one flank backing on to the sea and the other bordering on the desert, their only possibilities were a frontal attack on the flank or an encircling movement from inland, or to carry out both operations simultaneously or in succession. The tanks were hampered in their movements by dust and gravel, low-lying marshes, sandstorms and surfaces of jagged rock. The desert air was healthy but the ubiquitous mosquito carried nasty diseases. Over the vast, monotonous expanses where there were no landmarks, it was all too easy to lose one's way and lack of water soon became a matter of grave concern.

Montgomery was not much of an innovator; he preferred to act with extreme caution. Instead of trying to destroy the enemy tanks all at once, as Rommel did, he proceeded by nibbling operations and by frequently switching his line of attack, in one of those decisive breakthrough battles which Churchill compared to a naval battle but which was even more like an air battle; thus one by one the bases essential for the enemy tank operations

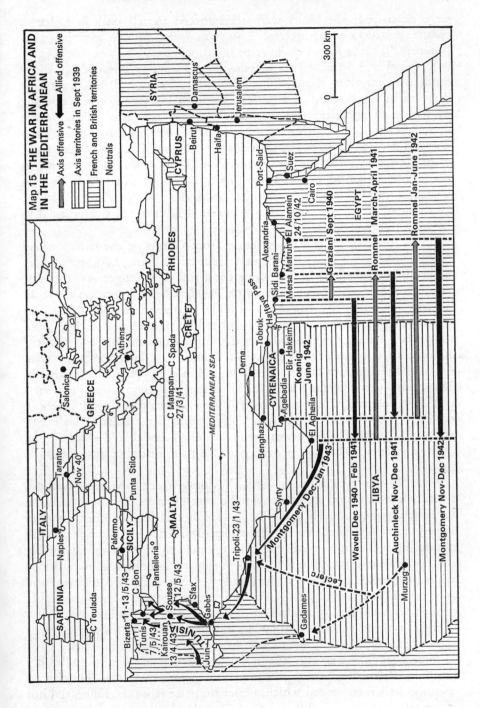

Map 15 THE WAR IN AFRICA AND IN THE MEDITERRANEAN

Axis offensive
Allied offensive
Axis territories in Sept 1939
French and British territories
Neutrals

300 km
0

SYRIA
Damascus
Jerusalem
Beirut
Haifa
CYPRUS
Port-Said
Suez
El Alamein 24/10/42
Cairo
Mersa Matruh
Sidi Barani
Graziani Sept 1940
EGYPT
Rommel March-April 1941
Rommel Jan-June 1942
Alexandria
Haifaya Pass
Tobruk
Derna
Bir Hakeim
Koenig June 1942
Agebadia
CYRENAICA
Benghazi
El Agheila
Wavell Dec 1940 – Feb 1941
LIBYA
Auchinleck Nov-Dec 1941
Montgomery Nov-Dec 1942
Syrty
Montgomery Dec-Jan 1943
Tripoli-23/1/43
Leclerc
Gadames
Murzug
C Matapan—C Spada 27/3/41
RHODES
CRETE
MEDITERRANEAN SEA
Athens
Salonica
GREECE
Taranto
Nov 40
ITALY
Naples
Palermo
SICILY
Punta Stilo
MALTA
Pantelleria
SARDINIA
C Teulada
C Bon
Bizerta 11-13/5/43
Tunis 7/5/43
Kairouan
13/4/43
TUNISIA
Juin
Sousse 12/5/43
Sfax
Gabès

were destroyed; the tanks were then forced to fall back in order to escape destruction themselves. This was what Monty meant by his phrase: 'I'll make Rommel dance to my tune.'

Rommel had protected his defence lines by laying hundreds of thousands of mines. On the evening of October 24, one British armoured division had succeeded in breaking through but another had scarcely made any advance; the situation was not very satisfactory. During the night of October 24-25, Montgomery and his lieutenants had a council of war and decided to carry out their plan at all costs. But at the same time, in order to be ready for any eventuality, Monty positioned troops in reserve. 'A leader who can act like this,' he wrote with a self-satisfaction which he took no trouble to disguise, 'is on the point of victory.' On the morning of October 25 the 10th Armoured Division also succeeded in crossing the minefields.

When Rommel made a hasty return from Germany, the situation had taken a disturbing turn; his deputy, General Stumme, had been killed. Fighting continued on his positions for a few days longer and then the 'desert fox' had to make himself scarce. He signalled the OKW on the night of November 2-3. They waited until Hitler was awake to tell him the bad news. The Führer's violent anger surprised no one. How had they dared to disobey him, he exclaimed, when the previous day he had ordered Rommel to 'conquer or die'? However, Rommel's aide-de-camp arrived at the OKW to justify his leader's decision: one had to accept the inevitable. Despite his preoccupation with the situation in Stalingrad and although disturbing concentrations of ships had been reported at Gibraltar, Hitler decided to reinforce the African Army with men, tanks and aircraft, apparently without any concern about the delays they would encounter on their way. In actual fact it proved possible to send only a few thousand men.

After 'de-mining Rommel's garden', Montgomery took great care not to launch into a wild race to cover the greatest possible distance in the shortest possible time. He had fully realised that in desert warfare supplies must follow on so as to avoid Pyrrhic victories. After each advance, he did not extend his lines, however great the temptation or however favourable the opportunity. He waited for the enemy counter-attack in positions which he himself had chosen; he boldly set up stocks of equipment and food supplies as near as possible to the front; he formed a 'forward supply group', with the task of equipping harbours and bases as he advanced.

Hitler's orders forbade Rommel to disengage in order to have room to regroup; he was to fight every inch of the way, which was exactly what Montgomery was wanting. But he could not find any line to establish a foothold. Petrol was arriving in ever-diminishing quantities. He clashed with the Italian command which, under pressure from the Duce, did not wish to be pushed so unceremoniously out of Cyrenaica and intended offering resistance at Sollum, then at Mersa el-Brega, short of the Great Syrtis, and finally at Bouerat outside Tripoli. However, these intentions were cancelled and contradicted by the Italian units which, after fighting bravely at El Alamein, became demoralised in retreat and broke up. And how was it possible to hold on firmly to a specific point with defeated troops who were not receiving any replacements either of equipment or ammunition?

Despite his steady succession of victories Montgomery was not free of anxiety; he could solve his supply problem only by capturing harbours which were in good condition. In January 1943 he wrote that if he did not reach Tripoli within ten days he would have to halt or even withdraw. But he arrived there before the fateful date and by a symbolic chance was joined there by the small Free French unit, ragged and wretchedly armed, which Leclerc had brought victoriously across the Sahara from Lake Chad. Nothing could now stop the Eighth Army. The conquest of Cyrenaica was followed by that of Tripolitania. Both Churchill and Montgomery noted it in their memoirs; 'Before El Alamein,' wrote one of them, 'we never had a victory; after El Alamein we never had a defeat'; which the other echoed when he wrote: 'For seventeen months we did not have one single failure.' The British victory in Africa was a replica of the American success at Midway; it was not due to a lucky chance, to a temporarily favourable combination of circumstances or to the genius of a military leader but to the superiority which the Allies had gained in armaments, manpower and organisation. And so the Mareth line, the gateway to Tunisia, had now been reached and other Allied troops, Americans this time, had come from the other side of the Atlantic to join hands with the Eighth Army.

VI OPERATION 'TORCH': THE ALLIED DECISION

In April 1942, the British and Americans had agreed on Operation 'Bolero', by which a powerful American force would be assembled in Britain, capable, at the earliest possible moment, of launching the full-scale attack across the Channel for which Stalin was continuing to clamour. If it were further delayed, there was a risk that either the Russians would be defeated or they would cut their losses with the Germans in order to put an end to the fighting in the east. A limited operation ('Sledge-hammer') had been contemplated for the summer of 1942 but calculations had shown that a landing would not really be possible before the spring of 1943 at the earliest (Operation 'Round-up').

However, Churchill had mapped out another plan which he had christened 'Gymnast'. Why not strike while the iron was hot and take advantage of the flourishing state of the North African front in order to gain victory by a landing in French territory? Churchill had a bee in his bonnet about bringing the French colonies back into the war; he saw all sorts of advantages in it: it would ensure the protection of Gibraltar, regain control of the Mediterranean, economise on shipping by avoiding detours round the Cape and very quickly bring down Italy, the weakest opponent.

The Americans, however, and Marshall particularly, were of a very different opinion. With their industrial power and their inexperience in military matters, they saw an offensive as an immense rationalised operation which would bring enormous amounts of equipment together at the right place and at the right time, thanks to meticulous planning and an exact timetable against which the Germans would have no adequate reply. The British, who were more empirical and wanted to husband their strength, were amused by this youthful impetuosity; for them the landing could only be the last and crucial blow against an enemy already worn down by a series of previous attacks.

It quickly became apparent that it was impossible to attempt to do anything across the Channel during the summer of 1942, because of the earlier delay in assembling men and equipment in Britain. The plan was to have a million men ready to embark in 2,200 special landing craft in the autumn of 1942; in fact, there were only 250,000 men and 400 craft. This was the result of the support given to MacArthur in the Pacific and Alexander in Egypt. Plans had to be revised.

Seizing his chance, Churchill, whose besetting sin was stubbornness, brought up 'Gymnast' again and since Marshall was still reluctant, he appealed to Roosevelt. On July 30, after several weeks of discussion, Roosevelt resigned himself to following his ally, on condition that the plan for a landing in Europe in the spring of 1943 was not abandoned.

Churchill, however, knew that his most authoritative military leaders were of the opinion that a landing in French North Africa in 1942 would make another landing in Europe in 1943 impossible. His silence on this point, as d'Hoop writes,[1] leads one to assume 'both an inveterate optimism and blatant dishonesty'. The experimental Dieppe raid on August 19, 1942 seemed to prove that he was right. Carried out with 6,000 men and one tank regiment, it needed 237 ships and landing craft and although a good deal was learnt from it, it ended in failure after revealing the full complexity of large-scale amphibious operations. Nevertheless, some Americans, in particular Admiral King, did not draw the same conclu-

---

1. 'Les Problèmes Stratégiques de la Grande Bretagne, juin '41–juillet' 42', *Revue d'histoire de la deuxième guerre mondiale,* July 1965.

sions from it as the British Premier: since it was impossible to attack in Europe, they said, they might just as well reinforce MacArthur in the Pacific, and since King was in charge of the allocation of ships, it needed all Roosevelt's authority to prevent Operation 'Torch' – the code name given to the landing in North Africa – from being deprived of essential shipping from the outset.

The fact nevertheless remained that 'Torch' was a makeshift operation, for which time was even more short because the date was fixed for the autumn, in order to prevent the Wehrmacht from taking advantage of the semi-truce in winter in the USSR by reorganising its troops in the west. Both the diplomatic and the military preparations – and the two were linked – would be bound to suffer from this.

Indeed the first problem which the preparations for 'Torch' had to solve was what kind of welcome the Allies would receive from the French troops and authorities; they were known to be loyal to Vichy – this they had proved at Mers el-Kebir, at Dakar, in the Middle East and in Madagascar – and very much against the British and the Free French. In order not to jeopardise the chances of coming to an agreement, it was therefore decided that it would be strictly an American operation, at least outwardly; it would be under an American general and, failing Marshall, whom Churchill suggested but whom Roosevelt wanted to keep by him, the choice fell on Eisenhower. It was also decided that General de Gaulle and Free France and even more the internal French Resistance should be kept out of the way and in ignorance – a decision which was all the more agreeable to Roosevelt because he denied that Free France had any right to represent France and because the American authorities had been greatly annoyed by the incidents of St-Pierre and Miquelon, which had been 'freed' by Admiral Muselier against the United States' wishes, and of New Caledonia, when the French commissioner Thierry d'Argenlieu had briefly taken to the jungle on the arrival of the Americans. Cordell Hull referred to them as the 'so-called Free French'.

But how were they to approach the Vichy troops in such a way as to neutralise them without at the same time divulging the secret of the expedition? The American diplomats made some discreet inquiries as to how they stood, with Murphy, the Consul-General at Algiers, playing the chief role. It seemed impossible to approach Pétain directly and dangerous to bring Admiral Darlan into it – even though he was Commander-in-Chief of the Vichy troops and even though he had made a few timid advances to the Americans after being removed from power in favour of Laval in April 1942; but he was the man of the 'Paris protocol' who supported French collaboration with the Axis. And the French Navy's hostility to the British was common knowledge. General Weygand continued to enjoy great prestige in French North Africa but he no longer had any official post and he declined the surreptitious advances which were made to him – he was above all else, he said, a disciplined soldier.

The Americans' choice therefore fell upon General Giraud, a man with a firmly established reputation in Africa as a good fighter, who had made a glorious escape from the fortress of Koenigstein and who had dared to stand up to Otto Abetz, the Reich's ambassador, when he came to ask him on behalf of the Führer to go back to his German prison, since otherwise he would make the French prisoners of war pay for it. The American diplomat Murphy had several conversations with Giraud, which ended in a vague agreement whose ambiguity was going to give rise to serious misunderstandings and tiresome confusion. The Americans recognised Giraud as the leader of the French Resistance; between de Gaulle the outcast and Pétain the untouchable they were, in fact, backing a 'third man'. They were relying on him to rally the French North African troops to the Allied cause and to avoid any bloodshed between the French and themselves. But whether he was intoxicated with his popularity or whether he had been deceived, General Giraud had completely different ideas; he thought that he was going to be put in charge of all the Allied troops in North Africa; he advocated a landing on the French Mediterranean coast, and no one told him bluntly that it was impossible; he set up a complete semi-clandestine network in the Armistice Army which he intended sending into the occupied zone. Sure that the Americans would support him, he had nothing but contempt for the French underground Resistance and he evaded the approaches which they made to him. To him, General de Gaulle was merely a brigadier-general, whose respect for discipline and rank required him to submit to his command. Some of Giraud's remarks give the impression that he saw himself as the head of the whole European Resistance movement. In fact, having been away from France for nearly two years, General Giraud had not gauged the development of French public opinion; he disapproved of collaboration for patriotic reasons; but he did approve of the National Revolution, for he had said so and put it in writing; he had complete and utter respect for Pétain.

VII THE PREPARATIONS IN NORTH AFRICA

Every step was taken to keep Giraud's arrival in Algiers till the last moment, so that it would cause the psychological shock that was hoped for; a British-controlled network in France, 'Alliance', was given the task of transporting him on a British submarine. In North Africa itself, the field had been prepared both by the Americans and by the General's emissaries; American consuls, who were sometimes nothing more than disguised special service agents, had established themselves in the big cities after an agreement with General Weygand at the time of his pro-consulate in Africa and had for some months been enlarging the number of necessary contacts. The Office of Strategic Services itself had set up a powerful branch in Tangier and established contacts with the intelligence and counter-espionage services of the Armistice Army which had rallied to Giraud. So a whole conspiracy could be set afoot in Algeria and Morocco.

The American consuls had found that on the whole the people of North Africa – officials, French settlers and natives – were loyal to the Vichy government. Free France had succeeded in recruiting only a small number of supporters in an offshoot of the metropolitan Resistance movement 'Combat', consisting primarily of academics. As for the army, its patriotism was as certain as its hostility to General de Gaulle; but since it was imbued with the official neutralism of the Vichy government, summed up in General Weygand's formula of 'fighting anyone who threatened the rights of France', there was no doubt that it would regard the Allied landing troops as aggressors and would open fire on them, unless their leaders gave them other orders in due course.

This barrel of gunpowder had therefore to be defused. The plot centred on a 'Group of Five', people of importance in favour of General Giraud, consisting of General Mast, the industrialist Lemaigre-Dubreuil, a leader of the Youth Work Camps, Van Hecke, an extreme right-wing journalist, Rigault, the officer Henri d'Astier de la Vigerie (two of whose brothers were on the side of General de Gaulle but who was himself a royalist), and the diplomat Tarbé de Saint-Hardouin. 'The Five' recruited accomplices in most of the services and in the large towns of North Africa. A double plot was hatched; in Algiers a putsch would neutralise those Vichy leaders who were assumed to be hostile, so that the American landing could be safely carried out; at Rabat, General Béthouart – the only leader who had achieved a French victory in 1940 at Narvik – would prevent any opposition from the Resident General Noguès, the GOC unless the latter were warned at the very last minute and joined the conspirators. In the meantime General Giraud would arrive in Algiers, take over command of the troops and the trick would have worked.

General Eisenhower sent his deputy, General Clark, by submarine to make contact with the Group of Five in the region of Cherchell in Algeria. The Five submitted to him their plan, which he approved, and presented him with a whole list of suggestions and *desiderata* which he did not exclude. They asked him for the arms they needed for the success of their attempt and they insisted on the landings taking place in the whole of North Africa, including Tunisia. Clark listened carefully and showed himself to be understanding but took good care not to give his companions the slightest inkling of the Americans' real plans, for fear of letting the cat out of the bag. The conspirators were to be forced to act alone, and virtually in the dark. From this point onwards a difference of views was apparent but no one thought it wise to emphasise it in case this made it worse: the resisters were acting from a specifically French point of view and with political aims which the Americans refused to go into or to understand; for them the only thing which mattered was the success of the military operation.

Indeed, the Allies had had some difficulty in deciding on a final plan. The British proposed simultaneous landings in Casablanca, Oran, Algiers and Bône; Admiral Cunningham, who was anxious to put an end to his trouble in the Mediterranean, wanted them to go as far as Bizerta, thus cutting off Rommel's rear, and the Axis would find it impossible to establish itself in Tunisia. The Americans, however, were more pessimistic; they were responsible for the operation and they knew that their resources were limited. They did not feel completely reassured about the behaviour of the French troops and they were afraid that they might continue offering strong resistance; finally, they were worried by Franco's attitude and by the possibility of a German reaction in the direction of Gibraltar. It was therefore important not to make the lines of the expedition too long.

In the end, the plan was not fully decided on until September 20. Three landing areas were fixed on, Casablanca, Oran and Algiers. The force operating in the west would be purely American; the one in the centre, against Oran, would be made up of American troops, convoyed by the Royal Navy and supported by an Anglo-American air force; the one in the east, against Algiers, would consist of troops from both countries, protected by the Royal Navy and supported by the RAF. They would all be under an American commander. There would be no landing east of Algiers until there was absolute certainty of success in the capital; only then would they advance towards eastern Algeria and if possible to Tunisia.

This was a wise but at the same time a complicated scheme; putting it into practice proved difficult. It required a great deal of time and it was precisely time that was lacking: there were only ninety days instead of the 360 which were deemed necessary. If one adds to this the fact that half the American troops had to be provided by the contingents which had arrived in Britain and that almost the whole of the available supply of troops had to be used, any large-scale operation across the Channel in 1943 became impossible.

Besides, the lack of experience of those carrying it out, especially of the Americans, gave rise to numerous problems. They have been carefully listed by Morison: some of the landing craft did not receive their engines until the day before they were due to sail; the crews had been recruited in a hurry and were bad at handling their craft; the aircraft-carriers which

were to escort them came almost straight from the shipyards; the troops
had not been trained to transfer at sea from the troop-ships to the landing
craft which had been provided to land them; the co-ordination of Army
and Navy was far from perfect; on September 9 Admiral Hewitt still did
not know what naval forces he would have at his disposal, and so on. In
short the chances were that this experimental interallied amphibious
operation would not be a brilliant one.

VIII THE LANDING

The American convoys had to cover 3,000 miles; those which had come
from Britain had the task of shipping men and provisions to Gibraltar –
they had been taken there by 340 troop-ships in the course of the previous weeks. Miracle number one: neither the Axis powers nor the Vichy
authorities detected these gigantic armadas until later: at the time, everyone thought that there was going to be an operation in the area of Dakar
or Malta.

The OKW's log-book mentions that on November 4, even though the
Germans knew that forces were being concentrated at Gibraltar, they were
not yet worried by it. On November 6 the convoys were sighted at sea;
Mussolini and Kesselring then expressed the opinion that they were heading for North Africa; but those in charge of German naval operations
thought that the landings which could now be expected would probably
take place in Tripoli, perhaps in Sicily and Sardinia and, as the last hypo-
thesis, in French North Africa. Besides, what could be done? Commitments on the eastern front were so heavy that all of the Wehrmacht's
forces were needed and a rapid survey made it plain that it was impossible
to send air forces to the Mediterranean. They therefore had to resign
themselves to strictly defensive measures – to putting into practice the
'Attila plan' for invading the unoccupied French zone, while in contradiction of this the shock units, notably the 6th Panzer Division, were transferred from France to Russia. Besides, an operation on French territory
did not seem such an alarming possibility; with their ears still ringing with
Laval's and Darlan's suggestions of collaboration, the Germans considered – as General Jodl said to Hitler on November 7 – that an Allied
landing on French territory 'would finally drive France into Germany's
arms'.

The landing troops' opponents, real or feared, were therefore taken
utterly by surprise. The first fortunate result of this was the complete
success of the Algiers putsch. On the night of November 7–8 a few hundred
young men, virtually unarmed, mostly Jews who had been joined by a
small handful of Arabs, took over the city without bloodshed. Most of the

officials were captured in their homes, notably General Juin, who commanded the troops, and Admiral Darlan, who had chosen an inopportune moment to come to Algiers to the bedside of his son who was suffering from poliomyelitis. The city's defences were thus disorganised and the Americans took advantage of this to land without difficulty. But they did so later than planned and at points known only to themselves. This removed any possibility of co-ordination with those who had carried out the putsch; at daybreak, the VIPs were freed and fighting broke out. As a last straw, General Giraud was not there; he was in Gibraltar arguing with General Eisenhower, for he had been greatly disappointed to learn that he was not the interallied Commander-in-Chief; a radio broadcast of a communiqué supposedly issued by him was inadequate compensation for his absence.

At the other end of the operation in Casablanca, the putsch, after a good start, had taken a bad turn. General Béthouart had used rebel troops to cut off the Residence; but General Noguès, who had been held prisoner for a short while, had succeeded in giving his orders through an uncut telephone link and loyal troops had come to free him. It was now General Béthouart's turn to be arrested and threatened with court martial. There, too, it had not been possible to prevent fighting and the French naval forces, under Admiral Michelier, were by no means negligible. Finally, at Oran a British attempt to force the harbour had failed and there was fighting there, too.

All the precautions which had been taken to avoid a Franco-Allied clash had therefore failed; the Americans' prime concern was to put an end to it as quickly as possible; but being unable to dictate their terms or to rely on General Giraud to make sure that they were accepted, they found themselves obliged to enter into discussions with the Vichy authorities, whom in any case they had nothing against, and they were forced to realise that Admiral Darlan alone, as Commander-in-Chief, had the power to call a cease-fire. So it was with him that an armistice was signed in Algiers at 6.45 p.m. on November 8.

But the fighting was continuing at Casablanca, where General Noguès, furious at his humiliating mishap, was even less disposed to put a stop to it because Marshal Pétain had appointed him commander of the troops, after disowning Admiral Darlan; the struggle was to continue until November 11, causing 2,000 casualties among the French, who lost all their fleet, among them the battleship *Jean-Bart*. The Americans' clumsiness had prevented them from achieving a rapid victory; their aircraft-carriers were so lacking in training that one of them lost twenty-one of its thirty-one planes, all as a result of accidents, except for one which was shot down; this same lack of experience cost them 150 landing craft out of the 347 intended to land on the Fedhala beach; the land fighting at Mehedia lasted longer and caused greater bloodshed because General Truscott, who had little knowledge of the capabilities of naval gunnery, failed to ask for its initial support.

When the cease-fire came, the landing had, however, been everywhere successful, although at a higher cost than had been anticipated. But politically the situation had taken a completely unexpected turn. When General Giraud arrived in Algiers, the dice were already cast and the other French military leaders refused to recognise his authority; they even severely criticised his behaviour. General Giraud accepted this state of affairs with equanimity; he was not interested in politics; he would be satisfied if the French Empire came back into the war and he was given command of an army. Admiral Darlan, on the other hand, the man of the 'Paris protocol' of May 1941, had made a spectacular comeback.

The fact was that he had succeeded in receiving Marshal Pétain's blessing, thanks to the French Admiralty's having kept a direct line with Vichy, thus allowing a certain amount of communication by telegram. One of these messages mentioned a 'secret agreement' of the Marshal's; the Admiral took advantage of it to explain away his sudden change as being authorised by the Head of State. He was not a rebel since Pétain approved of him and he claimed that he was only acting in accordance with the latter's secret intentions, which he was not in a position to divulge.

The exact meaning of this telegram has been hotly disputed; the Marshal's apologists have made great use of it in their campaign to rehabilitate him; they even draw attention to a task which Pétain was supposed to have given Darlan on August 4, 1940, which was obviously without any bearing on the totally unexpected situation of November 1942 and to which Admiral Darlan himself had never referred. General Schmitt and Dhers, by tracing the sequence of events very closely, have shown that this telegram was sent after they had taken place; not only did it arrive after Admiral Darlan had put an end to the fighting on his own initiative without being ordered to do so by Vichy, but it also referred to a previous phase, when the Admiral had informed Vichy of his intention of resisting the landing troops by force of arms. The 'secret agreement' thus concerned Darlan's original desire to fight and not his sudden swing over to the Allies; moreover, the Marshal's real thoughts had been expressed when he subsequently publicly disowned and formally condemned the Admiral.

This debate is important only from the strictly French viewpoint of the death-sentence passed on Marshal Pétain by the High Court of Justice in 1945 and the atmosphere of discord and passionate feeling which it continued to arouse in France. The important thing for the course of events is that Admiral Darlan, with the Marshal's consent, either real, assumed or invented, had reaffirmed his personal authority, forced an end to the fighting and retained power, which was reinforced by a *de facto* recognition of the Americans. The result was utter chaos.

One thing that does seem to be true is that the American landing put the Vichy government in a very difficult situation – even if some of its members and probably Marshal Pétain himself were delighted, in their heart of hearts. It gave no promise of a liberation of France in the near future and it exposed her to stern German reprisals. By losing control over the colonies, the Vichy government lost one of its chief assets and almost one of its *raisons d'être*; it looked as though it might deal the death-blow to the policy of collaboration advocated by Laval. Darlan's sudden swing could only confirm Hitler in his fundamental distrust of the French and his hostility towards them. What disasters might now be in store for France? The Marshal's policy, 'the gift of his person', had been dictated by the desire to reduce the misfortunes of the French and the firm belief that he was the only one who could do it. This was why he had refused to leave France in June 1940; this was why he refused again in November 1942, despite the urgings of some of those close to him, among them Admiral Auphan, and at the risk of upsetting a good many of his followers. His extreme caution, combined with the circumstances, prevented him from speaking his mind. It was therefore probable that the Marshal confined himself to accepting the *fait accompli* by letting Admiral Darlan follow a course, which he was in any case no longer in any position to prevent, and by remaining in France himself to save what he could from any possible disaster.

A 'secret agreement' with Admiral Darlan's sudden volte-face would have had some real meaning only if it had been accompanied by concrete measures which, it is true, would have had to be kept secret by reason of the circumstances. But no such measures were taken, either in Tunisia or in Toulon. The consequences of this were going to be very tiresome and even disastrous; yet it was not time which was lacking.

Indeed, no German reaction to the landing had been organised until November 10; it took the form on the one hand of the invasion of the southern zone by German and Italian troops and on the other hand the setting-up of a solid 'bridgehead' in Tunisia. There could be no serious objections to the first operation but the second was very risky and as the OKW had pointed out, it demanded a 'close and friendly' liaison with the French military authorities. This liaison worked perfectly, and no 'secret disagreement' occurred to disrupt it; furthermore, Vichy sent out a special envoy, Admiral Platon, the Colonial Minister, to negotiate it. In the face of this mutual determination, the Algiers discussions and the uncertainties arising from them reduced the French forces in Tunisia to inactivity, including those of their leaders who were sympathetic to the British and Americans.

So German transport aircraft were able to land on Tunis airfield without a single shot being fired against them; 'defence against anyone' did not operate against them at all. The French troops withdrew to the mountains west of Tunisia, as if their job had been to oppose a possible Anglo-American advance. Without meeting any opposition, the Germans were able quite happily to reinforce their advance-guard units by air and sea, to the point of despatching three German and two Italian divisions to Tunisia. They extended the perimeter of the occupied territories in the north by seizing Bizerta without firing a shot and capturing Admiral Derrien's small flotilla there; in the south they went to the aid of the *Afrika Korps*, which would thus be certain of being able to retreat westwards. It was not until November 19 that the French commander in Tunisia, General Barré, rejected the German ultimatum – in the meantime instructions to this effect had been received from Algiers, eleven days after the 'secret agreement' between Marshal Pétain and Admiral Darlan.

IX RESULTS OF OPERATION 'TORCH'

The Allied landing in North Africa therefore ended in semi-victory. It had clearly lacked boldness and breadth of conception but this was not realised until General Franco's complete inactivity had been confirmed. Above all, the American armies had shown how badly prepared they were for the enormous tasks awaiting them; all in all, Operation 'Torch', which had been restricted both in its area and in its risks, had been a good preparation for the crucial offensive across the Channel and the difficulty in carrying it out left one to suppose that a similar offensive in 1943 would very probably end in costly failure. It could therefore be argued that it was not just a huge waste of time, indeed quite the reverse.

In North Africa, on the other hand, the failure of the 'Giraud scheme' was creating a somewhat confused political situation. The recognition of Admiral Darlan, even though presented by President Roosevelt as a 'temporary expedient', nevertheless came as a shock to Allied public opinion, both American and British, and even more so to the French. It seemed that some kind of prize was being offered to the men who had upheld the policy of collaboration at the expense of volunteers – such as General de Gaulle – who had never given up fighting with the Allies even in their worst hours. In Africa, the Vichy government did not change its supporters or its laws – some of them inspired by Hitler, such as the abolition of the Crémieux Decree which had granted Algerian Jews French nationality. General de Gaulle made violent protest in London and the whole French underground Resistance followed suit; any contact with Darlan seemed to them dishonourable. Besides, did not Darlan disown those responsible for the Algiers conspiracy and anyone involved in it for disobedience to him, by demoting them from their posts and even imprisoning them? The ease with which the Admiral had obtained the support of West Africa and as a result the reinvolvement of the whole of French Africa in the war were small compensation for the troubled political situation which had been created and in which General Eisenhower struggled on as best he could but without always quite understanding the ins and outs of it all.

In France herself, the chief victim of the operation was the Vichy régime. A visit by Laval to Hitler's headquarters was unable to prevent the invasion of the southern zone, against which Marshal Pétain made a formal protest which had no practical effect. The plan drawn up by General Giraud was not carried out and the Vichy authorities ordered the Armistice Army not to resist the invader. Only General Delattre de Tassigny, in Montpellier, tried to take to the maquis, but scarcely anyone followed him and he was disowned by the government and imprisoned. The occupation of the southern zone was shared between the Germans and the Italians, with the Rhône as a boundary. All the cities were occupied without any difficulty. The Armistice Army which had at first been withdrawn to its barracks, was disarmed and then dissolved, except for one division which, together with the Navy, was given the task of defending the fortified port of Toulon, coming under the orders of the German formation called the 'Felber Group'.

The German authorities purported to regard the southern zone as still free; they did not set up any new districts within the zone of the kind which existed in the north. This was pure fiction; the semi-independence which the armistice had given the Vichy government was well and truly over. Robbed of its colonies, its army and its home territory and forced to break off diplomatic relations with the United States, Marshal Pétain's government could no longer even pretend to have a policy of its own, for it no longer had the means. This was the end of the experiment which began with the Rethondes armistice of a French government theoretically retaining a little independence and hoping to set the country on its feet again thanks to military neutrality offset by political and economic collaboration with the conqueror, and to the plan of reform called the National Revolution. There were only two possible cards left for the French to play: either full collaboration or Resistance. Most of the officers of the Armistice Army opted for the second; they did not, however, join the existing Gaullist Resistance movements; they tried via Spain to join the ranks of the new French army being formed in North Africa; those who stayed on in France made up the Army Resistance Organisation (ORA) which also wanted to depend only on this regular African army.

What would the Toulon fleet do? Admiral Darlan's invitation to come and join him in Algeria met with a resounding and vigorous refusal from its commander, Admiral de Laborde. Between their direct leader and Marshal Pétain, the sailors chose to obey the head of state. But there was the risk that they would allow themselves to be wholly or partly tempted by the call to arms. From November 16, Hitler decided, as a precaution, to neutralise the fleet and if possible to take control of it. The strictest secrecy was observed in order to prevent the Vichy government and even the Italians from learning about it. To reduce the risk, the French troops were withdrawn from Toulon, which the German shock units were stealthily approaching to the apparent unconcern of the French Admiralty. After all, Hitler had promised not to try to seize any ships.

At dawn on November 26, 1942, the German attack was launched. The French sailors were caught completely off their guard – Admiral Marquis, the port-admiral, was captured in bed. Since no sailing orders had been given, very few of the ships' commanders decided to make their escape, although it was not fuel that was lacking but only the orders or the will to do so. Only five submarines escaped, one of which was scuttled when it got out to sea while another went on to be impounded in Spain.

The other ships conscientiously obeyed the orders to scuttle which Darlan himself had issued a long time before. Thus four battleships, two of which had survived Mers el-Kebir, 7 cruisers, 17 torpedo-boat destroyers, 1 aircraft-transport ship, 6 sloops and 16 submarines were deliberately sunk – a total of 220,000 tons. In addition the Kriegsmarine took over in the Mediterranean ports 159 merchant ships amounting to 650,000 tons.

All that remained of the French fleet which had emerged unbeaten and intact from the fighting of 1939–40 had thus gone to the bottom without any benefit to France at all. It is true that Admiral de Laborde considered that honour had been saved. He had no difficulty in proving that Hitler had broken his word; why had he not given more thought to earlier cases when the Führer had similarly broken his word? This gentlemanly language had an anachronistic ring when referring to the men, the aims and the methods of Nazi Germany.

CHAPTER 3

The Battle of Stalingrad

IN 1942 Stalingrad was a city of 600,000 inhabitants, extending for nearly forty miles along the right bank of the Volga; it was a great industrial and communications centre. At this point, there was no bridge across this great Russian river, which was from half to one and a quarter miles wide and could be crossed only by ferries and boats. Hitler had ordered the Wehrmacht to capture and destroy the city. The strategic purpose was to cut the great connecting link from north to south formed by the Volga. But the very name of Stalingrad and its role in the Bolshevik revolution seem to have obsessed the Führer to such an extent that he attached a symbolic and almost mystical significance to conquering it. Since the Russians, for their part, were equally determined to retain the city, its approaches and later the centre itself were to be the scene of hard fighting for nearly five months followed by the most sensational reversal of any situation in the whole of the Second World War.

I THE GERMAN OFFENSIVE

Whereas the Germans – Halder, for example – say that the targets of the German summer offensive of 1942 had become known to the Russians, the latter claim that they were expecting it to take place in the direction of Moscow; according to them, it was this error of judgment which was responsible for the Wehrmacht's initial victories; but the Soviet Chief of Staff set about rectifying it as quickly as possible. As early as July 1942, he transferred two of the reserve armies to the Stalingrad front, which had been entrusted to General Yeremenko, with Nikita Khrushchev as party delegate and member of the Military Council.

In mid-July, when it became obvious that the attacker's aim was to capture the city, a line of defences was set up in the suburbs of Stalingrad, using a work-force of about 20,000 people. At the same time some of the city's inhabitants were taught how to handle AA guns and thousands of workers enlisted in a people's militia to defend the factories.

As the only railway line on the left bank was under enemy fire and the Volga itself was not safe, since the Luftwaffe had it covered, Stalingrad's industry was adapted to manufacture arms for its defenders; thus the tractor factory went over to assembling tanks which were sent straight from the testing bench to the front. But Stalingrad had still not become an entrenched camp nor a really fortified city.

In the first few months the Germans showed themselves almost irresistible, even though the Fourth Armoured Army had been withdrawn from the sector to be used in an attack on Rostov in the south. The Sixth Army, under Paulus, with two armoured and two infantry corps, was given the task of capturing Stalingrad and then of striking out towards Astrakhan in order to paralyse all traffic on the Volga. At the beginning of August it had reached the outer perimeter of the city's defences; some of their advances were most spectacular; thus the 14th Division advanced thirty miles in three days, from the Don loop to north of Stalingrad, reaching the Volga on August 23.

Instead of attacking the front at each end, so as to take the city from behind, the German command chose a frontal attack; it was letting itself in for a street battle. On August 25 the Soviet military on the Stalingrad front declared a state of siege, which did not prevent the Russian troops from having to be brought back inside the defensive perimeter on September 2. Paulus had eleven divisions, three of them armoured, against which Yeremenko could put up only five infantry divisions and two tank brigades. The Soviet command sent five divisions as reinforcements. In order to relieve the city it launched an attack in the north against the enemy units which had reached the Volga; this did not achieve any great success but gave the city a little breathing-space.

The Soviet reinforcements were being ferried across to the right bank of the Volga by the army flotilla; in this way 65,000 men and 24,000 tons of ammunition were convoyed across protected by armour-plated motor boats and floating batteries of artillery and AA guns; 35,000 wounded soldiers and 200,000 civilians who were of no use for the purpose of defence were taken back in the reverse direction.

However, on September 12 the front ran along a line varying from one to six miles from the built-up area. On the 13th the assault on the city began. Until the 26th the fighting took place chiefly in the centre and southern quarters; most of the industrial quarters in the north were not yet directly threatened. But the factories came under fire from the Germans and had to stop work and be evacuated. Since the Volga could no longer be used as a north–south communication line, the objectives fixed by Hitler in his directive of April 5, 1942 had been won. Thus any continuing attempts to capture the whole city were now only a matter of prestige.

However, on the Führer's orders the OKW decided 'to finish off the Battle of Stalingrad after mopping up the last parts of the city occupied by the enemy'. Hitler seems to have been irritated by the effect on world opinion of Stalin's communiqués extolling the heroic defence of the city which bore his name. Motives of vanity and propaganda thus took precedence over strictly military aims. The Germans also probably thought that the city's defenders, who had been driven back to the Volga, were in desperate straits. They had not calculated what quantities of men and equipment they might lose for every square yard they won in fierce fighting in a ruined city.

On September 27 fighting took place in the heart of the giant factories 'Red October' and 'Barricades'; every house became the scene of relentless fighting which took place with hand grenades and bayonets on every floor, in the rooms and in the lift-shafts; gaping holes in the walls enabled the defenders to pass from one block to another without being caught. In defying the enemy in this way, the Russians, fired by the feeling that they were fighting in their homes and for their belongings, showed unparalleled morale.

In fact, twelve German divisions wore themselves out in these exhausting battles, while thirty others were forced to cover their flanks, and yet in October the Russians still remained in control of most of Stalingrad. The Germans had not succeeded in preventing reinforcements from crossing the Volga. Their supply lines had become greatly extended while those of the Russians had shortened to their advantage. However, at the beginning of November, misinformed by their Air Force, whose inadequacies had become alarmingly obvious, Hitler and the OKW considered the Russians incapable of a counter-offensive. In his directive of October 14 Hitler decreed: 'The Russians will not be able to bring as many forces into the winter campaign as they did last year; whatever happens, the winter will not be a harder one.' A rash forecast!

II PREPARATIONS FOR A SOVIET COUNTER-OFFENSIVE

The Russians, wrote Marshal Yeremenko, had turned their setbacks to their own advantage by accumulating a wealth of experience; they had learnt to dispose their defences in depth, perfected the tactics of attacking the flanks of advanced enemy points and speeded up the transfer of reserves from quiet areas of the front to those sectors which were threatened; tanks had been better co-ordinated with the artillery and infantry and command of the large units simplified and streamlined by cutting out the intermediate echelons; the constant enemy attacks were blocked by concentrations of

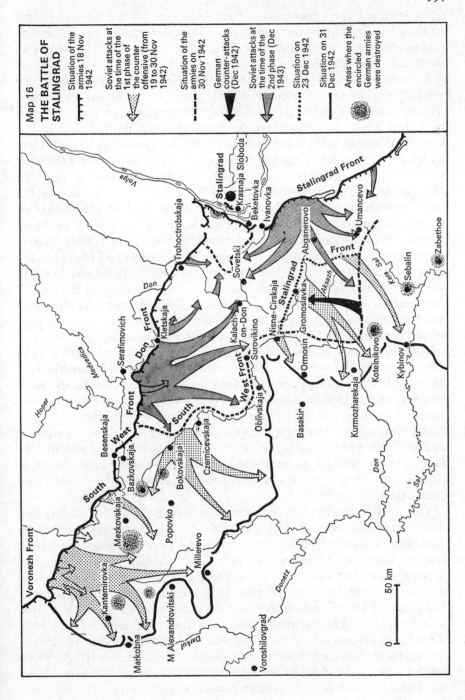

Map 16
THE BATTLE OF STALINGRAD

Situation of the armies 18 Nov 1942

Soviet attacks at the time of the 1st phase of the counter offensive (from 19 to 30 Nov 1942)

Situation of the armies on 30 Nov 1942

German counter-attacks (Dec 1942)

Soviet attacks at the time of the 2nd phase (Dec 1943)

Situation on 23 Dec 1942

Situation on 31 Dec 1942

Areas where the encircled German armies were destroyed

guns, so-called 'fists', concentrating as many as 200 guns every 1,000 yards or so. Above all the Soviet general staff were determined not to confine themselves to a static defence; any enemy advance must be checked by an immediate counter-offensive.

Since September 1942 a plan for a vast Soviet counter-stroke had been worked out in conferences at which Stalin met Zhukov, Voronov, Yeremenko and Vassilievskg. In October the weak points of the German positions, which had now become stabilised, had been detected. The German positions were based much more on the Don than on the Volga, which they had reached only at a few points. But even on the Don their situation was not favourable. Indeed, the Russians had retained or acquired bridgeheads on the right bank of the river, notably in the Serafimovitch sector; they had remained in control of the outlets of passages through a string of lakes. From some of the heights to which they had been clinging they could threaten the Sixth Army's flank. Above all, the corridor created by the advance of the German tanks between the Don and the Volga formed a narrow isthmus where any defence in depth was impossible. In short, the Soviet forces were enveloping the Fourth Armoured Army and what is more, the Sixth Army; and the latter was protected on its flanks only by satellite armies which were not very sound. Operation 'Stalingrad' rested on shaky foundations.

The plan for the Soviet counter-offensive provided first of all for the destruction of the German forces which had ventured directly into Stalingrad. The attacks were to be launched from the north by the army group from the Don in the direction of Kalach; from the south in the direction of Abganerovo by the group of armies from the Stalingrad front; this double enveloping movement would close like a vice on Paulus' Sixth Army. The battle to achieve this encirclement was to take four days; it was to be supported by minor diversionary attacks at Kalinin and Vyazma. The objective was therefore strictly limited and clearly defined.

The Soviet Armies found themselves facing the Italian Army, two Romanian Armies and the German Sixth and Fourth Armies, that is, fifty divisions, of which five were armoured and four motorised; but their reserves were dispersed as well as reduced in number. On the front as a whole the Russians did not have any real superiority, either in manpower or in armaments; the quality of their Air Force was even distinctly inferior. But in the Stalingrad sector they had mustered 25 per cent of their large infantry units and 60 per cent of their armoured and mechanised forces. They thus obtained a local superiority of two to one in men and eight to one in tanks. On their lines of penetration their superiority was much more marked and indeed overwhelming; thus the Fifth Armoured Army was attacking with odds of seven to two in manpower.

From June to December 1942, according to Marshal Rokossovski, the forces engaged by each camp changed as follows:

	June 1942			September 1942			December 1942		
	Men	Tanks	Air-craft	Men	Tanks	Air-craft	Men	Tanks	Air-craft
Soviet	187,000	360	337	590,000	600	389	854,000	797	1,035
German	250,000	740	1,200	590,000	1,000	1,000	846,000	770	1,066

The task of dispatching Soviet reinforcements became more difficult when the autumn rains caused the waters of the Volga to rise six and a half feet above normal and then a little later on when the river began to freeze. Russian engineers had to construct ten crossing-points.

On three occasions German raids damaged the cables on the left bank which were supporting the three footbridges by which pedestrians crossed the river. The steppe-like character of the terrain and the fact that built-up areas were few and far between meant that it was difficult to conceal the Russian troop concentrations; accordingly the units moved about only at night; in clear weather all movement was held up for twenty-four hours; during the day the men hid in the villages or, where there were none, at the bottom of gullies. This huge effort seems to have been badly assessed by the German general staff, although the Romanian general, Dimitrescu, several times expressed anxiety. But Paulus did not worry much about it and when the Soviet Army took up the offensive with considerably larger resources, it came as a disagreeable shock to the Wehrmacht.

III THE ENCIRCLEMENT OF THE GERMAN SIXTH ARMY

The Soviet attack began on November 19 on the Don front under the command of Rokossovski and continued on the 20th on the Stalingrad front under Yeremenko.

The movement along the Russian lines extended for more than 185 miles but the breakthrough was achieved over less than 125 miles. In order to destroy the enemy forces in depth the Russians had arranged their attacking troops in four successive echelons. After some eighty minutes of intensive artillery preparation, short but sharp, they launched their shock and mine-clearing units and the units of heavy tanks and self propelled guns, supported by the Air Force. These paved the way for the mobile groups of medium and light tanks and of motorised infantry, whose task was to exploit the initial success as quickly as possible by attacking the enemy's communication lines in order completely to disorganise its defence positions. Simultaneously, groups of all arms with mortars and flame-throwers were destroying any centres of resistance likely to provide a basis of local enemy counter-attacks. Finally, the light infantry, engineers and anti-tank groups widened the gap on the flanks and organised defence positions at suitable points to hold up any enemy counter-attack. The Russians moved over from the defensive to the offensive in all sectors with the result that they gained the enormous advantage of surprise. Their success was overwhelming.

In the north, by the evening of 19th, the armoured forces of the Don front had advanced twenty-two miles; after destroying the Romanian 1st Armoured Division, they reached the region of Kalach on November 22 and moved across to the left bank of the Don, while on the right bank they seized the most important enemy operational base at Kalach. On November 23 a Romanian group which had been encircled in the Raspopinskaya region was taken prisoner with all its 27,000 men.

For their part, the troops on the Stalingrad front in the south broke the enemy resistance in four days and on November 23 joined forces with the troops of the Don front at Sovietski.

Thus within the time laid down the Soviet offensive of November ended by encircling the German Sixth Army and part of the Fourth Army eighty-seven miles west of Stalingrad, that is, twenty-two divisions in all, numbering more than 300,000 men. In addition, the Romanian Third Army was smashed and the Fourth was in a bad way. From November 24 onwards the attack on the encircled forces began.

On November 19 Hitler was at Berchtesgaden; he was informed of the attack by the okw's new Chief of Staff, Zeitzler, the successor to Halder, who was himself at the Rastenburg headquarters in Pomerania. Although his information was inadequate and he was unable to assess the seriousness of the situation, the Führer's reaction was immediate and characteristic. He did not hesitate for one second to interfere in the details of operations. He notified Paulus that he should at all costs hold the western and southern ends of his positions. At the same time Hitler placed von Manstein, who was several hundred miles away in Vitebsk, in command of the armies on the Don. Von Manstein was held up by bad weather and was to be several days taking over his new command. As yet, Keitel, Jodl and Goering were entirely of the Führer's opinion: the Stalingrad position was much too important not to be held at all costs.

As for the Soviet general staff, they were hungry for more. In order to exploit to the full the success which had been achieved, a very large-scale operation had been devised. Golikov's armies on the southern Voronezh front and all Vatutin's on the south-west front would launch a large-scale

offensive in the direction of Rostov in order to destroy the entire south
wing of the German defences.

But in December the tired Soviet troops momentarily came to a halt. It
was then that von Manstein took up the initiative again to free the
German troops which had been encircled.

IV VON MANSTEIN'S COUNTER-OFFENSIVE

Von Manstein had the remainder of the Fourth Armoured Army and the
two Romanian Armies, four fresh Romanian divisions and one motorised
division; he divided them into two mass formations, each linked at the
rear by a railway, on both sides of the Don, at Ormosin and Kotelnikovo.
But he was not ready in time to take advantage of the tiredness of the
Russian troops. On December 3, according to Samsonov, he had a four
to one superiority in tanks; he decided, however, to wait for the LVII
Armoured Corps which was in the Caucasus. By the time he made up his
mind to attack, on December 12, the Russians had had time to be reinforced; the balance of forces had been restored.

At its most northerly point von Manstein's Don army was thirty miles
away from von Paulus' Sixth Army, which came under his command.
But realising that the Russians were firmly ensconced at this spot, von
Manstein decided to attack further to the south, at Kotelnikovo, seventy-
five miles from Stalingrad. He was going to use a more distant springboard, to give him greater impetus.

The German Don army's attack advanced until December 19 first as
far as the River Aksazh and then to the tributary of the Volga, the Mychtov, which it crossed, but was then held up.

At this moment a serious danger was beginning to threaten its rear. The
Soviet general staff had launched its huge operation. Once again it put
pressure on the satellite troops. On December 16, cut to pieces on the
south-west front, the Italian Eighth Army retreated and in eight days the
Russians advanced between 60 and 125 miles. Aware of the danger, the
German high command had to remove troops from other sectors and send
to France for the shock units which had now finished occupying the
southern zone. But the first result of this new Soviet offensive was to make
any further advance by von Manstein impossible. There was even a risk
of danger to the positions of the German units which had advanced into
the Caucasus.

Accordingly on December 23 General Hoth, who was in command of
von Manstein's tanks, realised that it was impossible for him to advance.
Worse still, on December 24 Yeremenko launched the Soviet Fifth Army,
under Popov, in an attack on Stalingrad. Hoth had to withdraw to his

starting-point, Kotelnikovo, which he lost on December 31. Von Manstein's counter-offensive had not succeeded.

V THE CAUSES OF THE GERMAN DEFEAT

What was the encircled Paulus doing in the meantime? After the war the Stalingrad disaster gave rise to long and lively controversy, both among the Germans who had taken part and among German and Soviet historians. Several German generals, including Zeitzler, vainly tried to take credit for having had the shrewdness to warn Hitler of the danger of clinging to Stalingrad at any price. Their clear-sightedness and courage in contradicting their Führer seems to have been greater after the event than at the time. Soviet historians vehemently criticise the German argument that by ordering a 'gradual withdrawal' in good time Hitler would have saved the Wehrmacht from the Stalingrad disaster; they showed that the Soviet offensive was strong enough and on a large enough scale, in the new circumstances which this withdrawal would have created, to advance just as quickly and successfully in other sectors, in Voronezh, for example; besides, if the German forces which had ventured towards the Volga had retreated, those which had advanced a long way into the Caucasus would have been exposed and forced into a hasty and more hazardous withdrawal. As for von Manstein and Paulus, they each, in their Memoirs, threw the responsibility for the defeat on to the other. Is it possible from these contradictory statements to determine what actually happened?

At the source of it all was Hitler's pigheadedness in regarding any withdrawal as a defeatist operation; it is certain that the Führer, who was in communication with Paulus over the head of the latter's superior officer, von Manstein, had ordered the commander of the Sixth Army not to abandon any of the positions he was occupying, in what he called the 'Stalingrad fortress'. But it seems equally certain that even in the autumn of 1942, the Wehrmacht's general staff, probably misled by the great successes of the summer, did not think that the Red Army was in a position to launch any major winter operations; after all, why should the Sixth Army not set up in the part of Stalingrad which it had conquered a strong-point capable of offering lengthy resistance to Soviet attacks?

The problem, then, was whether the encircled Sixth Army could be sufficiently well supplied to withstand the severe winter and to hold its own against the enemy. As there was no question of bringing supplies up by land, the task could be given only to the Luftwaffe. This was where Goering's personal responsibility came in. In his usual boasting way, the Field Marshal undertook to arrange for the daily lift of the 300 tons of various items which careful calculations showed to be the minimum needed by the Sixth Army in order to keep going. Did Goering, as Rohden writes, express this opinion against the judgment of the experts and air fleet commanders who argued that they now had a reduced number of aircraft, that the machines were the worse for wear and that the Russian winter presented unforeseen hazards? At all events, it is clear that Hitler, who wanted nothing better than to believe Goering, trusted him blindly, in spite of the unfortunate precedent of the failure of the Battle of Britain and the well-known boastfulness of the Luftwaffe's Commander-in-Chief; it is also probable that Goering, like a good courtier, had eagerly anticipated his Führer's wishes.

In these circumstances what else could Paulus do but obey? The head of the German Sixth Army did not lack character. In his sector he had of his own accord cancelled the orders for the execution of the Red Army's political commissars and the systematic extermination of the Jews. He was also an experienced tactician, conscientious to a fault. But this fine German general was imbued by tradition and by nature with the doctrine of respect for discipline; in addition, he did not have the overall view of the situation which could have enabled him deliberately to take initiatives which in any case went against his nature.

Accordingly on December 19, when Hoth's tanks came to within thirty miles of his own, Paulus did not move, since he had been refused permission to attempt a break-out which would have meant abandoning advanced positions which both the Führer and the OKW – the head of the German nation and his superior officers – ordered him to hold at all costs. To explain his failure to act, Paulus put forward psychological and technical arguments. Although the army corps generals had all been in favour of a sortie, he said, the officers and soldiers of the Sixth Army preferred to try to hold on to their positions. Furthermore, there was not enough petrol for the tanks to cover more than three-fifths of the distance separating them from those of Hoth. In short, Paulus could not have attacked even if he had wanted to, since the soldiers' reluctance and the lack of fuel made any advance very risky. Von Manstein refuted these arguments; an advance of a mere twenty miles or so, he wrote, which Paulus admitted to be feasible, would have enabled Hoth, by dint of a tremendous effort, to join up with him; however narrow, the corridor thus formed would have made it possible either for the Sixth Army to escape or for it to receive the supplies enabling it to keep going afterwards.

Manstein had told Paulus all this by telephone on December 23. The head of the Sixth Army therefore knew perfectly well how he stood and it was a struggle with his conscience which prompted him to act as he did. However much he sympathised with his soldiers' sufferings and despite his anxiety about their future fate, Paulus did not think it possible to disobey orders which he was told were necessary in order to prevent the south wing of the Wehrmacht's front from collapsing and to allow a new front to be established later on. He wrote: 'Is a responsible leader, when faced with the prospect of his own death or of the destruction or capture of his army, thereby released from his duty to obey orders?' And in his heart of hearts his answer to this question was 'no'. In these circumstances, von Manstein hardly had a right to criticise Paulus for not disobeying. He himself, who was his superior officer, had never given him any orders to this effect, since this would have involved an act of disobedience on his part. Paulus' drama was, in fact, at this moment that of the whole Wehrmacht which thought it its duty to obey the Führer of the German people *perinde ac cadaver*, despite the objections which everyone was beginning to raise in his own mind but which few had the courage to express.

VI THE DEATH THROES OF PAULUS' ARMY

Paulus had set the daily amount of supplies he needed first of all at 500 and then at 300 tons; this he never received. At the beginning, the aircraft were flying night and day and since the take-off areas were not very far from Stalingrad – about 125 miles – the load amounted to 137 tons per day for as long as Hoth's attempt to join up with the Sixth Army lasted. But when, following upon Hoth's withdrawal, the air bridge became longer, flying conditions grew more difficult because the pilots were hampered by fogs and storms and were subjected, in addition, to Russian AA fire which was becoming continually more powerful the closer it came. The Russians also raided the take-off bases and landing-strips; they sent up rockets similar to those used by Paulus to mark his landing-grounds, so as to throw the relief aircraft off course and shoot them down. The Sixth Army, for its part, lacked competent staff and its reception areas were becoming more and more restricted and dangerous as the Russian vice closed round them.

At the beginning of January, cold, fighting and disease had deprived Paulus of 80,000 men. The troops' rations had been reduced to just over five ounces of bread and one ounce of fat per man per day. The wounded could no longer be evacuated and on January 28 Paulus gave orders not to feed them any more so as to help keep up the strength of those who were fighting. In the second fortnight of January the amount brought in by air continued to decrease; it dropped to 70, 60 and even as low as 40 tons per day. It became more and more necessary to resort to parachute drops, for the planes could no longer afford to take such extreme risks; many containers were lost, either because they broke as they hit the ground or because they fell outside the reception area.

As its struggle to survive grew harder and harder, demoralisation set in in the Sixth Army and dissension in the German camp. Letters written by officers and soldiers shortly after Christmas and held back by order of the OKW showed that 57 per cent of the men no longer believed in victory; 33 per cent displayed indifference to the régime; 34 per cent were hostile. A general's son whose father had refused out of a sense of duty, to evacuate him from Stalingrad, violently reproached him and threatened to desert; a pianist was in despair because his hands were frostbitten; one officer wrote that this hell had caused him to lose his faith; fathers and husbands made known their last will and testament; perhaps through fear of the censorship, only one soldier dared to express his revolt; the rest sank into despair, which resignation did little to mitigate. The Sixth Army's general staff and Paulus himself had the feeling that their colleagues, and especially the Luftwaffe, had abandoned them; the Luftwaffe turned on the Wehrmacht and Hitler came down like a ton of bricks on both of them.

During this time the Russians did not remain inactive. Voronov was in charge of operations. On January 8, he sent an ultimatum which was rejected by Paulus on Hitler's orders. On January 10, more than 7,000 pieces of artillery, well over 400 to the square mile, started a massive softening-up process which was then completed by the bombers. In the evening, the first German line was broken through and the Russians advanced three to four miles. But it took two Soviet Armies three days to dislodge the second line of defence.

On January 17 Paulus' units poured into Stalingrad, some of them in disorder. On January 24, in order to spur the defenders on to greater efforts, Hitler showered them with titles and decorations; Paulus was promoted to field marshal. Goebbels' propaganda machine sang the praises of the men's heroism: 'The Red hordes smashed against their granite resistance.' This did not prevent von Seydlitz, Paulus' second-in-command, from suggesting that they accept the new Russian ultimatum. Disciplined to the last, Paulus rejected it, but he informed von Manstein that 'there is no longer any sense in prolonging the struggle; the catastrophe is inevitable; in order to save the men who are still alive I request immediate permission to surrender.' This permission was refused him; Hitler was categorical: against the Reds it was a case of conquer or die.

On January 25 street fighting began. Paulus gave permission for shock detachments to be formed and gave them a free hand to try to break out from their encirclement; but most of them failed. The area of resistance, the 'cauldron of Stalingrad', was gradually shrinking; on January 31 the last section surrendered in the south. On February 1 a report by the German VIII Air Corps read: 'Five aircraft have just returned from their mission; three did not find our troops; the fourth thought it caught sight of something; the fifth saw some lights.' A few hours later another message signalled: 'The course of our lines can no longer be made out; the enemy is on our former landing-ground.' On this day the German Sixth Army ceased to exist.

On February 2, the last section in the north surrendered, including Paulus. Ninety-one thousand men, among them 2,500 officers and twenty-four generals, were captured with hundreds of guns and tanks; 20,000 wounded came out of the cellars; since January 10 the encircled units had lost 100,000 men.

Germany declared three days of national mourning. But Hitler, in his funeral speech, had one last dig at Paulus: 'He could not succeed in crossing the threshold of immortality.'

VII THE SOVIET WINTER OFFENSIVE 1942-3

The victory of Stalingrad was the most outstanding episode of the Soviet offensive in the beginning of 1943 but in fact the whole of the front had been shaken, either simultaneously or sector by sector. The Wehrmacht had given ground everywhere.

Faced with being cut off, the German Armies whose task it was to seize the Caucasus had to make a hasty withdrawal of 375 miles in forty days. The Russians could not check their retreat until they had captured Stalingrad and restored rail communication out from the city. The German troops thus succeeded in withdrawing as far as Rostov; those which could not manage this were evacuated by sea. In this sector the Wehrmacht's order to withdraw had been given in good time, so as to avoid a second encirclement which would have turned the Stalingrad defeat into an irretrievable disaster. This success had been achieved in the nick of time, for Rokossovski's Don group of armies had advanced 125 miles southwards and on February 14 recaptured Rostov.

Further to the north, Vatutin, at the head of the south-west group of armies, had crossed the frozen Don and advanced as far as the Donetz.

On the Voronezh front, Golikov's group of armies had cut the poorly equipped and already demoralised Hungarian troops to pieces. In a matter of days one division had been destroyed and two more had to be withdrawn from the front. The first Soviet objective – to open up a gap in the German defences – was achieved in the course of two weeks in January 1943. The Hungarian Second Army had lost 140,000 men and eighty per cent of its equipment; the survivors were sent back to Hungary. In February, the Soviet line of advance had reached Kursk in the west, Kharkov further to the south and then ran along the Dnepr near Dnepropetrovsk. At the end of February a German counter-attack pushed the front line back to the Donetz but did not succeed in crossing it.

On the Moscow front the USSR capital was finally freed; the pocket held by the enemy at Rzhev and Vyazma was mopped up. Although the northern sectors remained quieter, on the Leningrad front Schlussenburg was reconquered.

Thus the Red Army had dealt a crushing blow to Hitler's hopes, to the OKW's calculations and to Goebbels' propaganda. Despite its losses, not only had it not been forced to remain on the defensive during the winter or compelled to restrict itself to small attacks but it had launched an almost all-out offensive more powerful than the previous year. One very good German army had been captured and four satellite armies destroyed; a considerable part of the Wehrmacht's artillery, engineering and reserve units had been obliterated. In spite of the particularly severe cold, the total advance was 125 miles on average and had sometimes attained 375 miles. An immense territory of 7,500 square miles – almost the area of France – including the northern Caucasus, Stalingrad, Rostov, Voronezh and most of the districts of Krasnodar, Voroshilovgrad, Smolensk and Orel, had been liberated.

VIII THE IMPORTANCE OF THE VICTORY OF STALINGRAD

The name of Stalingrad resounded all over the world, and Soviet historians rightly see the Red Army's brilliant success as the most crucial victory of the Second World War and one which marked its turning-point.

True, this was not yet final victory. Von Manstein was not entirely wrong in stressing that the Wehrmacht's southern wing had not been destroyed; to which Yeremenko replied that the Russians' hopes did not extend that far. The German Army had shown that its remaining forces were still formidable when, taking advantage of a somewhat hasty Soviet advance which had not been consolidated because of insufficient reserves, it had gone over to the offensive again at Kharkov. With the Nazis, you couldn't count your chickens before they were hatched. Nobody could foretell how the struggle between the armies would develop when the summer returned and which of the two would be in a position to take up the initiative.

It had nonetheless been proved that the Wehrmacht was not invincible and Hitler was the cause of its first great defeat. He had taken all the decisions privately with Zeitzler, the OKW's Chief of Staff, and he did not seem to grasp the full seriousness of the setbacks. At a conference of the OKW on January 23, 1943, while everyone was expecting Paulus to surrender at any minute, Hitler spoke of everything except Stalingrad; he seemed to be concerned only with future party meetings at Nuremberg and with the need to build a new hall. This lack of response to reality was not compensated for – quite the reverse – by the Führer's direct interference in the details of operations when he had neither the technical experience nor the necessary information to reach a decision. In short, although Hitler and his generals were not yet at loggerheads, the military leaders' confidence in him was beginning to suffer a few hard knocks.

Germany's allies were particularly affected. At the very moment when she was losing the last of her colonial empire, Italy had left her best equipment and her crack units in the USSR. Hungary had no army left and could not hope for any compensation for her defeats. General Antonescu wrote to Hitler that the Romanian Army, 230,000 strong in November 1942, had been reduced to 75,000 in January 1943. Both Count Ciano and the Romanian Foreign Minister, Mihaïl Antonescu, had begun to toy with the idea of breaking loose from the German yoke. Turkey, who had been both attracted and alarmed by Germany's great successes in the summer and was on the verge of rushing to help her to victory, crept back into her shell of neutrality.

It was not, of course, only at Stalingrad that a balance of forces had been reached which gave promise of a new era. But in the battle of the Atlantic convoys, this balance could well be upset by some technical invention of one of the belligerents and although it was full of promise for the future, the effects had not yet made themselves felt. At El Alamein the British victory showed yet again that the Italians were incurably weak and perhaps also that Germany had not sent sufficient forces to Africa. But at Stalingrad it was the full power of the Wehrmacht which had been beaten; the fact that tactical errors had been made did nothing to detract from the Red Army's extraordinary recovery. It had realised how to use the vast spaces of the USSR to the best advantage, how to retreat in order to come back more strongly and how to seize or create favourable opportunities. Its victory was due not only to 'General Winter' nor to the Russian soldier's dogged qualities and capacity for suffering. It had been able, at the right time and place, to provide manpower and equipment superior to those of its opponent; a new team of strategists had worked out the plans most appropriate to the circumstances and had carried them out in the field. The Soviet victory was the Red Army's victory, but it was also the victory of the Soviet economy and of the Bolshevik régime.

For the Communist party had completely identified itself with the Russian nation in order to give it leadership and train it for battle. Contrary to the hopes of the invaders, even after the first setbacks rebellion had not broken out either amongst the non-Russian population or among the peasants. Victory was going to knit the Russian people even more closely to its leaders who no longer appeared as having achieved power through a revolution stemming from national defeat but as the rightful heirs of the men, régimes and social classes which had built up the greatness of Russia.

Finally, this victory was Stalin's victory. Neither the failure of the policy of compromise with the Reich nor the setbacks of the first few months of the war had shaken his authority or weakened his determination. He had taken all responsibility, both political and military, upon himself, and had proved himself capable of shouldering it. His calm self-assurance, his nerves of steel, his realistic way of looking at things and his deep-seated cynicism, which was not bothered by principles or scruples, had enabled him to combine determination and efficiency.

The USSR gained enormous prestige throughout the world from a victory which she had achieved entirely on her own. The memory of the dubious era of the German-Soviet pact was fading away like a passing accident. She alone among the great Allied powers identified her cause with that of the oppressed peoples. She offered everyone the example of steadfastness in adversity, and by resisting the occupier she was pointing the road to victory. In every country she became a source of strength and pride to the Communist party, which was the spearhead of the underground struggle. The workers' strikes in northern Italy in March 1943 and the unification of the Resistance forces in France in the spring of the same year were not entirely unconnected with Stalingrad.

In short, the USSR seemed set to take advantage of any German defeat by filling the large vacuum that it would create in Europe. True, this defeat was not yet in sight; the Nazi Reich even strengthened its position by setting itself up as the champion of the struggle to oppose any revival of the threat of Bolshevism.

But the USSR, for her part, had earned the right to be more demanding with regard to her Anglo-Saxon allies. How was the 'strange alliance' which had been born out of the Nazi peril going to work?

BOOK THREE

THE DEFEAT OF ITALY

THE ALLIED WAR-MACHINE

BRITAIN, the United States and the USSR were associates in the same coalition by the fact of possessing common enemies rather than by mutual inclination. Britain and America had laid the foundations for close co-operation even before the war started and had built them up and defined them since, but Russia was exploring quite new ground in joining them – she had for twenty-two months been closely linked to their chief enemy, the Nazi Reich, and had even provided it with part of its fighting resources. It was obvious that, when added together, the human, economic and military potential of the three allies far surpassed that of the Axis powers, as long as they were entirely applied to the war effort and the armed forces thus produced were committed not in extended order but according to comprehensive plans based on mutual co-operation and jointly applied.

There were very powerful obstacles to the realisation of this indispensable co-operation. The USSR was not taking part in the war in the Pacific, but she was bearing the whole brunt of the Wehrmacht's attacks in Europe and her only concern was her struggle to survive. On the other hand, the United States had been attacked by Japan at a time when they were reserving their strength to strike, in the first place, against Germany. Britain, who had stood alone in bearing Nazi Germany's assault, was hoping to have a little breathing-space. How were these three rather reluctant allies going to harmonise their aims, co-ordinate their resources and conduct at one and the same time their own war and the common struggle? In short, how was the Allied war-machine going to be set up and put into operation?

CHAPTER I

The Anglo-American War

I THE BRITISH CONDUCT OF THE WAR

BRITAIN had been holding the fort since September 1939; she had gained experience which would benefit, but also put pressure on, the United States. The British conduct of the war was the result of one of those compromises, of which British history offers so many examples, between respect for tradition and forward-looking empiricism, as well as between the normal working of democratic institutions and that concentration of powers which produces efficiency.

For the whole of the war, the government remained responsible to Parliament and public opinion. Churchill thus from time to time had to face motions of censure from MPs, challenging the Cabinet. In point of fact, since the latter was composed of representatives from the two main political parties, it was practically certain not to 'fall' unless a large majority of public opinion came out against it.

The 'War Cabinet', consisting of five members, in a ministry which numbered sixty, was, with the consent of all the ministers, alone responsible for the conduct of the war. At the beginning, it met every day and any urgent business was immediately put before it while all important papers and telegrams were communicated to its members.

But little by little, this daily meeting seemed less and less necessary. In the end, there came into being what Churchill called the Monday parade which was attended, in addition to the members of the War Cabinet, by those ministers whose presence was required by the agenda, and the military leaders; weekly situation reports were then presented. The rest of the time, and very soon for the whole of the time, all the ministers, including those who belonged to the War Cabinet, confined themselves, as Churchill wrote, 'to relieving the Prime Minister of the burden of internal affairs and of party problems'. So, while the principle of collective responsibility of the Ministry for every decision remained sacrosanct, the whole conduct of the war was left to the Prime Minister. Churchill developed the habit of dealing directly with heads of foreign governments or of the dominions, and especially with Roosevelt, through messages which he himself drew up and only rarely communicated to the War

Cabinet. He likewise formulated British strategy and took the appropriate decisions directly with the Chiefs of Staff of the three services.

The fact was that the Prime Minister was also Minister for National Defence; his deputies, the Secretaries of State at the Admiralty, the Air Ministry and the War Office, confined themselves to administrative tasks, and did not attend either the meetings of the War Cabinet or those of the Committee of Chiefs of Staff. Since the members of these scarcely changed at all in the course of the conflict, a remarkable continuity in the conduct of the war was thus ensured.

The Chiefs of Staff – Army, Navy and Air Force – would study the situation in all its aspects and suggest solutions to the Prime Minister. When the latter had reached a decision after taking advice from his own general staff – which was at the same time the military office of the Secretary to the War Cabinet – the decisions adopted would go back for the Chiefs of Staff to carry out; they would give their instructions to the commanders of the British forces in the various operational theatres, to whom, as a general rule, they would allow a certain freedom of action by refraining from interfering in matters falling within the latters' province but without allowing them any power of initiative.

Thus the three levels of responsibility were clearly defined and graded; the government directed the political, diplomatic and military action; the general staffs drew up the overall strategy; and the commanders of the armed forces conducted the operations in their respective theatres. In actual fact, although there was nothing in writing to this effect, Churchill, with general agreement, intervened and imposed his will at every stage. The country's dramatic situation suited him down to the ground. Throughout the whole war his role of driving force was of incomparable importance. Although sometimes rash and impulsive, he was never downhearted, for he was immune to fatigue and never at a loss to concoct the boldest schemes.

II THE AMERICAN CONDUCT OF THE WAR

The same three grades of authority were to be found in the United States. At the top was the President whose powers were even greater than the British Prime Minister's, since, according to the Constitution, he was at one and the same time head of state, head of the government and commander of the armed forces.

Indeed the conduct of the war did not require any structural alteration in the peacetime government of the country. The White House remained a family residence, without formality and with no visible official staff. The team of Cabinet officers continued to lack uniformity, any differences of opinion being settled by the President. The President was still without any direct control over the congress and in order to put through his budgets and laws in the House of Representatives or in the Senate he had to negotiate with the leaders of the parties, whose considerable power remained undiminished. Above all he had to handle public opinion very carefully, for the state of war did not prevent the Constitution from operating in the normal way and the President's mandate expired at the end of his four years in office.

The American Chiefs of Staff corresponded almost exactly to their British counterparts. Their committee was presided over by Admiral Leahy but dominated by the personality of General Marshall, Chief of Staff of the Army. Their relationship was rather strained, owing to the old rivalry between the Army and the Navy. Moreover, the US Army Air Force, while theoretically part of the Army, was reluctant to let its squadrons be incorporated into the combined forces, where it would have no control over them and where they ran the risk of receiving orders which would not always take into account its special characteristics and approach. It wanted to be assigned only missions in general terms, so that it could then carry them out in its own way. As a result there were frequent clashes, both with the Army and the Navy.

Finally, in the field there were the commanders of each operational area; but the extent of their responsibilities and their remoteness from Washington often gave them a real independence to which their superiors took no exception, whereas the British found it excessive and were perturbed by it.

The actual conduct of the war therefore fell upon President Roosevelt. He was a complex person, a mixture of authoritarianism and familiarity, a man of great experience yet naïve. Eden used to say of him that 'he reminded him of a man deftly juggling with sticks of dynamite without realising their danger'. Everyone, indeed, fell under the President's spell. Roosevelt was less keen than Churchill on military affairs, a fact which led him to give a freer hand to his Chiefs of Staff than the British Prime Minister. Nevertheless, he knew quite well what he wanted, even though he disclosed little of what was going on in his mind, and he was both shrewd and skilful in achieving his aims. But he was not without his personal whims, and his dislikes were even stronger and more lasting than his likes. So he tended to play his own game, which he had carried out by people picked by himself outside the administration; for his missions, he chose men on whom he could rely, letting them deal with the most important issues directly with the authorities to whom they had been sent as delegates. Thus his friend Harry Hopkins acted secretly and efficiently as the power behind the throne; his opponents called him 'the Rasputin of the White House'. Hopkins was in poor health, like Roosevelt, but activated by the same sort of energy and intelligence as the President. He had not been one of the 'Brains Trust' of the 'New Deal', but he had served as Secretary of Commerce and director of the Public Works Administration and Federal Emergency Relief Administration; nevertheless it was only as Roosevelt's friend that during the war he accomplished his most important missions to Churchill and Stalin. It was he who distributed American equipment to Europe and Roosevelt hoped to make him a sort of economic dictator with the task of exploiting all the resources of the coalition.

III ANGLO-AMERICAN CO-OPERATION

Churchill and Roosevelt got on very well together. They were drawn together by a common culture, an identical religious attitude and a lofty and completely aristocratic sense of their office and authority. Both of them showed themselves determined to work hand in glove and they made no important decisions without prior agreement. Moreover, by means of a special code, they were in continuous communication by direct cable between Washington and the American embassy in London. Churchill reveals in his Memoirs that by this method he sent 950 messages to Roosevelt and received 800 replies. It was Churchill and Roosevelt who together took the main decisions committing the Anglo-Saxon coalition; their meetings were therefore of the utmost consequence and they attended them accompanied by such a considerable staff that, in fact, their respective states travelled about with them.

To assist them, they set up a Combined of Chiefs of Staff, with permanent headquarters in Washington. The American Chiefs of Staff were members; their British counterparts, compelled to remain in London with their government, were represented by general officers, of whom the most outstanding was Sir John Dill. But they remained in daily, and often hourly, contact with their superiors in London, so as to be certain to represent their views. The Combined Chiefs met often – 200 times in all, according to Churchill; first of all, each national committee sat separately; then the two groups met to compare their points of view and reach their conclusions. They then submitted them to Roosevelt and Churchill, who either endorsed them or settled any points of difference.

Co-ordination of this sort between two great states was unprecedented; to be sure, it was made easier by the common language – although sometimes words took on a different meaning in English and American, giving rise to misunderstandings, which might start rather tartly before they ended in laughter.[1] In every area where British and Americans fought

1. Churchill tells how a long and animated discussion was started one day about the expression 'to table it'. In English, it meant that the plan in question would be considered immediately but in American it meant that they would shelve it. There ensued a sharp argument for some time which was dissolved in laughter when the mistake was realised.

together, combined staffs were appointed, sometimes not without trouble and after very careful apportioning of the rights, powers and responsibilities of each one; on the whole, they operated satisfactorily. The economic resources were likewise managed by mutual agreement, in an unusual way. Thus, in January 1942 the Combined Shipping Adjustment Board came into existence; its task was to allocate Allied shipping according to the civil and military supply requirements. It had charge of a 'pool' of Allied merchant navies flying about twenty flags and its decisions were enforced by two subcommittees, one residing in London and the other in Washington. In 1944, this organisation found itself controlling a merchant fleet of 65 million tons and a tanker fleet of 20 million tons – that is to say 90 per cent and 95 per cent respectively of the current world total at the time.

Obviously this complicated machine sometimes seized up and it did not function without some squeaks and groans. At first it moved slowly; the Allies were carrying on the war through external lines of communication over vast distances; the movement of troops took a long time, especially from the Atlantic to the Pacific operational theatres. Prolonged delays were involved before things could be made to run easily, for plans had to be carefully examined by both sides, frequently compared and were then subject to the agreement of the two leaders. They had to be very precise since the deployment of any forces required a very elaborate timetable which was too complicated to be easily altered once it had been decided on.

There was often a difference of view between the two partners because their war aims were not the same. The main subjects of disagreement were the fate of the colonial empires, relations with the USSR, the role and future of France, and the place and date of the landing in Europe – to mention but a few of the main problems which gave rise to animated discussions and misunderstandings and lasting friction.

However, opinions were also divided on purely military matters. Britain had to defend a Commonwealth that spread over the five continents; even by concentrating all her forces on one single point, she was unable to win a decisive victory over Germany. She would have run too great a risk of losing everything at once by 'putting all her eggs in one basket'. She therefore formulated an Allied strategy in keeping with her weakness and her interests, that is to say a peripheral strategy; its trump cards were the blockade and the Air Force but also repeated operations in remote minor areas, where German power would gradually be worn down until it could be dealt a decisive blow with less effort. But although the Americans had accepted the premise that the protection of Britain was essential for the defence of the United States, they had no desire to fight for her Commonwealth; they were furious that forces should remain unused, or, as they saw it, misused, to recapture Burma or to take possession of the Dodecanese Islands; according to them, this meant jeopardising the success of a concentrated attack, which the superiority of their united resources would make irresistible; backing the British at every point meant a dangerous and pointless dispersal of their forces, thus protracting the war.

In short, the British accused the Americans of thinking only of military victory and not concerning themselves enough with the political consequences of the war. The Americans were afraid of becoming involved in the Byzantine quarrels of old Europe and of playing into the hands of British imperialism.

These differences of conception were sufficiently serious to break up even the most solid alliance but they never prevented the British and Americans from always managing to reach agreement by means of mutual concessions and this owed a great deal to Roosevelt's understanding approach. In short, never before had two great nations been united by so close an understanding in a war of such magnitude. However, as the Americans progressively passed out of their novice stage and took an increasing and eventually predominant part in the combined operations, they were able to force their point of view more and more frequently on to the British who had no alternative but to accept it.

The Anglo-American alliance was so weighty, so carefully balanced and its united resources so considerable that the other nations fighting against Germany – with the exception of the USSR – could do nothing but submit to its decisions; General de Gaulle and the Polish government in London, among others, were to discover this to their cost.

At least in the Atlantic Charter they found no difficulty in agreeing amongst themselves upon the principles for which British and Americans were fighting.

IV THE ATLANTIC CHARTER

Off the shores of Newfoundland, to which they had each come on board a battleship, Churchill presented Roosevelt with the draft of a solemn joint declaration, in order, he said, 'to direct their policies on the same lines'. Roosevelt accepted the idea and introduced a few slight modifications into the text which, when signed by the two statesmen on August 12, 1941, became 'the Atlantic Charter'.

The United States and Britain first of all drew attention to the contrast between their own idealism and the ambitions of the Axis states; they asserted that they were not seeking any territorial or other aggrandisement and that they were opposed to 'any territorial change which did not conform to the wishes, freely expressed, of the peoples concerned';

expressed in broad terms, the statement meant that any annexations by the Axis states would not be recognised; it did not, however, imply any commitment to re-establish the territorial integrity of any conquered countries – Churchill had not even made this promise to de Gaulle with regard to France. The Allies went on to recognise 'the right of all peoples to choose the form of government under which they wish to live' – this was a condemnation of dictatorships.

Article 4 went even further, for, taken literally, it would have implied the sharing of world resources. Indeed, in it was stated that they would 'favour the access of all states, great or small, conquerors or conquered, to world trade and the raw materials necessary for their economic prosperity' – a reply to Axis propaganda which represented the war as the struggle of proletarian against wealthy nations.

For this to be achieved, 'the fullest international collaboration in the economic field' was necessary, as was also a lasting peace giving to all men 'the certainty of being able to end their days free from fear and want'. The freedom of the seas was a condition of such a peace and the renunciation of the use of force guaranteed its preservation. Finally, reference was made to 'a broader and more permanent system of general security', without making any mention of the existence of the League of Nations.

The Atlantic Charter, conceived in very general terms, might at times sound hollow. Yet it sounded a note of human solidarity and brotherhood and of national equality which stood out like a ray of hope against the violence, racial discrimination and exploitation of the weak perpetrated by the totalitarian régimes.

The document was signed by all the Allied nations, with some reservations on the part of the USSR, and became the programme for the peaceful reconstruction of the world; but respecting it and putting it into operation would be a different matter and more difficult than proclaiming it.

V THE ADOPTION OF A COMBINED STRATEGY

Immediately after the attack on Pearl Harbour, anxious about the turn United States strategy might take as a result of the disaster that had befallen their fleet, Churchill had gone to Washington to have discussions with Roosevelt. From December 22, 1941, to January 14, 1942, the two men and their staffs examined all the problems with which they were faced and reached complete agreement on the solutions. This conference, called 'Arcadia', was therefore of paramount importance for the conduct of the war, for from it dates the close co-operation between the British and Americans.

It was then that the decision was taken to set up the Combined

Chiefs of Staff and to pool all the military and economic resources of the two countries. They were to take joint responsibility for the conduct of operations, the distribution of forces and equipment, the co-ordination of means of communication, the utilisation of intelligence and the administration of the conquered areas.

Churchill was afraid that Roosevelt might be more anti-Japanese than anti-German. He was completely reassured; the Nazi Reich remained the United States' enemy number one. Without going into too much detail about the significance of this proposal, it was decided as a result of this to leave in the Pacific only those forces necessary to defend points of vital importance: Hawaii, Alaska, Australia, New Zealand and India, likewise Singapore and the Philippines – but the Malayan peninsula had already been nibbled at and the Philippine archipelago was half lost. Japan's hour of reckoning would strike after Germany's.

Against the latter, the Americans, conscious of their weakness, had provisionally adopted the British plan of wearing her down progressively by air raids, the blockade, commando raids and minor attacks on the periphery of Europe; it was contemplated making an operation in Tunisia in 1942. Churchill succeeded in adding help to the subversive movements in the occupied territories – a subject about which the Americans had absolutely no notion. During this time, invasion bases would be gradually established round the Reich and in 1943 a return to the Continent would prove possible from several directions, either simultaneously or in succession.

In the course of 1942 the Americans changed their ideas. They put forward, and the British reluctantly accepted, the 'Bolero–Round-up' plan of landing in Europe in the course of 1943, with Britain as its launching pad. Churchill fought hard to make them give up views which he considered over-simple and which proved to be premature; all that remained of 'Bolero' was the ill-starred raid on Dieppe. Returning to their peripheral strategy of 'Arcadia', the two allies, at Churchill's instigation, began a landing in North Africa: this was Operation 'Torch'.[1]

This time, however, the Americans had followed their allies with grave misgivings. Marshall was no more keen to send Sherman tanks to Auchinleck than Hitler to send Tiger tanks to the Italians. Admiral King and Secretary of War Stimson did not hide the fact that abandoning 'Bolero', together with the serious losses sustained by the convoys across the Atlantic, would in their opinion be bound to lead to a revision of American strategy and give priority to the Pacific. On two occasions, supported by Marshall, they approached Roosevelt to request this. But the President then showed that he was able to take vital decisions alone – if need be. Against the judgment of almost all his advisers – Eisenhower

1. See pp. 381–393.

spoke of 'the blackest day in history' – he supported Churchill and insisted on Operation 'Torch'.

In the course of 1942, at Roosevelt's suggestion, the two allies had carried out a worldwide division of responsibilities. They were agreed that the Pacific would be an American operational area; Australia and New Zealand would therefore leave the British zone of influence to place themselves under the protection of an outsider; the two dominions raised no objection but asked to be represented on the Combined Chiefs of Staff, a request which was refused to avoid overburdening the organisation. The Middle East and the Indian Ocean remained British theatres. As for Europe and the Atlantic, they were equally divided, which in the ordinary course of events would lead to an American command, in view of the growing disparity between the Allied forces as the United States took the lead.

However, this logical division of duties and responsibilities brought to light deep differences of opinion. Outside the metropolis, the chief British interests were in their Commonwealth, which area had been assigned to them; inevitably, they would make the most strenuous efforts to interest their partner in them. The Americans, however, were particularly drawn to the Pacific, although they had given priority to the war against Germany. They had to find the means of reconciling these two contradictory demands; both would obviously be jeopardised if they followed the British and sent their forces in yet another direction – the Mediterranean or Burma. The result was endless and sometimes heated discussions.

For the moment, however, the success of Operation 'Torch', which ought to be exploited to the full, was pointing in the direction which the British wanted. In their meeting at Anfa near Casablanca in January 1943, (called the Casablanca conference), Churchill and Roosevelt drew the appropriate conclusions. First of all, they could not avoid taking a very close interest in the French problems in French North Africa; each summoned his 'favourite', and Giraud and de Gaulle had to overcome their mutual dislike and shake hands in public for the record. Delighted at having got Roosevelt where he wanted him, Churchill did not conceal from de Gaulle that he would not support him against his American ally – 'Between Roosevelt and you,' he told him, 'I pick the big one.'[1]

On the other hand, it was confirmed that Germany remained the Allies' chief enemy. But how could she be reached from the shores of Africa? It was decided that a great anti-submarine offensive would be launched to protect Alantic shipping and increase its flow, a necessary prerequisite for any offensive. In the meantime, the Reich's territory would be relentlessly pounded by 'carpet bombing'. This was an admission of semi-impotence for an indefinite period. Was it in order to conceal this fact that one day,

1. Translator's note: in Churchill's pidgin French: 'Je choisis le large.'

to the amazement of the journalists present, Roosevelt launched his great idea of 'unconditional surrender' of the Anglo-Americans' opponents, Germany, Japan and Italy?

VI UNCONDITIONAL SURRENDER

Thus, on January 24, 1943, in Churchill's presence, Roosevelt stated:

> 'The President and the Prime Minister, after considering as a whole the operations of the world war, are more convinced than ever that the world can return to peace only by the total elimination of German and Japanese war power, which enables us to reduce the aims of the war to a very simple formula: the unconditional surrender of Germany, Italy and Japan. Unconditional surrender implies the firm intention of ensuring that peace reigns in the world for generations. It does not imply the destruction of the German people, nor of the Italian or Japanese peoples; but it does imply the destruction in Germany, Italy and Japan of a philosophy based on the conquest and subjugation of other peoples.'

Churchill's embarrassment during Roosevelt's speech was abundant proof that he was in no way its co-author. With a rather forced smile, he confined himself to a brief word of approval and proposed an unenthusiastic toast to unconditional surrender.

This declaration had therefore been thought up by Roosevelt alone; it was certainly not the result of a sudden illumination during the course of a meal, as his son Elliott relates, but of slow and mature reflection, as Hopkins confirms. Perhaps it was even a last fruit of his collaboration with Wilson, to which he was so fond of referring. He had set his heart on it, for he repeated it on several occasions; in Christmas 1943, he made it even clearer when he stated that 'the United Nations had no intention of turning the German people into slaves', but it was not until May 1944 that he toned it down and then only in favour of the Axis satellites in eastern Europe, whom Stalin was very anxious to placate as the Red Army approached them.

As it stood, the call for unconditional surrender, together with the disaster of Pearl Harbour, formed one of the stalking-horses of Roosevelt's opponents after his death. They blamed it for the unsatisfactory conclusion of the armistice with Italy, for Nazi Germany's willingness to go on fighting right up to the last minute and for Japan's delay in capitulating. In short, they laid at its door all the sins of Israel.

It is likely that Roosevelt was wanting to please Stalin, who was only half-satisfied by Operation 'Torch', for in his eyes it did not really open up a second front. He also had in mind to give reassurances as to the American war aims to the resisting nations of Europe, who must inevitably be worried by Darlan's promotion and the policy of co-operation with all kinds of Quislings that this seemed to represent. Also, as Calvet was right in stressing, there was the important role played by Roosevelt's recollection of the conditions imposed upon the Southerners by General Grant and the religious and moral motivation, always dear to the American heart, which gave the current war the character of a crusade. We must also remember that it was essential to remind American public opinion that now that it was involved in the war it would have to see it through to the end.

But whatever Roosevelt's reasons, they are less important than the consequences of his decision. It is hardly true that it deprived the British of all diplomatic freedom of action. To believe this would be to forget that negotiating with Germany and Japan meant recognising the whole or a part of their conquests and probably of their political régimes. Nor did it doom the Resistance movements in the Axis countries to failure. The Italian Resistance at all events continued; and no one had ever discovered the existence of any Resistance in Japan. As for German opposition to Hitler, it had hitherto proved most disappointing; and Roosevelt's decision did not prevent the assassination attempt of July 20, 1944, from coming within a hair's breath of succeeding: besides, there was nothing in it likely to discourage possible German Resistance, indeed quite the reverse, since the United States President differentiated very clearly, much more clearly than the Pope, for example, between the régimes on which he was making war and the peoples to whom he was offering peace. To state, as Liddell Hart has, that the call for 'unconditional surrender' was 'the biggest blunder of the war' is, in my opinion, to make two mistakes: it forgets the existence of national Resistance movements swamped by the occupation, to whom Roosevelt was throwing a life-line; and it also misunderstands the essential nature of the Nazi régime and the Japanese faction then in power; whatever the Allied proposals, they were led by fanatics who were utterly determined to fight to the bitter end and to be destroyed, preferring to drag their country down with them if necessary rather than surrender.

VII ITALY, THE NEXT ALLIED OBJECTIVE

At Casablanca, the Anglo-American strategists were forced to realise that they would not have enough shipping for an attack across the Channel in

1943. They therefore reverted to the alternative of Mediterranean or Pacific.

Within the Chief of Staffs' Committee, Admiral King aggressively supported the second solution: while forced to accept that major operations against Germany should receive priority, he refused to release ships for minor operations in Europe. He considered that the war there should be concluded within a reasonable period of time in order to leave the United States sufficient forces to beat Japan. He was afraid that with the help of the jungle and the ferocity of her men, the latter might have time to build up an impregnable position. He suggested making use of available resources to open up the route to Burma so as to prevent the collapse of China.

Admiral King was supported by General Marshall, to whom he returned the favour by giving him his backing for an offensive across the Channel; and both of them were strongly against an extension of operations in the Mediterranean area.

They were, however, compelled to acknowledge two things. The first was that the Allies were involved in campaigns which it was essential to bring to a successful conclusion: the conquest of Tunisia, the offensive in Tripolitania of the British Eighth Army reinforced by American equipment, and additional aid to the USSR. It was impossible to send men as well as equipment to Britain without jeopardising the success of these campaigns. Secondly, there were the prospects opened up by the success in Africa: pressure on neutral states such as Turkey and Spain; retaining the strategic initiative; keeping the Suez Canal permanently open; the possibility of putting Italy out of action; forcing Germany to disperse her forces or transfer them from one front to another.

President Roosevelt was particularly alive to those prospects. He was also anxious to consolidate the friendship with Britain by showing regard for her vital interests – and the Middle East fell into this category. After guiding his advisers along the lines he desired, he excelled in giving them the impression that they were the ones who had made the decision and he was equally skilful in bringing them back to his chosen path when they showed signs of straying from it. He arranged for very careful examination to be given to all the possible consequences of the successful landings in North Africa as, for example, an invasion of Spain, which was supported by Admiral Leahy but opposed by General Marshall, or the idea of a landing in the Balkans across the Adriatic which Churchill was beginning to put forward. In short, he was, or pretended to be, convinced that major successes in the Mediterranean would make the final offensive across the Channel easier, even if they were not its necessary prerequisite. And when Marshall and King returned to the charge and suggested shifting the centre of gravity of American strategy to the Pacific, he gave a categorical refusal. One of his chief concerns was probably that if the Americans moved out of Europe, this might pave the way for German success in the USSR or drive Stalin to a reconciliation with Hitler.

In May 1943, a new interallied conference took place in Washington under the code-name of 'Trident'. The Americans were now very worried about the way the war was developing in the Pacific; they had no difficulty in eliciting the concession that the fighting there should be slightly stepped up. Since there could be no question about Hitler's continuing to remain enemy number one, the only alternative was to cut down operations in the Mediterranean. So Marshall agreed to their being continued but on that condition only. The British gave way, or pretended to. They accepted the date of the spring of 1944 for the landing in north-east Europe; by then, they would have had time to see how things were going. For the moment, even the smallest Mediterranean operations were important: the conquest or Tunisia and Tripolitania, the landing in Sicily and the free movement of shipping in the Mediterranean. If the Italian tree were given a thorough shake it might not be impossible to bring down Mussolini and perhaps even uproot him. After all, the defeat of even the weakest of the Axis powers was not an aim to be spurned. And Churchill had more than one trick up his sleeve when he wanted to bring up for a second time matters which, theoretically, had been already settled but to which he had not given his full approval.

In any case, there was ample proof that a grand Allied strategy was possible only with vast equipment; the construction of troop-ships and freighters, for example, was of paramount importance. A huge output would be necessary to cope with every eventuality – the great distances, enemy submarine attacks, blocking of ports, diversity of cargoes, the need to operate simultaneously in very remote areas – and to draw up in advance the complicated plans for putting the necessary men with their arms and supplies in the right place at the right time. It was to this end that the United States, following the policy laid down by Roosevelt, were in the process of becoming, as he put it, 'the arsenal of democracy'.

CHAPTER 2

The American Arsenal

In the course of the war, the United States provided the Allied coalition with more than half its armaments – thirty-five per cent of those employed against Germany and no less than eighty-six per cent of those used to force Japan to her knees. However, this enormous industrial effort did not prevent her from mobilising twelve per cent of her total population, as high a percentage as Britain and lower only than the USSR; in 1944, her armed forces numbered 12,000,000 and more than 5 million of them were fighting thousands of miles from their homeland in almost every operational theatre except eastern Europe. While providing the British Commonwealth, the USSR and Nationalist China with arms and loans, at the same time she more than doubled her industrial output and her national income, and the individual standard of living rose. In the well-known formula, in contrast to Germany which had produced guns instead of butter, the States produced guns and more butter as well. Yet no fundamental change in their economic ideas or structures was needed to produce these truly extraordinary results.

I CHOICES AND PROGRAMMES

However, the war caught the United States almost completely unprepared; she had no army – 190,000 men in 1939, 50,000 of them overseas, and 329 light tanks – no stocks of arms or ammunition and barely a war industry, which represented only 2 per cent of the total output and labour force.

It is true that she had unlimited potential. In 1939, in Néré's words, 'She represented nearly 42 per cent of total world production of capital goods, as against 14 or 15 per cent by Germany, 14 per cent by Great Britain and less than 5 per cent by France.' But although she had come out of the deep slough of the depression, the American economy was still experiencing its aftermath; it was not working full out and was using only part of its potential raw materials, plant and labour force – there were almost 7 million unemployed; orders for armaments could thus be met and, as in the early years in Nazi Germany, provide a stimulus for the economy. On the other hand, this vast, thinly populated continent, as yet not being fully exploited, contained reserves of raw materials, energy and space that Europe, outside Soviet Russia, had long since lost. To these resources might be added the as yet untapped and little known resources of the States' geographical complement, Latin America.

But this peace economy had to be 'converted' into a war economy while not impoverishing the country. To do this, it was important to draw up armament production schedules, allocate orders, in proper priority, provide the necessary credit, ensure and increase the supply of labour to the right industries; and all this without giving rise to inflation or reducing the standard of living, in consequence by stabilising prices and wages. Now the American economy was ruled by the sacrosanct law of 'free enterprise'; how could production be co-ordinated and channelled towards the manufacture of armaments without imitating the rigid state-control of the totalitarian régimes, which was anathema to the American public, and when, moreover, these régimes were considered the complete antithesis of the American way of life and opposed on these grounds? The economic crisis had, however, induced the President of the United States, with his New Deal, to take certain tentative steps to increase the part played by the state in the economic sphere. These pointed the way; as a result, President Roosevelt's role was to be crucial in transforming the American economy into what he himself called 'the arsenal of democracy'.

It was he who insisted – and everything followed from this – on helping Britain at the time of her direst need, when the military were afraid that any such help might prove useless. The British in fact agreed that part of the new divisions that they were raising should use American equipment, thus providing the first boost to American war industry.

Later, this development in American industry came up against opposition both from the conservatives who disliked the increasing public expenditure and from the 'progressive' elements who had come to the fore through the New Deal and who thought that unproductive military expenditure could not fail to damage the economy or else cause an artificial boom. Roosevelt had to manoeuvre between the two trends and always got his way in the end.

Once the decision had been taken to help the democracies and, later on, just Britain, by providing arms, at the outset a choice had to be made: should such help have priority or should the American forces be rearmed first of all? Roosevelt's decision was emphatic: they should both be done together. 'We shall,' he said, 'allow the opponents of force the use of the material resources of our nation; and *at the same time*, we shall provide ourselves in America with equipment capable of meeting any defence needs.'

As a logical consequence of this, on July 7, 1941, the Secretaries of the

War and the Navy were instructed to 'explore the overall needs of production necessary to defeat our possible enemies'. From the mass of reports which he received, Roosevelt extracted a programme which he called the 'Victory Program'; it fixed the size of the expenditure on armaments and the number of divisions that the American Army would need. These estimates were almost entirely guesswork, because they had not been drawn up with any specific strategy in mind; they took no account of the resources of a possible enemy, as yet unknown, which would need to be met with superior resources; and they added together hypothetical needs without really assessing America's ability to meet them all. But Roosevelt particularly wanted to fire people's imagination and stimulate their energy; his decisions on economic matters were at one with the determination which he was at the same time showing against Japan.

Accordingly, after the attack on Pearl Harbour, the 'Victory Program', with Churchill's agreement, was expanded at the 'Arcadia' conference. At the beginning of 1942, Roosevelt announced a compulsory programme in words that brooked no discussion: 'Let no one say that this cannot be done; it must be done and we are committed to doing it.' The schedule for 1942–3 was laid down as follows:

	First estimates	1942	1943
Combat aircraft	31,000	60,000	125,000
Tanks	29,500	45,000	75,000
AA guns	8,900	20,000	35,000
Machine guns (both years)	238,000	500,000	
Merchant ships (tonnage)		6,000,000	10,000,000

But it still remained to work out the means of achieving these astronomical figures and then putting them into operation.

II ECONOMIC MOBILISATION

As early as 1939, Bernard Baruch, Roosevelt's trusty adviser, had worked out a plan for a complete economic mobilisation and state-controlled war economy. The President did not adopt it for technical, moral and personal reasons. Technically, the military were not in a position to draw up an overall programme when they did not know what war they would have to wage and against whom. Psychologically, American public opinion was not ready to accept such a straitjacket as long as 'their boys' were not yet under fire – and Roosevelt knew full well that he must not try to rush things. Morally, since the United States did not possess a body of senior civil servants free from personal interests and trained to serve the state, the men capable of running such a cumbersome machine would perforce have to be borrowed from the large concerns which would themselves be involved and they would be exposed to the danger of being unable to forget their origins and former links. And finally, Roosevelt disliked the thought of relinquishing some of his own powers.

Jean Monnet and Arthur Purvis, the heads of the French and British purchasing commissions, had vainly pleaded for a minimum amount of co-ordination of American industrial production in order to facilitate their task. In 1941 and 1942, complete anarchy reigned; expenditure had no sooner been authorised by Congress than the orders poured out, simultaneously if not in self-contradiction, without the military authorities who placed them showing any concern as to their feasibility or having any means of meeting them. As a result there were long delays, shortages of raw materials and transport bottlenecks. It was impossible to cope at the same time with the demands of the American Army, the war against Japan and of lend-lease, even when they were as urgent as supplies for the USSR, and all this at a time when the Allies were suffering one disaster after another in the Pacific, Africa and eastern Europe. The allocation of the arms produced could be settled only month by month and for each item separately; the beneficiaries never knew in advance what they would receive, which made it impossible for them to draw up advance plans; a unit under training would suddenly lose its equipment to a division embarking for England or to a convoy leaving for Murmansk. In the midst of all this chaos, Roosevelt imperturbably continued to issue orders that every need must be met, convinced that the US economic machine, once launched, would prove inexhaustibly powerful through the determination and drive of the American people.

However, the early results did raise the question of whether the President's programme was not too ambitious; experts asked themselves if it was feasible and concluded that, on a number of points, it was not. For their part, the military were demanding that priorities should be worked out after a more thorough examination of their plans and they were taking steps to acquire the means necessary to satisfy them. In a word, the authorities in Washington were gradually taking over control of the war industry, a process which reached its peak in 1943.

The chief role of the organisations created for this purpose was the purchase of products and services – what the military called procurement – and channelling and directing productivity. In fact, however large the margin of control allowed, deliberately and as it were on principle, to the manufacturers, it was still necessary, in order to achieve the intended aims, to allocate the raw materials and labour force required and to keep an eye on the wage and price structures, the amount of profit and the question of taxation. After all, prices governed the movement of raw materials and by affecting profits, spurred on productivity. In order to make raw materials available where they were most needed, it was in fact necessary to ban their use in other sectors of the economy. Finally, coercive measures, ranging from compulsory orders to buying out businesses, could be expected against those firms which refused to toe the line or proved inefficient.

In short, at the end of the day the Federal authorities were poking their nose into everything and first of all providing themselves with the necessary bodies to do so. Thus, when a problem became urgent, they created, *ad hoc*, the appropriate agency to deal with it, without always worrying about the existing machinery. This led to permanent confusion and endless rivalry arising from conflicts over terms of reference; but another result was overall flexibility which left a great deal of scope to the initiative and imagination of those in charge. Moreover the various bodies gradually sorted themselves out and found their right level of importance.

Thus the Production Executive Committee, under Charles E. Wilson's chairmanship from September 1942 onwards, was given the job of supervising the orders placed by the military in order to assess their effect on the economy. The Controlled Materials Plan set up in November 1942 had the task of keeping an eye on essential raw materials – the ones most in demand were always the same, steel, aluminium and copper. The CMP would intervene to prevent industrialists from excessive stockpiling and thus 'freezing' a raw material for months on end. On the instigation of the trade union leader Walter Reuther, at the beginning of 1942 Roosevelt had already cut back production of cars for civilian use and restricted the production of refrigerators.

But the most important agency was the office of War Mobilization which came under Donald Wilson in the spring of 1943; it did not concern itself with the day-to-day running of the economy but it suggested to the President at the highest political level the long- or short-term decisions deemed necessary for the war economy and thus for the economy as a whole, since an adequate output of arms could no longer be reconciled with unrestricted 'civilian' production. A commission presided over by Senator Truman investigated cases of fraud and examined contracts.

Thus every branch of the American economy gradually fell under state control. For example, ports were placed under the authority of a high-ranking officer, generally a peacetime transport expert dressed up as a general.

But these were temporary structures, created solely by the state of war. From February 1944 onwards, the Baruch-Hancock report prepared for the reconversion to a peacetime economy. Shortly afterwards, the Office of War Mobilization added to its title the significant words 'and Reconversion', heralding a not too distant future for which everyone earnestly longed.

III ECONOMIC STABILITY

Being good disciples of Lord Keynes, the American economists had great confidence in the effectiveness of indirect controls in maintaining economic stability, that is by financial and monetary means and restricting purchasing power. Threatened inflation was thus held in check first of all by traditional means.

From 1939 to 1944 state expenditure rose from 13,000 to 71,000 million dollars. The switching of part of the civilian production to war production could not fail to lead to an excess of demand over supply, which was assessed at 17,000 million dollars in 1942. In 1944, it rose to 93,000 million. The first thing was to increase taxes relying, on the public spirit of the Americans. During the war federal revenue rose sevenfold almost entirely thanks to a steady increase in income tax. Another measure was to withdraw excess cash from circulation by directing it towards savings that at times were practically compulsory; the result was an increase in the public debt of 230,000 million dollars, although the rate of interest on the loans never exceeded three per cent. Such policies could be followed only if wage-earners retained a decent standard of living and if price stability and confidence in the dollar led subscribers to hope that after the war their savings held in war bonds would enable them to buy more goods than during the war.

Nevertheless inflationary pressures were not removed but only held temporarily in check – the same thing happened in occupied France. The massive sums taken out of circulation by taxation and loans were never sufficient to meet the increasingly massive expenditure on the war; from 1939 to 1945, the deficit on the Budget was greater than the sum total of Federal expenditure for the previous 150 years. Individual savings and the inflated cash liquidity of firms succeeded in holding in check an inflationary movement that proved irresistible after the war.

Galloping price increases were another inevitable danger. In the course of 1941, the consumer price index rose ten per cent and food prices twenty per cent. Price control had to be instituted and this automatically entailed the fixing of wages; the first measure was opposed by most of the members of Congress, usually the defenders of private interests, particularly those of farmers. The workers' trade unions opposed the second on the grounds of existing legislation.

On April 28, 1942, the Office of Price Administration fixed a price ceiling for most current consumer goods. Fraud became so widespread – especially by bringing out new articles slightly different from those falling within the regulations – that the Office of Price Administration found its task of inspection and price-fixing becoming more and more complicated. In the second half of 1942 it did, however, succeed in holding down price increases, which had risen sharply at the beginning of that year.

But wages were following an exactly opposite curve; from the first to the second half of 1942 the index of increase rose from 0·6 to 1 per cent. President Roosevelt then put through the Stabilization Act empowering him to publish before November 1, 1942, 'a general order stabilizing prices, wages and remuneration affecting the cost of living' at the level of September 15 of that same year. The Office of Economic Stabilization was set up to implement this decision under the chairmanship of the Supreme Court judge James Byrnes.

Rising prices and their race with wages were temporarily halted. In April 1943, the increase in prices reached four per cent and in wages three per cent. On April 8, 1943, Roosevelt issued the order to hold the line and froze prices and wages and forbade the Office of Price Administration to increase the former. In the summer of 1943, there was further federal intervention; a subsidy of 400 million dollars was offered to farmers to reduce commodity prices. At the same time, sugar, meat, fats, coffee and petrol were put on ration. These measures were effective and the rise in the cost of living was almost completely checked until the end of the war, with wholesale prices being held down rather better than retail prices. After the end of hostilities their upward curve began again until by 1948 they were double those of 1939, the increase being most marked in textiles and foodstuffs and least in fuel and rents. This did not, however, prevent the gross national product – after adjustments for price and tax increases – from rising by fifty per cent during the same period.

The fact remained that where one was dealing with new models continually being improved, the prices of arms and war equipment could not be fixed in the abstract without grave risk of error. In order to prevent firms from making excessive profits, the Army drew up contracts with them that were flexible enough to enable prices to be fixed in the course of manufacture, based on actual costs. The obverse of this was that firms had no incentive whatsoever to reduce their prime costs. President Roosevelt introduced the revolutionary measure of revision of contracts, thus contravening the principle of non-retrospective legislation. This was called renegotiation, which meant going into prices again after they had previously been fixed, thereby restricting the firms' profit margins. In this way nearly 10,000 million dollars were saved. This curbed the more scandalous fortunes being made by war profiteers; but firms working on national defence contracts were still doing sufficiently well on the one hand for the United States war costs to be markedly higher, proportionately, than Britain's and secondly to justify the workers' trade unions in protesting against the discrepancy between the increase in employers' profits and the blocking of wages and salaries.

IV MANPOWER

In the autumn of 1943, full employment had been practically achieved; the seven million unemployed had filled the places left empty by those who had joined the armed forces or taken the new jobs created in the armaments industry; there was already a noticeable shortage of skilled labour, particularly in New England and California.

Once again a number of members of Congress raised the old question that had been settled by one of Roosevelt's earlier decisions; isolationism reared its head again under the formula: 'weapons not men' – based on Churchill's statement: 'Give us the tools and we shall finish the job.' The campaign was led by a former President, Herbert Hoover, who had a reputation as an economic pundit. He was afraid that production might fall because of labour shortages; he pointed out that the enemy had been weakened; he thought that lack of shipping made it impossible to send large numbers of troops overseas. Many congressmen and senators followed in his wake, for electioneering purposes – one provisionally exempted conscript meant one extra vote.

Stimson, the Secretary of War, backed the general staff who were opposed to any reduction in manpower in the armed forces. He advocated 'national service', empowering the government to control all civilian employment. After seeking advice from various committees of 'wise men', Roosevelt ordered a reduction in the armed forces of a few hundred thousand men, which turned out to be an opportune measure, since the Army could not manage to enlist all the men whom it theoretically had the right to.

However, perhaps owing to the trade unions' reluctance – the mistake had been made of not associating them sufficiently closely with the war effort – or else out of respect for the rights of free citizens, Roosevelt did not introduce the 'national service' requested by Stimson, which was under consideration in 1944 but had been opposed by bodies representing the interests of the family as well as feminist organisations. Consequently, the employment of manpower and experts was never subject to one direct control, in fact not even handled in accordance with any definite policy. Responsibility was spread out between many bodies – the Civil Service Commission, the War Manpower Commission, the Department of Labour, etc. The result was that neither the military nor industry were ever fully

satisfied and at the end of the war there were 44 million American men and
women without a job or not looking for one.

The government confined itself to *ad hoc* remedies which turned out to
be barely adequate: employing blacks – in 1941, Roosevelt set up the Fair
Employment Practices Committee to prevent any discrimination against
coloured people in the labour market; taking on 60,000 Mexicans in the
agricultural sector; setting to work 125,000 of the 425,000 German and
Italian prisoners interned in the United States; bringing retired people and
invalids back into employment. The proportion of women employed did
not increase as much as it might have done.

Another grave concern was the strict observance of social legislation
in order not to cause strikes. Powerful employers like Fords refused to
have anything to do with this in their factories and the Army was hesitant
to give them contracts for fear that social strife might cause work stoppages. In fact, in 1941 a big strike almost paralysed the aeronautical industry; the government was reluctant to use legislation to restrict the right
to strike and preferred to offer to mediate.

Pearl Harbour brought an outburst of national feeling. The trade unions
patriotically pledged themselves not to stir up further strikes. Yet some
did occur, which were blamed on 'irresponsible elements' and in 1943
called forth a reaction from the government in the form of a law insisting
on thirty days' notice of withdrawal of labour and giving the President the
right to take over factories needed for national defence purposes.

V AMERICA'S MIGHT

Despite the Army's needs and the unproductive expenditure that this
entailed, America's output of goods of every sort continued to rise
throughout the war. Within the space of three years, more industrial plant
was built than during the ten previous years. Bauxite mines were discovered and exploited and production of aluminium increased sixfold;
that of synthetic rubber went from 50,000 to 70,000 tons; the wheat
harvest rose 33 per cent and coal output by 32 per cent. For that matter,
civilian consumption rose continually as well, despite a slight reduction in
motor cars and domestic appliances.

Throughout the war, national unity was the rule although there were
outbreaks of racial violence, notably in Los Angeles and Detroit. The
foreign policy was approved by both parties and Wendell Wilkie, Roosevelt's unsuccessful opponent in the presidential elections, became his
trusty representative on foreign missions. However, civil rights were
fully respected; the press remained free; elections took place as in peace-

time. The United States was an example of a democracy that did not turn its back on its principles whilst overcoming totalitarian régimes.

At the same time she provided herself with the most powerful army in the world, even though she had to create it from scratch within the space of a few months and recruiting, training and equipping all had to be undertaken simultaneously. Those who were called up were allocated to posts most suited to their intellectual ability and civilian occupation; the better educated were fed into the Air Force and the ancillary services; as a result difficulty was experienced in finding the 136,000 officers needed for the Army, 112,000 of them in 1942 and 1943; quality was often sacrificed to quantity and the problem of training the higher-ranking officers was never completely solved.

A man's initial training lasted only thirteen to seventeen weeks, including enlisting, medical examination, basic training and specialised training; once he had joined his unit, it became painfully obvious how inadequate his preparation was; the remedy was to set up military training establishments in Britain and, later on, in France. Training also suffered from shortage of arms and equipment and the lack of experienced officers and NCOs; it proved necessary for equipment to be used according to a rota system and to recall officers from fighting units.

When a new division was being formed, its commanding officer, his deputies and 200 senior officers were detailed three months in advance; they followed various courses; then they joined up with a thousand men who had already been trained in a parent division; next they were joined by the remaining officers and NCOs, who for the next fortnight or so took over the divisional equipment and prepared to receive the 13,000 to 15,000 other ranks. The group then had thirty-five weeks to turn itself into a fighting unit; but it did sometimes happen that divisional commanders went into action without ever having had the chance of taking their unit on manoeuvres.

As a rather rough and ready guess, in 1940 Lieutenant-General Wedermeyer at Roosevelt's request had estimated the American Army manpower requirements at 8,800,000 men, including the Air Force. He turned out to be just about right. On the other hand, planning errors occurred in the structure of the Army; for example, AA had been overplayed and there had to be a massive reallocation of AA crewmen. Above all, out of the 200 scheduled divisions, sixty-one were supposed to be mechanised and fifty-one motorised. It proved necessary to reduce this somewhat, as such a task was beyond the powers even of American industry.

Eventually, by the end of 1940, 23 divisions were operational; 13 were raised in 1941; in 1943, their number had risen to 91, comprising 67 infantry, 3 cavalry, 16 armoured and 3 airborne divisions.

Their equipment mirrored America's economic power. In all, the Army had at its service 96,000 tanks, 61,000 field guns, 7 million rifles, 2,300,000 lorries, 1,200,000 radio sets, 20,000 radars. More than 5 million men went overseas, including 2,700,000 to the Pacific, together with 11 million of the 21 million tons' total output of munitions. At Christmas-time 1944, the post handled 2,600,000 bags of Army mail via New York and 750,000 via San Francisco.

In particular, the Air Force had started from nothing. After the Munich agreement, Roosevelt had asked Hopkins to undertake a broad investigation of the possibilities of the American aeronautical industry. He wanted it to reach a productive capacity of 20,000 aircraft per year and an actual output of 10,000. But the American officers had no idea of air warfare; when the new Air Force commander General Arnold asked his deputies to assess their demands, they asked for 1,500 aircraft – but between 1940 and 1945 more than 300,000 were going to be built, as well as 800,000 engines.

As usual, Roosevelt wanted to stimulate output by drawing up a huge manufacturing programme: 18,000 aircraft and one million men by October 1, 1942. But a great deal of time elapsed between choosing a prototype, manufacturing it and going into mass production; the B 17 was on the drawing-board in 1938 and not delivered until 1941.

Roosevelt gave his approval to the plan put up by the Air Staff to create a Strategic Bomber Command; it had to be built, armed and trained entirely from scratch. By the end of November 1941, the Air Force comprised 300,000 men and 9,000 aircraft; by the end of the war, there were more than 100,000 planes being serviced by one million mechanics and flown by 200,000 pilots, including 1,500 women pilots on transport and meteorological flights.

As for shipbuilding, in less than two months, from June 1941, in order to counter the havoc caused by submarines 140 shipyards were started up in Delaware Bay, round Puget Sound, on the Mississippi and along the shores of the Great Lakes. They were assembly yards which put together parts that had been produced by factories in all the states of the Union and delivered by rail. By the maximum use of standardisation, it proved possible to halve the number of hours required to produce some types of craft – Liberty Ships, for example. The output of boats rose from 746 in 1942 to 2,242 in 1943 and 2,161 in 1944.

This immense achievement was, on the whole, the result of the usual American method of the 'profit motive', combining massive government expenditure, widespread purchasing power and price-fixing that encouraged production; the correctives were restraint on excessive profits, a restriction of competition through compulsory co-operation and the establishment of priorities in raw materials and credit facilities. The Americans were, of course, a very rich people at the start and their impetus was not slowed down by the privations inflicted on Europe; nor did they ever suffer any war damage and they were never under any threat of invasion.

Yet they still seem not to have exploited their economic and demographic potential to the full. They could perhaps have gone further by adopting at the outset an authoritarian system of state control on the lines advocated by Bernard Baruch. They would doubtless have thereby avoided a great deal of confusion and gained time. But it would have meant going against their convictions and their traditions of voluntary co-operation and free initiative – what Mossé has called 'America's Promethean spirit'. It is not certain that other methods, appealing more to a sense of discipline and obedience and less to joy in action and creativeness might not have damped their enthusiasm and their eagerness to produce.

There is, however, the opposite view: although it had become the dominating factor in the economy, the War Department had changed neither structures, social relations nor people's mentality. The New Deal and its left-wing trend were not revived. If the underprivileged social strata – coloured people, workers, farmers – did benefit somewhat from the war, it was more as a result of the strains on the labour market than of any deliberate action on the part of the authorities. At the end of the day, the boom created by the war basically benefited the richer regions and better off social classes.

All the same, economic analysis progressed to everyone's benefit; prosperity was based on monetary expenditure and Budget deficits which before the war would have been considered as heading straight for bankruptcy; the lessons thus learnt greatly helped full employment and the handling of economic crises after the war. Finally, whereas the pre-war years of depression had stifled scientific research and prevented inventions from being developed, the 'mobilisation of brain-power' brought about scientific advances, the most spectacular of which and the most fraught with consequences for the future was the discovery of the use of nuclear energy in the atom bomb.[1] So technology prospered and, as a result, the welfare of the American people.

VI LEND-LEASE

President Roosevelt certainly did not consider his slogan 'America, the arsenal of democracy' as mere propaganda. At the end of 1941, he decided that three-quarters of American armament production would be sent to

1. Cf. p. 768, et seq.

the countries benefiting from lend-lease – the American general staff considered this proportion too high and felt that it might jeopardise the arming of the American forces. The attack on Pearl Harbour forced a change of outlook and it proved necessary after all, within certain limits, to fall back on to the formula 'America First'.

Lend-lease aid rose progressively from 189 million dollars in 1941 to 3,200 million dollars in 1942, 6,600 million in 1943, 7,300 million in 1944 and then went back to 3,000 million in 1945.

The chief beneficiary was Britain; but the Soviet Union also received a not inconsiderable share[1] and the new French Army raised in North Africa was fitted out with American equipment.[2] In 1941 the Americans provided the British with 1,000 tanks and 5,194 aircraft; in 1942 with 4,389 tanks and 6,847 aircraft. Total lend-lease aid represented 16 per cent of American production but it was as high as 38 per cent of their output of tanks. Arms were the main item supplied but aid also included raw materials, industrial plant, food, charter shipping and services such as ship repairs, etc.

VII LATIN AMERICA

As early as the spring of 1940, Roosevelt had stated: 'For the United States to maintain their security and political and economic position in the western hemisphere' it was necessary 'to ensure economic prosperity in Central and South America and establish this prosperity within the framework of co-operation and economic interdependence within that hemisphere'. In fact, the United States imported from Latin America 90 per cent of their coffee, 85 per cent of their sugar, 78 per cent of their bauxite, 70 per cent of their tungsten, 39 per cent of their tin, 25 per cent of their copper and lead and 30 per cent of their crude oil. It was important to keep this important source of supplies and to make sure that the Axis powers had no access to it. At the military level it was not out of the question that Nazi Germany might stir up trouble or even gain a foothold in some South American republic, thanks to a dictator sympathetic towards Fascism. With the lapse of time the Monroe doctrine had not become merely a distant memory; it still lived on in the minds and hearts of the Americans; in recalling and even magnifying the danger of economic, political and military penetration into South America by Germany, Roosevelt was sure of striking a sympathetic chord with his compatriots; the 'Victory Program' had included the formation of an armed force

1. Cf. p. 474.
2. Cf. p. 499.

equipped to take part in any hostilities that might break out in that part of the world.

German propaganda lent fuel to these fears. It was stressing the exploitation of South America by American capitalists and distributing quantities of literature and film strips in Spanish on the theme of the struggle for liberation of states under Yankee oppression, particularly Puerto Rico and Cuba. It was clever enough not to attack democracy but American plutocracy and imperialism. The German propaganda services had acquired a radio station in Montevideo which was intended to broadcast to the states bordering the River Plate.

There were, moreover, a number of countries which were already in difficulties with the United States. Mexico had expropriated the American oil companies and the United States was proclaiming the existence of 'Communist and National Socialist plots' in that country; in May 1940, the American naval attaché wrote that the Mexican government was ready to expel any American agents who might be reported to them and that it was expecting a German victory to strengthen Mexico's position vis-à-vis the United States. In Brazil, in June 1940, President Vargas had informed the German ambassador of his firm intention of maintaining Brazil's independence, his personal sympathy for the totalitarian states and his dislike of the democratic system. In the Argentine, British interests and French cultural influence were predominant; but German propaganda appeared on the radio, in the cinema and in the newspaper *Pampero*. However, the Foreign Affairs Minister, Cantilho, was very anti-German; but after the defeat of France, through fear of falling too closely under the control of the United States, the Argentine government assured the Reich that it intended to follow a purely Argentine policy, maintain good relations with all the belligerents and in particular retain Germany's friendship.

The United States thus had to overcome the handicap of latent hostility and a backlog of distrust, although this was not everywhere the case; her relations with Chile, Uruguay and Panama were excellent. She set out to develop both political and economic solidarity between the two halves of the continent; on November 15, 1939, she set up a body of experts, the Inter-American Financial and Economic Committee, in Panama; then she called a series of pan-American conferences, held in Rio de Janeiro in January 1942, in Washington in June of the same year and in Mexico in February 1945, when the 'Chapultepec act' laid the foundations for effective joint co-operation.

Roosevelt appointed Nelson A. Rockefeller the 'co-ordinator for inter-American affairs'. Between September 1939 and December 1941, the Import-Export Bank authorised loans of 225 million dollars to sixteen Latin American countries who were admitted to the lend-lease club. Purchases by the United States rose to 2,300 million dollars and in 1945 their sales reached 3,000 million dollars, that is one-third of their total exports. American technical experts were sent out to modernise the economy of various countries. Spectacular projects took shape, such as the Inter-American Highway, a pan-American road joining Alaska and Patagonia.

In fact, the grip of American capital on Latin America merely grew tighter. It was American capital that provided Brazil with her first large metallurgical concern, Volta Redonda, situated in the heart of the forest. In Chile, it ousted European interests and secured for itself a monopoly in copper, as it did also for lead in Peru. Standard Oil provided up to 72 per cent of Venezuela's national income and 95 per cent of its exports; it built steel works and railways. American investments in Mexico tripled; 90 per cent of her imports came from the United States and 72 per cent of her exports went there. In Cuba, the Americans had the monopoly of sugar production and iron ore. In Central America, all the exports of agricultural produce were in the hands of the United Fruit Company.

Some difficulties were not smoothed out. In February 1944 the United States refused to recognise the Farrell government in the Argentine. They froze Argentine credits and recalled their ambassador; Colonel Peron became leader of a national socialist movement which was Fascist but socialistic in inspiration, and bought out the foreign owners of the public services. An undercurrent of nationalism persisted throughout the whole of Latin America.

On the whole, however, the United States maintained and increased her control. The South American states benefited from this; Brazil's industrial output increased fourfold; new sources of wealth were being exploited everywhere; the Yankee firms brought high wages and improved hygiene and health. But the essential problem had not been solved; indeed, it had become more difficult: the new profits went into the hands of the ruling class, of European origin, and the native population remained primitive and wretched.

The Americans remained indifferent if not hostile to any attempts at social reform, such as the distribution of land to Indians in Colombia organised by President Lopez or the workers' buildings put up by President Medina Angarita in Venezuela. They even viewed them as a dangerous Communist influence. In fact, true Communism did take root in Latin America during the war; a Communist central office was opened in Montevideo as early as August 1942; the Confederation of Latin American workers was infiltrated by Communist parties; in Guatemala, the government passed into the hands of trade unionists in 1944; in Cuba, three Communists joined the government in 1945.

Thus the United States had aroused two kinds of opposition, one based on social grounds, the second on xenophobia; they had also not always succeeded in obtaining the support of the ruling classes while being identified with them in the eyes of the oppressed classes. However, during the war this dual hostility did not give rise to any serious incidents. On the contrary, the various countries of Latin America, in their haste to support the winning side, meekly declared war on Germany and Japan with varying delays – Mexico in May 1942, Brazil in August 1942, Bolivia in April 1943, Colombia in November 1943, Paraguay, Ecuador, Peru, Chile and Venezuela in February 1945. Only the 'colonels' government' in the Argentine under Peron proved somewhat obstreperous, so much so that the USA and Britain withdrew their ambassadors from Buenos Aires; Peron decided to join the war in March 1945, so as to earn admission to the UN.

VIII BRITISH WAR PRODUCTION

Between the wars, as early as 1929, academic economists and Treasury experts had worked out a doctrine for a war economy, complete in every point; it was based on the principle that inflation must be curbed at the outset by means of ruthless taxation, a system of loans and, above all, as its principal novelty, sharply different from the American system, by widespread government control in fixing prices and wages, cutting down profits, introducing rationing and directing foreign trade. On the economic level, Britain was thus ready for war and the theory only needed to be applied.

But it was not applied at the right time and here, as in the diplomatic sphere, Neville Chamberlain's leadership proved disastrous. Right up to the declaration of war, the government showed reluctance to demand too great an effort from the country; for fear of financial difficulties, it slowed down and postponed the conversion of industry to armament production as an urgent priority; only seven per cent of the national income was devoted to the rearmament programme after the Munich agreements, when the full danger from Hitler could surely have been easily assessed.

When war broke out, the government gave itself three years to mobilise the resources of the country completely; its chief concern was to ensure financial stability and conserve the dollar reserves, which looked likely to run out rather rapidly. Accordingly, orders for armaments from the United States were restricted as much as possible. It was not until January 1940 that merchant shipping was requisitioned; in June 1940 there were still one million unemployed.

Once Winston Churchill was in power, financial concerns moved into the background; like Clemenceau, he made war in order to win and everything else was subordinated to victory. But there was a good deal of leeway to make up. In June 1940, industrial conscription was introduced by law. The number of people employed in the war industry increased by 2,000,000 in the space of six months and by July 1941, forty per cent of the active population were either mobilised in the Army or else conscripted for industry. The nation was committed to the war more resolutely than in any other country and the public spirit and patriotism of the British meant that the government had no need to employ coercion, as there were enough volunteers to satisfy every need. The system of direction of labour was organised in such a way that a worker could avoid military service only by being employed in the war industry; thus becoming a miner was an alternative to having to join the armed forces.

Scientists were not forgotten. They were grouped into a Directorate of Miscellaneous Weapon Development, otherwise known as the 'wheezers and dodgers', under the Canadian engineer Charles Goodeve. For five years they worked under constant prodding from Churchill; most of their inventions were practical – machines for producing drinking water for troops fighting in the desert, methods of camouflaging ships and rivers, artificial harbours and floating roads. But some of them belonged rather to science fiction, such as an enormous rocket-propelled drum full of high explosive to destroy the Atlantic wall, which was abandoned because of the grave danger to those actually using it.

This immense effort of a whole people deriving more from their wholehearted devotion than from their resources and economic potential, produced results that were sometimes excellent but frequently inadequate. Thus the struggle against inflation almost achieved perfection thanks to taxation, the reduction in imports and also to a fall in the standard of living – fourteen per cent overall compared with 1938 and twenty per cent in food consumption.

These restrictions and the ensuing privations were spread equally throughout the whole population thanks to rationing, price control, taxation, the development of utility articles and subsidies to stabilise the cost of living. There was no under-nourishment nor any increase in the death-rate, not even any deterioration in health. Social justice and the absence of any organised black market were the distinguishing characteristics of the British economy in time of war; wages kept up with prices; even while the war was still on, wide-ranging social reforms were worked out, such as the Beveridge plan of national insurance in December 1942, which was going to provide the model for more or less all the systems of social welfare introduced into various countries after the war.

To meet the food requirements of the nation, arable farming was given priority over sheep and cattle breeding. Seven million acres of pasture were put under the plough; grain production doubled. Production of iron and bauxite increased and, despite the destruction caused by German air raids, industrial output continued to rise, at least until 1943, without causing any very marked fall in the production of consumer goods.

However, these positive results were offset by three failures, in the spheres of employment, coal-mining and armament production, which showed that their leader Winston Churchill was asking the British people for an effort beyond their means, however great the need for it in the critical situation in which they found themselves.

In 1941 a shortage of skilled labour became apparent; from 1942 onwards, this shortage became a general one; it proved necessary to fix a ceiling for the Army of roughly 2 million men. The lack of competent manpower became worse and worse, although in 1944, fifty-five per cent of all the active adult population were working in the war industries. The low birthrate reduced the number of young men liable for national service every year; it proved necessary to increase working hours, introduce compulsory national service for women between twenty and thirty years old, employ Irishmen in spite of their dislike of the English – a dislike that was heartily reciprocated – and put 200,000 German POWs to work.

However, the shortcomings could not be made good in every important sector and output ceased to rise after 1943. The fact that Bevin, a member of the Labour Party, was Minister of Labour had ensured the greatest possible co-operation of the trade unions. Bevin disliked authoritarian methods of forcing workers to switch jobs in accordance with the needs of the war industry but he was obliged to resign himself to the official direction of labour. He did not succeed in satisfying every need nor did he prevent strikes from occurring, although the number of hours lost in this way was lower than in 1914–18.

At the moment when Britain needed the greatest possible supply of power, she went through a serious crisis in the coal industry owing to antiquated mining equipment and the erroneous calculation that the disappearance of exports would always ensure an adequate output for internal needs. From 1940 to 1945, coal production fell from 224 to 180 million tons and the danger of shortage was looming as early as 1941. Till then the government had only exercised indirect control through professional organisations. It had to change its methods. In June 1941 it set up the Ministry of Fuel and Power which increasingly intervened in matters of technology, wages and social questions; mechanisation, open-cast mining and coal rationing were some of the methods used. Mines were requisitioned and placed under government control but the owners continued to draw their dividends.

Indeed, feeling amongst the miners remained very strained. Thus the idea of nationalising the coal industry made headway. In 1944 Bevin, himself a miner's son, suggested this, at the same time as establishing state control of urban development and the main public services. In March

1945, the Reid Report, a technical examination of the matter by engineers, reached the same conclusions.

Manpower shortages, difficulties in the coal industry and in transport, the increasing size of the armed forces and their ever-increasing needs; all these weaknesses and contradictory requirements could not fail to affect the armaments industry. Moreover, in the Purvis Programme, similar to the American 'Victory Program', in order to provide an incentive for itself the industry had set its sights very high, indeed too high. Nor was it ever organised in a completely satisfactory way, for the equipping of each of the three services came under three separate government departments. Planning errors also occurred such as building long-range bombers, on the basis of a 'peripheral strategy' which proved to be impossible owing to lack of the necessary industrial potential and was partly overtaken once the Americans' strategic plans were adopted; but the mistake caused harm to 'combined operations' which were now becoming the rule. Above all, unlike the Americans, the British had too little time to work out a long-term armaments programme; they were always having to cope with emergencies – small ships to counter the submarine danger in 1940, tanks for Libya in 1941. The repeated changes in types of weapon, plus the small number of large factories, made mass-production methods difficult.

As a result, an output of only 626 tanks a month was reached in 1941, far fewer than the Army wanted. In 1942, an ambitious production schedule of 2,300 aircraft per month was drawn up but no more than 2,000 were ever built. The factories turned out 8,611 tanks in 1942 but only 7,476 in 1943 and still fewer in 1944. Similarly, aircraft-production reached its ceiling of 26,000 in 1943 and 1944.

From 1944 onwards, it became more and more obvious that industry was running out of steam, to such an extent that the government's chief concern was to obtain America's agreement to start reconverting the economy even before the war was over and turning it over to peacetime needs during the period between Germany's and Japan's surrender, which was assumed likely to be lengthy. The atom bomb curtailed this period; in September 1945, President Truman cut off Britain's lend-lease aid. Not only had Britain not obtained results proportionate to the immense effort, she was going to be hurled into a sea of trouble in which it proved impossible to keep her footing.

IX THE COMMONWEALTH

However, aid had not failed to be forthcoming from the Commonwealth, although it had turned out to be far less than had been anticipated at the beginning of the war and in the long run it was counter-balanced by the irresistible movement tending to draw the Commonwealth away from Great Britain.

In Canada, indeed, Prime Minister Mackenzie King proclaimed unswerving attachment to the mother country. A Canadian army was raised which was on active service from 1942 onwards, took part in the Dieppe raid, in the fighting in Italy, the Normandy landings and the ensuing campaigns in France and Germany. Canada also provided herself with a merchant fleet by building shipyards on the Great Lakes; in 1945 this merchant navy was as large as France's in 1939.

But loyal though he was, the Canadian Premier saw the Dominions' partnership in terms of free consultation and not of rigid centralisation, which was still the ideal of two such unabashed imperialists as Churchill and Alanbrooke. On occasion, problems of internal policy adversely affected Anglo-Canadian co-operation. Thus the French Canadians were opposed to the principle of conscription; seventy-two per cent of them voted against it on April 27, 1942, whereas eighty per cent of the rest of the country voted in favour. French Canadians who did join up were unhappy about the small number of French Canadian officers, as commands were given in English. It was in order to satisfy this French-speaking minority that the Canadian government maintained links with Pétain and a diplomatic representative in Vichy.

The Pacific coast provinces on the other hand felt themselves almost part of the United States, who, quite logically, sought to utilise Canada's resources for their own industrial effort and invested enormous capital there; new factories grew up all around the Great Lakes and in the Vancouver district, without too much regard for the national frontier. In August 1940, Canada linked her defence with that of her powerful neighbour; on April 20, 1941, by the Hyde Park Convention, it joined its economy to the United States. Since Britain was so far away, henceforth almost all Canada's trade transactions were with the United States; many French Canadians went to work in New England, particularly in Vermont.

However, Canada was constantly concerned to retain her own charter and preserve her national unity in the American world of which she was becoming part. Marshal Smuts' statements that after the war the world would be ruled by the Great Powers caused alarm in Canada. The Atlantic Charter had also offended her susceptibilities by the way in which it seemed to represent an Anglo-American bid for supremacy.

All the same, Canada remained entirely loyal and she participated most actively in the war; on December 31, 1944, her armed forces had risen to more than 1 million men, that is forty per cent of her male population between eighteen and forty years old. But war meant emancipation for Canada and was leading her to wish for greater flexibility in the organisation of the Commonwealth.

Despite her earlier reluctance, South Africa nevertheless fought in the operational theatres in Africa but in these alone. After the capture of Ethiopia, two divisions won fame in the Eighth Army against Rommel; one brigade occupied Madagascar; twenty-seven squadrons were based in the Middle East in 1944, which was more than Britain's contribution. South African losses were heavy: 13,000 prisoners were taken in Tobruk. In 1945, 220,000 volunteers were demobilised. But this effort was largely the personal achievement of Field Marshal Smuts as Prime Minister, Defence Minister and Foreign Minister. Public opinion was not whole-heartedly behind him because there was a powerful nationalist party in favour of taking South Africa out of the Commonwealth; moreover, the army contained two-thirds Afrikaners against one-third British.

Australia was more loyal; Prime Minister Curtin even wanted to strengthen the Commonwealth by setting up a permanent secretariat. Australia raised an army and built eighty ships of 700 to 13,000 tons. But after Japan's aggression, the Australian forces were kept for defending their own country; they fitted into the American defence arrangements and fought under American generals; it was also United States plant and equipment that enabled Australia to modernise and enlarge her industries, harbours and means of transport.

The situation was similar in New Zealand, except that Prime Minister Savage was anxious to be consulted and not be reduced merely to an executive role in the Commonwealth. When it became clear that Britain could no longer guarantee her defence, New Zealand provided herself with diplomatic representation in Washington. However, she took part in the common effort to the fullest extent of her powers; in July 1942, her armed forces numbered 154,000 men, that is one-tenth of her population.

Only in India did Britain meet really serious failure. Yet in the hour of danger, the Indian nationalists had sown sympathy. 'We are not seeking,' Gandhi had said, 'to base our independence on England's ruin.' But the Congress party's request in July 1940 for a provisional national government to be formed under the control of a viceroy met with a flat refusal from Churchill. It needed the fall of Singapore for Sir Stafford Cripps to be entrusted with reopening talks; the suggestion that the British government should issue a statement promising India dominion status was compared by Gandhi and Nehru at that time to 'a postdated cheque drawn on a bankrupt Empire'.

However, the British played on the rivalry between the Congress party, the Moslem League and the princes, as well as on the ethnic, social and regional differences in that enormous country. In 1939, the Indian Army totalled 353,000 men; on October 1, 1944, it had reached 2,641,000 men; but with a few exceptions, the Indians were never promoted to the higher ranks. At the same time, India was being exploited by the British in a

US WAR ECONOMY AND PRODUCTION

	1939	1941	1942	1943	1944	1945
Gross National Product (in 1000 million dollars)	91·4	126·4	161·6	194·3	213·7	215·2
Industrial Production (1935–1939=100)	109·0	162·0	199·0	239·0	235·0	203·0
Retail prices (1935–1939=100)	99·4	105·2	116·5	123·6	125·5	128·4
Wholesale prices (1926=100)	77·1	87·3	98·8	103·1	104·0	105·8
Workers (in millions)	45·7	50·3	53·7	54·5	54·0	52·8
Working hours (per week)	37·7	40·6	43·9	44·9	45·2	43·4
Stock Exchange (prices of 416 shares; 1935–1939=100)	94·2	80·0	69·4	91·9	99·8	121·5
Budgetary income (in 1,000 million dollars)	6·7	15·7	23·2	39·6	41·6	43·0
Budgetary expenditure (in 1,000 million dollars)	9·0	20·5	56·1	86·0	95·6	84·8
Public debt (in 1,000 million dollars)	42·0	58·0	108·2	165·9	230·6	278·0
Purchases of goods and services by the state (in 1,000 million dollars) including:	13·1	24·7	59·7	88·6	96·5	82·8
National defence (in 1,000 million dollars)	5·2	13·8	49·6	80·4	88·6	76·0
Personal income (in 1,000 million dollars)	72·6	95·3	122·7	150·3	165·9	171·9
Strength of the armed forces on January 1[1] (millions of men)	0·4	1·5	5·0	6·8	7·2	7·4
Production: of ships (in millions of tons)	1·5 (1940)	2·5	7·0	16·0	16·3	
of tanks	346 (1940)	4,052	24,997	29,497	17,565	20,000 (approx)
of aircraft	2,141 (1940)	19,433	47,836	85,898	96,318	46,000 (three-quarters)

1. Army and Air Force only and including only actual armed fighting personnel; including Navy and various ancillary services, 12 million men were mobilised.

shocking and even tragic manner; India's scanty rolling-stock was used to equip the railway running from Iran to the Caspian Sea and when, in 1942, the British halved their shipping traffic in the Indian Ocean, which was 100 ships a month before the war, famine ensued which caused the death of 1,500,000 people in Bengal in the summer of 1943.

*

Thus it was apparent from 1943 onwards that, left to herself, Britain would not be capable of winning the war. She was maintaining her position in the Allied coalition thanks only to lend-lease and to Roosevelt's kindness in pretending to continue considering Britain as an equal partner with the United States. History could hardly seem less moral, for Britain had held the breach, courageously and alone, against Nazi Germany; she had fought on by herself in order that peoples might be free. As a reward she had to face the sight of her capital and customers melting away all over the world, her empire crumbling, her industrial potential weakened and the admission of an irretrievable diminution of her power.

On the other hand the war was surely leading the United States to the summit of power; she had joined in after everyone else, after others had foundered in her absence; she was picking up the pieces of the legacy left by Britain; it was clear that she was becoming the *deus ex machina* to resolve the world drama that had started in 1939; Britain's dependence on her, her growing strength, military as well as economic, could not fail meanwhile to give her the most important voice, first of all in the interallied discussions on the conduct of the war and later at the conference tables where the world would be given its post-war shape.

But in 1943, her time had not quite come; it was still the Soviet Union that was bearing the brunt of the Wehrmacht's attacks.

CHAPTER 3

The Soviet War

I THE CONDUCT OF THE WAR

IT is not easy to find out how the war was directed and conducted in the Soviet Union. It is true that Soviet historians offer a good deal of detail as to the nature and role of the bodies that exercised the real power within the structure of Soviet institutions. But they are very sparing of information regarding their functioning; when reading them it would seem that these bodies were never split by dissension, that their members always knew unhesitatingly what needed doing and that, in fact, they were uplifted by such strong patriotic feeling that they saw everything with complete lucidity and were inspired by unswerving determination and mutual understanding. Soviet historians are even more discreet about the personal part played by the men in charge of these various bodies; more accurately, until Stalin's death, they showed them as all completely dominated by the giant figure of Lenin's successor, who became a legend in his own lifetime; once the campaign against 'the personality cult' started, Stalin's role was discussed more but still not closely examined or assessed and, apart from Khrushchev for a few years, his colleagues still remain overshadowed by Stalin. On the other hand, the Soviet Communist party always comes in for unstinting and undifferentiated praise; every single success is attributed to it but it is referred to as an anonymous mass and the individuals who formed part of it remain completely unidentified; its exact role is all the more difficult to analyse as some of its constituent bodies – the Comintern for example – are locked in impenetrable secrecy, not to mention the secret police and the intelligence services.

Thus, in the Soviet Union more than anywhere else, there is appearance and there is reality. In principle, Soviet institutions remained in force and continued to function: the Supreme Soviet of the USSR approved the Budget and ratified agreements but it does seem that, in essential matters, it had practically been reduced to inactivity; its Praesidium promulgated a large number of resolutions; the Councils of the People's Commissars of the various republics took countless decisions but only in the civilian sphere, in short, in routine matters.

The conduct of the war and the solution of its enormous problems were entrusted to new bodies, set up as early as June 1941 by the Central Committee of the Party. It is not easy to see the reason for these bodies because in the USSR the Communist party was solidly established in every senior post, at every executive level; in fact, even before the war, in every sphere of government, every avenue led back to Stalin, who was leader of the Party as well as of the government. Nor does it seem as if the Party which had suffered numerous purges in consequence of the suspicious and spiteful nature of its ambitious Secretary-General, was in any way basically reshuffled during the war by dismissals as a punishment for individual failures. The new bodies probably enabled more efficient centralisation of the new tasks into fewer hands and gave increased power to a few carefully selected leaders, chosen in accordance with principles which escape us but, in all probability, mainly because Stalin trusted them.

In any case, the conduct of the war in all its aspects was the responsibility of the State Defence Committee under Stalin's chairmanship. It had the power to issue edicts having the force of law for the duration and its authority extended to all state and party organisations. One cannot fail to be reminded of the French Revolutionary Committee of Public Safety, but minus the *Convention*: the State Defence Committee was answerable only to itself.

All the other bodies were restricted to a purely executive capacity. However, the SDC did not set up any new services of its own; it exercised its authority through the normal machinery of state; thus it controlled the planned economy, directed towards war production by means of the Commission of the Plan (Gos Plan); but it took direct decisions on matters which it considered urgent and which in normal times might have seemed of minor importance – for example the laying of an oil pipeline over Lake Ladoga to supply Leningrad during its siege.

The State Defence Committee also controlled the armed forces with the help of the General Headquarters (*Stavka*) on which there sat officers representing the forces but also high party officials, promoted to be Marshals of the Soviet Union for the purpose – for example, Bulganin. This GHQ worked out strategy, allocated units to the various fronts and controlled the strategic reserves; its decisions were carried out by the armed forces' general staff, composed entirely of service representatives.

The State Defence Committee poked its nose into everything. It sent plenipotentiary delegates to the various republics, to the different fronts, to industrial concerns – for example, to settle a crisis in the coal industry in Karaganda in 1943; here again, one is reminded of the 'special missions' of the representatives of the *Convention*.

The other new bodies were given only minor tasks of local importance, or morale-boosting missions. Thus, in areas where the situation was becoming dangerous – for example, at Stalingrad – local defence committees were set up. When the need was felt, the SDC formed fresh people's commissariats or ministries, as for the production of tanks and mortars.

At grass-root level, the local soviets, trade unions, Komsomols and production co-operatives had the task of providing the necessary official backbone for the population and spurring it on to satisfy the war needs. Thus the soviets, with a million members in all, collected warm clothing for the troops, helped to look after their families but also to maintain law and order and good discipline. The trade unions worked to increase output; and the Komsomols, with 9 million members, were the constantly replenished rearing-ground of half-trained recruits. Other new bodies with special aims but with the same general purpose were set up – for example, the body 'for the defence and advancement of aeronautics and chemistry'.

II STALIN'S ROLE

What part did Stalin play in all this? For an accurate assessment we would have to discover what share he had in planning the decisions taken by the SDC and determine those which he approved and accepted responsibility for when others had provided the idea; this is impossible to assess in the present state of knowledge, at least in France. He was certainly a very clever man, indeed a crafty one, but within a tightly closed world which he had been able to organise to his own advantage and bring under his thumb: the Russian Communist party. Outside this world, he was astonishingly lacking in knowledge; he had never been outside the Soviet Union; he knew no foreign languages; his ideas were as dull as his style; in a word, he seemed to deserve the title of the 'most insignificant of Lenin's comrades' which had earned him the post of Secretary-General of the Party, because of the fears aroused in his colleagues by Trotsky's strong personality. From this central position, he had patiently spun his spider's web and he controlled all its threads from the confined space of a few rooms in the Kremlin where he lived in austerity and from which he ruled the greatest empire in the world – the USSR and her Communist partners. To achieve this degree of power and stay there, Stalin had had to show few scruples and great gifts of guile, deceit, intrigue and brutality; by bringing them into disrepute with his astounding accusations, Stalin had gradually eliminated all his opponents, real or imaginary; he had placed men whom he could trust in every important post in the machinery of government. His efficient management and the terror which he inspired had thus consolidated his authority by ensuring that it would be permanent.

But his policy had now suffered a setback of the utmost gravity; he had proved unable either to foresee or to prevent German aggression; his policy had led to such major reverses that his authority seemed in danger of foundering and the Bolshevik Revolution of disappearing; the Soviet Union herself was threatened with disruption. It seems that Stalin was able to manoeuvre so that at one and the same time he managed to establish his power even more strongly, protect himself against any backlash from either his enemies or those who had suffered at his hands in the Party and rally the whole population behind himself and the Communist régime.

He was and remained head of government and leader of the Party; in addition, he became Marshal Stalin, head of the armies of the Soviet Union and Chairman of the State Defence Committee. Thus, everything that took place began or ended with him. Not one important measure was taken without his having inspired or approved it. It was he who dealt, directly and personally, with Roosevelt and Churchill. It is, incidentally, a somewhat surprising fact that, in the British parliamentary democracy as well as in the American presidential democracy and the Soviet socialist democracy, the conduct of the war and thus the leadership of the nation fell to a civilian leader issuing his orders to the military, as in the totalitarian régimes of Germany and Italy; paradoxically it was only under the Japanese military dictatorship that some corporate authority existed. In any case, in the Soviet Union Stalin's role was certainly predominant. But although, in Churchill's or Roosevelt's actions, it is possible to distinguish the proportion of mistaken and successful ideas, any similar analysis of Stalin is impossible.

The new bodies seem to have had a triple function; they allowed Stalin to gather round himself the indispensable professional advisers, scientists for example, even if they were not long-standing Communists, without having to go through the cumbersome and slow governmental, administrative or Party channels. They put the ordinary Soviet institutions into a state of suspended animation; these were possible sources of opposition or rivalry and, however slight their importance might have been, they needed no longer to be taken into account; and now these new organisations removed any hope of playing a larger part in affairs as they might have been tempted to do in view of the new situation arising from the Russian setbacks. Finally, these new bodies seemed to show that the régime was changing its nature; it was identifying itself more with the nation; it was ceasing to be tyrannical and revolutionary in order to become merely the voice and instrument of the will of the peoples of the Soviet Union to repel the invader.

Accordingly, a superficial façade was created to inspire confidence in the Soviet leaders, both inside and outside the country – a confidence which the latter had good reason to believe was far from widespread. So we find a determined propaganda machine installing loudspeakers even in the depths of the country, to blare out Stalin's reassuring fatherly voice, giving advice and instruction at times of crisis or real danger. One particularly widespread image of him represented him as an amiable, smiling, confident 'Father of his People', full of quiet strength. This conception seems even to have misled the British and Americans who met him; they expected to see a despot with cruelty written all over his face and they discovered a jolly good sort, a hard drinker, shrewd but accessible and frank, in short, a very likeable man. This is the picture and impression that Eden and Hopkins conveyed in their reminiscences. Churchill and Roosevelt expressed the same idea in their war correspondence by the familiar nickname 'Uncle Joe'.

It was important for the international Communist party to achieve, like its leader, in its internal as well as its external image, the greatest possible support by disarming the animosity that it had aroused hitherto.

III RUSSIAN NEO-NATIONALISM

In any case, even before the war, the danger from Hitler had induced the Soviet political leaders, in contradiction with the early days of the régime, to stress national unity and patriotism. Thus a sort of mythical pantheon of illustrious Russians had been created: Alexis Tolstoy had extolled the work of Peter the Great; Eisenstein had recalled that of Ivan the Terrible. Tolstoy and Tchaikovsky were rehabilitated because they had written about and celebrated the story of the Holy War against Napoleon. In France, the Communist party had ceased to advise people to refuse to fight for their country; they no longer condemned outright the illustrious deeds and works of the past as being for the benefit of a small number of people at the expense of the workers but claimed that the people as a whole could take credit for them. Thus Thorez had shown that French cathedrals or the Château of Versailles belonged to the people because, after all, it was the people who had built them.

This trend had been momentarily brought to a halt by the German-Soviet pact; but the break between the signatories gave it fresh vigour and urgency. On November 6, 1941, Stalin told the troops massed in Red Square: 'The war you are fighting is a war of liberation, a just war, in which you can seek inspiration from our great forefathers, Alexander Nevski, Dimitri Donskoy, Alexander Suvorov, Michael Kutusov.' On July 29, 1942, the Supreme Praesidium decreed that the Kutusov and Alexander Nevski decorations should be reinstated, and to these was added the Order of Lenin as their normal and natural successor in the history of the one and same Russian people.

Inversely, if the invaders continued to be described as 'Fascists', a word that incidentally became synonymous with bandits, they were above all accused of wishing to seize the USSR's wealth – especially her wheat and oil – and turn her inhabitants into slaves; so that the citizens of the Soviet Union were fighting for their possessions as well as for their self-respect and these included the Bolshevik régime that had given them the one and the other. It was, of course, Soviet national feeling but, above all, it was Russian: at the end of the war, Stalin, a Georgian, sang the praises of the Russian people and gratefully recognised it as the principal element and instrument of Soviet victory.

The power of religious feeling was not neglected; the Metropolitan Serge exhorted the Orthodox Russians to fight for Holy Russia, whereas the Bolshevik régime had been against religion. The 'Internationale' cased to be the USSR's national anthem. In one of his poems, Simonov spoke of 'the Fatherland . . . country roads traced by our forefathers with wooden crosses on Russian graves'.

In the Red Army, old traditions were revived; the ranks of general and marshal made their appearance again together with the epaulettes that in 1917 the revolutionaries had torn off the uniforms of the Czarist officers. In the thick of the battle of Stalingrad the 'political commissars', whose task was to ensure that the Army remained subordinated to the Party, became 'deputy commanders in charge of political matters', and so were less embarrassing for the military commanders.

Laran has analysed a whole popular literature written by 'soldier authors' – M. Sholokhov, B. Polojov, A. Tvarkovskiy, M. Tikhonov – who extolled the qualities of the Russian fighting man; there were many songs celebrating the exploits of the 'Katyushas'; 'the bogatyrs of the Russia of Kiev have been roused from their long slumber to fight once more against the invader'; the jet rocket-gun was nicknamed 'Ivan the Terrible'. The government sponsored and encouraged this upsurge of feeling through the 'Pansoviet House of Popular Creation'. In a word, an immense patriotic fervour, half spontaneous, half officially inspired, filled the hearts of all the peoples of the Soviet Union.

IV THE DISSOLUTION OF THE COMINTERN

On May 15, 1943, a long resolution was passed by the Praesidium of the executive committee of the Communist International dissolving the body commonly known as the Comintern which had been directing from Moscow the action of Communist parties all over the world. Although not the first in date – it had been preceded by the International Association of Communist Trade Unions, Profintern, and The International Peasants'

Association, Krestintern – the disappearance of this body was completely unexpected and it caused a sensation. Annie Kriegel has pointed out that though the members of the executive committee of the Comintern learned the news on reading *Pravda*, the decision had been maturing since the German-Soviet pact when Stalin was taking care not to alarm Hitler. So it was Stalin who had taken the decision, after a minimum of indispensable consultation.

It was Stalin himself who explained the event for foreign consumption in an interview which he granted to Reuter's correspondent.[1] He pointed out that this step put an end to 'the lie according to which the USSR interfered in the internal affairs of other states'; the decision would show how unfounded were the slanders describing 'the Communist parties of the different countries as not acting in accordance with the interests of their own people but obeying instructions from abroad'; it would enable 'patriots in freedom-loving countries to bring together all the progressive forces of their country . . . against Fascism'; as between nations themselves it would facilitate the establishment of 'an international front against the threat of Hitler'. But the decision had such a symbolic significance that, despite Thorez's vain attempts to justify it by reference to Marx's and Engels' dissolution of the 'League of Communists', according to Marty old revolutionaries 'shed tears as they signed it'; but they all submitted and gave their acceptance.

This measure seemed to put an end, at least for the moment, to the Soviet Union's aims of world revolution. Although it could partly be explained by certain difficulties in the functioning of the Comintern, it had certainly been taken with a view to reassuring foreign countries and first and foremost the Soviet Union's allies, the British and Americans and the non-Communist Resistance movements in occupied countries. It represented, in fact, the Soviet Union's contribution to the National Fronts. Goebbels was not mistaken when he denounced it as yet another monstrous act of collusion between Bolshevism and plutocracy. Although Churchill evinced some scepticism as to Stalin's intentions, Roosevelt and Hopkins certainly interpreted it in this way. As for the French Resistance, here are some of the views of its underground organisations, non-Communist and in some cases anti-Communist, on this sudden switch in USSR policy. 'Dissolving the Comintern,' wrote *Défense de la France*, 'means that the USSR has given up the idea of issuing revolutionary directives to the Communist parties of the various countries; these parties will now be able to fit in with the ordinary lines of internal policy.' *Franc-Tireur* drew attention to Stalin's statements that 'the USSR wanted to let the liberated peoples have the right to rule themselves as they chose'.

1. A. Kriegel, 'La Dissolution du Komintern', *Revue d'histoire de la deuxième guerre mondiale*, Oct. 1967.

A 'Secret Army' paper, *La Quatrième République*, criticised those who persisted in thinking that 'Stalin wants to bolshevise the world, for the Soviet statesmen are too intelligent to follow such a will o' the wisp'. In short, the Resistance considered that there was no longer any obstacle to a lasting alliance between France and the USSR; it was even highly desirable.

Stalin wanted the Soviet Union to cease being a bogy in the world, just as he wanted Communist parties to become respectable in their own countries; and he had achieved his aim. But the disappearance of the Comintern for purely tactical reasons did not mean that the Kremlin's hold over international Communism was in any way weakened; it was merely an internal transfer of responsibility.

V THE SOVIET UNION AND THE COMMUNIST PARTIES

In fact, even before the Comintern was dissolved, the Communist parties in the various countries had already taken up 'national' attitudes in accordance with instructions received from Moscow. Ever since July 1941, the British Communist party had organised lectures and meetings to stimulate war production; it proclaimed that British workers should group themselves solidly behind the coalition government and the colonised peoples should play down their claims and realise that the immediate task was to beat Hitler. It deplored Gandhi's obstinate persistence in his narrow-minded attitude, a criticism echoed by an Indian Communist party manifesto which in the course of the party's first non-clandestine meeting in September 1942 proclaimed that 'India was ready to serve the Allied cause'. The British Communist party failed to join the Labour Party after having asked to do so only because the latter refused to let it in.

The US Communist party advised the blacks to put an end to their campaign for 'equal pay for equal work' in the war industry which, if implemented, would have jeopardised production. The Socialist leader Norman Thomas who called on the blacks to continue their struggle for equal rights was accused by the Communist newspaper, the *Daily Worker*, of advocating Fascism. One American Communist leader wrote that there were no longer any economic classes in the USA, but merely the American people. The 'America, Peace, Mobilisation' movement was merely changed to 'American People's Mobilisation' – the initials remained the same and the message was reversed.

All over the world, instructions from Moscow continued to be transmitted by radio to the Communist parties of various countries; thus Maurice Thorez, André Marty and Jean-Richard Bloch addressed the French people on Radio Moscow; but other more secret messages were picked up by the central committee of the underground French Communist party.

The groups of exiled Communists remained at Stalin's beck and call in Moscow. He kept them out of the way or brought them into the limelight as pawns in his game of chess. Although the Finn Kuusinen was put back into his box after his failure in Finland, Bierut the Pole, the Romanian Anna Pauker, Rakosi the Hungarian, the Italian Togliatti, the Germans Pieck and Ulbricht, Gottwald the Czech and the Bulgarian Dimitrov were all kept in reserve, to bide their time. The Comintern had not really disappeared, it had been naturalised as Russian; the directives addressed to the various Communist parties were no longer issued by a theoretically independent international body but by an office of the Soviet Party's Central Committee; and these instructions were no longer issued on behalf of world revolution but of the Soviet Union; her salvation offered the only hope that one day the fight to achieve world revolution might start again.

The role of the non-Russian Communist parties was to encourage national Resistance movements likely to relieve the pressure that the Wehrmacht was exerting on the Red Army and, in each country, to form teams to share or take over power at the Liberation. Greater importance would be granted to those parties in territories which the Red Army itself reconquered. But except for Yugoslavia – and there with certain reservations only – every Communist party approved wholeheartedly and at all times the Soviet Union's policies and loyally supported her *vis-à-vis* her allies, in particular for the opening of a second front.

The French Communist party's underground press, for example, never ceased supporting the Soviet Union on every issue, whatever changes in policy she might make. *L'Humanité* sang the praises of the Russian soldier as 'a citizen defending his land, his liberty, his life and his mother-country'. The war being waged by the USSR was a 'holy war for the freedom and dignity of mankind'; the 'Fascist' argument that the Bolshevik régime was attacking private property was 'bad propaganda which should not deceive anyone'. As for the liberty of nations, the USSR had 'no territorial ambitions with regard to other nations . . . she had more than once shown her respect for the right of nations to self-determination'. From all this, Jacques Duclos drew the conclusion that 'France, with one voice, wants a treaty with the USSR similar to the one signed by Czechoslovakia'.

The fact remained that, in taking part in this patriotic struggle, in recruiting new members more on the basis of their participation in the Resistance than of their political convictions, in placing in the forefront those who owed their fame to their militant partisan activity, and in preaching and practising the principle of the broadest possible national unity, it was impossible for the Communists not to change their nature somewhat. The military leaders in the occupied countries were not always going to be in agreement with the exiles who had lived too long in the Soviet Union not to have rather lost touch with their own country. As a sign of the shape of things to come, Kriegel has drawn attention to an appeal by Togliatti, which he made as early as July 1943, for 'polycentrism', called for co-operation between Communist parties after the war and suggesting regional agreements that could be developed only at the cost of weakening the links with Moscow. But could the Russian Communist party itself fail to be affected by the patriotic struggle in which its members were unstintingly giving their all with the deep satisfaction of identifying themselves with the most fundamental aspirations of the peoples of the Soviet Union? In particular, it had played a preponderant role in ensuring that the high-quality armaments needed by the Red Army were produced in the right quantities and at the right time.

VI SOVIET ECONOMIC LOSSES THROUGH THE OCCUPATION

In 1940, the USSR produced nearly 30 million tons of iron ore, 15 million tons of cast iron and more than 18 million tons of steel, 166 million tons of coal, 31 million tons of oil and 48,000 million kilowatts of electricity. In certain sectors – the mechanical and machine-tool industries – plant was modern and output high; the enormous reserves of iron ore, coal or oil opened up unlimited possibilities.

But in the period immediately preceding the war, this economic potential was not being used to manufacture sufficient armaments to equip the Red Army properly. Nowadays Soviet historians blame Stalin for this, since they claim that it was not until June 6, 1941, that he issued a programme for the mobilisation of war production, which was not ready to start before the end of 1942. So in 1940, Germany's output of modern aircraft was 10,250 as against a few dozen by the Soviet Union. Soviet tank production was better – nearly 2,800 in 1940 – but still less than what was needed. Production of the 47-mm anti-tank gun had been stopped and Stalin has been held responsible for this, too, whilst the 57-mm gun which had been approved was still in the manufacturing stage.

Most of the Soviet Union's metallurgical industry was concentrated in factories in the western areas of the country, chiefly round Leningrad and Moscow, and in the Ukraine; their occupation, the fighting that took place there and the deliberate demolition undertaken in the course of the 'scorched earth' policy, cost the USSR 31,000 industrial concerns – factories, workshops, warehouses – over 40,000 miles of railway, 175,000 machine tools, 34,000 power hammers and forging presses, 62 blast-furnaces, 213 Martin furnaces and 45,000 looms. In towns held by the enemy, fifty per cent of the apartment blocks had been destroyed or badly damaged; 98,000 kolkhozes, 1,800 sovkhozes and 2,890 machinery and tractor depots had been devastated.

In six months, from June to November 1941, total industrial production fell to forty-eight per cent of the pre-war level; in particular output of ferrous and non-ferrous rolled sheet metal and of ball-bearings, indispensable for armaments, had been almost entirely brought to a stop in the turmoil.

This disastrous drop in production was accentuated in the course of 1942. Coal output fell from 142 million tons in 1941 to 75 million; production of cast iron from 18 million tons to 5; steel from 13·8 to 4·8 million tons.

The usual deliveries between regions or from coal mine to factory came to an abrupt stop; some factories outside the enemy's reach were no longer receiving any coal; others were unable to despatch their product for lack of transport. In the country there was a return to primitive methods of agriculture: hand-ploughs, home-made equipment; everywhere the most trivial articles and the most ordinary products became worth their weight in gold. In this catastrophe, the USSR was saved by her geography, her leaders' decisions and the courage and long-suffering nature of her inhabitants.

Her enormous size put large areas of the country beyond the reach of enemy operations, from the Urals and beyond; the problem was to have time enough and find the way to move men and machines into these areas and to enlarge the industrial concerns already sited there as a result of the Five Year Plans. Her population gave the Soviet Union equally unlimited reserves of manpower but it was necessary to turn women and peasants into skilled workers – in 1937 the active population still included 40 million rural workers. The government doubled its loans to discover raw materials in non-occupied areas; it gave priority to certain sectors of industry – special steels, for example; it sited new factories close to mining areas. In short, it sought to channel and direct production; but there remained two immense problems: the evacuation of workers and their machines eastwards and the mobilisation and training of manpower.

VII THE EVACUATION OF FACTORIES EASTWARDS

On June 24, 1941, only three days after the start of the war, the Party's Central Committee set up an Evacuation Committee, under Kaganovitch and later Svernik, helped by Kosygin; on June 27, the general outline of the programme was laid down by government decree and the first measures promulgated. The rapid anticipation and speed of these decisions are somewhat surprising; factories began to be evacuated well before they were threatened. As Girault remarks, 'Either the government organisations quickly became aware of the collapse of the front lines and reacted with great speed ... or else they were following deliberate tactics ... of fighting far back in the interior of the country.' It is certain that such far-reaching and complicated decisions could not have been deliberately worked out in the space of a few days; the vast amount of planning required must have been devised and worked out in advance; so one is led to wonder whether the Soviet counter-attacks in July 1941 had the purpose of enabling these plans to be carried out; in this respect therefore, Stalin seems to have acted wisely and he must be given a good mark despite the chorus of disapproval which now surrounds his memory.

It is true that the evacuation was made easier by the lines which the Soviet economy had been following before the war, the Five Year Plans, the development of natural resources and their conversion on the spot, in the Urals, Siberia and Turkestan. 'Twins' of factories sited in the west – in the mechanical, chemical and oil industries – had been built there; so some concerns found vacant places ready and waiting to fit them in; for example, the Kirov factory in Leningrad and the diesel engine factory at Kharkov merged with the tractor factory at Cheliabinsk to become the largest tank factory in the Soviet Union.

All the same, a gigantic effort was required. The Evacuation Committee split into three groups, each responsible for the transfer of the factories, the despatch of personnel and transport respectively; but in fact, the three sectors were inextricably linked. When the decision was taken to evacuate Moscow on October 16, 1941, the evacuation of government departments and 150,000 people had to be organised within twenty-four hours, using even Underground trains.

Between July and November 1941, 1,500,000 railway carriages were used to move 1,520 firms, including 1,300 very large ones, to the east, as well as 10 million people, more than 2 million of them from the Moscow region; 450 firms were set up in the Urals, 210 in western Siberia and 250 in central Asia. During these six months, the main factories in Dnepropetrovsk, Zaporozhye, Krivoy Rog, Kharkov, the Donetz (at times under enemy bombardment), Byelorussia, Leningrad and Moscow were dismantled and set up elsewhere; it is impossible to say how many fell, more or less intact, into German hands. A second, smaller wave was set off by the German offensive in the summer of 1942; it affected the centres of Stalingrad, Voronezh, Rostov and Krasnodar. When the new arrival was grafted on to an already existing factory, production restarted rapidly; Soviet historians quote the example of a factory from the Dnepr which was functioning again twenty days after being dismantled; one aircraft factory began to turn out aircraft again a fortnight after it had arrived, dismantled, at its new site; towards the end of 1941, the Leningrad factories in the Urals were sending heavy tanks to the front. But some of the industrial complexes were too large to be transported as they were and they were split up into specialised sections; thus, the Moscow ball-bearing factory, the largest in Europe, was set up at Kuibychev, Saratov and Tomsk; each section was intended to provide specific finished products, but the period of adaptation was bound to be that much longer.

Building new factories obviously took longer but it took place at a speed unknown before the war; thus, blast-furnaces which would have taken two and a half years to erect before the war, took only eight months at Magnitogorsk.

Results were not slow in coming. By March 1942, war production had caught up with that of June 1941; by the end of 1942, it had overtaken it. By that time, the Soviet Union was building more armaments than Germany; only slightly more tanks and aircraft but four times as many artillery guns; more than 6,000 miles of new railway lines had been laid. It was an undoubted success; as an American journalist put it, 'Magnitogorsk had defeated the Ruhr.'

This immense effort was to modify enormously the economic geography of the Soviet Union according to the programme drawn up by Voznessenski, chairman of the 'State Planning Commission' (Gosplan) and as such the man best qualified to adapt current changes to the former or intended state of affairs. If, by reason of their remoteness, progress was quantitatively rather limited in Siberia and central Asia – although local production increased more than tenfold – by the end of the war the Urals were completely transformed. The old factories, some of them dating back to the eighteenth century, had been modernised; nearly a dozen blast-furnaces and dozens of other new furnaces and rolling-mills were erected; the output of cast iron in the Urals almost doubled; steel output rose sixty-five per cent and sheet iron fifty-five per cent.

This economic victory certainly owed a great deal to government organisations and Soviet scientists; it had been made possible only by the sweat and suffering of the people; it had exacted a very heavy toll of human effort.

VIII THE HUMAN EFFORT

Soviet historians certainly do not minimise this effort; on the contrary, they magnify it and see it as a demonstration of the gratitude and affection of the people of the Soviet Union towards the Soviet régime at the same time as an affirmation of their unquenchable patriotic feeling. However, they stress the productive exploits of the Stakhanovites rather than the sufferings endured by the human beings involved, where the picture they paint would seem rather to conflict with the good conduct marks which they very properly allot to the organisers of the evacuation and consequently to the Party, which is given the credit for every success.

Certain facts do exist which enable us to form some idea of these sufferings, and Girault has very efficiently collated and drawn attention to them. There was the Party meeting at Zlatoust on December 13, 1941 when the secretary was accused of incompetence for not supplying adequate provisions for the workers; there was the decision of the Party's Central Committee in April 1942 which shared out the agricultural production of sovkhozes to various factories whose workers went out to work on the land on their rest-days; there was another decision authorising workers to undertake market gardening on their own account – doubtless many of them had not waited to receive this permission; at the end of 1942, 5 million new gardeners were listed. The number of working hours was increased and holidays cancelled; thus the number of working days per year for an adult kolkhoze worker rose from 255 in 1940 to 350 in 1944; to stimulate production, considerable differentials in wages and rations were introduced.

If one accepts the statement of the Soviet historian Cadaev that in the Soviet Union prices dropped by 230 per cent between 1943 and 1945, one is impelled to ask oneself what rises there had been earlier and to imagine that they must have been so steep that wages had found it impossible to keep pace. Material living conditions – accommodation, hospitals, food-supplies, heating, schools – were all the less likely to be satisfactory, at least until 1943, because they had not been given priority in the existing schemes, because 10 million people were involved and because the proportion of unproductive elements amongst them was considerable – there were 600,000 children from Moscow and 300,000 from Leningrad. As Girault wrote, an honest account of these inevitable sufferings would 'in no way detract from the heroism of the Soviet people, in fact quite the reverse'.

The problems involved were, in fact, colossal and they had to be solved both quickly and in a co-ordinated manner. It was not sufficient just to transfer labour; it had to be allocated in the best possible way – switched from one type of activity to another – employees in the tertiary sector became workers in factories engaged in war production, the gaps in the essential industries had to be filled by taking on whole social categories; this makeshift labour force then had to be adequately trained to ensure that the product was of the required quality.

The requirements were immense. In September 1940, there were

20,500,000 workers and employees in the Soviet Union; 6 million of them lived in the areas that were invaded; skilled workers were evacuated to the east in order of priority, but in insufficient numbers. Thus qualified manpower was in short supply in those activities where it was most needed; in heavy industry the number of specialist workers fell from 450,000 to 240,000; in the aeronautical industry, skilled manpower was no more than one-third of what it had been at the beginning of 1941. At the end of 1941, the 'Committee for the Census and Allocation of Manpower' spelt out its needs thus: there was a shortage of 215,000 workers in the evacuated factories, including 45,000 in the tank factories and 64,000 in the ordnance factories. This shortage could not fail to grow worse in view of the increased manpower demands of the Red Army and its losses which would require the mobilisation of civilian workers as the only means of meeting the first and replacing the second.

This shortage remained a constant factor in the Soviet war economy; in 1945, the numbers working in the economy as a whole were still only 27 million as against 30 million in 1940, that is 87 per cent; industrial workers and employees 9·5 as against 11 millions, that is, 86 per cent; ordinary workers 6·3 as against 8·3 million, that is 76 per cent. In 1942 the drop was particularly steep and alarming: the number of workers and employees in the heavy metallurgical industry fell to less than half that of 1940 and the shortage of trained personnel – engineers and technicians – was even greater and more serious than that of workers. The situation did not begin to recover until 1943 and it never became entirely satisfactory.

Increasing the number of working hours had been a temporary remedy at first but its inevitable consequences had been a falling-off in individual output. The movement of employees from the tertiary to secondary sectors was also of some help but its scope was bound to be limited. Directing labour to work of special priority was another remedy: thus the labour force employed in the armament industry was increased at the expense of the consumer industries; although at the end of 1942 the number of workers in the aircraft industry was moving towards that employed in 1940, in the textile industries it was only fifty per cent; that is to say, the standard of living was being forced down. True, the workers' enthusiasm and competitive spirit were stimulated by an intensive campaign in which the Komsomols played the leading part; but its effects were bound to be moral rather than practical; there is a limit to human strength.

The solution was thus to bring new social categories into the labour force. Here too the movement had started before the war when the Ukraine kolkhozians had been switched to the mines. We must leave aside the forced-labour camps and resign ourselves to ignorance as to their number and size, as Soviet historians are very discreet on the subject and although they are no longer taboo as a subject for discussion, they are still taboo as a subject for study. On February 13, 1942, a decree mobilised all the able-bodied urban population; it applied to men from 16 to 55 years of age and women from 16 to 45. They were put under the control of the 'Labour Force Statistics and Allocation Committee'. Twelve million new workers thus became available for productive work, most of them women and young people. In 1940, women represented 38 per cent of the entire labour force; at the end of the war this proportion had risen to 55 per cent; in agriculture it had reached 71 per cent by 1943. Three million women became factory workers; they formed nine-tenths of the textile labour force but they also worked in the mines, in the petro-chemical industries, turning, welding, etc. As for the young people, the proportion of under-18s employed in the economy was 15 per cent in 1942; 750,000 girls were directed to the mines, railways and metallurgical industries.

This labour force was not mobilised in their home towns but assembled in certain urban and industrial centres; most of the time, to save transport, this labour force was made up from those living in the vicinity of the towns, but sometimes the call-up concerned one particular branch of activity – the whole population of one region, for example, was directed into coal-mining. By the end of 1942 nearly 800,000 urban workers had been called up for full-time employment; but there were in addition more than 1,400,000 seasonal workers; 800,000 young men had been directed into technical schools since it was clear that the qualifications of this make-shift labour force left a good deal to be desired.

Building huts, digging and working in the fields was relatively easy. But when a factory had been rebuilt and had received and reassembled its plant, you still had to have workers capable of running it; and in the Moscow factories in January 1942 out of 280,000 workmen, barely 15,000 had received adequate professional training; so in 1942, the Moscow Central Party Committee opened eleven schools of metallurgy and thirty-nine of various other trades in Moscow itself.

The result was a mixed success. Overall, between 1941 and 1945, 2,500,000 skilled workers, or described as such, received training. In fact, it had not been possible always to set high standards; the newcomers had often merely been put into a gang and the foremen or older workers undertook to teach them the practice. In the schools, theoretical training was limited to six months; the rest was picked up in the factories. In certain branches of industry, where the work was of a particularly delicate nature, the shortcomings of the training were never made good.

Organisation was not everything and enthusiasm even less. It is difficult to agree with Rascate when he speaks of 500-per cent or even 1,000-per cent increases in production. But perhaps he is talking about special cases and levels that were particularly low in 1940. But it is a fact that war production in the USSR did increase considerably and that its workers did succeed in producing, at the right time 'the steel that wins a war'.

IX WAR PRODUCTION IN THE USSR

Soviet war production thus falls very clearly into a series of phases of development. After war was declared, the year 1941 was spent in the gigantic evacuation of factories to the east; it was thus bound to be marked by a sharp fall in output; factories had to be built or adapted and machinery reassembled; the necessary power resources were often lacking. It was from this point of view that 'General Winter' saved the Soviet Union; it is true that he made reconstruction slower and more difficult but he did not stop it, whereas he had put a stop to the Wehrmacht's all-conquering advance which, had it continued, would have made any reconstruction impossible – or pointless as a result of the defeat of the Red Army.

The evacuation continued in 1942 but the factories that had been moved were now beginning to go into production and an enormous labour force had been mobilised, trained and set to work. However, at the beginning of the year, production reached its lowest point; it rose in the spring and by the summer it had reached the 1940 level. Barring grave military setbacks – and this was the great importance of the battle of Stalingrad – economic victory was in sight.

From 1943 onwards, the impetus had been given and development was swift and steady. But overall the economy was stagnant, if not indeed in regression; certain losses were irretrievable; the switch to the east was no wonder-cure and would never lead to a revival; it was merely a last resort to ensure essentials.

And the essential thing was the output of armaments, and this continued to rise. To begin with, improved methods or greater skill on the part of workers frequently shortened production schedules: a fighter aircraft which took 20,000 hours to produce in 1941 needed only 12,500 in 1943 and a howitzer 2,400 hours compared with 4,500; the T 34 tank, 3,700 hours as against 8,000. These do not seem to be exceptional figures but they cannot have been the rule.

But an increasing number of weapons for the services certainly was the rule. By 1942, the USSR was producing 25,400 aircraft, 24,600 tanks and almost 30,000 field guns, as compared with the German output of 15,400, 9,300 and 12,000 respectively. Above all, the output of Stormovik tactical aircraft and T 34 tanks, both of which had proved their worth, moved to top priority – from July to December 1942 the T 34 tanks represented sixty-one per cent.

In 1943 production figures rose to 34,900 aircraft (11,193 of them

Stormoviks), 24,000 tanks and 130,000 guns. In 1944, these figures were 40,000 aircraft, 29,000 tanks and 122,000 guns.

According to Colonel Kravchenko, between 1941 and 1945, the USSR thus produced 142,800 military aircraft, 102,500 tanks or armoured cars, 490,000 guns of which 92,000 were of more than 75-mm calibre. These figures are second only to those of the United States; they greatly exceed Britain's and Germany's. From 1943 onwards, the Red Army not only possessed superiority in numbers over the Wehrmacht but also a superior quantity of equipment of equally good quality. As there was no lack of fighting spirit and high competence amongst young Russian marshals either, the way to victory lay wide open.

It is clear that Russia's immense size and climate had prevented her from being smashed by the German Blitzkrieg as France had been. But these were only positive assets inasmuch as they gained time for the Russians. The Soviet leaders undoubtedly took maximum advantage of them. If Stalin is to take his share of blame for the setbacks it seems only fair to give him his credit for the successes. But the Communist party probably deserves the greater share: one Soviet writer after another says this and keeps on saying it, and although propaganda may play some part, there is truth in what they say. However, it is not Marxist-Leninist doctrine which was the cause of their success; that had been temporarily shelved. And it was only partly the earlier achievements of the régime because these had been largely conquered or destroyed by the invader. But the Party had provided the perfect framework and the enthusiasm needed by the whole population; more accurately, the economic machine began to function as a whole once the Party had been completely reformed after the losses caused by mobilisation. This was the result of the immense propaganda effort and the fine example of the 3 million Communists scattered throughout the Soviet Union, preaching the good word as well as showing the way.

The Party was able to share out the various tasks and by appealing to national feeling ensure that everyone gave of his best. The Soviet people learned to work in suffering, to hope in disaster and to build while fighting. Not only were no scandalous gains made from the national misfortune – economic collectivisation saw to that – but it is difficult to see how anyone could have failed to bear his share of the national burden either by suffering under the occupation or as a soldier at the front or as a producer on the home front. Greater equality began to exist between the regions, between Russia in Europe and Russia in Asia. But above all, as Girault writes, 'the peoples of the Soviet Union were united in their suffering and their struggle, their troubles and, in the end, their joys.' In the eyes of the Russian people both the régime and the Party benefited by being identified with the salvation of immortal Mother Russia.

SUMMARY TABLE OF SOVIET WAR PRODUCTION

	1940	1st half of 1941	1942	1943	1944	1945 (10 months)
Cast iron (millions of tons)	14·9	9·1	5	5·5	7·2	8·8
Percentage from the east	28					
Steel (millions of tons)	18·3	11·4	4·8	8·4	10·8	12·2
Percentage from the east	37					
Rolled sheet (millions of tons)	13·1	8·2	5·4	5·6	7·8	8·4
Military aircraft (modern)	A few dozen	3,950 (2nd half of 1941)	25,437	34,900	40,300	26,478
Tanks (and machine-gun carriers)	2,794	4,742	24,668	24,000	29,000	22,590
Artillery (guns)			29,561	130,000	122,000	77,000
Labour force (in millions)	30	26·2	18·4	27·5		

CHAPTER 4

The Strange Alliance

HITLER turned the Soviet Union first into Britain's ally and then into the ally of the United States. These reluctant allies were all aware of the need to maintain their agreement throughout the war and to continue it after it was over. But their reasons for fighting and their aims were as entirely different as their mentality and behaviour. Hence understanding was difficult and there was deep distrust, mutual suspicion and frequent clashes.

The alliance required constant adjustment and it never functioned with perfect smoothness. Moreover these reluctant allies did not all have the same opponents. Stalin had to press Churchill for several months to make Britain declare war on the Axis satellites; he himself waited until 1945 before declaring war on Japan; the United States never broke with Finland, and the Soviet Union only intervened in Bulgaria in order to divert her from the Anglo-Saxons. By its very existence, therefore, the alliance set permanent problems and the leader of the American mission in Moscow, General John R. Deane, well placed to see how it worked, called it the strange alliance.

In view of the individual role that each leader played in his own country, the proper working of this strange alliance would clearly depend first of all on Churchill's, Roosevelt's and Stalin's conception of it, on their aims and on the relationship that they managed to establish between themselves.

I THE RELATIONSHIP BETWEEN CHURCHILL, ROOSEVELT
AND STALIN

Their correspondence, which deals with all sorts of subjects, enables us to see this relationship from inside. Churchill and Roosevelt were attempting to bring Stalin into their circle of trust and friendship; they wrote to him on a personal note and they spared no pains to win him over. 'I consider our personal relations of the greatest importance,' Churchill wrote to him, and he passed information on to him which he described as confidential and which he asked him to keep to himself, as if the request had some chance of being met. Roosevelt was so convinced of his persuasive charm that in May 1943 he suggested a private talk between the two of them, with only an interpreter and a typist present. Whenever they met him, the two Anglo-Saxons were convivial and unceremonious, and the Georgian cleverly responded; thus he made the impression, particularly on Roosevelt, of being a 'good fellow' who could be trusted and whose frankness was attractive, even if tinged with toughness; in any case, pleasanter and more open than that Siberian block of ice, Molotov.

Churchill and Roosevelt were convinced – like Hitler and Ribbentrop before them – that the time when the Politburo was preparing world revolution was past and that patriotism would henceforth be stronger than Communism in the USSR – Communistic patriotism seemed a contradiction in terms. Roosevelt went furthest in this direction; he believed that his personal relationship with Stalin would put an end to the Soviet's distrust of capitalism – a happy result which, in his view, Churchill would be unable to achieve since he was the champion of imperialism based on a system of monarchy. Consequently, the President of the United States considered that the clever thing to do was to maintain a balance between his partners; thus the appearance of the Soviet Union on the scene sometimes threatened the good understanding existing between Britain and America. Wendell Wilkie, his unsuccessful opponent in the presidential elections who became his envoy in the USSR, also stated, after being two days in Moscow, that 'there was not all that much difference between the American and Russian viewpoints'.

So in their correspondence we can see the two Western statesmen persistently wooing their heaven-sent ally, towards whom they felt a certain embarrassment because they were leaving him to bear the brunt of Hitler's attack on his own and they were prepared to accept and bear with his perpetual dissatisfaction; they took care not to rake up his recent shady associations but they were frequently brought up short by Stalin's cold realism. The latter never minced his words; he reminded Churchill that 'Britain would never have been able to continue the war without the help of the USSR' and when the British Premier complained of his correspondent's rather uncharitable criticisms of him, Stalin replied: 'It's a matter of personal contacts, so I speak my mind and you cannot regard it as an insult.' Stalin constantly displayed a touchy national pride and he persistently brought the correspondence back to the points which concerned him and to meeting his requests.

Consequently, little by little, mutual distrust grew up between them, irresistibly. A political and social rift separated the two Allied camps; it was made deeper by religious feeling: American Roman Catholic circles had expressed themselves against any collaboration with atheistic Communism. For his part, Stalin misjudged the importance and the role of American public opinion. The head of the American mission in Moscow, General Deane, very quickly realised the deep lack of understanding between the three leaders, despite the superficial cordiality of the correspondence which merely skated over the surface; he did not succeed in establishing personal relations with the Soviet military leaders with whom he had to work; in two years not one of them dared to invite him to his home; he did not even meet them except on very special occasions. This is how he described his disappointment to Marshall: 'We never make any request or suggestion that is not greeted with suspicion; the Soviets have absolutely no idea that any one can give without wanting to receive, with the result that even our gifts arouse their distrust.'

In fact, their reasons for lack of understanding and for distrust were deep-rooted. The Soviet Union, which had suffered invasion and which was for a long time the underdog, or even at bay, believed that her allies were not averse to letting her grow weaker, indeed were perhaps even doing it deliberately in order to impose their own terms on her when peace came. Even though they did not mention it, the British and Americans had not forgotten the German-Soviet pact; they were afraid that Hitler and Stalin might think it in their interest to revert to it and conclude a separate peace or at least reach a compromise to put an end to their hostilities. Against this sufficiently gloomy background, the Polish problem was going to cast so heavy a shadow as to make any permanent sweetness and light between the two parties impossible.

However, there was one point on which the three great powers were in agreement and this was that the decisions which committed the Allies must be taken by the three of them alone, like members of a sort of exclusive club. They exchanged envoys with each other who enjoyed their complete confidence; they paid visits to each other; and they met in conferences to take the major decisions required by the defeat of Germany and the advent of peace – at Teheran, Yalta and Potsdam. Thus the alliance jogged along until the surrender first of Germany and then of Japan.

II THE ANGLO-RUSSIAN ALLIANCE

At the time of the Wehrmacht's invasion, Stalin had been afraid lest Britain might have been notified of Hitler's peace proposals and jumped at the opportunity of extricating herself from the conflict on honourable terms. For their part, the British wondered whether the USSR would really fight and Lord Beaverbrook asked Maisky, the Soviet ambassador in London: 'Won't what happened in France happen to you?' Churchill immediately reassured the Soviet leader's fears; on July 3 he wrote to Stalin: 'We shall do everything to help you that time, geography and our growing resources permit' and on July 12 an alliance for the duration of the war was agreed upon in principle. The stubborn fighting of the Red Army provided the British with the reply to their question.

But Stalin would not be satisfied with words: he called for the signing of a properly drawn-up treaty of alliance. He thought that Britain could despatch forty or so divisions to the Continent without further delay, to France, Archangel or the Balkans, since the Wehrmacht had denuded western Europe of troops, and he told Churchill so in a letter of July 18. He demanded supplies of equipment and gave a detailed list of his requirements, not only to the British ambassador, Cripps, but also to Roosevelt's envoy, Hopkins, at a time when the United States had not yet entered the war.

The Americans were hesitant about cutting down their supplies to the British in favour of the Russians, and the first convoy for the USSR did not leave for Archangel until August 12. As for the British, seeing the speed of the German advance, they wondered whether the Soviet Union had not already lost the war in Europe; this was doubtless what Churchill had in mind when he suggested sending Wavell, the Commander-in-Chief of the Indian operational theatre, to Moscow – would they not be reduced to planning for Anglo-Russian co-operation in Asia?

The fact remains that when they signed the Atlantic Charter the British and Americans systematically ignored the Soviet Union; certain clauses as to the 'right of self-determination of peoples' and 'the renunciation of territorial advantages' seemed to apply just as much to their ally as to their enemy. A trip to Moscow by Eden in the second half of December 1941 did not clear up all the misapprehensions. True, Churchill had previously written to Stalin that 'the fact that Russia was a Communist state did not present any obstacle to working out a proper plan to ensure our mutual security and legitimate interests'. But, at a time when the German offensive against the capital had barely been halted – and nobody knew how long for – Stalin had already listed to Eden in Moscow some of his peace claims: restoring Russian influence in the Baltic countries and redrawing the Polish frontier along the 'Curzon line' – which meant recognition by the Allies of the territorial gains acquired by the Soviet Union as a result of the German-Soviet pact (in return, Stalin recognised Britain's right to establish and maintain bases in France, Belgium, Holland, Denmark and Norway).

However, realising that he had done the wrong thing, Stalin did not insist on this delicate point. At the beginning of 1942, he signed the United Nations Pact, a new version of the Atlantic Charter. But in exchange he asked for the immediate opening of a second front and remained unconvinced by Churchill's arguments that he lacked the necessary shipping, aircraft and manpower.

The United States' entry into the war opened up new prospects but brought no immediate change; in Washington, the British and American military leaders realised that there was no possibility of landing in Europe in 1942. It was poor consolation when on May 26, 1942 Churchill signed an Anglo-Soviet treaty of co-operation for twenty years with Stalin. The first part of the pact confirmed the alliance signed on July 12 for the duration of the war, plus the pledge that neither party would open separate negotiations with Hitler's Germany – this was the great fear that each had with regard to the other. The second part foreshadowed post-war co-operation to preserve peace and ensure their mutual security against any further German aggression.

However, there were two articles which showed that there were limits to the trust between the two countries; each of the contracting parties pledged herself not to make any territorial acquisitions on her own account and not to intervene in the internal affairs of other states. Churchill offered his own paraphrase of the articles in a statement he made to Eden in October 1942: 'It would be a disaster if Russian barbarism swamped the culture and independence of the countries of Europe.' Yet it was necessary to help the Soviet Union not to succumb beneath the hammer-blows of the Wehrmacht; so the USSR was admitted to the lend-lease club.

III LEND-LEASE AND THE USSR

Harriman, Roosevelt's special envoy in Moscow, somewhat incautiously promised Stalin 400 tanks and 300 aircraft to be delivered in two convoys per month, starting in July 1942; but the difficulties of shipping them were enormous and the risks very great.

First of all there was the shipping problem. As the Soviet Navy was in no position to provide the necessary protection, the Royal Navy had to take over the task, although Britain had accepted no commitment on this score. The Admiralty declared itself unable to guarantee more than two convoys of twenty-five ships a month or three convoys of twenty-five or thirty-five ships every two months. This had to be accepted as a beginning. Thus, at great cost to themselves, the British and the Americans intended to deliver to the Russians' own ports equipment that the recipients always considered to be inadequate or unsuited to their needs and while never ceasing to clamour for it, they denied that it had any beneficial effect on the course of the fighting.

The shortest way was the Great North Circle although New York was separated by 4,500 miles from the Soviet port of Murmansk, which was ice-free in winter. But as it passed through the Orkneys, the Phaeroes, Jan de Mayen and Bear Island, this shipping route ran along the southern limits of the ice-pack; the cold, the fog, the Arctic night and the icebergs made it arduous and dangerous. In the spring, danger came from German submarines and warships – the *Scharnhorst*, the *Gneisenau*, with their escorts, were sent up north after escaping from Brest. After being promised since August 1941, the first of the tanks – twenty of them in all – did not arrive until October; far from being effusively grateful, Stalin complained that they were badly crated and came in dismantled form.

At the end of May 1942, a convoy carrying 125,000 tons lost a fifth of its cargo – 7 ships out of 35, 147 tanks and 77 aircraft. At the end of June, out of 36 ships, only 11 reached their destination, with 164 tanks, 37 aircraft and 896 vehicles of various sorts. The fourteenth convoy which sailed during the period of the midnight sun, which acted as a magnificent searchlight for the submarines, had to turn back; and in view of this Churchill preferred to cancel the next one. At the end of 1942 results were rather disappointing; either because he failed to appreciate or refused to see the difficulties Stalin let loose a flood of recriminations especially attacking the reductions in some supplies – in particular tin and copper – which had been needed for the war in the Pacific.

There was another safer route joining the Persian Gulf with the Caspian Sea via Iran, a neutral state; but it was much longer – the Iranian ports were 13,000 miles away from the ports on the American Pacific coast. In addition, there were a large number of active and influential Germans in Iran – according to Israelian they maintained 4,000 agents there. On August 25, 1941 the Russians and the British asked the Shah to expel the Germans; on his refusal to do so, without any ultimatum troops of the two Allies converged on Teheran, forced the Shah to abdicate and leave the country and signed a treaty of alliance with his successor guaranteeing his independence.

Anglo-Russian co-operation had proved satisfactory. Later on, difficulties arose; when tribal leaders revolted against the central government, the British suspected the Russians of supporting the Kurdish independence movement in the north of the country. Next, after the British had obtained oil concessions in the zone they were occupying, it was the Russians' turn to claim equivalent privileges in theirs and they unleashed their propaganda against the Iranian government when it refused.

As for transporting American equipment to the USSR, which was the prime aim of the occupation of Iran, this met with enormous obstacles. Building a road was beyond the capacity of the British; there was only one railway and it was a single line from Teheran to the north of Iran. The British commandeered rolling-stock from India, where it was in short

supply anyway, thus providing plenty of fuel for the Indian nationalists'
anti-British propaganda. It was quite plain that this route was too slow
and complicated to be used effectively by the Anglo-Saxons to supply the
USSR.

However, the former thought that it could be used to provide the
Soviet Union with military assistance, an aspect which was strongly
stressed by the British ambassador, Stafford Cripps. One way would be
first of all to relieve the USSR of the task of occupying Iran; Churchill
suggested to Stalin taking over the occupation entirely with British
troops, thus releasing some four to six Soviet divisions; Stalin saw this
suggestion as the desire of the British to take the whole of Iran under their
protection and a refusal to fight except vicariously through their allies. The
second way consisted of sending troops to the Caucasus; Churchill
suggested two divisions at the beginning of 1942 and Roosevelt a few
squadrons. Stalin again refused; he wanted no foreign western troops on
Soviet soil; this reluctance showed itself in constant tiresome interference
with the British sailors at Murmansk, which caused great resentment. The
only exception he made was for Free France; after having suggested
sending a brigade which was kicking its heels in the Middle East waiting
for the British to use it, de Gaulle sent the *Normandie-Niemen* Air Force
regiment to the USSR.

Far from solving the difficulties between the Allies, lend-lease only
added to them. Soviet historians play down the generosity of their allies;
Israelian has written that the rate of delivery was ridiculously slow and
that the Anglo-Saxons were less keen on helping to strengthen the Red
Army than in letting it exhaust itself against Germany. Colonel Kravchenko assessed Anglo-Saxon aid at 8·9 per cent of the Soviet's own production of tanks and 1·5 for all other supplies; during the last year of the
war, the percentage reached a level of less than 3 per cent.

Nevertheless, Allied supplies to the USSR, almost entirely from America,
amounted in the course of the whole war to the not inconsiderable total of
11,000 million dollars, a sum never repaid. By the northern route alone,
from July 1943 till March 1944 5,000 tanks, 7,000 aircraft and 7,000 cars
and lorries were shipped; by the southern route, 2,000 locomotives. In
addition to armaments, munitions and vehicles, there were all kinds of
products which were in short supply in the Soviet Union – medical
supplies for example. This aid did not save the Russians in their moment
of greatest crisis – they had restored the situation on the Moscow front
before it reached them and its use set them certain problems; by itself, it
could not ensure their victory; and it was not a great deal compared with
the giant effort of their own population. While all this is true, nonetheless
it was of value to them, above all during the difficult summers of 1942 and
1943, although its usefulness declined in 1944. Stalin was not merely

being polite (this was not his habit anyway) when he told Roosevelt at the Teheran conference: 'Without American supplies we should have lost the war.' Previously, in February 1942, he had already expressed his gratitude for the two 1,000 million dollar loans that the US had granted the USSR.

IV THE PROBLEM OF THE SECOND FRONT

As early as September 1941 Stalin had made an urgent request which from then onwards 'was the leitmotif of his whole relationship with his two allies. 'The USSR is fighting on her own and is in mortal danger; the only thing to do is to pin down thirty German divisions elsewhere' – something which the tiny operational theatre of Cyrenaica was plainly incapable of doing. His double statement was amply confirmed by facts and figures. According to captured German documents, Soviet historians estimate the number of German divisions committed in the USSR as follows: in June 1941, 190; on November 1, 1942, 266; on July 1, 1943, 232; on May 1, 1944, 259; on May 1, 1945, 206. This meant that, on those dates, the percentage of enemy forces opposing the Red Army alone was respectively: 70, 72, 66, 53, 60. The pressure relaxed somewhat in the course of time but never completely; from the beginning to the end of the war, ever since she had joined in, the USSR bore the heaviest share of the joint struggle.

True, Stalin was quite happy to forget that before June 1941 Britain and France had faced Germany alone, whilst the USSR was congratulating the latter on her success and providing her with equipment; and that France had foundered in the uneven struggle. Once and for all, he had adopted the attitude of a creditor claiming his due. It was quite obvious that he had no conception of the difficulties of a landing and the enormous resources needed for its success. Churchill was forced to tell him: 'You have so much land that you do not find it easy to understand that we can only live and fight as our sea-links permit.'

Although he told Cripps that, after all, 'Stalin was only reaping what he had sown', Churchill was keen to relieve his exacting partner; as early as the summer of 1941, he was contemplating an operation in Norway and his military advisers were hard put to it to prove how impossible it was.

In April 1942, Roosevelt asked Stalin to send Molotov to Washington. All that Stalin's right-hand man could talk about was the second front. But when Roosevelt suggested cutting down on the equipment being sent to the USSR in order to increase the resources needed for a second front and hasten its opening, Molotov was annoyed; he wanted both together. After consulting Marshall, Roosevelt promised that the second front would be opened in the course of 1942; the 'Bolero–Round-up' plan was then worked out to satisfy Stalin.

When the plan proved not to be feasible and was replaced by Operation 'Torch', Churchill, who was responsible for the decision, had the unwelcome task of informing Stalin. He went to Moscow in the course of the summer of 1942. Stalin made no bones about his displeasure; he realised the strategic importance of 'Torch', but 'in the plainest possible terms, he could not agree that the opening of the second front should be put off till 1943'.

When the situation of the Soviet armies at Stalingrad became critical the Americans proposed a scaled-down version of 'Bolero' which they called 'Sledgehammer'. But the British were afraid that even this reduced version might jeopardise the success of 'Torch'; they were also scared of a costly failure which would have serious consequences and the indifferent results of the Dieppe raid seemed to justify their view. However, when the landing in French North Africa proved a success, Stalin was generous in his congratulation of the Allies; he approved everything they did, even the 'exploitation of Darlan'; 'you must know how to use the Devil and his grandmother', he wrote to Roosevelt.

But with his success at Stalingrad to support him, he quickly returned to the charge: when was there going to be a real second front? He demanded that it be opened by the spring of 1943 at the latest. It was partly in order to satisfy him that in Casablanca Roosevelt invented the formula of the 'unconditional surrender' of their common foes. But Stalin was greatly disappointed that the only direct attack against Germany was going to be an intensification of the bombing; he considered that the Tunisian campaign and the subsequent landings in Sicily were not really the second front that was required, any more than 'Torch' had been.

So in February 1943, Churchill promised that the landing across the Channel would take place in August or September 1943. But by that date, although the fall of Italy seemed near, preparations for 'Overlord' were far from complete and once again the promise had to be cancelled. What was Stalin's attitude going to be when faced by this fresh evasion? Roosevelt and Churchill were worried, and to straighten things out, they suggested meeting Stalin.

The Russians had no doubt about the intentions of the Anglo-Saxons; they were administering just enough oxygen to prevent the Russians from suffocating without making them really strong. Thus Ambassador Maisky wrote that after the Soviet successes at Stalingrad, the Allies estimated that the USSR was out of danger and could look after herself. This was certainly not in Roosevelt's mind or in those of his military advisers; but it is not certain if it was not in Churchill's mind. In any case, the British Premier was a past master in the art of diverting the Americans from their own plans in order to lead them on to objectives more in line with British interests. His behaviour did not escape the notice of the Russians who began to look to Roosevelt to satisfy their wishes. But any closer understanding between the British and Americans and the USSR presupposed a satisfactory solution to the deep rift between the Polish exile government in London and the one in Moscow.

V THE POLISH PROBLEM BEFORE STALINGRAD

Britain had entered the war to defend the integrity and independence of Poland and after the defeat of their armies, the Poles had continued to fight, within and without the frontiers of their country. Now Poland had been dismembered, oppressed and depopulated as much by the Russians as by the Germans. Hitler's aggression against the USSR had abruptly brought the Poles and the Russians together into the same camp; but it very quickly became apparent that although they were allies, their war aims and specifically those concerned with Polish territory were so diametrically opposed as to make them irreconcilable enemies. The British and Americans were thus caught between two of their allies; in addition, the British were bound by their pledges towards Poland; the Americans were freer in that respect; but how could Roosevelt reconcile his crusade for every sort of freedom with the sacrifice of a small state to the ambitions of a larger one because it was an ally of the United States – in a word, to let Stalin have something that he had refused Hitler?

The Polish-Soviet rift was as simple as it was dramatic: Poland wanted to return to her 1939 frontiers after the war; Stalin intended to hold on to the eastern Polish territories that he had been able to annex through the German-Soviet pact.

General Sikorski's government in London was composed of representatives of the four democratic parties that had opposed Marshal Pilsudski's dictatorship; but this did not make it pro-Russian. However, Sikorski realised that the entry of the USSR into the Allied camp was an important new factor that had to be reckoned with. He therefore set about trying to reach an agreement with Stalin; he felt that he was being sufficiently magnanimous in not claiming any compensation or reparations for the damage caused by the Russians in Poland and demanding only his rights: recognition of the eastern frontier of Poland as laid down in the Treaty of Riga – the 1939 frontiers – and the release of all the Polish citizens captured, deported or interned in the USSR, which he calculated at 1,500,000.

Stalin would accept only a vague formula that the 'Soviet-German treaties were no longer valid'; this did not amount to a guarantee; but, under pressure from the British, the Poles pretended that it was satis-factory, though not before three ministers had expressed their disagree-ment by resigning. However, in August 1941 a military agreement between Poland and Russia provided for the raising of a Polish army from amongst the Polish prisoners taken by the Red Army, which the USSR would equip and supply with the American equipment granted to Poland under lend-lease.

But in December 1941, the Russians showed their hand. Stalin suggested to Eden that a protocol should be added to the projected Anglo-Russian agreement, recognising the rights of the Soviet Union to the Baltic states and east Poland. Churchill's reaction to this was extremely sharp: 'this transfer of territories', he wrote to Eden, 'would be contrary to the aims which we are fighting for; there can be no question of drawing up fron-tiers before peace is signed.' Stalin did not insist – after all the Germans were at the gates of Moscow: he even signed the Atlantic Charter, but with a significant reservation which was expressed verbally by his delegate, the Soviet ambassador in London, who signed on his behalf, 'that the Charter would necessarily have to be adapted to historical conditions, needs and particular circumstances.'

General Sikorski was realistic enough not to apply pressure at the sore points. During a visit to Moscow he confined himself to emphasising by the way, as something self-evident, that 'the 1939 borders must not be revised'. But the implementation of the military agreement was not all that easy. Stalin quite plainly had no great liking for this Polish army that was being released in rags and tatters from Soviet prisons and camps in order to be armed by its gaolers. Instead of the Polish units fighting in Europe with the Red Army and one day returning to Poland with them, Sikorski was forced to agree to their being transferred to Iran and trained and equipped by the British. The commander of the new army, General Anders, was surprised to find so few officers among the 180,000 released prisoners of war. Sikorski expressed his amazement to Stalin who merely replied that they had all, in fact, been released. Despite the chill caused by Anders' discovery, an assistance pact was signed between Poland and Russia providing in vague terms for 'friendly collaboration after the war'. It was not perfect harmony but neither was it a breakdown of relations between them.

However, the exiled Polish government in London had put forward to the Czech government under Beneš a proposal for a Polish-Czech federa-tion as a first step towards the later amalgamation of the two countries, thus putting a stop to the old enmity which had been further fanned by Poland's participation in the dismemberment of Czechoslovakia after the Munich agreement. Beneš agreed only to a confederation of the two separate states, provided, however, with certain joint organisations such as a committee of ministers, general staff, foreign policy and parliamentary delegations. In January 1942, the two governments issued a joint declaration of agreement in principle and called on other European nations to join them. The Soviet government immediately evinced their hostility to what seemed to it to be a resurrection of the *cordon sanitaire* that had been set up immediately after the First World War. Beneš did not succeed in pacifying it by proposing tripartite collaboration between the Soviet Union, Czechoslovakia and Poland; on the contrary, this broader proposal met with opposition from the Poles. This veto by the Kremlin nipped the confederation in the bud; Beneš retreated to his tent and Polish-Soviet relations were manifestly not improved.

But if the Soviet Union's intentions towards Poland were so blatant at a time when the Wehrmacht was threatening Russia's very existence, what would they be after Stalingrad, when the danger seemed to be over?

VI THE POLISH PROBLEM AFTER STALINGRAD

In fact, at the beginning of 1942, Stalin took two further measures. On the one hand, he issued a decree whereby the hundreds of thousands of displaced Poles from eastern Poland who had moved into the Soviet Union became Soviet citizens – and the Polish government, under pressure from the British, decided not to protest. On the other hand, he formed the Union of Polish Patriots under Wanda Wasilevska, a Polish Communist writer married to a Soviet Ukrainian and herself a colonel in the Red Army. A Polish organisation in Moscow functioning independently of the legal Polish government could only mean a threat to set up a dissident movement. This time the Polish government complained bitterly to its British and American allies; but they seemed relatively unmoved.

The fact was that, impelled by an obvious sad but inescapable necessity, their views were gradually changing: how could they continue to demand that the USSR bear the brunt of the German onslaught almost alone and not keep their promises with regard to the opening of a second front, yet still refuse her any satisfaction with regard to her future frontiers in the west – a satisfaction which might in any case be given at the expense of Germany, since the latter was by definition excluded from benefiting from the Atlantic Charter? In this web of opposing interests, it was hardly possible that the weakest of all, Poland, should fail to be the scapegoat.

Moreover, the British themselves were beginning to find the attitude of the Poles in London rather tiresome. Their press was continually attacking the USSR; they confessed to Eden their hope and ambition that with the Soviet Union weakened and Germany crushed, Poland might become the most powerful central European western state. When he went to visit

Roosevelt at the beginning of 1943, Sikorski made no bones about his wish to abolish the Polish corridor and the east Prussian enclave for the aggrandisement of Poland; he spoke of the Oder as Poland's western frontier without relinquishing any of his claims in the east.

In March 1943 Eden and Roosevelt came to an agreement that after the war the Soviet Union should keep Bessarabia and the part of Finland which she had conquered in 1940; true, Romania and Finland were enemy countries and Roosevelt vigorously refused to make any concession regarding the Baltic states; nevertheless, it was a first step towards recognising the Soviet's June 1941 frontiers.

But in April 1943, there came a bombshell. After the discovery of the corpses of several thousand Polish officers buried at Katyn, the Germans launched a big anti-Soviet campaign. Were they the bodies of the officers that Anders had been vainly looking for in Russia? Polish diplomats had previously been arrested in Moscow; two leaders of the Polish Jewish Socialist Party, the Bund, who had taken refuge in the USSR and, at the Soviet Union's request, had founded an anti-Fascist Jewish World Committee, had been accused of complicity with the Nazis and executed – covered with abuse and murdered, like all Stalin's enemies. General Sikorski asked for an investigation by the International Red Cross which the Soviet Union rejected. However, an investigation did take place, conducted by the Germans; it concluded that the Soviet Union was guilty and the Poles accepted its findings. *Pravda* replied by accusing Sikorski of being Hitler's accomplice – an accusation for which no evidence was offered – and Stalin broke off relations with the Polish government in London. For the British and Americans, as for neutral public opinion, there was hardly any doubt that the horrible crime was the work of the Russians, committed either by Stalin's deliberate wish to destroy the Polish officer class or by subordinates who panicked at the time of the German attack.

Stalin now raised the Kosciusko Division in the USSR, which received Polish uniforms and was officered by Poles from the annexed Polish territories who had served in the Red Army – in fact, a sort of rival to Anders' army. He granted official Soviet support to Wasilevska's Union of Polish Patriots, which was joined by a number of Polish Communists who had hitherto been reduced to silence when not interned – an embryonic Polish government for the future and perhaps the only one that the Soviet Union would one day recognise.

The British and Americans realised that they must at all costs achieve some compromise. But on July 4 Sikorski was killed in an air crash. His successor, Mikolajczyk, was a moderate but he lacked his predecessor's authority and his War Minister, Soznkovski, was an obdurate anti-Communist.

Accordingly, when in September 1943 Eden put forward the compromise proposal agreed between the British and the Americans in Quebec, giving the Russians the Curzon line as their frontier in the west but offering Poland the compensation of east Prussia and part of Silesia, Mikolajczyk turned down the bargain; he had no right to lop off part of Poland by a revision of her eastern frontiers; such a plan, he said, not without foresight, would only lead to Poland's becoming a Soviet satellite.

The Polish problem, together with that of the second front, was to be in the forefront of the discussions that the three great powers decided to hold at Teheran in the autumn of 1943.

VII SECRET NEGOTIATIONS?

However, the 'strange allies' were mutually suspicious that each was trying to negotiate with the enemy behind the other's back. In February 1943, Moscow had been disturbed at contacts made in Geneva by a high-ranking ss officer, the Prince of Hohenlohe, with Allen Dulles, the head of the American intelligence services in Geneva.

In March 1943, the American State Secretariat was made aware of vague proposals coming from Romania via the Argentine ambassador in Paris – a circuitous route. These referred to Hitler's desire to come to terms with the British and Americans so as to conserve his forces for the struggle against Communism. Cordell Hull made no attempt to follow them up; but no mention of them seems to have been made to the Russians.

On roughly the same date, Himmler is said to have enquired of the Americans, via the Swedes, as to the exact meaning of the formula 'unconditional surrender'; he received no reply; and although this step is authenticated by a despatch sent to Roosevelt by Harrison and published by the Americans, the Swedes deny it.

On their part, at the beginning of 1943 the Hungarians had begun to bargain with the British to negotiate their withdrawal from the war, save the régime and protect Hungary from a Soviet occupation by joining in the fight against the Germans. One cannot say whether the Russians were informed of these approaches.

But as a rule they were kept very well informed by their agents. They themselves had been sounded by one of Ribbentrop's collaborators, Peter Kleist, who had confided in a businessman called Clauss of undefined nationality, who frequented the Soviet embassy in Stockholm and whom Kleist has described as a Soviet agent. The Germans are said to have informed the Russians, via Clauss, that they were prepared to come back to the 1914 frontiers in the east – another way of settling the Polish problem by private arrangement between Germany and Russia.

Molotov informed Harriman of these contacts but only some months later and describing Clauss as a German agent.

In January 1944, it was the Russians' turn to be alarmed. We find *Pravda* referring to talks between Ribbentrop and the British in Cairo. Churchill had to write to Stalin categorically denying these rumours.

Were these really attempts at 'secession' or merely the sort of contacts that countries at war always maintain even in the thick of the fighting, by means of more or less official agents, in order to keep their finger on their opponent's pulse? In any case, none of these attempted negotiations came to anything; that they should be known and should continue could, however, only aggravate the third reason for disagreement between the Allies, in addition to the second front and the Polish problem. This was the fear of each of the parties that one of them might negotiate a separate peace and leave the other holding the baby and compelled to settle their joint account with Hitler's Germany all alone.

PART II

THE ITALIAN SURRENDER

CHAPTER I

The End of the War in Africa

BOTH because of their own lack of daring and because of their reduced strength, for which they blamed Operation 'Torch',[1] the Allies did not manage to seize the whole of French North Africa at once, and this enabled the Germans to send an expeditionary force first by air lift and then by sea and succeed in establishing themselves in Tunisia and joining hands with the *Afrika Korps*. Far from being brought to an end by the two brilliant operations of El Alamein and the American landing, the war in Africa was thus going to be continued at the point of intersection of these two great successes, by a difficult and costly campaign in Tunisia. Then again, Eisenhower's acceptance of Admiral Darlan, with Roosevelt's approval, was going to disturb the French and cause further dissension amongst them at the very moment when everyone capable of fighting was siding with the Allies, thus wiping out the memory of the Rethondes armistice. The shortlived reign of Admiral Darlan and then General Giraud's government, both supported by the Americans, were characterised by a very sharp opposition between the Algiers authorities and General de Gaulle in London; but the latter was relying on the underground Resistance. In the absence of any real reconciliation between the hostile elements of the French forces, it was going to take months of bitter discussion to bring them together in a French government under General de Gaulle in Algiers. At least this strife did not prevent a French army from being reborn and fitted out with modern equipment by the Americans. But it had lent fuel to a vigorous upsurge of local national feeling strong enough to undermine the French Empire, which up to now, despite the setbacks suffered by the mother country, had remained quiescent.

I FRENCH 'INDECISION' IN TUNISIA

The best that one can say is that the behaviour of the French troops in Tunisia was ambiguous. They were probably motivated by contradictory

1. See p. 387.

feelings; on the one hand, the spirit of revenge against Germany certainly still lingered on; but on the other hand, they were steeped in the Vichy mystique, according to which France no longer had any allies, since the British in particular were suspected of wanting to seize her colonies. This mystique was expressed by the slogan 'France and France alone' and in North Africa by Weygand's orders to 'defend the Empire against all comers'. In Tunisia it was obviously the Germans who were the aggressors; but they were only replying to other aggressors in the rest of French North Africa, the British and Americans. An admiral is said to have asked out loud the question in everyone's mind: 'Who's the enemy?' Since the leaders had not been given any information or instructions, they decided to wait and see; they took no action against the Germans until the situation in Algiers had been cleared up and until they had received unequivocal orders to do so. Time was thus lost that would never be recovered and the Germans took the fullest possible advantage of this.

General Barré, the commander of the armed forces, took great care not to collaborate with the Germans as he was ordered to do by Admiral Darlan on the morning of November 9 and also by the civil authorities under the Resident General, Admiral Esteva, and yet again by the commander of the Bizerta base, Admiral Derrien – seven destroyers and nine submarines were captured undamaged by the Germans. But he took no action against them. He had withdrawn from Tunis without fighting, so that German paratroopers and later the transport aircraft were able to land on El Aouina airfield without a shot being fired against them. Barré had taken his troops up into the mountains which dominated the Medjerda in the west in order, he wrote, to 'hold the road for the Americans'; but none of the enemy forces was in a position to seize this road, which did not need holding and this operation had not in any way been prearranged with the Americans. In other words, it could just as well have been directed against them to block their approach to Tunis, according to how the situation developed in Algiers.

General Barré also wrote that he had 'left' his rearguard in Tunis under Colonel Le Couteulx de Caumont with the task of 'waiting until the night of November 13–14 for reinforcements which it was hoped would come from the west'. But what forces were left in Tunis? What were they supposed to do? In any case, what action were these units capable of now that they had been left behind by their main forces? And why not leave all the units in Tunis? With orders to fire on 'all comers'?

It is true that General Barré referred to 'a plan which had been in existence for several months', according to which Tunis had been considered indefensible. The question was: against whom? Against a powerful Allied landing force supported by a strong fleet, certainly; but not against a few German paratroopers who could be picked off in mid-air.

To justify the Vichy troops' withdrawal, General Koeltz, who knew all about these events because he had played an important part in them, painted a telling picture of the troops' weakness and shortages; they had no anti-tank sections, no AA guns and no heavy batteries; there were not enough European officers and NCOs to lead the native troops; for want of petrol, engines were running on alcohol; there were no spare parts or even tyres. But the entire African Army was in the same parlous state; this had not prevented it from fighting against the British and Americans in Algiers, Oran and Casablanca; but it had stopped it from resisting the Germans, who were much less strong, in Tunis and Bizerta.

Moreover, another contradiction now emerges. Vichy propaganda had always presented the armistice as the only solution enabling France in June 1940 to keep an army which would one day be able to resume the fight against the Germans. On the other hand, General Weygand had managed to get round the clauses of this armistice and he was rightly given the credit for keeping more troops and weapons in Africa than he had a right to. What was the point if, when the time came, these troops were unable to defend a position as important as Tunis on their own and if they could not resume the fight against the Germans – the very fight for which the Vichy leaders had had the foresight to keep and train them – unless the Allies immediately flew to their aid those same Allies whom they had fought in Algiers, Oran and Casablanca, with the unfortunate result of hindering and delaying the advance eastward which they were supposed to be so eagerly awaiting?

For their part, General Anderson's British troops, which had been given the task of forestalling the Germans in northern Tunisia, had not advanced very quickly; although Bougie had been captured on November 11, the Djidjelli airfield was not taken until the 13th; owing to lack of air cover at Bougie many Allied boats were sunk by Axis aircraft; the lines of communication were very long, the terrain was mountainous and roads were few and narrow. No co-ordination with the French had been possible: General Giraud had not wanted to place his troops under British command. If, then, the British had advanced very quickly, as General Barré wished, in what circumstances and with what instructions would Franco-British liaison have been established with a view to their later mutual co-operation for the recapture of Tunis? No one knows.

General Anderson noted that the French mayors and leading French officials made no secret of their hostility to the Allies; the Arabs were indifferent; the French population was sympathetic but passive. Once Bône had been captured on November 12, both by sea and by paratroopers, on the 13th Anderson was joined by reinforcements from Algiers, but his whole command never amounted to more than one brigade. He occupied

Tabarka but on November 18 he had to face an enemy attack at the Djebel Abiod. Till then General Barré's 12,000 men do not seem to have given him the slightest assistance; it was not until November 19 that Barré rejected the German ultimatum. At that time there were still very few German troops; 1,000 men in Tunis, according to Anderson, and 4,000 in Bizerta; but they were near to their airfields, which the French had abandoned without a fight, and this gave them air superiority. At the end of November, Anderson was relieved to see French officers whom he considered to be sympathetic to the Axis leave General Barré's staff; he noticed that the older French officers were either hesitant or hostile, while the younger ones were keener and more sympathetic to the Allies. By this time it was too late; at the end of November, British dilatoriness and French 'indecision' had enabled the Italian and German troops to occupy the whole of Tunisia and join hands with the *Afrika Korps*; a hard campaign was going to be needed to make up for the great opportunity which they had lost, even though the German operation had been carried out with meagre resources and for a limited objective – the evacuation via Tunisia of the forces which were retreating from Tripolitania.

II THE TUNISIAN CAMPAIGN

On December 1 and 2, General Anderson was at last in a position to attack in the direction of Tunis; he was repulsed. The Germans, under von Arnim, even counter-attacked, but their forces were inadequate and they were checked. Another Allied offensive was planned for December 22 and 23; torrential rains made it impossible; the roads were impassable. General Eisenhower finally cancelled it on December 24, and it was replaced by an operation in the south in the direction of Sfax, where the roads were wider. The Allies had lost the first round.

However, the French had formed a line in the centre of Tunisia. Starting from Tebessa, under the command of the GOC General Juin they had occupied the passes in the mountain ridges which run across Tunisia, in order to seize the outlets on to the Kairouan plain. As a result of this operation they might be able to cut off the German forces in Tunisia from those of the *Afrika Korps*.

In the course of January, in order to check this danger, General von Arnim launched his tanks against the French positions; for a month the French withstood the attack virtually on their own and with inadequate resources; they had heavy casualties – 5,000 men – but they lost only the eastern ridge. General Giraud then agreed to incorporate the French troops into the Allied defences – which he had to do in order to receive a

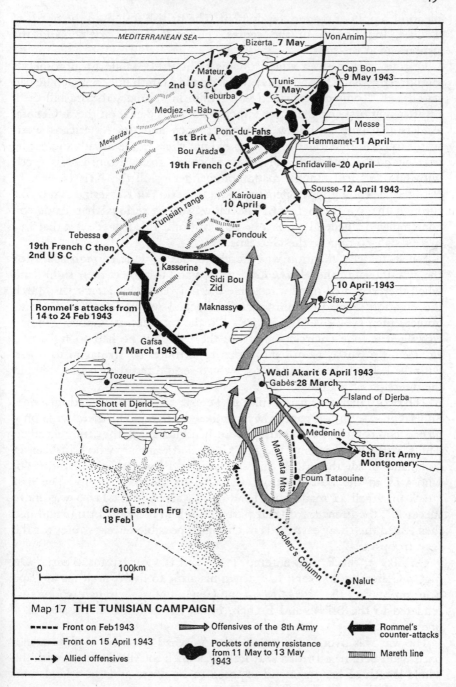

MEDITERRANEAN SEA

Bizerta 7 May

Von Arnim

Mateur
2nd U S C
Teburba
Medjez-el-Bab

Tunis
7 May

Cap Bon
9 May 1943

Medjerda

1st Brit A
Bou Arada
19th French C

Pont-du-Fahs

Hammamet 11 April

Messe

Enfidaville 20 April

Kairòuan
10 April

Sousse 12 April 1943

Tunisian range

Tebessa
19th French C then
2nd U S C

Fondouk

Kasserine

Sidi Bou
Zid

10 April 1943

Maknassy

Sfax

Rommel's attacks from
14 to 24 Feb 1943

Gafsa
17 March 1943

Tozeur

Wadi Akarit 6 April 1943
Gabès 28 March

Island of Djerba

Shott el Djerid

Medenine

Matmata Mts

8th Brit Army
Montgomery

Foum Tataouine

Great Eastern Erg
18 Feb

Leclerc's Column

Nalut

0   100km

Map 17 **THE TUNISIAN CAMPAIGN**

- - - - - Front on Feb 1943

———— Front on 15 April 1943

- - - -▶ Allied offensives

▓▓▓▓▶ Offensives of the 8th Army

⬛ Pockets of enemy resistance
from 11 May to 13 May
1943

◀━ Rommel's
counter-attacks

▨▨▨ Mareth line

plentiful supply of modern equipment. The British fought in the north of Tunisia, the French in the centre – under General Koeltz – and the Americans in the south.

Fearing an American attack on his right flank, while Montgomery's Eighth Army launched a frontal attack on the Mareth line to which he had withdrawn, Rommel persuaded von Arnim in February to forestall them by attacking first and the latter inflicted a serious defeat on them. General Anderson had to withdraw both the French and the Americans westwards to Kasserine. But von Arnim did not press home his advantage; he even withdrew one of his divisions from the front. Rommel disagreed with him and had himself made commander of all the Axis troops. In February he took up the offensive in the direction of Kasserine and broke through the American front. The blow was so serious that Anderson contemplated a general retreat; he now had only one brigade left that was in a fit state to oppose the Germans.

But Rommel's intention was merely to clear a wide enough space for the withdrawal of the *Afrika Korps* troops and to protect their right flank when they retreated northwards. He did not renew his attack; in March the situation seemed to him to be deadlocked and he left Africa. Montgomery then took over the initiative in the direction of Gabès. He had envisaged a wide encirclement from the west but he had to fight two eighteen-day battles in order to open up a route. He managed to do so with the help of the French corps, which recaptured the eastern ridge in the direction of Kairouan.

The two Italian-German armies in Tunisia were now formed into one, under von Arnim; on paper they numbered 250,000 but there were only 90,000 combat troops and they were hemmed in at the bridgehead in Tunis, with their backs to the sea. General Alexander, who had been in command of all the Allied forces since 14 February, gave Anderson, who was in the best position, the task of mopping it up. The first attack on April 22 made little headway. A second on May 6 was more successful; the French, for their part, had seized the Fahs bridge and had then edged their way eastwards to cut off all possible retreat routes for the Axis troops.

On May 7, the British entered Tunis and the Americans Bizerta. On May 9 General von Vaerst laid down his arms to the Americans at Cape Bon; on May 13 the *Afrika Korps* and General Messe's Italian troops surrendered to the British and French. In all, the Allies took 250,000 prisoners.

The war was over in Africa and the Axis had lost; the Mediterranean once again became a British sea; Italy was open to Allied attack, with the whole length of her mainland exposed to bombers and the islands and southern Italy to landing fleets.

III DARLAN'S REIGN

The scuttling of the Toulon fleet and the Tunisian defeats had been very damaging to Admiral Darlan's prestige and authority; it was a heavy blow. Yet he continued to wield complete power, civil and military, on behalf of Marshal Pétain, who was committed to stay in France by his promise not to leave the French and was said in Algiers to be in a situation where it was impossible for him to express his thoughts publicly. The Admiral claimed that he had been authorised to interpret them and was doing so faithfully. Although he had been disowned by Pétain and deprived of all his titles, while his photograph was disappearing from the many places in the Southern Zone where it had been displayed beside the Marshal's, the Admiral had received the allegiance of all the men in charge in North Africa – except for those in Tunisia. Governor-General Boisson had placed French West Africa under his authority; the only territories over which he had no hold – among those answerable to the Vichy government – were Indochina and the French West Indies, which were governed, however, by two admirals who owed their posts to him, Decoux and Robert. Admiral Godfroy, who was in command of Force x in Alexandria, was still hesitating about whether to join him.

Admiral Darlan had kept on all the Vichy officials, even those most heavily compromised by their collaboration. On the other hand, he had put the Algiers Gaullists in prison and banned their newspaper *Combat*; he had dismissed the ringleaders who, on behalf of Giraud, had organised the putsch of November 8, and some remained under threat of prosecution; but others had apparently joined him and he had given them important posts – for example Henri d'Astier de la Vigerie was put in charge of the police.

The Admiral governed with a council of colonial governors – the 'Imperial Council'. Although disowned by his peers, General Giraud's prestige and the American support earned him command of the armed forces, a post which fulfilled his every wish and to which he intended to confine himself. Relations between the French administration and the Allied forces were governed by an agreement which the Admiral had made with General Clark, Eisenhower's deputy, an agreement which was much more favourable to the Americans, especially as far as the rate of the dollar was concerned, than those which had previously been negotiated by Lemaigre-Dubreuil on behalf of General Giraud.

The American consul Murphy maintained his support for Darlan, who was being violently attacked by Free France, the underground Resistance and the American press, and whom President Roosevelt had half-disowned by treating him as a 'temporary expedient'. On December 23,

1942, the Admiral was assassinated by a young Gaullist, Bonnier de La Chapelle, perhaps influenced by the chief of police himself, after a chaplain had given him absolution. A wind of panic immediately swept over Algiers; Murphy and Giraud thought that they were threatened; Bonnier de La Chapelle was immediately brought before a council of war, deserted by his protectors and executed.

There was so much upset in men's minds that the Count of Paris thought that his hour had come; he had been bitterly disappointed in Vichy, where he had hoped for a moment that Marshal Pétain would become a French General Monk; he had supporters in Algiers, even in Darlan's government, and an actual conspiracy had been hatched on his behalf; in the first stage he was to be declared 'lieutenant of the realm'; his supporters and the Count himself considered that this was the only solution capable of uniting the warring factions which were splitting the French among themselves. But although General Giraud, whom the members of the 'Imperial Council' had quickly and unanimously named as Darlan's successor, showed himself very well disposed towards the Count of Paris, he held out no hope. Not that he was a convinced republican or a determined opponent of monarchy; these constitutional problems were of little importance to Giraud; but it was his firm belief that while the war lasted, they must not risk dividing the French even more by political reforms and decisions which would commit them for the future and which they would regard as having been forced on them.

IV GENERAL GIRAUD'S GOVERNMENT

Thus for six months the colonies which had re-entered the struggle were to be governed by a man with the strange title of 'Civil and Military Commander', who had accepted this responsibility only out of a sense of duty and who regretted that he was now unable to confine his activity to fighting, which in his opinion was the only thing he was qualified to do. General Giraud was a very fine man and a brave fighter and he had a great reputation in French North Africa – the Arabs used to say that he had 'baraka'. But he had no experience of government and he quickly showed that he was unable to cope with political and social problems. Refusing even to examine them, he declared that he was pursuing 'only one aim: victory', but he could not prevent these problems from arising.

In actual fact, the General's origins and upbringing tended to make him a great admirer of the National Revolution – he had said so to Marshal Pétain both verbally and in writing. He therefore preserved its legislation in Africa; the Crémieux decree was not restored, neither were republican laws and institutions; on the other hand, he retained the censorship, the corporate organisation of the economy, the ban on freemasonry and political parties and the Vichy organisations of the Legion of Ex-Service-men, with its 'police force' (SOL). Giraud had freed the men whom Vichy had imprisoned for opposition to the régime; but on the other hand all the officials appointed by this same régime remained in office. In doing this, Giraud indubitably had the backing of the African Army and administra-tion and in France of the officers and NCOs of the dissolved Armistice Army. But he clashed violently with General de Gaulle and Free France, which was supported by the underground Resistance. It is true that on the other hand he enjoyed the almost unconditional support of the Americans.

Indeed, President Roosevelt had a genuine dislike for General de Gaulle at whom he was always poking fun and making nasty digs, as well as telling racy stories about him which were untrue. He found the General's policy and behaviour 'intolerable'; he considered that he was afflicted with a 'Messiah complex'. As far as his exasperation allowed him to express political views, Roosevelt refused, as long as the war lasted, to identify France with any committee; from now on he would not discuss or even negotiate with anyone but local authorities. Giraud was in power in North Africa: he came to an agreement with him. In Equatorial Africa it was de Gaulle: he granted him lend-lease aid. This principle led him to the conclusion that all power in North Africa, both civil and military, should be in the hands of the Allied Commander-in-Chief; if a French Committee was set up it would be by agreement between himself and Churchill, without taking French opinion into account or even asking for it; at the Liberation, France would be under Allied occupation and military government for at least six months. In the meantime Roosevelt strangely dissociated de Gaulle not only from the French Resistance but also from Free France – and he suggested appointing him 'Governor of Madagascar'.

Churchill was too conscious of his debt to Roosevelt and his dependence on him to cross him and he made no secret to General de Gaulle that 'between the President of the United States and him he picked the big man'. But he did not make the same blatant mistakes as his partner about the situation in France and the attitude of the French; he knew that de Gaulle was 'the symbol of the Resistance'; although he said that he found him 'impossible' and even that he was 'disgusted' by him, he continued to support him and delayed dismissing him until later.

Each being backed by a 'Big Power', Giraud and de Gaulle had put up a show of being reconciled at Anfa and had established mutual liaison bodies. But their relationship remained touchy and tense. De Gaulle criticised Giraud for giving in to the Americans and for the fact that the aftermath of Vichy lived on in Algiers; above all, he ridiculed Giraud's indifference to political problems; 'is there a single country,' he said, 'which can make war without pursuing political ends?'

In this de Gaulle had the unanimous backing of the underground Resistance. At his instigation, Jean Moulin had succeeded in grouping together representatives of all the important movements of the two zones, of the political parties – including Communists – and of the two main trade union central committees into a 'National Resistance Council', over which he presided. In the course of its first meeting in Paris on May 27, 1943, the Council had come out unequivocally in favour of an agreement between the two generals which would give Giraud command of the armies but leave political control to de Gaulle. The fact was that de Gaulle had promised to let the French people decide their own fate after the Liberation; while waiting for this expression of opinion regarding any possible changes, the laws of the Republic would be brought back into force – this had been done at Réunion as early as the end of 1942. Giraud's behaviour caused the Resistance movements to fear that the Vichy régime, against which they were fighting and having to defend themselves, would continue after the Liberation.

Giraud's views themselves had changed in the course of these discussions; he had declared himself a believer in the Republic and recommended that at the Liberation they should bring in 'the Treveneuc law' which aimed at giving power to representatives on *Conseils Généraux* in the event of Parliament's being prevented from sitting – an arrangement which all thoughtful people in the Resistance considered to be impracticable. Giraud could also not go on indefinitely rejecting the advances of General de Gaulle, who was suggesting a meeting between them to achieve an agreement between Frenchmen on their own, independently of any protection or interference from outside. A mission by General Catroux in Algiers cleared the ground and General de Gaulle arrived in North Africa on May 30, 1943.

V THE FRENCH NATIONAL LIBERATION COMMITTEE

Together with General Giraud he formed the French National Liberation Committee under their joint chairmanship, in which they were each represented by an equal number of supporters, with Giraud retaining command of the troops. The strength of the two monarchs was, however, obviously far from equal; in population, troops, wealth or foreign sympathy and support, General Giraud had far and away the advantage over his rival who was now his colleague. Roosevelt persisted in choosing to recognise no one but him; he wrote to Churchill on June 10, 1943, that if de Gaulle managed to secure control of French West Africa he would contemplate sending 'several regiments and some warships to Dakar'; he regarded de Gaulle as a troublemaker 'who is jeopardising the Allies' war effort and constituting a very serious threat to them . . . the situation is intolerable; we shall have to break with de Gaulle'.

However, the armed forces of the two dissident parties were gradually combined and a joint general staff was set up. But apart from differences in mentality, the amalgamation was made difficult by the fact that the Free French had been equipped by the British and the North African troops by the Americans. In France the Army Resistance Organisation, which had developed out of the Armistice Army, did not join up with the other Gaullist underground movements and regarded itself as an offshoot of the North African Army. The most difficult of all to amalgamate were the secret services in Algiers – the London Central Intelligence and Action Office and the Armistice Army's Intelligence and Counter-Espionage Services, which had both gone over to General Giraud; the second of these regarded the first as amateurs while they, in their turn, despised the others as Vichyists. They were all combined in a new organisation, the General Directorate of Special Services (DGSS); but Giraud considered that this organisation was of a military nature and should depend on him, while de Gaulle regarded it as having a political role and wanted to make it answerable to the head of government. In the end, de Gaulle succeeded in having one of his own men, Jacques Soustelle, appointed as head of the DGSS.

Behind this bitter and unpleasant quarrel between two men loomed the future of France and this was the real significance of this clash of ambitions. If de Gaulle succeeded, the Resistance would take over power at the Liberation and the National Resistance Council set about drawing up an immense programme of economic reform; whilst Giraud would aim at bringing in a substitute for the Vichy régime or at all events conservative forces. The DGSS, whose task it would be to arm and officer the Resistance, had a vital role to play which was by no means purely technical.

However, even in North Africa itself public opinion was swinging over to General de Gaulle, who had won favour by the integrity of his behaviour since the armistice, the soundness of his views and the wide-ranging scope of his programme, to say nothing of the quality of his style. Beside a man of this stature, Giraud cut a poor figure. Many more were joining the Free French Forces, with the aura of their prestige gained at Kufra and Bir-Hakeim, than the North African units; furthermore, soldiers were deserting the latter to join the former; in New York, the sailors on the battleship *Richelieu*, in a state of semi-revolt, enlisted to fight in the Free French Navy; a number of Giraud's right-hand men, such as Jean Monnet, deserted him; General Delattre de Tassigny, who had come from France after escaping from prison, also went over to General de Gaulle.

Accordingly, Giraud gradually ceased to take any part in politics. When

called upon to choose between his office as co-president of the French
National Liberation Committee and that of Commander-in-Chief, he
opted for the latter; but in so doing he came under the orders of the
government and its leader; the result was that he was given the title of
Inspector General of the Armed Forces; he found this demotion intolerable and handed in his resignation; deeply embittered, he withdrew to
Morocco; he even accused General de Gaulle of wanting to have him
assassinated.

The French National Liberation had not yet become the French
government and was not recognised as such by the Allies: but it was
going to behave as if it were. It set up a Consultative Assembly to advise
it, presided over by Félix Gouin and representing those territories which
came under its administration, the Free French, those living abroad and
all shades of the underground Resistance. In every field it repealed the
Vichy legislation and brought back that of the Republic; the *Conseils
Généraux* started meeting again in Algeria; the Jews regained French
citizenship.

The Committee was actively preparing for the liberation of France. It
formed a whole body of new officials – Commissioners of the Republic
and Prefects – who were appointed by agreement with the underground
Resistance. At the same time the latter set up departmental Liberation
Committees to co-ordinate the underground Resistance and act as general
councils at the Liberation; they worked under the aegis of the National
Resistance Council which they took as their model. The French National
Liberation Committee drew up a complete programme of sanctions to be
applied to collaborators and Vichy officials at the Liberation; they ranged
from suspension from duty to 'loss of civil rights' and being brought to
trial in courts of exceptional jurisdiction; Pétain and his ministers were
to be judged by a High Court of Justice. As a beginning, Pucheu, who
was guilty of having sent Frenchmen to the German firing squad, was
sentenced to death and executed in Algiers in March 1944.

The French National Liberation Committee protested against the
Allied plans to have France run by a military government (AMGOT) after
the Liberation and to force her to accept an occupation currency. It embarked on an independent foreign policy; it asked to take part in decisions
on Italy. After first of all refusing to meet Marshal Badoglio, who was an
enemy of his, General de Gaulle declared that Franco-Italian friendship
must overcome past differences. To make this statement, he went to
Ajaccio which had now been freed; this new 'Latin' emphasis was
clearly aimed at preventing British and American control from becoming
too overbearing.

The French National Liberation Committee went one step further and
taking the view that the Allies really had no business to interfere in

French politics, on May 26, 1944 it declared itself the provisional government of the French Republic. By that time it had a proper army with very modern equipment; this it owed to the Americans and it was to a large extent the work of General Giraud.

VI THE REBIRTH OF THE FRENCH ARMY

The operation offered immense difficulties; the diversity of the troops which had to be equipped – blacks from French West Africa, Moslems from French North Africa, French Africans, Free French, those who had escaped from France; the language barrier; the diversity of eating habits; the lack of shipping and the small number of harbours equipped to receive, store and redistribute equipment; the small number of French technicians. These difficulties caused delays, bitter discussions and feelings of lasting resentment. In addition, trainees, in particular pilots, had to be sent to American schools and British equipment exchanged for American equipment, and it was necessary to arrange for the troops' supplies which the French were unable to provide. The equipment which had been unloaded had to be assembled at French bases; thus a conveyor-belt system was set up on the Algiers parade ground, where 2,700 vehicles of various types were assembled in one week, but whole companies needed to learn the necessary techniques.

The channels through which the French demands were met were also very complicated. On the French side the requirements were determined by a permanent military committee; missions were sent to the United States to see that they were fulfilled – General Béthouart and Lemaigre-Dubreuil in December 1942 and General Giraud himself in July 1943. But on the American side, the machinery was intricate; the commander-in-chief of the particular theatre submitted the French plans to the joint Chiefs of Staff in Washington with his recommendations; when they had made their decision, the plan came back to the Allied Commander-in-Chief, who passed it on to the Secretary of War for execution; then began complicated transactions which went from the operations department to the equipment depots via the ordnance departments or the various branches of the armed forces and a number of specialist committees; all that then remained to be done was to find the necessary ships, choose the loading harbours and form convoys. On this complex and circuitous route, progress was slow; the process of passing on and studying the files was still further delayed by differences of conception and language difficulties.

However, the Americans wanted to please General Giraud, even though they had been a little disappointed by his outdated strategic views; they regarded him as 'the only military representative of French interests', a formula which once again showed their lack of concern for General de Gaulle. Although General Eisenhower was full of goodwill, for him the task of arming the French took second place to arming his own troops and would have to wait until normal communications had been resumed and the necessary arrangements made.

As for General Giraud, he made considerable demands, but his ideas belonged to the pre-1939 era. Convinced that when peace came, the success of the Allied nations in achieving their war aims would depend on the strength of their armies, he wanted to raise and equip as many units as possible. In Washington General Béthouart presented a plan on his behalf which made provision for forming one general staff at army level, three army corps general staffs, three armoured divisions and eight infantry divisions, with an air force of 1,000 aircraft – 500 fighters, 300 bombers and 200 transport aircraft. In theory, the Americans accepted these figures; but Giraud then asked for two further divisions which they refused. Then, since the French National Liberation Committee had decided to turn Leclerc's division into an armoured division, Giraud suggested having four armoured divisions instead of three, that is to say a total of twelve divisions instead of eleven. And one armoured division required five times as much equipment as one infantry division. The Americans suggested looking at the whole plan again, so that in the course of the summer of 1943 the great divergence of views between the French and American nations suddenly burst into the open and there began the long discussions which have been called 'the battle of the services'.

The French were wanting to arm and send into the field as many men as possible; in addition, they wanted to obtain the maximum amount of resources from the Americans while at the same time retaining comparative freedom of action for their army, for example by allocating to it the air units which were arriving already equipped from across the Atlantic. The Americans criticised these suggestions for showing a lack of understanding of modern warfare. In their view the latter required very considerable logistical services; they had calculated that in the air force, aircrew did not amount to more than a tenth of the manpower employed on the ground and they had learnt in the Pacific that a large number of soldiers never went into action. They were thus going back to the medieval conception of an army: a small number of fighting men and a large number of ancillaries. They had set up the 'Army Service Forces', which was, in fact, a ministry for armaments, transport and all the needs of an army – recruiting, tests, finances, billeting, supplies, transport, chaplaincies, laundries, theatres, etc. In addition, they noted that because of the predominance of coloured troops, the French lacked officers and NCOs, in spite of the thousands of men who had escaped from France and arrived in French North Africa via Spain, and they lacked an even greater number of experts able to take care of the logistic services. Moreover, they refused to use their bases for supplying the French Army or to accept any responsibility for this task and for all the problems which it raised; the Army would have to work all this out for itself.

The squabble took a political turn when the French refused to be incorporated into the American Army. In this attitude the Americans thought they detected the influence of Free France and its touchy nationalism; they suspected it of lacking loyalty and gratitude to them and even of being undisciplined – they had been shocked by the 'desertions' to it from the African Army. In short, in December 1943 there was a distinct stiffening among the Americans at all levels. Even Eisenhower suggested cutting off supplies from the French unless they proved more amenable; Roosevelt was all the more inclined to agree with him because he was extremely angry that despite his intervention on Giraud's behalf, the latter had been gradually ousted. In his general report, General Marshall summed up the American point of view about the French when he wrote that they had fought well when there were no political questions involved.

In the end the French were forced to give in. They agreed to their Air Force becoming part of the Allied air 'pool'; they resigned themselves to the fact that the Americans would arm only five infantry and two armoured divisions, with a third armoured division – Leclerc's – to be formed later on. In these circumstances, the Americans agreed to provide France with equipment worth 3,000 million dollars, that is to say eight per cent of the lend-lease, and consisting of 1,400 aircraft, 160,000 rifles, 30,000 machine guns, 3,000 guns and 5,000 tanks. They refitted a large part of the French war fleet, equipping it with radar.

The French, for their part, were able to raise and equip 560,000 men outside their own country, of whom 300,000 were natives of North Africa, black Africa and the South Sea Islands; 163,000 were employed in ancillary services; there was a reserve force of 50,000 men; 256,000 went to form the various expeditionary forces. The French National Liberation Committee decided to place the Italian one under General Juin, to send Leclerc's armoured division to England and to form a second army under Delattre de Tassigny to operate in the south of France.

VII TOWARDS A FRENCH RECOVERY

Thus in Algiers, the temporary capital of France, the French National Liberation Committee was recovering or acquiring all the attributes of sovereign power. It was going to have an army which, thanks to American equipment, was more powerful than that of 1939, in spite of its small numbers. A last blow was dealt to the myth propagated by the Vichy régime that France could have recovered from her disaster of 1940 completely on her own or even become an arbitrator between exhausted antagonists by adopting a wait-and-see policy with a hint of collaboration. This French recovery constituted a personal triumph for General de Gaulle – although most of this army's officers and NCOs were still hostile to him – for he had constantly stated his view that by staying in the Allied camp France could still play a part in the war; he had never stopped working for this and events were proving him right. Through his intransigence in defending French interests he was enabling France to find her place again while at the same time preventing her from being made into a satellite by her powerful allies.

With her new-found freedom France had to be modernised – she was not making war, said General de Gaulle, in order to become a 'whited sepulchre' again. The Consultative Assembly in Algiers and the National Resistance Council in France were working out vast programmes of reform; they were planning for a controlled economy, the nationalisation of sources of energy and credit, the switch from an agricultural rural society to an industrialised urban society; the extension of education by democratising the schools and raising the school-leaving age; better training and increased efficiency in the civil service; an increase in the active population; the mechanisation of industry; the improvement of public health through social welfare services, etc.

But many people feared that France might be permanently weakened by defeat and occupation and that the damage they had caused would be a further burden for outworn economic structures and the rigid mentality which had produced them. Surely there was some hint of this in the fact that the rebirth of the Army had been possible only with American aid? Already the old structure of the colonial empire was showing signs of creaking – a prelude, perhaps, to breaking up altogether.

VIII THE EMPIRE: ITS DEVELOPMENT

The population of the Empire had behaved with amazing calm after the defeat of 1940, for even the leaders of the weak nationalist movements had not fully appreciated its seriousness. But the fratricidal strife in Dakar and Syria and then the American landing and the resulting friendly but nonetheless foreign occupation of French North Africa had made French authority lose face and for six months even removed it completely from

Tunisia. The difficulties experienced by France had revived the ambitions and intrigues – thoroughly outdated, of course – of British authorities such as the Colonial Office and the Intelligence Service. Above all, the Americans, and Roosevelt in particular, set themselves up as the champions of decolonisation, which, through a strange historical error, they believed had begun with American Independence, forgetting the extermination of the Indians and the slave trade out of which the United States had grown. Roosevelt considered that the colonial system implied war and that one could not fight Fascist slavery while doing nothing to free people from colonial slavery. The United States would set an example by 'freeing' the Philippines. On this particular point American capitalism strangely coincided with the views propounded by Soviet Communism. Moreover, Roosevelt condemned the British Empire just as much as the French Empire. He had informed Churchill that America would not help Britain merely to enable her to continue her brutal domination of colonial peoples. But the British Empire was taking an active part in the war, so that this was not the moment to undermine it. This was not the case with the French Empire. Elliott Roosevelt has told how in the course of a dinner at Rabat, to the growing embarrassment of Churchill, his father had first of all surprised and then tempted the Sultan of Morocco by opening up vistas of a post-war period in which the resources of Morocco would be developed by American aid and colonial exploitation by the French would come to an end.

General de Gaulle and the French Resistance were of a very different opinion; they were fighting to save France and they had no intention of losing any of her possessions; they had criticised the Vichy régime for giving up territory to Japan in Indochina, and General Giraud for being too submissive to their American ally in French North Africa; to a large extent, the Free French volunteers were also officers of the colonial army, overseas administrators or colonial settlers; the Communists themselves, eager to blow Déroulède's trumpet in order to win over all possible support inside the nation, had toned down their anti-colonial propaganda almost to the extent of praising the civilising influence of France in her Empire and contrasting it with Nazi racialism.

However, a change was taking place. In Equatorial Africa which had joined Free France, the work of Governor-General Félix Eboué, a negro from French Guyana, had earned General de Gaulle's approval when he gave more scope to African-born leaders and showed respect for customs and traditional social structures instead of continuing the policy of imposing the French way of life. During his anti-Giraud campaign, de Gaulle, speaking from London, had given the French North Africans a promise that he would improve their lot. In the Middle East, although the mandate which had been given to France by the League of Nations remained in existence until the end of the war, Free France had committed itself to granting independence to Syria and the Lebanon.

In October 1943 the governments of these two countries, secretly stirred up by British agents who had dreams of an Arab world united under British rule, asked that public services which were under the direct management of French officials should be handed over to them. The French National Liberation Committee refused and pointed out that no change of status in the mandated territories could be made until after the war. Going even further, the Lebanese government had a bill passed by Parliament to modify the Constitution, which had been granted them by France. The chief French representative, J. Helleu, took a strong line; he had the President of the Lebanese Republic and three ministers arrested, dissolved the House and set up a provisional government.

This gave rise to a serious Franco-British crisis at the very moment when the French National Liberation Committee's difficulties with the United States about arming the French troops required it to stay on the best of terms with the British. While the Egyptian and Iraqi press were unleashing attacks on 'French oppression', in November 1943 the British government actually sent an ultimatum to the French National Liberation Committee; it demanded the recall of Helleu and the freeing of the imprisoned leaders; otherwise British troops would take over the government of the Lebanon and Syria. The French National Liberation Committee tried to find a way out of the difficulty but eventually caved in; having advised its representative to be 'firm', it now cancelled his decisions, re-established the *status quo* and renewed its promise to grant independence to the two states.

In North Africa the nationalists were also beginning to stir again. In Morocco the leading personalities who had joined forces to form the traditionalist Istiqlal movement were becoming reconciled with the Sultan, to whom they had hitherto been opposed. In Tunisia Bourguiba, the leader of the Neo-Destour, had gone over to the Axis and had spoken to his countrymen over Radio Bari; after the capture of Tunis the French National Liberation Committee had dismissed the Bey and put someone else in his place.

But the most striking and alarming changes had taken place in Algeria. Until then the nationalists had restricted themselves to demanding greater integration of the natives, and in 1936 Farhat Abbas had even declared that there was no such thing as an Algerian nation and never had been. In May 1941 he had made only moderate demands to the Vichy régime: equality of Frenchmen and natives in the Army, the abolition of the military régime in the southern territories and agricultural reform. But he continued to militate in favour of 'assimilating' the natives, which met with opposition from the French 'settlers' who were anxious to keep their distance from the latter. Although the Ulemas' movement was more traditionalist, being Moslem and Arab orientated, and Messali Hadj's 'People's Party' which had been momentarily linked with the Communists, was more inclined to take violent action, no serious agitation had occurred.

The American landing sparked off an irresistible chain of events. The only response to an appeal to the natives by Admiral Darlan to take an active part in the war was a letter from Farhat Abbas on December 20, 1942, demanding the drawing up of a political, economic and social statute which would make the masses aware of their rights and their duty to take part in the war effort. On February 10, 1943, the matter was taken a step further in 'the Algerian people's manifesto' which condemned colonisation and denounced assimilation, which had been Farhat Abbas's objective up to then, as a 'lie'. The manifesto called for 'complete freedom and equality for all inhabitants of Algeria, the recognition of Arabic as the official language and real and immediate participation for Moslems in their country's government'. In June 1943 this first step was followed up by a programme which was presented to the French National Liberation Committee, with the aim of forming an Algerian government composed half of Moslems and half of Frenchmen, and of making all posts open to Moslems.

General Catroux, the State Commissioner for Moslem Affairs in the French National Liberation Committee, rejected the programme with the declaration that 'the French will never agree to grant independence to Algeria, which is an integral part of France'; the nationalist leaders then refused to sit in the 'Finance Delegation', which led to their arrest for 'stirring up unrest in time of war'.

But on December 11, 1943, the French National Liberation Committee decided to retreat and brought in a certain number of reforms in favour of the Moslems. These were announced by General de Gaulle on the following day in Constantine in a speech which excited worldwide interest. The élite of the native population would be granted French nationality without, however, giving up their personal status as Moslems; Moslems would have increased representation in the Assemblies and play a greater part in government; an immense programme of legislation and public works would improve their social and material situation. The 'Constantine Programme' was rejected both by the nationalists, who denounced it as a revival of the outmoded 1936 'Blum–Violette Plan', and by the French Algerians, who made no secret of the fact that they regarded it as the work of people who knew nothing at all about Algeria and that they would make no bones about repealing it once the French had gone back to their own country. Even men who had been Gaullists from the earliest days, like the Dean of the Law Faculty in Algiers, Viard, declared that they disagreed with the Moslem policy of the President of the French National Liberation Committee. As a result, Farhat Abbas became reconciled with the Ulemas and Messali Hadj. The manifesto became the charter for Algerian demands. The 'Friends of the Manifesto' soon numbered some several hundred thousand supporters and they launched a weekly paper, *Egalité*. The Algerian nationalists were turning from the peaceful and law-abiding development which they had been advocating hitherto to plans for violent action.

Black Africa was not moving so quickly. The French National Liberation Committee decided to hold a huge conference in Brazzaville to study its future. At the beginning of 1944 it was under the chairmanship of René Pleven and General de Gaulle took part in the final session and announced its conclusions. The conference had worked out a vast programme of social and economic reform to ensure gradual advancement for the natives; this programme aimed at africanising the administration and granting internal autonomy to territories for the future by providing them with assemblies which would gradually take over the running of the country. But there was no thought of granting any of these territories independence; in any case, the only people attending the conference had been colonial administrators.

*

Apart from its military consequences, the end of the war in Africa had thus brought France back into the concert of nations. At the same time this comeback was the beginning of a profound change in the political, economic and imperial structure of France. In the midst of her misfortunes, France was turning over a new leaf; her liberation would also be a rebirth. Nevertheless, the meaning and purpose of this development were not yet very clear, nor were they unanimously accepted; the only definite conclusion to be drawn was that the Vichy régime had been condemned, its laws abolished and its leaders punished. On the other hand, the Allies still did not look upon France as an equal, nor did they regard the French National Liberation Committee as her legal government. The Italian campaign was going to enable the Committee to establish itself rather more firmly and set its sights a little higher, thanks to the expeditionary force which was to have a share in the Allied victories.

CHAPTER 2

Italy Surrenders

I THE SICILIAN CAMPAIGN

IN May 1943 in Washington, at the suggestion of the British and in spite of American reluctance, the Allies decided to follow up their success in Africa by putting Italy out of action. However, because of shortage of shipping and lack of experience, in order also not to jeopardise the major landing across the Channel, which still had priority, an operation of minor importance was planned; any landing near Rome or even at Naples was considered too risky and the idea was ruled out; an operation in Sardinia would have had the advantage of making it possible to follow up by bombing the industrial centres of northern Italy; but since it was open to converging counter-attacks both from Corsica and from the Italian coast, it seemed too hazardous.

They therefore settled for a landing in Sicily; this would have the main advantage of ensuring a completely free east–west passage through the Mediterranean. Throughout June there were raids on both Sicily and on the little island of Pantelleria, fifty miles from Tunisia and some sixty miles from Sicily. Mussolini loudly boasted that Pantelleria was impregnable; but on June 12, 1943 the garrison's 12,000 men surrendered merely as a result of air raids, after losing only 56 dead and 196 wounded. This hardly showed a strong will to fight on the part of the Italians.

Operation 'Husky', the code name given to the landing in Sicily, needed very intricate gearing, for it involved the Army, Navy and Air force, and both British and American troops – the French did not take part. The dispersal of the general staffs showed how complicated it was: the American General Eisenhower, the interallied commander, was in Algiers; but the British General Alexander, who was responsible for the operation, had established himself in Tunis, while the naval general staff were based on Malta and the Army set up its own base in Sicily as soon as the landing started. All this did not make communication any easier and caused delay in making the decisions. But the Allies were sufficiently well co-ordinated for an American naval officer, for example, to take command of a sector which had been allocated to the British fleet.

The landing took place during the night of July 9–10, 1943, and although it could not achieve any surprise effect, it was nevertheless virtually a complete success. An army of 160,000 men, half Americans under Patton and half British and Commonwealth troops under Montgomery, set foot on land without meeting any great resistance. They were covered by 1,000 aircraft and transported by 3,200 ships – among which use was made for the first time of landing craft, flat-bottomed boats which could be beached without damage and were provided with a swing-door in the bows. They also were supported by 1,700 guns and 600 tanks, while paratroopers seized airfields inland. The timing of the convoys had been so well co-ordinated that a Canadian division from Scotland took over its landing barges which had come from Tripoli at 1.30 a.m. as planned, within sight of the Sicilian coast. The only difficulties arose from 'false beaches' which they had failed to detect or banks of pebbles not properly reconnoitred, on which some craft were smashed; some paratroopers were dropped too soon and fell into the sea.

But there was virtually no reaction from the enemy. And yet the Italians had ten divisions in Sicily; it is true that their strength had been reduced and that half of them belonged to the type called 'coastal', that is to say that they consisted of older men. The Germans had sent 70,000 men to northern Sicily, one of which was a crack division, the Hermann Goering ss Division. However, the coastal batteries did not open fire; the Italian headquarters were destroyed by raids and the base of Augusta was abandoned the day before the British arrived.

Accordingly, the troops landed and advanced without much trouble. In the west, on July 22 the Americans occupied Palermo; in the east, the British seized Syracuse on the 12th, but were stopped outside Catania; nevertheless on the 21st they joined up with the Americans. In his usual presumptuous and boastful way, Mussolini had declared that 'no enemy will leave the island alive'; in actual fact the Italian troops had stampeded; only the Germans clung on to Etna long enough to enable their troops to be evacuated from the island, a move which for once Hitler himself had decided upon, since he was anxious not to let the enemy coils close around them as in Tunisia.

On August 5 the British entered Catania; on the 16th the Americans entered Messina. Although they achieved their objective, their success was not complete because the Germans managed to bring back almost all their troops and equipment to the Italian mainland, that is to say 50,000 men and 10,000 vehicles; the 200,000 prisoners were Italians.

Being unable to prevent this evacuation was the only comparative failure of the Allies in this Sicilian campaign. Once again they had proved over-cautious; they had thought it impossible to land in the north-east of Sicily, which was the only way they could have reached the Straits of Messina before the Germans could cross it. They had also not dared to send their battleships to the straits in case they came under fire from the powerful batteries on both sides. In addition, they made mistakes which with better co-ordination could have been avoided; for example, the big bombers which would have done a great deal to hinder the evacuation had not been concentrated in time; General Alexander had not even called his subordinate commanders together to make an overall plan of action.

In short, the Allied force proved irresistible only against the Italians; with the Germans it was a different matter. Hitler made no secret of his apprehensions to Mussolini, whom he met at Feltre on July 19. It was absolutely necessary that Italy should hold on, he said, now that the Soviet offensive had been launched. The Duce promised everything the Führer wished; but he was no longer in a position to prevent the collapse of Fascist Italy. And his days were numbered.

II THE COLLAPSE OF FASCIST ITALY

By July 1943 there was no longer any shadow of doubt that the war was a disaster for Italy. Not only had she not achieved any of the objectives for which she had entered it but she had lost her empire; her Navy had been driven out of Mare Nostrum and was not safe even in the bases in the northern part of the country where it remained immobilised; the industrial centres were being flattened by increasingly massive raids; the enemy had conquered Sicily and the whole length of the peninsula was vulnerable and open to attack; the enemy's only difficulty was to choose where to thrust home.

From the economic point of view, industrial output had dropped by 35 per cent since 1939 and agricultural output by 20 per cent; imports had decreased by 78 per cent and exports by 54 per cent; the national debt had risen from 146,000 million lire to 405,000 million and currency circulation from 28,000 to 79,000 million. The state budgetary deficit, which reached 12,000 million lire in 1939, had risen to 87,000 million in 1943 and income now covered only 36 per cent of expenditure. Thanks to strict control, prices had theoretically only doubled, but a black market in every commodity was flourishing in all regions; and the population was suffering from a growing scarcity of foodstuffs. Corn was being sown in public squares; by this symbolic gesture, which those in power extolled as an assertion of the will to fight, the country was proving the depth of misery created by inefficiency and neglect.

This disaster was shown in the Duce's physical condition. His stomach ulcer made him anxious and nervous and necessitated a debilitating diet and long periods of rest which were not really compatible with a position of absolute power. He had less will-power and even his reflexes seemed to have slowed down; his relatives were astonished to see a strange inertia, an almost complete apathy come over the old warrior; he seemed to be more and more indifferent, as if resigned to what was happening to him and to what lay in store for him. He retained the demagogue's confidence in words; he continued to believe that a speech was action; he took refuge in commonplaces and superficial judgments; he excused his failures by lashing out against the Italian people who had to be 'driven into battle by kicks up the behind'.

The régime which Mussolini had created had fallen into a similar decline; the sixty-year-old Duce was setting an example of moral corruption by flaunting his love affair with the young Claretta Petacci, who was burdened with a family greedy for honours and wealth. All around him things were breaking up. Senise, the chief of police, painted a picture of permanent public despondency, of impotence and chaos among those in power and of disobedience at every level. Only the militia and some young Fascists still believed in the régime and its leader; the most intelligent officials turned from ironic criticism to scepticism and moral defection; they were wondering how to desert the sinking ship in time with their weapons and kit. 'Fascism was dead long before 1943,' wrote Guido Leto, the chief of the Fascist secret police, the OVRA.

Everyone was full of grievances against Germany and these were frequently justified. She had not kept her promise to provide Italy with coal and the Romanian oil which she had agreed to send her had arrived only in driblets; for her the war in the Mediterranean had always taken second place and she had refused to provide the resources for the capture of Malta, which could have had far-reaching consequences; in the USSR the Italian Eighth Army which had had 220,000 men when it had arrived now numbered only 80,000, and the Wehrmacht had no scruples in assigning it dangerous tasks, at the same time covering it with sarcasm. The humiliating thing was that both in Greece and in Africa it was only the last-minute intervention of the Germans which had saved the Italian troops, and this the Italians found difficult to swallow. Relations between the two armies were characterised by a display of arrogance, brutality and contempt on the part of the German officers which the Italians' pride and sensitivity found impossible to tolerate. Personal diplomatic relations were no better. And on top of that the Germans no longer made any bones about their designs for annexing the Italian Tyrol.

Mussolini chafed because he had become Hitler's henchman, no longer had any active say in joint decisions and had to dance attendance on the Führer. However, the personal bonds between the two men remained firm; disaster had not impaired their friendship nor affected their trust in each other. They realised that their fates were sealed. Hitler, in spite of the Duce's setbacks and his own irritation at some of Mussolini's decisions

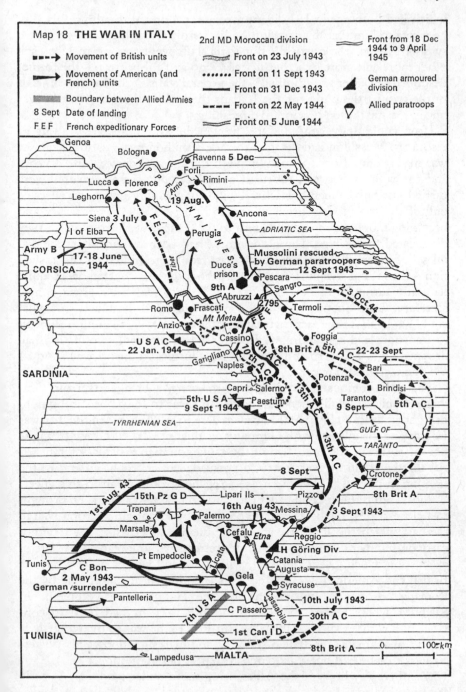

Map 18 **THE WAR IN ITALY**

2nd MD Moroccan division

- **=-→** Movement of British units
- **—→** Movement of American (and French) units
- ▓▓▓ Boundary between Allied Armies
- 8 Sept Date of landing
- FEF French expeditionary Forces

- ≈≈≈ Front on 23 July 1943
- ••••• Front on 11 Sept 1943
- ——— Front on 31 Dec 1943
- ---- Front on 22 May 1944
- ≈≈≈ Front on 5 June 1944

- ≈≈ Front from 18 Dec 1944 to 9 April 1945
- ▲ German armoured division
- ⛱ Allied paratroops

which had been particularly inappropriate, continued to admire his ally; he wrote to him that 'by carrying on his heroic struggle he had become a symbol for the whole world'. But their staffs were coming to hate each other more and more, whether it was Ciano and Ribbentrop – the former described the latter as a criminal – the general staffs or the leading officials of the two parties. And for the Italians themselves the word *tedeschi* was once more taking on a pejorative meaning.

How could Italy continue the fight? She was desperately short of resources. Mussolini had decided to raise a million men; national service was made compulsory for men between the ages of fourteen and seventy and for women between fourteen and sixty; but these measures were carried out rather unenthusiastically and they would have been effective only if the Italians had been willing to fight; but they were weary and becoming more and more indifferent to the 'Fascist war', from which they dissociated themselves. The government had been reshuffled by the dismissal of those ministers who took least trouble to hide their dissatisfaction – Ciano and Grandi; but those who had been ousted were quite naturally turning to open hostility. The Party had been given a new secretary, Carlo Scorza, a man who was devoted to the Duce. But what could he do about the fact that Allied submarines were making it difficult to transport lead and antimony from Sardinia, that tank production had dropped almost to zero and that the metallurgical industry was short of ore and electrical power?

The only obvious solution was *sganciamento*, a breakaway from Germany. Could Mussolini persuade Hitler to agree to Italy's becoming non-belligerent again? How would he even dare to ask him, when the war was *his* war and the alliance with Germany *his* alliance? To withdraw from the one or to break the other would be tantamount to a denial of himself. All that he could do was to try to persuade Hitler to put an end to the fighting in the USSR. On March 25, 1943, he wrote to him to this effect: 'I think I am right in saying that the Russian chapter can now be brought to a close, if possible by a separate peace or by setting up a strong wall in the east which the Russians would be unable to cross. . . . We cannot carry on summer offensives and winter retreats without reaching a state of exhaustion which, even if mutual, will in the end benefit no one but the British and Americans.' The Duce was encouraged in this course by the Romanian Foreign Minister and by the Hungarian government. In Salzburg, where he had met Hitler in April 1943, he had tried to convince him without success. In Feltre, on July 19, he was so overcome by a feeling of shame at the Italian setbacks and of resignation at his powerlessness that he had not even dared to repeat his suggestions.

Was there any hope of the Allies being more understanding? As early as December 1942 Franzoni, the Italian minister in Lisbon, had made discreet approaches to Eden and Cordell Hull, with the approval of Ciano, who had not consulted his father-in-law; this contact had been maintained up to July 1943 without any result. In July 1943 Bastianini, the Under-Secretary of State for Foreign Affairs, had returned to the attack; he thought he was acting with the tacit approval of Mussolini, since the latter had not replied to his request for permission. It was a matter of saving the Duce. The British categorically refused; what other answer could they have given after the decisions reached in Casablanca?

Moreover, in the Allied camp it was the British who were keeping up 'the hard line' towards Italy; they did not think that there was any other solution to Fascism; they wanted the disturbances in Italy to be sufficiently serious to warrant the intervention of the Wehrmacht; it would thus help the British 'peripheral strategy'. For the same reason, they were in favour of intensive air raids, which Allied propaganda said were caused by the presence of the Germans in Italy, so as to stir up the Italian population against the *tedeschi*.

The Americans were said to be in favour of less hostile measures, in order to make it easier for Italy to join the Allied camp; they would have liked to restrict the bombing and to reassure the Italians as to their intentions once the Fascist régime had disappeared. This was the point of view expressed by Roosevelt, who was more inclined to be well-disposed towards Italy, the foe, than towards his ally, Free France.

The USSR was happy to stir the pot in this discussion. She intended having her say in the decisions about Italy; she continually accused her partners of wanting to present her with a *fait accompli* and on the whole she had much in common with the British point of view. The debate ended with the Allied bombing of Rome on July 19; it aroused intense emotion in all Italian circles. It proved that the approaches made by the Fascist régime to the Allied side had no more chance of success than Mussolini's suggestions to Hitler. It was up to the Italians and the Italians alone to find a solution to the two interrelated problems of the existence of Fascism and of Italy's participation in the war; and as a necessary prerequisite, Mussolini had to be ousted.

III THE ITALIAN RESISTANCE

Since the King, the aristocracy, the Church, the industrialists, the big landowners and a large part of the liberal middle classes had given their support to Fascism, for a considerable time the opposition had been confined to a few thousand scattered refugees leading a precarious existence in France, England and the United States. For a long time Mussolini's successes made the Italian people turn a deaf ear to their propaganda; their action was limited by the French and British policy of friendship with the Duce before the war; and the final factor which paralysed them completely was their own internal divisions.

However, three factors had helped them to regroup. The first was the work of a group of intellectuals led by the Rosselli brothers – who were murdered near Bagnoles-de-l'Orne by hired assassins of OVRA. They founded a movement called 'Freedom and Justice' whose aim was to use anti-Fascism to bridge the gap between Marxists and liberal democrats. The second factor was Stalin's anti-Nazi policy during the years 1935–8; this brought the Communists – who, moreover, in Italy, with Gramsci and Togliatti, had constantly displayed a certain amount of independence with regard to Moscow – closer to other political parties. The Spanish war was the final melting-pot in which they mingled together; 3,100 anti-Fascist Italians fought in the International Brigades; fighting in a sort of civil war on foreign soil, it was they who repulsed the 'black shirts' at Guadalajara; 700 of them were killed and 1,000 wounded.

'The Popular Union of Exiles' in France comprised 70,000 supporters and its newspaper, *La Voce degli Italiani*, even penetrated into Italy, where hitherto only the Communists had maintained an underground network which OVRA had not succeeded in breaking up. Communists, Socialists and supporters of 'Freedom and Justice' joined together to form an 'Action Front'; the Christian Democrats with Dom Sturzo remained on the fringe, since the behaviour of the Pope and the high Italian clergy made things awkward for them – Dom Sturzo had advocated peace in Spain. While the Action Front declared itself republican, since the King was both upholding Fascism and profiting from it, the Christian Democrats and the liberals who were hostile to the régime but had remained in Italy set their hopes on the monarchy and the Army to overthrow it.

The Action Front was broken up by the German-Soviet pact; some Socialists, like Saragat and Tasca, became irreconcilable opponents of the Communists. Then Italy's entry into the war plunged everyone into a moral dilemma: was opposing the government not the equivalent of treason? France's defeat was nothing short of a disaster; the exiles who had settled there were imprisoned or had to hide or even escape to America. There as elsewhere the Wehrmacht's invasion of the USSR brought the Communists back into the paths of righteousness; three times a week on Radio Moscow, Togliatti urged the people to unite with the Allies in the name of peace, freedom and independence. Once again, notably in France, common fronts were formed between Communists and Socialists like Pietro Nenni or Silvio Trentin. In all the Allied countries the anti-Fascist exiles worked to persuade the governments and public not to confuse the Italian people with the régime which was oppressing it. They tried not to restrict themselves to purely destructive action; in New York Count Sforza drew up an 'Eight-Point Manifesto', a programme for post-Fascist Italy, which had the unanimous approval of the 'Pan-American Congress of Free Italians' which met in Montevideo in August 1942.

Italy's defeats brought the exiled leaders back to their own country. All were agreed that if Italy retained her ties with Germany she had lost the war in any case, for a victorious Germany would bring her under her yoke. The only way out was first to get rid of Fascism and then to side with the Allies. But how could this be done? Some Christian Democrats continued to hope that the King would recover his constitutional powers and bring about a legal revolution which would cut the losses and avoid chaos by making the whole of Italy swing over to the Allied cause in the hope of not losing any of her territory.

But this was not the opinion of the Socialists and the new Action party which had been formed by the merging of 'Freedom and Justice' with young liberal intellectuals, and had a republican and socialistic programme. The Communists took up a more flexible line; they were trying above all to unite the anti-Fascists. In 1943, on their initiative, a liaison committee of the six anti-Fascist parties was formed – Communist, Socialist, Action party, Christian Democrat, Liberal and Democrat Labour – this last party consisting merely of a few of Bonomi's friends. The programme was simple: to destroy Fascism and to hold over the solution of political problems until after the Liberation.

Thus in Italy, unlike France, the Resistance was not formed into new bodies of separate Resistance movements but incorporated into the former political parties, with the addition of the Action party. The strength of these parties varied greatly. Only the Communists had any sort of military organisation; the Christian Democrats could count on the lower clergy and 'Catholic Action'; but the Socialists had greater difficulty in re-forming their party, while the Action party was only a skeleton structure made up of intellectuals; as for the Liberals, virtually their only asset was the prestige of having Benedetto Croce as a member. Although the strikes in northern Italy in March 1943 had shown that anti-Fascism was becoming popular, in July 1943 the Italian Resistance was not a force to be reckoned with; it had not taken root throughout the country; it had no institution similar to the National Resistance Council in France; it had no armed forces; it had not really infiltrated the Italian civil service; and if one adds to this the fact that it was not known to the Allies and that it had not played any part in Sicily, it is obvious that it was incapable of overthrowing and replacing the Fascist régime on its own, however shaky and discredited the latter might be.

IV THE PLOT AGAINST MUSSOLINI

Since the underground Resistance was not in contact with other organisations, three groups were going to endeavour to bring down Mussolini.
They made no attempt to co-ordinate their action; they each had only a
few scraps of information about the plans and programme of the others;
as a result, though the operation succeeded it was going to cause chaos
all over Italy, split the country up between various authorities and lead to
civil war.

The first and weakest group was the one formed by former politicians
from pre-Fascist days; in actual fact there were two of them, Orlando and
Bonomi. The former still had a great reputation abroad but in his own
country his prestige had fallen considerably; the King referred to him as a
'ghost from the past'; but he had a great name which was likely to win the
Allies' confidence; he was also only one man. Bonomi, on the other hand,
had woven a spider's web; he was linked with the underground Resistance – he was relying especially on the Christian Democrat de Gasperi –
but he was equally welcome at the royal palace and he had not broken
with a few Fascists who were on the road to repudiating their party,
realising that the cock would soon be crowing for them.

King Victor Emmanuel had the constitutional power to dismiss Mussolini – after all, the Duce was only the president of the Council summoned
by him – and he was the titular commander of the armed forces which,
if they followed him, would be capable of controlling any possible violent
reaction by the last hard core of Fascists. But Victor Emmanuel had seriously compromised himself with the régime and he had never at any time
protested against its excesses. On the other hand, he was a very cautious
and secretive man; he would advance only by stealth, after making sure
that all the odds were on his side and without revealing anything of his
intentions. Amongst his entourage, Duke Acquarone, the minister of the
Royal Household, was a safe and loyal henchman, more resolute than his
sovereign.

On the military side, the ringleader was General Castellano, the
Deputy Army Chief of Staff, an excellent look-out man who was aggressively anti-German. His first successful move was to get rid of Cavallero,
the new scapegoat for Italy's failures, and to replace him by General
Ambrosio, who had not compromised himself too much with Fascism,
had a well-established reputation for honesty and was highly thought of
by the King; the Duce's dismissal would depend on his resolution. It is
true that at the very top of the military world there was still Marshal
Badoglio, who was no longer playing any active part but his prestige
remained great; if he took sides, the Army would follow him.

The third group was formed by anxious Fascists who had been ousted – Ciano and Grandi in the van, supported by the 'principal secondary characters' Bottai, Federzoni, Farinacci. Ciano was the most active, and also the most rash; he was in contact with General Castellano. Grandi, who had been ambassador in London, thought he enjoyed the confidence of the British and Americans; he was hoping to become Foreign Minister of the new government and thus make it easier for Italy to change sides. These Fascists were, of course, relying on benefiting from the national union which would follow their leader's downfall; they would thus save their skins and perhaps their portfolios.

The King had tried to contact the Allies. In the summer of 1942 the Italian consul in Geneva had spoken to his British counterpart, on behalf of the Duke of Aosta. As proof of the plot against Mussolini the British demanded that a prince of the House of Savoy should set up a government in Sardinia ready to collaborate with them. It is not known what Victor Emmanuel thought of this condition but it was not followed up. The Princess of Piedmont, the wife of the heir to the throne, had for her part approached the British Minister to the Vatican. Then she had asked Salazar to act as mediator, which the Portuguese dictator had agreed to do. The Allies had remained very cautious towards these advances, no doubt because the decisions they had taken in Casablanca compelled them to be firm; but they had not turned their back on a change of government made on the King's initiative; although they had not wanted to disclose their intentions and had not co-operated in any way, their silence was calculated to encourage Victor Emmanuel.

The defeats in Sicily speeded things up; urgent action was necessary before the war set the whole of Italy ablaze. This was what Bonomi went to explain to the old King: they must dismiss Mussolini and arrest him, he told the King – Castellano had worked out a plan to this effect – to form an anti-Fascist cabinet under a military man, denounce the German alliance and make contact with the Allies. If Germany did not react, Italy would return to a state of neutrality; if Germany attacked Italy, the latter would go over to the Allies. Half-convinced, the King took a few more days to think it over; on July 15 he summoned Badoglio; he seemed to be merely sounding him but the two men understood each other without spelling things out.

The failure of the Feltre interview on July 19 had caused Ambrosio to make up his mind once and for all and he controlled the Army, which was the engine-room of the plot. The Führer had continued to insult the Italians, while at the same time refusing them the aid they were pleading for – besides, he did not know where to get hold of the 2,000 aircraft for which they were asking. The Italians, said Hitler, had to decide to make war like the Germans, 'with a fanatical will to win'. Bastianini, Alfieri and

Ambrosio had vainly laid siege to the Duce to make him admit to Hitler that Italy could no longer continue the fight; Mussolini said not a word. He could definitely not be relied upon to rescue Italy from her hornet's nest; the only answer now was to get rid of him.

The bombing of Rome on July 19 acted as a spur. On July 22 Grandi visited the Duce; he tried to persuade him to resign of his own free will; he found him convinced that Germany was soon going to win the war with the aid of a new weapon. That same day Acquarone and Castellano met: the King had decided to act. On July 24 Acquarone, Ambrosio and Castellano visited Badoglio on his behalf and told him that the King had decided to place him at the head of the government. They handed him the declaration which he had to read and which Orlando had drawn up at the King's request. Badoglio approved and said: 'Everything's all right.' The die was cast.

Two distinct plots were thus developing simultaneously, each only partly aware of the other; true, one alone was enough to bring down the Duce, who was both gullible and overcome by inertia. But what about afterwards? They had at one and the same time to avoid civil war, prevent or forestall the wrath of the Germans and win the confidence of the Allies. Was this not attempting the impossible? Hypocrisy and secrecy could not be the complete answer, even though Victor Emmanuel seemed to be establishing a kind of record for duplicity; on July 22, having already decided to have Mussolini arrested, he told him that he would be 'the last person to desert him'.

V THE FALL OF MUSSOLINI

On July 23 the Fascist rebels drew up the motion which Grandi presented the next day at the meeting of the Fascist Grand Council; Mussolini had been warned. It was clear that if this text was adopted the time had come for him to disappear from the scene. Yet he passively waited to see what would happen.

At 5.15 p.m. on July 24 the members of the Grand Council met attired in Fascist ceremonial dress – the dress of the political movement whose demise they were plotting – black tunic, grey-green breeches and boots. Mussolini's statement was a long, rambling lukewarm speech in his defence; those present were struck and perhaps encouraged by the Duce's weariness, his ashen face and his obvious resignation. Mussolini's conclusion, however, was quite clear: the grave failures had been due to the fact that the Army had not always obeyed him.

Grandi replied with an indictment of the way in which the régime, which, he said, was completely out of touch with the country, was slowly collapsing and disintegrating. He held Mussolini responsible; he accused him of failing to give any real direction to his policy through having taken on too many minor tasks. He then read his motion, which suggested 'a return to the Constitution' in order 'to unite all Italians morally and materially in this hour of crisis for the nation's future', that is to say that the King should again take over actual command of the armed forces and 'complete initiative in any decisions'. Mussolini would devote himself solely to being leader of the Party; he would make it once again into a 'block of granite' which would one day be able 'to over-come their difficulties'.

The régime's senior officials were therefore not bent on self-destruction; they were trying to extricate themselves from dire straits by changing their navigator. It was not for them but for the King to decide whether or not Mussolini continued to be Prime Minister; they probably reckoned that the King could not break completely with a régime to which he owed so much. Moreover, they all solemnly protested their friendship for the Duce whose burden they said they merely wished to lighten. Mussolini could have proposed an amendment to the motion and even refused to let it be put to the vote. He did no such thing; the result of the vote, which was taken verbally, was nineteen in favour and eight against with one abstention. Mussolini did not seem to have any illusions about its mean-ing. He stated: 'You have plunged the régime into a state of crisis,' and he refused the traditional 'Salute to the Duce' when he closed the meeting after ten hours of dramatic discussion. It was 2.30 in the morning and July 25; what was he going to do?

This was only the first act. After all, an opposition group of nineteen people – even if important figures – was still not the whole party. One faithful supporter, Galbiati, the commander of the Fascist militia, sug-gested having the nineteen arrested – a few of them had taken fright and gone back on their vote – calling in the Germans under Himmler and moving the front back to the lower Alps; he produced this surprising formula: 'Just as France, by fighting on, will save the honour of the French, so a Mussolini movement will save the honour of the Italians.' Mussolini refused. In the afternoon he meekly answered the royal sum-mons; he was therefore placing his fate in the hands of his King, who owed him so much and had always continued to show him friendship – even though he took a malicious pleasure in humiliating him by taking precedence over him when they were both present at official ceremonies.

Victor Emmanuel knew what had happened at the meeting of the Grand Council – Grandi had told Acquarone about it. He knew that from now on Mussolini was alone, abandoned by everyone and weary of everything, and that he could now strike at him without risk. To make himself look taller, this dwarf of a man put on military uniform for the occasion.

Mussolini trusted the King implicitly and came without any special protection; he had completely failed to grasp what was happening that day; he was not only paralysed but blind. The interview lasted twenty minutes. The King informed the Duce that he was dismissing him and replacing him by Badoglio – the Grand Council meeting had put him one day ahead of his schedule. Then, under the pretext of ensuring his safety he had him arrested in the Quirinal gardens by a captain of the *carabinieri*; the Duce meekly got into the car which left the Quirinal by a back exit while his escort was waiting calmly at the main gate, convinced that the King had invited his Prime Minister to stay to dinner. For his 'safety', Mussolini was to be imprisoned first in one of the Lipari Islands and then in a chalet in the Gran Sasso in the Apennines.

What were his followers going to do? At 11.30 Galbiati learned that the Duce was no longer in office, that Senise, who had previously been dismissed by him, had taken over again as Chief of Police and that Scorza, the party secretary, had fled. The chief of the militia summoned his friends and collaborators; only two of them suggested 'punitive action' which Galbiati brushed aside with the simple question: 'Against whom?' And without even trying to call together or even warn the members of the militia who were scattered around Rome, without appealing, as he had one moment thought of doing, to the armoured division of the militia, which was considered to be absolutely loyal to the Duce and was stationed some twenty miles from the capital, Galbiati meekly allowed Badoglio to oust him from his command. Fascism was well and truly dead.

For the nineteen it was a Day of Dupes. For Grandi, who thought that he was back in favour with the King and did not know that the latter had decided to call Badoglio, there was nothing to do but flee. Ciano did the same but had the unfortunate idea of taking refuge in Munich, right in the mouth of the German lion. Both men were doubtless afraid of bearing the brunt of the people's anger after the outburst of joy in the working-class districts of Rome at the announcement of Mussolini's fall. They had not collected their thirty silver pieces and several of the nineteen were going to pay for their betrayal with their lives.

The King had successfully brought off his palace conspiracy. But Italy was at war and it was no longer up to him to decide her fate; this depended on two formidable unknown quantities: how were the Germans going to react and what did the Allies want?

VI THE ITALIAN SURRENDER

Mussolini's fall was a great moral and political victory for the Allies; it had considerable symbolic significance – had not the Duce, the founder of

European Fascism, declared that the twentieth century would be Fascist? The Italian Resistance had achieved its objective; it was in the logic of events that Italy should once again become a democracy in which the political parties would alternate in power. But the King did not wish to move so quickly; he confined himself to freeing the anti-Fascists who had been imprisoned and to restoring the trade unions, freedom of the press, freedom of assembly. Badoglio formed a purely military ministry which could be no more than a caretaker government and bore no resemblance to the face of post-Fascist Italy; besides, its members had been instruments of the fallen régime.

On the military plane, Mussolini's fall brought no benefits, for the Allies failed to take advantage of it. In order to appease the Germans and gain time, Badoglio declared that the war would continue; he wanted to avoid any violent German reaction which would be impossible to fend off and 'back out' only once he was sure that the Allies would be able to land considerable forces and reach Rome first. So on August 6 in Tarvis, Guariglia, the new Foreign Minister, met Ribbentrop who made no secret of his anxiety – according to the interpreter Schmidt he was even afraid of being kidnapped. Unruffled, Guariglia gave his companion his word of honour that Italy was not negotiating with the Allies and was remaining on Germany's side; yet he knew quite well that it had been decided to send an Italian emissary, General Castellano, to Lisbon to 'contact' the Allies. He added, however, that Italy was at the end of her tether. Badoglio just as bravely gave the same reassurance to Kesselring.

But Hitler was not taken in. Even before the Feltre interview, in the course of a naval conference on July 17, he had not concealed his distrust with regard to 'undesirable Italian elements'; a sort of court martial, he said, would have to be set up in Italy. And he laid down what measures were to be taken if the worst should happen. He regarded the fate of his friend Mussolini as a personal insult. Without more ado the German troops replaced the Italians guarding the railways and bridges – a sign of how quickly they would intervene if the occasion arose; one Panzer division crossed the Brenner. Hitler had contemplated abandoning the south of Italy but the Allies' inactivity made him decide to hold on there.

Badoglio, however, had succeeded in gaining time. On August 5 secret negotiations with the Allies had begun in Sicily. On August 18 in Quebec, Churchill and Roosevelt had drawn up the Allies' policy and strategic plans with regard to the new Italian government; Eisenhower was to seize Corsica and Sardinia and secure air bases close to Rome and if possible beyond; but at the same time, paradoxically, units and boats were taken away from his command, the former for the great attack across the Channel and the latter for the Pacific. In these circumstances Eisenhower thought it impossible to achieve the objectives which he had been set.

On the diplomatic level, there was a difference of views between Americans and British. The Americans would have liked to leave Eisenhower a free hand to impose a military armistice on the Italians as he thought fit, in order to retain the possibility of securing their help and to ensure the most favourable conditions for landing on the peninsula. But the British, who agreed with the Soviets on this point, attached scarcely any importance to Italy's contribution to the Allied war effort; they wanted to inform Italy straightaway of the harsh punishment she deserved – the desire to secure control of the sea in the Mediterranean was not far from British minds.

They compromised. Eisenhower was to deliver a brief and strictly military text to the Italians. A second document consisting of forty-four articles and containing the political and economic terms would be communicated to the Italian negotiators in Malta on September 29; in the meantime the landing would have taken place and the Italians put to the test.

But in any case, whether long or short, the armistice was a *Diktat* in which the Italians had no say and which was presented to them on August 31 in the form of an ultimatum; it was take it or leave it. This was a blow for the King and the Badoglio government: they were being no better treated than Mussolini would have been; however, they submitted; they were hoping that the Allied landing would take place north of Rome and that the capital would be occupied by an airborne division. The Allied general staff insinuated that this would be the case; but it mistrusted these Italians who had changed sides so easily and refused to lift the veil on its intentions; yet it knew perfectly well that with the forces at its command, there was no hope of reaching Rome.

On September 3 the armistice was signed in Cassibile; the terms remained secret; they would not be disclosed until the day of the landing. The Italians thought they had several days in which to find their feet and make preparations; they hoped particularly to separate the Italian troops from the German troops who were around Rome and to take control of the airfields on which the expected Allied division would be dropped. And on September 8 the Allied general staff suddenly informed Badoglio that they would announce the armistice that very evening and invited him to do the same on his side. During the night the landing took place, but a long way from Rome, south of Naples, in Salerno.

It was obvious that the Allies had merely wished to avoid being fired on by the Italians, but they were in for a nasty shock, for they found the Germans forewarned and firmly ensconced. As for Badoglio's government, it was caught off-guard and as far as it was concerned the affair was a failure. It considered that it was in no position to defend Rome against the Germans, who occupied it immediately; Badoglio himself left for

Brindisi with the King. Worse still, on September 16 ss commando went to free Mussolini in the Gran Sasso: the *carabinieri* who were guarding the Duce let the planes land and the ss advance towards them without firing a shot. With German support Mussolini was to try to reunite the last followers of Fascism on the side of the Germans in a movement which he called 'Fascist, Republican and Revolutionary'. Italy was going to be ravaged by civil war.

Guariglia was not wrong to hold the Allies responsible for the failure of the Italian 'secession', and it quickly proved a total failure. The hundreds of thousands of Italian workmen who had gone to work in Germany became so many hostages; suspects were imprisoned; those presumed to be dangerous were confined in concentration camps.

Almost everywhere the Italian troops, demoralised and abandoned, allowed themselves to be disarmed and captured; in Toulon several thousand soldiers were made prisoner by a handful of German sailors. But on the Greek island of Cephalonia, the Italian units, when consulted by their leader, General Gandin, decided to break with the Axis; fighting broke out between the former allies, with the Germans gaining the advantage after seven days, thanks to their air superiority. All the Italian officers, including General Gandin, were massacred after they had surrendered; nearly 3,000 soldiers were packed on to pontoons in an area that was mined and died in the resulting explosions.

The hardest fighting took place in the Dodecanese. In Rhodes the 7,000 Germans, who were better armed and concentrated in a main striking force, overpowered 36,000 Italians, though not without a fight and not until after the Italian ships had left the island. On Leros the British were able to land 4,000 men; they were bombed without being able to defend themselves properly and in November they surrendered to enemy paratroopers. The British also sent small garrisons to Cos and Samos; they fared no better. The British were putting into practice their conception of peripheral strategy, hoping in this way to influence Turkey. But General Eisenhower was against using large forces; by the end of November 1943 all the Cyclades were occupied by the Germans; Campioni and Mascherpa, the two Italian admirals who were in command there, were handed over by the Germans to the special tribunal of the Fascist Republic, which sentenced them to death for desertion.

Only the Italian war fleet was able for the most part to escape from the Germans because as early as September 6 the admirals knew the clauses of the armistice and the part they were supposed to play; the large ships were ordered to go to Malta, the smaller ones to Palermo. The Germans captured a few units which were tied up in harbour, under construction or being repaired – 3 cruisers, 8 destroyers, 22 torpedo-boats and 10 submarines. Their aircraft attacked the large ships which had set out from La

Spezia and sank the battleship *Roma*. But the ships based at Taranto and Pola came into harbour safe and sound – that is to say, two 35,000-ton battleships, three 24,000-ton cruisers, 8 fast cruisers and 10 destroyers, in all 126 units, plus 90 merchant ships, one of which was a liner, 300,000 tons of shipping in all. Except for the cruisers, all these ships that had escaped were to be used by the Allies in the Atlantic.

Italy was too heavily committed in Hitler's war to withdraw from it without loss. For her, the armistice brought anything but peace; for eighteen months, throughout its length and breadth, the peninsula was to be the theatre of desperate fighting between the Allies and the Germans, but also between the Italians.

VII THE WAR IN THE ITALIAN PENINSULA

On the same day on which the armistice with Italy was made known, two divisions of the British Eighth Army had crossed the Straits of Messina under the protection of four battleships and 400 guns, which started firing as soon as they left the coasts of Sicily; they occupied Reggio and gained a foothold in Calabria. Other units landed in Taranto and advanced on Bari and Foggia.

But it was further to the north in Salerno that the main Allied effort took place, with General Clark's American Fifth Army; this spot had been chosen because it was at the limit of the radius of action of the fighter air force based in Sicily. In theory Clark should have found himself confronted only by Italian units which had been neutralised by the armistice; he was reckoning on having no difficulty in making his way to Naples – a large port which was vital for receiving supplies – and in cutting off the enemy's route to the heel and toe of Italy. But this time the Germans had detected the convoys at sea and had dug themselves in; the landing troops were greeted by a hail of gunfire and were counter-attacked before they had taken up their positions.

On the 10th Clark nevertheless captured Salerno; but on the 13th, because of the raids by the German Air Force based in Foggia, things had come to such a pass that he was almost compelled to re-embark; Admiral Cunningham's fleet had to come in very close to support him and commit the whole of his naval air force. However, the Germans had been tied down by the running sore of Salerno; they had withdrawn in the south and on September 27 the Eighth Army occupied the Foggia airfields – from where raids could be carried out on Austria and south Germany. On October 1 the Germans evacuated Naples.

Once again the attack had not been a surprise; but the Allies had had a little more practice in amphibious landing operations. In Tunisia and

Sicily, the commander of the ground troops had complained at the belated arrival of support from an air force which was not under his control
and with which communications were rather unreliable. After the
Salerno landing, where this lack of co-ordination could have been fatal, a
first attempt towards a solution was made by bringing the Army and Navy
headquarters closer together; this was developed further by placing a
certain number of aircraft at the armies' immediate disposal but with most
of them remaining under the overall command of the Air Force.

The successive stages in the tactical use of the Air Force had now been
worked out: up to D-day–7 the attacks were concentrated on the enemy
airfields in order to achieve mastery in the air; from D-day–6 to D-day–1
their aim was to isolate the area under attack and rain bombs upon the
enemy positions; on D-day all the available air forces supported the landing units; a varying percentage wrecked the lines of communication
leading to them. From D + 4 onwards only twenty per cent of the aircraft
continued to support the landing; the rest were engaged in tasks required
by the extension of operations.

The Italian campaign thus became a test for the crucial operation across
the Channel; but in Italy itself the Allies were going to make slow progress because their plan was to attract and tie down as many German
troops as they possibly could; and these troops were able to dig themselves in very skilfully on the mountain barriers and behind the deep
valleys which had been cut by the rivers at right angles to the coast. The
Allies had only two tactics to choose from: a frontal attack, which would
not make the most of their tank superiority, or a landing behind the enemy
lines; but the narrow beaches and steep coastline prevented them from
deploying their troops in great numbers and breaking through. In both
cases their advance was slow and very gradual. However, by October 14
the Fifth Army had captured Capua, established its lines on the Volturno
some thirty miles north of Naples and joined hands with the British
Eighth Army on its right. It was going to be a long, long way to Rome.

VIII   THE LIBERATION OF CORSICA

The Germans had regrouped their troops at the crucial spot in order to
meet the danger; as early as September 9 they had began to evacuate
Sardinia via Corsica and Leghorn. The French were not going to let a
chance like this slip through their fingers.

In Corsica public opinion was unanimously against the Italians, who
had had 80,000 men occupying the island since November 1942. The Corsicans did not consider themselves in the least as Italians and had no wish
to become so. Fred Scamaroni, one of General de Gaulle's envoys, had
been sent from London to work on this grist to the Resistance mill; he

had been arrested by OVRA and had either committed suicide in prison or else was tortured to death.

It was easier to help the Corsican Resistance from Algiers than from London, and General Giraud took over the task. The submarine *Casabianca* under Commander Lherminier, which had escaped from Toulon when the fleet had been scuttled, carried out several missions to put agents and weapons ashore. Without referring the matter to the French National Liberation Committee, since he considered it to be a military operation which depended on him alone, General Giraud armed only one Resistance organisation, the National Front, without realising that it was Communist-inspired. At the same time he had formed a 'shock battalion' under Commander Gambiez, as the advance guard of a French Army landing which he had asked General Juin to plan – without referring the matter to General Eisenhower and knowing full well that the latter did not want it.

On September 9 the National Front announced the Corsican uprising; it set up a Liberation Committee in Ajaccio; the Corsicans laid a few ambushes for the German troops who were retreating northwards from the south; they were obviously not very strong. It is true that the *Casabianca* had transported a few hundred men and that the 'shock battalion' was at the ready as early as September 14. But General Eisenhower refused to deplete the Allied pool of ships in order to transport to the island the expeditionary force which Giraud had placed under General Martin; he also refused to lend any aircraft.

The liberation of Corsica was therefore a purely French affair. The French troops arrived without any heavy equipment in merchant ships and also in warships – which, in the Allies' opinion, could have been put to better use by keeping watch on the area round Bastia in order to hinder the Germans' evacuation of the island. The latter had recaptured Bastia; they held the whole of the route across the plain; they had tanks. All that the *maquisards* and shock battalions could do was threaten them from the passes of the mountain ridge. One thing in their favour was the attitude of General Magli's Italian troops who, without attacking the Germans, helped the French by placing lorries, radio links, mules and ambulances at their disposal.

The landing troops advanced towards Bastia through the mountains, guided by the whole population; not until after September 24 were they supported by a few aircraft. The Germans were blocking the Golo valley and defending Bastia to protect their evacuation. Preparations were made to attack the town, with the French and Italians co-operating; the American air force then intervened at the last minute to make things easier – and destroyed Bastia just as the enemy was abandoning it; only the harbour was captured undamaged before demolition of it had begun.

The liberation of Corsica was only a minor feat of arms – the French lost 70 dead and 270 wounded. But it had considerable repercussions in France; the island had been liberated, symbolically, by the joint effort of internal resisters and French forces from outside; the BCRA immediately made it a base for sending agents to the south of France.

In Algiers this personal initiative on the part of General Giraud did not improve his relationship with General de Gaulle, even less so as, to everyone's surprise, Corsica, which before the war had had only a tiny minority of Communists, woke up to find that the National Front had given it provisional Communist municipal councils voted in by acclamation in the public squares. Communist propaganda used Corsica as an example of how a popular rising could be successful at very little cost.

On the military plane, thirteen airfields were equipped, and although the island had very few plains, and these were small ones, she became a springboard for air raids against northern Italy and Bavaria; she was also a base for the landings on the French Mediterranean coast.

Corsica, moreover, was not the only region in which the Italian armistice had helped the Allies. In Yugoslavia Tito's followers had seized many of the stores belonging to the Italian occupation troops; they thus grew into an army of more than 200,000 men; they had been joined by a few Italian units and many individual volunteers. Tito now felt that he was strong enough completely to overthrow Mihailović, whom the British decided to desert; in November 1943, in Jajce in Bosnia the second session of the Yugoslav Anti-Fascist Council decided that the future state of Yugoslavia would be a Socialist democracy organised on a federal basis; it conferred the title of Marshal on Tito and forbade King Peter II to return to his country until the people had made up its mind about his fate. The Yugoslav Resistance felt that it had come of age and acted accordingly.

From November 1943 the Italian troops were evacuated from Albania via Valona. There again Communist supporters had taken advantage of the fact that they had been disarmed and had enlisted a few of them in their ranks; it was the same in the Greek maquis with a few survivors from Cephalonia.

Italians were thus showing that they had not changed sides merely out of opportunism; they were taking up their positions on the battlefield itself. However, the situation in Italy had become too confused for any common line of conduct to be adopted throughout the country.

IX THE DIVISION OF ITALY

By the autumn of 1943 the whole of the southern part of Italy was clear of Germans. It was under Allied military control, but administered by the legal Italian authorities: the King and Marshal Badoglio's government. Although this government had been reshuffled in November by the admission of civilians, it continued to consist of top-ranking officials and technical experts, without any representatives from the political parties. However, these parties had built up their strength again in the area and were asking to be admitted to the government; but they were pursuing their propaganda in the politically and socially least developed part of Italy and it was not fostered by the xenophobia and patriotism which the presence of the Germans aroused behind the front line. By definition there cannot be a Resistance in an area where there is no Occupation; Naples, moreover, was the only place where from September 27 to October 1 the people had revolted at the news that the Germans wanted to deport male adults and destroy the harbour. Nowhere else had any action been taken to prepare the ground for the Allied troops or make it easier for them to advance.

In these circumstances the Liberation Committees which had been set up by a coalition of anti-Fascist parties could take action only in internal politics; with varying degrees of enthusiasm they attacked the King and the government, whom they saw as the aftermath of Fascism; they thus made the impression of being revolutionary organisations in the eyes of the local population who had remained very much under the thumb of a conservative Church and over whom the big landowners had a great deal of influence. They also worried the Allies, particularly Churchill, who was anxious for Italy to remain a monarchy. Concerned above all to avoid disorder and ensure security, the Allied military command had formed a body of officers, 'the Allied Military Government of Occupied Territories' (AMGOT), which administered the territory and took care of the essential matter of supplies for the population. The Allies had drawn up a list of eminent Italians whom they considered to be deserving of a political role, but their choice was not always to the liking of the anti-Fascist parties.

Since the King and Badoglio were continually proclaiming their goodwill and giving increasing proof of it, they were gradually granted more and more actual power. On September 30, the Allies formally recognised the new Italian government's position as 'co-belligerent in the war against Germany'; and on October 13, 1943, this government declared war on Germany. How could it now be refused the attributes of a sovereign power? The Allies granted it permission to raise an army of limited strength, without, however, making any promise about Italy's future; and they allowed it to extend its powers equally to occupied Italy.

But in this region the government's departure had left room for the Resistance. Because of the presence of the Germans, the Resistance no longer confined itself to internal political action: its first objective, the fall of Fascism, had been achieved; from now on it was fighting to liberate the country from foreign occupation; it thus resembled the other national Resistance movements of occupied Europe. The anti-Fascist leaders had remained in Rome and they formed the 'National Liberation Committee' under the chairmanship of Bonomi, representing the Action party, the Christian Democrats (Gasperi and Gronchi), the Socialists (Nenni and Saragat), the Workers (Ruini), the Liberals (Soleri) and the Communists (Amendola). Regional Liberation Committees were set up in all the occupied provinces.

The resisters had taken up the struggle against the occupier more or less everywhere; when the Germans had occupied Rome, fighting had broken out even in the city streets and civilians had taken part. In the Abruzzi, in Umbria, the Marches, the Ligurian Apennines and the Slovenian Carso, groups of supporters had been formed by disbanded soldiers and anti-Fascists freed from jail, joined by young men from the towns.

The National Liberation Committee could feel that it was representing the living forces of the country; moreover, it had its seat in the capital. On October 16, 1943, it demanded that the struggle be directed against the Germans and the Fascists; this was tantamount to calling for the King to step down and the dissolution of the Badoglio government. But the Allies did not see it in this light; they fully accepted help from an Italian Resistance but on condition that it restricted itself to military action which was in keeping with their views and did not encroach on the political sphere. They did not sympathise with the Liberation Committee's revolutionary designs and since they considered that it was itself illegal and had only the authority which it had arrogated to itself, they did not grant it recognition. In addition, they wanted the Resistance to confine itself to carrying out small acts of sabotage on their instructions and they distrusted a general uprising, which in their eyes was synonymous with weakness and anarchy.

The King and Badoglio also had no intention of giving up their authority; they created a 'Military Intelligence Service' (SMI) which was set up in the centre; in Rome itself an underground military group under Colonel Montezemolo continued to be attached to the regular Army and not to the Liberation Committee. Finally, the latter's prestige was diminished by the authority of the Holy See; the Pope was making great efforts to have supplies provided for the population. He gave refuge to many anti-Fascists who were being pursued. He intervened with the Allies to prevent the city from being bombed. The people were growing used to the idea of Rome being governed from the Vatican.

Thus although Bonomi was a judicious chairman and was attempting to reconcile all Italians, the National Liberation Committee was not the major authority in the city, despite its title. Its counterpart in Upper Italy, which had its seat in Milan, was not at all the same sort of thing. True, it had the same structure as the one in Rome and in theory it agreed to take its orders from it; but the situation and social context were completely different.

Northern Italy was in fact the seat of the great Italian industrial centres. Here Communism and Socialism had long been firmly rooted. What they did could influence the masses, who followed them faithfully. Whereas the great Italian political movements, starting with the Risorgimento, had been the work of the bourgeoisie alone, for the first time workers, artisans and peasants became aware through and in the Resistance of the part they had to play.

This was going to make a tremendous difference to the Resistance. As far as the fighting was concerned it was going to be able to assert itself even in the cities, by means of mass demonstrations, acts of industrial sabotage, attacks on the enemy and strikes. But it did not limit its objectives merely to freeing territory; it had social and economic revolution in mind, the first stage of which was the struggle against the republican Fascists. In southern Italy the Resistance castigated the government; in Rome it claimed to be the government; in the north it was engaged in a patriotic and revolutionary civil war. It is true that the Liberation Committee of Upper Italy, whose authority extended as far as Florence, was joined by men of all views and from all walks of life; but it was not moderates like Bonomi who were in control of it but Communists and revolutionary intellectuals of the young Action party; and although some of the military continued to look to the Brindisi government, it was too far away to be able to govern effectively; and as for the Allies, at the end of 1943 they were preoccupied above all with their fighting in central Italy.

Thus not only did the Liberation Committee of Upper Italy become the leading wing of the Italian Resistance but it provided the framework for a vast revolutionary movement which was rousing the masses in Florence, Milan, Turin and Venice and laying the foundations for an Italy very different from the pre-war one, which in the south of the country continued to exist unchanged.

BOOK FOUR

THE DEFEAT OF GERMANY

THE ALLIED OFFENSIVE

CHAPTER I

The Bombing of Germany

FOR the Allies the end of the war in the Mediterranean and Italy's surrender were obviously welcome events and augured well for the future; but they still left Germany's military might untouched; indeed, to some extent, they relieved her of an embarrassing ally, more of a liability than an asset. It was plain that by a sort of tacit agreement between the opponents Italy would remain a minor operational theatre. The Germans were hanging on there, with the minimum of troops required, merely to keep the British and Americans as far away as possible from their own territory; the Allies were not perturbed by the slowness of their advance because their only aim was to afford some relief to the USSR and to force the Wehrmacht to withdraw troops from western Europe where they still intended to put the main weight of their effort. Until they were able to do so the USSR would continue to stand alone against the Wehrmacht which was not greatly weakened by the absence of the units left behind in Italy. For their part, in implementation of the Casablanca decisions, the British and the Americans were going to apply themselves above all to destroying Germany's industrial potential; basically, they were putting into effect the plan devised by Britain and France as early as 1939; but the American arsenal provided them with incomparably more powerful means of carrying it out and thus made it finally possible. We must examine the conceptions underlying the use of these means, the methods employed and the results which the Allies hoped to achieve. First and foremost what should be the targets? On the German side, what was the political and economic situation in the autumn of 1943, in this war of attrition that had set in on the Russian steppes as well as in the Italian mountains, in the Atlantic as well as in the skies over Germany?

I THE FINANCING OF THE NAZI WAR

The keystone of the Reich's economic legislation with regard to the war was a decree dated September 4, 1939. It introduced for the duration of the war a fifty per cent rise in income tax and an increased consumer tax for certain products; in addition, local communities were bound to transfer part of their tax revenue to the state. Other decrees, notably one in October 1941 and another in April 1942 laid down that excessive profits could be absorbed by taxation.

These fiscal measures did not suffice to finance the German armaments programme. To cover the expenditure of 657,000 million marks incurred during the five years of the war, revenue provided at most 315,000 million marks, that is rather less than one half. The balance came from the occupied countries amongst whom France's share was the largest, since it amounted to forty per cent of all the resources contributed to the Reich by the whole of conquered Europe.

But whilst subjecting the German nation to a considerable fiscal strain, the Nazi régime, for propaganda reasons, endeavoured to prevent prices from rising; against the advice of the general staff, Hitler decided to increase the production of consumer goods, at the expense of armaments, after the defeat of France in June 1940; until 1943 at least, the Germans' standard of living remained higher than that of the British.

So to make good the deficit more and more paper money was printed and the national debt rose considerably. It stood at 37,000 million marks at the beginning of the war and Schacht thought it too high then; by 1945, it had reached 380,000 million; it was clear that such a sum, even in the event of a German victory, could not have been paid off except by openly resorting to inflation.

Despite the swollen purchasing power, the régime cleverly avoided arousing doubts in the population and for four years maintained the stability of the currency. It owed its success to strict regulations governing the distribution of the vital commodities so that nobody went short, and also to very close supervision of wages and prices – price increases were subject to extremely heavy penalties. To counteract the effects of the increased purchasing power brought about by inflation – the deposit accounts of the Issuing Institute rose from 55,000 million marks in 1938 to 237,000 million at the end of 1944 – the government resorted only sparingly to taxation and loans; thus, in 'socialist' Germany, large fortunes paid less income tax than in 'plutocratic' Britain. As for loans, they also aroused a sense of coercion, since patriotic propaganda made it difficult to refuse to subscribe. The German government preferred to use a 'quiet method of financing' by forcing those organisations holding capital funds – banks, savings banks and insurance companies – to make them available to the state. Most Germans thus became state creditors, often without realising it.

But it was clear that the whole system could last only as long as the Germans had confidence in their leaders, that is as long as the Wehrmacht's successes promised final victory for Germany.

At least, up to 1944 the war economy was being financed in the least unpalatable way. True, in 1945, the Reich was at the end of her financial tether; but it was the dilapidated state of her economy that had revealed her financial plight to the Germans.

II THE ORGANISATION OF THE GERMAN WAR ECONOMY

Germany had entered the war with a modernised industry, armaments production double that of Britain, reserves of raw materials, not unlimited but considerable, and with her factories dispersed to the four corners of the land in a way which partly compensated for the vulnerability of the Ruhr. Nonetheless, she was equipped and organised for a short war and this situation persisted until 1942. By that date, in fact, her armament production had been overtaken by Britain's; and no restrictions of any importance had been placed on civilian needs.

In fact, despite the application of the *Führer-Prinzip* from top to bottom of Nazi society, the organisation of war production was a complete shambles. It was true that it was mainly in the hands of Goering, the dictator in charge of the Four Year Plan and as such responsible for the Ministries of Economics, of Labour and of Food. But Todt controlled the Ministry of Armaments, as well as the enormous organisation of major construction works which bore his name; the two were more or less autonomous. Hitler himself issued instructions of paralysing effect: he thought that he could achieve his objectives one after the other without lowering the German standard of living too much; he did not wish to sacrifice agricultural production; on principle, he considered that the place of the German woman was in the home – this prohibition was going to inhibit the employment of female labour until the end of the war. In 1940 and 1941, the civilian sectors of industry were allocated almost as much steel as the armaments factories.

Thus, in 1941, Germany produced 12,400 aircraft and 5,100 tanks and Britain alone 20,094 and 4,841 respectively; in 1942, comparative production was 15,409 aircraft and 9,400 tanks in Germany as against 23,672 and 8,611 in Britain. At that rate, with the help of American production, the Germans' early advantage was soon to become a thing of the past. And in the USSR the war was becoming long drawn out and turning into a war of attrition; Germany needed shaking out of the semi-lethargy into which she had sunk.

On February 15, 1942, Todt was killed in an air crash. To replace him Hitler called on the architect Speer; he took over Todt's two functions but at the same time he remained responsible for the 'central armament-planning programme' and a member of the Central Planning Committee.

Henceforth, absolute priority would be given to the armaments industry, in the allocation of both raw materials and manpower. Sauckel was put in charge of recruiting the masses of humanity in the appropriate numbers for Speer's needs.

Speer organised his ministry with the sole object of increasing output. He put industrialists in the important positions while still leaving them in charge of their own businesses, to avoid any director-manager dichotomy which has the unfortunate result of creating delays and squabbles. Under him, German output of armaments did not cease rising until 1945. He was able to do virtually anything he wanted except when he clashed with Himmler and the ss. He formed a special commission for the allocation of raw materials and machinery; he appointed well-tried experts; he made ever-increasing use of mass-production and assembly lines. This planning was to bear fruit.

By the autumn of 1943, German consumption had still not been reduced. By drawing on occupied Europe, above all France, Belgium and Holland in various ways[1] for raw materials, manufactured goods and foodstuffs, Germany increased her own resources by a quarter.

Coal output, which was 402 million tons in 1941, rose to 429 million in 1943. Steel production which reached 32 million tons in 1942 rose to only 34·6 million tons in 1943: Germany was paying dearly for Hitler's blunder in 1938 when he rejected the idea of building blast furnaces and sacrificed everything to the immediate manufacture of armaments. Aluminium production reached 367,000 and 378,000 tons in those same years. There was no shortage of rare ores: Turkey was letting Germany have her chrome and Spain and Portugal their wolfram. Crude oil output rose from 1,520,000 tons in 1940 to 1,989,000 tons in 1943; motor fuel and synthetic oils reached 1,900,000 tons in 1940 and set up a record in 1943 with 3,834,000 tons.[2]

There was thus a constant improvement but not sufficient to keep pace with the need of the armaments industries; the Reich's war industry never reached the levels of the Americans' arsenal.

III THE MANPOWER PROBLEMS

After four years of war, by the autumn of 1943, Germany had lost nearly 4 million men, killed, missing, wounded or captured, the great majority on the Russian front. At the same date, the total strength of her armed forces, not counting satellite troops, amounted to 11 million men. It was

1. See pp. 234 and 249.
2. Including 1,130,000 and 1,917,000 tons respectively of synthetic petrol.

difficult to increase it; indeed, it had dropped by 200,000 men in a few months and the physical condition of the most recent recruits had proved not completely satisfactory. The high command had been forced to reform a certain number of divisions by reducing their strength, a reduction which had not been compensated for by an increase in their fire-power, in fact, quite the reverse.

The civilian labour force of German origin at that time amounted to 30,300,000 persons. Nearly 8 million were employed in industry, of whom only 280,000 were women. These figures could hardly be increased; they had even dropped by 2 million since 1940 to fill the gaps in the Wehrmacht. By means of compulsory labour service, by the autumn of 1943 Sauckel had succeeded in commandeering for work in the Reich a labour force of 6,300,000 men and women, half of them voluntary, half forced labour; it could not be indefinitely increased beyond this figure; throughout occupied Europe, refusal to undertake forced labour was becoming widespread; those commandeered often did not have the necessary training or ability; they were not all reliable; their different origins and languages and their varying skills hindered their full productivity.

Speer turned to the labour reserve of prisoners of war and the inexhaustible supply offered by the concentration camps. Although asserting his respect for the Geneva Convention which protected prisoners of war, he was nevertheless going to employ them in illegal ways and the Convention did not stop him from using Soviet prisoners, since the USSR was not a signatory. On July 8, 1943, a personal decree from the Führer himself laid down that 300,000 Soviet POWs should be set to work in the coalmines, even if they were partisans between the ages of 16 and 55; before this they were shot; they were to be placed under the control of civilians, who would have the right to punish them if they misbehaved.

In April 1943, 200,000 French prisoners were transformed into civilian workers; the Vichy government urged officers to accept this change, though the Convention exempted them from having to work. A move in the other direction was when 300,000 Dutch prisoners of war who had been allowed to go home were recalled in the same month by their German jailers but most of them managed to obtain false papers and avoided having to go back to Germany. After September 1943, 400,000 Italian workers who had freely opted to work in Germany became military internees and lived in conditions similar to those of POWs; but as they were not servicemen, they were sent without more ado to work in armaments factories.

In February 1944, the number of prisoners of war who had been set to work was 1,930,000; to these must be added the Polish prisoners who, having lost their nationality, had been reduced to the status of slave labour; thus, with the French 'converted' POWs, the total was 2,500,000 or

8 per cent of the Reich's labour force. This did not include the Soviet prisoners employed in the occupied areas of the USSR (in all 5 million Soviet soldiers were captured during the war). A large part of this force worked as farm labourers, which required no special skills; but more than a million of them kept the wheels of the principal German industrial concerns turning.

The labour force from the concentration camps was both less reliable and less sound. Himmler would have liked to set up factories inside the camps and this was sometimes done, on a small scale, in Dachau, Buchenwald and Mauthausen; Speer pointed out both that it would be impossible to transport machine tools to the camps and that output would be higher elsewhere; and in September 1942, Hitler approved this. So instead it was the concentration camps or rather their large *kommandos* which were sited close to the factories. But Speer did not succeed in obtaining permission for the Jews to work in armament factories; Nazi racialism took precedence over armament manufacture and they were excluded in 1943 and sent off to Birkenau.

Internees from concentration camps were used, as were prisoners of war, by all the large German firms, in aircraft factories as well as in the underground factories where the secret weapons were assembled, in Dora, Laura and Ebensee. It seems to have been I. G. Farben which employed the greatest number, about 60,000, in its synthetic-rubber factories near Auschwitz. Their contribution was inconsiderable in extent and minimal in value. It was, however, significant for the evolution of the Nazi régime during the war that the ss, from having the task of exterminating the enemies of the Reich, should have become a purveyor for her industries; this did not, however, prevent the industrial labour force from increasing only at a very inadequate rate from 1939 to 1945.

IV SPEER'S PRIORITIES

However, in the autumn of 1943, the Greater Reich lacked neither soldiers nor manpower, any more than she lacked raw materials or motor-fuel, and she was still waging war from her own territory. But the war had taken on such vast proportions that she could not possibly cope with everything at once; she had to choose, and it was Speer's task to fix the priorities and to see that they were adhered to. The first casualty was agriculture, which was sacrificed to industry.

In the field of armaments, too, a choice was made in accordance with the immediate needs of the moment, that is of the war in the USSR. It still seemed possible to win this war but henceforth there was a risk of losing it and this risk must be minimised. But the war in the USSR was more like that which was waged in the Argonne or at Verdun in 1916–17 than the Blitzkrieg of 1940 when aircraft zoomed triumphantly overhead as the tanks careered ahead below; the Russian war brought millions of men face to face, fighting desperately to hold their ground, who needed to be adequately provided with the necessary supplies and equipment of the right quality.

Speer adopted the OKW's forecast of needs and met its requests. He granted absolute priority to guns, mortars, machine guns, small-arms ammunition, anti-tank weapons, motorised vehicles and tanks, in short everything that enabled armies to hold on to their positions or to advance. Thus in 1943, the output of guns was double that of 1942; it was going to increase by more than half in 1944.

Similarly, the output of tanks rose from 9,395 in 1942 to 19,885 in 1943 and 27,300 in 1944; it increased almost threefold in two years. Guderian alleged that this numerical increase took place at the expense of their quality. According to him, the expert tank officers would have liked the German designers to learn from the Soviet T 34 model but they were 'too proud of their own powers of invention'; they were also hampered by a shortage of 'steel alloys'. It would seem, in fact, that Speer was above all anxious to simplify production by reducing the number of types of tank; with Hitler's approval, he gave instructions that henceforth only Tigers and Panthers should be built; this last model was not yet being mass-produced. Guderian considered that this decision explained the defeats on the Russian front, especially in that it stopped the manufacture of Mark IV. This remark looks very much like an alibi; although the Tiger was too high, inadequately powered and with an insufficient range of action, on the other hand the Panthers had proved satisfactory; furthermore, at the end of 1944, powerful new models were going to appear, superior to their opponents, such as the 68-ton *Königstiger* with a 600-h.p. engine, armed with an 88-mm gun and two machine guns; it really seems difficult to blame Speer for the Wehrmacht's defeat.

Since the OKW considered that in the USSR the air force had become merely an auxiliary branch of the army, it was natural for it to suffer from Speer's decisions, since, although aircraft production did not come within his terms of reference, he was in a position to reduce their supplies of raw materials. Goering could hardly raise any opposition, since, while his own mountebank claims had regularly promised success, the successive failures of the Luftwaffe from the Battle of Britain to that of Stalingrad had considerably reduced his prestige and consequently, the trust and power that the Führer placed in him.

Speer put an end to the excessive efforts being expended on synthetic petrol production: in 1942 building had started on factories that could not be finished owing to lack of men and equipment. He considered that the discovery of a large oil field in the region of Zistersdorf in Austria would provide adequate compensation; moreover, over the next two years, Romanian oil would cover Germany's needs, estimated at 6,970,000 tons in 1943. Also, if the Caucasian oil wells were captured, the problem would be settled once and for all.

He similarly refused to allow the aircraft industry any priority in manpower, despite the storm of protest raised by Goering and Milch; as a young industry, the aeronautical industry also had a young labour force, and consequently the one best fitted for military service. The time was certainly past when Goering bragged – and Hitler believed – that the Luftwaffe would win the war on its own.

V GERMAN AIRCRAFT PRODUCTION

For the manufacture of aircraft, programmes had been drawn up with a short war in mind. Goering had decided to concentrate only on prototypes capable of going quickly into mass-production, with the emphasis on models of most immediate use for the fighting. The logical conclusion of this decision was to stop further research.

The length of the war thus condemned Germany to manufacture unimproved types of aircraft which thus became progressively outdated, as opposed to the completely modern ones being produced by the Americans. In this way, from the end of 1941, the Luftwaffe had had to give up night bombing, since the RAF night fighters inflicted heavy losses on the German bombers; on the other hand, the latter's range of action which had not been extended, became progressively inadequate as the battlefield spread over the enormous distances of Russia. Nor had the aircraft been planned to withstand either the Russian cold or the torrid Saharan heat.

The case of the Junkers 88 was a good illustration of the stagnating German aeronautical industry: it came out in 1936; its speed was 333 m.p.h. and it could carry two tons of bombs 1,250 miles; at that time, it outclassed any of its possible opponents; accordingly it was put into mass-production; between 1939 and 1945 its armament was improved and its pay-load increased by half; 15,000 of them were built; but its speed remained the same; by 1943, it was considerably inferior to its American counterparts and very vulnerable to their fighter attack.

In fact, it took an aircraft five years to go from drawing-board to full-scale production; new research in 1940 could have borne fruit in 1943–4; in this kind of production, the important thing therefore was not to be left behind at the start. In 1944 when Speer arranged for certain earlier projects to be started up again, it was too late; the most serious consequence of this initial blunder was that the manufacture of jet aircraft, having once been halted, never caught up again.[1]

In order to take advantage of Germany's initial air superiority, Goering did not devote any time to organising the structure of the aeronautical industry. Far from being specialised, the aircraft manufacturer built every type of aircraft: fighters, bombers, transports, etc. Instead of carefully choosing one type and employing every possible means to bring it out quickly, a number of them were followed up at once – in 1942, Heinkel were manufacturing three different engines at the same time. Thus they ignored the rules of large-scale mass-production, with all the economies achieved by the rational use of raw materials, machine tools, manpower, upkeep, storage, etc. At every level and with every means they could, the manufacturers defended the interests and prestige of their own firms; this led to endless debate and, above all, to an excessive number of types of aircraft being manufactured: twenty-four in 1942, twenty-three in 1943 and twenty-seven in 1944.

The top men in the Luftwaffe had not received the necessary training, least of all Goering. They were not technical experts but famous pilots, like Udet; they were not always able to realise the significance of certain technical questions or of decisions that lay outside their experience; attracted by the sporting nature of dive-bombing attacks, Udet had been responsible for increasing the number of medium bombers, the Stukas, at the expense of heavy bombers. Jeschonnek, the Chief of Air Staff, had backed him by assuring everyone, to Goering's great satisfaction, that thus armed, the Luftwaffe would be irresistible. Their blunders led them both to commit suicide, Udet after the failure of the Battle of Britain, Jeschonnek after the Battle of Stalingrad. This tragic exit did not make up for their mistakes.

In September 1942, Goering ordered a reduction in the time taken between working out a prototype and putting it into mass-production; it was easy to give an order, but carrying it out was another matter. The clumsy bureaucratic procedure in any case really precluded cutting any corners; the result of his order was that aircraft were brought hurriedly into service and proved unsuitable, or else that aircraft fell short of their estimated performance; in both cases, production had to be stopped and the delays grew longer.

It was not until March 1944 after Goering's disgrace when his incautious slogan that the 'German skies were inviolable' was given a devastating lie by Allied air raids, that Speer was able to take over aircraft production through his deputy Saur. It was very late in the day.

The first result of this state of affairs was that the gradual and continuous increase in German aircraft production was misleading: the proportion of

1. Cf. pp. 655 et seq.

new types of aircraft was low. Thus, out of 18,000 bombers actually delivered to the armed forces from 1942 to 1945, less than half were new types; the others had been used in the battles of 1939, 1940 and 1941 and more or less improved in the meantime.

The second result was that the Luftwaffe found it impossible to meet all its commitments; this was not due to lack of funds, since they had risen from 3,000 million Reichsmarks in 1939 to 12,000 million in 1944; but the proliferation and diversity of its tasks made it necessary to choose between certain imperative but contradictory needs, and the Führer could not make up his mind. Defending German air space against the British and American Air Forces in order to protect the armament factories and provide weapons for the armed forces fighting on the eastern front was the first need, and that required more and better fighter planes; but supporting the troops fighting in the USSR meant providing medium bombers, reconnaissance aircraft and transport planes in addition to fighters; finally, it was possible to give the Allies tit for tat only by bombing their home territory by using heavy bombers, the output of which had been held back as a deliberate policy since the beginning of the war.

General Milch, whose task was to handle the Air Force's economic problems, wanted to give priority to fighters; his programme provided for an output of 1,000 planes per month in 1942, 2,000 in 1943 and 3,000 in 1944. It was a defensive conception of air warfare as unattractive to Hitler as a retreat on the Russian front by German troops. He had 1,000 bombers per month added on to the programme, so that neither figure was achieved.

Above all, the intensified Allied air raids seemed an outrageous insult to the Führer. He had dreams of bombers flying at over 45,000 feet appearing over London on a sort of conveyor-belt system and equally capable of flying out to destroy the Russian factories in the Urals. Heinkel designed a four-engined bomber with a speed of 360 m.p.h. and a range of nearly 4,000 miles; a formidable aircraft, but it was the spring of 1944 before the first of them took to the air. It was not until July 1944 that Hitler categorically ordered a reduction in the number of types of aircraft, at the cost of sacrificing models in current production. By this time he had at last come out in support of new weapons, including jet aircraft; but this decision would begin to take effect only in 1945.

But by the middle of 1944, a report by Saur showed that the manpower resources of the allied and occupied countries were exhausted and that the production of machine tools was dropping irretrievably. It was too late to improve the operational performance of the aircraft and difficult even to prevent it from declining, for want of certain items of equipment, radio communications or armament.

Thus in 1944 the Luftwaffe, which had enabled the Wehrmacht to achieve its successes in 1939, was to prove unequal to all its tasks, whether in support of the ground forces fighting in the USSR, preventing the landings in Italy or France or, even as early as 1943, providing effective protection of the vital industrial centres against Allied air raids.

VI THE BRITISH AND THE BOMBING OF GERMANY

Unlike Hitler, Churchill saw victory in the future, not in the present; this induced him to take decisions that were all the more risky because they were not based on an analysis of a given situation but on a sort of prophetic outlook. Thus he had firmly gambled on the effect of bombing Germany. In any case, before 1943 the only way left to the British was to carry the war into enemy territory and, up to 1942, to prove British determination; the only way, also, until the Normandy landings, of helping the Soviet Union by tying down German fighters and flak away from her territory.

Despite requests, whose urgency he fully understood, both from the Navy, which wanted better air cover for its convoys, and the Army which preferred tactical aircraft to support ground operations, despite, too, Alanbrooke's pessimistic view that by trying to do everything at once you ran the risk of losing all over the board, Churchill pushed through his idea of increasing the output and operational use of heavy bombers; he was held back by the shortcomings of the British aeronautical industry; but American help renewed his hopes and confirmed him in his attitude.

So from 1941 onwards the British brought into action a strategic bomber force, Bomber Command. The first phase was unsuccessful; most of the bombs fell a long way from their targets. Moreover, for want of long-range fighters, the bombers were operating at night; their targets were selected more by reason of their proximity or because of the weather conditions prevailing at the time than for their military importance. The results were disappointing; even on a moonlit night accurate bombing proved impossible; navigational errors were frequent; the crews were misled by dummy fires lit by the enemy; if they did reach their target, they came away with an exaggerated idea of the extent of the damage. At the end of 1941, it became clear that only one-fifth of the bombers were dropping their bombs within a radius of three and a half miles of the spot they were aiming at.

Various technical devices enabled this performance to be improved. By 1942, the radar research centre at Malvern College had achieved miracles; the pilot could be led on to his target without actually seeing it. Churchill had ordered that during raids 'window' should be dropped; these were strips of silvered paper which jammed the enemy's radar screens and made it difficult to distinguish between friendly and enemy aircraft. But it was not until 1944 that British radar using VHF, which had been tried out in the previous November, came into general use and enabled the bombers actually to see their target; instead of merely recording the echo sent back by an object, aircrew could see a picture of the city or district on their screen.

From 1943 onwards, Bomber Command had perfected its tactics of massive night attacks on a large target with a force of 1,000 aircraft; they were first used in a raid on Cologne on May 30, 1942. A few minutes before zero hour, the targets were marked by flares dropped by aircraft; all kinds of interference and deceptive devices ensured surprise; the bombers then came in at timetabled intervals of twenty-five to thirty minutes. A photograph of the bombed area was taken automatically at the moment the bombs were released; next day, a scrutiny of the log-books of the pilot, the flight engineer and the radio operator enabled any errors to be discovered, so as to prepare the raid better next time; before each raid, the crews were assembled for briefing and each member was given the appropriate intelligence: weather conditions, detailed flight plans, the siting of the enemy AA on the route, details of the target, conventional landmarks.

But though the British had found the right method, they lacked the means of applying it profitably; they were short of heavy bombers: these were going to be provided by the Americans.

VII THE AMERICANS AND CARPET BOMBING

In Casablanca Roosevelt had readily been convinced by Churchill of the effectiveness of air warfare: was it not the only possible way to employ American equipment in Europe without further delay? Its purpose was threefold: to destroy the military, industrial and economic potential of the Reich; undermine German morale; and prepare the landing across the Channel by weakening the enemy's defence capability.

American air force bases were set up in Britain, and they were steadily reinforced. The American B 17 and B 29 aircraft were air cruisers, 'Flying Fortresses'; powerfully armed to defend themselves without help against fighters and thus not requiring any fighter escort, possessing a very long range, capable of carrying many tons of bombs and provided with devices – the gyroscopic bomb sight – enabling them to bomb accurately from heights out of the range of AA; in a word, invulnerable, at least in theory. The B 29 went into mass-production in July 1943; it weighed sixty-one tons and carried nine tons of bombs, over a distance of more than 3,000 miles, at 360 m.p.h. and at a height of nearly 40,000 feet.

The British and Americans shared the tasks out between themselves; the former continued night operations; as it was difficult to hit an exact target, they bombed large areas, that is urban centres; it was a 'terror offensive' which caused great ruin and devastation and above all affected the civilian population. The Americans flew by day; they endeavoured to attack key targets with the maximum likelihood of hitting them; but it was, of course, important to pick out these targets and establish an order of priority.

The choice of town was no problem; one after the other, they were all carpet bombed, some of them several times, starting with Hamburg. In 1943, 135,000 tons of bombs were dropped on Lübeck, Rostock, Bremen, Stuttgart, Nuremberg, the industrial centre of the Ruhr, and above all Berlin, where 50,000 tons of bombs caused havoc over an area of more than ten square miles, rendering a million people homeless. In 1944, as the Allied air bases in Italy and France came nearer and nearer to German territory, the bombers penetrated further and further into the heart of Germany. Every evening, as a sort of uplifting litany the BBC announced that 1,000 RAF bombers had buried yet one more German city under blazing rubble. Italian-based American aircraft landed in the USSR to avoid having to make the round trip, outside their range. The losses were not excessively heavy: in three successive raids on Hamburg, fifty-eight bombers out of 2,650 were lost, that is 2¼ per cent; over Berlin which was further away and better defended, they were heavier – nine per cent in the raid of December 1943. The heaviest was ten per cent in the attack on Leipzig in February 1944. They dropped almost to nothing when the German jamming stations were destroyed in October 1944.

The peak of this method of war was reached with the bombing of Dresden on February 13, 1945. It lasted fourteen hours and 135,000 people were killed – more than at Hiroshima. Appalling scenes took place; charred corpses were enveloped in sheets of flame; shapeless masses of blood, flesh and bones showed where groups of people had clung together in a vain attempt to seek shelter; the attackers suffered practically no losses.

Dresden was not an industrial town and it was badly defended. Discovering industrial targets was another matter. In fact, the Allies were completely ignorant of the layout of Germany's industry; its siting was known only very roughly. An analysis of Germany's industrial potential made at the outbreak of hostilities by British economists who were experts on Germany and which had been accepted by Churchill had seriously underestimated it by roughly a half; it was also clear that the Germans' exploitation of Europe had upset the initial premises.

In 1943, the Ruhr was the main target because of its proximity and the high density of its industries; German war production seemed to be hardly affected. Selected targets were then chosen; several raids were made on the ball-bearing factory at Schweinfurt, not far from Frankfurt, whose production was considered essential for the Wehrmacht's motorised vehicles. Other targets were submarine bases, notably at Lorient, and submarine shipyards and repair shops. From the spring of 1944 onwards, the large synthetic petrol factories were attacked, the oil works at Ploesti some thirty times or more. The same thing happened to electricity generating stations, marshalling yards, hydro-electric dams, etc.

Each of these attacks entailed heavy losses: the one on Schweinfurt in October 1943 led to the loss of twenty per cent of the aircraft engaged; the first raid on Ploesti, 54 aircraft out of 177; the successful destruction of the Moehne dam caused fifty per cent losses. In a few months, the American Eighth Air Force based in Britain lost 4,700 aircraft; the average life of a bomber aircraft was estimated to be 160 days; the pilots knew that they too were doomed.

The result was that the Luftwaffe had to be destroyed by attacking aircraft factories; but they were dispersed, camouflaged, often hidden underground and thus difficult to detect and hit.

This state of affairs was becoming critical when suddenly in the middle of 1944 a breakthrough was made. The Flying Fortresses, which had proved more vulnerable than might have been supposed, were provided with fighter escort by American P 51 Mustangs and long-range Lockheeds and Thunderbolts. Thus the Battle of Britain began again but this time over Germany: Allied fighter aircraft sought out and destroyed the German fighters, either in combat or on their airfields, on their home ground. The results were quickly seen: American bomber losses fell from nine per cent in October 1943 to 3½ per cent in March 1944.

However, Allied air supremacy was never absolutely complete; it did sometimes happen that, adventitiously, by a concentration of forces, the Luftwaffe regained a local advantage; but generally it was beaten by day and by night; bombing techniques were being continually improved, Allied losses fell and greater and greater havoc was wrought. The lesson to be drawn was that, in the air as on the ground, victory was not to be had for the asking.

VIII THE EFFECTIVENESS OF THE BOMBING

The Allies consistently overestimated the effectiveness of their bombing; they mistook the rubble for serious damage. From the point of view of morale, they did indeed achieve some, albeit not decisive, success. Goebbels used the propaganda slogan of 'barbarous Anglo-Saxons attacking the civilian population' in order to whip up the fighting spirit of the Germans. When towns in occupied countries were raided, the population was greatly upset by the senseless destruction caused by the 'liberators', which gave the lie to the BBC's assurances that only military targets were being hit. The entire Resistance movement in Provence violently protested against a raid on Marseilles and pointed out that given the necessary instructions and explosives they could have done the job better and at less cost themselves. One FFI leader from Brittany described the result of a massive and ill-directed raid, as follows: 'Effect on the population, terrifying; on the friends of the Allies, depressing; on their opponents, nil.' However, in the large German cities that had been rendered uninhabitable, millions were forced either to leave or go on living in miserable conditions which in the long run could not fail to wear down their physical resistance, undermine their determination and sap the morale of the fighting services when they heard of it.

On the economic level, the results were not as good as had been hoped. The view that the destruction of sixty 'key targets' would suffice to bring Germany to her knees proved to be mistaken. Tank and aircraft production was made more difficult and perhaps slowed down, yet it continued to rise until the end of 1944, thanks to Speer's dispersal of the factories. When at the end of August 1944, the Russians occupied the Ploesti area, five out of the fourteen refineries were still working and producing one-third of the quantity of oil being produced before the raids; similarly, the output of synthetic rubber did not fall, although it did not increase according to plan; these effects were certainly not negligible but they were not decisive; it was not until 1945 that the Luftwaffe began to run short of fuel.

GERMAN ARMAMENT PRODUCTION[1]

1940	1941	1942	1943	1944
17,847	24,520	36,804	71,692	106,258

BOMBS DROPPED ON GREATER GERMANY[2]

1940	1941	1942	1943	1944
13,000[3]	31,700[3]	48,000[3]	207,600[4]	915,000[5]

1. Heavy artillery, tanks and aircraft, in numbers of units.
2. In tons.
3. By the RAF alone.
4. Including 44,000 by the American air force.
5. Including 389,000 by the American air force.

It is important to note that:

1. It is impossible to distinguish between the raids made in support of operations and those against German industrial targets.
2. The bombs dropped from aircraft based in southern Italy after October 1943 do not figure in the totals.
3. Although German armament production still rose in 1944, this was primarily during the first six months; output fell sharply in the second half of the year.

In most cases, German ingenuity and hard work made good the damage. The example of Schweinfurt was significant; the first few raids badly damaged a number of workshops; the last one had little effect; Speer had had the time to protect, hide and disperse the workshops; ball-bearing factories remained top-priority targets for the Allied air staff but nobody knew where they were and until 1945 their output rose steadily. Could the Allies have done any better?

It is difficult to agree with General Spaatz in blaming the Allied authorities for these rather meagre results, compared with the means employed and the results expected; according to him, the authorities did not give the Air Force all the necessary equipment because they did not understand 'the revolutionary possibilities of strategic bombing'. This is the point of view of the man in charge who is inclined to believe that he is never properly understood or adequately backed. In fact, Roosevelt and Churchill did believe in the effectiveness of the strategic air force and they supported it lavishly.

Must one then share Colonel Tarlet's view that the 530,000 tons of bombs dropped on the towns were wasted and that better use could have been made of the 2 million tons that fell on Germany as a whole? Colonel Tarlet considers that the Allies should have reserved their bombs for two targets: motor-fuel and transport. This opinion seems contradicted by the course of the operations; strategic bombing paid off in certain circumstances: Allied air supremacy, superiority in aircraft, accessible targets, concerted action with the ground forces meant anything could be destroyed, as was seen by the successful attacks on the v-1 and v-2 factories and launching ramps. Earlier, any more specific choice of target would hardly have reduced the effectiveness of the Luftwaffe and the German flak – far from it, since the targets selected would have been better protected. Any attack on communications before June 1944 would in any case have had little point since there was no Allied army yet hammering on the gates of Germany and needing protection against the bringing up of massive enemy reinforcements.

In fact, strategic bombing had great importance, but indirectly and its action was delayed; a great number of workers were diverted from production to repair work; there was a considerable demoralising effect, difficult to assess, on service men who were worried about the fate of their families and possessions; from 1943 onwards almost 2 million men were immobilised in the flak depots and batteries and they could have been used at the front; the whole deployment of the Luftwaffe was upset: in June 1941, sixty-five per cent of Germany's air forces were concentrated in the east as against only thirty-two per cent three years later.

GREATER GERMANY'S WAR EFFORT

	1939	1940	1941	1942	1943	1944
Coal output (in millions of tons)	332·8	364·8	402·8	407·8	429·0	432·8
Steel output (in millions of tons)	22·5	21·5	31·8	32·1	34·6	28·5[1]
Synthetic motor-fuel (in millions of tons)		4,650	5,540	6,360	7,510	5,400[2]
German labour force (in thousands)	39,100	34,800	33,100	31,300	30,300	29,000
German labour employed in industry (in thousands)	10,855	9,745	8,861	8,011	7,948	7,515
Foreign labour employed in the whole German economy (in thousands)	300	1,150	3,020	4,120	6,260	7,130
Foreign labour employed in industry (in thousands)	104	236	644	1,001	2,061	2,367
Armed forces (in thousands)	1,336	5,600	7,400	9,400	11,235	12,385
Guns produced		5,500	7,000	12,000	27,000	41,000
Tanks produced	2,000	2,200	5,120	9,395	19,885	27,300
Aircraft produced including:	8,296	10,247	12,400	15,409	24,807	37,950
Bomber aircraft	2,886	3,952	4,350	6,537	8,589	6,468
Fighter aircraft	1,856	3,146	3,744	5,215	11,738	28,925

1. From 9·2 million tons in the first quarter, production dropped to 3·9 million in the last quarter.
2. Goering planned for an output of 10 million tons in 1945; in February 1945, it was 1,000 tons.

It is true that strategic bombing was not enough to win the war, as had been believed in France and England in 1939, and as Churchill still hoped in 1943. But when it was combined with large-scale ground operations, it worked admirably. From June 1944 onwards, it enabled the armies who landed to rely on complete control of the air; inversely, as they advanced, the bombers could penetrate more deeply and wreak greater havoc. These two causes were mutually helpful in increasing the effect. But the Luftwaffe had long since been forced back on the defensive, despite Hitler's fury and his occasional vain attempts to manufacture heavy bombers; by 1943, the attacks were all one-sided; the Germans could now only hope that one day their flying bombs would pay their opponents back, with dividends.

In short, in order to win the war, it was not enough to destroy German towns and factories; it was also primarily necessary for the Allied armies to fight and win their battles, first and foremost in the USSR.

CHAPTER 2

The Soviet Offensive.
The Teheran Conference

(July 1943–May 1944)

FROM the summer of 1943 onwards, the Red Army launched a series of offensives which broke like waves, at first intermittently and then in continuous succession; they were to stop only when Germany was defeated; in contrast to the earlier German offensive, they were not governed by the seasons and their impetus was maintained summer and winter; they would halt in one sector only long enough to enable the bulk of the troops and their equipment to catch up with the forward elements and build up a solid springboard for a fresh advance. The Germans were powerless to withstand this relentless tide; they were able to regain the initiative only in local attacks for a limited period and if they sometimes succeeded in winning back a little ground or clinging on to some point that they felt to be important, they never succeeded in breaking up the Soviet advance, although they might slow it down; even when they met initial success, their convulsive effort was short-lived because at the same time, in other operational theatres on the immensely long front, they had been forced to retreat and they finally had to bring all their forces into line on new positions, not of their choice but those to which their units had been forced to retreat.

In their memoirs, the German generals have put the blame for their defeats on Hitler's 'mistakes' and the Russians' 'qualities'. After blindly obeying their Führer for four years and falling over themselves to sing the praises of his military genius, they had discovered that he was self-taught, or half-taught; in short, a corporal left over from the First World War. It was a matter of granting to a man, in the painful hours of adversity, the authority and status which until then he had only possessed in times of victory and success.

According to these German chroniclers, the 'qualities' of the Russians were, first of all, the climate, represented by 'General Winter' who always arrived earlier than expected, who was harsher than he had ever been before and whose main target of attack was Germans; then the inexhaustible reserves of manpower of the USSR, who, backed by American equipment, overwhelmed the Wehrmacht; finally, the backward nature of the Soviet's economy and population, the lack of roads that hamstrung motorised units and the wild determination of the 'Asiatics' which enabled them to fight to the last on an empty stomach and even when surrounded.

Explanations of this sort have the advantage of leaving untarnished the myth of the strategic superiority of the Wehrmacht generals and the fighting quality of their troops; they were defeated by an unbeatable combination of adverse circumstances, but not by soldiers who were better than they were. But these explanations are self-contradictory. Without adequate logistical backing, how can one explain the Russians' ability to concentrate enormous masses of artillery at the right time and place? 'Tartar hordes' are not able to mount a series of interrelated offensives, with clockwork precision, hundreds of miles apart, each interlocking with the other in such a way as to overwhelm, irresistibly, the defence positions set up by the military geniuses of the OKH. Why should the winter and lack of roads have hindered the Germans and not the Russians, whether advancing or retreating?

In fact, the Germans were beaten by superior opponents; superior in number, of course, but also in equipment and quality. They were beaten by the Soviet's economic potential capable of manufacturing more arms, despite the loss of the richest areas of the USSR – American lend-lease contributed about eight per cent of the Russian production; they found themselves face to face with a mass of human beings fired with greater fervour and pugnacity than their own, whether the reason was love of their native soil or defence of a political system; finally, they were forced to bow to strategic thinking and logistical organisation better than theirs because it was completely adapted to the conditions of warfare in the USSR by an amazing generation of youthful army marshals.

I HITLER AND THE WAR IN THE USSR

In July 1943, there was no change in the German higher command; the Führer was still the supreme political and military leader; there was still an OKW and an OKH; in fact, as General de Cossé-Brissac has emphasised, these two bodies 'no longer had one subordinated to the other but existed side by side'. The Soviet war had become the concern of the OKH whose Chief of Staff, General Zeitzler, was at Hitler's beck and call. The latter had taken over command of operations and he interfered in the details of their course; thus he sometimes impeded the executive officers who did not dare decide on the spot to take the measures they deemed necessary because the Master might disown them.

Hitler was obsessed with one idea: any retreat was to be condemned because in his view it meant a lack of determination or indeed defeatism. He was also anxious to hang on to his gains: manganese, iron, coal, wheat. Yet he was not entirely deaf to reason; after an interview with von Manstein, he authorised him to withdraw some thirty miles; he made amends to Guderian by recalling him after he had dismissed him because he had ventured to contradict the Führer and he appointed him Inspector General of the Panzer division.

It seems unlikely that the Führer still thought it was possible to win the war by crushing the USSR. What he wanted was to keep the front as far away as possible from Germany hoping that the exhaustion of the Red Army, the probable break-up of the 'strange alliance' caused by the British and Americans' refusal to make a landing, and bringing into service the new weapons which had now reached the production stage, would give him back a sufficiently decisive advantage to enable him to dictate his own terms.

But he no longer had the means to carry out his policy. True, the morale of the Wehrmacht and of the German people was still high despite the failure at Stalingrad; some isolated figures, Treschkow and Schlabrendorff, were hatching vain plots against the Führer's life but they were not able to enlist sufficient support for their plans to be anything but abortive. In March 1943, after Stalingrad, local counter-attacks at Kharkov and Byelgorod achieved success in the freezing cold, the mud and the snow.

But they were short-lived and they did not succeed in destroying their opponents, solidly entrenched in positions behind the Donetz, which was beginning to thaw. Yet the Wehrmacht still had more than 5 million men and 206 divisions along the Russian front, plus 10 Romanian, 6 Hungarian and the Waffen SS divisions, out of a total, for the whole of the armed forces, of 320 divisions (24 in the Balkans, 22 in Italy, 50 in France and Holland, 18 in Denmark and Norway). The German effort seemed to have reached its peak: only 15 divisions were under training; henceforth it would not be possible, through lack of reserves, to fill the gaps left by the fighting in the USSR.

The German Army was not without powerful weapons. Their heavy and medium Tiger and Panther tanks gave them great hopes; the first of these weighed 60 tons and was armed with an 88-mm gun and two machine guns; the second, 45 tons, had one 75-mm gun and two machine guns; the self-propelled gun Ferdinand weighed 70 tons and had armour-plating nearly eight inches thick. Tanks and self-propelled guns together totalled nearly 6,000.

But the front held by these forces stretched for 2,500 miles and more than 1,250 miles of it were vulnerable – only the front north of Leningrad was static. Each division had to hold an average of well over six miles;

the armoured divisions now had only 60 to 100 tanks each which made them more mobile but less powerful. Hitler preferred to form new ones, thus increasing their numbers, rather than bring the old ones up to strength, which would have provided a useful blend of old soldiers and raw recruits. No longer, as in the period from 1939 to 1942, were they backed by an air force commanding complete air supremacy; 70 per cent of the fighters were allocated to the defence of the homeland against the Anglo-American bombing; the number of aircraft permanently engaged on the Russian front barely reached 3,000; a few heavy bombers were sent to raid the remote rear areas of the USSR, the Jaroslav rubber factories, the Saratov petrol refineries and the Astrakhan petrol storage depots; being practically out of reach, Soviet war production was hardly affected. At the front, aircraft concentrations over the battlefield were few and far between as well as inadequate; the Germans never massed more than 1,000 aircraft.

It was thus obvious – all that was needed was to count – not only that the Wehrmacht could no longer launch any more large-scale offensives as in previous summers, but that it would find it extremely difficult to keep its front line intact. The OKH timidly put forward the idea of shortening the line as a precautionary measure. But Hitler decided to regain the initiative by launching a new attack against the 'Kursk salient'.

II SOVIET WARFARE

In July 1943 the Red Army totalled more than 6 million men; it thus had superiority in numbers over the Wehrmacht, not an overwhelming one but sufficient to enable it to switch certain forces and deploy them elsewhere, thus considerably increasing their forces in a particular sector; above all, its reserves were practically unlimited. In addition, it had a greater number of tanks, aircraft and, above all, of guns, than its foe – 100,000 guns, nearly 6,000 tanks and more than 8,000 aircraft. It had brought into service a new 100-mm anti-tank gun and the fighter LA 5 which carried two cannons, six rockets and 450 lbs of bombs at a speed of 375 m.p.h.

The Soviet command had the advantage of being concerned only with one front and thus being able to work out a long-term strategy, without having to take into consideration possible developments in other operational theatres. Soviet historians distinguish three phases in the organisation of the command; in the first, the phase of defeat, with commanders more or less left to themselves in each sector; in the period of stabilisation, the *Stavka* exercised control by sending delegates to spread the gospel in the field; while during the period of continuous offensive the High Command itself took charge on every front.

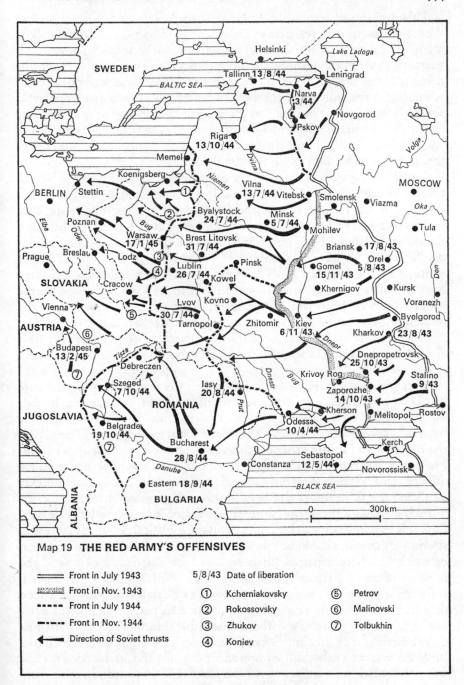

Map 19 **THE RED ARMY'S OFFENSIVES**

═══ Front in July 1943	5/8/43 Date of liberation
▓▓▓ Front in Nov. 1943	① Kcherniakovsky ⑤ Petrov
----- Front in July 1944	② Rokossovsky ⑥ Malinovski
─·─· Front in Nov. 1944	③ Zhukov ⑦ Tolbukhin
← Direction of Soviet thrusts	④ Koniev

This division of responsibility raises the problem of 'Marshal' Stalin's personal role; nowadays, Soviet historians tend to play it down. It does seem, however, that no decision was made without his approval; his personal share in the planning is more difficult to assess but it cannot be denied. Even though he is no longer considered 'the leading light of science and the military theoretician of genius', as Marshal Vassilevski among others, described him in *Pravda* on March 9, 1953, it must be noted that the harsh judgments passed on him now concern the period of Russian setbacks and not their successes; it is difficult to blame him for all the first and refuse him credit for the second.

Soviet strategy was adapted to the enormous length of the front which precluded any decisive breakthrough in narrow sectors of the enemy's defence, on the lines of that at Sedan. To achieve a decisive result, care had to be taken not to push forward dangerously extended 'probes' into the enemy's defence positions, but to keep on striking at them over their whole length. This was achieved by successive frontal operations in depth, so close together as to be continuous. Offensives were launched over broad sectors, more than 300 to 600 miles long, by several army groups – Soviet historians called them 'fronts'. But on the carefully limited line chosen for the decisive attack, the attacker, launching his surprise assault at night with concentrated forces, had an unanswerable advantage. For every mile of front, the Russians used 3,000 to 5,000 men, 8 to 15 tanks and 60 to 100 guns.

After penetrating 120 to 300 miles, when the enemy, to plug the gap, had been obliged to strip other sectors of the front, the advance halted; but meanwhile their greater reserves, inexhaustibly renewed thanks to the teeming population of the Soviet Union, as well as their mobility, enabled the Russians to prepare other offensives which took over the good work. Moreover, when one section of the front had been set moving, the others did not remain static; secondary attacks prevented the enemy from quickly localising the main thrust and slowed down his counter-stroke.

Such a strategy presupposed great powers of manoeuvre by enormous forces. It required complete mastery of all the logistical problems involved, since every advance could be continued only once the sparse rail and road network had been repaired (in particular, the Russians had solved the problem of crossing rivers by means of artificial fords and 'sunken bridges'). It forced the Germans to fight a type of war different from that for which they had been trained. True, tanks continued to play an important part; but they no longer achieved the decisive breakthrough; like giant primeval beasts, they became locked in obscure struggles in which the Russians strove to exhaust their opponents. As for the Soviet Air Force, it was committed in its entirety over the battlefield – fighters, bombers and tactical aircraft; its commander at the end of the war, Marshal Novikov, defined its tactics as follows, apparently paraphrasing a maxim of Stalin's: 'It is possible to win victory on a front only by close collaboration between all branches of the services; consequently the essential task of the Air Force consists in helping and supporting the armed forces.'

In contrast to the Luftwaffe in 1939 and 1940 and the British and American Air Forces, the Soviet Air Force did not at first set out to bomb the enemy's immediate or remote rear areas in order to destroy the lines of communication or even the enemy's economic potential. One of the characteristics of Soviet strategy was that it sought to paralyse the enemy's rear areas by the employment of 'partisan' units, not small groups of saboteurs but actual divisions formed with whatever means were available; they were scattered over wide areas, under direct radio control by *Stavka*, and operated as the Red Army approached and in co-operation with it.

Such defence methods were simple, robust and constantly adaptable. Basically, they were not very different in conception, albeit far more powerful, from those of 1914–18; Russian strategists have provided a sort of posthumous justification for their unfortunate French colleagues: artillery and infantry actually did once again become 'the lord of battles', with the important difference that they could not have done so without the support of tanks and a better air force.

Thus the Russians considerably developed the power of their artillery, to an almost unlimited extent. In particular, they used to the fullest possible advantage batteries of jet-rockets to which the troops gave the affectionate nickname of *Katyusha* and the sycophants 'Stalin's organ'. Their advantages were the suddenness and concentration of their fire-power, their very rapid deployment and the speed with which they could be made ready to fire. From 1943 onwards, divisions of self-propelled heavy weapons were formed; by the end of 1943, there were seven of them, plus 13 autonomous brigades and 117 independent regiments.

In general, fighting began with a barrage, each weapon firing off eight rockets at once; in this way, the enemy were softened up before the tanks attacked, followed by the infantry, who occupied the terrain while the sappers prepared defence positions. When the success had been consolidated, *Katyushas* were used against any enemy counter-attacks, especially against tanks; they broke up enemy concentrations and made it difficult to occupy new lines of defence. Targets between two and a half to four miles away were sometimes totally wiped out by rocket fire, thus enabling their immediate occupation by the infantry.

III OPERATION 'CITADEL'

As the winter of 1942–3 came to an end, on the southern sector the German front had been forced back from the Don to the Donetz and its junction with the central sector followed a winding course; in the region of Orel and Kharkov the German line bulged eastwards; but between the two the Russians had made a deep penetration towards the west; this pocket was to become known in history as the 'Kursk salient'.

Hitler decided to reduce it. In contrast to Guderian and von Manstein, who wished to launch only a limited attack, not later than May, with the intention of upsetting and delaying the expected Russian offensive – the Germans seemed, in fact, to have taken over the delaying tactics which till then had been a Russian prerogative – the Führer, backed by Zeitzler, who never said no, decided to commit half his armour. In all, 33 divisions were concentrated, including 9 armoured and 2 motorised divisions, with a total of 900,000 men supported by 2,700 tanks and 2,000 aircraft.

The preparation of this large-scale attack took time, so that, though originally intended for May, it did not start until July. The Russian command had wind of it; it knew of the existence of the Tiger and Panther tanks, some of which had been captured and their weak points detected; it was prepared for their onslaught. It was thus able to set up defence positions in depth and group 11 ordinary armies, 3 tank armies and 3 air armies, which represented 4 divisions for every fifteen miles, and 40 tanks and over 200 mortars for every five miles in the central sector. Nor was it wrong about the composition of the opposing troops, the direction of their attack, its assessment of their strength and their timetable for the attack; fifty per cent of the automatic rifles, machine guns and anti-tank rifles were reserved for use against aircraft; infantry troops had been trained on specially prepared terrain; the Soviet command detected changes in its opponent's troop concentrations and adapted its own accordingly. It was difficult to be better prepared to meet the onslaught.

Marshal Vassilevski gave Stalin the credit for the Soviet plan – but this was before 'destalinisation'. After rejecting a scheme which had been submitted to him for an immediate attack on Gomel and Kharkov, in order to forestall the German attack and force the crossing of the Dniepr, Stalin is alleged to have decided to check its impetus first and then force the enemy into a battle of attrition and break them. After this first defensive phase, indeed even before it was completed, offensive operations would be launched from Smolensk to the Sea of Azov. This direction had been chosen because of the rich gains offered by the south-western territories, and also in order to ensure that the forces defending the Caucasus were not cut off from those advancing from Stalingrad.

Both camps were thus perfectly aware of the importance of the battle they were about to join. In his order of the day to the Wehrmacht, Hitler stressed that 'the fate of the war might depend on its result'; in fact, it would cancel or confirm the battle of Stalingrad. But of the two antagonists it was the Russians who this time had worked out the most ambitious scheme in all its successive stages.

The battle of Kursk began on July 3, 1943. The Russians took the initiative by an artillery counter-barrage to hamper the enemy's expected attack. Then the German attack broke loose. By the evening of July 5, the Germans had carved out a pocket four or five miles deep in the sector of the Soviet Thirteenth Army; but at the end of July 8, they seemed to have lost their momentum and their progress slowed up; the pocket was only seven and a half miles deep.

IV THE 'AFFRAY' AT PROKHOROVKA

On July 9, the Germans achieved their deepest penetration – twenty-two miles towards Oboion; they then tried to skirt Kursk to the south and thus it was that on July 12 the great tank battle which Soviet historians call the 'affray at Prokhorovka' was fought.

More than 1,000 tanks on each side, backed by artillery and aircraft, came to grips on a restricted terrain. The Russians' orders were to 'bleed the enemy white'. It was in-fighting and this deprived both the Tiger tank and the Ferdinand gun of the advantage of their power – the latter, having no secondary armament, proved to be a giant with feet of clay when attacked from close in. Amidst clouds of smoke and dust and an indescribable, deafening turmoil, armour-piercing shells smashed through the armour-plating of the opposing tanks, blowing up ammunition and smashing turrets to pieces.

Almost no infantry was engaged on either side; the tanks did battle with each other alone over an area only two and a half miles deep. Apart from isolated guns and anti-tank batteries, the artillery could play hardly any part, so inextricably interlocked were the opponents. Similarly, no bombers took any direct part in the 'affray', since they were incapable of distinguishing friend from foe; they reserved their blows for the supply columns, outside the fighting area. Colonel Constantini has rightly pointed out that a tank battle on such a colossal scale had no precedent in World War Two and was not to be seen again.

Although they had done their utmost the Germans' attack had not succeeded. On July 13 von Kluge and von Manstein were summoned to the Führer's GHQ. On July 17, the OKH withdrew two armoured corps from the Kursk front, because of Soviet attacks elsewhere. At the same time, the Allied successes in Sicily and the fall of Mussolini were monopolising the Führer's attention. Operation 'Citadel' was the Wehrmacht's last attempt to regain and hold the initiative in the east. It ended in failure.

V THE SOVIET SUMMER AND AUTUMN OFFENSIVE, 1943

But although for a moment the Germans thought that they had rendered the Russians incapable of launching any large-scale attack, they were not long in realising their mistake. The whole front, from north to south, was gradually to start moving.

In order to keep open the possibility of despatching forces to Italy, Hitler ordered withdrawal to a certain 'Hagen line', which in fact, existed only on paper, since the Führer had forbidden any fortifications to be built on the Dniepr, fearing that this might encourage his generals in their defensive mentality to which he considered them too prone in any case.

The Soviet armies were strung out in army groups or 'fronts'. The Volchov, north-west and Kalinin fronts, from Lake Ladoga to Smolensk, remained static. But from Smolensk to the Black Sea a vast steamroller movement began, under the leadership of various hitherto unknown Soviet generals whose names have now gone down in history for their glorious achievements.

The first attack was launched on July 12 on the left wing of the 'western front' which was under the command of Sokolovsky – a brigadier in 1939; Smolensk was taken on September 27.

The 'Briansk front' under Popov relieved the north of the Kursk salient from any risk of attack; he took Orel on August 5 and Briansk on the 17th; by the end of September he was close to Mohilev. On his left, he was supported by the 'central front' under Rokossovski – a veteran who had fought against Admiral Koltchak and was a cavalry brigadier in 1939.

Yet it was south of the Kursk salient that, after taking Byelgorod, the Soviet offensive made its widest sweep, although it did not begin until August 3, after recovering from the wounds inflicted by Operation 'Citadel'. The 'Voronezh front' under Vatutin, one of those responsible for Paulus' defeat, and the 'steppes front', under Koniev, a peasant's son and political commissar in 1917, launched a joint pincer operation with Kharkov as its target. The town was taken on August 23.

Further south, the 'south-west front' was commanded by Malinovski who had served in the French Foreign Legion, and the 'Don front' by Tolbukhin, another peasant's son who had been a private in 1915. The former took Stalino at the beginning of September; the latter advanced along the Sea of Azov.

Everywhere the Germans were beating a retreat; nowhere were they able to hold their ground; they could commit only 1,500 aircraft permanently on the eastern front and the aircrews needed a rest; as a precautionary measure, the Luftwaffe's repair shops and supply depots had been moved back into Poland.

On October 1, the front line had reached Gomel, ran west of Chernigov and was close to Kiev, Cherkassy, Dnepropetrovsk, Zaporozhye and Melitopol. Only the attempts to cross the Kerch straits and fan out into the Crimea had failed. Stalin decided to leave the Crimea alone for the moment and told Tolbukhin to head for Odessa; once isolated, the Crimea would fall like a ripe fruit.

Throughout the autumn, the Soviet offensive suffered scarcely any interruption – just enough to enable each of the army groups to regroup its forces while its neighbours pressed on in turn.

By October 7, three bridgeheads had been established on the Dniepr, two of them north and south of Kiev. On the 14th, Zaporozhe was taken, on the 25th, it was Dnepropetrovsk's turn. The German army in the bend of the Dniepr was in great danger of being encircled; it managed to break out, thanks to the solid resistance of the strongpoint at Krivoy Rog which was under siege by Koniev.

Tolbukhin took Mariopol and then Perekov; Stalin's plan had been achieved and the Crimea was cut off; Kiev fell on November 6. On November 15, the entire front started advancing simultaneously. In the north, Sokolovsky was approaching Vitebsk; Rokossovski took Gomel and Vatutin Zhitomir.

On November 17, von Manstein launched a delaying counter-attack; he retook Zhitomir but lost it again after failing to reach Kiev. By the end of 1943, the Russians had advanced some 190 to 250 miles from Smolensk to Kherson; they had destroyed or badly mauled 100 enemy divisions. And, contrary to Hitler's hopes, there had been no break in the alliance between the USSR and her British and American allies.

VI THE 'BIG THREE' AT TEHERAN

After their Foreign Ministers had cleared the ground in Moscow in October 1943 and Churchill and Roosevelt had had talks with Chiang Kai-shek in Cairo, the three leaders, each of whom, in accordance with his different status, temperament and methods in fact was in charge of the alliance in his own country, met for the first time, from November 28 to December 1, in Teheran; hitherto they had confined themselves to sending each other letters and emissaries – only Churchill had had private discussions with each of his two partners.

On the face of it, it seemed that Roosevelt and Churchill, linked by so many ties of personal friendship, might often be led to form a common front against Stalin, who was beginning slightly to lift the veil on the USSR's war aims and claims. In fact, in Stalin's presence the British and Americans were embarrassed by their awareness of the fact that they were not keeping their pledge of opening a second front, for which the Italian operations were only a pale substitute. On the other hand, that 'old political flirt', as General de Gaulle called Roosevelt, set out to make Stalin's conquest, and the Russian leader was only too happy to oblige, delighted to have a friendly hearing from the President of the United States, whom he had invited to chair the meeting.

Roosevelt had even thought of seeing Stalin alone without Churchill. He had suggested to him 'a meeting of twin souls . . . somewhere in the extreme north of the Pacific'. He had told Bullitt: 'Stalin wants security for his country; if I give him everything I possibly can without asking anything in exchange, *noblesse oblige*, he will not attempt to annex anything and he will work for the foundation of peace and democracy in the world.'[1]

Roosevelt told Frances Perkins, his Secretary of Labor, how he had broken the ice with Stalin:

> For the first three days I made absolutely no progress. I couldn't get any personal connection with Stalin, although I had done everything he asked me to do . . . He was correct, stiff, solemn, not smiling, nothing human to get at . . . I felt pretty discouraged because I thought I was making no personal headway . . . I thought it over all night and made up my mind I had to do something desperate . . . As soon as I sat down at the conference table, I began to tease Churchill about his Britishness, about John Bull, about his cigars, about his habits. It began to register with Stalin. Winston got red and scowled and the more he did so, the more Stalin smiled. Finally, Stalin broke out into a deep, hearty guffaw, and for the first time in three days, I saw light. I kept it up until Stalin was laughing with me, and it was then that I called him 'Uncle Joe' . . . From that time on our relations were personal . . . The ice was broken and we talked like men and brothers.

For his part, Stalin had shown Roosevelt every consideration and invited him to live in the Soviet embassy, where he gave up his own quarters for him. At the end of the day, the two Anglo-Saxons, after a great deal of toasting and drinking and junketing, found their Slav partner a jovial, good-humoured man and, on the whole, a good sort – apart from one alarming statement, made in a deadpan voice, that it would be necessary to shoot 50,000 German officers to rid the world of Prussian militarism, a statement which Stalin eventually described as a joke but which provoked indignant protest from Churchill.

The leaders of the Big Three made the following statement when they parted: 'We came here with hope and determination; we are leaving as

---

1. When Churchill heard of this amazing plan and was deeply surprised by it, Roosevelt blamed it . . . on 'inferiors'.

friends in fact, in spirit and in intention.'[1] In reality, Stalin had been able to play on the sufferings of the Soviet people and the Red Army's successes to obtain what he wanted on many points.

VII THE DECISIONS TAKEN AT TEHERAN.
THE SECOND FRONT

Churchill expounded his 'Mediterranean strategy' to his partners. He suggested advancing as quickly as possible in Italy and, either simultaneously or later, carrying the war into the region of the Bosphorus and the Balkans. He did not state exactly where; but the British were at that time placing great hopes in Tito, whose fighting spirit had been favourably assessed by the Prime Minister's own son, Randolph Churchill, and in whose favour they had just completely abandoned Mihailović, after putting him to the test. Churchill found Stalin and Roosevelt joining forces against him on this point. Stalin strongly stressed that landings in force in France should be given priority, both across the Channel and the Mediterranean, with the cover names of 'Overlord' and 'Anvil' respectively.

Not until the third meeting of the conference and after Stalin and Churchill had had a private meeting alone, was the decision taken to launch 'Overlord' in May 1944. In order to bring pressure to bear on his partners, Stalin had at first stated that the Soviet offensive would take place only *after* the landing, but he then promised that it would begin at approximately the same time and that it would be launched in various sectors so as to pin down the maximum number of enemy divisions in the east. Close contact was to be established between the general staffs of the three powers.

This vital decision finally crystallised the British and American strategy in the west once and for all; Stalin had settled their differences. Henceforth, Italy would be a secondary operational area.

Stalin's interest in the Balkans did not pass unnoticed by his partners; it was clear that the Georgian wanted to make them a Russian sphere of influence. It was for the same reason that he opposed the idea of a 'Danubian federation' put up by Churchill. Stalin was looking a long way ahead; and although the others were not fools, they did not think at that time that the Red Army would one day be sufficiently powerful to give concrete reality to such vast and distant aims. Stalin seemed to justify their attitude by not showing much support for Tito; it was Eden who asked him to send a mission to the Yugoslav partisans, and not he who suggested it.

1. The British, especially Eden, were however much less optimistic than the Americans.

On other points Stalin had given a glimpse of the cloven hoof. He obtained recognition for the USSR's right of access to the warm waters of the Pacific, and Roosevelt even hinted that she might recover Port Arthur and Dairen, something which he had been careful not to mention to Chiang Kai-shek a few days earlier. Stalin made the formal stipulation that, in addition to having to hand over Petsamo to the Russians, Finland should revert to her 1940 borders, break with Germany, drive the German troops out of her territory herself and pay the USSR reparations amounting to one year's national income. Roosevelt vainly went to the defence of the Finns, who had been the only country to pay back all their debts to the USA and against whom the American government had not declared war. About the annexation of the Baltic states by the USSR, Stalin used a phrase that hinted that the question had been settled once and for all – 'by the will of the people'.

As for western Europe, Stalin plainly showed that he was not interested. He approved what the British and Americans were doing in North Africa and Italy; he conceded that Gibraltar's territory might be enlarged. Whilst he had encouraged the French Communists to side with de Gaulle without breaking with Giraud, he stated that in his view, Pétain still represented France, 'whose ruling classes were rotten to the core'. This amounted to inviting the British and Americans not to be too greatly concerned with respecting France's territorial integrity; Stalin even suggested that Bizerta and Dakar should become international bases.

The fact was that he was holding back all his strength in order to obtain what he wanted in Poland and Germany.

VIII THE POLISH PROBLEM

According to the Polish Premier Mikolajczyk, before leaving for Moscow Eden had confided in him that the only hope of re-establishing good relations between the USSR and Poland was for Poland to give up the territories occupied by the Russians in 1939. Justifiably alarmed at this, Mikolajczyk tried to discover more about Britain's intentions and he made an effort to meet Churchill and Eden before they left for Teheran. But the British refused to meet him; they were all the more embarrassed by their 1939 ally because they had already reached a decision against her interests. All that the Polish Prime Minister could do was to express firm hostility to any territorial encroachment at Poland's expense; if this happened he would immediately denounce the Polish-Soviet agreement.

Thus the decisions concerning Poland that were taken at Teheran remained secret.[1] In fact, Stalin's proposals had been accepted. Poland was to be 'pushed' westwards, at Germany's expense; she would receive east Prussia, Pomerania including Stettin and German Silesia; but she would abandon to the Russians the territories they had gained by the pact signed with the Germans; Stalin added Koenigsberg, stressing that 'he would then be holding Germany by the throat' and that the USSR had no warm-water harbour in the north-west; he also demanded Lvov – it did not matter who his partners were or whom he was talking to, Stalin could never be persuaded to change his political objectives.

Churchill and Roosevelt agreed to everything. The former, with three matches and much cynicism, even sketched out the new frontiers of eastern Europe; he merely made his acceptance dependent on that of the Polish government; he also suggested that the agreement should not become definite until Poland and Russia had resumed diplomatic relations, but Stalin remained silent on this point; he had his own ideas on the matter and the others took care not to encourage him to spell them out.

So the fate of Poland, the first casualty of Hitler's aggression, was settled in her absence and without her knowledge, and her territory was going to be amputated with the consent of Britain, who had declared war in order to defend its integrity. Once again she was the subject of a secret agreement between three great powers; she had been standing in the way of their agreement and they were sacrificing her in order to maintain it. Churchill was in no hurry to make Britain's breach of faith public; he did not mention it to Mikolajczyk until January 1944; it was in vain that Mikolajczyk reminded him that, at the time, Britain had supported the Polish frontier as drawn according to the Treaty of Riga in 1921 and not the 'Curzon line' of 1919 which she was supporting at the moment.

On February 22, 1944, Churchill informed the House of Commons of the general terms of the decisions involving the Polish frontier; this was equivalent to saying that the decision was final. However, he did plead with Stalin on behalf of the Poles to have some discussion about the possibility of a Polish-Soviet frontier somewhere between the one laid down at Riga and the Curzon line. Stalin bluntly refused. In this whole affair, the United States had made an exception to their principle of leaving territorial problems until after the peace; they were leaving the solution of the Polish question to the interested parties, which amounted to abandoning Poland to her fate. Poland made a request for her western frontier to be guaranteed; Churchill and Stalin promised that this would be done, but at the same time Churchill revealed to the Polish govern-

1. Roosevelt insisted very strongly on preserving this secrecy; he was moving into a pre-electoral period and did not wish to alienate the millions of American electors of Polish origin.

ment a further Soviet demand: its composition would have to be gone into and changed. It was difficult to flout the solemn principles of the Atlantic Charter more fundamentally.

IX THE GERMAN PROBLEM

The Polish settlement was a foretaste of the fate of Germany, because it deprived her of territory that had been inhabited by Germans from time immemorial and it provided for a mass exodus of the population of German origin. This was only one aspect of the severity with which the Reich was going to be treated by her conquerors – and on this point they were at one.

Roosevelt advocated carving Germany up into six self-governing regions: Prussia, Hanover, Saxony, Hessen and the south Rhineland, Bavaria and Baden-Würtemberg; two areas would remain under the protection of the United Nations: Kiel-Hamburg and Ruhr-Saar. In a word, he wished to deprive Germany of the bases of her inveterate imperialism: Prussian leadership, territorial unity and her economic power in which the Ruhr and Hamburg were the principal factors. Cordell Hull had worked out a scheme for the military occupation and tripartite administration of the whole of Germany, complete denazification and demilitarisation and heavy reparations. Going even further, Morgenthau advocated banning all industry in Germany and reducing her to a purely agricultural economy – the fate that she herself had intended for the countries she had conquered.

Churchill also thought that Prussia was the breeding-ground of Pan-Germanism; however, he was afraid that the little states that Roosevelt proposed reviving might be stillborn. He suggested a kind of revival of the Hapsburg Empire by creating a 'large Danubian Confederation as peaceful as a cow', containing Bavaria, Baden, Saxony and Würtemberg, together with Austria and Hungary.

Stalin's policy was more ambiguous and his designs more mysterious. Officially, in his speeches, he had always distinguished between 'German Fascists' and the 'best Germans'. He refused 'to identify the Hitler gang with the German people' because 'Hitlers come and go but the German people remains'. It was thus not Germany that had to be destroyed but 'Hitler's state'. Stalin did not forget that the war was not over and the Germans must be prevented from remaining loyal to Hitler to the bitter end either through fear or fanatical patriotism. This was why, although agreeing in principle to unconditional surrender, he had expressed some reservations.

But to his partners, away from the public eye and out of earshot of any Germans, he expounded different views. As early as December 16, 1941, when the Wehrmacht was still hammering on the gates of Moscow, he talked to Eden about dismembering Germany. At Teheran, he spoke out in favour of Roosevelt's plan – he would even have preferred splitting her up into smaller and thus weaker parts – and against Churchill's proposal of a confederation in which he saw the danger that the Germans might be reunited. 'The Germans,' he said, 'are all the same, there is no difference between the northerners and the southerners; they all fight like wild beasts.'

At Teheran, Germany was as yet not a source of discord between the three allies but on the contrary cemented their union – at Poland's expense. And beyond the fate in store for her there loomed the fate of the whole of eastern Europe, which was the preserve of the Red Army and the USSR.

X THE SOVIET WINTER AND SPRING OFFENSIVE, 1944

The Soviet winter offensive of 1944 was more localised than that in the summer of 1943 but it continued without pause; no sector remained static; *Stavka* strengthened the positions it had won and prepared for the big summer offensive, the direction of which had been dictated by political reasons; it was to be launched southwards, in order to hit at the states of the Danubian basin, while their leaders were plunged into anxiety by the Wehrmacht's defeats.

In the north, Leningrad had been finally relieved of all danger; the various German strongpoints had been taken in February; in the course of March, the Red Army reached Narva and Lake Peipus.

After recapturing Zhitomir, Vatutin advanced towards the Pripet in the north and the Bug in the south; in January a local counter-attack by von Manstein held him up at Vinnitza. Vatutin was replaced by Zhukov, a peasant's son and former factory worker who had been an NCO in 1917 and was a member of his regiment's soviet. He had organised the defence of Moscow and co-ordinated the battle of Stalingrad. Together with Koniev, he concerted a large-scale attack in the direction of the Carpathians, which was launched on March 15.

The thrust was so powerful and so broad that the whole German front gave way. In March, Koniev took Uman, crossed the Bug and then the Dniestr. On his left, after finally putting an end to resistance in Krivoy Rog in February, Malinovski took Odessa on April 10 and similarly reached the Dniestr on the 13th. The Romanians had lost Transnistria and their ambitions were all vanishing into thin air. Worse still, they were having to defend themselves in Bessarabia and Bukovina; but how could they when Hitler was firmly withholding their seven last divisions in the Crimea?

The Führer was in fact refusing General Jaenecke permission to open up a withdrawal route northwards by forcing the 'Perekop gap' and was paying no heed to Antonescu's anguished pleas. In doing this, Hitler was following Doenitz's advice that the loss of Sebastopol would seriously affect the situation in the Black Sea; the latter considered it possible to supply the garrison by sea and thus enable it to hold on for a considerable period. Hitler was also influenced by Goering's fears that the Romanian oil wells would be bombed from the Crimea – this was one of the Führer's recurrent nightmares. He was also afraid of the repercussions of any evacuation of the Black Sea on such wavering allies as Romania and Bulgaria and a hesitant neutral, Turkey. But after the fall of Odessa, the Red Army attacked the Crimea from the north; the whole peninsula was lost in under a week; three-quarters of the artillery were abandoned. Hitler authorised the evacuation of the wounded and nobody else; as he needed a scapegoat, he sacked Jaenecke. But on May 8 the garrison had to be hurriedly evacuated; 150,000 left in complete chaos; on May 12, Sebastopol fell. Some thousands of miles from the front, Hitler had once again taken far-reaching decisions with no knowledge of the real situation.

Hitler dismissed von Manstein and replaced Zeitzler by Guderian who had earlier also been dismissed. But switching responsibility did not prevent the Germans from making a disorderly withdrawal to a line running through Kovel, Lutsk, Tarnopol, Stanislawow, Iasi and Tiraspol.

The Russians took a breather and swiftly made good the destruction in White Russia and the Ukraine – particularly the communications. As early as 1943, this reconstruction had become the main concern of the Defence Committee. During 1943 and 1944, 25,000 miles of railway and the principal electricity generating stations had been repaired; the coal mines were again producing 44 million tons of coal and the blast furnaces nearly 3 million tons of steel and the same amount of iron. Soviet historians calculate that the total output of the liberated areas increased three-fold during these two years.

As manpower and machines were short, the Defence Committee arranged for direct liaison between the concerns which were to be rebuilt and the new ones which had taken over their function in the 'eastern provinces'; every factory in the Donbass was thus twinned with a similar factory in the Urals which provided it with tools, even if this restricted its own output; another big exodus took place but this time in the other direction. Requisitioning did the rest; 120,000 kolkhozians were transferred to the coalmines.

The organisation of the Soviet state and the driving power of the Communist party were not the only explanations for such military and economic feats. A great upsurge of popular feeling had been involved which also found expression in the partisan movement.

XI PARTISAN WARFARE

Hitler fancied himself as a disciple of Clausewitz; but in his famous formula 'war is the extension of politics', Clausewitz meant by politics a rational unified conception of needs and aims. And 'the liquidation of the USSR' was not rational, nor was it an aim but a means – both immoderate and wrong. An unlimited war was not a policy; in fact, the means was overriding the aim. It was just such a deviation that Clausewitz warned against when he wrote that one should beware of the 'dynamics of war', by which one is led to forget the reasons that gave rise to the war by concentrating on day-to-day fighting, where the aims are moulded by defeats and victories.

The Führer had not achieved a consistent attitude towards the anti-Communist elements or the national feeling of the non-Russian racial minorities in the USSR. There was, indeed, a school for propaganda workers at the Dabendorff camp under the 'National Russian Committee' created by Vlassov; this committee published newspapers intended for Soviet prisoners of war and for its supporters; its membership was thereby increasing. But on hearing that in the course of the Kursk fighting deserters had gone over to the Soviet Army again in their thousands, Hitler flew into a rage and ordered Vlassov's units to be transferred to the west within forty-eight hours! Jodl insisted that Vlassov should sign an open letter to his supporters approving this transfer. According to Peter Kleist, the total strength of the 'eastern battalions' at the beginning of 1944 was 650,000 men, including 110,000 Turcomans, 110,000 Caucasians, 35,000 Tartars and 60,000 Cossacks. But they had no sort of autonomy; they were scattered throughout all the German forces and serving in every sector – in France, they could be found in Lyon, Lorient, Rodez, Oléron, etc. It is true that they had been recruited in many different ways; but in treating them purely as mercenaries, the Germans made it impossible for them to provide the seeds of revolt amongst the peoples of the USSR.

On the other hand, the extortionate behaviour of the Germans would in itself have been enough to unite the peoples of the USSR against the occupying power. Their organisation came from disbanded units of the Red Army which the Wehrmacht had not bothered to take prisoner as they advanced but had been content merely to break up. It seems that both the Communist party and the Red Army were surprised by the spontaneity of the partisans' reaction and the size of their forces in their fight against the Germans; the Party had been disorganised by the Germans' repressive action and the Red Army was suspicious – like all regular armies – of these anarchical bands of undisciplined volunteers.

The first Resistance leaders were often without party affiliations, that is, they were isolated individuals. The Communist party set about organising their activities from Moscow. Instructions were broadcast by radio, newspapers printed and dropped by parachute and militant Communist organisers were sent out to join them. Gradually, the Party came to control the movement at every level; even meetings were organised. The indoctrination of the partisans was in the hands of political commissars. One of their shrewd moves consisted in considering that the partisans had shown themselves worthy to be Communists, that they had, as it were, received the call to become members of the Party.

Liaison with the Red Army was, in theory at least, all the easier because Lenin had defined the rules of subversive warfare and instruction in it had been provided in the Soviet military training establishments before the war; there had been exercises where regular had co-operated with irregular units. However, the partisans' general staff, under General Ponomarenko, retained a certain independence; according to him, he had met with hostility from Beria, the big white chief of the Soviet secret police. *Stavka* is also said to have shown a certain scepticism about the effectiveness of the partisans.

In any case, some decentralisation was made necessary by the size of the country and the depth of the German penetration; but by the second half of 1943, organisation from the centre had been more or less completed. From this time onwards, as the Red Army advanced, it took over the control and deployment of the partisans in the areas close to its operations; it dropped them weapons and sent them instructions; their leaders attended special courses in Moscow, Leningrad and Stalingrad.

The Soviet Resistance movement thus showed originality inasmuch as it tried to co-ordinate its activities with a regular government and a regular army, not situated abroad but in the country itself. It is rather difficult to assess its importance. For one reason, Soviet historians have very little to say about collaboration in the USSR, which is inseparably connected with the Resistance, since the latter was its antidote. Moreover, some of the accounts of the Resistance are not free from propaganda bias. The Communist party saw it as a link in the struggle of the people for their liberation, somewhere between anti-capitalism and anti-colonialism.

One thing is certain, however: it was a vast activity. It liquidated mayors and other authorities appointed by the occupier, it surreptitiously took over the organisations that replaced the kolkhozes, so as to supply the partisans, and it passed on instructions issued by Radio Moscow. Above all, as early as 1942, it turned to direct action, in the form of large-scale sabotage carried out by units sometimes several thousand strong; their targets were railway stations and railway lines, reservoirs, German depots and bridges. In addition, sabotage of industrial installations greatly reduced the occupier's output of coal, iron and manufactured goods in the

Donbass. At the end of 1942, there were 19,000 partisans operating in the district of Smolensk and 20,000 round Briansk. Over large areas the partisans succeeded in re-establishing Soviet institutions – fifty-eight rural soviets at Viazma – and more than 500 places were 'liberated' in an area of nearly 4,000 square miles round Briansk, during the same period. Leningrad was supplied by convoys which the partisans triumphantly escorted through the German lines into the town – one convoy consisted of 220 carts. One unit composed of Leningrad students raided 24 airfields, derailed 23 trains, destroyed 140 vehicles and captured 800 rifles. The partisans also attacked small garrisons, even when they were several hundred strong, so that during the winter the Germans abandoned most of the villages.

When the Red Army took the offensive, partisan activity assumed strategic importance. Thus the Kursk fighting was preceded by sabotage behind the German lines. The Red Army even systematically directed its attacks towards areas under partisan control. Sometimes, on the other hand, the partisans switched from one district to another to join up with the advancing regular troops. Their role in such circumstances was a dual one: they destroyed the enemy's supply lines but they also built bridges, repaired roads and occupied points of tactical importance.

One thing that was equally certain was that the Germans were taken completely by surprise by this sort of warfare. In July 1941, Hitler had stated that 'partisan warfare would enable hostile elements to be destroyed', but one year later, far from being pleased, he noted that these same partisans represented 'a grave threat in the east'. In theory the security police (SD) were in charge of preventive action and the repression of small groups while the Wehrmacht was responsible for major operations. In fact, the two bodies were forced to co-operate, more or less willingly. The Army formed a special staff and employed an increasing number of troops – von Manstein wrote that in the army under his command it was the equivalent of an army corps. The SS divisions, the Hungarians and other special units as well as regular divisions – eleven in 1943 – were thus taken out of the front line in order to fight an internal enemy, who was often impossible to locate.

Reprisals against the population only increased their hatred of the occupier; cleaning-up operations needed large forces and produced poor results; the net always had a hole in it somewhere, or else, having been tipped off, the birds had flown. Few German generals found any effective reply; in the Briansk sector, General Schmidt put a Russian civilian, Kaminski, in command of a militia; he distributed land, farms and cattle to the peasants and tried to persuade them to defend their property against the partisans. Other officers organised anti-guerrilla forces by amalgamating the best German soldiers with local collaborators. The lessons of these experiments were collected into a 'Manual of Anti-Partisan Warfare' in May 1944. In this way good results were obtained but they were not very common, and collaborators had no really convincing reasons for fighting; moreover, the Red Army's successes regularly reduced their numbers as well as the influence they exercised on the population.

XII SOVIET ESPIONAGE

The USSR had ideological supporters all over the world and thus benefited from excellent intelligence sources. But her 'special services' had not escaped Stalin's massive purges and they had not yet been completely reorganised by the beginning of the war. It is difficult to assess the activity of her spy rings; only the ones uncovered by the enemy are known and they were not necessarily the best organised or the most reliable; no one knows how much the intelligence passed on by various sources, generally differing amongst themselves or even contradicting each other, affected the decisions of the authorities who received it. Much has been written, both by specialists and by authors of bestsellers, blurring rather than illuminating the true state of affairs – usually as a result of exaggeration but also by omissions dictated by reasons of personal or national security.

It is known that in December 1941 the Abwehr uncovered a Soviet spy-ring in Belgium. In Berlin itself, another ring, *Rote Kapelle*, which was broken up in August 1942, should have been able to send back useful information on the German offensive in the summer of 1942 – but Soviet historians say that it took the Red Army by surprise.

In Switzerland, the activity of the *Rote Drei* ring is said to have been so important that two authors felt able to write, quite bluntly, that 'the war was won in Switzerland'. Yet it is difficult not to be sceptical when one reads that Swiss army intelligence passed information on to these Soviet spies and stopped doing so when Moscow showed an unhealthy curiosity concerning the Swiss armed forces – for what purpose? The Russians are also alleged to have had agents – including Philby – in the British Intelligence Service itself.

Counter-espionage made great strides during the war by using lorries equipped with detecting devices which enabled a radio transmitting station to be accurately pin-pointed; the only way of avoiding them was for the agent to change his position frequently; but this meant having a large number of centres and a wide circle of well disposed natives, which was easier for a Resistance network, with local sympathisers, than for a group of professionals.

It is certainly true that the Communists in the occupied countries

would have been very happy to inform the USSR of everything they knew –
after June 1941 this had become a patriotic duty. But what did they know?
Although extraordinary cases of infiltration have been disclosed by post-
war revelations, the social composition of the Communist parties as well
as the mistrust surrounding them before the war meant that they had little
chance of achieving high positions of responsibility. In the light of the
notorious post-war 'defections to the east', one may well wonder what
active sympathy the USSR benefited from during the war, particularly
amongst atomic scientists.

One thing which is beyond doubt is that crypto-Communists or self-
styled renegades joined Fascist party organisations, including the Nazi
party. This is what happened in the case of the most amazing and famous
Second World War spy, the German journalist Sorge. As press attaché at
the German embassy in Tokyo, Sorge gained the confidence both of the
ambassador and a certain number of high-placed Japanese, and he used
the services of a few Japanese Communists fanatical enough to betray
their country in time of war. It was thanks to him that Stalin is said to
have had complete confidence concerning Japan's intentions towards
Siberia. As Sorge was found out, his activity is fairly well-known; but his
most recent biographers have shown that he mixed false information and
unreliable predictions with correct ones; can we really be certain that he
did not occasionally mislead the people he was trying to help?

Were there other spies like Sorge in Greater Germany and Greater
Asia? This is not unlikely but they remain unknown and will probably
never be known. One thing is certain and that is that intelligence supplied
by spies is always scanty and incomplete; it is very dangerous for a
government or a general staff to base their decisions solely on such information; the Wehrmacht's movements in the USSR, for example, could be discovered more accurately and surely by air reconnaissance than from
scraps of information picked up by some official in a Berlin office. It is
also plain that, among the three major Allies, the USSR enjoyed a special
and formidable position. She was, of course, a country of vast dimensions
and large population, with a powerful economy and a valiant army; but
Moscow was also the Rome of a universal Communist church, the fabric
of which had not been entirely destroyed by the suppression of the
Comintern. As her regular troops began to beleaguer the German stronghold, other fighting units which were demolishing it from within were
going to come into the open, first of all in the occupied countries but also
in countries allied with Germany.

CHAPTER 3

Soviet Victories.
The Desatellisation of Greater Germany

(June–December 1944)

I N their offensive of June 1943, the Red Army's aims had been economic, like those of the Wehrmacht the year before; once again, the stakes were the grain-growing areas of the Ukraine and the Donbass mines. In June 1944, the Soviet attacks were dictated by political aims; they advanced on the southern end of the front towards the Danubian countries. This was not the shortest route to Berlin. Did Stalin want to forestall his allies in this sector, in which Churchill had shown such great interest at Teheran? Or did he think that the German satellites could easily be detached like dead branches from an ailing tree? Or yet again did he turn his attentions in that direction because of the difficulties raised by the Polish problem further north, which was going to culminate in the Warsaw uprising?

In any case, one after another, the states allied to Germany were going to be invaded, occupied and swiftly turned against her. At the same time, Communist parties which had generally been of little importance before the war made their appearance in force on the arrival of the Red Army and assumed power. In the areas that were still occupied, other Communists tried to involve as many patriots as possible in the struggle against the occupier, by co-operating with the Red Army in ways that had been perfected in partisan activity in the USSR.

I ALARM AMONGST THE SATELLITES

Romania was the first country to try to put an end to her subjection to Germany. Queen Helen, young King Michael's mother, was the moving spirit behind all the intrigues. Mihaïl Antonescu, the Foreign Minister, had contacted the Nuncio and the Swiss, Portuguese, Swedish and Turkish ministers; but these contacts did not bring him into touch with the Allies. Then in May 1943 he worked out a complete plan of action with Bova Scoppa, the Italian minister in Bucharest, who was also convinced that the Axis powers were losing the war; Mussolini must be made to see the light; Ciano's successor, Bastianini, expressed agreement; but the Duce refused to negotiate 'under the shadow of defeat in Africa'; he did, indeed, contemplate calling a general conference but only in two months' time; he even dared to suggest that it might be held whether Hitler was present or not. In the end, he said nothing about the scheme to Hitler on July 19 at Feltre; and on the 25th, he was deprived of all his power.

The Romanian government then recognised the Italian Fascist Republic, although King Michael, who was keeping his distance from the Axis, refused to receive its representative. In March 1944, he sent Prince Stirbey on a mission to Ankara and then Cairo, but with no result. Two months later, the Allies called on the Axis satellites to surrender 'unconditionally'. Mihaïl Antonescu vainly pleaded for an 'honourable settlement' and pointed out that Romania was not at war with Britain or America and that she was not waging an ideological war but merely trying to recover her lost provinces. The Allies replied by bombing Ploesti and Bucharest.

In Bulgaria, King Boris' sudden death put the young Simeon II on the throne, with a council of regency to assist him; a period of political instability began and the Bulgarian press started talking of the 'historical friendship' linking the Bulgarians and the Russians with whom they were not at war. As for the Sofia government, in January 1944 it made overtures to London and Washington.

In Hungary, Premier Kallay also made contact with the British and Americans in Istanbul. In September 1943, he contemplated the possibility of Hungary's surrendering unconditionally on a date fixed by the British and Americans with the Russians' knowledge and consent; he promised that Hungary would not allow herself to be occupied by the Germans. Kallay recognised the representative of Badoglio's government and sent gold to a Swiss bank. To avoid the imminent occupation by the Germans which would be precipitated by the Russian advance, with the accompanying danger that Hungary's traditional enemies, the Romanians, would also enter Hungarian territory, General Zsombalethy asked Keitel to leave the defence of the Carpathians to Hungarian troops only. Keitel was suspicious and refused, demanding instead that German troops should be allowed to pass through Hungary.

In fact, Hitler had seen through the Hungarians' game. On March 18, 1944 he sent for Admiral Horthy and demanded Kallay's dismissal, general mobilisation of the Hungarians, German control of the country's economy and communications and the free passage of German troops into and through Hungary.

Horthy gave in and Kallay went, to be replaced by General Sztojay. The new government banned political parties, closed down a number of newspapers, arrested some well-known personalities suspected of being opponents of the régime, placed the trade unions under the control of government commissars and replaced senior civil servants whose allegiance was uncertain. The Germans demanded and obtained still more: a 'joint armament programme', 50,000 workers to be sent to Germany, Hungary to take over the occupation costs of the German troops, an increased credit for Germany in the clearing bank, the delivery of 700,000 tons of grain and similar quantities of oil and bauxite.

Hungary also put into operation anti-Semitic measures likely to please the Germans. Although these measures were delayed – the wearing of the yellow star was made compulsory only on March 29, 1944 – the decisions were then implemented very rapidly. By the beginning of April, Eichmann and Veesenmayer were beginning to force the Jews into ghettoes. On May 15, 150,000 Jews were deported; it was planned that another 200,000 should follow them. For a short while, Horthy opposed the deportation of the Budapest Jews and then gave in. After this attempt to free herself, Hungary was now yoked more closely than ever to the German cause.

Finland had also begun negotiations with the USSR, this time through Sweden. But the Soviets' terms seemed too harsh and the talks had broken down.

Thus, by the spring of 1944, on the diplomatic level, Germany had made good to the best of her ability the effects of Italy's downfall and her own defeats in the USSR. She had plastered over the cracks of the anti-Communist coalition; there had as yet been no defections but the satellites were at the end of their tether and were liable to break away at any moment. They were held back by the Allies' decisions at Teheran and the British and Americans' insistence that they must discuss their method of exit from the war with the USSR. How much longer would they remain passively obedient? Had not Turkey, which was more independent, already shown that she considered that the die was cast by halting supplies of chromium to Germany?

II THE COMMITTEE FOR FREE GERMANY

For his part, Stalin thought that the stability of Nazi Germany herself had been sufficiently shaken for her to be weakened still further by skilfully fomenting disorder. He could rely on the devoted services of the Germans who had been exiled in the Soviet Union since 1933; these included Walter Ulbricht and Pieck; but these refugees had no hold over their compatriots. In Moscow in July 1943 a 'National Committee for Free Germany' was set up, under the nominal chairmanship of the writer Erich Weinert, assisted by a certain number of officer POWs, such as

Lieutenant von Einsiedel, a descendant of Bismarck's who had drawn up an appeal in May 1943 addressed to 20 generals and 300 officers captured at Stalingrad, encouraging them to join in the struggle against Hitler; he was wasting his time and succeeded only in being regarded as a traitor by his brother officers.

The organisers of the new Committee called a conference of 300 or 400 'delegates' from prisoner-of-war camps, not elected but chosen by the prisoners; they wanted to appeal to the mass of soldiers on every front and also to civilians living in Germany. They had a simple programme: 'anti-Hitler and in favour of immediate peace and a free and independent Germany'. The leaders were elected by acclamation – the list, very carefully compiled and prepared in advance, contained one-third Communists, one-third officers and one-third other ranks. In every occupied country, the Communists now began to appeal to the German soldier by means of tracts written in Germany and specially intended for him; but their activity was not helped, as in the USSR, by the presence of several hundred thousand prisoners demoralised by defeat and captivity. The 'Free German Committee in the West' was set up only at a much later date and had only limited appeal, although the BBC broadcast its instructions.

In the USSR, the Free German Committee published a newspaper, *Freies Deutschland*, which was distributed to POWs and dropped over the German lines; it received permission to send representative delegates to the various Soviet armies; at the front itself, they appealed to their German comrades by radio and loudspeakers, without much result. Discipline was still too strong in the Wehrmacht and fear of the 'Reds' too great.

In view of the poor results and against the advice of the Committee, the Soviet authorities made a direct appeal to the captured German generals who had till now remained aloof. In September 1943, General von Seydlitz, who had been in favour of refusing to obey Hitler's orders at Stalingrad and was apparently obsessed by the memory of Yorck at Tauroggen, was put in charge of a 'League of German Officers'. He was hoping to counteract the Communist influence in the Committee and encourage the generals to revolt against Hitler. Possibly the Russians made certain promises to von Seydlitz. According to Bodo Scheurig, General Melnikov had assured him that Germany would return to her pre-1938 frontiers, including Austria, if the Wehrmacht leaders revolted against Hitler. If such a promise was made it would have probably been before the Teheran Conference, but it was in contradiction with its conclusions.

Paulus' attitude towards the League, which was theoretically a branch of the 'Free German Committee', was very reserved although von Seydlitz staunchly asserted that he was not in the pocket of the Communists. However, Paulus eventually joined, together with fifty other generals, on hearing the news of the attempt on Hitler's life on July 20, 1944, which had been instigated by his peers, who were serving officers. But despite this splendid addition to its ranks, the League did not achieve much success. Perhaps this was because, as Einsiedel has pointed out, it was received with scepticism and, later, hostility from the Red Army. Or perhaps its foundations were undermined by the failure of the attempt on Hitler's life on July 20 and by the subsequent savage repression of the opponents of Nazism, including some of its members' own families.

It seems more likely, however, that as the Red Army advanced towards Germany and the German troops still continued to offer fierce opposition, the Soviet leaders lost interest in such an unreliable body which was gradually becoming pointless. They reserved their support for the militant wing of the Free German Committee represented by the Communists and joined by a few generals with the request for courses in political training. Finally the Russian authorities dropped their mask and in November 1945 abolished both the Committee and the League, leaving only the Communist party, to which they handed over the administration of those parts of Germany occupied by the Red Army – with the help of other more or less reconstituted 'anti-Fascist' parties.

III THE RED ARMY SUMMER OFFENSIVE OF 1944 – FINLAND

During the first half of 1944, Soviet factories turned out 16,000 aircraft and 14,000 tanks for the Red Army; the opening of the second front gave them great superiority in manpower – 7 million men against 4 million; according to Soviet historians, this superiority was even greater in armaments: fifty per cent more tanks and four times as many combat aircraft. In addition the new heavy tank Joseph Stalin outclassed its German counterpart.

The Russians thus had the means of launching a still more powerful offensive than previously; on June 23, as Stalin had promised at Teheran, the attack began on a 750-mile front. In the Carelian Isthmus, twenty-nine divisions grappled with eight Finnish divisions, reinforced by one German division; and Ryti, the President of the Finnish Republic, sent a letter to Hitler pledging himself not to negotiate a separate peace.

But although they relaxed their pressure in Carelia, the Russians advanced in Estonia towards Nerva and then into Latvia; Finland's right flank was threatened and she had no way of defending it. On August 1, President Ryti resigned and Marshal Mannerheim was unanimously elected to succeed him. On August 17, Mannerheim informed Hitler that Finland considered herself free to act independently; on September 2, he accepted the Russians' terms: Finland handed over the whole of Carelia,

gave up Petsamo and informed the Reich that any German soldiers remaining in Finland after September 15 would be interned.

The Russians showed great moderation; it is true that they had other
fish to fry; perhaps they were keen not to annoy Roosevelt who had
warmly supported the Finns at Teheran? They did not occupy Finland;
they were content to set up a control commission and insist that a government should be formed on which they could rely; its leader was Paasikivi
whom they had found the most amenable negotiator.

It only remained to settle the fate of the German Twentieth Army out
in the tundra, which Hitler had yet again ordered not to retreat. The
Russians attacked in October by landing troops in its rear; the Finns then
pursued the remnants as far as their frontier with Norway.

Meanwhile Bagramyan had taken Vitebsk and Govorov, another
peasant's son, took Narva. The Red Army crossed the Dvina and liberated
Tallinn on August 13; Memel was attacked on October 10 and Riga fell
on the 13th. Until then, General Schoerner, who had barely thirty divisions at his disposal, had been able to do nothing but retreat. But when
the Russians entered east Prussia, Hitler ordered him to counter-attack.
The Führer wanted to prevent German soil from being 'defiled by the
Reds'; he also wanted to cling on to the Baltic coast, where the secret
weapons were being produced which were the magic charm to lure victory
back into the German camp. So he left eight divisions in Courland which,
though supplied by sea and gradually encircled, fought on until the end
of the war; they would have been of more use elsewhere. By November 1
the Russians had occupied all the Baltic countries, including Lithuania.

IV POLAND

However, from the start of its offensive, the Red Army had directed the
main weight of its attack against Byelorussia, doubtless in order to complete the liberation of the whole of Soviet territory, including the areas
taken from Poland in September 1939. Four 'fronts' comprising 2,500,000
men supported by 45,000 guns, 6,000 tanks and 7,000 aircraft were faced
by 1,500,000 Germans under von Busch, backed by only 17,000 guns,
1,500 tanks and 2,000 aircraft.

Soviet superiority was so great that, despite the number of wide rivers
to be crossed, the Russians advanced an average of twelve to fifteen miles
a day as far as Minsk and eight to ten miles a day thereafter. The front
extended for nearly 450 miles; the Russians had little difficulty in breaking
through the enemy's defence positions and their mobile units skirted the
isolated pockets of resistance and attacked the Germans from the rear,
making it quite impossible for them to stabilise their lines.

During this advance, the partisans played an effective strategic role. The OKH had mistaken *Stavka*'s intentions; in the spring of 1944, they had used the strategic railway, the only one that existed, to move their reserves from north to south; the partisans let them go through without interference in accordance with the Red Army's instructions; but when the OKH realised its mistake and tried to bring their units back by the same route, the partisans sabotaged the permanent way – so much so that according to Colonel Teske, the head of Army Group Centre's transport, 'the German troop movements were paralysed'.

So the Russians managed to reach the Beresina on June 29, Minsk on July 5, Vilna on the 13th and Bialystok on 27th; on August 1, they had reached Kovno and by the 14th the Narev. As he headed for Warsaw, Rokossovski took Lublin on July 26 and Brest-Litovsk on the 31st. On August 1, he reached Praga, a Warsaw suburb on the right bank of the Vistula. He had covered 375 miles in little more than a month and he was still depending for his supplies on railway termini situated on the Dniepr; the few railway lines in conquered territory had not only been destroyed but also had had to be modified for the Russian gauge. The Germans now received reinforcements, including the Hermann Goering Division from Italy; Rokossovski was counter-attacked and had to retreat, which he took as a warning. He therefore halted his advance at the gates of Warsaw and this halt was to produce one of the most dramatic and violent incidents of the war.

The situation was that the Resistance movements which recognised the authority of the London government had gradually formed themselves into the 'Home Army' (AK), while a Communist Resistance movement had started up in Poland as a result of the creation of the 'Union of Polish Patriots' in Moscow. The Polish Communist party, harried in German-occupied Poland and until June 1941 banned in the Russian-occupied zone, had found it very difficult to build itself up again after the invasion of the USSR. First of all, it appeared in the form of small groups – 'The Hammer and Sickle', the 'Society of Friends of the USSR', which lacked any connection with each other and were mutually suspicious. Gradually unity was restored, thanks to militant organisers dropped by parachute from Moscow at the beginning of 1942.

Having arrived on the scene later than the 'Home Army', the 'People's Guard' formed by the Communists found some difficulty in recruiting supporters and obtaining weapons. It was not until the middle of 1943 that the Russians began to drop them arms by parachute. In the same period, the 'Union of Polish Patriots' in Moscow acquired an army corps intended to compete with Anders' army, which took its orders from London. The first division, called the Kosciusko Division, was formed in the middle of 1943 and was reinforced in January 1944 by a whole army corps commanded by General Berling and trained near Smolensk; by March, it was 40,000 strong.

To co-ordinate the guerrilla warfare, a Polish partisan general staff was formed in May 1944 in Rovno in the Ukraine; when the Soviet offensive was launched, the Red Army treated the Polish Communist partisans as it had treated the Soviet ones and provided them with arms and officers. The instructors were Poles from Berling's army corps.

The 'People's Guard' now became the 'People's Army' (Armja Ludowa or AL); in June 1944, it was strong enough for its underground fighters to resist several thousand German troops for some days in the region of Zamosc, close to the USSR; they suffered heavy losses.

The Polish government in London was disturbed by this underground activity which was outside its control and it accused the AL of behaving in an irresponsible manner. But it was not excessively concerned; most of the Polish Resistance came under the AK and in certain districts AL units had even joined up with it.

But on July 21, 1944, in Lublin, that is in territory liberated by the Red Army, a 'Polish Committee of National Liberation' was set up under the 'left-wing Socialist' Osubska-Moravski as an enlarged form of the 'Union of Polish Patriots'. It called on the Polish people to rise up against the Germans and demanded that the mother-country should be given back 'the former Polish lands of Pomerania and Silesia', specifying that these lands extended as far as the 'Oder-Neisse line', which thus made its first appearance in history. The Committee agreed to hand over the eastern Polish territories to the USSR in accordance with the principle of 'self-determination of the Byelorussian and Ukrainian peoples'. At the same time, it assumed the role of a government by ordering the mobilisation of all Poles to form a national army, into which Berling's army corps and the People's Army were incorporated. The balance of power in the Polish Resistance was thus suddenly altered – the Lublin Committee hoped to obtain 200,000 men from conscription. As it referred to the London government as 'usurpers', it was clear that, on the strength of USSR support and the presence of the Red Army, it was setting itself up as the government on the spot. This became plain when it decided to introduce immediate agrarian reform by confiscating large properties without compensation and fixing the size of every farm, old and new, at $12\frac{7}{8}$ acres; it was relying on this measure to win over the rural population to its cause.

V THE WARSAW UPRISING

The Red Army's advance into the disputed territories had faced the Polish government in London with a cruel predicament; it no longer had any diplomatic relations with the USSR and the Lublin Committee offered a rival government, already set up in Poland. General Bor-Komorovski, the head of the Home Army, proposed – and his proposal was accepted – that the leaders of the Polish Resistance government should approach the Russians as representing the legitimate Polish government and suggest concerted action against the occupier; but in no circumstances should they agree to be incorporated in Berling's army corps. At the same time, all the non-Communist Resistance groups had informed London of 'the desire of the Polish nation to resist the new Soviet aggression in order to preserve its freedom and the freedom of Europe'; they were opposed to handing over any territory. The Polish government was thus far from being restricted by its partisans in its relations with the Soviet Union.

The Red Army leaders, either through lack of precise instructions or on the principle that every little helps, seem to have raised no difficulties in granting the Polish Resistance groups the status of regular units when contact was first made; indeed, there was mutual congratulation and decorations were awarded. But subsequently all Poles were simply incorporated into Berling's forces and anyone who refused was interned. The Red Army was now interested only in the Lublin Committee.

At this juncture, Bor-Komorovski pointed out to the London government the danger of leaving the Communists to take the initiative of launching an insurrection in Warsaw while accusing the Secret Army of inertia. On July 25, the London government gave him full power to take any action he might consider appropriate. On July 29, the Moscow and Lublin radios broadcast a call to revolt. 'People of Warsaw, take up your arms . . . a million Poles must become a million soldiers.' Bor-Komorovski thought that the time had come and that he must not allow himself to be forestalled; he fixed the start of the uprising for August 1.

The Home Army commander was sure of the approval of the Polish authorities on the spot and he had received a blank cheque from his government; his decision was only part of a plan for a vast national uprising, called Operation 'Tempest'. All the same, he had acted somewhat in the dark and without full knowledge of the international situation; neither the British and Americans nor the Soviets had been consulted or even informed; they were all faced by a *fait accompli*. At the time, Mikolajczyk, the head of the Polish government, went by plane to Moscow to discuss the 'liberation' of Poland with Stalin. If he imagined that the Warsaw uprising would put him in a position of strength in his talks with the formidable Stalin, he made a grave mistake.

Yet things started off quite promisingly. Did Stalin think that Rokossovski would take Warsaw quickly? He merely told Mikolajczyk that the uprising had been 'premature'. He put him in touch with Bierut, a Polish Communist who had been living in the USSR since 1927 and was the real leader of the Lublin Committee: Bierut suggested to Mikolajczyk setting up a united national government in which the lion's share would go to the Lublin Committee with fourteen members as compared with the four allotted to the London government. On August 9, Stalin once more promised his guest that the offensive against Warsaw would start again as soon as possible – we know all this from Mikolajczyk himself, who can hardly be accused of kindly feelings towards Stalin.

And then suddenly things went wrong. Without warning, Stalin refused to send aid to the insurgents and Radio Moscow began to heap abuse and insults on them, in particular accusing them of 'provocation'. It seems that the extent of the uprising had taken Stalin by surprise; not only was the whole population of Warsaw totally involved, but even the Communists had joined in and placed themselves under Bor-Komorovski's leadership. On the other hand, the uprising had acted like a magnet in attracting German reinforcements. In short, not only would it now be a more risky operation for Rokossovski to capture Warsaw but it would also be difficult for him, if he succeeded, not to recognise the fact that power would actually be in the hands of the triumphant and victorious Home Army. And its power was opposed to the Communists inside the country and to the USSR outside.

Having been unable to forestall his opponents and refusing to strengthen their position, Stalin cold-bloodedly let the Germans crush the uprising. He stated that 'he dissociated himself from a reckless and terrible adventure', which had been instigated by 'criminals'. Not only did he refuse to provide any support for his allies fighting against a common foe but, as at the time of the big trials of his rival Bolsheviks, he even covered them with abuse and slander.

Churchill was more anxious to help the Poles than was Roosevelt, 'who was afraid of hindering the overall development of the war', in other words, of upsetting Stalin. But only the Americans had the heavy bombers capable of reaching Warsaw – but they could not make the return journey without refuelling. Eden suggested that they should fly on to the USSR; Stalin refused. The result was that the insurgents were abandoned by their allies because either they would not or could not come to their help.

At the end of August, Stalin changed his tune again; Rokossovski was now, in fact, ready to attack; the insurgents were no longer strong enough to be embarrassing but there were still enough of them to be useful. On September 14 the Russians took Praga; on the 16th, Berling tried to cross the Vistula but was repulsed. Not until September 18 did 104 Flying Fortresses drop arms and ammunition and much of it failed to reach their recipients. It was too late; on October 2, Bor-Komorovski surrendered; 50,000 inhabitants of Warsaw had been killed, wounded or taken prisoner; 350,000 were deported to Germany; the town was in ruins and the victorious Germans systematically destroyed what was left.

Polish Communist historians – particularly Kirchmayer – blame the Polish government in London for its 'Jagellonian approach', that is to say, its desire to expand eastwards and its hostility to Russia. What would have happened if it had accepted the Curzon line? It is doubtful whether Stalin would have been as gentle towards Poland, whom he wanted to exist only as a satellite state to provide a defensive barrier against Germany, as he had been towards Finland from whom he had nothing to fear, both because of her outlying position and her lack of strength. But at least time would have been gained and as a result the tragedy might have been averted; for their part, the British and the Americans – first and foremost Roosevelt – would have been less embarrassed in dealing with Stalin and under greater compulsion to support the Poles. But could the Polish government give up Polish territory?

Stalin's duplicity towards the heroic insurgents earned him worldwide public censure. He is unlikely to have been greatly perturbed. Poor Poland had lost her second battle of independence.

Under pressure from Churchill and Eden, Mikolajczyk nevertheless agreed to go back to Moscow in October 1944. He was then informed by Stalin and Churchill, who was there as well, that Poland would have to accept the Curzon line. Thereupon the Lublin Committee demanded and indeed insisted that Lvov, which had never been Russian, should be handed over to the USSR; all the Polish oil is found in that area. In addition, Mikolajczyk had to accept a compromise over the composition of a government of national unity in which the Lublin Committee was in the majority, although he himself would be its head; Churchill sweetened the pill by stating that democratic elections would take place after the war. On his return to London, Mikolajczyk was unsuccessful in persuading his colleagues. He resigned and was replaced by an extremely anti-Communist Socialist, Arciszewski. But what hope was there for the Polish government in London, short of a dispute between the Allies and a Third World War? It was a high price indeed to pay for a revival of Poland as she was in 1919.

On December 27, 1944, Stalin wrote to Roosevelt that 'the elements controlled by the Poles in London had committed the most heinous crimes'. He hinted that the Lublin Committee, the only one containing decent and honest Poles, would become the provisional government.

VI CZECHOSLOVAKIA

On July 15, Koniev attacked south of the Pripet marshes. On July 30 he took Lvov, crossed the Vistula in August, established a bridgehead at

Sandomir which he managed to hold despite Model's counter-attacks but came to a halt at the Carpathians.

The Czech Communist party, which had concentrated its main effort in Bohemia and Moravia, had been seriously weakened by the arrests of some of its members in August 1943 and January 1944; it nevertheless continued its activity in the Beskides and the region of Olomouc.

Its failures in the field were compensated for by the political success of an agreement signed with the London government under Beneš. Unlike Tito, the Czechoslovak Communists continued to implement the instructions of the Comintern, even after it had been dissolved; some of them were members of the Beneš government in London. In December 1943, Beneš signed a pact with the Communist leaders Gottwald and Slansky in Moscow; he described the Liberation as 'a national revolution combined with a social revolution'; he spoke of the 'necessity of nationalising certain sectors'; he agreed that a Communist should be the head of the first united Czechoslovak government after the war. Beneš was sincerely convinced that Czechoslovakia's future could only be guaranteed by and with the friendship of the Soviet Union.

The Red Army's approach brought Slovakia into the limelight. This woody and mountainous region was well suited to guerrilla warfare; however the early groups were unsuccessful; the mass of the peasantry remained aloof and the Central Committee of the Communist party was arrested in 1943. Slovakia was also a clerical, anti-Czech country with Fascist tendencies; political traditions and social structure were unsuitable for organising an uprising.

But this state which had been brought into being by the Nazis was falling apart; in 1943 there were mass desertions from the Slovak units fighting in the USSR – a whole regiment 2,000 strong, led by its officers, went over to the Red Army; 800 others joined the Ukrainian partisans. The Russians began to send arms and agents trained in Kiev into Slovakia; they also set up a Czechoslovak unit in the Red Army; similarly Soviet partisans sometimes crossed the frontier to join the Slovakian partisans.

The Communist party's problem was to provide the peasants with the necessary organisation to encourage them to revolt. But the London government was also anxious to control the uprising; it intended to make it a purely military operation and it despatched two generals to lead it. Some of the officers in the Slovak Army were strongly nationalistic and were ready to change sides if Slovakia was guaranteed her independence. The Communists did not hesitate to establish contact with these officers; they stated that, even though Czechoslovakia certainly existed, she consisted of two absolutely equal peoples, Czechs and Slovaks – on this point they seemed rather ahead of Beneš.

In July, the Slovak uprising took place, on a grand scale; bands of escaped prisoners of war joined in, including some French. All over the country 'National Committees' were set up, as had been decided in the agreement concluded between Gottwald and Beneš. The small German garrisons were attacked, as well as road and rail convoys. A 'Slovak National Council' was established at Banska-Bystrica; it seemed to have achieved a very broad spectrum of unity – even the Slovak Communists were slightly nationalistic.

The Slovak government launched several attacks against the rebels; they came to nothing. But then the Germans came on the scene and the insurgents were driven out of the plains into the mountains. There were harsh repressive measures. The uprising failed because it had not received the help that it had expected from the Red Army. It was in fact not until mid-November that Petrov crossed the Carpathians and entered sub-Carpathian Ukraine; and then he moved off obliquely towards Hungary.

The motivation and course of the Slovak uprising were not always clear; the Communists in Slovakia and those who were dropped from Russia disagreed as to who should take the credit, and then blamed each other for the failure; one can vaguely discern a pattern of suspicion to-wards the Czechs on the part of the Slovaks anxious to assert the weight of their majority; the part played by the generals despatched from London and their tragic fate are also not very clear. It seems, however, that the Communists who insisted, in France for example, that mobility was the essence of guerrilla warfare, here made the mistake of setting up 'central mobilisation strongholds' as in the Vercors. Tactics which were possible in the vast spaces of Russia became a trap when applied to more restricted areas. But henceforth it was difficult for the Germans to retain any confidence whatsoever in the Slovaks.

VII ROMANIA

The Slovakian mountains were hardly suitable terrain for the Russian tanks; accordingly, the Red Army had decided to strike hardest towards Romania. When the front stopped short at the Carpathians, it continued its advance in the south.

In the spring of 1944, the German army group south of the Ukraine had started to withdraw from the Dniepr to the Dniestr, where it set up a defensive front; but to hold this front, some 400 miles long, it could pro-vide only two German and two Romanian armies; the fighting spirit of the latter was suspect and they had been sandwiched between the Ger-mans; it was thought that this would prevent the collapse of large areas of front, as on the Don. On the other hand, Marshal Antonescu, though militarily subordinated to the German command, jealously guarded his privileges as head of the Romanian government and there were frequent clashes between the allies – more particularly over the evacuation of the Crimea.

In order to meet the Soviet attacks in the north, Hitler had withdrawn eleven divisions from this sector, including four out of the six Panzer divisions, and they had not been replaced. In addition, General Schoerner who was familiar with the troops and the terrain, had relinquished his command to General Friesner, who knew nothing about either. Friesner had noticed that the right wing of his positions had an excessive bulge and was open to attack from the north southwards; he asked permission to shorten his line by withdrawing from the Dniestr to the Danube; Hitler refused.

The Russians attacked on August 20 from Iasi and Tiraspol; once again, they pounced on the enemy's weak point, the two Romanian armies, so as to encircle the German Sixth Army which was sandwiched between them. By the evening of the 20th they had crossed the Dniestr; by the 22nd, their manoeuvre had succeeded, although Friesner, with Antonescu's approval, had given the order to withdraw before receiving Hitler's permission. The Führer then insisted that the Focsani–Galatz–Danube delta line should be held in order to protect Bulgaria, which was restless and causing him concern.

But on August 23 a palace revolution broke out in Bucharest. King Michael, who must have been reflecting on Victor Emmanuel's example, had Antonescu arrested and formed a government of national unity under General Zanatescu, including Communists; previously, the elder statesmen Maniu and Bratianu had once more appealed to the British and Americans who had referred them to the Russians.

Hitler bombed Bucharest, thus enabling King Michael to declare war on Germany on August 24; the Romanians immediately invaded Transylvania to take it back from the Hungarians. On August 28, the Red Army entered Bucharest where they at first behaved as enemies. Then on September 12, the Russians granted an armistice on moderate terms – the war was not over – and the Romanians benefited from their timely switch. The USSR took back Bessarabia and north Bukovina from the Romanians and returned Transylvania, at the Hungarians' expense. Molotov came to Bucharest and promised that the Romanian political and social structure would remain unchanged; but an 'Allied Control Commission' was set up in Romania under the Russians.

The situation of the German forces had become critical; they could now escape only over the mountain passes of the Carpathians. 'There's no longer any general staff and nothing but chaos,' wrote Friesner, 'everyone, from general to clerk, has got a rifle and is fighting to the last bullet.' The result was the surrender of nearly 200,000 men and the loss of the oil wells so crucial for the Luftwaffe. The operation carried out at Iasi by Malinovski and Tolbukhin was one of the most successful of the war.

VIII BULGARIA

In Bulgaria in the summer of 1944, pro-Russian feeling was running high. The 'Fatherland Front' contained Communists, Socialists and representatives of the 'People's Agrarian Union'; it operated through many hundreds of underground committees. As early as 1942, groups of partisans were carrying out sabotage in the Pirin, Rila and Rhodope districts and in the Balkans. From 1943 onwards units deserted from the Army to join the underground Resistance fighters who by 1944 numbered 18,000 men. Mass demonstrations and strikes followed thick and fast in Sofia and Plovdiv.

The Bagrianov government withdrew its troops from Greece and Yugoslavia; at the same time it sought the protection of the British and Americans; whilst the Red Army was preparing to invade Bulgaria, it sent a delegation to Cairo. It received the same answer as the Romanians: the Bulgarians should seek a settlement with the Russians. The latter had in any case not waited before sending an ultimatum which the Bulgarians were compelled to accept.

On September 5 Muravief formed a new government which asked the Russians for an armistice, although the Bulgarians were not at war with them. But on August 26 the 'Fatherland Front' had decided on a national uprising which began in Sofia on September 9; mutiny broke out in the Army; street fighting took place in Sofia where the 'Fatherland Front' seized power. On September 8 the Red Army suspended its operations and on the 18th marched into Sofia. Bulgaria mobilised, declared war on Germany and sent 150,000 men to fight side by side with their Red Army comrades.

IX YUGOSLAVIA

The policy of the British and Americans was thus clear and consistent; they considered that they should do nothing to embarrass the USSR in the Red Army's own operational theatres. Moreover, apart from Poland, the Russians behaved with apparent moderation; they confined themselves to reversing the situation to their advantage; they set up governments of national unity which they controlled from within by their Communist members and from without by armistice commissions, theoretically interallied but under Russian control. Bent only on ending the war with Germany, they did not seem to be including Communist revolution in their baggage-train.

The Russians were also ignoring Greece which, by agreement with the British, did not come into their zone of influence. But on September 6, they joined up with Tito's partisans in an atmosphere of extraordinary enthusiasm; though Tito may have disobeyed Stalin, he and his followers had always considered the Soviet Union as their elder sister, Slavs as well as Communists, and the Red Army as their natural ally. All that Hitler could now do was to order von Weich's Army Group E to retreat from Greece and southern Yugoslavia, a difficult operation when hemmed in by Greek and Yugoslav underground fighters who were growing in numbers and aggressiveness as they scented victory.

The Red Army could be supplied via Romania's ports and railway system, none of which had been destroyed and which would not have been available had it been advancing from Warsaw towards Berlin; strategic needs as well as problems in Poland had thus turned the countries in the Danube basin and the Balkans into a Russian preserve, whereas previously the governments in these parts of Europe had been anti-Soviet.

Until now Tito had been backed and armed only by the British and when King Peter showed signs of returning to his country using two British aircraft that he was hoping to lay hands on, he was stopped by them. They forced him to dismiss Mihailović and replace his Prime Minister Purić by Subasić, a member of the Croatian Peasant party who had gone to see Tito on the island of Vis in June 1944. An agreement was signed, sponsored by the British; Tito pledged himself not to raise any questions concerning the political régime for the duration of the war – though in fact in the areas under his control he had already taken certain measures that would be difficult to reverse; two of Tito's partisans joined the London government; in exchange, Subasić urged the members of all the Resistance movements in Jugoslavia to join the partisans.

In August, Churchill met Tito in Naples; if he hoped to find him meek and grateful, he quickly had to change his tune. Tito talked to His Majesty's powerful Prime Minister as equal to equal, if not even with arrogance. At that time he had conquered the whole of Serbia after defeating the combined forces of his enemies in the area round Toplica and Jablanica – roughly 30,000 men, Bulgarians, Nedić's and Mihailović's Chetniks, Ustashis and Germans. He had obviously forgotten the time when he had been saved from a mass German parachute drop at Drvar in Bosnia by nearly 1,000 sorties by the Allies – although it was not very long ago, in May 1944. The massive aid represented by British war equipment did not seem to carry much weight, although it had been made possible by the Balkan Air Force which had been formed in Italy and by the priority that the British had given to Yugoslavia in arms deliveries over other European Resistance movements; and it was through this help that Yugoslavia had acquired the equipment which enabled her to transform her guerrilla bands into an army that even had tanks and aircraft, driven and piloted by men trained in Italy by the British.

Tito categorically refused to agree to King Peter's return to Yugoslavia; he claimed Trieste and Istria; he bluntly rejected any idea of British or American operations in Yugoslavia, even going as far as to say that he would resist them by force, thus spelling the doom of Churchill's schemes aimed at the 'soft underbelly of Europe'. He would not pledge himself not to set up a Communist régime in Yugoslavia.

The Red Army's successes were obviously not unconnected with this stiffening of Tito's attitude; unlike King Michael and the Regent Horthy, Tito was far from being scared by the approach of the Red Army. At the beginning of September, without informing Churchill, he had flown to Moscow to see Stalin although the Russians had been the last to despatch a mission to him and had not yet provided him with any material aid. Tito gave the Red Army 'permission to enter Yugoslavia'; it undertook to withdraw as soon as it had accomplished its task.

Churchill now bitterly regretted the support he had provided for the ungrateful Tito. He did not know that the interview between Tito and Stalin had been a stormy one. The latter had asked him to reinstate King Peter; when Tito reacted violently, he became more explicit: 'Not for always, just for the time being; if he gets in your way, at the first opportunity just stab him gently in the back.'

Meanwhile, on October 4, Tolbukhin reached the Morava; helped by partisans, he entered Belgrade on the 19th; the partisans freed the rest of Yugoslavia by themselves and threatened Trieste. The Germans forming the Löhr Group, about 350,000 men, were beating a laborious retreat, harassed at night by partisans and by day by Allied bombers – a large-scale joint operation had been laid on to attack the whole of Yugoslavia's communication routes.

But having accomplished his mission, Tolbukhin moved back northwards; he crossed the Danube and joined up with Malinovski. In order to protect the road to Vienna, Hitler had decided to make his stand in Hungary.

X HUNGARY

Both the Hungarians and Romanians had based their whole policies on establishing their 'rights' in Transylvania; they had both been equally anxious to convince the Germans on the subject; and now that the Wehrmacht was a broken reed, they had both set out to gain the good graces of the Allies. The Hungarians lost; the arrival of the Red Army in Romania had given her the advantage; once the Romanian Army had marched into Transylvania, the only thing left for Hungary to do was to fight it; but by doing this, she found herself sucked into the German camp – the losing side.

The Hungarians had made another miscalculation: they thought that they could hold up the Russians on the ridges of the Carpathians long enough to enable the British and American forces from Italy to arrive in Hungary first. But Romania's sudden change of sides rendered Hungary vulnerable from the east and the south.

Admiral Horthy now tried to revive his July plan: Hungary should re-assert her sovereignty *vis-à-vis* the Germans and ask the British and Americans for an armistice. On August 29, he replaced Sztojay's govern-ment by a military cabinet under General Geza Lakatos; but his anti-Communism prevented him from making contact with the Russians at the right time, although Harrison, the American ambassador in Switzerland with whom he was in touch, had informed him of his government's view that he should do so. When he finally resigned himself to sending a delegation to Moscow at the end of September the Germans had had the time to collect their thoughts and work out a plan of campaign in which Hungary was an essential pawn.

On October 11 the Hungarian delegation in Moscow finally signed the preliminaries to an armistice, the terms of which were approved by Churchill who was also in Moscow; this agreement laid down that Hungary should break with Germany and declare war on her. Horthy carried out only half of it; on October 15 he disclosed his request for an armistice to Rahn and Veesenmayer, the German diplomats in Budapest, but he promised not to attack German troops. Fearing internal political repercussions, he also refused to come to an agreement with the anti-German groups in Hungary. He relied solely on the Army.

But the first result of the Regent's apparent indecision was to im-mobilise the Army. The Germans had Szalassí and the Arrow Cross up their sleeves; aided and abetted by sympathisers in the Army, this con-tingent took control of the Army by neutralising the officers who were hostile to them and Szalassy seized power. German troops occupied the strategic points in the city and the radio stations. Horthy was left with his castle in Buda and his bodyguard; he hesitated and finally decided not to use this last line of defence; he resigned, was arrested and taken away to Germany.

Meanwhile, Malinovski had reached the Tisza, taken Szeged on October 7 and then, after a ten-day siege, Debreczen; but instead of finding friends in power ready to open up the gates of Budapest to them, as in Bucharest, the Russians found themselves compelled to set about besieging it. In order to weaken the Hungarian opposition, the Russians encouraged the formation of a provisional government at Debreczen on December 24 under General Dalnoki Miklos, who called for a national uprising against the Germans and the Arrow Cross government. On January 25, 1945, he signed an armistice with the Red Army.

<h2 style="text-align:center">XI THE AGREEMENT OF OCTOBER 1944
BETWEEN CHURCHILL AND STALIN</h2>

Churchill was more alarmed than Roosevelt at Russia's dominance in the Danube basin which seemed likely to result from the Red Army's successes. He had suggested to his allies dividing Europe into zones of influence, an idea which Cordell Hull had rejected out of hand as a matter of principle, but which the more pragmatic Roosevelt, overriding his Secretary of State, had accepted for a provisional three months' period, so that the British gave Russia a free hand in Romania in return for a free hand in Greece, on the old system of tit-for-tat.

This agreement was never put into writing and was based on a few words exchanged between Eden and the Soviet ambassador Gusev. In any case, it was due to come to an end in September. Tito's unexpectedly pro-Soviet attitude increased Churchill's alarm. He suggested another meeting of the Big Three, which Roosevelt refused to attend, since presidential elections were impending; all he could do was to send Harriman as his delegate, but purely as an observer with no power to take any decisions binding on the USA.

So Churchill and Stalin met in Moscow in October 1944 for one of those private talks of which they were both so fond. They easily reached agreement on the armistice terms to be imposed on Hungary. As for Poland, Stalin was adamant and Churchill had to be content to pass on his partner's wishes to Mikolajczyk; but Stalin on the other hand raised no difficulties about making compensatory concessions to Poland at the cost of the Germans – Stettin and the 'Oder-Neisse line', that is to say that Poland would gain nearly 40,000 square miles in the west and lose 70,000 square miles in the east, though this was poorer land.

As for the fate of the Danubian and Balkan countries, Churchill and Stalin came to a very strange agreement, rather like thieves disposing of the swag. This is how Churchill tells the story:

The moment was apt for business, so I said:

Let us settle about our affairs in the Balkans. Your armies are in Roumania and Bulgaria. We have interests, missions and agents there.

Don't let us get at cross-purposes in small ways. So far as Britain and Russia are concerned, how would it do for you to have ninety per cent predominance in Romania, for us to have ninety per cent of the say in Greece and go fifty-fifty about Yugoslavia?' While this was being translated I wrote out on a half-sheet of paper:

	(per cent)
Romania	
Russia	90
The others	10
Greece	
Great Britain	90
(in accord with USA)	
Russia	10
Yugoslavia	50–50
Hungary	50–50
Bulgaria	
Russia	75
The others	25

I pushed this across to Stalin, who had by then heard the translation. There was a slight pause. Then he took his blue pencil and made a large tick upon it, and passed it back to us. It was all settled in no more time than it takes to set down. .... After this there was a long silence. The pencilled paper lay in the centre of the table. At length I said, 'Might it not be thought rather cynical if it seemed we had disposed of these issues so fateful to millions of people, in such an offhand way? Let us burn the paper.' 'No, you keep it', said Stalin.

Next day Eden and Molotov had a lively discussion to 'revise' these percentages and the Russian Foreign Minister managed to raise the Soviet Union's interests in Hungary and Bulgaria to eighty per cent. This procedure was all the more extraordinary since these figures did not lend themselves to any exact interpretation, either in territorial terms or in the proportion of pro-British or pro-Russians in the post-war governments of these countries.

In addition, this agreement violated the previous decision reached at Teheran, whereby the Allies had agreed that a 'European Consultative Commission' should examine all territorial problems that needed settling at the end – but only after the end – of the war and make suggestions to the Allies jointly approved by representatives of all three powers. The Americans and first and foremost Roosevelt, attached great importance to this formula; their failure to react, as a result of the extraordinary power vacuum created by the untimely occurrence of presidential elections in the middle of a war, allowed two unrepentant imperialists to carve up

Europe on their own, as their counterparts had done in Africa in the nineteenth century. For the two confederates, however, it was a straight-forward bargain: it meant that Britain was washing her hands of Bulgaria and Hungary, was resigned to the effects of Tito's sudden switch, was determined to maintain an interest in Romania and intended to keep Greece under her thumb, while Bulgaria would no longer be pressing Greece for an opening on to the Aegean.

Stalin and Churchill also discussed the fate of Germany. Shortly be-fore, in Quebec, Churchill had approved the Morgenthau plan to destroy Germany's heavy industry in favour of those countries which had suffered from Hitler's ambitions. This plan was also approved by Stalin; any scheme likely to impede Germany's recovery was immediately attractive to him. The question thus once more arose of placing the Ruhr and the Saar under 'international control' – no more explicit interpretation of the term was offered. Churchill again raised his idea of a federation of Ger-many's southern provinces with Austria, which was, he suggested, the natural historical counterweight to Prussian influence; Stalin showed less hostility to this plan than before, perhaps because he had received the *quid pro quo* of a free hand in south-east Europe. But he made no pledges; in any case, it was impossible not to wait for Roosevelt's views on all these matters that did not require an immediate solution; accordingly, it was decided to leave the question to be examined by the 'European Consultative Commission'.

XII GREECE

The Communist underground in Greece was much stronger than their associates and rivals, because they had been able to lay hands on the stocks of arms left behind by the Italians when they surrendered. In March 1944, ELAS had formed a National Liberation Committee fore-shadowing the government which it intended Greece to have after the Liberation. The movement had even contaminated the armed forces of the Greek government in Cairo; in April 1944 mutiny had broken out in the Greek fleet commanded by Admiral Alexandris which made up one-third of the Allied naval forces in the Mediterranean; the mutineers asked for ELAS representatives to be admitted to Tsouderos' conservative exile government; the rebellion had to be forcibly overcome and the partici-pants disarmed and interned.

This incident was not without significance and it alarmed Churchill sufficiently for it to be a possible explanation of his trip to Moscow and his agreement with Stalin. A preliminary measure was to persuade King George to widen the basis of his government. The liberal leader, Papaan-

FORCES EMPLOYED IN THE SOVIET COUNTER-OFFENSIVES

Operational theatres	Length of front (in miles)	Numbers (in thousands of men)	Guns and mortars	Tanks and self-propelled guns	Combat aircraft
1. Winter campaign 1941-42	3,000	4,200	32,000	2,000	3,700
Moscow offensive	625 (24%)	1,000 (25%)	8,000 (25%)	720 (35%)	1,170 (32%)
In depth	60–160				
2. Winter campaign 1942-43	3,860	6,120	77,800	7,000	3,250
Stalingrad offensive	500 (13%)	1,000 (18%)	14,000 (18%)	1,325 (19%)	1,115 (34%)
In depth	60–100				
3. Summer campaign 1943	2,700	6,400	103,000	10,000	8,400
Byelgorod-Kharkov-Orel operations	375 (12%)	2,300 (38%)	34,000 (34%)	5,000 (50%)	3,700 (44%)
In depth	160–190				
4. Campaign of first half of 1944	2,750	6,160	92,600	5,360	8,500
Ukraine offensive	750 (27%)	2,370 (39%)	28,900 (31%)	2,040 (38%)	2,400 (28%)
In depth	350–375				
5. Summer campaign, 1944	2,780	6,420	92,600	7,750	13,450
Operations in Byelorussia	750 (26%)	2,500 (40%)	45,000 (48%)	6,000 (70%)	7,000 (53%)
In depth	350–375				
6. Spring campaign, 1945	1,500	6,530	108,000	12,900	15,600
Vistula-Oder operation	315 (21%)	2,200 (33%)	39,000 (36%)	4,500 (36%)	5,050 (33%)
In depth	362				

1. From Colonel Constantini's translation into French of an article by General Pavlenko in the Soviet Review of Military History, March, 1966.

dreou, was brought from Athens, and in September 1944 he summoned a conference in Beirut of all shades of opinion of the Greek Resistance movements. Whether or not it was a result of the tacit understanding between the British and Russians at the time, the Greek Communists showed themselves much less demanding than their Polish counterparts; they agreed to dissolve the National Liberation Committee and to be in a minority by providing only five members of the government of national unity.

German troops evacuated Greece on October 18 and the Papaandreou government was set up in Athens. By an interallied agreement signed at Caserta, all the Greek troops came under the command of the Allies and the Greek government attempted to disband the armed Resistance groups. But ELAS refused to hand over their weapons and a general strike was declared in Athens. It is unlikely that the USSR either ordered or even encouraged these two events and her delegate with ELAS probably tried to prevent them; they may well have been caused by Tolbukhin's advance and probably also by Tito's example in Yugoslavia at the same time.

However this may have been, Papaandreou's government was in no position to put down the revolt. Churchill dealt with it, as he had dealt with the Greek sailors' mutiny in Alexandria. British troops landed in Greece and 'restored law and order' in Athens; both Churchill and Alexander had considered the situation serious enough to warrant a visit to the Greek capital. Neither Roosevelt nor Stalin protested against this display of force.

Nonetheless, it was the final act of an extraordinary reversal in the state of affairs. In countries in which the Communists had been a weak minority before the war, the Soviet Union was finding little difficulty in establishing a dominating position that seemed likely to last a long time, either because of the internal Resistance movements or because of the Red Army's success and mostly owing to both these factors. On the other hand, Britain was losing on every score: she had been obliged to abandon Poland to her fate, although she had entered the war on behalf of the Poles; and in Greece, Churchill, the very man who had championed resistance, had succeeded in maintaining Britain's position only by using British soldiers against the Greek Resistance forces. For their part, the United States were already showing blatant and symptomatic indifference towards territorial problems whose solution would create the shape of things to come in post-war Europe. Were the British not paying the price for their delay in opening the second front and for the fact that the Red Army had enjoyed too long a monopoly of success against the Wehrmacht?

CHAPTER 4

The War in Italy
(September 1943–December 1944)

In Teheran Churchill had not dwelt too much on the fact that he regarded the Italian front as of prime importance; he had spoken chiefly about the Dodecanese expedition; this had come to a lamentable end, but the British resources used in the undertaking had been small and he was hoping to begin again with Turkish and above all American support. Now that the landing across the Channel was no longer in doubt, the Americans were quite willing to admit the importance of Mediterranean problems for their allies. They had approved of the Anglo-Turkish treaty of 1943, which seemed to indicate that Turkey would enter the war; they were delighted at being able to bomb the southern regions of Germany from the airfields in the south of Italy. But they were quite determined that the Mediterranean must continue to be a minor operational area; Marshall categorically refused to give up men and boats for that 'damned country', as he called the Dodecanese; and when Roosevelt, whom Churchill could twist round his little finger, contemplated replacing the divisions which had been taken from Italy for 'Overlord', Marshall was so violently opposed to it that the President backed down.

In these circumstances, the Allied armies in Italy were going to slog their way all the way up the boot – 'like a bug on one leg', said Churchill. And so the disorder which had become rife in the country dragged on and grew worse until it degenerated into civil war. But since Churchill was doggedly persistent and did not easily admit defeat, there were going to be endless interallied discussions on the final direction of the Anglo-American attack which would make Nazi Germany give in.

I THE MILITARY OPERATIONS

In terrain broken by steep mountain chains dropping precipitously into narrow valleys, Todt had packed the narrowest part of the Italian peninsula between the Garigliano and the Sangro with trenches, casemates, mines and pill-boxes. This was the Gustav line, which blocked access to Rome and kept the Allies at a standstill in front of it throughout the winter of 1943.

The Germans had left about thirty divisions in Italy, under two separate commands: Rommel was responsible for maintaining law and order in the occupied part from Rome to the Alps; the Air Force general, Kesselring, was facing General Clark's Allied troops, which since November had been swelled by General Juin's French Expeditionary Force, originally two and then later four divisions strong.

Every frontal attack against the German defences ended in failure. In January 1944, in order to outflank them, the Americans attempted a landing on a limited scale – two divisions and eighty-eight boats, without any intensive preparation. The place they chose was Anzio, right behind the enemy lines, short of Rome. Churchill, on the contrary, had advocated a big operation to the north of Rome using large numbers of men and quantities of material. These would have had to be taken from those intended for 'Overlord' and were consequently refused him. Although the landing succeeded without any great difficulty, General Lucas did not consider that he was strong enough to advance inland; he confined himself to fortifying his positions while waiting for the American Fifth Army to reach him. Kesselring, who had for a moment thought of undertaking a complete withdrawal, realised that the Allies had let a great opportunity slip through their fingers; he endeavoured to fling the landing troops back into the sea and it was only after a month of hard fighting and thanks to the support of the Navy with their guns that they managed to hold on.

But they did not break through the Gustav line, despite having captured a few hills, among them the Belvedere, which was taken by the French. The German defence line ran through the famous Monte Cassino monastery, after the monks and art treasures had first been evacuated. Americans, New Zealanders and Hindus launched attacks on the position, but to no avail. In February 1944 bombers destroyed the monastery but again all to no purpose; the ruins acted as shelters for the defenders; the tanks of the attacking forces were held and the infantry attacks all failed.

General Clark insisted on continuing his frontal attacks. Yet the Allies had superiority in men – twenty-one divisions as against fourteen – and even more in equipment, tanks and aircraft; but the German defences were impregnable; it was a return to 1915 trench warfare.

In the spring General Juin devised an operation across the mountainous region of the Araunci mountains, whose size seemed in fact to preclude the possibility of any military operations. But the French Expeditionary Force included Moroccan troops who were equipped and trained to operate in mountains; with their mules General Sevez's *goumiers* climbed some 4,850 feet on to a group of mountains which the Germans had not bothered to fortify, in the belief that it was inaccessible; from there, on May 15, 1944, they pounced on the Germans from behind.

At the same time the Poles and the British seized Monte Cassino; the troops who had landed in Anzio also attacked. Because General Clark had disobeyed Alexander in an attempt to be first to enter Rome the Germans escaped encirclement but had to evacuate Rome, which the Allies entered on June 4 – just at the moment when German propaganda had stuck magnificent posters of a crawling snail all over the walls of Paris to illustrate the slowness of their advance.

The Germans withdrew to other fortifications built by the Todt organisation. These barred the way up the peninsula over a distance of 125 miles between Pisa and Rimini; they lay along the Tuscan Apennines, which was the last obstacle before the plain; this was the Gothic line, consisting of trenches, anti-tank barriers and concrete pill-boxes at both ends and in the passes.

At the end of August, the British Eighth Army attacked in the area of Rimini, which was stormed by the Greeks on September 2. The American Fifth Army in its turn seized Pisa and Lucca; in the centre the Indians had advanced into the mountains; Forli was captured on November 10 and Ravenna on December 5. But the advance was checked by bad weather before the Allies could emerge on to the plain. They had to spend the winter where they were; there was nothing else for the troops in Italy to do, weakened as they were through having been compelled to hand over men for the Normandy operation.

In the meantime, on June 17 the French First Army under General Delattre de Tassigny had got its hand in by seizing Elba and capturing 2,000 prisoners. Conquering the island enabled them to prevent enemy ships from using the channel which separated it from the Italian mainland.

II THE ALLIES AND ITALY

The British and Americans were not yet ready to hold out a welcoming hand to Italy, who had shed her Fascism all too quickly; certainly, the people welcomed their troops so warmly that the saying that 'Italy numbers 40 million Fascists and 40 million anti-Fascists' had become a by-word. The Americans had recognised that British interests had priority in Italy but the British were torn between conflicting demands.

As soon as the political pattern of post-war Europe began to emerge, Churchill's inherent conservatism came to the fore. He considered that twenty years under a Fascist régime had deprived the Italian middle classes of any sense of democracy; the only factions now remaining were therefore the King and the aristocracy on the one hand – the former had to some extent redeemed himself by getting rid of Mussolini – and Communism on the other, with which Churchill rather hastily lumped together the whole of the Italian Resistance. British sympathy and support was therefore reserved for the King and Badoglio; they wanted them to strengthen their authority throughout the kingdom and allowed them to raise a small army; they refused to look upon the Resistance volunteers as anything but a few extra soldiers, or even a possible source of disorder. At times Churchill gave free rein to personal feelings of resentment as, for example, when he refused to have any dealings with a politician of the stature of Count Sforza. Thus in Italy as in Greece the British were in favour of seeing the leading conservative and reactionary elements remain in power, despite the fact that they had compromised themselves with Fascism and even with Nazi Germany; and they were opposed to their natural allies – the Resistance.

But at the same time, long-term calculations led the British to want a weak post-war Italy in the middle of the Mediterranean; it was only in driblets that they restored Italy's strength and a minimum of disorder in the country was not entirely against their wishes.

American policy, too, was not without its contradictions. Contrary to what had happened in North Africa and Yugoslavia – where they had supported Giraud and Mihailović – in Italy the Americans respected the distinction which they had committed themselves to making between the Italian people and the Fascist régime. Noticing the impotence of Badoglio and the growing energy of the anti-Fascist parties, perhaps motivated by a traditional feeling of hostility towards monarchies and anxious not to repeat the blunder they had made with Darlan, they gradually showed themselves in favour of a revival of Italy once she had wiped her slate clean of Fascism. Their chief support was for the Church and Christian Democracy, which reassured them against any possible dangers of subversion. They also wanted to set the Italian economy on its feet again, even if only to relieve themselves of the burden. But they had allowed inflation to race ahead until prices, which stood at the level of 600 per cent of 1938 values in July 1943, soared to 3,500 per cent in April 1944.

In September 1944 the British and Americans issued a declaration which somewhat mitigated the harshness of the armistice clauses; they relaxed their control of the Italian administration and agreed to the Italian government's accrediting representatives to them.

Disappointed by the behaviour of the British and Americans when he was hoping to achieve a quick switch from foe to ally, Badoglio looked to the USSR to redress the balance; in January 1944 Prunas, the Secretary-General at the Ministry of Foreign Affairs, met Vyshinsky in Naples; the Russian appeared understanding, in accordance with the USSR's constant political line of bringing together all anti-German forces; the Italian Communist party, as well as Tito in Yugoslavia, was invited by Moscow to show a conciliatory attitude towards the King.

For its part, the French National Liberation Committee, after adopting a very unforgiving attitude towards Badoglio's government – the French Resistance remained very hostile to Italy — showed signs of wanting reconciliation. In Ajaccio after its liberation, General de Gaulle said a few words to disperse the clouds of the past and recalled the deep historical roots of 'Latin friendship'. In July 1944 he met Prunas, assured him that France was not making any territorial claims against Italy and spoke to him about a European federation, the keystone of which would be Franco-Italian reconciliation. Couve de Murville, the minister in Algiers, was appointed French ambassador in Rome in order to carry out this plan, which was not without ulterior motives with regard to the powerful British and Americans.

III THE SALO REPUBLIC

After he had been freed from the Gran Sasso by ss troops, who may have been informed and helped by Senise, his former police minister, Mussolini had taken up the fight again on the German side 'to defend Italian honour and national patriotism'. He declared an 'Italian Social Republic' with its seat on the shores of Lake Garda in Salo. He ordered mobilisation, which could only mean, in fact, remobilisation, and he placed the command of the armed forces in the hands of Marshal Graziani.

Fascism was thus breaking with the monarchy; it must, said the Duce, return to its origins, the Republic, Socialism and the struggle against capitalism; it must refresh itself at its source and set off afresh in the right direction.

In actual fact the new state lacked any constitutional foundations. At its very first meeting the Council of Ministers decided to call a special Constituent Assembly but had to postpone its meeting until after the war. The ideological principles were defined in a Fascist party programme which was drawn up in October 1943. The Italian Social Republic recognised the pre-eminence of labour, guaranteed private property, which 'fulfilled a man's personality', placed all public services in the hands of the state and amalgamated all professional groups into a General Labour Confederation; although the masses were thus recognised as having a right to social justice, they were given no democratic power and the party retained its complete monopoly of political life.

The Neo-Fascist party recruited 250,000 partisans and raised four infantry divisions which were trained in German camps. In actual fact it had hardly any support in northern Italy – even though eminent persons like Cardinal Schuster in Milan dealt with Mussolini to the very last as the rightful holder of power. The industrialists who had financed Fascism in its initial stages were worried by the demagogic propaganda put out by *L'Italia del Popolo* and towards the end they stood aloof from it. The working masses ignored the Fascist delegates in industrial concerns and stepped up their strikes and attacks. As for the administration, its power was purely one of fact, not of right, and this greatly encouraged traditional feelings of provincial independence.

Moreover, the Party leaders were not in agreement among themselves. The old hands like Farinacci, Pavolini and Buffarini outbid each other in their servility to the Germans; they were worried by *L'Italia del Popolo* and succeeded in having it suppressed; they even conspired against the Duce. The younger men were more fanatical; they introduced an atmosphere of harshness and puritanism of which the victims were black marketeers and renegades like Count Ciano; the latter was handed over by the Germans, tried by court martial, sentenced to death and executed in Verona with four accomplices, among them de Bono. The whole trial had been conducted under constant threat from an excited crowd which had forced the judges' hands as well as Mussolini's, Ciano's father-in-law. Among these impassioned Neo-Fascists, Prince Borghese fought the Allies to the bitter end, at the head of the group of naval launches called 'Mas'; some young people sacrificed their lives to the very last day for the Duce and Fascism. But they were only a minority.

Besides, the Salo Republic's only real strength was that the Germans chose to allow it to exist. And the Germans no longer trusted any of the Italians; Hitler himself had not wanted Mussolini to stay in Rome nor had he wanted the troops raised by the Social Republic to fight the Allies. Liaison was maintained by Ambassador Rahn on the German side and Ambassador Anfuso for the Italians; but Mussolini himself was kept under lock and key by Lieutenant Dicheroff, a German aide-de-camp who was lent by the Führer and who behaved like a real major-domo.

The Wehrmacht leaders treated Italy like an occupied country and all Mussolini's protests when he considered that his authority was being too obviously flouted remained a dead letter. Leading Fascists were not even given permission to move about; when Marshal Graziani arrived in Udine he was asked by a German officer what he was doing there. The Propaganda Minister, Pavolini, was in Trieste for several weeks waiting for permission to hold a conference and when he announced that Trieste was Italian, he was ordered to leave.

The Germans often behaved with extreme brutality. Not only did they bring the anti-Semitic laws into full operation and deport Italian Jews, who till then had not been persecuted with any great vigour, but they adopted the practice of indiscriminate collective sanctions. On March 23, 1944, there was an attempt against a coach-load of German policemen in Rome. General Maelzer, the governor of the city, wanted to blow up the surrounding houses and their inhabitants with dynamite. Himmler's idea had been a mass evacuation of the people accompanied by massive demolition. Hitler decided that twenty Italians should be shot for every German who had been hit; Kesselring reduced the figure to ten. Kappler, the chief of the SD in Rome, had 335 hostages executed in the Fosse Ardeatine. Hitler had long wanted to annex the Julian Veneto and now ordered that it, together with Trieste and the south Tyrol, should be administered by two Gauleiters, Raines and Hofer; according to the established practice, the Italian language disappeared from all public buildings and even from tombstones.

In the eyes of its German allies and protectors, Neo-Fascism was only an auxiliary militia, intended to ensure internal law and order; its troops were employed only in civil war against the partisans.

IV THE LIBERATION COMMITTEES

In the disorder and atmosphere of civil war which were now becoming rife in Italy, the Liberation Committees were able to extend and consolidate their authority. But their only point of agreement was their opposition to Fascism and the Germans. In March 1944 the Milan Committee took a firm stand against Badoglio's government; it demanded that a 'special government' be formed, 'by all the anti-Fascist parties which had joined the Resistance, giving them full constitutional powers'. The Milan Committee was thus announcing its intention of taking over the leadership of the new Italy on behalf of the Resistance, and its claim was justified by the forces under its control and by its hard struggle against the Germans and the Neo-Fascists.

The Rome Committee followed suit; it demanded that Victor Emmanuel should abdicate and a regency be set up under his son, Prince Umberto. But in the course of the negotiations which now began, the King held his ground, backed by the British. He received unexpected support from the Communists; Togliatti, who had just come back from Moscow, announced that the solution to the problem of the monarchy must wait; he agreed to collaborate with Badoglio in a coalition government of national unity.

This announcement came as a bombshell to the other anti-Fascist parties which took their lead from Count Sforza, but the Communists carried so much weight that they gave in. The King promised to hand over his powers to the Crown Prince after the liberation of Rome, and this was a perfectly constitutional solution. Some changes were made in the government, however; on April 21, 1944, Badoglio formed the first government of politicians, which was called 'the six-party government'; this was a concession to the anti-Fascist parties, but the Socialists and the Action party were dissatisfied with it and rejected the compromise; this resulted in tension and led to Bonomi's resignation as president of the Liberation Committee. The Allies' entry into Rome came just in time to bring the legal solution they were hoping for: Prince Umberto became Lieutenant-General of the Realm and promised not to influence the nation's choice of the institutions it would like the country to have when peace came. Badoglio resigned and was replaced by Bonomi. This was a victory for democracy and showed itself in a stringent purge, which hit thousands of officials, big and small, who were guilty of having made their career as Fascists and as a result of Fascism.

In actual fact, all the anti-Fascist parties were divided. Coexisting alongside the Action party were the progressives of 'Freedom and Justice' and liberals who supported a radical type of democracy and economic liberalism. The Christian Democrats contained representatives of conservative clerical trends which were closely linked with the Catholic hierarchy, but also men from the *sinistra christiana*, some of whom even described themselves as 'Catholic anti-clericals'. In the Communist party a 'tough' section published a newspaper in Salerno entitled *Il Soviet*, which criticised Togliatti's national coalition policy.

These differences often caused disagreement between the leaders and the people at the bottom; the first had a better understanding of the value of compromise; the second, with their lack of political experience, were more rigid and unbending in their condemnation of the fallen régime. But another difference was emerging among those in power, a generation gap, in fact an actual conflict between the older men who had returned from exile, who were sectarian and formalistic, and the younger ones who had been through the fighting since 1943 and had a more realistic outlook on things.

The Liberation Committees, which were party coalitions, had even more reason to be torn by internal strife. The Communists wanted to make them revolutionary assemblies, by means of which they would be able to broaden their recruitment and increase their membership; the moderates, on the contrary, regarded them as makeshift organisations which should step down in favour of governmental authority when the Liberation came. Consequently, the committees did not work out any coherent doctrine; they merely made promises to the workers that Fascist paternalism would disappear and that a people's social democracy would be set up; in order not to jeopardise the coalition which was necessary for the war, the Communists themselves said very little about their intentions;

in particular, no programme of reform was announced for the peasants, who were merely asked not to sell any of their produce to the Germans – a serious omission in a country whose population was mainly rural.

V THE PARTISANS

In northern Italy, which was under the heel of the Nazi occupier and his Neo-Nazi accomplices, the position of the resisters had become very different from that in the liberated areas; they were still at war; what is more, they were the only ones at war, holding down eight German divisions out of the twenty-six which were fighting in Italy. In March 1944, the National Liberation Committee of Northern Italy successfully organised week-long strikes in all the industrial cities. It controlled the 'patriotic action groups' which carried out acts of sabotage and other attacks in towns and 'patriotic action squads' which operated in the rural areas – they had begun in Emilia.

It is true that the Resistance was not the exclusive achievement of any one particular social class; in the maquis, students, regular soldiers and members of the liberal professions fought side by side with workers; castles or churches frequently offered refuge to resisters on the run; when the Turin Military Committee was arrested, a general, a university professor and a worker stood trial side by side.

But on the whole the most numerous, the best organised and the most active elements belonged to the Communist party – these were the 'Garibaldi' groups, about forty per cent – and to the Action party, that is to say the 'Freedom and Justice' groups, comprising about thirty per cent; the others were Socialist, military or independent. In the Liberation Committee of Upper Italy, Bonomi's Liberal party was not even represented.

Consequently, it was the revolutionary element inspired by the Action party which carried the day; it would not agree to returning purely and simply to the former political and economic structures even if they were purged of Fascists and of the spirit of Fascism; it wanted to bring about 'a revolution' and transform the state and society; it advocated calling an Assembly of the Liberation Committees, which would assume power immediately after the people's uprising. The Communists and Socialists were in less of a hurry, for they considered that the presence of the Allied troops made it an inopportune moment for a programme as bold as this; but they did accept the programme. As a result, the Liberation Committee of Upper Italy clashed both with the Rome government and with the Allies.

It asked the Bonomi government for permission to have power to act on its behalf but this was refused: there could not be two governments in Italy. But the Socialist ministers and those of the Action party held dif- ferent views from those of the President of the Council on this point and for several months they left the government. In the end it was agreed to postpone solving the political problems until after the war; the Commun- ist party played a conciliatory role in this compromise, as did also Bonomi. The Liberation Committees, however, won the right to carry out a purge, each one in its own field, during the period of insurrection.

The Northern Committee had formed one single underground army: the 'Volunteer Freedom Corps'. To lead it, the Rome government sent General Cadorna, who was in favour with the Allies. The Northern Committee did not question Cadorna's honesty or quality but recognised his authority only as a military adviser. There again the Communist party acted as mediator: in October 1944 Cadorna was accepted by all as leader of the insurrectionary army but he was to be assisted by F. Longo, a Communist, with Ferruccio Parri from the Action party acting as Chief of Staff; the three men were in turn assisted by representatives of the Committee of Upper Italy; this reaffirmed the Committee's central control and authority.

The Allies had little confidence in these rebel troops with such strong political motivations and they would have liked to restrict them to acts of sabotage decided on by themselves. In November 1944, General Alexander, realising that he would have to halt his offensive before emerging on to the Po plain, asked the groups of partisans to demobilise. How could they do this without putting themselves completely unarmed in the hands of the Germans and Neo-Fascists? But inversely, how could they continue to fight without Allied equipment?

In December 1944, four delegates from the Liberation Committee of Upper Italy went to Rome. General Maitland Wilson, acting on behalf of the British and American governments, eventually recognised the Liberation Committee of Upper Italy as having actual authority – on con- dition that the Committee promised to maintain law and order, safeguard economic resources, carry out the orders of the Allied command and hand over to it the running of the liberated areas; in short, that it would fight but it would not start a revolution.

The Bonomi government followed in the footsteps of the Allied mili- tary leaders. It delegated to the National Committee of Upper Italy the power to represent it in that part of the country which was still occupied; the Committee would act on behalf of the Rome government whom it accepted as the only rightful authority.

Thus Italy was fighting her way out of the Fascist era on the side of the Allies and gradually regaining her independence. But her future was not yet clearly defined; she did not know what terms would be imposed when peace came and at the end of 1944 the desire for rebirth which inspired the Resistance had already been somewhat blunted. Although the liberation of the whole of the country had slowed down, was it at least within sight?

VI THE DISPUTE BETWEEN BRITISH AND AMERICANS OVER STRATEGY

Before and during the Italian campaign, the British and Americans had continued to carry on endless discussions and arguments about the best way to win the war. Ralph Ingersoll, who has disclosed this permanent tension, summed up the points of view as follows: 'The Americans were trying to destroy the enemy's armed forces in the shortest possible time and by the most direct method.'[1] The British, it is true, were striving for the same goal 'but by means of a strategy which would safeguard the military and political interests of the British Empire'. Since the Americans held the means of action in their hands – the shipping, the weapons and to an increasing degree, the men – in theory the British had come round to their way of thinking: the landing across the Channel would have overall priority; this would be the crucial, final operation and it was given the name of 'Overlord', a word full of implications.

In actual fact, at every opportunity, at Anfa, at the Trident Conference, in Teheran and again in Algiers in January 1944, Churchill had tried to have the plans of this operation modified. What he advocated, sometimes directly and sometimes by the roundabout way of a minor operation – in the Aegean Sea, for example – was an extension of the war in Italy by launching an attack against the Balkans which he strangely called 'the soft underbelly of Europe', an inaccurate image, if ever there was one, for a region bristling with awkward mountains crossed only by one or two bad roads. It seems Churchill wanted to forestall the Russians in central Europe. This was certainly not his aim when he put forward his plan for the first time in 1943 – at that time he thought that the Red Army was worn out and would not advance beyond the frontiers of the USSR and what he feared most of all was a new agreement between Hitler and Stalin. It was later on, in the midst of the 'cold war', that he found difficulty in denying that he had had such a brilliant premonition.

In actual fact, when it came to comparing and discussing them, the British and Americans were putting forward two conceptions of strategy which were dictated by their material resources and their historical experience – inspired, in fact, by the inherent characters of the two peoples.

1. Ralph Ingersoll, *Top Secret*, New York, Harcourt Brace, 1946.

The American conception was that of a young nation who was sure of herself and whose conduct of the war was determined by her industrial power. The United States had no war aims, nothing to regain and nothing to take from anyone else. Accordingly, she wanted to end the war as soon as possible and preferred grand and rapid solutions. She built her plans on military considerations only; Cordell Hull, the Secretary of State, was never invited to a meeting of Roosevelt's 'little cabinet', that intimate group of advisors in whom the President had most confidence; the American military were afraid that the British would force them to disperse their forces; the politicians feared that by following their ally 'into the Balkans', they would become involved in complicated and tortuous European squabbles in the wake of the British imperialists; in general they mistrusted European politicians, whom they considered to be 'crafty'. Basically, although the Americans had become the major world power, they had as yet no overall global policy; the old substratum of isolationism remained solid and intact; their plan was simple; they would win the war as quickly as possible and when the job was done, the boys would go back to their homes.

For their part, the British, over their long history, had learnt to appreciate the cost of failure and the virtue of patience. They were afraid of the bloodshed which would result from an attack across the Channel, leaving Britain enfeebled, and they criticised the Americans for excessive and juvenile optimism, if not even of thoughtlessness, which made them minimise the difficulties of the enormous undertaking which they wanted to launch, to the exclusion of any other. Alanbrooke considered that the Americans' reasoning was rigid and over-simplified and that they did not appreciate the magnitude of the problem of building ships, equipping and training troops and transporting vast quantities of equipment. Accordingly, he and Churchill always advocated the same programme: threaten Germany from both north and south, bomb her to smithereens, let her exhaust herself against the Russians and then finish her off at the last moment, thus saving oneself excessive effort and useless slaughter. Beyond that, Churchill wanted Britain to retain her world power at the very moment when she was losing the means to do so; he was thinking of Europe after the war was won and even more of the British Commonwealth.

Both sides suspected the other of ulterior motives and there was a certain amount of mutual contempt. The British generals had a poor opinion of the American generals, who had never fought in India; the latter, born in the motor, tank and aircraft age, looked upon their colleagues as rather pretentious back-numbers. However, the discussions and the procrastination have been exaggerated after the event in the memories of those taking part and by historians of the two countries who have followed in their wake. In actual fact, agreement was always reached; the British historian

Ehrmann was hardly overstating the case when he wrote that 'there was a general atmosphere of harmony between the Allies, each one considering that it was fully satisfied with the decisions which had been taken'.

The last squabble, while the fighting in Italy was still very active, was about the landings in the south of France which had been decided upon in Teheran. It would be completely meaningful only if they coincided with those in Normandy. But could one stop victorious troops? The generals in command in Italy – Alexander, Clark and Juin – did not surrender their resources willingly; they showed that, if they were allowed to hold on to them, the road to the Brenner and the Tarvis were at their mercy; beyond lay Bavaria and then Vienna. Churchill succeeded in having 'Anvil' – the code name for the landing in the south of France – delayed. But when at the beginning of August he tried to have the operation cancelled, he aroused general opposition because this cancellation would have jeopardised the outcome of 'Overlord'.

For 'Overlord' had become sacrosanct; enormous resources had been assembled for its success and these gigantic efforts must at all costs be crowned by victory.

CHAPTER 5

The Liberation of France

I THE ALLIED VICTORY IN THE ATLANTIC

FROM the spring of 1943 onwards the Battle of the Atlantic was moving towards final victory for the Allies. Their convoys had increasingly strong escorts consisting either of newly built aircraft-carriers or of converted merchant ships, carrying sixteen fighter planes and twelve torpedo aircraft; 138 escort aircraft-carriers were built in the United States between 1941 and 1945 and the Americans gave thirty-six of them to the British. The number of destroyers and frigates was also growing; there was an average of six to eight per convoy with the purpose of pursuing submarines, once detected, for hours or even days on end. The torpedo-aircraft were armed with rockets and the technique for their use did not take long to perfect: a fast fighter plane neutralised the submarine's AA armament with its cannon while another plane came in and sank it with its rockets. The increasing number of very long-range bombers, the Liberators, also meant that convoys could be protected by land-based aircraft far out at sea. Aircraft and ships were manned by crews increasingly well trained and materially and psychologically armed for anti-submarine warfare.

They were being provided with a whole arsenal of technical devices which were continually being increased and perfected, such as the 'Hedgehog' which launched quick-sinking depth-charges ahead of the escort vessels. The most effective device, however, was a new VHF radar which had been invented by the British and perfected at the Massachussets Institute of Technology; aircraft were provided with it as well as ships and it was not until the spring of 1944 that the German submarines began to be able to protect themselves against it. Up to then they were taken so much by surprise that for a short while Doenitz had ordered them to remain surfaced and fight it out with the aircraft. These proved to be very costly tactics: in May 1943 six submarines were sunk crossing the Bay of Biscay; between May and August 1943, out of the fifty submarines engaged in the Atlantic twenty-eight went to the bottom; the Allied aircraft losses were also heavy, but the American arsenal could stand it.

GERMAN SUBMARINES

	Strength[1]	Number built	On operations	Losses
1940	58	48	10 to 12	30[2]
1941	76	195	22 to 91	35
1942	236	239	91[3]	70
1943	405	283	212[3]	237
1944	451	234	168[3]	263
1945	420	78[4]		120[5]

German submarines could no longer come within the right distance from the convoys; it became dangerous for them to surface at night to recharge their batteries. 'The means of attack by naval and air forces were so heavily concentrated,' wrote Masson, 'that it was possible to destroy a submarine by keeping it submerged for nearly forty hours at a time, thus exhausting its batteries.'[6]

Admiral Doenitz decided to continue the submarine war, not in order to destroy the convoys but to keep as many Allied forces as possible at sea, especially aircraft, so as to help reduce the heavy air raids over Germany. The German submarines thus remained at sea right up to the end of the war and the crews remained brave and dashing to the last; but the losses – 380 submarines in less than two years – were excessive in comparison with the results achieved – less than 1 million tons of Allied shipping were sunk during the same period, despite the use of acoustic torpedoes and guided bombs.

However, there was hardly any reduction in the output of submarines. In the spring of 1943 Hitler had given Doenitz the means he needed and the Allied raids on bases and workshops had proved a failure. But the submarines now had to be equipped to fight against the new enemy weapons, and modifying the prototypes involved delays in building. As a result, at the end of 1943 the German shipyards were turning out only twenty to twenty-five submarines per month, instead of the thirty to forty which had been expected. In May 1944, Doenitz informed Hitler that the monthly rate of production had fallen to twelve; the only thing they could now do to protect the workshops against the increasingly

1. On January 1.
2. Between September 1939 and the end of 1940.
3. On average.
4. From January to March.
5. From January to April.
6. Philippe Masson, 'Les grandes étapes de la bataille de l'Atlantique', *Revue d'histoire de la deuxième guerre mondiale*, Jan. 1968.

frequent air raids was to disperse them and this gave rise to further delays in assembling the submarines.

The Germans could no longer concentrate their attacks on poorly defended sea areas for there no longer were any – except in the Indian Ocean, which had no strategic importance. In February 1944 eleven German submarines were sunk, whilst twelve Allied convoys got through safe and sound. This failure taught Doenitz a lesson; in March he withdrew the U-boats from the centre of the Atlantic in order to regroup them in the north Atlantic or to re-equip them in the Baltic. Accordingly, in 1944 Allied merchant shippings losses became insignificant, whilst the quantity of new vessels rose to 13 million tons.

Consequently, ships, men and equipment were able to cross the Atlantic in vast numbers from Canada and above all from the United States – 75,000 boats, 268 million tons of shipping and 4,300,000 soldiers. Thus the British Isles had become the springboard for the crucial attack against the 'fortress of Europe'.

II THE COMMAND OF 'OVERLORD'

In spite of their willingness to co-operate, the British and Americans did not always find it easy to co-ordinate their actions and even less to combine their forces. For example, they never succeeded in appointing a Supreme Command for the Battle of the Atlantic! But for the purpose of the landing a joint general staff was formed and its complexity and carefully calculated composition left its efficiency unimpaired.

For the head of the gigantic operation there was unanimous agreement on the name of General Marshall; but President Roosevelt valued his services too highly to part with him. Churchill toyed for a moment with the hope of having Alanbrooke appointed, for the Americans were torn between two fears: that a British Commander-in-Chief would do his best to delay the date of D-day and that if an American took charge of 'Overlord', this would automatically mean a British commander of the Mediterranean operations, thus making it easier for Churchill to carry out his plans for the Balkans.

In the end, the choice fell on the American General Eisenhower who had proved himself in North Africa as an organiser. He was given command of the tactical ground, naval and air forces which were concentrated for the invasion but of only a part of the strategic air forces. Although Eisenhower's Chief of Staff was General Bedell Smith, an American, his other deputies were British: Admiral Sir Bertram Ramsay and Air Marshal Sir Trafford Leigh Mallory commanded the naval and air forces. The British would also have liked a special commander to be appointed for the ground armies, who would have been Montgomery; Eisenhower agreed to Monty's assuming this command in the initial stages of the landing but he decided to take it over again himself once the latter had succeeded, for according to him it would then be duplicating the post of Commander-in-Chief. This decision was to have repercussions throughout the campaign.

Eisenhower's joint general staff (SHAEF) reached considerable dimensions, with representatives from both nations existing side by side in every department and at every level. In July 1944 it numbered 4,914 people; by February 1, 1945 there were 16,000, of whom 2,700 were officers; at the end of the war it had 30,000 soldiers and civilians – of whom 996 were accredited Allied war correspondents.

It was a cumbersome piece of machinery and fitting it out was a complicated process. Inevitably, there arose frequent misunderstandings and differences of opinion, because the two armies were not organised in the same way and the two governments sometimes had different notions. It is true that the Americans had a weighty argument for pressing their points of view: by the end of 1944 there were sixteen American divisions engaged on the front as against eighteen from the British Commonwealth, ten French and one Polish. Thus Eisenhower really did exercise undoubted power; but he was careful not to abuse it; he took pains to avoid meeting his allies head on; an organisation so extraordinarily complicated needed an exceptional kind of leader and Eisenhower fitted the bill.

Indeed, he was without precedent. He was a general who had never held a command in the field and very seldom went to the front line. He carried out his duties like the chairman of a board of directors of Ford, who is not required to know how to assemble the parts of an engine. He was moreover a modest and honest man, without malice or ill feeling, who was perfectly aware of his shortcomings and he had an easy-going temperament. As a general rule he hesitated to foist his views on people; he tried to obtain the opinion of everyone concerned in order to fuse widely differing opinions into a compromise solution. His talent lay in maintaining the cohesion of the Allied armies and sometimes of their governments in moments of very great tension. Churchill and de Gaulle had the habit of communicating with the British and French military leaders over the head of the Commander-in-Chief. Whilst pointing out that this was contrary to American custom, Eisenhower had the good sense not to be offended by it. With him there were none of those strokes of genius in the field which you could expect from a Montgomery or a Rommel, because this Commander-in-Chief was only incidentally a military man. He was even more, and simultaneously, the representative of the Allied governments, of the American government – Marshall was still its direct head, the head of the Allied Civil Affairs section and the head of the Allied Military Government. He had to settle difficult economic and political problems – supplies to liberated peoples, control of means of transport, requisitions, legal problems concerning the status of Allied troops on friendly territory and censorship of the press and radio. In short, his duties illustrated the full complexity of modern warfare. But he was sometimes physically and mentally too remote from the military operational areas always to seize strategic or tactical opportunities as they arose; on the other hand, his training was too exclusively military for him to feel completely at ease in the civilian aspects of his post.

In the end he triumphed over every obstacle. It is true that he was unstintingly given all the resources he required and that he was allowed sufficient freedom of action to carry out the task whose grandeur and simplicity is echoed in the instructions which he had received: 'You will enter the continent of Europe and, in conjunction with the other United Nations undertake operations aimed at the heart of Germany and the destruction of her armed forces.'

III THE PREPARATION OF 'OVERLORD'

At Anfa it had been decided to form a joint organisation, COSSAC, to prepare for 'Overlord'. In August 1943 in Quebec Roosevelt and Churchill gave their approval to the programme which had been drawn up by COSSAC. Normandy was chosen as the theatre for the landing; it is true that the Straits of Dover were shorter to cross and the turn-round of ships and movement of troop-carriers would have been quicker and air support would have been continuous; but this was the part of the coast best defended by the Germans. The Allies therefore came down in favour of Le Cotentin; it had fewer German airfields and Allied airfields would be easier to set up; the *bocage* would make it difficult for enemy tanks to move up and the Allied craft would be better sheltered from the west winds by the Cotentin peninsula.

Success depended on three main conditions: a force of eighteen divisions must be able to hold out for the two or three months required to capture a large harbour and bring it back into operation – Cherbourg in the first instance and then St-Nazaire and Nantes; the enemy air force must be whittled down to a minimum at the moment of the attack and the attacker must take the greatest possible advantage of surprise; and finally, the enemy forces must remain inferior to the landing forces throughout the initial stages of consolidation, which presupposed that enemy reinforcements would be harassed and delayed as much as possible.

THE LIBERATION OF FRANCE

It is impossible to give more than a few details about the preparation of 'Overlord'. One is rightly amazed by the complexity of the operation, the large resources employed and the minute detail of their co-ordination.

The total strength initially provided for by COSSAC – three landing divisions and two airborne brigades on the first day – was steadily increased, at Churchill's and Montgomery's request, until it became five landing divisions and three airborne divisions. The vast resources needed to ship them were assembled, that is to say, 4,300 landing craft, 500 warships and 300 minesweepers.

The first major item to COSSAC's credit was drawing the right conclusions from the Dieppe raid, which had proved both disappointing and costly; but it had shown the need to give the attacking troops strong close support and to 'saturate' the landing beaches with gunfire at pointblank range – and above all it had shown the impossibility of seizing a harbour undamaged.

Starting from these conclusions, the ingenuity of the British worked wonders. For example, they perfected an extraordinary number of different types of armoured vehicles: armoured bulldozers for clearing the beaches, armoured vehicles provided with flails for opening up paths through minefields, armoured footbridges for crossing ditches, tanks which hurled massive explosives against concrete walls, armoured flame-throwers, turret-less tanks to give other tanks a lift across dikes, amphibious tanks. Above all, they devised and built the two 'Mulberries', the code name given to the artificial harbours each of which were the size of Dover harbour and intended to provide shelter for cargo ships as they unloaded, until Cherbourg was captured and brought back into service. But American industrial power did the rest: for example, in the United States 500 Sherman tanks were turned into amphibious tanks in the space of a few months.

Soils were studied and tides calculated with the utmost precision; a special device was produced to guard against the possibility of running aground and the landing was timed exactly for a day when mid flood tide would be forty minutes after daybreak, on a night when the moon would rise between 1 and 2 a.m., after taking account of local variations.

As for reconnoitring the terrain, suffice it to say that one year in advance aircraft had begun to take photographs of the coasts, from the Netherlands to Spain. In particular, from April 1 to June 5, 1944, 4,500 air-reconnaissance sorties took place, adding their information to the thousands of reports provided by the French Resistance. Thus the coastal defences, bridges, airfields, marshy areas, enemy depots, roads, railway stations, etc. were known with great accuracy. The head of each landing unit was provided with plans and photographs of the place where he would be operating; even trees were marked on them.

The use of the air force raised very delicate problems. Should priority be given to bombing the landing areas, as Eisenhower wanted, or the German factories and plants further away, as recommended by Harris and Spaatz, the commanders of the British and American strategic air forces? Eisenhower won; General Koenig, the representative of the French provisional government, gave his consent, since this was the high price to be paid for the liberation of France. It was decided to concentrate on attacking workshops, engineering depots and stations and on machine-gunning trains; eighty targets were chosen in the north and Belgium. For its supplies, the Wehrmacht in France needed 100 trains per day from Germany: in April 1944 the average number in transit fell to 60 and in May to 32; this hindered the building of the Atlantic wall and also the stockpiling of ammunition and petrol. Then the bridges over the Seine and the Oise were bombed – on June 5 eighteen were destroyed and three damaged. All the airfields within a radius of 125 miles of the coast were heavily raided in order to prevent the Luftwaffe from using them and to make it move or disperse its planes.

The needs of the landing were enormous. Forty-five cargo ships and tank-carriers plus escort vessels were needed to land one armoured division which would then need 600 tons of supplies per day; calculations showed that each day after D-day, 12,000 tons of provisions and 2,500 loaded vehicles of all shapes and sizes, not to mention the troops, would have to be landed.

IV THE DISPARITY BETWEEN THE FORCES INVOLVED

German strategy had been authoritatively laid down once and for all by Hitler himself from the depths of his bunker on the eastern front. To give any ground whatsoever always seemed to him a harbinger of defeat and weak acceptance of its imminence. Accordingly, he ordered the German army to fight the crucial battle along the Atlantic wall in defensive positions along the coast. The enemy's attempts at invasion were to be smashed before and during the landing and the landing forces destroyed on the spot in local counter-offensives. The German military leaders were therefore denied any freedom of strategy or the exercise of any thought or initiative.

Besides, who was in command of the German armies? In theory it was Marshal von Rundstedt. But his subordinate Rommel had precedence over him since he was the man who inspected and co-ordinated all the coastal defences from Denmark to Gascony and he made his reports to Hitler, merely keeping his immediate superior informed. In administrative matters the military commanders in Belgium, the Netherlands and

France were answerable to the general staff of the Wehrmacht. Intelligence, the security of the rear areas and the police were the province of the ss, who regarded Himmler as their only leader. The Todt organisation followed the directives of the Minister of Munitions. The Navy and the Luftwaffe took their orders from Doenitz and Goering; the latter exercised his command from somewhere in east Prussia. In all matters of training and organisation the general in charge of the armoured corps came under the Inspector General, Guderian.

Thus, paradoxically, whilst Eisenhower, the head of the armies of a coalition which had differing views on the scope and aims of the war and on the strategy to be used, had very real powers of command over all the forces which he was deploying in the operation, Hitler had systematically split up the command of the German armies. The orders he gave were not adapted to a mobile situation and he was ready to risk further Stalingrads in the hope of another Dunkirk. It is true that he was not unaware of the importance of 'Overlord' and he agreed to withdraw a few forces from the east to check the invasion. But he was misinformed about the real scope of the Dieppe raid and the Anzio landing and thought that 'Overlord' was doomed to failure; an immediate counter-attack would be enough, he considered, to drive the enemy back into the sea. He would then turn his attentions back to the USSR; and he would finally crush his Western enemies in Britain itself with the wonder weapons which were now being manufactured.

Von Rundstedt was convinced that the Führer was wrong; together with Jodl he considered that the Germans' only chance of success lay in forming a large strategic reserve capable of waging the crucial battle in any area where the landing troops might be concentrated after their initial success – which seemed to him impossible to prevent. But the old Marshal was resigned to keeping quiet when the Führer thundered. Accordingly, up to and including June 6 the Germans had no very clear idea of what line of conduct they should follow, at the very time when they were expecting a landing at any moment.

Concentration of forces and minute preparation in the democratic camp; division and uncertainty on the side of the dictatorship: Goebbels' propaganda could no longer disguise the attackers' advantage which was to become even worse as a result of the discrepancy between the forces involved.

In the Navy and Air Force the Germans were spectacularly weak. Against the 500 Allied warships the Kriegsmarine could put up only some fifteen torpedo boats and a few dozen motor-boats; before D-day, thirty-eight large ships were damaged by Allied bombing raids on Le Havre; on the announcement of the landing, forty submarines were supposed to return from the Atlantic; only six managed to do so.

In the air the Luftwaffe now had only 500 aircraft in the west, 90 of which were bombers and 70 fighters, as against 2,000 Allied aircraft. There had been a reversal of the situation since 1940 and the German Air Force had now disappeared from the sky. As a result, both while the landing was being prepared and while it was being carried out there were no serious attacks against Allied convoys either at sea or in the air.

As for the ground forces, the disproportion was less marked. In June 1944, on the whole of the western front, von Rundstedt had 59 divisions under him, 41 of which were north of the Loire. In the Channel, Rommel had 24 infantry and 5 armoured divisions; 6 infantry divisions and 1 armoured division were stationed near the landing zone. But the men were for the most part either old or else too young and above all they were immobilised and dispersed all along the Atlantic wall.

With regard to this wall, one can only wonder whether Hitler himself had not fallen for Goebbels' propaganda, which praised it as 'powerful and unbroken, ready to go fully into action during the stage of the actual landing, which is particularly crucial for the attack'. In point of fact, in spite of Rommel's improvements on the actual seashore itself, the wall was a linear fortification stretching over a distance of 2,500 miles; although very strong at a few points, thanks to powerful batteries, more often than not it represented only improved field fortifications with no second line of defence and with its operational bases several miles apart. The wall could impede or slow down an invasion, but it could not prevent one.

V PREPARATIONS FOR D-DAY

On D-Day, therefore, the Allies apparently had overwhelming superiority and if one considered merely the men and the figures, they seemed certain of success. But the gods of war demand more than this and the Allied leaders knew it. As soon as they began to concern themselves with the more distant future, their calculations became more pessimistic. They considered that the disparity of forces would be reversed: from having eight Allied divisions against six German divisions on D-day, twenty days later there would be twenty-four Allied against thirty German divisions. They must therefore at all costs prevent the numerical advantage of the enemy from gradually turning in their favour, that is to say they must make the Germans disperse their forces for as long as possible.

Surprise thus became one of the essential factors in the outcome of the attack. From this point of view it was a complete success. Up to and including June 4 there were twice as many air raids north as there were south of the Seine, in order to make the enemy think that the landing would take place in the Straits of Dover. As a further deception, messages to Montgomery, which were picked up by the Germans, went via the county of Kent. Accordingly, the German command placed a second line of supporting divisions only from Le Havre to Calais. In the end, on D-Day the German forces were equally divided: fifteen infantry and three armoured divisions were stationed between the Seine and the Scheldt and exactly the same number between the Seine and the Loire.

As for the date, after first thinking that the invasion attempt would take place on May 18 the Germans now considered that it would not be possible before August. On June 4 Rommel had left for Ulm; he was to be back at his command post at 5 p.m. on June 6; but the attack had begun the previous night and Rommel had declared that 'the first twenty-four hours would be crucial'.

But the inherent weakness of 'Overlord' was the delicate accuracy of its timetable; the various elements were closely interlocked; everything must be on the minute and the slightest delay would risk jamming the whole mechanism. And however strong the fleets and however sagacious their captains, they could not command the winds; on June 4 there was such a gale that Eisenhower delayed the departure; on June 5 a temporary calm made him take a risky decision. The initial success of 'Overlord' may in the end have been due to a weather forecast which was accurate for a few hours.

VI D-DAY

There have been many accounts of June 6, 1944, in all its details. We shall confine ourselves to the main points and to summing up its stages as they took place simultaneously or in succession.

The huge fleet crossed without incident, apart from seasickness. At 2 a.m. the American Rear-Admiral Moon's Naval Force U began to position its 1,000 ships transporting the 30,000 men and 3,500 vehicles which were to land during the day some twelve miles from Le Cotentin in the Utah sector. There was little reaction from the German coastal batteries and radars, which were bombed and jammed both from the air and from the sea. At 6.30 the first amphibious unsinkable tanks arrived with the infantry and took the Germans by surprise. By 9 o'clock the outer shell of the Atlantic wall had been broken through over a stretch nearly two miles long.

Things were not going quite so well in the next sector which was called Omaha; the amphibious tanks sank and the men set foot on land seasick and without protection; the boats were firing blind for weather conditions were dreadful and visibility bad; the beaches were congested; by 9.30 the attacking regiments were still only 100 yards from the shore, except in the region of Colleville where they had advanced just over a mile.

The British had less difficulty in their sectors but their objectives were ambitious; their job was to protect the flank of the Americans, who had the task of capturing Cherbourg; they themselves had to reach Bayeux and Caen during the day, set up a bridgehead for the Air Force to the east of the Orne and advance twelve to thirteen miles inland. In the Gold sector, there was complete success. But in the Caen sector, where the landing had been made later, the Germans gave them a warmer reception; the fortifications had not been destroyed and the 4th Panzer Division was in Caen, so that any idea of capturing it had to be abandoned. In the Sword sector, on the left wing of the defences, the tide had risen faster than had been expected and water covered the beaches; instead of advancing, the troops dug themselves in on the spot.

Three airborne divisions had been dropped beforehand: two American divisions at the base of Le Cotentin and one British near Caen; their task was to seize the crossing points behind the enemy lines and to block the way for reinforcements; they achieved a varying measure of success. One American division was dispersed by German flak over an area twenty-five miles by twelve; the second remained better grouped and cut off the Cherbourg–Carentan road, but did not succeed in blowing up the bridges. They had for a moment contemplated moving right across the Cotentin peninsula and cutting off Cherbourg but this plan proved infeasible; nevertheless, one German division had been withdrawn from the coastal defences to be put into action inland, so that the diversion had been a partial success. The British division had seized the two bridges over the Orne which had to be kept intact and had destroyed five over the Dives, as planned.

The Germans were completely taken by surprise; they did not detect the Allied fleet by sonar until it was twelve miles from shore. When it was clear that it was a major operation, General Blumentritt asked for permission to commit the armoured divisions; Jodl refused, speaking on behalf of the Führer; headquarters could not yet quite make out the real centre of attack. In Rommel's absence Speidel hesitated to accept responsibility for committing the reserves; in the end, one Panzer division went into attack in the morning but another was lost on its way to Deauville; a third did not leave Caen until 3 p.m., in order to check the British infantry; it was not until 4 p.m. that Hitler ordered the armoured reserves to retake the bridgehead and then it was too late. The bulk of the German reserves were between the Seine and the Loire, more than a day's journey from the battlefield; moreover, the first tanks, which arrived on D + 1, were short of petrol and were held up by the Air Force.

For the Allied Air Force enjoyed an arrogant air supremacy, making 10,500 sorties during the day against the Luftwaffe's 319 and not losing one single plane by the latter's action. In 1940 the Wehrmacht were using

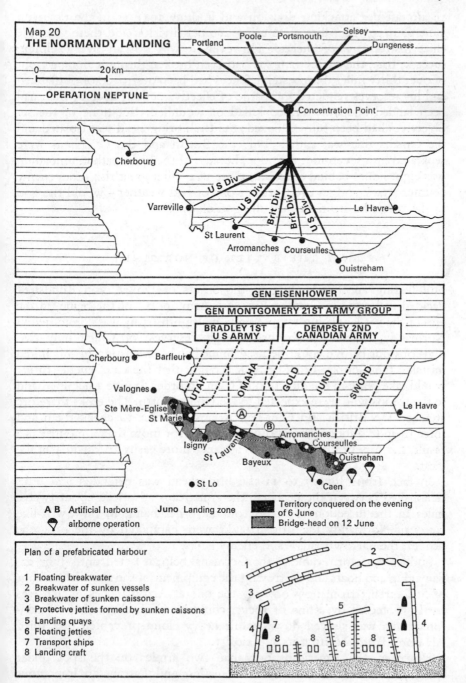

Map 20
THE NORMANDY LANDING

0   20km

OPERATION NEPTUNE

Portland   Poole   Portsmouth   Selsey
Dungeness

Concentration Point

Cherbourg

U S Div
U S Div
Brit Div
Brit Div
U S Div

Varreville

Le Havre

St Laurent
Arromanches   Courseulles
Ouistreham

GEN EISENHOWER

GEN MONTGOMERY 21ST ARMY GROUP

BRADLEY 1ST U S ARMY	**DEMPSEY 2ND CANADIAN ARMY**

Cherbourg   Barfleur

Valognes

UTAH
OMAHA
GOLD
JUNO
SWORD

Ste Mère-Eglise
St Marie
(A)
(B)
Arromanches
Isigny
Courseulles
St Laurent
Ouistreham
Bayeux

St Lo
Caen

Le Havre

A B Artificial harbours   **Juno** Landing zone

airborne operation

Territory conquered on the evening of 6 June

Bridge-head on 12 June

Plan of a prefabricated harbour

1 Floating breakwater
2 Breakwater of sunken vessels
3 Breakwater of sunken caissons
4 Protective jetties formed by sunken caissons
5 Landing quays
6 Floating jetties
7 Transport ships
8 Landing craft

19 aircraft per attacking division and in June 1941 25 in the USSR; on June 6, 1944, the Allies were using 260 per division and these were the chief instruments of success. However, it was not an overwhelming success; true, the enemy rampart had been broken through along a front of over thirty miles, his coastal defences had been destroyed or outflanked and his reserves rendered incapable of effective action; 200,000 men had been landed and only 11,000 killed or wounded. But none of the set objectives had been fully achieved; the Utah bridgehead was isolated and the Omaha one was rather frail; the British and the Canadians were separated by a seven-mile corridor; because of the bad weather, unloading was eight hours behind schedule; there was still a great risk of an enemy counter-attack and an even greater one of bad weather – would the god of the winds be stronger than the god of war?

VII THE BATTLE OF NORMANDY

Still fearing another landing in the Straits of Dover, von Rundstedt decided to leave the German Fifteenth Army north of the Seine, in the area of the v-1 launching ramps; only the Eighth Army was committed in Normandy, together with the strategic reserves, of which only two divisions out of five could be used immediately. Persisting in this initial mistake, the German Chief of Staff thought that the chief enemy thrust would take place in the direction of Caen, in order to give a helping hand to the troops who were expected to land in the north. The tanks therefore attacked the British and Canadian troops in order to check them and force them to adopt a static positional battle for more than a month; as a result, the Americans were able to advance more easily and swiftly in the west.

In fact, from June 7 to 11 the bridgehead was extended and links established between the beaches; the Americans advanced about twelve miles in the direction of St-Lô; on the other hand, in the Swiss-like *bocage* of Normandy the British tanks were hampered by the hills, the hedges, the narrow roads – and enemy tanks.

Suddenly, a storm came to the Germans' help; it lasted until June 22, damaging 400 boats and destroying the equipment of the artificial harbour of St-Laurent; from now on only the one at Arromanches, which was partly protected by a line of rocks, could be used; the arrival of reinforcements was slowed down, while heavy cloud prevented the Allied Air Force from asserting its superiority.

However, the Americans now had two armies on the spot under Bradley, a former teacher of mathematics, and Patton, an impetuous athlete who had taken part in the Stockholm Olympic Games. On June 18 they reached Barneville on the west coast of Le Cotentin; the peninsula was sealed off and 40,000 Germans were surrounded at the top end. The destruction of one artificial harbour and the deteriorating state of the other made it even more urgent to capture Cherbourg.

Once again, when Rommel, who was no longer receiving any reinforcements, suggested concentrating his forces on defending Cherbourg, Hitler ordered him not to withdraw and all that Rommel could do in Le Cotentin was to draw up a thin thirty-mile-long line of defence, which was quickly pierced. On June 20, the Americans reached the outskirts of Cherbourg and then the sea to the east of the town; one by one they destroyed and captured the fortifications on the ridges; on July 1 the fighting came to an end; 39,000 Germans were taken prisoner. But the harbour was unusable.

In Caen in the meantime the battle had continued hammer and tongs. According to the programme worked out by COSSAC the crucial attack would take place between Caen and Falaise, in open fighting. Eisenhower had set his heart on this, putting into practice the tactical method which Marshall had defined as follows: 'Go straight in and punch them right on the nose.' But Montgomery changed all that; he wanted to force the Germans to disperse and then encircle them on the spot, 'and deprive them of the means of resisting our invasion of Germany'.

Rommel, for his part, had suggested taking the Seventh Army back behind the Seine and bringing up the armies in the south of France to the rescue, in order to establish and hold a new front 'from the Seine to the Swiss frontier'. Hitler would not hear of it; he replaced von Rundstedt by von Kluge and ordered Rommel to attack at Caen with all his armour. Thus, by the deliberate choice of both opponents, the area around Caen became the theatre of fierce fighting.

The Allied plan stipulated that the Canadians would form a sort of pivot on the left on which the British and more particularly the Americans would hinge – the latter had fourteen divisions in Le Cotentin against the Germans' seven. The British and Canadian forces attacked Caen from the front and bombed it to smithereens – so much so that they found it difficult to advance through the rubble; but the German defence had had time to be deployed to a depth of ten miles; on July 10 the Allied advance was checked; not until the 18th was a bridgehead established to the east of the Orne; true, it was a short advance but the British had immobilised most of the German forces – including seven out of the nine armoured divisions.

The Americans were the ones to benefit from this drain on the enemy forces. From July 19 to 25 their attack was delayed by bad weather. At first the advance was slow; for one hour the Allied Air Force pounded away at a rectangle of about four miles long by one mile wide, so that the tanks which were following up had to pick their way between the bomb-holes. The Americans launched tanks, motorised artillery and bull-dozers; the tanks were fitted with the Rhinoceros, a device consisting of four powerful steel teeth for cutting down the hedges in the *bocage*; one officer in front remained in permanent liaison with the Air Force; when they came up against an obstacle the tanks sent up a smoke-shell and the air-craft immediately intervened. The day of July 27 was crucial; on the 28th Coutances was captured; on July 30 and 31 it was the turn of Granville and Avranches. The breakthrough had been achieved; at the base of Le Cotentin stretched the wide open spaces allowing broad sweeping manoeuvres where tanks could roll forward in all directions.

VIII THE BATTLE OF FRANCE

At 6 p.m. on June 6, 1944 General de Gaulle addressed the French people over the BBC after two days of bitter and difficult discussions with the Allies, when the landing had already begun the night before and there were very few Frenchmen directly involved in it. He produced one of those slogans for which he had a special gift, summing up a whole policy and outlining the future: 'This is the Battle of France and it is France's battle.'

The great importance which General de Gaulle and his government attached to a strategic commitment of the 'Fighting French' was expressed in Algiers in November 1943 when an 'Action Committee for France' was set up. Under the chairmanship of General de Gaulle, it provided for regular meetings of the Commissioner for Internal Affairs and the Com-missioner for War; its secretary was the head of the executive body, the Special Services Directorate General; this was *Comidac*, the decision-making body.

In occupied France, at the beginning of 1944, similar patient effort had led to all the military groups of the underground Resistance, armed or not, being united at least in principle in the 'French Forces of the Interior', which were provided with a national general staff and a regional or often even a departmental command.

But the FFI troops were made up of volunteers who, as a result of habits acquired in the underground and a natural concern for security, were inclined to recognise only those movements from which they had sprung. Accordingly, in February 1944 liaison between the underground military forces and the political organisation for co-ordination set up in the spring of 1943, the 'National Resistance Council' (CNR), was provided by forming an 'Action Commission' in France, the *Comac*, in which were represented, together with de Gaulle's Secret Army, the Communist *Francs-Tireurs et Partisans* and Giraud's 'Army Resistance Organisation'.

Because the underground, inevitably limited in its knowledge, could not be integrated into the Allied defences all on its own; because it had to be saved from immediate decapitation by the occupier; and finally because it was in London and Algiers that a French state, government and army had been in existence since June 1940, General de Gaulle considered that the FFI should be commanded from outside. This was why in April 1944 General Koenig was appointed commander of all the French forces stationed in Britain – namely, General Leclerc's 2nd Armoured Division and the special services of the BCRAL – and at the same time of the French Forces of the Interior who would be fighting with the Allied landing troops. To officer the FFI General Koenig despatched a complete skeleton staff to France, called the Military Delegation; it was a general staff without any troops – the latter came under the FFI's national general staff – but it was the principal organisation dispensing those sinews of war, arms and money. In theory, the military delegates were not in command of the internal Resistance; they informed it of the orders of the general staff in London; in actual fact, in practice they were allowed, or took for themselves, certain powers of initiative.

This appointment of the hero of Bir-Hakeim was highly symbolic; it asserted the unity of fighting France to the eyes of the world; it was carrying out the decision made known to the Allies by de Gaulle from the rostrum of the Consultative Assembly in Algiers on March 18, 1944: 'The Resistance will go into action on the orders of the French command.' The Allies had apparently accepted this view. In reality, there still existed wide divergence of opinion.

Indeed, the military leaders – and the Americans more than the British – had always regarded the Resistance, and not only the French Resistance, as a somewhat if not completely undesirable force whose aims and methods gave rise to anxiety and which they considered as of negligible military value in the industrial war which they conceived as being on a world scale.

As far as France was concerned, the politicians were just as suspicious as the military men: did not arming the Resistance mean helping to impose General de Gaulle on the French people, which was what Roosevelt in particular wanted to avoid at all costs? The secret services had vainly pleaded the cause of the underground, which they had discovered was effective. Churchill had been partly convinced; but even in January 1944 he had asked d'Astier de La Vigerie: 'Can you guarantee that the resisters will obey Eisenhower and that the arms which they receive will not be turned against each other?'

The provisional Government of the French Republic could, of course, organise the Resistance and claim that it was under control; but it was not responsible for arming it, because this depended on the willingness of the Allies who were the only ones with equipment, arms and aircraft. Also, it had been allowed no say in Allied strategy, any more than it had any say in the use of the Resistance, either in choosing the moment or the way in which it would be used.

IX THE ACTION OF THE RESISTANCE

In these circumstances the organisation which, in London and afterwards in Algiers, drew up the plan of action for the underground Resistance now united in the FFI, could work only in the dark and on conjectures. The achievements of the 'BCRA Planning Section' (*Bloc Planning*) were therefore all the more remarkable for the accuracy of most of the conclusions it reached at the end of March 1944.

Having established the obvious fact that 'the Resistance was better able to carry out acts of sabotage and surprise attacks and to harry the enemy secretly than to undertake large-scale armed action', the Planning Section concluded that before the landings the Resistance must be used for supplying intelligence and for carrying out selected acts of sabotage; after the landings its role would be 'to act in the enemy's rear', 'paralysing their means of transport and damaging their war economy'; in addition it would ensure that the enemy did not destroy harbours or tunnels and bridges which might be used by the landing troops.

In practice, plans had been worked out in the most minute detail. During the ten to fifteen days which were thought necessary to set up a bridgehead under the 'Green Plan', acts of sabotage were to be repeatedly carried out to paralyse enemy movement by rail; under the 'Blue Plan', electric grids were to be cut above ground and under the 'Purple Plan', the underground lines a long way from post office centres; finally, the aim of the 'Bibendum Plan' was to delay enemy units arriving by road by setting up large numbers of obstacles, sabotaging bridges and attacking convoys. In the view of the Planning Section, although 'underground action had to be directed from outside by a very strictly centralised command', 'the actions of the partisans', on the other hand, 'were by their nature decentralised'. Hence they planned for the Resistance to intervene in various areas and at different times in conjunction with the Allied operations.

On one point, however, probably for political reasons, the Planning Section drew up vast schemes whose success entailed a generous dose of optimism. It intended setting up 'strongholds' in the Alps, the Massif Central and the Pyrenees as bases from which to launch raids outside the operational zone and centres to attract support from the surrounding population. They could become 'mobilisation points' through which Frenchmen might perhaps be able, on their own, to liberate parts of the national territory which would then quite naturally be taken over by the Algiers government. This scheme, though broad in scope, had been worked out in detail, and communicated to the military delegates in the form of microphotos, together with orders for putting it into practice appropriate to the geographical and economic characteristics of the particular regions. The commencement of operations would be announced in the conventional way by messages over the BBC; a preliminary warning message would be followed forty-eight hours later by the message to go into action.

The British special services had been informed of this whole vast project and they had given their approval from a technical point of view. But its tactical organisation depended on the Allied high command, with which the French had no links, and its outcome would depend on the use to which the high command wanted to put it; in particular, the Planning Section had specifically stated that 'the troops mobilised in the strongholds would have to receive heavy weapons and the support of parachute units from the French and the Allies'; but only the Allied command could take the decision to dispatch them and without them success was impossible.

However, there was one principle on which Anglo-Saxons and French seemed to agree: the Resistance would go into action only with great caution and forethought. But on June 1 and 2, 1944, apparently without any consultation with the general staff of the FFI in London, which was simply informed of the decision, the BBC broadcast the preliminary warning messages and gave the word to mobilise; this message was addressed to the whole of the Resistance and concerned every sphere of activity as specified in the plans which had been prepared. During the night of June 5–6 all the messages to begin immediate action were sent out, thus setting all the plans into operation everywhere simultaneously. Thus, after hesitating for a long time whether to recognise and arm the Resistance, the Allied high command, probably with the idea of causing uncertainty and hesitation amongst the enemy, was suddenly launching it into an immense strategic operation for which it was in fact ill-prepared.

Indeed, at that date General Koenig's FFI general staff had hardly been formed; when he arrived in London on April 30, only five weeks before the landing, General Koenig had been very much hindered by the 'ban' that is to say the security measure by which the British Isles were completely isolated, thus preventing him from communicating directly with his government in Algiers. He had spent the whole of May incorporating the Allied special services which were theoretically attached to him from now on; it was not until June 6 that his command was finally complete and accepted by the Allies.

In France the amalgamation of the FFI had scarcely begun and in many cases it had failed. The Communists, with a large part of the FTP behind

them, considered that their responsibility to General Koenig was purely
symbolic and saw him simply as a mouthpiece for Allied orders. *Comac*,
which refused to be dependent on anybody but the National Resistance
Council, had declared itself the FFI's highest organ of command, asking it
'to carry out its directives and operational orders with iron discipline'.

For its part, the Army Resistance Organisation considered that it was
under the orders of the French military command in Algiers. It was not
until June 23 that it became fully and completely subordinate to General
Koenig.

Finally, the 'general uprising' which they were ordered to launch
caught the FFI unprepared and sometimes completely at a loss. There
was a huge discrepancy between the tasks they were called upon to
perform and the resources they had been given to carry them out.
Generally, although they had been provided with good sabotage equipment, even though it was not standardised and there was not enough of it,
the arms they had been sent were not always adapted to the conditions
in which they were fighting; moreover their numbers were utterly
inadequate and they were always short of heavy weapons.

Thus in the Orne, that is to say just behind the landing zone, out of
1,800 FFI recruits only 600 were armed and these had only one sub-
machine gun with 150 cartridges for every four men and one machine
gun with 200 cartridges for thirty men. In the Eure, except for 200
members of the '*Surcouf*' maquis the 5,000 FFIS were unarmed. By June
21, in this same department, not one parachute drop had taken place; the
departmental head of the FFI had no idea where the explosives and
ammunition reserves were sited nor could he find out which acts of sabotage were considered the most urgent and the most useful to the Allied
general staff.

Thus in spite of many sacrifices, timely and judicious research and basic
co-ordination, the FFI's operations were bound to be hurried and inadequate. They were off to a bad start.

In these circumstances there could have been complete and utter
failure and it would be pointless to deny that there were many blunders,
some of them serious. Willingness and determination did not make up for
ignorance, and many acts of sabotage were carried out somewhat at
random. Above all, the general call to insurrection addressed to the whole
Resistance movement brought about a general mobilisation which was
half spontaneous and half official, and which was greatly increased by the
collective psychological phenomenon of all the resisters thinking that
their particular region was to be the decisive theatre of operations. Consequently, groups of unarmed men, possibly in their thousands, wearing
arm-bands which could lead only to their condemnation, were executed
when they happened to come up against units of the occupation Army.

But such was the upsurge of patriotism that, temporarily forgetting all causes of dissension in the unity of battle, the underground Resistance exhausted its meagre stocks of equipment and ammunition in a few days. Accordingly, on June 10 General Koenig telegraphed to the military delegates to 'restrain guerrilla activity as much as possible because of the impossibility of sending them supplies; everything possible must be done to break off contact'. At all events the Allies were the first to be surprised by the dash and vigour of this force, for they, like the Germans who were attacked by it, had underestimated it.

Because of its very nature, it is difficult to assess the results obtained by guerrillas in a battle of this magnitude: they conquered no territory, took few prisoners and won no decisive victory and their activity was dispersed in many local skirmishes; accordingly, to assess the part played by the Resistance in the Battle of France, it is better to let its enemies and its allies speak.

Here are a few extracts from reports from the occupation Army Corps' Intelligence Departments: 'Aurillac, June 7: "Our troops are continually being attacked." On June 9 in the High Pyrenees: 'Our troops are continually being attacked; these bands are jeopardising the safety of our troops.' On June 10 in the Dordogne: 'Every day the 11th Armoured Division is having to grapple with the terrorists all over the Dordogne.' On June 10: 'After fighting, the Clermont-Ferrand-Limoges (sic) region is completely in the hands of the terrorists; throughout the region rail traffic is at a total standstill; we are having great difficulty in moving troops from one place to another,' etc. The attacks against the Mont Mouchet 'stronghold' had started as early as the end of May.

For its part, the Allied command announced at the end of June that the results had surpassed all its hopes. General Eisenhower assessed the FFI's contribution as equivalent to fifteen divisions. They were in fact paratroopers who had already landed by the time the crucial moment arrived.

General Koenig had estimated that the programme had been sixty per cent carried out. Often it was only lack of equipment which held up the FFI: for want of explosives, for instance, they had to cut down trees with a woodcutter's saw in order to erect obstacles across roads.

If it had been better armed, better understood and better prepared the French Resistance would have done even more and even better. The French had everything to learn about subversive warfare; they had discovered the rules by practising it. As for the Allies, they had found themselves confronted with a problem which they had not properly appreciated and with a force which they had underestimated. One cannot say that, when it came to the point, they were exactly brimming over with imagination or that they immediately rushed to put right their mistakes.

If it had been otherwise, it is not certain whether even the Mont Mouchet and Vercors 'strongholds', which met a tragic end, might not have turned out differently, at least if linked up with the landing in Provence on August 15.

X THE ADVANCE TO THE SEINE. FALAISE

Despite the bad weather the Allied reinforcements had continued to pour in, even though Cherbourg harbour had remained virtually unserviceable until the beginning of August; 54,000 tons were arriving every day – 6,000 in the prefabricated harbour of Arromanches, but most of them on the beaches. American technology had worked wonders; at low tide coasters were beached and unloaded direct into lorries. During the first seven weeks only five troop-ships were sunk; 1,500,000 men – that is to say thirty-six divisions – 330,000 vehicles and 1,600,000 tons were landed. During the same space of time the Germans despatched only twenty divisions into Normandy, the majority under strength and in poor shape. Speidel continued to believe that the forty-two divisions which had been massed in Britain were going to swarm across the Straits of Dover; he took only three divisions from the Fifteenth Army north of the Seine. It was to no avail that the Reich's factories were producing even more tanks than the Wehrmacht was losing: they were no longer arriving at the front in time nor were they fully ready to be used.

The Allies therefore maintained their superiority in arms and equipment and were safely over the hump of D + 20. In the air the Luftwaffe had not reappeared. Although the mass-bombing raids had turned out to be of relatively slight tactical value, especially compared to the heaps of rubble which they caused, on the other hand the co-operation of the armoured columns and aircraft had worked like clockwork from beginning to end; each tank unit had four fighter planes on reconnaissance for it; if any obstacle proved too troublesome, the bulk of the Air Force was immediately summoned to the rescue.

By July 20, 1944, there was not one single bridge intact between the Loire, the Seine and the Paris–Orléans line. Each time the enemy convoys moved by day they were discovered and bombed; they had to proceed at night and by road and the nights were short and fuel scarce. The enemy tanks were advancing at an average of barely eighteen miles per day.

As early as August 2 four American armoured divisions moved forward into the bottleneck of Avranches and split up in two directions, one towards Brest and the other to Nantes. Patton raced ahead like greased lightning; on August 4 Rennes was captured, on the 6th they reached Brest and on the 10th Nantes; the fighting for St-Malo lasted from the

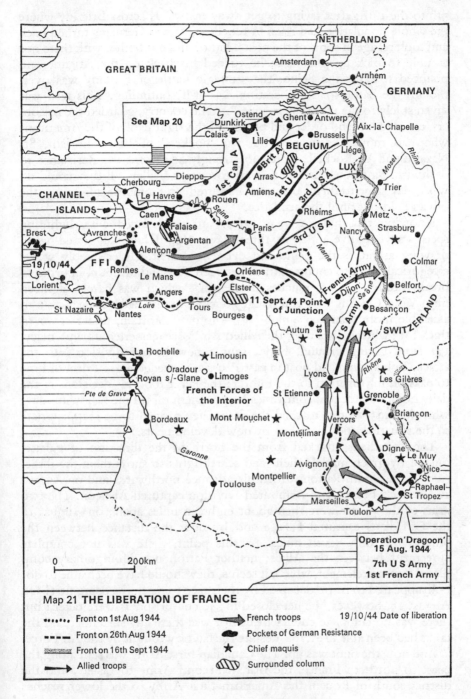

Map 21 THE LIBERATION OF FRANCE

- •••••• Front on 1st Aug 1944
- – – – – Front on 26th Aug 1944
- ≈≈≈≈≈ Front on 16th Sept 1944
- ──▶ Allied troops
- ◢◤◤▶ French troops
- ⬮ Pockets of German Resistance
- ★ Chief maquis
- ▨ Surrounded column
- 19/10/44 Date of liberation

Operation 'Dragoon'
15 Aug. 1944
7th U S Army
1st French Army

0   200km

9th to the 14th; after trying to get away eastwards across Brittany where the whole population had risen in rebellion, 75,000 Germans turned back and took refuge in some of the ports. Patton did not bother with them nor trouble to pick up prisoners; he turned his back on the Atlantic and pounced towards the Seine; the strategic battle of Brittany was over, though the battle for its liberation was still continuing. This task was given solely to the FFI; they mopped up the country, guarded the prisoners, ensured law and order and protected the right flank of the Americans who had moved eastwards. But the 'pockets' of Brest, Lorient, St-Nazaire and La Rochelle were too strongly armed for the Resistance to deal with. Since they had neither air force nor artillery all they could do was to lay siege to them. Brest was captured after a month's fighting; the others held out until the armistice.

Knowing that his rear was safe, Patton advanced with lightning speed – seventy-five miles in three days. Von Kluge suggested withdrawing as far as the Seine and even beyond it. Hitler's reply was a categorical order to counter-attack between Vire and Mortain, in order to break through the 'Avranches bottleneck', which was barely eighteen miles wide. On August 7 von Kluge attacked but he had not been able to assemble more than 200 tanks. He recaptured Mortain, under cover of thick fog; when it dispersed, the Allied Air Force reasserted its supremacy. Far from giving ground, Hitler sent a new Panzer division into the attack. In his command post in east Prussia, it needed a great deal of time to pass on information to the Führer; the latter took his decisions at the daily noon conference; sometimes he put them off till the following day; when his instructions reached the front they proved to be inappropriate to the situation and overtaken by new developments.

The Canadians attacked from the north in the direction of Falaise, guided by green marker shells and searchlights to show them the direction. In the south Patton turned his advance northwards and on August 12 Leclerc's French 2nd Armoured Division captured Alençon. The two arms of the pincer were then about eighteen miles apart; on August 16 the Canadians captured Falaise and by now the distance between the pincers was only seven miles. At this point, there was not complete agreement between the Allies; neither Patton nor Montgomery completed the encirclement, which, it seems, they should have been able to do; both appeared to be preoccupied by their race to reach the Seine first! On August 19, however, the net closed in; 50,000 prisoners were taken; but there was no complete encirclement nor was there any surrender and the tanks had been able to escape, despite the havoc wrought by the Air Force.

And now the hunt was up. The Canadian First Army was sent along the coast to northern France, the British Second Army to Lisieux and the district south of Rouen, the American First Army to the lower reaches of the Seine and the Third to the upper reaches, one on each side of Paris, whose liberation now seemed only a matter of days; Orléans had been liberated on the 17th and Chartres on the 18th.

XI THE ALLIES AND THE PROVISIONAL GOVERNMENT

In the Battle of Normandy the Germans had been given a thorough trouncing; they had lost nearly 500,000 men, including 250,000 prisoners; out of 2,300 tanks, only just over a hundred had crossed back over the Seine, on ferry-boats and a number of pontoon-bridges between Elbeuf and the sea, and sometimes on rafts made of cider barrels; almost all their heavy equipment had had to be jettisoned; the infantry made off on all kinds of odd means of transport commandeered from the inhabitants – old motor vehicles, carts and even bicycles. Since the Allied Mediterranean landing of August 15 had in the meantime also been crowned by complete success, the hour had come for a general withdrawal. Model, whom Hitler had dubbed the 'saviour of the eastern front' and now appointed to replace von Kluge, announced that he was pulling back to the Somme; in order to hold on there he asked for thirty infantry and twelve armoured divisions which the OKW was quite unable to provide. The Germans could see that any possibility of defending themselves on the Seine was fading away and gave up the idea.

After discovering a footbridge at Mantes on August 19 and setting up another bridgehead at Melun the Americans then conceived the idea of a broad encirclement from north and south of Paris. They wanted to skirt Paris rather than go through it, both in order to gain time, to avoid the responsibility of having to provision the inhabitants at the expense of their own troops, and also to prevent their troops from succumbing to the temptations of the big city.

It was in this strategic context that the Resistance tried to launch an uprising of the people of Paris; this rising was one episode in the war which set General de Gaulle against the Americans; it was also going to bring the internal quarrels of the underground Resistance out into the open.

The Allies did not, indeed, recognise the provisional government of the French Republic. They wanted to impose a military government on Allied France as on enemy Italy; they had even issued an occupation currency; they paid their troops with francs printed in America which the Normans distrusted and got rid of by paying their taxes in advance. These measures called forth violent protests from the Algiers government which had obtained permission to set up an administrative liaison mission directed by Hettier de Boislambert to work with the Allied military authorities. It particularly wanted to take over the administration of the liberated areas – a special ministry had been set up to this effect and General Koenig in the northern zone and General Cochet in the southern zone provided the FFI with large numbers of senior civilian officers as well as military general staffs. As soon as he was able, General de Gaulle went to Bayeux to install Coulet as the first of the commissioners of the Republic; Triboulet was appointed as the first sub-prefect. De Gaulle described the occupation francs as 'counterfeit currency'. The Resistance organisations everywhere were trying to place their own men in the prefectures and town halls, appointed more or less with the agreement of the Algiers government but intended in any case to replace the Vichy officials; but the Allies were keeping the latter in their positions, or else reinstating them.

The task of the Resistance was to be made easier by two unforeseen events. The first was the total collapse of the political structures of the Vichy régime. None of its leaders tried to hold on to their positions but they handed them over of their own accord to Resistance men, whether the Allies wanted it or not. The second event was General Patton's discovery of the effectiveness of a Resistance about which he knew nothing: he had even given orders to shoot anyone not in uniform who was carrying a rifle and he showed more concern for the German prisoners of war who were protected by the Geneva Convention than for the ragged FFI whose lives were not guaranteed by any treaty. But these mysterious FFI fought and fought well. If they were being left to complete the liberation of Brittany, how could one do otherwise than hand over its administration to them, too?

As a result the authority of the Algiers government became established everywhere, amidst general rejoicing; it was a real plebiscite. But what was going to happen in Paris? There were a large number of complicated Resistance organisations there; the National Resistance Council had its seat in Paris, but this was the territory of a powerful vassal, the Paris Liberation Committee, which had a Communist majority. The Algiers government was represented by a general delegate with the rank of minister, Parodi, and by a military delegate, Chaban-Delmas; but the two men had only the authority which their title gave them, without the means to enforce it. The real power still belonged to the men of Vichy, who were prefects of the Seine, chief commissioners of police and presidents of the municipal and general councils, which had control of the administration and the police. The FFI under the Communist Rol Tanguy, were few in number and badly armed; it is true that the Resistance had recruited supporters in all the official departments; the next watch was ready to take over.

XII THE LIBERATION OF PARIS

On August 16, in accordance with the tactics of the Communist party, the Paris Liberation Committee ordered an uprising; the National Resistance Council and the Delegation followed suit. The Communists and the other resisters whilst bound together by the solidarity of comrades-in-arms, were also suspicious of each other. The Algiers government had not been consulted, although its instructions had been not to start the uprising without its orders. It was now faced with two problems; the first, a military one, was not to allow the FFI to be crushed; the second, a political one, was not to find another government installed in Paris when it entered the capital, whether it sprang from the rising or was a result of obscure negotiations, of which it had had wind, between the Americans and Pierre Laval, in which Camille Chautemps and Edouard Herriot had been involved – the latter reluctantly, but he was not free to act as he wished.

General von Choltitz commanded a small German garrison which was largely made up of veterans and administrative services. He had received orders to blow up the bridges so as to delay the Allied advance and some of the latter had been mined. But von Choltitz was very concerned about the responsibility which he would incur in the eyes of the world if he destroyed part of Paris; he did not feel strong enough to fight a proper battle; and although he had the resources to crush a rising which he knew to be weak, he lacked the firm determination to do it. He was approached on the matter and this forced him to face up to his responsibilities; he knew that he could not hope to receive any reinforcements; he was ready to accept any 'honourable solution'.

On July 14, at various points, processions had taken place, flying tricolour flags; on August 10 the railwaymen went on strike; from the 15th onwards there was no *Métro* and on that day the police, too, went on strike, followed on the 18th by the Post Office.

The tricolour was hoisted on public buildings, several town halls were occupied by the resisters and there were skirmishes in the Latin Quarter, in the 18th and 19th *arrondissements* and also in the suburbs. The Resistance police took over the police headquarters, where it admitted the new prefect, Luizet, while the National Resistance Council, following the tradition of Paris revolutions, seized the Hôtel de Ville.

On the 19th Nordling, the Swedish consul, negotiated a truce which lasted only forty-eight hours, since *Comac* decided that the Resistance should not keep it. From the 22nd onwards a Liberation press began to appear; the Resistance had seized possession of the radio and the ministries, where a secretary general took over each department; barricades went up virtually everywhere. The Wehrmacht remained confined in a few bases; a few tanks were despatched to attack police headquarters and a few brief street battles broke out at various points.

The Germans' superiority was such that the FFI were in danger of being crushed. After receiving a mission from Paris, the Americans gave in to the entreaties of General de Gaulle and General Koenig and authorised Leclerc's division to march on the capital. Captain Dronne's detachment reached the Porte d'Italie and made its way to the Hôtel de Ville on the evening of August 24. On August 25, the troops of the 2nd Armoured Division entered through the southern and western gates of Paris, their task being made easier by the action of the FFI, who had localised the enemy centres of resistance. In the afternoon General von Choltitz signed the act of surrender of the German garrison. On August 26, while militiamen – or supposedly so – fired on the crowd from rooftops and inside Notre-Dame, General de Gaulle walked in triumph down the Champs-Elysées.

The liberation of Paris was only a small episode in the gigantic confrontation of enemy armies and did not influence the outcome of the war. But the meeting of the French Forces of the Interior and Leclerc's soldiers in the French capital had a symbolic significance and a moral importance which aroused tremendous echoes all round the world – in Montevideo there was dancing and singing in the streets.

XIII THE DECISION TO LAND IN THE MEDITERRANEAN

Until the very last moment Churchill had tried to prevent the landing in Provence which had been planned at Teheran. But when, in the thick of the Battle of Normandy, Eisenhower called for it to be carried out, Churchill had given in; Wilson was ordered to be ready for August 5. However, after the breakthrough at Avranches the British Premier, who was never at a loss for new ideas, suggested a diversionary operation in Brittany; Eisenhower, Hopkins, Marshall and then Roosevelt himself on his return from the Pacific, were all against him; having run out of arguments, Churchill was reduced to relying on divine providence: 'I pray God that you may be right.' He had fought to the last to carry his point of view and he would take the matter up again at the earliest opportunity.

Eisenhower and Marshall considered that the port of Marseilles was absolutely vital to bring into France the forty divisions still stationed in the United States which were needed to ensure the German defeat. Roosevelt backed his generals when he summed up their plans in the formula: 'A straight line is the shortest distance between two points.'

The British, on the other hand, thought that the landing in Provence would not produce the hoped-for results. Once it was launched the Germans would have no fears of any other major operations elsewhere; its preparations would mean that large units would have to remain inactive for a number of crucial weeks. And Alexander considered that the conquest of Italy could be over by the end of August; after which the Ljubljana gap would be at the mercy of the victors.

Both sides finished up by attaching excessive importance to a minor operation. Wilson even went so far as to write that the continuation of the war in Italy and its development in the Balkans would bring about Germany's defeat in 1944, while carrying out the 'Anvil' plan would delay it until 1945. Clearly, at this state of the war politics came before strategy, and preparing the post-war world took precedence over bringing the war to the successful conclusion which was now almost a certainty.

On the American side internal politics had never lost their importance; with consummate skill Roosevelt had succeeded in making his people accept the necessity of war against the Axis and first and foremost against Nazi Germany. But there were limits to his persuasive powers; only a rapid and decisive victory could justify sending millions of Americans so far from the mother country. Roosevelt was convinced that American public opinion would not have tolerated any diversion likely to delay this victory, particularly since, after Germany, they would still have to defeat Japan.

Churchill's thoughts, however, were from now on obviously concerned with the shape of Europe as it was gradually emerging out of the clash of armies. Although the alliance with the USSR had seemed to him necessary in order to defeat Hitler – which had led him to accept as an obvious and inescapable fact that 'Russia would become the greatest military power after the war' just as he recognised it again in September 1943 – he did not intend to sit back and let the USSR dominate Europe politically. On May 4, 1944, he declared that 'the moment is drawing near when the western powers and the Russians will have to lay their cards on the table . . . If our conclusion is to resist Communist infiltration we must say so without beating about the bush, as soon as military events present us with a favourable moment.' In the political context, the offensive from Italy towards central Europe took on its full significance, which was not merely to hasten Germany's defeat.

Roosevelt was not unaware of the dangers of Soviet expansion. But being preoccupied above all with maintaining a lasting peace once hostilities were at an end, he thought there was more to be won from remaining on friendly terms with Stalin than from open hostility. He placed all his hopes for the post-war period on an international organisation which would be effective only if the victors joined it and remained united within it. This was why he refused to modify unilaterally the plans which had been agreed upon at Teheran with Stalin, in order not to antagonise the latter.

In actual fact, the Americans had sized up the growing weakness of Great Britain and her dependence on them. What was the significance of a balance of power in Europe – the traditional aim of British diplomacy – when the Red Army's mastery extended unchallenged as far as the Elbe, given the fact that France and Germany would fade into the background for a long time to come? In such a situation what did the Knights of St George and the Royal Navy represent, these traditional forces of British power which had now been greatly reduced? Only American strength could provide a balance to the power of the Russians, on condition that the American public realised the fact and wanted it.

The Americans' determination was echoed equally strongly by General de Gaulle, who for once was in agreement with his allies from across the Atlantic.

XIV FRENCH PARTICIPATION

France had gone a long way between June 6 and August 15.

General de Gaulle was not invited to the political-strategic conferences of the British and American heads of state and the French command was not asked to the proceedings of the joint general staffs. The president of the provisional government refused to accept this reduction in status; he considered 'that no French force could be employed in any operational area without the order of the French government'; since 'France was not taking part in the Allies' discussions', he felt justified in acting 'whenever necessary in the interests of France alone, independently of others'.

At the end of June 1944 General de Gaulle informed his Allies that 'the French troops would not be able to stay in Italy after July 25 or to go beyond the Arno'. In this way France contributed for the first time to determining Allied strategy; after this General de Gaulle was regularly kept informed of the programme of operations, to which he gave his approval.

The French First Army numbered 260,000 men and contained seven divisions, two of which were armoured; it was completely motorised. As soon as he took over, Delattre regarded himself as French supreme commander, not subordinate to the Allied command; on April 18, 1944, after fruitless negotiations, the provisional government had unilaterally confirmed this attitude; in the end, the Allies came to an agreement among themselves that after the landings, French headquarters would assume tactical command of the First Army. The army which took part in the landing was therefore a modernised French army but also an independent national army directly answerable to the French government.

Preparations had also been made for the uprising of the 'French Forces of the Interior'. In Algiers General Cochet had been appointed as their commander in the southern operational area; the French First Army included a liaison service with them; an FFI department functioned at the French War Ministry.

The importance which the Americans themselves now attached to the French Army of the Interior had been confirmed by the outcome of a mission to Algiers undertaken by Colonel Henri Zeller, a resister who had succeeded in convincing the authorities there that the landing troops would be able to advance more quickly with the help of the maquis, if they took the Route Napoléon so that their main thrust was toward Grenoble.

XV THE LANDING OF AUGUST 15

At first sight the wild, rocky coast of Provence, with its sheer cliffs and its tiny beaches, was hardly a suitable place for a fleet to approach and land an army; a succession of mountain ranges blocked the road inland. But a fifty-five-fathom line near the coast offered the fleet an anchorage protected from mines and would enable its guns to fire at close quarters; the proximity of Corsica meant that the tactical air force could be used. The coastal defences of Marseilles and Toulon were formidable – 200 guns in each; the 'Mediterranean wall' consisted of a series of blockhouses, mines, obstacles and barbed-wire entanglements. The beaches of Hyères and Le Lavandou were dismissed, for they would be under fire from the batteries in St-Mandrier; those of the bay of St-Tropez could not be used until afterwards because of mines. The landing thus took place from Cap Nègre to Agay, along some forty-five miles of rocky coast.

For the benefit of the Normandy front, three infantry and two armoured divisions had been taken from the German Nineteenth Army under General Wiese; it now numbered ten divisions, one of which was committed against the maquis in the Alps and another stationed in Bordeaux; in addition there were large numbers of units which were not formed into divisions; in all 250,000 men, many of them ex-casualties or of non-German origin – Armenians, Croats, Georgians, etc. The Navy had only eight submarines and the Air Force 230 aircraft of which seventy were fighters.

The Allied forces numbered 500,000 men, transported in 450 freighters and 230 warships and supported by 1,500 aircraft. This fleet had sailed from Brindisi, Taranto, Naples and Oran, and although it took five days to assemble, it completed the process without detection.

During the night of August 14–15, paratroopers were dropped behind

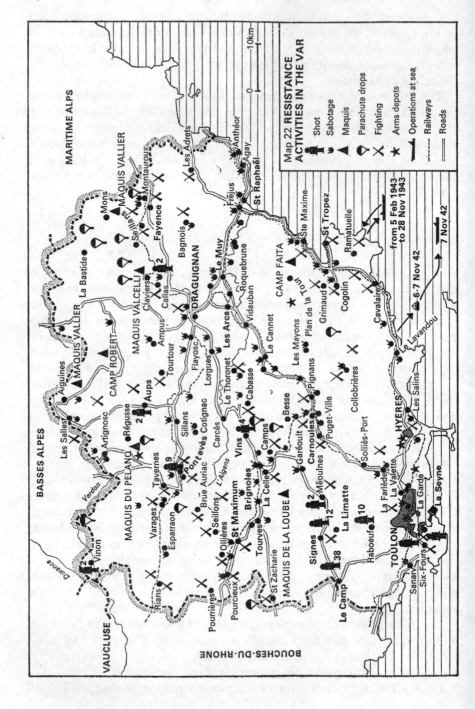

Map 22 RESISTANCE ACTIVITIES IN THE VAR

Shot
Sabotage
Maquis
Parachute drops
Fighting
Arms depots
Operations at sea
Railways
Roads

the Maures in the region of Le Muy; at the same time commandos surprised and captured enemy batteries sited on the cliffs. General Patch's three divisions landed at five points: Cavalaire, Pampelonne, Ste-Maxime, Fréjus and Le Drammont; matters were simplified by the fact that there was no tide.

Everything went off as planned. General Blaskowitz – who was Commander-in-Chief in the south of France – and General Wiese would have liked to withdraw immediately; Hitler ordered them to hold on as long as possible; but the Führer had to resign himself to the inevitable: on August 19 the order was given for a general retreat.

The Americans made their way to the Route Napoléon, leaving the French First Army with the task of capturing Toulon and Marseilles; for the former the timetable was D + 20, for the latter, D + 40. But on August 20, without waiting for the heavy weapons which were still at sea, General Delattre de Tassigny launched Larminat's corps against Toulon and at the same time, contrary to plan, that of Montsabert against Marseilles. As it turned out, this boldness paid off: Toulon was captured on August 27 and Marseilles on the 28th – respectively eight and twenty-seven days earlier than planned: 35,000 Germans were taken prisoner.

Operation 'Anvil' therefore ended in total success. As a result, General Eisenhower praised it as 'the most decisive contribution to the complete defeat of the Germans'. General Clark, on the contrary, who was in command in Italy and could not bear having to play second fiddle, denounced 'Anvil' as 'one of the biggest *political* mistakes of the war', for he saw it as the origin and cause of Soviet expansion in central Europe. Clark's judgment was made after the war, with hindsight; moreover, it is by no means certain that the Red Army's advance would have been checked if the troops in Italy had advanced further; one American historian, Matlof, has even calculated that it might perhaps have reached the Rhine first if the Anglo-Saxons had not kept their commitments to the USSR and released the latter from her commitments to them!

Nevertheless, it may be doubted whether Operation 'Anvil' was a determining factor in the German defeat at the time it was launched, since the matter had already been decided in Normandy. Afterwards, reassured about the development of the war in Italy, the Germans were able to transfer three divisions from there to the Rhine. Had it been launched at the same time as 'Overlord', 'Anvil' would certainly have had quite a different importance.

XVI THE RHONE CAMPAIGN

The retreating German units avoided the Massif Central and went through the Rhône valley. On the right bank of the river the French First Army pushed on towards Lyon and reached St-Etienne on September 2, while at the same time despatching patrols to Languedoc. On August 22, the Americans reached Grenoble, on the 23rd Valence and on the 26th Briançon.

Lyon was attacked from various directions and was captured on September 3, while one French unit was already at Lons-le-Saunier; the landing troops were two months ahead of schedule; this rapid advance was partly due to the support of the French Forces of the Interior.

This time the Resistance had been fully engaged everywhere. It had spread its activity over a large number of small operations which it would be impossible and in fact tedious to list; all that we can do is to try to give an idea of their pattern. First, even before August 15, it carried out acts of sabotage all over France. In the Côte-d'Or, for example, there were 168 acts of sabotage of railway lines or equipment, 11 of waterways, 16 of high-voltage power-lines and 38 of telephone wires. In the Isère, rail traffic was at a standstill between Grenoble and Chambéry.

After August 15, guerrilla attacks increased; there were more than a hundred in the department of the Var alone. Most of them took place systematically outside the built-up areas, on minor roads; they consisted of brief ambushes followed by swift disengagement. In Toulon, however, as early as August 18 it had become difficult for the German convoys to cross the city.

These clashes paid off particularly well when it was possible to establish co-operation with the landing troops. To the north of Montélimar two FTP battalions held the Germans back for nearly thirty-six hours until the bombs of the American air force were able to pin the convoy down on the road. On two occasions in the Hérault the intervention of Allied aircraft forced some thousand German soldiers to surrender.

Indeed, the enemy's demoralisation was probably the most important result of the way in which it was being harassed. In Hyères the Armenians who had enlisted in the Wehrmacht had become so unreliable that the Germans disarmed them; 110 of them, however, co-operated with the maquis. In Giens 158 Germans surrendered to thirty-eight of the maquis, whose leader promoted himself to colonel for the occasion. Also in the Var, their guerrilla activities enabled the FFI to seize more German weapons than they themselves had possessed when the fighting began.

As a result, there were certain areas where the Germans no longer dared venture, as for example in the Cévennes, Aigoual, Lozère, the Upper Loire and the Upper and Lower Alps. Almost everywhere else they gave up their drive against the maquis. Consequently, in very many places power had changed hands long before the landing troops arrived; the decrees posted up in the town halls were now signed by the authorities who had grown out of the Resistance.

Conversely, the landing troops were, as it were, swept along by the general wave of enthusiasm. Fearing the effect that the demoralising atmosphere of a city in a state of chaos might have on his troops, Delattre did not want to go straight into Marseilles, where the FFI had decided on an uprising as early as August 19. In fact, this uprising made a costly siege unnecessary; all that the Germans could do was to take refuge in a few remaining strongpoints.

The FFI had attacked isolated groups everywhere; they had sometimes destroyed but sometimes also saved tunnels and bridges; they had provided information about the Germans' defences and intentions; and they had acted as guides to the landing troops, whose lines of communication they were protecting; after which they had mopped up the enemy pockets of resistance.

The FFI's part in the Allied victory is difficult to assess. It is certain, however, that it was only a contribution, albeit an important one; both British and American historians are agreed on this fact; Eisenhower had shown the way in stressing that 'without the FFI the liberation of France and the enemy's defeat in western Europe would have taken a great deal longer and been much more costly'.

XVII LIBERATED FRANCE

The Allies had been surprised by the speed of their advance; they had even been somewhat embarrassed by it, for their supplies were still coming to them by road from Bayeux and the first train which left the liberated zone did not arrive in Paris until August 30. At the beginning of September, Cherbourg harbour was only just beginning to come into use; Le Havre was still occupied and although the Dieppe harbour had been captured in good condition on September 1, it could not be brought into use until a week later. The Allies were hindered by the destruction they had caused, particularly with regard to bridges.

How were they to keep up a rapid rate of advance in spite of these supply difficulties? Eisenhower's plan was to move forward all his pawns at once: to push on north-eastwards in the direction of Antwerp, so as to seize the harbours and V-1 launching pads and threaten the Ruhr; and *at the same time* to reach the Saar via Lorraine and join up the armies from the north of France with those from the south; the ultimate aim was to occupy the whole length of the Rhine in order then to launch the crucial attack against the very heart of Germany.

Montgomery objected that it was better to choose one single line of penetration in order to exploit any successes to the full; given that the Germans could not hold the whole of the front from the North Sea down to Switzerland, he suggested launching the great offensive from the plains in the north between the sea and the Ardennes, and he asked to be made responsible for the tactics of the operation – that is to say he asked for the American First Army to be placed under his orders.

Eisenhower stuck to his guns; since Patton, for his part, refused to give Montgomery the reinforcements he needed, the British and Canadian group of armies was given only theoretical priority; in actual fact the Allied advance took place on all fronts at once but it was held up by the shortage of petrol – which for Patton began as early as August 30, for he had advanced as far as possible in order to confront Eisenhower with a *fait accompli* and make it impossible for Montgomery's plan to be adopted.

In these circumstances the Canadian First Army advanced along the coast, cutting off the ports of Boulogne, Calais and Dunkirk, and shutting in the German garrisons; on September 8 it captured Ostend. The British Second Army marched on Lille, Brussels and Antwerp; on September 4, thanks to intelligence provided by the Belgian Resistance, this great port was captured intact, but in order to be able to use it they had to clear all enemy forces from the mouth of the Scheldt. The American First Army had crossed the Meuse at Dinant and captured Liège. Since the bridges were undamaged the tanks sometimes advanced at a rate of twenty-eight miles an hour; Belgium was thus liberated without any destruction and the maquis defences which had been prepared in the Ardennes proved unnecessary.

General Patch's American Seventh Army and the French First Army advanced simultaneously towards Besançon-Belfort-Colmar and towards Dijon-Epinal, the point being to close the net round the German units who were flocking in from the south-west by joining up with the American Third Army. The Germans stood their ground in Burgundy; from September 3 to 13 the Allies had to battle with them round Chalon-sur-Saône and Autun. On September 12 'Overlord' and 'Anvil' joined up at Montbard; and it was highly symbolic that it was French soldiers from Leclerc's 2nd Armoured Division and from Delattre's French First Army who embraced on a French road. Some German forces, however, had been able to escape via Beaune and Dijon; but others, harried by the FFI who, under Colonel Schneider, had been sent to pursue them, surrendered – including the 17,000 men of the 'Elster column' at Issoudun.

On September 6 Patton's American Third Army crossed the Moselle; on the 15th it seized Nancy. But they were too short of numbers to hold a broad front and achieve the necessary concentration opposite the fortified points. Although the Germans were flocking back in complete chaos – two divisions demoralised, wrote the American historian Cole, a third with good morale but no equipment and a fourth consisting of odd elements and poorly trained – Patton was held in check by the fortified positions west of the Moselle. The autumn rains and mud bogged him down.

XVIII THE FRENCH REVIVAL

By November 1944 only Alsace and part of Lorraine still remained to be liberated. Everywhere else France was rising like a Phoenix out of the ashes. Of course, the war was not over; more than a million prisoners, 600,000 men who had been taken away to forced labour as well as nearly 200,000 in concentration camps were still dying in dreadful conditions in Germany; the task of reconstruction was immense; but apart from a handful of collaborators who had followed the German troops, national unity was greater than it had ever been before and the masses were stirred with enthusiasm and a new will to live.

General de Gaulle had reshaped the Algiers government by admitting members of the National Resistance Council; but at the same time he had abolished the temporary institutions which the Resistance had set up, and re-established the traditional state structures. His authority was fully accepted everywhere; wherever he went the praise and approval of the people acclaimed him as leader; but the country was still in a state of great moral and material chaos.

At every level the Resistance had put in men of its own choice who were not always prepared for the tasks which they were given. The violence and anger of the people had shown itself in looting and brutality – women who had 'collaborated' had had their hair shorn off; there were many imprisonments and summary executions, sometimes dictated by the desire to pay off old scores. The Liberation Committees took charge of the administration of departments and communes; they legislated, requisitioned, purged, taxed commodities and tried to solve the thousand and one problems raised by an effervescent situation.

There was intense unrest, especially in the south-west which had remained outside the Allied troops' field of action and where the Resistance wielded full power; this unrest did not last long, however; thanks to the measures which had been planned in the underground gradually everything began to function normally again. Outbursts of spontaneous repression by the people were channelled and restricted by special courts – courts martial and above all civil courts and courts of justice; estimates of the number of victims caused by such disturbances vary greatly and are extremely arbitrary; what can be said with certainty is that the figure was not equally high in every region and that the blaze of revolution soon died down.[1]

1. A collective inquiry has been undertaken by the *Comité d'Histoire de la deuxième guerre mondiale* in order to ascertain the most accurate figures possible.

National unity showed itself in the fact that the Communists, the Socialists and a third big party which had come out of the Christian Resistance – the 'Popular Republican Movement' (MRP) – were taking part in the government; the traditional Right were also represented in it, but only by certain outstanding individuals; the Right was the chief casualty of the collapse of the Vichy régime which had received, on the whole, the support of the right-wing electorate.

Of the Vichy régime, nothing was left; its laws were all abolished, its leaders imprisoned. In Sigmaringen, where they had been transferred by the Germans against their will, Pétain and Pierre Laval refused to allow themselves to be given any semblance of authority. Until such time as the French could be consulted about what régime they wished the country to have, when the war was over and the prisoners had returned, the laws of the Third Republic were brought back into force, in so far as they did not impede the war effort. But the pre-1939 legislative assemblies were not summoned; the government was not subjected to parliamentary control; it had merely broadened the Consultative Assembly which had advised it in Algiers.

The Communist party was the first to urge the working masses to go back to work, to give up their claims and make no use of the right to strike for the time being – once salaries and wages had been properly set to rights again. Living conditions in France nonetheless remained difficult and the French continued to face restrictions on foodstuffs and vital goods.

The national uprising had enabled France to take her place once more amongst the Allies; they had at last recognised the provisional government of the Republic. As it was, the French First Army and the 2nd Armoured Division formed a complex medley of veterans from Narvik, Lake Chad and Bir-Hakeim, the African Army which had been brought back into the fold, natives and Frenchmen from the Empire as well as men who had 'escaped' from France. Their ranks were going to be swollen by volunteers from the FFI in every region – among them, most symbolically, Parisians from 'Colonel Fabien's' group; he was the Communist worker who had been the first to make a deliberate attack against a German officer on a *Métro* platform. In September the number of FFI volunteers joining the regular army was 40,000, by October 15 it was 60,000 and in November 137,000; only the shortage of weapons occasionally held back this enthusiasm; some fought in the Alps or against the pockets of German resistance on the Atlantic coast; the others were amalgamated into the French First Army and went on to play their part in the victory in Alsace and beyond the Rhine.

General de Gaulle's statement that 'the French were fighting a single battle for a single country' had thus become a reality. Now that it had

Allied recognition, was supported by popular acclaim and provided with institutions and armed forces, the government of the Republic was going to have greater power to make its voice heard in the Allied coalition, whether in matters of strategy or of diplomacy.

XIX THE FIGHTING OF AUTUMN 1944

Hitler had recalled von Rundstedt to the command of the German armies in the west, since he had rehabilitated himself in his eyes by meekly agreeing to become president of the Wehrmacht's 'Court of Honour' which had punished the accomplices of the conspirators of July 20. The Führer's intention was to hold on during the winter on the Moselle and in the Vosges. But von Rundstedt had only twenty-five divisions to defend 375 miles, plus 135,000 men taken from garrison battalions, training regiments and the Luftwaffe paratroopers who were now without a job. With fourteen armoured brigades each of thirty to ninety tanks he could not possibly form a reserve strong enough to prevent a new Allied breakthrough. Again, since 1940 the Siegfried line had not been occupied by troops or maintained; weapons, mines, barbed-wire entanglements and radio communications had been partly dismantled; some of the defence installations were no longer suited to the calibre of the latest weapons.

The Allies had drawn up their plan of attack, which was not to change for the rest of the war; after Montgomery's group of British and Canadian armies north of the Ardennes came Bradley's group of American armies – the First, Third and the recently formed Ninth Armies; south of the Eifel, General Devers commanded a Franco-American group of armies. The overall total was fifty-four divisions.

Once again Montgomery thought that the moment had come to push on to Berlin via the Ruhr, which he felt to be within his reach, particularly as the tactical air force based in Britain would be able to support his advance. Yet again Eisenhower refused to give him the reinforcements he needed. His HQ was still in Granville and he remained in liaison with his immediate subordinates not by teleprinter like Hitler, but by radio; he continued to believe, from rather far away, that his armies would be able to capture the Ruhr and the Saar and to break through the Siegfried line as well; he was also reluctant to deprive Patton, who had become the popular idol of the Americans, of his reinforcements and supplies.

Having pointed out that the Siegfried line stopped in the north-west but that the Meuse and the two arms of the Rhine formed a broad barrier, Montgomery won approval for an immense airborne operation on Arnhem passing over the top of the obstacles presented by the rivers. On

September 17, 1,000 transport aircraft and 500 gliders dropped three paratroop divisions which had the task of opening up a fifty-mile corridor; since there were not enough aircraft for all the men involved to be dropped in one operation, it was absolutely essential that the weather should remain fine.

At the beginning all went well; preceded by 1,000 bombers and protected by 1,000 fighters, the transport planes deposited their human cargoes; one bridge over the Meuse was captured; one armoured brigade, although using only one road, was able to join up with the paratroop units; but by mistake an Anglo-Polish division had been dropped a few miles to the north; following on this, the second wave of gliders which had lost their way in the fog, either went astray or made a bad landing. As it happened, a German Panzer division happened to be unexpectedly on the spot – this unfortunate accident was for a long time attributed to treachery. The persistent bad weather prevented their air force from intervening before the 24th; and that same day, short of provisions, the paratroopers had had to withdraw in darkness, rain and wind. Seven months were to elapse before the British were able to return to Arnhem. Nevertheless, it had proved possible to establish and maintain bridgeheads on the Meuse and the Waal and to create a large salient about sixty miles long protecting Antwerp.

Montgomery still did not admit defeat; he put up a plan for crossing the Rhine which was examined by a good thirty generals at Versailles, where Eisenhower had established himself. While his plan was accepted in theory, it was decided that it would not be put into operation until the port of Antwerp had been properly freed so that it could be used to handle all the supplies needed for a big offensive. There was nothing for Montgomery to do but to carry out mopping-up operations in his rear and on the mouth of the Scheldt; the Canadians had captured Le Havre and then Boulogne and Calais, but the Liberty ships were not able to use these harbours until mid-October.

On the banks and islands of the Scheldt estuary the Germans had set up strong coastal batteries which prevented ships from entering and were difficult to attack from the sea. The key to Antwerp was the island of Walcheren; the Allied tactics were to bomb the dikes in order to flood the island. It then took fifteen days of fierce fighting, sometimes hand-to-hand fighting in trenches, to reduce the various small forts and blockhouses; finally, it took about a hundred minesweepers three weeks to clear the seventy-mile channel which linked Antwerp with the North Sea; the first convoy did not enter Antwerp until November 28; the Germans had gained precious time.

But the British had not completely wasted their time; with the southern part of the Netherlands freed, they moved along the whole of the lower

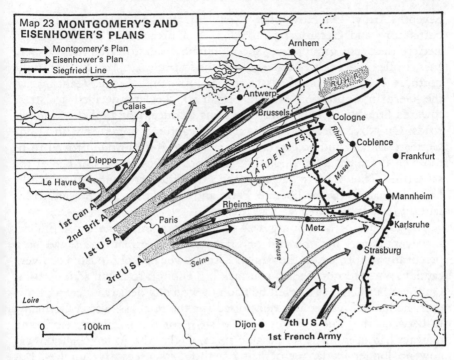

Map 23 **MONTGOMERY'S AND EISENHOWER'S PLANS**

➤ Montgomery's Plan
➤ Eisenhower's Plan
⊤⊤⊤ Siegfried Line

course of the Meuse. On October 21, after eight days of hard fighting, Hodges and his Americans had reached the Siegfried line and captured Aix-la-Chapelle; but the Germans had entrenched themselves behind the Roer which was in spate; since the Ruhr could not be besieged, the only alternative was to bomb it regularly; these raids were destructive without producing any major positive results, for the armaments factories had been evacuated.

Bradley had taken it upon himself to authorise Patton's offensive, the latter having undertaken to capture the Saar in a few days; but his tanks were stopped by the mud; on November 22 they reached Metz; however, the forts held out until December 13. Bridgeheads were established along the Saar, in contact with the Siegfried line; this was not the promised breakthrough, only a nibbling operation.

In the south, on November 14 Delattre had attacked by skirting Belfort; the French First Army emerged into upper Alsace in the rear of the German Nineteenth Army; on November 19 it reached the Rhine and the French had the privilege of firing the first Allied shells on to the German side; on the 20th Mulhouse was captured; but the Germans clung on in central Alsace, in the 'Colmar pocket'.

The most spectacular feat of arms in the campaign was achieved by Leclerc's 2nd Armoured Division, which was attached to the American

Seventh Army. On November 13 it had attacked in the direction of Sarrebourg and Gérardmer; on the 19th a breach was made at Cirey; Leclerc then sent groups over the mountain roads towards the Valsberg pass, while others skirted Sarrebourg; the last of these, still further to the north, reached the plain of Alsace and swooped on Saverne. Realising that the German opposition was disorganised, Leclerc decided to strike towards Strasbourg from four directions at once, using all the available roads. On November 23, Strasbourg was captured, together with 15,000 German soldiers and 20,000 civilians; but the Kehl bridge proved to be too well defended by a whole line of blockhouses to be stormed at the same time. Thus Leclerc had kept the splendidly arrogant oath which he had taken at Kufra, to liberate Paris and Strasbourg; as he said to his faithful followers, 'Now we can die.'

The capture of Strasbourg was of enormous importance for France; however, it was not the end of the war: the German front had been practically re-formed on the Rhine. Eisenhower had obviously been very cautious; he had not made any attack big enough to entail serious risks. On the other hand, as a result he had not won any decisive victory; however, he had all his armies well poised for the final assault on Germany. In between the time had not been wasted, for the harbours, roads and railways had been made serviceable again, so that the Allied coalition was now no longer in danger of being without its necessary supplies. But further campaigns were to be needed in order to penetrate into the heart of the German fortress.

PART II

THE CAPITULATION OF GERMANY

CHAPTER I

The Final Convulsions of the Nazi Reich

I GERMAN OPPOSITION TO HITLER

WITHOUT any doubt, the most dramatic theatre of operations against the Hitler régime lay in Germany herself. The Nazis had come to power legally, through the workings of the electoral system; afterwards they had retained it by illegal means, through violence, but they had thus nipped any organised opposition in the bud by imprisoning their most determined opponents in the first concentration camps set up especially for that purpose; even before the war anti-Nazism had thus been very much weakened in Germany by the repressively preventive measures of those in power.

When war broke out, Hitler's great initial success unquestionably won him the support of the large majority of the population. His opponents were confronted with a tragic dilemma of conscience: was hostility to one's country's government in time of war tantamount to putting one's ideological preferences before the national interest? Did it not mean supporting the enemy of the Fatherland? In order to assert itself as anti-Nazi, German patriotism had to be backed by the very highest moral fervour and in apparent contradiction to the German nation's immediate interests.

In these circumstances it was impossible for there to be more than a few German resisters. Moreover they inspired very little trust in the other resisters in the occupied countries who quite simply denied that they existed and more often than not refused to make a distinction between good and bad Germans. The Allies, too, had no faith in their effectiveness and the fact that the German refugees were divided among themselves confirmed their mistrust, which had been expressed most clearly in the demand for unconditional surrender, a demand full of consequences for the future.

From the moment when the Wehrmacht became bogged down in Russia and the German people began to suffer more keenly, passive hostility to the régime tended to develop. It is difficult to determine whether it was the result of a deliberate intention or the bitter fruit of discouragement, the sum total of individual initiative or the result of proper organisation. How can one know the motives of the thousands of German soldiers who were punished for behaviour contrary to good order and discipline?

However, active opposition had been enlisted and organised in various circles; the Communists had carried out acts of sabotage and collected information for the USSR; students – e.g. Hans and Sophie Scholl's 'White Rose' – had distributed leaflets; the 'Kreisau Circle' led by Helmut von Moltke brought together aristocrats, Jesuits and Social Democrats. None of this could nor did go very far. Not only had the German opposition to Hitler not 'gone underground' or carried out widespread acts of sabotage – it had not even published a clandestine press of any magnitude – but, with the exception of the Communists, it did not succeed in defining an ideology or even a plan of action able to replace Nazism; it could not formulate either war or peace aims which would be likely to modify Allied policy towards it and its influence on the German public remained slight.

Also, since they came from all walks of life and were united only by their hostility to Hitler, the opponents of the régime were not in agreement about methods either; some – the former political and trade union leaders – tended to favour the use of propaganda and an approach to the masses, a method which was necessarily rather conspicuous and therefore vulnerable; others thought that they should strike at the top and rid Germany of her Führer; but the pacifists refused to resort to murder and a palace revolution would involve coming to an understanding with leading figures who were compromised with the Nazis and many found this distasteful.

Within Nazi Germany there were two forces which had retained some independence and a certain amount of influence over the people: the churches and the army. It is true that the prelates were far from being all anti-Nazi; had not Bishop Hudal in 1936 stressed Catholic influence within National Socialism? By his servility to the régime, Mgr Groeber had earned the nickname of the 'brown archbishop' of Freiburg in Breisgau. Accordingly, both the Evangelical and Catholic hierarchies discouraged people from refusing to serve Nazism, as was commonly done by minor sects such as Quakers, Mennonites and Jehovah's Witnesses: Zahn has discovered, all in all, seven Catholic conscientious objectors – but also a chaplain who refused to give one of them the last sacrament. Condemnation of Nazism from the pulpit was generally limited to a denunciation of neo-paganism and even with men like Cardinal Faulhaber or Mgr Galen that was often partly cancelled out by prayers 'for the German people and its Führer'. It was nevertheless a fact that Catholics and Protestants formed a milieu which was receptive to anti-Nazism and that it was they who suffered persecution – for example, priests were deported to Dachau.

It was the Army – that is to say the high command – which had benefited most from Hitler's success and it had meekly carried out his decisions, but defeats had undermined its confidence in him and affected its
relationship with its Führer. The defeats on the eastern front had caused
quite a turnover of generals; Manstein, for instance, had fallen from grace
three times and von Rundstedt twice; Hitler had developed the habit of
intervening more and more in the detail of operations; at the beginning of
1944 the prerogatives of the army leaders had been still further reduced
when *Nationalsozialistische Führungsoffiziere*, that is, in reality, Nazi
political commissars, had been assigned to every staff down to battalion
level. The military leaders could not punish a member of the Waffen ss
without referring the matter to Himmler and they had even less power
over the sD and the Gestapo. With their authority reduced and themselves frequently an object of sarcasm for the Führer, the army leaders were
worried as to what lay in store for Germany at the hands of her Master
when defeat began to seem more and more likely; some of them, anxious
to limit the effects of this defeat, decided to get rid of Hitler.

II THE PUTSCH OF JULY 20, 1944

With General Beck and Marshal Witzleben at their head, they resolved to
seize power by surprise and establish themselves in the leading positions
of authority in the state – this was the 'Valkyrie Plan'. The conspirators
approached the principal German military leaders cautiously and often in
veiled terms; their preliminary enquiries convinced them that they would
receive quite considerable backing, which, even if it proved passive, gave
them some hope of success – for example, Marshals von Kluge and
Rommel, without committing themselves formally, let it be understood
that they approved, while the military commander in France, von
Stülpnagel, gave his full support.

The conspirators let civilians, like Goerdeler, the former Mayor of
Leipzig, into their secret; they even made indirect contact with the
Socialist, Leber, but he was arrested and the military, influenced also by
class consciousness, made no further effort to attract any broader popular
participation in their plot; they confined themselves to operating through
official channels, while speculating on the masses' growing dissatisfaction
with the National Socialists.

On the other hand, proper preparation for their plan involved making
contact with staunch Nazis who were still in office, such as von Helldorf,
the Chief of Police in Berlin, and through Popitz, the former Finance
Minister, with Himmler himself! One wonders how in these circumstances the plot could have failed to be discovered and averted.

Although small, the group was thus a very mixed bag. Consequently, its views lacked unity. Some thought that they could bring Hitler round to better ways by making him more receptive to the advice of the general staff; others contemplated restricting him to honorary duties – this seems to have been the idea which was suggested to Himmler; a number, more daring, wanted to follow the lead given by Badoglio in his treatment of Mussolini and take the Führer by surprise; a small group led by Colonel von Stauffenberg was even more determined and considered that the only way to put an end to Hitler's hold over the German people was to eliminate him.

What the conspirators intended to do once the operation had been successful is not very clear. They knew of the decision taken by the Allies in Casablanca demanding Germany's unconditional surrender; accordingly, they could hardly entertain any hope of a compromise peace. Some, it seems, would have liked to come to an agreement or even reach an armistice with the British and Americans, so that they could then turn all their energies against the USSR. Von Stauffenberg, on the other hand, appears to have been in favour of establishing relations with the National Committee of Free Germany in Moscow. However that may be, no contact was made with any foreign country before the putsch. The days following it would therefore be full of uncertainty; at least the conspirators could hope to show the world that the Nazi Reich was not the only Germany; they doubtless considered that enough was enough and wished to free their consciences from having been too closely and too long subservient to a criminal régime.

On July 20, 1944, von Stauffenberg placed a bomb in a room of the Führer's HQ in Rastenburg during one of Hitler's working conferences. He was able to leave the room in time, heard the explosion, concluded that Hitler was dead and succeeded in fleeing to Berlin. The conspirators then carried out their programme and troops moved in to neutralise the ss and take over positions of authority – sometimes those responsible had no very clear idea of what was expected of them and sometimes they were even completely in the dark. In Paris the ss were quite simply put under arrest.

But Hitler had been protected by a heavy table and by the body of one of the men beside him, and although he was badly shaken by the explosion he came out of it alive. The conspirators were too heavily committed to turn back; nevertheless the determination of some of them weakened; those who were wavering immediately changed their tune, beginning with Fromm, the head of the Home Army; to crown it all, a major by the name of Remer went to see Goebbels and was easily persuaded by him to proceed to arrest the leaders of the conspiracy whom it was his very task to protect.

In the end the affair was a total failure; too few of the conspirators held an actual command: and on the other hand there were too many young officers who were fanatically devoted to Hitler. The people, in the first place out of ignorance, but above all from lack of organisation, made no move. In Paris, the military and the ss, by mutual agreement, chose to forget the incident and tossed off glasses of champagne to celebrate their reconciliation, pretending to have been merely victims of a misunderstanding. But in Berlin and then throughout Germany, the plot ended in a blood-bath.

III NAZI FANATICISM

Once they had recovered from the shock, the Nazi leaders took advantage of the event to get rid of their rivals, the military leaders, once and for all. The official argument was that the attempt was the work 'of a small clique of ambitious, stupid, criminal and unscrupulous generals'; but Hitler told the Gauleiters that three-quarters of the army officers and NCOs were corrupt and could never lead Germany to victory. The Nazis first of all had the delight of seeing the military tear each other to pieces – Beck was forced by Fromm to 'commit suicide' and von Rundstedt agreed to preside over a military court which proceeded with great severity. Then a 'people's court' under Roland Freisler, a fanatical Nazi who humiliated and insulted the accused – Marshal von Witzleben appeared before his judges holding up his trousers with both hands because they were too big and his braces had been cut – sentenced thousands of people to be deported or hanged. Von Kluge and von Stülpnagel committed suicide; Rommel was forced to do the same in order to avoid being indicted. Admiral Canaris, chief of the Abwehr, died in the Oranienburg camp. Himmler had cheerfully ordered children to denounce their parents; the bodies of the leaders of the conspiracy executed by Fromm (who did not, however, thereby, save his own skin) were dug up and burnt and their ashes scattered to the four winds.

Nazi leaders took over command of the armies – Himmler was put in charge of the Home Army; at last the Nazis were going to be able to transform the aristocratic Wehrmacht into a people's army, inspired by the pure spirit of Nazism. The first measure concerned potential deserters: their families would be shot; any soldier absent without leave would be executed. It was announced that a mass levy would take place and old men and adolescents were enrolled in the Volkssturm; invalids were mobilised like everyone else – one battalion was formed of men suffering from stomach complaints.

Hitler's health had been affected by the assassination attempt; it aggravated the nervous illness from which he had been suffering for the last year; the trembling of his left arm and leg grew worse and he showed signs of deafness. This strengthened his distrust of everyone – except his astrologer-cum-doctor; he immersed himself in his bunker, talked to himself all the time, no longer listened to anyone, rejected any objections out of hand and even refused to hear a report through to the end; his outbursts of rage increased, followed by bouts of depression. But his determination and his faith in victory were as strong as ever.

Goebbels became the second man in the Reich, with responsibility for mobilising the people. Although his propaganda was still churning out the old themes of the Jewish-Bolshevik conspiracy, the threat of the destruction of Western civilisation and the danger that the Aryan race would die out, he began to place more stress on the need for total terror and the possibility of an epic end, a 'twilight of the gods'. Hitler pointed the way for his faithful spokesman; more than ever, he rejected the idea of giving up or even of retreating; he thought of denouncing the Geneva Convention and of putting Germany to fire and sword; he declared: 'If the war is lost, the nation must perish.' Germany's leaders thus made the people fear the worst, in order to galvanise their energies into one wild final effort. But they did not relinquish all hope of victory: did they not possess secret weapons capable of reversing the military situation in their favour?

IV GERMANY'S SECRET WEAPONS

Indeed, German science and technology had perfected inventions which were going to revolutionise air and naval warfare; since they were not available to the ground forces, they made no difference to the fighting in the east; but they aroused great anxiety in the British and Americans in the west.

Nothing much had been gained from early improvements made to the submarines, whether it was a question of using oxygen peroxide as fuel so as to be able to submerge more quickly, or the acoustic torpedo, or launching buoys called 'Aphrodites' intended to deceive enemy airmen through false radar echoes, or finally of explosives which, when they went off, gave the impression that the hunted submarines had been destroyed and thus led to the pursuit being called off.

This was not the case with the 'snorkel', which came into use in the middle of 1944. Through a double vertical tube submerged submarines were able to breathe air from the surface and to discharge waste gases; consequently, the submerged submarine was able to use its diesel motors instead of electric propulsion, which had only a small range of action; it could thus remain submerged for an almost indefinite period; moreover, it was virtually impossible for aircraft to spot it; the disadvantages were that it could not submerge to any great depth because of the limited length of the tube and that its cruising speed was reduced to six knots.

Thus at the last moment the submarine war suddenly flared up again in a way which constituted a dangerous threat to the Allies. It was not until September 1944 that the last U-boats had disappeared from the Mediterranean – before that the Germans had succeeded in evacuating 37,000 men from Crete and the Aegean islands. Allied convoys were to suffer losses in British coastal waters as late as April 1945; since the aircraft were returning from their missions empty-handed, the number of escort boats had to be increased. Even in March 1945 Admiral Doenitz sent a group of six submarines to the east coast of the United States; the American Intelligence Service discovered the *kommando*, but four aircraft-carriers and forty destroyers had to be employed to destroy five out of the six submarines.

The danger to the Allies was therefore not inconsiderable; but the number of German submarines equipped with a snorkel was never very high; production was held up and eventually stopped altogether as a result of the incessant bombing raids on naval shipyards. Consequently the new German inventions, against which it is difficult to see how the Allies would have been able to protect themselves, were in practice unable to go into action in time or in any great numbers. And these inventions were impressive; Doenitz had ordered more than 100 electrically powered submarines of 1,600 tons capable of a speed of fifteen knots while submerged and carrying three times the amount of electrical equipment of ordinary submarines so that they were able to cover 15,000 miles while submerged and were fitted, besides, with torpedoes with homing heads which found their targets of their own accord. But in May 1945 they were still in the experimental stage in the Baltic; only eight were in service between the British Isles and Norway.

Besides, from the end of 1944 onwards the naval war had lost its strategic importance; six months earlier this certainly would not have been the case. This confirmed both Hitler's miscalculation at having sacrificed everything to a short war as early as 1938 and the Allies' wisdom in giving the Germans priority over Japan as enemies.

The jet aircraft was another example of an invention which came into operation too late and once again Hitler was personally responsible for the delay. Propeller aircraft had reached the limit of their development, since above a certain speed the blades were no longer gripping the air. As early as August 1939 a Heinkel aircraft had used the inrush of air into the engine to expel it more quickly than it had entered; this jet propulsion produced speeds and heights which had never been achieved before –

560 miles an hour and a height of 35,000 feet reached in three minutes. The first flight of a British aircraft of this kind did not take place until May 1941; as for the Americans, they had completely neglected this aspect of aeronautics.

But Hitler was not greatly interested in this invention. In 1939 and again in 1940, convinced that the victory on which he was staking everything was close at hand, he reduced the allocations for new research and ordered an increased output of current models. Afterwards, when Allied bombers were beginning to reduce Germany to rubble, the Führer could think only of reprisals; he did take an interest in jet aircraft, particularly in those built by Messerschmitt, but only as bombers; when it became evident that the jet aircraft's speed was heavily reduced when it was loaded with bombs and that it consumed too much fuel to have the range of action needed to reach Britain, Hitler broke into one of his familiar violent rages which may have intimidated men but had no effect on machines.

It was not until June 1944 that he authorised the building of jet fighters, and not until November that he gave orders for it to have priority over all others; after superseding all the experts of the Air Force, among them General Galland, Inspector General of the fighter Air Force, he put Himmler, who was totally incompetent, in charge of the operation. In the meantime Messerschmitt had perfected another revolutionary aircraft, rocket-propelled, the first trials of which dated back to 1941. At the end of 1944 both types of aircraft began to be produced in numbers and caused a sensation by their manoeuvreability and their attacking possibilities; in March 1945 Allied formations which had been sent to bomb Berlin suffered unexpectedly heavy losses. As usual, success filled Hitler with wild hopes; he imagined the streets of Berlin cleared of their ruins to become runways for the ME 162 and 163, whose mass intervention would reverse the situation against the Russians – but there was to be no 'new miracle of the house of Brandenburg'.

It was too late. The Allied bombers had reduced the assembly works to rubble, despite the fact that Speer had ordered them to be dispersed; carpets of bombs had also been dropped on the revolutionary aircraft's enormous takeoff areas, which could be easily spotted; then the advance of the Allied armies had made it possible for both to be occupied. In no other field had Hitler's blunders and the ignorance of the Nazis so hampered and then cancelled out the Germans' amazing technical superiority and lead over their opponents.

Hitler was, however, more interested in von Braun's flying bombs. The V-1s (the initial of the German word *Vergeltungswaffe*, an instrument of reprisal) were small, jet-propelled, pilot-less aircraft; they flew at 2,900 feet at 375 miles an hour and could carry half a ton of explosives over a distance of about 185 miles. They were employed in the landing battle on June 13, 1944 but solely against London, not during the actual fighting. Seven thousand five hundred were launched in three months; half of them exploded in flight, missed their target or were intercepted by fighter aircraft; but the other half made Londoners relive the worst day of the 1940 blitz by destroying 25,000 houses in the British capital and killing 6,000 people; afterwards the port of Antwerp was used as the sole target for the V-1s.

The Allies had been informed about the new weapon by the French and Polish Resistance – some of the V-1 components were manufactured in the underground factories employing deported men, in particular Dora; in August 1943 they were thus able to detect, bomb and destroy most of the launching ramps in France before they were used, followed by the factories on the island of Peenemünde – the most important bombing raids of the whole war; finally, their advance on the mainland put British soil out of the range of V-1s, at a time when, at the end of 1944, Germany was producing 2,000 of them a month.

The V-2s which came next in September 1944 proved formidable in a different sort of way; they were rockets propelled by gases produced by the combustion of alcohol and liquid oxygen. The V-2s were launched vertically, rose to a height of twenty-five miles, flew at a speed of 310 miles per hour and then fell free at some 950 miles per hour; they were faster than sound and exploded before they were heard; the fighter planes and the AA were powerless against them. London received more than 500 of them and Antwerp more than a thousand.

All that the Allies could do was to attack the launching pads and factories. Fortunately for them the V-2s did not reach large-scale production until November 1944; it was then held up by the Germans' difficulty in procuring the necessary alcohol and liquid oxygen; in addition, Hitler was obsessed by his fixed idea of reprisals and had reserved the V-1s for London, while according to the British Air Marshal Joubert, if they had been launched against the Portsmouth–Southampton area they would have made it extremely difficult for the convoys to cross the Channel, while if they had been used six months earlier they might have constituted a serious threat to the success of the landing.

The Germans did not have time to finish the A-9, a V-2 fitted with wings which enabled it to cover more than 1,250 miles, the A-10, an eighty-five-ton rocket missile – the V-2 weighed thirteen tons – nor the A-14, with a virtually unlimited range of action. They were unable to use a whole arsenal of poison gases, the trilons, which were extremely dangerous and were still being worked on in May 1945. Finally, in the manufacture of the atom bomb, the ultimate weapon of the age, they went off on the wrong course and were forestalled by the Americans.

The new German weapons added an extra dimension to the war and gave a glimpse of an apocalyptic future; they showed that in the future an army's success would depend on a scientific discovery and consequently the work of the secret services would from now on be concerned exclusively with scientific and industrial espionage. But at the same time it became apparent that inventions would inevitably depend on technological advance and industrial power in order to be turned into effective weapons. Henceforth strategy would be bound up with the rate of production; success would be a result of the leaders' ability to choose between possibilities which could be only half assessed – what was later to be called 'prospection'. It is easy for the survivors of Nazi Germany to heap blame on Hitler today for his unfortunate decisions,[1] which he alone had to take among the heads of the countries at war. In any case, Germany did not have, or no longer had, the human and economic potential needed to conduct efficiently both a war of numbers on the Russian front and a push-button war against the British and Americans. All that Hitler could now do was to try to force the hand of fate by attempting to achieve a victory as sudden and decisive as his first triumphs. For the scene of this victory he chose the Ardennes, where the utter defeat of the French Army four years previously seemed a good omen.

V HITLER'S LAST THROW

Once again Hitler had to force his generals to accept his plan; Model and von Rundstedt admitted that a counter-attack would be useful but they thought it would be possible only for reducing the salient at Aix-la-Chapelle in order, at best, to reach the Meuse and capture Liège. Hitler rejected this 'paltry solution'. He ordered an offensive by three armies on a sixty-mile front; the main effort would take place in the north, towards Antwerp; a minor thrust would be carried out in the centre, in the direction of Brussels; and the whole campaign would be protected in the south by a cover operation. Commanded by Skorzeny, an ss brigade dressed in American uniforms would seize bridges over the Meuse and create havoc in the enemy's rear by acts of sabotage. Afterwards further operations would be launched in the direction of Maestricht and Breda and from Colmar in the direction of Strasbourg. The attack was planned for December 16; according to the weather forecast there would be several days of thick fog at this time which would keep the American air force grounded.

1. Messerschmitt wrote that 'if they had listened to him 10,000 V-1s per month could have been built, at the right time' – but this was said after the war.

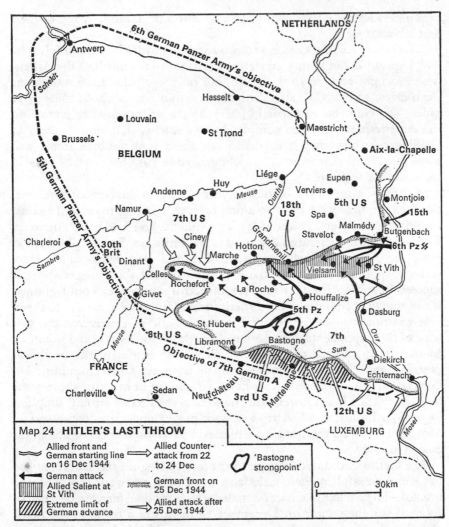

Map 24   HITLER'S LAST THROW

Allied front and German starting line on 16 Dec 1944

Allied Counter-attack from 22 to 24 Dec

'Bastogne strongpoint'

German attack

Allied Salient at St Vith

German front on 25 Dec 1944

Extreme limit of German advance

Allied attack after 25 Dec 1944

0   30km

Hitler explained to his generals that the main thing was to make the British and Americans lose the complete confidence in victory which had buoyed their hopes since June 6. But he also entertained the hope of an outright success which would put an end to the enemy supplies through the port of Antwerp and even cut off and isolate the British and Canadian group of armies in the north, as had once happened with the British Expeditionary Force at Dunkirk. For the purpose of this ambitious objective twenty-eight divisions were assembled in the Ardennes and six in Alsace – the latter under Himmler; all the available tanks were re-grouped, but their petrol was rationed; it was hoped that fuel could be captured from the enemy, who had vast stores of it within reach of their first advance.

Eisenhower had disposed his troops so as to launch an early offensive; he had, logically enough, massed sixteen divisions to the north of the Ardennes mountains and ten to the south, but only five behind the mountains themselves, so that they stretched out in a thin line of about ninety-five miles. The Germans succeeded in keeping the operation very secret and the Americans were taken completely by surprise, despite the scraps of intelligence which they had picked up; these were misinterpreted and made them think that an attack on a limited scale was going to take place in the direction of Liège.

In the first stage of the battle everything went in the Germans' favour, even though they were moving along narrow, winding roads and against the flow of the rivers. Preceded by V-1s launched on Liège and Antwerp, the five German armoured divisions advanced according to plan. However, the Americans held on in St Vith and Bastogne – which were real strongpoints in the Germans' positions – and the Panzers did not succeed in seizing the vast reserves of petrol which they could glimpse almost under their wheels; the Americans just had time to set fire to them.

It was not until December 18 that the Americans discovered the vast scale of their opponents' plans and realised the seriousness of the situation. In the south Patton's offensive, which was to begin on the 21st, was cancelled and, despite his protests, one division was taken from him; but General de Gaulle refused to abandon Strasbourg in order to shorten the lines, in spite of Eisenhower's threats to stop the French armies' supplies; in the north all the Allied troops were placed under the command of Montgomery, who was not a little pleased with himself at being cast in the role of saviour.

The Germans did not manage to capture Bastogne; the saboteurs had been unsuccessful in their tasks and most of them were captured and unmasked by having to answer detailed questions on American baseball or football and then shot; on December 24 there was a break in the dense cloud, sufficient to enable operations by the Allied Air Force, which immediately took control of the sky. However, the Germans had arrived within about four miles of Dinant; Hitler intervened in the battle and gave orders not to continue in this direction, in spite of the success which had been achieved, but to advance northwards, because the objective was Antwerp and also because the commander in this sector was the ss Sepp Dietrich, to whom the Führer wanted to give the chance of brilliant success which would redound to the credit of the régime.

When the British and American counter-attack began, Hitler was opposed to any withdrawal; what is more, on January 1 Himmler attacked as planned in the direction of Strasbourg, which de Gaulle ordered

Delattre to defend inch by inch, whereas the Americans would have liked to retreat to the Maginot line. Himmler succeeded only in establishing a small bridgehead and in advancing to within twelve miles of Strasbourg. On January 5 the situation was reversed; in the Ardennes, Montgomery attacked in the north and in the west; on January 15 the German withdrawal was complete; Hitler's 'last throw' had failed, even though the battle for Strasbourg lasted until January 21.

From now on the Wehrmacht was reduced to waging a desperate defensive battle; all its best equipment had been lost and the fact that some generals had been superseded and Himmler promoted to be Commander-in-Chief on the Vistula did little to make good the losses! There was one last hope, one final thought: could Hitler rely on a split among his opponents? The French and Americans and the Americans and British had indeed been somewhat at loggerheads. Montgomery in particular had claimed all the credit for their success and had started arguing the point with Bradley on the subject at a press conference. Goebbels cleverly seized upon the incident; through Radio Arnhem, which was still available, he broadcast anti-American statements which were attributed to Montgomery and which the Americans thought came from the BBC! The best proof of the solidity of the coalition lay in its success. If Hitler had thought for a moment that 'the strange alliance' would break up as the danger which had brought it into being diminished, the Yalta Conference was going to strip him of his last illusions.

CHAPTER 2

The Yalta Conference

FEELING that victory was near and dreading a post-war period in which they were not bound by any agreement – apart from Churchill's and Stalin's shady deals in October 1944 – the three great allies were anxious to meet again. But Roosevelt, who had been re-elected in November 1944, was not available until February 1945; he it was, in fact, who fixed the date of the meeting. As for the place, they had to take into account both Stalin's wish not to leave the USSR and Roosevelt's desire to take advantage of the occasion to have talks with various important people on the shores of the Mediterranean; this was why the Crimea was chosen, and, in the Crimea, Yalta. The 'Big Three' therefore continued their talks among themselves, as at Teheran, without thinking it worthwhile to involve the smaller powers in their discussions and bargainings; so France was not invited and General de Gaulle gave public expression to his resentment.

I THE CIRCUMSTANCES AND ATMOSPHERE OF THE CONFERENCE

It was a favourable moment for the Russians; three-fifths of the German forces were fighting against them and yet their winter offensive was developing with majestic and relentless efficiency, while the British and Americans were recovering from the heavy blow they had received in the Ardennes and had not yet crossed the Rhine. Everyone, however, knew that Nazi Germany's days were numbered and was thinking of the future; but each was looking at it in his own way. The Russians had already secured certain pledges in Europe – in Poland, Romania and Bulgaria; they had reached the Oder, some forty-five miles from Berlin and some eighty from Vienna; what they were concerned with was the fate of defeated Germany and first and foremost that of her satellites. The British and Americans were thinking of the strenuous second lap in which they would need to launch all their strength against Japan; the assistance of the USSR would be useful, if not even essential, if they were to succeed – Roosevelt did not yet know what progress was being made in making the atom bomb and it was only in March that he learned that it was nearing completion. Finally, Churchill was more worried than Roosevelt about the Red Army's advance into central Europe and the unilateral measures taken by the USSR in Poland. In short, the British and Americans who at Teheran had thought it advisable to restrict themselves to preliminary discussions and vague conclusions about the big problems which would arise when peace came, because they felt guilty towards the Russians for not yet having opened up a proper second front, were going to find themselves faced at Yalta with Soviet proposals or demands, which were not only very specific but which Stalin clung to very firmly – in most cases the USSR would be capable of carrying them out on her own, whatever her allies might feel about it.

Moreover, the British and Americans did not put up the same unified front against the Russians as against the Germans. Churchill was quite determined not to be 'the gravedigger of the British Empire', an Empire which for him was not confined to the territories over which flew the Union Jack. He thought the Mediterranean formed part of it; since December, British soldiers had been intervening in the Greek civil war and even in the street fighting in Athens – Churchill had cabled General Scobie that if necessary he should behave in the Greek capital 'as he would in a conquered city'; as King George had failed to win ELAS over to his views, Churchill had forced him to step down for the time being in favour of the very popular Archbishop Damaskinos, who became Regent. In Europe Germany's collapse and the weakness of France left room for Russian predominance, something which upset the balance that had always been the basis of British continental policy. But since Stalin had respected the 1944 agreement with regard to Greece, the British Premier was obliged in return to temper his reactions towards Soviet behaviour in Poland; but he did not find it easy.

Roosevelt had not made any protest against his partners' cynical deal, which had been concluded in his absence if not even behind his back; but he was nonetheless bound by it and as Cordell Hull has very rightly stressed, it weakened his position *vis-à-vis* Stalin. He had protested against the British operation in Greece without being able to prevent it but he was quite determined not to subordinate United States policy to defending British imperialism, which Stettinius said was prepared 'to lay hands on land anywhere, even if it was only a few isolated rocks or sandbanks'.

American experts thought that the Anglo-Soviet conflict which was emerging could lead to a third world war. Roosevelt had set himself the task before he died of making this impossible. He had come to Yalta very ill, knowing that his days were numbered; his adviser Hopkins was also seriously ill with cancer; if the American President was not very well acquainted with all the documents and sometimes intervened irrelevantly, it was because he was thinking of the post-war period more than of the war itself. Above all he wanted to keep the Allies united and to persuade the USSR to take part wholeheartedly in the newly restored League of Nations in which he placed all his hopes for preserving peace in the future. Was this naïvety or was it blindness born of optimism? Roosevelt saw Stalin as a potential liberal; he said to Bullitt: 'I have a kind of impression that all that Stalin wants is to ensure the security of his country. I think that if I give him everything I possibly can without demanding anything in return, then noblesse oblige, he will not attempt to annex anything and will work to build a peaceful and democratic world.' And to Mikolajczyk: 'It must be remembered that the Soviet régime has only two years' experience in international relations; I am certain, however, that Stalin is a realist and not an imperialist.'

The 'wily Georgian' was going to play on his position of strength and even on his good health in masterly fashion; he showed growing consideration for Roosevelt and stepped up his drinking sessions with Churchill. While thinking that he was acting as arbitrator between Great Britain and the USSR, the American President often came down in favour of measures which were exactly what the latter wanted.

II THE FATE OF DEFEATED GERMANY

With regard to Germany, whose ultimate defeat everyone accepted as a matter of course, the agreements which were concluded concerned the co-operation of the Allied armies to ensure and hasten victory, the occupation and dismemberment of Germany after her defeat, the amount of reparations which would be demanded from her and how they would be extracted.

In actual fact, on the military level they confined themselves to mutual congratulations – since the Russian spokesman Antonov had not failed to stress that the Soviet winter offensive had been a great help to the Anglo-Saxons, as was shown by the sudden appearance on the eastern front of German troops from the Ardennes, Churchill expressed 'his deep admiration for and his gratitude to' the Red Army. The real problem now, however, was not how to launch simultaneous offensives which henceforth would continue uninterrupted on both sides but to take appropriate measures now that the Anglo-American and Soviet armies were drawing close to each other and would shortly join hands. For the time being it was a question of deciding on a 'bombing line' which would have to be adjusted as each advanced; and they could not reach agreement on where to place it, since the Russians refused to reveal their daily positions to their allies.

As for ground operations, a British proposal to co-ordinate them by means of a tripartite mission in Moscow was rejected by the Russians. It was obvious to Stalin and to Churchill that the troops' advance into the heart of Germany raised political problems – Stalin had shown this quite clearly by stipulating that Vienna would be an objective reserved for the Red Army. But the Americans refused to see anything but the military aspect of the war; they therefore left it to the Commander-in-Chief to take the necessary measures as and when required; Eisenhower could therefore come to direct agreement with Stalin on this point, over the heads of the British and American governments. But for the time being, no tactical co-ordination was arranged; there was not even an exchange of information about operational plans; Churchill was alarmed but Roosevelt washed his hands of it.

The fact that the whole of Germany would have to be occupied was beyond any shadow of doubt; but how, by whom and for how long? Stalin wanted her to be occupied by the Big Three alone, to the exclusion of France 'who,' he said, 'had opened her gates to the enemy' – no one asked him what the USSR was doing at that moment. Churchill, who knew that what the American people wanted most urgently was for the boys to go back home as soon as possible and who was consequently afraid that the United States would quickly come to lose interest in Europe as they had done after the First World War, supported France's demand and defended her right to occupy a part of Germany – he probably thought that if France became a great power again she would provide a counter-balance to Soviet power on the Continent. Stalin agreed that a portion of the British and American zones should be administered by the French. He was the only one to raise the problem of creating a unified government of Germany, but the question remained unanswered and no decision was taken on the matter. It was simply agreed that for the time being each country would administer its own zone and Berlin be subject to joint occupation and military government.

That Germany must be dismembered was also generally agreed. But how many parts? Stalin was in favour of an immediate decision on this point; but he found himself faced with an American plan to divide her up between five or six states and a British plan to isolate Prussia by internationalising the Rhineland and setting up a Danubian Confederation – 'as peaceful as a cow', in Churchill's words. The problem was set aside for examination by a special committee under Eden's chairmanship. Although Stalin had not put forward any plan, he had not been opposed to the dismemberment, far from it – he had in particular declared his determined opposition to any regrouping of the Danubian states.

It was he who proved toughest with regard to the reparations to be demanded from a conquered country which was quite rightly to be treated as guilty. He called to mind the dreadful havoc suffered by the USSR and provided evidence with huge figures that had been arrived at by a special commission under Maisky which had been working since 1943. It concluded that German heavy industry must be reduced by 80 per cent and that factories, machines and men must be starved of capital; afterwards, there would be levies on production for a period of ten years. The total was to amount to 20,000 million dollars, half of which would go to the USSR.

According to Maisky, Roosevelt is said to have been surprised at the USSR's moderation; he was expecting to see her demand 50,000 million dollars! In actual fact Roosevelt and Churchill were afraid of making Germany too poor and afterwards having to pay to keep her and set her on her feet again. However, they accepted the figure of 20,000 million dollars as a basis for discussion and a special commission in Moscow was given the task of replacing this preliminary assessment by more accurate figures.

It did not occur to anyone that the Germans ought to be called in to discuss their fate in some way or another; the demilitarisation and the denazification of the Reich as well as the punishment of war criminals were also taken for granted by the Big Three. Although victory was in sight, the bonds created by the war were still too close and too essential for Germany yet to have become a bone of contention between them. This was not the case with Poland.

III THE POLISH PROBLEM

The Polish question was brought up at six out of eight of the Conference's plenary sessions and at all the meetings of the Foreign Ministers. The Soviets emphasised that in the course of history Poland had been the corridor through which Russia's invaders had poured in. Indeed, two problems arose as far as she was concerned: that of her new frontiers and that of her government and her régime. An attempt to reach a joint solution to the first of these problems had already been made at Teheran and in the interallied talks which had followed that conference; the second was stated in terms unilaterally defined by the Russians because of their recognition of the Lublin government and this government alone.

Where the eastern frontiers of Poland were concerned, Stalin's position was very strong both in law and in fact. The population of the territories he was demanding was mostly Byelorussian and Ukrainian; it was difficult for the British not to recognise the fact since this had been the point of view of their negotiator Lord Curzon in 1920; besides, the Allies had admitted it at Teheran: how could they now go back on their opinion? In actual fact these territories were already occupied by the Red Army and practically annexed to the USSR; how could she be turned out except by force? The Curzon line was therefore unanimously accepted by the Allies; the USSR, with a generosity which cost her little, promised to look into the possibility of readjustments of a few miles or so if the Poles wished.

On the compensation to be granted to Poland in the west at Germany's expense there was also no disagreement. But where should the new frontier run? The Oder had already been accepted as the natural boundary and, further upstream, the Neisse; but which Neisse? The western or the eastern one? Stalin advocated the western Neisse, since he was anxious to show his generosity to the Poles at the expense of Germany. But the British and Americans were afraid of the eternal Polish-German conflict which, to use Churchill's vivid expression, would result from 'stuffing the Polish goose with German lands' – a conflict which Stalin obviously wanted to be as bitter and prolonged as possible. In the end it was decided to consult the new Polish government and to postpone the decision until the Peace Conference. So, on this point, the Soviets had not had their own way and referring the question to the Peace Conference could only in the long run enable the Germans to have their say in the matter one day.

But what would be the composition of this new Polish government which was now a further factor in the problem? It was this point which gave rise to the most heated discussion. Normally, the Atlantic Charter should have provided the solution, as set forth by the Big Three's declaration of principle which wound up their meeting and which stated that 'the liberated peoples would be assisted in forming provisional governments widely representative of all democratic elements and pledged to establishing through free elections and as soon as possible governments corresponding to the will of the people.' On this point Roosevelt proved firmer than Churchill, who had shown a very strange way of putting this principle into practice in Greece.

But though there was agreement on what was said, there was disagreement about what was meant. The Soviets regarded the Lublin Committee as the national government and the Polish government in London as composed of refugees cut off from their country; the idea of free elections, which had never been carried out in the USSR in the same way as in the west, did not have the same crucial significance as it had for the British and Americans.

After endless discussions, the Russians obtained satisfaction on the main point: the Lublin Committee would provide the framework for the new Polish government; it would be joined by 'democratic leaders who were at present abroad'. The new government would institute elections which Roosevelt stipulated 'should be like Caesar's wife, above suspicion', and which Molotov promised to organise within a month – in a country completely occupied by the Red Army and where the Polish Communists whom it had placed in power would be in control.

IV THE WAR AGAINST JAPAN

Roosevelt considered that the war in the Pacific was a strictly American affair; he did not want the British or the French to play any important part in it for their objective would be to re-establish their domination in Burma and Indochina and he considered that the two colonial powers had never done anything for the natives in their empires. On the other hand, he thought that he would need the help of the USSR against Japan and that this help would be disinterested. Had his military advisers not told him that the war in Asia would last another eighteen months after it was over in Europe? They were also afraid that the split between the Kuomintang and the Communists in China would become worse and the only way to avert this was good understanding between themselves and the USSR.

In short, in a private interview with Stalin, behind Churchill's back, this disconcerting President of the United States concluded an actual secret agreement of the very kind which he condemned in others. The USSR promised to go to war against Japan three months after the surrender of Germany – the time needed to move her forces from Europe to Asia. In return she would receive the Kurile Islands, the southern part of Sakhalin, a lease on Port Arthur and the Manchurian railways, and the maintenance of the *status quo* in Outer Mongolia. Thus both in Asia and in Europe Stalin was proving to be a worthy successor of the Czars and was making up for their defeats in 1905 and 1917. But what is one to think about Roosevelt who, contrary to all his principles and to the Atlantic Charter, was allocating to one of his allies territories which belonged to someone else – at this juncture it was Chiang Kai-shek – without first of all consulting him? How and on what grounds would he have been able to make a successful stand later on against Soviet demands in Europe? It is true that in Cairo Roosevelt had offered French Indochina to Chiang Kai-shek; that time it was France, the first great power to have fought against Germany virtually on her own and the first to have paid dearly for it, who was paying the price of the American President's mixture of guile and idealism.

This same anxiety of Roosevelt's to please Stalin, at whatever cost, had been shown with regard to the right of passage through the Dardanelles; it was decided that the statute of Montreux should be revised in favour of the USSR, 'who must not be dependent on the control of the Turks' – who were thus punished for not having emerged from their cautious neutrality until a very late hour.

The fact was that Roosevelt's main idea, perhaps even his obsession, was to set up a new and tougher League of Nations which, by perpetuating the agreement of the Big Three, would make world wars impossible for good and all.

V THE UNITED NATIONS ORGANISATION

Continuing in the line of American idealists in which his most famous predecessor was Wilson, Roosevelt thought that relations between states could and must be ruled by international law and not by violence. He realised that the era of selfish isolationism was over for the United States. He saw them as playing a dominant role as members of a second League of Nations which would thus not be weakened, as the first had been from the very start, by their absence. 'America,' he said, 'is the only power which can keep peace in the world.'

It was obvious that international co-operation would be fatally jeopardised if the USSR stayed out and even more if she were hostile. She too had for a long time held aloof from Geneva, although in her case it was because of the opposition of the other great powers. Roosevelt had no regard for the Soviet régime; both by upbringing and character he tended to view it with mistrust and even with incomprehension – it was the complete antithesis of the American way of life. But he had been greatly struck by the strength which the USSR had shown in the war and by the resilience of a régime which emerged from the storm stronger than ever. He was doubtless exaggerating the significance and permanence of internal changes which were brought about largely by force of circumstance and by guile; but in a way which was again typical of the American temperament, he wanted to draw an optimistic cheque on the future and he was openly speculating on a relationship of trust and co-operation between the Russians and the Americans after the war.

Stalin and Churchill were also in favour of a 'United Nations Organisation' but they did not see it in quite the same light as Roosevelt. The first had in mind above all to set up a solid bulwark against a revival of German imperialism by discouraging any idea of seeking revenge; the second was essentially concerned with maintaining British power to the greatest possible extent and the Yalta Conference had confirmed that from now on it was far inferior to that of the USSR and the United States.

The question of when and where the constituent assembly would sit was settled without any trouble. It was decided that the United States would send invitations for a meeting in San Francisco on April 25, 1945.

No one could say whether or not the war would be over by that date and the decision was therefore an important indication of the attitude of the victors of 1945. Israelian is quite right to point out that in their concern to preserve international security above all else they were very different from their predecessors of 1918, whose first thought had been to settle the fate of the defeated nations.

The choice to decide which nations to be represented in the United Nations Organisation also presented very little difficulty. Since it had been born out of the war, it was obvious that, at least to begin with, it would include only those states which had fought against the Axis states; for even more obvious reasons the latter were excluded from it. The only controversy arose from the USSR's request made as early as the autumn of 1944 that the sixteen Republics of the USSR should be represented in the same way as, according to the Russians, the Dominions of the Common-wealth. The Americans raised the objection that the United States were also a federal state but that they did not demand that all the states of which they were composed should have a seat in UNO. In the end, Stalin agreed that only Byelorussia and the Ukraine should have a separate vote from the USSR; if American public opinion demanded it he promised to support at San Francisco an American request for two extra votes – a request which for some reason the Americans never made.

The only real problem in the end was how UNO would work in such a way as to respect the rights of the smaller nations without at the same time impairing the efficiency of the organisation and reducing it to the state of powerlessness which had so hampered the League of Nations' efforts to keep the peace. The Big Three came to an agreement quite easily, albeit from different motives. They did not for one moment think of setting up a super-state with powers of coercion which would in fact deprive the member states, that is to say themselves, of part of their sovereignty. They believed they had solved the contradiction by setting up two organisations; in the General Assembly, all the nations, even the smallest, would sit with equal rights; but the great powers would hold a permanent seat in the 'Security Council', a more restricted organisation which, as Roosevelt said, 'would have the main responsibility for main-taining international peace and security'.

The great powers were easily named: China and France were promoted to join America, the USSR and Britain. It remained to be decided how they would take their decisions. Since in actual fact none of those taking part in the Yalta Conference envisaged for one moment the possibility of not retaining complete power in his own country, it was decided by common consent that any decision of the Security Council must have the unani-mous agreement of the five great powers. This meant establishing for each of them a right of veto which could paralyse the institution.

VI CONCLUSIONS ON THE YALTA CONFERENCE

In their great concern not to endanger their agreement, those taking part in the talks steered clear of a few minor subjects which were nonetheless capable of giving rise to bitter discussions, such as the occupation of Iran, the forming of a united Yugoslav government or the setting up of a Balkan federation for which a Bulgarian-Yugoslav treaty seemed to have paved the way. Accordingly, they parted, feeling very pleased with themselves. Roosevelt spoke of 'a new period in world history'; Churchill talked lyrically 'of the splendid possibilities for the future and of the wide sunny plains of peace and happiness'; in his cold, taciturn way, Stalin was equally enthusiastic; in the USSR large meetings took place to celebrate the agreements and the editorial of *Izvestia* stated that 'the conference would go down in history as a new example of how understanding had been reached on the most complex questions in the interests of peace, democracy and progress.' American public opinion shared this enthusiasm: Herbert Hoover wired to his old opponent Roosevelt that it had given 'great hope to the world'. The *New York Times* said that 'the conference was a milestone in the road of history and peace', and other newspapers 'that it had laid the lasting foundations for a peace based on international justice' and 'swept away for ever any doubts one may have had as to the possibility of the Big Three's co-operating in peace as in war.' Only the French government, left out of decisions which were shaping the post-war world, remained gloomy amidst the general rejoicing.

Today, on the other hand, in the light of the cold war, opinions on Yalta have greatly changed. Although Soviet historians continue to praise Yalta as being in the spirit of the golden rule of international relations – 'the possibility of fruitful co-operation between states with different social systems', wrote Israelian – and to regard Roosevelt as a 'progressive' statesman, his American opponents have pitilessly attacked the President of the United States. They have violently condemned his weakness towards Stalin, which seemed to be confirmed by the latter's satisfaction: a 'fool's bargain', a 'wartime Munich', a 'diplomatic Waterloo', a 'sell-out', even 'treason', have become current expressions in American historical literature with regard to Yalta. Roosevelt's advisers have tried to stem this tide of criticism and Stettinius stated that the Conference 'was a diplomatic triumph for the United States'. All in vain: Yalta still has a bad press in the United States.

In France the Yalta Conference is generally presented as a supreme example of the type of agreement between two super-powers which must at all costs be avoided in the future, as expressing a desire for world domination at the expense of smaller powers. It is apt to be described as ending in a 'partition of the world'. It is obvious that all these contradictory opinions are inspired by emotion and by the way events have developed since the end of the war. What is one to think?

In the first place, it is an exaggeration to say that Roosevelt had made concessions to the USSR without asking anything in return. True, his trust in Stalin and his liking for him had made him neglect the plentiful warnings of more pessimistic advisers such as Ambassador Harriman and General Deane; he had pinned a great deal of faith in his charm and his skill in handling situations and relied too much on man-to-man talks of which he was so fond. But surely this was the way he had always behaved with Churchill and it was by this means that he had succeeded in consolidating the Anglo-American alliance, avoiding offending or humiliating his partner whilst remaining very firm on what he considered to be essentials – 'Overlord' for example? He had acted in exactly the same way with Stalin; but the essentials for him at that moment were to maintain the 'strange alliance' right to the end and for the USSR to become a member of the United Nations Organisation. For the rest, Byrnes is right to stress that he had never given anything away for nothing; for example, the territorial concessions at China's expense had been repaid by Stalin's promise not to support the Chinese Communists against Chiang Kai-shek, and Molotov even went so far as to say to General Hurley that 'the Chinese Communists were not really Communists at all'. Stettinius is also right to point out that on many questions Stalin had given ground in relation to his original demands. Even while the conference was going on Hopkins wrote to Roosevelt: 'The Russians have made so many concessions that we must not annoy them.'

In what ways then did the Russians ultimately benefit from the Yalta Conference? Their most substantial gains were on the German problem but at this juncture the Soviets' attitude to this question was not very different from that of the Anglo-Saxons; the dismemberment, occupation, demilitarisation and denazification of Germany, the punishment of war criminals, the control of industry, reparations, all these were common sanctions in the war aims of all the members of the coalition. On the other hand, the USSR's partial failure with regard to Germany's eastern frontier was obvious; the final decision on the boundary had been postponed till peace came, since they had been unable to choose between the two Neisses; but it was a failure without any practical significance, since Poland's new frontiers as a whole had been accepted by everyone, just as no one had questioned the USSR's *faits accomplis* – this would have been impossible without breaking with her.

Roosevelt had set what was perhaps an unprecedented example of a statesman who, with virtually no diplomatic traditions to act on, no historically determined political line to follow, no territories to claim or interests to defend, had raised an international conference to the very highest plane: to bring the war to an end as soon as possible and to ensure a lasting peace for mankind. On the first point he had succeeded: Yalta had marked the culmination of the Allied coalition. On the second point he had been too optimistic when on his return to the United States he had announced to Congress that 'in the post-war world there would be no more need for spheres of influence, alliances, balance of power or any of these special agreements by which in the unhappy past nations tried to ensure their security or promote their interests'. Can he be blamed for this?

In actual fact, at the beginning of 1945 the war situation and the areas held by the Red Army made it possible for the USSR to do what she liked – first of all in Europe and then in Manchuria. To prevent her would have meant coldly contemplating a third world war. No one had dared to mention even the possibility of such a thing. Besides the Soviets had already achieved their expansion towards the west; a war might have checked it – at what cost? – but it would not have prevented it. It was obvious, moreover, that world public opinion, and above all American public opinion, would not have accepted this, and Roosevelt knew it; it is equally evident that if the Allies had not been united at Yalta this would have merely played into the Nazis' hands by prolonging the war.

Why then were Roosevelt's hopes disappointed? Did he die too soon? Or, as Stettinius surmises, had the Politburo disowned Stalin? The one thing which is certain is that the USSR ruthlessly laid down the law in the territories 'liberated' by the Red Army, without worrying very much about or taking into account her partners' reactions. This was probably in the end the chief reason why 'the spirit of Yalta' came to nothing – the Conference having after all been no more than a temporary diplomatic resting place on the way to a new balance of power, one of those ruthless assertions of might which no treaty in the course of world history has ever been able to prevent or even restrain. Perhaps Roosevelt's mistake was, then, to see the future too much in terms of the past; he had foreseen only the risk of an Anglo-Russian conflict; he had not foreseen that at the end of the war, with the collapse of Germany and Japan, with France and Italy fading into the background and with Great Britain weakened, a victorious USSR would necessarily become one of the two great world powers, whatever her political and social régime, and that this advance would make her a powerful and potentially hostile rival of the United States. But were not the human relationships which he had established, the atmosphere of trust which he had endeavoured to create and finally the United Nations the best if not the only means of warding off this danger?

CHAPTER 3

The Death Throes of Nazi Germany

A T the beginning of 1945 Hitler had, on paper, 10 million men, of whom 7,500,000 were in the armed forces forming 290 divisions, that is to say twice as many units as in May 1940. But these figures are deceptive; the divisions were not up to strength; the number of tanks in the Panzer divisions had been reduced and the men were morally and physically exhausted; because of Allied bombing raids and despite the fact that distances had been shortened, the Wehrmacht had virtually lost the great advantage it had had up to now of moving its forces from one front to another by advancing along internal lines of communication; owing to shortage of petrol, the motorways were deserted and the railways, with their dilapidated installations and equipment, were running at a third of their normal capacity.

The blind confidence which the Führer placed in the new secret weapons led him to minimise the enormous danger Germany was in because of the growing inferiority of her armies on all fronts, both in numbers and in equipment. On several occasions, stubbornly persisting in a line of conduct in which he refused to make the slightest change even though he was committing one blunder after another, he had not allowed Guderian to cut his losses by evacuating minor operational areas – Norway, the Balkans and Italy. In order to protect the Baltic shipyards where the new submarines were being built, he kept some thirty divisions immobilized in Courland with their backs to the sea and practically encircled and useless.

In particular, Hitler stubbornly refused to recognise the tremendous strength of the Red Army which had been proved on the field and thus belied all the Nazi propaganda slogans. He declared that it was only bluff, 'the biggest since Gengis Khan'. He had withdrawn troops from the eastern front in order to counter-attack the British and Americans in the Ardennes at the very moment when the Russians were going to launch a great winter offensive.

I THE SOVIET OFFENSIVE OF JANUARY–FEBRUARY 1945

The Red Army had overwhelming superiority: from the Drave as far north as Courland, taking into account its inexhaustible reserves, it was capable of launching 5 million men, against only 1,800,000 Germans who were virtually without any hope of reinforcements and had no fortifications in which they could make a stand – Hitler considered that it would be demoralising to build any. The Russians had 7,000 tanks against 3,500 – according to Bauer, the forty-six-ton Joseph Stalin heavy tank, which had a range of 150 miles, was 'the most formidable caterpillar-tracked engine of war built by the belligerents'; and more than 50,000 guns were pounding away at 4,000 German guns, some of which had been taken from the flak, which was becoming less and less effective in protecting the cities of the Reich against Allied air raids. Finally, the sky was almost empty of German aircraft, since virtually all the fighters were being kept for defending the home front.

After halting for a while and even suffering a defeat outside Budapest at the beginning of the year, the Red Army now took and kept the initiative without pause, in a gigantic series of staggered operations. Abandoning its steamroller tactics, which meant advancing along the whole length of the front simultaneously and uniformly, *Stavka* concentrated its forces at the heart of the enemy defences, with Berlin as its objective. The chief task would thus fall to the first Byelorussian front under Zhukov and, at its southern end, to the first Ukrainian front under Koniev; in these two sectors *Stavka* concentrated 2 million men, 4,500 tanks and 40,000 guns, 2,500 of them self-propelled. The tactics were to ensure overwhelming superiority at the breakthrough points, where the concentration of forces sometimes reached a density of one infantry division, 240 guns and 100 tanks to every 1,100 yards – on the opposing side, one German division sometimes had to hold a good twelve miles. The Russians anticipated rapid success; with their first forward leap, spread out over a fortnight, they hoped to advance by 155 to 190 miles in order to reach the line Bromberg–Poznan–Breslau–Vienna; the second stage, with Berlin as its goal, was to take thirty days; the German resistance was therefore going to be finally broken in forty-five days. The Anglo-Saxons, delayed by their mishaps in the Ardennes, would probably be far outstripped in this interallied competition to occupy the vital centres of Germany.

After an artillery barrage, the Soviet offensive began on January 12 on the first Ukrainian front, in two waves of tanks following in the wake of caterpillar-tracked guns; by the time night fell they had advanced between 10 and 15 miles but darkness did not stop them; by the third day they had covered 28 miles and after completely breaking down the enemy defences, the chase was now on. Two days later a new leap of over sixty miles brought Koniev's tanks beyond Czestochova; next Cracow was captured and Breslau threatened.

On the first Byelorussian front, the attack began on January 14 first under Rokossovski and then under Zhukov, who was appointed by

Stalin on January 20 – an appointment which showed the vital importance which Stalin attached to this sector. Two days later the Russians
were at Radom, thirty-eight miles away, and Warsaw, threatened with
encirclement, had fallen. On January 21, Poznan was in sight some 145
miles west of Warsaw and it was encircled. On these two fronts the objectives of the offensive had therefore been achieved ahead of schedule.

Hitler had returned to Berlin to take over the control of operations. His
first concern was to punish the generals who had taken it upon themselves
to decide on a withdrawal – he even had Colonel von Bonin arrested for
having given up the hopeless task of defending the ruins of Warsaw with
the four meagre battalions at his disposal; he forbade any attempt to
evacuate the population; he was concerned above all with appointing
staunch Nazis as generals in especially critical points – Schoerner in
Silesia, for example; he turned the Gauleiters into Commissioners for the
Defence of the Reich with very extensive powers. Now in desperate
straits, Germany was resorting to Nazi fanaticism as her final weapon.

The Soviet breakthrough in the centre had hustled the Germans out of
their defences. In the north, the advance was slower; however, Rokossovski had arrived on the borders of east Prussia and Chernyakovsky had
reached the Baltic. It was only south of the central Slovakian mountain
range that the German front, with its salient in Budapest, remained unbroken and indeed, was not even seriously weakened.

At the end of January an examination of the military situation showed
Stavka that the Germans had massed reinforcements in Pomerania; also,
the advance varied according to the sectors; this left a wide gap between
the second and the first Byelorussian front; in addition, the Soviet armies
were not completely motorised and the infantry had not followed up;
finally, the leading units were beginning to be short of ammunition and
fuel, since their stores were still in the Warsaw region.

In the end it was decided that Zhukov's armies must be given a breathing space before being launched against Berlin. Stalin then ordered
Koniev to advance north-westwards; the plan was to capture Berlin in the
vice of the Byelorussian and Ukrainian armies, with the two jaws closing
in from the north and the south so as to complete the encirclement of the
city from the west. February was therefore spent in mopping-up operations; east Prussia was completely cut off from the rest of Germany; all
that was left was the 'strongpoint' of Koenigsberg. With his right flank
thus protected, Zhukov advanced to the Oder and set up bridgeheads on
the left bank as a preliminary to launching another offensive. Koniev
seized the whole of Upper Silesia, where the last of the German forces were
making a stand in Breslau.

Thus Silesia, Germany's last great industrial area, which Hitler had
ordered to be defended at all costs, had to be abandoned; the Russians

even seized three newly built factories producing *ersatz* petrol. Hitler at last resigned himself to evacuating Courland and Forster, the Gauleiter of Danzig, belatedly organised the withdrawal of more than a million refugees. The Führer gave Himmler, whose competence did not extend further than blind devotion to the régime, command of the armies on the Oder; he was hoping – and Goering and Jodl shared this hope – that the British and Americans would be horrified by the Soviet advance, with its implied threat of revolution, and that they would give favourable consideration to a compromise with the Reich. But after squabbling for a while about what strategy to adopt, as was their wont, the British and Americans were equally ready, for their part, to launch a final offensive which they intended to be irresistible.

II THE ANGLO-AMERICAN DISCUSSIONS – THE MALTA CONFERENCE

Hardly was the Ardennes crisis over when the excitement aroused by the mauling they had received added fresh fuel to the perennial controversy between the British and Americans as to the quickest way to defeat Germany. The British insisted on the need to strike the enemy at his most vulnerable point: the great northern plain. They were afraid of dispersing their forces and thereby making it easier for the enemy to defend himself, and they therefore asked for considerable reinforcements to be transferred to the north of the joint front; since Montgomery was in command there they would naturally come under his control. And since it would have to be a co-ordinated operation, why not give the command of all the ground troops on the whole of the front to the man responsible for the chief, decisive operation, that is to say, to Montgomery himself?

But the Americans did not see things in this light. The correlation established by the British between their plan and a British command made them suspicious, the more so as they were intensely irritated by the superior manner Monty had adopted ever since he had had American troops under his control. Eisenhower considered that because of the importance of the Ruhr the enemy would concentrate his forces in the north and fight to the death. In his view the essential first stage was to destroy the bulk of their armies; if this was successful, everything else would follow without trouble; the second stage would be to cross the Rhine, but it would be wiser to undertake this crossing at several points, in the lower course of the river, naturally, but also in the region of Frankfurt; finally, once the Allied armies had occupied the whole length of the Rhine, they would decide on the best way to invade Germany according to the situation and the various opportunities that offered; this might perhaps be the northern plain – but not necessarily, and it was certainly not a foregone conclusion. To begin with, therefore, some time would have to be spent, which would not be wasted, in destroying the enemy forces on the left bank of the Rhine by attacking all of them at once. Eisenhower was thus hoping not to run the risk of irreparable failure which might occur if he placed all his eggs in one basket; he wanted to retain the initiative in the operation and to keep enough forces in hand to exploit the breach wherever it occurred.

This matter was heatedly discussed in Malta, where, on the way to Yalta, the British and American military leaders took counsel together from January 30 to February 2, 1945; both sides became so excited that the debate finished up in camera as a small committee. Churchill had cunningly persuaded Roosevelt to agree to the replacement of Eisenhower's deputy, Tedder, an airman, by Alexander, also British, but an army man; under the supreme command of Eisenhower, the British would thus acquire the sole command of the ground armies which they had so greatly coveted – the objections which might apply against the stormy Montgomery could have no foundation or validity against the sagacious and reasonable Alexander. But the Americans saw through the trick; Marshall threw all his weight into the balance and Eisenhower, who had not come to Malta, in the end remained both Commander-in-Chief and the man responsible for ground operations; he also retained the right to choose which course to take; he merely promised not to let slip any opportunities which arose in the north, even if this should cause his original plan to suffer; and he agreed that five divisions which had been withdrawn from Italy should be given to Montgomery without delay; this formal concession having been made, in the end it was once again the American plan which prevailed.

III THE COLMAR POCKET – THE BATTLE OF THE RHINELAND

Eisenhower had 90 divisions – 60 infantry, 25 armoured and 5 airborne – and 6,000 tanks, against which von Rundstedt could put up only 65 divisions, among which were theoretically 8 Panzer divisions with a total of about a thousand tanks, to hold a front 470 miles long. The British and American armies had the advantage of being very powerfully equipped, and they were almost completely motorised – they were the only armies of which this was so throughout the whole war. But the Pershing tank, which had replaced the Sherman, did not prove superior to the German tanks and it would have been very inferior to the mammoth tanks which

the arsenals of the Reich were now not going to have time to mass-produce. On the other hand, the Allied Air Force held complete mastery of the
skies; not one inch of German territory was beyond its range; the fighters
were protecting the bombers wherever they chose to raid and as they were
in the air for a short time only, they were able to play a more intensive
part in the fighting. The invisible chink in the Allied armies was that
common for all coalitions; they were a loose collection rather than an
integrated whole, consisting as they did of 60 American, 14 British and 5
Canadian divisions, 4 brigades (Belgian, Dutch, Polish and Czech) and 14
French divisions – 4 of them keeping guard on Dunkirk, Lorient, Royan
and the Alps. But Rundstedt's more serious weakness in weapons and
manpower was increased by the fact that Hitler was forcing him to fight
on the left bank of the Rhine instead of shortening his lines by 60 miles or
so and strengthening his positions by putting a ditch some 90 to 300 yards
wide between himself and his foe from Hüningen to Wesel. The Germans
were therefore accepting the battle of attrition which Eisenhower was
aiming at; they would be fighting with their backs to the Rhine.

The Allied armies were deployed as follows: in the north, Montgomery
commanded the Canadian First Army (General Crerar), the British
Second Army (General Dempsey), the American Ninth Army (General
Simpson) and the First Airborne Army (General Brereton). In the centre,
Bradley had under him General Hodges' and General Patton's American
First and Third Armies. In the south, Devers commanded Patch's
American Seventh Army and Delattre de Tassigny's French First Army;
Montgomery had therefore been greatly favoured in the allocation of men
and resources. Eisenhower now systematically set in motion four succes-
sive pincer operations with the object of wiping out the German resistance
on the left bank of the Rhine, so that the whole of the Allied forces could
occupy the river between Karlsruhe and Wesel and seize and exploit the
first opportunity to cross.

The French began by reducing the 'Colmar pocket', with the aid of an
American army corps. On January 20 – the battle of the Ardennes was
only just coming to an end – Béthouart's I Army Corps attacked between
Mulhouse and Thann; the hilly terrain, the mined forests, the rivers and
the cold helped the defence; since the enemy forces were thus being drawn
southwards, Montsabert's II Army Corps launched the main attack from
west to east with the Rhine as its chief objective; on January 27 Colmar
was captured, while in the centre Béthouart liberated Guebwiller on
February 4. On February 5, Neuf-Brisach fell. From Colmar the 5th
Armoured Division proceeded through the Vosges towards Munster and
mopped up the Hardt forest. On February 9, the Colmar pocket was
finally eliminated.

The battle of the Rhineland had already begun north of the Eifel with

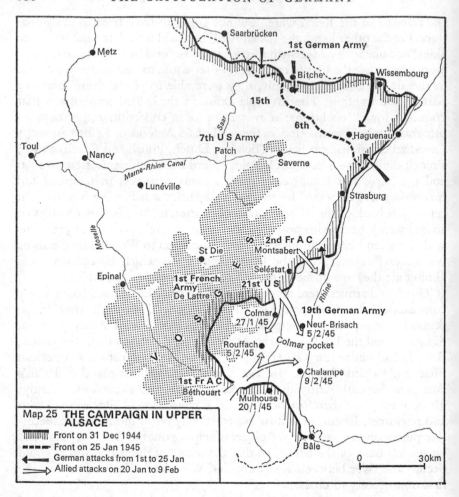

Map 25 **THE CAMPAIGN IN UPPER ALSACE**
- ‖‖‖‖ Front on 31 Dec 1944
- ▬▬▬ Front on 25 Jan 1945
- ◄━━ German attacks from 1st to 25 Jan
- ━━▷ Allied attacks on 20 Jan to 9 Feb

the Canadians. Their advance was checked by the small forts of the Siegfried line, the thaw and the floods, plus the high concentration of German forces, which Eisenhower had foreseen; in eleven days only about fifteen miles were covered. But from the south the American Ninth Army advanced northwards ahead of the Canadians and on March 2 reached the Rhine opposite Düsseldorf. The British Second Army had no need to intervene. However, the German First Army of paratroopers had been able to withdraw behind the Rhine.

As early as February 23 the third pincer had been launched in the Eifel, even though Montgomery had asked once again for the attack to be delayed so that reinforcements could be sent to him. The American First Army came down from the north after forcing its way across the Roer, the level of which the Germans had kept high by jamming the locks; on March 7 it captured Cologne; on its right Patton's Third Army had stormed, one by one, the forts on the Siegfried line hidden in the woods and gullies; on March 11, they joined hands. This time whole German units were being taken prisoner.

Persisting in his blind obstinacy, Hitler once again thought that he could force the hand of fate by changing the actors; von Rundstedt was disgraced, for the third time, and replaced by Kesselring. The latter was unable to prevent the fourth Allied pincer from closing in on the Palatinate with remarkable speed, thanks to Patton, who in two days emerged on to the plain of Mainz, reached the Rhine on March 13 and then turned the Siegfried line, which Patch's Seventh Army was approaching at the same time. This was the most unequivocal success of the campaign; 70,000 German prisoners were taken.

Eisenhower had thus won his bet; in six weeks he had occupied the whole length of the Rhine; he had conducted the battle as he had decided, in successive interlocking operations. The British are good losers and congratulated him; Alanbrooke, who had attacked him most bitterly of all, was the first to do so. The Germans had fallen into the trap, prompted by what Eisenhower called 'the conquerors' complex' – that is to say the fear, as he said, 'that the loss of the smallest piece of conquered territory would cause the collapse of the worm-eaten pedestal of the myth of Teutonic invincibility'.

The bombers had played the part which the Russians gave the artillery on the eastern front. They had caused such heaps of rubble ahead of the armies' advance that the latter had sometimes been unable to advance, notably in Cleves, where they had had to wait for the bulldozers to clear the road for them. Above all, on February 22 they had launched Operation 'Bugle', the largest bombing raid of the whole war; in one week 10,000 aircraft dropped 55,000 tons of bombs – some of them weighing ten tons – on German railways; they hit 200 major targets, as well as thousands of minor ones – important viaducts, marshalling yards, concentrations of rolling-stock, points, signals and bridges. The Allies were thus hoping to force the Germans to reserve rail transport for military needs at the expense of their economic requirements and to increase road transport, thus exhausting their last petrol supplies. They did in fact achieve this result but not the additional psychological effect which they expected: although the German people's morale was affected, there were neither strikes nor riots. But the Reich no longer had a coherent railway system.

Eisenhower, who was the lucky winner all along the line, had benefited in addition from the fact that the Remagen bridge had been miraculously captured intact, a happy chance which was going to decide the direction of the Allied thrust.

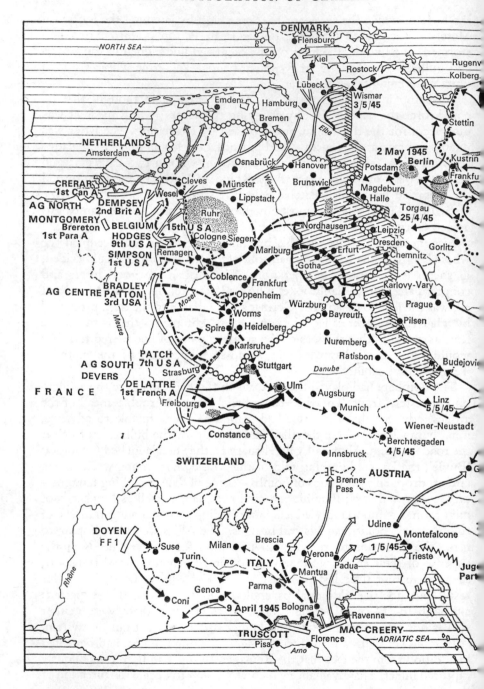

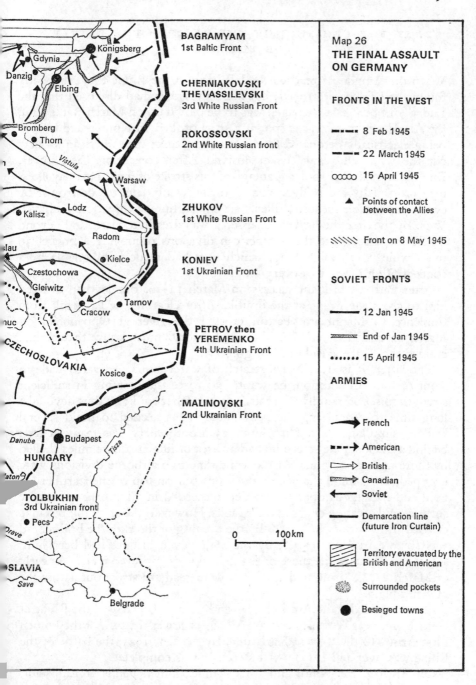

BAGRAMYAM
1st Baltic Front

CHERNIAKOVSKI
THE VASSILEVSKI
3rd White Russian Front

ROKOSSOVSKI
2nd White Russian front

ZHUKOV
1st White Russian Front

KONIEV
1st Ukrainian Front

PETROV then
YEREMENKO
4th Ukrainian Front

MALINOVSKI
2nd Ukrainian Front

TOLBUKHIN
3rd Ukrainian front

Map 26
**THE FINAL ASSAULT
ON GERMANY**

FRONTS IN THE WEST

---- 8 Feb 1945

--- 22 March 1945

ooooo 15 April 1945

▲ Points of contact
between the Allies

\\\\\ Front on 8 May 1945

SOVIET FRONTS

—— 12 Jan 1945

End of Jan 1945

•••••• 15 April 1945

ARMIES

→ French

---→ American

⊐⊃ British

Canadian

← Soviet

—— Demarcation line
(future Iron Curtain)

Territory evacuated by the
British and American

Surrounded pockets

Besieged towns

0   100 km

Königsberg
Gdynia
Danzig
Elbing
Bromberg
Thorn
Vistula
Warsaw
Kalisz   Lodz
Radom
lau
Kielce
Czestochowa
Gleiwitz
Tarnov
Cracow
nuc
CZECHOSLOVAKIA
Kosice
Danube   Budapest
HUNGARY   Tisza
aton
Pecs
rave
SLAVIA
Save
Belgrade

IV THE CROSSING OF THE RHINE – THE BATTLE OF THE RUHR

When the Americans reached the left bank of the Rhine they frequently found the bridges destroyed; but after a prisoner had disclosed that the Ludendorff bridge at Remagen was to be blown up on March 7 at 4 p.m., the Americans were on the spot at 3.50; a broken wire prevented it from being electrically detonated from the other bank; the American sappers cut the wires and sank the explosives. After consulting Eisenhower, Bradley immediately took advantage of this stroke of luck; next day 8,000 men crossed by the bridge. The Germans vainly tried to destroy it by every conceivable means, artillery, air attack, human torpedoes and even V-2s. By the time the bridge collapsed it was already too late; and beyond the Rhine there were three American divisions occupying a pocket 30 miles wide by 10 miles long, which they had made impregnable by a concentration of guns of every kind.

After Patton's brilliant success on March 12–16, Bradley had ordered him to cross the Rhine at the double. After clearing the left bank from Coblence to Mannheim, Patton crossed the river at Oppenheim on March 22 and declared that 'the whole world must know that he had crossed the Rhine ahead of Montgomery'.

The latter, it is true, had a stretch of water some 550 yards wide in front of him. In addition, he wanted to force the crossing in sufficient strength to set off rapidly afterwards on the other bank; he thus devoted a long time to assembling the heavy equipment needed to build several bridges simultaneously. On March 23 Montgomery was ready at last; behind a thick smoke screen he had an area of fifteen square miles shelled by more than 2,000 guns. At the same time two airborne divisions were dropped, not behind the enemy positions but on top of their artillery, a bold and dangerous operation which succeeded in taking the enemy by surprise and creating chaos in their ranks. However, the amphibious tanks crossed the river on their own. By the evening of the 24th the bridgehead was some thirty miles deep; by the 26th, seven bridges had been built across the Rhine, while those over the Issel were captured intact. As early as March 28, six armoured divisions were ready to strike out across the Münster plain.

On the same day the American Seventh Army also crossed the Rhine at Gernsheim, near Worms. Next, on March 31 it was the turn of the French First Army, to the west of Karlsruhe. By April 1, 1945, the battle of the Rhine was over and Eisenhower's victory was complete.

On April 2, the Ninth and First Armies joined hands at Lippstadt, closing up the Ruhr pocket where eighteen German divisions under

Model were shut in amongst the jumble of towns and factories; Model had not even tried to disengage from the enemy – where could he go? A siege war began, which Eisenhower entrusted to a new American army, the Fifteenth, under Gerow.

Eisenhower now systematically set about adding to and strengthening the bridges over the Rhine. American engineers worked wonders; eleven days after the capture of Wesel they had already built a bridge with a railway line; stores were piling up on the right bank; they could begin the pursuit in all directions at once, as Eisenhower wanted; the terrain no longer presented any great obstacle; the German motorways were wide open to the tanks and could not be defended, for they skirted the built-up areas where the enemy might make a stand; the straight stretches could even be turned into runways for aircraft.

Germany's defeat was practically complete; British and American disagreements were now a thing of the past. The problem now was to coordinate and to join hands with the Red Army; there were two sides to this; Eisenhower only considered it from the military angle, but Churchill was concerned above all with its political aspect.

V THE BATTLE OF BUDAPEST – THE USSR AND SOUTH-EAST EUROPE

While the Soviets were advancing in Pomerania and Silesia they had been marking time south of the Carpathians for some considerable time; but this semi-failure by their armies was amply compensated for by their political success in all the countries which the Red Army had entered.

At the beginning of December 1944 the Russians had with some difficulty advanced as far as Budapest and the shores of Lake Balaton. During December, Malinovski in the north and Tolbukhin in the south had attacked in conjunction with each other and had broken through the line of fortifications which had been hastily set up by the Germans round Budapest. By the end of the year street fighting had even begun in Pest.

The Hungarian Fascist Arrow Cross government had set about fortifying the city by mobilising the population to build defence works; since there were many desertions, public executions became a common event. Hitler was greatly interested in this operational area, for there were ss generals in command there. He ordered them to defend the city house by house, forbade them to attempt to leave and threatened to shoot as a deserter anyone who tried to join the German forces in the west. The Russians were therefore forced to lay siege to Pest and to the heights of Buda, where 70,000 men were making a stand.

In January 1945 General Gille's ss armoured corps tried in vain to relieve the beleaguered city. The garrison then began to run short of provisions, since the attempted parachute drops made on a small area in bad weather had had no greater success than at Stalingrad; they were so short of petrol that their crews had to blow up seventy immobilised tanks.

On January 15, the Russians reached the main streets of Pest; they advanced along the underground railway and the Germans withdrew, blowing up the Danube bridges as they did so. On January 19, Gille made a renewed attack to relieve Buda, but in vain; the citadel was being pounded by Soviet artillery; completely demoralised, some Hungarian units went over to the Red Army. On February 11, the garrison surrendered – only 20,000 men succeeded in escaping. But Malinovski's advance towards Bratislava and Vienna as ordered by *Stavka* had been delayed by more than fifty days by this unexpected siege.

Meanwhile, the Germans continued to attack on both sides of the Danube. Against Guderian's advice Hitler decided to send reinforcements from the Ardennes to General Sepp Dietrich because the latter, a former butcher, was a long-standing Nazi. On March 6, the Germans began three simultaneous concentric counter-attacks with the main thrust taking place towards the Danube, south of Budapest, from the isthmus between Lake Balaton and Vehenezi. A breach was made on the first day, but through lack of experience the raw German recruits failed to stick close enough to the tanks; the latter soon ran out of petrol and even of shells; after an advance of some eighteen miles they came to a halt.

On March 16, Malinovski and Tolbukhin took up the offensive together; their objective was Vienna. On March 27, the German position collapsed and on March 29 the Russians reached the Austrian frontier.

As the Red Army moved on, all the countries liberated by them rapidly underwent tremendous changes. First of all, as they drew near, Communist-controlled guerrilla activity broke out so as to pave the way; the Russians dropped arms, officers and instructors to the partisans by parachute; skirmishes started up again in Slovakia as early as February; in Hungary the Committee of National Unity, on which the Communists were represented, only just failed in an attempt at revolt which, had it succeeded, would have conspicuously shortened, if not entirely prevented, the siege of Budapest; but partisans were fighting both ahead of and behind the Red Army's lines.

At the same time armies were being raised in Romania (350,000 men) and in Bulgaria, which were incorporated into the Red Army to fight against the Germans. But above all the governments of the liberated countries contracted an alliance with the USSR as well as being reshuffled in accordance with the latter's wishes. In Yugoslavia a national coalition government was formed in Belgrade on March 7, 1945; with Tito as president, it contained twenty-three Communist members out of twenty-eight, and all the key positions were in the hands of Titoists. In a letter to King Peter of Yugoslavia, Churchill recognised that 'events had disappointed his heartfelt desires and that he was no longer in a position to prevent what was happening in Yugoslavia'.

For his part, President Beneš had started negotiations both with the Czech Communists who had taken refuge in Moscow and with the USSR. They ended in the 'Kosice Programme' and the agreement of March 31, 1945. according to which the Czechoslovaks would be mobilised and armed by the USSR and a coalition government would be formed to which Communists would be admitted. Between the western powers and the USSR, Czechoslovakia under Beneš, who had not forgotten the Munich betrayal, had resolutely opted for the USSR.

But the most memorable and, for the British and Americans, the most worrying events had taken place in Romania. At the end of February Vyshinsky, Moscow's former public prosecutor and now the USSR's deputy Foreign Minister, had come to Bucharest barely sixteen days after the end of the Yalta Conference. The Communists' programme of expropriation, confiscation and nationalisation had split the Democratic National Front, from which Bratianu and Maniu had withdrawn. General Radescu's government, which had been gradually deprived of its powers, had proved powerless to prevent the spontaneous partition and redistribution of country estates, the collapse of the administration and the assumption of direct control of immense areas by the Red armies. Vyshinsky came and put the government out of its misery. He immediately went to the royal palace outside which Soviet armoured cars were carrying out manoeuvres, while other Russian units were disarming the Romanian security forces. King Michael put up a show of resistance and Vyshinsky gave him twenty-four hours to dismiss Radescu and replace him by Petru Groza, who belonged, indeed, to a wealthy bourgeois family but who hastened to give the Ministry of the Interior to a Communist, thus causing a wave of arrests.

Representations by London and Washington made no difference to this situation. Roosevelt suggested to Stalin forming a tripartite commission with the task of implementing in Romania the decision which had been taken unanimously at Yalta to allow each liberated people freely to choose its own institutions. On March 17, Stalin rejected the suggestion outright, on the pretext of military necessity.

VI CHURCHILL'S ANXIETIES AND PROPOSALS

Churchill, for his part, had carried out his policy in Greece and installed men of his own choice. The elections of March 31, 1945 were supervised by British and American observers; fifty-four per cent of the votes went to the monarchists. The resulting royalist government, led by Tsaldaris, held a referendum: out of 1,500,000 votes cast, 1,162,000 were in favour of the monarchy. But the National Liberation Front (EAM) refused to accept this popular verdict and came out against the return of King George; it was determined to prevent it by force if necessary.

As far as the behaviour of the USSR was concerned, Churchill had expressed his anxiety even before Yalta. Whereas he had thought that the Red Army would be exhausted and stop once their national territory had been liberated, there they were advancing on Berlin, Vienna and Prague. For the British Premier, who was heir to a long diplomatic tradition of striking a balance of power in Europe, the war was beginning to take on a different look; the USSR was becoming a potential enemy. On the military plane, the advance westwards had to be stopped by a British and American counter-advance as far eastwards as possible; he urged Eisenhower to take action to achieve this. On the political plane he wrote to Roosevelt 'that all the great problems causing a division between Western and Eastern Europe must be settled before the armies of the democracies dissolve. I do not see why we should put on sack-cloth and ashes if by a mass surrender in the west we can reach the Elbe, or even beyond.' For him, the gloomy outlook ahead made it important to make an immediate return to the schemes which the British had always been advocating: to push on northwards as fast as possible, first of all in order to prevent the shores of the North Sea, Denmark and Norway from being taken over by the Russians and secondly and above all so that the British and Americans could be the first to enter Berlin, in order, wrote Churchill to Roosevelt on April 5, 'to show the Russians that there are limits to the amount of insults we can stand'. In the south, where the Russians were advancing more slowly through the wooded mountains of Slovakia, it was necessary to reach Prague before them 'so that Czechoslovakia would not follow the example of Yugoslavia', and also in order to be on an equal footing with them in Austria, since it was now impossible to prevent them from winning the race to Vienna.

Churchill was not absolutely convinced that Soviet policy would take a completely hostile turn; but he considered that the only way to prevent this was for the British and Americans to make a firm stand; the best way to maintain the alliance of the Big Three on an equal footing was for the Allied armies to advance as far as possible into eastern Europe. 'If the Red Army entered Vienna and Berlin at the same time,' he said, 'it would be convinced that it had played an overwhelming role in the joint victory and this would create great difficulties for the future.'

Churchill appealed once more to Roosevelt: 'Our friendship is the rock on which the future of the world will be built.' But the American President by this time was in the last stages of his long illness; a great empty space had appeared in the White House which could not be filled by the slowly dying Hopkins or the inexperienced Truman; Roosevelt was no longer able and Truman did not know how. In the circumstances, the State Department was anxious above all to avoid a showdown with the Russians. It was the military men – that is to say Eisenhower, covered by Marshall, who was speaking on behalf of the President – who replied as military men to the political proposals and anxiety of Churchill.

While recognising that Berlin was 'the symbol of what remained of German power' and that there was nothing in their agreements with the Russians to prevent the British and Americans from trying to get there first, Eisenhower replied to Churchill that 'Berlin in itself was no longer an objective of primary importance'. Bradley thought that an advance on Berlin from the Elbe would cost him a hundred thousand lives and that his lines were too extended for the operation not to offer risks. The American point of view was put forward very decisively by Marshall, on behalf of Roosevelt: 'Our only aim must be to achieve a rapid and complete victory.'

For that purpose Eisenhower considered that it was necessary to join hands with the Russians as soon as possible in order to prevent the German armies from re-grouping. In addition, it was important to seize the areas where winter might help to protract the struggle, namely in Norway and above all in Austria, where there were some signs that Hitler was preparing his last stronghold for a stiff German resistance. The main British and American advance therefore took place not towards Berlin, but further to the south, towards Leipzig and Dresden, where the Russians were nearest, taking advantage of the narrower rivers; after that two related thrusts would be launched; in the north towards the Baltic and in the south towards the Tyrol. At the end of March, without more ado, Eisenhower communicated his plans to Stalin, as Commander-in-Chief to Commander-in-Chief, as if Stalin had not been in addition the political leader of the USSR.

Anglo-American exchange of opinions was turning into a series of monologues. Churchill realised the fact and with his amazing adaptability he apparently submitted to events which he was now no longer in a position to control. He was well aware that Britain could not do much on her own, without the support of the USA; moreover, the British Commonwealth was providing only a quarter of the forces invading Germany. Roosevelt's death had put an end once and for all to the relationship of friendship and trust which in spite of the discrepancy between their forces, had enabled Britain so often to put her point of view to the USA and even to impose it on her. On April 19, Churchill gave up the idea of capturing Berlin: "The Russians have two million five hundred thousand soldiers in the sector and the Americans have only twenty-five divisions on a huge front.' He nevertheless still thought it possible to outpace them in the direction of Lübeck in the north and Prague and Linz in the south. But in actual fact Eisenhower was from now on free to act as he chose, and his views had not changed.

VII THE BATTLE OF BERLIN

It is probable that the steps taken by Churchill, or at least what they knew of them, confirmed the Russians' fear that the British and Americans wanted to be the first to reach Berlin. Soviet historians of 'the great patriotic war' even allege that the Germans were prepared to open their defences to the British and American armies to enable them to forestall the Russians in their capital, even though they were nearly 190 miles away and the Red Army only about 45. There is no doubt in these circumstances that the Russians were making the capture of Berlin their chief objective and that they speeded up their operations in order to win the race against their allies. But the first requirement for success was for Zhukov's right flank to be protected against German counter-offensives from Pomerania. At the beginning of March Rokossovski (second Byelorussian front) reached Közlin on the Baltic. Then on March 19 Zhukov (first Byelorussian front) also arrived on the Baltic at Kolberg; the Germans had to evacuate part of their troops to the left bank of the Oder by sea. The Russians then set about conquering the mouth of the Vistula; on March 28, Gdynia was captured with the battleship *Gneisenau*; on March 30, Danzig fell. Further to the north Vassilevski (third Byelorussian front) reduced the German pockets of resistance in Brandenburg; Koenigsberg fell on April 10.

All the encircled positions which were pinning down Soviet forces were stormed one after another: Poznan, Graudenz and Glogau; only Breslau resisted until May 7. At the same time Zhukov extended the Küstrin bridgehead on the left bank of the Oder, which was the springboard for the crucial offensive.

At the end of March the attack on Berlin was finally ready to be launched. Zhukov was given command of the operation. South of Berlin Koniev was to reach the Elbe in the direction of Dresden; in the north, Rokossovski was to protect Zhukov and then swoop down on Stettin and beyond. D-Day was fixed for April 16.

In all, the Red Army were deploying two million men, 41,000 guns, 6,300 tanks and 5,000 aircraft on a 250-mile front. But the stronghold of Berlin covered an area of some 350 square miles; the *U-Bahn* and other underground tunnels and bridges gave the defenders great possibilities of manoeuvre; blocks of houses, bridges and canals formed natural pockets of resistance. In the relative lull, which was really the eve of battle, from March 12 to April 10, Hitler had grouped two armies on the Oder under General Heinrici and a considerable reserve force between Frankfurt and Berlin. Once again Guderian was in disgrace, and had been replaced by Krebs. Once again Hitler forbade any retreat; the order was: save Berlin and the enemy shall be crushed. The moment had come for the Führer to carry out the decision which he had expressed as early as November 1939: 'I will never surrender.' But Hitler was now no more than a shadow of his former self; he had lost the use of his right arm and his sense of balance; he was in a general state of physical decay; his body was kept going only by dint of pills and hypodermic injections of strychnine and hormones – as many as six a day. Gerhard Bolt, one of Guderian's aide-de-camps who had seen him in April 1945 described his hesitant walk, his bent body, his flaccid handshake, his anguished expression and his obvious senility. Germany's Führer had reached the point of exhaustion to which he had condemned his own people.

Soviet superiority was beyond dispute; on the lines of their intended thrust, respectively twenty-seven and twenty-two miles long, Zhukov and Koniev had concentrated 7,080 and 7,170 guns respectively. The attack began on April 12 at Küstrin and on the Neisse; it was checked for one day and then began again on the 13th. On April 16 the Berlin sky was darkened by clouds of Stormoviks. On April 19 its encirclement began. On the 22nd Zhukov's and Koniev's troops joined hands both to the east and to the west of the city, which was now completely surrounded. Voronov then set up a circle of 25,000 guns, nearly 1,000 to the mile, and hurled 25,000 tons of shells on to the city. On several occasions the Germans, who fought savagely to the bitter end, broke out of the encirclement but the Russians closed it up again. On April 29, the street-battle began; the Russians had built a whole armoury of special equipment – for example, tanks with ladders for forcing barricades. One by one the blocks of houses were captured; the Soviet Red Star was hoisted over the Brandenburg Gate.

Hitler kept his oath: 'I shall not under any circumstances survive my people's defeat.' On April 30, when he now ruled over only the few square yards of his underground bunker, the Führer put a bullet through his head and committed suicide together with Eva Braun, his constant companion, whom he had married; according to his wishes, both their bodies were burnt; the Russians were only 500 yards away. Goebbels did the same, after poisoning his wife and six children! At the moment of his death Hitler was virtually alone, abandoned by all his henchmen from happier days: Keitel, Jodl, Himmler, Ribbentrop and Speer.

On May 2 General Weidling handed over to Chuikov, who had defended Stalingrad, the last 70,000 defenders of Berlin. By this time all the German fronts had collapsed.

VIII THE END OF THE FIGHTING IN ITALY

In the middle of January 1945 the Germans had tried to sound out the British and Americans in order to separate them from the Russians; to this end Ribbentrop had sent delegates to Berne and Stockholm, but without success. In February 1945 a fresh attempt was made; the ss General Wolff made contact with the American secret services in Switzerland and then with the headquarters of Alexander, Wilson's successor in Italy. The British and Americans had not rejected these overtures which might have brought fighting in the peninsula to an end more quickly. But they demanded an unconditional surrender, as they informed the Russians on March 12. Stalin reacted very sharply; Molotov demanded an immediate end to the talks and a promise from the British never to restart them. In the end, since Wolff had probably been disowned by Himmler, and Kesselring, who was rather in favour of the talks, was replaced by von Vietinghoff, the contacts were broken off.

Nevertheless Stalin continued to show that he was not pleased. His greatest fear of all was obviously of a limited German surrender in the west, for this would have been a sort of replica of the German-Soviet pact. He accused his partners – saying that he knew all about it – of having negotiated with Kesselring for a rapid advance eastwards in exchange for concessions to Germany, once peace came.

For once Roosevelt was indignant that he could have been credited with such dark designs; his correspondence with Stalin took on an unusually sharp tone; he complained of having been 'basely wronged'; he stated his conviction that a break between the Russians and the Americans at this juncture would be 'an historic tragedy'. Stalin then calmed down and the incident had no serious consequences. On the contrary, one of Roosevelt's last messages to Churchill on April 12 reaffirmed the United States President's desire 'to minimise the Soviet problem as a whole because most of the day-to-day difficulties could be settled.' His successor, Truman, went even further and considered that the British and Americans must keep their promises to the Russians, even if the Russians did not keep theirs.

The only result of the incident was to delay the Allied offensive in Italy. The Allies had kept only twenty-three divisions on this minor front, the most hybrid collection imaginable – Americans, British and Commonwealth troops, Poles, Brazilians, Jews and Italians. Opposing them were

German troops of almost equal strength – including the Italians from Salo – but they were short of petrol and they were fighting with their backs to the Po. Alexander and Clark decided to break through along the Adriatic in the direction of Ferrara, between two flooded zones.

The offensive was launched on April 9; then on April 14 the Fifth Army attacked in the direction of Bologna. On the 20th the German withdrawal began; on the 23rd the Allies crossed the Po. At the same time there was a general uprising of the Italian partisans which was particularly effective in the cities. They had seized control in Milan and Venice; in Genoa they captured the 4,000 men in the garrison. For their part the Yugoslav partisans had occupied Klagenfurt, Zagreb, Split and Zadar and were advancing towards Trieste – which Tito had his eye on but which the British and Americans had promised to the Italians.

On April 24, Wolff reappeared in Switzerland, this time with full negotiating powers. Churchill informed Stalin, asked him to send representatives and stipulated that Alexander would receive an unconditional surrender from the enemy of an exclusively military nature. On April 29, when Hitler was still alive, the surrender was signed – not without some squabbling between Kesselring and von Vietinghoff who threatened each other with arrest. The surrender covered Carinthia, the Vorarlberg, the Tyrol, Salzburg and Italy as far as the Isonzo.

IX THE END OF THE FIGHTING IN GERMANY

Contrary to all logic the Germans had not evacuated the Ruhr. On March 31, Eisenhower sent out an appeal to Model 'to put an end to the butchery'; since Model did not reply, the Ruhr was hemmed in by the Allied Air Force, and systematically pounded with bombs. Model vainly tried to break out of the ring of fire; on April 14, the pocket in which he was enclosed was cut in two; on April 18, the whole garrison surrendered – 320,000 prisoners, of whom thirty were generals; Model committed suicide.

By this time, the British and Americans had not encountered any organised resistance for the last ten days and were advancing more quickly than the Russians, against whom the German soldiers were continuing to fight stubbornly. But Eisenhower, who was completely covered by Marshall – the American military authorities were left to their own devices as a result of the gap left in the White House by Roosevelt's death – was concerned solely with ensuring to the best of his ability that they should join up with the Russians. He continued to communicate his plans to Stalin – but Stalin did not do the same for him. Eisenhower suggested that the armies should meet on the middle Elbe; he consequently gave Bradley priority for an advance across the centre of Germany, the operational argument being that the rivers were less wide and would be more easily crossed. Bradley therefore found himself in command of the Ninth Army, which had been taken away from Montgomery, and the Fifteenth Army which had been made available after the surrender of the Ruhr. The advance in the north and the south of Germany took second place to joining hands with the Red Army.

However, the British Second Army was pushing forward strongly towards Lüneberg, Hamburg and Bremen; on April 5, it crossed the Weser, on the 19th it reached the Elbe and on the 26th, Bremen; that same day a bridgehead was established on the Elbe; on May 1, Hamburg surrendered; on May 2 it was Lübeck's turn and on May 3 the British Army crossed the Kiel canal.

During this time the Canadian First Army had advanced between the Weser and Holland; on April 16 Groningen was captured. But the Germans blew up the dikes on the Zuyder Zee; Holland was cut off and experienced an unprecedented famine – people were dying in thousands. The Allies then entered into talks with Seiss Inquart, the Reich's High Commissioner; on April 28 a truce was agreed upon, enabling supply convoys to arrive.

In the centre Bradley and his Americans, advancing along the motorways, were going even faster, raking in prisoners while leaving behind a few pockets of resistance, in particular in the Harz. On April 10, Simpson captured Hanover; on the 13th he reached the Elbe but was unable to cross it; on the 18th he seized Magdeburg and joined hands with Hodges who had advanced seventy-five miles in five days. On April 14, Patton had entered Leipzig.

On April 25, the most spectacular event of the war occurred. At Torgau on the Mulde elements of the American Third Army met some Russians; on both sides cameras recorded for posterity a perfectly genuine display of joy and friendship. Every precaution had been taken to avoid incidents, since the language difference made it impossible to use radio – aircraft had already been firing on each other; flight lines were fixed, a system of identification was adopted and the dividing-line for the troops on the field was clearly marked out. For the American soldiers the event meant that the war was over and that they would soon be able to return home. The Russians had taken care to stipulate that they intended to take charge of mopping-up on the right bank of the Elbe and the banks of the Voltava, that is to say that they were reckoning on liberating Prague; on April 30 Eisenhower replied to them that he took note of the fact.

In the south, Patch had advanced between the Main and the Neckar, captured Nuremberg on April 19 and crossed the Danube on the 25th; on

May 2 Munich fell and on May 4 Leclerc was able to hoist over Hitler's Eagle's Nest in Berchtesgaden the flag which he had brought back from Kufra. Meanwhile, Delattre had advanced into the Black Forest, where he encircled 40,000 Waffen ss; Béthouart had reached the Swiss frontier at Schaffhausen and entered the Vorarlberg; Montsabert had surrounded Stuttgart, thus sparking off a major Franco-American incident, for the city was in the Americans' operational zone. Eisenhower asked the French to evacuate it; de Gaulle's reply was curt and uncompromising; at the same moment, in the Alps the French had entered the Aosta valley and refused to leave, despite the orders of Alexander and the protests of the Italians. 'De Gaulle showed himself to be over-sensitive and extraordinarily obstinate on what seemed to us minor points,' wrote Eisenhower; in order to make the French give in they had to be threatened with having their food supplies cut off.

However, the event most pregnant in consequences had occurred in Bohemia. On May 4, the American Third Army was making ready to attack Pilsen, while the Russians were still in Moravska Ostrava and Brno; the Americans were within some sixty miles of Prague; the Russians were more than 100 miles away; the Russians asked their allies not to go beyond Pilsen; on his own initiative Eisenhower agreed, again covered by Marshall who did not want to 'shed blood for political motives'; Truman himself gave his approval; Churchill had protested to the President, and then again on May 7 to the Commander-in-Chief, but in vain; the American troops halted and then turned back.

A few days previously the Czechs had formed a National Council with Albert Prazak as president; it was half recognised by the occupation authorities. On May 5 an insurrection broke out; the Communist party took control of it; barricades went up all over Prague. The Germans set about repressing the revolt and between the 5th and the 8th they had very little trouble in dealing with the insurgents who had been left to fight all alone. It was only on May 8 – after the general armistice – that General Schoerner, the last of the Nazis still to be fighting – signed the document arranging for his troops' withdrawal. It was not until the 9th that the Red Army entered the city; thus the Russians completed the occupation of Czechoslovakia which the Americans had left in their hands. By this time the German surrender had become effective everywhere.

X THE GERMAN SURRENDER

In March and April the Germans had again begun to make approaches to the western powers through their ambassador in Stockholm and then unexpectedly by Himmler in person. On April 24, this sinister individual had informed Count Bernadotte that he was ready to surrender in the west, adding that he was in no way disposed to do the same in the east, for 'he still remained the sworn enemy of Communism'; the fate of those detained in concentration camps served as a basis for the negotiations, since Himmler had contemplated and perhaps even ordered that they should be totally exterminated. The British and American governments replied that they would accept nothing but an unconditional surrender on all fronts. Churchill informed Stalin, who for once proved satisfied.

In the north of Europe Marshal Busch, the commander in Norway, had made it known that General Lindemann, the commander in Denmark, and he were ready to surrender when the Allies reached the Baltic – while the Swedish general staff were examining the possibility of intervening in these two countries. On May 3, Admiral von Friedeburg suggested to Montgomery the idea of accepting the surrender of three armies which were fighting against the Russians; Montgomery refused. Thus the Wehrmacht was falling apart on all sides, but wherever possible on the side of the British and Americans. However, there was still a central authority, since Hitler had made Admiral Doenitz his successor; when the Admiral learned that he had been appointed he quickly surveyed the situation and realised that there was obviously no way out – even although on May 7 German units were still making bayonet charges shouting 'Heil Hitler'.

While army group commanders were urging him to allow them to surrender, Doenitz's only objective now was to enable as many German soldiers and civilians as possible who were fleeing from the Red Army to be captured by the British and Americans. Eisenhower had allowed his deputies to accept the surrender only of the German forces with whom they were in contact. In these circumstances, the armies in Denmark, Holland and the Friesian Isles surrendered to Montgomery on May 4. On May 5 Kesselring surrendered to Devers near Munich, Brandenberger to the Americans and French at Innsbruck and Lohr to Alexander.

That same day Marshal Keitel gave orders to offer no further resistance in the west, while Doenitz dissolved the Werwolf, which was theoretically in charge of guerrilla activity, and forbade acts of sabotage. However, more than a million Germans had been made prisoner in Italy and in Germany $2\frac{1}{2}$ million had been captured by the British, French and Americans in only a few days. Many of them were men who had been fighting on the Russian front.

On May 5, Doenitz had sent Admiral von Friedeburg to General Eisenhower's headquarters in Rheims, hoping to gain a little time. Eisenhower immediately told him that he would accept only a general surrender on all fronts and he informed the Russians of the fact. They replied that even if this was not the case Doenitz's offer should be rejected.

Doenitz then sent General Jodl to explain to Eisenhower that a surrender on all fronts was not desirable. Eisenhower threatened to drive the German civilians and soldiers who were fleeing from the Red Army back eastwards. Jodl submitted and Doenitz grudgingly gave in. After some difficulty in finding and drawing up a text which had in fact been ready since the end of April, at 2 a.m. on May 7 in Rheims, Jodl signed the act of surrender on all fronts, on behalf of the German high command.

Eisenhower had kept the Soviets informed and had asked them if they wanted any particular arrangement. The Soviets said that Zhukov would receive the German surrender in Berlin the next day. On reflection, Eisenhower saw no point in beginning the signing ceremony all over again and sent his deputy Tedder as a delegate. At about midnight, after several hours of discussion between the Allies to decide in what capacity and in what way Spaatz and Delattre would sign on behalf of the Americans and French, Keitel set Germany's signature on the document which sealed her defeat.

Other partial surrenders took place some time later, because of the remoteness or isolation of the troops. In Norway, while Terboven and several Nazi leaders committed suicide, 300,000 to 400,000 men who had been virtually wasted throughout the war surrendered on May 8. In Courland, delegates from the National Committee of Free Germany were brought in by motor-boat on May 9; General Hilpert took advantage of the breathing-space to evacuate 25,000 men – which was more difficult than he had expected, since Sweden had not supplied the coal which she had promised. The Heligoland garrison did not surrender until May 11.

In the west, the Dunkirk pocket which had been cut off by widespread flooding and by-passed by the French, was not liberated until the armistice. On the other hand, in Royan the FFI under General Larminat had finished mopping up the pocket there and had captured the island of Oléron. On May 9 the ports of La Pallice, La Rochelle and Rochefort had been handed over by the occupiers; the next day it was the turn of Lorient and St-Nazaire; in the islands the garrisons gave themselves up to their own French prisoners. It was also on May 9 that the 22,000 soldiers in the Channel Islands ceased being occupiers and became captives instead.

Thus 'the strange alliance', formed under the pressure of circumstances and strengthened by Hitler, although it had never asserted itself in really concerted action, had held good to the last, thanks to the stubbornness of the Germans and in spite of the cracks which had been appearing in it since Yalta. Neither the vicissitudes of war nor differences of opinion nor enemy operations had succeeded in breaking it up. Was it going to continue when peace came, now that Roosevelt, the man chiefly responsible for instigating it, was dead? Was there not a risk that Germany would become a bone of contention among its members? It is true that one last enemy still remained to be beaten – Japan. In order to try to settle the controversial issues and prepare for victory in the Pacific the Big Three met for the last time, in Potsdam.

CHAPTER 4

The Potsdam Conference

ALTHOUGH the Big Three had depicted the Yalta Conference as representing a climax of friendship and trust, relations between them had considerably deteriorated since then. What were the reasons for this and is it possible to assign responsibility for it?

Churchill's distrust of the USSR was plainly in some ways inherent and in any event already existed before Stalin's suspicious policies could have aggravated it further. But since the Normandy landing, Britain's importance in the coalition had greatly diminished and her impetuous and much-admired leader now had only a semblance of equality of power and decision with his partners. Both in strategy and diplomacy, it was Roosevelt's opinions which had carried the day in the Anglo-American alliance; whether he wanted to or not, Churchill had had to resign himself to endorsing them: relations between the 'Big Powers' were therefore now becoming increasingly nothing but a dialogue between the USSR and the United States.

Roosevelt cannot be held responsible for the new atmosphere which arose after Yalta. Although it is probable that he had sometimes been sorely disappointed, he had overcome his disappointments and had not changed his opinions. His death, however, had put an end to his personal influence which had acted as a sort of charm and there was nothing to replace it. Although his less sophisticated successor, Truman, had listened more readily to the Cassandras of the White House – Harriman, Deane and Leahy above all – even to the extent of cancelling the USSR's lend-lease privileges a few hours after the signing of the armistice[1] – he had nevertheless not turned his predecessor's goodwill towards the USSR into systematic hostility. The hints of strain or failure to maintain agreements did not come from his side.

The same obviously cannot be said for Stalin. After Yalta, he had looked after the interests of the USSR by going against virtually all the agreements and even commitments which he had approved of or endorsed. What is surprising is that this had surprised the British and Americans. Yet it was obvious that although they had all used the same words, they did not all

---

1. As a result of Stalin's energetic protests, the measure was explained away as a mistake and withdrawn.

understand them in the same way. As regards the smaller powers, had Stalin not suggested that they should support 'the political leaders who had taken an active part in the struggle against the German invaders'? Was this not admitting that he deliberately intended not to leave them the freedom to choose their own régime and government? Stalin had no idea of a western-type democracy based on free consultation with the people – and he said that he felt nothing but scorn for it. Besides, how could one suppose that the man who held the people of the USSR tightly in his iron grasp and refused to grant them any freedom, might behave any differently towards non-Soviet peoples whose territory had been conquered by the Red Army and who in addition had taken part in Hitler's anti-Bolshevik crusade? Surely they deserved to be punished, at least at the start? Just as he recognised unreservedly his partners' right to behave as they wished in their zones of occupation or influence, so Stalin had not the slightest doubts about his power to act exactly as he wanted in his zones. Whether he was motivated by a feeling of nationalism rooted deep in Russian history or by a justifiable distrust of Germany and a desire for revenge or by the wish to impose his conception of Communism on western Europe, or by all these reasons put together, Stalin was determined to be Stalin both inside and outside the USSR. A tragic mistrust had grown up between him and his partners, although fortunately, and thanks above all to Roosevelt, this did not have any serious consequences until after the war. Perhaps both sides had in fact been victims of mutual ignorance and of the mistakes to which it gave rise. In these circumstances the slightest dispute could not fail to become embittered.

I MATTERS OF DISPUTE

Some concerned Germany, which was a new and worrying factor; others were concerned with USSR policy in the territories controlled by the Red Army; the most serious of all, however, was still Poland.

In Germany, Admiral Doenitz had asked on May 5 for a sort of free enclave to be left on the Danish frontier so that his government and general staff could take their decisions with a semblance of independence; Doenitz had, strangely enough, referred to the precedent of the Vichy régime and the semi-freedom which it had been granted. Although Montgomery categorically rejected this request, he had in actual fact satisfied it: British troops had occupied the area around Flensburg but not the town itself, where Doenitz was. What is more, the admiral and his officers kept their weapons and still remained in command of a few groups of soldiers and sailors even after the total surrender of the Wehrmacht.

This method of procedure, which may have been dictated solely by courtesy but more probably by the desire to bring about the surrender as quickly as possible by making the fullest use of the authority enjoyed by Hitler's successor, was no longer justifiable after May 9. The Americans were surprised and sent Murphy to see Doenitz. The Russians at once suspected their allies of hatching a plot, since it was Murphy who had thought up or carried out the idea of using Darlan in Algiers. On May 22, the British put an end to the incident by arresting Doenitz, Admiral von Friedeburg and Jodl; von Friedeburg, who was one of the signatories of the act of surrender in Rheims, committed suicide as a result.

Had Churchill something in the back of his mind? It would seem so in the light of his insistent suggestion to Truman that they should check the Soviet thrust in the west.

Otherwise [he wrote to Eden on May 4] there will be no hope of achieving a satisfactory result and very little of avoiding a third world war. It would be one of the blackest events in history ... without precedent ... and completely unforeseen by the Allies ... if the Russian frontier started from the North Cape, crossed the Baltic east of Lübeck, cut across the whole breadth of Germany and extended from Czechoslovakia and the Isonzo.

How could this disaster be prevented? By negotiating knock for knock? Partly at Churchill's instigation and partly for military reasons Eisenhower had agreed that no line of contact with the Russians should be marked out in advance: both fronts would be free to shift as the fighting required; afterwards the necessary adjustments would be made, in keeping with the boundaries of the occupation zones which had been decided on at Yalta – boundaries, moreover, about which Churchill now began to make reservations, which was perhaps a hint that he was going to ask for them to be revised. Thus the Anglo-American armies had considerably overflowed into part of the future Soviet occupation zone.

Churchill intended that it should not be the military alone who should decide that the Anglo-American troops should return to their own zones. As early as April 27 he had informed Stalin, calling him 'my dear friend', that he considered it as a matter for the governments; but on May 2, Stalin had pretended not to understand. On May 5, the Polish question seemed to have reached a complete deadlock; it was Churchill's attitude, said Stalin, which made it impossible to reach an agreement. On May 6, Churchill suggested to Truman: 'We must not move from the positions which our armies have already occupied, or are in the process of occupying in Yugoslavia, Czechoslovakia and Austria, on the main American front in the centre and on the British front as far as Lübeck, including Denmark. Afterwards we must show the Soviets exactly what we have the power to grant or refuse them.' And Churchill was already envisaging Soviet concessions in Poland, on the Danube and in the Balkans in exchange for benefits in the Black Sea and in the Baltic.

On May 12, Churchill gave to the world the famous expression: 'An iron curtain has fallen on the Soviet front', and he drew the conclusion 'that it is vital to reach an agreement with the Russians before we fatally weaken our armies or withdraw them to the occupation zones'. But Truman did not follow his ally's recommendations. On June 21, he suggested to Stalin that the American withdrawal should begin without more ado. On July 1, hundreds of thousands of German refugees followed the British and American troops who evacuated Thuringia, Saxony and Mecklenburg. On the other hand, on July 3, the British and Americans established themselves in Berlin; the Russians first of all refused to hand over their powers to them and to give up premises in the sectors which they were to occupy; they had to take them over at night and almost by force; the French arrived a few days later and on July 11 the quadripartite Allied government of Berlin came into being. The fact that they were established in Berlin gave the British and Americans a bargaining counter; but everywhere else in central Europe the dice were loaded in favour of the USSR.

In Czechoslovakia, which before the war had been the most liberal democracy in Europe, the Communists held eight ministerial posts – among them the Ministry of the Interior and the Ministry of Information – in the government under the presidency of the Socialist Fierlinger, who was in favour of amalgamating his party with the Communist party.

In Austria the USSR had put the old Socialist, Renner, the former Chancellor, in power; in his government the Communists also held the key post of Minister of the Interior. As in Berlin, the Russians, under various pretexts, were opposed to the western powers' sending any missions; but once again Stalin eventually gave in and the Quadripartite Interallied Commission was set up. But the Russians supported the Yugoslav demands and they were occupying the richest part of Austria; they regarded it as German land, which meant that its wealth would be war booty for them to take.

In Italy Tito was hoping to keep Trieste, which his supporters had entered at the same time as the New Zealanders, since when each had settled himself in his own positions. However, in the Julian Veneto the Yugoslavs were behaving as if they were in an annexed country, changing the names of the villages and expelling eminent Italians. By doing this Tito was breaking the interallied agreement which in January 1945 he had at first endorsed, whereby the administration of all Italian territory was put in the hands of the Allied military command. Truman sent an actual ultimatum to Tito – even though the affair took place in a part of the world which the British regarded as their sphere; Tito submitted, or at least pretended to.

All these quarrels did not, after all, lead to a break. Stalin, who had been satisfied in Poland, Czechoslovakia and Austria, probably put pressure on Tito, while at the same time supporting his demands. A sign that a new era was approaching was that the antagonism between the British and Russians which Roosevelt had been so much afraid of was turning into a confrontation between Russia and America and that relations remained strained even though a working agreement was beginning to be achieved. The Polish problem was not developing in a way likely to straighten matters out.

II THE POLISH PROBLEM

Poland had not been included when, in the autumn of 1944, Churchill and Stalin had sat at a table in Moscow and divided Europe up into zones of influence. The Big Three had only promised to set up a provisional representative government which would proceed to hold free elections. The first stage of the Polish problem therefore merely amounted to amalgamating the exiled government in London with the Lublin Committee; the fate of Poland would obviously depend on the relative proportions of these two components.

In fact, the Russians had done everything within their power to ensure a comfortable majority for their protégés, whereas the latter most certainly did not represent more than a tiny minority of the Polish population. Churchill for his part had used all his weight to persuade Mikolajczyk to accept the Yalta decisions and he had succeeded in extracting a statement from him 'that a close and lasting friendship with Russia should form the keystone of Polish politics'. It quickly became plain that Stalin's attitude would not be altered by a few reassuring statements from people whom he regarded as his inveterate enemies. He seemed to have persuaded himself of two things, of which he remained firmly convinced: that it was absolutely necessary for the USSR to have as neighbour a Poland which was to some extent her vassal and that, apart from a few Communists, the Polish nation could only be hostile to the USSR.

On the one hand Stalin was going to stand out strongly against any foreign intrusion in Poland, which from now on was regarded as strictly his sphere and his alone. The names of the members of the London government suggested by his allies were challenged by him as being guilty of anti-Sovietism. He was even opposed to sending British and American observers to Warsaw on the pretext that 'the Poles would see this as an insult to their national dignity'; the first result of this was that there was delay in repatriating the Wehrmacht's prisoners of war who had been freed by the Red Army – French and Yugoslavs particularly.

At the same time the Lublin Committee's authority was reinforced by its protector both inside and outside the country. Stalin summoned leaders of the Secret Army and of the non-Communist Polish parties to Moscow; he gave them safe-conducts; they accepted his invitation, confidently expecting that their journey boded well for the forming of a new and acceptable Polish government. No sooner had they arrived in Moscow than the unfortunate men were accused of acts of hostility to the Red Army, imprisoned, tried by a Soviet military tribunal and sentenced to years of imprisonment. With a treachery that would not have disgraced a Tartar Khan, Stalin had simply lured them into a trap. Having thus rid the Lublin Committee of its opponents, he wanted to make it the sole representative of Poland at the San Francisco Conference, at which the United Nations Organisation was to take shape.

Churchill and Roosevelt had been stupefied by their partner's behaviour; but the American President at first refused to make any energetic protest; the British Premier was therefore reduced to appealing to Stalin's better feelings; he cabled to him that the future of the world was being built 'on the rock of their friendship'; he reminded him that he had been the first to accept the Curzon line as the USSR frontier in the west; he beseeched him 'not to strike a fatal blow against the hand of friendship which he was holding out to him, with an eye to assuming world control'. This sort of language was too much out of keeping with Churchill's temperament not to be regarded by Stalin as an admission of great weakness; he stuck to his guns and handed back to the British and Americans the responsibilities which they were trying to load on to him.

Roosevelt then broke his silence. At the end of March he addressed himself directly to Stalin, made no secret of the fact that he was worried and took refuge behind American public opinion which was very alarmed and which 'no government action could change' – a statement which had very little chance of being understood by a head of state who paid so little heed to the reactions of his own people. However, although Stalin did not give ground on essentials, Roosevelt's reaction did seem to make an impression on him; his reply was even rather encouraging, since he agreed, on certain conditions, that Mikolajczyk should come and see him in Moscow. But Roosevelt died before he was able to turn this ray of hope into a reality.

Truman quickly adopted a tougher tone. He curtly told Molotov that 'for the American people the Polish question had become the symbol of the future development of international relations'. The Russian reaction was one of violent protest. Stalin replied that he would accept in the Polish government only people 'who had given proof of their friendship towards the USSR' – which apparently excluded the whole of the London government. So each side remained obstinately deaf to the other; Churchill could not see any way out except by another meeting of the Big Three 'before the American Armies left Europe; otherwise there was no hope of achieving a satisfactory result and very little of avoiding a third world war'. But could 'the spirit of Yalta' be revived?

III THE POTSDAM CONFERENCE – THE POLISH PROBLEM

On July 17, 1945, the Big Three therefore met at Potsdam, in the former summer residence of the Crown Prince. The situation was no longer the same as at Yalta; the war was over in Europe and the British and Americans no longer needed to be so careful in their handling of the USSR; but it was still going on in Asia, where they did need her; moreover, at Yalta the USSR had promised to join in three months after the German surrender; the time was therefore nearly due.

In these circumstances the balance of power in Europe was all the more favourable to Stalin because there were numerous indications that the Americans wanted to repatriate their armies as quickly as possible. As early as May 7 Eisenhower had cabled to the joint general staff that 'his task was fully accomplished'. When he was unexpectedly called on to appear before several thousand American soldiers and did not quite know what to say to them, he had roused their enthusiasm by promising to have them back home in half the time by doubling the number of passengers on each boat – with part of them on deck and the rest below. How could one avoid the conclusion that America was sinking back into her original isolationism from which Roosevelt had had such difficulty in temporarily rousing her? The British would certainly not be taking her place. In the very middle of the conference and, it seems, to the absolute amazement of Stalin, to whom there was no risk of such a thing happening, Churchill was defeated in the elections and replaced as Prime Minister to represent Britain by his old Labour opponent, Clement Attlee. True, Attlee knew more about the problems involved than Truman did when Roosevelt died; but he was far from possessing his predecessor's pugnacity – Churchill said of him that he was 'a sheep in sheep's clothing'. Above all, the real meaning of the Labour victory was that the British people were very weary, which was yet another indication of Britain's weakness.

It is true that the Americans had a formidable weapon for exerting pressure on the USSR: on the very day on which the conference opened, Truman learned that the atom bomb had just been added to the American arsenal of weapons. But despite the fact that he regarded his Soviet companion from now on as a possible opponent, far from trying to make him more amenable by brandishing this terrible weapon as a possible threat,

Truman confined himself to mentioning it to him 'incidentally', without dwelling on it. 'The United States,' he said simply, 'possessed an extraordinarily powerful weapon.' Had Stalin been told by his intelligence sources – it is possible that he had some even among the team of atomic scientists working in the United States – or did he underestimate the importance of the information? He replied only by expressing the hope that good use would be made of the new weapon against Japan. And no more was said about it.

The Soviets were therefore filling up their own the huge power vacuum which had been left in Europe by the collapse of Hitler's dreams. Certainly France was in no position to provide a counter-balance – quite the contrary, for General de Gaulle was playing the card of Soviet friendship in order to stand up to the dominance of the British and Americans, which bitter experience had taught him could be all too heavy. In these circumstances, what else should Stalin do but lay down the law and be prepared, if he did not obtain complete satisfaction, to create a *de facto* situation which would be irreversible and which his partners would one day be reluctantly forced to accept?

So it was with Poland. The discussion as to where her western frontier was to lie – on the western or the eastern Neisse – which had not been settled at Yalta, soon turned out to be purely a matter of form at Potsdam. Stalin revealed that 'he had not been able to prevent the Poles from taking over the administration of the area up to the western Neisse'. Truman and Churchill vainly protested that a fifth occupation zone had thus been set up and Churchill deplored the fact that Germany was deprived of her 'source of wheat'. The Poles pleaded – and on this point there was agreement between Bierut of the Lublin Committee and Mikolajczyk of the London government – that the ethnic and economic balance of Poland required her to expand into this region, otherwise she would have a smaller surface area than in 1939. One indisputable argument was that 8 million Germans had been, or were in the process of being, expelled. All that Truman and Attlee could do now was to accept the situation; their only resource was to postpone the question of the final definition of the frontier until the Peace Conference. This made no difference to the actual situation; since the German territories which the USSR had handed over to a Polish administration under the protection of the Red Army lay outside the scope of the Interallied Council responsible for the administration of Germany, did they still belong to Germany or were they now part of Poland? No one thought it wise to clear up this legal point; the evasiveness of the British and Americans was ill-disguised by their humanitarian concern that the population should be transferred 'in an orderly and humane way'. Besides, this was asking a great deal of the Poles and the Czechs, whom the Germans had been oppressing and exploiting for the last five or six years. In the meantime Bierut rejected as an insult any idea that the Polish elections should be under international supervision.

Since matters had not reached breaking-point on the more serious problems, the Big Powers had no great trouble in reaching agreement on matters of minor importance: the Austrian occupation zones and the organisation of free elections, which did actually take place; the evacuation of Iran, after a period of time; the opening of Russo-Turkish negotiations for revising the Montreux Convention; and the maintenance of an international zone in Tangier. A few points of disagreement which they preferred to leave undecided were not pressed: the Soviet desire for part of the Italian colonies; Molotov's request that British action in the Near East should stop; freedom of navigation on all international waterways, to which, to everyone's amazement, Stalin was opposed; and Soviet policy in Romania and Bulgaria, where Stalin waved aside Churchill's accusations as being mere 'fairy tales'.

The immediate interest of the Conference lay elsewhere. It was a question of deciding the fate of Germany in defeat and preparing for that of Japan.

IV THE FATE OF GERMANY

As far as rendering Germany harmless was concerned and the way to set about it, the Big Three were in agreement – if the British treatment of Doenitz betrayed that Churchill had had some ulterior motive at the back of his mind, he kept it well hidden. It was repeated that Germany would be decentralised, that a revival of democratic life would be encouraged at regional level and that, at the right moment, provincial authorities would be established through elections. It was something of a contradiction in terms to divide Germany up politically and then to say that she would form an economic unity; but the Americans were already taking action to prevent trade from coming to a standstill so that they would not find themselves obliged to make up the deficit in the trade balance of the occupied territories.

In order to prevent any fresh burst of desire for revenge, Germany would remain disarmed and demilitarised; all military and paramilitary forces would be dissolved and all arms and munitions of war would be handed over or destroyed.

Denazification would entail dissolving and barring all Nazi works and organisations and, more positively, by reinstating and putting into practice all the essential freedoms – freedom of speech, religious freedom and freedom for the trade unions. Although this whole programme was very clear as a statement of principle, it remained very vague when it came to carrying it out.

The Allies also intended that the Germans should be punished for the crimes of Nazism and that as far as possible they should make amends. It was decided that as soon as it was possible to identify all the offences, the war criminals – the Nazis, but also the military – should be brought before tribunals in the liberated countries. For the leaders of the Party and those holding posts of responsibility in the Wehrmacht, an Interallied Special Tribunal would be set up, with its seat in Nuremberg, consisting of four judges and four deputies. To this tribunal would be referred crimes against peace, war crimes or violations of the laws and customs of war, and 'crimes against humanity' – deportation, persecution and extermination.

So the German people were not being entirely dissociated from their leaders. They would need a long time to pay their debts – the reparations. This was one of the few problems dealt with in any detail at Potsdam. The Russians, moreover, had not waited for the meeting before helping themselves in their occupation zone; they were systematically dismantling factories and machinery so that they could transport the parts to the USSR and reassemble them there. This unilateral action was naturally recognised as their right – how could one prevent them? – and the Poles were also allowed to help themselves in the territories under their administration. But the Russians' appetite – which was increased by their desire to restore the Soviet economy as quickly as possible – caused them to cast covetous eyes on their Allies' zones. And after Yalta, at the Reparations Conference in Moscow, the Russians and Americans had crossed swords on two points: the Americans asked for exact statistics in order to work out correctly the total amount that they would demand, since the figure of 10,000 million dollars had been taken only as a basis for discussion; they were also opposed to making levies on current production while the German economy was still not strong enough to stand them. They were equally divided at Potsdam; but here again the Russians had shown that an ounce of practice was worth a pound of theory. It was decided that each power would satisfy its requirements by requisitioning in its own zone; in addition, the USSR would receive twenty-five per cent of the industrial equipment of the British and American zones. In such circumstances it was of little use stipulating that 'the payment of reparations should leave the German people with enough resources to subsist without aid from outside'; this clause was a mere formality; someone had to help the Germans to their feet again, that is to say had to give them with one hand what was being taken away from them with the other, and who else could this be but the United States?

Now well launched, the Russians went on to ask if they could take part in the administration of the Ruhr which at Teheran Roosevelt had suggested should be internationalised. Molotov stated the Russian requirements very clearly: 2,000 million dollars worth of equipment from the region should be allocated to the USSR and the industrial investments of Rhein-Westfalen as well as its internationalisation should thus be shared exclusively among the Big Three. This time the USSR really was trespassing on her partners' zones of influence. Since Stalin was still concerned with remaining in control in his own country, he thought it wise to withdraw this suggestion at the last sitting; had he persisted, he would surely have risked provoking his partners to meddle in the affairs of the Soviet zone of influence.

So Germany was going to have to pay, and pay a high price. The unfortunate experience of 1918 did not seem to have taught the Potsdam negotiators to exercise caution in that field. Neither were they greatly deterred by the obvious contradiction of demanding large amounts of goods from a country which was deprived of its means of production. Germany would pay, but which Germany, or which Germanies? Till now it had been intended that the Reich's territory should be dismembered and the only question to be discussed was the number of parts and their boundaries. But since Yalta the USSR had changed her points of view; Gusev, her representative at the Special Commission in London, had indicated that the division of Germany was not an end in itself but merely a means of rendering her harmless. What was the explanation for this change in the Soviets' attitude? Probably, as Castellan has pointed out,[1] the fact that the Politburo gradually realised the tremendous possibilities which the end of the war offered the USSR. Now that the German danger had been removed once and for all by the revival of Poland with her extended western boundaries (and therefore friendly to the USSR) and by the demilitarisation of the Reich, why not hold on to the great asset offered by Germany if she entered the Soviet orbit – a mutilated Germany, of course, but united and peaceful?

Accordingly, at Potsdam Stalin did not offer any opposition to setting up a German central government as suggested by Churchill, provided that it was controlled by the Allies; it was Truman who was against it. Provision was made only for 'central administrative departments' which would be more economic than political; secretaries of state would thus control finances, transport, communications, foreign trade and industry.

For the moment, then, the real authority would belong to the Control Council formed by the Allied military leaders of the four occupation zones who would meet from time to time in Berlin. This was an unprecedented situation and a real leap in the dark. On the one hand the occupation zones had been determined by the advance of the Allied armies; they were completely without unity; on the other hand the four Allies were going to

1. G. Castellan, 'La politique allemande de l'URSS', *Revue de l'histoire de la deuxième guerre mondiale*, January and April 1956.

be forced to settle complex problems by unanimous agreement at the very moment when their relationship was beginning to be marred by growing mistrust and misunderstanding which were soon to become a permanent state of affairs.

The Potsdam negotiators, and particularly the Americans, were not unaware of the disadvantages or even the dangers of this situation. But they all thought that this makeshift solution would be only temporary. The task of preparing a permanent peace treaty was given to the Foreign Ministers; the Germans would be forced to accept it but would play no part in the negotiations; it would automatically bring about the political unity of Germany. Unable to see how to overcome their present difficulties, the Allies were therefore postponing them until a later date, while being no clearer on how they would set about solving them in the future.

As at Yalta, the Potsdam negotiators separated feeling pleased with themselves. Truman told Forrestal 'that he did not find it difficult to get on with Stalin'; but according to Murphy he had apparently resolved never to meet the latter again. This contradiction reflects that of Russo-American relations at that time: the two Allies had successfully ended their war against their common enemy; now that the task was complete they were coming to realise what they had refused to contemplate up to then, namely, that a whole world divided them. Actually the first blow to the Potsdam agreements came not from the contracting parties but from General de Gaulle who had not been invited to the meeting. Indeed, he spoke out categorically against setting up any central administrative services again in Germany; he had not given up the idea of detaching the Rhineland and the Ruhr. The emotions aroused by the war were still running too high even for the prophets to foresee that if Germany ceased to exist, she would one day have to be reinvented.

V THE ULTIMATUM TO JAPAN

Since the Allies were still at war with Japan she was discussed at Potsdam solely as an enemy. Churchill was the only one to put forward the idea of leaving the opponent with 'some means of saving his military honour', but Truman replied that this honour had been lost for ever at Pearl Harbour, and Stalin was of the same opinion.

After Chiang Kai-shek had been consulted and given his approval, an ultimatum was sent to Japan, which was drawn up without consultation with France. The Japanese leaders were informed that their country would be 'neither destroyed as a nation nor reduced to slavery nor deprived of essential liberties'. But her armies would have to surrender unconditionally – the decisions which had been taken at Casablanca would be carried out to the very last; otherwise 'she would lay herself open to complete and utter destruction'. There was no chance of this allusion to the atom bomb being understood by the Japanese. In July 1945 they were in serious and almost desperate straits; but no one knew how much longer they would go on fighting nor how they could be forced to stop. These apprehensions were not unfounded; although the Japanese fleet and Army had been defeated many times since Midway, they had nonetheless continued to fight tooth and nail.

BOOK FIVE

THE DEFEAT OF JAPAN

CHAPTER I

Strategy and Forces in Asia

T H E Allies had decided to pursue the war against Japan on a comparatively restricted scale until the defeat of Germany; the experts' view was that at least a year would then be necessary to bring Japan to her knees. On the whole this strategic planning on a global scale was observed; the operational theatres in Asia and Europe were kept separate; it was only when discussions between the British and Americans were marking time that the latter, especially the Navy, at times contemplated reversing the order of priorities and even despatched troops and equipment to the Pacific instead of across the Atlantic; those were little tiffs of no real importance.

Although deferred, the vast offensive against Japan had nonetheless to be prepared long in advance and this preparation came up against immense difficulties. The most serious sprang of course, from the nature of things: the enormous distances, the need to create from scratch the essential economic structures (harbours, roads, bases, stocks, workshops), the destructive climate. But other more unworthy difficulties, whose solution depended solely on human effort, were no less awkward; as in Europe, the British and the Americans had to work in unison in a joint war; but, in Asia, another discordant note was provided by the presence of a third partner, China, as enormous as she was weak, led by Chiang Kai-shek, who was both demanding and disappointing. In addition, in the Pacific where they had sole control over all decisions and operations the Americans, particularly the Army and Navy, had even greater difficulty in coming to an agreement amongst themselves over the way to proceed and the assignment of tasks.

Accordingly, until the atom bomb cut the Gordian knot, the Allied staffs were not successful in working out an overall plan acceptable to everyone like 'Overlord' in Europe. They were continually divided between those who wanted slowly to strangle Japan to death through air raids and submarine operations and those who were in favour of making a landing; even by the end of 1944, the latter were still discussing the best way to reach Tokyo. These hesitations and the failure to follow a strong line led to the general belief in the need for Soviet help. They explain why Stalin's Teheran proposal, later confirmed at Yalta and Potsdam, supporting Soviet intervention was received with general satisfaction; but they meant that operations in 1943 were doomed to uncertainty of purpose, undertaken at random and were sometimes merely reactions provoked by enemy initiatives.

I THE SITUATION AT THE BEGINNING OF 1943

At this time, MacArthur had ten divisions at his disposal – four American and six Australian; his schemes were as ambitious as his resources were limited: not only was he determined not to abandon one single inch of territory and preserve Australia from any contamination by the enemy, but he also intended to forestall the Japanese in New Guinea and the Solomon Islands archipelago. But conditions were appalling in those areas; the hot damp climate caused dysentery, typhus and little-known fevers; mosquitoes, leeches and jiggers without number spread disease and were relentless and all-pervading in their hostility; the mountainous terrain, intersected by steep gullies and crossed by treacherous rivers always ready to flood, was the greater hindrance because no accurate maps existed. Everything had to be fetched in from outside, that is from more than 6,000 miles away. The American troops, perpetually at a loss, were in addition completely in the dark as to their enemy's intentions and movements; counter-intelligence was entirely inoperative; in order to interrogate Japanese prisoners of war, Japanese living in the States had to be sent for to act as interpreters; the only way to communicate with the natives was to learn their language.

The Japanese had gradually seized the string of Solomon Islands which cut off the Americans' route to Australia between the Bismarck Islands and the New Hebrides. To defend the Australian continent, it was essential to reopen this route. This is why the Guadalcanal operation had been agreed on in July 1942; it had been entrusted to Admiral Ghormley, after long and lively discussion between the American Army and Navy. The island was nearly 100 miles long and roughly 30 miles wide, extremely hilly and covered in almost impenetrable jungle.

The operation began with a few battalions capturing the small island of Tulagi. Then began month after month of fierce fighting as the Americans in a series of operations captured beaches, ridges and small forts. The Americans at first deployed 11,000 men, which by the end of 1942 had risen to 60,000, including the ancillary services. Their losses were not very heavy but they only succeeded in overcoming the stubborn resistance of the Japanese because of the superiority of their equipment. When the fighting finally came to an end in February 1943, Japanese prisoners of war totalled only 1,000 as against 14,000 dead. Guadalcanal was a foretaste of what the war would be like in the Pacific islands; a long, bloody and vicious war of attrition, never decisive, continually flaring up, unable to open up broad horizons, moving at a snail's pace towards an uncertain and distant victory. It is amazing that the Americans did not immediately draw the obvious conclusions.

At the Casablanca conference, Churchill and Roosevelt decided on a series of small-scale operations in Asia, difficult to synchronise, because of the remoteness of theatres and the special circumstances of each of them. Operation 'Watchover', started at Guadalcanal and in New Guinea, was to be continued towards the Bismarck Islands with the aim of taking the Japanese base at Rabaul; in the extreme north, the enemy would be flushed out of the Aleutians; and an advance would begin towards Timor. To these operations the British succeeded in adding the possibility of re-taking Burma, for which they completely lacked any resources. In sum, the Allies' 'offensive' plans boiled down to maintaining the *status quo* on the perimeter where the Japanese advance had been halted.

II THE DEFENSIVE STRATEGY OF THE JAPANESE

The Japanese general staff was perfectly happy with this situation. At the beginning of 1943, everyone in Japan was convinced that the war had been won. The important thing was to organise and exploit, politically, militarily and economically, the immense territories that had been conquered. Japanese strategy thus became deliberately defensive.

Tokyo fixed the defensive perimeter on a line passing through the Marianas, Truk, the middle of the Solomon Islands, the west of New Guinea and Timor. In the area threatened by the Americans, the Japanese intended merely to delay and damp down the enemy's offensives; munitions were thus stockpiled in the Bismarck archipelago, Bougainville, the Gilbert and the Marshall Islands and their garrisons were reinforced; the pivot and bastion of these defences was the base at Rabaul. To maintain freedom of passage in the straits between New Guinea and the Indian archipelago, seventeen new airfields, in addition to the seven already in existence, were to be built in New Guinea.

The Japanese were not giving up all idea or plans of attack but they were delaying their execution till the spring of 1944. Then they would make raids in depth in both the central and south Pacific, so as to disrupt the enemy's preparations and dislocate his defences by continually cutting his communications.

The success of the Japanese plans depended on their being able to keep open their own sea lines of communication, which were particularly vulnerable by reason of their number and length. And the Americans had set up submarine bases at Port Darwin in Australia and, nearer to their targets, at Milne Bay in New Guinea; they had put right certain defects in their weapons, such as those affecting the exploding of their torpedoes. By the beginning of 1943, the danger could not be ignored; American submarines had already sunk a million tons of Japanese merchant shipping, more than their naval shipyards had built in the course of 1942.

The Japanese drew their conclusions from this fact, as they had from the lessons of Midway. They stopped building giant battleships and speeded up the construction of aircraft-carriers; five extremely large vessels, called Taiho, were put on order; at the same time, ships of the line, seaplane supply-ships and cargo steamers were converted into air-craft-carriers. A total of twenty-one aircraft-carriers was planned but the final decisions had been delayed and they would take a long time to implement; in addition, as the aircraft-carriers came from different sources, the fleet could not fail to be uneven in quality and performance; the decision to provide battleships with a flight deck was merely a makeshift.

The Japanese aircraft-carriers were inferior to their American counter-parts, particularly in AA; they had nothing to compare with the Swedish Bofors gun and their 127 gun fired ordinary shells whereas the American equivalent was equipped with rockets; as a result, American gunnery was much more effective. Nor did the Japanese succeed in providing their ships with adequate radar or even proper radio links – a very serious handicap when the operational command and staff were generally on board aircraft-carriers.

After Midway, the Japanese Navy feverishly set about replacing the aircraft and trained personnel that had been lost. It produced a few new aircraft, for example the dive-bomber Judy and the torpedo-aircraft Jill; but right up to the end of the war it proved incapable of producing a better aircraft to succeed the Zero fighter which was a long way behind its American rivals.

Comparison between the results of Midway and Guadalcanal showed that the greatest victories in the Pacific war would be at sea; it would be an air and naval war. The surprising thing was that the Americans took so long to draw the practical conclusions from this and assign tasks accord-ingly; their vision was clouded by service rivalry and internal squabbles.

III THE SEARCH FOR AN ALLIED OFFENSIVE STRATEGY

The map showed four ways leading to Tokyo. The shortest was from the Aleutians; but it was a cramped springboard and the cold and foggy cli-mate precluded any proper preparation; in this sector, all that could be done was to eject the Japanese and make a few submarine raids. That case was swiftly despatched.

Another access route was via the Malacca Straits. This had the advan-tage of support from strong Allied bases in India but the disadvantages were enormous, for as British interests predominated in this area, this way could be used only after concluding one of those joint agreements between the British and Americans which experience in Europe had shown to be difficult both to reach and to implement.

The two other approaches could be used only by the Americans; theoretically, this should have made their choice easier but paradoxically they proved incapable of making one. In the south, there was a sort of land route, with some gaps, under MacArthur's command; in fact, it consisted of a series of islands and moving from one to the other required considerable help from the Navy. And the latter had opted for advancing largely by sea across the Pacific – the shortest route, straight for the target.

The only thing that was plain from the outset was that using all three approaches at once would require enormous resources which could not be made available until after Germany was defeated; it would also mean having to disperse the American forces and this would play into the hands of Japanese defence policy; finally, it would not be taking advantage of the vulnerability of the Japanese resulting from the immense areas that they were required to defend. In a word, attacking from all directions at once meant approaching the vast Japanese stronghold along its whole perimeter instead of trying to discover and exploit the weak spots that were bound to exist. This was exactly what should not have been done; yet it was what the Allies tried at first to do.

At Casablanca, a sort of theoretical priority had been given to operations in the Indian Ocean. This was when the British found it fairly easy to force their opinions on the inexperienced Americans, who had not yet achieved their overwhelming superiority in equipment on which the British would gradually come to depend. Churchill saw it as a means of defending India by recapturing Burma; as British interests in the area predominated, the Americans agreed that the Supreme Commander in the area should be Lord Mountbatten. For Roosevelt, it was important to provide supplies to China, about which country the American leaders and the American public long cherished extraordinary illusions; the fact was that, in view of the insufficient number of British and American forces, the only army fighting against the Japanese was the Chinese Army; it could hardly be expected to win victories or even launch an offensive. But action was necessary to ensure that it could continue in existence and pin down the greatest possible number of Japanese troops so that there would be all the fewer in the other sectors.

As only the Americans had sufficient resources to come to China's aid, more particularly with aircraft, they meant to keep sole control of that part of the enterprise, including the command of the Air Force; Chiang Kai-shek's pretensions were a final extraordinary complication in the problems concerning the command and conduct of operations in this area where the means were never adequate for the enormous objectives being pursued.

IV THE ALLIED COMMAND IN THE CHINA—BURMA SECTOR

In this immense sector, there were basically two distinct operational theatres; it was difficult to refuse Chiang Kai-shek the right, at least in theory, to take charge of the operations in China and nobody questioned Mountbatten's authority in India and, later on, in Burma. The complication arose from the fact that on the one hand the Americans expected to supervise, if not indeed to command, the Chinese Army which existed only by their grace and favour; on the other hand, they wished to have complete control of the strategic air force which alone was capable of taking positive action and which consisted solely of aircraft made in the United States – the B 29. There arose an overlapping of the various services and an intertwining of responsibility which led to completely intractable situations. Let the reader judge for himself.

The American General Stilwell was Chiang Kai-shek's Chief of Staff and commander of the American troops in China, Burma and India. His first two functions meant that he was torn between the Chinese and the joint Chiefs of Staff in Washington, and this caused him serious difficulties. But his last two functions – in India and Burma – caused him still greater embarrassment; he was, indeed, subordinate there to Lord Mountbatten, and during the latter's absence he took over the command of the whole operational theatre, which was a reasonable solution; but at the same time he had direct command over north Burma, because that was the only region that actually concerned the Americans and, in so doing, he came under the commander of the interallied ground forces, General Gifford – who, however, became subordinate to him in Mountbatten's absence. In such circumstances, how was it possible for Stilwell to avoid sometimes making suggestions to his American superior officers that were diametrically opposed to Chiang Kai-shek's wishes and Mountbatten's plan? The latter, moreover, being British, depended on the joint British Chiefs of Staff through whom he had to go if he wished to approach the American general staff; thus he was sometimes left in ignorance of the instructions issued by the American planning staff in Washington to their generals in Asia; on the other hand, he was never sure that his own requirements were fully understood in Washington, which, in view of the virtual disappearance of the British presence in Asia, was the only source able to supply the equipment that he needed. Mountbatten indeed lacked neither competence nor character; but how could he fail to be hamstrung by such a tangled pattern of command?

The same complicated overlapping of command existed in the Air Force. The Americans wanted complete strategic and operational control; B 29s were still rather scarce in 1943 and they were suspicious of the way the British might use them. The American Joint Chiefs of Staff thought that the best solution would be to control the Air Force from Washington through General Arnold, the Supreme Commander of the American air arm, whose Chief of Staff was General Hansell. The British protested and asked for a proper joint general air staff to be set up on the spot under Mountbatten, as was the case in Europe; this staff would control the operations of the whole air force, American as well as British. But there were practically no British aircraft in Asia and the American arguments easily carried the day. So Lord Mountbatten was in supreme command, theoretically, of everything except the Air Force, which was the only force capable of fighting.

All that remained was to organise the air force commands in the various sectors. In India and South-east Asia, Mountbatten's deputy, Sir Richard Peirse, was appointed air chief, with the American General Stratemeyer as his second-in-command – the latter received his orders directly from Washington although he was supposed to receive them from the British.

In the China–North Burma sector, the command was apparently simplified by the fact that Stilwell was in sole charge with another American, General Chennault, as his air deputy. But Stilwell's supplies came from India; as they were of purely American origin, General Stratemeyer was at one and the same time subordinate to the British and the 'adviser' to another American general in another sector. As for the B 29s, the subject of the whole dispute, they were put under their own commander, the American General Wolfe, who took his orders from Arnold in Washington.

In practice, the Americans tried to simplify matters but the chain of command was still tortuous and complicated:

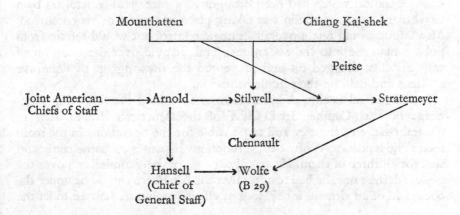

Nevertheless, although the relationship between the Allies and the co-ordination of their efforts took a long time to work out and never achieved perfection, in fact, behind this ostensible chain of command there gradually emerged the reality that there was only one organised and effective force in the whole area – the American B 29s.

V THE AMERICAN COMMAND IN THE PACIFIC

The Guadalcanal operation had given rise to some criticism of the American command. Admiral Ghormley was blamed for having made insufficient use of the Air Force while the admiral himself complained that he had not been supported by the Army as much as he would have liked. Thus the Americans who were perfecting the most delicate piece of mechanism imaginable, i.e. a logistical system capable of transporting hundreds of thousands of men and millions of tons of equipment to the right place at the right time, had at the start met that old stumbling block, lack of understanding and even ill-will between those two most important services, the Army and the Navy, whose co-operation was essential for victory and even, indeed, for waging war; and they were to have the greatest difficulty in making them work together. The dispute was all the more acrimonious because it concerned at one and the same time command, strategy and personalities.

The Navy started by claiming sole command over the whole Pacific on the excuse that the Army had it in Europe, but it had to relinquish this exaggerated, if not puerile, claim. The squabble started up again when the series of operations against the Solomon Islands was being planned, to follow on the capture of Guadalcanal. The Navy wanted to be in charge of these operations, arguing that they were the continuation of the Guadalcanal operation which had been brought to a successful conclusion by a naval man; since the action was taking place in an area of his command, MacArthur would retain overall strategic control but would refrain from poking his nose into the operations. This dispute over the question of responsibility dragged on and prevented the drawing up of definitive schemes and held up their implementation.

In the central Pacific, Admiral Nimitz combined the following functions: he was Commander-in-Chief of the American Pacific fleet, in general charge of the area and responsible for the operations in the main sector; he tended to confuse these functions by using the same command staff for all three of them. He was always appointing admirals all over the place. All the same, he had to agree that the Air Force should be under the command of an airman, for reasons of efficiency, but he refused to let the training of landing troops be undertaken by a general. It was not until September 1943 that Nimitz set up a joint general staff which included airmen and soldiers under the command of his deputy, who was, of course, an admiral. This was as far as he would go; for him, the Pacific war was and must remain a naval matter.

These squabbles over questions of power, and even of precedence, were both childish and dangerous in the face of the enemy. Marshall and King tended to share the opinion of their particular services but they had enough intelligence and a sufficiently lofty view of the interests of the nation, particularly Marshall, to be able to keep their personal preferences under control. However, they realised that they could not change in a few days systems and habits of thought that had been formed over dozens of years. They endeavoured to ensure that all branches of the forces were represented on the various staffs so as to make for better understanding that could eventually lead to real co-operation. But they were forced to relinquish the idea of justifying one party at the expense of the other and American strategy in the Pacific was thus bedevilled by chronic rivalry between generals and admirals and constant unstable compromise.

MacArthur advocated adopting one route to the exclusion of all others: he called it the New Guinea–Mindanao route and it involved making a detour via the Philippines, where he had sworn to return, before the American armies reached Japan. He requested that most of the fleet as well as the amphibious troops should be brought under his command. He considered that Nimitz's plan would take too long and entailed too many risks because the islands that were to be captured like so many stepping stones were very far apart; moreover, the Japanese with their newly constructed airfields could sink any naval forces that ventured to sail into that area.

Admiral Nimitz refused to confine himself to covering MacArthur's northern flank. He pointed out that any accumulation of American forces in the South Pacific islands would leave the Japanese freedom of action over the rest of their defensive perimeter. He maintained that the war would be won more quickly by a series of combined air and naval actions. These would enable a series of strategic air raids to be launched against vital points in Japan, which would be impossible solely from the ground in the South Pacific; aircraft-carriers and long-range aircraft would achieve victory at less cost.

Neither MacArthur nor Nimitz sat with the Chiefs of Staffs where the decisions were taken. But MacArthur was less well supported by Marshall (who was anxious to keep in the good books of the Navy since it would be providing him with the necessary resources for the landings in Europe) than Nimitz was by Admiral King. Nimitz's plans also had the ear of Arnold, the commander of the Air Force, the role of which would have been confined under MacArthur's scheme to supporting land operations.

As the sailors were not opposed to MacArthur's advancing along the route he advocated, because their own plans and schemes did not require the services of ground forces except once they were within sight of Japan and a landing eventually proved necessary, a rough and ready compromise was reached satisfying the pair of them and, through them, the services they represented. Instead of being a single plan conceived with the sole purpose of achieving a successful result, American Pacific strategy thus bore the marks of a sort of compromise between two great feudal lords forcing their own rivalry on a nation under arms.

VI AMERICAN NAVAL AND AIR SUPERIORITY

Not only were the methods advocated by the Navy less costly in time and men but, by the beginning of 1943, proof had been shown of the Americans' great superiority at sea one that MacArthur was going to find difficult to demonstrate on land – and then only at great cost. This superiority was due to their aircraft-carriers, of which thirty-nine were completed and brought into service in 1943.

Immediately after the battle of the Coral Sea, the American Navy had worked out the naval tactics which were to ensure their success. Aircraft-carriers were positioned in the middle of the squadron in conjunction with which they provided a formidable concentration of AA fire-power; these carriers were refuelled and rearmed at sea, which enabled attacks to be made on very remote targets and spread over a number of days. By the end of 1942, the number of aircraft on board each carrier had risen from twenty-six to thirty-six and the fighters, whose range of action had been increased, were in a position to protect the raiding bomber and torpedo-aircraft over long distances.

On the other hand, the radar system had been improved so that it was possible to identify friendly or hostile aircraft at long range; a central operations room on board each ship enabled the operations of the aircraft and AA fire to be co-ordinated. Methods of air attack had similarly been precisely worked out; the aircraft were guided by radio right on to the target; operating in waves of thirty aircraft apiece, they could bombard any warship with bombs, however well protected it might be by its guns.

This use of warships and aircraft-carriers combined into Task Forces, the exact composition of which was worked out in accordance with the task to be completed, proved to be the keystone of the American victory in the Pacific. These Task Forces, preceded by long-range land-based aircraft which also provided cover and supplied with short-range reconnaissance by their own ship-borne aircraft, were able to extend their action over enormous areas; their flexibility was unlimited, they were far superior to US Army Air Force in attacking any enemy air force; they destroyed more than half the Japanese aircraft and they were also effective against submarines. In contrast to MacArthur's 'flea hops' from one atoll to the next and one beach after another, which entailed unremitting, exhausting and bloody fighting, Task Forces represented giant leaps which would lead them straight to the heart of the Japanese Empire.

They could also have reduced to a minimum the China and Burma campaigns in which vast quantities of equipment and not inconsiderable amounts of money were being swallowed up without any very serious effect on the enemy.

CHAPTER 2

The War in China and Burma

THE British and American objectives in South-east Asia were not identical; although the Americans had agreed to let the former command in that area, they were not going to allow themselves to be sacrificed in order to resuscitate the British Empire. When Churchill suggested conquering Burma from the south by air and naval operations, aimed first at Rangoon with Singapore as the ultimate target, Roosevelt replied that, first and foremost, Chiang Kai-shek needed help and that this could only be done from North Burma.

Churchill's plans required considerable action by the British fleet, would have ensured the defence of India and, in a word, restored Britain's prestige and authority by making the best use, to her own advantage, of the resources that the USA would make available to her. Accordingly, the British Prime Minister raised objection after objection to the American plans, stressing the difficulties offered by the high mountain barrier, the dense jungle and the torrential monsoon rains. But Roosevelt dug in his heels; in any case, the direct subordination of the B 29s to General Arnold gave the Americans the exclusive use of the only force ready for action in 1943.

Accordingly, from November 23 to 25, 1943 in Cairo, Roosevelt and Churchill – especially the former – promised a delighted Chiang Kai-shek to supply him with the means to step up his resistance to the Japanese and even to go over to the offensive. It was understood that Manchuria and Formosa should be returned to China and that Korea should become independent. In return, Chiang Kai-shek promised everything his partners wanted, and more.

I CHINA'S WEAKNESS

Relying on his 'hunches', Roosevelt wanted at all costs to help Chiang Kai-shek, because the latter had made a great impression on him. Moreover, the Chinese cause was very popular in the United States; public opinion was very sympathetic towards the first country that had suffered the aggression of the hated 'Japs'. In the course of frequent trips, lectures and conversations, Chiang Kai-shek's wife and her brother, the banker Song, had woven a skilful web of contacts, in business circles as well as amongst intellectuals; thus a real pressure group, a lobby in fact, had been formed in support of China, and Roosevelt had to take this into account.

The American President overestimated the importance of China's war effort and Chiang Kai-shek easily brought him round to his point of view by vague threats of making a separate peace with Japan. In fact, had China stopped fighting, the course of the war would have been in no way changed; in order to maintain their own law and order in that immense country the Japanese would have had to keep there all the forces they had already sent. But Roosevelt thought differently. In any case, he was faced with a sort of choice between defending British colonialism in India and liberating China from the Japanese yoke; he did not hesitate for one second; he wanted to make China one of the great powers in the post-war world and one of the pillars of the United Nations Organisation; he was toying with the idea of handing over French Indochina to her.

Indeed, the Chinese Army was, on the face of it, an enormous force; in proportion to her population, its total strength should have been immense and, on paper, it comprised 324 divisions, 60 independent brigades and 89 guerrilla units. Closer inspection showed it was a farce; because of the restricted quantities of arms and ammunition that were coming in slowly and sparsely now that Indochina had been occupied by Japan, it had proved possible to equip only twenty-three divisions of 10,000 men each and two of 8,000, that is in all 350,000 men. On the other hand, a distinction had to be made between the regular army under Chiang Kai-shek, which was relatively well disciplined, and the provincial armies commanded by 'war lords' which were merely bands, 'great companies', more concerned with living off the country and even looting it than fighting the invader.

As a result, fighting had almost come to a halt in China. Their shortage of troops and their excessively long lines of communication precluded any further large offensives by the Japanese. For its own part, the Chinese Army, with its poor supplies, poor arms, poor food and poor officers was largely standing easy; its health situation was not good and its soldiers were inadequately trained. Thus a Chinese army theoretically containing twelve divisions did not even try to attack the single Japanese division facing it, which was spread out over a long front. Chiang Kai-shek was aware of his weakness and of his inability to beat the Japanese; that was why he did not wish to fritter away his meagre forces; he was holding them in reserve to re-establish his authority after the Japanese had gone, to bring to heel the provincial leaders who had become practically independent, and to beat Mao Tse-tung's People's Army.

Chiang's American adviser, General Stilwell, who could see this inaction and general slovenliness, kept sending Washington pessimistic reports couched in the most violent terms. He abused the Chinese generals 'who give orders and then warn their inferiors not to carry them out . . . and who pay their soldiers when they feel in the mood'; he reported that whole companies were deserting or going over to the Communists; he accused Chiang Kai-shek of starting negotiations with the Japanese and of trying to sell himself to the highest bidder – he was haggling with the Americans for a 1,000 million dollar loan in exchange for the promise to launch an offensive in the direction of the Bay of Bengal.

Stilwell's reports and Stilwell himself were appreciated for their courage and frankness. But he was also known to be an irascible, abrupt man and diplomacy was not his strong point. In any case, the Americans had decided to accept any sacrifice that might be required to keep China in the Allied camp and to use her as best they could. The Americans' permanently starry-eyed view of Chiang Kai-shek and his régime, despite the repeated warnings provided both by men and by events, is one of the most amazing aspects of the Second World War.

II AMERICAN AID TO CHINA

To remove all suspicion as to his intentions, Roosevelt decided to give up the United States' extra-territorial rights in certain parts of China. He took the decision against the advice of the State Department and his ambassador at Chungking, Gauss, who pointed out that the Chinese were always ready to receive but never inclined to give away anything at all. He also had to overcome the reluctance of the British, who were fully alive to the great losses they would incur through this step, especially in Shanghai. Ultimately, in January 1943, Chiang Kai-shek signed a treaty in Washington with the Americans and with the British in Chungking which handed back to China all the powers she had signed away in certain areas of her territory by granting 'concessions' to foreign powers. However, with that pragmatism which often contradicts their idealism, the Americans immediately insisted on her signing another treaty, protecting their soldiers in China from the normal processes of the law – a privilege justified by the exigencies of war and, indeed, strictly limited to the duration of hostilities.

Roosevelt had big ideas for China. Stilwell was given the Herculean task of modernising the Chinese Army. He set about it with his customary gusto; in agreement with the British, he organised an officers' training school at Ramgarth in India; he held the view, indeed, that the Chinese soldier was brave and that young officers could be taught; on the other hand, he considered the senior officers a dead loss. The first important thing, therefore, was to form a new generation of officers.

Chiang Kai-shek, as usual, was exploiting American goodwill to the full. He asked for 1,000 aircraft and equipment for thirty divisions – and this was only the beginning. How would they reach him? Quite simply, Chiang replied, sketching the map of a road and a railway line from India to China. This scheme met with only half-hearted approval from the British; they politely refused the 100,000 Chinese volunteers whom Chiang Kai-shek suggested sending them; they thus roused Stilwell's wrath, who violently criticised them for their lack of activity – 'they have 70,000 men drawing rations and 12,000 men at the front; you find corps commanders at every level, each one doing a captain's job or else nothing at all.'

Opening a proper route would be a long process; meanwhile, because of the immense distances – New Delhi was about 2,200 miles from Chungking – the only possibility was an air-bridge, despite the height of the mountains that would have to be crossed. The logistical problems were tremendous; on the one hand, despite their long range, the B 29s would need refuelling by other aircraft; on the other, many other things had to be done: constructing bases in the Calcutta area and airfields round Chungking, transporting equipment and supplies to India and thence to China, by sea, rail, road and air, equipping the Indian harbours to receive the anticipated 6,000 tons per month, and maintaining and repairing on the spot the aircraft and rolling-stock.

From November 1943 onwards, five existing airfields in Bengal were brought up to date; the work was completed in April 1944. In Chungking, American dollars, disbursed at a rate of exchange very favourable to the Chinese, were used to employ 400,000 coolies on building four runways, using the Chinese method of little baskets and stone-breaking by hammers, with the workteams faithfully reflecting the social hierarchies of their villages.

At the same time, with a copious use of manpower combined with modern American equipment, the land was cleared for the road to Ledo, joining the Assam railway to that part of the 'Burma road' that had not fallen into Japanese hands.

The results were not commensurate with the immense effort expended. True, Stilwell did succeed in airlifting 60,000 Chinese soldiers into India where they were trained by American instructors at Ramgarth. But Chiang Kai-shek was complaining that he was not receiving the promised equipment – meanwhile he had increased his requests to enable him to arm fifty Chinese divisions. The British were becoming impatient because so many men and so much money and equipment were being exclusively and uselessly expended in an area entirely without interest for them whereas other easier operations were not only possible but necessary, aimed at Rangoon and Singapore. As for Stilwell, he was annoyed with everybody. He wrote: 'I am fighting against the British and the Chinese; occasionally, against the Japanese'; he criticised Chiang Kai-shek and his generals for their poor use of the officers who had come back from Ramgarth and for their bad choice of those who were sent there – there were hardly any students amongst them.

The only solution of some magnitude was to retake North Burma so as to reopen the whole of the 'Burma road'. Stilwell set about this task, using principally two Chinese divisions that had been forced by a Japanese attack to take refuge in India and which, trained and re-equipped, had then been placed under his command. But the British suggested stopping the operation in order to recapture the Dutch East Indies – and Stilwell had to despatch reports to Washington saying the exact opposite of what was being suggested by his superior, Admiral Lord Mountbatten. For his part, despite his promises, Chiang Kai-shek failed to bring up the seventeen divisions which, theoretically, were under his command in the Yünnan province.

It was left to the Japanese to compel their opponents to come to an agreement between themselves by their threatening attacks against north-east India, in January 1944 against the Arakan front and against Imphal in March 1944. Once their advance had been halted, in August 1944, Stilwell succeeded in driving them out of the centre of Myitkyina, where the road from Assam joined the old Burma road; it thus became possible to improve supplies to Chiang Kai-shek – in particular petrol was brought as far as Myitkyina by pipeline. Nevertheless, it was not the big success that had been anticipated; it was clear that, in this operational theatre, the grand plans that had been contemplated required considerable resources which would have had to be taken from other sectors considered more important for the Allied strategy. In addition, the Japanese, disturbed by the development of the situation, had started to attack the Chinese troops again.

III THE WAR IN CHINA

Even though it was not possible to launch the Chinese masses against the Japanese, at least B 29s could take off from Chungking's runways and drop their bombs on Japanese installations in China and one day on the Japanese archipelago itself; it was a way of taking from the rear the Japanese defences that MacArthur and Nimitz were attacking from the front. Although they were inadequate to modernise the Chinese Army, the supplies that were being brought in from India by land and air at least provided the bombers with the necessary petrol, bombs and spare parts. This was the cause of another squabble among the Americans, this time between Stilwell and his deputy Chennault, the Air Force commander.

The subject of the quarrel was the size of the air attack and its targets; Stilwell refused to allow Chennault sole control of the allocation of the supplies which he had requested, thereby depriving Chiang Kai-shek's armies; and for his part, MacArthur was opposed to bombing the Philippines. Agreement was reached to attack Japanese river transport on the Yangtse-Kiang; this was only a minor target and the results were limited.

These attacks were nonetheless sufficient to alarm the Japanese. One of their permanent aims was to ensure the safe possession of the Peking–Canton railway and the branch line at Henyang which went towards Liuchow and Kweilin; it was a route joining north China with Indochina and its importance was growing as sea links became progressively less safe and more difficult to keep open. The Japanese advanced so far that in the summer of 1944, Chennault's air bases had to be evacuated.

Chiang Kai-shek was alarmed and asked Stilwell to withdraw from the Burmese border to Chungking. Marshall then suggested to Stilwell that he should take over command of the Sino-American forces in China; this was the fifth job that Stilwell had been allotted but its terms of reference were no clearer or easier than the previous ones: how could his powers be reconciled with those of the Chinese Supreme Commander? Who should be allocated the resources provided by lend-lease? Stilwell could not envisage accepting any responsibility without the authority that went with it, and Chiang Kai-shek refused to allow him any; Chiang appealed to Roosevelt to decide; the latter sent first of all a general and then Wallace, the Vice-President of the United States. Wallace heard nothing but recriminations against Stilwell, from Chiang, Mountbatten and Chennault. In October 1944, Stilwell, the Cassandra whom no one appreciated, was recalled and replaced by Wedermeyer in China and Sultan in Burma.

Wedermeyer's functions and posts were more exactly defined: he became Chiang's Chief of Staff and he commanded the American forces in China, apart from the strategic air force, that is 27,000 men in all, a large number considering the difficulties of supply and reinforcing them, but inadequate for an action of any size.

Meanwhile the Japanese had increased their pressure towards Kweiyang with the intention of cutting the Burma road. Fearing that Chungking itself might one day be attacked, despite its natural fortifications of encircling mountains and fogs, Wedermeyer asked for fighting in Burma to be brought to a halt, for the Chinese divisions there to be sent back to China and for any schemes to reconquer central and south Burma to be dropped. Very fortunately, without the Chinese having done anything to hinder them, the Japanese came to a stop of their own accord, through exhaustion, and withdrew, not without providing a full quota of murder, rape and looting.

Wedermeyer then set about providing sixteen Chinese divisions, at

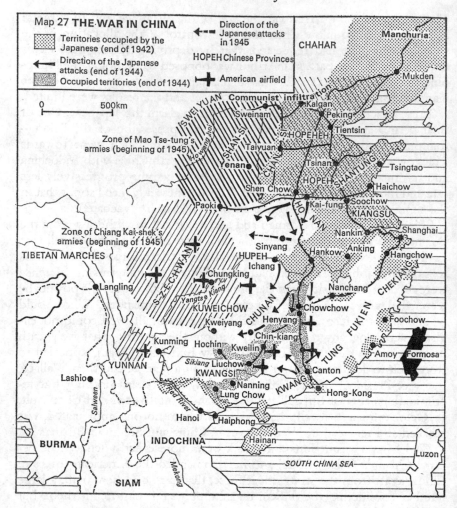

Map 27 **THE WAR IN CHINA**

⬚ Territories occupied by the Japanese (end of 1942)

← Direction of the Japanese attacks (end of 1944)

▨ Occupied territories (end of 1944)

◀--- Direction of the Japanese attacks in 1945

HOPEH Chinese Provinces

✚ American airfield

regimental level and above, with American 'advisers' who would see that equipment was properly distributed, the troops paid, the food improved and training completed. He even thought up an ambitious scheme to capture a Chinese port on the south-west coast using only Chinese troops; he was not able to put the scheme into operation and he had to be content with a defensive success, quite a decisive one, however, when for once the Chinese forced the Japanese to retreat – they had tried to capture an American airfield in the direction of Chinkiang.

So the Chinese nationalist armies took part in hardly any fighting. More serious than this inactivity was the decay of the Kuomintang administration and the uselessness of its leaders for organising guerrilla warfare in the Japanese rear. The fact was, as Bianco wrote, that 'the rural masses could not be mobilised, organised and led without reducing the powers of the local notables' – on whom the Kuomintang were relying for support. If one adds that the 'war lords' forced conscription only on the poor – the wealthier Chinese bought themselves out by bribery – that conscripts had barely sufficient rations to avoid starving to death, that the Chinese leaders made raids on their own compatriots as much as if not more than on the Japanese, it was difficult for the nationalists to expect a popular uprising to support their own efforts. Sometimes the peasantry even attacked isolated soldiers. Thus the war accentuated the conservative nature of the Kuomintang and as a result favoured the Communists' propaganda and activity in the vast areas under their control.

IV COMMUNIST CHINA

In the Shen-si province where he had first established himself and then gradually throughout the whole of north China, Mao Tse-tung's Communist party had gradually replaced the Kuomintang's administration, either because the latter ceased functioning out of patriotism when the Japanese arrived or else because it continued to exist only by coming to terms with them. Considerable effort was made to win over the support of the mass of the peasants, both by social reform and by appeals to national feeling.

The Communist party had abandoned most of its revolutionary programme; it had given up the idea of expropriating the big landowners, of whom there were anyway fewer in the north than in the centre or south; it restricted itself to placing a limit on the rate of ground rent, which appealed to the tenant farmers, and reduced interest rates and taxation, which satisfied the small landowners, who were the largest class and chronically in debt to money-lenders or the state. This plan of reform caused no great concern. But at the same time the Communists organised the peasantry who thus came to experience mass democracy; instead of the local despot who enforced his own notions, the party delegate tried to understand the villagers' grievances; he did not hold them to ransom; he brought them together so that they could realise what their problems were and decide together on what joint solution they could find for them.

At the national level, Mao Tse-tung put himself forward as the successor to Sun Yat-sen. He constantly referred to his desire to 'save the country' which took on a very specific meaning in an area regularly held to ransom by the Japanese. Japanese atrocities – poison fed into tunnels where the population had taken refuge, the extermination of whole villages, 'mopping-up' operations that left not one person alive and every house burnt to the ground – were the best recruiting sergeant for the partisans.

In the areas occupied by the invader, power in village communities waxed and waned according to the time of day – the day belonged to the occupier or collaborator, the night to the Communists.

This mixture of nationalism and moderate social reform – combined with the formation of a people's army and the appearance of a peasant democracy – explained the success and increasing spread of the Communist party. From 1 million peasants in 1937, its authority had spread to 90 million in 1945; over the same period the Red Army grew from 80,000 to 600,000 men; and the Party from a few thousand members to more than a million. And in contrast to the European Communist parties, at no time did Chinese Communists anywhere become compromised with capitalist democratic governments or armies; Mao negotiated no agreements with Roosevelt or Churchill as Stalin had been forced to do.

V PREPARATIONS FOR THE BURMA CAMPAIGN

Meanwhile, in the operational theatre of South-east Asia, the Allies had now achieved considerable superiority in men and weapons; by the end of 1944, Mountbatten could count on more than a million men – including the 180,000 Americans under Sultan – as against barely 300,000 Japanese. The latter had never recovered from the war of attrition in the Imphal plain which had extended over several months and had been a great trial for them owing to the weather, the mud and inadequate supplies – they had lost almost 100,000 men.

In addition, the Allied logistical bases had been completed so that reinforcements of all sorts could be swiftly despatched to any sector; the ancillary services were organised and first and foremost, the medical services; the proportion of sick to wounded had sunk from 120 to 1 in 1943 to only 6 to 1 in 1944. Allied air superiority was overwhelming; it enabled them to supply units that had ventured far into the depths of this vast country even when they were cut off, and to bomb the enemy's depots and lines of communication. Whole corps could be airlifted in record time and this made the Allied armies so mobile that they might almost be described as ubiquitous.

The Japanese on the other hand could move only on roads constantly under attack by bombs; this did not reduce their fighting spirit and they always chose death rather than capture. But they were operating far from their bases and they were obliged to leave behind their dead and wounded and their equipment. Marshal Terauchi's troops were exhausted and ill-equipped when, from July 1944 onwards, they beat their retreat. The boldness and initiative needed for victory had changed sides.

On the whole the Burmese had tended to sympathise with the Japanese invaders, except those living in the mountains who provided the British with fine guerrilla forces; under General Wingate they continually harassed the Japanese and created a great sense of insecurity behind their lines. In addition, with the ripe experience of their long imperial past, the British were skilful in winning the goodwill of their Burmese opponents; when they returned to Burma they punished those who had been responsible for atrocities but they did not interfere in internal problems and they allowed the nationalists who had supported the Japanese to join their ranks – General Aung Sang for example, with whose co-operation they turned the Burmese irregulars into a proper Burmese army.

Finally, the departure of the stormy petrel Stilwell enabled the general staff organisation to be simplified by forming the Allied forces in South-east Asia into one command under Sir Oliver Leese, who had under him Indians, Africans, British, Chinese and Americans.

Henceforth, the Allies were to attack unceasingly in Burma; even the wet monsoon did not stop them; the Japanese were given no chance to take a breather.

VI THE RECONQUEST OF BURMA

The plan that was adopted aimed at thrusting towards central Burma from the west as well as from north to south. This second operation, which included Chinese troops, advanced towards the Irrawaddy across the Bhamo plain; it freed the Ledo region and made it possible to start using the China road again. A light convoy reached Kunming in January 1945 and the road proper was opened to large convoys in February.

The Japanese offensive in south-east China put a stop to the use of Chiang Kai-shek's Chinese troops and Wedermeyer's Americans in Burma. Henceforth the British conducted the whole campaign themselves, with the benefit of amphibious equipment which was beginning to arrive from Europe, whilst the Allied victories made the Burmese nationalists decide to make their definitive choice and rebel against the Japanese throughout the country.

At the same time the advance continued along the coast of the Bay of Bengal towards Akyab, in order to capture the airfields which had been built by the Japanese and which could be used to support the thrust in central Burma; Mandalay was taken on March 20. During that month Allied aircraft transported 27,000 men and 78,000 tons of equipment, ranging from a rifle, if not a packet of needles, to bulldozers and railway engines, dismantled for reassembly.

It was still more than 300 miles to Rangoon. The British despatched three columns; one followed the railway line, the second the Irrawaddy;

the third, from Akyab, made the quickest progress and reached Rangoon on May 2, in a threefold air, sea and land attack, which Churchill, never at a loss to invent a word, described as 'triphibious'. The Japanese had already evacuated the town by the time Slim, the general responsible for the operation, landed there in the aircraft which he had found to be the most suitable command post; this shows the importance of the air force in an area as big as France but infinitely less well provided with roads.

Till the very last the Japanese fought back ferociously, leaving only one wounded man for every hundred dead. In the very last days, in the battle of Sittang, only 740 prisoners were taken as against 6,000 killed. The survivors managed to escape via Siam.

Although not involving large numbers of men, the Burma campaign had been one of the most arduous of the whole war; its only result was to enable the British, with great effort and heavy losses, to recapture a country with they would have recovered in any case when the Japanese surrendered and for which the Burmese nationalists' 'Anti-Fascist People's Freedom League' immediately claimed independence from their liberators by demanding the withdrawal of the liberation army which they were anxious not to see assume its former role of guardian of the British Empire.

CHAPTER 3

The War in the Pacific

MACARTHUR'S advance was parallel with Nimitz's. But whilst Nimitz was operating in the wide spaces of the Pacific, seeking the decisive naval battle that would destroy Japan's fleet and toll the knell of her defeat, MacArthur began by becoming bogged down in the countless islands of Polynesia. He waged a series of obscure but bloody battles in order to seize minor targets; the soldiers called it the 'palm and coconut war', an accurate description because Japanese snipers were often perched at the top of a tree.

The Japanese practised what General Chassin calls 'the strategy of drawing blood'. They fortified the tiniest atoll and hid in trenches and underground dugouts, making the enemy pay dearly for the smallest advance; the struggle was often agonising; taking full advantage of the superiority of their equipment, the Americans would begin by saturating the enemy positions with bombs from their aircraft and shells from their ships; under cover of this powerful barrage, their crack infantry – the marines – would be put ashore; the first few hours or even days were very tough because the Japanese were well dug in and could pick off their opponents huddled on the beach or under the flimsy protection of some fold in the ground. After that, the landing troops would advance blindly, through jungle, swamps and tropical undergrowth, without maps or any detailed intelligence, over terrain that was usually covered in booby-traps. Gradually the Japanese would be winkled out of their lookouts and dugouts; usually, it ended in hand-to-hand fighting; often mines and flame-throwers blasted the last defenders out of their bunkers like human torches. In this bitter fighting, it was difficult to evacuate the wounded and their medical treatment was rudimentary; the Japanese fought till they dropped and the Americans were not over-anxious to encumber themselves with prisoners; this wild rage was doubtless not unconnected with racial feeling.

To husband his resources and save time, MacArthur gradually perfected his 'leap-frog' tactics. They consisted in by-passing the enemy's stronger positions except when absolutely necessary and attacking his weak points; the Japanese thus found themselves blockaded in their own fortresses, which were still intact and indeed impregnable, under siege

---

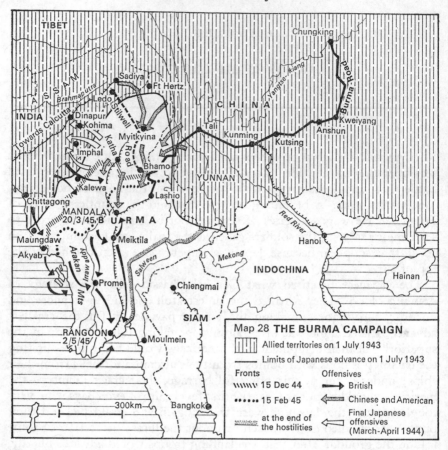

Map 28 THE BURMA CAMPAIGN

not by the enemy but by the sky and sea; lacking any means of communication, they became their own prisoners. The American advance could move on round these strongholds that were no longer of the slightest use, assuming that, in his own area, Nimitz had destroyed or neutralised the Japanese fleet.

Wherever the Americans gained a foothold, they established airfields which their bombers could use as bases for a new leap forward. These methods necessitated perfect co-operation between the three services; it was achieved without much trouble, as a result of the complementary role played by the Navy and Air Force; the Navy moved troops from one island to another, as well as their supplies and confined itself to supporting them during the fighting; the Air Force, having no strategic targets, functioned entirely as flying artillery, dive-bombing the enemy's positions very close to their own landing troops – in New Guinea sometimes little more than 100 yards away. The experience gained in this way was to prove very useful to them in Europe when preparing 'Overlord'.

I THE FIGHTING IN PAPUA AND NEW GUINEA

In February 1943 General MacArthur's plan was, once Guadalcanal had been captured, to invest the large Japanese base at Rabaul from the Solomon Islands and New Guinea. His first target was the base at Lae which General Imamura, the commander of the Japanese Army in the south-west and Admiral Kusaka, the commander of the Rabaul base, had decided to hold at all costs; with this in mind, a convoy carrying some ten thousand Japanese troops was despatched thither.

This convoy was spotted and attacked by the US Amy Air Force on March 3 and 4. The Japanese were afraid of a torpedo attack and made the mistake of sailing straight towards the attacking aircraft; as a result, many of the bombs, dropped at a range of only 160 yards, hit their target: four Japanese destroyers and eight cargo vessels were sunk; the flagship and four more destroyers were damaged and turned back to Rabaul; several thousand men intended for Lae were drowned and only 850 reached their destination. This most successful operation cost the Americans only two bombers and three fighters; MacArthur claimed that this clash of air force versus navy, which took place off the Bismarck Islands, was 'the decisive air operation of the South Pacific'.

Reassured at their enemies' inability to bring up reinforcements, between June and October 1943 the Americans set out systematically to flush out the Solomon Islands. They took the Munda base and then the one in New Georgia. Throughout October, Bougainville was attacked incessantly by some hundred aircraft of the fleet air arm and was finally captured in November after a naval battle at night in which the Japanese ships were forced to withdraw. Whereas at Guadalcanal the Americans were well over 600 miles away from Rabaul, they were now within 160 miles and they started bombing it before the end of 1943.

Meanwhile in New Guinea MacArthur had advanced very slowly from his bases in the extreme eastern end of the island. He moved west-wards in a series of leaps, making landings at roughly sixty-mile intervals, occasionally using paratroops. He was to take more than five months to cover the 1,250 miles to the western end of the island. His chief enemies were mountains – some of which were nearly 13,000 feet high – and the climate, which caused malaria, dysentery and beriberi. More than 100,000 Japanese remained scattered over the large island and they were hunted down by the Australians. MacArthur set up a large base at Finschhafen, near New Britain, where he landed in the middle of December; by the

746   THE DEFEAT OF JAPAN

Map 29 THE AMERICAN OFFENSIVE IN THE PACIFIC

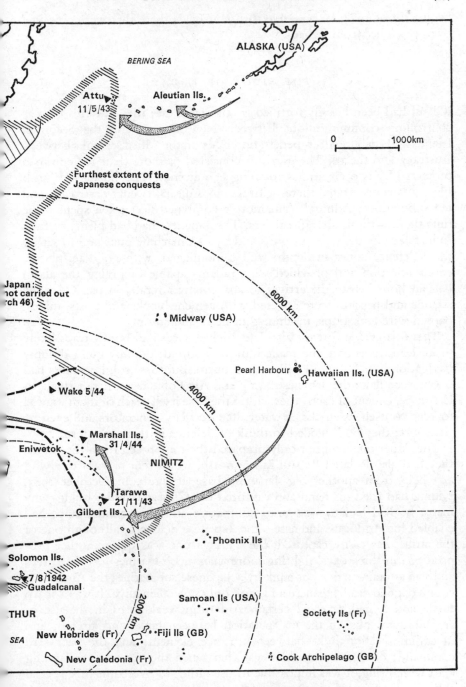

ALASKA (USA)

BERING SEA

Attu
11/5/43

Aleutian Ils.

0   1000km

Furthest extent of the
Japanese conquests

Japan:
not carried out
ch 46)

6000 km

Midway (USA)

Pearl Harbour
Hawaiian Ils. (USA)

Wake 5/44

4000 km

Marshall Ils.
31/4/44

Eniwetok

NIMITZ

Tarawa
21/11/43
Gilbert Ils.

Phoenix Ils

Solomon Ils.

7/8/1942
Guadalcanal

Samoan Ils (USA)

Society Ils (Fr)

THUR

2000 km

SEA   New Hebrides (Fr)   Fiji Ils (GB)

New Caledonia (Fr)

Cook Archipelago (GB)

beginning of 1944, he was able to use airfields there that were only just over 300 miles from Rabaul.

II THE SIEGE OF RABAUL

Rabaul had been heavily fortified by the Japanese; they saw this base as controlling communications between New Guinea and the Solomon Islands and enabling deep-penetrating raids on the Allied sea links between Australia and the US. The garrison consisted of more than 100,000 men protected by two air armies totalling 600 aircraft. The Japanese Eighth Fleet was concentrated there, with its ten cruisers, twenty destroyers and ten submarines; Admiral Yamamoto's combined fleet often spent some time there with his aircraft-carriers. The Japanese had had plenty of time to install more than 100 AA guns and 250 AA machine guns and to set up three defence zones in depth, well camouflaged, with good telephonic communication and provided with radars capable of giving the alarm half an hour before the arrival of any enemy aircraft; in particular the strands and beaches were covered with cement blocks and posts, mines, barbed wire tank traps, machine-gun nests and so on.

This formidable fortress also had trick devices and booby-traps likely to mislead the enemy and make him look stupid: dummy guns, dummy navigation lights, dummy villages, all lit up. But these solid defences had one unseen flaw: the Japanese Navy and Air Force were, if not rivals, at least independent of each other within the base itself; each of them wanted to keep to itself its stocks of water, its electricity generators and even its transport; they both tended to think of defence in their own terms.

The Americans had not only prepared their approach from the south; they had also isolated Rabaul in the north, to prevent it from receiving any help from another big Japanese base at Truk. In October 1943, Nimitz had tried his hand and captured the Gilbert Islands; lacking any maps, he had had to wait until submarine and air reconnaissance had enabled him to locate and assess the Japanese defences; although one of the atolls was easily captured, the Turawa one was quite another proposition; in three days' fighting more than 3,000 marines lost their lives and one aircraft-carrier was sunk by a Japanese submarine; the Americans counted 4,690 dead Japanese and took only seventeen alive. It was a sharp tussle and it had revealed certain American weaknesses in the use of amphibious tanks, in the co-operation between tanks and aircraft, and in communication links between advance elements and the backward command; one of the troubles was that when the guns on the landing craft were firing, it was impossible to use radio; to overcome this, special ships were equipped as advance command posts.

One of the results of capturing the Gilbert Islands was to facilitate air raids against the Marianas which had hitherto been within range only of land-based bombers, which had had to cover some 1,200 to 1,700 miles. Another result was to provide a springboard for the conquest of the Marshall Islands, or more accurately the atoll of Kwajalein, which was chosen as the first stronghold in the archipelago. It was taken by assault in January 1944 at the cost of 330 dead and 1,400 wounded as against 8,500 Japanese dead. From the Gilbert and Marshall Islands Nimitz's next stage loomed up ahead in the direction of the Marianas; but at the same time the Japanese base at Truk, whose reserves were running out as a result of the relentless inroads of the enemy, was bombed and rendered harmless. The immediate consequences of this was the complete isolation of Rabaul, the key to the whole defence system of the Japanese perimeter.

Indeed, from the middle of 1943 onwards, Rabaul had been regularly attacked by nearly 800 land- or carrier-based aircraft. American air superiority continued to assert itself, both qualitatively, as for example in radio communications and speed – the Japanese fighters could not fly much faster than the American bombers – and then very soon, quantitatively, as the number of American aircraft steadily increased while the Japanese were not always able to replace their losses. At the beginning of 1944, the Japanese Air Force recognised defeat and evacuated the base.

Although the base continued to defend itself, it was in a hopeless situation; in its turn, the naval force was withdrawn to avoid inevitable and futile destruction. For the first time in the history of warfare, Rabaul was subjected to a blockade maintained purely from the air. The Americans experimented more or less successfully with phosphorus bombs, fragmentation bombs suspended from parachutes, radio-controlled pilotless aircraft and so on. The 80,000 entrenched Japanese, besieged from the air, now found their escape cut off; they could receive nothing from outside nor send anything out; they were reduced to being bombed, having to stand by and see their AA defences destroyed gun by gun or rebuilding their small forts which were immediately demolished again; worn out, doomed to defeat and knowing it full well, they grew weaker and weaker; but they still remained full of fight, and managed to hold out until the end of hostilities.

III THE NAVAL BATTLE IN THE MARIANAS

By September 1943, the Americans had penetrated deep into the Japanese defensive perimeter. With the Aleutians, the Solomons and now eastern

New Guinea lopped off, this perimeter had been reduced by an Imperial Conference to a 'sphere of unconditional national defence', whose eastern boundary passed through the Kuriles, the Bonins, the Marianas, the Dutch East Indies and Burma; it was decided that there would be no retreat beyond that line and impregnable defence positions would be built all along it. Retention of this area was considered the most essential Japanese war aim; losing any part of it would mean not winning the war in the way that was intended when it was declared. So for the moment, it must be successfully defended in the hope of going over to the offensive later on, forcing the Americans to cease their attacks and acquiesce in a Japanese victory which would, after all, be no more than a moral defeat for them.

The news from Europe – Italy's surrender and the assault on the fortress of Europe that was just beginning – showed the Japanese that there was no relief to be expected from that quarter. On the other hand, their naval losses were increasing as a result of the growing number of American submarine and air attacks as they gradually drew nearer; it was becoming more and more difficult, without inordinate losses, to supply the remoter outposts and to ship to Japan the goods needed by her industry and her population; it was thus important to stabilise the lines of communication with the Indian archipelago, the principal source of raw material and oil; a network of shipping links was drawn up on the map which convoys were to be obliged to follow, under the protection of a special escort fleet depending directly on the Imperial General Staff; but the strength and responsibilities of this new squadron were restricted to avoid encroaching on the domains of the admirals already in command in the various operational theatres.

At the beginning of 1944, the Japanese schemes for a big spring offensive proved abortive as a result of their failures in the Gilberts and Rabaul. Nevertheless the Japanese continued to believe in a successful outcome to the conflict; true, they had had to resign themselves to the fact that the Americans had penetrated into a vital part of their defences, if not into their inner lair itself; but they pinned their hopes on a big naval battle, a sort of repetition of Pearl Harbour, which would give them back mastery of the seas and restore their situation. This crucial battle for which they longed was called, optimistically, *Sho*, which means victory.

So the Japanese Admiralty built up another impressive strike force under Admiral Ozawa, including nine aircraft-carriers with 450 aircraft – 50 more than for the attack on Pearl Harbour. It also included five battle-ships and was based on Guam. When on June 15, 1944, the Americans began their landings on the island of Saipan, close to Guam in the Marianas, they seemed to have jumped into the lion's mouth. Admiral Toyoda, who had just taken over command of the Japanese Navy, ordered

Ozawa to attack with no thought of retreat; as at Pearl Harbour and Midway, everything was to be thrown in; once more the war was being decided by the toss of a coin; it was all or nothing.

But Admiral Mitscher's Task Force 58, which included 15 aircraft-carriers, 900 ship-borne aircraft and 7 battleships was far superior to the Japanese armada; in particular, its new Hellcat fighters outclassed their Japanese equivalents and the American pilots were also far more skilled than their counterparts, whose training had had to be curtailed.

The decisive battle for mastery of the skies was waged on June 19; 400 Japanese aircraft were intercepted and shot down by American fighters with such ease that the American crews talked about its being just a 'big turkey shoot'. During this time, American submarines sank two Japanese aircraft-carriers.

Deprived of air cover, since he had only forty-seven aircraft left, Admiral Ozawa had no other choice than to retreat. That night Admiral Mitscher's reconnaissance picked them up 250 miles away; on June 20 200 American bombers set off on the attack again, sank another Japanese aircraft-carrier and damaged four others. On June 21 the rest of the Japanese fleet succeeded in scattering but it had suffered irreparable losses – five or ten times more than its enemy.

This naval victory enabled the Americans to finish off their conquest of the Marianas undisturbed; Washington had decided on this operation because from there, with their range of well over 3,000 miles, the B 29s which were now coming into service would be able to raid the Japanese archipelago. For this operation, the Americans deployed 100,000 men, the largest landing force that had ever assembled. At Saipan, things did not go very smoothly; there was a pile-up of men and equipment on the beaches which caused heavy losses and two generals disagreed about their respective roles; the island was not captured until August 6 after a fight lasting twenty-five days and with casualties of twenty per cent.

On the other hand, the capture of Tinian ended in complete success. Whilst the Japanese expected the attack to be made on the only large beach on the island, the Americans achieved the technical accomplishment of landing in their rear, in good order, on two beaches only just over 200 yards long overall. Taken by surprise from behind, the Japanese counterattacked savagely, as usual, although a lucky hit had been scored by the Americans on their command post. Within a week, it was all over and the Americans had won, thanks above all to the use, for the first time, of napalm bombs, which created havoc. By August 1, the 9,000 men of the garrison were dead; many of them committed suicide with hand-grenades.

Finally, it was the turn of Guam, which eventually fell on August 10, 1944, after a struggle lasting twenty days. Nimitz set up his forward command post there; airfields were equipped with runways long enough for B 29s; on October 12, 1944, the first mission of these formidable heavy bombers took off: their target was Tokyo.

IV FORMOSA OR THE PHILIPPINES?

After their respective successes, achieved in any case more or less jointly with the one supporting the other, the controversy between MacArthur and Nimitz had sprung up again. The sailors wanted to exploit their victory in the Marianas as soon as possible and press on towards Formosa, since the Japanese archipelago was still too far away to be attacked directly; from Formosa while the B 29s were battering the Japanese industry and defences, landing forces would make a fresh leap forward to the Ryu-Kyu Islands, whence would be launched the final assault.

But MacArthur persisted in wanting to make a detour via the Philippines and use them as the springboard for the crucial attack. It had become a matter of personal concern for him – he had promised the Filipinos to return and he had to keep his word, if only out of consideration for the Resistance movements which, relying on his promise, were battling against the invader; he went even further, and claimed that not only his own but the honour of the United States was at stake. At a more practical level, he pointed out that Formosa, where the Japanese were strongly established in force, was a very different proposition from the Philippines, which were further from Japan and inwardly crippled by a network of resisters working in collusion with the Americans.

This time, the two objectives could not possibly be pursued together; it was clear that opposition from the Japanese would become keener and stronger as it became concentrated over a smaller area and now that Japan herself was at stake. A choice must thus be made. At no time during these discussions was any consideration given to the possible use of the atom bomb, although it was now being manufactured.

In July 1944, Roosevelt, MacArthur and Nimitz met at Pearl Harbour; Admiral King, whose basic dislike of MacArthur still continued unabated, had not been invited, so that MacArthur could put forward his point of view in peace. He succeeded in convincing Roosevelt, and also, rather more unexpectedly, Admiral Nimitz – the President's acquiescence was not without influence on the latter. All the same, no official decision was taken, although in practice the die was cast.

At the Quebec conference in September 1944, MacArthur and Nimitz worked out the timetable of their joint advance. They agreed to co-operate in the invasion of Leyte in December 1944. However, the decision concerning an attack on Formosa, with its saving in time and distance but also its great difficulties, was taken only after the unexpected success of an aircraft-carrier operation against the Philippines by Admiral Halsey; he went very close inshore almost under the eyes of the Japanese, and destroyed airfield installations and enemy aircraft, without any loss to himself; it was a remarkable demonstration of Japanese weakness in the Philippines; equally it spelt the doom of any schemes against Formosa.

On October 4, the final plan was adopted: Luzon and Manila would be liberated first; next they would launch out against Iwo Jima in January 1945; and finally, in March, on Okinawa; so Okinawa replaced Formosa or the Chinese coast as the last stage before Japan.

V JAPAN'S GROWING WEAKNESS

As a result of a law ordering 'general mobilisation of the country' promulgated by Prince Konoye in 1938, capital, industrial plant and external trade in Japan were taken over by or brought under the control of the state. Although this law had not been fully implemented because of the lively opposition from very powerful trusts, war production had grown regularly during the war – taking 1941 as 100, the index had risen to 339 in 1944. But remarkable though this was, it was not sufficient, especially since 1944 marked a peak that was going to be followed by an increasingly sharp decline.

Japan's economic potential suffered from certain natural weaknesses which were difficult if not impossible to remedy. The first was a lack of manpower, not in numbers but in skill, despite the extremely tough use of prisoners of war;[1] another one was the lack of concentration of industry; there were too many small factories working on army contracts and their organisation quickly proved chaotic; thus, in the aeronautical industry, fuselage production had increased sixfold whereas that of engines had increased only fourfold. For agriculture, no plan had been drawn up; in theory, the number of people living in the country had risen; in fact, the surplus came from refugees from towns living with and on the peasants and as a result of mobilisation the actual number of farmers and the amount of land under cultivation had dropped, by roughly ten per cent.

The government realised only too well all the inherent shortcomings of the Japanese economy; it was, indeed, in order to obtain coal, iron, bauxite, rice, rubber and oil that her armies and fleet had set out to conquer a Greater Asia and at first their efforts had been completely successful. But it was only worthwhile exploiting these conquered territories if their produce could be safely shipped back to Japan. And after the

1. In one camp near Singapore 6,000 prisoners died out of 10,000; in another, the Japanese put up a memorial stone to 15,000 POWs who died building a railway.

Americans had captured the Marianas, Japan's shipping links became hopelessly disorganised.

Indeed the Merchant Navy's losses had risen steadily since 1943. A hundred or so American submarines were permanently on patrol, especially on the tanker routes between Borneo and Japan; but even the seas in the proximity of Japan and China were no longer a Japanese lake free from danger; ships were being sunk off Yokohama, Kobe or Nagasaki; that year, a total of 1,800,000 tons went to the bottom.

In 1944, the campaign became even more deadly. More than 3,800,000 tons were sunk; there were 150 American submarines, operating in packs, in liaison with the Air Force, which was now based close to its targets: in February 1945, ship-borne and land-based aircraft alone sank 180,000 tons at Truk. From a tonnage of more than 4,000,000 in 1943, by 1944 the Japanese Merchant Navy had dropped to 3,000,000. Trade was shrinking at a frightening rate. Apart from home waters and continental coastal traffic, the only safe route was the one to Singapore. In the words of an American admiral quoted by Reussner, 'Japan's commercial fleet was being worn out sooner than the empire that it was serving'.

Protective measures were somewhat improved in August 1944 by a decision to place all escort vessels under the control of the Navy. It was too late and the number of escort vessels – 167 of very different types – was inadequate. Thus, the wealth that had been gained by conquest stayed where it was or went to Davy Jones' locker; at all events things were becoming short in Japan; imports of oil, the most valuable of all, fell from 1,500,000 barrels a month in 1943 to 300,000 in 1944.

The decline in output was accentuated by a variety of related causes, all reacting on each other in a vicious spiral. For want of iron ore, steel production fell from the record figure of 5,600,000 tons in 1943, to 4,230,000 in 1944; but from 1941 to 1944 the reserves had melted away from 4,470,000 tons to 450,000. Consequently the naval shipyards were no longer producing the number of ships required. The Navy had, indeed, taken over all naval shipbuilding operations in 1942; it built new shipyards and dockyards, reduced the number of types of vessel, cut down on delays and gave priority to tankers. In 1944 production at 1,500,000 tons was ahead of schedule – this would have been wonderful if losses had not been twice that amount.

Aircraft production suffered a similar spectacular fate: schemes were drawn up, textile factories converted to aeronautics; yet, over nearly four years, only 65,000 aircraft were produced while every year more than 10,000 planes were being lost and, increasingly, experienced pilots were not being replaced.

For lack of shipping, Japanese industry was short of iron which, in turn, meant building fewer ships; and then these ships could no longer get the fuel they needed; consequently, imports of iron were still further reduced and, as a result, the number of ships on the stocks fell, too: it was a vicious circle. The only inevitable conclusion was that Japanese military power was crumbling as the danger to their islands was drawing nearer; the islands were increasingly less well protected by the fleet and the Air Force; seasoned soldiers were not available for their defence as they were tied down in the vast conquered spaces of Greater Asia; bombing was going to hasten the disorganisation of the Japanese economy and, little by little, reduce it to utter chaos.

VI THE BATTLE OF LEYTE

To recapture the Philippines, MacArthur, in addition to his ground forces, had an air squadron under General Kenney and a naval force under Admiral Kinkaid; Admiral Halsey's Third Fleet was to be in support but it remained under Admiral Nimitz's command. This complicated organisation did not lead to any unfortunate consequences; the real problems, once again, were the immense distances and the amount of shipping required.

After having first thought of landing on Mindanao, MacArthur chose the island of Leyte; as usual, he wanted to set up a large naval and air base from which he could launch out to recapture the whole of the Philippines. The landing took place in October 1944, two months earlier than anticipated, and encountered little difficulty – only fifty men killed. The first Japanese reaction was an air attack; it was limited to 200 bombers and half of them were shot down.

The Japanese then decided to risk their all in one big naval and air battle. They had hesitated between two operations: the first was to concentrate their fleet in their home waters and keep it safe; but this meant completely giving up the resources of Greater Asia and, in fact, acquiescing in its loss. The other operation, which was the one adopted, consisted in dividing the fleet into two: one based in Japan, the other in Malaya and the Indian archipelago; the difficulty then would be to bring these two very widely separated halves together at the right time and place.

Yet this was what Admiral Toyoda decided to try. He ordered the two fleets to converge on Leyte; Admiral Ozawa's fleet of aircraft-carriers from the north and the Singapore fleet comprised of two groups of unequal size under Admirals Kurita and Nishimura. The Japanese fleet air arm was inferior to the Americans' and the former had no airfields at hand; in addition, their various combat groups had bad communication links and were unable to co-ordinate their actions.

The battle of Leyte, which Morison has described as 'the greatest naval battle in history' consisted of various episodes, practically simultaneous but separate. On October 24, in the north, Admiral Halsey's aircraft-carriers, as usual, defeated Admiral Ozawa's in the battle of Cape Engano; Ozawa lost four aircraft-carriers and one cruiser; he went about and, applying the principle of naval warfare which says that the chief aim of a fleet commander is the destruction of the opposing fleet, Halsey set out in pursuit; but his intelligence was faulty. He looked for Ozawa in the wrong place and failed to regain contact; so despite his heavy losses, the Japanese admiral had fulfilled his mission which was to draw the American aircraft-carriers away from Leyte.

In fact, in the Japanese plans, the chief role was that of Admiral Kurita who was to use his four battleships – including two of mammoth proportions, *Musashi* and *Yamato* – and eight cruisers to destroy the American amphibious forces off Leyte. On October 25, this Japanese fleet clashed with the escort of aircraft-carriers, under Admiral Sprague; the large warships – this was the constant lesson of the Pacific war – were once again powerless giants against the clouds of aircraft supported by only a few destroyers; one-third of the Japanese fleet was destroyed during that day and another third in the night – this time by old American battleships repaired after Pearl Harbour, thus adding a little extra spice of revenge to the American victory. Without waiting for any more, Admiral Kurita turned and fled.

The Japanese fleet had lost three battleships, four aircraft-carriers, ten cruisers and eight destroyers. The part played in the battle by suicide pilots – the Kamikaze – who crashed their aircraft on their opponents' ships, certainly proved the very great courage of the indomitable Japanese; but this introduction of samurai ideas and methods into modern warfare could not redress the balance of material strength. Like the Wehrmacht later in the Ardennes, the Japanese fleet had staked its all; henceforth, it was no longer capable of fighting. The conquest of the Philippines could pursue its course.

VII THE RECONQUEST OF THE PHILIPPINES

Marshal Terauchi, trained in Germany and one of the most ferocious Japanese commanders in the conquest of China, described by Marshall as the 'perfect example of a Japanese jingo', commanded an immense operational theatre covering the Philippines, Malaya, the Indian archipelago and Borneo; he had set up his headquarters in Manila. In theory, he had ten armies under his command totalling nearly a million men; in fact, his forces were fragmented and tied down. Unable to switch them from place to place or to receive any further reinforcements, he was condemned to meet superior enemy forces wherever they might wish to attack him.

Yet the capture of Leyte proved extremely arduous and needed far more resources and time than had been anticipated; the American intelligence service had underestimated the enemy's strength; the rain-soaked valleys had turned into swamps thus making it impossible to build roads and airfields, so that runways had to be abandoned almost before they had been laid out; the Americans straightaway lost their air superiority and reinforcements were held up; in such circumstances the Japanese attack had a vim and vigour that was not always to be found on the American side. They made no bones about going into the ricefields and harrying the Americans at night, whilst the attacks by the US Army Air Force sounded more effective then they were. The Americans took time to concentrate all the resources and forces necessary to re-establish their supremacy.

A small number of Japanese succeeded in escaping from Leyte; out of 70,000 defenders, 50,000 had been killed; the Americans had deployed more than 250,000 men. As MacArthur had predicted, the capture of Leyte ensured a firm foothold for the Americans in the Philippines; in addition, communications between Japan and the countries of the south Pacific were now severed once and for all.

In the new American objective of Luzon, General Yamashita had only 150,000 men, hardly any air support and was forced to rely on static defence, with no possibility of launching a successful counter-attack. MacArthur landed in the Lingayen Gulf in January 1945; the Japanese had evacuated the beaches and their only reaction was from the Kamikaze, who succeeded in sinking a score of ships and damaging some fifty more, but were unable either to prevent or even delay the American advance.

After taking Clark Field airfield, MacArthur advanced on Manila, which he reached on February 2; but he had to take the town sector by sector and this street-battle lasted until the beginning of March. All that remained was to capture the entrance to the bay, that is the Batan peninsula and the tiny island of Corregidor – the position as it was in 1942 was now reversed, with the Americans attacking the fortifications that they had previously been defending. It took 40,000 Americans a month to overcome all the resistance of the 4,000 Japanese at Bataan. As for Corregidor, after being shelled from the sea and bombed from the air, it was captured on February 27 by a combined operation of landing-parties and paratroops.

Next the Americans had to mop up the south and the north of Luzon; furious fighting took place there right up to the end of the war; especially in the north, which was extremely mountainous, and where there were still 50,000 Japanese continuing the struggle in August 1945; by that time, of course, the Americans had already withdrawn, some months previously, the majority of their forces in order to launch them against Japan itself, leaving the pursuit of the last Japanese in the archipelago to Filipino guerrillas whom they had at first rather distrusted but later provided with arms. There were about 100,000 of them – the Asian counterpart to General Larminat's FFI, which at that moment were being given the task of mopping up the pockets of resistance on the Atlantic.

VIII IWO JIMA

The American plans had been finalised at the San Francisco conference at the end of September 1944. Iwo Jima in the Bonins was to be attacked even before the Marianas had been retaken; they would serve as a staging-post for the big bombers based on Saipan in the Marianas in their raids on Japan and as a fighter base to enable them to be escorted throughout their attack. Afterwards Okinawa, in the Ryu-Kyu Islands, was intended as the great naval and air base for the Pacific 'Overlord' – the landing on Honshu.

Before this, the British and Americans had to settle a problem which once more put their co-operation to the test and which deeply wounded British pride. The British were anxious to re-establish after the war the influence in South-east Asia which had been greatly compromised by their defeats and inglorious forced withdrawals in that area, and so they wanted to play an active part in the final crucial battles in the Pacific. The fighting in Europe would shortly be coming to an end and the battle of the Atlantic would finish even sooner, thus releasing most of their fleet; Mountbatten's additional resources and his successes in Burma would provide the necessary basis for the transfer of forces from Europe to the Far East.

But the Americans were not keen on sharing their laurels with late arrivals and they did not intend to be anybody's catspaw. They limited the British to retaking Singapore and then Indochina and the Indian archipelago, whereas Churchill wanted to return in triumph to Hong Kong. MacArthur agreed to take a British squadron under his command – it would be one less for Nimitz. But Admiral King was vigorously opposed to any such thing; he pointed out that the British Navy was 'short-legged', that is to say that they would have to return to their bases, which were a long way off, after only a fortnight's operations at the most; on the contrary, the American Navy was so equipped as to be able to remain at sea for months on end and declined to give up any part of its logistical resources to help an ally of whom it had no need. The American sailors wanted to wage their own war in the Pacific until final victory and they were determined that it should be a strictly American war and an American victory from beginning to end.

For the first time in history the help of the Royal Navy had been considered useless in a war that involved Britain; this was a humiliation which Roosevelt was anxious to spare Churchill; against the advice of his staff, he decided that the British Navy should take part in the attack on Okinawa.

Iwoshima was a little island just under five miles long and two and a half miles wide nearly 900 miles from Honshu. Three marine divisions were landed there in February 1945. The Japanese had had time to reinforce their defences, both in manpower and guns, which were very well protected. A swarm of Kamikaze planes hurled themselves on the attackers, sinking and damaging nearly 250 craft but sacrificing a good thousand pilots and aircraft, most of them shot down before they reached their targets. The Americans took a month to overcome the opposition, at a cost of 6,821 dead and more than 17,000 wounded. As might be expected, the warlike spirit of the Japanese was far from diminishing as the threat to their homeland drew nearer.

IX OKINAWA

The Japanese expected the attack on Okinawa, which had been constantly raided since October 1944 and even more from January 1945 onwards. They had concentrated nearly 100,000 men on the island, in the southern part of which they had constructed a large number of well camouflaged interconnected tunnels which were vulnerable only to a direct hit; they had made full use of reverse slopes and enfilading fire.

For their part, the Americans had brought together a force of hitherto unprecedented size in the war in the Pacific. The Tenth Army under General Buckner had been specially formed, comprising three marine and four infantry divisions, 180,000 men in all, with 1,200 landing-craft and 110 warships to protect them – including twenty-two British. As a preliminary, the Ryu-Kyu Islands had been isolated by means of submarines and aircraft; then the Kerama and Keise Islands, close to Okinawa, had been occupied without trouble; they were intended to provide shelter for the Navy and long-range guns had been set up on them. Finally, the landing was preceded by bombing raids of fiendish intensity which lasted continuously for more than a week. The Japanese made no reply and 60,000 men were able to come ashore from April 1 onwards almost without a fight.

If the Americans imagined for one moment that they had destroyed or demoralised their opponents, they soon learnt their mistake. The Japanese had merely adopted the tactics advocated by von Rundstedt in Normandy: let the enemy commit himself in order the better to destroy him afterwards and leave him with no possibility or desire to start again. They landed Kamikaze attacks one after the other; by using these romantically suicidal attacks, the Japanese general staff not only intended to assert Japan's indomitable will but cause permanent damage, at a price, to the enemy's war potential, so as to delay any landing on Honshu or even render it impossible. The Kamikaze planes sank more than thirty vessels and damaged more than a hundred, sometimes causing more than a thousand casualties on the same craft – thus one radar ship was attacked twenty-two times and hit by six Kamikaze and four bombs! But although a number of aircraft-carriers and one battleship were put out of action, the Americans' resources were such that they could immediately plug any gaps in their defences – their depots and bases were bulging with stocks and stores and they had supplies for 210 days.

After some hesitation, the Japanese made up their minds to sacrifice what remained of their war fleet – after Leyte, they had hidden the surviving ships by dispersing them in the innumerable bays along their coastline and they had even put their crews ashore. Admiral Toyoda issued the order that 'every sailor must consider himself a Kamikaze'. Eventually, the Japanese managed to assemble one cruiser and eight destroyers, led by the monster battleship *Yamato*, reputedly unsinkable with its 65,000 tons and 150 AA guns; but they no longer had any aircraft-carriers. Opposing them were 27 aircraft-carriers, 10 battleships and 9 heavy cruisers; in addition, another fleet of 15 aircraft-carriers and 8 battleships was lying off, ready to interevene. The balance of forces had greatly changed since Pearl Harbour; it had come into line with industrial power.

On April 8, despite low cloud, the Japanese fleet was attacked by 900 aircraft. It was obliged to turn half-circle without being able to attack the enemy fleet; the *Yamato* was sunk; out of nearly 3,000 officers and other ranks, only 269 were saved.

This disaster at sea failed to destroy the Japanese determination on land; as early as five days later, they counter-attacked. After failing to throw the landing forces back into the sea, they resolutely awaited attack in their underground fortifications. The Americans vainly tried to demolish them with 1000- and 2000-pound bombs and by shelling them from their battleships; although under fire from every direction, the Japanese held out. They had to be winkled out of their bunkers, attacked one by one with tanks and infantry using explosive charges; mostly the defenders were burnt alive or suffocated by tank-mounted flame-throwers, with a range of 100 yards, or else by floods of flaming petrol – 600 gallons were pumped into one of the underground tunnels.

The American attack was stopped for a time by an unexpected Japanese ally: rain, which turned the island into a quagmire where even the tanks' caterpillar tracks became bogged down. But at the beginning of June, the fine weather returned; on the 22nd the Japanese General and his Chief of Staff committed hara-kiri following the appropriate rites. It had been a hard and bloody struggle; the Japanese had lost 110,000 men, 23,000 of them by burning, and several thousand aircraft,[1] mostly flimsily built machines. The Americans had 12,500 dead, including General Buckner, and 400 boats were damaged; they took only 7,400 prisoners.

If the Japanese were defending their advance-posts with such desperate fanaticism, what would happen beyond the archipelago, when it was the turn of Honshu and her sacred cities to be attacked?

[1] From various American sources.

CHAPTER 4

The Japanese Surrender

I AIR RAIDS ON JAPAN

EVEN before the outbreak of hostilities, the Americans had assigned an important role to the B 29 bomber in their war plans in the Pacific; in fact, it had been conceived as a means of attacking Japan from far-distant bases; but strategic bombing was such a complex and rigidly organised operation and such a long time was required for its preparation that B 29s did not come into intensive use until the spring of 1944.

First of all, it took a long time before it was built; it was on the drawing board in January 1940 but an experimental prototype did not fly for the first time until September 21, 1942; the first mass-production aircraft came off the assembly lines in the middle of 1943 and it was not until 1944 that the Air Force was able to put into operation an actual wing of 150 planes.

Calculations showed that the B 29 would be capable of bombing Tokyo from Formosa, Saipan and eastern China—all in the possession of the Japanese. It was plain that the course of the operations would dictate the final choice of the take-off base or bases. This was another reason – added to the Americans' determination to keep this outstanding weapon completely to themselves – for not restricting the B 29 to any one operational theatre; they formed a special strategic 'Twentieth Bomber Command' coming directly under General Arnold and the American Joint Chiefs of Staff.

In view of their inability to fly as far as Japan, the Americans considered the possibility of using B 29s in the first instance from bases in Ceylon, Calcutta and Port Darwin against Burma, Siam, Indochina and Japanese shipping. Roosevelt decided on Operation 'Matterhorn', which was to provide support for China. The logistical problems presented by this plan were immense and difficult to solve: shipping personnel by air via Natal and Karachi or by sea cross the Pacific or round Africa; building runways at great expense by employing hundreds of thousands of Chinese coolies; bringing up fighters to these makeshift airfields in order to defend them; building up stocks of fuel and ammunition, which could only be brought in by B 29s themselves, so that each gallon of petrol on the airfield needed several gallons to fetch it in.

The results were out of all proportion to these titanic efforts; they were frankly disappointing; aircraft became bogged down; the pilots lacked training; the first raids missed their targets and valuable aeroplanes were shot down and not replaced; one of the purposes – to spur Chiang Kai-shek and his troops into action – was obviously not achieved; and, finally, Tokyo was still out of reach from Chungking.

The capture of the Marianas provided the right solution: from Saipan all the towns in Honshu could be reached. American strategists indulged in wild and wonderful speculations; on the assumption that each B 29 squadron could undertake five missions a month and that they would have forty squadrons available towards the end of 1945, they calculated that 168 squadrons a month could completely destroy Japan's economic and military potential in one year. The concentration of industrial targets and the vulnerability of the densely populated areas of wooden houses surrounding them led to preference being given to incendiary bombs; careful calculation worked out that 1,700 tons of M 69 bombs – an eight-pound incendiary bomb which was very effective against light structures – would be the amount of explosive required totally to destroy each of the twenty main cities of Japan. After that, all that would be needed would be to land and pick up the prisoners from amongst the smoking ruins.

Although he had an order of priorities in which the most important targets were aircraft factories, in February 1945 General Arnold decided, as an experiment, to destroy by fire, systematically, a certain number of extensive urban areas. The towns chosen were Tokyo, Nagoya, Osaka and Kobe. In each town an area some four miles by three was marked out where the population reached a density of 128,000 to the square mile. The raids took place by night, using radar, because observation had shown that in Japan cloud often dispersed at the end of the day and the wind dropped somewhat.

On March 8, 1945, Tokyo was hit by 2,000 tons of bombs dropped by 334 B 29s. A quarter of the town – 260,000 buildings – was burnt down, leaving a million people homeless; it took twenty-five days to clear away the rubble and dig out the 83,000 dead; the holocaust had been made worse by the panic-stricken attempts of many of the inhabitants to escape through the flames; the American pilots summed up their mission laconically and triumphantly in the message: 'Target bombed visually; observed extensive fires; moderate flak; no fighter opposition.'

Less than thirty hours after Tokyo, Nagoya was visited, again at night, by 317 B 29s. On March 13, 1,700 bombs wiped out eight square miles of Osaka in three hours; on March 16, it was Kobe's turn to be hit by

2,300 tons of bombs. In ten days, the Twentieth Bomber Command had made 1,600 sorties, dropped nearly 10,000 tons of bombs and destroyed nearly forty square miles of Japanese towns, at the low cost of under one per cent of the aircraft engaged.

II JAPAN'S EXHAUSTION

In these circumstances, it was clear that at this rate Japan's economy would be rapidly destroyed. Would this destruction force Japan to surrender unconditionally, as Roosevelt and Churchill had decided at Casablanca and reasserted, together with Stalin, at Potsdam?

In the spring of 1945, imports into Japan of coal, iron ore, bauxite and petrol had practically ceased. The lack of raw materials plus the effects of the air raids caused the output of steel to drop to 500,000 tons between April and July and that of aluminium to 10,000, that is, barely a quarter of the 1943 production.

Aircraft factories were paralysed by the lack of duralumin; during the first half of 1945, the naval dockyards turned out only 180,000 tons of shipping; by April, the Merchant Navy had been reduced to 2,370,000 tons and in August, it was only 500,000. Petrol stocks were so low that the warships lying camouflaged in the bays along the coast could no longer put to sea and aircrew training had to be restricted to half the time required to produce a properly skilled pilot – it was this that led to the Kamikaze.

Schemes for mass-production by building giant new factories had at last been completed after years of economic anarchy but they could not now even begin to be put into operation. The Japanese government considered dismantling factories and shifting them to Manchuria or Korea; but in June 1945 in the 'Emperor's Council', that is, in the presence of the Emperor, the ministers had to admit that a total breakdown of communications was imminent.

Feeding the people was also a serious problem. Whereas 2,400 calories per day were considered necessary for a Japanese, the authorities could provide a ration of only 1,200 to 1,400. So while there was no shortage of men, they were no longer able to work or fight satisfactorily.

However, there were millions of valiant soldiers, cut off from their homeland, who continued to occupy the greater part of the territories conquered by the Japanese; these soldiers belonged to armies that were still formidable but which from now onwards would have to fend for themselves and receive no supplies from outside. Native nationalists, even the most firmly devoted to Japan's cause, began to question their relationship with her or deserted her; in Burma, they made no bones about changing sides; in Malaya, at the beginning of 1945, nationalist guerrillas, led by the British, joined the Communist guerrillas to fight the Japanese, while still retaining their own identity and highly suspicious of their allies. In China, the Japanese command had been forced gradually to withdraw its forces to the essential coastal ports of Canton, Shanghai and Tientsin; through his opponent's exhaustion Chiang Kai-shek was thus able to do what he had always planned: to free China with a minimum of fighting and at the lowest possible cost.

In order to ensure communications between their forces in Siam and China, the Japanese issued an ultimatum on March 9, 1945, putting an end to the relative autonomy that had been enjoyed by French Indochina by demanding that the army, the police, administration and transport should come entirely under their control. When Admiral Decoux gave an answer that was considered unsatisfactory, the French troops were disarmed and interned, in some places before the ultimatum had expired; sometimes the garrisons were massacred and the French officers beheaded in front of their native troops; French civilians were humiliated, interned and ill-treated. Now at last the nationalists thought that their time had come; they obtained arms from Japanese deserters and negotiated agreements with the Japanese generals, as Asians working together against the Europeans.

The Japanese were thus being prevailed on to prepare for the independence of enormous areas that they had at first thought of annexing. Since the end of 1944, Indonesia had had the right to its own flag and to its own army; the nationalist leaders gradually took over control of the mass movements, as well as of the Japanese-inspired youth movements. In March 1945, a mixed commission was set up with the task of leading Indonesia forward to independence; while Tokyo was in favour, these developments were held back by the local army commanders, who were unwilling to admit the full gravity of the situation. But there was no going back; in June 1945, the nationalists and Moslems formed into one mass movement, in which the former predominated.

The Japanese Empire, reeling under attack from without, was breaking up internally; the Japanese economy was at the end of its tether; the Navy and Air Force out of action. Would the Americans nonetheless have to conquer Japan island by island? And what price would they have to pay?

III CONQUEST OR SURRENDER?

After the Normandy landings and the prospect of a swift defeat of Germany, a few timid voices had been raised in Japan in favour of negotiating with the Americans; they belonged to eminent personalities who had lived abroad and were not blinded by fanatical jingoism; amongst them were Marquis Kido Koichi, Privy Keeper of the Seal and the Emperor's secret informer; Prince Konoye; Yoshida, the former ambassador in London, and Okada, the former Premier; their idea was to persuade Hirohito to abandon the passive role to which he had been restricting himself since the Meiji era and take over the actual leadership of Japan during this difficult time when her fate was in the balance – it was, *mutatis mutandis*, what the conspirators had asked Victor Emmanuel to do in Italy.

While refusing to exceed his legal powers – the constitution contained no provision to allow him to intervene in politics – the Emperor had accepted Tojo's resignation and his replacement by Koiso, another soldier but one who as governor of Korea had played no active part in launching Japan into the war nor in its conduct. A newspaper editor made discreet contact with the Swedish minister in Tokyo but the new government did not dare to speak out openly in favour of actual negotiations. The only man to take a definite stand at this time was Prince Konoye, who sent a minute to the Emperor in February 1945; without beating about the bush, he stated that Japan had lost the war and that the inevitable conclusions must be drawn. The Emperor merely confined himself to listening to all the parties, without adopting any position and even without expressing any personal view; in any case, some of his advisers were saying that he should not undertake any initiative which might compromise the dynasty and as a result jeopardise Japan's traditional social and political structures.

However, the defeat at Okinawa caused Koiso to give way to Admiral Kantaro Suzuki. The new Prime Minister understood the overriding necessity of putting an end to the struggle; but he was unable to bring the military to accept unconditional surrender; he confined himself to creating an atmosphere conducive to peace negotiations. He was unable to prevent Anami, the War Minister, from ordering the arrest of 400 people accused of pacifist propaganda, including the ambassador Yoshida and Judge Sawada, a lawyer of international repute; in the Council of Ministers, the Chiefs of Staff of the Army and the Navy declared themselves in favour of fighting to the bitter end; they were convinced that any American landing in Honshu would end in bloody defeat, thanks to which Japan would be able to obtain better peace terms.

Nevertheless, one of Suzuki's agents made contact with American representatives in Berne and was told that the question of unconditional surrender was not open to discussion. Approaches to Chiang Kai-shek to put an end to the war in China foundered on the question of Manchuria, which Japan wished to retain and China wished to recover.

On June 20, the Imperial Conference decided to approach the USSR to ask her to act as mediator; was she not still bound with Japan by a non-aggression pact? These approaches would at least provide information as to whether there was still hope that Russia would continue to remain neutral in the Far East. Instructions were issued to the Japanese ambassador in Moscow; should the first contacts prove favourable, a special envoy would hold himself in readiness to fly from Tokyo – Prince Konoye. But the Japanese proposals were very vague, in order not to give the impression that Japan was at the end of her tether and also not to offend the military, who had agreed to the approach only on condition that it did not mean accepting any sort of ultimatum. In any case, the USSR replied with a downright snub which left little doubt as to her early intentions.

On the American side, neither government circles nor, above all, public opinion was in favour of making any concession whatsoever towards Japan; indignation at the Pearl Harbour attack was still very much alive and no punishment was considered too severe for those responsible. Only the ambassador Grew expressed loudly and clearly his view that Japan must be convinced that the US did not want either her complete destruction or the end of the imperial régime. But the American armed forces had in fact begun to achieve this destruction by their air raids and were anxious to see it through to the end; as for the Emperor, many Americans rated him as a war criminal who would have to be put on trial with the others.

It was in this mood that the American general staff was preparing its final assault. No one doubted that the price would be extremely high. As always, the first problems to be solved were not so much technical ones as those concerning rivalries between the services and between personalities. As there would now be only one final operational theatre, it was clear that the partitioning of the Pacific between the Army and the Navy could no longer be retained. But how could MacArthur be subordinated to Nimitz or vice versa? One solution which was considered was to appoint MacArthur ambassador in Moscow and put Marshall in charge, under whom Nimitz would have agreed to serve. But MacArthur would not agree to be robbed of his victory when the laurels were just about to be placed on his brow and Marshall's presence in Washington was still considered indispensable. It was thus decided that MacArthur should take command of the ground forces and Nimitz of the naval forces; the strategic air force would retain its independence under General Spaatz. Thus, when the war came to an end, there were still three American commands in the Pacific, subordinated only to the Joint Chiefs of Staff, some thousands of miles away.

Such an organisation could not fail to give rise to problems; to begin with, it did not make the choice of plan any easier. The Navy, led by Admiral King, considered that blockade and bombing would suffice to compel Japan to give up the struggle; and in fact, on July 14, warships subjected the Japanese coastal defences to a merciless shelling without producing any real reaction. In such circumstances, the crucial role would be played by the Navy and the final victory of America would be its victory.

MacArthur raised the objection that it would take a long time slowly to strangle Japan. He advocated a series of landings; it would be an entirely American operation; British and French contingents, as suggested by their governments, would be accepted only on the condition that they would be entirely subordinate to the American command and would not come into operation until July 1946 – after it was all over.

President Truman was afraid of the heavy losses that would be caused by these landings and the ensuing fighting – they were assessed at a million dead and it was calculated that the Japanese still had 5 million men spread out over their islands. In fact, he never reached a final decision between the two plans. He decided that the blockade and the raids on Japan should continue; at the same time, the attack on Kyushu would be launched in November 1945; the attack on Honshu, the heartland of Japan, was not planned to take place until after March 1946. But the success of the first atom bomb explosion upset all these schemes and cut down all these schedules.

IV THE ATOM BOMB

Shortly before the war, European scientists, including the Joliot-Curies, had succeeded in proving experimentally that the atom could be split. From all over Europe, atomic scientists fleeing Nazi persecution had taken refuge in the USA – the Hungarian Leo Szilar, the Italian Fermi, the Germans Fuchs and Frisch, the Dane Bohr – and Einstein had no trouble in convincing Roosevelt of the paramount importance of forestalling Germany in this field of research. In 1942, Roosevelt decided to form a research centre, the 'Manhattan Project' which was set up in Los Alamos in New Mexico, provided with immense material resources and unlimited funds and brought together an extraordinary community of scientists working under Robert Oppenheimer. In 1945, there were 4,000 persons working at Los Alamos and more than 2,500 million dollars had been devoted to making the atom bomb without anyone being able to say with certainty that this concentration of grey matter would lead to any positive result.

Fortunately, the German scientists had taken the wrong turning by concentrating on the heavy water process; they were thus lagging behind and this was aggravated by the destruction of the heavy water installations and reserves in Norway by sabotage and air raids; still later the raids on her industrial installations put Germany out of the atomic energy race before the end of the war in Europe. For her part, Japan had not yet started or even contemplated starting any work in this field.

All the same, at the time of the Yalta Conference, producing an atom bomb still seemed, in Hopkins' words, a 'remote possibility' this was why the possibility of its use had not been taken into account in the plans to deal with Germany or Japan; all that had been done was to set aside a group of B 29s in preparation for dropping it if necessary and to draw up a list of priority targets. Before his death Roosevelt had been informed that work on the bomb was reaching a successful conclusion but he did not have to take any decision regarding it. The secret had been so well kept that even Truman, the Vice-President of the United States, was told about it by the Secretary of War Stimson only when he succeeded Roosevelt.

Anxious to be fully informed before taking a decision which, according to the American constitution would be his and his alone, Truman set up a commission composed of some of his colleagues – Stimson and Byrnes – and four atomic scientists, including Fermi and Oppenheimer. The members of the commission reported disagreement; Stimson and Byrnes were for its earliest possible use against Japan, without giving her the slightest warning – in his memoirs the Secretary of State claims the sole credit for having succeeded in urging Truman to accept this viewpoint. On the other hand, the scientists, appalled by the deadly implications of their invention, now that any danger from Hitler, which was their justification, had disappeared, were of the opinion that the atom bomb should first of all be tried out on some uninhabited spot – an atoll; at the same time, an ultimatum should be sent to Japan and the bomb would only be dropped on a Japanese city if she rejected this ultimatum. One of the scientists, Frank, a German Nobel prizewinner, supported by Einstein, even wanted the use of the bomb to be placed under an effective international control for atomic weapons but this would obviously not be possible for some time to come.

But the USA had only three atom bombs. How could the risk possibly be taken of wasting one on an atoll? The first one was successfully tested at Alamagordo in New Mexico on July 16. Truman consulted his military leaders; all of them – Marshall, King and Arnold – were in favour of dropping the bomb. Only Admiral Leahy, who considered himself an expert on explosives, expressed some reservations, of a technical nature, not of principle. All were agreed that it was impossible to warn Japan, because no one could guarantee that the bomb dropped on the atoll would explode properly and that its effects would thus be sufficiently convincing for the Japanese government.

Churchill readily agreed, as did Stalin in Potsdam, the latter being merely asked incidentally. The Potsdam ultimatum threatened Japan with sudden and total destruction without further details – but the weight and number of air raids left no other fate open to the Japanese, so they did not need to give thought to any other appalling source of destruction. Without waiting for the Japanese to reply, the second bomb was shipped to the island of Tinian by cruiser – which was sunk after it had landed it.

On August 6, it was dropped on Hiroshima; it was more powerful than 20,000 tons of ordinary high explosive; 71,000 people were killed out of a population of 250,000 and the number of casualties who died from wounds and leukemia afterwards was never discovered.

The effects were terrifying. A witness told an American journalist

> ... that he had heard a voice coming out of the undergrowth asking: 'Have you anything to drink?' He saw a uniform. Thinking that there was only one soldier there, he brought some water. When he went into the undergrowth, he saw about a score of them, all in the same dreadful state: their faces burnt all over, their eye sockets empty, their eyes liquefied all over their cheeks. (They must have been looking upwards at the time of the explosion; they may have been part of an AA battery.) Where their mouths should have been there was just an open wound swollen and covered in pus and so painful that they could not even open their lips wide enough to put the spout of the tea-pot into it.[1]

The explosion terrified the Japanese but apparently had no effect on the determination of their military leaders. On August 9 the third bomb – and the last, but the Japanese were not to know – was dropped on Nagasaki, as cloud-cover had protected another town that had been previously selected; this one killed 80,000 people.

Truman does not seem to have felt any qualms of conscience. The Japanese had to be defeated as soon as possible and his advisers had decided with one voice on the most expeditious means; war was war and after all, it was the Japanese who had started it. On the other hand, the scientists, first and foremost Oppenheimer and Einstein – were filled with consternation. Later on, during the electoral campaign, the Republicans blamed the Democrats for their decision which Baldwin described as making them the 'successors of Gengis Khan'. But at the time, the American leaders of whatever party were in agreement.

Did Truman want to impress the Russians? This is what Soviet propaganda claimed during the angry days of the cold war; it was intended as an implicit threat to the USSR as well as a warning to the Japanese. In fact, the Americans did nothing to delay the Red Army's entry into the

---

1. J. Hersey, *Hiroshima*, Paris, Editions Laffont, 1947.

war against Japan, as they had requested. But it is possible that the announcement of the bomb followed by its successful dropping may have induced the Red Army to speed up its preparations and hasten its intervention.

V THE RED ARMY'S CAMPAIGN AGAINST JAPAN

Immediately after Pearl Harbour, MacArthur had expressed the wish that the Soviet Union should take action against Japan. But American approaches in Moscow met with no success: Stalin refused any talks, any information, any sort of co-operation whatsoever, however confidential it might be. It was not until the danger to the USSR from Germany was on the ebb that Stalin revised his position; on October 31, 1943, when Cordell Hull was on a mission to Moscow, he told him that the USSR would declare war on Japan once Germany was beaten; Cordell Hull was as delighted as he was surprised.

At that time, the American Chiefs of Staff were all agreed in wanting the Soviet Union to intervene against Japan in Manchuria; it would be useful if it took place before the costly landings in the Kyushu Islands and on Honshu, for which they reckoned eighteen months' preparation would be required after victory in Europe; thus the greatest possible number of Japanese troops would be pinned down in fighting outside Japan.

By October 1944, however, Soviet-American military co-operation against the Japanese, although agreed on in principle, had made no progress at all. Stalin merely informed Churchill and Eden in Moscow that the Soviet Union would begin operations three months after the German surrender. Moreover, he stated his price – his territorial claims in China which first of all Roosevelt accepted in Yalta and then Truman in Potsdam.

By this time, the American military leaders were less concerned than a year ago at the risk of meeting desperate Japanese resistance in their landings on the islands. In their view, Soviet support had lost much of its importance – after all, the troops confined in Manchuria were not really dangerous; the crucial action would take place on Honshu. However, they did not reject such support – they were in no position to do so anyway. But they insisted that any Soviet action must be swift and take place before the landing on Kyu-Syu.

At Yalta, talks between experts were begun; they did not go very smoothly, because of the Russians' distrust; up to now, Stalin had declined to undertake any real co-operation with the Allies; at best, he had agreed to some sort of joint timetable for their respective campaigns in Europe; but he had never wanted the Americans to set foot on Soviet soil for any reason whatsoever, apart from a few aircrew who left straight-away from the airfield where they had landed after raiding German territory. So no agreement was concluded.

In April 1945, the American Joint Chiefs of Staff had changed their mind; Soviet intervention now seemed entirely unnecessary – and Roosevelt was no longer there to put these military considerations into their proper perspective with a mind to Soviet-American post-war co-operation. But Stimson and Forrestal, the Secretaries of War and Navy, considered that the USA was in no position to ban the Russians from entering Manchuria and that it was out of the question to get there before them; it would thus be polite to let them do what they had in any case been asked to do.

However the Americans' trust in the USSR and in Stalin had been badly shaken by the Russians' behaviour in Romania and Poland. It was not far-fetched to fear that something similar might happen in Manchuria, this time at China's expense – and the United States had, in fact, been drawn into war against Japan by China, which they intended to restore to her full power and sovereign territorial rights and which they did not want to become Communist. Before the Potsdam Conference, Hopkins made a final trip to Moscow to sound Stalin on this subject. On May 28, 1945, he cabled a report from Moscow to Washington calming the Americans' apprehensions. Stalin, he said, 'had stated categorically that he would do everything in his power to bring about Chinese unity under Chiang Kai-shek'; he made it clear that 'there was no Communist leader strong enough to unite China'; he declared that he had no territorial ambitions in Manchuria or in Sinkiang and that the Red Army would everywhere respect Chinese sovereignty and restore Chinese government; he also gave his agreement to a trusteeship of Korea exercised by the USA, Britain, China and the USSR. Could one imagine anything more accom-modating?

These statements forestalled any American objections which in any case would have had no practical effect. Accordingly, agreement was reached in Potsdam concerning the manner of the Soviet Union's entry into the war in the Far East, which was to take place in August. There was one point, however, which embarrassed the Russians – they were bound to Japan by a non-aggression pact. One of Byrne's assistants, Benjamin Cohen, whispered the solution in Molotov's ear: the great powers would invoke the United Nations Charter – not yet ratified – to launch a concerted operation against Japan 'in order to maintain peace'.

The USSR intervened on August 9 – three days after the first atom bomb had been dropped; it may be surmised that their action was hastened by that news from the fact that Stalin did not wait for the conclusion of talks which had begun with Chiang Kai-shek, on the lines laid down in Hopkins' report. The Soviet Union had a joint frontier with territories controlled by the Japanese well over 2,000 miles long, and its course plainly dictated the Red Army's decision to launch an enveloping operation to encircle the Japanese troops. Marshal Vassilevski's forces were three times the size of those of the Japanese, whose so-called Kwangtung Army comprised roughly 750,000 men, supported by 1,000 aircraft.

Despite torrential rain and the barriers of wide rivers and wooded ridges, the Russians advanced swiftly – the tanks covered as many as 100 miles a day; however, at certain points the Japanese offered stubborn resistance, as always. Kharbin was not taken until August 20. One day before, the Red Army had joined hands with the Chinese People's Army.

On August 17, Marshal Vassilevski had issued an ultimatum to the Japanese; he dropped paratroops on Mukden and the Soviet fleet occupied the coastal ports and prevented any evacuation by the Japanese troops; where would they have gone to anyway? At 4 p.m. on August 20, the Japanese command gave orders to its troops to lay down their arms and the Japanese units gathered at the appointed places. That same day, Mukden was taken; Port Arthur fell on the 23rd, Sakhalin on the 28th; on September 1, the Russians landed on the Kuriles.

Soviet historians assert that the speed and completeness of this victory was the major cause of Japan's surrender. They contrast this ten-day campaign, leading to the capture of 500,000 Japanese soldiers, with the slow and largely ineffectual fighting of the Americans over a period of three years. It is clear that in so doing they had proved that to a greater degree even than in eastern Europe, the Red Army was capable of implementing in Manchuria the policy decisions of the Kremlin, whatever the reservations or even the hostility of the British and Americans. However, the importance attaching to this great victory would only have been deserved beyond any doubt had it taken place before the atom bomb had been dropped. In fact, when the Japanese troops in Manchuria stopped fighting on August 20 the Emperor had already informed the Americans six days earlier that he would agree to an unconditional surrender. The only question which now remained was whether the Japanese military would accept the Emperor's decision.

VI THE JAPANESE SURRENDER

The Allies' determination to demand unconditional surrender from Japan had been further strengthened by Stalin's statements to Hopkins; no doubt fearing that an agreement between America and Japan might be negotiated behind his back just as he had several times thought that he detected signs of similar intentions by his partners in Europe with regard

THE DEFEAT OF JAPAN

to Germany, Stalin had insisted on the necessity of 'destroying once and for all Japan's military might'; if, in order to induce them to recognise their defeat as soon as possible, it proved tactically necessary to let the Japanese hope for relatively gentle peace terms, later on, during the occupation of their country – in which the USSR certainly had hopes of taking part – the greatest severity would need to be shown; indeed, Stalin said 'if the war lords, the leading industrialists and the politicians are allowed to retrench themselves in Japan with their armies unconquered, their navy not entirely destroyed and their industrial plant partly intact, they will straightaway start preparing their war of revenge.' This desire to weaken Japan seems to Morison a plot by Stalin to import Communism into Japan, but this view probably originates from the atmosphere prevailing during the 'cold war'. In fact, Stalin was perfectly well aware that the occupation of the Japanese islands would be primarily undertaken by the Americans and that the United States would see that their ideas prevailed. Another possibility is that Stalin wished to set Japan definitely apart from the continent of Asia, which he hoped to transform into a vast private preserve for international Communism and Soviet expansion – starting with China; but this is equally improbable. Stalin's confidence in Chiang Kai-shek at this period does not seem to have been a pretence; nor does the fundamental role that he considered the Americans, and the Americans alone, should play in setting China on her feet again. He knew full well – he had told Hopkins so – that it would take the USSR years to recover from the injuries she had sustained. The USSR had none of the entirely justified grievances towards Japan that she had towards Germany; but both in Europe and Asia, it seemed to Stalin that the utter defeat of his opponent was the best guarantee against any temptation to have another try.

On the part of the Americans, there had been little relaxation in their refusal to allow Japan any concessions; the ambassador Grew had had difficulty in having Hirohito's name removed from the list of war criminals; nor was this any guarantee that the Japanese dynasty would be maintained. Japan's failure to reply to the Potsdam ultimatum was hardly likely to arouse feelings of indulgence towards her; without publicly refusing, the Japanese government had in fact allowed the press to offer an uninhibited commentary on the Allies' solemn declaration. If there was any chink in the determination of the Japanese it was extremely well hidden.

The atom bomb precipitated events; it was plain that the apocalypse had come for Japan and that the massacre must be halted. At the Council of Ministers on August 9 there was unanimous desire to end hostilities. But though the Prime Minister Suzuki, the Foreign Minister Togo Shigenori and the Minister for the Navy Yonai were in favour of accepting the ultimatum unreservedly, the War Minister Anami and the Army and Navy Chiefs of Staff, General Umezu and Admiral Toyoda, wanted to discuss the terms; they were against the occupation of the whole of Japan and her complete disarmament. The Council of Ministers was too divided to take a decision; it placed the decision in the hands of the Emperor.

In the night of August 9–10, Hirohito at last broke his silence; he decided against the military leaders who continued to assert that an enemy landing would cause such bloodshed amongst the landing troops that Japan might obtain 'honourable terms'. The Emperor stated that continuing the war would destroy the nation; the problem was to safeguard the imperial dynasty as a guarantee of Japan's long-term revival. In reply to the note expressing these ideas, the Allies replied that the 'Emperor's authority would be exercised under the supervision of the interallied C.-in-C.'; this was both something of an assurance and a deep humiliation for the sacrosanct Emperor who would henceforth come under a foreign occupying power. More royalist than the Emperor, the military leaders advocated refusal. Once again, and this time brooking no refusal, the Emperor asserted his will; on August 14 Japan accepted the Allied terms.

The question remained of whether the young Japanese officers would be prepared to submit. Several times in the past, they had not hesitated to execute their own leaders when they considered them guilty of not doing what they considered the right thing. Would they dare to revolt against the Emperor? On August 11, with the tacit connivance of the War Minister, this thought was in the minds of some of them, and during the night of August 14–15 they decided to act, by trying to bring out a guards' division in rebellion with them; the attempt failed. The only result was an outbreak of hara-kiri, set off by Anami. But Hirohito knew of the danger and was able to assess it, and this may explain his delay in taking his decision, a delay which caused great harm to Japan by prolonging the sufferings of her people and adding to the destruction.

If the officers' putsch had succeeded, what support would they have found amongst the public? Immediately after dropping the first atom bomb, the Americans had produced a technically remarkable piece of propaganda; millions of copies of a pamphlet translated into Japanese, drawn up after 'talks' between Washington and Hawaii using radio photography and secret telephone, were printed in Saipan, put into special bombs and dropped in vast quantities by B 29s over every Japanese town. It is true that Japan's dense population helped the dissemination of such a message and her dramatic situation made the Japanese all the more open to suggestion. Yet the political effect of the operation must remain in doubt; nothing in their history or their habits had prepared the Japanese for such an event. In any case, since it emanated from the enemy, it carried much less weight than the Emperor's message broadcast to his people on August 14 announcing his decision. But the fact that, for the first time, the Japanese masses had been called upon to know their fate, by their past leaders and future rulers, both from within and without, with no power left to decide for themselves, heralded fundamental changes in their political rules and customs.

When Hirohito had spoken, the Japanese military leaders submitted one after another; but their remoteness made it impossible to synchronise the surrenders in every operational theatre, so these took place in stages throughout the month of September. The main surrender, which Mac-Arthur was determined to make solemn, spectacular and symbolic, took place on board the battleship *Missouri* on September 2, 1945, off Tokyo. In full dress uniform and accompanied by obsequious civilians, Lieutenant-General Torashivo Kawabe signed the act of surrender for all the armed forces in the name of the Emperor. The countries which had been temporarily beaten by Japan – Britain, the Netherlands and France – were all represented, France by General Leclerc; their face had now been saved if not their empires; at the same time throughout their conquered territories, the Japanese were handing over their power and their weapons to the native nationalist leaders.

VII THE CAUSES OF THE JAPANESE DEFEAT

The protagonists and the historians disagree about the real cause of the Japanese defeat. Those responsible for the strategic bombing assert that Japan's destruction would have been completed by the end of 1945, even without the atom bomb. Admiral Nimitz continued to believe that it was America's complete naval supremacy that enabled victory to be achieved and that it alone would have sufficed; the Soviet thesis has found unexpected support from General Chennault, who was in charge of air operations in China: in his view, the Red Army's intervention was the determining factor and would have been so without the atom bomb. But no one has attributed the victory to Chiang Kai-shek, except himself.

The liveliest debate has been on the subject of the atom bomb – a debate not unconnected with electoral propaganda as well as the genocidal character that it gave the end of the American war. While recognising that it shortened the conflict by more than a year and saved more lives than it cost, Morison deplores the fact that by hastening Russian intervention, it increased the anarchy reigning in China and that, in Indonesia as elsewhere, it prevented the American troops from taking the situation in hand, which they were only able to do after the Japanese had handed over their authority, thus creating a situation for which there was no redress; but could these troops have done anything but recognise the actual power already granted to the nationalists by the Japanese?

It would seem that it is the sum of all these causes that first led up to and then precipitated the Japanese defeat. But there were two permanent and overriding factors which meant that the writing was already on the wall: first and foremost, Japan's economic weakness – she had only fifteen per cent of America's potential – which made it impossible for her to produce a vast military effort and at the same time exploit an equally vast empire, when each of these two operations assumed that the other was, if not complete, at least progressing favourably. The inferiority of the Japanese could only have been compensated for by the Americans' inability to take advantage of their great superiority at the right time or their excessive tardiness in doing so; from this point of view, the American decision to give priority to Germany could have presented an insurmountable handicap. But the Americans – and this is the second decisive factor – succeeded in mobilising and using their strength magnificently; it was the Pacific rather than the European war which was a triumph for the Americans' capacity for organisation, forward planning and the deployment of their giant strength. Not without pride, Morison stresses the fact that American strategy in Asia was faultless – once personal squabbles, command problems and inter-service rivalry had been settled.

So the fact that this superiority culminated in the appalling apotheosis of the atom bomb is a secondary consideration; only the circumstances, the formulation and the timing of the solution were altered, not the basic problem itself.

Thus whilst the United States were precipitately withdrawing from the hornet's nest of Europe, they were becoming deeply involved in Asia – the Pacific was becoming an American lake, with its shores in Australia and the Japanese archipelago as well as in California. But they had not been so successful on the continent as they had been at sea, nor in the archipelagos of the south Pacific, where they had not really obtained a foothold. Similarly their anti-colonialist policy was going finally to bring down the existing structures without putting anything constructive in their place. China, now left to herself, was the first great post-war riddle; but the liquidation of the colonial empires that had already begun was a foretaste of others to come; the United States had only temporarily succeeded in lifting herself out of the backwash set off by the Japanese attack on Pearl Harbour.

BOOK SIX

THE WORLD AT THE END OF THE WAR

CHAPTER I

The Aftermath

No war had ever caused such immense havoc, material and moral, as the Second World War. If one compares it with the First, one sees that the fighting took place over the greater part of the globe, on land, sea and in the skies; that new methods or weapons, such as massive air raids and the atom bomb, were shown to be incomparably more deadly; that, in addition to the losses sustained in the fighting, ideological and revolutionary warfare involved the destruction of whole categories of people. However, of all the continents, Europe was the hardest hit; the greatest battles were fought over her territory; and the most fundamental and lasting upheavals took place in European countries.

I THE BLOODSHED

The number of casualties can only be approximately assessed; accurate figures are lacking for China and Japan; elsewhere the destruction of civilian records, the use of false identities, displaced populations and deliberate disappearance (as of war criminals or prisoners of war who remained in the country in which they were held) make it difficult, if not impossible, to count up exactly the number of deaths or to make comparisons, in each individual country, between pre-war and post-war population figures. Also, after the cessation of hostilities, there were many deaths attributable to the suffering due to the war: e.g. leukemia as a result of the atom bomb or deaths from 'concentration camp sickness'.

As a result, assessments vary between 40 and 50 million people, that is roughly four times as many as between 1914 and 1918. Other differences compared with the First World War were that half the casualties were civilians, including many women and children, and that a very large number, for which only an approximate figure can be given, lost their lives without their death having any direct relation with the needs of war – millions of Jews and concentration camp inmates.[1]

1. The *Comité d'Histoire de la deuxième guerre mondiale* has been trying for the last ten years to find out the exact number of French subjects sent to Nazi concentration camps; it has been compelled to acknowledge that it is impossible to trace them all, although it has 200,000 classified individual index cards.

In Europe, the losses sustained by the belligerents depended on the harshness of the German occupation or whether it took place early or late in the war, as well as on how their armies had fared. As a large part of her territory suffered grievously under the ss and as she used large numbers of infantry, the USSR heads this spectacular list with roughly 20 million dead, that is almost twelve per cent of her population. Poland's losses were proportionately even higher: 6,000,000 men, that is twenty-two per cent of her population, only 600,000 of whom fell in battle; the others were mainly exterminated in concentration camps, in particular almost all the Jews; but many hundreds of thousands were transplanted to the USSR and shared the difficult living conditions of the Soviet people, or suffered under Stalin's harshness. In Yugoslavia, the partisan war was very hard fought, with its accompaniment of mutual reprisals: out of 1,500,000 people missing, 1,200,000 were civilians. The proportion was roughly the same in Greece, where circumstances were similar: 20,000 armed forces and 140,000 civilians.

In western Europe, the losses were noticeably lighter. Belgium, Holland and Norway each lost a few tens of thousands of men, most of them in Nazi concentration camps and from starvation during the last few months of the war in the Netherlands. In France, the number of people missing is assessed at 600,000, of whom 200,000 were soldiers killed in the campaigns of 1939–40 and 1944–5 and 400,000 civilians – deportees, people executed or killed in air raids. It is plain that these enormous differences between eastern and western Europe spring from the relatively 'moderate' treatment shown by the occupying power, at least until 1944.

Although taking part in the fray from beginning to end, Britain had only 326,000 military casualties; but for the first time in her modern history, she experienced the horrors of war on her own territory and 62,000 civilians were entombed beneath the heaps of rubble caused by the Luftwaffe. However, it was in the USA that men's lives were placed least at risk, because they were the only belligerents whose territory was left completely unscathed and their mechanised armies fought with weapons rather than cannon-fodder: in all they had 300,000 dead, all of them in the armed forces, divided almost equally between the European and Asian operational theatres.

Relatively few Italian troops were engaged in fighting and Italy made her exit from the war soon enough for her casualties to amount to only 310,000 dead, half of them civilians; 70,000 soldiers were reported missing in the USSR. As for Germany, her direct war losses totalled nearly 8 million, comprising 4,400,000 soldiers – including Austrians and *Volksdeutsche* – and 2,000,000 civilians killed in Allied air raids; three-quarters of her military casualties died on the eastern front.

In Asia, China's losses were estimated at between 6 and 8 million men and Japan's at 3 million, including 600,000 civilians. But no figures can be adduced for India and Pakistan[1] or for the countries occupied by Japan.

In these figures, the total number of Jews killed can be only approximately assessed, as the Nazis took great care to leave the least possible trace of their abominable crimes. However, a report prepared at Himmler's request in the spring of 1943 spoke of 'a decrease of four million in the number of European Jews'. In view of the fact that there were ghettoes and work camps of considerable size still existing in occupied Poland at that date and that deportation had not yet started in several countries, in particular Hungary, Israeli statisticians have arrived at the figure of 6 million Jews killed by the Nazis' anti-Semitic measures; moreover, the same total is reached if one adds together the 'output' of the great slaughterhouses where this genocide was being perpetrated or if one compares the population of the Jewish communities before and after the war.

To these 'direct' losses must be added the 'indirect' losses caused by the fall in the birth-rate and the increase in the death-rate; exhaustion, resulting from undernourishment amongst the civilian population, for example, continued to take its toll several years after the end of hostilities, in the form of rickets or tuberculosis; in Germany, for example, this 'excess' death-rate has been estimated at 3 million people between 1939 and 1950.

Germany's case is indeed a peculiar one; the heavy conscription of men over a period of more than six years caused a marked discrepancy between the sexes amongst the German population – in the Federal German Republic in 1960 there were still 126 women for every 100 men. During the war itself, however, the birth-rate did not fall, as a result of the enforced presence in the Reich of millions of prisoners of war or workers in the forced labour camps.

As a rule, also, the losses were made up more quickly than after the First World War; in France, the birth-rate started picking up as early as 1942. However, in every country the number of old people in the population rose above that of younger adults; the average life-span decreased; the discrepancy between ages and sexes did not disappear for a number of years. All these factors were not without effect on the economy and on society: the drop in manpower held back production; in the belligerent countries, the active population had to carry a heavier burden after the war than in the neutral countries, in order to maintain the old people, children or those disabled by the war. Many women were unable to marry and start a family and this was probably one of the causes of the increase in illegitimacy; the scarcity of men at home also explains the increasingly

1. In particular, for deaths due to famine.

frequent employment of women on arduous tasks as well as the rapid promotion of young people, insufficiently mature, to take over from the lost generation of older men.

II POPULATION MOVEMENTS

Immense migrations took place as a result of military operations, sometimes induced by fear (the civilian exodus in France in 1940 to escape from the Wehrmacht or in east Germany in 1944–5 to escape the Red Army), and others caused by the war itself and lasting at least as long (there were 12,000,000 prisoners of war at the very least and large numbers of people were transferred to increase armament-production in central Germany or beyond the Urals); even the United States experienced the migration of labour from the south and the middle west to the industrial areas of the north-east. But it was only Europe which experienced the upheaval caused by massive population movements ordered by the belligerents.

During the war the main transfers concerned the *Volksdeutsche*, whom Hitler repatriated to Germany in implementation of a series of bilateral agreements: German speakers from south Tyrol; German minorities from the Baltic states, Bukovina and north Dobruja, Croatia and Bulgaria. Italy, the USSR, Romania, Croatia and Bulgaria agreed to these movements which affected some 600,000 people in all but only roughly one-third of the various populations of German origin or culture; the German communities of Transylvania, the Banat and Hungary largely stayed where they were; as for the Tyroleans, many of those who opted for Germany were not repatriated, as Hitler considered it more expedient to annex the region after the fall of Mussolini.

In the reverse direction, the Germans tried to colonise the Ardennes and above all Alsace-Lorraine, the Lorrainers being expelled into France and many Alsatians sent to Germany. Above all German settlers drove out 3 million Poles from the Poznan region in the General Government, as well as 80,000 Slovenes from Carinthia and 70,000 Czechs from Sudetenland. However, they failed, primarily through lack of time, to settle more than a few thousand Dutch or Danes in the Ukraine.

During the war, Stalin also instigated considerable movements of population, either as a matter of policy or as a precaution. He raised no difficulties in letting the Germans move out of the territories annexed in 1939–40 and later on he thought it wise to deport the German colony on the Volga, the Tartars in the Crimea and the Kalmuks in Caucasia to Siberia; he dispersed Estonians, Lithuanians and above all Poles, probably more than a million in all, throughout the vast spaces of the Soviet Union. In exchange, 200,000 Romanians moved out of Bessarabia, 140,000

Magyars out of Transylvania and 250,000 Karelians left their country to seek refuge in Finland.

But the main flood of migration took place at the end of the war as a result of the Red Army's advance into central Europe, and here the Germans were the main sufferers. At first Hitler tried to stop the inhabitants from leaving the areas threatened by invasion but he succeeded only in delaying them, and the impending German defeat brought about a general exodus. The first to leave were the most recent settlers in the Crimea and the Ukraine; then members of communities that had been established for several centuries in Romania, Yugoslavia and Hungary – more than a million people in all.

The two main currents were those from Bohemia and Poland, draining away almost all the Germans. In Sudetenland, out of almost 3 million Germans, only 170,000 remained; two-thirds of them went into the British and American occupation zones, the other third into the Soviet zone, despite the reluctance of the authorities. By 1945, $1\frac{1}{2}$ million Czechs had taken their place.

In Poland, more than $1\frac{1}{2}$ million Germans first of all evacuated the General Government where they had settled. But in face of the Russian steamroller, the Prussians, Pomeranians and Silesians took to their heels. After the Potsdam Conference, the expulsion of the Germans, already started by the *de facto* Polish authorities set up by the USSR, became systematic, either with the tacit approval of the British and Americans or else because they were powerless to stop it. About 5 million Germans abandoned their houses and towns that had been built by their ancestors. They were gradually replaced by Poles repatriated from Siberia or from the former Polish provinces which, with the consent of the Lublin Committee, had now finally become Russian. In all, 10 to 12 million Germans completely without resources sought asylum in the British, American or French occupation zones, where there was little more than ruins to greet them.

The number of persons euphemistically described as 'displaced' has been assessed at 30 million. In fact, no European country went entirely unscathed; Norwegians and Swedes moved out of Lapland when fighting broke out there; Greeks left Bulgarian Macedonia and Bulgarians occupied Dobruja.[1] Most of the time the same population ebbed and flowed over the same territory. But the large population movements at the end of the war were irreversible. The ethnographical map of central and western Europe was completely transformed; the Slav peoples had moved westwards almost to the Elbe, which had been their limit in the Middle Ages. Thus Prussia made its bow from world history, an event of

1. With the help of UNRA, by 1947, 7 million persons had been repatriated.

capital importance. Equally, Germany was shrinking visibly at the very moment that she was becoming overpopulated; the influx of refugees posed immediate big problems of food and lodging and later on would create political and economic difficulties.

In these migrations of peoples swept away by the tide of events, there were in 1945 some who either could not or would not find asylum anywhere: these were survivors of concentration camps who had lost everything and who longed to escape from Europe, many of them to Israel; there were also the exiles from countries annexed by the USSR – the Poles in Anders' army for example; and finally there were all those who feared that they might be in trouble with the law in their own countries by reason of their actions during the war – the 'collaborators'. In all, there were more than 900,000 human beings packed into makeshift internment camps where most of them languished for several years.

III THE MATERIAL HAVOC

Destruction was chiefly caused when fighting was bitter and prolonged over the same area; above all when, as in the USSR, the opponents successively conquered and then lost the same territories. Allied air raids were an equally powerful factor but their effect was mainly felt in areas where landings took place and in German towns, those in the west suffering more frequently and in the early stages in the war. By comparison, 'scorched earth' tactics, Resistance sabotage, the occupying power's reprisals or acts of vengeance by the victors caused less serious but more widespread damage; in Germany, the worst was probably avoided by not implementing Hitler's policy of total destruction. In Asia, only Japan suffered heavy damage from air raids; as a rule, the fighting took place in relatively unpopulated regions, except in China.

Thus it was Europe which suffered most from the war. It is more difficult than it might appear to establish exact figures of the amount of material destruction: how, for example, can one assess the loss of working hours, reduced output, the abnormal wear and tear of badly maintained plant? However, in all the countries that were occupied, 'reparations' commissions drew up statistics, sometimes extremely detailed, of buildings destroyed, damage caused, goods commandeered and art treasures stolen, in order to be able to quote chapter and verse when claiming repayment from Germany.

In the USSR, the statistical year book for 1962 mentioned the total or partial destruction of 1,710 towns, 70,000 villages and 6 million houses; in addition, the Germans had destroyed or damaged 31,850 industrial concerns, 40,000 miles of railway track, 98,800 kolkhozes and 2,890 tractor depots; they appropriated and despatched to Germany 7 million horses and 17 million cattle. It was agriculture that suffered most, as industry was partly saved by dismantling factories and transferring them to the east; it was the richest land which was devastated, to the point where cultivation had been reduced to manual labour by families as a result of the disappearance of mechanical equipment.

In Poland, a report by the 'War Reparations Bureau' assessed the destruction of transport and scientific and industrial equipment at 80 per cent, agricultural implements and buildings at 50 per cent, whilst nearly 620,000 acres of forest were completely devastated; 10 per cent of Warsaw was destroyed in 1939 and 70 per cent in 1944. In all, these losses are assessed at 31 per cent of the national wealth; in 1945, grain production had dropped to 39 per cent of the 1938 figure; there were 1,500,000 cases of tuberculosis. If, quantitatively, it was Russia that suffered most, it is clear that proportionately it was Poland that was hardest hit.

Yugoslavia, infinitely less rich, suffered more grievously than Britain and almost as much as France; 20 per cent of her houses were destroyed, as well as 30 per cent of her orchards and 50 per cent of her livestock; her railway installations and rolling-stock were reduced to 20 per cent and her industrial potential to 36 per cent. This destruction was countrywide, with no region escaping unscathed; but it made the underdevelopment of Bosnia and Montenegro even worse.

In France, far less blood was shed than in 1914–18; on the other hand, the material losses extended over the whole country, with the south-west as the only region relatively unscathed; many areas of towns were nothing but rubble; in particular, all the harbours had been systematically bombed or sabotaged and were blocked by sunken ships. Out of nearly 51,000 miles of railway track more than 23,000 miles were damaged, as well as 1,900 bridges and tunnels and 4,000 road bridges; rolling-stock was reduced to a quarter of the number of locomotives and carriages existing in 1938 – the others were either destroyed or had been sent to Germany; communications between Paris and south-western and south-eastern France were not re-established until September 10, 1944. More than a million buildings suffered damage; stocks of coal and ore dwindled to practically nothing; industrial output sank to almost half the 1938 figure. In the agricultural sector, in the course of the whole war, Cépède assesses the losses caused by destruction and demolition at 118 per cent for wheat, 200 per cent for potatoes and 112 per cent for wine, compared with an average harvest. In addition, thousands and thousands of acres of beaches and clearings as well as fields had been covered with 13 million mines and pounded by 17 million shells. A number of branches of the German forces specialised in looting works of art; and 60 per cent of France's machine tools were transferred to Germany. Destruction on such a scale

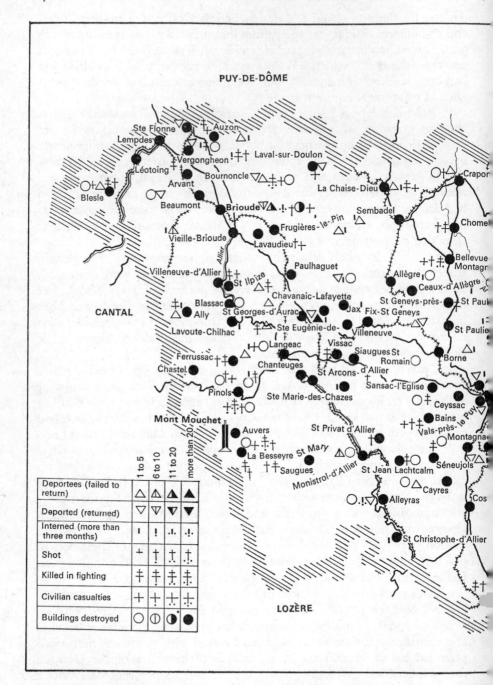

PUY-DE-DÔME

Ste Florine
Lempdes
Léotoing
Arvant
Blesle
Beaumont
Vergongheon
Bournoncle
Auzon
Laval-sur-Doulon
La Chaise-Dieu
Crapor
Brioude
Vieille-Brioude
Lavaudieu
Frugières-le-Pin
Sembadel
Chomel
CANTAL
Villeneuve-d'Allier
St Ilpize
Blassac
Ally
St Georges-d'Aurac
Chavanaic-Lafayette
Paulhaguet
Allègre
Ceaux-d'Allègre
St Geneys-près-
Bellevue
Montagr
St Pau
Lavoute-Chilhac
Ferrussac
Chastel
Pinols
Langeac
Chanteuges
Ste Eugénie-de-
Jax
Fix-St Geneys
Villeneuve
Vissac
Siaugues St
Romain
St Arcons-d'Allier
St Paulie
Borne
Sansac-l'Eglise
Ceyssac
Bains
Vals-près-le Puy
Montagna
Séneujols
Cos
Mont Mouchet
Ste Marie-des-Chazes
Auvers
La Besseyre St Mary
Saugues
Monistrol-d'Allier
St Privat d'Allier
St Jean Lachtcalm
Cayres
Alleyras
St Christophe-d'Allier
LOZÈRE

	1 to 5	6 to 10	11 to 20	more than 20
Deportees (failed to return)	△	◭	◮	▲
Deported (returned)	▽	▿	▾	▼
Interned (more than three months)	!	!	.!.	.!.
Shot	+	†	‡	.†.
Killed in fighting	‡	‡	.‡.	.‡.
Civilian casualties	+	+	‡	‡
Buildings destroyed	○	◖	◑	●

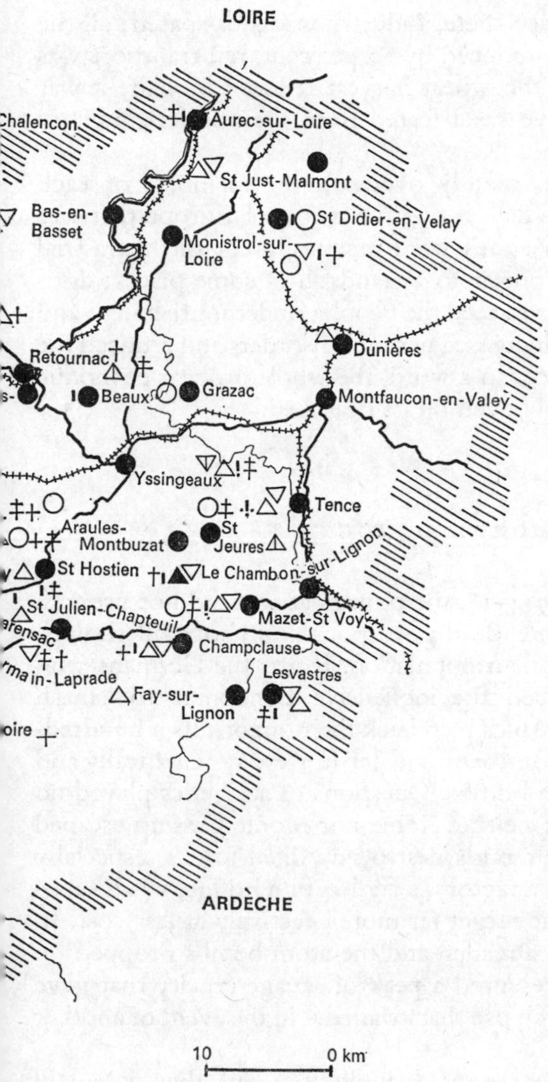

LOIRE

Chalencon

† Aurec-sur-Loire

▽ St Just-Malmont

Bas-en-Basset

St Didier-en-Velay

Monistrol-sur-Loire

▽ I †

Retournac †

Dunières

Beaux ○ Grazac

Montfaucon-en-Valey

Yssingeaux ▽ △ I †

Tence

Araules-Montbuzat

St Jeures △

St Hostien †I △ ▽ Le Chambon-sur-Lignon

St Julien-Chapteuil

Mazet-St Voy

Champclause

Lesvastres

Fay-sur-Lignon

ARDÈCHE

10   0 km

Map 30

THE ORDEAL OF A FRENCH DEPARTMENT

Statistics
Casualties in the fighting at Mont Mouchet from 31 May to 11 June 1944

	Combatants	Civilians	Total
Haute-Loire	55	27	82
Cantal	64	35	99
Lozère	6	7	13
Sum totals	125	169	194

Area : 5000 km 2

Population : (approx. number of inhabitants 250,000)

Confirmed arrests: 1504

Deportees: 234 (including 83 foreigners)

Children: 21 ; Men: 171 ; Women: 42

Returned : 58 (including 5 foreigners)

Failed to return : 176 (including 78 foreigners)

Resisters : 60

Hostages and picked up in raids : 24

Racial : 94 (including foreigners)

Political : 27

Criminal : 9

Unspecified : 19

Died in Battle : 313 (total)

Killed or shot : 232 (including 82 round Mont Mouchet)

Civilian Casualties : 74 (including 4. in June 1944)

Buildings destroyed : 66 (including bridges)

Interned for more than 3 months : 208

Killed during the final fighting in June 1940: 2

Survey made in 1967 (comprising 90 communes)

was unprecedented. But the needs of the war required rapid repairs and many sectors had recovered before the end of the war, with American aid.

On the whole, despite having been first an aggressor and then a beaten country, Italy suffered less than France because although the northern plain, the richest region, experienced air raids and guerrilla warfare, no conventional fighting took place there. Industry was thus spared; all the same, the national wealth was reduced by 20 per cent, rail transport was 50 per cent disorganised and the wheat harvest reduced by half; it was obviously less than might have been feared from the political, military and moral fiasco of Fascism.

Of course, this devastation mainly overtook the members of each country; but at the end of the day, it was the whole of Europe that was weakened. Relations between states were practically cut off; industrial output was reduced if not brought to a standstill in some places; agriculture was no longer adequate to feed the people; undernourishment and the strains and stresses of war increased nervous disorders and reduced the productivity of the labour force. In a word, the whole pre-war economic system was disabled or possibly even on its deathbed.

IV MORAL HAVOC

Unlike their predecessors in 1914–18, the powers at war did not use gas. But they did employ far more deadly weapons and above all showed complete disregard for the civilian population. It was the Germans who started this when they bombed the inoffensive Londoners to 'smash British morale'. Later on, the Allies paid back their opponents a hundred-fold. The chief cities of Italy, Germany and Japan were systematically and indiscriminately pounded with bombs. Questions of aesthetics played no part in this 'terror bombing'; neither Rome nor Monte Cassino escaped unscathed. Far worse, such air raids destroyed Allied towns, especially French ones, in order to hit at a factory, a station or a bridge, when sabotage would have dealt with the target far more effectively at less cost. In this respect, the flattening of Dresden and the atom bombs dropped on Hiroshima and Nagasaki represented a peak of savage cruelty that gave mankind a glimpse of the apocalypse that awaited it in the event of another world war.

But though these weapons were increasingly powerful, they were still being used in a military context. But because of the Nazis, the war became in addition a conflict of ideologies, a religious war as well as an international civil war, in which the Spanish war had been the first episode. The Nazis felt themselves entrusted with a mission which Himmler's brutish troops were to carry out; in all the territories conquered by the Wehrmacht, the ss followed up – half secretly in western Europe and quite openly in the east – to impose their own idea of 'law and order'. Whole categories of people came under their jurisdiction, not because they were criminals but because of what they were by nature, almost by divine call. Jews and Communists had first priority but Socialists, Democrats, Freemasons, Christians, in a word, anyone or everyone, were similarly treated as born enemies. When the population of the conquered territories began to show unrest, it was the German army itself which applied the monstrous system of hostages against real or supposed offenders, punishing innocent people by death because it was unable to find out who was guilty. Nor did it respect the Geneva Convention regarding prisoners when dealing with the Red Army, on the pretext that the USSR was not a signatory; the poor wretches were crammed into makeshift camps, exposed to epidemics and starvation and then despatched to a lingering death in concentration camps.

In every occupied country the Germans recruited lackeys to carry out their dirty work; in addition, by their skilful propaganda they misled a good number of people. As a result the population was induced to split into two camps and fly at each other's throats, as collaborators or resisters. Thus in 1940, one half of the French population denounced the other; the Vichy régime punished whole classes of Frenchmen and sometimes condemned them without trial. In reply, the resisters stepped up their attacks against the *collabos*; in 1944, they subjected them to summary justice; they indulged in large-scale 'purges', sometimes in an atmosphere of civil war. When the Red Army entered Germany, their officers gave their troops free rein to wreak their vengeance and take their pleasure in countless instances of rape, looting and wanton destruction.

But even here it might be argued that these were the consequences of war and difficult to avoid. But in addition, the war allowed the Nazis to apply a large-scale system of coercion with complete impunity, a system built up on their dreams of power and the logical consequences of their racialist doctrines of violence and inhumanity. Concentration camps were the crowning glory of Nazism and their apotheosis was genocide. In every territory which the Wehrmacht conquered, the ss set up concentration camps. It is plain that these would have become a permanent institution in a Nazi-dominated world, had they won. Into these camps, they flung all their enemies, real or imaginary: Communists, resisters, Jews, gypsies, conscientious objectors, believers in non-violence; but they also sent their anti-social criminals, sexual offenders and murderers as well as those in temporary disfavour, such as black marketeers or prostitutes found guilty of soliciting, even collaborators who had given cause for complaint; and then there were the hostages, those who had attempted to evade forced labour, prisoners of war who had 'defiled the German race', everybody, in fact. In the camps there were old people, children, pregnant women; at the Liberation a whole gang of children from Buchenwald who had forgotten even their names and nationalities and who had worked out a sort of common, utility language, ran loose under one of their number whom they had chosen as leader. Before being sent to the gas chambers, the Jews had been covered in scorn, stripped of their possessions and outlawed from Hitler's Germany because they represented the counter-myth to the triumphs of Nazism.

The most serious aspect of the pernicious nature of Nazism was perhaps the way it perverted men of science. It is true that in every country, scientists put themselves entirely at the service of the state, as a duty to their country; in the United States a team of distinguished atomic scientists, many of them victims of Nazi tyranny, worked uninterruptedly to win the race to make an atom bomb, on which victory, as a result, the fate of the world, might depend; afterwards, appalled at having opened Pandora's box, they suffered grave pangs of conscience. Nothing similar seems to have happened to German scientists and learned men; eminent lawyers felt no compunction in drawing up the Nuremberg Laws that turned thousands of their compatriots into pariahs, talented architects designed concentration camps, of which they must have known the purpose in order to make them 'functional'; outstanding chemists produced *Zyclon-B* gas which they can surely not have imagined was going to be used only against rats; in the camps themselves, 'doctors' undertook 'experiments' on human guinea-pigs, often out of pure sadism. Thus a great people with a glorious past which before the war had won Nobel prizes and given to the world musicians and philosophers of the highest repute, allowed crime to become the rule within its own frontiers and by a strange deviation, many of its members to become criminals, through a perverse application of excellent principles of conduct – discipline, patriotic duty and even duty to society. Rarely has Rabelais' well-known adage been more amply proved that *science sans conscience n'est que ruine de l'âme*.[1]

It cannot be known what stains these monstrous crimes have left on the conscience of mankind. The violence unleashed by the war took more overt forms in its usual aftermath: a wave of immorality, a mad urge to live after so many restrictions and alarms, the break-up of families after too long a separation of husband and wife, excessive profits made by black marketeers or collaborators, over-rapid promotion to adult responsibilities of insufficiently mature young people, exacerbated nationalism and ideological conflict, a thirst for money and pleasure; a heavy legacy.

1. 'Knowledge without morality is death to the soul.'

V THE ECONOMIC CONSEQUENCES

The war had brought about a prodigious boom in death-dealing industries; firms had been modernised, factories built and shipyards opened. The US and Canada had been the main countries to gain from this boom but it had also benefited Chile, the Argentine, Brazil, Sweden and Australia; the USSR had considerably developed its productive capacity in Asia; in these privileged countries, techniques had been improved and output increased. The economic problems of the world were thus of a double nature: in the countries enriched by the war, the economy had to be reconverted to peacetime conditions; in those which had been impoverished, an immense effort was needed to built up former prosperity again.

These second countries were to have greater difficulty than the first, so vast were the problems, which were, moreover, almost identical everywhere. They were all in debt; their budgets were in chronic deficit as a result of the costs entailed by the occupation which had been succeeded by the expenses of reconstruction; there was a grave danger of considerable depreciation of the currency, where this had not already occurred; there was little possibility of saving or floating public loans. Excessive quantities of paper money were chasing too few goods, thus causing a rise in prices and a continuing black market. One way of reducing the excessive amount of currency could be by increased taxation or even confiscation of illicit profits; this method combined a sense of justice and propriety with the needs of a sound financial policy. But more money had to be drawn off than could be done by this method alone, in order to reduce purchasing power by official action. The most savage use of such authoritarian methods was made in Belgium by Finance Minister Gutt in October 1944: bank deposits and savings accounts were blocked and each person could change a limited sum of the former currency into the new one. The USSR also issued a new rouble worth ten old ones – collective enterprises were given a specially favourable rate. Later on, similar measures were to be taken in Italy, Denmark, the Netherlands, France, Japan, Czechoslovakia, Hungary and Greece – where inflation had been particularly disastrous, one new drachma being worth a million old ones. Only Britain was able to keep down inflation by heavy taxation, without affecting the pound.

So regulations and state control were retained and even increased almost everywhere. In countries liberated by the Red Army and where Communists had taken over, such methods were a matter of doctrine. In the liberal democracies, a mixed economy emerged, half liberal, half state-controlled, by means of taxation combined with some nationalisation, leading to a sort of semi-state capitalism. Thus the liberal democracies, by the greater importance that they were giving to the state in cutting back the power of financial oligarchies and in introducing wider social legislation, were drawing nearer to the Socialist democracies, now no longer represented by the USSR alone.

Social upheavals went hand in hand with these economic changes. During the war, farmers had been given favourable treatment, not quantitatively but relatively; they had suffered less than city dwellers from shortages and air raids; however, neither their equipment nor methods had improved. Of greater importance was the increase in the number of industrial workers and the general use of female labour. Above all, the ruling classes had changed; either they had become poorer as in England or been exterminated by the Nazis as in Poland, or been compromised by having collaborated with the enemy; in the central and eastern European countries occupied by the Red Army, as well as in Germany, Japan or Italy, new rulers had in theory completely replaced the old ones.

Without outside help, the recovery of those countries that had been impoverished was in danger of being very slow. But those which had formerly been highly industrialised, such as Germany and France, now had nothing to export in exchange for the food, raw materials or equipment which they lacked. Those which exported agricultural produce, such as Denmark or Holland, could no longer obtain the necessary foreign currency on the London market, since Britain had lost a large part of her foreign investments.

VI THE COLLAPSE OF GERMANY

In 1945, the German people found themselves paying very heavily for Hitler's megalomania. Its industrial, railway and road system had completely collapsed as a result of the air raids, the fighting, the resiting of factories as well as their capture by the Allies and subsequent dismantling and confiscation; out of 948 river bridges, 750 had been destroyed, and 2,400 railway bridges and well over 2,000 miles of permanent way;[1] out of 16 million homes, 2,340,000 had been rendered uninhabitable and 4 million damaged; only a quarter of the city of Berlin remained more or less unscathed. Hamburg alone suffered more damage than the whole of Britain.

However, industrial installations suffered less than the widespread heaps of rubble might have led one to suppose; synthetic petrol factories suffered most, as about half of them were destroyed; but the losses in the textile industry were only 20 per cent, in the mechanical industries 15 per cent and in the mines only 10 per cent. This limited destruction was due

1. Solely in the zones occupied by the British, French and American armies.

to the dispersal of the factories, their camouflage and the work of specially trained repair squads; above all, stocks of machine tools had on the whole been hidden or sufficiently well protected not to be destroyed. Germany's economic potential had thus suffered less than was apparent and the chief target of the persistent Allied attacks, her heavy industry, had suffered least of all!

But in 1945, Germany was in a general and spectacular state of chaos. Any revival was made difficult by the lack of raw materials, the population movements, the scarcity of skilled labour, the breakdown of communications, the collapse of government – officials had either disappeared, gone into hiding or been arrested by the Allies. There was no longer any state or any Germany, only Germans demoralised by the extent of the disaster, the absence of 3 million prisoners of war, the discovery not of Hitler's crimes but of their immensity and their monstrosity, and the hatred towards them expressed by the occupied countries, as shown by the hostility of the victorious armies. Inflation, which had been contained or disguised for a considerable time, took its toll: the amount of money in circulation rose from 40 million marks in 1938 to 407 million in 1944; it was the middle classes who were the chief sufferers and their downfall coincided with the increasing cost of living and the general spread of the black market. In Piettre's words, 'industrial output had fallen to the level of 1860'; only 39 million tons of coal were mined in 1945 and in 1946 only 3 million tons of steel were produced; the Ruhr was working at twelve per cent of its capacity.

The population exodus made the situation still worse; in the east, it was the great change-over between Slavs and Germans; in the west, it was overpopulation, with the population rising from 40 to 45 million inhabitants; in the British occupation zone, there were nearly 640 people to the square mile. Families were crammed into cellars and moral standards were slipping everywhere; if the Allies had not taken the necessary steps, famine would have threatened and there was a real danger of epidemics. In a word, for Germany this was the darkest moment; in the heart of Europe, utter chaos was setting in.

In principle the Allies had made preparations well beforehand as to how to run Germany after her defeat but discussions in the European Consultative Commission set up after the Moscow Conference in October 1943 had more or less come to a standstill and had not resulted in any joint proposals. Consequently, the Potsdam decisions concerning Germany were ambiguous: they proposed the abolition of 'excessive' economic concentration without defining 'excessive'; they named no figure for the amount of 'authorised' production; they allowed Germany to remain an 'economic entity' but surrounding the question with reservations that could more or less cancel it out.

Map 31
THE OCCUPATION
OF GERMANY AND
AUSTRIA
Occupied zones
French
British
American
Soviet

As a result, the only positive agreement was in drawing up the boundaries of the occupation zones; this was done in accordance with the British proposals made at the beginning of 1944, later somewhat modified by granting the US ports on the North Sea coast which had previously belonged in the British zone, and providing France with a zone carved out of the American and British zones. It had been decided that Berlin would be administered by the four main Allies and that the four Allied Commanders-in-Chief would act jointly for the whole of the occupied territories; but there was nothing in writing to lay down the powers of each commander in his own zone; this could not fail to lead to a great diversity of decisions.

At the beginning, the four Allies were united in their single desire to punish Germany; this had been shown by the harsh behaviour of the armies of occupation – above all, by the Red Army's shock troops, and was confirmed on November 20, 1945, when the big international trial of war criminals opened in Nuremberg; it also showed itself in stern measures in dismembering or nationalising firms. It led to territorial claims: Denmark claimed Schleswig, the Netherlands the island of Borkum and an area close to Aachen (over 600 square miles); the Poles, Frankfurt-on-the-Oder and the island of Usedom. But it was France who suggested the biggest territorial rearrangements: on September 10, 1945, General de Gaulle asked that the Rhineland should be permanently separated from Germany and placed under the political and military control of Britain, France, Belgium and the Netherlands; the Ruhr should also be separated from the Reich and internationalised.

The practical disadvantages of the zone boundaries very soon became apparent, for they bore no relation to natural regions. The British zone was industrially the richest but also the least well balanced as it was both overpopulated and lacking in food resources. The American zone could more easily subsist on its own but had taken in large numbers of refugees. As France refused to admit any of these into her zone, it was the most self-sufficient for food although the least rich of the three. The Soviet zone had suffered less from air raids because the resiting of factories organised by Speer had provided it with an industrial potential matching its agricultural resources; but the inhabitants were deserting it and the Russians were dismantling its machines. The behaviour of each of the occupying

GERMAN OCCUPATION ZONES

	West Germany (three zones) (per cent)	Berlin (per cent)	East Germany (Soviet zone + the ceded territories) (per cent)
Area (compared with 1937)	52·3		47·7
Population (compared with 1937)	49·0	6·0	45·0
Industry (value of the 1936 output)	60·5	8·7	30·7
Agriculture (area under cultivation)	52·0		48·0[1]

1. Table taken from A. Piettre's *L'économie allemande contemporaire*, p. 74.

powers very soon assumed its own particular form. The Russians seized plant, nationalised firms and confiscated the large landed properties; as early as September 1945, Zhukov set up a regional government and the frontier with the other zones was hermetically sealed; only four political parties were recognised; considerable power was given to workers' trade unions, and Communist officials took over the chief administrative posts.

The French were equally strict; they insisted that reparations should be handed over according to schedule, they resolutely opposed any attempt to set up a central government and were even against the administrative regions laid down in the Potsdam agreement.

FRANCE'S LOSSES

Requisitioned by the Germans:	corn and derivatives	3 million tons
	other cereals	2·4 million tons
	meat	0·89 million tons
	potatoes	0·5 million tons
	sugar	0·3 million tons
	horses and mules	690,000
	dairy produce	5,775 million gallons
	wine	2,625 million gallons
	coal	63 million tons
	iron ore	42 million tons
	electricity	16,000 million kWh
	locomotives	3,288, i.e. 20 per cent of the 1938 rolling-stock
	carriages	335,000, i.e. 50 per cent
	motor cars	750,000, i.e. 32 per cent
	merchant ships	973,000 tons
	forced labour in France	735,000 men in June 1944
	forced labour in Germany	723,000 men in June 1944
Destroyed:	dwellings completely destroyed	279,000
	dwellings partly destroyed	1,084,000

The British Labour government confiscated the Krupp factories without further ado. But the Americans were scared by the difficulties that might arise if Germany were reduced to destitution and by the revolutionary decisions taken by their allies; they suggested unifying the zones to avoid bankruptcy and anarchy which, to their mind, would be the forerunners of Communism; they stopped requisitioning and dismantling factories and soft-pedalled denazification.

Thus Germany was tending to be split by a line running north and south. But throughout the whole territory a transformation of society of paramount importance was taking place; the big country landowners and industrial tycoons were vanishing in the east and dwindling in the west; the Prussian-style army, the bulwark of authoritarian régimes, had also been destroyed. Whether it were Socialist in the east or liberal in the west, a true democracy could now be established in Germany – assuming that her penitent attitude would leave no room for a recurrence of Nazism and the horde of refugees did not become a permanent source of unrest.

It was clear that in 1945, in Asia as in Europe, the centres of wealth and the axes of power would never again be the same as in 1939; the fabric of trade and commerce, political trends and social hierarchies had been deeply disturbed. How could the new balance of power fail to be affected by all this?

CHAPTER 2

The New Balance of Power

WHEN the guns fell silent, the results of the fighting and the power of the armies that had achieved them joined forces with economic potential to decide the new balance of power in the world. The weakness of western Europe in every field was manifest, whereas in 1939 the four great western European nations could have been considered the most powerful in the world; Germany was weak in the extreme; Italy only slightly less so; France's weakness had been partly stemmed and Great Britain's was already visible despite her triumphant victory. Europe had obviously lost her leading role for a long time to come; as a consequence, the domination that she had exerted over whole continents through her colonial empires was breaking down; the monsoon countries of Asia, the Arab world and black Africa were being shaken up in varying degrees by the turmoil from which new nations would emerge. With a foot in both Europe and Asia, the USSR, that colossus, had built herself a new sort of empire, based on a common ideology, shut in on itself yet ever ready to proselytise other countries, if not to launch crusades. But the only power to emerge intact and strengthened from the storm was the United States; financially and economically she was in a position to lay down the law; militarily and, even more, diplomatically, she moved less confidently. In any case, the threat of new conflicts, even more colossal than the one which had just ended, cast its shadow over the future of mankind.

I GREAT BRITAIN

Britain's stubborn courage, embodied in Winston Churchill, had saved freedom for the world and earned universal acclaim; but the price was so high that Britain's power was shaken to its very core, although her losses in human lives and material destruction were less than those of other countries – France, for example. It is indicative of the disruption of her economy that food crops, insignificant before the war, increased at the expense of stockfarming, and that on the other hand, the output of the textile industry, which provided exports, was now reduced by half; no less significant was the decrease in the Merchant Navy by more than 6 million tons; it was now barely a third of the size of the American fleet, whereas in 1939 it had been half as large again. The battle of the Atlantic, although it ended in victory, showed that the time was past when the Royal Navy ruled the waves.

Britain no longer possessed the financial strength to meet the needs of her reconstruction, to provide other work for the 2 million people employed in the war industry and to find new civilian jobs for the 4 million demobilised soldiers; during the war, she had borrowed £14,000 million, £3,500 million of this abroad – primarily from the United States and then from the dominions but also from India and Egypt, those poor relations of the Commonwealth. The national debt represented more than three times the national income; foreign assets had been reduced by half; with every nerve strained in the war effort and cut off from the outside world by the German blockade, Britain had lost her best customers.

The hoped-for recovery was jeopardised by the weak balance of payments situation, since invisible exports no longer made up for the traditional trade deficit. Consuming more than she produced and spending more than she earned, in short, living above her means, Britain was threatened by permanent inflation. The first cure was heavy taxation to mop up surplus income; but this causes pressure on prices; another weapon was import control but then the result was to increase internal demand, that is, to aggravate inflationary pressures.

In her efforts to find a solution to this vicious spiral Britain was no longer under a national coalition government, led by Winston Churchill, but by a Labour ministry under Attlee.[1] In his electoral programme of May 1945, Attlee had opted fairly and squarely for state control: full employment, nationalisation of key industries, stabilisation of the standard of living. He set about producing an economic and social transformation, without coercion or violence, for a rational organisation of industry, implementing the Beveridge plan of a generous social welfare scheme, increasing the wealth of the workers and improving their living conditions. This ambitious scheme assumed that Britain's weakness caused by the war would be remedied; to achieve this would entail increasing production, that is, the amount of work done, and having to put up with austerity for a considerable time; the trade unions' workers disliked this and their conservatism resisted the revolutionary ideas of their rulers. And it was necessary, too, that the last remaining major sources of profit

1. On 5 July 1945 the Labour Party obtained nearly 12 million votes against the 9 million Conservative votes.

for Britain's prosperity should not dry up; but social legislation made British products more costly and jeopardised their sale overseas; as for the resources available in the Commonwealth, they depended on colonial domination to which the Labour party wished to put a stop and which in any case was tending to crumble of its own accord.

In addition, as inheritors and caretakers of Britain's greatness, the Socialists had not entirely given up the heavy responsibilities of a prestige policy: occupying Germany, maintaining naval and air bases at the main communication centres all over the world, wishing to play the part of a world power for which she lacked the means. All this involved the risk of tying Britain to the United States' apron-strings as foreshadowed by the loan that Washington granted London in December 1945; its apparent generosity was barely able to disguise its onerousness: a straight cancellation of lend-lease debts and the loan of £4,400 million for fifty years at 2 per cent.

Belgium came out of the war relatively well. Armies had twice crossed her territory but this had happened quickly and she had suffered little destruction; thanks to the Congo and the port of Antwerp, the Allied armies were in her debt. But she was shaken by a grave political crisis. The Communist and Socialist parties opposed the return of King Leopold, who had been freed by the American Army; he was called upon to abdicate and the government did not hesitate to resign in order to bring pressure to bear on him; he therefore placed the decision in the hands of the nation and meanwhile a regency was set up. This dispute put another, more serious, one into the background but the penalties inflicted on collaborators hinted at the serious nature of the question: the *flamingant* movement, the most vigorous supporter of Flemish nationalist claims, had cut itself off from the nation by coming to terms with the occupier.

Holland had to face a grave economic crisis – her imports were ten times as large as her exports; although no difficulty was experienced in re-establishing traditional institutions as the Resistance movement stepped down without any question in favour of Queen Wilhelmina, the traditional parties underwent changes, although they continued to exist; they lost their hitherto preponderantly religious nature; the working classes, whose strikes had been the main weapon against the occupier, played a more important role in a new 'Labour party'; the Communist party made its bow on the political scene.

But the Belgian-Dutch customs union, which had been agreed on in London in September 1944, under the name of Benelux, had not yet got off the ground. Together with Denmark and Norway, Belgium and Holland remained within the British orbit – at Yalta, Stalin had sketched out for Churchill a British zone of influence in Europe, grouping these four small states together.

II FRANCE

In France, after the total collapse of the Vichy régime, the Resistance had had no difficulty in staking its claim on all the roads to power and all positions of control. The unanimous acceptance of General de Gaulle, the fact that the Communist party had put liberation and victory before revolution, as well as the presence of Allied troops, had enabled her to be spared the horrors of civil war, although here and there, there had been sharp internal tussles and harsh purges. National unity lasted for two years under General de Gaulle's leadership.

Nonetheless, the traditional political forces were thrown completely into confusion; the Right suffered from having supported Vichy, and temporarily disappeared from the political scene; by failing to play an active part in the Resistance, the Radical Socialists lost their pre-eminent position; the big Roman Catholic party, the *Mouvement républicain populaire*, drew members from these two discredited parties; the Socialists merely took up their pre-war position. New factors were the discovery of the strength of the Communist party and the continuing support for de Gaulle among the general public.

The Communist party became more powerful than its Socialist rival; it had members in the government and it had placed its own men in the administrative machinery of the country; it continued to be a leading light in the Resistance organisations, the National Council and the Liberation Committees of the *départements* and when it proved necessary it used them as pressure groups. Above all, it dominated the reunified CGT, which in 1945 contained more than 5 million members as compared with 700,000 in the CFTC. But the Party was using this power in the service of the nation; it co-operated with the other parties; it urged the working classes to produce more; it advised against strikes; it seemed to expect that by legal means and universal suffrage it would achieve power all in good time. It worked to bring this about by suggesting joint action with the Socialist party and by manoeuvring within the organisations that had originated in the Resistance, in order to achieve this coalition on terms favourable to itself.

General de Gaulle had no organised force behind him apart from his loyal Free French supporters and the various Resistance networks, but his personal prestige was enormous; his feeling for the state reassured many Frenchmen who looked on him as a bulwark of political and social order. The General strove above all to restore France to her former greatness and independence, by means of internal reforms combining 'reason and novelty' and a policy of maintaining a balance between the major Allies.

In a series of orders in council, the coal mines, the firm of Renault and air transport were nationalised; the printing and distribution of the press and the running of the radio were turned into public services. Nationalisation did not mean state control; in theory, the nationalised industry was to remain a commercial undertaking with its own budget and independent management; it was not subject to the budgetary and accounting control of the government services; however, the state held the majority of shares and appointed the directors. A system of quotas, of import and export licences, combined wth exchange control, also ensured government control of foreign trade; in any case, quite apart from any doctrinaire reasons, such measures were rendered inevitable by the enormous budget deficit – an expenditure of 500,000 million francs and a revenue of only 192,000 million, as well as 620,000 million francs circulating in paper money.

While Vichy's 'corporative' régime was abolished and freedom restored to the trade unions, a complete social welfare programme was drawn up, as well as a scheme for modernisation and industrial re-equipment worked out by Jean Monnet. Wages were increased by between 30 and 50 per cent. But in order to combat inflation and rising prices, the government did not adopt Pierre Mendès France's plan of calling in bank-notes, blocking accounts, massive taxation and maintenance of a strict system of regulations; instead a classical large-scale funding operating was launched.

In foreign policy, General de Gaulle worked for a rapprochement with Italy.[1] But above all, he went to Moscow to obtain a double guarantee: against a revival of danger from Germany and against excessive subordination to his British and American liberators. He endeavoured to persuade Stalin to let France occupy the Rhineland; in exchange, he expressed himself in favour of the Curzon line and the Oder-Neisse frontier, without, however, going so far as to recognise the Lublin Committee, as Stalin requested. But the latter refused to commit himself; he did not wish to cause trouble with his allies and he advised France to join in the 1942 Anglo-Soviet treaty, which de Gaulle refused to do, for fear of being in a subordinate position with regard to Britain. Despite her spectacular recovery and the fact that her armies had taken part in the victory, France was not yet completely recognised by the other victorious powers as one of themselves; she was not one of the 'big' powers; she had had no voice in the Yalta and Potsdam decisions and she remained excluded from certain of their implementations and consequences.

---

1. In February 1945, an agreement on Tunisia was signed between Couve de Murville and de Gasperi, by which Italy gave up any claim to special privileges for her subjects.

III ITALY

Ravaged by war, whose havoc extended from top to bottom of the peninsula, shaken by revolutionary movements, and under military government
by the Allies, Italy had been plunged into a grave state of crisis; the budget
deficit was more than 400,000 million lire, which was the same amount as
the money in circulation, while the national debt was 1,200,000 million
lire; for her finances and her reconstruction as well as for her supplies and
her final fate when peace was signed, Italy was entirely at the mercy of her
conquerors.

The government was completely hamstrung by the opposing tendencies
of its constituent parties. Since it was not possible to assess their strength
by a general election, they were all equally represented in the *Consulta*, the
consultative assembly that met in Rome in September 1945 to prepare for
the election of a Constituent Assembly. Deeper than all the divergences
between the Resistance groups there remained the gap between Fascists
and anti-Fascists throughout the whole country. It showed itself principally
in the question of the fate of the monarchy; the Action party was most
virulent in demanding the proclamation of a republic, as a punishment
on the King for having served Fascism too loyally. Churchill's pro-
monarchical sentiments provided opposition to this movement for some
considerable time but Labour's success in the elections opened the way
for Victor Emmanuel's abdication.

The continuing existence of Fascism was shown by the appearance and
success of a curious movement called *L'Uomo Qualunque* after the name of
Guglielmo Giannini's newspaper which reached a circulation of almost a
million readers from the moment of its publication in December 1944. In
vindictive terms, Giannini attacked 'the liberators', the 'Liberation Committees' and the 'new state'. Without rehabilitating Fascism, he ran down
its conquerors and this explained his success with the Church, business
circles and the middle classes.

In September 1945, a Council of Foreign Ministers discussed what
terms should be imposed by the victors on Italy, which was defeated yet
co-belligerent. No agreement was reached; whereas the British and
Americans wanted to let Italy keep Trieste, the USSR wanted it to go to
Yugoslavia; at least, Italy lost only a limited amount of home territory.
On the other hand, it was decided to strip her of her colonial empire,
although Bidault, the French delegate, suggested leaving her in precarious
control of it in the form of a mandated territory. Molotov had asked for the
USSR to have a share in Tripolitania – 'the USSR should occupy the position
due to her in the Mediterranean'; but Byrnes and Bevin had declared

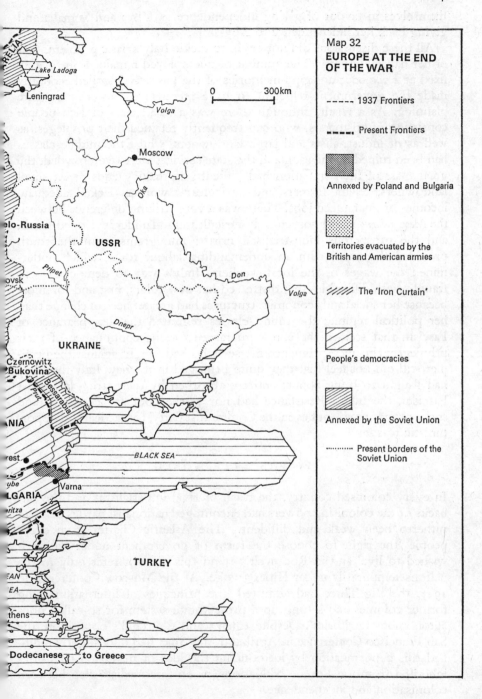

Map 32

EUROPE AT THE END OF THE WAR

----- 1937 Frontiers

▬▬▬ Present Frontiers

Annexed by Poland and Bulgaria

Territories evacuated by the British and American armies

////// The 'Iron Curtain'

People's democracies

Annexed by the Soviet Union

·········· Present borders of the Soviet Union

themselves in favour of giving independence to Libya and Somalia and giving back her independence to Abyssinia.

All these discussions did not begin to tackle Italy's basic problem, that of her natural poverty. The number of unemployed remained obstinately fixed at 2,000,000; unhappy memories of the Fascist-controlled economy made the government reluctant to have recourse to austerity or state planning. As a result, although there was a small class of rich people consisting of aristocrats, who had frequently retained their privileges, as well as of industrialists and large landowners, whilst the middle classes had been ruined by inflation and the state services were overcrowded, the great mass of the population had difficulty in making ends meet; small landowners, tenant farmers and agricultural workers lacked adequate incomes or guaranteed jobs. There was a very striking difference between the *Mezzogiorno*, the almost entirely agricultural and underdeveloped south, and the prosperous industrialised north; immigrants from the south provided the north with an undemanding labour force, which undermined the wages of the local workers. Italy's way to democracy was fraught with difficulties that distressed her new rulers, first and foremost because her social and economic structures had greater need of change than her political régime; the ruling classes regretted the disappearance of Fascism that seemed the surest guarantee for the continuance of their privileges; the underprivileged masses who had fought against the occupier still did not feel that they quite belonged in the new Italy that they had fought to bring about; entirely absorbed by their struggle against Fascism, the Italian Resistance had not worked out any economic and social programme – not even the Communist party, for tactical and opportunistic reasons.

IV THE ARAB WORLD

In every colonised country, the clash of rival imperialisms and the setbacks of the colonising powers had encouraged nationalist parties that had hitherto been weak and diffident. The Atlantic Charter gave every people 'the right to choose the form of government under which it wished to live' and in Roosevelt's mind this did not refer only to the nations temporarily under Hitler's yoke. At the Moscow Conference in 1943, the Big Three had admitted 'the principles of internationalising former colonies and setting up a protectorate system for so-called non-autonomous territories'. Despite Eden's and Churchill's opposition, the San Francisco Conference in April and May 1945 had only slightly mollified this condemnation by introducing the idea of mandated territories inherited from the League of Nations, as an intermediate step between colonisation and independence.

Nowhere did these prospects arouse more excitement and hope than in the Arab world. In fact, the war there had taken place in various stages, each of which, from the native point of view, had the advantage of causing one colonial power to lose face; first the French, then the Italians and finally the British had been either beaten or in danger or even ousted from their possessions – had in fact come in their turn under the protection of others, like the French in North Africa as a result of the Americans' arrival after November 1942. At the same time, war had brought them relative prosperity; cotton, oil and sugar had been fetching better prices; armies quartered on their territories had produced an inexhaustible flow of dollars and sterling; providing roads, railways, airfields, harbours and water-supplies had increased the possibilities of all forms of trade and commerce. What is more, the colonisers had mobilised the natives; in a way they had called on them for help; in return, how could one turn a deaf ear to requests that were all the more urgent because they were based on conviction, on a feeling of greater strength and a better knowledge of the possibilities?

Moreover, in the Middle East there were states which were independent in theory, which had been promised, in principle, that they would actually become so and whose hopes had been, as it were, enshrined by their membership of the new United Nations Organisation.

In the grave peril threatening their empires, the colonial powers had in any case cut their losses. Faced by the Iraqi revolt, in May 1941 Anthony Eden had asserted Britain's intention of giving 'the most complete support' to a plan for Arab unity. The French Committee of National Liberation had promised and later granted independence to the Near Eastern countries; it had decided to introduce reforms in the status of the natives of Algeria. A common language and religion, the awareness of racial unity, memories of a rich and ancient culture and the existence of cultivated minorities who had studied in European schools provided the ferment of pan-Arab agitation, which was made all the more topical by the threat of a 'home for the Jews' in Palestine which the Grand Mufti of Jerusalem had denounced as a 'deadly peril'.

The British tried both to satisfy this movement and to make use of it for their own ends. In February 1943, Eden spoke out in favour of an 'economic, cultural and political union of the Arab countries'. Nuri As-Said, the Iraqi Prime Minister, was probably anticipating Britain's wishes when he suggested that Syria, Lebanon, Jordan and Palestine should form one single state with Iraq – to the exclusion of Egypt. In reply, in the middle of 1944 Nahas Pasha, the Prime Minister of Egypt, called the first pan-Arab conference in Alexandria. Out of this meeting came the 'Arab League' which was not a union but a movement of co-operation in which the countries could meet without prejudicing the national sovereignty of any of them. When Saudi Arabia joined in March 1945, the League comprised six states, with a total population of 28 million inhabitants, torn by personal and sectarian rivalries but bound together by a double aversion to western imperialism and Zionism.

The League had its seat in Cairo; thus Egypt, with the strength afforded by her population, her past and her central position, assumed the leadership. She meant to make Britain pay for Egypt's loyalty, which had hung by a thread – Nahas Pasha – at the time of Rommel's advance towards the Nile delta. In February 1945, Egypt declared war on the Axis in order to have the right to join the United Nations Organisation; at the same time, she asked for certain frontier modifications in her favour in Libya. Later on, she went further and raised the question of her sovereignty over the Anglo-Egyptian Sudan, requesting its return to her. King Farouk as well as the rival factions of the old Nationalist party, the Wafd, outbid each other in their nationalistic claims, yet public opinion – led by the Moslem brotherhood, the students and the army – accused them of being too moderate. On July 30, 1945, Egypt sent a note requesting a revision of the treaty of alliance with Britain; it was a sign of the times that she threatened, should Britain prove recalcitrant, to seek backing from Moscow.

Egypt was supported in this struggle by the Arab League, which also adopted an anti-French attitude in the Near East. In gratitude, the constitution of the new independent Syria proclaimed 'the Syrian people's desire that the Arab nation be one day united into one single state'. Britain's action thus proved a double-edged weapon and the United States was the first to take advantage of her troubles. Roosevelt had put Arabia on the list of nations to benefit from lend-lease. When he met Ibn Saud in February 1945, he told him that 'the colonial era is at an end'; he pledged to give him weapons and he promised to support the efforts of the Arab states to achieve their emancipation. In exchange, Ibn Saud granted Aramco, an American company, a sixty-year lease of territory, and the sole right of prospecting and exploiting the oil.

American influence similarly replaced British influence in Iran. Roosevelt had met the Shah in Teheran; as with the Sultan of Morocco a few months before, he had spoken to him of the possible development of arid territories, thanks to American techniques, and he had severely condemned Britain's monopoly of Persian oil; Iran had a perfect right to assert her independence and to dispose of her natural wealth as she saw fit. American experts and financiers then arrived and the result was an agreement in September 1944 between the Anglo-Iranian Oil Company and Standard Oil to develop new oilfields. In order not to be ousted, the USSR asked for a mixed Soviet-Persian company to be set up in the north of the country. In face of this concerted threat, in December 1944, urged on by Dr Mossadegh, the Iranian Parliament passed a law banning any fresh concession until foreign occupation of the country had ceased. But neither at Yalta nor at Potsdam could the Big Three come to an agreement to leave Iran; they confined themselves to evacuating Teheran. When the war had ended, the Iran government again asked for its territory to be evacuated in September 1945; only the Americans showed themselves willing to accede to this request; Britain and Russia, rivals and accomplices as in 1907, turned a deaf ear. However, the British companies had given up their monopoly of constructing pipelines to an American concern.

Thus, in this effervescing Arab world, interests were shifting all round, new nations were asserting themselves and new groups were beginning to take shape. French North Africa did not escape this unrest, despite the promises of the CFLN. In January 1944 in Morocco, Allal el Fassi re-formed the Independence party with the approval of the Sultan and asked for the abolition of the protectorate, without going so far as to claim immediate independence. In Tunisia Bourguiba, the Neo Destour leader, handed the Resident General the 'notables' manifesto. It asked for an elected parliament, responsibility for government, political freedom, in a word, a considerable measure of independence for Tunisia, on the lines of French institutions. In Algeria events were more dramatic; on May 1, a strike began, followed by riots which caused hundreds of casualties at Sétif and Guelma, amongst the French and Algerian 'collaborators'. They were harshly repressed by the Foreign Legion; the nationalists took full advantage of this in their propaganda; thus, a sort of routine of atrocity tended to become the rule. But the French government and the French people were still too elated by the enthusiasm which they had shown in freeing their country to contemplate relinquishing any part of their power over their overseas territories – the French population in French North Africa were in any case unanimously opposed to any such action.

Although black Africa remained calm for the moment, the break-up which was threatening empires almost all over the world could not fail eventually to arouse her as well. Even now, the victories of Japan and her subsequent defeat had created a revolutionary situation in Asia, favoured not only by the mere presence, as allies, of the Americans, who were sympathetic if not active supporters of native claims, but also by the remoteness of the colonial powers – Britain, France and Holland.

V JAPAN AND CHINA

Although up to 1943 Japan had experienced increasing prosperity, in the happy days of Greater Asia, by August 1945 she had become economically a moribund country which had been forced to surrender by the atom bomb. Her losses were comparable only to Germany's; more than 2 million buildings and well over 30,000 miles of railway track had been destroyed, forty per cent of her urban area lay in ruins, her merchant navy had been reduced from 8,000,000 to 500,000 tons; her industry, which had been highly concentrated, had been largely paralysed before it had been possible to disperse the factories, and output was less than thirty per cent of that of 1943.

The fanatical and warlike spirit which had characterised her until the very last minute – in 1945 the schools had been closed and the pupils automatically sent to work on the land or in the factory – had been succeeded by complete prostration. The myths and beliefs of her people had all collapsed; in all her misery Japan could see no gleam of hope; all that remained was her Emperor but he was a fallen god. The exodus of the urban population into the country was causing famine but not preventing unemployment; and poverty was giving rise to banditry.

However, the Americans were not at a loss; ever since 1942, they had been studying the problems that would arise from the occupation of Japan, defined the powers of the military command and laid down the principles of their Far Eastern policy. They had hesitated for some considerable time before determining what treatment they should mete out to the Emperor; eventually they had decided to keep him under close supervision and force him to delegate his powers to the American military authorities, so that they would be more willingly accepted by the Japanese people.

Being anxious to keep the occupation in their own hands, since it was the fruit of their victory, the Americans rejected a Soviet proposal to set up a 'Big Four' Control Commission, as in Germany; instead they set up a broader commission comprising the eleven countries which had fought against Japan and granted it only consultative status. When the Emperor, departing from traditional principle, informed the Diet that Japan must become a 'peaceful nation', MacArthur, like a real proconsul, laid down the principles that would underlie the occupation: abolition of militarism, trial of war criminals, purging of officials and democratisation of institutions. Thus began a co-existence between victor and vanquished without precedent, the former helping both in the recovery and the re-education of the latter.

Although one of the victors and considered as a great power by her allies, China was not much better off; more than 40 million of her inhabitants had been 'displaced'; most of her factories, merchant navy and railway network destroyed; the national debt was out of control; central government had practically disappeared. What would happen to China now that peace had returned? In theory, she had been reunited after the Japanese surrender at Nankin; apart from Hong Kong and Port Arthur, there were no longer any foreign enclaves on her territory; Formosa and

Manchuria were to be given back to her; her troops were occupying northern Indochina.

One bogy that was represented by the USSR had been removed. It was
true that the USSR had managed to penetrate into Sinkiang and even as far
as Tibet, where she had supported her own candidate for the post of
Dalai Lama; she still occupied Manchuria and she was demanding that
Outer Mongolia should remain independent, but in a treaty of alliance and
friendship signed on August 24, 1945, she recognised the Chungking
government as the government of the whole of China and promised not
to interfere in her affairs. Even more, she exerted pressure on Mao Tse-
tung to bring the civil war to an end. First Chou En-lai, and then Mao
himself, went to Chungking and proposed forming a coalition government. An agreement was reached on paper; but Chiang did not want to
share his power with anyone; although the Communists took part in
disarming the Japanese, open hostility remained between the two parties.

Thus Chiang Kai-shek wished neither to share power nor to initiate any
wide-ranging reforms. But the Kuomintang, national China's single party,
on which he depended for support, was falling apart; one sector of it did
not wish to go beyond the teaching of Confucius; the generals, who had
won their victory without actually fighting, had gone back to being local
potentates; only a minority of technical experts and teachers wanted
western-style reforms, democratic as well as economic; but this minority
carried no weight against the graft and corruption of the officials or the
conservatism of the landowners. Before the end of 1945, civil war flared
up again.

VI SOUTH-EAST ASIA

In the Pacific, the coloured population was too small and backward to be
roused from their torpor by the war; the two white strongholds of
Australia and New Zealand had remained untouched by the Japanese
tide of war; but as the immense ocean became, thanks to the Task Forces,
an American lake, the two dominions had become progressively more
dependent on their American protector; their links with the Commonwealth were now only theoretical and traditional.

On the other hand the teeming masses of South-east Asia had vibrated in
sympathy with the Japanese victories, which had brought loss of face to
the colonising powers; but their incorporation into Greater Asia had been
far from having very happy economic consequences for them; in addition,
Japanese military domination had proved burdensome; but the nationalist
movements had been able to come into the open and even develop
through this domination; when they left, the Japanese forces had handed

over power to them and often their arms as well. And in all these countries there existed educated minorities – of intellectuals, minor officials and businessmen – who thought that their time had come; even before the war, they had claimed, without success, a greater share in the government of their country; but their efforts had been met by the blank incomprehension of the rural masses, who, though unable to see further than their daily handful of rice, were yet sensitive to the virus of zenophobia which dragged them out of their torpor.

In French Indochina the Japanese had encouraged anti-French nationalist movements such as the Cao Daist sect; even before the war, they were subsidising the 'League for the Independence of Annam'; they had achieved less success with the 'League of Revolutionary Organisations of Vietnam', inspired by the Communists and anti-Japanese as well as anti-French. On March 9, 1945, in a sudden coup, the French troops were disarmed, colonial administration abolished and thousands of nationalists released from prison. The preparations being made by the Indochinese Resistance movement in conjunction with the Free French bases in Calcutta and Yünnan were nipped in the bud. The most active nationalist movement, with the widest network of cells, the Vietminh under Ho Chi Minh, extended its hold over the country. When the Japanese collapsed, the Americans, because of their anti-colonialism, did not call on the French but let the conquered Japanese maintain law and order and their Chinese allies, with their agreement, occupied the north of the country; the British were to occupy the south. The Vietminh formed a provisional government, with the emperor Bao Dai as adviser, after his abdication, and seized weapons from the Japanese armouries. Ho Chi Minh informed France through Jean Sainteny, the head of the French mission in Yunnan, of the Vietminh's programme: election of a parliament by universal suffrage; independence within five to ten years; while France would be granted 'economic concessions'. So the matter was open to discussion; but in Paris, as a result of the failure to make a proper assessment of the strength of the movement for independence, preparations were under way to reconquer the country.

In Indonesia, on August 17, 1945, Soekarno proclaimed his country's independence. As in Indochina, Roosevelt was not willing to restore the previous colonial domination and as in Cochinchina, it fell to the British to accept the Japanese surrender. The Japanese had pledged themselves not to modify the *status quo*; but in fact they recognised the provisional republican government, turned a deaf ear to Mountbatten's request that they should dissolve it and handed over their arms to the nationalists. When the British landed, they had no difficulty in disarming the Japanese and releasing the Dutch prisoners but found themselves up against a native militia strong enough to force them to recognise Soekarno's government. The Dutch in Indonesia thus found it impossible to take over the administration of the country; the native population was solidly opposed to them. But the Dutch government wanted to reconquer its rich colonial empire; it had despatched a brigade to Singapore; an armed confrontation was in sight.

India had been no more than threatened by Japan and, on the whole, she had remained steadfast even in Britain's darkest hours; it is true that 60,000 nationalists had been thrown into gaol. But in 1945, strikes, popular revolts and mutiny in the armed forces all flared up together; the native civil servants offered passive resistance. The Labour government realised that it was going to run up against insurmountable difficulties; at the same time, it realised that the Congress party consisted of Hindus and the League of Moslems; the movements' leaders did not want a violent and complete break; they considered that they still needed the British to develop their country's economy. For their part, the British felt too weak when faced by their united opposition; on the other hand, they could take advantage of any lack of unity; they thus started negotiations with the nationalists with a view to arranging both independence and partition.

In all this unrest, Russian influence was little seen; in any case, she did not add fuel to the fire; but the case was different in central and eastern Europe.

VII THE USSR AND THE COMMUNIST WORLD

When the USSR entered the war, she was isolated and for a long time the Red Army withstood the Wehrmacht's attacks alone; the policy of reconciliation with Germany, however understandable from the Russian point of view, had aroused general disapproval; later on, no country had endured such suffering or sustained such losses as the USSR. However, in 1945 she was the only major Allied country which had extended her power beyond her 1939 borders; her prestige and her international reputation were enormous. Her recovery was prodigious.

First of all, Russia had kept all the territories which she had annexed as a result of her pact with the Reich: Karelia, the Baltic countries, Polish White Russia, Bessarabia and northern Bukovina. In Asia, she added the Kuriles, south Sakhalin, Dairen and Port Arthur; in Europe, Koenigsberg, east Prussia and sub-Carpathian Ruthenia. But through her armies, she had extended her influence much further. In Asia, they were occupying Manchuria and north Korea, as well as Persian Azerbaidzhan; in Europe, they lorded it over Poland, Romania, Hungary, Bulgaria and Czechoslovakia; they were laying down the law in half of Germany and Austria. Still further afield, the USSR was claiming certain districts of Turkish

Armenia and a settlement in her favour of rights of passage through the
Dardanelles; she meant to play her part in running the Ruhr, the administration of Tangier or the trusteeship of the Italian colonies; she was
encouraging Yugoslavia to cast eyes on Trieste, asking for a trading base in
the Dodecanese and demanding to take part in the occupation of Japan.

However, her economic recovery set immense problems; not everything, of course, had been wasted through the war effort; coal output had
not decreased and that of rare ores had increased; the steel industry in the
Urals and central Asia was booming; new electricity generating centres
had been built and new oilfields exploited; even as early as 1945, some
branches of industry had reached their 1938 level of production. But the
plight of the population of the devastated areas remained wretched; the
USSR had only her own resources to rely on for her recovery. And war
had brought to light two grave shortcomings in the Soviet economy: the
scarcity and poor quality of her communications, roads and railways, and
her inadequate production of consumer goods, since previous Five Year
Plans had put emphasis on heavy industry; in 1945, the people of Soviet
Russia lacked even the bare necessities; although the demobilisation of the
American Army left the Red Army as the only large one in the world, its
armament would be soon outclassed unless it possessed atomic weapons;
part of her resources of men, money, raw materials and machines would be
needed to manufacture these; the vast area under occupation made it
necessary to keep a large number of conscripts under arms; finally –
although this was denied – the collaboration of the local population with
the occupiers was not always wholehearted, and rebel bands – in particular
those of Bandera – were still causing disorder over large areas of territory.

These lasting handicaps did not prevent the USSR from playing a large
part in the affairs of the world. At times, she seemed to be pursuing Czarist
dreams and getting her revenge on Japan for 1905; going further back
still, the destruction of Prussia had cancelled the work of the Teutonic
Knights. At others she recalled that Moscow had been the capital of the
Greek Orthodox religion: the Metropolitan, Serge, was sent to Jerusalem to renew links with the Orthodox communities of the Holy Places.
But pan-Slavism was also an agent of expansion against Germanism, and
the presence of 20 million Moslems in Soviet Asia justified setting up
consulates in the Near East and attracting Arab students to Tashkent.

The USSR was thus playing, in masterly fashion, all the trumps which
her history and geography afforded. However, her most loyal and influential political allies were provided by international Communism. Not
only had the national parties of occupied Europe hastened to her help in
her hour of greatest peril but they would now be holding important posts
in the post-war governments both of central and western Europe; they
controlled the trade unions in every country; in the countries liberated by

the Red Army, they held the chief ministerial posts and their numbers had increased tenfold; in addition, it was Communists who had lived through the whole of the war in USSR who now returned to take over the leadership of their Party, full of Kremlin directives and prepared to carry them out to the letter: Thorez in France, Togliatti in Italy, Anna Pauker in Romania, Ulbricht and Piek in Germany, Bierut in Poland, etc. The Communist International was more solid than ever before; and more than ever before, it was directed from and by Moscow.

In addition, the USSR had gained a wider hearing from the Resistance movements of every country. This was because, alone amongst the Big Three, the USSR had conducted Resistance warfare on her own soil. She put forward the Resistance as part of a great international fight in favour of oppressed peoples; by her own example, she showed how it was both a national war and a revolutionary struggle; she gave it a place in world history between workers' uprisings against capitalist oppression and the efforts of coloured peoples to free themselves from the colonial yoke, to whom she was setting an example.

Nevertheless, Moscow did not fully become once again the Mecca of world revolution. Principally concerned with tending his own country's wounds and perhaps with completely restoring the authority of his own régime, Stalin restricted his activity outside the borders of the USSR; in any case he had no hold over India, black Africa or the Scandinavian and Anglo-Saxon countries; still entirely obsessed by the thought of the danger from Germany, his relations with his allies were entirely dictated by the desire to forestall any revival of it; his conception of international policy was still that of dividing Europe into areas of influence, as he had worked out with Churchill in Moscow; he tried to have this policy adopted by the United Nations Organisation; in return, he intended to do as he pleased in those parts of Europe that had been exposed to Soviet pene-tration by the Red Army's victories.

In 1945, Czechoslovakia, Poland, Romania, Hungary, Bulgaria, Albania and Yugoslavia represented nearly 352,000 square miles and 70 million inhabitants. All these countries had to face the same problems: rebuilding a ruined economy; transferring population; combating in-flation; and adapting transport facilities to newly drawn frontiers. In all of them, the behaviour of the Communist parties and the policy of the USSR were more or less the same. The Communist parties, strongly in the minority before the war, did not seize power completely, as the presence of the Red Army would have enabled them to; they formed coalition governments, which were based on the Resistance organisations, and in which they kept the key posts for themselves. Agreement was reached on a short-term programme: setting the country on its feet again without calling on external capitalist aid; punishing collaborators, a term including almost all the former ruling classes; social reform by redistributing land to the peasants, without immediate collectivisation; nationalisation of industry and a government-controlled economy.

Thus countries that had had a liberal economy before the war fell into line with Soviet ideas of collectivisation and planned economy. They also adopted Stalin's régime of dictatorship and oppression. In fact, far from persevering in the policy of liberalisation that his allies had been led to expect by some of his measures, dictated purely by circumstances, as soon as the war was over Stalin immediately brought back his régime of personal power and police terror. The famous military leaders, as possible rivals, were covered with honours and put on the shelf, starting with Zhukov. No party congresses were called and the Party itself was run in dictatorial fashion by its Secretary-General; propaganda, run by Zhdanov and the political police, was the chief machinery of power. Nor were there words fulsome enough to glorify 'the Father of the People' and he was surrounded by toadies each trying to outdo the other.

In theory, the USSR did not intervene in the internal changes taking place in the satellite countries, which were officially proclaimed as being in response to the heartfelt wishes of the masses. But she was ready to guard against any deviation, as she showed in Romania. In every country, she took over German property, which had achieved monstrous proportions through the occupation and which she looked on as the spoils of war; she forced her former enemies to pay out large sums in reparations, despite the fact that they had become her friends; she requisitioned machines, plant and stocks of all sorts and despatched them to Russia; she formed joint companies, such as 'Sovrom Petrol' in Romania, whose power extended to a great variety of sectors: coal, steel, wood, crude oil, chemical products; commercial transactions between the satellite countries were cut down to make way for direct trading by each of them with the USSR; the price of the produce traded was fixed at a level extremely favourable to the USSR: thus Poland had to deliver coal at £23 a ton whereas Sweden was offering her over £90, while Czechoslovakia bought wheat from the Soviet Union at double the price she would have paid for it from the USA. The new governments accepted these harsh conditions; they even agreed to hand over territory, as Czechoslovakia did in sub-Carpathian Ukraine; they signed treaties of alliance directed against Germany, which turned them into Russian satellites; this meekness can, of course, be explained by the fact that they were Communist-led; but the ever-present memories of German oppression also worked in Russia's favour, as well as the desire to retain the advantages that Germany had been forced to grant in defeat – the Oder–Neisse frontier or Sudetenland.

However, Stalin kept to the agreement that he had made with Churchill over Greece and he got nothing out of Turkey despite his pressure on her.

VIII THE AMERICAN TITAN

While Europe was licking her wounds and Asia and Africa were hesitatingly building for themselves an uncertain future, the United States was bubbling over with wealth and optimism. Although they had deployed larger forces against Germany than had the Commonwealth and had borne the burden of the war against Japan almost single-handed, their losses in men were insignificant in proportion to their population and the population curve had continued to climb; this saving in human lives sprang from their methods of fighting; they made machines do the fighting for them – they were one war ahead of their partners. The number of unemployed dropped from 7 million in 1939 to 700,000 in 1945; national income had more than doubled and despite war debts the budget had been balanced, because the internal loans were less than the profits being made.

Output had made giant strides in every sector: 33 per cent up in agriculture, 32 per cent more coal, 40 per cent more crude oil, 400 per cent more iron ore. The United States was producing 684 million tons of coal and 244 million tons of crude oil; one half and two-thirds of the total world output respectively. They had sufficient capability to produce 95 million tons of steel and one million tons of aluminium. Perhaps the most remarkable indication of their power was the size of their merchant navy which, at 57 million tons, was two-thirds of the world total and 60 per cent of the tankers (as compared with 21 and 24 per cent in 1939); their shipbuilding yards could launch twice as many ships as were sunk by German submarines in their most successful year. But in addition the United States had the only fleet of trans-ocean aircraft in the world; their 15,000 long-range aircraft guaranteed them an almost complete monopoly of intercontinental air transport.[1]

So seven per cent of the earth's surface and population was wealthier, by itself, than the rest of the world put together. As monetary proof of this wealth, sixty per cent of the gold and precious metals of the whole world lay in the vaults of the Federal Reserve Bank. The result was that, despite its proliferation, the dollar was the only real gold currency in the world – henceforth, the pound would have difficulty in staying at its old level. The American trade balance had a considerable surplus and the balance of payments an even larger one, thanks to the investment of capital overseas (nearly 4,000 million dollars). The United States was thus in a position to fix prices unilaterally on world markets; it was clear that Europe could be

1. The possibilities offered by this power were demonstrated when entire nationalist Chinese divisions were lifted thousands of miles to receive the Japanese armies' surrender.

rebuilt and the new nations put on a sound basis only with her help. Her economic strength gave her formidable political power.

In the first instance, it was the American continent itself which both benefited and suffered from this double power. Canada had followed her neighbour's example; after having hitherto been a supplier of food products and wood, she had now also became a supplier of munitions; her steel output had doubled, her trade balance had increased fivefold but her meat production had also increased considerably. In South America mining and oil resources were being far more intensively exploited – tin in Bolivia, bauxite in Brazil, oil in Venezuela. But industry had also developed to replace European manufactured products in the textile and steel industry; and chemical industries had been started up. After having been her debtors, Argentina, Brazil, Chile and Uruguay had now become Europe's creditors; the sale of British assets had relieved them of part of their debts; their banks had been able to build up gold reserves which opened up prospects of equipping and developing their own industries.

This prosperity owed a great deal to the United States. It was she who had provided Canada with fuel and ore and she became the largest purchaser of raw materials from South America, where her manufactured products had filled the gap left by those from Europe. But above all, it was the Americans who supplied the capital with which to build the new factories. American or joint companies thus owned nickel or bauxite refining firms as well as steel and chemical industries in Canada and three-quarters of the Venezuelan crude-oil production; the same thing happened in the railways and public services. True, it was private capital and not a systematic policy of exploitation by a new colonial system. The results were the same: the American continent had become an essential producer and customer for United States production. The other countries, cut off from an impoverished Europe, could dispose of their surplus production only in their markets; thus the strongest country established a complete financial and economic hegemony.

This situation brought political and military consequences in its train. United States ambassadors intervened in the internal affairs of countries, for or against governments that were considered pro- or anti- American – in Buenos Aires, Spruille Braden endeavoured to overthrow Colonel Peron. The American Army had obtained the use of bases in Mexico, on the Galapagos Islands and in Panama. In March 1945, by the Chapultepec agreement, the United States undertook to co-ordinate the defences of the Latin American countries.

Although Canada adopted a style of life based on her neighbour's, with high wages and a high standard of comfort, in Central and South America only the ruling classes really benefited from the economic boom. The urban and rural masses remained ignorant and poverty-stricken. However, a new dawn was beginning to appear. In Mexico, Torrès Bodet launched an immense programme to provide schools for the Indian population and adapt them to a technical civilisation. Although he abolished the workers' right to strike, President Vargas did try to allocate the resources of Brazil more fairly over all areas of the country. In Argentina, Colonel Peron reduced working hours, increased wages and forced employers to recognise the *aguinaldo* – a thirteenth month in the working year.

American experts had greatly feared the transitional period between the final phasing-out of the war economy and the complete return to a normal economy. They thought that when the orders placed by the state came to an end, under-production and under-employment would occur at the very moment when demobilisation would be throwing millions of men on to the labour market. They assessed the probable number of unemployed at between 5 and 10 million, and the drop in national income at 9,000 million dollars. Obsessed by memories of the slump of the thirties, they had sought ways and means to prevent its recurrence; even before the end of the war, immense orders placed by the War department had been cancelled, requisitioned firms had been freed and most controls abolished.

The American economy was thus going back to a *laissez-faire* policy which industry was most anxious to see reinstated and which seemed necessary since an appeal was about to be made to the consumer. But the trade union leaders, fearing a drop in wages as a result of unemployment and a rise in the cost of living due to inflation, backed a policy of regulating prices and incomes and their support in the elections had enabled the Democrats to remain in power.

President Truman thus launched a completely empirical policy. Whilst abolishing all rationing and freeing overseas trade, he maintained price control for a limited period on certain important goods, on the understanding that it should not be rigid and that increases might be allowed. He continued to use state intervention to increase production where the need arose; he provided for ex-servicemen; he gave priority to the re-equipping of the car industry; he replaced private enterprise by state in order to avoid unemployment and, above all, he launched a vast programme of public works. On September 6, 1945, Truman announced to the nation a whole programme to guarantee work for 60 million people: building roads and houses; geological surveys; hydraulic installations on the Missouri, Colorado and Columbia to irrigate the west and produce electrical power; removal of the locks to open up the Great Lakes to ocean shipping, etc.

So any fall in production was limited and short-lived and prosperity was never jeopardised. However, there were more gloomy sides to the picture; increased prosperity had not been evenly spread throughout every region; the upsurge in prices had not been entirely kept under control and the discrepancy between wages provoked large-scale strikes among workers; above all, the distribution of wealth had been very uneven and had left millions of underprivileged: blacks and Indians, the more or less clandestine immigrants from Mexico, French Canadians in Vermont; thus sharply divided class divisions existed in the United States but there was little class feeling and the war had not given rise to a class struggle, indeed quite the opposite; on the whole, the number of poor families had fallen; a poor black American would seem well off if he were transplanted to Africa. In 1945, despite racial and social disturbances, considered as inevitable in a period of transition, the American public was more or less unanimous in thinking that the American way of life was the best possible.

However, since Roosevelt's death the United States had not yet clearly decided upon their international policy; Truman was too unsure of himself not to be content to follow the lead laid down by his illustrious predecessor. But once military operations had come to an end, this had disappeared. What would Roosevelt have done once the Soviet's power, ambitions and hostility had become obvious? Would he have continued to follow the path on which he had embarked at Yalta? The former Vice-President, Wallace, was convinced that this would have been the case and he advocated adopting a friendly attitude towards the USSR and over-coming the resentment caused by this deep disillusionment. But other people, led by the experts in 'Kremlinology', considered that the time had come to be firm or else a very grave situation would arise. Between these two policies, Truman remained undecided: would not the first result of firmness mean putting a stop to demobilisation, which could not fail to be unpopular? For the moment, it was Byrnes' experience and vigilance which dictated White House policy: remain on guard, of course, but keep up a dialogue with the USSR, sometimes obtaining a *quid pro quo* for any concessions that might have to be made and at other times refusing to give in to her.

IX PROBLEMS AND DISAGREEMENTS

As long as Germany and Japan had not surrendered, the Allies, in order not to jeopardise their victory, had avoided fanning the flames of any disagreement which might exist between them elsewhere in the world; but the end of the hostilities brought these disagreements into the open and gave rise to others. The euphoria of the early days of the great alliance was succeeded by the suspicions aroused by its methods of application and, gradually, by open hostility; but in the autumn of 1945, this had not gone beyond the stage of skirmishing, as if the opponents were fencing for position before tackling each other full on.

Between August and September 1944, an interallied conference met in

Paris to settle the question of Tangier; Spain was called upon to evacuate the zone and at once did so; the international administration was restored, with the addition of American and Soviet delegates. The USSR asked that Spain should be excluded, as a punishment for her Fascist régime, but the Americans, British and French opposed this on the grounds that the population of the zone was largely Spanish, and the USSR did not press the point.

As for Italy, France had made known her territorial claims; they affected only a few mountain ridges and two villages in the Mercantour region, with the consent of the inhabitants. Italy gave her agreement and promised to grant a certain autonomy to the French-speaking Aosta valley. But she was more obdurate with regard to her rights on the Julian Alps, which were entirely occupied by Yugoslav troops; under pressure from the British and Americans, these troops moved out of Trieste in June 1945 and here too, although the Russians supported Yugoslavia, they left their allies free to enforce their views.

But this conciliatory attitude changed as soon as the territories freed by the Red Army were concerned. In Romania and Bulgaria, the British and American missions vainly endeavoured to see that free elections were held in accordance with the principle decided upon at Yalta. In Poland, on June 29, 1945, 'a provisional Polish government of national unity' had been formed under Osubka-Moravski, with Mikolajczyk as Vice-President and the key posts in the hands of the Communists; the United States, Britain and France had reluctantly agreed to recognise this government, in the hope that free elections would be held; but without waiting for these elections, Poland was bound to the USSR by a treaty of mutual assistance. Only in Hungary did General Miklos reject the Soviet suggestion of drawing up a single list for the elections; the result was that in November 1945, 245 'small landowners' were elected as against only 70 Communists; but the latter retained the Ministry of the Interior and Moscow did not fail to draw the moral of this unfortunate experience.

The territorial rivalries between countries that had now entered Russia's zone of influence were settled by the USSR on her own; thus, while awaiting a proper treaty drawn up in due form, Romanian troops continued to occupy Transylvania; on the other hand, Bulgaria retained the south of Dobruja; the Russians exerted strong pressure on the Hungarians to make them agree to an exchange of population with Czechoslovakia, who was anxious to expel the Hungarian subjects living in Slovakia and obtain the return of Slovaks from Hungary; as for the question of navigation on the Danube, although Moscow agreed that it should be free, it was claimed that it must be under the control of the Danubian countries alone.

It was in Turkey, however, that the situation seemed gravest. Faced by the Soviet Union's demands for a permanent base in the Dardanelles and the return of the Armenian vilayets that had been held by Turkey since the Treaty of Brest-Litovsk, the Turks suspended the demobilisation of their armed forces. In these circumstances, the granting by the United States of a 500-million dollar loan was the equivalent of diplomatic backing. Similarly, in Greece the Regent, Damaskinos, found himself called to order by Attlee because he was relying on support from reactionary elements who were former collaborators and looked on the Resistance fighters as brigands; the American ambassador openly supported the Regent.

So in the autumn of 1945, three major consequences of the war were appearing. The first was the declining importance of Britain; she was still concerned in a few minor military operations, based on her former imperialist attitudes, as for example in the Near East, where Colonial Office agents were trying to oust the French by stirring up the native nationalists; but she was soon going to be absorbed in her own serious internal problems. The second was the immense area in central and eastern Europe that despite her exhaustion the USSR had taken over as her own preserve. Last but not least, was the fact that, albeit hesitantly, the United States was intervening more and more openly in world affairs; this was in contradiction with their previously stated intention of repatriating and demobilising their armies; but on the other hand, it represented the wish of certain military leaders such as Patton and MacArthur and economic experts who advised President Truman to come to the financial and economic aid of Europe, in the interests of the United States themselves.

The world was thus tending to be divided between two great powers, still of unequal strength. Each of them had supporters in the countries where they did not exercise any direct authority; each was eyeing the other with growing distrust and suspecting the other of hatching the darkest plots. They seemed to be opposed on every point and their hostility was thus fundamentally ideological in nature. The United States' power was based on a liberal economy, a presidential democracy and private enterprise; her strength came first and foremost from her wealth. The USSR was an authoritarian régime in which public opinion counted for nothing, in which everything was owned by the state and one political party had the monopoly of power. Her strength lay in her ideology. The greatest naval and commercial power in the world stood face to face with the greatest land power. Could these deep-rooted differences, affecting the form of government, political, economic and social structures, the role of the individual and conceptions of politics and morality, still leave open any possibility of discussion? At the point where this study ends, the answer was yes; but even at this stage, on many points, the Allies preferred not to face each other for fear of crossing swords and to postpone indefinitely questions which needed settling. The war was over but no one, in the autumn of 1945, would have dared assert that peace had been won.

CHAPTER 3

The Task of Reconstruction

THE Second World War was a total war: in order to defeat the enemy, every country had mobilised her economic potential, human resources, intelligence and creative powers to the full. This militarised society and economy, this 'war civilisation' in fact, which came into being in all the belligerent countries – one of the reasons why France was defeated was that she was slow to adapting herself to it – left very little room for pure research, disinterested intelligence, art for art's sake or imaginative literature. Machines, bodies and brains had to co-operate to produce works of destruction.

Yet while still in the thick of the fighting, the Allies were preparing for the post-victory period; they were looking for ways of preventing such disasters from happening again and of leading men away from fratricidal strife towards a new solidarity: out of these concerns was born the United Nations Organisation with all its dependent organisations. On the other hand, the research which had been carried out to meet the needs of the armies and to produce decisive weapons led to such important discoveries in science and technology that this was to speed up the task of rebuilding and make it much easier, while vast new horizons were opening up for the human race once it was at peace.

I THE UNITED NATIONS ORGANISATION

The idea of replacing the League of Nations by a more effective international organisation came into being in the Atlantic Charter of August 26, 1941; this was an American initiative, taken before the United States entered the war. It was also the American State Department which prepared the United Nations' Declaration in January 1942, by which the powers at war with the Axis promised to remain united when peace returned; the USSR having given her assent in October 1943, the Teheran Conference set up a group to study the question, with its headquarters naturally in Washington, in view of the fact that the Americans were the prime movers in having the plan adopted and put into operation.

It was at Dumbarton Oaks, also in the United States, that in September and October 1944 the four great powers (the USA, Great Britain, the USSR and China – France had not been invited) reached agreement on the broad lines on which the United Nations Organisation would be organised. They envisaged it as being controlled by two main institutions: a General Assembly and a Security Council of which the five major Allies (including France) would have the right of permanent membership. The Yalta Conference endorsed these proposals and decided that the Security Council could not make a decision until there was unanimity among the major powers, which amounted to giving each of them the right to veto.

All the powers at war with the Axis (forty-nine in all) – some, like the Argentine, had hurriedly declared war so as not to be left out – were summoned to the UN Constituent Assembly, which was held from April 25 to June 15, 1945, still in the United States, in San Francisco. In contrast to what happened in 1918, the task of setting up the world Organisation was kept distinct from that of drawing up the peace treaties, which was to be dealt with separately. The USSR did not succeed in having the 'democratic government' of Poland or 'the World Trade Union Organisation' accepted – 'the conference was the concern only of governments', in Attlee's words. By unanimous agreement the conference set forth a certain number of principles: equality between peoples and the right of each one to self-determination; the need for international co-operation and non-interference in the internal affairs of other states; the settling of disputes by peaceful methods.

Article 73 laid down that the colonial powers must 'recognise the overriding importance of the inhabitants of colonial territories' and help them 'gradually to develop their free political institutions'. This was inviting the development of nationalism in subject countries; even before it came into being, the UN showed itself to be inspired by a spirit of anti-colonialism – a result of the fact that on this particular point the Russians and the Americans were of one mind.

Another agreement, this time between the British and the Soviet Union, was not so successful; extrapolating from the conclusions reached by Churchill and Stalin in their talks of October 1944, they would have liked to divide the world up by organising it into three large territorial sectors: Eurafrica, America and Eurasia; obviously, in this way Great Britain, the United States and the USSR would each allocate themselves an immense zone of influence. The United States and the smaller powers were opposed to dividing the world up like this; the UN was confirmed as a united organisation with ecumenical equality for its members.

In the end all 'peaceful' states who would accept the UN charter were allowed to take part in the General Assembly – which amounted to excluding for the time being only the Axis states and their allies. The

General Assembly had some power; it elected the non-permanent members of the Security Council, it admitted new members and could exclude those who violated the charter; but as a general rule its role remained a consultative one; on important problems it could only set up inquiries and move recommendations for the Security Council.

The leading role in the Organisation devolved on the latter, which was composed of eleven members, five of them permanent. The Council had to prevent or resolve any conflicts which presented a threat to international peace; it could suggest negotiation or mediation; but it also had the task of applying to those who violated the charter through acts of aggression retaliatory measures ranging from diplomatic sanctions (breaking off relations) or economic sanctions (severing communications, blockades) to military intervention by 'national contingents of armed forces'. In order that it should face up to its obligations, it was arranged that the Council should sit very frequently and take its decisions by a majority of seven votes, including the five votes of the permanent members; on this last point the USSR had stood firm, perhaps frightened by the obviously dominant influence of the United States in the UN or else anxious not to bind herself, in order to remain in control in the areas of influence which the Red Army's victories had carved out for her. Through the expedient of the veto, therefore, a sort of federation of the big powers was being set up to control the world, but one which would be paralysed by any disagreement among its members.

II THE NEW INTERNATIONAL ORGANISATIONS

There was no doubt whatsoever that the UN represented a step forward as compared with the League of Nations; the membership of the United States and the USSR made all the difference to its strength; while the General Assembly preserved the rights of the smaller nations, the Security Council introduced a realistic concept of unequal powers; it was plain, however, that the Organisation would work only if the big powers, and, in the first instance, the two biggest, were in agreement; the veto which was given to each of them merely expressed this fact in legal terms; how, except by war, which was exactly what they were trying to avoid in the future, could the will of a majority be imposed on a big power which was determined to defend its national interests? The world Organisation would be what its leading members wanted it to be.

As it stood, however, the UN offered great hopes for the future. Although its main aim was to preserve peace, it has also declared its determination to defend the basic rights of men and nations, irrespective of race, sex or religion. And in order that its principles should not remain a dead letter, it promised 'to promote social progress and to bring about better living conditions, together with greater freedom'. In order to achieve these aims, provision was made to set up a whole group of international organisations.

A 'Trusteeship Council' was formed to administer the territories formerly held under mandate by the League of Nations, those taken away from enemy countries or any others which might ask for protection from the UN – which was a way of helping the colonised peoples on the road to independence.

An 'International Court of Justice' was constituted on the lines of that of the International Permanent Court of Justice in the Hague; it is true that it could only put forward opinions; but it was the highest court of appeal to arbitrate between states which were anxious to settle their differences peacefully.

The General Staff Committee was in charge of preparing for possible cases of intervention by UN forces and all the member powers promised to put the necessary armed forces at the Security Council's disposal on request.

Above all, the Economic and Social Council, consisting of eighteen members, had the task of bringing about world co-operation in the field of economics, social and intellectual matters, health, etc. It was a vast, indeed even an unlimited programme. In order to carry it out, the Council provided itself with specialised institutions without any limits of number.

Thus UNRRA (United Nations Relief and Rehabilitation Administration) was set up as early as 1943 and entrusted with ensuring supplies of provisions to nations impoverished by war and with speeding up the repatriation of displaced persons; over a period of two years it would supply 25 million tons of commodities to seventeen different countries.

The International Labour Organisation replaced the League of Nations' former International Labour Office as early as October 1944. Its aim was to strive for social justice through full employment, by raising the standard of living and by co-operation between employers and employed.

UNESCO (United Nations Educational, Scientific and Cultural Organisation), the idea of which went back to the London meetings of the Ministers of Public Instruction of the exiled governments, was to encourage co-operation in the field of culture, art and science, and in particular to provide increasing aid from the wealthy powers to the underdeveloped peoples, such as treatment for endemic diseases, improved education and help in progress towards self-government.

The United Nations Food and Agriculture Organisation, which came into being in Hot Springs, Virginia, in 1943, set itself the task of raising the standard of living of the peoples of the world by drawing up worldwide programmes against famine and agricultural underproduction.

The Civil Aviation Organisation and the European Continental Transport Organisation were intended to go into the question of co-ordinating the methods and rules operating in the various countries – rights of passage, landings, signals, timetables, etc.

In July 1944 in Bretton Woods, the International Bank for Reconstruction and Development was set up. Its aim was to finance the rebuilding and equipping of countries which had suffered disaster, to encourage a return to international investment and to foster peaceful interchange; poor countries could thus receive the financial aid essential for their recovery. To complement the Bank there was the International Monetary Fund, also set up at Bretton Woods, with the task of ensuring stability of exchange rates, with the aid of a reserve fund formed by the associate states which would make it possible to lend foreign currency to countries suffering from a temporary deficit in their balance of payments; the states which had signed the agreement promised, in addition, not to devalue their currencies unilaterally.

All these international organisations had originated during the course of the war itself: they had been initiated by the Americans and it was the United States which provided them with the greater part of their means of carrying out the tasks with which they were entrusted. The richest country in the world, which had emerged from the war richer than ever, was thus helping to set the poorer countries on their feet again. Their convalescence was also going to be helped by scientific discoveries and technological progress.

III THE COMMITMENT OF WRITERS AND ARTISTS

The triumph of Nazism had plunged Germany into intellectual darkness; Goering's famous phrase 'When I hear the word culture, I reach for my revolver', was not an idle quip; works and their creators who fell foul of the masters of the Third Reich had been banned, interned or used for an *auto-da-fé*; the only thing the artist or the writer could do was to flee his country in order to remain free,[1] keep silent in order to escape persecution or prostitute himself in order to live. The Wehrmacht's victories extended this dead hand all over Europe. Material difficulties – shortage of paper and printers' ink, of tubes of paint for the painter and of film for the film-director – were made worse by strict censorship and propaganda slogans until at last the whole of intellectual Europe lay under the same yoke. With paintings and sculptures being removed and confiscated, conditions were hardly favourable for exhibitions, nor did power cuts

1. This happened with Freud, Einstein, Thomas and Heinrich Mann, Stephan Zweig, Hindemith, Béla Bartók and others.

and the curfew do much to promote theatrical performances, cinema shows or concerts.

Some of the writers and artists, either through lack of awareness, greed or for ideological reasons, chose collaboration with the present master; the latter moreover was able to reward those who served him – or to dupe the gullible ones – by financing travel, giving subsidies and publicity or by placing orders for their works. Drieu La Rochelle, Abel Bonnard, A. de Chateaubriant, R. Brasillach, Paul Chack, Georges Claude and many others, to mention merely those in France, sang the praises of the Nazi order; R. Benjamin and H. Pourrat made their name by defying Marshal Pétain.

Others chose to keep silent and these were often the greatest writers: Alain, André Gide, Jean Giraudoux, Romain Rolland, Henri Bergson, Julien Benda; or they left for shores where the spirit still breathed freely – like André Maurois, Henri Bernstein, Jules Romains, St-John Perse, André Breton, Jacques Maritain, Georges Bernanos, Louis Jouvet and René Clair. Some were clever enough to produce ambiguous works in which everyone could find what he was looking for: Jean Anouilh won praise for his *Créon* during the occupation and for his *Antigone* after the Liberation; Claude Vermorel achieved the same double success with *Jeanne avec nous*.

But in any case it was no longer a time for art for art's sake, stylistic devices or subtleties of thought; writers and artists had to join in the national struggle, which for them was also a personal one. No group was free of internal dissension; thus, within the small circle of existentialist philosophers, Heidegger had a weakness for Nazism while Jaspers was viewed with suspicion by its followers and Sartre and Camus fought against it.

The majority of writers realised that it was their own *raison d'être* that was at stake – freedom of thought and expression. Their pens became swords and their fellowship a fighting unit; in France, within the single *Comité national des Ecrivains* and through the medium of a single publisher, *Éditions de Minuit*, François Mauriac, Louis Aragon, Paul Eluard, J. Vercors, André Malraux, Georges Duhamel, Jean Guéhenno, André Chamson, Jean Paulhan, Claude Aveline, Louis Martin-Chauffier, Jean Cassou, etc., enlisted on the same side of the barricades – the barricade of the Resistance for which Robert Desnos, Georges Politzer, Jacques Decour, Jean Prévost and many more gave their lives.

This mobilisation of writers and artists took place in every country that was at war with the Axis: Dos Passos extolled the efficiency of American industry, Dreiser cried out that 'America must be saved', while Ilya Ehrenburg bewailed the fall of Paris and Shostakovitch composed the *Song of the Woods* as a homage to the partisans; Frank Capra explained to the American people in pictures 'why he was fighting', Friedrich Ermler related the epic of Stalingrad and David Lean praised the cause in *In which we serve*.

Thus, in every country, patriotic feeling became the chief inspiration of literary and artistic works which all made, in their own way, their contribution to victory. In these circumstances, the development of aesthetics and philosophies of artistic creation, such as surrealism, came to a standstill. It was hardly an era likely to produce great and original works on themes other than those based on events, neither was there much opportunity for powerful intellects to make their mark; in order to regain or find their identity, they had to bow to the pressures of war.

There could hardly be any secret painting or sculpture and it would have made little impact; on the other hand the times favoured the growth of the politico-philosophical essay and even more of the pamphlet, as well as of poetry which, owing to its somewhat mysterious nature, was allowed to be openly published. Feeling was running at such a pitch that culture could only suffer; must one cease to love Bach, Beethoven, Goethe and Schiller because they were Germans and because the *Propagandastaffel* was misusing their fame for its own purposes? On the other hand, was it not right and proper to glorify such and such an author of dubious talent merely because he was a victim of the new order?

At all events the commitment of writers and artists helped to promote national unity, and when peace came contributed to maintaining a drive and a will to survive which proved fruitful in the period of reconstruction; the intellectual freedom which had been all too long suppressed was then able to explode in all directions.

IV GIANT STRIDES IN PHYSICS[1]

The war witnessed immense advances in the field of electronics, with all its unlimited possibilities of application. Although the first electron microscope had been built in 1931, ten times more powerful than its predecessors, now it was possible to achieve a resolution of 1/100,000 mm; this made many viruses visible which are at the extreme limit of living matter, the macromolecules which go to form plastic materials.

In the field of aircraft detection, by 1944 research in Germany had reached the stage of experimenting with infra-red rays; in the United States the sniperscope, with its infra-red projected image, had been adapted to the rifle and made it possible to see some fifty or sixty yards in the dark without the enemy's knowledge. These discoveries, when applied to the radio-telescope, allowed far speedier observation and

1. Messrs. Taton and Grmek have kindly re-read pp. 831 to 839. I am very grateful to them.

increased its strength to make it possible to see burnt-out stars that were still warm and enable objects to be examined at very high temperatures – such as aircraft engines.

In the field of two-way radio communications, considerable progress had been made; transmitter-receivers had been gradually reduced in size and had become less sensitive to damp, heat and shock; this made it possible to produce sets which were not much larger than a small parcel. Remarkable progress was made also as a result of the development of the multiplex technique, by means of which one single wave could carry several telephone conversations simultaneously – a technique employed both in broadcasting and in telephonic communications, especially by using co-axial cables linking together two transmitters and receivers. The world's short-wave broadcasting network was considerably developed. Not only were the national networks – the BBC, for example – able to broadcast for several hundred hours each day, but research made it possible to select the best frequency for a given transmission, according to the date, time and prospective audience. Studio techniques were also revolutionised by magnetic recording and the use of tape-recorders. Only frequency modulation and television lagged somewhat behind during the war; the former had proved expensive and of no importance for the war; the latter was to reap full benefit after the war from the manufacture of cathode-ray tubes and the general adoption of radar; thus the quality of the picture was thereby greatly improved.

It was radio navigation, however, both at sea and in the air, which made the greatest advance. After the discovery of radar, methods of radio goniometry and blind-landing techniques had been perfected and had gained in accuracy by the use of very short wavelengths; thus the landings in the summer of 1944 had been directed by a system called 'Decca'. Again, from 1940 onwards, in Switzerland, turbo-electric engines were first tried out.

The whole process of developing electronic equipment had followed on from the progress made in the technique of electronic valves, of which the total world production rose during the war to several hundred million – miniature valves lodged in the head of a missile and firing the detonator close to the target, oscillating magnetrons providing continuous radiation, klystrons used as oscillators, amplifiers and frequency multipliers or travelling-wave tubes which could amplify frequency bands of any width.

Electronics had made it possible to construct either arithmetical or algebraic calculating machines, able to repeat operations at great speed and to deal with numbers virtually beyond the capabilities of the human brain, in view of the length of time required and the inevitable mistakes which this would involve. The various operations were translated into figures. Thus in May 1944 an electronically programmed machine called

Mark I worked out calculations of range tables and aerodynamics a hundred times faster than man. Beams of electrons replaced perforated bands and numbered wheels and the first electronic brain came into use in 1945; it worked out the calculations which led to the manufacture of the atom bomb – using 100,000 electrical impulses per second.

Although Lawrence had constructed a cyclotron at Berkeley as early as 1934, it was the work of Fermi and Joliot-Curie which made it possible to move from the laboratory to the industrial stage, to show that matter was a permanent source of energy and to split the atom. Forestalling the German, Heisenberg, who originated the idea of describing the atom in terms of matrices but who lacked good assistants and was inadequately supported by the Nazis, the brilliant international team of 'Manhattan Project' successfully developed the two ways leading to the manufacture of nuclear explosives: the main American university laboratories succeeded in separating the isotope uranium 235; at almost the same time atomic piles using graphite or heavy water began to produce plutonium. They followed up the first of these processes, since it seemed to lend itself better to the chain reaction leading up to the explosion: two 700-gram blocks of uranium were joined by a delayed-action fuse; the chain reaction split up a steadily increasing number of atoms and released an immense and uncontrollable force which devastated everything within range.

Mankind was thus provided with an unlimited power of destruction; scientists did not forget the positive, creative aspect, but these achievements were for the future; they had to learn to control the energy, build atomic power stations which would obediently supply the required number of kilowatts and protect users against harmful radiation. For the moment man had turned devil and was not yet a god. At first, President Truman selfishly thought of keeping this fabulous secret for his own country by preventing the spread of information about it. But responsible scientists did not share this view; some, supported by certain Protestant movements, even wanted the United States to give up the atomic bomb; but would this not mean leaving the field open for possible opponents? The American government was divided; although some of its members were happy to accept an arms race in which the United States had such a lead that it seemed certain that it would never be caught up, others, Stimson among them, suggested holding talks with the USSR which could lead to co-operation in working for peaceful ends.

This was the solution adopted by Truman, which he announced to the country in a message to Congress on October 3, 1945. On November 10 preliminary talks opened in Washington between Americans, British and Canadians – the partners in manufacturing the bomb. The conclusions differed from the premises: fearing that if information spread it would lead to an arms race before any efficient system of safeguards had been

established, the three allies confined themselves to suggesting setting up a
UN commission – and kept their secret to themselves. Ot at least, so they
thought; in fact, a great deal of information had already been circulated
which the USSR was going to put to advantage.

V GIANT STRIDES IN CHEMISTRY

Inorganic chemistry, which had lagged behind organic chemistry, caught
up with it thanks to the use of new products in industry. Large-scale
hydrogenisation of coal was used to convert it to petrol; likewise, by a
direct industrial process of combining carbon with hydrogen, it had been
possible to produce light hydrocarbons. Hydrogen peroxide had been
used in German rockets. As for organic chemistry, it continued to expand
and had discovered, in particular, thousands of colouring agents.

New chemical elements had been isolated and classified, such as nep-
tunium, discovered by the Americans MacMillan and Abelson, and
plutonium, which had been produced by Seaborg as early as 1940 and was
later to be used to replace uranium in atom bombs.

In Germany, the USSR and the United States the scarcity of natural
rubber had led to its replacement by synthetic rubber made from acetylene
(German buna) or by cracking crude oil (Russian rubber); this synthetic
latex had the advantage of being more resistant to wear and to heat than
natural rubber.

Artificial resins were produced to compete with plastics of vegetable or
mineral origin and very soon became more widely used; materials
produced by the polymerisation of ethylene, which resisted corrosion and
possessed great insulating properties, had been used in making radar sets.
Even before the end of the war plastic materials, easy to cut up or mould,
had become widely used both for ordinary everyday objects and for
industrial equipment.

Although nylon was being made as early as 1938 by the firm of Dupont,
the manufacture of parachutes had given it a new impetus; similar to
steel in toughness, it was yet finer than silk. Synthetic fibres such as the
American vinyon and French rhovyl, all produced from vinyl acetate,
were used for chemical filters, surgical threads and fishing nets.

Desert warfare had made it necessary to distill sea-water; a lightweight
apparatus that removed chlorides and sulphates was issued to sailors and
soldiers; it had likewise proved possible to precipitate out calcium and
magnesium salts, which had made some fresh water unusable.

There was no field of chemical research which did not progress by
leaps and bounds during the war; in most cases it is difficult to date these
advances, since discoveries followed on one from another slowly as a

result of imperceptible improvements; but in the field of medicine, chemists, biologists and bacteriologists had joined forces to achieve extraordinary results. This was because they had had to face a recrudescence of disease.

VI DISEASE DURING THE WAR

Poverty and malnutrition, made worse by inadequate hygiene, new weapons, huge population movements and crowded living conditions, had caused outbreaks of new diseases and the reappearance of epidemics which had previously disappeared.

One disease which was due to a kind of rickets and had been found only in Queensland, Australia (Q. fever), had spread among both the Allied and the Axis armies in Libya and Greece, countries which they had occupied in turn; it was as if they were passing the germs on to one another. Exanthematous typhus had wrought havoc in Naples, the Balkan countries, the USSR and above all in the concentration camps – notably Dachau, Buchenwald and Bergen–Belsen – where the liberators found the ground littered with thousands of dead bodies. Endemic tetanus had ravaged the Germany army; malaria became widespread; fevers and skin and intestinal diseases from the Far East made their appearance in Europe.

In those countries which had been plundered or devastated, malnutrition had aggravated tuberculosis and revealed itself in the deficiency diseases which attack people compelled to live in a perpetual state of undernourishment: extreme emaciation, reducing people to skin and bones, chilblains, growing troubles in children, decalcification causing proneness to fractures, rickets, irregular menstruation, etc.

Undernourishment, the cold, lack of privacy, excessive work, fear and loneliness had caused former prisoners of concentration camps to suffer from an actual disease which Professor Richet and Dr Maas have described as 'post-concentration-camp', characterised by chronic asthenia, nervous exhaustion and premature ageing – between 1945 and 1955 14,000 French deportees died from the after-effects of the camps.

Air raids, the use of napalm and explosions involving petrol had considerably increased the proportion of burned among the wounded, with deeper burns covering a larger area of skin – second- and third-degree burns became a common occurrence. Collapsing buildings, explosions and derailment had produced a syndrome causing bone disease, a local loss of fluid and damaged kidneys; in particular, the blast of explosions gave rise to lung and stomach complaints with bleeding and acute oedema of the lungs.

Finally, the radioactive effects of the atom bomb in Japan caused damage to all the tissues of the human organism and caused loss of hair, sterility, miscarriages, loss of teeth, stomach ulcers, diarrhoea and vomiting, extreme fatigue and, above all, leukemia.

VII IMMENSE DEVELOPMENTS IN MEDICINE AND THERAPY

The ss warned concentration camp internees that they had to observe high standards of hygiene by a pithy notice saying: 'One louse and you're dead', but although German doctors knew how to prevent typhus by means of vaccines, they did not know how to arrest it. From 1943 onwards DDT, a Swiss insecticide which had already been used in the Swiss Army, was used by the Americans on a vast scale on their troops and on the population of the countries in which they were living. DDT proved harmless to man but fatal to flies, bugs, mosquitoes and lice; at the same time, the aerosol spray came into being. Other insecticides such as the German DFDT, the French HCH, Dr Slade's gammexane and lethane 384, were also used but proved less powerful or more awkward to use. At all events, radical means of delousing thus became available and were used for disinfecting clothes, bedding and premises; better still, immense areas of the Pacific were rid of malaria; battle could also now be successfully waged against the plague, sleeping sickness and yellow fever.

In order to protect their troops against malaria, from 1940 onwards the Americans devoted vast sums to research to find substitutes for quinine and were able to isolate three effective components, chloroquine, pentaquine and paludrine.

Sulphonamides derived from sulphur were known before the war both in Germany, through work on colouring matters, and in France, where the Pasteur Institute had demonstrated their sterilising effect on bacteria. The widespread use of these sulphonamides led to the discovery and industrial manufacture of groups which made it possible to counteract purpuric fevers, gonorrhoea, pneumonia, colibacilli, staphylococci, etc.

Penicillin had been discovered by Fleming as early as 1928, through the culture of moulds, but no further work had been done on it. After 1942 it was produced industrially, having proved to be the most effective agent against infection. In 1944 Waksman succeeded in isolating streptomycin, which had the power to inhibit the growth of Koch's bacillus; three other antibiotics were shown to be effective against the pneumococcus, staphylococcus and streptococcus. Mass tests were carried out at the time of the Italian and French campaigns; instead of restricting themselves to ineffectual orders putting certain districts in towns out of bounds, the American army medical authorities began a successful campaign against one of the oldest and most formidable scourges of the human race – syphilis.

The regrettably frequent necessity of amputating called for and led to the discovery of new anaesthetics, such as pentathol. Curare extract was first applied to the treatment of tetanus, then in preventing traumatism and finally, after 1942, for muscular relaxation during serious operations thus making light anaesthesia possible. The improvements in anaesthesia which led, for example, to improved techniques to control breathing were going to enable surgeons to carry out the most daring operations, since the level of intoxication of the patient was reduced to a minimum.

A large number of vitamins was already being investigated in 1939: during the war some were produced by chemical synthesis and others were added to the list, such as vitamin Bc which was isolated in spinach leaves, or vitamin H, which was identified as a factor in growth. It proved possible to confirm the effect of vitamins on the human body. In order to combat the effects of malnutrition on children, synthetic vitamins were distributed in the schools of the occupied countries, disguised in sweets or biscuits. These vitamins had been shown to counteract scurvy, pellagra and rickets. The products called antivitamins which were made by transforming live vitamins proved useful in preventing pathological conditions.

In order to counteract the effects of shock which could lead to death by anoxemia, transfusion (of blood, saline solutions and serums) and oxygen treatment techniques were successfully evolved. As it became impossible to provide supplies of fresh blood in every case, the needs of war considerably extended the use of stored blood, serum and plasma. A whole range of therapy, combining sulphonamides, antibiotics and transfusions succeeded in saving a great many lives of people who were burnt or had suffered from crashes or explosions. These discoveries were particularly useful in an age of heavy motor traffic. But they were also used in pre- or post-operative care and in cases of anaemia, haemorrhage and poisoning.

It was probably surgery, however, which, together with the control of infectious diseases, made the most progress, improving its methods by intensive practice and by taking advantage of the discoveries of biology and medicine. Thus as early as 1942 pleuralisation made it possible to close off the ends of bronchi. From 1943 onwards, arterial surgery seemed capable of curing diseases arising from poor blood circulation and on October 14, 1944 Crafoord became the first man to stitch up an aorta. In 1944–5, the surgical anastomosing of large blood-vessels made it possible to treat congenital deformities by transferring the blood from one part of the body to another which was short of it, thus curing the 'blue' disease, caused by a restricted flow of blood to the lungs through the pulmonary artery.

Even when it was producing unprecedented devastation, the atom bomb was providing medical science with rays far superior to those obtained from radium, either for physiological examination or for therapy, e.g. for leukemia.

In 1941 the British had perfected a process against toxic war gases which fortunately was not needed during the war but which, in the form of ointments or in solution, proved strong enough to remove arsenic from tissues. It was to counteract the effects of such gases that in 1943 Gilman discovered the first chemical radiomimetic bodies capable of acting on cancers. In the treatment of this scourge, which in 1940 was limited to X-rays, an advance was made in the use of hormones – the first cure was recorded in 1941; in 1943 research was undertaken on the treatment of breast cancer by male hormones.

In France Halpern discovered in 1942 antergan as the basis of curing or preventing asthma. In 1940 an Australian, Gregg, discovered the link between German measles in mothers and cataract or congenital heart disease in children. Later research showed that the consequences could also be deafness, dumbness or mental backwardness. This was the beginning of a great breakthrough into the hitherto unexplored field of embryology. Many cases of congenital malformation of the brain could be attributed to the toxoplasma, an intracellular parasite. Through the study of blood groups, in 1940 Landstein and Wiener discovered that the proteins in the blood were strictly specific; mishaps arising during transfusions or births were due to mixtures which could now be avoided by classifying individuals according to the 'rhesus factor'; it thus became possible to remedy, in the last months of pregnancy or in the first few days after birth, the situation caused by a couple's incompatible blood group; in serious cases children were even provided with a complete change of blood at birth.

In the USSR teams working under Negovsky had improved methods of resuscitation; the serum known as Bogomoletz's serum was used in transfusions; the surgeon Bogoraz had pointed the way for the complete rebuilding of vital parts of the body such as the hand. The ophthalmologist Tilatov had shown by his studies of the treatment of tissues that living cells placed in normally unfavourable conditions could stimulate regeneration.

All these discoveries were not the fruit of brilliant intuitions but of steady teamwork. They showed how medicine was dependent on observation and measuring instruments, the detection of electrical phenomena, chemical analysis, the study of the atom, recording techniques, psychology laboratories, improved surgical equipment, experiments on animals, etc. The progress which had been achieved seemed to offer unlimited possibilities and to be full of infinite promise; the doctor's role was no longer so much to cure illnesses as to detect them. For once, social development was in line with scientific progress; by putting all these wonder drugs within the reach of every purse, social welfare programmes considerably improved the living conditions of under-privileged peoples and classes; it was truly a revolution, but one in which violence played no part. Death retreated because its recuiting agents were being destroyed; human suffering was reduced; the average life-span was spectacularly lengthened; as a result, the population of mankind inevitably increased at a rate which could well prove disastrous if techniques of production are unable to provide work for everyone and the necessary means of subsistence.

VIII THE AGE OF SCIENCE AND TECHNOLOGY?

Scientific discoveries did not remain at the theoretical stage for long during the Second World War; military needs required them to be put into practice and new products to be mass-produced as quickly as possible. This speed was made possible by the combination of a number of factors: the action of public authorities in planning and directing the economy; the provision of vast sums for the appropriate programmes; dictatorial methods of directing labour and brainpower; the industrial power required to convert or build the factories geared for production. Thus the number of research laboratories and research workers considerably increased; pure research was closely linked with applied research or technology; a whole series of practical processes made it possible to pass quickly from the drawing board to production by making the most of a discovery which was then gradually improved. Within one and the same concern, two opposite tasks had to be pursued at the same time: more and more elaborate specialisation, enabling people to deepen their knowledge, and co-ordination, first of all between teams and then between disciplines, so that everyone could benefit from the progress of each one.

But in actual fact, in 1945 only the United States and to a lesser extent the USSR had all the assets needed for entering fully into the scientific and technological era; America had the advantage over Russia of being able to introduce the most recent technological innovations into everyday life without delay – whether it was a question of consumer goods, household equipment or relaxation. In both countries scientists were in a similar position; they had considerable power and stood at the top of the social ladder – immediately after the Wehrmacht surrendered the two countries had competed to 'liberate' German scientists – but they held neither political or economic power; in the United States they were working for capital, in the USSR for the state; they were not completely free either in their choice of research or in the use to which their work would be put. And despite the fact that peace had returned, the first consequence of scientific progress was to increase the possibilities of destruction should there ever be another war.

The limitation of scientific advance to a particular civilisation increased the disparity between the developed and the underdeveloped nations. Since communication had become both faster and more effective through the radio and the promise of television, and the problem of distance had been reduced and almost eliminated by aircraft which were flying farther and faster all the time, it became possible to spread knowledge more quickly over greater areas, while contacts between societies of very different levels of development increased. The presence of armies in the poor countries of Asia, Africa and the Mediterranean had produced a false prosperity and created new needs which the local economies were unable to satisfy; a vast appetite for a higher standard of living welled up in countries which were either without the means or did not know how to exploit their wealth, at the same time as the war gave many colonial territories the hope of self-determination in the near future.

The problems facing the political leaders still remained, of course, those bequeathed by history: disputed frontiers, clashes of interests, racial, social and religious dissensions and antagonism. But there were other bigger problems, existing on a different level, which concerned the whole of mankind; the question was whether science, which was now bringing wealth and power, would benefit everyone or whether it would, on the contrary, create a new form of imperialism in which the financier and the ideologist would take over from the soldier and the coloniser.

The solution would obviously be provided by the unlimited productivity offered by continuous technological progress. As it was, industrial building methods, prefabricated housing and new building materials – plastics, aluminium, synthetic wood – as well as the fact that many architects and town-planners were now thinking in social terms, made it possible to foresee first of all that new buildings would speedily arise from the ruins and that later the cancer of slums would be excised, giving a promise of wellbeing for all.

But geochemistry was also improving knowledge of the constituents of minerals and by explaining their properties making possible a more rational treatment of metals. Geophysics, with the help of radioactivity, could study strata down to a very great depth, and this made prospecting the resources of the subsoil more efficient. There was thus every chance that the earth's natural wealth would be better exploited. In industry mechanisation increased output, lowered the cost of manufacture, made better use of by-products and reduced human effort; in the mines, mechanised methods which had originated in the United States increased

capacity. The steel industry succeeded both in achieving increased purity
of the end product and in producing numerous new varieties of alloys.
But the greatest and most rapid changes occurred in the chemical industry,
where synthetic products competed with even the most traditional ones
in a never-ending chain-reaction of invention.

Man was beginning to be absolute master of matter; he could now see
no limits to his power. This technological age will probably lead to the
standardisation of society and of ways of life, and to simplification, perhaps
even to impoverishment, of individual civilisations. But this will go hand
in hand with the defeat of mankind's real enemies: cold, hunger, disease,
ignorance and superstition. If men can control their passions, their
antagonisms and their more or less outdated divisions, the age of science –
in spite of the crimes and havoc produced by Hitler's madness – can lead
to progress for all men.

Conclusion

THE Second World War began in the guise of a return match for the First, as a conflict between great European powers; then it broadened out into a world war and the stake had become world domination. But even before it started, from the time of the Spanish Civil War, international Fascism had given it the character of an ideological crusade, which had been further emphasised by the USSR's entry into the lists. However, it was the liberation of the Nazi-occupied countries which had revealed its full significance; mass slaughter, concentration camps and genocide would have become institutionalised in a world dominated or inspired by the Nazis; the war had thus been waged on behalf of civilisation against barbarism, whose evil deeds were only aided and abetted by science; this was why, in spite of their widely differing views and their past struggles, democrats in the tradition of the age of enlightenment, Christians imbued with the teaching of the Gospel and Marxists striving for an end to the exploitation of man by man had all found themselves on the same side of the barricade in the 'strange alliance' or in the underground Resistance movements; they had fought to put an end to the reign of violence, racialism, political and social inequality and destructive nihilism, so that mankind might emerge from a long period of spiritual darkness.

The world had been so shaken to its foundations, the efforts of the belligerents had been so herculean, that when military operations finally ceased the overall impression was one of a completely topsy-turvy world, a complex kaleidoscope of antagonism and uncertainty. No one could be sure when and to what extent the tremendous material and moral havoc would be put right; no one would dare to say that the agreement amongst the victors and the rainbow of frail international institutions supporting it would be a guarantee that 'the thunder was over'.

What was certain was that the decline of western and central Europe, impoverished and drained of its life-blood, was becoming more marked; that Asia was in a turmoil of change; that Africa, particularly the Arab world, and South America were shaking off their slumber and beginning to stir; and that the colonial empires were in danger. The combination of vast open spaces, huge populations – they were, in fact, continents – and an unprecedented economic and military potential caused two 'super-states' to arise out of the chaos, the United States and the USSR; the financial power of the former was balanced by the widespread ideological attraction of the latter. These two giants appeared to be different in every way; in actual fact there was a basic similarity between them, founded on the common hope in the future with the aid of the benefits of science and technology; but their more obvious differences caused them for the time being to drift apart and oppose each other.

The decline of western Europe was also the decline of liberal democracy, for every western European country had been organised on a system of controlled economy which gave the state more and more extensive powers. The victory of the USSR was also the victory of international Communism; not only had it taken over control of eastern and central Europe but in many countries of the world – especially in China, France and Italy – it aimed at achieving power and was ready to do so; nevertheless, for the time being, it wore the mask of Stalinism, whose damaging totalitarianism was more frightening than attractive. As for the United States, her unparalleled wealth was powerful evidence that she was thriving on liberal capitalism; however, in 1942 Burnham had forecast that it would develop towards a state capitalism in which the real authority would belong to the economic and managerial experts – it was the beginning of the 'age of technocrats'.

The most visible change in men's lives was that distances were shortened and the earth seemed smaller as a result; for example, air flights – and the possible use of intercontinental rockets – revealed an unexpected route over the North Pole. But paradoxically, as peoples came to know each other better and became neighbours linked together by trading and other exchanges, they seemed deliberately to sink back into a touchy nationalism and took pleasure in isolating themselves and asserting their originality. 'A world of contradictions': this, it seems, is how one might define the world which emerged from the war: productivity had become potentially limitless but never before had the gap between rich and poor, whether peoples or individuals, been wider; the pace of events had speeded up and for the developed countries life was improving at a breakneck speed, but whole continents were still plunged in the unchanging lethargy of times immemorial; the advance of knowledge could refine the intelligence, spread good taste and increase toleration, but radio and cinema loudspeakers and ideological propaganda were also capable of producing mass stupidity, of whipping up emotions and of turning the simplest problems into complex and insoluble ones; in some countries it had been discovered how to overcome physical and social diseases; but in others hunger – indeed, starvation – still held sway unchallenged, together with ignorance, slavery, physical wretchedness, the exploitation of the weak, etc.

The panacea for all these ills was no longer an illusion, for science could provide it; it had just shown that it was capable of rapid and unlimited progress. In actual fact, science gave both good and evil equal chances of fulfilment, by means of its greatest discovery, the one most full of promise and at the same time the most formidable: nuclear energy. Although it opened up grandiose vistas – the levelling of mountains, the irrigating of deserts, providing the poor countries with inexhaustible power supplies at low cost, 'wonder drugs', etc. – at the same time the sun of Hiroshima was also the portent of an apocalyptic future; unless mankind could control its passions, instincts and appetites, it now possessed the means of resolving its contradictions by wiping itself out completely. Through the 'Bomb', Mother Earth had become mortal and Man had the power to bring her to an end.

Appendix

Progress in the Production and Performance of Fighter Aircraft[1]

Country	Date	Number of front-line aircraft	Monthly output	Make[2]	Armament[3]	Max. speed (mph)[4]	Range (in miles)[5]
FRANCE	September 1939	578 (a)	200 (b)	Morane Saulnier 406 1939	1 20-mm C, 2 7·5-mm MG	302	596
	June 25, 1940 (c)	637 (c), 1,484 (d)	330 (b)	Dewoitine 520 1940	1 20-mm C, 4 7·5-mm MG	332	547–949
BRITAIN	September 1939	608	93	Supermarine Spitfire I, 1939 (e)	8 7·7-mm MG	362	410
	April 1945[6]	47,500	900 (approx.)	Gloster Meteor III 1945 (f)	4 20-mm C	494	1,332
USSR	June 1941	4,080 (of all types, mainly old)	580 (approx.)	Polikarpov I 16 1936 (g)	2 20-mm C, 2 7·62-mm MG, 6 R	326	248–435
	April 1945[6]	8,000 (approx.), 70,000 (approx.) (h)	1,500 (approx.)	Lavochkin LA 7 1944	3 20-mm C, 4 40 B or 6 R	415–430 (i)	394
USA	December 1941	300 (approx. at Pearl Harbour)	312 (j)	Curtiss P 40B Tomahawk 1941	2 12·7-mm MG, 2 7·5-mm MG	353	732–852
	August 1945	98,703 (k)	2,785 (L)	Republic P 47N Thunderbolt 1944 (m)	8 12·7 MG, 1,985 B or 10 R	460	803–2,097
				North American P 51H	6 12·7-mm MG, 1,985 B	488	1,070–1,527

Remarks

(a) As at October 1, 1939.
(b) Not including American Curtisses.
(c) As at May 10, 1940.
(d) From September 3, 1939 to June 25, 1940 not including 158 imported.
(e) 20,351 Spitfires of all types built.
(f) Fitted with 2 jet engines.
(g) Used by the Spanish republicans in the Civil War.
(h) Approx. 10,000 fighters received from USA and 3,000 from Britain.
(i) Second figure with auxiliary rocket propulsion.
(j) Average between July 1940 and December 1941.
(k) From July 1, 1940 to July 31, 1945.
(m) 15,660 P 47s built of all versions.

Country	Date			Aircraft	Armament		
	April 1945[6]	2,367 (n) / 55,503 (q)	2,325 (r)	1938 (o) Focke Wulf 109 D 9	2 20-mm C / 2 13-mm MG	438	613
				Messerschmitt 262 A1a Sturmvogel 1945 (s)	430-mm C	541	652
ITALY	June 1940	656	270 (t)	Macchi C 200 Saetta 1940	2 12·7-mm MG	312	553
	September 1943	555 / 11,500 (v)	240 (u)	Fiat G 55 Centauro 1943	3 20-mm C / 2 12·7-mm MG	385	750-990
JAPAN	December 1941	370 (w)	650 (x)	Mitsubishi A 6M2 Zero Sen (Zeke 21) 1940 (y)	2 20-mm C / 2 7·7-mm MG / 265 B	335	1,275-1,938
	August 1945	3,250 / 65,400 (z)	2,557 (aa)	Mitsubishi J2 M3 Raiden 21 (Jack) 1944	4 20-mm C / 265 B	380	652
				Nakajima KI 84 Ia Hayate (Frank)	2 20-mm C / 2 12·7-mm MG / 1102 B	390	1,020-1,820

or 1939.

(o) Used by the Spanish nationalists during the Civil War, 30,753 Messerschmitt 109s built of all versions.
(p) As on June 6, 1944.
(q) Including night fighters and 1,774 jet fighters.
(r) As in November 1944.
(s) Fitted with twin jet engines.
(t) 1940 average; military aircraft of all types.
(u) 1943 average, military aircraft of all types.
(v) Military aircraft of all types produced from January 1 to August 31, 1943.
(w) Fleet air arm only.
(x) Military aircraft of all types in December 1941.
(y) First used in operations against China in August 1940. 10,094 Zero Sen built of all versions.
(z) Military aircraft of all types built from December 1, 1941 to August 1945.
(aa) All types in November 1944; 1,023 in July 1945.

Explanatory Notes:
1 Table drawn up with the help of Mr Davel (and Colonel Costantini for the USSR).
2 For Japanese aircraft the Allied code-name is in brackets. The year is when the aircraft made its first operational flight.
3 Abbreviations: C: cannon; MG: machine gun; B: bombs (in lbs); R: rocket.
4 At cruising height.
5 The second figure is with supplementary fuel-tanks.
6 The second figure, after that of first-line aircraft, shows the number of aircraft built during the whole war.

Progress in the Production and Performance of Bomber Aircraft[1]

Country	Date	Number of front-line aircraft	Monthly output	Main Types							Remarks[^]
				Make and type[2]	No. of engines	Wing-span (ft)	Max. weight (lbs)	Bomb load (lbs)	Max. speed[3] (mph)	Range[4] (miles)	
FRANCE	September 1939	219 (a)	22 (b)	M. Bloch 210 BN 5 1939	2	75	21,340	6,300	230	930	(a) On October 1, 1939, metropolitan France only. (b) Plus 10 for fleet air arm, 4 of them imported from USA (average for September to December 1939).
	June 25, 1940[5]	242 (c) 753 (d)	174 (e)	Loire-et-Olivier 451 B 4 (1939)	2	74	25,076	6,300	298	1,370	(c) On May 10, 1940, metropolitan France only. (d) Not including 309 imported from USA and on May 31, 1940, 119 for fleet air arm, 39 of them imported from USA. (e) Average from May 1, 1940 and June 20, 1940, not including 72 imported from USA and, in May 1940, 73 fleet air arm, 23 of them

Country	Date			Aircraft type	Engines					
	April 1945	2,094 / 27,720 (h)	713 (i)	1939 / Avro Lancaster III 1943 (j)	4	102	65,000	14,000	270	1,125
USSR	June 1941	6,300 (of all types)	120	Petlyakov Pe-2 1941	2	157	18,746	2,200	335	620
	April 1945	15,000 (of all types)	3,700 (of all types in 1944)	Tupolev Tu-2 1944	2	61	28,260	5,000	345	870
USA	December 1941	400 (approx.)	264 (k)	Boeing B 17D Fortress 1941	4	104	48,500	4,014	323	2,000
	August 1945	96,847 (l)	2,157 (m)	Boeing B 29 Superfortress 1944	4	142	135,280	20,050	350	3,250
GERMANY	September 1939	1,556	218 (n)	Heinkel III P 1939	2	74	24,640	4,410	255	1,120
	April 1945	1,350 (o) / 30,808 (p)	636 (q)	Arado 234 B 2 Blitz 1945	2 (r)	46	20,240	2,200	472	990

arm and 320 22 (squadrons) in reserve or employed on training.

(g) Average from September to December 1939.

(h) From September 1939 to end of June 1944.

(i) Average of first six months of 1944.

(j) 7,337 Lancasters of all types built.
Approx. 3,870 bombers supplied by the USA.

(k) Average between July 1940 and December 1941.

(l) From July 1, 1940 to July 31, 1945.

(m) Average of first 7 months of 1945.
12,677 B 17 of all types built.

(n) Average of last 4 months of 1939.

(o) In January 1945.

(p) Including single-engined fighter/bombers and 214 Arado jets.

(q) 1944 average, including fighter/bombers.

(r) Jet engine.

Progress in the Production and Performance of Bomber Aircraft—*continued*

Country	Date	Number of front-line aircraft	Monthly output	Make and type[2]	No. of engines	Wing-span (ft)	Max. weight (lbs)	Bomb load (lbs)	Max. speed[3] (mph)	Range[4] (miles)	Remarks
ITALY	June 1940	783	217 (s)	Savoia Marchetti S.M. 79 1937 (t)	3	70	24,860	2,760	270	1,240	(s) 1940 average, military aircraft of all types. (t) Used in the Spanish Civil War.
	September 1943[5]	276 11,500 (u)	241 (v)	Pioggio P.108 B 1942	4	105	64,782	7,720	270	1,550	(u) Military aircraft of all types produced from January 1, 1940 to August 31, 1943. (v) 1943 average; military aircraft of all types.
JAPAN	December 1941	450 (w)	650 (x)	Mitsubishi Ki 21 II b Type 97 (Sally) 1941 (y)	2	73	21,490	2,200	297	1,344	(w) Fleet air arm, 362 aircraft. (x) Military aircraft of all types in December 1941. (y) Approx. 1,800 built.
	August 1945	65,400 (z)	2,350 (aa)	Mitsubishi Ki 67 Ib Type 4 Hiryu (Peggy) 1944	2	74	30,350	1,760	333	2,360	(z) Military aircraft of all types built from January 1, 1941 to August 1945. (aa) All types in November 1944, 1,023 in July 1945.

Explanatory Notes:
1 Table drawn up with the help of Mr Davel (and Colonel Costantini for the USSR).
2 For Japanese aircraft, the Allied code-name is given in brackets. The year is when the aircraft made its first operational flight.
3 At cruising height.
4 With full bomb load as indicated.
5 The second figure, after that of first-line aircraft, shows the number built during the whole war or during the period indicated.

General Bibliography[1]

1. The works relating particularly to the USSR, Japan and the United States are indicated in the list of works consulted for the chapter on the entry of each of these states into the war.

Bibliographies

A quarterly bibliography which is kept regularly up to date and is virtually exhaustive is included in each number of the *Revue d'histoire de la deuxième guerre mondiale*, published by the Presses Universitaires de France, Paris. A selective bibliography has been published by HenriMICHEL and J.-M. D'HOOP: Bibliographie sélective de l'histoire de la deuxième guerre mondiale, in *Les deux guerres mondiales*, Brussels, Brepols, 1964, pp. 163–242. Mrs Janet ZIEGLER has listed all the works which appeared in English in *World War Two Books in English (1945–1965)*, Hoover Institute Press, 1971, and has gathered together all the bibliographies in two articles in the *Revue d'histoire de la deuxième guerre mondiale* (nos. 63 and 81).

Chronologies

R. CERE, C. ROUSSEAU: *Chronologie du conflit mondial*, Paris, S.E.F.I., 1945
P. BELPERRON and ANDERSEN: *La deuxième guerre mondiale*, Paris, Plon, 1945
P. LIMAGNE: *Ephémérides de quatre années tragiques*, Paris, Editions Bonne Presse, 1945–47, 3 vols
Chronologia della seconda guerra mondiale, Rome, Faro, 1959
M. H. WILLIAMS: *Chronology 1941–1945*, Office of the Chief of Military History, Washington, 1960
TOLDO: *La seconda guerra mondiale giorno per giorno*, Rome, A.V.E., 1966

Documents

The most important series of documents is still that of the *International Military Tribunal, Trial of the Great War Criminals*, Nuremberg, 1949, 42 vols. The extent to which diplomatic documents have been published varies from country to country. The German Foreign Office secret archives are appearing in three editions; up to now, Vols. VIII and IX have appeared in a French edition under the title *Les archives secrètes de la Wilhelmstrasse*, in two books each (Sept. 4, 1939–June 22, 1940), Paris, Plon. The English edition, entitled *Documents on German Foreign Policy*, London, HMSO, series D, has brought out four volumes (X, XI, XII, XIII; Sept. 1940–Dec. 11, 1941). The German edition, *Akten zur deutschen Auswärtigen Politik* (Baden-Baden, P. Keppler Verlag) consists of eleven volumes in series D (1937–45).

The ninth series of the *Documenti diplomatici italiani* (Ministerio degli affari esteri, La libreria dello Stato, Rome) numbers five volumes (Sept. 4, 1939–October 1940).

The third series of the *Documents on British Foreign Policy*, London, HMSO, is limited for the time being to five volumes relating to the year 1939.

The American series *Foreign Relations of the United States Diplomatic Papers* numbers 64 volumes, 43 of which concentrate on the period 1941–1945.

The only French documents published are concerned with the *Délégation française auprès de la Commission allemande d'Armistice* (5 vols., June 29, 1940–December 21, 1941), Paris, A. Costes.

Documents on Polish-Soviet Relations 1939–1945, 2 vols., London and Toronto, Heinemann, 1967

Correspondence Between the Chairman of the Council of the Ministers of the USSR and the Presidents of the USA and the Prime Ministers of Great Britain, 2 vols., Moscow, 1957

Le Saint Siège et la guerre en Europe, Lettres de Pie XII aux évêques allemands, Le Saint Siège et la situation religieuse en Pologne et dans les pays baltiques 3 vols., Cité du Vatican, 1965, 1966, 1967

General Histories

Maurice CROUZET: *L'époque contemporaine*, 'Histoire générale des civilisations', Paris, Presses Universitaires de France, 1957
J. PIRENNE: *The Tides of History*, London, Vol. I, *From the Beginning to Islam*, 1962. Vol. II, *From the Expansion of Islam to the Treaties of Westphalia*, Allen and Unwin, 1965
Henri BERNARD: *La guerre et son évolution à travers les siècles*, Vol. II, *De 1939 à aujourd'hui*, Brussels, Ecole Royale Militaire, 1957
M. MOURIN: *Histoire des grandes puissances de 1918 à 1958*, Paris, Payot, 1958
A. LATREILLE: *La seconde guerre mondiale*, Paris, Hachette, 1966
E. BAUER: *Histoire controversée de la deuxième guerre mondiale*, Paris, Rombaldi, 1967, 7 vols.
BATTAGLIA: *La seconda guerra mondiale*, Rome, Ed. Riuniti, 1960
GIGLI: *La seconda guerra mondiale*, Bari, Laterza, 1964
H. A. JACOBSEN: *Der Zweite Weltkrieg*, Frankfurt, Fischer, 1965
Andreas HILLGRUBER: *Probleme des Zweiten Weltkriegs*, Cologne-Berlin, 1967
C. WILMOT: *La lutte pour l'Europe*, Paris, Fayard, 1953
Gordon WRIGHT: *The Ordeal of Total War*, New York, Harper and Row, 1968

Military History

E. BAUER: *La guerre des blindés*, Paris, Payot, 1962, 2 vols.
General CHASSIN: *Histoire militaire de la deuxième guerre mondiale*, Paris, Payot, 1954
F. H. HINSLEY: *Hitler's Strategy*, London, Cambridge University Press, 1951
J. F. L. FULLER: *The Conduct of the War*, New Brunswick, Rutgers University Press, 1961
B. COLLIER: *The Second World War, a Military History from Munich to Hiroshima*, Gloucester, Mass., Peter Smith, 1967
C. MACDONALD: *The Mighty Endeavour, American Armed Forces in the European Theatre in World War II*, New York, Oxford University Press, 1970
Sir Basil LIDDELL HART: *History of the Second World War*, London, Cassell, New York, Putnam, 1970
La Guerre en Méditerranée: report of a conference held in Paris in 1969, Editions du CNRS, 1971
Particular attention should be given to *Grand Strategy* by J. R. BUTLER, J. M. GWYER, J. EHRMAN and M. HOWARD in the official British history *History of the Second World War*, HMSO
K. VON TIPPELSKIRCH: *Geschichte des zweiten Weltkriegs*, Bonn, Athenaum Verlag, 1951
G. BUCHEIT: *Hitler der Feldherr. Die Zerstörung einer Legende*, Rastatt, Grote, 1958

F. GILBERT: *Hitler Directs his War; the Secret Records of his Daily Military Conferences*, New York, University of Pennsylvania Press, 1950, Oxford University Press, London, 1951

A. HITLER: *War Directives, 1939–1945* (ed. H. Trevor-Roper), Sidgwick and Jackson, London, 1964

Istorija Velikoj Otecestvennoj Vojny Suvestskogo Sojuza 1941–1943, 6 vols., Moscow, Ministry of Defence, 1960–1965

Air Force

Sir Charles WEBSTER and Noble FRANKLAND: *The Strategic Air Offensive Against Germany*, London, HMSO, 1961, 4 vols.

G. BOWMANN: *War in the Air*, London, Evans, 1956

S. FEUCHTER: *Der Luftkrieg*, Frankfurt am Main, Athenaum Verlag, 1965

A. GALLAND: *First and Last: German Fighter Force in World War II*, translated by M. Savill, London, Methuen, New York, Ballantine, 1970

Wesley F. CRAVEN and J. L. CATE: *The Army Airforces in World War Two*, Chicago, 1948–1958, 7 vols.

The Royal Airforce 1939–1945, 3 vols., London, HMSO

N. MACMILLAN: *The Royal Air Force in the World War*, London, Harrap, 1950

General SANTORO: *L'aeronautica italiana nella seconda guerre mondiale*, Rome, Domesi, 1950, 3 vols.

D. RICHARDS, H. st. G. SAUNDERS: *The R.A.F. in the Second World War*, London, HMSO, 1954, 3 vols.

R. GENTILE: *Storia delle operazione aeree nella seconda guerra mondiale*, Rome, Associazione cultura aeronautica, 1952

Navy

Captain ROSKILL: *The War at Sea*, London, HMSO, 1954–56, 3 vols.

Admiral BARJOT: *Histoire de la guerre aéro-navale*, Paris, Flammarion, 1961

Führer conferences on naval affairs, Brassey's naval annual, 1948

Admiral RUGE: *Sea Warfare, 1939–1945; a German Viewpoint*, London, Cassell, 1957

M. SALEWSKI: *Die deutsche Seekriegsleitung 1935–1945*, Frankfurt

Admiral de BELOT and A. REUSSNER: *La puissance navale dans l'histoire*, Vol. III *1914–1959*, Paris, Editions maritimes et d'outre-mer, 1960

S. E. MORISON: *History of the United States Naval Operations in World War Two*, 15 vols, Boston, Little, Brown, London, Oxford University Press, 1962

POTTER, NIMITZ: *Sea Power, a Naval History*, New York, Prentice Hall, 1960

BRAGADIN: *Che ha fatto la marina italiana*, Milan, Garzanti, 1955

Army

H. A. JACOBSEN: *Deutsche Kriegsführung, 1939–1945*, Hanover, Hannoversche Druck und Verlag, 1961

W. ERFURTH: *Die Geschichte der deutschen Generalstab*, Göttingen, Musterschmidt Verlag, 1957

J. WHEELER-BENNETT: *The Nemesis of Power, 1918–1945*, London, Macmillan, 1954, New York, St Martin's Press, 1964

H. A. JACOBSEN: *Kriegstagebuch des Oberkommandos der Wehrmacht*, Frankfurt, Bernard und Graefe, 1965

Colonel STACEY: *Official History of the Canadian Army in the Second World War*, Ottawa, 1957–1960, 3 vols.

United States Army in World War Two, 71 vols., Washington, Dept of the Army

W. WARLIMONT: *Inside Hitler's Headquarters, 1939–1945*, London, Weidenfeld and Nicolson, 1964

Diplomatic History

J.-B. DUROSELLE: *Histoire diplomatique de 1919 à nos jours*, Paris, Dalloz, 1953

P. RENOUVIN: *Histoire des relations internationales*, Vol. VIII, Paris, Hachette, 1958

E. WISKEMANN: *The Rome–Berlin Axis*, London, Oxford University Press, 1966

Sir Llewelyn WOODWARD: *British Foreign Policy in the Second World War*, London, HMSO, 1962, 1970, 1971, 3 vols.

M. MOURIN: *Les tentatives de paix séparées pendant la deuxième guerre mondiale*, Paris, Payot, 1949

J. A. LUKACS: *The Great Powers and Eastern Europe*, New York, American Book Company, 1958

A. HILLGRUBER: *Die Sowjetische Aussen Politik 1939–1945*, D. Geyer, 1971

Germany

W. HOFER: *Le national-socialisme par les textes*, Paris, Plon, 1963

W. SHIRER: *The Rise and Fall of the Third Reich: a History of Nazi Germany*, Vol. II, New York, Simon and Schuster, London, Secker and Warburg, 1960

A. HITLER: *Table Talk 1941–4*, translation by W. Cameron and R. H. Stewart, London, Weidenfeld and Nicolson, 1953

H. A. JACOBSEN and W. JOCHMANN: *Ausgewählte Documente zur Geschichte des Nazionalsozialismus*, Bielefeld, Verlag Neue Gesellschaft, 1961, 5 vols.

H. MAU and H. KRAUSNICK: *German History, 1939–45: an Assessment by German Historians*, translated by E. and A. Wilson, London, Wolff, 1959

W. BLEYER, K. FORSTER and G. HASS: *Deutschland von 1939 bis 1945*, East Berlin, Deutscher Verlag d. Wissenschaften, 1969

W. BLEYER: *Staat und Monopole im totalen Krieg*, ibid, 1970

Italy

F. CHABOD: *A History of Italian Fascism*, London, Weidenfeld and Nicolson, 1963

L. SALVATORELLI and G. MIRA: *Storia del fascismo, l'Italia dal 1919 al 1945*, Rome, Edizioni di novissima, 1953

G. PERTICONE: *L'Italia contemporeana dal 1871 al 1948*, Milan, Mondadori, 1962

R. BERNOTTI: *Storia della guerra nel Mediterraneo*, Rome, Terrena, 1962

H. GALLO: *L'Italie de Mussolini*, Paris, J. Perrin, 1964

F. CATALANO: *Dalla crisi del primo dopoguerra alla fondazione della Repubblica*, Turin, U.T.E.T., 1960

G. QUAZZA: *Fascismo e Societa italiana*, Turin, Einaudi, 1971

E. SANTARELLI: *Storia del movimento et del regime fascista*, 2 vols., Rome, Ed. Riuniti, 1967–1972

'L'Italie dans la deuxième guerre mondiale' special number of the *Revue d'histoire de la deuxième guerre mondiale*, October 1973

Biographies

A. BULLOCK: *Hitler: A Study in Tyranny*, New York, Harper, 1960 and London, Penguin, 1969

Helmut HEIBER: *Joseph Goebbels*, Berlin, Colloquium Verlag, 1962

w. FRISCHAUER: *Himmler, the Evil Genius of the Third Reich*, New York, Belmont, 1962

R. MANVELL and H. FRAENKEL: *Hermann Goering*, New York, Simon and Schuster, London, Heinemann, 1962

J. WULF: *Martin Bormann*, Gütersloh, Sigbert Mohr, 1962

G. ROUX: *Mussolini*, Paris, Fayard, 1960

MONELLI: *Mussolini; an Intimate Life*, London, Thames and Hudson, 1953

L. BROAD: *Sir Anthony Eden*, London, Hutchinson, 1956

Memoirs

Sir Winston CHURCHILL: *The Second World War*, 6 vols., London, Cassell, 1948–54, Boston, Houghton Mifflin

MONTGOMERY OF ALAMEIN: *The Montgomery Memoirs*, Collins, London, 1958

Viscount ALANBROOKE: See A. BRYANT:
   The Turn of the Tide, 1939–43, London, Collins, 1957
   Triumph in the West, 1943–6, London, Collins, 1959
   (Studies based on the diaries and autobiographical notes of Viscount Alanbrooke)

A. EDEN: *The Eden Memoirs*, Vol. II, *Full Circle*, London, Cassell, 1962

Lord ISMAY: *The Memoirs of General Lord Ismay*, London, Heinemann, 1960

Air Vice-Marshal J. E. JOHNSON: *Full Circle: the Story of Air Fighting*, London, Pan Books, 1969 (3rd impression)

Field Marshal F. E. VON MANSTEIN: *Lost Victories*, translated by A. G. Powell, London, Methuen, 1958

Field Marshal KEITEL: *Memoirs*, ed. with an introduction and epilogue by w. GORLITZ, London, Kimber, 1965

Field Marshal KESSELRING: *The Memoirs of Field Marshal Kesselring*, translated by L. Hudson, London, Kimber, 1953

Admiral K. DOENITZ: *Memoirs: Ten Years and Twenty Days*, translated by R. H. Stevens and D. Woodward, London, Weidenfeld and Nicolson, 1959

A. ROSENBERG: *Letzte Aufzeichnungen*, Göttingen, Plesse Verlag, 1958

F. VON PAPEN: *Memoirs*, translated by B. Connell, London, André Deutsch, 1952

J. VON RIBBENTROP: *The Ribbentrop Memoirs*, London, Weidenfeld and Nicolson, 1954

E. VON WEIZSAECKER: *Memoirs*, London, Gollancz, 1951

F. HALDER: *Hitler als Feldherr*, München, Münchener Dom Verlag, 1949

General H. GUDERIAN: *Panzer Leader*, London, Michael Joseph, 1970 (10th impression), New York, Ballantine, 1972

Admiral RAEDER: *Struggle for the Sea*, London, Kimber, 1959

General de GAULLE: *War Memoirs*, London, Weidenfeld and Nicolson, 1959, New York, Simon and Schuster, 1964

General D. EISENHOWER: *Crusade in Europe*, London, Heinemann, 1948

Harold MACMILLAN: *The Blast of War*, London, Macmillan, 1967, New York, Harper and Row

Periodicals

France: *Revue d'histoire de la deuxième guerre mondiale*, the only periodical dealing solely with the history of the Second World War. By January 1974 it had reached its 94th issue, including 20 special numbers.

Germany: *Vierteljahrshefte für Zeitgeschichte*, Stuttgart

Italy: *Il movimento di liberazione in Italia*, Milan

Works Consulted

Book One THE WAR IN EUROPE (September 1939–June 1941)

Part 1 THE PRELUDE IN POLAND AND SCANDINAVIA

CHAPTER 1 THE OBLITERATION OF POLAND FROM THE MAP OF EUROPE

In addition to the general works listed on pp. 851–855.

General HALDER: *Kriegstagebuch*, Vol. I, Stuttgart, Kohlammer, 1962

C. BECK: *Dernier rapport, politique polonaise (1926–1939)*, Paris–Neuchâtel, La Baconnière, 1951 (*Final Report*, New York, Robert Speller, 1958)

General ANDERS: *Mémoires*, Paris, La Jeune Parque, 1948

L. NOEL: 'L'agression allemande contre la Pologne', Paris, Flammarion, 1946 (pp. 385–503)

Basil SPIRU: *September 1939*, Berlin-Est, 1959

MOCZULSKI: *Wojna Polska*, Poznan, 1972

Studies

R. JARS: *La campagne de Pologne*, Paris, Payot, 1949

V. GROSZ: *La vérité sur le drame polonais*, Paris, Éditions du Pavillon, 1951

N. von VORMANN: *Der Feldzug in Polen*, Weissenburg, Prinz Eugen Verlag, 1958

E. BAUER: *La guerre des blindés*, Vol. I, Paris, Payot, 1962, pp. 51–57

CIALOWITZ: 'Le siège de Varsovie', *Cahiers Pologne—Allemagne*, April 1963

ZGORNIAK: 'Les préparatifs allemands d'attaque contre la Pologne', *Revue d'histoire de la deuxième guerre mondiale*, no. 77, January 1970

A great many works have been published in Polish, either in Poland, or in London through the efforts of the Sikorski Institute. On these last, see:—

J. B. NEVEUX: Sur la bataille de Pologne, *Revue d'histoire de la deuxième guerre mondiale*, no. 34, April 1959, pp. 20–6, and the review of General KOPANSKY'S book by M. BORWICZ, *ibid.*, no. 60, October 1965. A very large number of studies or reminiscences which were printed in Warsaw have also been summarised in the *Revue d'histoire de la deuxième guerre mondiale*, notably General KIRCHMAYER'S books, in nos. 40, 46 and 52.

CHAPTER 2 THE PHONEY WAR (October 1939–10 May 1940)

In addition to most of the works indicated in the bibliography to Chapter 1, see:

W. N. MEDLICOTT: *The Economic Blockade*, Vol. I, London, HMSO, 1959

A. HYTIER: 'La politique des Etats-Unis en Europe entre 1939 et 1941', *Revue d'histoire de la deuxième guerre mondiale*, no. 67, January 1967

M. DINCIC: 'La politique étrangère de la Yougoslavie', *ibid.*, no. 58, April 1965

H. A. JACOBSEN: 'Les buts et la politique de Hitler', *ibid.*, no. 63, July 1966

B. S. VIAULT: 'Les démarches pour le rétablissement de la paix (sept. 1939–août 1940)', *ibid.*, no. 67, July 1967

JON KIMCHE: *The Unfought Battle*, London, Weidenfeld and Nicolson, 1968, New York, Stein and Day, 1968

ROSSI-LANDI: *La drôle de guerre, la vie politique en France*, Paris, Colin, 1971

Henri MICHEL: *La drôle de guerre*, Paris, Hachette, 1971

III The Finnish-Soviet Conflict

H. A. JACOBSEN: *The Diplomacy of the Winter War*, Cambridge, Mass., Harvard University Press, 1961

Field Marshal C. G. E. MANNERHEIM: *Memoirs*, London, Cassell, 1953

C. TANNER: *The Winter War, Finland against Russia*, London, Oxford University Press, 1957

L. LUNDIN: *Finland and the Second World War*, Bloomington, Indiana University Press, 1956

A. F. UPTON: *Finland in Crisis, 1940–1941, A Study in Small Power Politics*, London, Faber and Faber, 1964

HEIKKI JALANTI: *La Finlande dans l'étau germano-soviétique*, Neuchâtel, Editions de la Baconnière, 1966

J. J. FOL: 'Les conversations finno-soviétiques (nov 1939–mars 1940)', *Revue d'histoire de la deuxième guerre mondiale*, no. 77, January 1970

M. HAIKIO and A. RUSI: 'La Finlande dans la seconde guerre mondiale', *Revue d'histoire de la deuxième guerre mondiale*, no. 93, January 1974

IV Mussolini's Hesitation

Hitler, Mussolini, Lettere e documenti, Milan, Rizzoli, 1946

Count CIANO: *Les Archives secrètes du comte Ciano*, Paris, Plon, 1948 and *Diary*, 2 vols., London, Methuen, 1952, Heinemann, 1947, New York, Dutton, 1953

D. ALFIERI: *Dictators Face to Face*, London, Elek Books, 1954, Doubleday, 1946

Marshal BADOGLIO: *Italy in the Second World War*, London, Oxford University Press, 1948

M. MAGISTRARI: *L'Italia a Berlino*, Milan, Mondadori, 1956

ANCHIERI and F. DEBYSER: Les rapports italo–allemands 'Sur la diplomatie italienne', *Revue d'histoire de la deuxième guerre mondiale*, no. 26, January 1959

F. DEBYSER: 'Un mémorandum inédit de Mussolini', *ibid.*, no. 14, January 1956

G. JUHASZ: 'La politique extérieure de la Hongrie', *ibid.*, no. 62, April 1966

V Franco-British Determination

P. REYNAUD: *In the Thick of the Fight, 1930–45* (abridged edition), London, Cassell, 1955

Envers et contre tout, Paris, Flammarion, 1963

General WEYGAND: *Memoirs*, Vol. III, *Recalled to Service*, London, Heinemann, 1952

General GAMELIN: *Servir*, Vol. III, *La guerre (sept. 1939–mai 1940)*, Paris, Plon, 1947

Les evénéments survenus en France de 1933 à 1945, Témoignages et documents recueillis par la Commission parlementaire, Presses Universitaires de France, 1947, 9 vols.

J. JEANNENEY: *Journal politique (sept. 1939–juillet 1942)*, Paris, Colin, 1972

Les relations militaires franco-belges, mars 1936–10 mai, 1940, Paris, CNRS, 1968

General ALBORD: 'Weygand devant le problème oriental', *Revue des Deux Mondes*, June 1, 1965

General CARPENTIER: 'Avec Weygand au Moyen Orient', *Revue Militaire générale*, February and April 1961

'Avec Weygand au Moyen Orient, la guerre des pétroles', *Revue Militaire générale*, January and February 1966

General CHASSIN: 'Un plan grandiose, l'attaque des pétroles du laucase', *Forces aériennes françaises*, December 1961
General de LARMINAT: *Chroniques irrévérencieuses*, Paris, Plon, 1942
J. BARDOUX: *Journal d'un témoin de la Troisième*, Paris, Fayard, 1957
M. MEGRET: 'Les origines de la propagande de guerre française', *Revue d'histoire de la deuxième guerre mondiale*, no. 41, January 1961
D. C. WATT: 'L'opposition allemande en face des Alliés', *ibid.*, no. 62, April 1966

VI Allied Relations with Belgium and Holland
General VAN OVERSTRAETEN: *Albert Ier, Léopold III, 20 ans de politique militaire belge*, Bruges, Desclée de Brouwer, 1949
Au service de la Belgique, Vol. I, *Dans l'étau*, Paris, Plon, 1947
M. VAN WELKENHUYZEN: 'L'alerte du 10 janvier, 1940', *Revue d'histoire de la deuxième guerre mondiale*, no. 12, October 1953
J. WILLEQUET: 'La politique d'indépendance de la Belgique', *ibid.*, no. 31, July 1958
Les relations militaires franco-belges, mars, 1936–10 mai 1940, Paris, CNRS, 1968

CHAPTER 3 THE WAR IN NORWAY

J. MORDAL: *La campagne de Norvège*, Paris, Editions Self, 1949
B. ASH: *Norway, 1940*, London, Cassell, 1964
J. WAAGE: *The Narvik Campaign*, London, Harrap, 1964
T. K. DERRY: *The Campaign of Norway*, London, HMSO, 1952
TRYGVE LIE: *Lave eller do Norge in Krieg*, Oslo, Norsk Forlag, 1955. (Review by General RENONDEAU, *Revue d'histoire de la deuxième guerre mondiale*, no. 27, July 1957)
General BETHOUARD: *Narvik, victoire française*, Sedan, Bellegarde, 1947
W. HUBATSCH: *Weserübung: Die deutsche Besetzung von Dänemark und Norwegen*, Göttingen, Musterschmidt Verlag
J. L. MOULTON: *The Norwegian Campaign. A Study of Warfare in Three Dimensions*, London, Eyre and Spottiswoode, 1966
C. A. GEMZELL: *Raeder, Hitler und Skandinavien*, Lund, 1965
General AUDET: 'L'expédition de Norvège, Namsos', *Revue historique de l'armée*, no. 1, 1957
Commandant ACCART: 'La Royal Air Force dans la campagne de Norvège', *Forces aériennes françaises*, July 1954
Magne SKODVIN: *Stridden one Okkupajconstyret in Norge*, Oslo, 1956. (Review by General RENONDEAU, *Revue d'histoire de la deuxième guerre mondiale*, no. 34, April 1959)

Part II THE DEFEAT OF FRANCE

CHAPTER 1 PLANS AND FORCES OF THE ANTAGONISTS IN MAY 1940

(In addition to the works listed on pp. 851–855).
Documents. In addition to the German Foreign Office secret archives, and the evidence and various documents published by the French Parliamentary Investigation Commission (see particularly, in Vol. V, the testimony of Generals Dassault, pp. 1459–1479; Bruneau, pp. 1163–1191; Bruché, pp. 1213–1253; Devaux, pp. 1325–1367), which have already been quoted, see the following:

Secret documents of the French General Staff,[1] Berlin, Deutscher Verlag, 1941

ROY J., tr. by R. Baldick: *The Trial of Marshal Pétain,* London, Faber and Faber, 1968

Foreign Relations of the United States, 1940, Vols. 1 and 2, Department of State, Washington

Memoirs (by Frenchmen)

General de GAULLE: *War Memoirs,* Vol. I, London, Weidenfeld and Nicolson, 1959

General WEYGAND: *En lisant les mémoires du général de Gaulle,* Paris, Flammarion, 1955

Camille CHAUTEMPS: *Cahiers secrets de l'armistice,* Paris, Plon, 1963

E. HERRIOT: *Épisodes 1940–1944,* Paris, Flammarion, 1950

Marc BLOCH: *Strange Defeat,* London, Oxford University Press, 1949

P. BAUDOUIN: *The Private Diaries, March 1940 to Jan. 1941,* London, Eyre and Spottiswoode, 1948

Léon BLUM: *Mémoires. La prison et le procès,* Paris, Albin Michel, 1955

Y. BOUTHILLIER: *Le Drame de Vichy,* Vol. I, Paris, Plon, 1950

E. BARTHE: *La ténébreuse affaire du Massilia,* Paris, Imprimerie P. Dupont, 1945

CHARLES-ROUX: *Cinq mois tragiques aux Affaires étrangères,* Paris, Plon, 1949

A. FEVRIER: *Expliquons-nous,* Paris, Wast, 1946

A. LEBRUN: *Témoignage,* Paris, Plon, 1945

J. MONTIGNY: *Toute la vérité sur un mois dramatique,* Clermont-Ferrand, 1940

Léon NOEL: *Un Témoignage, le diktat de Rethondes et l'armistice franco-italien,* Paris, Flammarion, 1945

Tony REVILLON: *Mes carnets (juin-octobre 1940),* Paris, Odette Lieutier, 1945

General LAFFARGUE: *Justice pour ceux de 1940,* Paris, Lavauzelle, 1952

General PRETELAT: *Le destin tragique de la ligne Maginot,* Paris, Berger-Levrault, 1950

General ROTON: *Années cruciales,* Paris, Lavauzelle, 1947

General RUBY: *Sedan, terre d'épreuve,* Paris, Flammarion, 1948

J. MINART: *P. C. Vincennes,* Paris, Berger-Levrault, 1945

General MONTAGNE: *La bataille pour Nice et la Provence,* Montpellier, Editions des Arceaux, 1952

General DOUMENC: *Histoire de la IXe Armée,* Grenoble, Arthaud, 1945

General ARMENGAUD: *Le drame de Dunkerque,* Paris, Plon, 1948

J. BEAUX: *Dunkerque (1940),* Paris, Presses de la Cité, 1967

O. DIVINE: *Les neuf jours de Dunkerque,* Paris, Calmann-Lévy, 1964

General BEAUFRE: *1940: The Fall of France,* London, Cassell, 1967 and New York, Knopf, 1968

General d'ASTIER de LA VIGERIE: *Le ciel n'était pas vide,* Paris, Julliard, 1952

P. A. BOURGET: *De Beyrouth à Bordeaux: la guerre 1939–1940 vue du P. C. de Weygand,* Paris, Berger-Levrault, 1946

General REQUIN: *Combats pour l'honneur,* Paris, Lavauzelle, 1946

Louis MARIN: 'Contribution à l'étude des prodromes de l'armistice', *Revue d'histoire de la deuxième guerre mondiale,* no. 3, July 1951

Memoirs (by Englishmen)

W. CHURCHILL: *The Second World War,* Vol. II, London, Cassell, 1949

General SPEARS: *Assignment to Catastrophe,* Vol. I, London, Heinemann, Boston, Houghton Mifflin, 1948

Lord GORT: *2nd Despatch from 1 Feb. to 31 May 1940,* supplement of the *London Gazette*

1. The List of French documents seized by the Germans at La Charité-sur-Loire.

Memoirs (by Belgians) ·

General VAN OVERSTRAETEN: *Albert Ier, Léopold III*, Bruges, Desclée de Brouwer, 1949

Au service de la Belgique, Paris, Plon, 1960

Lieutenant-General MICHIELS: *Dix-huit jours de guerre en Belgique*, Paris, 1947

Baron JASPAR: 'Carnets de route', *Revue des Deux Mondes*, May 15, 1961 (cf. J. WILLEQUET: Critical bibliography on 'Le rôle de l'armée belge en 1940', *Revue d'histoire de la deuxième guerre mondiale*, nos. 10–11, April–July 1953)

Memoirs (of Germans)

General HALDER: *Kriegstagebuch*, Vol. I, Stuttgart, Kohlhammer, 1962. (Extracts have been published in the *Revue de Paris* (July 1958), and the *Revue d'histoire de la deuxième guerre mondiale*, April–July 1953)

Sir B. H. LIDDELL HART: *The other side of the hill: Germany's generals, their rise and fall, with their own account of military events, 1939–1945*, London, Cassell, 1948

Kurt ASSMAN: *Deutsche Schicksalsjahre; Historische Bilder aus dem Zweiten Weltkrieg und seiner Wahrgeschichte*, Wiesbaden, Brockhaus, 1950

P. SCHMIDT: *Hitler's Interpreter*, London, Heinemann, 1951, New York, Macmillan, 1951

Marshal ROMMEL: *Rommel's Papers*, London, Collins, 1953

LISS: *Westfront, 1939–1945*, Neckargemünd, Kurt Vowinkel Verlag, 1959

Memoirs (of Italians)

R. GUARIGLIA: *Ricordi*, Naples, Ed. Scientifiche italiane, 1950

G. CARBONI: *Memorie segrete, 1935–1948*, Florence, Parenti, 1955

French studies

Colonel H. LUGAND: 'Les forces en présence au 10 mai 1940', *Revue d'histoire de la deuxième guerre mondiale*, nos. 10–11, May–July 1953

General COSSE-BRISSAC: 'L'armée allemande dans la campagne de France', *ibid.*, no. 53, January 1964

'Combien de chars allemands contre combien de chars français', *Revue de défense nationale*, July 1947

Colonel PAQUIER, Lieutenant-Colonel COSSE-BRISSAC, Lieutenant-Colonel LYET: 'Combien d'avions allemands contre combien d'avions français', *ibid.*, June 1948

Colonel LESQUEN: 'L'armée de l'air française en 1940', *ibid.*, January 1952

M. VAN WELKENHUYZEN: 'Le premier plan allemand pour l'attaque à l'Ouest', *ibid.*, no. 22, April 1956

J. BENOIST-MÉCHIN: *Sixty days that shook the West*, London, Cape, 1963. (See also the review of L. MARIN, *Revue d'histoire de la deuxième guerre mondiale*, no. 31, July 1958)

Colonel de BARDIES: *La campagne 1939–1940*, Paris, Fayard, 1947

Colonel GOUTARD: *The Battle of France, 1940*, London, F. Muller, 1958

General KOELTZ: *Comment s'est joué notre destin*, Paris, Hachette, 1957

P. DHERS: *Regards nouveaux sur les années 1940*, Paris, Flammarion, 1958

Hervé CRAS: *Dunkerque*, Paris, Editions France-Empire, 1960

Lieutenant-Colonel LYET: *La campagne de France*, Paris, Payot, 1947

LERECOUVREUX: *L'armée Giraud en Hollande*, Paris, Nouvelles Editions Latines, 1951

General PAQUIER: *L'aviation de bombardement française en 1939–1940*, Paris, Berger-Levrault, 1948

SALESSE: *L'aviation française au combat (1939–1940)*, Paris, Berger-Levrault, 1955

Admiral AUPHAN and J. MORDAL: *La Marine française pendant la seconde guerre mondiale*, Paris, Hachette, 1958

Commandant VAUQUIER: 'L'action des forces cuirassées', *Revue d'histoire de la deuxième guerre mondiale*, nos. 10–11, June 1953

Lieutenant-Colonel GOASTER: 'L'action des forces aériennes', *ibid.*

Admiral de BELOT: *La marine française pendant la campagne (1939–1940)*, Paris, Plon, 1954

Colonel MERGLEN: 'La surprise aéroportée sur le canal Albert', *Revue historique de l'Armée*, no. 3, 1960

Colonel VILLATTE: 'L'entrée des Français en Belgique et en Hollande en mai 1940', *Revue d'histoire de la deuxième guerre mondiale*, nos. 10–11, May–July 1953

General ROLLOT: 'La bataille de Sedan', *ibid.*, no. 32, October 1958

Colonel FOX and Commander d'ORNANO: 'La percée des Ardennes', *ibid.*, nos. 10–11, May–July 1953

Colonel LE GOVET: 'La percée de Sedan', *ibid.*, no. 59, July 1965

A. REUSSNER: 'Le changement de commandement du 19 mai', *ibid.*, nos. 10–11, May–July 1953

Lecuir, FRIDENSON: 'L'organisation de la coopération franco-britannique (1935–mai 1940) *Revue d'histoire de la deuxième guerre mondiale*, January 1969

Colonel CAILLOUX: 'La contre-attaque qui n'eut jamais lieu', *Revue historique de l'Armée*, no. 3, 1966 (cf. General Koeltz's testimony to the French Parliamentary Investigation Commission. Vol. IX, p. 2804–2806)

'La bataille de Menton', *Cahiers d'information des troupes de montagne*, 1st quarter, 1960

H. AZEAU: *La guerre franco-italienne*, Paris, Presses de la Cité, 1967

Leon NOEL: 'Le projet d'union franco-britannique', *Revue d'histoire de la deuxième guerre mondiale*, no. 21, January 1956

Colonel GOUTARD: 'Hitler et l'armistice', *Revue de Paris*, October 1960

Colonel LYET: 'A propos de Sedan 1940', *Revue historique de l'Armée*, no. 4, 1962

A. GOLAZ: 'L'offensive allemande en Alsace', *Revue historique de l'Armée*, no. 3, 1963

F. DEBYSER: 'Bibliographie des ouvrages parus en France sur la guerre 1939–1940 et l'armistice', *Cahiers d'histoire de la guerre*, January 1949

J. VIDALENC: *L'exode du mai–juin 1940*, Paris, Presses Universitaires de France, 1957

A. TRUCHET: *L'armistice de 1940 et l'Afrique du Nord*, Paris, Presses Universitaires de France, 1955

R. ARON: *The Vichy Régime, 1940–44*, London, Putnam, 1958

Henri MICHEL: *Vichy, année 40*, Paris, Robert Laffont, 1966

E. BERL: *La fin de la IIIème République*, Paris, Gallimard, 1968

M. LAUNAY: *L'armistice de 1940*, Paris, Presses Universitaires de France, 1972

Dutch studies

General NIERSTRAZ: 'L'évolution du plan d'opérations néerlandais en 1939–1940', *Revue générale belge*, mai 1960

C. T. de JONG: 'Les préparations de l'attaque allemande sur la Hollande, en 1940', *Revue d'histoire de la deuxième guerre mondiale*, no. 20, October 1955

'La campagne de mai 1940 dans l'historiographie néerlandaise', *ibid.*, nos. 10–11, May–July 1953

L. de JONG: *Het Koninkryk der Nederlanden in Tweede Vereldsorlog*, Gravenhage, 1969

862 BIBLIOGRAPHY

Belgian studies

L'armée, la Nation, special number, Brussels, May 1955

M. CHAMBORD: *Ombres et clartés de la campagne belge de 1940*, Brussels, F. Wellens-Pay, 1946

M. FOUILLIEN and J. BOUHON: *Mai 1940, La bataille de Belgique*, Brussels, Editions Universelles, 1946

Commandant HAUTECLER: 'La bataille de la Meuse', *Revue générale belge*, November 1962

Colonel DINJEART: 'L'armée belge au cours de la deuxième guerre mondiale', *L'armée, la Nation*, July–August–September 1951

General ROLLOT: 'Les rapports franco-belges au moment de l'offensive', *Revue d'histoire de la deuxième guerre mondiale*, no. 38, April 1960, and replies by M. VAN WELKENHUYZEN and Commandant HAUTECLER, *ibid.*, no. 42, April 1961

H. J. L. CHARLES: *Les forces armées belges au cours de la 2ème guerre mondiale*, Brussels, La Renaissance du Livre, 1970

General NUSSENS: 'La contre-offensive qui n'eut jamais lieu', *L'armée, la Nation*, May 1, 1953

English studies

A. TOYNBEE: *The Initial Triumph of the Axis*, London, Oxford University Press, 1958

L. F. ELLIS: *The War in France and Flanders*, London, HMSO, 1953

Captain ROSKILL: *The War at Sea*, Vol. I, *1939–1941*, London, HMSO, 1954

D. RICHARDS and H. SAUNDERS: *The RAF in the War*, Vol. I, *The Fight at Odds (1939–1941)*, London, HMSO, 1954

Commander SAUNDERS: 'L'évacuation par Dunkerque', *Revue d'histoire de la deuxième guerre mondiale*, nos. 10–11, May–July 1953

W. SHIRER: *The Collapse of the Third Republic*, New York, Simon and Schuster, 1969, London, Heinemann, 1970

German studies

H. A. JACOBSEN: *Fall gelb, der Kampf um den deutschen Operationsplan zur Westoffensive 1940*, Wiesbaden, Franz Steiner Verlag, 1957

Dokumente zur Vorgeschichte des Westfeldzuges 1939–1940, Göttingen, Musterschmidt Verlag, 1965

'L'erreur du commandement allemand devant Dunkerque', *Revue historique de l'Armée*, no. 3, 1958

R. JOUAN: *La marine allemande dans la deuxième guerre mondiale*, Paris, Payot, 1949

A. HILLGRUBER: *Hitlers Strategie, Politik und Kriegsführung*, Frankfurt, Bernard und Graefe, 1965

MUELLER-HILLEBRANDT: *Das Heer 1933–1945, Entwicklung des organisatorischen Aufbaues*, Frankfurt-am-Main, Mittler und Sohn, 1956

W. HUBATSCH: *Hitler's War Directives, 1939–1945*, London, Sidgwick and Jackson, 1964

H. BOHME: *Der deutsche-französische Waffenstillstand im Zweiten Weltkrieg*, Stuttgart, 1966

CHAPTER 2 THE BREAKTHROUGH AT SEDAN

See pp. 858–862.

CHAPTER 4 THE ARMISTICE

See pp. 858–862.

Part III BRITAIN STANDS ALONE

CHAPTER I THE BATTLE OF BRITAIN

R. WHEATLEY: *Operation Sea-Lion*, Oxford, Clarendon Press, 1958
B. COLLIER: *The Defence of the United Kingdom*, London, HMSO, 1957
P. FLEMING: *Operation Sea-Lion*, New York, Simon and Schuster, 1957
D. WOOD and D. DEMPSTER: *The Narrow Margin: the Battle of Britain and the Rise of Air Power, 1930–1940*, London, Hutchinson, 1961
A. KAMMERER: *La passion de la flotte française*, Paris, Fayard, 1951
P. BELL: 'Prologue à Mers el-Kébir', *Revue d'histoire de la deuxième guerre mondiale*, January 1959
Admiral ASSMAN: 'L'opération Seelöwe', *Revue Maritime*, October 1953
Sir Frederick PILE: 'Report on the British air defence', Supplement of the *London Gazette*, December 16, 1947
M. T. WEREX: 'Le radar dans la bataille d'Angleterre', *Forces aériennes françaises*, December 1959
A. CALDER: *The People's War*, London, Carne, 1969, New York, Pantheon, 1969

Commonwealth
N. MANSERGH: *Documents and Speeches on British Commonwealth Affairs, 1931–1952*, London, Oxford University Press, 1953
L. G. ELLIOTT: *A Role of Honour. The Story of the Indian Army*, London, Cassell, 1965
J.-C. SMUTS: *Jean-Christian Smuts*, London, Cassell, 1952
F. H. SOWARD: *The Mackenzie King Records*, Vol. I, Toronto, Oxford University Press, 1960
C. C. LINGARD and R. G. TROTTER: *Canada in World Affairs*, Toronto, Oxford University Press, 1951
M. WADE: *The French Canadians*, London, Macmillan, 1955
S. J. BUTLIN: *War Economy, 1939–1942*, Canberra, Australian War Memorial, 1955
H. G. GELBER: *Problems of Australian Defence*, London, Melbourne and New York, Oxford University Press, 1970
H. T. V. BAKER: *The New Zealand People at War*, Wellington, Department of International Affairs, 1965

VII The Exiled Governments – Free France
Henri MICHEL: *Histoire de la France libre*, Paris, Presses Universitaires de France, 1963
Les mouvements clandestins en Europe, Paris, Presses Universitaires de France, 1961
E. BENES: *From Munich to New War and New Victory*, London, Allen and Unwin, 1954

Colonel PASSY: *Mémoires*, Vols. I and II, Monaco, R. Solar, 1947 and 1948
J. SOUSTELLE: *Envers et contre tout*, Vol. I, Paris, Robert Laffont, 1947
Dr TEMPEL: *Nederland in London*, Haarlem, 1946
Henri MICHEL: *European Resistance Movements*, London, Pergamon, 1964

VIII   The Involvement of the United States

Foreign Relations of the United States, 1941, Vol. II, *Europe*, Washington, Department of State

W. LANGER and S. E. GLEASON: *The World Crisis and American Foreign Policy*, Vol. I, *The Undeclared War*, New York, Harper, 1953

W. S. COLE: *America First, the Battle against Intervention*, Madison, University of Wisconsin Press, 1953

D. W. BROGAN: *The Era of Franklin Roosevelt*, New Haven, Yale University Press, 1950

R. E. SHERWOOD: *Roosevelt and Hopkins: an Intimate History*, New York, Harper, 1950

Basil RAUCH: *Roosevelt from Munich to Pearl Harbour*, New York, Creating Age Press, 1950

Sumner WELLES: *Seven Decisions that Shaped History*, New York, Harper, 1951

W. NEWMAN: *Making the Peace: The Diplomacy of Wartime Conferences*, Washington, Foundation for Foreign Affairs, 1950

H. W. BALDWIN: *Great Mistakes of the War*, New York, Harper, 1950

J.-B. DUROSELLE: *From Wilson to Roosevelt; Foreign Policy of the United States, 1913–1945*, London, Chatto and Windus, 1964

J.-B. DUROSELLE: 'Roosevelt, chef de guerre', special number of *Revue d'histoire de la deuxième guerre mondiale*, April 1971

J.-B. DUROSELLE: 'L'évolution des Etats-Unis vers la guerre', *Revue d'histoire de la deuxième guerre mondiale*, no. 18, April 1955

CHAPTER 2   THE BIRTH OF HITLER'S EUROPE

A. and V. TOYNBEE: *Hitler's Europe, Survey of International Affairs*, London, Oxford University Press, 1954, 2 vols.

A. JACQUEMYNS: *La société belge sous l'occupation allemande*, Brussels, Nicholson and Watson, 1950, 2 vols.

J. WILLEQUET: 'Le procès Falkenhausen', *Revue d'histoire de la deuxième guerre mondiale*, no. 3, June 1951

G. JUHASZ: 'La politique extérieure de la Hongrie de 1939 à 1943, *ibid.*, no. 62, April 1966

'L'occupation allemande en Pologne', special number, *Revue d'histoire de la deuxième guerre mondiale*, no. 40, October 1960

S. HOEL: *Meeting at the Milestone*, London, Secker and Warburg, 1951 (on Norway)

H. PROST: *Destin de la Roumanie (1918–1954)*, Paris, Berger-Levrault, 1954 and *Documenta Occupationis*, Poznan, Zachodni Institute, 7 vols.

GRUCHMANN: *National-sozialistische Grossraumordnung*, Stuttgart, Deutsche Verlag-anstalt, 1962

CIUREA: 'L'effondrement des frontières roumaines', *Revue d'histoire de la deuxième guerre mondiale*, no. 20, October 1955

P. HAYES: 'Quisling et le gouvernement de la Norvège', *ibid.*, no. 66, April 1967

'La Roumanie pendant la guerre', *ibid.*, special number, April 1968

IV The Vichy Government

Documents

Journal officiel (June 1940–June 1941), Vichy, Imprimerie Nationale

La gazette du Palais, Législation de l'occupation, Imprimerie du Palais, Vols. I, II, III, 1940–44

La Délégation française auprès de la Commission allemande d'armistice, Imprimerie Nationale, 5 vols., 1955

Messages aux Français de Philippe Pétain (analytically classified), edited in 1941 by the Ecole nationale des Cadres d'Uriage

Dommages subis par la France et l'Union française, du fait de l'occupation allemande, Imprimerie Nationale, 1950, 8 vols.

Documents on German Foreign Policy, Vols. X and XI, London, HMSO, Vol. X, 1957; Vol. XI, 1961

Memoirs

O. ABETZ: *Mémoires d'un ambassadeur, histoire d'une politique franco-allemande,* Paris, Stock, 1953

P. L. BRET: *Au feu des événements,* Paris, Plon, 1959

F. de BRINON: *Mémoires,* Paris, La Page Internationale, 1949

J. CARCOPINO: *Souvenirs de sept ans,* Paris, Flammarion, 1953

DU MOULIN DE LA BARTHÈTE: *Le temps des illusions,* Geneva, Editions du Cheval-Ailé, 1946

Admiral FERNET: *Aux côtés du maréchal Pétain,* Paris, Plon, 1953

R. GILLOUIN: *J'étais l'ami du maréchal Pétain,* Paris, Plon, 1966

M. MARTIN DU GARD: *La carte impériale,* Paris, Bonne, 1949
          La chronique de Vichy, Paris, Flammarion, 1958

P. NICOLLE: *Cinquante mois d'armistice,* Vol. I, Paris, Bonne, 1947

Marcel PEYROUTON: *Du service public à la prison commune,* Paris, Plon, 1950

SARRAZ-BOURNET: *Témoignage d'un silence,* Paris, SELF, 1948

SCAPINI: *Mission sans gloire,* Morgan, 1960

General SERRIGNY: *Trente ans avec Pétain,* Paris, Plon, 1959

X. VALLAT: *Le nez de Cléopâtre, Souvenirs d'un homme de droite,* Paris, Les Quatre Fils Aymon, 1957

Studies

PLUMYENE: *Pétain,* Paris, Editions du Seuil, 1964

P. FARMER: *Vichy, Political Dilemma,* London, Oxford University Press, 1955

Marquis d'ARGENSON: *Pétain et le pétinisme,* Paris, Créator, 1952

P. ARNOULT: *Les finances de la France sous l'occupation,* Paris, Presses Universitaires de France, 1959

Henri MICHEL and others: *La France sous l'occupation,* Paris, Presses Universitaires de France, 1959

A. HYTIER: *Two Years of French Foreign Policy, Vichy 1940–1942,* Geneva, Droz, 1958

Y. DANAN: *La vie politique à Alger de 1940 à 1944,* Paris, Librairie générale de Droit et de Jurisprudence, 1963

Guy RAISSAC: *Un soldat dans la tourmente (le général Weygand),* Paris, A. Michel, 1963

A. MALLET: *Pierre Laval,* Paris, Amiot-Dumont, 1954, 2 vols.

H. COLE: *Laval, a Biography,* London, Heinemann, 1962

WARNER: *Pierre Laval and the Eclipse of France,* New York, Macmillan, 1968, London, Eyre and Spottiswoode, 1968

J.-M. BOPP: *L'Alsace sous l'occupation allemande,* Clermont-Ferrand, Alsatia, 1945

General SCHMITT : *Les accords secrets franco-britanniques, histoire ou mystification*, Paris, Presses Universitaires de France, 1957

P.-J. STEAD : *Second Bureau*, London, Evans, 1959

L. SEREAU : *L'armée de l'armistice*, Paris, Nouvelles Editions Latines, 1961

In the *Revue d'histoire de la deuxième guerre mondiale*, cf. particularly:

'Problèmes de la jeunesse', no. 56, October 1964 (articles by E. MAILLARD, R. JOSSE, H. MAVIT, A. BASDEVANT)

'Problèmes de l'emploi', no. 57, January 1965 (articles by P. DURAND, H. DELVINCOURT, A. SAUVY, A. HIRSCHFELD)

J. P. COINTET, R. BOURDERON, P. GOUNAND, Y. DURANT and D. BOHBOT, M. LUIRARD, 'Sur la collaboration', *Revue d'histoire de la deuxième guerre mondiale*, no. 91, July 1973

Henri MICHEL : *Vichy, année 40*, Paris, Robert Laffont, 1966

Henri MICHEL : *Pétain, Laval, Darlan, trois politiques*, Paris, Flammarion, 1972

A. S. MILWARD : *The New Order and the French Economy*, London and New York, Oxford University Press, 1970

J. MIEVRE : *Le système Ostland en France durant la 2ème guerre mondiale*, Université de Nancy, 1971

J. EVRARD : *La Déportation des travailleurs français dans le IIIème Reich*, Paris, Fayard, 1972

Robert O. PAXTON : *Vichy France*, New York, Alfred Knopf, 1972

IX Spain

F. DOUSSINAGUE : *España tenía razon*, Madrid, Espasa Calpe, 1950

Sir Samuel HOARE (Viscount Templewood): *Ambassador on Special Mission*, London, Collins, 1946

Serrano SUNER : *Entre Henduye et Gibraltar*, Geneva, Editions du Cheval-Ailé, 1948

The Spanish Government and the Axis, Washington, State Department, 1946

D. DETWILLER : *Hitler, Franco und Gibraltar*, Wiesbaden, F. Steiner Verlag, 1962

B. BURDICK : *Germany's Military Strategy in World War Two*, New York, Syracuse University Press, 1968

HALSTEAD : 'Un Africain méconnu, le Cl. Beigbeder', *Revue d'histoire de la deuxième guerre mondiale*, no. 83, July 1971

CHAPTER 3   THE FIGHTING IN AFRICA AND THE BALKANS

II Naval War in the Mediterranean. The Antagonists

I Documenti diplomatici italiani, Vol. V *June 11–October 28 1940*, Rome, Istituto poligrafico dello Stato, 1965

J.-M. D'HOOP : 'Les problèmes stratégiques de la Grande-Bretagne (juin 1941–juillet 1942)', *Revue d'histoire de la deuxième guerre mondiale*, no. 59, July 1965

Viscount CUNNINGHAM : *A Sailor's Odyssey*, London, Hutchinson, 1951

Admiral GODFROY : *L'aventure de la Force X à Alexandrie*, Paris, Plon, 1953

La marina italiana nella seconda guerra mondiale (Vol. IV, 10 June 1940–13 March 1941) Rome, 1970

La guerre en Mediterranée, (International symposium) Paris, CNRS, 1971

General CATROUX : *Dans la bataille de la Méditerranée*, Paris, Julliard, 1949

M. GABRIELLE : *Operazione Malta*, Rome, Ufficio storica della marina militare, 1965

D. MACINTYRE : *The Battle for the Mediterranean*, London, Batsford, 1964

Admiral ASSMANN : 'La stratégie navale en Méditerranée', *ibid*.

General A U D E T : 'Stratégie allemande en Méditerranée', *Revue de la Défense nationale*, December 1951

Commandant C A R O F F : 'La marine italienne pendant la guerre', *Revue d'histoire de la deuxième guerre mondiale*, nos. 39 and 42, July 1960 and April 1961

Admiral B A R J O T : 'Les sous-marins italiens pendant la guerre', *Revue Maritime*, June 1955

V The War in East Africa

M. V I T A L E : *L'opera dell' esercito*, Vol. III, *Africa settentrionale*, Rome, Istituto poligrafico dello Stato, 1964

Field Marshal Lord W I L S O N : *Eight Years Overseas*, London, Hutchinson, 1950

C. B A R N E T T : *The Desert Generals*, London, Kimber, 1960

A. H E C K S T A L L - S M I T H : *Tobruk*, London, Anthony Blond, 1959

E. F. M O E L L H A U S E N : *La carta perdente*, Rome, Sestante, 1949

E. V O N R I N T E L E N : *Mussolini als Bundesgenosse*, Tübingen, Rainer Wunderlich Verlag, 1951

V O N E S E B E C K : *Rommel et l'Afrika Korps*, Paris, Payot, 1950

Lutz K O C H : *Erwin Rommel*, Paris, Correa, 1950

D. Y O U N G : *Rommel*, Collins, 1950

General P E S E N T I : *Fronte Kenya*, Borgo San Dalmazzo, 1952

Major-General P L A Y F A I R and others: *The Mediterranean and the Middle East*, London, HMSO, 1954

G. K I R K : *The Middle East in the War*, London, Oxford University Press, 1953

I. L I P S C H I T Z : *La politique de la France au Levant (1939–1941)*, Amsterdam, Keesing, 1963

General L A F F A R G U E : *Le général Dentz*, Paris, Les Iles d'Or, 1954

R. R A H N : *Ruheloses Leben*, Düsseldorf, Diederichs Verlag, 1949

U. C A V A L L E R O : *Commando supremo*, Rome, Cappelli, 1948

General I N G O L D : *L'épopée Leclerc au Sahara*, Paris, Berger-Levrault, 1945

J. B. S C H E C H T M A N : *The Mufti and the Führer*, New York, Thomas Yoseloff, 1965

Colonel G O U T A R D : 'La réalité de la menace allemande sur l'Afrique du Nord', *Revue d'histoire de la deuxième guerre mondiale*, no. 44, October 1961

A. B A R K E R : *Erythrea, 1941*, London, Faber and Faber, 1966

A. V E R D E : *In Libia con i meii Soldati*, Milan, 1971

A. S W I N S O N : *The Raiders: Desert Strike Force*, New York, Ballantine, 1968, London, MacDonald, 1969

VII Italian Setbacks in Greece

C E R V I : *Storia della guerra di Grecia*, Milan, Sugar, 1965

D. M. D A V I N : *Crete*, Wellington, N.Z., 1953 and London, Oxford University Press, 1954

J. H. S P E N C E R : *Battle for Crete*, London, Heinemann, 1962

I. M C D. G. S T E W A R D : *The Struggle for Crete*, London, Oxford University Press, 1966

C. B A U D I N O : *Una guerra assurda, la Campagna di Grecia*, Milan, Istituto Editoriale Cisalpino, 1965

A. C L A R K : *The Fall of Crete*, New York, Morrow, 1962

F. K U R O V S K I : *Der Kampf um Kreta*, Herford, Maximilian Verlag, 1965

David A. T H O M A S : *The Battle at Sea*, London, André Deutsch, 1972, *Crete 1941*, New York, Stein and Day, 1973

G. Z A N E T T E : *Tempesta sulle Alpi albanese*, Milan, 1967

Colonel VERNIER: 'La guerre italo-grecque (d'après des documents grecs)', *Revue d'histoire de la deuxième guerre mondiale*, no. 38, April 1960
C. BURDICK: 'L'Axe Berlin–Rome et la campagne italo-grecque', *Revue historique de l'Armée*, no. 3, 1960

IX   The Crushing of Yugoslavia

W. DEDIJER: 'Sur l'armistice germano-yougoslave', *Revue d'histoire de la deuxième guerre mondiale*, no. 23, July 1956
Letter from M. Tsvetkovich to the *Figaro*, April 4, 1950
P. FABRY: *Balkan Wirren, 1940–1941*, Darmstadt, Wehr und Wissen, 1966
STUGAR: 'Aperçu bibliographique sur la Yougoslavie', *Revue d'histoire de la 2ème guerre mondiale*, no. 87, July 1972
W. DEAKIN: *The Embattled Mountain*, London and New York, Oxford University Press, 1971

XI   The Battle of Crete

See Section VII, p. 867.

Book Two   THE WORLD WAR (June 1941–January 1943)

Part I   THE GREATER REICH

CHAPTER I   THE BREAK BETWEEN GERMANY AND RUSSIA

Documents
General HALDER: *Kriegstagebuch*, Vol. III, Stuttgart, W. Kohlhammer, 1963
H. SCHILLER: '*Erinnerungen und die deutsche Zeitung im Ostland*', in *Baltische Hefte*, April 1941 (the newspaper of the occupying authorities)

Reminiscences
G. GAFENCO: *Prelude to the Russian Campaign*, London, Muller, 1945
P. KLEIST: *The European Tragedy*, Douglas, I.O.M., Times Press, 1965 and London, Gibbs and Phillips
F. HOSSBACH: *Infanterie im Ostfeldzug*, Osterode, Giebel und Dehlschagel, 1951
M. LITVINOV: *Notes for a Journal*, London, André Deutsch, 1954
C. KALINOV: *Les maréchaux soviétiques parlent*, Paris, Stock, 1950
General RENDULIC: *Gekämpft, gesiegt, geschlagen*, Heidelberg, Verlag Weisermühl, 1952
General MESSE: *La guerra al fronte russo*, Milan, Rizzoli, 1947
General DOERR: *Der Feldzug nach Stalingrad*, Frankfurt am Main, Mittler, 1957
G. ZHUKOV: *Memoirs*, New York, Delacorte, 1971, London, Cape, 1971
C. MERETSKOV: *Serving the People*, London, Central Books, 1971

General Studies
'L'URSS en guerre', *Revue d'histoire de la deuxième guerre mondiale*, no. 43, July 1961
Various articles in *Recherches internationales à la lumière du marxisme*, nos. 9–10
J. ERIKSON: *The Soviet High Command, 1918–1941*, London, Macmillan, 1962
F. C. BARGHOORN: *Soviet Russian Nationalism*, New York, Macmillan, 1956
GOUDIMA: *L'Armée Rouge dans la paix et la guerre*, Paris, Défense de la France, 1947
B. LIDDELL HART: *The Red Army, 1918–1945*, New York, Harcourt, 1956

ASHER LEE: *The Soviet Air Force*, London, Duckworth, 1950
A. CLARK: *Barbarossa. The Russian-German Conflict*, New York, Morrow, 1965
G. BUCHEIT: *Hitler, chef de guerre*, Paris, Arthaud, 1961
Istorija Velikoj Okecestvennoj Vojny Sovetskog O Sajuza, 1964, 6 vols., (cf. Marc Ferro's
article in *Revue d'histoire de la deuxième guerre mondiale*, January 1961)
A. SEATON: *The Russo-German War (1941–1945)*, London, Arthur Barker, 1971,
New York, Praeger, 1971

The Break
A. ROSSI: *The Russo-German Alliance*, London, Chapman and Hall, 1950
G. HILGER and A. G. MEYER: *The Incompatible Allies; German-Soviet Relations,
1918–1944*, New York, Macmillan, 1953
General WEINBERG: *Germany and the Soviet Union, 1939–1941*, Leyden, E. J. Brill,
1954
P. W. FABRY: *Der Hitler–Stalin Pakt*, Darmstadt, Fundus Verlag, 1962
P. GOSZTONYI: 'Über die Vorgeschichte des deutschen Angriffs auf die Sowjet-
union im Juni 1941', *Allg. Schw. Mil. Zt.*, June and July 1966
F. SCHNEIDER: 'Rétrospective historique, les variations de Hitler en 1940 et
l'opération Barbarossa', *Revue militaire générale*, June 1966
T. HIGGINS: *Hitler and Russia, The Third Reich in a Two-Front War (1937–1943)*,
New York, Collier-Macmillan, 1966, London, 1967
*Auf Antisowjetischen Kriegskurs, Studien zur militarischen Vorbereitung des deutschen Imperia-
lismus gegen die U.R.S.S. (1933–1941)*, Berlin, Deutscher Militärverlag, 1970
B. LEACH: *German Strategy against Russia 1939–1941*, Oxford, Clarendon Press, 1973,
New York, Oxford University Press, 1973

Military operations
G. ERIKSON: 'The Red Army before June 1941', *St Anthony's Papers*, Oxford, 1962,
no. 3
General GUILLAUME: *Pourquoi l'Armée Rouge a vaincu*, Paris, Juilliard, 1948
Colonel LEDERREY: *La défaite allemande à l'est, les armées soviétiques en guerre de 1941 à
1945*, Paris, Lavauzelle, 1951
A. WERTH: *Russia at War, 1941–5*, London, Barrie and Rockliffe, 1964
L. GOURE: *The Siege of Leningrad*, Stanford, Stanford University Press, 1962
Le Operazioni del C.S.I.R., Rome, 1947 (War Office official history)
A. VALORI: *La campagna di Russia*, Rome, 1951
Colonel CONSTANTINI: 'La bataille de Smolensk', *Revue d'histoire de la deuxième guerre
mondiale*, July 1965
'Opérations en Crimée de mai à juillet 1942', *Revue historique
de l'Armée*, no. 1, 1965
General de COSSE-BRISSAC: 'La campagne de Russie', *Revue historique de l'Armée*,
nos. 2 and 3, 1949
P. CHERNIAVSKY: 'Corporal Hitler, General Winter and the Russian Peasant',
The Yale Review, Summer 1962
General DITTMAR: 'La guerre de Laponie', *Irish Defence*, December 1948
General BOURCART: 'La guerre en Finlande', *Revue d'histoire de la deuxième guerre
mondiale*, January 1953
General BOLTINE: 'La bataille de Moscou', *Recherches internationales à la lumière du
marxisme*, nos. 9–10, Sept.–Dec. 1958
S. CHAMPEAUX: 'La leçon du front russe', *Revue de défense nationale*, Nov. 1952
E. KERN: *Kampf in der Ukraine*, Göttingen, 1964
W. P. MOROSOW: *Westlich von Voronesh*, Berlin, Deutscher Militärverlag, 1962

General POPJEL : *In schwerer Zeit*, Berlin, Deutscher Militärverlag, 1962

W. HAUPT : *Baltikum 1941*, Neckargemünd, K. Vowinckel, 1963

Colonel HUAN : 'Les opérations en Crimée (1941–1942)', *Revue Maritime*, January 1964

A. M. SAMSONOV : *Die grosse Schlacht vor Moskau*, Berlin, R.D.A., 1959. (Translated from the Russian)

A. CONSTANTINI : *L'union soviétique en guerre (1941–1945)*, Paris, Ministère des Armées, Imprimerie Nationale, 3 vols., 1968, 1969, 1970 (resumés of Soviet publications)

E. W. MOLLER : *Die Tagebuch Aufzeichnungen entstanden im südabschnitt der Russischen Front*, Osnabruck, Russisches Tagebuch, 1971

The Occupation

A. DALLIN : *German Rule in Russia, 1941–1945*, London, Macmillan, 1957
    The German Occupation of the USSR in World War Two, bibliography, Washington, 1955

R. ILNYTZKYJ : *Deutschland und die Ukraine*, Munich, Osteuropa Institut, 1958, 2 vols.

W. THORWALD : *Wenn sie verderben wollen*, Stuttgart, Steingruben Verlag, 1952
    Die ungeklärten Fälle, Stuttgart, Steingruben Verlag, 1952

I. KAMENETSKY : *Hitler's Occupation of the Ukraine*, Stuttgart, Steingruben Verlag, 1952 and Marquette University Press, 1956

W. SAMARIN : *Civilian Life under the German Occupation*, New York, 1954

Le Crime méthodique, Moscow, foreign language edition, 1963

N.B. There are a very large number of Soviet publications. My knowledge of them is through partial translations, resumés, or analyses published in the *Revue d'histoire de la deuxième guerre mondiale*.

CHAPTER 2   THE WEHRMACHT'S VICTORIES IN THE USSR

See also pp. 868–870.

International Military Tribunal at Nuremberg, Vol. IV (pp. 459–461); Vol. III (p. 249); Vol. IX (Ohlenders' evidence, p. 39)

A. D. BAGREEV : *The Art of War in Capitalist Countries*, Moscow, Ministry of Defence, 1960. (In Russian. Review by A. BESANÇON, *Revue d'histoire de la deuxième guerre mondiale*, no. 47, July 1962)

M. BATAILLON and K. KIRITCHENKO : 'Le ravitaillement de Leningrad pendant le siège', *Recherches internationales à la lumière du marxisme*, Sept.–Dec. 1958

M. HORVATH : 'The Destruction of the Hungarian Second Army in the Don region', Budapest, 1959. (In Hungarian. Review by P. GOSZTONYI, *Revue d'histoire de la deuxième guerre mondiale*, no. 68, October 1967)

E. KORDT : *Wahn und Wirklichkeit*, Stuttgart, Union Deutsche Verlagsgesellschaft, 1950

A. NEKRITCH : *Soviet Historians and the German Invasion*, translated by V. Petrov, University of South Carolina Press, 1968

CHAPTER 3   THE DOMINATION OF EUROPE

1. In addition to the works quoted on p. 864, there are large numbers of publications on this theme throughout central Europe, particularly in Poland; only those which have been reviewed in some detail in the *Revue d'histoire de la deuxième guerre mondiale* are mentioned here.

H. LAUFENBURGER : *Les finances de 1939 à 1945*, Paris, Librairie de Médicis, 1948, 2 vols.

SCHWERIN VON KROSIGK: *Es geschah in Deutschland*, Tübingen, R. Wunderlich-Verlag, 1951. (The memoirs of the Reich's Finance Minister)

R. DUBAIL: *L'Allemagne socialiste et son économie*, Paris, Société anonyme de Publications, 1962

A. MILWARD: *The German Economy at War*, London, Athlone Press, 1965

M. DAVID: *Le marché noir*, Paris, S.P.I.D., 1945

A. SCHWEITZER: *Big Business in the Third Reich*, London, Eyre and Spottiswoode, 1964

K. BRANDT, O. SCHILLER, F. AHLGRIMM: *Management of Agriculture and Food in the German Occupied and Other Areas of the Fortress Europe*, Stanford, Stanford University Press, 1953

S. D. ZAGOROV: *The Agricultural Economy of Danubian Countries, 1925–1945*, Stanford, Stanford University Press, 1955

E. COLLOTTI: *L'occupazione nazista in Europa*, Rome, Editori Riuniti, 1964

D. PETZINA: 'La politique financière et fiscale de l'Allemagne pendant le deuxième conflit mondial', *Revue d'histoire de la deuxième guerre mondiale*, no. 76, October 1969

On France

'Aspects de l'occupation', special number of the *Revue d'histoire de la deuxième guerre mondiale*, no. 55, April 1964. (H. MICHEL: 'Aspects politiques'; F. BOUDOT: 'Aspects économiques'; M. de BOUARD: 'La répression allemande')

M. CEPEDE: *Agriculture et alimentation en France pendant la deuxième guerre mondiale*, Paris, Génin, 1961

'Apurement des comptabilités financières et règlement définitif des budgets (1939–1945)', in *Statistiques et études financières*, supplement no. 75, March 1955

L. BAUDIN: *L'économie française sous l'occupation allemande*, Paris, Editions politiques, économiques et sociales, 1945

La fiscalité pendant la guerre, Paris, Presses Universitaires de France, 1946

P. DURAND: '*La S.N.C.F. pendant la guerre*', Paris, Presses Universitaires de France, 1968

A. MUNZ: *Die Auswirkungen der deutschen Besetzung und Wahrung und Finanzen Frankreichs*, Tübingen, 1957

H. KISLENMACHER: *Die Auswirkungen der deutschen Besetzung auf die Ernährungswirtschaft Frankreichs*, Tübingen, 1959

P. CATHALA: *Face aux réalités, la direction des Finances publiques sous l'occupation*, Paris, Editions du Triolet, 1948

X...: 'Le marché noir en France', *Cahiers d'histoire de la guerre*, no. 4, May 1950

La France économique de 1939 à 1946, Paris, Recueil Sirey, 1948

H. W. EHRMANN: *French Labor, from Popular Front to Liberation*, New York, Oxford University Press, 1947

Organised Business in France, Princeton, Princeton University Press, 1957

'Aspects de l'économie française sous l'occupation', *Cahiers d'histoire de la guerre*, no. 4, 1950

'La France économique de 1939 à 1946', *Revue d'économie politique*, Sept.–Oct. and Nov.–Dec. 1947

J. HORNUNG: Bibliography on 'L'économie française pendant la guerre', *Revue d'histoire de la deuxième guerre mondiale*, no. 57, January 1965

International Tribunal at Nuremberg, Vol. XXXVII, interrogation of Dr Globke

'Aspects de la reprise économique en France après l'armistice', *Revue d'histoire de la deuxième guerre mondiale* (especially J. MIEVRE, 'Les débuts de l'Oxtland en Meurthe-et-Moselle'), no. 7a, July 1970

D'HOOP: 'La main d'oeuvre française au service de l'Allemagne', *Revue d'histoire de la deuxième guerre mondiale*, no. 81, January 1971

On other countries
Recueil de documents établi par le secrétariat du Roi concernant la période 1936–1949, 1950, 7 vols. (i.e. King Leopold)
J. GERAR-LIBOIS, J. GOTOVITCH, *L'an 40, la Belgique occupée*, Brussels, CRISP, 1971
Luxembourg Martyr (1940–1945), Luxemburg, Imprimerie Pierre Linden, 1946
L. de JONG: 'Les Pays-Bas et la seconde guerre mondiale', *Revue d'histoire de la deuxième guerre mondiale*, no. 50, April 1963
CONSTANTINESCU: 'L'exploitation et le pillage de l'économie roumaine', *La Roumanie pendant la deuxième guerre mondiale*, Bucharest, Academy of Science, 1964, pp. 105–129
U. KRAL: *The Economic and Social Evolution of the Czechs*, Prague, 1959, 3 vols. (In Czech. Review by P. OSUSKY, *Revue d'histoire de la deuxième guerre mondiale*, no. 51, 1963.)
G. RANKI: 'L'occupation de la Hongrie par les Allemands', *ibid.*, no. 61, April 1966
D. KITSIKIS: 'La famine en Grèce, les conséquences politiques', *Revue d'histoire de la deuxième guerre mondiale*, no. 74, April 1969

On Poland
W. MARKERT: *Osteuropa Handbuch: Polen*, Köln-Graz, Böhlau Verlag, 1959
Text of the 'Generalplan Ost' published in *Polish Western Affairs*, Warsaw, 1962, Vol. III, no. 2, pp. 401–442
Text of the note from Himmler to Hitler in *Vierteljahreshefte für Zeitgeschichte*, no. 2, 1957
Text of Dr Wentzel in *Cahiers Pologne-Allemagne*, July–Aug.–Sept. 1960
J. DATNER: 'L'appareil militaire allemand de répression en Pologne', *Cahiers internationaux de la Résistance*, March 1960
J. DULCZEWSKI: 'Les migrations de guerre sur les territoires occidentaux', *La Pologne et les affaires occidentales*, Vol. I, 1965, pp. 168–196
S. SAWICKA: 'Un pillage scientifiquement organisé', *Cahiers Pologne-Allemagne*, July–Aug.–Sept. 1960
H. FRANK: *Im Angesicht des Galgens*, Munich, Fr. A. Beck Verlag, 1953
C. MADAJCZYK: *Politika IIIè Rreszy w Okuprawonej Polsce*, 2 vols., Warsaw, P.W.N. 1970
'La Pologne pendant la guerre', special number, *Revue d'histoire de la deuxième guerre mondiale*, no. 78, April 1970
M. BROSZAT: *Nationalsozialistische Polen Politik, 1939–1945*, Stuttgart, 1961

CHAPTER 4   CONCENTRATION CAMPS AND GENOCIDE

I Nazi Anti-Semitism

J. TENENBAUM: *Race and Reich, the Story of an Epoch*, New York, Twaine Publishers, 1956
H. ARENDT: *The Origins of Totalitarianism*, New York, Harcourt Brace, 1951, Meridian Books, 1958, London, Allen and Unwin, 1961
Daniel GASMANN: *The Scientific Origins of National Socialism. Social Darwinism in Ernst Haeckel and the German Monist League*, London, MacDonald, New York, American Elsevier, 1971

Eliamm Ben ELISSAR, *La diplomatie du IIIème Reich et les Juifs (1933–1939)*, Paris, Juilliard, 1965

Georges L. MOSSE: *Germans and Jews*, New York, Howard Fertic, 1970, London, Orbach and Chambers, 1971

Magie und Manipulation ideologischer Kult und politische Religion des National-Sozialismus, Göttingen, Vandenhoeck u Ruprecht, 1971

Erns NOLTE: *Three Faces of Fascism*, New York and London, Holt, Rinehart and Winston, 1966

II The SS

E. CRANKSHAW: *Gestapo, Instrument of Tyranny*, London, Putnam, 1956

J. de la RUE: *The History of the Gestapo*, London, Macdonald, 1964

G. REITLINGER: *The S.S., Alibi of a Nation 1932–1945*, London, Heinemann, 1956

F. BAYLE: *Psychologie et éthique du national-socialisme*, Paris, Presses Universitaires de France, 1953

H. BUCHHEIM: *Die S.S., das Herrschaftsinstrument*, Olten und Freiburg im Breisgau, Walter Verlag, 1965

Totalitäre Herrschaft, Munich, Kunsel Verlag, 1962

E. VERMEIL: 'Himmler', *Revue d'histoire de la deuxième guerre mondiale*, no. 17, January 1955

R. MANVELL and H. FRAENKEL: *Heinrich Himmler*, London, Heinemann, 1965

Waffen S.S. im Bild, Göttingen, Plesse Verlag, 1957

G. STEIN: *The Waffen S.S.; Hitler's Elite Guard at War, 1939–1945*, New York, 1966

E. CALIC: *Himmler et son Empire*, Paris, Stock, 1966

H. HOHNE: *Order of the Death's Head: the story of Hitler's SS*, London, Secker and Warburg, 1969, New York, Coward McCann, 1970

E. GEORG: 'Die wirtschaftlichen Unternehmungen der SS', *Vierteljahrhefte für Zeitgeschichte*, Munich

III The Concentration Camps

F. BAYLE: *Caducée contre croix gammée*, Paris, published by the author, 1950

E. KOGON: *The Theory and Practice of Hell: the German Concentration Camps and the System Behind Them*, London, Secker and Warburg, 1950

D. ROUSSET: *A World Apart*, London, Secker and Warburg, 1951

Les jours de notre mort, London, 1947

O. WORMSER and Henri MICHEL: *Tragédie de la déportation*, Paris, Hachette, 1954

Témoignages strasbourgeois: de l'Université aux camps de concentration, Paris, Editions Belles-Lettres, 1947

'Le système concentrationnaire', special number of the *Revue d'histoire de la deuxième guerre mondiale*, nos. 15–16, July–September 1964

L. MAURY: 'Aperçus sur le comportement des diverses nationalités à Neuengamme', *Revue d'histoire de la deuxième guerre mondiale*, no. 17, January 1955

M. de BOUARD: 'Mauthausen', *ibid.*, nos. 15–16, July–September 1964

'GUSEN', *ibid.*, no. 45, January 1962

A. PIRIE: *Operation Bernhard*, London, Cassell, 1961

G. TILLION: 'Le système des camps de concentration', *Revue d'histoire de la deuxième guerre mondiale*, no. 6, April 1952

'Réflexions sur l'étude de la déportation', *ibid.*, nos. 15–16, July–September 1964

R. PHILLIPS, editor: *War Crimes Trials, the Belsen Trial*, Vol. II, London, Hodge, 1949

Les Français à Ravensbruck, Amicale de Ravensbruck, Gallimard, 1965

C. RICHET and A. MANS: *Pathologie de la déportation*, Paris, Plon, 1956

ANTHONIOZ (G. de Gaulle): 'Les enfants à Ravensbruck', *Revue d'histoire de la deuxième guerre mondiale*, no. 45, January 1962

J. BILLIG: *L'hitlérisme et le système concentrationnaire*, Paris, Presses Universitaires de France, 1967

GRYN and Z. MURAVSKA: *Camp de concentration de Majdanek*, Lublin, 1966

Olga WORMSER: *Le système concentrationnaire (1933–1945)*, Paris, P.U.F., 1968

Joseph BILLIG: *Les camps de concentration dans l'économie du Reich hitlérien*, Paris, P.U.F., 1973

Germaine TILLION: *Ravensbruck*, Paris, Le Seuil, 1973

T. MUSIOL: *Dachau (1933–1945)*, Katowice, Ed. Slask, 1968

IV   The Fate of the Jews

J. BILLIG: *L'Allemagne et le génocide*, Paris, Editions du Centre, 1950
  Le commissariat aux questions juives, Paris, Editions du Centre, 1955–60, 3 vols.

G. REITLINGER: *The Final Solution. The Attempt to Exterminate the Jews in Europe*, London, Vallentine, Mitchell, 1953

L. POLIAKOV and J. WULF: *Le IIIe Reich et les Juifs*, Paris, Gallimard, 1959

R. KEMPNER: *Eichmann und Komplizen*, Zürich, Europa Verlag, 1961

Faschismus, Ghetto, Massenmord, Dokumentation über Ausrottung und Widerstand der Juden in Polen, Berlin, Rutten und Loenig, 1961

J. WULF: *Das dritte Reich und seine Vollstrecker. Die Liquidation von 500,000 Juden*, Berlin, Arani Verlag, 1961

E. RINGELBLUM: *Chronique du ghetto de Varsovie*, Paris, Laffont, 1959

H. G. ADLER: *Theresienstadt*, Tübingen, J. Mohr, 1955

Le dossier Eichmann et la solution finale de la question juive, Paris, Corréa, 1961

M. BORWICZ: *L'insurrection du ghetto de Varsovie*, Paris, Juilliard, 1966

STROOP: *The Report of Stroop Jurgen*

J. SEHN: *Le camp de concentration d'Oswiecim*, Birkenau, Warsaw, 1957

L. POLIAKOV: *Auschwitz*, Paris, Juilliard, 1964

R. HOESS: *Commandant of Auschwitz; the Autobiography of R. Hoess*, London, Weidenfeld and Nicolson, 1959

Témoignages sur Auschwitz, Paris, Editions de l'Amicale des Déportés d'Auschwitz, 1946

'La condition des Juifs', special number of the *Revue d'histoire de la deuxième guerre mondiale*, no. 24, October 1954

H. G. ADLER, et al.: *Zeugnisse und Berichte*, Frankfurt, Europäische Verlag, 1961

J. ROBINSON and P. FRIEDMAN: *Guide to Jewish History under Nazi Impact*, New York, Yivo Institute for Jewish Research, 1960

Nira FELDMAN: *Guide to Unpublished Materials of the Holocaust Period*, Jerusalem, The Institute of Contemporary Jewry, 1972

Jacob ROBINSON: *La Tragédie juive sous la croix gammée à la lumière du procès de Jérusalem*, Paris, CDJC, 1969

Tuvia BORZYKOWSKI: *Between Tumbling Walls*, Tel Aviv, Hakkibbutz Hamenchad, 1972

G. WELLERS: *L'Etoile jaune à l'heure de Vichy*, Paris, Fayard, 1973

IX   The Silence of the Vatican

M. SCHEINMANN: *Der Vatican im Zweiten Weltkrieg*, Berlin, Dietz, 1954

Saul FRIEDLANDER: *Pius XII and the Third Reich*, London, Chatto and Windus, 1966

C. FALCONI: *The Silence of Pius XII*, London, Faber and Faber, 1970

F. L'HUILLIER: 'Le Vatican dans la crise mondiale', *Revue d'histoire de la deuxième guerre mondiale*, no. 28, October 1957

'La politique du Vatican dans la crise mondiale', *ibid.*, no. 63, July 1966

Actes et documents du Saint-Siège relatifs à la seconde guerre mondiale, Vol. I, *Le Saint-Siège et la guerre en Europe*, 1965, Vol. II, *Lettres du Pie XII aux évêques allemands*, 1966, Vols. III and IV, *Le Saint-Siège et la situation religieuse en Pologne et dans les pays baltes*, 1967, Rome, Libreria Editrice Vaticana. (The first volume has appeared in an English edition: *Records and Documents of the Holy See Relating to the Second World War*, Vol. I, *The Holy See and the War in Europe*, London, 1968)

P. LAPIDE: *The Last Three Popes and the Jews*, London, Souvenir Press, 1967

P. LAPIDE: *Le Saint Siège et la guerre mondiale, 1941, octobre 1942*, 1969

Actes et documents du Saint Siège relatifs à la 2ème guerre amondiale, (nov. 42–dec. 43), vol. 7, 1973

Mgr GROCHE et P. SAINT-GERMAIN, *Pie XII devant l'histoire*, Paris, Laffont, 1972

CHAPTER 5   COLLABORATION

II Goebbels' Propaganda

L. P. LOCHNER, editor: *The Goebbels Diaries*, London, Hamish Hamilton, 1948

E. EBERMAYER, H. O. MEISSNER: *Evil Genius: the Story of Joseph Goebbels*, London, Allen Wingate, 1953, and Panther, 1958

R. SEMMLER: *Goebbels – the Man Next to Hitler*, London, Westhouse, 1947

L. FRASER: *Propaganda*, London, Home University Library, 1957

Z. A. B. ZEMAN: *Nazi Propaganda*, London, Oxford University Press, 1964

J. WULF: *Presse und Funk im dritten Reich*, Gütersloh, S. Mohn, 1965

E. K. BRAMSTERD: *Goebbels and National Socialist Propaganda*, Ann Arbor, Michigan State University Press, 1965

R. MANVELL and H. FRAENKEL: *Doctor Goebbels* (revised ed.), London, Heinemann, 1968 and N.E.L., 1968

W. VON OVEN: *Mit Goebbels bis zum Ende*, Buenos Aires, 1949, 2 vols.

H. GLASER: 'La mise en condition nationale-socialiste', *Documents*, March–April 1961

R. CLOET: 'Les directives de Goebbels', *Revue d'histoire de la deuxième guerre mondiale*, no. 64, October 1966 (special number devoted to propaganda)

A. SCHERER: 'Joseph Goebbels', *ibid.*, no. 19, July 1955

III The Collaborators in Occupied Europe

M. COTTA: *La collaboration*, Paris, A. Colin, 1964

Procès de la radio, Paris, Albin Michel, 1947

Procès de la collaboration, Paris, Albin Michel, 1948

J. QUEVAL: *Première page, cinquième colonne*, Paris, Fayard, 1945

J. DUQUESNE: *Les catholiques français sous l'occupation*, Paris, Grasset, 1966

R. SOUCY: 'Le fascisme de Drieu la Rochelle', *Revue d'histoire de la deuxième guerre mondiale*, April 1967

'International Fascism', *Journal of Contemporary History*, no. 1, London, 1966

P. HAYES: 'Bref aperçu de l'histoire de Quisling', *Revue d'histoire de la deuxième guerre mondiale*, no. 66, April 1967

A. H. PAAPE: Le mouvement national-socialiste en Hollande, *ibid.*

J. WILLEQUET: 'Les fascismes belges et la deuxième guerre mondiale', *ibid.*

'La collaboration', special number, *Revue d'histoire de la deuxième guerre mondiale*, no. 80, Oct. 1970, (C. LEVY on France; L. BINDSLOV on Denmark; Van der LEEUW on Hollande; Mme de BENS on Belgium)

SAINT-PAULIEN: *Histoire de la collaboration*, Paris, L'Esprit nouveau, 1964

IV The Satellites

M. MOURIN: *Le drame des Etats satellites de l'Axe*, Paris, Berger-Levrault, 1957

G. BARBUL: *Mémorial Antonescu*, Paris, Editions de la Couronne, 1950

S. KERTESZ: *Diplomacy in a Whirlpool; Hungary between Nazi Germany and Soviet Russia*, Indiana, University of Notre-Dame Press, 1953

C. A. MACARTNEY: *A History of Hungary 1929–1949*, Vol. II, New York, Praeger, 1957

M. VIETOR: 'Evolution de l'Etat slovaque', *Revue d'histoire de la deuxième guerre mondiale*, no. 52, October 1963

M. LACKO: 'Les Croix-Fléchées', *ibid.*, no. 62, April 1966

BROSZAT: *Der kroatische Ustascha-Staat*, Stuttgart, Deutsche Verlaganstadt, 1964

K. DINCIC: 'L'Etat Oustacha de Croatie', *Revue d'histoire de la deuxième guerre mondiale*, no. 74, April 1969

J. SCHRODER: 'L'Allemagne et ses Allies', *Revue d'histoire de la deuxième guerre mondiale*, no. 88, Oct. 1972

T. GEORGESCU: 'La cinquième colonne en Roumanie', *Revue d'histoire de la deuxième guerre mondiale*, no. 70, April 1968

GORNENSKY et KAMENOV: 'La politique intérieure de la Bulgarie en guerre', *Revue d'histoire de la deuxième guerre mondiale*, no. 72, Oct. 68

DIMITROV: 'La mort du roi Boris III', *Revue d'histoire de la deuxième guerre mondiale*, no. 83, July 1971

V Collaboration in the Soviet Union

J. THORWALD: *Wenn sie verderben wollen*, Stuttgart, Steingruber Verlag, 1952

A. JUNIN: 'La défaite psychologique allemande sur le frontde l'Est', *Revue d'histoire de la deuxième guerre mondiale*, no. 46, April 1962

G. FISCHER: *Soviet Opposition to Stalin*, Cambridge, Mass., Harvard University Press, 1952

J. A. ARMSTRONG: *Ukrainian Nationalism 1939–1945*, New York, Columbia University Press, 1955

G. FISCHER: 'Le cas Vlassov', *B.E.P.I.*, suppl. to no. 89, May 1953

Commandant X: *Formation des unités de l'Est par le haut-commandement allemand*, March 1957

VII The Friendship of Spain

J. STAVNIK: 'L'Espagne pendant la guerre', *Revue d'histoire de la deuxième guerre mondiale*, no. 5, January 1952

P. VILAR: *ibid.*, no. 6, April 1952

O. DANKELMANN: *Franco zwischen Hitler und den Westmachten*, Berlin, Deutscher Verlag, Wissenschaften, 1970

C. B. BURDICK: *Germany's Military Strategy and Spain in World War II*, New York, Syracuse University Press, 1968

B. CROZIER: *Franco: A Biography*, London, Eyre and Spottiswoode, 1967, Boston, Little, Brown, 1968

VIII Swedish Supplies

F. LA RUCHE: *La neutralité de la Suède*, Paris, Nouvelles Editions Latines, 1953

P. JEANNIN: 'La Suède pendant la guerre (les livres blancs suédois)', *Revue d'histoire de la deuxième guerre mondiale*, no. 13, January 1954

F. SCOTT: *The United States and Scandinavia*, Cambridge, Mass., Harvard University Press, 1950

S. ABRAHAMSEN: *Sweden's Foreign Policy*, Washington, Public Affairs Press, 1957

CHAPTER 6   RESISTANCE MOVEMENTS BEGIN

Henri MICHEL: *Les mouvements clandestins en Europe*, Paris, Presses Universitaires
de France, 1961
> 'Aspects de la Résistance européene', *Cahiers d'histoire de la guerre*,
> Paris, no. 3, 1950

Henri MICHEL: *The Shadow War*, London, André Deutsch, 1972, New York, Harper
and Row, 1973

General REDELIS: *Partisanenkrieg*, Heidelberg, K. Vowinckel, 1959

European Resistance Movements, London, Pergamon, Vol. I, 1960, Vol. II, 1964

Proceedings of a Conference on British and European Resistance, Oxford, St Anthony's
College, 1962

II   The Allies and the Resistance

B. WITTEK: *Der brittsche Ätherkrieg gegen das dritte Reich*, Münster, Faule, 1962

R. LOCKHART: *Comes the Reckoning*, London, Putnam, 1947

J. L. CREMIEUX-BRILHAC: 'Les émissions françaises à la B.B.C. pendant la
guerre', *Revue d'histoire de la deuxième guerre mondiale*, no. 1, November 1950

M. FOOT: *L'aide (anglaise) à la résistance en Europe*, *Revue d'histoire de la deuxième guerre
mondiale*, no. 90, April 1973

III   Resistance in Western Europe

L. de JONG: 'Les Pays-Bas dans la seconde guerre mondiale', *Revue d'histoire de la
deuxième guerre mondiale*, no. 50, April 1963

L. LEJEUNE: 'Tableau de la Résistance belge', *ibid.*, No. 31, July 1958

General GERARD: *Armée secrète*, Brussels, La Renaissance du Livre, 1962

O. LAMPE: *The Savage Canary, the Story of Resistance in Denmark*, London, Cassell, 1957

Inventaire de la presse clandestine conservée en Belgique, Brussels, Archives générales du
Royaume, 1966

H. BERNARD: *La Résistance*, Brussels, La Renaissance du Libre, 1968

IV   The French Resistance

Henri MICHEL: *Histoire de la Résistance française*, Paris, Presses Universitaires de
France, 1951
> *Les courants de pensée de la Résistance*, Paris, Presses Universitaires de
> France, 1962
> *Jean Moulin, l'unificateur*, Paris, Hachette, 1964
> *Bibliographie critique de la Résistance*, Paris, Hachette, 1964

R. HOSTACHE: *Le Conseil national de la Résistance*, Paris, Presses Universitaires de
France, 1958

C. TILLON: *Les F.T.P.*, Paris, Julliard, 1962

M. R. D. FOOT: *S.O.E. in France*, London, HMSO, 1966

Special numbers of the *Revue d'histoire de la deuxième guerre mondiale*: 'Aspects de la
Résistance française' (November 1950); 'Sur la Résistance en zone nord' (April 1958);
'Sur la Résistance française' (July 1959), 'Aspect de la Résistance française' (January
1966 and January 1972)

V   Resistance in Central Europe

Czechoslovakia

V. KRAJINA: 'La Résistance tchécoslovaque', *Cahiers d'histoire de la guerre*, no. 3, 1950

La Résistance et la Révolution, Prague, Czechoslovak Committee of the History of Anti-
Fascist Resistance, 1965

Poland

General BOR-KOMOROVSKI: *The Secret Army*, London, Gollancz, 1950

ZAMOJSKI: 'Recherches sur la Résistance polonaise', *Cahiers internationaux de la Résistance*, no. 1, Nov. 1959

E. DURACZYNSKI: 'La structure sociale et politique de la Résistance anti-hitlerienne en Pologne', *Revue d'histoire de la deuxième guerre mondiale*, April 1970

Z. MANKOWSKI: 'L'historiographie polonaise consacrée à la politique de l'occupant et à la Résistance', *Revue d'histoire de la deuxième guerre mondiale*, April 1970

VI Resistance in the Balkans

Yugoslavia

W. DEDIJER: *Tito Speaks, his Self-Portrait and Struggle with Stalin*, London, Weidenfeld and Nicolson, 1953

Sir F. MACLEAN: *Eastern Approaches*, London, Jonathan Cape, 1949 (reissued 1966)

J. ROOTHAM: *Miss Fire, the Chronicle of a British Mission to Mihaïlovic*, London, Chatto and Windus, 1946

M. DINCIC: articles in *Revue d'histoire de la deuxième guerre mondiale*, January 1958, April 1959, April 1960, April 1961

F. TRGO: 'L'armée de libération nationale', *Revue d'histoire de la deuxième guerre mondiale*, July 1972

M. APOTOLSKI: 'La guerre de libération en Macedoine', *Revue d'histoire de la deuxième guerre mondiale*, July 1972

Greece

F. NOEL-BAKER: *Greece, the Whole Story*, London, Hutchinson, 1946

General SARAFIS: *Greek Resistance Army*, London, Birch Books, 1951

C. M. WOODHOUSE: *Apple of Discord, a Survey of Recent Greek Politics*, London, Hutchinson, 1948

A. KEDROS: *La Résistance grecque*, Paris, Laffont, 1966

E. SCHRAMM VON THADDEN: *Griecherland und die Grossmächte im Zweiten Weltkrieg*, Wiesbaden, Steiner, 1955

Part II JAPAN'S GREATER ASIA

CHAPTER I THE BREAK BETWEEN JAPAN AND THE UNITED STATES

C. BEARD: *President Roosevelt and the Coming of the War*, New Haven, Yale University Press and London, Oxford University Press, 1948

H. FEIS: *The Road to Pearl Harbour*, Princeton, Princeton University Press, 1950 and Oxford, Oxford University Press, 1951

VULLIEZ: *Tonnerre sur le Pacifique*, Paris, Fayard, 1966

Foreign Policy of the United States, 1941, Vols. IV and V: *The Far East*

Basil RAUCH: *Roosevelt from Munich to Pearl Harbour*, New York, Creative Age Press (Farrar, Straus), 1950

R. BUTOW: *Tojo and the Coming of the War*, Princeton, Princeton University Press, 1961

E. KORDT: *Nicht aus den Akten*, Stuttgart, Union Deutsche Verlagsgesellschaft, 1950

G. CASTELLAN and D. A. JARS: 'La diplomatique allemande et la guerre du Pacifique', *Revue d'histoire de la deuxième guerre mondiale*, no. 2, April 1951

Marc BENOIST: 'Les Etats-Unis devant la question japonaise', *ibid.*
S. TOGO: *The Cause of Japan*, New York, Simon and Schuster, 1956
LEQUILLER: *Le Japon*, Paris, Sirey, 1966
H. PERRY: *The Pannay Incident: Prelude to Pearl Harbor*, 8 vols., New York, Macmillan, 1969
Nobutaka IKE: *Japan's Decision for War: Records of the 1941 Policy Conference*, New York and London, Stanford University Press, 1967

II   The China War

General CASSEVILLE: *De Tchang Kaï-chek à Mao Tsé-toung*, Paris, Lavauzelle, 1950
F. F. LIU: *A Military History of Modern China*, Princeton, Princeton University Press, 1956
Dr MIGOT: *Mao Tsé-toung*, Paris, Planète, 1966
E. O'BALLANCE: *The Red Army of China*, London, Faber and Faber, 1962
Tchang-Fou JOUEL: 'Sur la guerre sino-japonaise', *Revue d'histoire de la deuxième guerre mondiale*, October 1969
L. BIANCO: *The Origins of the Chinese Revolution, 1915–1949*, New York, Stanford University Press, 1971, London, Oxford University Press, 1971
LEMERY: *D'une République à l'autre*, Paris, La Table Ronde, 1965
Admiral DECOUX: *A la barre de l'Indochine*, Paris, Plon, 1949
Testimony of General MARTIN in *The Trial of Marshal Pétain*
General SABATIER: *Le destin de l'Indochine*, Paris, Plon, 1952
J. LEGRAND: *L'Indochine à l'heure japonaise*, Cannes, 1963
General MORDANT: *Au service de la France en Indochine*, Saigon, Editions Ifom, 1950
General MARCHAND and J. ROLLET: *L'Indochine en guerre*, Paris, Les Presses Modernes, 1954

VI   The Attack on Pearl Harbour

Admiral THEOBALD: *The Final Secret of Pearl Harbor*, London, Holborn Publishing Co.
W. LORD: *Day of Infamy*, London, Longman, Green, 1957
R. WOHLSTETTER: *Pearl Harbor, Warning and Decision*, Stanford, Stanford University Press, 1962
H. L. TREFOUSSE: *What happened at Pearl Harbor*, New York, Twaine, 1958
J. C. BUTOW: The Hull Nomura Conversation; a Fundamental Misconception, *American Historical Review*, July 1960
P. BURTNESS and OBER: 'Problem of Pearl Harbor Intelligence Reports', *Military Affairs*, Winter 1961
A. HOEHLING: *The Week before Pearl Harbor*, New York, Norton, 1963
H. WALLIN: *Pearl Harbor: Why, How: Fleet Salvage and Final Appraisal*, Washington, 1968

CHAPTER 2   JAPAN'S LIGHTNING WAR

D. H. JAMES: *The Rise and the Fall of the Japanese Empire*, London, G. Allen, undated
Major-General KIRBY: *The War against Japan*, Vol. II, London, HMSO, 1958
Major-General WHITNEY: *MacArthur, his Rendezvous with History*, New York, Knopf, 1953

C. A. WILLOUGHBY and CHAMBERLAIN: *MacArthur: 1941–1951: Victory in the Pacific*, London, Heinemann, 1956

D. MACARTHUR: *Reminiscences*, London, Heinemann, 1965

J. TOLAND: *But Not in Shame. The Six Months after Pearl Harbor*, New York, Random House, 1962

K. EGUCHI: 'Compte-rendu de plusieurs ouvrages japonais', *Revue d'histoire de la deuxième guerre mondiale*, April 1972

W. F. CRAVEN and J. L. CATE: *The Army Air Forces in World War Two*, Chicago, University of Chicago Press, 1948

S. HAYASHI and A. COX: *The Japanese Army in the Pacific War*, Quantico, Marine Corps Association, 1959

On strategy

A. REUSSNER: 'La marine marchande, la stratégie et l'économie de guerre japonaises', *Revue d'histoire de la deuxième guerre mondiale*, no. 2, April 1951

S. FALK: 'The Japanese command in World War Two', *Political Science Quarterly*, Dec. 1961

'Japanese strategy in World War Two', *Military Review*, June 1962

Admiral BARJOT: 'La stratégie aéronavale japonaise', *Revue Maritime*, Aug. 1952

L. MORTON: Command in the Pacific, *Military Review*, Dec. 1961

Lieutenant-Colonel MERGLEN: 'Les opérations aéroportées japonaises dans la deuxième guerre mondiale', *L'armée*, Sept. 1960

Louis MORTON: *Command decisions, United States Army in World War Two*, Washington, 1962

M. MATLOFF and E. SNELL: *Strategic plans for coalition warfare, 1941–1942*, Washington, Department of the Army, 1953

L. MORTON: *Strategy and Command: The First Two Years*, Washington, 1962

On logistics

C. B. A. BEHRENS: *Merchant Shipping and the Demands of War*, London, HMSO, 1955

R. M. LEIGHTON and COAKLEY: *Global Logistics and Strategy*, Washington, Department of the Army, 1955

R. LECKIE: *Strong Men Armed: the US Marines Against Japan*, New York, Random House, 1962

On operations

S. MORISON: 'The Great Battles of the Pacific War', *History of U.S. Naval Operations in World War II*, London, Oxford University Press, 1947

Captain S. ROSKILL R.N.: *The War at Sea*, London, HMSO, Vol. I 1954, Vol. II 1956

Admiral SHERMAN: *Combat Command, the American Aircraft Carriers in the Pacific War*, New York, Dutton, 1950

L. MORTON: *The Fall of the Philippines*, Washington, Government Printing Office, 1952

S. FALK: *The March of Death*, New York, Norton, 1962

EDMONDS: *They Fought with what They Had*, Boston, Little, Brown, 1951

Captain GRENFELD: *Main Fleet to Singapore*, London, Faber and Faber, 1951

Sir John SMYTH: *Percival and the Tragedy of Singapore*, London, MacDonald, 1971

Major-General KIRBY, et al.: *The Loss of Singapore*, London, HMSO, 1957

D. CONGDON: *Combat, the War with Japan*, New York, Dell, 1962

General CHASSIN: 'Rabaul', *Forces aériennes françaises*, April 1949

A. G. VROMANS: 'Les Indes néerlandaises', *Revue d'histoire de la deuxième guerre mondiale*, no. 50, pp. 27–36

Admiral HELFRICH: *Mémoires*. (In Dutch. Review by C. T. de JONG, *Revue d'histoire de la deuxième guerre mondiale*, nos. 10–11, June 1953)

Commandant de FOUQUIÈRES: 'La campagne de Birmanie', *Forces aériennes françaises*, May 1948

Field Marshal SLIM: *Defeat into Victory*, New York, MacKay, 1961

C. ROMANUS and R. SUNDERLAND: *China, Burma, India Theater*, Washington, Department of the Army, 1953

FELLOWES-GORDON: *The Battle for Naw Song's Kingdom*; *General Stilwell's North Burma Campaign and its Aftermath*, London, L. Cooper, 1971, *The Magic War: Battle for North Burma*, New York, Scribners, 1972

CHAPTER 3   THE SPHERE OF CO-PROSPERITY

F. L. JONES, H. BORTON and B. P. PEARN: *The Far East, 1942–6*, London, Oxford University Press, 1955

W. ELSBREE: *Japan's Role in South-East Asian Nationalist Movement (1940–1946)*, Cambridge, Mass., Harvard University Press, 1953

Richard STORRY: *The Double Patriots; a Study of Japanese Nationalism*, London, Chatto and Windus, 1957

VASILJEVOVA: 'Le nationalisme japonais et la deuxième guerre mondiale', *Pensée*, Aug. 1966

On various countries

CHINN KEE ONN: *Ma rai El*. London, Harrap, 1953 (Malaya)

Spencer CHAPMAN: *The Jungle is Neutral*, London, Chatto and Windus, 1952 (Malaya)

Thakin NU: *Burma under the Japanese*, London, Macmillan, 1954

T. FRIEND: *Between Two Empires: The Ordeal of the Philippines*, New Haven, Yale University Press, 1965

M. A. AZIZ: *Japan's Colonialism and Indonesia*, The Hague, Martinus Nijhoff, 1955

H. BENDA: *The Crescent and the Rising Sun: Indonesian Islam under Japanese Occupation*, New Haven, Institute of Pacific Relations, 1958

J. KOE: 'Soekarno and the Japanese Occupation', *Eastern World*, May 1963

R. THOMAS: 'Educational Remnants of Military Occupation: The Japanese in Indonesia', *Asian Survey*, November 1966

D. JAJANAMA: *Thailand im Zweiten Weltkrieg*, Hamburg, 1970

M. C. GUERRERO: 'Les Philippines, la propagande japonaise', *Revue d'histoire de la deuxième guerre mondiale*, April 1972

LI-OGG: 'Les Japonais et la langue coréenne', *Revue d'histoire de la deuxième guerre mondiale*, January 1973

IV China Under the Chungking Government

Foreign Relations of the USA, 1942, China, Washington, 1956

B. SCHWARTZ: *Chinese Communism and the Rise of Mao*, Cambridge, Mass., Harvard University Press, 1951

MAO TSE-TUNG: *Strategic Problems of China's Revolutionary War*, Peking, 1954
          The Dictatorship of the People's Democracy, New Haven, Yale University Institute of Far Eastern Languages (Mirror Ser., C.5), 1951

MAO TSE-TUNG: 'Talks at the Yenan Forum on Art and Literature', *Selected Works*, Vol. IV, London, Lawrence and Wishart, 1956

A. YOUNG: *China's Wartime Finance and Inflation*, Cambridge, Harvard University Press, 1965

CHANG-FOU-JOUEI: 'Sur la guerre sino-japonaise', *Revue d'histoire de la deuxième guerre mondiale* (summary of Chinese books from Formosa), no. 76, October 1969

R. COLLENOT: 'Les communistes chinois et le conflit mondial', *ibid.*, no. 13, Jan. 1954

\   *Part III*   THE WATERSHED OF THE WAR

CHAPTER I   A BALANCE OF FORCES IN THE WAR AT SEA

II The Coral Sea and Midway

S. E. MORISON: *History of United States Naval Operations in World War II*, Vol. IV, *Coral Sea, Midway and Submarine Actions*, Vol. V, *The Struggle for Guadalcanal*, London, Oxford University Press, 1950–52 and Boston, Little, Brown, 1947

M. FUCHIDA and M. OKUMIYA: *Midway, the Battle that Doomed Japan*, Annapolis, US Naval Institute, 1955

Colonel BERNARD: *La bataille de Midway: Tournants de la guerre, op. cit.*, p. 69–75

Admiral SMITH: *Midway, Turning-Point of the Pacific*, New York, Thomas J. Crowell, 1966

Commandant ACCART: 'La bataille de Midway et l'avenir du porte-avions', *Forces aériennes françaises*, Nov. 1946

S. MILNER: *Victory in Papouasie*, Washington, Department of the Army, 1957

W. LORD: *Incredible Victory*, New York, Harper and Row, 1967, London, Hamish Hamilton, 1968

V German Submarine Successes in the Atlantic

S. CONN and B. FAIRCHILD: *The Framework of Hemisphere Defence*, Washington, Office of Chief of Military History, 1960

S. CONN, R. ENGELMANN and B. FAIRCHILD: *Guarding the United States and Its Outposts*, Washington, Office of Chief of Military History, 1964

P. BRODIE: *La stratégie navale et son application dans la guerre (1939–1945)*, Paris, Payot, 1947

C. FARAGO: *The Tenth Fleet*, New York, Obolensky, 1962

R. KUENNE: *The Attack Submarine*, New Haven, Yale University Press, 1965

Admiral ASSMANN: *Deutsche Seestrategie in zwei Weltkriegen*, Heidelberg, Vowinckel, 1957

G. BIDLINGMAIER: *Einsatz der schweren Kriegsmarineeinheiten im ozeanischen Zufuhrkrieg*, Neckarsgemünd, Vowinckel, 1963

Admiral DOENITZ: *Memoirs; Ten Years and Twenty days*, Weidenfeld and Nicolson, 1959

Führer Conferences on Naval Affairs, London, Admiralty, 1947, 7 vols. (roneo)

A. MARTIENSSEN: *Hitler and his Admirals*, New York, Dutton, 1949

Admiral RAEDER: *Struggle for the Sea*, Vol. II, London, Kimber, 1959

K. PUTTKAMMER: *Die unheimliche See*, Vienna, Kühne, 1952

H. SOHLER: *U-Bootkrieg und Völkerrecht*, Berlin, Mittler, 1956

S. E. MORISON: *The Battle of the Atlantic*, London, HMSO, 1946

C. BEKKER: *Swastika at Sea: the Struggle and Destruction of the German Navy, 1939–1945*, London, Kimber, 1953

Admiral de BELOT: *The Struggle for the Mediterranean, 1939–1945*, Princeton, Princeton University Press, 1951

Air Ministry: *Coastal Command*, London, HMSO, 1943

E. B. POTTER and C. W. NIMITZ: *The Great Sea War*, London, Harrap, 1960

R. JOUAN: *La marine allemande dans la seconde guerre mondiale*, Paris, Payot, 1949

W. KARIG, E. BURTON and L. FREELAND: *The Atlantic War*, New York, Farrar and Rinehart, 1946

D. MACINTYRE: *The Battle of the Atlantic*, London, Batsford, 1961

S.E. MORISON: *The Battle of the Atlantic, Sept. 1939–May 1943*, Boston, Little, Brown, 1947

T. ROSCOE: *United States Destroyer Operations in World War Two*, Annapolis, United States Naval Institute, 1953

Captain S. ROSKILL R.N.: *The War at Sea*, Vol. I, 1954, Vol. II, 1956, London, HMSO

F. RUGE: *Sea Warfare, 1939–1945; a German Viewpoint*, London, Cassell, 1957

A. THOMAZI: *La bataille de l'Atlantique*, Paris, Plon, 1949

F. BUSCH and H. J. BRENNECKE: *La tragédie des cuirassés allemands*, Paris, Payot, 1950

D. WOODWARD: *The Secret Raiders*, London, Kimber, 1955

R. GRENFELL: *The Bismarck Episode*, London, Faber and Faber, 1948

J. MORDAL: *À la poursuite du Bismarck*, Paris, Les Deux Sirènes, 1948

D. POPE: *The Battle of the River Plate*, London, Kimber, 1956

A. VULLIEZ and J. MORDAL: *Battleship Scharnhorst*, London, Hutchinson, 1958

HILARION: *S et G*, Paris, France-Empire, 1957

L. PEILLARD: *Sink the Tirpitz*, London, Jonathan Cape, 1968

G. BLOND: *Ordeal below Zero*, London, Souvenir Press, 1956

Sir Peter GRETTON: *Convoy Escort Command*, London, Cassell, 1964

F. REISENBERG: *Sea War*, New York, Rinehart, 1956

E. ROMAT: *La guerre sous-marine en Atlantique*, Paris, de Gigord, 1946

B. B. SCHOFIELD: *The Russian Convoys*, London, Batsford, 1964

C. BEKKER: *Radar*, Paris, France-Empire, 1960

M. BOUGARAN: 'La lutte contre les sous-marins', *Revue Maritime*, March 1966

P. BELL: 'La guerre sur mer à l'Ouest', *Revue d'histoire de la deuxième guerre mondiale*, no. 39, July 1960

A. MASSON: 'Les grandes étapes de la bataille de l'Atlantique', *ibid.*, no. 69, January 1968

P. K. KEMP: 'La protection des convois britanniques', *ibid.*

J. ROHWER: 'La radiotélégraphie, auxiliaire du commandement dans la guerre sous-marine', *ibid.*

Further material is contained in the bibliography drawn up by the Bibliothèque de documentation internationale contemporaine and printed in the special number of the *Revue d'histoire de la deuxième guerre mondiale*, 'La bataille de l'Atlantique', January 1968

CHAPTER 2   THE GERMANS HALTED IN AFRICA

A. Bryant: based on the diaries of Viscount ALANBROOKE: *The Turn of the Tide, 1939–1943*, London, Collins, 1957

General ALEXANDER, edited by John North: *The Alexander Memoirs, 1940–45*, London, Cassell, 1962

Field-Marshal MONTGOMERY: *El Alamein to the River Sangro*, London, Hutchinson, 1948

I. S. O. PLAYFAIR, F. C. FLYNN, *et al.*: *The Mediterranean and Middle East*, Vol. II, *The Germans came to the Help of their Allies*, London, HMSO, 1956

C. E. L. PHILIPPS: *Alamein*, Heinemann, London, 1962

M. CARVER: *El Alamein*, London, Batsford, 1962

J. CRAWFORD: *Objective Alamein*, John Spencer, London, 1964

Admiral ASSMANN: 'La stratégie navale en Méditerranée', *Revue Maritime*, March 1954

Commandant CAROFF: 'La marine italienne pendant la guerre', *Revue d'histoire de la deuxième guerre mondiale*, nos. 39, July 1960, and 42, April 1961

Colonel GOUTARD: 'La réalité de la menace allemande sur l'Afrique', *Revue d'histoire de la deuxième guerre mondiale*, no. 44, October 1961

Silla CAVALIERE: 'La politica egiziana dal 1936 à 1951', *Rivista di studi politici internazionali*, April–June 1953

J. MORDAL: *Bir-Hakeim*, Paris, Amiot-Dumont, 1951

'Le Destin d'Erwin Rommel', *Revue de Paris*, July 1954

Admiral DI SQUADRA: *La difesa del traffico con l'Africa Settentrionale*, Rome, Officio Storico, 1964

La Marina italiana nella seconda guerra mondiale, Vols II and VII, Rome, Officio Storico, 1958

P. CARELL: *The Foxes of the Desert*, London, Macdonald, 1960

P. CACCIA DOMINIONI: *Alamein, 1933–1962; an Italian Story*, London, Allen and Unwin, 1966

F. MADJALANY: *The Battle of El Alamein*, London, Weidenfeld and Nicolson, 1965

G. KOENIG: *Bir-Hakeim*, Paris, Robert Laffont, 1971

B. MANCINELLI: *Del fronte dell'Africa settentrionale all'abbandono del la Libia*, Milan, Rizzoli, 1970

VII   The Preparations in North Africa

Henri MICHEL: 'Darlan et le débarquement allié en A.F.N.', *Cahiers d'histoire de la guerre*, no. 1, Jan. 1949

A. KAMMERER: *Du débarquement africain au meurtre de Darlan*, Paris, Flammarion, 1949

A. FUNK: *Eisenhower, Giraud and High Command of Torch*, Military affairs, Oct. 1971

S. E. MORISON: *Operations in North African Waters, Oct. 1942–June 1943*, Vol. II of U.S.

History of Naval Operations in World War II, Boston, Little, Brown and London, Oxford University Press, 1947

G. F. HOWE: *North-West Africa, Seizing the Initiative in the West*, Washington, Gov. Printing Office, 1957

General GIRAUD: *Un seul but, la victoire*, Paris, Julliard, 1949

Marshal JUIN: *Mémoires*, Vol. I, Paris, Fayard, 1959

G. ESQUER: *Le 8 novembre, premier jour de la Libération*, Paris, Charlot, 1946

G. MAST: *Histoire d'une rebellion*, Paris, Plon, 1969

CRUSOE: *Vicissitudes d'une victoire*, Editions de l'Ame française, 1946

Y. DANAN: *La vie politique à Alger de 1940 à 1944*, Paris, Librairie générale de Droit, 1963

R. MURPHY: *Diplomat Among Warriors*, New York, Doubleday, 1964

General SCHMITT: *Les accords secrets franco-britanniques*, Paris, Presses Universitaires de France, 1957

P. DHERS: *Regards nouveaux sur les années 40*, Paris, Flammarion, 1958

K. PENDAR: *Le dilemme France-Etats-Unis*, Montreal, Beauchemin, 1946

H. NOGUERES: *Le suicide de la flotte française à Toulon*, Paris, Laffont, 1961

CHAPTER 3   THE BATTLE OF STALINGRAD

Marshal PAULUS: *Paulus and Stalingrad*, London, Methuen, 1963, New York, Citadel Press, 1964

P. GORLITZ: *Die Schlacht um Stalingrad*, Stuttgart, Methuen, 1951

V. RHODEN: *Die Luftwaffe ringt um Stalingrad*, Wiesbaden, Limes Verlag, 1952

Lettres de Stalingrad, Paris, Buchet-Chastel, 1957

M. FENYO: 'The Allied Axis Armies and Stalingrad', *Military Affairs*, no. 2, Summer 1965

L. GOURE: *The Siege of Stalingrad*, Stanford, Stanford University Press, 1962

H. A. JACOBSEN: 'Zur Schlacht von Stalingrad', *Allg. Schw. Mil. Zeit.*, Feb. 1963

Marshal YEREMENKO: *Stalingrad*, Paris, Plon, 1963

Marshal CHUIKOV: *Stalingrad Anfang des Weges*, Berlin, Deutscher Militärverlag, 1962

G. ZHUKOV: *Memoirs*, New York, Delacorte Press, 1971, London, Cape, 1971

V. NEKRASSOV: *Dans les tranchées de Stalingrad*, Paris, Presses de la Cité, 1963

Marshal VORONOV: 'Operation Ring', *Z.F. Militärgeschichte*, no. 2, 1962

TELPUKHOVSKY: 'La victoire de Stalingrad', *Revue d'histoire de la deuxième guerre mondiale*, no. 43, July 1961

Marshal ROKOSSOVSKI: 'Reminiscences', *Polityka*, May–June 1965. (In Russian)

A. M. SAMSONOV: *Stalingradskaya Bitva*, Moscow, 1960. (In Russian. Review by A. BESANÇON, *Revue d'histoire de la deuxième guerre mondiale*, no. 53, January 1964.)

ADLER BRESSE: 'Le maréchal Paulus et la bataille de Stalingrad', *Revue d'histoire de la deuxième guerre mondiale*, no. 48, October 1962

Book Three   THE DEFEAT OF ITALY

Part I   THE ALLIED WAR-MACHINE

CHAPTER I   THE ANGLO-AMERICAN WAR

Foreign Relations of the USA, The American Republics, Vols. VI, 1963 and VII, 1962; *1942*, Vol. VI, 1963; *1943*, Vols. V and VI, 1965

R. E. SHERWOOD: *Roosevelt and Hopkins; an Intimate History*, New York, Harper and Row, 1950

The White House Papers of Harry L. Hopkins, London, Eyre and Spottiswoode, Vol. I, 1948, Vol. II, 1949

Admiral W. D. LEAHY: *I Was There*, London, Gollancz, 1950 and New York, Whitlesey House

E. ROOSEVELT: *As He Saw It*, New York, Duell, Sloan and Pearce, 1946

R. INGERSOLL: *Top Secret*, New York, Harcourt Brace, 1946

S. FALK: 'Military Strategy in World War Two', *Military Review*, June 1962

S. CONN: 'Changing Concepts of National Defense in the USA', *Military Affairs*, Spring, 1964

E. J. KINGSTON-MCCLOUGHRY: *The Direction of War*, London, Jonathan Cape, 1955

M. MATLOFF and E. SNELL: *Strategic Planning for Coalition Warfare 1941–1942*, Washington, US Government Printing Office, 1953

Strategic Planning for Coalition Warfare, 1943–1944, Washington, US Government Printing Office, 1960

R. LEIGHTON: 'Overlord revised; an interpretation of American strategy in the European war', *American Historical Review*, July 1963

GREENFIELD: *American Strategy in World War Two, a Reconsideration*, Baltimore, Johns Hopkins Press, 1963

S. E. MORISON: *American Contributions to the Strategy of World War Two*, London, Oxford University Press, 1958

F. C. POGUE, A. BLUM, F. B. MISSE, R. W. COAKLEY: 'Roosevelt, chef de guerre'. Special number, *Revue d'histoire de la deuxième guerre mondiale*, April 1971

R. A. DIVINE, *Roosevelt and World War Two*, Baltimore, John Hopkins Press, 1969, London, Penguin Books, 1970

H. CALVET: 'Roosevelt et la deuxième guerre mondiale', *Revue d'histoire de la deuxième guerre mondiale*, no. 3, July 1951, pp. 82–5
      'La reddition inconditionnelle, idée rooseveltienne', *ibid.*, no. 20, October 1955, pp. 43–9

J. NERE: 'Logistique et stratégie de l'alliance anglo-américaine', *ibid.*, no. 27, July 1957, pp. 1–19

Sir Ian JACOB: 'La direction de la guerre chez les Anglo-Saxons', *Revue de défense nationale*, June 1961

J. EHRMAN: *Grand Strategy*, London, HMSO, 1956, 2 vols.

M. MOURIN: 'Reddition sans conditions', *Revue de défense nationale*, Jan. 1953

Lord HANKEY: *Politics, Trials and Errors*, Oxford, 1949

A. ARMSTRONG: *Unconditional Surrender; the Impact of the Casablanca Policy upon World War II*, New Brunswick, New Jersey, Rutgers University Press, 1961

O. GROEHLER: 'Probleme der allierten Koalition', *Z.F. Militärgeschichte*, no. 2, 1965

F. O. MIKSCHE: *Unconditional Surrender*, London, Faber and Faber, 1952

M. HOWARD: 'La pensée stratégique britannique', *Revue d'histoire de la deuxième guerre mondiale*, April 1971

CHAPTER 2 THE AMERICAN ARSENAL

R. PALMER, B. WILEY, W. KEAST: *The Army Ground Forces; the Procurement and Training of Ground Combat Troops*, Washington, US Government Printing Office, 1948

B. GOLD: *Wartime Economic Planning in Agriculture*, New York, Wiley, 1950

R. H. CONNERY: *The Navy and the Industrial Mobilisation in World War Two*, Princeton, Princeton University Press, 1951

J. CRAFT: *A Survey of the American Economy*, New York, North River Press, 1947

P. HOMAN: 'Economics in the War Period', *American Economist Review*, 1946, pp. 855–71

H. MURPHY: *The National Debt in War and Transition*, New York, McGraw Hill, 1950

L. V. CHANDLER: *Inflation in the United States, 1940–1948*, New York, Harper, 1951

F. WITNEY: *Wartime Experiences in the National Labor Relations Board*, Urbana, 1949

R. ELBATON SMITH: *The Army and Economic Mobilization*, Washington, Department of the Army, 1959

B. FAIRCHILD and J. GROSSMAN: *The Army and Industrial Manpower*, *ibid.*, 1959

D. NELSON: *Arsenal of Democracy, the Story of the American War Production*, New York, Harcourt Brace, 1946

D. NOVICK, M. ANSHEN, W. TRUPPNER: *Wartime Production Controls*, New York, Columbia University, 1950

L. CHANDLER and D. WALLACE: *Economic Mobilisation and Stabilisation*, New York, Holt, 1951

SCITOVSKY, E. SHAW, L. TARSHIS: *Mobilising Resources for War*, New York, McGraw Hill, 1951

E. JANEWAY: *The Struggle for Survival, a Chronicle of Economic Mobilisation in World War Two*, New Haven, Yale University Press, 1951

F. WALTON: *Miracle of World War Two; How American Industry Made Victory Possible*, New York, Macmillan, 1956

R. LEIGHTON and R. W. COAKLEY: *Global Logistics and Strategy, 1940–1943*, Washington, Department of the Army, 1955

J. D. MILLETT: *The Army Service Forces*, Washington, *ibid.*, 1954

C. GREEN, M. THOMSON, P. ROOTS: *The Ordnance Department*, Washington, 1955

W. F. CRAVEN and J. L. CATE: *The Army Air Forces in World War Two*, 6 vols., Chicago University Press, 1965

S. CONN and B. FAIRCHILD: *The Framework of Hemisphere Defense*, Washington, US Government Printing Office, 1960

J. BRIGANTE: *The Feasibility Dispute, Determination of War Production Objectives for 1942 and 1943*, Washington, Committee on Public Administration Cases, 1950

W. RUNDELL: *Black Market Money*, Baton Rouge, Louisiana University Press, 1964

R. MOSSE: 'La mobilisation économique aux Etats-Unis', *Revue d'histoire de la deuxième guerre mondiale*, no. 12, October 1953 (pp. 1–9)

J. NERE: 'Points de vue sur l'économie de guerre aux U.S.A.', *ibid.*, no. 17, January 1954, pp. 37–47

        'Logistique et stratégie de l'alliance anglo-américaine', *ibid.*, no. 27, July 1957 p. 1–19

R. M. LEIGHTON: 'Les armes ou les armées', *ibid.*, no. 65, January 1967, pp. 7–25

A. BLUM and J. GROSSMANN: 'Le problème de la main d'œuvre industrielle', *ibid.*, pp. 25–37

E. SMITH: 'La mobilisation économique', *ibid.*, pp. 37–75

T. B. WORSLEY: 'La stabilisation économique', *ibid.*, pp. 75–94

J. KIRK and R. YOUNG: *Great Weapons of World War Two*, New York, Walker and Co., 1962

VIII British War Production

M. HANCOCK, and M. GOWING: *British War Economy*, London, HMSO, 1949

J. D. SCOTT and R. HUGHES: *Administration of War Production*, London, HMSO, 1950

M. M. POSTAN: *Design and Development of Weapons*, London, HMSO, 1964
        British War Production, London, HMSO, 1951

J. HURTSFIELD: *The Control of Materials*, London, HMSO, 1953

R. TITMUS: *Problems of Social Policy*, London, Longman, Green, 1950

D. N. CHESTER: *Lessons of the British War Economy*, London, Cambridge University Press, 1951

W. H. B. COURT: *Coal*, London, HMSO, 1951

R. J. HAMMOND: *Food*, London, HMSO, 3 vols., 1951, 1956, 1962

R. S. SAYERS: *Financial Policy*, London, HMSO, 1956

SNOW: *Science and Government*, Cambridge, Mass., Harvard University Press, 1961

H. PARKER: *Manpower*, London, HMSO, 1957

K. MURRAY: *Agriculture*, London, HMSO, 1955

E. HARGREAVES and M. GOWING: *Civil Industry and Trade*, London, HMSO, 1952

S. FERGUSON and H. FITZGERALD: *Studies in the Social Services*, London, HMSO, 1954

P. INMAN: *Labour in the Munitions Industries*, London, HMSO, 1957

W. HORNBY: *Factories and Plant*, London, HMSO, 1958

Statistical Digest of the War, London, HMSO, 1951

F. DONNISON: *Central Organisation and Planning*, London, HMSO, 1966

B. SABINE: *British Budgets in Peace and War (1932–1945)*, London, Allen and Unwin, 1970, New York, Verry, Lawrence, 1971

A. CALDER: *The People's War; Britain 1939–1945*, London, Cape, 1969, New York, Pantheon, 1969

Mrs GOWING: 'La mobilisation économique', *Revue d'histoire de la deuxième guerre mondiale*, April 1973

A. MARWICK: 'L'impact de la deuxième guerre mondiale sur les Britanniques,' *Revue d'histoire de la deuxième guerre mondiale*, April 1973

CHAPTER 3   THE SOVIET WAR

I   The Conduct of the War

J.-J. MARIE: *Staline*, Paris, Editions du Seuil, 1967

M. RASCATE: 'L'Etat soviétique pendant la grande guerre patriotique', *Revue d'histoire de la deuxième guerre mondiale*, no. 68, October 1967

J. STALIN: *On the Great Patriotic War of the Soviet Union*, Moscow, 1944 and London, Hutchinson, 1945

N. VOZNESSENSKI: *L'économie de guerre dans la période de la guerre nationale*, Paris, Librairie Médicis, 1948

J. HALPERIN: 'L'économie soviétique pendant la guerre', *Revue d'histoire de la deuxième guerre mondiale*, no. 6, April 1952

A. BELIKOV: 'Transfert de l'Industrie soviétique vers l'Est', *ibid.*, no. 43, July 1961, pp. 38–48

G. GIRAULT: 'L'effort humain de l'arrière pendant la première partie de la grande guerre patriotique', *ibid.*, no. 68, October 1967

P. SORLIN: *La Russe soviétique*, Paris, Colin, 1964, and summary of various Soviet works: *Revue d'histoire de la deuxième guerre mondiale*, no. 51, July 1963

C. BETTELHEIM: *L'économie soviétique*, Paris, Sirey, 1950

N. LIPATOV: *The Metallurgical Industry in the Urals During the Great Patriotic War*, Moscow, Academy of Science, 1960. (In Russian. Review by R. PORTAL, *Revue d'histoire de la deuxième guerre mondiale*, no. 51, July 1963)

R. CAMPBELL: *Soviet Economic Power*, Boston, Houghton-Mifflin, 1966, London, Macmillan, 1967

Ray MEDVEDEV: *Let History Judge*, London, Macmillan, 1972, New York, Knopf, 1972

C. CONSTANTINI: *Les grands chefs militaires soviétiques*, Paris, Ministère de la Défense Nationale, 1971

III   Russian Neo-Nationalism

M. LARAN: 'Le Folklore soviétique 1941–1945', *Revue d'histoire de la deuxième guerre mondiale*, no. 68, October 1967

A. KRIEGEL: La dissolution du Komintern, *ibid.*

Jane DEGRAS: *The Communist International*, Vol. III, London, Oxford University Press, 1965

A. BURMEISTER: *Dissolution and Aftermath of the Comintern; Experiences and Observations*, New York, Research Programme on the USSR, 1955

J. HERNANDEZ: *La grande trahison*, Paris Fasquelle, 1953

M. THOREZ: *Son of the People*, London, Lawrence and Wishart, 1938

A. MARTY: *L'affaire Marty*, Paris, Deux Rives, 1955

U. VLAKHOVITCH: article in *Est-Ouest*, no. 216, pp. 16–31, May 1959

R. MAZAUD: 'Signification politique de l'armée soviétique', *Revue militaire d'information*, February 1959

CHAPTER 4   THE STRANGE ALLIANCE

Stalin's Correspondence with Churchill, Attlee, Roosevelt and Truman, 1941–5, 2 vols. in 1, London (USSR pr.), 1958. (Summary by Henri MICHEL, *Revue d'histoire de la deuxième guerre mondiale*, no. 34, April 1959, pp. 1–8)

H. FEIS: *Churchill, Roosevelt, Stalin*, Princeton, Princeton University Press, 1957

P. A. SOROKIN: *Russia and the United States*, London, Stevens, 1950

General J. DEANE: *The Strange Alliance*, London, Murray, 1947

Admiral STANDLEY and A. AGETON: *Admiral Ambassador to Russia*, Chicago, 1955

W. P. and Z. COATES: *A History of Anglo-Soviet Relations*, Vol. II *1943–1945*, London, Lawrence and Wishart, 1958

V. ISRAELIAN: *The Coalition Against Hitler*, Moscow, Mezdunerodnye otnosenija, 1964. (In Russian. Review by M. FERRO, *Revue d'histoire de la deuxième guerre mondiale*, no. 41, January 1964, pp. 29–40)

I. MAISKY: *Before the Storm: Recollections*. (Extracts were published in *Le Figaro*, March 18–24, 1965)

J. TRISKA and D. FINLEY: *Soviet Foreign Policy*, London and New York, Macmillan, 1968

L. FISCHER: *Russia's Road from Peace to War*, New York, Harper and Row, 1969

'Le second front', *Recherches internationales à la lumière du Marxisme*, Sept., Dec. 1958

General ZHILIN: *Rôle et place du front germano-soviétique dans les opérations militaires*, *ibid.*

G. KENNAN: *Russia and the West under Lenin and Stalin*, New York, New American Library, 1962

E. R. STETTINIUS: *Lend-Lease, Weapon for Victory*, New York, Macmillan, 1944

H. D. HALL: *North American Supply*, London, HMSO, 1955

Admiral SCHOFIELD: *The Russian Convoys*, London, Batsford, 1964

Sir Reader BULLARD: 'Persia in the Two World Wars', *The Royal Central Asian Society Journal*, Jan. 1963

L. KOGAN: *The Struggle for Germany*, Edinburgh, Edinburgh University Press, 1963

Sikorski Institute: *Documents on Polish-Soviet relations*, Vol. I, 1939–1943, London, Heinemann, 1961

W. KOWALSKI: 'Les puissances occidentales et la frontière polono-allemande pendant la deuxième guerre mondiale', *La Pologne et les Affaires occidentales*, Zachodni Institute, Poznan, nos. 1 and 2, 1965

H. de MONTFORT: *Le massacre de Katyn, crime russe ou allemand?* Paris, La Table Ronde, 1966

P. WANDYCZ: *Czechoslovak Polish Confederation and the Great Powers*, Bloomington, University of Indiana, 1956

E. BENES: *From Munich to New World and New Victory*, Cambridge, Riverside Press, 1954

P. KLEIST: *The European Tragedy*, Douglas, I.O.M., Times Press, London, Gibbs and Phillips, 1965

S. KOT: *Polish Ambassador to the USSR*, London, Oxford University Press, 1963

Part II   THE ITALIAN SURRENDER

CHAPTER I   THE END OF THE WAR IN AFRICA

General ANDERSON: Report in *Supplement to the London Gazette*, Nov. 1946

General KOELTZ: *Une campagne que nous avons gagnée*, Paris, Hachette, 1959
article in *Revue de Paris*, April 1959

General MESSE: *La prima armata italiana in Tunisia*, Milan, Rizzoli, 1960

General BARRE: *Tunisie 1942–1943*, Paris, Berger-Levrault, 1950

BLUMENSON: *The Kasserine Pass*, Boston, Houghton, Mifflin, 1967, *Rommel's Last Victory: Battle of the Kasserine Pass*, London, Allen and Unwin, 1968

K. MACKSEY: *Crucible of Power, the Fight for Tunisia*, London, Hutchinson, 1969

III Darlan's Reign

Foreign Relations of the United States, 1943, Vols. I and IV; *1944*, Vols. I and V

A. DARLAN: *L'amiral Darlan parle*, Paris, Amiot-Dumont, 1953

R. MURPHY: *Diplomat Among Warriors*, London, Collins, 1964

General JUIN: *Mémoires, Alger, Tunis, Rome*, Vol. I, Paris, Fayard, 1959

General GIRAUD: *Un seul but, la victoire*, Paris, Julliard, 1949

J. SOUSTELLE: *Envers et contre tout*, Vol. II, Paris, Laffont, 1950

Henri MICHEL: 'Le giraudisme', *Revue d'histoire de la duexième guerre mondiale*, no. 35, July 1959

C. PAILLAT: *L'échiquier d'Alger*, Vol. II, Paris, Laffont, 1967

General CATROUX: *Dans la bataille de Mediterranée*, Paris, Julliard, 1949

Admiral ROBERT: *La France aux Antilles*, Paris, Plon, 1950

A. ANNET: *Aux heures troubles d l'Afrique française*, Paris, Conquistador, 1952

P. TOMPKINS: *The Murder of Admiral Darlan*, London, Weidenfeld and Nicolson, 1965

M. VIGNERAS: *Rearming the French*, Washington, US Government Printing Office, 1958

'Le réarmement des Français', *Revue historique de l'Armee*, no. 2, 1957

Commissioner MONDIN: 'Le réarmement en A.F.N. en 1943', *Forces aériennes françaises*, July 1949

LERECOUVREUX: *Résurrection de l'armée française*, Paris, Nouvelles Editions Latines, 1955

Commandant PETITJEAN: 'Le réarmement des troupes françaises en 1942', *Revue historique de l'Armée*, no. 4, 1953

A. FUNK: *Charles de Gaulle, the Crucial Years*, Norman, University of Oklahoma, 1959

D. WHITE: *Seeds of Discord; De Gaulle, Free France and the Allies*, New York, Syracuse University Press, 1964

M. VIORST: *Hostile Allies; F.D.R. (F. D. Roosevelt) and Charles de Gaulle*, New York, Syracuse University Press, 1965

General SCHMIDT: *Toute la vérité sur le procès Pucheu*, Paris, Plon, 1963

R. RAINERO: 'Il movimento nazionalista e la situazione dell, Algeria dal 1940 à oggi', *Oriente moderno*, Nov. 1954

J. de LA ROCHE: *Le gouverneur général Félix Eboué*, Paris, Hachette, 1957

R. ARON: *Histoire de l'épuration*, Vol. I, Paris, Fayard, 1967

Y. DANAN: *La vie politique à Alger de 1940 à 1944*, Algiers, Librairie de Droit et de Jurisprudence, 1963

R. BOUSCAT: *De Gaulle-Giraud, dossier d'une mission*, Paris, Flammarion, 1967

MACMILLAN: *La grande tourmente*, Paris, Plon, 1967

A. KASPI: *La mission de Jean Monnet à Alger*, Paris, Editions Richelieu, 1971

CHAPTER 2   ITALY SURRENDERS

I The Sicilian Campaign

A. B. CUNNINGHAM: 'The Invasion of Sicily', *Supplement to the London Gazette*, April 25, 1950, pp. 2077–97

A. GARLAND, Lieutenant-Colonel MCGOW, H. SMITH, M. BLUMENSON: *Sicily and the Surrender of Italy*, Washington, Department of the Army, 1965

H. POND: *Sicily*, London, William Kimber, 1962

M. BLUMENSON: 'Sicily and Italy, Why and What For?', *Military Review*, Feb. 1966

R. LEIGHTON: 'Planning of Sicily', *US Naval Institute Proceedings*, May 1962

C. CIGLIANA: 'Le operazioni anglo-americane in Italia nell' autumno del 1943', *Rivista militare*, Dec. 1963

H. POND: *Salerno*, London, Kimber, 1961

J. WERSTEIN: *The Battle of Salerno*, New York, Crowell, 1965

U. CAVALLERO: *Commando supremo*, Bologna, Capelli, 1948

III   The Italian Resistance

Cf. the collection of *Movimento di liberazione in Italia*, Milan

C. DELZELL: *Mussolini's Enemies*, Princeton, Princeton University Press, 1961

F. PARRI and F. VENTURI: *The Italian Resistance and the Allies, European Resistance Movements*, London, Pergamon, 1964

R. BATTAGLIA: *The Story of the Italian Resistance*, London, 1957

G. VACCARINO: *Problemi della Resistenza italiana*, S.T.E.M., Mucchi, Modene, 1966

F. CHABOD: *A History of Italian Fascism*, London, Weidenfeld and Nicolson, 1963

M. SALVADORI: *Storia della Resistenza italiana*, Venice, Neri Pozza, 1955

E. COLLOTTI: 'L'occupation, la Resistance et les Allies', *Revue histoire de la deuxième guerre mondiale*, October 1973

M. LEGNANI: 'La Societé italienne et la Resistance', *Revue d'histoire de la deuxième guerre mondiale*, October 1973

L. VALIANI, G. BIANCO, E. RAGIONIERI, *Azionisti, Cattolici e communisti nella Resistenza*, Milan, 1971

IV   The Plot against Mussolini

F. DEBYSER: 'La chute du régime', *Revue d'histoire de la deuxième guerre mondiale*, no. 26, April 1957, pp. 24–59

P. PUNTONI: *Parla Vittorio Emanuele III*, Rome, Palazzi, 1958

G. BOTTAI: *Vent 'anni e un giorno*, Milan, Garzanti, 1949

General ROSSI: *Come arrivammo al armistizio*, Milan, Garzanti, 1945

SENISE: *Quando ero capo della polizia*, Rome, Ruffolo, 1946

E. GALBIATI: *Il 25 luglio e la MVSN*, Milan, Bernabo, 1950

W. F. D. DEAKIN: *The Brutal Friendship*, London, Weidenfeld and Nicolson, 1962

M. VAUSSARD: *La conjuration du Grand Conseil fasciste contre Mussolini*, Paris, Del Duca, 1965

E. DOLLMANN: *Roma nazista*, Conganelli, 1951

E. von RINTELEN: *Mussolini als Bundesgenosse*, Leins, 1951

R. RAHN: *Ruheloses Leben*, Düsseldorf, Diederichs Verlag, 1949

V. ARALDI: *La crisi italiana dell' 1943*, Milan, Silva, 1964

G. BIANCHI: *25 luglio, crollo di un regime*, Milan, Mursia, 1963

E. BASTIANINI: *Uomini, Cose, Fatti*, Vitigliano, 1959

VI   The Italian Surrender

M. GUARIGLIA: *Ricordi*, Naples, Editions Sc. It., 1949

I. BONOMI: *Diario di un anno*, Milan, Garzanti, 1947

H. SMITH: 'The Armistice of Cassibile', *Military Affairs*, Spring 1948

R. ZANGRANDI: *1943, 25 luglio, 8 settembre*, Milan, Feltrinelli, 1964

Mario TOSCANO: *Dal 25 luglio all' 8 settembre*, Florence, Lemonnier, 1966

C. VIDAL: 'La marine de guerre italienne et l'armistice du 3 septembre', *Revue d'histoire de la deuxième guerre mondiale*, no. 2, April 1951

Admiral FRANCO: *Pennello nero*, Rome, 1945

P. PIERI: 'La storiografia italiana relativa al 25 juglio e all' 8 settembre', *Movimento di liberazione in Italia*, Oct., Dec. 1964

MUSCA: *La verità sull' 8 settembre 1943*, Milan, Garzanti, 1965

General CASTELLANO: *Come firmai l'armistizio di Cassibile*, Milan, Mondadori, 1945

VIII   The Liberation of Corsica

J. A. LIVRELLI: *L'occupation italienne de la Corse*, Ajaccio, Freschi, 1949

General MAGLI: *Le truppe italiane in Corsica*, Lecce, Typographia Schola, 1953

R. SEREAU: *La libération de la Corse*, Paris, Peyronnet, 1955

Commandant J. LHERMINIER: *Casabianca: the Secret Missions of a Famous Submarine*, London, Miller, 1953

CHOURY: *Tous bandits d'honneur*, Paris, Editions Sociales, 1956

E. PIQUET WICKS: *Four in the Shadows: a True Story of Espionage in Occupied France*, London, Jarrolds, 1957. (On Scamaroni)

General MARTIN: 'Aspects militaires de la libération de la Corse', *Revue historique de l'Armée*, Feb. 1959

I. GRIFFI: 'Mission spéciale en Corse', *Revue de la France libre*, Nov. 1954

GAMBIEZ: *La libération de la Corse*, Paris, Hachette, 1973

IX   The Division of Italy

Marshal BADOGLIO: *Italy in the Second World War*, London, Oxford University Press, 1948

H. S. HUGHES: *The United States and Italy*, Cambridge, Mass., Harvard University Press, 1953

N. KOGAN: *Italy and the Allies*, Cambridge, Mass., Harvard University Press, 1956

C. R. S. HARRIS: *Allied Military Administration of Italy*, London, HMSO, 1957

P. SECCHIA and P. FRASSATI: *La Resistenza e gli alleati*, Milan, Feltrinelli, 1962

LIZZARDI: *Il regno di Badoglio*, Milan, Avanti, 1963

F. CATALANO: *L'Italia della dittatura alla democrazia*, Milan, Lerici, 1962

General SCALA: *La riscossa dell'Esercito*, Rome, 1948

La Marina dall' 8 settembre 1943 alla fine del conflitto, Rome, Officio storico, 1962

Documenti relativi ai rapporti tra l'Italia e le nazioni unite, Rome, Ministry of Foreign Affairs, 1945

A. ESPINOSA: *Il regno del sud*, Rome, Migliaresi, 1946

Le concours italien dans la guerre contre l'Allemagne, Rome, Ministry for Foreign Affairs, 1946

V. PETROV: *Money and Conquest*, Baltimore, Johns Hopkins Press, 1967

G. A. SHEPPERD: *The Italian Campaign*, London, A. Barker, 1968, New York, Praeger, 1968

G. BOULLE: *Le corps expéditionnaire français en Italie*, Paris, Imprimerie Nationale, 1973

'L'armistizio, gli Alleati e il governo Badoglio', *Movimento di liberazione in Italia*, nos. 54 to 57, 1960

Book Four   THE DEFEAT OF GERMANY

Part I   THE ALLIED OFFENSIVE

CHAPTER I   THE BOMBING OF GERMANY

I   The Financing of the Nazi War

Dieter PEZINA: 'La politique financière et fiscale de l'Allemagne pendant la deuxième guerre mondiale', *Revue d'histoire de la deuxième guerre mondiale*, no. 76, October 1969

Fritz FEDEREAU: *Der Zweite Weltkrieg; seine Finanzierung in Deutschland*, Tübingen, 1962

Friedrich LÜTGE: 'Die deutsche Kriegsfinanzierung im Ersten und Zweiten Weltkrieg', *Festschrift für Rudolf Stucken*, Göttingen, 1953

Schwerin von KROSIGK: 'Wie wurde der Zweite Weltdrieg finanziert', in *Bilan des Zweiten Weltkrieges*, Oldenburg, 1953

II   The Organisation of the German War Economy

Die deutsche Industrie im Kriege, Berlin, Duncker und Humblot, 1954

B. KLEIN: *Germany's Economic Preparation for War, 1933–1942*, Cambridge, Mass., Harvard University Press, 1959

A. MILWARD: *The German Economy at War*, London, Athlone Press, 1965

W. BIRKENFELD: *Der syntetische Treibstoff, 1933–1945*, Göttingen, Munterschmidt Verlag, 1964

E. HAMPE: *Der zivile Luftschutz im Zweiten Weltkrieg*, Frankfurt am Main, Bernard und Graefe Verlag, 1963

S. VON KROSIGK: *Es geschah in Deutschland*, Tübingen, Rainer Wunderlich Verlag, 1951

E. GEORG: *Die wirtschaftlichen Unternehmungen der S.S.*, Stuttgart, Deutsche Verlagsanstalt, 1963

H. E. KANNAPIN: *Wirtschaft unter Zwang*, Cologne, Deutsche Industrie Verlag, 1966

E. HEINCKEL: *A l'assaut du ciel*, Paris, Plon, 1955

R. DUBAIL: *L'Allemagne nationale socialiste et son économie*, Paris, I.P.D., 1962

I. ESENWEIN-ROTHE: *Die Wirtschaftsverbände von 1933 bis 1945*, Berlin, Duncker und Humblot, undated

L. DAVIN: *Les finances de 1939 à 1945*, Vol. II *L'Allemagne*, Paris, Librairie Médicis, 1949

Joseph BILLIG: 'Les prisonniers de guerre dans l'économie de guerre allemand', *Revue d'histoire de la deuxième guerre mondiale*, no. 37, January 1960, pp. 53–77

A. PIRIE: *Operation Bernhard*, London, Cassell, 1961

Wolfgang BLEYER: *Staat und Monopole im totalen Krieg 1943*, Berlin-Est, 1970

Joseph BILLIG: *Les camps de concentration dans l'economie du Reich hitlérien*, Paris, P.U.F., 1973

A. SPEER, *Inside the Third Reich*, New York, Macmillan, 1970, London, Weidenfeld and Nicolson, 1970

Gregor JANSSEN: *Das Ministerium Speer. Deutschlands Rustung im Krieg*, Berlin, Frankfurt/M., Vienna, Verlag Ullstein, 1968

J. M. D'HOOP: 'La main-d'oeuvre française au service de l'Allemange', *Revue d'histoire de la deuxième guerre mondiale*, no. 81, January 1971

Karl Heinz LUDWIG: 'Fabrications de fusées et strategie', *Revue d'histoire de la deuxième guerre mondiale*, no. 84, October 1971

VI   The British and the Bombing of Germany

Der Luftkrieg über Deutschland, München, Deutscher Taschenbuch Verlag, 1963

C. WEBSTER and Sir Noble FRANKLAND: *The Strategic Air Offensive Against Germany*, London, HMSO, 4 vols., 1961

G. QUESTER: 'Bargaining and Bombing during World War Two', *World Politics*, no. 3, April 1963

H. RUMPF: *The Bombing of Germany*, London, Muller, 1963

Lieutenant-Colonel STACEY: 'The Bombing of Germany', *Revue militaire générale*, July 1963

D. IRVING: *The Destruction of Dresden*, London, 1963, revised and updated 1966 (Corgi Books)

M. CAIDIN: *The Night Hamburg Died*, New York, Ballantine Books, 1960
Black Thursday, New York, Dutton, 1960

J. DUGAN: *Ploesti, the Great Ground Air Battle of 1st August 1943*, New York, Random, 1962

Colonel TARLE : 'Bombardements stratégiques', *Forces aériennes françaises*, Sept. 1948
Lieutenant-Colonel CHEMIDLIN : 'La guerre des ondes dans l'aviation', *ibid.*, Dec. 1946
Colonel VENOT : 'Stratégie britannique et bombardements', *ibid.*, April 1948
Commandant GAROT : 'Bombardement tactique dans la R.A.F.', *ibid.*, Jan. 1949
T. WEBER : 'Evolution de la tactique du radar', *ibid.*, Dec. 1959
R. BARKER : *The Thousand Plan*, London, Chatto and Windus, 1965
Marshal TEDDER : *With Prejudice; the War Memoirs of the Marshal of the Royal Air Force*, London, Cassell, 1966
A. VERRIER : *The Bomber Offensive*, London, Batsford, 1968, New York, Macmillan, 1969

CHAPTER 2   THE SOVIET OFFENSIVE. THE TEHERAN CONFERENCE
(July 1943–May 1944)

C. FISCHER : *The Life and Death of Stalin*, New York, Harper, 1952
I. DEUTSCHER : *Stalin; a Political Biography*, London, Oxford University Press, 1949
M. TANSKY : *Joukov, le maréchal d'acier*, Paris, Laffont, 1955
M. CHERNIAVSKY : 'Corporal Hitler, General Winter and the Russian Peasant', *The Yale Review*, Summer 1962
A. CLARK : *Barbarossa; the Russian-German Conflict, 1941–5*, London, Hutchinson, 1965 and Penguin, 1966
A. FONTAINE : *History of the Cold War*, Vol. I, London, Secker and Warburg, 1968
General COSSE-BRISSAC : 'La campagne de Russie, de Kharkov à Berlin', *Revue historique de l' Armée*, no. 4, 1949
Colonel PAVLENKO : Article on the weapons and units of the Red Army, *Revue historique militaire soviétique*, March 1966. (Summary by Colonel COSTANTINI)
PROKHORKOV and TRUSOV : 'L'artillerie à réaction soviétique', *ibid.*, Jan. 1966. (Summary by Colonel COSTANTINI)
G. CASTELLAN : 'La politique allemande de l'U.R.S.S.', *Revue d'histoire de la deuxième guerre mondiale*, nos. 21 and 22, January and April 1956
S. XYDIS : article on the Churchill–Stalin agreement, *Journal of Central European Affairs*, Oct. 1955

III   Operation 'Citadel'

General KUROCKI : *Inter-Service Co-operation in Attack*, Moscow, 1966. (In Russian. Review by Captain NOULENS, *Revue d'histoire de la deuxième guerre mondiale*, no. 67, October 1967)
A. HILLGRUBER : *Die Räumung der Krim*, Berlin, Mitter und Sohn, 1959
Colonel CHAMPEAUX : 'Les leçons du front russe', *Revue de défense nationale*, Nov. 1952
J. MARKIN : *Die Kursker Schlacht*, German Democratic Republic, Berlin, Ministry of Defence, 1960. (Translated from the Russian. Analysis by Colonel COSTANTINI, *L'Union Soviétique en guerre*, Paris, Imprimerie Nationale, Vol. 3, 1968)
Colonel COSTANTINI : 'La bataille de chars de Prokhorovka', *Revue historique de l'armée*, no. 4, 1965
Colonel ACCART : 'Bataille dans le ciel russe', *Forces aériennes françaises*, no. 19, April 1948
General BOURCART : 'La guerre en Finlande', *Revue d'histoire de la deuxième guerre mondiale*, no. 9, January 1953
W. REHM : *Jassy*, Neckargemünd, Kurt Vowinckel, 1959

H. KISSEL: *Die Katastrophe in Rumänien*, Darmstadt, Wehr Wissenverlagsgesellschaft, 1964

Colonel LEDERREY: 'Entre Don et Donetz, les opérations de von Manstein en Russie de Sud', *Revue militaire suisse*, Nov. 1956 and Nov. 1959

E. KLINK: *Das Gesetz des Handelns: die Operation Zitadelle*, Stuttgart, Deutscher Verlag, 1966

VI The 'Big Three' at Teheran

J. M. BLUM: *From the Morgenthau Diaries*, Vol. III, Boston, Houghton Mifflin, 1967

H. FEIS: *Churchill, Roosevelt, Stalin; the War they Waged and the Peace they Sought*, Princeton, Princeton University Press, 1957

Frances PERKINS: *The Roosevelt I Knew*, New York, 1947

M. MISSE: 'Le rôle des Etats-Unis dans les Conferérences de Caire et de Téhéran', *Revue d'histoire de la deuxième guerre mondiale*, July 1968

J. M. BRUGEL: 'Teheran, Yalta und Potsdam aus sowjetischer Sicht', *Europa Archiv*, November 25 1966

'Die Konferenz von Teheran zwischen den Oberhäuptern der drei Grossmächte', *Die Aussenpolitik*, Sept.–Oct. 1961

R. BEITZELL: *The Uneasy Alliance, America, Britain and Russia*, New York, Alfred A., Knopf, 1972

XI Partisan Warfare

A. FEDOROV: *L'obkom clandestin au travail*, Paris, Les Editeurs français réunis, 2 vols., 1951

Brigadier DIXON and Dr O. HEILBRUNN: *Communist Guerrilla Warfare*, London, Allen and Unwin, 1954

C. KIZIA: 'La lutte du peuple ukrainien', *Revue d'histoire de la deuxième guerre mondiale*, no. 43, July 1961, pp. 21–35. (Analysis by Colonel COSTANTINI, *L'Union Soviétique en Guerre*, Paris, Imprimerie Nationale, Vol. 3, 1968)

E. von DOHNANY: 'Combatting Soviet Guerrillas', *Marine Corps Gazette*, Feb. 1955

M. ADLER-BRESSE: 'Témoignages allemands sur la guerre des partisans', *Revue d'histoire de la deuxième guerre mondiale*, no. 53, Jan. 1964, pp. 51–60

J. ARMSTRONG: *Soviet Partisans in World War Two*, University of Wisconsin, 1964

C. ANDRIANOV: 'La lutte armée des partisans sovietiques dans la grande guerre nationale', *Revue historique de l'Armée*, no. 1, 1973

XII Soviet Espionage

W. F. FLIKE: *Agenten funken nach Moskau*, Kreuzlingen, Neptun Verlag, 1954

General C. A. WILLOUGHBY: *Sorge: Soviet Master Spy*, London, Kimber, 1952

H. O. MEISSNER: *The Man with Three Faces* (on R. Sorge), London, Evans Bros., 1955

G. PERRAULT: *The Red Orchestra*, London, Arthur Barker, 1968

F. W. D. DEAKIN: *The Case of Richard Sorge*, London, Chatto and Windus, 1966

J. BOURCART: *L'espionnage soviétique*, Paris, Fayard, 1962

R. DEACON: *A History of the Russian Secret Service*, New York, Taplinger, 1970, London, Garden City Press, 1972

CHAPTER 3 SOVIET VICTORIES. THE DESATELLISATION OF GREATER GERMANY
(June–December 1944)

I Alarm amongst the Satellites

R. BOVA SCOPPA: *Colloqui con due dittatori*, Rome, Ruffolo, 1949

G. RANKI: 'L'occupation de la Hongrie', *Revue d'histoire de la deuxième guerre mondiale*, no. 62, April 1966, pp. 37–53

I. POPESCO-PUTURI: 'L'importance historique de l'insurrection armée d'août 1944', *Nouvelles Etudes historiques*, 1965

K. MENEGHELLO-DINČIČ: 'L'Etat oustacha de Croatie', *Revue d'histoire de la deuxième guerre mondiale*, no. 74, April 1969

I. DIMITROV: 'La politique extérieure du gouvernement d'Ivan Bagrianov', *Revue d'histoire de la deuxième guerre mondiale*, no. 13, January 1974, and 'La mort du roi Boris', *ibid.*, no. 83, July 1971

II The Committee for Free Germany

B. SCHEURIG: *Free Germany; the National Committee and the League of German Officers*, Middletown, Conn., 1969

E. WEINERT: *Das Nationalkomitee Freies Deutschland*, Berlin-Est, Rutten und Loening, 1957

Heinrich Graf von EINSIEDEL: *The Shadow of Stalingrad; Being the Diary of Temptation*, London, Alan Wingate, 1953

J. von PUTTKAMER: *Irrtum und Schuld: Geschichte des Nationalkomitee Freies Deutschland*, Berlin, Michael Verlag, 1948

General KORKES: 'Nationalkomitee Freies Deutschland', in *Juni 1941*, Berlin, German Democratic Republic, 1961

V The Warsaw Uprising

H. HUBERT: *Borem Lasem*, Warsaw, Ministry of Defence, 1958

Ksiega Zolnierza Polskiego, Warsaw, Ministry of Defence, 1958. (Review by KRAWIEC, *Revue d'histoire de la deuxième guerre mondiale*, no. 46, April 1962)

General KIRCHMAYER: *Some Polish Problems*, Warsaw, Ministry of Defence, 1959. (In Polish. Review by J.-B. NEVEUX, *ibid.*)

General BOR-KOMOROVSKY: *The Secret Army*, London, Gollancz, 1950

The Polish Armed Forces in the Second World War, London, Sikorski Institute, Vol. III, Armia Krajova, 1956. (In Polish)

Ludnosc ci jwilna W. Postaniu Warszawskim (The civilian population in the Warsaw Uprising), Warsaw, 1974, 4 vols.

J. SOLC: 'Le mouvement slovaque des partisans', *Revue d'histoire de la deuxième guerre mondiale*, no. 52, October 1963, pp. 61–79

F. JANACEK: 'La stratégie et la tactique du parti communiste tchécoslovaque dans la lutte de libération nationale contre l'occupant fasciste', *Ceskolovensky Casopis Historicky*, Vol. 4, no. 1, 1956. (Summary by OSUSKY, *Revue d'histoire de la deuxième guerre mondiale*, no. 45, Jan. 1962)

F. BEER, et al.: *An Historical Crossroads. The Slovak National Uprising, its Prelude and Results*, Bratislava, V.P.P., 1964. (In Czech and in Slovak. Review by M. L. LIPTAK, *Revue d'histoire de la deuxième guerre mondiale*, July 1967)

Admiral ALEXANDRIS: *Our Navy During the War Years*, Athens, Aetos, 1952. (In Greek. Summary by M. MARGARITIS, *Revue d'histoire de la deuxième guerre mondiale*, no. 13, January 1954)

R. KENNEDY: *German antiguerrilla operations in the Balkans*, Washington, US Government Printing Office, 1954

G. GHEORGUIEV: 'Annales de l'héroïsme', *Bulgarie d'aujourd'hui*, no. 6, 1967

V. BOZHINOV: 'La libération de la Bulgarie du fascisme et de la domination capitaliste', *Etudes historiques*, Sofia, 1960

CHAPTER 4 THE WAR IN ITALY
(September 1943–December 1944)

I The Military Operations

Lord ALEXANDER: *The Italian Campaign*, Report, London, HMSO, 1951
E. LINKLATER: *The Campaign of Italy*, London, HMSO, 1951
M. PUDDU: *Guerra in Italia*, Rome, Nardini, 1965
H. M. WILSON: *Eight Years Overseas*, London, Hutchinson
Field Marshal KESSELRING: *The Memoirs of Field Marshal Kesselring*, London, Kimber, 1953
General M. CLARK: *Calculated Risk*, New York, 1950
M. BLUMENSON: *Anzio, the Gamble that Failed*, Philadelphia, Lippincott, 1963
Lieutenant-Colonel MERGLEN: 'Anzio', *Revue historique de l'Armée*, no. 1, 1965
Charles CONNELL: *Monte Cassino*, London, Elek, 1963
R. BOHMMLER: *Monte Cassino*, Paris, Plon, 1956
Lieutenant-Colonel G. W. L. NICHOLSON: *The Canadians in Italy* (*Official History of the Canadian Army in the Second World War*, 2), Ottawa, 1957
E. FISCHER: Rome, an Open City, *Military Review*, August 1965
D. ORGILL: *The Gothic Line, the Autumn Campaign in Italy, 1944*, London, Heinemann, 1967
General CARPENTIER: *Les forces alliées en Italie*, Paris, Berger-Levrault, 1949
Marshal JUIN: *La campagne d'Italie*, Paris, G. Victor, 1962
M. BLUMENSON: *Bloody River: Prelude to the battle of Cassino*, London, Allen and Unwin, 1970, Boston, Houghton Mifflin, 1970
H. GREINER: *Kampf im Rom. Inferno am Po. Der Weg der 362 Infanterie-Division*, Neckar-Gemund, Kurt Vowinckel, 1970
W. G. F. JACKSON: *The Battle for Rome*, London, B. T. Batsford, 1969, New York, Scribners, 1969

III The Salo Republic

G. PERTICONE: *L'Italia contemporanea*, Milan, Mondadori, 1962
E. COLLOTTI: *L'amministrazione tedesca dell' Italia occupata*, Milan, Lerici, 1963
G. FOGAR: *Sotto l'occupazione nazista nelle provincie orientale*, Udine, Del Bianco, 1961
G. VALABREGA: 'Appunti sulla persecuzione antisemita in Italia durante l'occupazione tedesca', *Movimento di liberazione*, Jan.–March 1964
E. CIONE: *Storia della Republica sociale italiana*, Rome, Latinita editrice, 1950
E. AMICUCCI: *1600 giorni di Mussolini*, Rome, Faro, 1949
G. PINI: *Itinerario tragico*, Milan, Edizione Omnia, 1950
E. ANFUSO: *Da Palazzo Venezia al lago di Garda*, Rome, Cappelli, 1957
G. DOLFIN: *Con Mussolini nella Tragedia*, Milan, Garzanti, 1950
F. GALANTI: *Socializzazione e Sindicalismo nella R.S.I.*, Rome, Magi-Spinetti, 1949
R. MONTAGNA: *Mussolini e il processo di Verona*, Milan, Edizione Omnia, 1945
Processo Graziani, Rome, Ruffolo, 1950, Vols. II and III
A. REPACCI: 'Le procès Graziani', *Revue d'histoire de la deuxième guerre mondiale*, no. 9, January 1953
F. W. D. DEAKIN: 'Le Congrès de Vérone', *ibid.*, no. 26, April 1957
F. CATALANO: 'Le Fase de formazione della R.S.I.', *Movimento di Liberazione*, Oct., Dec. 1964

V The Partisans

Dati sulla lotta partiziana, Documenti di vita italiana, Presidenza del Consiglio dei Ministri, Rome, April 1954
G. QUAZZA: *La Resistenza italiana*, Torino, Giappichelli, 1966

M. BENDISCIOLI: *Antifascismo e Resistenza*, Rome, Studium, 1964

R. BATTAGLIA: *Trento anni di vita di lotta del P.C.I.*, Rome, Quaderni di Rinascita, 1953

G. MASTROBUENO: *Le forze armate italiane nella resistenza e nella guerre di liberazione*, Rome, 1965

G. PANZA: *La Resistenza in Piemonte, guida bibliographica*, Torino, Giamichelli, 1965

G. BOCCA: *Una republica partigiana*, Milan, Il Saggiatore, 1964

U. BRANCA: *La Resistenza in Toscana*, Mulino, Bologna, May–June 1963

R. PERRONE CAPANO: *La resistenza in Roma*, Napoli, Macchiaroli, 1963, 2 vols.

C. FRANKOVITCH: *La Resistenza a Firenze*, Florence, La nuova Italia, 1962

A. BRAVO: *La Republica partigiana dell'Alto Monferrato*, Turin, Giappichelli, 1964

G. PANSA: *Guerra partigiana tra Genova e il Po*, Latenza, 1967

G. ROCHAT: *Atti del commando Generale del C.U.L.*, preface by Ferrucio Parri, Milan, Franco Argeli, 1972

CHAPTER 5   THE LIBERATION OF FRANCE

I The Allied Victory in the Atlantic

F. POGUE: *The Supreme Command, European Theatre of Operations*, Washington, US Government Printing Office, 1954

J. EHRMANN: *Grand Strategy*, Vol. V, *August 1943–September 1944*, London, HMSO, 1956

R. RUPPENTHAL: *Logistical Support of the Armies*, Vol. I, Washington, US Government Printing Office, 1953

D. EISENHOWER: *Eisenhower's Own Story of the War; the Complete Report by the Supreme Commander on the War in Europe*, New York, Arco, 1946
    Crusade in Europe, London, Heinemann, 1948

General Bedell SMITH: *Eisenhower, Six Great Decisions, Europe, 1944–5*, New York, Longmans, Green, 1956

General O. BRADLEY: *A Soldier's Story*, New York, 1951, London, Eyre and Spottiswoode, 1951

General ARNOLD: *Global Mission*, New York, Harper and Brothers, 1949

J.-B. DUROSELLE: 'Le conflit stratégique anglo-américain (juin 40–juin 44)', *Revue d'histoire moderne*, July–Sept. 1961, pp. 161–184

L. FARAGO: *Patton, Ordeal and Triumph*, New York, Obolensky, 1963

Field Marshal MONTGOMERY: *Normandy to the Baltic*, London, Hutchinson, 1947

General PATTON: *War As I Knew It*, Boston, Houghton Mifflin, 1947

Captain BUTCHER: *My Three Years with Eisenhower*, New York, 1946

L. F. ELLIS: *Victory in the West, the Battle of Normandy*, London, HMSO, 1962

F. POGUE: *George Marshall: Organiser of Victory, 1943–1945*, New York, Viking Press, 1973

EISENHOWER FOUNDATION: *D-Day: The Normandy Invasion in retrospect*, University Press of Kansas, 1971

III The Preparation of 'Overlord'

Hans SPEIDEL: *We Defended Normandy*, London, H. Jenkins, 1951

Admiral RUGE: *Rommel face au débarquement*, Paris, Presses de la Cité, 1960

E. KENNETH: *L'opération Neptune*, Paris, La Jeune Parque, 1947

Cornelius RYAN: *The Longest Day, June 6, 1944*, London, Gollancz, 1960

C. F. A. STANFORD: *Force Mulberry*, New York, William Morrow, 1951

Colonel de LESQUEN: 'Le mur de l'Atlantique', *Revue du génie militaire*, May–June 1952

Admiral LEMONNIER: *Paisible Normandie*, Paris, La Colombe, 1954

Lieutenant-Colonel CHEMIDLIN: 'La guerre des ondes', *Forces aériennes françaises*, Dec. 1946

Commandant CHEVALIER: 'Applications de la météorologie en temps de guerre', *Revue Maritime*, no. 56, November 1956

P. BOUSSEL: *D-Day Beaches Pocket Guide*, London, Macdonald, 1965

Major BROU: 'Le miracle technique des ports artificiels', *L'Armée, la Nation*, August 1, 1954

von SCHWEPPENBURG: 'Reflections on the invasion', *Military Review*, February–March 1961

STJERNEFELT: *Alerte sur le mur de l'Atlantique*, Presses de la Cité, 1961

Admiral LEMONNIER: *Les cent jours de Normandie*, Paris, France-Empire, 1971

S. L. A. MARSHALL: *Night Drop: The American Airborne Invasion of Normandy*, Boston, Little, Brown, 1962, London, Macmillan, 1962

IX   The Action of the Resistance

Henri MICHEL: 'L'aide apportée aux Alliés par la Résistance clandestine française', *Revue politique et parlementaire*, Jan. 1963

M. BAUDOT: *L'opinion publique sous l'occupation*, Paris, Presses Universitaires de France, 1960

C. TILLON: *Les F.T.P.*, Paris, Julliard, 1962

A. DANSETTE: *Histoire de la Libération de Paris*, Paris, Fayard, 1959

Lieutenant-Colonel TANANT: *Vercors*, Grenoble, Arthaud, 1948

Robert ARON: *De Gaulle before Paris: the Liberation of France, June–Aug. 1944*, London, Putnam, 1962

De Gaulle Triumphant: the Liberation of France, Aug. 1944–May 1945, London, Putnam, 1964

A. PARODI: 'Témoignage sur trois décisions historiques', *Le Figaro*, August 19, 1964

E. POUSSARDIE: *Il y a 20 ans, Viombois*, Raon L'Etape, 1964

Les maquis dans la Libération de la France, special number of the *Revue d'histoire de la deuxième guerre mondiale*, no. 55, July 1964 (articles by M. M. LEROUX, LOMBARD, BOULADOU, CLÉMENDOT)

H. DENIS: *Le Comité parisien de Libération*, Paris, Presses Universitaires de France, 1963

P. BERTAUX: *Libération de Toulouse et de sa région*, Paris, Hachette, 1973

P. BECAMPS: *Libération de Bordeaux*, Paris, Hachette, 1973

E. DEJONGHE and D. LAURENT: *Libération du Nord et du Pas-de-Calais*, Paris, Hachette, 1973

H. INGRAND: *Libération de l'Auvergne*, Paris, Hachette, 1974

H. ROMANS-PETIT: *Les maquis de l'Ain*, Paris, Hachette, 1974

R. BOURDERON: *Libération du Languedoc*, Paris, Hachette, 1974

Y. DURANT and R. VIVIER: *Libération des pays de la Loire*, Paris, Hachette, 1974

G. GUINGOUIN: *Quatre ans de lutte dans le Limousin*, Paris, Hachette, 1974

J. GIRARD: 'L'organisation et les opérations à caractère militaire des F.F.I. dans les Alpes-Maritimes de mars à août 1944', *Revue d'histoire de la deuxième guerre mondiale*, no. 85, January 1972

X   The Advance to the Seine. Falaise

S. E. MORISON: *The Atlantic Battle Won*, Boston, Little Brown, 1954 and London, Oxford University Press, 1956

M. BLUMENSON: *European Theatre of Operations. Break Out and Pursuit*, Washington, US Government Printing Office, 1962

J. MORDAL: *La bataille de la France*, Paris, Arthaud, 1964

C. M. COLE: *Lorraine Campaign*, Washington, US Government Printing Office, 1950

C. HIBBERT: *The Battle of Arnhem*, London, Batsford, 1962

General de LANGLADE: *En suivant Leclerc, d'Alger à Berchtesgaden*, Paris, Laffont, 1964

E. BELFIELD and H. ESSAME: *The North-West Europe Campaign, 1944–5*, Aldershot, Gale and Polden, 1962

M. BLUMENSON: 'Beyond the Beaches', *Military Review*, Sept. 1962

E. FLORENTIN: *Battle of the Falaise Gap*, London, Elek Books, 1965

A. MCKEE: *Caen, Anvil or Victory*, London, Souvenir Press, 1964

M. DEVILLIERS: *Objectif Anvers*, Brussels, 1964

J. MORDAL: 'Le Dunkerque allemand de l'Escaut', *Revue militaire d'information*, May 1963

von CHOLTITZ: *Soldat unter Soldaten*, Frankfurt, Europa Verlag, 1951

XV   The Landing of August 15

Admiral LEMONNIER: *Cap sur la Provence*, Paris, France-Empire, 1954

Colonel BOUVET: *Ouvriers de la première heure*, Paris, Berger-Levrault, 1954

Captain MAIGNE: 'Les forces françaises et la jonction Overlord-Dragoon', *Revue d'histoire de la deuxième guerre mondiale*, no. 19, July 1955, pp. 17–34

M. MATLOF: 'Was the invasion of southern France a blunder?', *Naval Institute*, July 1958

P. GUIRAL: *La libération de Marseille*, Paris, Hachette, 1974

F. RUDE: *La Libération de Lyon*, Paris, Hachette, 1974

G. GRANDVAL and A. J. COLLIN: *La Libération fe l'Est de la France*, Paris, Hachette, 1974

F. L'HUILLIER: *La libération de l'Alsace*, Paris, Hachette, 1974

XVII   Liberated France

A. FUNK: 'La reconnaissance du CFLN', *Revue d'histoire de la deuxième guerre mondiale*, no. 33, January 1959

General de GAULLE: *War Memoirs*, Vol. III, London, Weidenfeld and Nicolson, 1960

A. PHILIP: 'Réformes économiques de structure', *Etudes et documents*, March–April 1945

General de GAULLE: *Speeches*, Oxford, Oxford University Press, 1943

E. GIRAUD: 'Le gouvernement du général de Gaulle, un échec relatif, *Revue politique et parlementaire*, Feb. 1948, March 1948, April 1948, May 1948, June 1948, Oct. 1948, Nov. 1948, Jan. 1949

Robert ARON: *Histoire de l'épuration*, Vols. I and II, Paris, Fayard, 1967

B. CHENOT: *Organisation économique de l'Etat*, Paris, Dalloz, 1965

MALEZIEUX: 'Index des travaux constitutionnels de l'Assemblée Consultative provisoire et de l'Assemblée nationale constituante', *Revue de droit public et de la science politique*, April–June 1946

M. BAUDOT: 'La Résistance française face aux problèmes de repression et d'épuration', *Revue d'histoire de la deuxième guerre mondiale*, no. 81, January 1971

P. NOVICK: *The Resistance Versus Vichy: The Purge of Collaborators in Liberated France*, New York, Columbia University Press, 1968, London, Chatto and Windus, 1968

A. W. DEPORTE: *De Gaulle's Foreign Policy 1944–1946*, Harvard University Press, 1968, London, Oxford University Press, 1968

Part II THE CAPITULATION OF GERMANY

CHAPTER I THE FINAL CONVULSIONS OF THE NAZI REICH

I German Opposition to Hitler

G. RITTER: *The German Resistance: Carl Goerdeler's Struggle Against Tyranny*, London, Allen and Unwin, 1958

German Resistance to Hitler, published by the Press and Information Service of the Federal Government, Bonn, Berto Verlag, 1960

Inge SCHOLL: *Six Against Tyranny*, London, John Murray, 1955

Günther LEWY: *The Catholic Church and Nazi Germany*, London, Weidenfeld and Nicolson, 1964

H. ROTHFELS: *The German Opposition to Hitler: an Assessment*, London, Wolff, 1962

W. ABENDROTH: 'Recherches sur la Résistance en République fédérale allemande', *Cahiers internationaux de la Résistance*, Nov. 1959

'L'opposition allemande à Hitler', special number of the *Revue d'histoire de la deuxième guerre mondiale*, October 1959

T. PRITTIE: *Germans Against Hitler*, London, Hutchinson, 1964

P. HOFFMANN: *Widerstand, Staatsstreich, Attentat: Der Kampf d. Opposition gegen Hitler*, Munich, R. Piper, 1969

K. ZENTNER: *La Résistance allemande 1933–1945*, Paris, Stock, 1968

G. VANROON: *German Resistance to Hitler, Count von Motke and the Kreisau Circle*, New York and London, Von Nostrand Reinhold Company, 1971

II The Putsch of July 20, 1944

M. BAUMONT: *La grande conspiration contre Hitler*, Paris, Del Duca, 1963

E. REMER: *20 juillet 1944*, Hamburg, Verlag deutscher Opposition, 1951

W. von SCHRAMM: *Conspiracy Among Generals*, London, Allen and Unwin, 1956

F. von SCHLABRENDORFF: *Revolt Against Hitler*, London, Eyre and Spottiswoode, 1948

Dieter EHLERS: *Technik und Moral einer Verschwörung, 20 Juli 1944*, Frankfurt-Bonn, 1964

P. BERBEN: *L'attentat contre Hitler*, Paris, Laffont, 1962

G. BUCHHEIT: *Soldattum und Rebellion, Die Tragödie der deutschen Wehrmacht*, Rastatt, Grote, 1961

H. KIRST: *La révolte des soldats*, Paris, Laffont, 1965

IV Germany's Secret Weapons

Admiral BARJOT: 'Synthèse de la guerre sous-marine', *Revue Maritime*, Dec. 1951

A. N. GLENNON: 'The Weapon that Came Too Late', *US Naval Proceedings*, March 1961

R. LUSAR: *German Secret Weapons of the Second World War*, New York, Philosophical Library, 1959

G. PAWIT: *The Secret War 1939–1945*, London, Harrap, 1956

C. BURDICK: 'L'avion à réaction allemand', *Revue d'histoire de la deuxième guerre mondiale*, no. 44, October 1961

E. HEINKEL: *Stormy Life: Memoirs of a Pioneer of the Air Age*, New York, Dutton, 1956

B. COLLIER: *The Battle of the V-Weapons*, London, Hodder and Stoughton, 1964

Major-General W. DORNBERGER: *V-2*, London, Hurst and Blackett, 1954

Air Marshal JOUBERT: *Rocket*, New York, Philosophical Library, 1957

E. ROMAT: 'L'histoire de la bombe volante V 1, *Forces aériennes françaises,* Nov. 1946

J. W. ANGELL: 'Guided missiles would have won', *The Atlantic,* Jan. 1952

Captain COLLOMP: 'Les Trilons', *Forces aériennes françaises,* Oct. 1949

J. MACGOVERN: *Crossbow and Overcast,* London, Hutchinson, 1965

Admiral LEMONNIER: 'Les armes secrètes d'Hitler et celles des Alliés', *Revue de la défense nationale,* July 1960

D. IRVING: *The Mare's Nest,* London, Kimber, 1964

K. H. LUDWIG: 'Fabrications de fusées et stratégie', *Revue d'histoire de la deuxième guerre mondiale,* no. 84, October 1971

M. BORNEMANN: *Geheimprojekt Mittelbau. Die Geschichte d. dt. V. Waffen Werke,* Munich, J. Flehmann, 1971

V   Hitler's Last Gamble

J. W. TOLAND: *Battle: the Story of the Bulge,* London, Muller, 1960

J. NOBECOURT: *Le dernier coup de dés de Hitler,* Paris, Laffont, 1962

H. M. COLE: *The Ardennes, Battle of the Bulge,* Washington, Department of the Army, 1965

H. KESSLER: *Der letzte coup, die Ardenneoffensive,* Berlin, Deutscher Militärverlag, 1966

Franklin DAVIS: *Breakthrough; the Epic Story of the Battle of the Bulge,* Derby, Monarch Books, 1961

M. DEVILLERS: *Objectif Anvers 1944,* Brussels, Brepols, 1964

B. HOOD: 'Operation greif', *Military Review,* Jan. 1960

R. MERRIAM: *The Battle of the Ardennes,* London, Souvenir Press, 1958

H. JUNG: *Die Ardennen Offensive 1944–1945. Ein Beispiel für die Driegsfuhrung Hitlers,* Göttingen, Zürich, Musterschmidt, 1971

J. STRAWSON: *The Battle for the Ardennes,* London, B. T. Batsford, 1972, New York, Scribners, 1972

P. ELSTOV: *Hitler's Last Offensive,* London, Secker and Warburg, 1971, New York, Macmillan, 1971

CHAPTER 2   THE YALTA CONFERENCE

I   The Circumstances and Atmosphere of the Conference

H. FEIS: *Churchill, Roosevelt, Stalin. The War they Waged and the Peace they Sought,* Princeton, Princeton University Press, 1957

W. MACNEILL: *America, Britain and Russia, their Co-operation and Conflicts,* London, Oxford University Press, 1953

G. KENNAN: *Russia and the West under Lenin and Stalin,* Boston, 1961

G. CASTELLAN: 'La politique allemande de l'URSS', *Revue d'histoire de la deuxième guerre mondiale,* nos. 21 and 22, Jan.–April 1956

L. KOCHAN: 'L'URSS et le partage de l'Allemagne en zones d'occupation, *ibid.,* no. 47, April 1962

A. FONTAINE: *Histoire de la guerre froide,* Vol. I, Paris, Fayard, 1965

WOODWARD: *British Foreign Policy in the Second World War, 1943–1945,* 3 vols., London, HMSO, 1971

Louis FISCHER: *The Road to Yalta: Soviet Foreign Relations, 1941–1945,* New York, Harper and Row, 1972

F. B. MISSE: 'Roosevelt et le department d'Etat', *Revue d'histoire de la deuxième guerre mondiale,* no. 82, April 1971, pp. 1–26

II The Fate of Defeated Germany

E. STETTINIUS: *Roosevelt and the Russians: the Yalta Conference*, Garden City, Double-day, 1949 and London, Jonathan Cape, 1950

J. F. BYRNES: *Speaking Frankly*, New York, Harper, 1947
All in One Lifetime, New York, Harper, 1954

J. SNELL, POGUE, DELZELL, LENSEN: *The Meaning of Yalta*, Baton Rouge, Louisiana State University Press, 1956

V. ISRAELIAN: 'L'URRS et la Conférence de Crimée', *Revue d'histoire de la deuxième guerre mondiale*, no. 68, October 1967, pp. 45–66

Sikorski Institute: *Documents on Polish-Soviet Relations*, London, Heinemann, 1961 and 1967

ROZEK: *Allied Wartime Diplomacy, a Pattern in Poland*, New York, J. Wiley, 1958

W. KOWALSKI: *La Pologne et les affaires occidentales*, Vol. I, Warsaw, 1965

R. SONTAG: 'Reflections on the Yalta Papers', *Foreign Affairs*, July 1955

F. DEBYSER: 'Sur la conférence de Yalta', *Revue d'histoire de la deuxième guerre mondiale*, no. 39, July 1960

C. BOHLEN: 'Echo of Yalta', *U.S. News and World*, July 1959

J. VLOYANTES: The Signification of Pre-Yalta Policies, *Western Political Quarterly*, June 1958

'Les conférences de Yalta et de Potsdam', *La vie internationale*, Moscow, 1965

J. Lewis GADDIS: *The United States and the Origins of the Cold War*, New York and London, Columbia University Press, 1972

A. SMITH: 'Churchill et l'armée allemande (1945)', *Revue d'histoire de la deuxième guerre, mondiale*, no. 93, January 1974

CHAPTER 3 THE DEATH THROES OF NAZI GERMANY

I The Soviet Offensive of January–February 1945

Jurgen THORNWALD: *Das Ende an der Elbe*, Steingruben Verlag, 1950

D. IRVING: *The Destruction of Dresden*, London, Kimber, 1963

GOSTONY: 'La bataille de Budapest', *Revue d'histoire de la deuxième guerre mondiale*, no. 60, October 1965, pp. 21–45

General RENDULIC: *Gekämpft, gesiegt, geschlagen*, Heidelberg, K. Vowinckel, 1952

S. E. MORISON: *The Invasion of France and Germany*, Boston, Little Brown, 1957

J. DOLEZAL, J. KREN: *La Tchécoslovaquie en lutte*, Prague, Académie des Sciences, 1961

K. BARTOSEK: *The Prague Uprising*, Prague, Artin, 1965. (Review by M. TAPIÉ, *Revue d'histoire de la deuxième guerre mondiale*, no. 46, April 1962)

J. TOLAND: *The Last 100 days*, London, Arthur Barker, 1966

Colonel POSTEL: 'L'opération Clairon', *Revue historique de l'Armée*, Dec. 1950

Colonel CHABANNIER: 'Le front de Courlande', *Revue historique de l'Armée*, no. 3, 1963

Colonel CHAMPEAUX: 'Les leçons du front russe', *Revue de défense nationale*, Nov. 1962

'La Roumanie en guerre', special number of the *Revue d'histoire de la deuxième guerre mondiale*, April 1968

von AHLFEN NIEHOFF: *So kämpfte Breslau*, Munich, Verlag Graefe und Unzer, 1959

R. BECKER: *Niederschlesien 1945*, Bad Nauheim, Pozdun Verlag, 1965

G. HAAS: *Brände an der Oder*, Ring Verlag H. Cramer, 1962

K. JONCA: 'The Destruction of Breslau', *Polish Western Affairs*, no. 2, 1961

J. TEGLU: 'La participation de l'armée roumaine à la guerre antihitlérienne', *Revue roumaine d'histoire*, no. 1, 1962

Maria ERELISKA: 'Le mouvement de résistance en Bulgarie', *Revue d'histoire de la deuxième guerre mondiale*, October 1968

J. M. D'HOOP: 'Eisenhower et le problème de Berlin en mars 1945', *Revue d'histoire de la deuxième guerre mondiale*, no. 88, October 1972

B. DOLATA: *Wyzwolenie Polski, 1944–1945*, Warsaw, MON, 1971, (cf. *Revue d'histoire de la deuxième guerre mondiale*, no. 94, April 1974, p. 94, by C. Gervais)

I. S. KONEV: *Year of Victory*, London, Central Books, 1970

Karl HNILICKA: *Das Ende auf dem Balkan 1944–1945*, Gottingen, Zurich, Frankfurt, Musterschmidt, 1970

VII The Battle of Berlin

A. TULLY: *Berlin, Story of the Battle*, New York, Simon and Schuster, 1963

H. TREVOR-ROPER: *The Last Days of Hitler*, London, Macmillan (3rd ed.), 1956

W. HAUPT: *La dernière bataille de Hitler*, Paris, France-Empire, 1966

Cornelius RYAN: *The Last Battle*, London, Collins, 1966

T. PLIEVIER: *Berlin*, Paris, Flammarion, 1954

E. KUBY: *The Russians and Berlin, 1945*, London, Heinemann, 1968

F. D. VORB'EV, I. V. POROT'KINE and A. N. CHIMANSKI: *Poslednijchturm, Berlinskaya operatsiya*, Moscow, Institute of Military History, Ministry of Defence USSR, 1970, (cf. *Revue d'histoire de la deuxième guerre mondiale*, no. 88, October 1972, pp. 106–111, by F. Conté)

V. CHUIKOV: *The Fall of Berlin*, London, McGibbon, 1967, New York, Halt, 1968

X The German Surrender

K. KOLLER: *Le dernier mois*, Paris, Payot, 1950

LUDDE NEURATH: *Les derniers jours du IIIe Reich, le gouvernement de Doenitz*, Paris, Berger-Levrault, 1950

G. ROSANOV: *Das Ende des dritten Reiches*, Berlin, Dientz, 1965

J. MORDAL: 'Les poches de l'Atlantique', *Revue historique de l'Armée*, no. 4, 1961

R. HANSEN: *Das Ende des dritten Reiches*, Stuttgart, E. Klett, 1966

CHAPTER 4 THE POTSDAM CONFERENCE

Z. STYPULKOWSKI: *Invitation to Moscow*, London, Thames and Hudson, New York, Mckay, 1951

H. TRUMAN: *Memoirs*, Vol. I 1955, Vol. II 1956, London, Hodder and Stoughton *Documents on Polish-Soviet relations*, London, Heinemann, 1961

Foreign Relations of the United States; the Conference of Berlin, Washington, US Government Printing Office, 1961, 2 vols.

A. KLAFKOWSKI: *L'accord de Potsdam du 2 août 1945*, Warsaw, Pax, 1964

H. FEIS: *Between War and Peace, the Potsdam Conference*, Princeton, Princeton University Press, 1960

J. W. BRUGEL: 'Die Sudetendeutsche Frage auf der Potsdamer Konferenz', *Vierteljahrsh F. Zeitgeschichte*, Jan. 1962

Potsdam 1945, Quellen zur Konferenz der Grossen Drei, Munich, Deutscher Taschenbuch Verlag, 1953

'Secrets of Potsdam', *U.S. News and World Reports*, May 13, 1961

'Les conférences de Yalta et de Potsdam des dirigeants des trois grandes puissances', *La vie internationale*, Moscow, nos. 6–9, 1965

G. ALPEROVITZ: *Atomic Diplomacy, Hiroshima and Potsdam*, New York, Simon and Schuster, 1965

W. T. KOWALSKI: 'La Pologne et les Alliés (1939–1945)', *Revue d'histoire de la deuxième guerre mondiale*, no. 78, April 1970

W. T. KOWALSKI: 'Potsdam after twenty five years', *International Affairs*, July 1970

Ernst DEUERLEIN: *Deklamation oder Ersatzfrieden? Die Konferenz von Potsdam, 1945*, Stuttgart, Kohlhammer, 1970

Book Five THE DEFEAT OF JAPAN

CHAPTER 1 STRATEGY AND FORCES IN ASIA

I The Situation at the Beginning of 1943

M. MATLOFF: *Strategic Planning for Coalition Warfare*, Washington, Department of the Army, 1959

J. MILLER: *Guadalcanal, the First Offensive*, Washington, Department of the Army, 1949

General CHASSIN: 'Le plan Matterhorn', *Forces aériennes françaises*, Oct. 1954

L. MORTON: 'Command in the Pacific', *Military Review*, Dec. 1961

S. E. MORISON: *American Contributions to the Strategy of World War Two*, London, Oxford University Press, 1958

Camille ROUGERON: 'Porte-avions ou bases terrestres', *Forces aériennes françaises*, Feb. 1953

L. MORTON: 'Japanese policy and strategy in mid war', *U.S. Naval Institute Proceedings*, Feb. 1959

'Crisis in the Pacific', *Military Review*, April 1966

W. F. CRAVEN and J. L. GATE: *The Army Air Force in World War Two, Guadalcanal to Saipan*, Chicago, University of Chicago Press, 1950

A. P. STAUFER: *The Quartermaster Corps; Operations in the War against Japan*, Washington, Department of the Army, 1956

B. MACCANDLESS: 'The San Francisco Story', *U.S. Naval Institute Proceedings*, Nov. 1958 (an episode of the battle of Guadalcanal)

R. W. TREGASKIS: *Guadalcanal Diary*, New York, Popular Library, 1962

G. WEEMS: 'Salomons battle logistics', *U.S. Naval Institute Proceedings*, Sept. 1962

A. WATTS: *Japanese Warships of World War Two*, London, Ian Allan, 1967

D. BARBEY: *Les forces navales amphibiés de MacArthur*, Annapolis, US Naval Institute, 1969

CHAPTER 2 THE WAR IN CHINA AND BURMA

J. K. FAIRBANK, A. CRAIG, REISCHAUER: *East Asia, the Modern Transformation*, Boston, Houghton Mifflin, 1965

C. ROMANUS, R. SUNDERLAND: *The China–Burma–India Theater*, Washington, Department of the Army, 1959

S. HAYASHI and A. COX: *The Japanese Army in the Pacific War*, Quantico, Marine Corps Association, 1959

Louis ALLEN: *Sittang, the last battle. The end of the Japanese in Burma, July-August 1945* London, MacDonald, 1973

III The War in China

L. BIANCO: *Les origines de la Révolution chinoise*, Paris, Gallimard, 1967

R. PELISSIER: *The Awakening of China, 1793–1949*, London, Secker and Warburg, 1967

J. K. FAIRBANK: *The Unites States and China*, Cambridge, Mass, Viking Press, 1962

Chalmers JOHNSON: *Peasant Nationalism and Communist Power*, Stanford, Stanford University Press, 1962

R. NORTH: *Moscow and Chinese Communists*, Stanford, Stanford University Press, 1963

CHIANG KAI-SHEK: *China's Destiny and Chinese Economic Theory*, London, Dobson, 1947 and New York, Macmillan, 1947

L. K. ROSINGER: *China's Wartime Politics, 1937–1944*, London, Oxford University Press and Princeton, Princeton University Press, 1944

H. FEIS: *The China Tangle: the American Effort in China from Pearl Harbour to the Marshall Mission*, London, Oxford University Press, 1954 and Princeton, Princeton University Press, 1953

C. ROMANUS and R. SUNDERLAND: *Stilwell's Command Problems*, Washington, Department of the Army, 1956

General J. W. STILWELL: *The Stilwell Papers*, London, Macdonald, 1949

L. L. LIU: *A Military History of Modern China*, Princeton, Princeton University Press, 1956

E. O'BALLANCE: *The Red Army of China*, London, Faber, 1952

A. CHENNAULT: *Chennault and the Flying Tigers*, New York, P. S. Erikson, 1963

Y. GUILLERMAZ: *Histoire du parti communiste chinois*, Paris, Payot, 1968

Milton E. MILES: *A Different Kind of War: The Little Known Story of the Combined Guerilla Forces Created in China by the US Navy and the Chinese during World War II*, Garden City, N.Y., Doubleday, 1967

V Preparations for the Burma Campaign

P. KHERA and S. PRASAD: *The Reconquest of Burma*, 1959

General KIRBY: *The Reconquest of Burma*, London, HMSO, Vol. I 1958, Vol. II 1961

Admiral MOUNTBATTEN: *Report to the Combined Chiefs of Staff*, London, HMSO, 1951

Field Marshal SLIM: *Defeat into Victory*, New York, David MacKay, 1961

Commandant de FOUQUIÈRES: 'La reconquête de la Birmanie', *Forces aériennes françaises*, May 1948

G. EVANS: *The Desert and the Jungle*, London, Kimber, 1959

H. FUWA: 'Japanese Operations in Hukaway Valley', *Military Review*, Jan. 1962

J. MASTERS: *The Road past Mandalay*, New York, Harper, 1961

W. PEERS and D. BRELIS: *Behind the Burma Road, the Story of America's Most Successful Guerrilla Force*, Boston, Little, Brown, 1963

Gerd LINDE: *Burma 1943 und 1944: Die Expeditionen Orde C. Wingates*, Freiburg, Verlag, Rombach, 1972

CHAPTER 3 THE WAR IN THE PACIFIC

S. E. MORISON: *Victory in the Pacific, 1945*, New York, Little Brown, 1960

M. ITO and R. PINEAU: *The End of the Imperial Japanese Navy*, Washington, Norton, 1962

W. P. CRAVEN and J. L. CATE: *Matterhorn to Nagasaki*, Chicago, University of Chicago Press, 1953

M. HASHIMOTO: *Sunk: the Story of the Japanese Submarine Fleet*, New York, Holt, 1954

General KENNEY: *The MacArthur I Know*, New York, Duell, Sloan and Pearce, 1951

L. MORTON: 'The Long Road of Unity of Command', *Military Review*, Jan. 1960

George ODGERS: *Air War Against Japan 1943–1945*, Canberra, War Memorial, 1957

L. C. F. TURNER, GORDON, CUMMINGS and BETZLER: *War in the Southern Oceans 1939–1945*, Cape Town, London and Toronto, Oxford University Press, 1961

II   The Siege of Rabaul

D. DEXTER: *The New Guinea Offensives*, Canberra, Angus and Robertson, 1961

S. MILNER: *The War in the Pacific, Victory in Papua*, Washington, Department of the Army, 1957

General CHASSIN: 'Rabaul', *Forces aeriénnes françaises*, April 1949

Guy SEVERAC: 'La bataille de la mer de Bismarck', *ibid.*, Nov. 1952

P. CROWL and E. G. LOWE: *Seizure of the Gilberts and Marshall*, Washington, Department of the Army, 1955

W. HOFFMANN: *The Seizure of Tinian*, Washington, Historical Division, Marine Corps, 1950

P. CROWL: *Campaign in the Marianas*, Washington, Department of the Army, 1960

S. FALK: 'Japanese Strategy in World War Two', *Military Review*, June 1962

R. SMITH: *The Approach to the Philippines*, Washington, Department of the Army, 1953

IV   Formosa or the Philippines?

H. CANNON: *Leyte, the Return to the Philippines*, Washington, US Government Printing Office, 1954

R. SMITH: *Triumph on the Philippines*, Washington, 1963

S. E. MORISON: *Leyte, June 1944–January 1945*, Boston, Atlantic Little, 1958
    Liberation of the Philippines, New York, Little Brown, 1959

S. FALK: *Decision at Leyte*, New York, Norton, 1966

General KRUEGER: *From Down Under the Nippon*, Washington, Combat Forces, 1955

S. SMITH: *The Battle of Sawa*, New York, MacFadden, 1962

Admiral LOCKWOOD and Colonel ADAMSON: *Battles of the Philippine Sea*, New York, Crowell, 1967

VIII   Iwoshima

R. NEWCOMB: *Iwojima*, New York, Holt, Rinehart and Winston, 1965

M. NICHOLS and H. SHAW: *Okinawa, Victory in the Pacific*, Washington, US Government Printing Office, 1948

R. APPEMAN, J. BURNS, *et al.*: *Okinawa, the Last Battle*, Washington, US Government Printing Office, 1948

Admiral de BELOT: 'La fin du Yamato', *Revue des deux mondes*, Sept. 1958

Admiral YOKOI: 'Thoughts on Japan's Naval Defeat', *US Naval Institute Proceedings*, Oct. 1960

R. WHEELER: *The Bloody Battle for Suribachi*, New York, Crowell, 1965

CHAPTER 4   THE JAPANESE SURRENDER

II   Japan's Exhaustion

A. REUSSNER: 'La marine marchande, la stratégie et l'économie de guerre japonaise', *Revue d'histoire de la deuxième guerre mondiale*, March 1951

J. L. CATE: 'Global Command: the Double Cross', *The Journal of Modern History*, Dec. 1951

Genichi ABE, Shigeto KAWANO, Yoshio ANDO: articles in *Studies on the End of the Pacific War*, Tokyo, Nihon Gaikogaku Kai, 1958. (In Japanese. Summary by P. AKAMATSU, *Revue d'histoire de la deuxième guerre mondiale*, no. 48, October 1962)

J. SUNDERMAN: *World War in the Air; the Pacific*, New York, Watts, 1962

A. HARA: 'L'Economie japonaise pendant la deuxième guerre mondiale', *Revue d'histoire de la deuxième guerre mondiale*, no. 89, January 1973

David BERGAMINI: *La conspiration de Hiro-Hito. Le Japon dans la seconde guerre mondiale, 1941–1945*, Paris, Fayard, 1973

J. TOLAND: *The Rising Sun. The Decline and Fall of the Japanese Empire, 1936–1945*, New York, Random House, 1970

IV The Atom Bomb

H. FEIS: *The Atom Bomb and the End of the War in the Pacific*, Princeton, Princeton University Press, 1961

R. JUNGK: *Brighter Than a Thousand Suns*, London, Gollancz, 1958

L. GROVES: *Now It Can be Told*, New York, Harper, 1962, London, André Deutsch

L. MORTON: 'The Decision to Use the Atomic Bomb', *Foreign Affairs*, Jan. 1957

L. GIOVANNITTI and F. FREED: *The Decision to Drop the Bomb*, New York, Coward MacCann, 1965

F. ASHWORTH: 'Dropping the Atomic Bomb on Nagasaki', *U.S. Naval Institute Proceedings*, Jan. 1958

R. BARTHCHELDER: *The Irreversible Decision*, Boston, Houghton Mifflin, 1962

A. GROOM: 'US Allied Relations and the Atomic Bomb', *World Politics*, Oct. 1962

S. GROUEFF: *Manhattan Project; the Untold Story of the Making of the Atomic Bomb*, London, Collins, 1967

VI The Japanese Surrender

R. T. BUTOW: *Japan's Decision to Surrender*, Stanford, Stanford University Press, 1954

T. KASE: *Mission to the Missouri*, New Haven, Yale University Press, 1950

L. MORTON: 'Soviet Intervention in the War with Japan', *Foreign Affairs*, July 1962

F. DEBYSER: 'La genèse de l'intervention russe contre le Japon', *Politique étrangère*, Dec. 1955

H. HUAN: 'Vingt-cinq jours de guerre navale soviéto-japonaise', *Revue Maritime*, July 1961

Lester BROOKS: *Behind Japan's Surrender*, New York, McGraw-Hill, 1966

William CRAIG: *La chute du Japon*, Paris, Laffont, 1969

TAKASHI: 'La fin de la deuxième guerre mondiale dans les puissances de l'Axe', *Revue d'histoire de la deuxième guerre mondiale*, no. 89, January 1973

R. GARTHOFF: 'Malinovski's Manchurian campaign', *Military Review*, Oct. 1966

Book Six THE WORLD AT THE END OF THE WAR

CHAPTER I THE AFTERMATH

I The Bloodshed

M. REINHARD and A. ARMENGAUD: *Histoire générale de la population mondiale*, Paris, Montchrestien, 1961

R. LANNES: 'Les conséquences démographiques de la deuxième guerre mondiale', *Revue d'histoire de la deuxième guerre mondiale*, July 1955

G. FRUMKIN: *Population Changes in Europe Since 1939*, New York, Kelly, 1951, London, Allen and Unwin, 1952

M. KULISCHER: *Europe on the Move, War and Population 1917–1945*, London, Oxford University Press, New York, Columbia University Press, 1946

POLIAKOV: 'Note sur le chiffre total des victimes juives', *Revue d'histoire de la deux-ième guerre mondiale*, no. 24, October 1956

R. LUZA: *The Transfer of the Sudeten Germans*, London, Routledge and Kegan Paul, 1964

E. ARAB-OGLY: 'Les conséquences démographiques de la guerre', *La nouvelle revue internationale*, Aug. 1962

J. de LA ROBRIE: 'Transferts de population', *Revue historique de l'armée*, January 1948

M. DULCZEWSKI: 'Les migrations de guerre sur les territoires occidentaux', *La Pologne et les affaires occidentales*, Warsaw, 1965

G. WOODBRIDGE: *The History of the United Nations Relief and Rehabilitation Administration*, 3 vols., New York, Columbia University Press, 1950

L. MADAJCZYK: 'La guerre et l'occupation en Pologne comme instruments de la destruction d'un peuple', *Revue d'histoire de la deuxième guerre mondiale*, no. 78, April 1970

        'Principes généraux et caractères des transferts de population opérés par les nazis', *Studia Historiae Oeconomicae*, vol. 8, Poznan, 1973

Arthur EISENBACH: 'Operation Reinhard, Mass Extermination of the Jewish Population in Poland', *Polish Western Affairs*, Poznan, vol. III, 1962

Le Crime méthodique: Documents éclairant la politique de l'Allemagne nazie en territoire soviétique de 1941 à 1944, Moscow, Ed de langues etrangères, 1963

III   The Material Havoc

La Maison Consultative des Réparations: *Dommages subis par la France et l'Union française du fait de la guerre et de l'occupation ennemie*, 7 vols., Paris, Imprimerie Nationale, 1947–50

Statement on War Losses and Damages of Poland, Warsaw, 1947

M. CEPEDE: 'L'influence de la guerre et de l'occupation sur les récoltes', *Economie contemporaine*, Oct. 1951

Les marines marchandes mondiales, *Notes documentaires et études*, Paris, Documentation Française, July 1946

Zachodnia agencja prasowa, Warsaw, no. 3, 1957

Institut National de Statistiques et d'Enquêtes Economiques: 'Pertes humaines subies par les belligérants, destructions causées par la guerre', *Études et conjonctures, Economie mondiale*, 1947

V   The Economic Consequences

J. CHARDONNET: *Les conséquences économiques de la guerre*, Paris, Hachette, 1947

        L'économie mondiale au milieu du XXe siècle, Paris, Hachette, 1952

A. BETTELHEIM: *Esquisse d'un tableau économique de l'Europe*, Paris, Domat-Mont-chrestien, 1948

UNO: *Economic Report. Salient Features of the World Economic Situation*, New York, 1948

A. J. BROWN: *The Great Inflation, 1939–1951*, London, Oxford University Press, 1955

'Cinq ans d'évolution économique', *Economiste européen*, no. 2487

Anon: 'Comparison de l'évolution industrielle et agricole de 1938 à 1945 en France et en divers pays', *Etudes et conjonctures*, Paris, Oct. 1946

Anon: '*Problèmes de l'électricité*', *Etudes et documents*, Paris, March–April and May–June, 1945

J. SINGER-KEREL: *Le coût de la vie à Paris de 1840 à 1954*, Paris, A. Colin, 1961

G. PIROU: 'Le problème monétaire en France depuis la Libération', *Revue d'économie politique*, Feb. 1945

P.-H. DOUBLET: *Confiscations des profits illicites et des biens mal acquis*, Paris, Librairie Générale de Droit et de Jurisprudence, 1945

'Problèmes économiques d'après-guerre en Grande-Bretagne', *Bulletin de documentation*, Agence Française de Presses, Feb. 23, 1946

'La France économique de 1939 à 1946', *Revue d'économie politique*, Sept.–Oct. and Nov.–Dec. 1947

'Inventaire économique de l'Europe', special number of *Etudes et conjonctures*, 1947

M. M. POSTAN: *An Economic History of Western Europe 1945–1964*. London, Methuen, 1967, New York, Barnes and Noble, 1967

Maurice CROUZET: *European Renaissance since 1945*, London, Thames and Hudson, 1970, New York, Harcourt Brace, 1971

VI   The Collapse of Germany

A. PIETTRE: *L'économie allemande contemporaine (Allemagne occidentale)*, 1945–1952, Paris, Librairie Médicis, 1952

D. SCHMIDT: *Der Statist auf die Galerie, 1945–1950*, Bonn, 1951

M. VIRALLY: *L'administration internationale de l'Allemagne du 8 mai 1945 au 24 avril 1947*, Paris, Pedone, 1948

P. MOSELY: 'Dismemberment of Germany', *Foreign Affairs*, April 1950
    'The Occupation of Germany', *ibid.*, July 1950

L. CLAY: *Decision in Germany*, Garden City, Doubleday, 1950

Recueil de textes à l'usage des conférences de la Paix, Paris, Imprimerie Nationale, 1946

Richard CASTILLON: *Les réparations allemandes, deux expériences*, Paris, Presses Universitaires de France, 1953

CHAPTER 2   THE NEW BALANCE OF POWER

I   Great Britain

K. HUTCHINSON: *The Decline and Fall of British Capitalism*, London, Cape, 1951

J. L'HOMME: *La politique sociale de l'Angleterre contemporaine*, Paris, Presses Universitaires de France, 1953

J.-P. MARTIN: *Les finances publiques britanniques (1939–1955)*, Paris, Genin, 1956

A. L. MORTON and G. TATE: *The British Labour Movement, 1770–1920: a History* London, Lawrence and Wishart, 1956

J. de SAILLY: *Politique économique du Royaume-Uni et du Commonwealth depuis la guerre*, 3 parts, Paris, Les Cours de Droit, 1962

A. MARWICK: 'L'impact de la deuxième guerre mondiale sur les Britanniques', *Revue d'histoire de la deuxième guerre mondiale*, no. 90, April 1973

A. CALDER: *The People's War: Britain 1939–1945*, London, J. Cape, 1969, New York, Pantheon Books, 1969

P. HUET: *La politique économique de la Grande-Bretagne depuis 1945*, Paris, Colin, 1969

II   France

M. DUVERGER: *Partis politiques et classes sociales en France*, Paris, Colin, 1955

J.-M. JEANNENEY: *Forces et faiblesses de l'économie française (1945–1956)*, Paris, Colin, 1956

J. FAUVET and A. DUHAMEL: *Histoire du Parti communiste français*, Vol. II, Paris, Fayard, 1965

Gordon WRIGHT: *Rural Revolution in France*, Stanford, Stanford University Press, 1964

J. CHAPSAL: *La vie politique en France depuis 1940*, 3 parts, Paris, Les Cours de Droit, 1961

J. LECLERC: *La percée de l'économie française*, Paris, Arthaud, 1963

R. ARON: *Histoire de l'épuration*, Vol. II, Paris, Fayard, 1967

H. COPELAND: *The Resistance and the Post-Liberation French Politics (1940-1946)*, Ithaca, New York, Cornell University Press, 1966

Marcel BAUDOT: 'La résistance française face aux problèmes de répression et d'épuration', *Revue d'histoire de la deuxième guerre mondiale*, no. 81, January 1971

A. W. DEPORTE: *De Gaulle's Foreign Policy, 1944-1946*, Harvard University Press, Cambridge Mass., and London, 1968

G. BOUTHILLIER: *La nationalisation du gaz et de l'electricitè en France. Contribution à l'étude des décisions politiques*, Paris, Fondation Nationale des Sciences Politiques, 1968

III Italy

F. CALAMANDREI, A. BATTAGLIA, CORBINO: *Dieci anni dopo (1945-1955)*, Bari, Laterza, 1955

M. GRINDROD: *The Rebuilding of Italy. Politics and Economics (1945-1955)*, London, Oxford University Press, 1955

F. CATALANO: *L'Italia della dittatura alla democrazia*, Milan, Lerici, 1965

G. PERTICONE: *L'Italia contemporanea*, Milan, Mondadori, 1962

G. ROSSINI: *Dal 25 luglio alla Republica*, Turin, Eri, 1966

Massimo BONANNI: *La politica esteradella Republica italiana*, 3 vols., Milan, Comuntia, 1967

Raffaele COLAPIETRA: *La Lotta politica in Italia dalla liberazione di Roma alla Costituente.* Bologna, Patron, 1969

IV The Arab World

G. LENCZOWSKI: *The Middle East in World Affairs*, London, Oxford University Press, Ithaca, New York, Cornell University Press, 1952

W. SPENCER: *Political Evolution in the Middle East*, Philadelphia, Lippincott, 1962

F. W. FERNAU: *Moslems on the March*, London, Robert Hale, 1955

LE TOURNEAU: *L'Islam contemporain*, Paris, Les Editions internationales, 1950

C.-A. JULIEN: *L'Afrique du Nord en marche*, Paris, Julliard, 1952
Histoire de l'Algérie contemporaine, Paris, Presses Universitaires de France, 1964

P. SEBAG: *La Tunisie*, Paris, Editions sociales, 1951

A. AYACHE: *Le Maroc, bilan d'une colonisation*, Paris, Editions sociales, 1956

S. CAVALIÈRE: 'La politica egiziana dal 1936 al 1951', *Rivista di studi politici internationali*, April–June 1953

L. ELWALL-SUTTON: *Persian Oil: a Study in Power Politics*, London, Lawrence and Wishart, 1955

M. LAISSY: *Du panarabisme à la ligue arabe*, Paris, Maisonneuve, 1948

M. COLOMBE: *L'évolution de l'Egypte*, Paris, Maisonneuve 1951

H. GIBB: *Modern Trends in Islam*, Chicago, Chicago University Press, 1947

M. SETON-WILLIAMS: *Britain and the Arab States*, London, Luzac, 1948

S. BERNARD: *The Franco-Moroccan Conflict, 1943-56*, New Haven, Yale University Press, 1968

V Japan and China

B. LASKER: *Asia on the Move*, New York, H. Holt, 1945

M. ZINKIN: *Asia and the West*, London, Chatto and Windus, 1951

W. BALL: *Nationalism and Communism in East Asia*, Melbourne, Melbourne University Press, 1952, London, Cambridge University Press

G. PECK: *Two Kinds of Time*, Boston, Houghton Mifflin, 1950

J. F. FAIRBANK, E. O. RESCHAUER and A. M. CRAIG: *East Asia, the Modern Transformation*, Vol. 2 of *A History of East African Civilization*, Boston, Houghton Mifflin, 1965

J. CHEROY: *Où va le Japon?*, Paris, Hachette, 1954

H. BORTON: 'Preparation for the Occupation of Japan', *Journal of Asian Studies*, Feb. 1966

A. K. WU: *China and the Soviet Union*, London, Methuen, 1950

W. H. ELSBREE: *Japan's Role in South-east Asian Nationalist Movements*, Cambridge, Mass., Harvard University Press, 1953

A. ODASAKI: *Histoire du Japon: l'économie et la population*, Paris, Institut National d'études demographiques, no. 32, 1958

H. FEIS: *The China Tangle; the American Effort in China from Pearl Harbor to the Marshall Mission*, Princeton, Princeton University Press, 1953

E. MARTIN: *The Allied Occupation of Japan*, New York, Macmillan, 1948

J. LEQUILLER: *Le Japon*, Paris, Editions Sirey, 1966, pp. 358–458

E. O. REICHAUER: *Histoire du Japon et des Japonais*, Paris, Du Seuil, 1973, vol. 2: *De 1945 à 1970*

HO PING TI and TANG TSOU: *China in Crisis*, Chicago and London, University of Chicago Press, 1968

Jacques GUILLERMAZ: *History of the Chinese Communist Party (1921–1949)*, New York, Random House, 1972, London, Methuen, 1972

VI   South-East Asia

Tibor MENDE: *L'Inde devant l'orage*, Paris, Du Seuil, 1950
    South-East Asia Between Two Worlds, London, 1955

G. KAHIN: *Nationalism and Revolution in Indonesia*, Ithaca, New York, Cornell University Press, 1952

A. ROTHIER: La Birmanie nouvelle, Centre d'études de Politique étrangère, Paris, 1953

LE THANK KHOI: *Le Viêt-nam, histoire et civilisation*, Paris, Editions de Minuit, 1955

Paul MUS: *Viêt-nam, sociologie d'une guerre*, Paris, Editions du Seuil, 1952

P. DEVILLERS: *Histoire du Viêt-nam, de 1940 à 1952*, Paris Editions du Seuil, 1952

J. NEHRU: *Glimpses of World History*, London, Drummond, 1949

C. A. BUSS: *The Far East. A History of Recent and Contemporary Relations in East Asia*, New York, Macmillan, 1955

Y. THOMSON: *The Left Wing in South Asia*, New York, 1950

F. H. MICHAEL and G. E. RAYLOR: *The Far East in the Modern World*, London, Methuen, 1956

L. A. MILLS, *et al.*: *The New World of South Asia*, University of Minneapolis Press, 1949, London, Oxford University Press

V. P. MENON: *The Transfer of Power in India*, London, Longman, Green, 1957

J. VAN LEUR: *Indonesian Trade and Society. Essays in Asian Social and Economic History*, The Hague, Institute of Pacific Relations, for the Royal Tropical Institute, Amsterdam, 1955

The Development of Self-Rule in Burma, Malaya and the Philippines,
    Part I *Burma*, John F. Cady,
    Part II *Malaya*, Patricia G. Barnett,
    Part III *The Philippines*, Shirley Jenkins,
    New York, American Institute of Pacific Relations, 1948

Jacques DECORNOY: *L'Asie du Sud-Est*, 2 vols., Paris, Sirey, 1970
Jean SAINTENY: *Ho Chi Minh and his Vietnam*, New York, Regnery, 1972

VII The USSR and the Communist World

S. PROKOPOVICH: *Histoire économique de l'URSS*, Paris, Flammarion, 1953
C. BETTELHEIM: *L'économie soviétique*, Paris, Sirey, 1950
The Economist Intelligence Unit, Cartographic Dept: *The USSR and Eastern Europe*, London, Oxford University Press, 1956
M. FAINSOD: *How Russia is Ruled*, Cambridge, Mass., Harvard University Press, 1953
Max BELOFF: *Soviet Policy in the Far East*, London, Oxford University Press, 1953
N. VERE-HODGE: *Turkish Foreign Policy*, Geneva, 1950
Le continent américain et le déséquilibre mondial, Centre de Politique Étrangère, Paris, 1948
L. LAURAT: *Bilan de 25 ans de plans quinquennaux*, Paris, Plon, 1955
L'économie soviétique (1917–1957), Brussels, Institut de Sociologie, 1958
G. L. JARAY: *Tableau de la Russie jusqu'à la mort de Staline*, Paris, Plon, 1954
J.-B. DUROSELLE: *Les frontières européennes de l'U.R.S.S.*, Paris, Fondation Nationale des Sciences Politiques, 1957
Alexander WERTH: *Russia, the Post-War Years*, London, R. Hale, 1971, New York
Roy MEDVEDEV: *Let History Judge: Origins and Consequences of Stalinism*, New York, Alfred A. Knopf, 1972, London, Macmillan, 1972
G. MARTINET: *Les cinq communismes: Russe, Yougoslave, Chinois, Tcheque, Cubain*, Paris, Du Seuil, 1971
H. SETON WATSON: *The East European Revolution*, London, Methuen, 1950
R. BETH: *Central and South-East Europe (1945–1948)*, London, Oxford University Press, 1950
F. FEYTO: *Histoire des démocraties populaires*, Paris, Editions du Seuil, 1952
C. BOBROWSKI: *La Yougoslavie socialiste*, Paris, Colin, 1950
A. KORBONSKY: *Politics of Socialist Agriculture in Poland (1945–1960)*, New York, Columbia University Press, 1965
G. CASTELLAN: *D.D.R., Allemagne de l'Est*, Paris, Editions du Seuil, 1955
E. C. CIUREA: *Le traité de paix avec la Roumainie du 10 février 1947*, Paris, Pedone, 1954
S. KERTESZ: *The Fate of East Central Europe*, Notre Dame, Canada, University of Notre Dame Press, 1956
        Soviet and Western politics in Hungary 1944–1947, *Review of Politics*, Jan. 1952
M. DJILAS: *The Unperfect Society: Beyond the New Class*, New York, Harcourt Brace, 1969, London, Methuen, 1970
Laszlo NAGY: *Democrazie populari, 1945–1968*, Milan, Il Saggiatore, 1969

VIII The American Titan

D. GUERIN: *Où va le peuple américain?*, Paris, Julliard, 2 vols., 1950–51
R. FRANCK: *Histoire économique et sociale des Etats-Unis de 1919 à 1949*, Paris, Aubier, 1950
Marc de LOGERES: *Le mouvement des prix aux Etats-Unis durant la période de reconversion*, Paris, Colin, 1952
H. STAUB: *Le profit des grandes entreprises américaines*, Paris, Colin, 1954
F. BOURIEZ-GREGG: *Les classes sociales aux Etats-Unis*, Paris, Colin, 1954
L. REISSMANN: *Class in American society*, London, Routledge and Kegan Paul, 1960 and International Library of Sociology and Social Reconstruction, Free Press, New York Collier-Macmillan, 1959

E. F. GOLDMAN: *The Crucial Decade: America (1945–1955)*, New York, Alfred A. Knopf, 1956

J. K. GALBRAITH: *American Capitalism*, Boston, Houghton Mifflin, 1956, London, Hamish Hamilton, 1957

Raymond ARON: *République impériale. Les Etats-Unis dan le monde 1945–1972*, Paris, Calmann-Levy, 1973

South America

P. HORN and H. E. BISE: *Latin-American Trade and Economics*, New York, Prentice-Hall, 1949

K. SILVERT: *The Conflict Society: Reaction and Revolution in Latin America*, New York, American Universities Field Staff, 1966

F. MALLEY: *Inquiétante Amérique latine*, Paris, Editions du Cerf, 1963

J. GANTENBEIN: *The Evolution of our Latin American Policy*, New York, Columbia University Press, 1950

IX Problems and Disagreements

A. FONTAINE: *History of the Cold War*, Vol. I, London, Secker and Warburg, 1968

A. HUSSLER: *Contribution à l'étude de l'élaboration de la politique étrangère britannique (1945–1956)*, Geneva, Droz, 1961

F. GAETA: *La seconda guerra mondiale e i nuovi problemi del mondi*, Storia Universale, Vol. IV, Turin, U.T.E.T., 1967

J. FREYMOND: *The Saar Conflict, 1945–55*, London, Carnegie Endowment for International Peace, European Centre, 1960

W. REITZEL, M. CAPLAN and C. A. COBLENZ: *United States Foreign Policy (1945–1955)*, Washington, Brookings Institute 1956, London, Faber and Faber, 1956

R. FIFIELD: *The Diplomacy of South-East Asia (1945–1958)*, New York, Harper, 1958

A. L. SMITH Jr: 'Churchill et l'armée allemande (1945)', *Revue d'histoire de la deuxième guerre mondiale*, no. 93, January 1974

John GIMBEL: *The American Occupation of Germany*, Stanford and London, Stanford University Press, 1969

J. L. GADDIS: *The United States and the Origins of the Cold War, 1941–1947*, New York and London, Columbia University Press, 1972

Bruce KUKLICK: *American Policy and the Division of Germany: the Clash with Russia over Reparations*, Ithaca, Cornell University Press, 1972

CHAPTER 3   THE TASK OF RECONSTRUCTION

I The United Nations Organisation

V. ISRAELIAN: 'Les Conférences internationales de 1945', *Recherches internationales à la lumière du marxisme*, June–Dec. 1964

L. GOODRICH: *The United Nations*, London, Stevens, 1960

Foreign Relations of the U.S.A., Diplomatic Papers, 1944, Vol. I, and *1945*, Washington, US Government Printing Office, 2 vols., 1966 and 1967

Maurice CROUZET: *De la deuxième guerre mondiale à nos jours*, Paris, Flammarion, 1970

A. M. CORDIER: *Public Papers of the Secretaries-General of the U.N.*, Vol. I; *Trygve-Lie 1946–1953*, New York and London, Columbia University Press, 1969, 535 pp.

III The Commitment of Writers and Artists

Encyclopédie de la Pléiade, Vol. II, *Littératures occidentales*, Paris, Gallimard, 1956

R.-M. ALBERES: *L'aventure intellectuelle au XXe siècle*, Paris, La Nouvelle Edition, 1950

M. NADEAU: *The History of Surrealism*, London, Jonathan Cape, 1968

M. EHRHARD: *La littérature russe*, Paris, Presses Universitaires de France, 1948

A. CAZIN: *Panorama littéraire des Etats-Unis de 1890 à nos jours*, Paris, Robert Martin, 1952

J. BROWN: *Panorama de la littérature contemporaine aux Etats-Unis*, Paris, Gallimard, 1954

J. MAJAULT, et al.: *Littérature de notre temps*, Paris, Casterman, 1966

M. F. CUNLIFFE: *The Literature of the United States*, Harmondsworth, Penguin, 1967

P. H. SIMON: *Histoire de la littérature française au XXe siècle*, Paris, Colin, 2 vols., 1956

H. PERRUCHOT: *L'art moderne à travers le monde*, Paris, Hachette, 1963

R. GENAILLE: *La peinture contemporaine*, Paris, F. Nathan, 1951

P. FRANCASTEL: *Peinture et Société*, Lyon, Audin, 1951

P. LANDORMY: *A history of Music*, New York, Scribners, 1923

René JEANNE and Charles FORD: *Histoire du cinéma parlant*, Paris, Laffont, 1958

G. SADOUL: *Histoire du cinéma mondial*, Paris, Flammarion, 1959

IV   Giant Strides in Physics

A. PRYCE-JONES: *The New Outline of Modern Knowledge*, London, Gollancz, 1956

P. ROUSSEAU: *Histoire des Sciences*, Paris, Fayard, 1949

La science au XXe siècle, Paris, Hachette, 1954

R. TATON: *A General History of the Sciences*, Vol. IV *Science in the Twentieth Century*, London, Thames and Hudson, 1966

J. ROSTAND: *Les grands courants de la biologie*, Paris, Gallimard, 1952

R. BROCA: *Cinquante ans de conquêtes médicales*, Paris, Hachette, 1955

P. GUAYDIER: *Les grandes découvertes de la physique moderne*, Paris, Corréa, 1951

R. SIMONET: *Les derniers progrès de la physique*, Vol. II, Paris, Calmann-Lévy, 1948

A. CHAPLET: *Les prodigieuses réalisations de la chimie moderne*, Paris, Hachette, 1955

R. SIMONET: *Les derniers progrès de la technique*, Paris, Calmann-Lévy, 1950

J. FOURASTIÉ: *La civilisation de 1975*, Paris, Presses Universitaires de France, 1953

H. CARL: *Les secrets de la matière; physique et physiciens du XXe siècle*, Paris, Union Générale d'Edition, 1964

C. RICHET and A. MANS: *Pathologie de la déportation*, Paris, Plon, 1956

Index

Aachen, 797
Aandalnes, 75
Abbas, Farhat, 504, 505, 506
Abbeville, 108, 114, 115, 119
ABDA (unified Allied command), 331
Abelson, 834
Abetz, Otto, 174, 281, 289, 384
Abganerovo, 398
Abrial, Admiral, 121
Abruzzi, region, 529
Abwehr, 96, 208, 242, 252–4, 574, 659
Abyssinia, 19, 808
Acquarone, Duke, 516, 518, 519
Action Committee for France, 626
Action française, 282
Addis Ababa, 184
Admiral Scheer (German ship), 179
Admiralty, British, 65; war in Norway, 75, 79; French collapse, 114, 121; Atlantic war, 366–8
Adriatic Sea, 187, 426
Aegean Sea, 609
Afghanistan, 60
Africa, 6, 290, 357, 448; fighting in, 177, 181, 183, 188, 193–6; Germans halted, 371–93; end of war, 487–506; and Italian surrender, 507, 510; and post-war balance of power, 811, 817; see also Algeria, Morocco, Tunisia *etc.*
Afrika Korps, 194, 204, 289; Germans halted, 371–2, 374–7, 391, 487; end of African war, 490, 492
Agay, 641
Ailette Canal, 125
aircraft production, German, 542–5; American B29, 762
Aisne, R., 113, 125
Aix-la-Chapelle, 651, 664
Ajaccio, 498, 526, 603
Aksazh, R., 401
Akyab, 741, 742
Alain, 830
Alamagordo, 769
Alanbrooke, General, 130–1, 149, 447, 545, 610, 614, 687

Alaska, 344, 422, 442
Albania, 188, 190, 192, 527, 817; resistance, 305–6
Albert Canal, 20–3, 84, 88; phoney war, 54, 56–8, 74; Sedan breakthrough, 98, 100, 102n
Alencon, 634
Aleutian Islands, 332, 344, 345; Japanese attack, 360–1, and British strategy, 723, 724; American penetration, 749
Alexander, King of Croatia, 284
Alexander, General, 377, 382, 598; end of African war, 492; Italian surrender, 507, 509; landings in Italy, 600, 608, 611, 639, 698; replaces Tedder, 684; end of fighting, 699, 701, 702
Alexandria, 64, 150, 598, 809; fighting in Africa, 180–1, 186, 189, 192, 197; Germans halted, 372, 375, 376; end of African war, 493
Alexandris, Admiral, 596
Alfieri, Dino, 186, 517
Algeria, 385–6, 393, 498, 504–5, 809, 811
Algiers, 487, 507, 603, 609, 626; Germans halted, 383–92; end of African war, 488–9, 493–9, 501–2; liberation of Corsica, 526–7; government in, 629, 630, 635–7, 641, 647–8
Allied Air Force, 622, 625, 634, 666, 685, 699
Allied Expeditionary Force, 71, 76
Allied Military Government of Occupied Territories (AMGOT), 528
Allied Submarine Detection Investigation Committee (ASDIC), 65
Alps, 20, 49, 89, 131, 600, 628, 648, 685, 701
Alsace, 300, 647–8, 651–2, 665
Alsace-Lorraine, 17, 89, 147, 171, 245, 287, 784
Altgayer, Dr Branimir, 276
Altmark (German tanker), 71
Altmeyer, General, 130
Amann, Max, 277
Amboyna, 338

Ambrosio, General, 516, 517
Amendola, 529
America First Movement, 158, 324
American Army Air Force, 330, 417, 526, 644, 664; American arsenal, 437, 438; bombing of Germany, 546, 549n; in Asia, 728, 744, 745, 757
American Army, 160, 359, 501, 802, 816, 820; and Japan, 315, 331, 722, 728; Anglo-American war, 417, 430; American arsenal, 431, 436, 437
    First Army, 634, 646, 649, 685, 686, 690
    Third Army, 635, 646, 649, 685, 687, 700, 701
    Fifth Army, 524, 525, 600, 601, 699
    Seventh Army, 646, 652, 685, 687, 690
    Ninth Army, 649, 685, 686, 690, 700
    Tenth Army, 759
    Fifteenth Army, 691, 700
American Merchant Marine, 332, 365
American Navy, 160, 178, 417; Japan, 315–16, 320–1, 331, 338, 722, 728–30; Pacific War, 359–62, 744, 758
Amiens, 108
Amsterdam, 298
Anami, General Korechika, 766, 775
Andaman Islands, 341
Anders, General, 32, 34, 303, 480, 482, 582, 786
Anderson, General, 489, 490, 492
Anfa, 609, 616
Anfuso, Ambassador, 604
Angarita, President Medina, 442
Anglo-Egyptian Treaty, 141n
Anglo-French-Turkish Treaty (1939), 59
Anglo-Soviet Treaty (1942), 474, 804
Anglo-Turkish Treaty (1943), 599
Ankara, 292, 577
Anouilh, Jean, 830
Anti-Fascist Council of National Liberation (AVNOY Yugoslav party), 305
anti-semitism, 258–60, 266–72, 283, 288, 604
Antigone (J. Anouilh), 830
Antonescu, General, 166, 270, 276, 283, 408, 570, 588, 589
Antonescu, Mihaïl, Romanian Foreign Minister, 408, 576, 577
Antonov, General, 670
Antwerp, 56, 87, 98, 645–6, 650, 663–6, 802
'Anvil', Operation, 565, 611, 639, 643, 646
Anzio, 600, 601, 619
Aoki, Shuzo, 346
Aosta, Duke of, 183, 184, 517
Appleton, Sir Edward, 152

Arab League, 809, 810
Aragon, Louis, 830
Arakan, 736
Araunci Mountains, 600
'Arcadia' conference (1941–2 Washington), 421, 422, 430
Archangel, 473
Arciszewski, Thomas, 586
Arctic Ocean, 230, 332, 364
Ardennes, The, 20, 91, 250, 299; breakthrough at Sedan, 99, 100, 104, 109; end of fighting in Europe, 664–7, 669–670, 680, 681, 683, 685, 692
Argenlieu, Admiral Thierry d', 344, 383
Argentine, 441–3, 793, 820, 821, 826
Argonne, 124
Ark Royal (British aircraft carrier), 76, 179, 372
Arlon, 98
Armenia, 229, 816
armoured vehicles, 92–3
Army Resistance Organisation (ORA French), 392, 497, 626, 630
Arnhem, 649, 650
Arnim, General von, 490, 492
Arno, R., 640
Arnold, General, 438, 727, 729, 732, 762, 763, 769
Aron, Robert, 135
Arosa, 68
Arras, 114–15, 117–20, 123
Arromanches, 624, 632
As-Said, Nuri, 809
Asmara, 184
Assam, 735, 736
Assman, Admiral, 179, 375
Astier de la Vigerie, Emmanuel d', 300
Astier de la Vigerie, Henri d', 385, 493, 627
Astrakhan, 395, 556
Atelier (syndicalist party), 281
Athens, 189, 192, 305, 598, 669
Atlantic Charter, 420–1, 447, 473, 480, 481, 568, 673, 674, 808, 825
Atlantic Ocean, 6, 65, 97, 183, 299, 357, 500, 524; Norway, 71, 80; Battle of Britain, 155, 159, 161; Battle of the Atlantic, 177–9, 364–5, 367–8, 370, 372; Anglo-American war, 422, 423; allied victory, 612–14
atom bomb, 711, 717, 721, 768–71, 776
Attlee, Clement, 149, 711, 712, 801, 824, 826
Attolico, Bernardo, 50
Auchinleck, Claude, 372, 375, 376, 377, 422
Audacity (British aircraft carrier), 369

Aufban Ost plan, *see* Barbarossa
Aujourd'hui (anti-militarist party), 281
Auphan, Admiral, 390
Aurillac, 631
Auschwitz, 237, 257, 262, 270, 540
Australia, 155, 179, 330, 793, 813, 835; Japan's lightning war, 331, 332, 335, 338, 341, 344; Pacific war, 359, 360, 362, 748, 777; Anglo-American strategy, 422, 423, 448; and strategy in Asia, 722, 723
Austria, 36, 262, 524, 579, 694, 695; outbreak of war, 1, 14, 17; Nazi Europe, 245; German war economy, 542; Teheran, 568; post war plans for, 596; Potsdam, 707, 708, 709; and USSR, 815
Autun, 646
Aux cotés du maréchal Pétain (Fernet), 134n
Auxerre, 131
Avallon, 131
Aveline, Claude, 830
Avranches, 626, 632, 638
Azerbaidzhan, 229, 283, 815
Azores, 65, 161
Azov, Sea of, 560, 562

Baden, 267, 568
Badoglio, Marshal, 128, 187, 498, 577; plot against Mussolini, 516–18, 520–22; Italy surrenders, 528–9, 658; war in Italy, 602, 603, 605, 606
Baghdad, 195, 196
Bagnoles-de-l'Orne, 514
Bagramyan, Ivan, 581
Bahamas, 147, 160
Baku, 61, 62, 228, 229
Balbo, Marshal, 184–5
Bali, 338
Balkans, 197, 211, 426, 473, 565, 614, 680; allied plans in, 58–60; fighting in, 186–93, 207; German/Russian break, 206, 209; Soviet victories, 590, 591, 594; war in Italy, 609, 639; Potsdam, 708
Baltic Sea, 6, 70, 71, 168, 211, 212, 292; war at sea, 369, 614, 661; end of fighting, 682, 695, 696, 702; Potsdam, 708
Banat, The, 190, 784
Bandera, Stephen, 285, 816
Bandung, 339
Bangkok, 339, 347
Banska-Bystrica, 588
Bao Dai, Emperor, 814
Bapaume, 115
'Barbarossa', Operation, 204, 210
Bardia, 185, 371
Bari, 524

Barneville, 625
Barré, General, 391, 488, 489, 490
Bartók, Béla, 829
Barjot, Admiral, 75
Baruch, Bernard, 430, 439
Basch, Franz, 277
Basdevant, Pastor, 196
Bastia, 526
Bastianini, Giuseppe, 513, 517, 577
Bastogne, 666
Bataan, 334, 337, 757
Batavia, 338, 339
Battai, 517
Batum, 61
Baudouin, Paul, 111, 133, 136, 138, 139
Bauer, E., 29, 109, 114, 125, 203, 374, 681
Bavaria, 262, 527, 568, 611
Bayeux, 622, 636, 645
Bear Island, 475
Beaune, 646
Beaune-la-Rolande, 271
Beauvais, 124
Beaverbrook, Lord, 472
Beck, General, 657, 659
Beigbeder, General, 290
Beirut, 60, 598
Belfort, 131, 646, 651
Belgian Army, 84, 97, 98, 114–16
Belgian Congo, 57, 156, 802
Belgium, 17, 41, 42, 51, 211, 281, 373, 802; problem of, 20–3; allied relations with, 53–8, 68; May 1940, 83, 84, 87–9, 91–3; breakthrough at Sedan, 97–9, 100–1, 104, 107, 108, 274; French collapse, 116; armistice, 129; Battle of Britain, 151, 156; Hitler's Europe, 168, 169, 246; resistance, 297, 298; Soviet alliance, 473, 574; German war economy, 538; liberation of France, 618, 646; aftermath, 782, 793, 797
Belgrade, 49, 189, 190, 206, 268, 592, 692
Belin, René, 288
Belsen, 835
Benda, Julien, 830
Beneš, Eduard, 156, 301, 302, 480, 481, 587, 588, 693
Bengal, 735
Bengal, Bay of, 734, 741
Benghazi, 182, 289, 373
Benjamin, R., 830
Benoist-Méchin, 287, 289
Béraud, Henri, 134n
Berchtesgaden, 195, 257, 400, 701
Beresina, R., 218, 582
Bergen, 75
Bergeret, General, 142

Bergson, Henri, 830
Beria, Laurenti, 572
Berlin, 11, 41, 163, 205, 207, 209, 232 *et passim*
Berling, General, 583, 584, 585
Bermuda, 160
Bernadotte, Count, 702
Bernanos, Georges, 830
Bernard, Colonel, 119, 164, 228, 230, 363
Berne, 68, 766
Bernstein, Henri, 830
Besançon, 91, 131, 646
Bessarabia, 166, 482, 569, 589, 784, 815
Besson, General, 91
Béthouart, General, 76, 121, 385, 388, 499, 500, 685, 701
Béthune, 114
Beveland, 57
Beveridge Plan, 444, 801
Bevin, Ernest, 445, 805
Bhamo plain, 741
Bialystok, 245, 272, 582
Bianco, L., 738
Bichelonne, 289
Bidault, Georges, 805
Bierut, Boleslas, 459, 584, 585, 712, 713, 817
Bihac, 305
Bir-Hakeim, 373, 497, 648
Birkenau, 271, 540
Bilderding, Baron von, 235
Billig, J., 258, 261
Billotte, General, 91, 101, 114-17
Bismarck (German battleship), 3, 44, 179
Bismarck Islands, 344, 359, 722, 723, 745
Bizerta, 170, 174, 179, 181, 195, 373, 386, 391, 488, 489, 490, 492, 566
Black Sea, 60, 61, 212, 228, 230, 292, 562, 570, 708
Blanchard, General, 56, 117, 121, 122
Blaskowitz, General, 257, 643
Blitz, London, 153
Blitzkrieg, 54, 79, 94, 109, 541; in Russia, 204, 220, 239, 468
Bloch, Jean-Richard, 458
Blücher, Ambassador, 47
Blum, Léon, 16, 288
Blumentritt, General, 622
Bock, General von, 32; plans for invasion, 84, 86, 89; French collapse, 123, 125; war with USSR, 211, 222, 225, 228
Bodet, Torrès, 821
Boentsch, Lt Col., 8
Bohemia, 1, 32, 268, 587, 701; and Hitler's Europe, 164, 167, 246; resistance, 302; population migration, 785
Bohr, Niels, 768

Boislambert, Hettier de, 636
Boisson, General, 195, 493
'Bolero', Operation, 381, 422, 478
Bolivia, 443, 820
Bologna, 699
Bolt, Gerhard, 697
Bomber Command, 367, 545, 546
Bône, 386, 389
Bonin, Colonel von, 682
Bonin Islands, 750, 758
Bonnafous, Max, 277
Bonnard, Abel, 289, 830
Bonnet, Georges, 36n, 111
Bono, Emilio de, 604
Bonomi, Joseph, 515-17, 529, 530, 606-8
Bor, 250
Bor-Komorovski, Tadeusz, 584, 585
Bordeaux, 129, 133, 134, 178, 641
Bordeaux government, 136-43, 150; *see also* Vichy government
Borghese, Prince, 604
Boris, King of Bulgaria, 45, 577
Borkum, 797
Bormann, Martin, 39, 231
Borneo, 338, 346, 349, 754, 756
Bose, Chandrah, 341, 347
Bosnia, 305, 527, 591, 787
Bosphorus, 565
Boudienny, Marshal, 219, 224, 229
Bouerat, 381
Bougainville, 723, 745
Bougie, 489
Boulogne, 117, 153, 646, 650
Bourg, 131
Bourguiba, Habib, 282, 504, 811
Bouthillier, Yves, 111, 133
Brabant, 104
Bracher, Dietrich, 258
Braden, Spruille, 820
Bradley, Omar, 624, 649, 651, 667, 685, 690, 695, 700
Bragadin, 187, 371
Brandenberger, 702
Brandenburg, 696
Brasillach, R., 282, 830
Bratianu, 283, 589, 693
Bratislava, 164, 692
Brauchitsch, Walther von, 37, 41; invasion plans, 84, 86, 89; Battle of Britain, 151; war with Russia, 203, 204, 223
Brauer, Ambassador, 72, 77, 78
Braun, Werner von, 662
Bräutigam, Otto, 285, 286
Brazil, 441, 442, 443, 793, 820, 821
Brazzaville, 506
Breda, 56, 57, 87, 97, 664

Bremen, 547, 700
Brenner, R., 611
Brereton, General, 685
Breslau, 681, 682, 696
Brest, 131, 179, 366, 475, 632, 634
Brest-Litovsk, 216, 218, 582
Breton, André, 830
Briançon, 644
Briansk, 219, 562, 572
Briare, 132
Brindisi, 523, 641
Brisbane, 332, 364
Britain, 12, 287, 289; outbreak, 1, 2, 15, 17, 21, 23; shortcomings, 12; Poland, 32, 35, 37, 38; phoney war, 41, 42, 49, 51–3, 59, 63, 67–9; war in Norway, 71, 77; May 1940, 83, 84, 94; French collapse, 114, 123, 124; armistice, 135–7, 139–40, 142–3; Battle of Britain, 147–61, 196, 203, 206, 403; and Hitler's Europe, 162–3, 172–4, 176; Africa and Balkans, 177–9, 182, 184, 186, 193, 196–7; German/Russian break, 205–7; Wehrmacht in USSR, 217, 220, 225; Hitler's domination, 246, 290, 309; and resistance, 295, 296; and Japan, 312–13, 316–17, 330–2, 335, 344, 346, 352; war at sea, 366–7; war in Africa, 381, 382, 386–7, 503; American alliance, 413, 415, 419, 419–20, 422, 426; American arsenal, 428–9, 431, 435, 437, 440, 443, 450; war production, 445, 447–8, 468; Soviet alliance, 470–3, 477, 479; bombing of Germany, 535–7, 546, 552; Teheran, 566–7; and German satellites, 577, 595, 596, 598; war in Italy, 610; liberation of France, 619, 627, 632, 640, 649; end of European war, 661–2, 695; Yalta, 670, 676, 679; Potsdam, 705, 711; war in China/Burma, 732, 759, 772, 776; aftermath, 782, 787, 793, 794, 797; new balance of power, 800–802, 804, 809–11, 815, 823–4; reconstruction, 826; see also Royal Air Force, Royal Navy
British Army, 7, 83, 148, 446; French collapse, 120, 123; Africa and Balkans, 184, 289; Germans halted, 376, 377
    Second Army, 634, 646, 685, 686, 700
    Eighth Army, 426, 448; African war, 373, 375, 377, 381, 492; Italian surrender, 524, 525; war in Italy, 601
British Broadcasting Corporation (BBC), 295, 299, 369, 547, 549, 579, 626, 629, 667, 832

British Expeditionary Force, 51, 90, 100, 114, 117, 118, 119, 122, 130–1
British Guiana, 160
British Merchant Navy, 65, 66, 177, 801
British Somaliland, 183
Brittany, 634, 636, 638
Brno, 701
Brochard, General, 107
Bromberg, 31, 681
Brüning, Heinrich, 15
Brussels, 56, 373, 646, 664
Bucard, Marcel, 282
Bucharest, 49, 576, 577, 589, 594, 693
Buchenwald, 14, 262, 264, 540, 792, 835
Buckner, General, 759, 761
Budapest, 49, 578, 593, 594, 681, 682, 691, 692
Buenos Aires, 443, 820
Buffarini, 604
Bug, R., 233, 569
'Bugle', Operation, 687
Buisson, General, 125
Bukovina, 205, 232, 569, 784, 815
Bulganin, Nikolai, 452
Bulgaria, 45, 166, 247, 470, 570, 692, 784; Balkan war, 187, 188, 190, 192; German/Russian break, 205, 209; break with Germany, 577; Soviet victories, 589, 590, 594–6; and USSR, 713, 815, 817, 823
Bullitt, Ambassador William C., 124, 128, 564, 670
Bullock, Alan, 258
Bulson, 105
Buna, 362
Bureau central de Renseignements et d'Action, 299
Burgundy, 167, 646
Burma, 674, 735; Japan/US break, 312, 313, 318, 319; Japan's lightning war, 332, 335, 340–1; Japanese occupation, 346, 347, 348, 351, 352, 353; Anglo-American war, 419, 423, 426; Pacific strategy, 723, 725–7, 731, 732, 736–7, 741–2; war in Pacific, 750, 758; Japanese surrender, 762, 764
Busch, Marshal von, 581, 702
Butler, R., 52
Butow, R., 317
Bydgoszcz, see Bromberg
Byelgorod, 228, 555, 562, 597
Byelorussia, 218, 232, 233, 462, 581, 597, 676
Byrnes, James, 434, 678, 769, 772, 805, 822
Bzura, 34

Cadaev, 464
Cadorna, General, 608
Caen, 622, 624, 625
Cairo, 305, 348, 350, 484, 563, 577, 590, 596, 674, 732; fighting in Africa, 192, 197, 375, 377; Arab League, 810
Calabria, 182, 524
Calais, 120, 122, 123, 153, 621, 646, 650
Calcutta, 735, 762, 814
Calvet, 425
Cambodia, 318, 346
Cambrai, 115
Cameroons, 157, 299
Campinchi, César, 111, 132
Campioni, Admiral, 523
Camus, Albert, 16, 830
Canada, 154–5, 329, 365, 447, 614, 793, 820
Canadian First Army, 634, 646, 685, 700
Canaris, Admiral, 659
Canary Islands, 176, 291
Cantilho, 441
Canton, 311, 737, 765
Cape, The, 179, 181, 372, 382
Cap Nègre, 641
Cape Engano, 756
Capra, Frank, 830
Capua, 525
Carelian Isthmus, 46, 220, 580
Carentan, 622
Caribbean, 160, 368
Carinthia, 699, 784
Carol, King of Romania, 166
Casabianca (French submarine), 526
Casablanca, fighting in Africa, 386, 388, 489; Allied Conference (Jan 1943), 423, 425, 478, 492, 513, 535, 546, 658, 716, 723, 725, 764
Caserta, 598
'Cash and Carry' Bill (US 1939), 69, 160
Carpathian Mts., 587–9, 593, 691
Caspian Sea, 450, 475
Cassibile, 522
Casson, Jean, 830
Castellan, G., 715
Castellano, General, 516, 517, 518, 521
Catania, 508
Catalonia, 176
'Catapult', Operation, 150
Catroux, General, 196, 496, 505
Caucasia, 784
Caucasus, proposal to attack, 60–2, 64, 67; German/Russian break, 210; Wehrmacht victories, 219, 225, 228–30, 401–402, 406–7; Allied alliance, 476; Soviet offensive, 560
Caumont, Colonel Le Couteulx de, 488

Cavalaire, 643
Cavallero, Ugo, 187, 373, 375, 516
Celebes, 338, 349
Cépède, 787
Central Committee for Internal Resistance (UVOD Czech Resistance), 302
Cephalonia, 523, 527
Ceylon, 336, 341, 762
Chaban-Delmas, 636
Chack, Paul, 830
Chad, The, 184
Chalon-sur-Saône, 131, 646
Chamberlain, Neville, 12, 15, 18, 147, 443; phoney war, 42, 52, 67; war in Norway, 70, 80
Chambéry, 644
Champagne, 125
Champon, General, 120
Chamson, André, 830
Chang-kia-kow, 311
Channel Islands, 246, 703
Chapelle, Bonnier de la, 494
Chapultepec Agreement (US 1945), 820
Charles-Roux, François, 138
Chartres, 635
chasseurs ardennais, 99–100
Chassin, General, 61, 743
Château, R., 281
Chateaubriant, A. de, 830
Chautemps, Camille, 111, 135, 637
Cheliabinsk, 462
Chennault, General, 727, 736, 737, 776
Chemery, 104
Cherbourg, 131, 616, 617, 622, 625, 632, 645
Cherkassy, 563
Chernigov, 563
Chernyakovsky, Ivan, 682
Chen-si, 354
Chiang Kai-shek, 286, 674, 678; China war, 311–13, 315, 319; Chungking government, 352–4; Communism, 354, 356; Teheran conference, 563, 566; ultimatum to Japan, 716; fighting against Japan, 721, 725–6, 732–7, 772, 773, 776; Japanese surrender, 763, 765, 766, 774; postwar balance of power, 813
Chiers, R., 107
Chile, 441, 442, 443, 793, 820
China, 9, 205, 426, 674, 843; China war, 309–16, 319; and Japan's lightning war, 326, 335, 340, 341; Chungking government, 345, 352–4; Communist China, 354–6; American arsenal, 428; UNO, 676; Yalta, 678; Pacific war, 721, 725–7, 731–7, 741, 754, 756, 772, 776;

Japanese surrender, 762, 765, 766, 774, 777; and USSR, 771; aftermath, 781, 782, 786; new balance of power, 812, 813; reconstruction, 826; *see also* Communism

Chinese Army, 725, 726, 733, 734, 736
Chinkiang, 738
Choa, 183
Choltitz, General von, 637, 638
Chou En-lai, 354, 813
Chroniques irrévérencieuses (Larminat), 62n
Chungking, 311, 340, 734, 735–7, 763, 813
Churchill, Randolph, 565
Churchill, Winston, 12, 15, 18, 109, 291, 305, 740, 770; phoney war, 52, 62; Norway, 70, 72, 75, 77, 80, 297; French collapse, 114, 117, 118, 121, 122, 124; French armistice, 132, 135, 137; Battle of Britain, 147–52, 155–7, 160; Africa and Balkans, 182, 184, 188, 193, 197, 198; German/Russian war, 208, 220, 230; strategy in Asia, 725, 732, 742, 771; war against Japan, 315, 330, 339, 341, 758, 759; war at sea, 365, 366; North Africa, 372, 375–8, 381–3, 495–6, 503; Anglo-American alliance, 415–18, 420–4, 426, 427, 430; arms production, 443–5; Commonwealth, 447–8; USSR war, 454, 455, 457; Soviet alliance, 470–8, 480, 484; Italy surrenders, 521, 528; bombing Germany, 545–7, 550, 552; Teheran, 563–9; Soviet victories, 576, 585–6, 591–6, 598; landings in Italy, 599–602, 609–11; Overlord, 614–17; liberation of France, 627, 638–9; Yalta, 668–75, 677, 678; end of war in Europe, 684, 691, 693–6, 698–9, 701–2; Potsdam, 705, 707–13, 715–16; Casablanca, 723, 764; postwar balance of power, 800–802, 805, 809, 818; Moscow talks, 817, 826
Chuikov, 698
Ciano, Count, 19, 38, 39, 42, 147, 151, 375, 577; phoney war, 49, 51, 79; collapse of France, 128; armistice, 139, 141; Romania, 166; Libya, 184; Greece, 186, 187; dissatisfaction with Germany, 408; Italy surrenders, 512, 513, 517, 520; death, 604
Cirey, 652
'Citadel', Operation, 559–61, 562
Clair, René, 830
Clark, General, 385, 493, 524, 600, 611, 643, 699
Claude, Georges, 830
Clausewitz, Karl, 571
Clauss, 483, 484

Clemenceau, 111
Clerk, Staf de, 281, 283
Clermont-Ferrand, 131
Cleves, 687
Cluj, 166
Coastal Command, 178, 367
Coblence, 690
Cochet, General, 636, 641
Cochinchina, 814
Cognac, 365
Cohen, Benjamin, 772
Colombia, 442, 443
Cole, C. M., 646
Colijn, Hendrikus, 168
Colleville, 621
Colmar, 646, 664, 685
Cologne, 546, 687
Colombo, 336, 348
Combined Shipping Adjustment Board, 419
Comintern, dissolution of, 456–8, 575, 587
Comité d'Histoire de la deuxième guerre mondiale, IX, 647
Comité secret d'action revolutionnaire (Deloncle party), 282
Commonwealth, 419, 423, 428, 446–50
Communism, China, 354–5, 739, 740; concentration camps, 264, 265; Czechoslovakia, 587; France, 629, 637, 648, 803; Germany, 656; Greece, 596, 598; Italy, 514–15, 527, 530, 602, 603, 606–8; Japan, 311, 348, 349; Poland, 50; resistance organisations, 296–7, 301–3, 305; S. America, 442; USSR, 408–9, 452, 454–60, 468, 572, 574, 575, 580, 816, 817; Soviet victories, 231, 576, 579, 586
Compiègne, 254
Confederation Générale du Travail, 16
Courland, 581, 680, 683, 703
Constanza, 60
Controlled Materials Plan (CMP), 432
Constantine Programme (Algeria), 505
Constantin, Colonel, 561, 597n
Copenhagen, 72
Coral Sea, 730
Corap, General, 101, 102
Corinth, 193
Cork, Admiral, 76
Cornet, Matteo, 134n
Corregidor, 337, 757
Corsica, 2, 141n, 143, 373, 507, 521, 525; liberation of, 525–7; liberation of France, 641
Cos, 523
Cosne, 130
COSSAC (Allied organisation for 'Overlord'), 616, 617, 625

Cossé-Brissac, General de, 212, 554
Côte-d'Or, 644
Contentin, 616, 621, 622, 625, 626
Coulet, Camille, 636
Courageous (British aircraft carrier), 76
Courtrai, 118, 120
Coutances, 626
Couve de Murville, Maurice, 603, 804n
Coventry, 154
Cracow, 165, 246, 257, 272, 681
Craiova, 233
Créon (J. Anouilh), 830
Crerar, General, 685
Crete, 182, 192, 193, 339, 661
Crimea, 224, 227, 563, 569, 570, 589, 668, 784, 785
Cripps, Sir Stafford, 448, 473, 476, 477
Croatia, 79, 190, 246–7, 254, 274, 276, 284, 784
Croce, Benedetto, 515
Crozat Canal, 125
Cuba, 46, 441, 442
Cunningham, Admiral, 64, 150, 189, 193; Africa, 181–3, 386; Italy, 524
Cunningham, General, 184
Curtin, John, 448
Curzon, Lord, 672
Cyrenaica, 185, 194, 197, 371–2, 381, 477
Czechoslovakia, 17, 19, 20, 32, 36, 52, 148, 208, 459; resistance, 301–2; dismemberment, 480–1; and USSR, 586–8, 693, 694, 701, 707–9; aftermath, 793; postwar balance of power, 815, 817, 818, 823
Czernovitz, 218
Czestochova, 681

Dachau, 14, 262, 274, 540, 656, 835
Dabendorff, 571
Dahlerus, Birger, 42
Dairen, 566, 815
Dakar, 157, 170, 173, 174, 182, 195, 383, 387, 496, 502, 566
Daladier, Edouard, 42, 101; phoney war, 52, 54, 61, 63; French collapse, 111–12, 288
Dalmatia, 190
Damaskinos, Archbishop, 669, 824
Danish National Bank, 73
Danube, R., 60, 61, 589, 592, 692, 708, 823
Dantry, Minister, 13, 111
Danzig, 32, 696
Dardanelles, 205, 674, 816, 823
Darlan, Admiral, 6, 22, 74, 90, 393, 425; French collapse, 112; armistice, 134, 150; collaboration, 173–5, 287–9, 387;

in Africa, 195, 383, 388–91, 478, 487; end of African war, 488, 493, 494, 505, 602
Darnand, Joseph, 254
Darwin, Charles, 258
Davies, General, 306
Dauphiné, 131
D-day, 618, 620, 621; *see also* Overlord, France
Deane, General John R., 470, 472, 678, 705
Déat, Marcel, 281
Deauville, 622
Debreczen, 593, 594
Decour, Jacques, 830
Decoux, Admiral, 493, 765
Degrelle, Léon, 281, 283
Delattre de Tassigny, General, 110, 392, 497, 501, 601; liberation of France, 640, 643, 645, 646, 651; Strasbourg, 667; end of European war, 685, 701, 703
Delestraint, General, 301
Deloncle, Eugène, 282
Dempsey, General, 685
Denmark, 140, 156, 292, 618, 694, 702; war in Norway, 72–3, 78–9; German/Russian break, 211; occupation, 247, 248, 250; resistance, 298; Anglo-Russian alliance, 473; and USSR, 707; aftermath, 793, 794, 797; postwar balance of power, 802
Dentz, General, 196
Déroulède, Paul, 503
Derrien, Admiral, 391, 488
Desnos, Robert, 830
Derry, T. K., 75
Detroit, 436
Deuxième Bureau (French military intelligence), 8, 10
Devers, General, 649, 685, 702
Devèze, 53
Dhers, General, 389
Dicheroff, Lieutenant, 604
Diego, Suarez, 341
Dieppe, 230, 382, 422, 447, 478, 617, 619, 645
Dietl, General, 211
Dietrich, Sepp, 277, 666, 692
Dijon, 131, 646
Dill, General Sir John, 117, 131, 149, 189, 418
Dimitrescu, General, 399
Dimitrov, Georges, 459
Dinant, 86, 92, 105, 646, 666
Dives, R., 622
Djawa Hokokai (Association for the assistance of Java), 351, 352

Djibouti, 2, 184
Dnepropetrovsk, 211, 220, 406, 462, 563
Dniestr, R., 232, 569, 588, 589
Dobruja, 166, 784, 785, 823
Doctrine de guerre du Général Douhet, La (Vauthier), 18n
Dodecanese Ils., 420
Doenitz, Admiral, 7, 178, 570, 619, 706, 707, 713; war at sea, 365, 369, 370; Allied Atlantic victory, 612–14; final throes, 661, 702, 703
Don, R., 225, 228, 230, 395, 398, 399–401, 406, 559, 588
Donbass, 570, 573, 576
Donetz, R., 225, 235, 406, 407, 462, 555, 559
Doorman, Admiral, 338
Dora concentration camp, 262
Dordogne, 631
Dordrecht, 97
Doriot, Jacques, 282
Dormoy, Marx, 287
Dos Passos, John, 830
Douhet, Guilio, 8–9, 61, 152, 178, 367
Doumenc, General, 113
Doumergue, Gaston, 112
Dover, 122
Dover, Straits of, 65, 171, 178, 616, 620, 624, 632
Drancy, 271
Drave, R., 680
Dreiser, Theodore, 830
Dresden, 547, 695, 696, 790
Drieu la Rochelle, 279, 282, 830
Dronne, Captain, 638
Drvar, 591
Duclos, Jacques, 459
Dufieux, General, 93
Duhamel, Georges, 830
Dulles, Alan, 483
Dumbarton Oaks, 825
Dumoulin, G., 281
Dunkirk, 118–24, 130, 135, 152, 646, 685, 703
Durazzo, 187
Düsseldorf, 686
Dutch Army, 96, 97, 338
Dutch East Indies, 97, 313–15, 319, 331, 335, 337, 346; China/Burma war, 736, 750
Dutch Navy, 338
Dvorjetzky, 272
Dyle plan (KW line), 56, 57, 98, 101
Dyle R., 56, 87
'Dynamo', Operation, 121–3

Eben Emaël fort, 100

Eboué, Félix, 503
Economic Stabilization, Office of, 434
Ecuador, 443
Eden, Anthony, 52, 114, 417, 512, 671, 707; Africa and Balkans, 188–90; USSR, 455, 473, 474, 480–3, 594, 595; Teheran, 565, 566, 569; Warsaw uprising, 585, 586; Japan, 771; San Francisco conference, 808; Arab unity, 809
EDES (Greek non-Communist party), 305
Edward VIII, 148
Egypt, 155, 282, 358; North African war, 183, 184, 188, 189, 194, 195, 197; Germans halted, 371–8, 382; postwar balance of power, 801, 809; Arab League, 810
Ehrenburg, Ilya, 830
Eichmann, Adolf, 271, 578
Eifel, R., 649, 685, 686
Einsatzgruppen, 237, 267
Einsiedel, Lieutenant von, 579, 580
Einstein, Albert, 768–70, 829n
Eire, 155, 365
Eisenhower, General, 331, 422, 666, 707, 711; N. Africa, 383, 385, 388, 392, 487, 490, 500, 501; Italian surrender, 507, 521, 522, 523, 526; 'Overlord', 614, 615, 618, 619, 621, 625; liberation of France, 627, 631, 638, 643, 645, 646, 649, 650, 652; Yalta, 671; Battle of the Rhineland, 683–7, 690–91; and Russians, 694–6; end of fighting in Germany, 699–703; atom bomb, 769
EKKA (Psaros's party Greece), 305
El Agheila, 185, 372
El Alamein, 375, 381, 408, 487
ELAS (Greek Communist party), 305, 596, 598, 669
Elba, 601
Elbe, R., 640, 694–6, 699, 700, 785
Elbeuf, 635
El'brus, 229
Electra (British cruiser), 338
Eluard, Paul, 830
Emilia, 607
English Channel, 19, 125, 366, 425, 426, 507, 521, 525, 546, 565, 599, 609
Epinal, 646
Epirus, 186, 187, 246
Eritrea, 184
Ermler, Friedrich, 830
Estienne, General, 7
Esteva, Admiral, 488
Estonia, 45, 232, 580
Ethiopia, 51, 183, 184, 299, 448
Etna, 508

Eupen, 147, 245
Eure, R., 630
European Consultative Commission, 595, 596
Evatt, Dr, 344

Falaise, 625, 634
Falgade, General, 116, 130
Falkenhausen, General von, 169
Falkenhorst, General von, 78
Farinacci, 517, 604
Farouk, King of Egypt, 282, 810
Fascism, 601, 602; collaborators, 280–3, 293; Italy surrenders, 513–16, 518–21, 523, 529; Salo republic, 603, 604; war in Italy, 606–7; aftermath, 805, 808
Fassi, Allal el, 811
Faulhabier, Cardinal, 656
Feiling, Sir Keith, 67
Feltre, 509, 512, 517, 521, 577
Ferdonnet, 67
Fermi, Enrico, 768, 769, 833
Fernet, Admiral, 134n
Ferrara, 699
Fifth Column, 29, 31, 341
Fighter Command (RAF), 153
Fiji Islands, 344
Finland, 70, 220, 292, 459, 566, 785; Finnish/Soviet conflict, 45–9; allied plans in Scandinavia, 63, 64, 67; German/Russian break, 205, 207, 208, 210, 215; and Allied alliance, 470, 482; break with Germany, 578, 580, 581, 586 Finnish Army, 219, 285
Finland, Gulf of, 46
Finschhafen, 745
Flanders, 119, 124, 281
Flavigny, General, 107
Flemish Nationalist movement, 21
Flensburg, 706
Florence, 530
Flossenberg, 262
Foch, Marshal, 112, 141, 147
Foggia, 524
Forbach, 36
Ford, Henry, 158
Foreign Legion, 76, 811
Forli, 601
Formidable (British aircraft carrier), 193
Formosa, 326, 336, 364, 732, 752, 753, 762, 812
Forrestal, James, 716, 772
France, 281, 309, 330, 401, 447, 566, 571, 588, 603, 676, 776, 843; outbreak, 1, 2, 10, 12–13, 15, 17, 19–21; and Poland, 32, 35–8; phoney war, 41, 42, 48n, 51–4, 58–9, 63, 64, 67, 69; war in

Norway, 74, 77, 79; May 1940, 83–4, 89, 90, 92, 94; French line broken, 109–110; collapse, 111–28; armistice, 129–138, 140–43; Battle of Britain, 149, 150, 153, 156–8; Vichy government, 162, 167, 169, 170; exploitation, 172–3, 176; East Africa, 184; Syria, 195–6; German/Russian break, 211, 217; occupation, 245–8, 250, 251, 253, 254; anti-semitism, 266, 267, 270, 274; collaboration, 174, 282, 289, 290; resistance, 295, 297, 299–303, 409; and Chiang Kai-shek, 312, 313, 315; N. Africa, 373, 384, 385, 387, 389, 390, 392, 393; and Anglo-American alliance, 419, 421; American arsenal, 428, 437, 441; Soviet war, 455, 458, 459, 468; Soviet alliance, 472, 473, 477; end of N. African war, 488, 489, 493, 495, 497, 498, 501–5; Italy surrenders, 513–15, 519, 527; German war economy, 535, 536, 538, 545; bombing of Germany, 547, 552; landing plans, 565, 611; liberation of, 612–52; end of war in Europe, 657, 663; Yalta, 668, 669, 671, 674, 677, 679; Potsdam, 712, 716; aftermath, 782–4, 787, 790, 793, 794, 796, 797; postwar balance of power, 800, 803, 804, 811, 817, 823; reconstruction, 825, 826, 830; scientific discovery, 836, 838; see also Free French
French Army, 7, 68, 84, 90, 123, 132, 136
    First Army, 56, 87, 601, 685, 690; breakthrough at Sedan, 101, 104; French collapse, 117–18; liberation of France, 640, 641, 643, 646, 648, 651
    French Expeditionary Force, 600
    Fourth Army, 35, 130
    French Navy, 6, 134, 140, 142–3, 383
    French Air Force, 11, 35, 94, 134, 137, 142, 501
France au travail, La (anti-clerical party), 281
Franco, Francisco, 69, 111, 386, 391; Hitler's Europe, 174, 175–6; 244; collaboration, 290, 291
Franco-German compensation agreement, 173
Franco-Polish convention, 2
François-Poncet, 93, 125
Frank, Hans, 39, 165, 233
Frankfurt, 548, 683, 697
Frankfurt-on-the-Oder, 797
Franzoni, 512

Frauenwarte (paper of National Socialist women), 278
Free French, 156, 157, 184, 196, 299, 330, 331, 341; in Africa, 375, 381, 383, 385; Soviet alliance, 476; end of N. African war, 493, 495, 497–9, 501, 503, 504; Italy surrenders, 513
Free German Committee in the West, 579, 580
Freetown, 177
Freiburg, 656
Freisler, Roland, 659
Fréjus, 643
Fremantle, 364
Frenay, Henri, 300
French Compensation Bureau, 173
French Equatorial Africa, 157, 299
French Forces of the Interior (FFI), Battle for France, 626–31, 634, 636; liberation of Paris, 637, 638; liberated France, 644–6, 648, 703
French Guyana, 503
French Morocco, 176
French National Committee, *see* Free French
French National Liberation Committee, 496, 498, 500–502, 504–6, 526, 603
French Pacific Islands, 157
French West Africa, 157, 170, 182, 493, 496, 499
French West Indies, 493
Frère, General, 115, 118, 125
Freud, Sigmund, 829n
Freyberg, General, 192, 193
Friedeburg, Admiral von, 702, 707
Friesian Ils., 702
Friesner, General, 589
Fritt Folk (Quisling newspaper), 167
Fromm, Erich, 658, 659
Front Populaire, 13, 15, 16
Frossard, 135

Gabès, 492
Galapagos Ils., 820
Galbiati, General, 519, 520
Galen, Mgr., 656
Galland, General, 662
Gambiez, Commander, 526
Gamelin, General, 8, 18, 20, 22, 288; Poland, 35, 36n; phoney war, 51, 53–4, 56–8, 61; war in Norway, 74; forces May 1940, 87, 90, 93; breakthrough at Sedan, 100, 104, 107, 109; French collapse, 112, 113, 115, 123
Gandhi, Mahatma, 155, 341, 448, 458
Gandin, General, 523

Ganzer, Richard, 163
Garibaldi, General, 227
Garigliano, R., 599
Gascony, 618
Gasperi, Alcide de, 516, 529, 804n
Gaulle, General Charles de, 108, 173, 244, 384, 391, 476, 564, 566, 603, 666, 701; outbreak of war, 7, 8, 18; French collapse, 111, 119; in London, 135, 137; Free France, 156–7; in Africa, 196, 383, 385, 487; resistance, 299–301; Anglo-American alliance, 420, 421, 423; end of N. African war, 495–8, 500, 502, 503, 505, 506; liberation of Corsica, 525, 527; 'Overlord', 615; liberation of France, 626–7, 635–6, 638, 640, 647, 648; Yalta, 668; Potsdam, 712, 716; aftermath, 797; postwar balance of power, 803, 804
Gazala, 373
Gdynia, 35, 696
Gembloux 'gap', 56, 87, 98, 101
General Directorate of Special Services (French DGSS), 497
Generalplan Ost, 243
Geneva, 298, 483, 517
Geneva Convention, 210, 334, 539, 636, 660, 791
Genoa, 183, 699
Gensoul, Admiral, 150
Gentilhomme, General Le, 184
George, King of Greece, 192, 596, 669, 694
Georges, General, 35; phoney war, 52, 54, 56, 57; forces, May 1940, 87, 90, 93; breakthrough at Sedan, 102, 104, 107, 109; French collapse, 113, 118, 124
Georgia, 229
Gérardmer, 652
Germany, 12, 83, 97, 367, 447, 488, 576, 613, 616, 756, 777, 819; potential force, 1, 2, 6, 11, 14, 15, 19; Poland, 20, 31, 34, 37, 39; German-Soviet pact, 41, 42, 45; Finnish-Soviet conflict, 47–8; and Mussolini, 49–51; Balkan plans, 59–62; blockade, 64–5; phoney war, 68–9; war in Norway, 70, 71, 79, 80; French armistice, 135, 137, 138, 140–2; Battle of Britain, 147, 151, 154, 155, 157, 159; Hitler's ideas for Europe, 162–8; and Vichy government, 169, 171, 173; Spain, 176; Romania, 186; Balkans, 185, 189–90, 195, 197; German/Russian break, 203–6, 208; war with USSR, 214, 220, 231, 234, 235, 237, 317, 357; Nazi Europe, 239, 242, 244–51, 254, 255; concentration camps, 258, 260, 261,

Germany – (contd.)

265, 266–7, 273–4; collaboration, 278–
80, 283, 287, 290, 291–2; resistance,
298, 302, 303; relations with Japan,
310, 312, 313, 315, 316, 318–20, 324,
325, 327, 334, 335; end of war in N.
Africa, 373, 377, 380, 387, 488;
Stalingrad, 406, 408; Anglo-American
alliance, 413, 419, 420, 422–6; Allied
arsenal, 428, 440, 441, 443, 446; Soviet
war production, 454, 460, 463, 468;
Anglo-Soviet alliance, 472, 474, 476–8,
481, 483, 484; Italian surrender, 510,
512, 515, 517, 518, 521, 523, 524;
Allied bombing, 535, 547–51; war
economy, 536–45; Soviet offensive,
553, 555, 575; Teheran discussions,
566–9; desatellisation, 576–98; fighting
in Italy, 599, 610; liberation of France,
618, 625, 639, 640, 645, 647, 652;
opposition to Hitler, 655–60; secret
weapons, 660–4; last offensive, 664–7;
Yalta discussions, 668–74, 678–9; end
of war in Europe, 680–704, 725;
Potsdam, 706, 707, 712, 713, 715, 716,
721; atom bomb, 768–9; aftermath,
782–4, 786–7, 790–2, 794–9, 829; post-
war balance of power, 800, 802, 804,
811, 812, 815, 817, 818, 822; scientific
discoveries, 831, 834, 836
Wehrmacht, 2, 8, 17, 23, 276, 277, 369,
548, 555, 604, 659, 667, 709, 784;
Poland, 31, 32, 34, 36, 40, 41, 44;
phoney war, 54, 58, 60, 68; Norway,
72; plans/forces May 1940, 86, 89,
92, 95; French armistice, 139, 141,
147; Hitler's Europe, 162, 176, 252;
Africa and Balkans, 182, 185, 193,
197, 205, 206; break with USSR, 203,
209–14, 514; victories in USSR, 216–
238, 270, 291, 371, 376, 383, 387, 459,
576; domination, 239, 242, 257; and
SS, 261, 266, 271, 791; collaboration, 283, 285–7, 291, 292; resistance, 302–4; Stalingrad, 394, 399,
402, 404–8, 413; Soviet war, 450,
467, 468, 569; Anglo-Soviet alliance,
472, 473, 474, 481; Italian surrender,
510, 513; war economy, 535, 536,
539, 541, 544; Soviet offensive, 554,
556, 560–1, 571, 573, 575; Soviet
victories, 579, 593, 598, 655; fighting
in Italy, 604; liberation of France, 618,
619, 622, 632, 638, 644; and Nazi
regime, 659; end of war in Europe,
667, 680, 702, 706, 839; aftermath,
714, 829; see also Panzer division

First Army, 686
Fourth Army, 229, 395, 398, 400, 401
Sixth Army, 228, 395, 398, 400–6,
589
Seventh Army, 625
Eighth Army, 624
Fifteenth Army, 624, 632
Eighteenth Army, 97, 204
Nineteenth Army, 641, 651
Twentieth Army, 581
Luftwaffe, 3, 9, 10, 11, 104, 524, 590;
outbreak of war, 29, 31; Norway,
71, 74–6; German plans, 84, 91, 94;
collapse of France, 114, 119, 123–4;
Battle of Britain, 148, 151–4, 161,
782; Africa and Balkans, 178, 193,
195, 197; war with Russia, 204, 211,
218, 222, 223, 227, 365; Stalingrad,
395, 402, 403, 405; offensive by
USSR, 559, 562, 590; domination in
Europe, 239, 290; N. Africa, 371,
374; German war economy, 541–4;
Allied bombing, 548–52; liberation
of France, 618–20, 622, 632, 649
Kriegsmarine, 3, 43, 65, 151, 179, 225,
393, 619; war in Norway, 71, 79;
war at sea, 364, 365, 366, 369
German Armistice Commission, 173
German-Soviet pact, 1, 14, 15, 16, 88,
176, 197, 302, 314, 409, 455, 457, 472,
473, 514; Poland, 32, 34, 36, 38, 479;
phoney war, 43, 49, 59, 62, 64, 68;
German-Soviet break, 203, 207, 209,
312
Gernsheim, 690
Gestapo, 165, 242, 657; in Russia, 236,
237; Hitler's Europe, 253, 254; colla-
boration, 279, 290; resistance, 300, 302
Ghent, 56
Ghent canal, 23
Ghormley, Admiral, 722, 728
Giannini, Guglielmo, 805
Gibraltar, 6, 69, 180, 181, 183, 197, 290,
291, 566; Germans halted in N. Africa,
374, 380, 382, 386–8
Gide, André, 830
Giens, 644
Gifford, General, 726
Gilbert Ils., 335, 336, 341, 345, 723, 748–
750
Gille, General, 691, 692
Giraud, General, 56, 423, 487, 566, 626;
in Africa, 384, 385, 388, 389, 392; end
of African war, 489, 490, 493–7, 499–
501, 503, 602; liberation of Corsica,
526–7
Giraudoux, Jean, 67, 830

Girault, 462, 464, 468
Givet, 101
Globke, Dr, 245
Globocnik, 270
Glogau, 696
Glorious (British aircraft carrier), 76
Gneisenau (German battle cruiser), 3, 366, 475, 696
Godfroy, Admiral, 64, 150, 493
Goebbels, Joseph, 14, 154, 206, 211, 230, 231, 242, 243, 259; collaboration, 276–8, 282, 283, 285; resistance, 295; Stalingrad, 405, 407; Soviet war, 457; bombing of Germany, 548; 'Overlord', 619, 620; plot against Hitler, 658, 660; end of war in Europe, 667; death, 697
Goerdeler, Carl, 68, 657
Goering, Marshal Hermann, 3, 10, 96, 141, 369, 619, 829; phoney war, 41, 44, 62, 65; Battle of Britain, 152, 153; war with Russia, 204, 570; Stalingrad, 400, 402, 403; Nazi domination in Europe, 243, 245, 257, 290; German war economy, 537, 541–3, 551n; end of war in Europe, 683
Golikov, General, 400, 406
Gomel, 560, 563
Goodeve, Charles, 444
Gort, Lord, 51, 101, 114–21, 123
Gottwald, Klement, 459, 587, 588
Gouin, Félix, 498
Goutard, Colonel, 109
Goyet, Colonel Le, 105
Graf Spee (German battleship), 65
Graf Zeppelin (German airship), 153
Grandi, Dino, 512, 517, 518–20
Granville, 626, 649
Graudenz, 696
Gravelines, 122
Graziani, General, 140, 185, 603, 604
Grebbe line, 96
Greece, 59, 174, 274, 590, 835; fighting in, 186, 188–90; battle of Crete, 192, 194; German/Russian break, 204, 205, 206; Nazi domination, 246; resistance, 305; Italian weakness, 371, 510; Soviet victories, 591, 594, 595–6, 598; and Britain, 602, 669, 673, 693; aftermath, 782, 793, 818, 824
Greenland, 79, 161, 178
Greiser, Gauleiter, 256
Grenoble, 641, 644
Grew, Ambassador, 315, 767, 774
Groeber, Mgr., 656
Groningen, 700
Grossrosen concentration camp, 262
Group of Five (Giraud plot), 385

Groza, Petru, 693
Groznyy, 61, 225, 229
Guelder, 96
Gustav line, 599, 600
Guadalajara, 514
Guariglia, Raffaele, 521, 523
Guantanamo, 368
Guatemala, 442
Guebwiller, 685
Guderian, General, 8, 45, 125, 131, 213, 541, 619; breakthrough at Sedan, 102–104, 107–9; Wehrmacht victories in USSR, 216, 223, 555; Soviet offensive, 560, 570; end of war in Europe, 680, 692, 697
Gusev, 594, 714
Guadalcanal, 357, 362, 363, 722, 723, 724, 728, 745
Guam, 330, 335, 336, 750, 751
Guelma, 811
Guéhenno, Jean, 830
'Gymnast', Operation, 382

Haakon, King of Norway, 77, 78, 156, 167
Hacha, President, 302
Hague conventions, 252
Hague, The, 96, 246
Haiphong, 313
Halder, General, 41, 109, 119, 151, 162, 179; German plans 1940, 86, 88, 89, 95; break with USSR, 203, 204, 211, 212; Wehrmacht victories in USSR, 216, 218, 219, 223, 224, 227–30; Stalingrad, 394, 400
Halsey, Admiral, 753, 755, 756
Hamburg, 262, 547, 568, 700, 794
Hangkow, 311
Hankö peninsula, 46
Hanover, 568, 700
Hansell, General, 727
Harar, 183
Harriman, Ambassador, 474, 484, 494, 678, 705
Harrison, Ambassador, 483, 593
Hart, Admiral, 337
Hatta, Mohammad, 350
Hawaii, 332, 336, 344, 360, 422
Hawaiian Ils., 321, 330, 331, 360
Heidegger, 830
Heinkel, 76, 543, 544
Heinrici, General, 697
Heisenburg, 833
Helen, Queen of Romania, 576
Helleu, J., 504
Helsinki, 47

Hendaye, 175, 176, 290
Henyang, 737
Hersey, J., 770n
Herriot, Edouard, 134, 135, 637
Herzog, General, 155
Hessen, 568
Hewitt, Admiral, 387
Heydrich, Reinhard, 237, 252, 264, 268, 270, 302
Hilpert, General, 703
Himmler, Heinrich, 211, 483, 519, 605, 657, 790; Hitler's Europe, 163, 164, 167–8; Wehrmacht victories in USSR, 211, 231, 236, 237; Nazi domination, 242, 243, 255; genocide, 260, 261, 264, 268, 270, 271; collaboration, 282, 283; German war economy, 538, 540
Hipper (German cruiser), 65, 369
Hirohito, Emperor of Japan, 310, 328, 766, 774–6, 812
Hiroshima, 547, 770, 790, 844
Hiroshima (J. Hersey), 770
History of the Great Soviet War, 208
Hitler, Adolf, 443, 552, 567, 568, 613, 706, 707, 712, 784, 785; outbreak of war, 12–15, 17–19; Belgium, 21–3; Poland, 31–2, 34–40; German-Soviet pact, 41–3, 45–7; and Mussolini, 49–51; Balkans, 58, 62, 187–90; war in Norway, 70–2, 77, 78; plans 1940, 83–4, 86; French collapse, 119, 120n, 121, 125; French armistice, 135–6, 139–41; Battle of Britain, 147, 148, 151, 152, 154, 161; ideas for Europe, 162–76; Mediterranean and Africa, 178, 179, 182, 186, 194–8; break with Russia, 203–12; victories in USSR, 216, 217, 219, 222–5, 227–31, 233, 236, 291; Stalingrad, 394, 395–6, 400, 402, 403, 405–8; Soviet offensive, 455, 457, 458, 553–6, 560, 562, 563, 569, 570, 571, 573; domination of Europe, 243–6, 255; genocide, 258–62, 267, 269, 271, 273, 274; collaboration, 276–9, 282, 283, 285, 286, 289, 290; resistance, 297, 425; Japan, 320, 334; war at sea, 364, 366, 369, 370; N. Africa, 372–6, 378, 380, 387, 390–3; Anglo-American alliance, 422, 427; Anglo-Soviet alliance, 470–2, 479, 482, 483; Italy surrenders, 508, 509, 512, 513, 517, 518, 521, 524; financing war, 536–8, 540–2, 544, 545; desatellisation, 577, 579, 580, 581, 589, 592, 596; fighting in Italy, 604, 605, 609; liberation of France, 618–20, 622, 625, 634, 635, 639, 643, 649; opposition to, 655–9; Nazi fanaticism, 659–60;

secret weapons, 661–4; last offensive, 665–7; end of war in Europe, 680–3, 685, 687, 691, 692, 695, 699, 702, 703; death, 697
Hitoshi, General, 339
Ho Chi Minh, 348, 814
Hodges, General, 651, 685, 700
Hodja, Enver, 306
Hoepner, General, 223
Hoess, R., 237
Hofer, Gauleiter, 605
Hohenlohe, Prince of, 483
Holland, 21, 42, 50, 151, 211, 246, 248, 262, 473, 538, 702; allied relations with, 54–8, 64, 68; May 1940, 83, 84, 87, 89; invasion of, 96–7, 274; Hitler's Europe, 168, 250, 618, 700; anti-semitism, 266, 271; collaboration, 281; resistance, 297–9; aftermath, 782, 794, 797; postwar balance of power, 802, 811
Dutch Army, 96, 97, 338
Home Army (AK Polish Resistance), 582–585
Home Guard, 148
Hong Kong, 155, 330, 335, 336, 337, 346, 758, 812
Honolulu, 322, 323
Honshu, 758–61, 763, 766, 768, 771
Hood (British battleship), 179
Hoover, Herbert, 435, 677
Hopkins, Harry, 159, 695; American war conduct, 417, 424; American arsenal, 438; Stalin, 455, 457, 473; liberation of France, 638; Yalta, 669, 678, 769; Japanese surrender, 772, 773, 774
Horthy, Admiral, 68, 283, 284, 577, 578, 592, 593
Hossbach, Friedrich, 219, 220
Hoth, General, 401, 403, 404
Hudal, Bishop, 656
Huillier, F. L', 273
Hull, Cordell, 69, 207, 316, 319, 320, 383, 483, 513, 568, 594, 610, 669, 771
Hungary, 68, 166, 208, 225, 247, 483, 568, 692, 784, 785; genocide, 271; collaboration, 277, 283; Stalingrad, 406, 408; break with Germany, 577–8; Soviet victories, 588, 592–6; aftermath, 783, 793; postwar balance of power, 815, 817, 823
Hungarian Army, 225, 406
Hüningen, 685
Huntziger, General, 91, 251; break-through at Sedan, 101, 103, 104, 105, 107; French armistice, 130, 142, 143
Hurley, General, 678

'Husky', Operation, 507
Husseini, Hadj Amin al, 282
Hyères, 641, 644
Hytier, Adrienne, 114

Iasi, 570, 589, 590
Ibn Saud, 810
Iceland, 79, 161
Il Soviet newspaper, 606
Illustrious (British aircraft carrier), 182
Imamura, General, 745
Imphal plain, 736, 740
India, 155, 205, 313, 358, 610; Japan's
    lightning war, 330, 335, 340, 341, 344;
    and Japanese Empire, 347, 353; Anglo-
    American alliance, 422, 448, 450, 475;
    Pacific strategy, 724-7, 732-6; after-
    math, 783, 801; postwar balance of
    power, 815, 817
Indian Ocean, 6, 65, 179, 341, 423, 450,
    614, 725
Indonesia, 156, 205, 313, 330, 331, 359;
    and Japan, 349-51; Japanese surren-
    der, 765, 776; postwar balance of
    power, 814, 815
Indochina, 312-16, 318-19, 336, 339,
    493, 503, 674; and Japan, 345, 346,
    348; war at sea, 364; war in China/
    Burma, 733, 737, 758; Japanese sur-
    render, 762, 765; aftermath, 813, 814
Ingersoll, Ralph, 609
Inner Mongolia, 311
Innsbruck, 702
Interallied War Council, *see* Supreme
    Interallied War Council
International Bank for Reconstruction
    and Development, 829
International Labour Organisation, 828
International Monetary Fund, 829
International Red Cross, 273, 482
Iraq, 60, 61, 185, 195-6, 209, 809
Iran, 60, 230, 332, 450, 475, 476, 480, 677,
    713, 810, 811
Ireland, *see* Eire
Ironside, Field Marshal, 52, 114, 117
Irrawaddy, R., 741
Iskra, 235
Ismay, Lord, 149
Isonzo, R., 707
Israel, 259, 786
Israelian, Victor, 475, 476, 676, 677
Issoudun, 646
Istanbul, 577
Istria, 189, 592
Italia del Popolo, L', 604
Italo-German Conference (Innsbruck
    1940), 185

Italy, 79, 128, 148, 174, 478, 566, 582, 592,
    593, 680, 684, 698, 699, 702, 708, 784,
    843; phoney war, 59, 60, 64, 69;
    French armistice, 141; Hitler's Europe,
    163, 173, 246; Africa and Balkans, 179,
    180, 182, 186, 187, 189, 194, 197; break
    with Russia, 205, 207; collaboration,
    290; and Japan, 310, 313, 334; N.
    Africa, 371, 373, 382, 492, 498; Stalin-
    grad, 408, 409; Soviet offensive, 454,
    562, 565; Anglo-American alliance,
    424, 426; surrender, 507-30, 535, 545,
    547, 578, 679, 750; landings in, 599-
    611, 639, 640, 643; postwar balance of
    power, 800, 804n, 805, 808, 817, 823;
    aftermath, 782, 790, 793, 794
Italian Army, 371, 398, 401, 510
Italian Navy, 3, 180-2, 372, 509, 523
Italian Air Force, 182, 183
Italian Somaliland, 184
Iwo Jima, 753, 758, 759

Jablanica, 591
Jacobsen, H. A., 162
Jaenecke, General, 570
James, H., 334
Jan de Mayen, 475
Jany, General, 225
Japan, 9, 43, 68, 159, 163, 215, 503, 575,
    639, 661, 704, 772, 822; pact with
    Germany, 205, 209, 222; break with
    US, 309-25; lightning war, 326-44;
    occupied Empire, 345-56; reverse, 357;
    war at sea, 360-4; Anglo-American
    alliance, 413, 422, 424-6, 446, 448, 668,
    819; Allied arsenal, 428, 431, 443;
    Anglo-Soviet alliance, 470, 472; Yalta,
    674, 679; Potsdam, 712, 713, 716;
    strategy and forces in Asia, 721, 723,
    729, 730, 733; Pacific War, 743, 750,
    752-5, 757-8, 760; air raids on Japan,
    762-5; Emperor discusses surrender,
    765-8; atom bomb, 769, 770, 835;
    surrender, 773-7; and USSR, 771, 774;
    aftermath, 781, 783, 786, 790, 793, 794;
    postwar balance of power, 811-12,
    815, 816
Japanese Army, 310-11, 313, 317, 346,
        360, 717, 745; lightning war, 326-
        329, 335
    Sixteenth Army, 349
    Twenty-fifth Army, 349
Japanese Navy, 310, 313, 317, 319, 321,
        363, 717, 724; force, 326-8;
        conduct of war, 328-9; nature of
        Pacific war, 335; Japanese empire,
        346, 349; siege of Rabaul, 748;

Japan – (contd.)
    Marianas, 750; production for, 754
  Merchant Navy, 327, 346, 350, 754,
    764, 812
  Japanese Air Force, 335, 337, 341, 346,
    748, 749; Kamikaze, 756, 757, 759,
    760, 764
Jasenovać, 284
Jaroslav, 556
Jassy, 267
Java, 338, 339, 349, 350, 351
Je suis partout (Brasillach party), 282
Jean-Bart (French battleship), 6, 388
Jeanne avec nous (C. Vermorel), 830
Jezireh, 61, 62n
Jodl, General, 84, 89, 119, 213, 387, 697;
  armistice, 142; war with Russia, 204,
  216, 218, 571; Stalingrad, 400; libera-
  tion of France, 619, 622; end of war in
  Europe, 683, 703, 707
Johnson, Air Marshal, 154
Jordan, 809
Joubert, Air Marshal, 663
Jouvet, Louis, 830
Juin, General, 388, 490, 501, 526, 600, 611
Julian Alps, 823
Jutland, 72

K detachment, 99; *see also chasseurs
  ardennais*
Kairouan, 492
Kalach, 228, 398, 400
Kalinin, 222, 398, 562
Kallay, Premier of Hungary, 577
Kamikaze, *see* Japan
Kan-su, 354
Karachi, 353, 762
Karaganda, 452
Karelia, 815
Karlsruhe, 685, 690
Karmasin, F., 276
Kasserine, 492
Kattegat, 79
Katyn, 482
Kawabe, Lt-Gen. Torashivo, 776
Kayaerts, General, 102
Keise Ils., 759
Keitel, General, 44, 89, 141, 142, 172, 213,
  236, 577; *Nacht und Nebel* decree, 254;
  and Vlassov, 286; Stalingrad, 400;
  Battle of Berlin, 697; German sur-
  render, 702, 703
Kenney, General, 755
Kenya, 183, 184
Kerama Ils., 759
Keren, 184
Kertch, 224, 227

Kesselring, 371, 373, 378, 387, 521; war
  in Italy, 600, 605; end of war in Europe,
  687, 698, 699, 702
Key West, 368
Keyes, Admiral, 116
Keynes, Maynard, 433
Kharbin, 773
Kharkov, 224, 227, 233, 406, 407, 462,
  555, 560, 562, 597
Khrushchev, Nikita, 394, 451
Kherson, 563
Kiel, 568, 700
Kiev, 211, 212, 217–19, 233, 270, 286,
  563, 587
Kimmel, Admiral, 323
Kimura, General, 347
King, Admiral, 362, 382, 383; Anglo-
  American alliance, 422, 426; American
  Pacific command, 729; and Mac-
  Arthur, 752, 758; final assault, 767;
  atom bomb, 769
King, Mackenzie, 154, 447
Kinkaid, Admiral, 755
Klagenfurt, 699
Kleist, General von, 102, 103, 107–8, 123,
  227, 229
Kleist, Peter, 483, 571
Kluge, Gunther von, 224, 561, 625, 634–
  635, 657, 659
Kobe, 754, 763
Koch, Erich, 232
Koeltz, General, 489, 492
Koenig, General, 375, 618, 627, 629–31,
  636, 638
Koenigsberg, 567, 682, 696, 815
Koltchak, Admiral, 562
Koningshoyet, 98
Koenigstein, 384
Koichi, Marquis Kido, 766
Kolberg, 696
Kollontai, Madame, 47
Koniev, Ivan S., 562, 563, 569, 586, 681,
  682, 696, 697
Konoye, Prince, 313, 316–19, 329, 753,
  766, 767
Korea, 326, 732, 764, 766, 772, 815
Kosciusko Division, 582
Kosygin, Aleksei, 461
Kotelnikovo, 401, 402
Kovel, 570
Kovno, 582
Kowloon, 337
Közlin, 696
Krasnodar, 229, 407, 462
Kravchenko, Colonel, 468, 476
Kriegel, Annie, 457, 460
Kriegsmarine, *see* Germany

Krivoy Rog, 235, 462, 563, 569
Krosigk, Schwerin von, 248
Kufra, 184, 497, 652
Kuibychev, 463
Kunming, 741
Kupyansk, 228
Kurile Ils., 335, 674, 750, 773, 815
Kurita, Admiral, 755, 756
Kurusu, Saburo, 314, 319
Kusaka, Admiral, 745
Küstrin, 697
Kutno, 33
Kutusov, 220
Kursk, 228, 406, 560, 561, 562, 571, 573
Kuusinen, 46, 459
Kwajalein, 749
Kweilin, 737
Kweiyang, 737
KW line (Dyle plan), 98, 99, 100
Kyushu, 322, 768, 771

La Pallice, 178, 703
La Rochelle, 634, 703
La Spezia, 182
Laborde, Admiral de, 393
Lae, 745
Ladoga, Lake, 46, 222, 562
Lakatos, General Geza, 593
Lampson, Sir Miles, 376
Languedoc, 644
Laon, 108
Lapland, 220, 785
Larissa, 190
Larminat, General, 62n, 643, 703
Lashio, 341
Latin America, 429, 440, 441–3; see also
    Brazil, Chile, etc.
Latreille, M., 324
Latvia, 45, 218, 232, 580
Langer, W., 135
Langres, 131
Laurent, General, 99
Lausanne-Ouchy, 68
Laure, General, 112
Laval, Pierre, 15, 195, 383, 392; phoney
    war, 67, 79; armistice, 134, 150; Vichy
    government, 170, 173–4; collabora-
    tion, 251, 289, 290, 387, 390; resis-
    tance, 301; liberation of France, 637, 648
Le Casteau, 101
Le Drammont, 643
Le Havre, 125, 619, 621, 645, 650
Le Lavandou, 641
Le Luc, Admiral, 143
Le Muy, 643
League for the Independence of Annam,
    814

League of Nations, 63, 421, 503, 670,
    675, 676, 808, 825, 827, 828
League of Revolutionary Organisations
    of Vietnam, 814
Leahy, Admiral, 196, 417, 426, 705, 769
Lebanon, 196, 299, 504, 809
Lebed, Mykol, 285
Leclerc, General, 184, 381, 500, 501, 701;
    liberation of France, 627, 634, 638,
    646, 651, 652; Japanese surrender, 776
Lebrun, Albert, 112, 129, 135
Ledo, 735, 741
Lee, Admiral, 363
Leeb, Marshal von, 84, 86, 89, 211, 224
Leese, Sir Oliver, 741
Leghorn, 525
Leipzig, 68, 237, 547, 657, 695, 700
Lemaigre-Dubreuil, 385, 493, 499
Lemberg, 285
Lend-lease, 160, 431, 440, 441, 446, 450,
    476, 501, 554
Lenin, Nikolai, 356, 572
Leningrad, 45, 209, 211, 212, 219, 220, et
    passim
Leopold III, King of Belgium, 21, 101,
    156, 168, 802; allied relations with, 53,
    54, 57; Weygand's plan, 115–17;
    Belgian capitulation, 120–1
Leros, 523
Leto, Guido, 510
Léquérica, M. de, 138
Lens, 117
Leyte, 752, 755, 756, 757, 760
Lezaky, 302
Lherminier, Commander, 526
Liberation Committee of Upper Italy,
    607, 608
Libya, 148, 211, 217, 289, 299, 446, 835;
    N. African campaign, 182, 183, 187,
    194; Germans halted, 373, 374; inde-
    pendence, 808, Arab League, 810
Liddell Hart, Basil, 36, 425
Lidice, 302
Liège, 84, 98, 646, 664, 666
Ligurian Apennines, 529
Lille, 120, 300, 646
Lindbergh, Charles, 158
Lindemann, General, 702
Linz, 696
Lipari Islands, 520
Lippstadt, 690
Lisbon, 512, 521
Lisieux, 634
Lithuania, 37, 45, 218, 232, 581
Littorio (Italian battleship), 180
Liuchow, 737
Lingayen, 337, 757

Liverpool, 332
Ljubljana gap, 639
Lloyd George, David, 15, 149
Lodz, 33, 269, 271
Lofoten Ils., 297
Lohse, Heinrich, 232
Loire, R., 130, 131, 141, 621, 622, 632
Lombardy, Plain of, 20
Longo, F., 608
London, 78, 135, 137, 140, 149, 152 et passim; V1 bombs, 663
Lons-le-Saunier, 644
Lopez, President of Colombia, 442
Lorient, 178, 179, 548, 571, 634, 685, 703
Lorraine, 89, 645, 647
Los Alamos, 768
Los Angeles, 436
Louvain, 98, 101
Lübeck, 547, 696, 700, 707
Lublin, 37, 267, 270, 582–4, 672
Lublin Committee, 583–6, 673, 709, 710, 712, 785, 804
Lucas, General, 600
Lucca, 601
Luftwaffe, see Germany
Lüneberg, 700
Lutsk, 570
Lutjens, Admiral, 74
Luxemburg, 104, 245
Luzon, 337, 753, 757
Lvov, 218, 233, 267, 269, 271, 272, 567, 586
Lyet, Colonel, 110
Lyon, 125, 131, 571, 644
Lys Canal, 98, 117, 122

Maas, Dr, 835
Maestricht, 664
MacArthur, General, 318, 337, 344, 384, 771; war at sea, 359, 362, 382, 383; 1943, 722, 725, 728, 729–31, 736, 737; Papua/New Guinea, 743, 745; Formosa, 752; Battle of Leyte, 755; Philippines, 757–8; Japanese surrender, 767, 768, 776; postwar balance of power, 812, 824
Macedonia, 190
Macek, 59
Mackesy, General, 76
Mâcon, 131
Madagascar, 268, 299, 341, 383, 448
Madrid, 138, 291
Maelzer, General, 605
Magdeburg, 700
Maginot line, 20, 86, 91, 101, 104, 109, 125, 130, 131

Magli, General, 526
Magnitogorsk, 463
Maher, Ahmed, 376
Maidanek concentration camp, 257, 262, 270
Maikop, 225, 229
Main, R., 700
Maisky, Ivan, 209, 472, 478, 672
Malacca, 338, 340
Malacca Straits, 724
Malaya, 318, 320, 322; American strategy, 331; Japanese plans, 335, 337; Japanese conquest of, 340; Japanese occupation, 348; war at sea, 364, 372; Battle of Leyte, 755–6; Japanese surrender, 765
Malmédy, 147, 245
Malraux, André, 830
Malta, 6, 141n, 181, 182, 190, 194, 195, 684; N. African campaign, 371, 372–6, 387; Italian surrender, 507, 510, 522, 523
Malinovski, 562, 569, 590, 592, 593, 691, 692
Mallory, Air Marshal Sir Trafford Leigh, 614
Manchukuo, 312, 313, 345
Manchuria, 311, 315, 345, 679, 732, 764, 766, 771–3, 785; postwar balance of power, 813, 815
Mandalay, 341, 741
Mandel, Georges, 111, 136
Mangunkusumo, Dr Tjipto, 350
Manila, 316, 753, 756, 757
Mann, Heinrich, 829n
Mann, Thomas, 829n
Mannerheim, Marshal, 46, 47, 211, 220, 580
Mannheim, 690
Maniu, Juliu, 283, 589, 693
Manstein, von, 86, 88, 227, 657; Stalingrad, 400–4, 407, 555; Soviet offensive, 560, 561, 563, 569, 570, 573
Mao Tse-tung, 311, 354–6, 733, 739, 740, 813
Maranda, 372
Mariana Ils., 723, 749–52, 754, 758, 763
Marin, Louis, 111, 136
Marks, General, 204
Marquis, Admiral, 393
Marseilles, 125, 299, 549, 638, 641, 643, 645
Marshall, General, 149, 362, 501, 599, 614, 615, 625, 638, 756; break with Japan, 320, 324, 331; N. Africa, 382, 383; Anglo-American alliance, 417, 422, 426, 427; Soviet alliance, 472,

477; end of war in Europe, 684, 695, 699, 701; strategy in Asia, 729, 737; Japanese surrender, 767; atom bomb, 769

Marshall Ils., 341, 723, 749
Martin, Colonel, 286
Marty, André, 457, 458
Martin, General, 526
Marion, Francis, 287, 288
Mariopol, 563
Maritain, Jacques, 830
Mark, B., 271
Marle, 108
Martin-Chauffier, Louis, 830
Marne, R., 130, 131
Masjumi (Moslem association), 351
Massif Central, 628, 643
Masson, Philippe, 613
Mast, General, 385
Matsuoka, Japanese Minister of Foreign
    Affairs, 209, 314, 316, 317
'Matterhorn', Operation, 762
Maulde, R., 98
Mauriac, François, 830
Maurois, André, 830
Maurras, Charles, 174
Mauthausen, 262, 264, 271, 540
Maw, Ba, 347
Mazar, 269
Mecklenburg, 708
Mechelen, 57
Mediterranean, 6, 19, 60, 128, 150, 163,
    176 *et passim*
Mehedia, 388
Mein Kampf (A. Hitler), 31, 162, 230, 244,
    258, 279
Melitopol, 563
Melnikov, General, 579
Melnyk, A., 285
Melun, 635
Memel, 581
Mendès, France, Pierre, 804
Menton, 132, 246
Merignac, 365
Mers el-Kebir, 150, 157, 169, 173, 181,
    383, 393
Mersa-el-Brega, 381
Mersa Matruh, 194, 375
Messe, General, 224, 227, 229, 235, 238,
    371, 492
Messina, 182, 508
Metz, 184, 651
Meuse, R., 54, 57, 86, 87, 96–105, 107,
    109, 646, 649, 650, 651, 664
Meyer, Dr Konrad, 243, 244
Mexico, 441, 442, 443, 820, 821, 822
Mexico, Gulf of, 368

Michael, King of Romania, 166, 283, 576,
    577, 589, 592, 693
Michelier, Admiral, 388
Midway Ils., 332, 344, 357, 717, 724; war
    at sea, 360–3, 381, 751
Mihailović, Colonel, 304, 305, 527, 565,
    591, 602
Miklos, General Dalnoki, 594, 823
Mikolajczyk, Polish Premier, 482–3, 566–
    7, 584–6, 594, 670, 709–10, 712, 823
Milan, 530, 604, 699
Military Intelligence Service (SMI Italy),
    529
Milch, General, 542, 544
Milne Bay, 723
Milorg (Norwegian Resistance), 297
Minsk, 212, 218, 581, 582
Mindanao, 337, 729, 755
Missouri (American battleship), 776
Mitscher, Admiral, 751
Miquelon, 383
Moehne Dam, 548
Moerdyk, 97
Molotov, Vyacheslav, 45, 46, 47, 205,
    471, 698; Anglo-Soviet alliance, 477,
    484; Soviet victories, 589, 595; Yalta,
    674, 678; Potsdam, 710, 713, 714, 772
Moltke, Helmut von, 37, 213, 656
Model, 587, 635, 664, 691, 699
Mohilev, 218, 562
Monastir, 192
Mongolia, 312, 348, 349
Monnet, Jean, 804
Mons, 101
Mont Mouchet, 631, 632
Montargis, 131
Montauban, 299
Montbard, 646
Montcornet, 108
Monte Cassino, 600, 601
Montélimar, 644
Montenegro, 190, 305, 787
Montevideo, 65, 441, 442, 515, 638
Montezemolo, Colonel, 529
Montgomery, Field Marshal, N. African
    campaign, 377, 378, 380, 381, 492;
    surrender of Italy, 508; 'Overlord',
    615, 617, 621; liberation of France, 634,
    645, 646, 649, 650; end of war in
    Europe, 666–7, 683–6, 690, 700, 702,
    706
Montgomery (A. Moorehead), 377n
Monthermé, 105
Montoire, 173, 174
Montpellier, 392
Montmédy, 91, 125
Montsabert, General de, 643, 685, 701

Montreuil, 114
Moluccas, 338
Monnet, Georges, 111
Monnet, Jean, 135, 431, 497
Moon, Rear-Admiral, 621
Moorehead, Alan, 377
Morava, R., 592
Moravska Ostrava, 701
Moravia, 164, 246, 587
Morgenthau, Henry, 69, 568, 596
Morison, Admiral, 324, 365, 386, 755, 774, 776, 777
Moscow, 15, 32, 37, 38, 45, 208, 209 *et passim*
Moscow Conference (1943), 808
Moselle, R., 646, 647, 649
Mosquito (British light bomber), 10
Moslem movement, 350, 351
Mossadegh, Dr, 810
Moulin, Jean, 301, 496
Morocco, 244, 350, 385, 498, 503, 504, 811
Mortain, 634
Mountbatten, Lord, 725–7, 736–7, 740, 758, 814
Moulins, 131
Mouvement républicain populaire (MRP French Catholic party), 648, 803
Mukden, 773
'Mulberry' harbours, 617
Mulhouse, 651, 685
Munda, 745
Munich, 139, 443, 480, 520, 701, 702
Munster, 685
Muravief, 590
Murmansk, 211, 220, 366, 369, 431, 475, 476
Murphy, Robert, 383, 384, 493, 494, 707, 716
Musashi (Japanese battleship), 756
Muselier, Admiral, 383
Muslim League, 155; *see also Masjumi* and Moslem movement
Mussert, Anton, 168, 262, 281, 282, 298
Mussolini, Benito, 1, 3, 19, 39, 147, 213, 284, 427, 577; phoney war, 42, 45, 47, 49–51, 65; war in Norway, 71, 72, 79; Hitler's plans, 83, 84; French collapse, 125, 128; armistice, 139, 141; expansion in Europe, 163, 166, 167, 174, 176; Africa and Balkans, 179, 180, 184–8, 206; war with Russia, 207, 229, 238; and Hitler, 244, 246; N. Africa, 372, 373, 374, 378, 387; Italy surrenders, 508–10, 512–13; plot against Mussolini, 516–20; fall, 521–3, 561, 602, 658, 784
Mychtov, R., 401

Myitkyina, 736
Myth of the Twentieth Century, The (Rosenberg), 231

Nagano, Admiral, 321
Nagasaki, 754, 770, 790
Nagoya, 763
Nahas Pasha, 375, 376, 809, 810
Namsos, 75, 76
Namur, 56, 57, 98, 101
Nancy, 646
Nankin, 812
Nantes, 616, 632, 635
Naples, 182, 183, 507, 524, 525, 528, 591, 602, 641, 835
Narva, 569, 581
Narvik, 62, 63, 70, 74–8, 89, 121, 385, 648
Nasjonal Samling (Norwegian party), 71, 167
Natal, 762
National Committee for Free Germany, 578
National Liberation Army (ALNY Yugoslavia), 305
National Liberation Committee (Italy), 529
National Liberation Front (EAM Greece), 694
National Resistance Council (CNR France), 626, 630, 636, 637, 647
National Socialist Party (Germany), 15
Natzweiler-Struthof concentration camp, 262
naval treaty (German-British 1935), 3
Nazi party, 13, 166, 242, 272, 280, 281; and religion, 656; fanaticism, 659–60; moral aftermath, 790–2, 829; *see also* Germany, Goebbels, Himmler, Hitler, SS
Near East Expeditionary Force, 59, 60
Near Eastern Air Corps, 60
Neckar, R., 700
Nedić, General, 59, 591
Nehru, Pandit, 341, 348
Neisse, R., 673, 678, 697, 712
Nenni, Pietro, 514, 529
Nerva, 580
Neuengamme concentration camp, 262
Neuf-Brisach, 685
Neufchâteau, 103
New Britain, 745
New Caledonia, 330, 332, 341, 344, 383
New Deal (US), 429, 439
New Delhi, 735
New Georgia, 745
New Guinea, 336, 344–6; war at sea, 359, 362, 364; strategy in Asia, 722, 723,

729; fighting in, 744–5; siege of Rabaul, 748, 750
New Hebrides, 330, 722
New York, 332, 368, 475, 497, 515
New Zealand, 155, 331–2, 335, 422, 423, 448, 813
Newfoundland, 160, 178, 420
newspapers, resistance, 298, 300, 579
Nice, 141n
Nieuport, 123
Nimitz, Admiral, 359; war at sea, 360; strategy in Asia, 728, 729, 736, 743–4; siege of Rabaul, 748–9; Formosa, 752; Battle of Leyte, 755; Iwo Jima, 758; Japanese surrender, 767, 776
Niort, 131
Nishimura, Admiral, 755
Nile, R., 810
Noël, Léon, 32
Nomura, Admiral, 317, 318, 319, 320
Noguès, General, 136, 182, 385, 388
Nordling, Consul General, 63, 637
Norfolk (British cruiser), 179
Normandy, 167, 611, 632, 705; 'Overlord', 616; Battle of, 624–6, 635, 638, 641, 643
North Africa, 135, 136, 142, 174, 181, 194, 246, 426, 478, 566, 602, 614, 809; Allied campaign, 357, 358; Germans halted, 382–5, 387, 391, 422, 423, 440, 487; end of N. African war, 488, 493–5, 497, 499, 501–4; postwar balance of power, 811
North Bukovina, 166
North Sea, 62, 71, 108, 115, 119, 123, 168, 645, 650, 694, 796
Norway, 42, 46, 97, 140, 211, 339, 581, 661, 680, 694, 695; phoney war, 63, 64, 68; war in, 70–80, 88, 121, 178; Battle of Britain, 151; Hitler's Europe, 167, 168, 246, 291; collaboration, 280, 281; resistance, 297; war at sea, 366; Anglo-Soviet alliance, 473, 477; German surrender, 702, 703; aftermath, 782; postwar balance of power, 802
    Norwegian Army, 297
    Norwegian Merchant Navy, 78, 79
Novikov, Marshal, 558
Novorossiysk, 229
Nuremberg, 547, 700, 714, 796

Oboion, 561
Oder, R., 668, 673, 682, 683, 696, 697
Odessa, 211, 232, 233, 563, 569, 570
Oeuvre L' (M. Déat), 281
Oise, R., 110, 125, 618
Okinawa, 753, 758, 759, 766

OKH (Oberkommando des Heeres), 204, 212, 534, 561, 582
OKW (Oberkommando der Wehrmacht), 42, 49, 89, 99, 541, 554, 635; Africa and Balkans, 185, 188; war with Russia, 204, 232, 236; Stalingrad, 396, 400, 403, 405, 407; N. African campaign, 374, 380, 387
Oléron, 571, 703
Olomouc, 587
'On the border of two worlds' (H. Colijn), 168
Oppenheim, 690
Oppenheimer, Robert, 768, 769, 770
Oran, 176, 386, 388, 489, 641
Oranienburg-Sachsenhausen, 262, 659
Ordzhonikidze, 229
Orel, 222, 224, 235, 407, 560, 562, 597
Orkney Ils., 475
Orléans, 632, 635
Orne, R., 622, 625, 630
Osaka, 763
Oslo, 74, 77, 98, 167
Ormosin, 401
Ostend, 122, 123, 646
Osubska-Moravski, 583, 823
Otranto, Straits of, 183
Our, R., 103
Outer Mongolia, 813
'Overlord', Operation, 478, 565, 599, 600, 609, 611, 721; command of, 614–16; preparation of, 616–18; liberation of France, 619, 621, 643, 646
Overstraeten, General van, 21, 53, 57, 98, 99, 115, 116, 120
Ozawa, Admiral, 750, 751, 755, 756

Pacific Islands, 313
Pacific Ocean, 65, 159, 316, 331–2, 335–6, 344–5, 357, 500, 566, 721, 724–5, 728–30; war at sea, 359, 364, 373, 375; Anglo-American strategy in, 419, 422, 423, 426, 427, 431, 438
Pahang, Sultan of, 349
Pai-Yi, 345
Pakistan, 783
Palau Ils., 336
Palermo, 508, 523
Palestine, 15, 185, 809
Pampelonne, 643
Panama, 441, 820
Pantellaria, 161, 179, 507
Panzer division, 29, 31, 89, 91, 92, 117, 194, 239, 521; breakthrough at Sedan, 97, 103, 104; French armistice, 131, 137; in Russia, 225, 228, 387, 589; liberation of France, 622, 634, 650; end of war in Europe, 680, 684

Papagos, General, 187, 192
Papen, Franz von, 147n, 292
Paraguay, 443
Paris, 125, 142, 171, 172, 184, 254 *et passim*; liberation of, 637–8, 652, 659
Paris army, 130
Parti franciste (Bucard party), 282
Parti populaire français (PPF Doriot party), 282, 287
Parti social français, 111
Parri, Ferruccio, 608
Patagonia, 442
Patch, General, 643, 646, 685, 687, 700
Patton, General, 508, 824; liberation of France, 624, 632, 634, 636, 646, 649, 651; last German offensive, 666, 685, 687, 690; German surrender, 700
Paul, Prince of Yugoslavia, 59, 189
Panker, Anna, 459, 817
Paulhan, Jean, 830
Paulus, General, 188, 204, 225, 228–9, 562, 579; Stalingrad, 395, 398, 399–407
Pavlenko, General, 597n
Pavlevic, 254, 284
Pearl Harbour, 320–4, 327–8, 330–1, 335–7, 339, 344, 359, 365, 421, 424, 430, 436, 440, 716, 750, 751, 752, 756, 767, 771, 777
Peenemünde, 663
Peirse, Sir Richard, 727
Peipus, Lake, 569
Peking, 311, 737
Peloponnese, 192, 193
People's Army (*Armja Ludowa* AL Polish Resistance), 583
People's Guard (Communist Polish resistance), 582, 583
Perche hills, 130
Perekov, 563
Perkins, Frances, 564
Peron, Colonel, 442, 443, 820, 821
Peronné, 108, 115, 125
Perse, St-John, 830
Pershing, General, 160
Persian Gulf, 205, 217, 228, 475
Peru, 442, 443
Pesenti, General, 183
Petacci, Claretta, 510
Pétain, Marshal, 18, 93, 111, 112, 124, 157, 384, 447, 566, 830; French armistice, 132, 133–7, 139, 150; Vichy government, 170–1, 173–4, 249; French colonies, 182; Syria, 196; collaboration, 287–8; and resistance, 299, 300–01; war in N. Africa, 383, 388, 389–93, 493, 494, 498; liberation of France, 648

Peter II, King of Yugoslavia, 190, 304, 527, 591, 592, 693
Petsamo, 63, 205, 211, 566, 581
Phaeroe Ils., 475
Philippines, 46, 315, 322, 324, 330, 422, 503; American strategy, 331; Japanese conquest, 335, 337, 338, 341; Japanese occupation, 346, 348, 351; war at sea, 359, 364; war in China, 729, 737
Philipps, Admiral, 339
phoney war, 41–69
Picardy, 125
Pieck, Walter, 459, 578, 817
Piedmont, Prince of, 143
Piedmont, Princess of, 517
Pierlot, Hubert, 58, 116, 156
Prévost, Jean, 830
Pilsudski, Marshal, 479
Pilson, 701
Pirin, 590
Pisa, 601
Pithiviers, 271
Pinsk, 233
Pius XII, Pope, 49, 273–5, 529
Platon, Admiral, 390
Platt, General, 184
Pleven, Rene, 135, 506
Ploesti, 548, 549, 577
Plovdiv, 590
Poliakov, L., 271
Pohl, General, 265
Pola, 524
Poland, 54, 59, 66, 69, 84, 92, 124, 153, 156, 164, 217, 276, 562, 772, 826; outbreak of war, 1, 2, 8, 11, 17–19, 23; obliteration of, 29–40, 41, 42, 43, 48, 49, 50, 52, 53; Hitler's Europe, 164–5, 167, 245; German/Russian break, 208, 210, 216, 231, 237, 242; Nazi domination, 255–7; concentration camps, 262, 267, 270, 273; resistance, 295, 302–4; Anglo-Soviet alliance, 479–83; Teheran, 566, 567, 569; Soviet victories, 581, 582, 590, 591, 594, 598; Warsaw uprising, 583–6; Soviet gains in, 668, 669, 772; Yalta, 672–4, 678; Potsdam, 706, 708, 709, 710, 712, 715; aftermath, 782, 783, 785, 787, 794; postwar balance of power, 815, 817, 818, 823
Polish Army, 7, 33, 303
Politzer, Georges, 830
Polojov, B., 456
Polynesia, 743
Pomerania, 400, 567, 583, 682, 691, 696
Ponomarenko, General, 572
Pontarlier, 131
Po, R., 699

Popov, 401, 562
Popular Republican Movement, *see Mouvement républicain populaire*
Port Arthur, 566, 674, 773, 815
Port Darwin, 336, 723, 762
Port Moresby, 360, 362
Portal, Charles, 149
Portsmouth, 663
Portugal, 140, 538
Potsdam Conference, 472, 705–17, 721, 764, 770, 771, 772, 774, 785, 795, 798, 804, 811
Pound, Admiral Dudley, 149, 367
Pourrat, H., 830
Poznan, 31, 38, 245, 256, 681, 682, 696, 784
Praga, 582, 585
Prague, 270, 294, 694, 696, 700, 701
Prazak, Albert, 701
Prételat, General, 91, 131
Pretsch, 237
Price Administration, Office of, 434
Prinz Eugen (German battleship), 44
Provins, 131
Prioux, General, 117
Pripet, R., 212, 569, 586
Production Executive Committee (USA), 432
Prokhorovka, 561
Provence, 632, 638, 639, 641
Prunas, 602, 603
Prussia, 32, 245, 262, 483, 567–8, 581, 619, 634, 671, 682, 685; annexed by USSR, 815, 816
Psaros, Colonel, 305
Puchen, 287, 498
Puerto Rica, 441
Punto Stilio, 182
Purkaiev, General, 217
Purvis, Arthur, 431
Purvis Programme, 446
Putera (Indonesian non-Moslem party), 350, 351
Pyrenees, 628, 631

Qattara depression, 378
Quebec, 521, 596, 616, 752
Queen Mary (British liner), 367
Queuille, 111
Quezon, President of Philippines, 348
Quisling, Viakun, 71, 72, 77–8, 298; Hitler's Europe, 167, 168, 246; collaboration, 280, 281, 283
Quoi, Ngugen Ai, *see* Ho Chi Minh

Rabat, 385, 503
Rabaul, 336, 344, 723, 745, 748, 749, 750

radar, 152, 178, 180, 545, 546
Radescu, General, 693
Radom, 33, 682
Raeder, Admiral, 3, 6, 176, 373; war in Norway, 71; Battle of Britain, 151, 152; Atlantic, 179, 364, 366, 369, 370; Mediterranean, 194; war with Russia, 204, 225
Rahn, Ambassador, 593, 604
Raines, Gauleiter, 605
Ramgarth, 734, 735, 736
Ramsay, Admiral Sir Bertram, 614
Ramsgate, 151
Rangoon, 340, 341, 345, 732, 735, 741, 742
Rascate, 466
Rassemblement national populaire, 281
Rashid Ali, General, 195, 209, 282
Rastenburg, 658
Ravenna, 601
Ravensbruck, 262
Red Army, *see* USSR
Reggio, 524
Reichenau, General von, 237
Reichssicherheitshauptampt (RSHA), 252
Reinhard, General, 216
Remagen, 687, 690
Remer, Major, 658
Rennes, 131, 632
Reparations Conference (Moscow), 714
Repulse (British battleship), 340
Resistance movement, 293–306, 366, 425, 527, 598, 646, 802; French, 383–4, 391–2, 409, 457, 487, 493, 495–8, 503, 549, 603, 617, 626–31, 635–7, 644, 647, 663, 803, 830; Italy, 515–18, 521, 525–6, 528–30, 602, 605, 607, 609, 808; USSR, 571–4, 817; Poland, 582–4, 663
Rethel, 91, 110
Rethondes, 141, 143, 147, 169, 392, 487
Reussner, André, 363, 754
Reuther, Walter, 432
Revue d'histoire de la deuxième guerre mondiale, 382n, 613n, 715n
Reynaud, Paul, 8, 18, 157, 209, 288; phoney war, 52, 61; war in Norway, 70, 72, 77, 79; collapse of France, 111, 112, 118, 121, 128; armistice, 130, 132–6, 150
Reynaud-Simon agreement, 51
Rheims, 107, 702, 703, 707
Rhine, R., 90, 96, 102, 131, 643, 645, 648–52, 668, 683–7, 690, 691
Rhineland, 14, 21, 54, 568, 671, 685, 716, 797, 804
Rhodes, 523
Rhône, R., 246, 643

Ribbentrop, Joachim von, 78, 141, 185, 243, 471, 697, 698; Poland, 32, 34, 37, 38; phoney war, 44, 45, 47, 48–50, 65; Hitler's Europe, 166, 176; war with Russia, 207n, 222, 483, 484; propaganda, 276, 277; Japan, 314, 319; Italy surrenders, 521

Richardson, Admiral, 323

Richelieu (French battleship), 6, 497

Richet, Professor, 835

Riga, 218, 581

Riga, Treaty of, 479, 567

Rimini, 601

Rio de Janeiro, 441

Ritchie, General, 373

Rochefort, 703

Rockefeller, Nelson A., 441

Rodez, 571

Roer, R., 651, 686

Rokossovski, Marshal, 399, 406, 562, 563; Soviet victories, 582, 584, 585; end of war in Europe, 681, 682, 696

Rolland, Romain, 830

Roma (Italian battleship), 524

Romains, Jules, 113, 830

Romania, 11, 42, 59, 61, 68, 79, 270, 817; Hitler's Europe, 165–6, 186, 205, 247, 249, 250; German/Russian war, 208, 210, 232–3, 570; collaboration, 276, 283; Anglo-Soviet alliance, 482, 483; break with Germany, 576–7; Soviet victories, 588–90, 591, 593–6; Soviet gains in, 668, 713, 772, 815, 818, 823; end of war in Europe, 692, 693; aftermath, 784, 785

Romanian Army, 167, 398, 400, 401, 408

Rome, 143, 507, 513, 518, 520, 521 *et passim*

Rommel, Erwin, 35, 125, 131, 367, 600; N. African campaign, 194–7, 282, 289, 305, 358, 810; Germans halted, 371–8, 380, 386, 448, 492; liberation of France, 618, 620, 621, 622, 625; plot against Hitler, 657, 659

Roosevelt, Theodore, 46, 69, 125, 128, 188, 353, 365, 723, 810; Battle of Britain, 158–61; break with Japan, 315–20; Pearl Harbour, 323–5; forces in Japan, 330, 331; N. African war, 382, 383, 391, 487, 493, 495, 496, 501, 503; Anglo-American alliance, 415, 417–18, 420–7; American arsenal, 429–32, 434–41, 450; Soviet war, 454, 455, 457; Soviet alliance, 470, 471, 473–4, 476–9, 482, 483; Italian surrender, 513, 521; bombing of Germany, 546, 550;

Teheran Conference, 563–9, 581, 714; Poland, 585; Russian advance in Europe, 694, 695, 696, 698; landings in Italy, 599, 610; 'Overlord', 614, 616; liberation of France, 627, 638, 639; Yalta, 668–79; end of war in Europe, 684, 693, 694, 695, 698; relationship with USSR, 705, 709, 710; strategy in Asia, 725, 732, 733, 734, 737, 740, 814; death, 699, 703, 711, 822

Rosenberg, Alfred, 71, 72, 163; occupation of USSR, 231, 232, 233, 236; political domination, 243, 247; genocide, 259; and Goebbels, 277, 285, 286

Roskill, Captain, 6

Ross, Colin, 267

Rossoch, 228

Rostock, 547

Rostov, 228, 229, 395, 401, 406, 407, 462

'Round-up', Operation, 381, 422, 478

Rotterdam, 97

Rougeron, Camille, 10

Rouen, 125, 634

Rovno, 583

Royal Air Force (RAF), 10–11, 52, 96, 190, 339, 367, 542; war in Norway, 74, 76; force May 1940, 94–5; French collapse, 114, 122, 123; Battle of Britain, 151, 153, 154; N. African campaign, 376, 386; bombing of Germany, 547, 549n

Royal Navy, 65, 140, 326, 386, 474, 801; outbreak of war, 3, 6, 12; war in Norway, 71, 75, 76; Battle of Britain, 149, 151; Battle of the Atlantic, 177, 179, 366, 372; Crete, 193; Mediterranean, 197; Pacific war, 758, 759

Royan, 685, 703

Ruge, General, 297

Ruhr, 54, 83, 84, 229, 235, 303, 537, 547, 568, 596, 645, 649, 651, 683, 690, 699, 700, 714, 716, 795, 797, 816

Rumkovski, 269, 271

Rundstedt, General von, 32, 84, 86, 89, 92, 211, 657, 659, 664; French collapse, 119, 123, 125; Wehrmacht victories in USSR, 218, 223; liberation of France, 618, 619, 620, 624, 625, 649; end of war in Europe, 684, 685, 687

Ruthenia, 232, 815

Ryti, President of Finnish Republic, 580

Ryu-Kyu Ils., 752, 758, 759

Rzhev, 224, 407

St-Dizier, 131

St Étienne, 125, 644

St-Laurent, 624

St-Lô, 624
St-Malo, 632
St-Mandrier, 641
Ste-Maxime, 643
St-Nazaire, 178, 616, 634, 703
St-Pierre, 383
St Quentin, 108
St-Tropez, 641
St Valéry-en-Caux, 125
St-Vith, 666
Saar, 131, 596, 645, 649, 651
Saar offensive, 35–6
Sachsenhausen, 265
Sahara Desert, 299
Saint-Hardouin, Tarbé de, 385
Saint-Pierre-et-Miquelon, 299
Sainteny, Jean, 814
Saipan, 750, 751, 758, 762, 763, 775
Sakhalin, 674, 773, 815
Salazar, 517
Salerno, 522, 524, 525, 606
Salo Republic, 603, 604, 699
Salonica, 58, 59, 60, 188, 189, 190, 305
Salzburg, 512, 699
Samoa, 344
Samos, 523
San Francisco, 330, 332, 333, 675, 676, 758, 808, 826
Sang, General Aung, 741
Sangro, R., 599
Saragat, Giuseppe, 514, 529
Saratov, 463, 556
Sardinia, 387, 507, 512, 517, 521, 525
Sarrebourg, 652
Sarreguemines, 35
Sarrelouis, 36
Sartre, Jean-Paul, 830
Sauckel, Gauleiter, 251, 285, 538, 539
Saudi Arabia, 810
Saur, 543, 544
Savage, PM New Zealand, 448
Saverne, 91, 652
Sawada, Judge, 766
Saxony, 568, 708
Scamaroni, Fred, 525
Scandinavia, 62–4, 70, 71; *see also* Denmark, Norway, Sweden
Scapa Flow, 6, 66
Schaffhausen, 701
Scharnhorst (German battle cruiser), 3, 366, 475
Schekendorff, General von, 285
Scheldt, R., 23, 54, 98, 101, 621
Scheldt seaboard, 56, 114n, 115, 120, 646, 650
Scheurig, Bodo, 579
Schleswig, 73, 245, 797

Schlieffen plan (1914), 84, 87
Schlussenberg, 407
Schmidt, General, 229, 573
Schmidt, A., 276
Schmitt, General, 389
Schmundt, Colonel, 41
Schneider, Colonel, 646
Schoerner, General, 581, 589, 682, 701
Scholl, Hans, 656
Scholl, Sophie, 656
Schussler, W., 163
Schuster, Cardinal, 604
Schweinfurt, 548, 550
Schwend, F., 265
Scobie, General, 669
Scoppa, Bova, 576
Scorza, Carlo, 512, 520
'Sea-lion', Operation, 151–2
Sebastopol, 224, 225, 227, 570
Sedan, 86, 89, 91, 92, 96–110, 558
Seine, R., 130, 131, 618, 620, 621, 622, 624, 625, 632, 634, 635, 636
Seiss-Inquart, Arthur von, 168, 246, 281, 700
Selassie, Emperor Haile, 183
Semois, R., 103
Semur, 131
Senise, 510, 520, 603
Sens, 131
Serbia, 190, 304, 591
Serol, 111
Serrano-Suñer, Ramon, 69, 176, 290
Sétif, 811
Sevez, General, 601
Seydlitz, General von, 405, 579
Sfax, 490
Sforza, Count, 515, 602, 605
Shanghai, 311, 734, 765
Shen-si province, 739
Shetland Ils., 297
Shigenori, Togo, 774
Sholokhov, M., 456
Short, General, 323
Siam, 334, 339, 345–6, 742, 762, 765
Siberia, 222, 255, 256, 313, 317, 335, 462, 463, 575, 784, 785
Sicherungshaft (security detention), 254
Sicily, 179, 181–2, 195, 371, 427, 478; N. African war, 373, 376, 387; surrender of Italy, 507–9, 515, 517, 521, 524, 525, 561
Sidi-Barrani, 185
Siegfried line, 17, 32, 35, 89
Sigmaringen, 648
Sikorski, General, 156, 303, 479, 480, 482
Sikorski Institute, 36

Silesia, 32, 33, 38, 245, 483, 567, 583, 682, 691
Sima, Horia, 166
Simeon II, King of Bulgaria, 577
Simpson, General, 685, 700
Simović, General, 59, 190
Sin-Kiang, 353, 722, 813
Singapore, Japan/US break, 314, 315, 316, 318; allied strategy, 330, 331; conquest by Japan, 335, 338, 339, 340, 344; annexed, 346, 347; Anglo-American alliance, 422, 448; war in China, 732, 735, 753n, 754, 758; postwar balance of power, 815
Sittang, Battle of, 742
Skagerrak, 79
Skarzysko-Kamienna, 257
Skopje, 190
Slansky, 587
'Sledgehammer', Operation, 381
Slim, General, 742
Slovakia, 164, 247, 276, 587, 588, 692, 694, 823
Slovenia, 190, 245
Slovenian Carso, 529
Smigly-Rydz, Marshal, 33
Smith, General Bedell, 614
Smolensk, 219, 224, 286, 407, 560, 562, 563, 572, 583
Smuts, Field Marshal, 155, 447, 448
Sobibor, 272
Soekarno, 350, 351, 814
Sofia, 49, 590
Soissons, 125
Sokolovsky, 562, 563
Sollum, 185, 371, 381
Solomon Ils., 332, 336, 344, 345, 722; war at sea, 359, 362; Allied strategy, 723, 728; siege of Rabaul, 745, 748, 749
Somalia, 808
Somaliland, see British Somaliland
Somerville, Admiral, 150, 181
Somme, R., 84, 86, 113, 120, 124, 125, 137, 635
Song of the Woods (Shostakovitch), 830
Sonkowski, General Kasimir, 37, 482
Sorge, Richard, 208, 575
Soustelle, Jacques, 497
South Africa, 1, 155, 228, 448
Southampton, 663
Soviet Air Force, see USSR
Soviet Navy, see USSR
Soviet Review of Military History, 597n
Sovietski, 400
Spaak, Paul-Henri, 53, 54, 116
Spaatz, General, 550, 618, 703, 767
Spain, 1, 10, 19, 42, 69, 274, 392, 393, 426,

501, 514, 538, 617, 823; armistice, 136, 140, 141; Hitler's Europe, 175, 176, 247; collaboration, 290–1
Spanish Civil War, 9, 16, 175, 304, 514
Special Operations Executive (SOE), 296, 297, 298, 303
Speer, Albert, 213, 225, 662, 697; German war economy, 537, 538, 539, 541, 542; bombing of Germany, 549, 550; resiting of factories, 797
Speidel, Hans, 622, 632
Spitfire fighters, 153, 374
Spitzbergen, 365
Split, 699
Spoleto, Duke of, 284
Sprague, Admiral, 756
SS (Sicherheitsdienst), 31, 88, 540, 603, 619, 782, 791; war in Norway, 73; Nazi domination in Europe, 164, 242–3, 252, 254–5; in USSR, 231, 232, 236, 237, 270, 573; genocide, 260, 261, 262, 264, 265, 267, 269, 270–2; plot against Hitler, 658, 659; collapse of Germany, 664, 666, 691
Stalin, Joseph, 17, 286, 367, 381, 514, 609, 782, 784, 826; Poland, 32, 37, 38; phoney war, 43, 45–8, 50; break with Germany, 206–9; Wehrmacht victories in USSR, 216, 220, 230, 235; resistance, 303–5; Japan, 314, 354; Stalingrad, 396, 398, 409; Anglo-American alliance, 418, 424, 427; Stalin's role in Soviet war, 451–60, 462, 468; Anglo-Soviet alliance, 470–82, 484, 740; Soviet offensive, 558–60, 563, 574, 575; Teheran, 564–8, 721; Soviet victories, 576, 578, 580, 584, 585, 586, 591, 592, 594, 595, 596, 598; and Roosevelt, 639, 640; Yalta, 668–79, 802; end of war in Europe, 682, 693, 695, 698, 699, 702; Polish problem, 705, 706, 707, 708, 709–10; Potsdam, 711–13, 715, 716, 764, 770; declares war on Japan, 771–4; postwar balance of power, 804, 817, 818
Stalingrad, 212, 228, 229, 358, 380, 462, 572; Battle of, 394–409, 452, 456, 467, 478, 481, 541, 555, 560, 569, 579, 597
Stalino, 562
Stanislawow, 570
Staraya Russa, 224
Stark, Admiral, 160, 320
State Defence Committee (USSR), 452, 453, 454
Stauffenberg, Colonel, 231, 286, 658
Stavanger, 74, 178, 248
Stettin, 567, 594, 696

Stettinius, E., 160, 669, 677, 678, 679
Stilwell, General, 353, 726–7, 733–7, 741
Stimson, Henry, 324, 422, 435, 769, 772, 833
Stirbey, Prince, 577
Stockholm, 47, 483, 701
Stöhrer, Dr Eberhard von, 69, 138
Strasbourg, 184, 652, 664, 666, 667
Strasbourg (French battleship), 150
Strasser, Otto, 15
Stratemeyer, General, 727
Stroop, General, 272
Studnicki, Ladislas, 285
Stuka bomber, 9, 94, 100, 103, 152
Stülpnagel, General von, 171, 657, 659
Stumme, General, 380
Sturzo, Dom, 514
Stuttgart, 547, 701
Stutthof concentration camp, 262
Suarez, G., 281
submarines, 364–5, 612–13, 614, 660–1
Suda Bay, 192
Sudan, 183, 184, 810
Sudetenland, 14, 784, 785, 818
Suez Canal, 155, 177, 184, 197, 217, 373, 375, 426
Sultan, 737, 740
Sumatra, 338, 339, 349, 350
Sumner Welles, 52, 65, 208n, 318
Sun Yat-sen, 739
Supreme Interallied War Council, 51, 56, 63, 70
Surabaya, 330, 338
Sure, R., 103
Suvaja, 284
Suzuki, Admiral Kantaro, 766, 774
Svernik, 461
Svoboda, 228
Sweden, 2, 42, 45, 247, 298, 578, 703; Finland, 46, 47; phoney war, 62, 63, 64, 68; war in Norway, 70, 71, 78; collaboration, 291–2; aftermath, 793, 818
Switzerland, 15, 51, 89, 91, 92, 574, 593, 646, 698, 699, 832
Syracuse, 508
Syria, 61, 112, 174, 185, 195, 196, 299; end of African war, 502, 504; Arab unity, 809, 810
Szalassi, Ferenc, 284, 593
Szeged, 593
Szilar, Leo, 768
Sztojay, General, 577, 593

Tabarka, 490
Table-Talk (A. Hitler), 258
Tahiti, 330

Tai-yuan, 311
Tarlet, Colonel, 550
Tallinn, 218, 581
Talks on art and literature in Yenan (Mao Tse-tung), 356
Tangier, 69, 385, 713, 816, 823
Tanguy, Rol, 636
tanks, 92–3, 137, 211, 214, 398–9, 541, 555, 561
Tanner, Väinö, 46, 47
Taranto, 182, 183, 185, 524, 641
Tarnopol, 570
Tarvis, R., 521, 611
Tashkent, 816
Task Force, 360, 363, 730, 731, 751, 813
Tebessa, 490
Tedder, Sir Arthur, 684, 703
Teheran, 472, 475, 477, 483; Big Three Conference, 563–9, 576, 578, 579, 580, 581, 595, 599, 609, 638, 640, 668, 669, 672, 673, 714, 721
Teleki, Count, 68
Terauchi, Marshal, 740, 756
Terboven, Joseph, 78, 167, 246, 298, 703
Teske, Colonel, 582
Thames, R., 66
Thann, 685
Thailand, 313
Theobald, Admiral, 323
Theresienstadt, 268, 269
Thermopylae, 192
Thessaly, 192, 246
Thomas, Norman, 458
Thorez, Maurice, 457, 458, 817
Thrace, 60, 190
Thuringia, 708
Tibet, 348, 813
Tientsin, 765
Tikhonov, M., 456
Tikhvin, 219, 224
Tilburg, 57, 87
Time for Decision, The (Sumner Welles), 208n
Timor, 336, 338, 339, 346, 349, 723
Timoshenko, Semyon, 214, 219, 224, 227
Tinian, 751, 770
Tinjilap, 336
Tiraspol, 570, 589
Tirpitz (German battleship), 3, 365
Tiso, Josef, 164
Tisza, R., 593
Tito, Josip, 284, 565, 587, 603; resistance army, 304–5, 527; and Churchill, 591, 592, 594, 596, 598; coalition government, 692; Trieste, 699, 708, 709
Tobruk, 185, 194, 373, 375, 376, 448
Todt, Fritz, 537, 599, 601

Togliatti, Palmero, 459, 460, 514, 605, 606, 817
Tojo, General, 313, 316, 318–21; 329, 334, 346, 347, 351, 766
Tokyo, 68, 208, 314, 315, 318, 776 et passim
Tokyo, International Convention of, 254
Tolbukhin, Marshal, 562, 563, 590, 592, 598, 691, 692
Tonkin, 346
Tonningen, Rost van, 281
Top Secret (R. Ingersoll), 609n
Toplica, 591
Tomsk, 463
'Torch', Operation, 383–91, 422, 423, 425, 478, 487
Torgau, 700
Toulon, 390, 392, 393, 493, 523, 526, 641, 643, 644
Tours, 129, 130
Toyoda, Admiral, 750, 755, 760, 775
Trade Policy, Steering Committee for, 163
Transcaucasia, 229
Trans-jordan, 185
Transnistria, 233, 569
Trans-Siberia, 230
Transylvania, 68, 166, 186, 245, 276, 784, 785; and Romania, 589, 592, 593, 823
Treblinka, 272
Trieste, 592, 604, 605, 699, 708, 805, 816, 823
Trincomalee, 336
Trinidad, 368
Tripoli, 182, 373, 381, 387, 508
Tripolitania, 381, 426, 427, 490, 805
Trondheim, 75, 178, 365
Truk, 723, 748, 749, 754
Truman, Harry, 432, 446, 695, 833; German surrender, 698, 701; and USSR, 705, 707, 708, 710; Potsdam, 711, 712, 715, 716; Japanese surrender, 768, 771; atom bomb, 769, 770; postwar balance of power, 821, 822, 824
Truscott, General, 389
Trentin, Silvio, 514
Tuapse, 230
Tula, 222, 230
Tulagi, 362, 722
Tunis, 488, 489, 490, 492, 504, 507
Tunisia, 2, 19, 20, 49, 141n, 143, 170, 179, 196, 282, 289, 804n, 811; Germans halted, 381, 385, 386, 390, 391; Anglo-American alliance, 422, 426, 427, 487; end of war in N. Africa, 488–90, 492, 493, 503, 504; Italy surrenders, 507, 508, 524

Tuka, A., 164
Turawa, 748
Turin, 530, 607
Turkestan, 283, 353, 462
Turkey, 11, 43, 59, 61, 62n, 68, 217, 265, 292, 374, 426, 570; Balkan war, 184, 189; effect of Stalingrad, 408; Italy surrenders, 523; German war economy, 538, 578; Anglo-Turkish treaty, 599; and USSR, 818, 823, 824
Tvarkovskiy, A., 456
Tyrol, 605, 695, 699, 784

Udine, 604
Ukraine, 207n, 210, 244, 246, 283, 676, 784, 785; Wehrmacht victories, 218, 225, 232, 233, 235; collaboration, 285; economic exploitation, 460, 465; Soviet offensive, 570, 576, 597; Soviet victories, 583, 588; postwar balance of power, 818
Ulbricht, Walter, 459, 578, 817
Ulex, General, 257
Ulm, 621
Uman, 219, 569
Umberto, Prince, s. of Victor Emmanuel, 605, 606
Umbria, 529
United Nations Organisation, 676, 678–9, 710, 733, 772, 809, 810, 817; reconstruction, 825, 826–8
United Nations Educational, Scientific and Cultural Organisation (UNESCO), 828
United Nations Food and Agriculture Organisation, 828
United Nations Relief and Rehabilitation Administration (UNRRA), 829
United States, 2, 140, 213, 287, 357, 392, 513, 610, 617, 638, 661, 695, 842, 843; phoney war, 52, 69; Battle of Britain, 155, 158, 159–61; tripartite pact, 163; Vichy government, 169; Spain, 176; German-Russian break, 205, 206, 207, 217; and Japan, 312–19; Pearl Harbour, 321–4, 325, 328; Allied forces in Japan, 328–32, 334, 335, 344; and Japan's satellites, 346, 348, 352, 353, 355; war at sea, 178, 197, 359, 365, 368, 383; Anglo-American alliance, 413, 415, 416, 419–23, 426, 427; American arsenal, 428–43; Soviet war, 458, Soviet alliance, 470, 471, 473, 474, 477, 479; N. African campaign, 499, 503, 504; Teheran, 566, 567; Romania, 577, 594; Greece, 598; victory in Atlantic, 612, 614; Yalta, 669, 671, 674–7, 679;

Potsdam, 705, 709, 712, 714; strategy
in Asia, 726, 732, 734; Pacific war, 748,
752; Japanese surrender, 767, 772,
773–4, 777; atom bomb, 768–9; aftermath, 782, 784, 792, 793, 796; science,
831, 833, 834, 839, 840; reconstruction,
825–7, 829; postwar balance of power,
800, 801, 802, 810, 818, 819, 820, 822,
823–4; see also American Army, American Navy, American Air Force, lend-
lease etc.
Upper Silesia, 31, 682
Urals, 210, 211, 215, 357, 461–3, 544, 570,
784, 816
Uruguay, 441, 820
Usedom, 797
USSR, 11, 15, 32, 34, 37, 38, 148, 166, 169,
189, 310, 367, 373, 387, 624, 656, 658,
785, 842, 843; phoney war, 41, 43, 45,
47–50, 52; Turkey, 59; Caucasus operation, 62; Finland, 63, 70, 71, 79;
German-Soviet pact, 83, 88; Romania,
166; German invasion, 197, 274, 291;
break with Germany, 203–15, 291,
317, 357; Wehrmacht victories, 216–38,
319, 365, 371, 374, 376, 383; occupation, 245, 247, 254, 255; anti-semitism,
267, 268, 270; collaboration, 276, 282–6;
resistance, 295, 296–7, 302–4; Japan,
310, 312, 314, 332, 334, 354, 355, 766–7,
771–4; Stalingrad, 408, 409; Anglo-
American alliance, 413, 419, 420–1,
426–7; Allied arsenal, 428, 431, 440;
war in USSR, 450–4, 456–61, 463–5,
467–8; Anglo-Soviet alliance, 470–83;
Italy surrenders, 510, 512–14; German
war economy, 535, 537, 539–42, 545;
bombing of Germany, 547, 552; Soviet
offensive, 553–75; Soviet victories,
576–98, 655; war in Italy, 602, 609;
liberation of France, 619, 639, 643;
Yalta, 668–79; end of war in Europe,
692–5; Polish problem, 705, 706, 708,
709, 710; Potsdam, 711, 712, 714, 715;
atom bomb, 770, 833; aftermath, 782,
784, 786, 791, 793, 794; reconstruction,
825, 826, 827, 834–5; science, 838, 839;
postwar balance of power, 800, 805,
810, 811, 813, 815–18, 822, 823–4
Red Army, 43, 46, 47, 207n, 271, 285,
286, 355, 424, 569, 580, 584, 712,
791, 815, 816; German/Russian
break, 209, 212, 214; Wehrmacht
victories, 216–19, 222–4, 231–5;
resistance, 303, 304; Stalingrad,
358, 399, 402, 403, 407, 408;
conduct of USSR war, 424, 456,

459, 460, 465, 467, 468, 473, 476,
477, 480–2; Soviet offensive, 553,
555, 559, 565, 570, 571–4, 576;
victories, 581–3, 587–94, 598, 609,
640, 643, 670; in Europe, 669,
671, 673, 674, 679, 706; end of war
in Europe, 680, 681, 691, 692,
694, 696, 700–3; Japan, 770–3,
776; in Germany, 784, 785; aftermath, 793, 794, 796, 817, 823, 827
   Fifth Army, 401
   Thirteenth Army, 561
Soviet Navy, 474
Soviet Air Force, 216, 222, 227, 398,
   399, 558, 559
Utrecht, 96

V-1 flying bomb, 662, 663, 664n, 666
V-2 flying bomb, 663, 690
Vaerst, General von, 492
Valday plateau, 212
Valence, 644
Valona, 187, 527
Valsberg pass, 652
Vannes, 365
Vansittart, Sir Robert, 68
Vargas, President of Brazil, 441, 821
Vassilevski, Marshal, 398, 550, 560, 696,
   773
Vatican, 42, 68, 169, 273–5, 517, 529
Vatutin, Marshal, 400, 406, 562, 563, 569
Vauthier, Colonel, 18n
Veesenmayer, 578, 593
Vehenezi, 692
Venezuela, 365, 442, 443, 820
Venice, 530, 699
Vercors, J., 830
Vercors, 632
Vermeil, E., 162, 259
Vermorel, Claude, 830
Verona, 604
Versailles, 650
Versailles, Treaty of, 14, 32, 162, 245
Viazma, 573
Viborg, 46, 47, 219
Vichy government, 156–7, 170–76, 179,
   186, 195–7, 245, 254, 268, 281, 447,
   791; collaboration, 287–9, 290; and
   resistance, 299, 300; Japan, 313, 315,
   318, 331, 341, 345; N. African cam-
   paign, 373, 383, 385, 387–93, 488–9,
   493–6, 498, 502–4; German war
   economy, 539; liberation of France,
   636, 648; collapse, 803, 804
Victor Emmanuel, King of Italy, 19, 49,
   516–19, 605, 805
Victorious (British aircraft carrier), 179

Vienna, 60, 276, 592, 611, 668, 671, 681, 692
Vietminh (Independence Front), 348
Vietnam, 348
Vilna, 256, 582
Vincennes, 117
Vinnitza, 569
Vire, 634
Vis Island, 591
Vistula, R., 38, 246, 582, 585–6, 597, 667, 696
Vistula-Nareth line, 32
Vitebsk, 218, 400, 563, 581
Vittorio Veneto (Italian battleship), 180, 189
Vladivostock, 318
Vlassov, General, 286, 571
Volchov, 562
Volga, R., 210, 219, 228–30, 245, 256, 303, 394–6, 398–9, 401, 402, 784
Volodanskoe, 235
Vorarlberg, The, 699, 701
Voronezh, 225, 228, 400, 402, 406, 407, 462, 562
Voronov, 398, 405, 697
Voroshilovgrad, 407
Vosges, the, 171, 262, 649, 685
Vuillemin, General, 61, 90, 97, 112
Vyazma, 222, 224, 398, 407
Vyshinsky, Andrei, 602, 693

Waal, R., 96, 650
Waalhaven, 97
Waffen ss, 282, 555, 657, 701; *see also* ss
Wake Island, 330, 335, 336, 341
Walcheren Island, 57, 97, 650
Wallace, Vice President usa, 737, 822
Walter (German submarine), 364
Wang Tsing-wei, 311, 346
Wannsee, 270
Wanty, General, 100
War Cabinet (British), 415
War Mobilization, Office of (us), 432, 433
Warliment, General, 203, 204
Warsaw, 31, 33–5, 37, 165, 268, 271, 272, 576, 582, 584, 591, 682, 709, 787; uprising, 583–6
Wartheland, 256
Washington, 359, 418, 419, 421, 427 *et passim*
Wasilevska, Wanda, 481, 482
'Watchover', Operation, 723
Watt, Robert Watson, 152
Wavell, General, 184, 188, 193, 331, 338, 344, 473
Wavre, 57, 98, 101
Wedermeyer, Lt Gen., 437, 737, 741

Wehrmacht, *see* Germany
Weich, von, 228, 591
Weidling, General, 698
Weimar, 262
Weinert, Erich, 578
Werth, Henrik, 68
Wesel, 685, 691
Weser, R., 700
West Indies, 160
Wentzel, Dr, 255, 256
Weygand, Maxime, 18, 58, 59, 61, 62n, 93, 289, 393, 385; French collapse, 112–19, 122–5; armistice, 130–7, 142; and Hitler, 175; French colonies, 182, 195; N. African campaign, 488, 489
Weygand plan, 60, 189
White Committee (us), 158
White Russia, 210
Wiesbaden, 173, 287
Wiese, General, 641, 643
Wieterheim, General von, 229
Wilhelmina, Queen of the Netherlands, 97, 156, 802
Wilhelmshaven, 366
Wilkie, Wendell, 436, 471
Wilmot, Chester, 366
Wilson, President, 158, 424, 675
Wilson, Charles E., 432
Wilson, Donald, 432
Wilson, General Maitland, 608, 638, 639, 698
Wingate, General, 741
Winkelman, General, 96, 97
Wirth, Chancellor, 68
Wirtschaftskommandos (economic control groups), 234
Witzleben, Marshal von, 657, 659
Wolfe, General, 727
Wolff, General, 698, 699
World War I, 10, 17, 58, 69, 84, 92, 96, 298, 481, 781, 783
Wunthann (Burmese Buddhist party), 348
Würtemberg, 568

Yalta Conference, 472, 667, 668–79, 684, 693, 694, 703, 705, 707, 709, 711, 712, 714, 715, 716, 721, 769, 771, 802, 804, 811, 822, 823, 826
Yamamoto, Admiral, 321, 322, 360–2, 748
Yamashita, General, 337, 340, 757
Yamato (Japanese battleship), 756, 760
Ybarnegaray, Jean, 111, 133, 135
Yenan, 354
Yeremenko, General, 218, 394–6, 398–9, 401, 407
Yonne, R., 130
Yokohama, 754

Ypres Conference (May 1940), 115–17
Yser, R., 115, 116, 117
Yugoslavia, 11, 59, 68, 267, 274, 371, 459, 590, 602, 707; crushed by Germany, 189, 190, 192, 204, 205; Nazi Europe, 245, 250; resistance, 295, 297, 304–6; and Italy, 527, 603; Soviet victories, 590–92, 595, 598; German surrender, 692–4
Yünnan, 313, 736, 814

Zadar, 699
Zagreb, 190, 699
Zamosc, 583
Zanatescu, 589

Zaporozhye, 462, 563
Zeeland, 87, 97
Zeitzler, Kurt von, 400, 402, 407, 554, 560, 570
Zeller, Colonel Henri, 641
Zervas, General, 305
Zhitomir, 218, 563, 569
Zhukov, General, 222, 569; Stalingrad, 398; German surrender, 681, 682, 696, 697, 703; aftermath of war, 797, 818
Zisterdorf, 542
Zlatoust, 464
Zsombalethy, General, 577
Zuyder Zee, 700
Zweig, Stephan, 829n